HALLEY'S
BIBLE HANDBOOK

"The Bible is the most priceless possession of the human race."

HALLEY'S

BIBLE HANDBOOK

ZondervanPublishingHouse
Academic and Professional Books
Grand Rapids, Michigan

A Division of HarperCollins*Publishers*

Published by arrangement with Halley's Bible Handbook, ® Inc.

ISBN 0-310-48961-X

Requests for information should be addressed to:
Zondervan Publishing House, Grand Rapids, Michigan 49530

This edition is printed on acid-free paper and meets the American
National Standards Institute Z39.48 standard.

Library of Congress Card Number: 32-8057

PRINTED IN THE UNITED STATES OF AMERICA

THE PRINTING HISTORY

First Edition 1924 10,000
Second Edition 1925 10,000
Third Edition 1927 10,000
Fourth Edition 1927 10,000
Fifth Edition 1928 10,000
Sixth Edition 1929 10,000
Seventh Edition 1931 10,000
Eighth Edition 1932 10,000
Ninth Edition 1933 10,000
Tenth Edition 1934 10,000
Eleventh Edition 1936 10,000
Twelfth Edition 1938 10,000
Thirteenth Edition 1939 15,000
Fourteenth Edition 1941 30,000
Fifteenth Edition 1943 30,000
Sixteenth Edition 1944 30,000
Second Printing 1945 30,000
Seventeenth Edition 1946 30,000
Second Printing 1946 50,000
Eighteenth Edition 1948 60,000
Second Printing 1950 40,000
Nineteenth Edition 1951 30,000
Second Printing 1952 40,000
Third Printing 1952 40,000
Fourth Printing 1953 50,000
Fifth Printing 1954 50,000
Twentieth Edition 1955 50,000
Second Printing 1955 50,000
Third Printing 1956 50,000
Twenty-first Edition 1957 50,000
Second Printing 1958 60,000
Twenty-second Edition 1959 ... 60,000
Second Printing 1960 60,000
Third Printing 1960 60,000
Fourth Printing 1961 60,000
Twenty-third Edition 1962 60,000
Second Printing 1963 75,000
Third Printing 1964 75,000
Fourth Printing 1964 50,000
Billy Graham Edition
First Printing 1964 250,000
Second Printing 1964 250,000
Third Printing 1964 250,000
Twenty-fourth (Revised)
Edition 1965 75,000
Second Printing 1965 75,000
Third Printing 1966 75,000
Fourth Printing 1966 50,000
Fifth Printing 1967 50,000
Sixth Printing 1968 50,000
Seventh Printing 1969 50,000
Eighth Printing 1969 50,000
Ninth Printing 1970 60,000
Tenth Printing 1971 50,000
Eleventh Printing 1971 60,000
Twelfth Printing 1972 60,000
Thirteenth Printing 1972 75,000
Fourteenth Printing 1973 75,000
Fifteenth Printing 1973 75,000
Sixteenth Printing 1974 100,000
Seventeenth Printing 1975 ... 50,000
Eighteenth Printing 1975 50,000
Nineteenth Printing 1976 50,000
Twentieth Printing 1976 50,000
Twenty-first Printing 1976 ... 50,000
Twenty-second Printing
1976 50,000
Twenty-third Printing 1977 .. 50,000
Twenty-fourth Printing 1977 . 50,000
Twenty-fifth Printing 1978 ... 50,000
Twenty-sixth Printing 1978 .. 25,000
(Large Print Edition)
Twenty-seventh Printing
1978 50,000
Twenty-eigth Printing 1978 .. 50,000
Twenty-ninth Printing 1979 .. 50,000
Thirtieth Printing 1979 10,000
(Large Print Edition)
Thirty-first Printing 1979 10,000
Thirty-second Printing 1979 . 50,000
Thirty-third Printing 1980 .. 10,000
(Large Print Edition)
Thirty-fourth Printing 1980 .. 50,000
Thirty-fifth Printing 1980 50,000
Thirty-sixth Printing 1980 ... 10,000
(Large Print Edition)
Thirty-seventh Printing 1980 . 50,000
Thirty-eighth Printing 1980 .. 10,000
(Large Print Edition)
Thirty-ninth Printing 1981 ... 10,000
(Large Print Edition)
Fortieth Printing 1981 50,000
Forty-first Printing 1981 12,500
(Large Print Edition)
Forty-second Printing 1981 .. 50,000
Forty-third Printing 1982 50,000
Forty-fourth Printing 1982 ... 50,000
Forty-fifth Printing 1983 7,500
(Large Print Edition)
Forty-sixth Printing 1983 50,000
Forty-seventh Printing 1983 . 50,000
Forty-eighth Printing 1984 8,500
Forty-ninth Printing 1984 50,000
Fiftieth Printing 1984 50,000
Fifty-first Printing 1984 50,000
Fifty-second Printing 1985 ... 10,000
(Large Print Edition)
Fifty-third Printing 1984 50,000
Fifty-fourth Printing 1986 ... 25,000
Fifty-fifth Printing 1986 2,000
(Large Print Edition)
Fifty-sixth Printing 1986 35,000
Fifty-seventh Printing 1986 ... 3,000
(Large Print Edition)
Fifty-eighth Printing 1986 ... 50,000
(Continued)

Fifty-ninth Printing 1987 5,000
(Large Print Edition)
Sixtieth Printing 1987 12,000
Sixty-first Printing 1987 25,000
Sixty-second Printing 1988 5,000
(Large Print Edition)
Sixty-third Printing 1988 30,000
Sixty-fourth Printing 1988 50,000
Sixty-fifth Printing 1988 30,000
Sixty-sixth Printing 1989 5,000
(Large Print Edition)
Sixty-seventh Printing 1989 50,000
Sixty-eighth Printing 1990 3,000
(Large Print Edition)
Sixty-ninth Printing 1990 50,000
Seventieth Printing 1991 3,000
(Large Print Edition)
Seventy-first Printing 1991 30,000
Seventy-second Printing 1992 ...30,000
Seventy-third Printing 1992 25,000
Seventy-fourth Printing 1993 25,000
Seventy-fifth Printing 1993 7,200
(Large Print Edition)
Seventy-sixth Printing 1993 21,000
Seventy-seventh Printing 1994 ..30,000

Foreign Language Editions

Afrikaans
Chinese, 1954
French, 1979
Greek, 1964
Indonesian, 1964
Italian, 1964
Japanese, 1953
Bulgarian
Arabic/Coptic
Korean, 1940
Portuguese, 1964
Spanish, 1955
Thai, 1959
Russian
Swahili
Filipino Dialects (Cebuano, Hiligaynon, Ilocano, and Tagalog)
Romanian

"The vigor of our Spiritual Life will be in exact proportion to the place held by the Bible in our life and thoughts. I solemnly state this from the experience of fifty-four years.

"The first three years after conversion I neglected the Word of God. Since I began to search it diligently the blessing has been wonderful.

"I have read the Bible through one hundred times, and always with increasing delight. Each time it seems like a new book to me.

"Great has been the blessing from consecutive, diligent, daily study. I look upon it as a lost day when I have not had a good time over the Word of God."—*George Muller, of Bristol Orphanage fame, most outstanding example of Effectual Prayer in modern times.*

"I prayed for Faith, and thought that some day Faith would come down and strike me like lightning. But Faith did not seem to come.

"One day I read in the tenth chapter of Romans, 'Now Faith cometh by hearing, and hearing by the Word of God.' I had closed my Bible, and prayed for Faith. I now opened my Bible, and began to study, and Faith has been growing ever since."—*D. L. Moody.*

FOREWORD

This is the 24th Edition of this Bible Handbook. It is completely revised and up-dated, and reset in larger, more readable type. More recent photographs have also been substituted at several places in the volume.

This book has been a growth. It was started in 1924, as a 16-page leaflet. Next it was 32 pages. Then 40. Then 80. Then 120. Then 144. Then 160. Then 180. Then 200. Then 288. Then 356. Then 476. Then 516. Then 604. Then 676. Then 764. Then 768. Now 850.

It is not designed as a textbook, but rather as a handy brief manual, of popular nature, for the average Bible reader who has few or no commentaries or reference works on the Bible. However, many Bible classes use it; and many accomplished Bible scholars, possessors of large libraries, have been most cordial in acknowledging its helpfulness. Its usefulness may be enhanced by looking through it a good deal, so as to become familiar in a general way with its contents.

I could wish the type were larger. But that would make it a bulky volume. It is a "Pocket Handbook," covering a rather wide range of material. I think it is better that the type be small than that the book be large. The type used is quite clear. The paragraphs are, for the most part, short, and well separated, each having its own definite heading. It is, indeed, more readable than if it were in larger type set solid with little or no spacing, the way so many books are printed. All in all, it is, certainly, as readable as the average newspaper.

The book is built, quite largely, on a system of page, or double page, units, so as to exhibit before the eye, at a glance, a sort of general view of the topics or sub-topics.

In the main, it is a book of FACTS, Biblical and Historical. I have sought to avoid featuring my own opinions on controversial subjects.

By including, along with the Notes on Bible Books, an Outline of Archaeological Discoveries which bear on the Bible, and an Epitome of Church History, connecting Bible times with our own times, I have hoped to make the book a rather complete, though small, compendium of practical information, which Christians, who wish to keep themselves intelligent and well-instructed about their religion, may find useful and helpful.

In my efforts to familiarize myself with archaeological findings, it has been my good fortune to meet, or be in correspondence with, a number of archaeologists. I have been greatly impressed by their courtesy, and also by their openmindedness. They are men who deal with facts, and seem to be more free from dogmatic tendencies than many men of academic calling. For the archaeological Photographs I acknowledge with gratitude my indebtedness to: the University Museum of Pennsylvania; the Oriental Institute of Chicago University; the Field Museum of Natural History; the British Museum, London; the Ashmolean Museum of Oxford University; the Metropolitan Museum, New York; the Louvre Museum, Paris; the Cairo Museum, Egypt; the American Schools of Oriental Research; Dr. W. F. Albright; Sir Flinders Petrie; Dr. John Garstang; Mr. Francis Neilson; Dr. J. L. Kelso; Mr. Fahim Kouchakji, owner of the Chalice of Antioch; Rev. F. J. Moore; and Rev. Roderic Lee Smith.

I have tried to include enough Maps to make it easy to correlate events and places. For these I acknowledge grateful indebtedness to Mrs. Henry Berry.

This Handbook is dedicated to the proposition that Every Christian should be a Constant and Devoted Reader of the Bible; and that the primary business of the Church and Ministry is to lead, foster, and encourage their people in the habit.

H. H. Halley.

SOURCES OF INFORMATION

Archaeological

American Journal of Archaeology
American Journal of Semitic Languages and Literatures
Annuals of Archaeology and Anthropology, University of Liverpool
Annuals of the American School of Oriental Research
Annuals of the Palestine Exploration Fund
Antiquaries' Journal
Antiquity
Art and Archaeology
Bulletins of the American Schools of Oriental Research
Bulletins of the University Museum
Museum Journal
Oriental Institute Communications
Oriental Institute Reports on the Near East
Quarterly Statements of the Palestine Exploration Fund

* * * * * *

Adams, J. McKee, "Biblical Background"
Albright, W. F., "Archaeology of Palestine and the Bible"
Baikie, James, "History of Egypt"
Banks, E. J., "Bible and Spade"
Barton, G. A., "Archaeology and the Bible"
Breasted, J. H., "Oriental Institute," "History of Egypt"
Caiger, S. L., "Bible and Spade"
Cambridge Ancient History
Clay, A. T., "Light on the Old Testament from Babel"
Cobern, C. M., "New Archaeological Discoveries"
Cook, S. A., "Religion of Ancient Palestine"
Duncan, J. G., "Digging up Biblical History," "Accuracy of O T"
Ellis, W. T., "Bible Lands Today"
Field, Henry, "Field Museum-Oxford Expedition to Kish"
Fisher, C. S., "Exploration of Armagedaon"
Free, J. P., "Archaeology and Bible History"
Gadd, C. J., "History and Monuments of Ur"
Garstang, John, "Story of Jericho"
Grant, Elihu, "Haverford Symposium on Archaeology and Bible"
Guy, P. L. O., "New Light from Armageddon"
Hall, H. R., "Ancient History of the Near East"

Hammarton, J. A., "Wonders of the Past"
Hilprecht, H. V., "Exploration of Bible Lands"
Irwin, C. H., "The Bible, the Scholar and the Spade"
Jastrow, Morris, "Civilization of Babylonia and Assyria"
King, L. W., "History of Sumer and Akkad"
Kyler, M. G., "Explorations at Sodom," Articles in ISBE
Langdon Stephen, "Semitic Mythology"
Macalester, R. A., "Bible Sidelights from Gezer"
Marston, Charles, "New Bible Evidence"
Maspero, G. C., "Dawn of Civilization"
Newberry and Garstang, "Short History of Egypt"
Olmstead, A. T., "History of Assyria," "History of Egypt"
Olmstead, A. T., "History of Palestine and Syria"
Peake, Harold, "The Flood"
Petrie, Flinders, "History of Egypt," "Palestine and Israel"
Price, Ira M., "The Monuments and the Old Testament"
Robinson, George L., "Bearing of Archaeology on Old Testament"
Sayce, A. H., "Ancient Empires of the East"
Sayce, A. H., "Fresh Light from the Ancient Monuments"
Smith, G. & A. H. Sayce, "Chaldean Account of Genesis"
Wiseman, P. J., "New Discoveries about Genesis"
Woolley, C. L., "Ur of the Chaldees," "Ur Excavations"
Zondervan Pictorial Bible Dictionary

Biblical

Buckland's Bible Dictionary
Cambridge Bible for Schools and Colleges
Clarke's Commentary
Davis' Bible Dictionary
Dummelow's Commentary
Eiselen's Abingdon Commentary
Elliott's Commentary
Expositor's Bible
Gore's Commentary
Gray's Commentary
Hasting's Bible Dictionary
International Critical Commentary
International Standard Bible Encyclopaedia
Jacobus' Bible Dictionary
Jamieson, Faussett and Brown's Commentary
McClintock and Strong's Encyclopaedia
Moulton's Modern Reader's Bible

Peake's Commentary
Peloubet's Bible Dictionary
Piercy's Bible Dictionary
Pulpit Commentary
Schaff's Bible Dictionary
Schaff-Herzog's Encyclopaedia
Schaff-Lange's Commentary
Speaker's Commentary
Various Commentaries on Single Books
The BIBLE ITSELF

Church History

Cambridge Medieval History
Coxe's Ante-Nicene Fathers
Creighton's History of the Papacy
Crook's Story of the Christian Church
Duchesne's Christian Church
Fisher's History of the Christian Church
Fisher's Outline of General History
Fisher's The Reformation
Freeman's General Sketch
Hurlbut's Church History
Hurst's History of the Christian Church
Jenning's Manual of Church History
Kidd's History of the Church
Kurtz' Church History
Lindsay's History of the Reformation
McGlothlin's Church History
Moncrief's Short History of the Christian Church
Mosheim's Church History
Nagler's The Church in History
Neander's Church History
Newman's Manual of Church History
Nichols' Growth of the Christian Church
Ploetz' Epitome of Universal History
Robertson's History of the Christian Church
Sanford's Cyclopaedia of Religious Knowledge
Schaff's History of the Christian Church
Sheldon's History of the Church
Smith & Cheetham's Dictionary of Christian Antiquities
Zenos' Compendium of Church History

CONTENTS

PHOTOGRAPHIC ILLUSTRATIONS

MAPS

ARCHAEOLOGICAL NOTES

Alphabetically Arranged

NOTABLE SAYINGS ABOUT THE BIBLE

Abraham Lincoln: "I believe the Bible is the best gift God has ever given to man. All the good from the Saviour of the world is communicated to us through this book."

W. E. Gladstone: "I have known ninety-five of the world's great men in my time, and of these eighty-seven were followers of the Bible. The Bible is stamped with a Specialty of Origin, and an immeasurable distance separates it from all competitors."

George Washington: "It is impossible to rightly govern the world without God and the Bible."

Napoleon: "The Bible is no mere book, but a Living Creature, with a power that conquers all that oppose it."

Queen Victoria: "That book accounts for the supremacy of England."

Daniel Webster: "If there is anything in my thoughts or style to commend, the credit is due to my parents for instilling in me an early love of the Scriptures. If we abide by the principles taught in the Bible, our country will go on prospering and to prosper; but if we and our posterity neglect its instructions and authority, no man can tell how sudden a catastrophe may overwhelm us and bury all our glory in profound obscurity."

Thomas Carlyle: "The Bible is the truest utterance that ever came by alphabetic letters from the soul of man, through which, as through a window divinely opened, all men can look into the stillness of eternity, and discern in glimpses their far-distant, long-forgotten home."

John Ruskin: "Whatever merit there is in anything that I have written is simply due to the fact that when I was a child my mother daily read me a part of the Bible and daily made me learn a part of it by heart."

Charles A. Dana: "The grand old Book still stands; and this old earth, the more its leaves are turned and pondered, the more it will sustain and illustrate the pages of the Sacred Word."

Thomas Huxley: "The Bible has been the Magna Charta of the poor and oppressed. The human race is not in a position to dispense with it."

W. H. Seward: "The whole hope of human progress is suspended on the ever growing influence of the Bible."

Patrick Henry: "The Bible is worth all other books which have ever been printed."

U. S. Grant: "The Bible is the sheet-anchor of our liberties."

Horace Greeley: "It is impossible to enslave mentally or socially a Bible-reading people. The principles of the Bible are the groundwork of human freedom."

Andrew Jackson: "That book, sir, is the rock on which our republic rests."

Robert E. Lee: "In all my perplexities and distresses, the Bible has never failed to give me light and strength."

Lord Tennyson: "Bible reading is an education in itself."

John Quincy Adams: "So great is my veneration for the Bible that the earlier my children begin to read it the more confident will be my hope that they will prove useful citizens of their country and respectable members of society. I have for many years made it a practice to read through the Bible once every year."

Immanuel Kant: "The existence of the Bible, as a book for the people, is the greatest benefit which the human race has ever experienced. Every attempt to belittle it is a crime against humanity."

Charles Dickens: "The New Testament is the very best book that ever was or ever will be known in the world."

Sir William Herschel: "All human discoveries seem to be made only for the purpose of confirming more and more strongly the truths contained in the Sacred Scriptures."

Sir Isaac Newton: "There are more sure marks of authenticity in the Bible than in any profane history."

Goethe: "Let mental culture go on advancing, let the natural sciences progress in ever greater extent and depth, and the human mind widen itself as much as it desires; beyond the elevation and moral culture of Christianity, as it shines forth in the gospels, it will not go."

Henry Van Dyke: "Born in the East and clothed in Oriental form and imagery, the Bible walks the ways of all the world with familiar feet and enters land after land to find its own everywhere. It has learned to speak in hundreds of languages to the heart of man. Children listen to its stories with wonder and delight, and wise men ponder them as parables of life. The wicked and the proud tremble at its warnings, but to the wounded and penitent it has a mother's voice. It has woven itself into our dearest dreams; so that Love, Friendship, Sympathy, Devotion, Memory, Hope, put on the beautiful garments of its treasured speech. No man is poor or desolate who has this treasure for his own. When the landscape darkens, and the trembling pilgrim comes to the Valley of the Shadow, he is not afraid to enter; he takes the rod and staff of Scripture in his hand; he says to friend and comrade, 'Goodbye; We Shall Meet Again'; and, confronted by that support, he goes toward the lonely pass as one who walks through darkness into light." (*From* Companionable Books, *by Henry Van Dyke, through courtesy of its publishers, Charles Scribner's Sons.*)

CHRIST
is the
CENTER and HEART of the BIBLE

The Old Testament is an account of a Nation.

The New Testament is an account of a MAN.

The Nation was founded and nurtured of God to bring the Man into the world.

God Himself became a Man, to give mankind a concrete, definite, tangible idea of what kind of Person to think of when we think of God. God is like Jesus. Jesus was God incarnate in human form.

His appearance on the earth is the Central Event of all history. The Old Testament sets the stage for it. The New Testament describes it.

As a Man, He lived the most strangely Beautiful Life ever known. He was the Kindest, Tenderest, Gentlest, most Patient, most Sympathetic man that ever lived. He Loved people. He hated to see people in trouble. He loved to Forgive. He loved to Help. He wrought marvelous miracles to feed hungry people. For relieving the suffering He forgot to take food for himself. Multitudes, weary, pain-ridden, and heart-sick, came to Him, and found healing and relief. It is said of Him, and of no other, that if all the deeds of Kindness that He did were written, the world would not contain the books. That is the kind of man Jesus was. That is the kind of Person God is.

Then: He Died, on the Cross, to take away the Sin of the world, to become the Redeemer and Saviour of men.

Then: He Rose from the Dead: is Alive Now: not merely an historical character, but a Living Person: the Most Important Fact of History, and Most Vital Force in the world today.

The whole Bible is builded around this Beautiful Story of Christ, and His promise of Life Eternal to those who Accept Him. The Bible was written only that men might Believe, and Understand, and Know, and Love, and Follow CHRIST.

Christ, the Center and Heart of the Bible, the Center and Heart of History, is the Center and Heart of Our Lives. Our Eternal Destiny is in His hand. Our Acceptance, or Rejection, of Him, determines, for each of us, Eternal Glory, or Eternal Ruin; Heaven, or Hell: one, or the other.

The Most Important Decision any one is ever called on to make is to Settle, in his heart, once for all, the matter of his Attitude toward Christ. On that depends Everything.

It is a Glorious thing to be a Christian, the Most Exalted privilege of mankind. To accept Christ as Saviour, Lord, and Master, and to strive Sincerely and Devotedly to Follow in the Way of Life which He taught, is, certainly, and by far, the most reasonable, and most satisfactory way to live. It means Peace, Peace of Mind, Contentment of Heart, Forgiveness, Happiness, Hope, Life, Life Here and Now, Life Abundant, LIFE THAT SHALL NEVER END.

How can anyone be so blind, or so dumb, as to go through life, and Face Death, without the Christian Hope? Apart from Christ, what is there, what can there be, either for This World, or the Next, to make life worthwhile? We All have to Die. Why try to laugh it off? It seems like Every Human Being would Welcome Christ with Open Arms, and consider it the Proudest Privilege of his life to wear the Christian Name.

In the last analysis, the dearest, sweetest thing in life is the consciousness, in the inner depths of our motives, that we live for Christ; and, though our efforts be ever so feeble, we toil at our daily tasks, in hope of, in the final roundup, having done something to lay, in humble gratitude and adoration, as an offering at His feet.

THE BIBLE
IS
GOD'S WORD

Apart from any theory of inspiration; or any theory of how the Bible books came to their present form; or how much the text may have suffered in transmission at the hands of editors and copyists; apart from the question of how much is to be interpreted literally and how much figuratively, or what is historical and what may be poetical; if we will assume that the Bible is just what it appears to be, and study its books to know their contents, we will find there a Unity of Thought indicating that One Mind inspired the writing and compilation of the whole series of books; that it bears on its face the stamp of its Author; that it is in a unique and distinctive sense THE WORD OF GOD.

There is a present-day view, held rather widely in certain intellectual circles, that the Bible is a sort of age-long story of man's effort to find God: a record of man's experiences reaching after God, gradually improving his idea of God by building on the experiences of preceding generations. In those passages, so abundant in the Bible, in which it is said that God spoke, God, according to this view, did not really speak; but men put their ideas in language professing to be the language of God, while in reality it was only what men imagined about God. The Bible is thus reduced to the level of other books, and is made to appear, not a Divine book, but a human book, pretending to be Divine.

We reject this view utterly, and with abhorrence. We believe the Bible to be, not man's account of his effort to find God, but rather an account of God's effort to reveal Himself to man: God's own record of His dealings with men, in His unfolding revelation of Himself to the human race: the Revealed Will of the Creator of Man, given to Man by the Creator Himself, for Instruction and Guidance in the Ways of Life.

The books of the Bible were composed by human authors; and it is not even known who some of these authors were. Nor is it known just how God directed these authors to write. But it is asserted that God did direct them; and these books must be exactly what God wanted them to be.

There is a difference between the Bible and all other books. Authors may pray for God's help and guidance; and God does help and guide; and there are many good books in the world which unmistakably God has helped the authors to write. But even so, even the most saintly of authors would hardly presume to claim for his books that God wrote them. But that is claimed for the Bible. God Himself superintended and directed and dictated the writing of the Bible books, with the human authors so completely under His control that the writing was the writing of God. The Bible is GOD'S WORD in a sense that No Other Book in the World is God's Word.

It may be that some Bible utterances are "ancient thoughtforms" for ideas that we would now express in a different way; for they were expressed in language of ancient times. But even so, the Bible contains precisely the things that God wants mankind to know, in exactly the form in which He wants us to know them. And to the end of time the Dear Old Book will remain the one and only answer to humanity's quest for God.

The Bible, composed by many authors, over a period of many centuries, yet ONE BOOK, is, in itself, the outstanding Miracle of the Ages, bearing aloft its own evidence of its Superhuman Origin.

EVERYBODY ought to Love the Bible. Everybody ought to be a Regular Reader of the Bible. Everybody ought to strive to Live by the Bible's teachings. The Bible ought to have Central Place in the Life and Working of Every Church; and in Every Pulpit. THE PULPIT'S ONE BUSINESS IS THE SIMPLE EXPOSITORY TEACHING OF GOD'S WORD.

OUTLINE OF THE BIBLE STORY

God created Man, and placed him in the Garden of Eden, in southwest Asia, the approximate Geographic Center of the largest land portion of the earth's surface, indicated by the Black Square on Map 1.

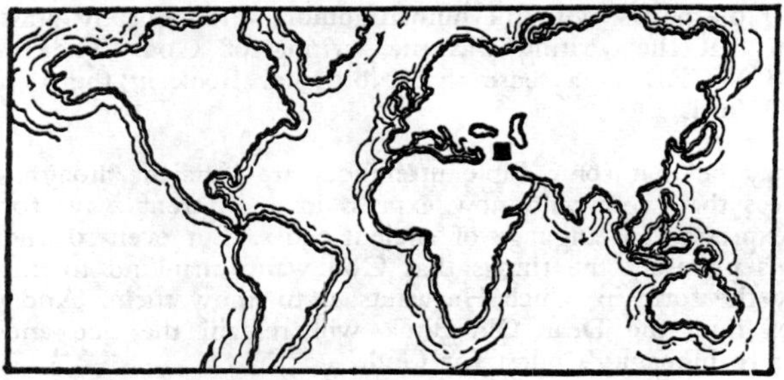

Map 1.

Man sinned, and fell from what God designed him to be. Then God inaugurated a Plan for Man's ultimate Redemption and Re-Creation, by calling Abraham to found a Nation through whom this would be accomplished. God let Abraham out of Babylonia into the land of Canaan. Abraham's descendants migrated to Egypt, and there grew to be a Nation.

Map 2.

After 400 years, they were led out of Egypt, under the direction of Moses, back into the Promised Land of Canaan. And there, in the course of some four or five hundred years, under the reigns of David and Solomon, the Nation became a Great and Mighty Kingdom.

Then, at the close of Solomon's reign, the Kingdom divided. The North part, Ten Tribes, called "Israel," lasted about 200 years, and was taken captive by Assyria, 721 B.C. The South part, called "Judah," lasted a little over 100 years longer, and about 600 B.C., was carried away captive by Babylon. A Remnant of the Captive Nation, 536 B.C., Returned to their own land, and re-established their national life.

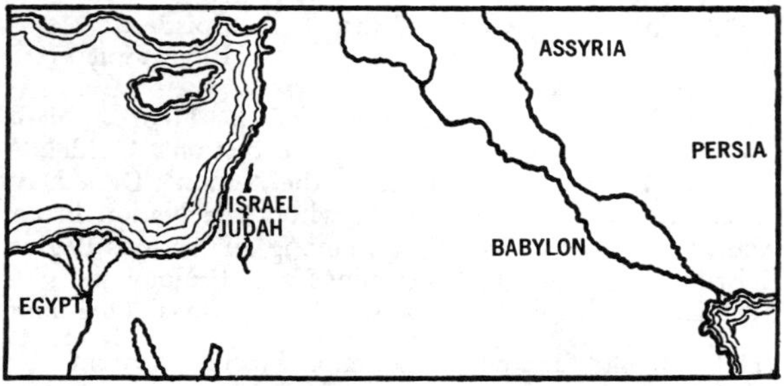

Map 3.

Soon thereafter the Old Testament closed. Four hundred years later, JESUS, the Messiah of Old Testament prophecy through Whom man was to be Redeemed and Re-Created, appeared, and did His work: Died for Human Sin; and Rose from the Dead; and commanded His disciples to carry the Story of His Life, with its Redemptive Power, to All Nations.

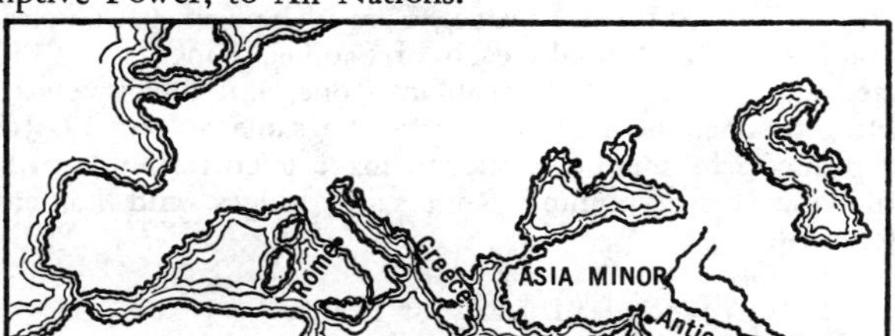

Map 4.

They went in every direction with the Glad News: mainly, westward, through Asia Minor and Greece, to Rome, along what was the backbone of the Roman Empire, which then comprised the known civilized world. With the work of Human Redemption thus launched, the New Testament closes.

BIBLE BOOKS
ARE IN
SEVEN GROUPS

OLD TESTAMENT	NEW TESTAMENT
17 Historical	4 Gospels
5 Poetical	Acts
17 Prophetic	21 Epistles
	Revelation

Historical:	Rise and Fall of the Hebrew Nation.
Poetical:	Literature of the Nation's Golden Age.
Prophetic:	Literature of the Nation's Dark Days.
Gospels:	The MAN whom the Nation Produced.
Acts:	His Reign among all Nations Begins.
Epistles:	His Teachings and Principles.
Revelation:	Forecast of His Universal Dominion.

The Hebrew Old Testament contains exactly the same books as our English Old Testament, but in different arrangement:

"Law," (5 books)	Genesis, Exodus, Leviticus, Numbers, Deuteronomy
"Prophets," (8 books)	4 Earlier: Joshua, Judges, Samuel, Kings 4 Later: Isaiah, Jeremiah, Ezekiel, The Twelve
"Writings," (11 books)	3 Poetical: Psalms, Proverbs, Job 5 Rolls: Song, Ruth, Lamentations, Ecclesiastes, Esther 3 Books: Daniel, Ezra-Nehemiah, Chronicles

By combining the 2 books each of Samuel, Kings and Chronicles into one, and Ezra and Nehemiah into one, and the Twelve Minor Prophets into one, these 24 books are the same as our 39. Josephus further reduces the number to 22, to make it correspond to the Hebrew alphabet by combining Ruth with Judges, and Lamentations with Jeremiah.

The five Rolls were read yearly at Feasts:
Song, at Passover, allegorically referring to the Exodus.
Ruth, at Pentecost, celebrating Harvest.
Esther, at Purim, commemorating Deliverance from Haman.
Ecclesiastes, at Tabernacles, most joyous of Feasts.
Lamentations, 9th of Ab, commemorating Destruction of Jerusalem.

The Septuagint Translators re-classified the Old Testament books according to subject-matter. English translators followed the Septuagint order, as we now have them.

THE 39 OLD TESTAMENT BOOKS

17 HISTORICAL	5 POETICAL	17 PROPHETIC
Genesis	Job	Isaiah
Exodus	Psalms	Jeremiah
Leviticus	Proverbs	Lamentations
Numbers	Ecclesiastes	Ezekiel
Deuteronomy	Song	Daniel
Joshua		Hosea
Judges		Joel
Ruth		Amos
I Samuel		Obadiah
II Samuel		Jonah
I Kings		Micah
II Kings		Nahum
I Chronicles		Habakkuk
II Chronicles		Zephaniah
Ezra		Haggai
Nehemiah		Zechariah
Esther		Malachi

THE 27 NEW TESTAMENT BOOKS

4 GOSPELS	ACTS	21 EPISTLES	REVELATION
Matthew	Acts	Romans	Revelation
Mark		I Corinthians	
Luke		II Corinthians	
John		Galatians	
		Ephesians	
		Philippians	
		Colossians	
		I Thessalonians	
		II Thessalonians	
		I Timothy	
		II Timothy	
		Titus	
		Philemon	
		Hebrews	
		James	
		I Peter	
		II Peter	
		I John	
		II John	
		III John	
		Jude	

SUBJECT OR LEADING THOUGHT OF EACH BOOK

Some of the books have a Principal Thought: Others are about a number of things.

Genesis	Founding of the Hebrew Nation
Exodus	The Covenant with the Hebrew Nation
Leviticus	Laws of the Hebrew Nation
Numbers	Journey to the Promised Land
Deuteronomy	Laws of the Hebrew Nation
Joshua	The Conquest of Canaan
Judges	First 300 years in the Land
Ruth	Beginning of the Messianic Family of David
I Samuel	Organization of the Kingdom
II Samuel	Reign of David
I Kings	Division of the Kingdom
II Kings	History of the Divided Kingdom
I Chronicles	Reign of David
II Chronicles	History of Southern Kingdom
Ezra	Return from Captivity
Nehemiah	Rebuilding Jerusalem
Esther	Escape of Israel from Extermination
Job	Problem of Suffering
Psalms	National Hymn Book of Israel
Proverbs	Wisdom of Solomon
Ecclesiastes	Vanity of Earthly Life
Song of Solomon	Glorification of Wedded Love
Isaiah	The Messianic Prophet
Jeremiah	A Last Effort to Save Jerusalem
Lamentations	A Dirge over the Desolation of Jerusalem
Ezekiel	"They shall Know that I am God"
Daniel	The Prophet at Babylon
Hosea	Apostasy of Israel
Joel	Prediction of the Holy Spirit Age
Amos	Ultimate Universal Rule of David
Obadiah	Destruction of Edom
Jonah	An Errand of Mercy to Nineveh

Micah	Bethlehem to be Birthplace of the Messiah
Nahum	Destruction of Nineveh
Habakkuk	"The Just shall Live by Faith"
Zephaniah	Coming of a "Pure Language"
Haggai	Rebuilding the Temple
Zechariah	Rebuilding the Temple
Malachi	Final Message to a Disobedient People
Matthew	Jesus the Messiah
Mark	Jesus the Wonderful
Luke	Jesus the Son of Man
John	Jesus the Son of God
Acts	Formation of the Church
Romans	Nature of Christ's Work
I Corinthians	Various Church Disorders
II Corinthians	Paul's Vindication of his Apostleship
Galatians	By Grace, not by Law
Ephesians	Unity of the Church
Philippians	A Missionary Epistle
Colossians	Deity of Jesus
I Thessalonians	The Lord's Second Coming
II Thessalonians	The Lord's Second Coming
I Timothy	The Care of the Church in Ephesus
II Timothy	Paul's Final Word
Titus	The Churches of Crete
Philemon	Conversion of a Runaway Slave
Hebrews	Christ the Mediator of a New Covenant
James	Good Works
I Peter	To a Persecuted Church
II Peter	Prediction of Apostasy
I John	Love
II John	Caution against False Teachers
III John	Rejection of John's Helpers
Jude	Imminent Apostasy
Revelation	Ultimate Triumph of Christ

RELATIVE SIZE OF BIBLE BOOKS

There are 1189 chapters in the Bible: 929 in the Old Testament; 260 in the New Testament.

The Longest Chapter is Psalm 119. The Shortest Chapter is Psalm 117, which is also the Middle Chapter of the Bible.

The Longest Verse is Esther 8:9. The Shortest Verse, John 11:35.

Inasmuch as Chapters vary in length, Relative Size of Books is indicated by Number of Pages rather than by Number of Chapters. This table, made from a Bible having 1281 pages, shows Relative Size of Books:

	Chapters	*Pages*		*Chapters*	*Pages*
Genesis	50	58	Nahum	3	2
Exodus	40	49	Habakkuk	3	3
Leviticus	27	36	Zephaniah	3	3
Numbers	36	51	Haggai	2	2
Deuteronomy	34	48	Zechariah	14	10
Joshua	24	29	Malachi	4	3
Judges	21	30	Matthew	28	37
Ruth	4	4	Mark	16	23
I Samuel	31	38	Luke	24	40
II Samuel	24	32	John	21	29
I Kings	22	36	Acts	28	38
II Kings	25	35	Romans	16	15
I Chronicles	29	33	I Corinthians	16	14
II Chronicles	36	40	II Corinthians	13	10
Ezra	10	12	Galatians	6	5
Nehemiah	13	17	Ephesians	6	5
Esther	10	9	Philippians	4	4
Job	42	40	Colossians	4	4
Psalms	150	98	I Thessalonians	5	3
Proverbs	31	34	II Thessalonians	3	2
Ecclesiastes	12	9	I Timothy	6	4
Song	8	6	II Timothy	4	3
Isaiah	66	57	Titus	3	2
Jeremiah	52	65	Philemon	1	1
Lamentations	5	7	Hebrews	13	12
Ezekiel	48	59	James	5	4
Daniel	12	18	I Peter	5	4
Hosea	14	8	II Peter	3	3
Joel	3	3	I John	5	4
Amos	9	6	II John	1	1
Obadiah	1	1	III John	1	1
Jonah	4	2	Jude	1	1
Micah	7	5	Revelation	22	19

In above mentioned copy

The Old Testament has	993 pages	Prophetic books	254 pages
The New Testament	288 pages	Pentateuch	237 pages
Historical books	552 pages	Gospels	129 pages
Poetical books	187 pages	Epistles	102 pages

THREE BASIC THOUGHTS OF OLD TESTAMENT

1. God's Promise to Abraham:

That in His Seed All Nations should be Blessed.

God founded the Hebrew Nation for the specific purpose of making it a Messianic Nation to the World, that is, a nation through which Great Blessings would come to All Nations.

2. God's Covenant with the Hebrew Nation:

That, if they would Faithfully Serve Him,
they would Prosper as a nation:
That, if they Forsook Him, and served Idols,
they would be Destroyed as a nation.

All nations worshiped Idols. There were gods everywhere: gods of the sky, gods of the earth, gods of the sea, gods of the land, gods of the cities, gods of the country, gods of the mountains, gods of the valleys, male gods, female gods, families of gods.

The Old Testament is an account of God's age-long effort to establish, in a world of Idol-Worshiping nations, the IDEA that there is ONE GOD by Building a NATION around the IDEA.

3. God's Promise to David:

That His Family should Reign over God's People Forever.

When God's Nation became a Great Nation, God chose One Family in the nation, the Family of David, and began to build around that Family His Promises, that, out of That Family there would come One Great King, who would Himself personally Live Forever, and establish a Universal Kingdom of Endless Duration.

Three Steps in Progress of Old Testament Thought:

1. The Hebrew Nation was founded that through them the Whole World should be Blessed. The Messianic Nation.
2. The way the Hebrew Nation would Bless the World would be through the family of David. The Messianic Family.
3. The way the Family would Bless the World would be through One Great King to be born in the Family. The Messiah.

Thus:

In founding the Hebrew Nation,
God's ULTIMATE object
Was to bring Christ into the world:
God's IMMEDIATE object
Was to establish, in a world of Idolatry,
As a background to the coming of Christ,
The Idea that there is One True Living God.

OLD TESTAMENT CHRONOLOGY

The "Received Chronology"

Dates found in margins of some Bibles are not a part of Bible text. They were worked out by Archbishop Usher, A.D. 1650. He dates Adam at 4004 B.C. The Flood, 2348 B.C. Abraham's birth, 1996 B.C. The Exodus, 1491 B.C. Solomon's Temple, 1012 B.C.

The Period from Adam to Abraham

In Genesis 5, the figures appear to make 1656 years from Adam to the Flood. In Genesis 11, the figures make 427 years from Flood to Call of Abraham. Total, 2083 years, from Adam to Abraham. (See pages 70, 84.)

The Septuagint, in Genesis 5, gives figures that add up to 2262 years, from Adam to Flood; and, in Genesis 11, figures that make 1307 years, from Flood to Abraham: total, from Adam to Abraham, 3569 years.

The Samaritan Pentateuch, in Genesis 5, gives figures that make 1307 years, from Adam to the Flood: and, in Genesis 11, figures that make 1077 years, from the Flood to Abraham: total, from Adam to Abraham, 2384 years.

Abraham's Date

Though variously placed between 2300 B.C. and 1700 B.C., Abraham's date is generally recognized as about 2000 B.C. Thus:

Adam's Date, about 4000 B.C.; or, according to the Septuagint, about 5500 B.C.; or, by the Samaritan Pentateuch, about 4300 B.C.

Flood's Date, about 2400 B.C.; or, according to the Septuagint, about 3300 B.C.; or, by the Samaritan Pentateuch, about 3000 B.C.

Other Interpretations

While the "received chronology" appears, in the main, and approximately, to harmonize with the text in our English Bibles, there are interpretations of these texts which would allow for earlier dates should discovery of new data so require. (See page 70.)

Bible Chronology and Modern Science

There is a widely held present day opinion that man has been on the earth much longer than the Bible indicates.

The two oldest civilizations are those of Babylonia and Egypt. Upon purely archaeological evidence, apart from Biblical statements, the beginning of the HISTORIC period in Babylonia is variously placed between 5000 B.C. and 2400 B.C., mostly about 3400 B.C. The beginning of the HISTORIC period in Egypt, between 5500 B.C. and 2000 B.C. most historians centering it around 3000 B.C. As for the PRE-Historic period in both countries, opinions vary from a few centuries to fanciful guesses of untold ages. The Euphrates and

Nile valleys are now known to have been of comparatively recent formation, not ante-dating 7000 B.C. Archaeology and history show that in these valleys man appeared rather suddenly, with a well-developed civilization right at the start. There are many scholars who think there is no conclusive evidence yet produced that man has been on earth longer than the traditional Biblical 6000 years.

The "Millennium-Sabbath" Theory

The Epistle of Barnabas, in the beginning of the Christian Era, mentioned a belief then held that, even as there had been 2000 years from Adam to Abraham, and 2000 years from Abraham to Christ, so there would be 2000 years for the Christian Era, and then would come the Millennium even as the 6 days of creation were followed by the Day of Rest. Inasmuch as we are now drawing toward the close of 2000 years of the Christian Era, it will soon be known for sure what there is to this belief. There are many things now on the horizon that seem to be saying that the Great Day may be nearer than we think.

Period from Abraham to the Exodus

645 years or 430 years. Exodus 12:40 says "430 years in Egypt." The Septuagint and Samaritan add, "and in Canaan." The period between Abraham's entrance into Canaan and Jacob's migration to Egypt was 215 years, Genesis 12:4; 21:5; 25:26; 47:9. But Genesis 15:13; Acts 7:6; and Galatians 3:17 seem to leave it uncertain whether to include the 215 years in, or add it to, the 430 years.

Date of the Exodus

This depends, in part, on how the figures in preceding and following periods are interpreted, and, in part, on its relation to Egyptian chronology. Opinion now seems to be pretty well divided between about 1450 B.C. and 1230 B.C. (See more fully pages 113–117.)

Period from the Exodus to Solomon's Temple

In I Kings 6:1 it is said that Solomon's 4th year was the 480th year since Israel had come out of Egypt. Accepting 1450 B.C. as a probable approximate date of the Exodus, and 970 B.C. as a probable approximate date of the 4th year of Solomon's reign, there are exactly 480 years between. However, the figures in the book of Judges, of alternate oppressions and deliverances, appear to make a total of 410 years. This, added to the 40 years of Wilderness Wandering, an unnamed number of years of Joshua's leadership, the judgeships of Eli and of Samuel, the 40 years of Saul's reign, and 40 years of David's reign, approximate a total of some 600 years. Some of these must have overlapped. (See page 168.)

IMPORTANT OLD TESTAMENT DATES

To fix in the memory

The earlier dates here given are in round numbers, and only approximate, and somewhat uncertain. (See preceding two pages.) They are, however, sufficiently accurate to show the historical sequence of events and persons; and they should be thoroughly memorized by every one who wishes to familiarize himself with the Bible.

Adam	About 4000 B.C.
The Flood	About 2400 B.C.
Abraham	About 2000 B.C.
Jacob	About 1900 B.C.
Joseph	About 1800 B.C.
Moses	About 1400 B.C.
The Exodus	About 1400 B.C.
Ruth	About 1150 B.C.
Samuel	About 1100 B.C.
Saul	About 1053 B.C.
David	About 1013 B.C.
Solomon	About 973 B.C.
Division of the Kingdom (See under I Kings 12)	About 933 B.C.
Galilee Captivity	About 734 B.C.
Captivity of Israel	About 721 B.C.
Judah Conquered by Babylon	About 606 B.C.
Jehoiachin's Captivity	About 597 B.C.
Destruction of Jerusalem	About 586 B.C.
Return from Captivity	About 536 B.C.
Temple Rebuilt	About 520 B.C.
Esther becomes Queen of Persia	About 478 B.C.
Ezra Goes to Jerusalem	About 457 B.C.
Nehemiah Rebuilds the Wall	About 444 B.C.

Periods

Ante-Diluvian World	About	1600 years	4000–2400 B.C.
Between Flood and Abraham	About	400 years	2400–2000 B.C.
Patriarchs: Abraham, Isaac, Jacob	About	200 years	2000–1800 B.C.
Israel's Sojourn in Egypt	About	400 years	1800–1400 B.C.
Period of the Judges	About	300 years	1400–1100 B.C.
The Kingdom: Saul, David, Solomon	About	120 years	1053– 933 B.C.
The Divided Kingdom	About	200 years	933– 721 B.C.
The Captivity	About	70 years	606– 536 B.C.
Period of Restoration	About	100 years	536– 432 B.C.

APPROXIMATE VALUES OF BIBLE WEIGHTS, MEASURES, MONEY

Bath, about 9 gallons, unit of liquid measure
Bekah, ¼ of an ounce
Cab, 2 quarts
Cubit, about 18 inches
Daric, gold, $5; silver, 64 cents (same as shekel)
Day's journey, about 20 miles
Denarius, 16 cents
Didrachma, 32 cents
Digit, ¾ of an inch
Drachma, 16 cents
Ephah, about 1 bushel, unit of dry measure
Farthing, ¼ cent, or 1 cent. Two different words for "farthing"
Fathom, 6 feet
Firkin, 9 gallons
Furlong, ⅛ of a mile
Gerah, 1/40 of an ounce
Half-shekel, 32 cents
Handbreadth, 3 inches
Hin, 6 quarts
Homer, 90 gallons liquid measure, 11 bushels dry measure
Kab, 2 quarts
Kor, 90 gallons, or 11 bushels
Lethech, about 5½ bushels
Log, 1 pint
Maneh, about 2 pounds
Mite, ⅛ of a cent
Omer, 7 pints
Pound, $16
Pound of silver, about $20, or $40. Two standards
Pound of gold, about $300, or $600. Ratio of silver to gold, 15 to 1
Reed, about 11 feet
Sabbath Day's Journey, about 1 mile
Seah, 1½ pecks
Shekel, ½ ounce, unit of weight
Shekel, 64 cents, unit of money
Span, about 9 inches
Stadium, about 1/7 mile
Talent, about $1000
Talent of silver, about 100 pounds, or 50 pounds; $1250, or $2500
Talent of gold, about 120 pounds, or 60 pounds; $20,000, or $40,000

CANAAN

The Land of Bible Story

South Half of East Border of Mediterranean Sea. About 150 miles long, North and South, average width, East and West, about 50 miles. A ribbon of fertile land between Desert and Sea.

Parallel to East shore of Mediterranean are two mountain ranges, with a valley between. Rains and rivers, provided by these ranges, make the fertile belt between Desert and Sea.

The Lebanon Mountains, opposite Tyre and Sidon, are the center and high point of these ranges. From their snow-covered peaks flow enormous quantities of water in all directions.

The Orontes river, flowing North, made Antioch. The Abana, flowing East, made Damascus. The Leontes (Litany), flowing West, made Tyre and Sidon. And the Jordan, flowing South, made Canaan, a "land flowing with milk and honey."

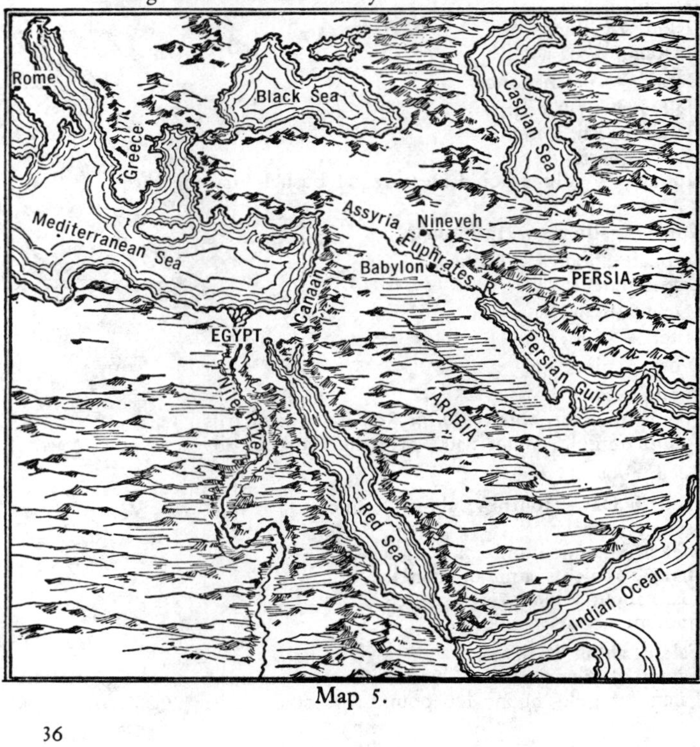

Map 5.

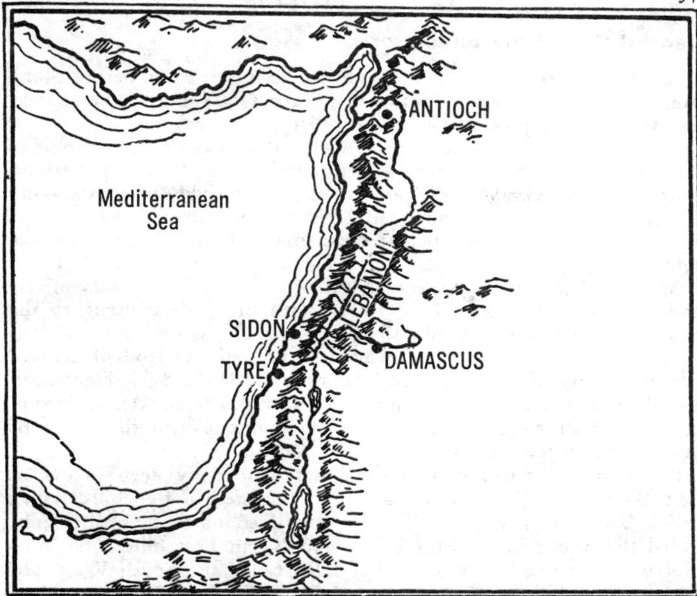

Map 6.

Canaan was on the highway between the Euphrates Valley and Egypt, the two principal Centers of Population in the ancient world. It was the geographic center, and meeting place, of Egyptian, Babylonian, Assyrian, Persian, Greek, and Roman cultures; a strategic and protected location, in the hub of these mighty civilizations that made ancient history. Here Israel was planted, to represent God among the nations.

The Euphrates Valley

Original Home of Man, was Seat of Three World Powers:
Assyria occupied the North part of the Valley
Babylon occupied the South part of the Valley
Persia was on the East border of the Valley
Egypt was a world-power 1600–1200 B.C.
Assyria was a world-power 900–607 B.C.
Babylon was a world-power 606–536 B.C.
Persia was a world-power 536–330 B.C.

Israel was:

Nurtured in Egypt in the day of Egypt's power
Destroyed by Assyria and Babylon in the day of their power
Restored by Persia in the day of Persia's power

JERUSALEM

Central City of the Bible Story

Jerusalem seems to have been chosen of God, even before Abraham came, to be Earthly Headquarters for God's work among men; for Melchizedek was already there (Genesis 14:18).

If, as Hebrew tradition holds, Melchizedek was Shem, survivor of the Pre-Flood world, oldest living man, priest, in the patriarchal period, of the whole living population of the earth—then, sometime previous to Abraham's coming, Melchizedek had already come out of Babylonia, to take possession, in the name of God, of this particular spot.

Melchizedek may have known Abraham as a boy, back in Ur, and may have had something to do with his Call to come to this Promised Land, which God had chosen for His work.

Jerusalem was located in the South center of the land of Canaan, on the summit of the water-shed between Jordan and Mediterranean, about 20 miles from Jordan, and about 40 miles from Mediterranean, in a region protected on the West by mountains, on the South by desert, and on the East by the Jordan gorge.

It was built on a mountain ridge, surrounded by deep valleys on East, South, and West sides. The ridge consisted of two hills, with a valley between. The East Hill was composed of three smaller hills, called the South East, Central East and North East hills. The West Hill was composed of two smaller hills, called the South West, and North West hills. And, being just off the Coastal Highway, where world civilizations met, it was well-suited to be chief seat of God's work among the nations.

Map 7. Air-View of Jerusalem Ridge, Looking Northwest.

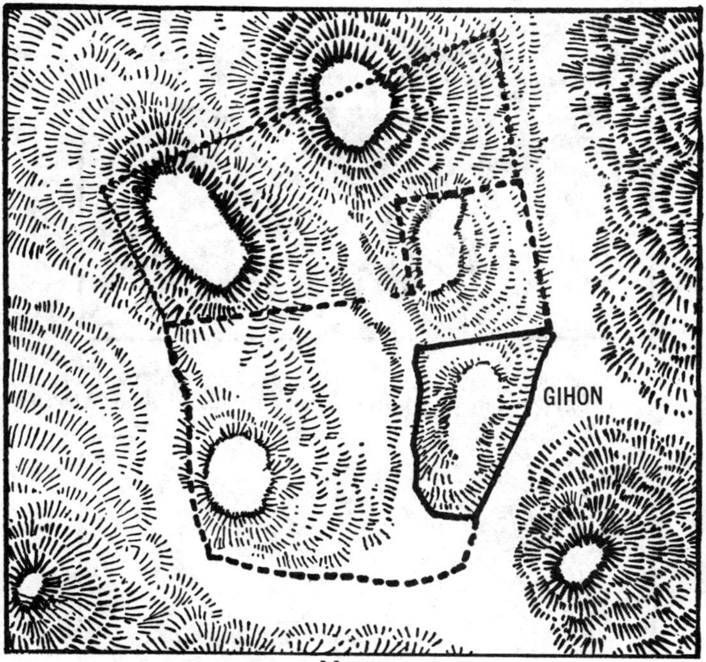

Map 8.

The city originally stood on the South East Hill. Its naturally impregnable position, with a spring of water, Gihon, at foot of hill, made it a very desirable location for a walled city.

On South East Hill stood Melchizedek's city. On Central East Hill, called Moriah, Isaac is said to have been offered; and on it, 1000 years later, Solomon's Temple was built. On the North East Hill, 1000 years still later, Jesus was crucified.

On the Map, the heavy line indicates the city of Melchizedek and Abraham. The dotted line above it indicates the larger city of David and Solomon. And the lighter dotted line further above shows the still larger city of Jesus' time.

From Jerusalem: Egypt was about 300 miles Southwest; Assyria, 700 miles Northeast; Babylon, 700 miles East; Persia, 1000 miles East; Greece, 800 miles Northwest; Rome, 1500 miles Northwest.

David made Jerusalem Israel's national Capital, 1000 B.C.; a magnificent city. Destroyed by the Babylonians, 586 B.C. Again it was a magnificent city in Christ's day. But MURDERED Him whom it was founded to bring forth. (See further page 655.)

WORLD POWERS OF BIBLICAL TIMES

Six Great Governments dominated the Pre-Christian World. Every one was connected, one way or another, with the Bible Story.

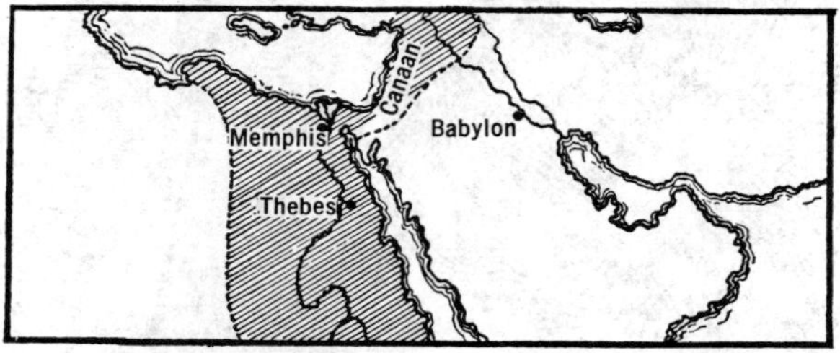

Map 9. Egyptian Empire, 1600–1200 B.C. Co-eval with Israel's Sojourn in Egypt. Here Israel grew from 70 souls to about 3,000,000.

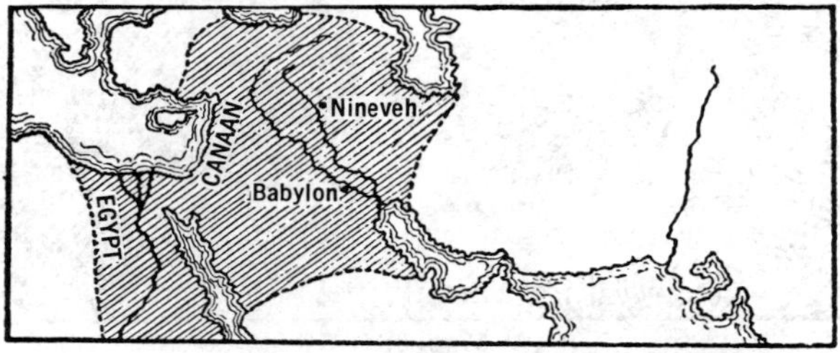

Map 10. Assyrian Empire, 900–607 B.C. Destroyed the Northern Kingdom of Israel, 721 B.C. And exacted tribute from Judah.

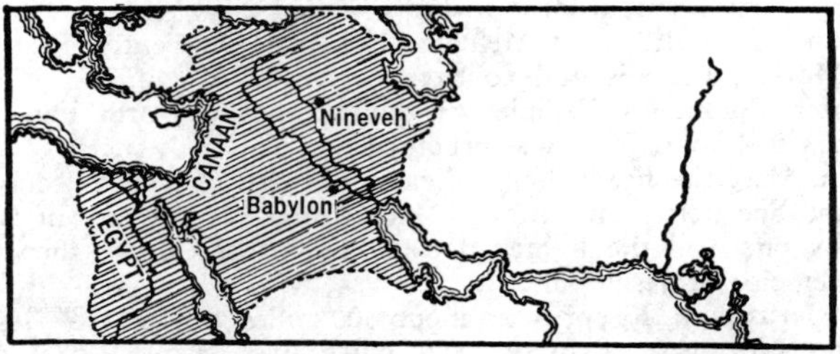

Map 11. Babylonian Empire. 606–536 B.C. Destroyed Jerusalem. Carried Judah away. Jews' Captivity co-eval with Empire.

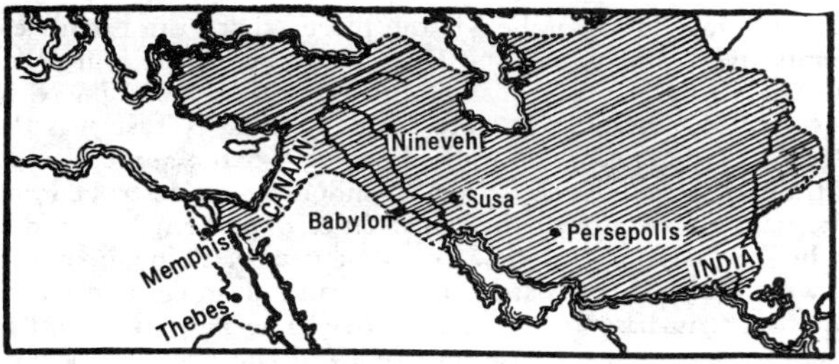

Map 12. Persian Empire. 536–330 B.C. Permitted Jews' Return from Captivity, and aided in their Re-Establishment as a Nation.

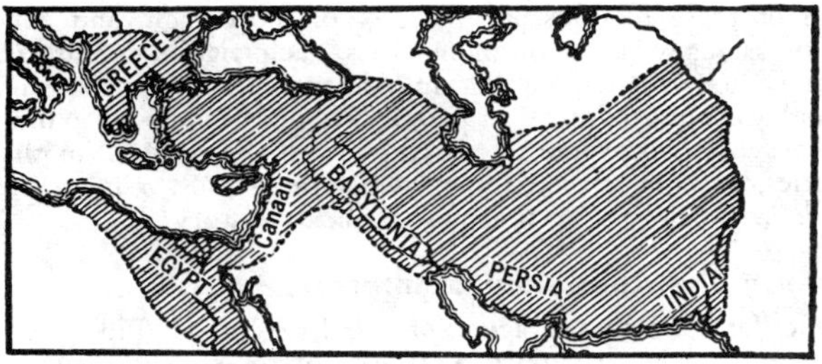

Map 13. Greek Empire. 330–146 B.C. Ruled Palestine in central period between Old and New Testaments. (See pages 402, 403.)

Map 14. Roman Empire. 146 B.C. to A.D. 476. Ruled the world when CHRIST appeared. In its day the CHURCH was formed.

ARCHAEOLOGICAL DISCOVERIES

The Euphrates Valley

The Euphrates-Tigris Valley is the place where the earth's earliest inhabitants lived, and where the Bible story begins. It is now dotted with mounds which are ruins of ancient cities, including the first cities ever built. These cities were built of brick. Refuse was thrown into streets, or dumped over walls. Houses, when repaired, would be brought up to street level. When abandoned, or destroyed in war, and afterward re-occupied, the ruins, instead of being cleared away, would be leveled off as a base for a new city. Being composed of brick, which would be partly broken and disintegrated, it would form quite a firm base for the city above. The new city would thus bury beneath itself the rubbish and relics of the previous occupation.

Thus the mounds grew higher and wider, city on top of city. When finally abandoned, the brick, beaten by rains, disintegrated; a coating of earth formed; and, covered by sandstorms, these mounds contain secrets of the life and civilization of the peoples who successively inhabited them.

Some of these mounds are 100 feet or more high, and cover remains of as many as 20 or more cities, each city a definite distinct stratum of its own, containing Implements, Pottery, Rubbish, Records, and various Relics of its people. Digging in these mound ruins, in recent years, archaeologists have gone to the bottom, to the very first cities, and uncovered things which in a most remarkable way Confirm, Supplement, or Illustrate Biblical History.

Beginning of Archaeological Interest

Claude James Rich, an agent of the British East India Company, residing at Baghdad, 50 miles Northeast of the site of ancient Babylon, his curiosity aroused by some inscribed bricks brought in by a fellow-agent, visited the site, 1811. He stayed 10 days; located, and charted, the vast collection of mounds which had been Babylon; and, with the help of natives, dug into the mounds, and secured a few tablets, which he carried back to Baghdad.

In 1820 he visited Mosul, and spent 4 months sketching a plan of the mounds just across the river, which he suspected were the ruins of Nineveh; and collected tablets and inscriptions which neither he nor any one else could read.

Paul Emil Botta, French consul at Mosul, began digging in these mounds, 1842; and in the following 10 years laid bare the magnificent palace of Sargon at Khorsabad.

Sir Austen Henry Layard, an Englishman, called the "father of Assyriology," discovered, 1845–51, at Nineveh and Calah, ruins of palaces of five Assyrian kings who are named in the Bible, and the great library of Assur-banipal, which is estimated to have contained 100,000 volumes.

Since then scores of expeditions, British, French, German, and American, have been digging in various mound ruins of the Euphrates-Tigris valley; and have found hundreds of thousands of inscribed tablets and monuments that were made in the early days of the human race. The work still goes on; and a steady stream of ancient inscriptions continues to pour into the great museums of the world.

These inscriptions were in a language that had long since passed out of use, and had been forgotten. But they were so important that scholars became greatly interested in their decipherment.

The Behistun Rock, Key to Babylonian Language

In 1835 Sir Henry Rawlinson, a British army officer, noticed, on Behistun mountain, 200 miles Northeast of Babylon, a great isolated rock, rising 1700 feet out of the plain; and, on the face of this rock, on a perpendicular cliff, 400 feet above the road, a Smoothed Surface with Carvings. He investigated, and found it to be an inscription, engraved, 516 B.C., by the order of Darius, king of Persia, 521–485 B.C., same Darius under whom the Temple in Jerusalem was rebuilt, as told in Ezra, the same year the Temple was completed.

This inscription gave a long account, in Persian, Elamite, and Babylonian languages, of the conquests of Darius. Rawlinson had some knowledge of Persian; and, assuming that it was the same inscription in three languages, with amazing perseverance, over a period of 4 years, he climbed the rock, and, standing on a ledge about a foot wide at the bottom of the inscription, with aid of ladders from below, and swings from above, he made squeezes of the inscriptions.

In 14 years more translations were completed. He had found the Key to the ancient Babylonian Language, and unlocked to the world the vast treasures of ancient Babylonian literature.

Map 15.

Fig. 1. Behistun Rock.
(*Courtesy University Museum.*)

Writing

Until recent years it was commonly believed that Writing was unknown in the early days of Old Testament history. This was one of the bases of the modern critical theory that some of the Old Testament books were written long After the events they describe, thus embodying only Oral Tradition. But now the spade of the archaeologist has revealed that WRITTEN records of important events were made from the dawn of history.

Ante-Diluvian Origin of Writing

Berosus related a tradition that Xisuthrus, the Babylonian Noah, buried the Sacred Writings before the Flood, on tablets of baked clay, at Sippar, and afterward dug them up. There was a tradition among Arabs and Jews that Enoch invented Writing, and left a number of books. An ancient Babylonian king recorded that "he loved to read the Writings of the age before the Flood." Assurbanipal, founder of Nineveh's great Library, referred to "inscriptions of the time before the Flood."

Ante-Diluvian Books

Some Pre-Flood inscriptions have been found. Figure 2 is a pictographic tablet found, by Dr. Langdon, at Kish, under the Flood deposit. Figure 3, seals found, by Dr. Schmidt, at Fara, under the Flood layer. Dr. Woolley found Pre-Flood seals at Ur.

Seals were the earliest form of writing, representing a person's name, identifying ownership, serving as a signature on letters, contracts, receipts, and various kinds of writing. Each person had his own seal. Seals were carved by delicate saws or drills on small pieces of stone or metal. In use they were impressed on clay tablets, while the clay was yet soft.

Fig. 2. Pre-Flood Tablet, Kish. (*Courtesy Ashmolean Museum.*)

Fig. 3. Pre-Flood Seals, Fara. (*Courtesy University Museum.*)

Pictographic Writing

Writing began when God put a "mark" or "sign" on Cain. That mark stood for an Idea. Thus "marks," "signs," "pictures" came to be used to record ideas, words and combinations of words. These pictures were painted or engraved on pottery or clay tablets. This is the kind of writing found in lowest levels of Pre-Historic cities of Babylonia. Pictures on clay tablets.

Original Extent of Writing

It seems that Writing, whenever it was invented, was used, at first, and for a while, only by scribes in main centers of population. As families migrated away from settled communities, into unsettled territory, there grew up, outside the sphere of Recorded events, all kinds of gross, pantheistic, idolatrous, and absurd traditions based on what had been original fact.

Cuneiform Writing

At first a certain kind of mark stood for a Whole Word, or Combination of Words. As the art of writing developed, "marks" came to stand for Parts of Words, or Syllables. This was the kind of writing in use in Babylonia at the dawn of the Historic period. There were over 500 different marks, with some 30,000 combinations. Generally these marks were made on soft clay bricks or tablets, from an inch to 20 inches long, about two-thirds as wide, written on both sides; and then sun-dried or baked.

Alphabetic Writing

Was a further development, in which "marks" came to stand for Parts of Syllables, or Letters; a greatly simplified form of Writing, in which, with 26 different marks, could be expressed all the different words which it had taken 500 of the Cuneiform marks to express. Alphabetic writing began before 1500 B.C. (See page 54.)

Writing Material

The words, "Writing," "Book," "Ink," are common to all branches of the Semitic language; which seems to indicate that Writing in a Book with Ink must have been known to the earliest Semites before they separated into their various races. In Babylonia it was mostly on Clay Tablets. The Egyptians used Stone, Leather and Papyrus. Papyrus, the forerunner of Paper, was made from reeds which grew in marshes, 2 to 3 inches in diameter, and 10 to 15 feet high. It was sliced, and placed crossways, in alternate layers, moistened, and pressed, and made into sheets, or rolls, usually about a foot wide, and 1 to 10 feet long. Broken Pottery was sometimes used for writing.

Pre-Abrahamic Books

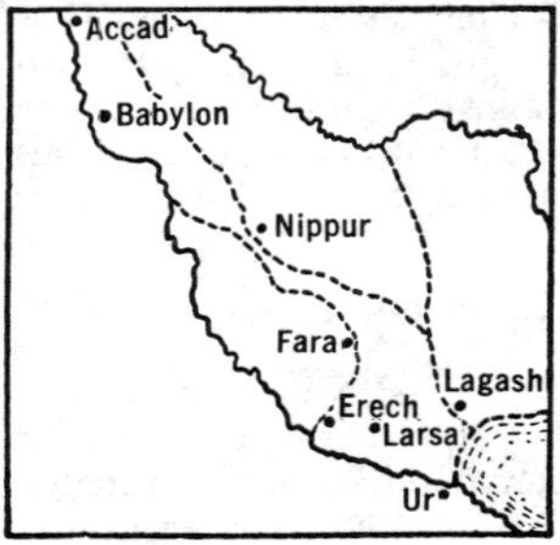

Map 16.

The earliest centers of population, after the Flood, as told on pages 85 and 86, were in Babylonia, at Kish, Erech, Lagash, Accad, Ur, Babylon, Eridu, Nippur, Larsa and Fara.

In ruins of these cities thousands of books have been found, which were written, on stone, or clay tablets, before the days of Abraham. Five of the more famous ones are here shown.

Annipadda's Foundation Tablet, Figure 4. This is a marble slab, 3 by 4 inches. It was found by Woolley, (1923) in a corner stone of a temple in 'Obeid, 4 miles west of Ur. It has this inscription: "Annipadda, king of Ur, son of Messanipadda, has built this for his lady Nin-Kharsag" (Mother-Goddess). This tablet is now in the British Museum. A replica is in the University Museum.

Fig. 4. Foundation Tablet.
(*Courtesy University Museum.*)

This inscription was hailed as the "Oldest Historical Document" ever found. Plenty of older tablets had been discovered. But this was the oldest WRITTEN RECORD of a CONTEMPORANEOUS EVENT. It marks the dividing line, in Babylonian annals, between the "historic" and "prehistoric" periods. (See further page 85.)

Ur-Nina's Family Portrait, Figure 5, king of Lagash, his sons and servants; grandfather of Eannatum, with inscriptions explaining it.

Stela of En-hedu-anna, Figure 6, daughter of Sargon, with inscription that she was priestess of the Moon Goddess at Ur.

Eannatum's Stele of the Vultures, Figure 7. Found at Lagash, by Sarzec. Now in the Louvre, at Paris. Records his victories over the Elamites, and depicts his way of fighting: leading his warriors in a wedge-like formation, armed with lances, shields and helmets.

Stele of Ur-Nammur, Figure 8. A limestone slab, 10 feet high, 5 feet wide. Found on the floor of the Hall of Justice in Ur. Now in the University Museum of Pennsylvania. Describes the building of the Ziggurat, when Ur was in its glory. Called "Stele of the Flying Angels," because angels are carved floating above the head of the king.

All this has a bearing on the human authorship of the early books of the Bible. It shows that the practice of Recording important events was in common use from the dawn of history, making it certain that the early events of the book of Genesis Could Have Been, and Most Likely Were, Recorded in Contemporaneous Documents; making it more and more easy to believe that from the very beginning, God formed the Nucleus of His Word, and watched over its transmission and growth from age to age.

Fig. 5. Ur-Nina. Fig. 6. Sargon's Daughter.
(*Courtesy of the University Museum of Pennsylvania.*)

Fig. 7. Stele of Eannatum. Fig. 8. Stele of Ur-Nammur.
(*Courtesy of the University Museum of Pennsylvania.*)

Books and Libraries of Primitive Babylonia

Babylonia was the Cradle of the Human Race, Site of the Garden of Eden, Scene of the Beginning of the Bible Story, Center of the Flood Area, Home of Adam, Noah and Abraham. Its early history is exceedingly interesting to Bible students.

Babylonia was at the mouth of the Euphrates and Tigris rivers; about 250 miles long, 50 miles wide; formed by alluvial deposit from these two rivers; drained marshlands of unbelievable fertility; for many centuries the center of a dense population. It is now, for the most part, a desert waste.

Accad

Also called Sippar, Akkad, Agade, Abu Habba. One of Nimrod's cities (Genesis 10:10). Capital of 8th Pre-Flood king (see page 72). Capital of Sargon's Empire (see page 87). 30 miles northwest of Babylon. One of the places where Hammurabi's laws were set up. "Sippar," one of its names, means "Book Town," which indicates that it was famous for its Libraries. It was the place where, tradition says, the Sacred Writings were buried before the Flood, and afterward dug up. Its ruins were excavated (1881) by Rassam, and (1894) by Scheil. 60,000 tablets were found, among them a whole library of 30,000 tablets.

Lagash

Also called Tello, Shirpurla. About 50 miles north of Ur. Capital of one of the first kingdoms after the Flood (see page 87). Excavated by Sarzec (1877-1901). A great Library center. More inscriptions found there than at any other place.

Nippur

Also called Nuffar, Calneh, 50 miles southeast of Babylon. One of Nimrod's cities. Excavated by the University of Pennsylvania under Peters. Haynes and Hilprecht, at intervals between 1888 and 1900, who found 50,000 tablets with inscriptions made in the 3rd millennium B.C., among them one library of 20,000 volumes; archives of kings; schools with large reference cylinders mounted on revolving stands, dictionaries, cyclopaedias, complete works on law, science, religion and literature. Figure 9 is a ruin where vast libraries were found.

Fig. 9. Nippur. (*Courtesy Museum of Pennsylvania.*)

Jemdet Nasr

A Pre-Flood City, 25 miles Northeast of Babylon. Destroyed by fire about 3500 B.C. Excavated (1926), by Field Museum-Oxford University Expedition. Here Dr. Langdon found Pictographic Inscriptions which indicated to him Original Monotheism (see page 62).

Weld Dynastic Prism

First known Outline of World History. Written 2170 B.C. by a scribe named Nur-Ninsubur, giving a list of kings from the beginning of the race to his own time, including the 10 long-lived Pre-Flood kings. It is a fine prism of baked clay. Was secured by the Weld-Blundell Expedition (1922) at Larsa, just a few miles north of Ur. It is now in the Ashmolean Museum at Oxford. It was in existence over 100 years before the time of Abraham, just a few miles from Abraham's home.

Fig. 10. Weld Prism. (*Courtesy Ashmolean Museum, Oxford.*)

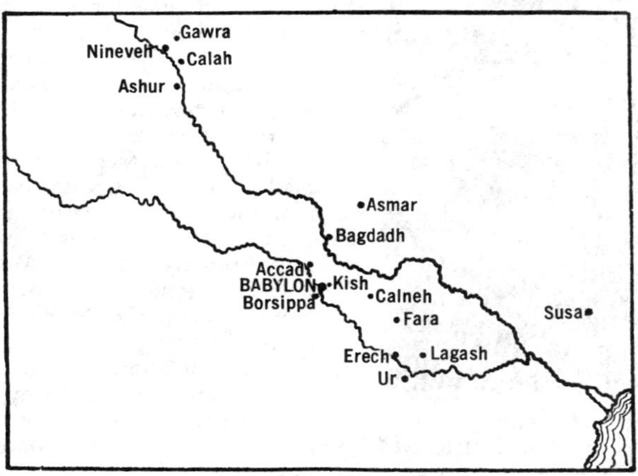

Map 17.

Books of Abraham's Day

It was at 'Obeid, 4 miles west of Ur, that Woolley found the "oldest historical" document (see page 46). Thus it is known that Abraham's community was a center of literary culture for generations before the days of Abraham.

Hammurabi's Code

Fig. 11. Hammurabi's Code. (*Courtesy Louvre Museum.*)

This Code was one of the most important archaeological discoveries ever made. Hammurabi, king of Babylon, about 2000 B.C. was a contemporary of Abraham. He is commonly identified by Assyriologists with "Amraphel" of Genesis 14, one of the kings Abraham pursued to rescue Lot. He had his scribes collect and codify the laws of his kingdom; and had these engraved on stones to be set up in the principal cities. One of these, which had been set up in Babylon, was found (1902) in the ruins of Susa by a French expedition under M. J. de Morgan. It is now in the Louvre Museum in Paris. It is a finely polished block of hard black diorite stone, 8 feet high, 2 feet wide, 1½ feet thick, somewhat oval in shape, beautifully cut, on all four sides, in cuneiform writing of Semitic Babylonian language. It has about 4000 lines, equal in subject matter to the size of the average Bible book; the longest cuneiform tablet yet discovered. It represents Hammurabi as receiving laws from the sun-god Shamash: laws dealing with the Worship of Gods, administration of Justice, Taxes, Wages, Interest, Money-lending, Property, Disputes, Marriage, Partnership, Public Works, Canal Building, Care of Canals, Regulations regarding Passenger and Freight Service by Canal and Caravan, International Commerce, and many other subjects. Here is a book, written on stone, not a copy, but the original autograph book itself, made in Abraham's day, still in existence, bearing testimony, not only to a well-developed system of jurisprudence, but also to the fact that as early as Abraham's time literary skill had reached a remarkably advanced stage.

Libraries in Abraham's Day

In Ur, Abraham's own city, in Lagash, Nippur, Sippar, indeed in every important city in Babylonia, in connection with schools and temples, there were libraries with thousands of books; Dictionaries, Grammars, Reference Works, Encyclopaedias, Official Annals, works on Mathematics, Astronomy, Geography, Religion and Politics. It was a period of great literary activity; produced many of the masterpieces which Assurbanipal had his scribes copy for his great library in Nineveh.

When Abraham visited Egypt there were millions of Inscriptions on Stone Monuments, Papyrus and Leather. In Canaan, near Hebron, city of Abraham, was a town called "Kiriath-Sepher," which means "scribe-town," indicating a people of Literary Tastes.

A School of Abraham's Day

In Ur, in the stratum of Abraham's time, Figure 12, was uncovered by Woolley, with 150 school Exercise Tablets, with Mathematical, Medical, Historical texts, and one large tablet in parallel columns with a Complete Conjugation of a Sumerian verb and its equivalent in Semitic. Abraham may have attended this school.

Abraham and the Sacred Writings

Beyond doubt Abraham must have received from Shem the Story of the Creation and Fall of Man, and of the Flood. He himself had a direct Call from God to become Founder of a Nation through which one day the whole race would be blessed. He lived in a society of Culture, Books, and Libraries. Abraham was a man of conviction and leadership. He surely must have made Careful and Accurate Copies of Accounts and Records which he had received from his ancestors; to which he added the story of his own life and God's promises to him; on Clay Tablets, in the cuneiform language, to be handed on for the Annals of the Nation which he was founding.

Fig. 12. School Room, Ur. (*Courtesy University Museum.*)

Writing in Egypt

Napoleon, in his expedition to Egypt (1798) took along about a hundred scholars. They brought back reports that aroused the interest of scientific men. J. G. Wilkinson, an Englishman, went to Thebes, lived there, and copied inscriptions on the great monuments (1821–33). He is called "Father of Egyptian Archaeology," and some of his works are still a standard of authority. Lepsius, a German, produced (1842) the first great scientific work on Egyptian Archaeology. Since then the enterprise has grown to enormous proportions.

The Rosetta Stone

Key to the Ancient Egyptian Language. The language of ancient Egypt was Hieroglyphic, picture writing, a symbol for each word. By 800 B.C. a simpler form of writing came into use, called "Demotic," which was nearer alphabetic, and which continued as the popular language till Roman times. And then both went out of use, and were forgotten. So these inscriptions were unintelligible, until the Key to their translation was found. This was the Rosetta Stone.

It was found by M. Boussard, one of the French scholars who accompanied Napoleon to Egypt (1799) at a town on the westernmost mouth of the Nile called Rosetta. It is now in the British Museum. It is black granite, about 4 feet high, 2½ feet wide, 1 foot thick, with three inscriptions, one above the other, in Greek, Egyptian Demotic, and Egyptian Hieroglyphic. The Greek was known. It was a decree of Ptolemy V, Epiphanes, made about 200 B.C., in the three languages, which were then used throughout the land, to be set

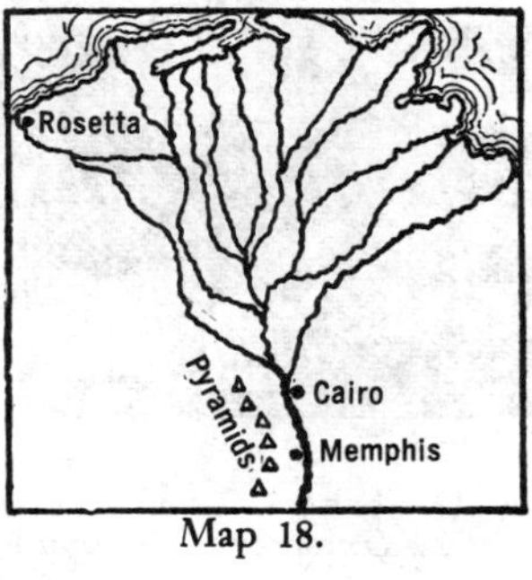

Map 18.

Fig. 13. Rosetta Stone.
(*Bettmann Archive*)

up in various cities. A French scholar, named Champollion, after four years (1818–22) of painstaking and patient labor, in comparing the known values of the Greek letters with the unknown Egyptian characters, succeeded in unraveling the mysteries of the Ancient Egyptian Language.

Literary Activity in Ancient Egypt

For a thousand years before the days of Moses the Literary Profession had been an important one, not only in Babylonia, but also in Egypt. Everything of importance was recorded. In Egypt it was on stone, leather and papyrus. Leather was used as early as the 4th dynasty. The exploits of Thothmes III, 1500 B.C. in Palestine, were recorded on rolls of very fine vellum. Papyrus was used as early as 2700 B.C. But records on stone were most durable; and every Pharaoh had the annals of his reign carved on his palace walls and monuments. There were vast libraries of state documents; and monuments galore covered with exquisite inscriptions. Figure 14 shows inscriptions on Queen Hatshepsut's Obelisk in Thebes.

Fig. 14. Hatshepsut's Obelisk.

© *Matson Photo*

The Tell-el-Amarna Tablets

In 1888 there were found in the ruins of Amarna, halfway between Memphis and Thebes, about four hundred Clay Tablets which had been a part of the royal archives of Amenhotep III and Amenhotep IV, who reigned about 1400 B.C. These Tablets are now mostly in the Museums of London and Cairo. They are from 2 to 3 inches wide, and 3 to 9 inches long, inscribed on both sides. They contain official correspondence from various kings of Palestine and Syria, written in Babylonian cuneiform script, to these two Pharaohs of Egypt. Like the Stone Tablet of Hammurabi, they constitute one of the most important archaeological discoveries of recent years.

Writing in Palestine and Border Regions

A great abundance of cuneiform inscriptions of ancient Babylonia, and hieroglyphic inscriptions of ancient Egypt, have been found; but comparatively few from ancient Palestine. This has been one of the bases of the critical theory that many of the Old Testament books were written long after the events they describe happened, thus embodying only Oral Tradition. There may have been many reasons why Hebrew kings did not go in for building vast monuments, with inscriptions to perpetuate their own glory, as others did. But in recent years many evidences have appeared that the Hebrews were a "writing" people.

Shechem. Here Sellin found Canaanite cuneiform tablets of the pre-Israel period, private documents, indicating a knowledge and use of Writing by the common people.

Earliest Alphabetic Script. In a Semitic temple, at Serabit, near the turquoise mines, in Sinai, Sir Flinders Petrie (1905) found, along with Egyptian hieroglyphic inscriptions, an inscription in Alphabetic language, the earliest Alphabetic writing known, made about 1800 B.C. This was in the country where Moses spent 40 years; and this inscription was made 400 years before Moses lived.

Gezer. Here Garstang (1929) found a jar handle of the period of 2000–1600 B.C. inscribed with letters of the Sinaitic script, indicating that the Sinaitic alphabet writing was thus early used in Palestine.

Beth-shemesh. Here Prof. Elihu Grant, of the Haverford College Archaeological Expedition (1930) found a fragment of a clay jar of about 1800 B.C. used as a memorandum with five lines of Semitic alphabetic writing in ink, similar to the Sinaitic writing.

Lachish. Here (1934) J. L. Starkey, of the Wellcome Archaeological Expedition, found an inscribed ewer, dating from about 1500 B.C. with the same Sinaitic alphabetic writing. Lachish is one of the cities that Joshua destroyed at the time "the sun stood still"; and here is a book, written on pottery, of the city before Joshua destroyed it.

Ras Shamra (Ugarit), North of Sidon, near Antioch, a Phoenician city, a seaport which linked the Euphrates with the Mediterranean, where civilizations met and mingled. A French Expedition (1929–) found a Temple Library, a school for scribes, a sort of theological seminary, with vast quantities of tablets, with dictionaries and works of reference, in 8 languages, Babylonian, Hebrew, Egyptian, Hittite,

Old Sumerian, some unknown languages, the Sinaitic script, and an alphabet of 27 letters far earlier than any previously known; many of them dating from middle of second millennium B.C.

Boghaz Keui, in Asia Minor, an early Hittite center. Here a library was found, on cuneiform and other tablets, classified and arranged in pigeon holes; in Sumerian, Accadian, Hittite, Midian, and other languages, with some bi-lingual tablets in cuneiform and Hittite.

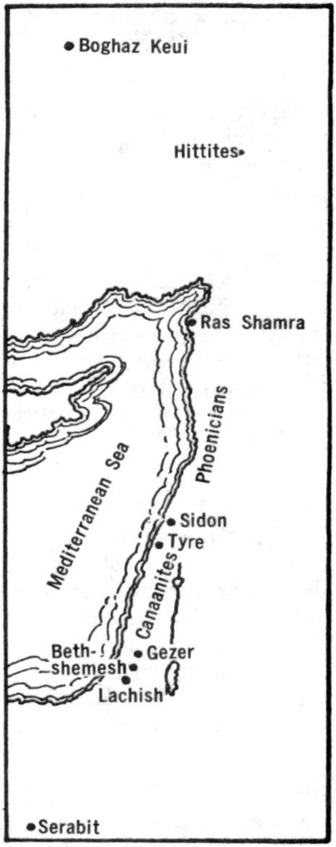

Map 19.

Thus, it is certain that writing was in common use in Palestine, Sinai, Syria and Phoenicia, for centuries before the days of Moses. Dr. W. F. Albright, leading authority on Palestinian archaeology, says, "Only a very ignorant person can now suggest that writing (in many forms) was not known in Palestine and the immediately surrounding regions during the entire second millennium B.C." (Bulletin No. 60 of the American Schools of Oriental Research, December 1935).

Hence, there is no reason why the events of the early Bible books could not have been recorded by their contemporaries.

Why, then, have these records been lost, while such vast quantities of Egyptian and Babylonian records have been preserved? Because of the perishable nature of the writing material; papyrus and leather. In Egypt also the papyrus and leather records, with a few exceptions, have perished. The Pentateuch, even if written originally on cuneiform tablets, as some have suggested, was soon translated into Hebrew and copied on leather. The ten commandments, the nucleus of the Law, were engraved on stones, but the rest written in "books" (Exodus 17:14). Thus early the Hebrews fell into the habit of using leather and papyrus, which had to be recopied as the older copies wore out.

Authorship of the Pentateuch

The Traditional View is that Moses wrote the Pentateuch substantially as we now have it, with the exception of the few verses at the close which give an account of his death, and occasional interpolations made by copyists for explanatory purposes; and that it is consistently historical.

The Modern Critical View is that it is a composite work of various schools of priests, made about the 8th century B.C. for partisan purposes, based on oral traditions, the principal redactors of which are called "J," "E" and "P." And although the critics differ widely among themselves as to just which sections to assign to these respective editors, the theory is put forth under the specious claim that it is the "assured result" of "modern scholarship." According to this view, it is not real history, but only a "patchwork picked out of a rag bag of scattered legends."

What Saith Archaeology? Archaeology has been speaking so loudly of late that it is causing a decided reaction toward the conservative view. The theory that writing was unknown in Moses' day is absolutely exploded. And every year there are being dug up in Egypt, Palestine and Mesopotamia, evidences, both in inscriptions and earth layers that the narratives of the Old Testament are true historical records. And "scholarship" is coming to have decidedly more respect for the tradition of Mosaic authorship.

This Much Is Certain: Moses could have written the Pentateuch. He was educated in the palace of Pharaoh; "instructed in all the wisdom and learning of the Egyptians," which included the literary profession. He probably knew more about previous world history than anyone now knows. He was leader and organizer of a movement which he believed to be of immense importance to all future generations. Could he have been so STUPID as to trust the annals and principles of his movement to ORAL TRANSMISSION alone? Moses did make use of writing (Exodus 17:14; 24:4; 34:27; Numbers 17:2; 33:2; Deuteronomy 6:9; 24:1, 3; 27:3, 4; 31:19, 24). As for Genesis, it seems he used records which had come down from previous generations. As for Exodus, Leviticus, Numbers and Deuteronomy; they all had to do with his own life work, and, no doubt, were written under his own personal direction. Phenomena of stratification in the record are abundantly accounted for by the use of earlier documents of such antiquity and sanctity, that Moses refrained from alteration or too damaging integration.

In What Language was the Pentateuch written? Possibly archaic Hebrew, which was in use among the Israelites in Moses' day, on leather rolls or papyrus. Or, possibly in the cuneiform language of Palestine and Syria, on clay tablets; and afterward translated into Hebrew: "its fragmentary and repetitious style, in parts, is exactly what would be expected in books translated from tablets, each of which was a book in itself." What became of the original copies? If on leather or papyrus, they wore out with use, and were replaced with new copies. If on clay tablets, possibly they may have been destroyed by some of Israel's idolatrous kings.

* * * *

From here on Notes on Archaeological Discoveries will appear in connection with Biblical Chapters on which they bear. There are over a hundred Archaeological Discoveries mentioned in this Handbook. They may be located by referring to the Alphabetical Table of Archaeological Contents at the beginning of the book or to the Summary of Archaeological Discoveries, pages 830–842 or to the Index, pages 855–860.

Many of these Archaeological Discoveries, made in recent years by those who have been digging in the ruins of Biblical cities, are records plainer than if written in a book. These records coincide exactly with Biblical narratives. Piece by piece the Old Testament is being confirmed, supplemented and illustrated. Even those things which seemed most like a myth are being shown to nave been factual.

Narratives that are susceptible to proof are being proved. Does not that enhance the trustworthiness of the Bible as a whole? And make it easier for us to rely on ALL that the Bible says? Even its wondrous promises, both for this life, and that to come.

The most important single statement in the Bible is that CHRIST ROSE FROM THE DEAD. This is the thing for which the whole Bible was written, apart from which it would mean nothing. It is the thing that gives meaning to life, apart from which life would mean nothing. It is the basis of our hope of Resurrection and Eternal Life.

Is it not comforting to know that the book which is builded around this event is being proved to be a consistently historical book? And thus make our "assurance doubly sure" that this MOST IMPORTANT EVENT of the ages is an ACTUAL FACT.

GENESIS

Beginning of World, Man, Hebrew Nation
Creation Flood Abraham Isaac Jacob Joseph

Authorship of Genesis

The age-old Hebrew and Christian tradition is that Moses, guided of God, composed Genesis out of ancient documents existent in his day. The book closes something like 300 years before Moses. Moses could have gotten this information only by direct revelation from God, or through such historical records as had been handed down from his forefathers.

Opening with the "Creation Hymn," there are then given ten "Books of Generations" which constitute the framework of Genesis. It seems that they were incorporated bodily by Moses, with such additions and explanations as he may have been guided of God to make. These eleven documents are as follows:

"Creation Hymn" (1:1–2:3).
"The Generations of the Heavens and Earth" (2:4–4:26).
"The Book of the Generations of Adam" (5:1–6:8).
"The Generations of Noah" (6:9–9:28).
"The Generations of the Sons of Noah" (10:1–11:9).
"The Generations of Shem" (11:10–26).
"The Generations of Terah" (11:27–25:11).
"The Generations of Ishmael" (25:12–18).
"The Generations of Isaac" (25:19–35:29).
"The Generations of Esau" (36:1–43).
"The Generations of Jacob" (37:2–50:26).

These eleven documents, originally family records of God's Chosen Line, and kindred families, which compose the book of Genesis, cover the first 2000 years of man's history, from the Creation of Man to the Settlement of God's Chosen People in Egypt.

The "Creation Hymn," 1:1-2:3

A poetic description, in measured, majestic movement, of the successive steps of creation, cast in the mold of the oft-recurring Biblical "seven." In all literature, scientific or otherwise, there is no sublimer account of the Origin of Things.

Who wrote the "Creation Hymn"? Used by Moses, but written, no doubt, long before, perchance by Abraham, or Noah, or Enoch or Adam. Writing was in common use ages before the days of Moses (see pages 44–55). Some of God's "commandments, statutes and laws" were in existence in the days of Abraham, 600 years before the days of Moses (Genesis 26:5).

How did the writer know what happened before man appeared? No doubt God "revealed to him the remote past as later the distant future was made known to the prophets."

Who knows but what God himself may have taught this hymn to Adam? And it may have been recited by word of mouth, around the family circle, or sung as a ritual in primitive worship (hymns constituted a large part of the very earliest forms of literature), generation after generation, till Writing was invented, God himself guarding its transmission, till finally, under the master mind of Moses, it took its place as the Opening Utterance of the Divine Book of the Ages.

If the Bible is GOD's Word, as we believe it to be, and if God knew from the beginning that He was going to use the Bible as a main instrument in the Redemption of Man, why should it be difficult to believe that God himself, co-eval with His creation of man, gave to man the germ and nucleus of that Word?

Chapter 1:1. Creation of the Universe

"In the Beginning" GOD Created the Universe. What follows, in the "Seven days," describes the Forming of substance already created, in preparation of the Earth's Surface for the Creation and Abode of Man. The creation of Man, according to Biblical chronology, was about 4000 B.C. But the creation of the Universe may have been countless ages earlier.

Who Made God?

Every child asks this question. And no one can answer it. There are some things beyond us. We cannot conceive of the Beginning of Time, nor the End of Time, nor the Boundaries of Space. The world has been in existence Always, or, it was Made out of Nothing; one, or the other; yet we can conceive of neither. This we do know: the highest of all things within reach of our thinking is Personality, Mind, Intelligence. Where did it come from? Could the Inanimate create Intelligence? In FAITH we accept, as the Ultimate in our thinking, a Power higher than ourselves, GOD, in hope that some day, in the beyond, we shall understand the mysteries of existence.

The Universe which God Created

Astronomers estimate that the Milky Way, the Galaxy to which our earth and solar system belong, contains over 30,000,000,000 suns, many of them immensely larger than our sun, which is a million and a half times larger than the earth. The Milky Way is shaped like a thin watch, its diameter from rim to rim being 200,000 light-years: a light-year is the distance that light travels in a year at the rate of 186,000 miles per second. And there are, at least, 100,000 Galaxies like the Milky Way, some of them millions of light-years apart. And all this may be only a tiny speck in what is beyond in the infinite, endless stretch of space.

Chapters 1:2 to 2:3. The Seven Days

Whether they were days of 24 hours, or long successive periods, we do not know. The word "day" has variable meanings. In 1:5 it is used as a term for Light. In 1:8, 13 it seems to mean a day of 24 hours. In 1:14, 16 it seems to mean a 12-hour day. In 2:4 it seems to cover the whole period of creation. In such passages as Joel 3:18, Acts 2:20, John 16:23, "that day" seems to mean the whole Christian era. In such passages as II Timothy 1:12 it seems to refer to the era beyond the Lord's Second Coming. And in Psalm 90:4 and II Peter 3:8, "one day is with the Lord as a thousand years, and a thousand years as one day."

This chapter is not a treatise on Science. Yet its harmony with present Biological and Zoological Knowledge is amazing.

First Day, 1:2-5

Light. Light must have been included in the "heavens and earth" that were created in the "beginning." But the earth's surface must have been still in darkness, because the cooling earthcrust, covered with boiling waters, must have sent up dense layers of mists and gases that completely shut out the sun's light. Light, and the Succession of Day and Night, were established on the Earth's Surface when the cooling processes had diminished the density of the fog sufficiently for Light to penetrate. However, the Sun itself did not become Visible till the Fourth Day.

Second Day, 1:6-8

The Firmament, called "Heaven," here means the Atmosphere, or Layer of Air, between the water-covered earth and the clouds above, made possible by the cooling of the earth's waters, still warm enough to make clouds that hid the Sun.

Third Day, 1:9-13

Land and Vegetation. The earth's surface, till now, it seems, had been wholly covered with water, because continual breaking of newly-formed thin crust must have kept the earth's surface smooth, as a liquid ball. But the crust, as it became cooler and thicker, began to buckle up, and islands and continents began to appear. No rains as yet; but dense mists watered the newly-formed land, which was still warm by its own heat. A tropical climate everywhere; and Vegetation must have grown rapidly and in gigantic proportions, which, under countless alternate submergences and upheavals, produced our present-day coal beds.

Fourth Day, 1:14-19

Sun, Moon, Stars. They must have been created "in the beginning." On the "first day" their light must have penetrated the earth's mists (1:3), while they themselves were not visible. But now, due to the lessened density of clouds, as a result of further cooling of the earth, they became Visible on earth. Seasons came when the earth's surface ceased to receive heat from within, and became dependent on the Sun as its only source of heat.

Fifth Day, 1:20-25

Sea Animals, Birds. Notice the progression: 1st, 2nd days, Inanimate things; 3rd day, Vegetable Life; 5th day, Animal Life.

Sixth Day, 1:24-31

Land Animals and MAN. The earth at last ready for Man's abode, God made Man in HIS OWN IMAGE. God saw everything that He had made, and it was "very good" (1:4, 10, 12, 18, 21, 25, 31). But soon the picture darkened. God must have known beforehand that it would, and must have regarded his whole work of the creation of man as but a step toward the glorious world that will yet issue from it, as told in the closing chapters of Revelation.

Seventh Day, 2:1-3

God Rested. Not absolutely (John 5:17), but from this particular creative work. This was a basis of the Sabbath (Exodus 20:11). It bears a mystical reference to Heaven (Hebrews 4:4, 9). On "Seven" see pages 139, 688. The number "Seven" may figure in the structure of the universe far beyond man's knowledge.

ARCHAEOLOGICAL NOTE: Babylonian Creation Stories

Epics of Creation, in various forms, on tablets which were in circulation before the time of Abraham, have been found in recent years in the ruins of Babylon, Nineveh, Nippur and Ashur, which are strikingly similar to the "Creation Hymn" of Genesis.

There are "seven" tablets (or epochs) of creation—"in the beginning" a "primeval abyss"—a "chaos of waters" called "the deep"—the gods "formed all things"—made the "upper and lower firmaments"—"established the heavens and the earth"—the 4th day "ordained the stars"—"made the grass and the green herbs to grow"—"the beasts of the field and the cattle and all living things"—on the 6th day "formed man out of the dust of the ground"—"they became living creatures"—"man with wife they dwelt"—"companions they were"—"in a garden was their dwelling"—"clothing they knew not"—the "7th" day was appointed a "holy day," and "to cease from all business commanded."

These Babylonian and Assyrian Creation stories are all grossly Polytheistic. But with so many points of similarity to the Genesis account, it would seem that they must have had a common origin. Are not these corrupted traditions a testimony to the fact of a divine original?

ARCHAEOLOGICAL NOTE: Original Monotheism

The Bible represents the human race as starting with a belief in ONE GOD, and that Polytheistic Idolatry was a later development. This is directly contrary to the present day theory that the idea of One God with a gradual development upward from Animism. The Bible view has received recent confirmation from Archaeology. Dr. Stephen Langdon, of Oxford University, has found that the earliest Babylonian inscriptions suggest that man's first religion was a belief in One God, and from that there was a rapid decline into Polytheism and Idolatry. (See Langdon's "Semitic Mythology," and the "Field Museum-Oxford University Expedition to Kish," by Henry Field, Leaflet 28).

Sir Flinders Petrie said that the Original religion of Egypt was Monotheistic.

Sayce announced (1898) that he had discovered, on three separate tablets in the British Museum, of the time of Hammurabi, the words "Jahwe (Jehovah) is God."

Leading anthropologists have recently announced that among all primitive races there was a belief in One Supreme God: (see Dr. Schmidt's "Origin and Growth of Religion—Facts and Theories").

"Generations of the Heavens and Earth," 2:4-4:26

Sometimes called the "Second Account" of Creation. It starts with a reference to the desolate condition of the earth (2:5, 6), which corresponds to the early part of the "third day" in the "first account" (1:9, 10); then gives some details omitted from the first account; and then proceeds with the story of Man's Fall. It is supplemental, not contradictory. Added details are not contradictions.

Who was the original author of this document? It carries the story down to the 6th generation of Cain's descendants (4:17–22), and closes while Adam was still alive (he lived to the 8th generation of Seth's descendants [5:4–25]). So everything in it happened in Adam's lifetime. If writing was not invented while Adam was yet alive, may it not be that Adam told these things over and over in his family circle, so that at least their substance took a sort of fixed form till writing was invented? May it not be that Moses recorded the story of Man's Fall, in the main, in the very words in which Adam himself had told it?

Chapter 2:4-17. The Garden of Eden

In chapter 1 the Creator is called "God" (Elohim), generic name of the Supreme Being. Here it is "The Lord God" (Jehovah Elohim), His personal name: first step in God's revelation of Himself.

"No Rain, but a Mist" (5, 6). This must mean that, for a while, the earth was watered by heavy fogs, because the earth's surface was so warm, and consequent vapors so dense, that cooling raindrops on the far outer fringes of the clouds would turn to vapor again before they reached the earth.

"Tree of Life" (9; 3:23) may have been an actual food of Immortality, indicating that Immortality is dependent on something outside ourselves. This Tree will again be accessible to those who have washed their robes in the blood of the Lamb (Revelation 2:7; 22:2, 14).

"Tree of the Knowledge of Good and Evil" (9, 17) was "good for food," "a delight to the eyes," and "to be desired to make one wise" (3:6). Whatever the exact nature of this Tree, literal, figurative or symbolic, the essence of Adam and Eve's sin, in part, at least, was this: Transference of Control of their lives from God to Themselves. God had, in substance, told them they could do Anything they wanted to, EXCEPT that One Thing. It was a Test of their Obedience. As long as they refrained, God was their Master. When, in spite of God's command, they did that One Thing, they made Themselves their Own Master. Is not that the Essence of Human Sin? From the beginning God designed Man to LIVE FOREVER, the one condition being Obedience to God. Man failed. Then began the long, slow process of Redemption, by a Savior, through Whom Man may regain his lost estate. Only in obedience to God is Life.

Chapter 2:18-25. The Creation of Woman

It had already been stated in 1:27 that Man was created "Male and Female." Here the manner of Woman's creation is more fully told. And here, at the start of the human race, at the outset of Sacred Writ, is ordained the divine origin and sanctity of Marriage: One Man and One Woman, One Flesh (24).

Scripture represents Marriage as an earthly counterpart of the relation between Christ and the Church (Ephesians 5:25-32; Revelation 19:7; 21:2, 9). The Church is called the "Bride" of Christ. Adam's bride was made from his side, while he was asleep (21, 22). This may be a primeval picture of the Church, Bride of Christ, being made out of "blood and water" that came from Christ's side, while He was in "sleep" on the Cross (John 19:34; I John 5:6, 8).

"Naked, and Not Ashamed" (25). It may be that they were enswathed in the ethereal Light of God, as Jesus was when he was Transfigured (Mark 9:3); and which vanished on the entrance of Sin, and which will one day again clothe the Redeemed (Revelation 3:4; 21:23). Of all God's creatures, as far as we know, Man alone wears Clothing, a badge of our sinful nature.

Location of the Garden of Eden

It was on the Euphrates and Tigris rivers, at their junction with the Pishon and Gihon (2:10-14). The Pishon and Gihon have not been identified. The Euphrates and Tigris rise in the Caucasus mountain region of southwest Asia, flow southeastward, and empty into the Persian Gulf (see map page 79).

Thus man may be said to have been created at about the center of the earth's surface; for this Caucasus-Euphrates region is approximate center of Eastern Hemisphere, which is the largest of the two Hemispheres (see Black Square on Map 1, page 24).

Ethnologists quite generally consider this region to have been the original home of all the present races of men. It was the region from whence came the ox, goat, sheep, horse, pig, dog, apple, peach, pear, plum, cherry, quince, mulberry, gooseberry, vine, olive, fig, date, almond, wheat, barley, oats, pea, bean, flax, spinach, radish, onion, and most of our fruits and vegetables. The cradle of the human race.

Babylonia

While there are some who think that the Armenian Highlands, on the headwaters of the Euphrates and Tigris, which may not have been as high above sea level as now (see map on page 79), might possibly have been the particular site of the Garden of Eden, the traditional and generally accepted site of the Garden of Eden, is Babylonia, near the mouth of the Euphrates.

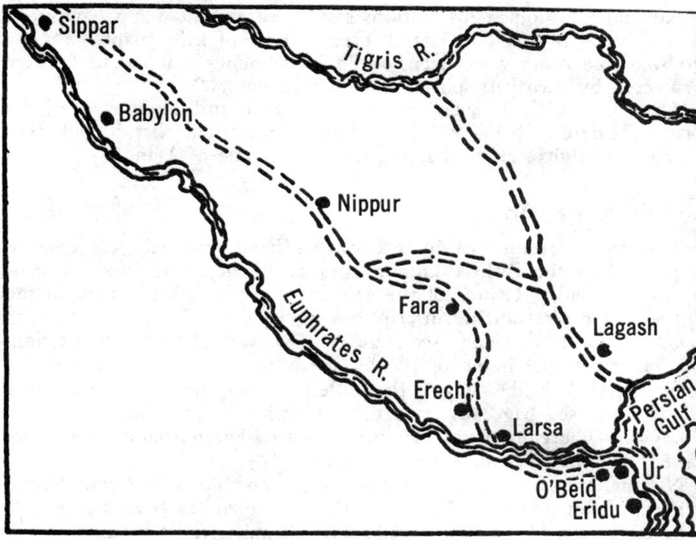

Map 20. Cradle of the Human Race

At present the Euphrates and Tigris unite about 100 miles above the Persian Gulf. In Abraham's day the Gulf extended inland as far as Ur, and the two rivers entered the Gulf by separate streams, as indicated by the Dotted lines on the map on this page. The whole Babylonian plain was made by alluvial deposit of these two rivers. The river beds changed their courses often.

In Adam's time, possibly, the two rivers may have united for a short distance, and divided again, before entering the Gulf; the Garden being on the united stream between the junction and separation of the rivers, thus making four branches, or "heads" (2:10); the two rivers continuing as the east and west coast of the Gulf, and called Gihon and Pishon. In ancient inscriptions the Persian Gulf was called a "river."

ARCHAEOLOGICAL NOTE: Eridu, Traditional Garden of Eden

The particular spot which tradition has fixed as the site of the Garden of Eden is a group of mounds, 12 miles south of Ur, known as Eridu (Abu Sharem). It was the home of "Adapa," the Babylonian Adam (see page 68). The Weld Prism says the first two kings in history reigned at Eridu (see page 71).

Ancient Babylonian inscriptions say, "Near Eridu was a garden, in which was a mysterious Sacred Tree, a Tree of Life, planted by the gods, whose roots were deep, while its branches reached to heaven, protected by guardian spirits, and no man enters."

The ruins of Eridu were excavated by Hall and Thompson, of the British Museum (1918–19). They found indications that it had been a prosperous city, revered as the Original Home of Man.

The Eridu Region

The region around Eridu, excavations have revealed, was densely populated in the earliest known ages of history, and was for centuries dominating Center of the World; a region where many of the oldest and most valuable inscriptions have been found.

Ur, home of Abraham (see pages 87, 88), was 12 miles from Eridu.

Fara, traditional home of Noah (see page 78) was 70 miles away. 'Obeid (Al 'Ubaid), where the oldest known historical document was found (see page 46), was only 15 miles from Eridu.

Lagash, where immense primitive libraries were found (see pages 48, 86) was only 60 miles from Eridu.

Nippur, library center (see page 48), was 100 miles from Eridu.

Erech, Nimrod's city (see page 87), was 50 miles from Eridu.

Larsa, where Weld Prism was found, 40 miles from Eridu.

Babylon was only 150 miles from Eridu.

Chapter 3. The Fall of Man

It was effected through the subtlety of the Serpent. The Serpent is represented as speaking as of himself. But later Scripture indicates that it was Satan speaking through the Serpent (II Corinthians 11:3, 14; Revelation 12:9; 20:2). Some have thought that originally the Serpent stood erect, and was very beautiful, and by nature fitted to be the tool of Satan. He inveigled Adam and Eve into Disobedience of their Creator. The dreadful work was done. And the pall of Sin and Gloom and Toil and Pain and Death fell upon a world which God had made beautiful.

Why Did God Make Man So That He Could Sin?

Well, is there any other way He could have made him? Could there be a Moral Creature without the power to Choose? FREEDOM is God's gift to man: Freedom to Think, Freedom of Conscience; even though man uses his freedom to Disobey God.

In a certain train wreck, the engineer, who could have saved his life by jumping, stuck to his post, and thereby saved the passengers, but lost his own life. They erected a monument, Not to the Train, for it did only what its machinery Forced it to do, but to the Engineer, who, of his own volition, Chose to give his life, to save the passengers. What virtue is there in obeying God, if, in our Nature there is no inclination to do otherwise? But if, of our Own Choice, and against the steady urge of our Nature, we obey God, there is Character in that.

But Did Not God Foreknow that Man Would Sin?

Yes; and He foreknew the fearful consequences; and He also foreknew the Ultimate Outcome. We suffer and suffer, and wonder and wonder, why God has made such a world. But one day, after all has come to Final Fruition, our Suffering will be Over, and our Wonderment will Cease, and, with the Redeemed of all ages, we will join in never-ending Hallelujahs of Praise to God for Creating us as He did, and for leading us on to Life, Joy and Glory, in the Endless Ages of Eternity (Revelation 19:1–8).

Effect of Sin on Nature

Here, in the opening pages of the Bible, we have a primeval explanation of Nature as it is today: common Hatred of Snakes (3:14, 15); Pain in Childbirth (3:15); and the earth's Spontaneous Production of Useless Weeds, while food-bearing vegetation has to be Toilsomely Cultivated (3:17–19). Also Foregleams of Christ, in the Seed of the Woman (3:15), and in Sacrifice and Atonement (4:4).

"Seed of the Woman," 15

Here, immediately after the Fall of Man, is God's prophecy that His Creation of Man would yet prove to be successful, through the "Seed of the Woman." This is the Bible's first hint of a Coming Redeemer. The use of "He" (15) shows that One Person is meant. There has been only ONE descendent of Eve who was born of Woman without being begotten of Man. Here, right at the start of the Bible story, is this foregleam of Christ; and, as the pages pass. Hints, Foregleams, Glimpses, Pictures and Plain Statements, become clearer and more abundant, so that, as we come to the end of the Old Testament, there has been drawn a fairly Complete Picture of Christ.

"The Mother of All Living" (20). On the Unity of the race in Adam is based the Atonement of Christ. One man's sin brought Death. One Man's Death brought Redemption (Romans 5:12–19).

ARCHAEOLOGICAL NOTES: Babylonian Traditions of Fall of Man

Early Babylonian inscriptions abound in references to a "tree of life," from which man was driven, by the influence of an evil spirit personified in a serpent, and to which he was prevented from returning by guardian cherubs.

Among these tablets there is a story of "Adapa," so strikingly parallel, to the Biblical story of Adam, that he is called the Babylonian Adam.—"Adapa, the seed of mankind,"—"the wise man of Eridu,"—"blameless,"—then he "offended the gods,"—"through knowledge," —then he "became mortal,"—"food of life he ate not,"—"sickness he imposed on the people,"—the gods said, "he shall not rest,"—"they clothed him with a mourning garment." See Price's "Monuments and the Old Testament."

There are two ancient Seals, figures 15 and 16, which seem to portray in Picture exactly what Genesis says in Words:

The "Temptation" Seal, Figure 15, found among ancient Babylonian tablets, now in the British Museum, seems definitely to refer to the Garden of Eden story. In the center is a Tree; on the right, a Man; on the left, a Woman, plucking Fruit; behind the Woman, a Serpent, standing errect, as if whispering to her.

The "Adam and Eve" Seal, Figure 16, found, 1932, by Dr. E. A. Speiser, of the University Museum of Pennsylvania, near the bottom of the Tepe Gawra Mound, 12 miles north of Nineveh. He dated the Seal at about 3500 B.C., and called it "strongly suggestive of the Adam and Eve story": a naked man and a naked woman, walking as if utterly down-cast and broken-hearted, followed by a serpent. The seal is about an inch in diameter, engraved on stone. It is now in the University Museum at Philadelphia.

Fig. 15. Temptation Seal
(*Courtesy of the British Museum.*)

These old records, carved on stone and clay, at the very dawn of history, in the original home of man, preserved under the dust of the ages, and now at last brought to light by the spade of the archaeologist, are evidence that the main features of the Biblical story of Adam became deeply fixed in the thought of primitive man.

Fig. 16. "Adam and Eve" Seal. (*Courtesy University Museum.*)

Other Traditions of the Fall of Man

Persian: our first parents, innocent, virtuous, and happy, lived in a Garden, where there was a Tree of Immortality, till an evil spirit in the form of a Serpent appeared.

Hindoo: In the first age man was free from evil and disease, had all his wishes, and lived long.

Greek: the first men, in the golden age, were naked, free from evil and trouble, enjoyed communion with the gods.

Chinese: had a tradition of a happy age, when men had an abundance of food, surrounded by peaceful animals.

Mongolians and Tibetans: had similar traditions.

Teutons: the primeval race enjoyed a life of perpetual festivity.

All Barbarous Races: have traditions of a more civilized state.

The original story of the Garden of Eden was, no doubt, told by Adam to Methuselah, and by Methuselah to Noah, and by Noah to his sons; and in the national cultures that followed it became variously and grossly modified.

Chapter 4. Cain and Abel

Assuming that Adam and Eve were created full-grown, Cain, when he killed Abel, must have been about 129 years old; for Seth was born soon after (4:25), at which time Adam was 130 (5:3).

Abel's Sacrifice (4:4) was acceptable, because he was righteous (I John 3:12), and because it was offered in faith (Hebrews 11:4). On the entrance of Sin, it seems, God had ordained such sacrifice. It appears to have been a sort of primeval picture of the Atoning Death of Christ.

Cain's Wife (4:17) must have been his Sister, for Eve was the "mother of all living" (3:20). Adam had unnamed sons and daughters (5:4); tradition says, 33 sons and 27 daughters.

Who was there for Cain to fear? (4:14) In the 130 years from Adam's creation to Abel's murder, a good many generations had arisen, with a total population probably of many thousands.

Cain's Sign (4:15). Whatever it was, the people must have understood what it meant. This may have been the origin of writing: the mark stood for an Idea: and, soon, different marks for different ideas.

Cain's City (4:17), somewhere east of Eden, was probably only a village of rude huts, with a wall for defense, to serve as a sort of headquarters for his outcast offspring.

Polygamy (4:19) soon followed murder, in Cain's family. God had ordained, at the start, that One man and One woman live together in marriage (2:24). But man soon managed otherwise.

ARCHAEOLOGICAL NOTE: Early Use of Metals

While Adam was yet living his descendants learned the use of copper and iron, and invented musical instruments.

Until recently the use of iron was thought to have been unknown previous to the 12th century B.C. The terms which historians and archaeologists have used to denote the successive steps in the advance of civilization are:

Palaeolithic: Early Stone Age; used unshaped stones.
Neolithic: Late Stone Age; used shaped stones, bone, wood.
Chalcolithic: Copper-Stone; transition from stone to metal.
Bronze Age: 2500–1200 B.C. Iron Age: 1200 B.C. onward.

In 1933 Dr. H. E. Frankfort, of the Oriental Institute, discovered, in the ruins of Asmar, about 100 miles northeast of Babylon, an Iron blade which had been made about 2700 B.C.; thus pushing back the known use of iron some 1,500 years.

Primitive inscriptions have revealed that Babylonia has never been inhabited with people unacquainted with the use of metals. Copper instruments have been found in the ruins of a number of pre-Flood cities, see under chapter 5.

The Weld Prism, which gives names of ten long-lived kings who reigned before the Flood, says that the 3rd, 5th, and 6th reigned at "Badgurgurru." This word means "city of workers in bronze." It may be a tradition of Cain's city, 4:17.

"The Book of the Generations of Adam," 5:1 to 6:8

The 3rd document composing the book of Genesis (see page 58). It carries the story to the 500th year of Noah's life (5:32). It may have been started by Adam, continued by Enoch and Methuselah, and completed by Noah. Copies of this and the two previous documents may have been made by Noah on clay tablets, and buried, as the tradition says (see page 44), at Sippar. Copies may have been taken into the Ark.

Chapter 5. Genealogy from Adam to Noah

Their ages are listed as follows: Adam, 930 years, Seth, 912 years, Enosh, 905 years, Kenan, 910 years, Mahalalel, 895 years, Jared, 962 years, Enoch, 365 years, Methuselah, 969 years, Lamech, 777 years, Noah, 950 years.

The Great Age to which they lived is ordinarily explained on the theory that Sin had only begun its malign influence on the race.

Figures in this chapter, with 6:6, indicate that there were 1656 years between Creation of Man and the Flood. Some think that, inasmuch as this genealogy, and that in chapter 11, each have 10 generations, they may be abbreviated, as that of Jesus in Matthew 1. But the formula, "lived–years, and begat–," is against such a theory.

Enoch, 21-24

He was the Best of Them. In a society of unspeakable wickedness, he "walked with God." Born 622 years after the creation of Adam, he was contemporary with Adam 308 years. "God took him" 69 years before the birth of Noah, while he was only 365.

The one other to be thus Translated, without having to die, was Elijah (II Kings 2): Enoch and Elijah, perhaps, being intended of God to be a sort of fore-picture of the happy fate of the saints who will still be in the flesh when the Lord Returns (I Thessalonians 4:17).

Arabs had a legend that it was Enoch who invented Writing. The New Testament refers to a Prophecy of Enoch (Jude 14).

Methuselah, 25-27

He was the Oldest of the ten (969 years), son of Enoch. His life overlapped that of Adam by 243 years and that of Shem by 98 years, thus forming a connecting link between the Garden of Eden and the Post-Flood world. He died the year of the Flood.

ARCHAEOLOGICAL NOTE: Primeval Longevity

Berosus, a Babylonian historian of 300 B.C. basing his history on archives in the Temple of Marduk, copied from primitive inscriptions, many of which have been found, named 10 long-lived kings who reigned before the Flood, each reigning from 10,000 to 60,000 years, as: Aloros, Alaparos, Amelon, Ammenon, Megalaros, Daonos, Eudorachus, Amenpsinos, Otiartes, Xisuthros. "In the time of Xisuthros," says Berosus, "the Great Deluge occurred."

The Weld Prism and Nippur Tablets (see pages 48, 49), assigning thousands of years to each reign, name the Pre-Flood kings as:

Alulim	Reigned at Eridu	28,000 years
Alalmar	Reigned at Eridu	36,000 years
Emenluanna	Reigned at Badgurgurru	43,000 years
Kichunna	Reigned at Larsa	43,000 years
Enmengalanna	Reigned at Badgurgurru	28,000 years
Dumuzi	Reigned at Badgurgurru	36,000 years
Sibzianna	Reigned at Larak	28,000 years
Emenduranna	Reigned at Sippar	21,000 years
Uburratum	Reigned at Shuruppak	18,000 years
Zinsuddu (Utnapishtim)		64,000 years

"Then the Flood overthrew the land."

These must be the same kings as those named by Berosus, known by different names after the Confusion of Tongues at Babel. The tablets that give these names were written after the Historic period began. It seems that the ancients, in speaking of their PRE-Historic times, fell into the same temptations that our moderns do, of exaggerating to vast dimensions the chronology of their primeval world.

Besides the Babylonians: Persians, Egyptians, Hindoos, Greeks, and others had traditions of the great longevity of earth's earliest inhabitants. Where could such traditions come from, except from the fact that the first men did actually live long?

ARCHAEOLOGICAL NOTE: Excavations in Pre-Flood Cities

The cities named at the top of this page, as the homes of Pre-Flood kings, have been identified, except Badgurgurru. Excavations in their ruins, and the ruins of other Pre-Flood cities, have brought to light many features of Ante-Diluvian life, and have made very real to us the world of the first few chapters of Genesis.

Among the Pre-Flood cities excavated are: Eridu, Obeid, Erech, Susa, Tepe Gawra, Ur, Kish, Fara (Shuruppak), Sippar (Accad), Larsa, Jemdet Nasr. In their ruins archaeologists have gotten very close to the beginnings of settled life in Babylonia.

Among the relics of Pre-Flood peoples found in these ruins are such things as painted pottery, flint implements, tools, turquoise vases, copper axes, copper mirrors, hoes, sickles, implements of stone, flint, quartz, fish hooks, models of boats, an underground kiln, beautiful vitrified pottery, cosmetics which pre-historic women used for darkening their eyebrows and eyelids, brick ruins of temples painted red or covered with plaster, pottery artistically painted in intricate geometric patterns and figures of birds, even a chariot, and architectural accomplishments that indicate an "astonishingly advanced civilization."

Chapter 6:1-8. Pre-Flood Wickedness

The "sons of God" (6:2) are thought to have been either fallen angels, to which there may be reference in II Peter 2:4 and Jude 6, or leaders in Sethite families who intermarried with godless descendants of Cain. These abnormal marriages, whatever they were, filled the earth with corruption and violence.

Jesus regarded the Flood as an Historical Fact, and likened the time of His Coming Again to the days of Noah (Matthew 24:37–39). What is going on in the world at the present time, makes us wonder, if, even now, those days may be returning.

The "120 years" (6:3) may mean respite to the Flood. Or, it may mean reduced span of life, from that referred to in chapter 5.

"The Generations of Noah," 6:9 to 9:28

The 4th document composing the book of Genesis (see page 58). It contains the story of the Flood, as told, and perhaps recorded, by Noah, and handed on by Shem to Abraham.

Chapter 6:9-18. Noah and the Ark

The Ark was about 450 feet long, 75 feet wide, 45 feet high. It had three decks, divided into compartments, with a window course around the top. It must have been very much the same size and proportion as ocean ships of today. Living on the banks of a great river, boat building was one of man's earliest accomplishments. Cuneiform tablets indicate that at the dawn of history the inhabitants of Babylonia engaged in river traffic. Noah's home, according to Babylonian tradition, was at Fara, on the Euphrates, about 70 miles from site of the Garden of Eden. So boatbuilding and river traffic must have been familiar to Noah from childhood.

Chapter 6:19 to 7:5. The Animals

In 6:19–21 and 7:2 it is explained that Seven pairs of Clean animals, but only One pair of each of the others, were to be taken into the Ark. Some have calculated that there was room in the Ark for 7000 species of animals.

It was a gigantic task to build the Ark, gather the animals and store the necessary food. Noah and his three sons could not have done it alone. Being grandson of Methuselah, and great grandson of Enoch, he may, as the Babylonian tradition says, have been a City-King; and may have employed thousands of men in the work. And he may have been the best part of 120 years doing it (6:3), and was undoubtedly the subject of unceasing ridicule, but undaunted in his Faith (II Peter 2:5; Hebrews 11:7).

Chapter 7:6 to 8:19. The Flood

"Fountains of the great deep were broken up, and the windows of heaven were opened" (7:11). The Euphrates Valley might almost be called the Isthmus of the Eastern Hemisphere, where the Mediterranean Sea and Indian Ocean approach each other. The Armenian Mountain country is almost like an island system, with the Caspian and Black Seas on the north, the Mediterranean on the west, and the Persian Gulf and Indian Ocean on the south. A cataclysmic subsidence of the region would cause the waters to pour in from these seas, as rain poured down from above.

Extent of the Flood

"All the high mountains that were under the whole heavens were covered. And all flesh died that moved upon the earth" (7:19, 21). This, doubtless, is the very language in which Shem related, or wrote, the story of the Flood to his children and grandchildren. He told it as he saw it. Are we to interpret his language according to his own geography? or present day geography? The whole race, except Noah and his family, were destroyed. To destroy the race it was necessary for the Flood to cover only so much of the earth as was inhabited. Accepting the Bible account as it is, there had been only TEN generations from Adam, the first man. How could ONE family, in TEN generations, with primitive modes of travel, populate the whole earth? Most likely the race had not spread far outside the Euphrates basin.

Time in the Ark

Noah went into the Ark 7 days before it began to rain (7:4, 10). It began to rain 17th day of 2nd month of Noah's 600th year (7:11). Rained 40 days (7:12). Waters prevailed 150 days (7:24; 8:3). Ark rested 17th day of 7th month (8:4). Removed Ark's Covering 1st day of 1st month of Noah's 601st year (8:13). Went out of Ark 27th day of 2nd month (8:14–19). In the Ark 1 year 17 days: 5 months floating, 7 months on mountain.

Mount Ararat

After floating some 500 miles or more from where it had started, the Ark rested on a peak in the mountains of Armenia, called Ararat, see Map page 8, about 200 miles north of Nineveh, Mt Ararat is 17,000 ft high. At its foot is a city called Naxuana, or Nakhichevan, which claims the tomb of Noah. The name means, "Here Noah settled."

Chapter 8:20 to 9:17. The Rainbow

It may be that the Flood produced a clarified air that made the Rainbow clearly visible. And God designated it as the Sign of His Covenant with mankind that there would not be another Flood (9:8–17). The earth's next destruction will be by Fire (II Peter 3:7).

Chapter 9:18-28. Noah's Prophecy

Descendants of Ham to be servant races; Shemites to preserve knowledge of the True God; Japhetic races to have largest portion of world, and to supplant Semitic races as teachers of God. It was fulfilled when Israelites took Canaan, Greeks took Sidon, and Rome conquered Carthage; and ever since Japhetic races have dominated the world, and have been converted to the God of Shem, while Semitic races have occupied a place of comparative insignificance; and Hamitic races a place of servitude. An amazing forecast!

Reported Discovery of Noah's Ark

It has been announced in a number of publications that certain Russian aviators, just prior to the Bolshevik Revolution, claimed to have seen the hulk of a gigantic ship high up in the inaccessible glacier fastnesses of Mt. Ararat; and that they reported their find to the Russian Government. Just then the Czarist Government was overthrown by the atheistic Bolsheviks, and these reports were never made public.

Babylonian Tradition of the Flood

Archives of the Temple of Marduk, in Babylon, as related by Berosus, 300 B.C., contained this story: Xisuthros, a king, was warned by one of the gods to build a ship, and take into it his friends and relatives and all different kinds of animals, with all necessary food. Whereupon he built an immense ship, which was stranded in Armenia. Upon subsidence of the Flood, he sent out birds; the third time, they returned not. He came out, builded an altar, and sacrificed.

Other Traditions

Egyptians had a legend that the gods at one time purified the earth by a great Flood, from which only a few shepherds escaped.

Greek tradition: Deucalion, warned that the gods were going to bring a flood upon the earth, for its great wickedness, built an ark, which rested on Mt. Parnassus. A dove was sent out twice.

Hindu tradition: Manu, warned, built a ship, in which he alone escaped from a Deluge which destroyed all creatures.

Chinese tradition: Fa-He, founder of Chinese civilization, is represented as having escaped from a Flood sent because man had rebelled against heaven, and his wife, 3 sons and 3 daughters.

England: Druids had a legend that the world had been re-peopled from a righteous patriarch who had been saved in a strong ship from a Flood sent to destroy man for his wickedness.

Polynesians have stories of a Flood from which 8 escaped.

Mexicans: One man, his wife and children, were saved in a ship from a Flood which overwhelmed the earth.

Peruvians: One man and one woman were saved in a box that floated on the flood waters.

American Indians: Various legends, in which 1, 3 or 8 persons were saved in a Boat above the waters on a high mountain.

Greenland: The earth once tilted over, and all men were drowned, except one man and one woman, who re-peopled the earth. (See International Standard Bible Encyclopedia.)

Universality of the Tradition

Babylonians, Assyrians, Egyptians, Persians, Hindus, Greeks, Chinese, Phrygians, Fiji Islanders, Esquimaux, Aboriginal Americans, Indians, Brazilians, Peruvians, and indeed every branch of the whole human race, Semitic, Aryan, Turanian—have traditions of a Great

Deluge that destroyed all mankind, except one family, and which impressed itself indelibly on the memory of the ancestors of all these races before they separated. "All these myths are intelligible only on the supposition that some such event did actually occur. Such a universal belief, not springing from some instinctive principle of our nature, must be based on an Historical Fact."

ARCHAEOLOGICAL NOTE: The Flood Tablets

George Smith, of the British Museum, found (1872), in tablets from the Library of Assur-banipal at Nineveh, accounts of the Flood curiously parallel to the Bible account, which had been copied from tablets dating back to the First Dynasty of Ur, a period about mid-way between the Flood and Abraham. Later, many of these ancient tablets were found. In these tablets these expressions repeatedly appear: "The Flood," "the age before the Flood," "inscriptions of the time before the Flood."

Babylonian Noah's Own Story of the Flood

It is part of what is called the Gilgamesh Epic. Gilgamesh was the 5th king of the Erech dynasty, which was one of the first dynasties after the Flood. This Epic gives the story of his adventures, one of which was a visit to the island abode of Utnapishtim, the Babylonian Noah. This visit is depicted on a seal (Figure 17) found recently at Tell Billa near Nineveh (see next page). In his reply to Gilgamesh, Utnapishtim (Noah) relates the story of the Flood and his escape from it. In substance, and in brief, it is as follows: "The assembly of the gods decided to send a Deluge. They said, On the sinner let his sin rest. O man of Shuruppak, build a ship, save your life. Construct it with six stories, each with seven parts. Smear it with bitumen inside and outside. Launch it upon the ocean. Take into the ship seed of life of every kind. I built it. With all that I had I loaded it, with silver, gold, and all living things that I had. I embarked upon the ship with my family and kindred. I closed the door. The appointed time arrived. I observed the appearance of the day. It was terrible. All light was turned to darkness. The rains poured down. The storm raged; like a battle charge on mankind. The boat trembled. The

Fig. 17. Gilgamesh Seal. (*Courtesy of the University Museum of Pennsylvania.*)

gods wept. I looked out upon the sea. All mankind was turned to clay, like logs floating about. The tempest ceased. The flood was over. The ship grounded on Mt. Zazir. On the seventh day I sent out a dove; it returned. I sent out a swallow; it returned. I sent out a raven; it alighted, it waded about; it croaked; it did not return. I disembarked. I appointed a sacrifice. The gods smelled the sweet savor. They said, Let it be done no more."

Fig. 18. Town pit where they found Flood Layer at Ur. (*Courtesy of the University Museum of Pennsylvania.*)

ARCHAEOLOGICAL NOTE: The Flood Deposit at Ur

These traditions of the Flood, though mixed with polytheism and some evident myth, show that the Flood had become a fixed fact in the memory of the early inhabitants of Babylonia. And now, within the last few years, an Actual Layer of Mud, evidently deposited by the Flood, has been found in three separate places: Ur, which was 12 miles from the traditional site of the Garden of Eden; at Fara, traditional home of Noah, 60 miles further up the river; and at Kish, a suburb of Babylon, 100 miles still further up the river; and, possibly, also at a fourth place, Nineveh, 300 miles still further up the river (see page 80).

At Ur, city of Abraham, the Joint Expedition of the University Museum of Pennsylvania and the British Museum, under the leadership of Dr. C. L. Woolley, found (1929), near the bottom of the Ur mounds, underneath several strata of human occupation, a great bed of solid water-laid clay 8 feet thick without admixture of human relic, with yet the ruins of another city buried beneath it. Dr. Woolley said that 8 feet of sediment implied a very great depth and a long period of water, that it could not have been put there by any ordinary overflow of the rivers, but only by some such vast inundation as the Biblical Flood. The civilization underneath the flood layer was so different from that above it that it indicated to Dr. Woolley "a sudden and terrific break in the continuity of history." (See Woolley's "Ur of the Chaldees.")

(For more about Ur Excavations, see pages 87–89.)

ARCHAEOLOGICAL NOTE: The Flood Deposit at Kish

Kish (Ukheimer, El-Ohemer, Uhaimir), on the east edge of Babylon, on a bed of the Euphrates which is now dry, was said, on the tablets, to have been first city rebuilt after Flood.

The Field Museum-Oxford University Joint Expedition, under the direction of Dr. Stephen Langdon, found (1928–29) a bed of clean water-laid clay, in the lower strata of the ruins of Kish, 5 feet thick, indicating a flood of vast proportions. In the center of Fig. 19 the flood layer is located just above the wall ruins. It contained no objects of any kind. Underneath it the relics represented an entirely different type of culture. Among the relics found was a four-wheeled Chariot, the wheels made of wood and copper nails, with the skeletons of the animals that drew it. (See "Field Museum-Oxford University Expedition to Kish," by Henry Field, Leaflet 28.)

Fig. 19. Ruins of Kish.
© *Matson Photo*

ARCHAEOLOGICAL NOTE: The Flood Deposit at Fara

Fara (Shuruppak, Sukkurru), home of the Babylonian Noah, about half way between Babylon and Ur. Once on the Euphrates, now 40 miles to the east. A low-lying group of mounds, beaten by the sands of the desert. Excavated (1931), by Dr. Eric Schmidt, of the Uni-

Map 21.

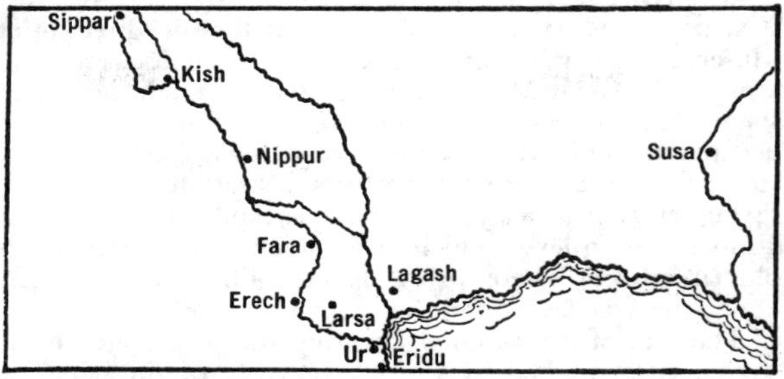

versity Museum of Pennsylvania. He found the remains of three cities: the top one, contemporaneous with the 3rd Ur dynasty (see page 87); the middle city, Early Sumerian; and the bottom city, Pre-Flood.

The Flood Layer was between the middle city and the bottom city. It consisted of yellow dirt, a mixture of sand and clay, definitely alluvial, water-laid, solid earth, without relics of human occupation, as illustrated in Figure 21. Underneath the flood deposit was a layer of charcoal and ashes, a dark colored culture refuse which may have been wall remains, painted pottery, skeletons, cylinder seals, stamp seals, pots, pans and vessels. Figure 20 shows Dr. Schmidt's men digging underneath the flood deposit. (See "University Museum Journal," September, 1931.)

Fig. 20. Under Flood Layer at Fara.

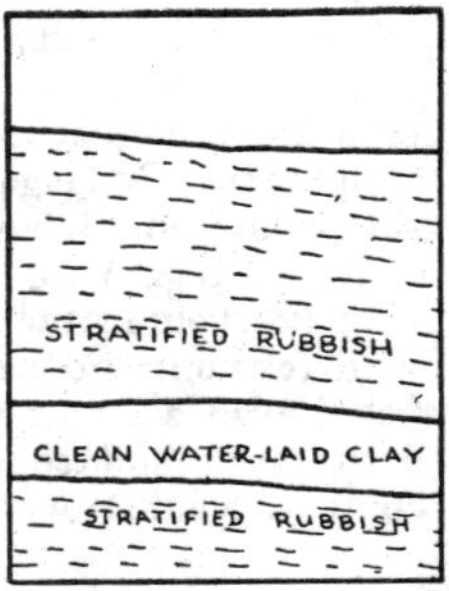

Fig. 21. Cross-section of Fara Mound.

(Courtesy University Museum.)

At Nineveh Also In "Annals of Archaeology and Anthropology," Vol. XX, pages 134–35, PI 73, M. E. L. Mallowan, director of the British Museum Excavations at Nineveh (1932–33), describing the sinking of a pit in the Great Mound, through 90 feet from the top to virgin soil, states that 70 feet of the 90 represented five pre-historic strata of occupation, and that about half-way down, between the 2nd and 3rd strata from the bottom, there was a stratum some 8 feet thick consisting of alternate layers of viscous mud and riverine sand with 13 distinct rises in level, which in his opinion, indicated a series of severe pluvial seasons. There was a distinct difference between the pottery under the wet layer, and that above it.

1. The fact of a vast flood covering the whole area of early civilization is established by the 8 foot layer of silt which cuts through the "culture levels" of all the Euphrates Valley sites.
2. Sumerian "King Lists" from Lower Mesopotamia retain the tradition of a Deluge. Phrases such as, "then the Flood swept over the earth" . . . "after the Flood," occur.
3. A Sumerian tablet of 2000 B.C. gives a full account of a Flood. One man is saved by the intervention of the gods, in a huge boat.
4. The Babylonian epic of Gilgamesh is based on this story, but is much more fully developed. The text again comes from the library of Ashurbanipal. The story in this poem is strikingly similar to the Genesis account.
5. Resemblances are factual: (i) Both accounts hold that the Deluge was a divine judgment on human transgression. (ii) That one man was warned and delivered by the device of a ship. (iii) Both accounts similarly describe the physical causes though the Bible account is more cataclysmic in its description. (iv) Both accounts speak of a mountain resting place, and two birds, the second of which fails to return. (v) Both accounts speak of worship by the survivor and blessing upon him.
6. The differences are moral, spiritual and vital: (i) The idea of God in the two accounts is vastly different—a noble conception of a righteous God against a crude polytheism. (ii) The notion of sin is different. Jehovah judges outrageous sin, but not in caprice, and with regard for the just.
7. Fact lies behind both accounts. In the Bible that fact is recorded with restraint and noble theological and ethical contents while the Babylonian account preserves a core only of the truth encrusted with myth and superstition and robbed of much of its moral content. Neither account derives from the other.

"The Generations of the Sons of Noah," 10:1 to 11:9

5th document composing Genesis (see page 58), prepared, probably, by Shem, and handed on to Abraham: Shem lived from 98 years before Flood till 150 years after birth of Abraham (11:10).

Chapter 10. Nations Descended from Noah

Noah's family dis-embarked from the Ark at Mt. Ararat, near the headwaters of the Euphrates. Then, it seems, they migrated back, 500 miles, to Babylonia, their Pre-Flood home. Then, 100 years later (10:25), were scattered by the Confusion of Tongues.

Descendants of Japheth, North Zone of Nations, 2-5

Japhethites went Northward, and settled in regions around the Black and Caspian Seas; and became progenitors of the great Caucasian races of Europe and Asia.

Descendants of Ham, South Zone of Nations, 6-20

Hamites went Southward. The names given seem to indicate South and Central Arabia, Egypt, the East Shore of the Mediterranean, and the East Coast of Africa. Canaan, son of Ham, and his descendants, settled, and gave their name to the land which later became the home land of the Jews. Egypt was called the "Land of Ham." Ham himself may have led the migration to Egypt. "Khen," an Egyptian god, was Egyptian equivalent of the Hebrew word "Ham." Egypt was called "Mizraim," the name of Ham's son. Nimrod was a Hamite (see next page).

Descendants of Shem, Central Zone of Nations, 21-31

Shemites included Jews, Assyrians, Syrians, Elamites, in north Euphrates Valley and its borders (see page 84).

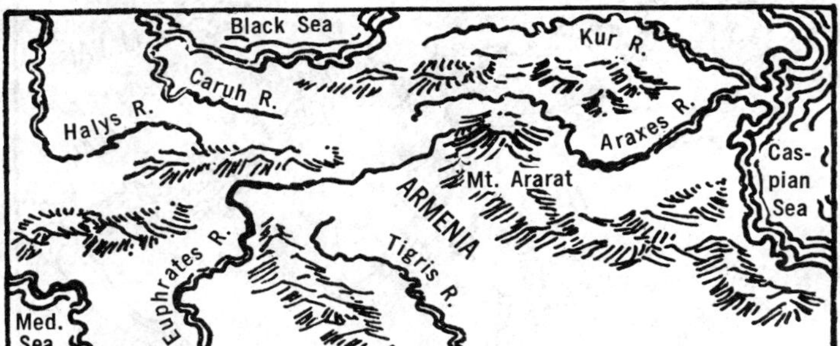

Map 22. Where Noah's Ark Landed.

Nimrod, 8-12

Nimrod was the most outstanding leader in the 400 years between the Flood and Abraham. Grandson of Ham (8), born soon after the Flood, judging by the ages mentioned in 11:10–16, he may have lived through the whole period. He was a very enterprising man.

His fame as a "mighty hunter" (10:9), meant that he was protector of the people at a time when wild animals were a continual menace. Early Babylonian seals represented a king in combat with a lion. This may be a tradition of Nimrod.

In his ambition to control the rapidly multiplying and spreading race, he seems to have been leader in the Tower of Babel enterprise (10:10; 11:9). And, after the Confusion of Tongues, and Dispersion of the People, Nimrod seems to have, later, resumed work on Babylon. Then he built three nearby cities, Erech, Accad and Calneh, and consolidated them into one kingdom under his own rule. This was the beginning of Imperialism.

Babylonia was long known as the "Land of Nimrod." He was afterward deified, his name being identical with "Merodach."

Still ambitious to control the ever-spreading race, Nimrod went 300 miles further north, and founded Nineveh (though one version says it was Asshur) and three nearby cities, Rehoboth, Calah and Resen. This constituted Nimrod's northern kingdom. For many centuries afterward, these two cities, Babylon and Nineveh, founded by Nimrod, were the Leading Cities of the World.

Cuneiform inscriptions state that Nineveh was colonized from Babylon; which is an archaeological confirmation of Genesis 10:11.

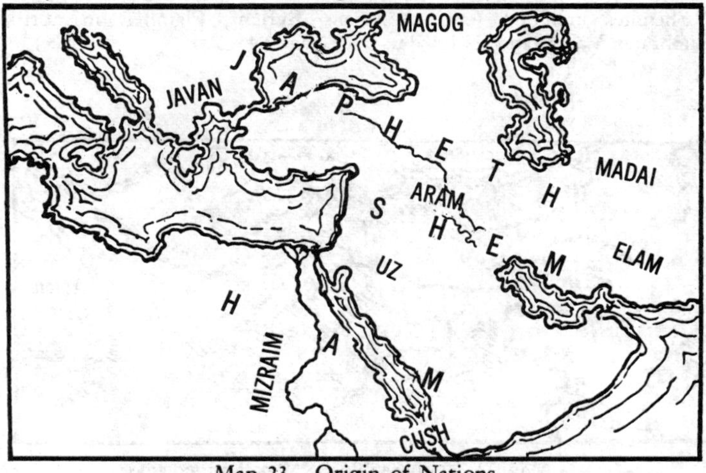

Map 23. Origin of Nations.

Fig. 22. Ruins, Tower of Babylon and Birs Nimrud.
© *Matson Photos*

Chapter 11:1-9. Tower of Babel

The Confusion of Tongues occurred in the 4th generation after the Flood, about the time of the birth of Peleg (10:25), which was 101 years after the Flood, and 326 years before the Call of Abraham (10:26). It was God's method of dispersing the race to its task of subduing the earth. It may, in part, account for the variety of gods, and the variety of names of Pre-Flood persons.

Work on the Tower of Babel was stopped temporarily; but was resumed by those who remained in Babylonia; and the Tower became the center around which Babylon was built. It became a pattern for similar towers in other Babylonian cities and may have suggested the form of Pyramids in Egypt.

ARCHAEOLOGICAL NOTE: Site of the Tower of Babel

The traditional Tower of Babel is at Borsippa, 10 miles southwest from the center of Babylon. Sir Henry Rawlinson found in a foundation corner in Borsippa a cylinder with this inscription: "The tower of Borsippa, which a former king erected, and completed to a height of 42 cubits, whose summit he did not finish, fell to ruins in ancient times. There was no proper care of its gutters for the water; rain and storms had washed away its brick, and the tiles of its roof were broken. The great god Marduk urged me to restore it. I did not alter its site, or change its foundation walls. At a favorable time I renewed its brick work and its roofing tiles, and I wrote my name on the cornices of the edifice. I built it anew as it had been ages before; I erected its pinnacle as it was in remote days." This seems like a tradition of the unfinished tower of Babel (Figure 22).

It is commonly thought by archaeologists that more likely the actual site was in the center of Babylon, identified with the ruins just north of the Marduk Temple (Map 48). G. Smith found an ancient tablet reading: "The building of this illustrious tower offended the gods. In a night they threw down what they had built. They scattered them abroad, and made strange their speech." This seems like a tradition of Babel. It is now an immense hole 330 feet square, which has been used as a quarry from which to take bricks. When standing it consisted of a number of successive platforms one on top of another, each smaller than the one below, a sanctuary to Marduk on the top.

The Tower of Babel

1. Genesis 11:4, "a tower with its top in heaven" is an expression of the vast pride of the first builders of "ziggurats," the artificial temple hills of Sumeria and Babylonia.
2. The notion was to concentrate, to build powerful groups and cities instead of obeying the command of Genesis 9:1. The old spirit of rebellion, the worship of man, and human pride was again in control.
3. The date of this scattering is not recoverable. Ussher's guesses are based on false premises. The genealogies of Genesis 5 and 11 are undoubtedly abbreviated. Many genealogies illustrate the habit of omission.
4. Ziggurats still exist in ruin at Ur and Erech (mod. Warka) and their construction illustrates Genesis 11:3, 4. Their whole purpose whenever found was idolatrous worship and herein lay the sin of the Babel builders.

NOTES:

(a) Languages fall into a few large families. Within the family, resemblances are apparent and development can be traced back sometimes for 3000 years. Between the major groups—e.g. Indo-European and Semitic there is no resemblance.

(b) Woolley in "The Sumerians" and "Ur of the Chaldees" describes in detail the amazing engineering of a ziggurat.

"The Generations of Shem," 11:10-26

6th document composing book of Genesis (see page 58). In 10:21-31, Shem's descendants are named. Here the line is carried straight from Shem to Abraham, covering 10 generations (427 years). Shem himself may have recorded this entire genealogy, for his life spanned the period covered by it. On page 85 is a table showing ages from Adam to the Flood, as given in chapter 5, (see pages 70, 71); and from the Flood to Abraham, as given here in chapter 11.

	Age at son's birth	Total age
Adam	130	930
Seth	105	912
Enosh	90	905
Kenan	70	910
Mahalalel	65	895
Jared	162	962
Enoch	65	365
Methuselah	187	969
Lamech	182	777
Noah, at Flood	600	950
	1656	

	Age at son's birth	Total age
Arpachshad, born after Flood	2	
Arpachshad	35	438
Shelah	30	433
Eber	34	464
Peleg	30	239
Reu	32	239
Serug	30	230
Nahor	29	148
Terah	130	205
Abraham, entered Canaan	75	
	427	

According to these figures:
It was 1656 years from Adam to Flood: 427 years, Flood to Abraham.
Adam's life overlapped Methuselah by 243 years.
Methuselah's life overlapped Noah by 600 years, Shem by 98 years.
There were 126 years between death of Adam and birth of Noah.
Noah lived 350 years after Flood; died 2 years before birth of Abraham.
Shem lived from 98 years before Flood till 502 years after Flood.
Shem lived till 75 years after Abraham entered Canaan.
Adam alive at birth of great-great-great-great-great grandchildren.
Noah lived to 9th generation of his own descendants.
In column at right, all but Peleg and Nahor, alive at birth of Abraham.
In such a period of longevity, population increased very rapidly.
Before Flood they lived to great age. Then, a gradual reduction.

"The Generations of Terah," 11:27 to 25:11

7th document composing the book of Genesis (see page 58). The story of Abraham, recorded, probably, by Abraham and Isaac.

Chapters 10 and 11. From Flood to Abraham

This Period in Babylonian History

Ancient Babylonian inscriptions, after naming 10 Pre-Flood kings, add, "Then the Flood overthrew the land" (see page 71).

Then, for the period between the Flood and Abraham, 100 kings, of 20 different cities, or dynasties, are named.

On the tablets, for the early part of this period, there is a sudden reduction in the length of reigns, from enormous to reasonable figures, marking the dividing line between "Historic," that is, records made of Contemporaneous Events, and "Pre-Historic," that is, records of Earlier Events made from Oral Tradition.

City-Kingdoms

At the opening of the historic period there were settlements at Kish, Lagash, Erech, Ur, Eridu, Nippur, Accad, Babylon, Larsa, Fara, and other places. These were small fortified cities, each ruled by a king or priest-king. They were in constant conflict with one another. Sometimes one city would gain control over others thus making a small empire. This domination would last for a while, and then dissolve, or pass to some other city or cities. These kings recorded their exploits on clay tablets, thousands of which have been dug up in recent years. The tablets, however, do not indicate to what extent the city-dynasties were contemporaneous, consecutive or overlapping. So the chronology of the period is very uncertain.

The Prinicpal Dynasties, according to these tablets, ruling in Babylonia, between the Flood and Abraham, are named on next page. Notice: these centers of population were clustered around Eridu, traditional Eden, and Fara, traditional home of Noah.

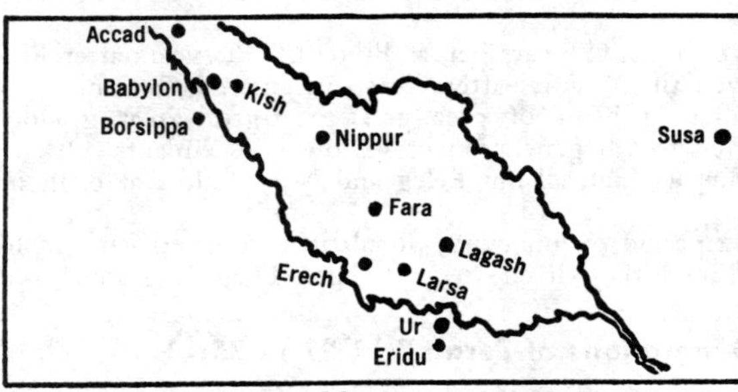

Map 24.

Kish Dynasty

Called on the tables the First Dynasty after the Flood. Kish was a suburb of Babylon, near the site of the Tower of Babel, earliest great Post-Flood city, main capital of Babylonia in the period immediately following the Flood. (See further page 78.) Here Dr. Langdon found remains of the Flood deposit.

Lagash Dynasty

Lagash was capital of the first Sumerian, or Hamitic, kingdom, after the Flood, in South Babylonia, as Kish was the capital of the first Semitic kingdom, in North Babylonia; about 100 miles apart. Lagash was a library center, excavated by Sarzec (1877–1901, see pages 46–48).

Erech Dynasty

Erech, also called Uruk, or Warka, one of Nimrod's cities, was only 50 miles from traditional Garden of Eden. One of its kings, Lugalziggissi, called himself "Lord of the World." Erech was excavated by Koldewey (1913), and Nöldeke and Jordan (1928–33). They found it to be one of earth's oldest cities, with 18 distinct pre-historic layers. It was the chief seat of Ishtar worship, where prostitution was compulsory.

Accad Dynasty

Accad, also called Sippar, another of Nimrod's cities, and another famous library center (see page 48), was about 100 miles northwest from Noah's traditional home, Fara. It produced SARGON I, most famous warrior of pre-Abrahamic times, who ruled from Elam to Mt. Sinai. He was a great conqueror, builder and promoter of learning. He founded a great library. He is thought to have been about contemporary with Cheops, builder of the Great Pyramid in Egypt.

Ur Dynasties

Only 12 miles from Eridu, Ur, for a while, after the Flood, was outstripped by other nearby cities. But by the time of Abraham it had grown to be the leading city of the world (see next two pages). Under two of its most famous kings, Ur-engur and Dungi, Ur ruled from the Persian Gulf to the Mediterranean.

Babylon Dynasty

About the time of Abraham's migration to Canaan (2000 B.C.), Babylon, under Hammurabi, came into supremacy. Hammurabi, a great warrior, who built temples and compiled a legal code, is commonly identified with "Amraphel" of Genesis 14:1. (See page 50.)

Chapters 10,11. From Flood to Abraham

This Period in Babylonian History

Excavations in Ur, the City of Abraham

Ur, also called Mugheir, and Mugayyar, was once a seaport, on the Persian Gulf, at the mouth of the Euphrates river, 12 miles from

Eridu, traditional site of the Garden of Eden (see map page 65). A Pre-Flood city; destroyed by the Flood; and rebuilt. Just preceding the time of Abraham, it was the most magnificent city in all the world; a center of manufacture, farming and shipping, in a land of fabulous fertility and wealth, with caravans going in every direction to distant lands, and ships sailing from the docks of Ur down the Persian Gulf with cargoes of copper and hard stone. Then, about the time of Abraham, it was eclipsed by Babylon, but remained an important city on down to the Persian period; by which time the Gulf had receded, and the Euphrates had changed its course, running 10 miles to the east; and Ur was abandoned to be buried by the sandstorms of the desert.

The Ruins of Ur, a number of cities, one upon another, Abraham's city near the bottom, consist of a tall mound, surrounded by lower subsidiary mounds, covering an area about 2 miles long northwest and southeast, and about ½ mile wide. Remnants of a surrounding wall, 70 feet thick, 80 feet high, have been traced for 2½ miles. The Sacred Area, occupied by Temples and Palaces, was surrounded by an inner wall, 400 yards long, 200 yards wide.

The University Museum of Pennsylvania and the British Museum, in a Joint Expedition, under leadership of C. L. Woolley, for 12 seasons (1922–34), each season lasting 4 or 5 winter months, with some 200 workmen each season, quite thoroughly explored the secrets of these ruins.

The Ziggurat, or Temple-Tower, patterned after the Tower of Babel, is now the tallest mound, and in Abraham's day was the most conspicuous building in the city. It was last rebuilt by Nabonidus, in the 6th century B.C., on the ruins of the Temple that had stood in Abraham's time, which itself, in turn, had been rebuilt over the foundations (which still remain) of one that had stood there in prehistoric times. The Tower, as Abraham saw it, was square, terraced, built of solid brick, the successive terraces planted with trees and shrubbery; at the top a sanctuary to the Moon-God.

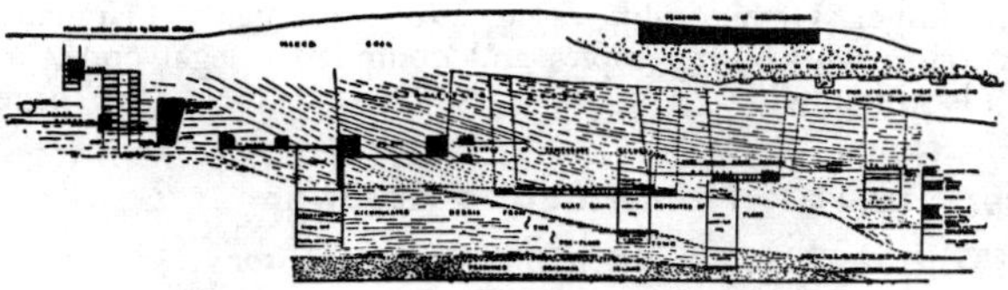

Fig. 23. Cross-section of the Mound, showing Flood Deposit. (*Courtesy of the University Museum of Pennsylvania.*)

Fig. 24. Ur.
General View of the Ruins Dating from the Time of Abraham.

Fig. 25. Ur.
Intrusive Neo-Babylonian Burials.
(Courtesy Matson Photo Service.)

The Temples. The two main Temples were those of the Moon-God, Nannar, and the Moon-Goddess, Ningal; in their glory in Abraham's day; a vast complex of shrines, small rooms, living quarters for the priests, priestesses and attendants: deities Abraham's father worshiped.

The Royal Tombs. One of the most amazing discoveries was the rich treasures of the tombs of Queen Shubad, Mes-kalam-dug, and an un-named King, in the lower levels of the Cemetery, of a time about midway between Abraham and the Flood. With the bones of the Queen were found a golden crown, head-dress, a great profusion of beads, necklaces, and ornaments of gold, silver, and semi-precious stones, cups, plates, saucers, toilet boxes, paint cups, a golden harp; the bones of 40 court servants who had been sacrificed at the burial of the Queen, with an endless variety of copper, bronze, stone and flint implements, to serve the Queen in the next world; the remains of a chariot with the bones of the animals that drew it. These may now be seen in the University Museum at Philadelphia. They bear witness to a very high degree of skill, thus early; and also to the practice of human sacrifice, and belief in a future life.

A Residence Section, of Abraham's time, was uncovered, homes, shops, schools and chapels, with thousands of tablets, business documents, contracts, receipts, hymns, liturgies, etc. The houses were built of brick, two-story, flush with the street, court on inside

Chapters 10,11. From Flood to Abraham

This Period in Egyptian History

While the Bible story starts in Babylonia, it soon shifts to Egypt, which ever afterward looms large in the Old Testament.

Egypt was founded, soon after the Flood, by Mizraim son of Ham. It was called the "Land of Ham."

While civilization was developing in Babylonia under Nimrod, Sargon and Hammurabi, it made greater strides in Egypt under the first 12 Dynasties, which covered the period between the Flood and Abraham.

Manetho's 31 Dynasties

Manetho, an Egyptian, about 250 B.C., wrote a history of Egypt, which he arranged under 31 dynasties, from Menes, first historical king, to the Greek conquest by Alexander the Great, 332 B.C.; and to this day ancient Egyptian history is commonly spoken of in terms of these 31 dynasties; and in the main their correctness has been corroborated by archaeological findings.

		Contemporary with
1st Dynasty	Menes	Nimrod?
2nd Dynasty		
3rd Dynasty		
4th Dynasty	Pyramids	Sargon?
5th Dynasty		
6th Dynasty		
7th Dynasty		
8th Dynasty		
9th Dynasty		
10th Dynasty		
11th Dynasty		
12th Dynasty	2000 B.C.	Abraham
13th Dynasty		
14th Dynasty		
15th Dynasty		
16th Dynasty	1800 B.C.	Joseph?
17th Dynasty		
18th Dynasty	1580–1340	Moses
19th Dynasty	1340–1200	
20th Dynasty	1200–1100	
21st Dynasty	1100– 950	David
22nd Dynasty	950– 750	
23rd Dynasty	750– 720	
24th Dynasty	720– 712	
25th Dynasty	712– 663	
26th Dynasty	663– 525	
27–31 Dynasties	525– 332 Persian	
Greek Period	332– 30 B.C.	Septuagint
Roman Period	30 B.C.–A.D. 300	Christ

At first Egypt was composed of a number of family groups, or small tribes, each called a "kingdom." They had their "pre-historic" period, that is, a period before written records were made of contemporaneous events; with traditions of primeval long-lived gods, demi-gods and kings. They knew the use of gold, silver, copper, lead and flint. They made boats and ships.

The Three Great Epochs of Egyptian History Were:

The Old Kingdom: Dynasties 3 to 6. Era of Pyramid Building. Variously placed at between 4000 B.C. and 2000 B.C., most commonly at about 2700 B.C. or 2400 B.C.

The Middle Kingdom: Dynasties 11 and 12. Era of Canal Building. Great Prosperity. About 2000 B.C. Time of Abraham.

The Empire Period: Dynasties 18 and 19. 1600–1200 B.C. The First World Empire. Ruled from Ethiopia to the Euphrates. This was the time of Israel's Sojourn in Egypt.

Egyptian Chronology

Is fairly well established back to 1600 B.C.; but beyond that it is very uncertain. Thus, Menes, the first historical king, is dated, by Egyptologists, variously as follows: Petrie, 5500 B.C.; Brugsch, 4500; Lepsius, 3900; Bunsen, 3600; Breasted, 3400; Meyer, 3300; Scharff, 3000; Poole, 2700; G. Rawlinson, 2450; Wilkinson, 2320; Scharpe, 2000. Thus, it may be seen, Petrie and Breasted, two of the most famous Egyptologists, differ by more than 2000 years as to the beginning point of Egyptian history. These same two men differ by 1000 years on the date of the pyramids, and 700 years on Hyksos period. Present tendency is to lower the dates, both of Egyptian and Babylonian chronology, placing the Great Pyramid at 2400 or 2500 B.C.

Bible Chronology and Egyptian Chronology. Egyptians had traditions of the Flood back in the Pre-Historic period. The Pyramid civilization developed after the Flood. Sufficient time for considerable increase in population from Noah's family had to elapse. The Bible text seems to place the Flood about 2400 B.C.; while the general average among Egyptologists for the beginning of the Egyptian Historical period is about 3000 B.C. (see above); thus placing 600 years Before the Flood events which must have come considerable time After the Flood. This seems like a conflict between Egyptian chronology and Bible chronology. But it may be noted, from the paragraph on Egyptian chronology, above, that some Egyptologists bring the beginning of the Egyptian historical period down to this side of 2400 B.C.; and it must be remembered that the Septuagint and Samaritan Pentateuch push the Bible date for the Flood back of 3000 B.C. (see under "Chronology," pages 32, 33). So, it is only some of the Egyptian chronological systems that are in conflict with some of the Biblical chronological systems; others are in perfect harmony.

Chapters 10,11. From Flood to Abraham

This Period in Egyptian History

1st Dynasty. Menes (Mena), first historical king, consolidated various tribes, and united Upper and Lower Egypt. Conquered Sinai, and worked its turquois mines. His name is identified by some scholars with Mizraim, the son of Ham. He may have been about contemporary with Nimrod; while Nimrod was laying the foundations of Imperialism among the small states of Babylonia, Menes was doing the same in Egypt. His tomb has been found at Abydos, and in it a vase of green glaze with his name. This dynasty had 9 kings.

2nd Dynasty. 9 kings. Semitic names indicate intercourse with Babylon. Mines of Sinai were worked.

3rd Dynasty. 5 kings. Kept up mining at Sinai. Built ships 160 feet long for Mediterranean trade; made sea-voyage to Lebanon. Beginning of Pyramid Era. Zozer built the "Step-Pyramid," at Sakkarah, 2 miles west of Memphis, with 6 receding stages, somewhat after the manner of Babylonian Temple-Towers. Snefru (Seneferu), next, imitated Zozer, but filled in the terraced stages, making smooth slopes, the first real pyramid, at Meydum, nearby.

4th Dynasty. 7 kings. Zenith of Pyramid Era. The Three Great Pyramids: of Cheops (Khufu), Khafre (Cephren), Menkure (Menkaura), at Gizeh, 8 miles west of Cairo. The largest was that of Cheops, one of Egypt's greatest rulers. Next was Khafre's, in connection with which he had the Sphinx carved out with a portrait of himself. Menkure's mummy was found in his pyramid.

5th Dynasty. 9 kings. Mining kept up in Sinai. Trading expeditions on the Mediterranean, to Phoenicia, Syria and Ophir.

The Egyptians had a strong belief in the future life. On the west side of the pyramid of Queen Khent-Kawes, of the 5th dynasty, a boat has been discovered, 110 feet long, 15 feet wide, which she had cut deep in the rock, to transport her soul to the other world. The tombs of the Pharaohs were well-stocked with the treasures of this world which they thought they were taking with them to the other world.

6th Dynasty. 6 kings. End of Old Kingdom. Pepi II, 5th king, reigned 90 years; longest reign in history.

7th, 8th, 9th, 10th Dynasties. 20 kings. Period of disintegration; many contending kingdoms.

11th Dynasty. 7 kings. Beginning of Great Middle Kingdom, which lasted through 12th dynasty.

12th Dynasty. 8 kings. Amenemhet III built the Temple of Serabit in Sinai where Petrie recently found the oldest alphabetic writing in the world. There was frequent intercourse with Syria. A canal was built from the Nile to the Red Sea. Senusert I built the Obelisk of On which is still standing. Senusert II is commonly thought to have been the Pharaoh when Abraham visited Egypt.

Egyptian Pyramids

Unlike Babylonian Temple Towers, which were built with shrines at the top on which to worship the gods, were merely Tombs, to perpetuate the glory of the Pharaohs who built them. Beginning in the 1st dynasty, the Pyramid craze reached its zenith in the 4th dynasty.

Fig. 26. Portrait of Cheops
(Courtesy of Sir Flinders Petrie)

The Great Pyramid of Cheops. Grandest monument of the ages. Covered 13 acres, 768 feet square (now 750), 482 feet high (now 450). Estimated to have contained 2,300,000 stones of an average thickness of 3 feet each, and an average weight of 2½ tons. Built of successive coats of rough-hewn blocks of limestone, the outer coat made smooth by exquisitely carved and close-fitting blocks of granite. These outer blocks have been removed and used in the building of Cairo. In the middle of the north side there is a passage, 3 feet wide, 4 feet high, which leads into a chamber cut in solid rock, 100 feet under ground level and exactly 600 feet under the apex; two other chambers halfway between this and the apex, with pictures and sculptures depicting the king's exploits. The mummy of Cheops was not there.

How Built. The stones were cut, with stone and copper instruments only, from a quarry 12 miles to the east, floated across the Nile during inundations, and then drawn up long sloping construction ramps of earth by endless gangs of men tugging at ropes, raised and brought into place by means of wedges driven alternately on one side and then the other of platforms with cradle-like bottoms. It is said to have required 100,000 men 10 years to build the causeway, and another 20 years to build the pyramid itself; all in forced labor; working classes and slaves, driven under the pitiless lash of the taskmaster.

The amazing thing about the Pyramids is that they were built at the dawn of history. Sir Flinders Petrie calls the Pyramid of Cheops "the greatest and most accurate structure the world has ever seen." The Encyclopaedia Britannica says, "The brain power to which it testifies is as great as that of any modern man."

Chapter 12:1-3. Call of Abraham

Here starts the story of Redemption. It had been hinted at in the Garden of Eden (3:15). Now, 2000 years after the Creation and Fall of Man, 400 years after the Flood, in a world lapsed into Idolatry and Wickedness. God called Abraham to become the founder of a movement having for its object the RECLAMATION and REDEMPTION of Mankind.

In that pioneer age of the earth, while nations were still not much more than tribal communities, prospecting and settling the more favored lands, Abraham, a righteous man, a believer in God, not an Idolater, one of the few still holding to the tradition of primitive Monotheism, was promised of God that his descendants:

1. Should inherit the land of Canaan.
2. They should become a Great Nation.
3. Through them ALL NATIONS SHOULD BE BLESSED.

This promise (12:2, 3; 22:18) is the foundation thought of which the whole Bible is a development. God first called Abraham in Ur (Acts 7:2–4; Genesis 11:31). Again in Haran (12:1–4). Again in Shechem (12:7). Again in Bethel (13:14–17). And twice in Hebron (15:5, 18; 17:1–8). The promise was repeated to Isaac (26:3, 4). And to Jacob (28:13, 14; 35:11, 12; 46:3, 4).

Abraham

It seems, from 11:26, 32; 12:4; Acts 7:2–4, that Abraham was born when his father was 130 years old, and was not the first-born, as might be inferred from 11:6. He was 75 when he entered Canaan. About 80 when he rescued Lot and met Melchizedek. 86 when Ishmael was born. 99 when Sodom was destroyed. 100 when Isaac was born. 137 when Sarah died. 160 when Jacob was born. He died at 175, which was 115 years before Jacob's migration to Egypt.

The Development of Idolatry

Abraham was not an Idolater. But he lived in a world of Idolatry. In the beginning man had had ONE God; and, in the Garden of Eden, had lived in rather intimate communion with God. But, with his sin and banishment, man lost his primeval knowledge of God; and, groping in his darkness for a solution of the mysteries of existence, he came to worship the powers of Nature which seemed to him to be the sources of life. Sex, because it was the means through which life came, played a very important part in early Babylonian religion. Cuneiform inscriptions have revealed that a large part of their liturgies were descriptions of sexual intercourse between gods and goddesses, through which, they thought, all things came into being. Then, too, the Sun and Rain and various forces of nature were Deified, because on them depended the life of the world. And Kings also, because they had power, came to be deified. Many cities and nations had for their chief god their founder: as Asshur, father of the Assyrians, became the chief god of the Assyrians; and Marduk (Nimrod), founder of Babylon, became chief god of Babylon. And, to make their gods more real, images were made to represent the gods; and then the images themselves came to be worshiped as gods. Thus, man took his nosedive from Original Monotheism into the abyss of innumerable polytheistic idolatrous cultures, some of which, in their practices, were unspeakably vile and abominable.

The Idolatry of Abraham's Day

Ur was in Babylonia; and Babylonians had many gods and goddesses. They were worshipers of fire, the sun, moon, stars and various forces of nature. Nimrod, who had exalted himself against God in building the Tower of Babel, was ever afterward recognized as the chief Babylonian deity. Marduk was the common form of his name; later became identical with Bel. Shamash was the name of the sun-god. Sin, the moon-god, was the principal deity of Ur, Abraham's city. Sin's wife was called Ningal, the moon-goddess of Ur. She had many names, and was worshiped in every city as the Mother-Goddess. Nina was one of her names, from which the city of Nineveh was named. Her commonest name in Babylonia was Ishtar. She was the deification of the sex passion; her worship required licentiousness; sacred prostitution in connection with her sanctuaries was a universal custom among the women of Babylonia. In connection with her temples were charming retreats or chambers where her priestesses entertained male worshipers in disgraceful ceremonies. In addition to these prostitute priestesses, every maid, wife or widow had to officiate at least once in her lifetime in these rites.

Abraham Believed in One God

His countrymen were Idolators. His father was an Idolater (Joshua 24:2). There are legends of his being persecuted as a child for refusal to worship Idols. How did Abraham know about God? No doubt, by direct revelation from God. And moreover, taking the figures in chapters 5 and 11 as they are, Noah's life extended to the birth of Abraham; and Noah's life was overlapped by Methuselah by 600 years while Methuselah's life was overlapped by Adam for 243 years. So Abraham could have learned directly from Shem Noah's account of the Flood and Methuselah's account of Adam and the Garden of Eden.

Chapter 12:4-9. Abraham's Entrance into Canaan

Haran, abut 600 miles northwest from Ur, 400 miles northeast from Canaan, was Abraham's first stopping place. He had set out from Ur, in search of a land where he could build a nation free from Idolatry, not knowing whither he was going (Hebrews 11:8). But Haran was already a well-settled region, with roads to Babylon, Assyria, Syria, Asia Minor and Egypt, along which caravans and armies constantly marched. So, after the death of his father Terah, Abraham, under the call of God, moved on in search of a more sparsely settled land.

Shechem, Abraham's first stopping place in Canaan, in the center of the land, was in a vale of surpassing beauty, between Mt. Ebal and Mt. Gerizim. Here Abraham built an altar to God, but soon moved on south in further exploration of the land.

Bethel, 20 miles south of Shechem, 10 miles north of Jerusalem, was Abraham's next stopping place. It was one of the highest points in Canaan, with a magnificent view in every direction. Abraham was following the top of the mountain range, probably, because the Jordan Valley on the east, and the Sea Coast Plain on the west, were already pretty well settled. In Bethel, too, he built an altar, as he did later at Hebron, and as he had done at Shechem, not only as an acknowledgement to God, but also as a publication of his Faith to the people among whom he had come to live. He must have liked Bethel; for that is where he settled when he returned from Egypt; till he and Lot separated.

Chapter 12:10-20. Abraham's Sojourn in Egypt

As he journeyed on south from Bethel, he must have passed close to Jerusalem; and, if Melchizedek was Shem, Abraham may have called on him, for he must have known him back in Babylonia. On account of famine, Abraham journeyed on into Egypt, to sojourn there till the famine was over. It came near to getting him into trouble. His wife Sarah was beautiful; and powerful princes had a practice of confiscating beautiful women for themselves; and killing their husbands. His cautious subterfuge of calling Sarah his "sister" was not exactly a lie. She was his half-sister (20:12). Marriages between near relatives was common in early ages, till the growth of families offered wider selection.

ARCHAEOLOGICAL NOTE: Abraham's Visit to Egypt. On the tomb of Senusert II, of the 12th dynasty, at Benihassen, who is thought to have been the Pharaoh at that time, there is a sculpture depicting a visit of Asiatic Semitic traders to his court. The patriarchal narratives clearly suggest a vigorous commerce with Egypt (Genesis 12:10–20; 37:25; 43:11; 46:6).

Chapter 13. Abraham and Lot Separate

Lot was Abraham's nephew. They had been together since they had left Ur years before. But now their flocks and herds and tents had become so extensive, and their herdsmen so quarrelsome over pasture lands, that it seemed best to separate. Abraham magnanimously gave Lot his choice of all the land. Lot foolishly chose the Plain of Sodom. Then Abraham chose Hebron, which was henceforth his settled home.

Chapter 14. Abraham Defeats Babylonian Kings

This was to rescue Lot. Abraham must have been something of a military genius. With 318 men of his own, and some help from neighbors, by a midnight surprise attack, he discomfited these four famous Babylonian kings. Armies then were small. Kings were tribal princes. Abraham was a sort of king, perhaps the head of a clan a thousand or more.

ARCHAEOLOGICAL NOTE: Hammurabi. "Amraphel" (1) is commonly identified as Hammurabi, most famous of early Babylonian kings, the discovery of whose celebrated Code of Laws has made his name a household word. Abraham may have known him personally when he was in Ur. Hammurabi's "Code of Laws" is a voice from the dust of Abraham's world. (See page 50.)

ARCHAEOLOGICAL NOTE: The "Way of the Kings" (5, 6). The places, named in verses 5, 6, by way of which the four Eastern kings came against Sodom, were so far east of the ordinary trade route, that Albright said that he once considered it an indication of the legendary character of the 14th chapter of Genesis; but, in 1929, he discovered a line of great mounds, in Hauran and along the east border of Gilead and Moab, of cities that flourished about 2000 B.C., indicating that it was a well-settled country, on the trade route between Damascus and the gold and copper regions of Edom and Sinai.

Melchizedek, 14:18-20

Priest-King of Salem (Jerusalem). Hebrew tradition says that he was Shem, survivor of the Flood, who was still alive, earth's oldest living man, priest, in the patriarchal age, of the whole race. If so, it is a hint that, thus early, right after the Flood, God chose Jerusalem to be the scene of Human Redemption. Whoever he was, he was a picture and type of Christ (Psalm 110; Hebrews 5, 6, 7).

Chapters 15,16,17. God's Promises to Abraham Renewed

With explanation that, before his seed should inherit Canaan, they would spend 400 years in a foreign land (15:13), meaning Egypt. When Abraham was 100, and Sarah 90, Isaac was promised; and the Covenant of Circumcision instituted, as a mark of God's nation.

Chapters 18,19. Sodom and Gomorrah

These cesspools of iniquity were only a few miles from Hebron, the home of Abraham, and from Jerusalem, the home of Melchizedek; yet so vile, their stench reached heaven. It had been only 400 years since the Flood, almost within the memory of men then living. Yet men had forgotten the lesson of that cataclysmic destruction of the race. And God "rained fire and brimstone" on these two cities, to refresh men's memories, and to warn of the wrath of God that is in store for wicked men; and, perhaps, to serve as a token of the earth's final doom in a holocaust of fire (II Peter 2:5, 6; 3:7, 10).

Jesus likened the time of His Return to the days of Sodom (Luke 17:26–32); as he did also to the days of the Flood. Both were periods of unspeakable wickedness. Today, on a scale never before known in history, with greed, brutality, beastliness and criminal instincts, in demons in the high places of earth, it does not require much imagination to see the end toward which we are heading, however much good men and statesmen may try to avert it. Unless there comes a world-movement of Repentance, the Day of Doom may not be far off.

Location of Sodom and Gomorrah

Either the north end or south end of the Dead Sea. "Sodom" (Usdom) is the name of the mountain at the southwest corner. There was persistent ancient tradition that great topographical changes took place around the south end of the Dead Sea when Sodom and Gomorrah were destroyed. Ancient writers generally thought that the sites of the two cities were buried beneath the Dead Sea.

The Dead Sea

The Dead Sea is about 40 miles long by 10 miles wide. The north end is very deep, in some places 1000 feet. The south third is nowhere deeper than 15 feet and in most places less than 10 feet. The water level is higher now than in Abraham's time, because of silting up by the Jordan and other streams, with no outlet. What is now the south third of the Dead Sea was then a plain.

ARCHAEOLOGICAL NOTE: In 1924, Drs. W. F. Albright and M. G. Kyle, directing a joint Expedition of the American Schools and Xenia Seminary, found, at the southeast corner of the Dead Sea, five Oases, made by fresh water streams, and, centrally located to them, on a plain 500 feet above the level of the Dead Sea, at a place called Bab-ed-Dra, the remains of a great fortified enclosure, evidently a "high place" for religious festivals. There were great quantities of potsherds, flints, and other remains of a period dating between 2500 B.C. and 2000 B.C.; and evidence that the population ended abruptly about 2000 B.C. This evidence that the region was densely populated and prosperous indicates that it must have been very fertile, "like the garden of God." That the population ceased abruptly, and that it has been a region of unmixed desolation ever since, seems to indicate that the district was destroyed by some great cataclysm which changed the soil and climate.

The opinion of Albright and Kyle, and most archaeologists, is that Sodom and Gomorrah were located on these oases, further down the streams, and that the site is now covered by the Dead Sea.

"Slime" (14:10) was bitumen, asphalt, pitch, a lustrous black petroleum product, which melts and burns. There are vast beds of it on both sides of the Dead Sea, more abundant at the south end, and great masses of it at the bottom. Considerable quantities of it have risen to the surface during earthquakes.

"Brimstone" (19:24). Kyle said that under Mt. Usdom there is a stratum of salt 150 feet thick; and above it a stratum of marl mingled

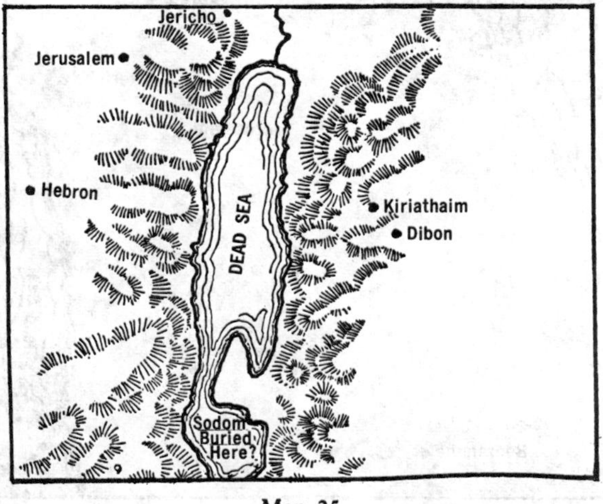

Map 25.

with free sulphur; and that at the proper time God kindled the gases; a great explosion took place; the salt and the sulphur were thrown into the heavens red hot, so that it did literally rain fire and brimstone from heaven. Lot's wife was encrusted in salt. There are many pillars of salt at the south end of the Dead Sea which have borne the name of "Lot's Wife." Indeed everything about the region seems to dovetail exactly with the Biblical story of Sodom and Gomorrah.

Chapter 20. Sarah and Abimelech

Though Hebron was his main home, Abraham, from time to time, moved from place to place, in search of pasture for his herds. In Gerar, a Philistine city, some 40 miles west of Hebron, near the sea coast, he had another experience like that with Pharaoh (12:10–20). Sarah must have been extremely beautiful, to thus attract the attention of kings, especially considering her age. Isaac and Rebekah had a similar experience with a later Abimelech, in the same city (chapter 26).

ARCHAEOLOGICAL NOTE: In towns named in connection with Abraham, Isaac, and Jacob: Shechem, Bethel, Ai, Gerar, Dothan: Albright and Garstang have found, in bottom levels of their ruins, shreds of about 2000 B.C. evidence that the towns did exist then.

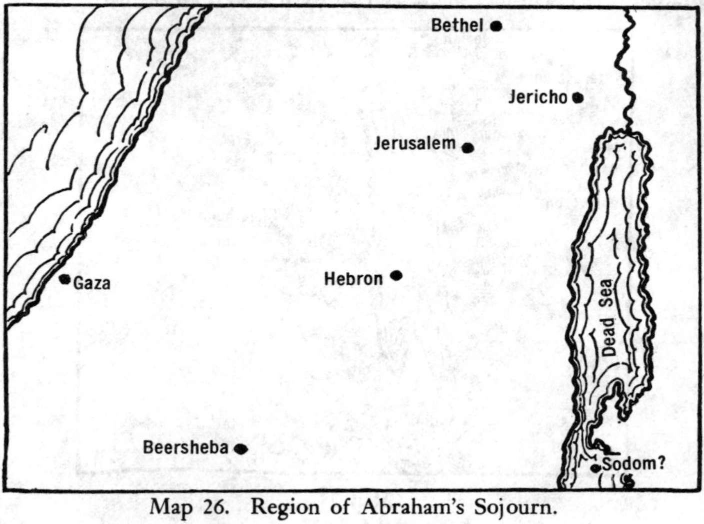

Map 26. Region of Abraham's Sojourn.

Chapter 21. Birth of Isaac

Ishmael, at the time, was about 15 years old (5, 8; 16:16). Paul used the story of these two children as an allegory of the Mosaic and Christian Covenants (Galatians 4:21–31).

Beersheba (30, 31), where Abraham, Isaac, and Jacob dwelt much of the time, was at the southernmost border of Canaan, some 20 miles southwest of Hebron, 150 miles from Egypt. It was a place of "seven wells." Wells in a semi-desert country like that were priceless possessions. The self-same wells are still there.

Chapter 22. Abraham Offers Isaac

"God enjoined it only to forbid it." It was a test of Abraham's faith. God had promised that Isaac should be the father of nations (17:16). Yet here God commands that Isaac be slain before he had any children. Somehow Abraham believed that God would bring him back to life (Hebrews 11:19). We do not know in what manner God made known the command to Abraham. But that it was the voice of God Abraham could not have doubted; for surely he would not have set out to perform a task so cruel and revolting without being certain that God had commanded it. The idea originated with God, not with Abraham.

The Offering of Isaac was a Picture-Prophecy of the Death of Christ. A Father offering his Son. The Son Dead for Three Days (in Abraham's mind, 4). A Substitution. An Actual Sacrifice. And it was on Mt. Moriah, the very same place where, 2000 years later God's Own Son was Offered. Thus, it was a Shadow, in the birth of the Hebrew nation, of the Grand Event the nation was born to bring about.

Chapter 23. Sarah's Death

The Cave of Machpelah, where Sarah was buried, is on the west slope of Hebron, in a mosque, under Mohammedan control, who permit no Christian to enter. In 1862 the Prince of Wales, by special permit of the Sultan, entered. He saw stone tombs of Abraham, Isaac, Jacob, Sarah, Rebekah, and Leah; and a circular opening into a cavern below, which was supposed to be the real Cave of Machpelah, and which was said to have been un-entered for 600 years.

Chapter 24. Betrothal of Isaac and Rebekah

Rebekah was Isaac's second cousin. Abraham's purpose in sending back to his own people for a wife for Isaac was to keep his posterity free from Idolatry. If Isaac had married a Canaanitish girl, how different the whole history of Israel might have been. What a lesson for young people in the matter of chosing a mate.

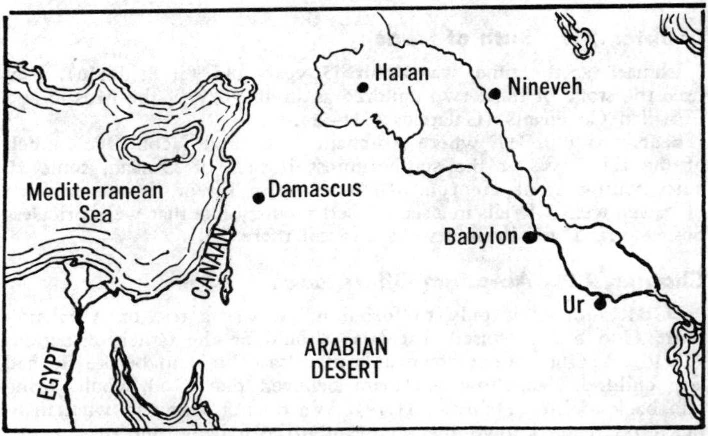

Map 27. Abraham's World.

Chapter 25:1-11. Abraham's Death

Sarah had died at the age of 127, at which time Abraham was 137. He lived for 38 years after that, in which time he married Keturah. She bore him six sons, of whom came the Midanites. It was a Midianite woman that Moses married, 500 years later (Exodus 2:16–21). On the whole, Abraham was the "greatest, purest, and most venerable of the patriarchs, revered by Jews, Mohammedans and Christians." "Friend of God." "Father of the Faithful." Generous. Unselfish. A Superb Character, with Unbounded Trust in God.

"The Generations of Ishmael," 25:12-18

8th document composing Genesis (see page 58). Ishmael was Abraham's son by Hagar, Sarah's Egyptian handmaid (chapter 16). Ishmaelites made Arabia their home, and became known generally as Arabians. Thus, Abraham was the father of the present Arab world. Rivalry between Isaac and Ishmael has persisted through the centuries in the antagonisms between Jews and Arabs.

Arabia is a peninsula, 1500 miles long, 800 miles wide, about 150 times the size of Palestine (see Map 5). It is mostly desert, with scattered oases, sparsely inhabited by nomadic tribes.

"The Generations of Isaac," 25:19 to 35:29

The 9th document composing the book of Genesis. The story of Isaac and Jacob, handed on by Jacob to his sons.

Chapter 25:19-34. Birth of Jacob and Esau

Esau, the first-born, was Isaac's natural heir, and inheritor of the Abrahamic Promises. But God, knowing, before they were born, the qualities of the two men, chose Jacob to be transmitter of the precious heritage, which He hinted to their mother (23); which was the background of Jacob's deal with Esau (31).

In the Line of Promise, all Abraham's sons were eliminated, except Isaac. Of Isaac's sons, Esau was eliminated, and Jacob only chosen. With Jacob the eliminating process stopped; and all Jacob's descendants were included in the Chosen Nation.

Chapter 26. Isaac's Sojourn among the Philistines

Not much is told of Isaac's life, beyond this incident of Abimelech and Rebekah, and the strife over wells. He had inherited the bulk of his father's extensive flocks and herds; was prosperous and rich; peaceable; and his life uneventful.

Isaac was born when Abraham was 100, and Sarah 90. He was 37 when his mother died. 40 when he married. 60 when Jacob was born. 75 when Abraham died. 137? when Jacob fled. 157? when Jacob returned. 167 when Joseph was sold. He died at 180, the year that Joseph became ruler of Egypt.

Abraham lived 175 years. Isaac, 180. Jacob 147. Joseph, 110.

IMPORTANT: God's "Commandments, Statutes and Laws" (5). This looks very much like Biblical evidence that the beginnings of God's Written Word were already existent in Abraham's day.

Chapter 27. Jacob Obtains His Father's Blessing

He had already bought the Birthright from Esau (25:31–34). It was now necessary to get his father to validate the transfer. This he accomplished by deception. In evaluating the moral quality of Jacob's act, a number of things need to be considered. 1. His mother put him up to it. 2. He earnestly desired the Birthright, channel of God's promise of blessing to the whole world. 3. He probably could have obtained it in no other way. 4. Esau cared nothing for it. 5. Jacob paid dearly for his fraud (see under chapter 29). 6. God Himself, laying the foundation of gigantic world plans (Romans 9:10–13), made the choice before the boys were born (25:23).

Isaac's Predictions (29, 40). God must have put these words into Isaac's mouth; for they did come true. Jacob's descendants did attain a dominant position among the nations; and in time produced Christ, through Whom they are marching onward to universal empire. Esau's descendants, the Edomites, were subservient to Israel; and in time, they did throw off Israel's yoke (II Kings 8:20–22), and, they have disappeared from history.

Chapter 28. Jacob's Vision at Bethel

The transfer of the Birthright from Esau to Jacob had been validated by Isaac. It is now validated in Heaven, God Himself giving assurance to Jacob that henceforth he is to be the recognized vehicle of the Promises. The Ladder was a hint that the Promises would culminate in something that would bridge Heaven and Earth. Jesus said that HE was the Ladder (John 1:51).

Jacob is thought to have been 77 at this time. He was 15 when Abraham died. Was 84 when he married. 90 when Joseph was born, 98 when he returned to Canaan. 120 when Isaac died. 130 when he went to Egypt. 147 when he died.

His first 77 years were spent in Canaan. The next 20 in Haran. Then 33 in Canaan. The last 17 in Egypt.

Chapters 29,30. Jacob's Sojourn in Haran

Haran was 400 miles northeast of Canaan. It was the place where Jacob's mother, Rebekah, had been raised, and from which his grandfather Abraham had migrated years before. Laban was Jacob's uncle. Jacob was there 20 years. They were years of hardship and suffering. A wife, whom he did not want, was forced on him by deceit, just as he had gotten his father's blessing by deceit. He had begun to reap what he had sown.

Jacob's Family

He had two wives and two concubines, whom, except one, he did not want, and who were forced on him. Of these, 12 sons were born.

Of Leah: Reuben, Simeon, Levi, Judah, Issachar, Zebulun.
Of Rachel: Joseph, Benjamin.
Of Zilpah, Leah's handmaid: Gad, Asher.
Of Bilhah, Rachel's handmaid: Dan, Naphtali.

This polygamous family, with many shameful things to their credit, was accepted of God, as a whole, to be the beginning of the Twelve Tribes which became the Messianic Nation, chosen of God to bring the Savior into the world. This shows:

1. That God uses human beings as they are, to serve His purposes, and, so to speak, does the best He can with the material He has.
2. It is no indication that every one that God thus uses will be eternally saved. One may be useful in serving God's plans in this world, and yet fail to qualify for the eternal world in the day when God shall judge the secrets of men for final disposition (Romans 2:12–16).
3. It is a testimony to the Truthfulness of Bible writers. No other book narrates with such utter candor the weaknesses of its heroes, and things so contrary to ideals which it aims to promote.

Chapters 31,32,33. Jacob's Return to Canaan

He had left Canaan 20 years before, alone and empty-handed. Now, he was returning, a tribal prince, rich in flocks, herds and servants. God had kept His promise to Jacob (28:15). Jacob's parting with Laban (31:49), originated the beautiful Mizpah benediction, now so widely used, "The Lord watch between me and thee, while we are absent one from another."

Angels, on Jacob's departure from Canaan, had wished him God-speed (28:12). Now, on his return, Angels welcome him home (32:1).

Isaac was still living. Abraham had been dead about 100 years. Jacob was now entering his inheritance in the Promised Land of Canaan. God had been with him thus far. He felt he needed God more than ever (32:24–30). Esau had vowed to kill him (27:41). Jacob was still afraid. They met, and separated, in peace.

Chapter 34. Dinah Avenged by Simeon and Levi

Shechem was Jacob's first stopping place in Canaan, on his return. There he bought a parcel of ground, and erected an altar to God, as if planning to make it his home, temporarily at least. But the bloody act of Simeon and Levi made him odious to his neighbors. And soon he moved on to Bethel.

Chapter 35. God Renews the Covenant at Bethel

Bethel was the place where, 20 years before, in his flight from Canaan, Jacob had seen the Heavenly Ladder, and God had made him heir to the Abrahamic Promises. Now God reassures him that those Promises shall be fulfilled. Then Jacob moved on to Hebron, the home of Abraham and Isaac.

"The Generations of Esau," Chapter 36

The 10th document composing the book of Genesis (see page 58). A brief account of the origin of the Edomites.

Esau, in personal character, was "profane," irreligious; "despised" his birthright: Jacob, compared to Esau, was more fit to be the father of God's Messianic Nation.

Edomites and Land of Edom. (See page 361. Map page 142).

Amalekites (12) were a branch of Esau's descendants. They were a wandering tribe, centering mainly about Kadesh, in the north part of the Sinai peninsula, but roaming in wide circles, even into Judah and far to the east. They were the first to attack Israel on departure from Egypt; and oppressed Israel in time of the Judges.

"Jobab" (34) is thought by some to have been "Job" of the book of Job. "Eliphaz" and "Teman" (10, 11) are named in book of Job. This chapter may supply the setting for book of Job.

"The Generations of Jacob," 37:2 to 50:26

The 11th, and last, document composing Genesis. The story of Joseph, and Israel's Migration to Egypt: incorporated, no doubt, with family records they had received from Abraham; and sacredly guarded through the years of their sojourn in Egypt.

Chapter 37. Joseph Sold into Egypt

The "coat of many colors" (3) was a badge of favoritism, possibly indicating Jacob's intention to make Joseph heir to the Birthright.

Reuben, Jacob's first-born, was natural heir to the Birthright; but he was disavowed because of his illicit relation with one of his father's concubines (35:22; 49:3, 4; I Chronicles 5:1, 2). Simeon and Levi, second and third in line of succession (29:31–35), were passed over because of their crime at Shechem (34:25–30; 49:5–7). Judah, 4th son, was next in line; and, it may have been expected, in family circles, that the Birthright would fall to him.

But Joseph, though Jacob's 11th son, was Rachel's first-born. Rachel was Jacob's best-loved wife; and Joseph was his favorite son (37:3). So the "coat" looked suspicious. And Joseph's dreams of his own ascendancy (5–10), aggravated the situation.

Thus, Judah and Joseph appear to have been rivals for the Birthright. This may explain Judah's active part in selling Joseph into slavery (26, 27). The rivalry between Judah and Joseph passed to their descendants. The tribes of Judah and Ephraim (Joseph's son) were contenders for supremacy. Judah took the lead under David and Solomon. Then, under lead of Ephraim, Ten Tribes seceded.

Chapter 38. Judah's Children

This chapter is inserted, probably, because Judah was progenitor of the Messiah; and it was in accord with Old Testament purpose to preserve family registers all along the line of succession, even though they contained some things not very praiseworthy.

Chapter 39. Joseph Imprisoned

Joseph was of unblemished character, unusually handsome, with an exceptional gift for leadership, and ability to make the best of every unpleasant situation. He was born in Haran, 75 years after the death of Abraham, 30 years before the death of Isaac, when his father was about 90, and 8 years before they returned to Canaan. At 17 was sold into Egypt. 13 years in Potiphar's house, and in prison. At 30 became ruler of Egypt. Died at 110.

ARCHAEOLOGICAL NOTE: Joseph and Potiphar's Wife. The "Tale of Two Brothers," on an ancient papyrus now in the British Museum, written in the reign of Seti II, shortly after the Exodus, has such close resemblance to the story of Joseph and Potiphar's wife that the editor of the English edition of Brugsch's "History of Egypt" surmised that it must have been worked up from the incident, which must have been recorded in the annals of the Egyptian court: A married man sends his younger brother, who was unmarried, and to whom he had entrusted everything about his place to his home, to bring some seed corn. The wife tempts him. He refuses. She, angered, reports to her husband that he had tried to force her. The husband plans to kill him. He flees; and later becomes king of Egypt.

Chapters 40,41. Joseph Made Ruler of Egypt

Joseph married a daughter of the priest of On; and, though he had a heathen wife, and ruled a heathen kingdom, and resided in a center of vile Idolatry, he maintained his childhood faith in the God of his fathers, Abraham, Isaac and Jacob.

ARCHAEOLOGICAL NOTES:

Joseph's Palace in On. Sir Flinders Petrie (1912), discovered ruins of a palace thought to have been that of Joseph.

The Seven Years' Famine. Brugsch, in his "Egypt under the Pharaohs," tells of an inscription which he calls a "very remarkable and luminous confirmation" of this. In a family rock-cut tomb of a certain Baba, governor of the city of El-Kab, south of Thebes, erected in the 17th dynasty, which was contemporary with the 16th dynasty in the north, under which Joseph ruled, there is an inscription in which Baba claims to have done for his city what the Bible says Joseph did for all Egypt: "I collected corn, as a friend of the harvest god. And when a famine arose, lasting many years, I distributed corn to the city, each year of the famine." Brugsch says: "Since famines in Egypt are of the very greatest rarity, and since Baba lived about the same time as Joseph, there remains but one fair inference: that the 'many years famine' in the days of Baba are the 'seven years of famine' under Joseph."

Chapters 42 to 45. Joseph Makes Himself Known

This has been called one of the most beautiful stories in all literature. The most touching incident in the story is where Judah, who, years before, had been leader in selling Joseph into slavery (37:26), now offers to become hostage for Benjamin (44:18–34).

Chapters 46,47. Jacob and His Family Settle in Egypt

God had planned that Israel should be nurtured, for a while, in Egypt, which was the most advanced civilization of that day. As Jacob passed out of Canaan, God gave him assurance that his descendants would return (46:3, 4).

Chapters 48,49. Jacob's Blessing and Prophecy

Jacob seems to have split the Birthright, designating Judah as channel of Messianic Promise (49:10); yet pronouncing national prestige on Joseph's son Ephraim (48:19–22; 49:22–26; I Chronicles 5:1, 2).

Jacob's Prophecy about the Twelve Tribes, to a remarkable degree, parallels the subsequent history of the Tribes. "Shiloh" (10) is commonly taken to be a name for the Messiah. The tribe of Judah produced David; and David's family produced Christ.

Chapter 50. Deaths of Jacob and Joseph

Jacob's body was taken back to Hebron for burial. And Joseph exacted an oath, of his brothers, that when Israel returned to Canaan, they would carry his bones. This belief that Canaan would be their homeland was not forgotten; and, 400 years later, when they set out for Canaan, they took Joseph's bones along (Exodus 13:19).

EXODUS

The 400 Years in Egypt
The Going Out of Egypt
The Ten Commandments
The Tabernacle

Moses had written Genesis out of previously existing documents. With Exodus begins the story of Moses himself. His own life and work comprise the subject matter of Exodus, Leviticus, Numbers and Deuteronomy. He himself wrote these books. The story of Moses constitutes about one-seventh of the whole Bible, and is about two-thirds as large as the New Testament.

Chapter 1. Israel in Egypt

There is a gap between Genesis and Exodus of nearly 300 years, from the death of Joseph to the birth of Moses; or a total of 430 years from Jacob's migration to Egypt till the Exodus (12:40, 41). In this time the Israelites had increased exceedingly (1:7). After the death of Joseph a change of dynasty made them a race of slaves. At the time of the Exodus there were 600,000 men above 20, besides women and children (Numbers 1:46). This would total about 3,000,000. For 70 persons to reach this number in 430 years it would be necessary to double about every 25 years, which would be easily possible. The growth of the population in the United States, in 400 years, from nothing to more than a hundred million, not altogether by immigration, makes credible the statement about the growth of the Israelites.

The family records of Abraham, Isaac and Jacob, no doubt, had been carried to Egypt, and through the long years of bondage there was steadfastly cherished the Promise that Canaan would one day be their national home.

Egypt and the Bible

In the first place, Egypt was settled by the descendants of Ham. Abraham spent some time in Egypt. So did Jacob. Joseph was ruler of Egypt. The Hebrew nation, in its childhood, was 400 years in Egypt. Moses was the adopted son of a Queen of Egypt, and, in his preparation to be Israel's Law-Giver, he was instructed in all the wisdom and learning of Egypt. The religion of Egypt, Calf-Worship, became the religion of the Northern Kingdom of Israel. Jeremiah died in Egypt. From the Captivity till the time of Christ there was a considerable Jewish population in Egypt. The Septuagint Translation of the Old Testament was made in Egypt. Jesus spent part of his childhood in Egypt. Egypt became an important early center of Christianity.

Egypt

Map 28.

A valley, 2 to 30 miles wide, with an average width of about 10 miles; and 750 miles long; cut by the Nile, through the east end of Sahara Desert, from Aswan (see Map, page 117), to the Mediterranean; with a desert plateau on either side about 1000 feet high.

The floor of the valley is covered with black alluvial deposit of rich soil from Abyssinian highlands, of unparalleled fertility, ever renewed by annual overflow of the Nile.

Irrigated from the dawn of history, with a vast system of canals and reservoirs. The Aswan Dam, recently built by the British, now controls the overflow of the Nile, and famines are a thing of the past.

"Surrounded, and protected, by the desert, here developed the First Great Empire in history, and nowhere else have witnesses of ancient civilization been so well preserved."

The population now is about 24,000,000; in Roman times, 7,000,000; probably about that, or less, in the days of Israel's sojourn.

The Delta, a triangle, the spread-out mouth of the Nile, is about 100 miles north and south; and about 150 miles east and west, from Port Said to Alexandria (see Map page 125). It is the most fertile part of Egypt. The land of Goshen, main center of Israelite habitation, was the east part of the Delta.

The Religion of Egypt

Sir Flinders Petrie, famous Egyptian archaeologist, says that the Original religion of Egypt was Monotheistic. But before the dawn of the historic period a religion had developed in which each tribe had its own god, represented by an animal.

Ptah (Apis) was god of Memphis, represented by a Bull.
Amon, god of Thebes, was represented by a Cow.
Mut, the wife of Amon, by a Vulture.
Horus, sky god, by a Falcon. Ra, sun god, by a Hawk.
Set (Satan), god of the east frontier, by a Crocodile.
Osiris, god of the dead, by a Goat. Isis, his wife, by a Cow.
Thoth, god of intelligence, by an Ape. Heka, a goddess, by a Frog.
Nechebt, goddess of the South, by a Serpent.
Nile was sacred. (See further, page 122).
Bast, a goddess, by a Cat.
There were many other gods. The Pharaohs were deified.

Chapter 1. Israel in Egypt

Contemporary Egyptian History

During Israel's Sojourn in Egypt, about 1800–1400 B.C. Egypt grew to be a World-Empire. With Israel's departure, Egypt declined, and became, and remained a second-rate Power. (For earlier Egyptian History see page 92.)

PERIOD Between JOSEPH and EXODUS, about 1800-1400 B.C.

13th, 14th, 17th Dynasties: 25 kings: Ruled in the South.

15th, 16th Dynasties: 11 kings: Ruled in the North. These were the Hyksos, or Shepherd kings, a Semitic line of conquerors from Asia, kin to the Jews, who pressed in from Syria, and unified the rule of North Egypt and Syria. Apepi II, about 1800 B.C. of the 16th Dynasty, is thought to have been the Pharaoh who received Joseph. Under the Hyksos Israelites were favored. But when the Hyksos were driven out by the 18th Dynasty, Israelites were reduced to Slavery.

PERIOD of MOSES and the EXODUS

18th Dynasty, 13 kings; 19th Dynasty, 8 kings; 1500–1200 B.C. These made Egypt a World-Empire. Their Names are as follows:

Amosis (Ahmes, Ahmose) I. 1580 B.C. Drove out Hyksos. Made Palestine and Syria tributary to Egypt.

Amenhotep (Amenophis) I. (About 1560 B.C.)

Thotmes (Thothmes, Thutmose) I. (1540 B.C.) Ruled to the Euphrates. First Royal Rock-cut Tomb.

Thotmes II. 1510 B.C. Hatshepsut, his half sister and wife, was real ruler. Made frequent raids to Euphrates.

Thotmes III. (1500 B.C.) Queen Hatshepsut, his half sister, was regent the first 20 years of his reign; and, though he despised her, she completely dominated him. After her death he ruled alone for 30 years. He was the greatest conqueror in Egyptian history. Subdued Ethiopia, and ruled to the Euphrates, first Great Empire in history. Raided Palestine and Syria 17 times. Built a Navy. Accumulated great wealth. Engaged in vast building enterprises. Recorded his achievements in detail on walls and monuments. His tomb is at Thebes. His mummy is at Cairo. Thought to have been the Oppressor of Israel. If so, then Famous Queen Hatshepsut may have been the Pharaoh's Daughter who rescued and brought up Moses.

Hatshepsut. Daughter of Thotmes I. Regent for Thotmes II and Thotmes III. First Great Queen in history. A most remarkable woman, and one of Egypt's greatest and most vigorous rulers. Had many of her statues represent her as a man. Extended the Empire. Built many monuments; two great obelisks at Karnak, the great Temple at Deir el Bahri, furnished with many statues of herself. Thotmes III hated her, and on her death, one of his first acts was to take her name off all monuments and destroy all her statues. Those at Bahri were broken to pieces, flung in a quarry, covered by drifting sands, and recently found by the Metropolitan Museum.

Amenhotep II. (1450–1420 B.C.) Many scholars think he was the Pharaoh of the Exodus. He maintained the empire founded by Thothmes III. His mummy is in his tomb at Thebes.

Thothmes IV. (1420 B.C.) Chariot in which he rode has been found. His mummy is now at Cairo.

Amenhotep III. (1415 B.C.) Greatest splendor of Empire. Repeatedly raided Palestine. Built vast temples. Mummy at Cairo.

Amenhotep IV. (Akhenaten). (1380 B.C.) Under him Egypt lost her Asiatic Empire. He attempted to establish Monotheistic Sun-Worship. If the Exodus occurred under Amenhotep II, some years previous, then this Monotheistic move may have been an indirect influence of Moses' Miracles.

Semenka. (1362 B.C.). A weak ruler.

Tutankhamen. (1360–1350 B.C.) Son-in-law of Amenhotep IV. Restored the old religion. Was one of the lesser rulers of Egypt, at the close of the most brilliant period of Egyptian history; but famous now for the amazing riches and magnificence of his tomb, which was discovered by Howard Carter (A.D. 192). His mummy is still in the tomb. The inner coffin which contains the mummy is of solid gold. His chariot and throne were there. First unrobbed tomb of a Pharaoh to be discovered.

Ay (Eye), Setymeramen. (1350 B.C.). Two weak rulers.

Harmhab (Horembeb) (1340 B.C.). Restored Amon worship.

Rameses I. (1320 B.C.)

Seti (Sethos) I. (1319 B.C.) Palestine recovered. Began the Great Hall at Karnak. Mummy now at Cairo.

Rameses II. (1300 B.C.) Ruled for 65 years. One of the greatest of the Pharaohs, though inferior to Thothmes III and Amenhotep III, but a great builder, a great advertiser, and something of a plagiarist, claiming credit, in some cases, for accomplishments of his predecessors. He re-established the Empire from Ethiopia to the Euphrates. Raided and pillaged Palestine repeatedly. Completed the great Karnak Hall, and other vast works, fortifications, canals and temples, built by slaves taken in war, or throngs of captives from the far South, along with the native working class, toiling in gangs in the quarry or brick fields, or dragging great stone blocks over soft earth. Married his own daughters. Mummy at Cairo.

Merneptah. (1235 B.C.) Thought by some to have been the Pharaoh of the Exodus. His mummy is at Cairo. His throne room in Memphis has been uncovered by the University Museum of Pennsylvania. (See further the following four pages.)

Amenmeses, Siptah, Seti II. (1220–1200 B.C.) 3 weak rulers.

(For later Egyptian Dynasties see page 90.)

Chapter 1. Israel in Egypt

Who was the Pharaoh of the Exodus?

There are two leading opinions: Amenhotep II (1450–1420 B.C.), or Merneptah (1235–1220 B.C. See page 114.)

If the Exodus was under Amenhotep II, then Thothmes III was the great oppressor of Israel, whose sister brought up Moses. This sister was the famous Queen Hatshepsut. How wonderfully do the facts of her reign fit in with the Bible story. She was interested in the mines of Sinai, and restored the temple at Serabit, of which Moses may have had the oversight, with opportunity to familiarize himself with the Sinai region. Then too, when Moses was born Thothmes III would have been an infant, and Hatshepsut regent; and on her death the oppression of Israel grew more bitter, and Moses fled. It would also explain, in part, Moses' prestige in Egypt.

If the Exodus was under Merneptah, then Rameses II was the great oppressor of Israel, whose daughter brought up Moses.

Thus, Moses was brought up either under Thothmes III, or under Rameses II, both of whom were among Egypt's most famous kings.

And Moses led Israel out of Egypt either under Amenhotep II, or under Merneptah.

Whichever it was, the MUMMIES of ALL FOUR have been found. So, we may now see the actual face of the Pharaoh of Moses' day, with whom Moses himself had very intimate dealings.

Discovery of the Mummies

In 1871 an Arab discovered, in a rocky inaccessible cliff, back of Thebes (see page 117), a tomb filled with the treasures and the coffins of 40 of the Mummies of the kings and queens of Egypt. He kept his secret for 10 years, selling the treasures to tourists. Cartouches and scarabs of the greatest of the ancient kings began to appear in circulation. The Cairo Museum authorities went to Thebes to investigate. They found the Arab, and by bribery, threats and torture, made him reveal the place. The Mummies were not in their original tombs. They had been removed ages before to a secret hiding place, on account of the early appearance of professional tomb robbers. These Mummies were removed to Cairo.

Chapter 1. Israel in Egypt

Pharaoh of the Exodus: Amenhotep II? or Merneptah?

Indications for Amenhotep II. The Amarna Letters, written to Amenhotep III and Amenhotep IV, urging help from Pharaoh, indicate that at that time (the earlier date), Palestine was being lost to the "Habiri." Here are some excerpts: "The Habiri are capturing our fortresses; they are taking our cities; they are destroying our rulers. They are plundering all the country of the king. May the king send soldiers quickly. If no troops come this year the whole country is lost to the king." The "Habiri" are taken by many scholars to mean "Hebrews," and, accordingly, that these letters contain a Canaanite description of Joshua's Conquest of Canaan. Those scholars who hold to the later date for the Exodus think that the "Habiri" may have been an earlier invasion or emigration (I Chronicles 4:21–22; 7:21).

Fig. 27.
Hall at Karnak.
© *Matson Photo*

Archaeological evidence that Jericho fell about 1400 B.C. Dr. John Garstang, who made thorough excavations at Jericho, is very confident on this point. (See page 159.)

Fig. 28. Mummy of Amenophis II in the Royal Tomb of Thebes.
© *Matson Photo*

Indications for Merneptah.

Fig. 29. Merneptah's "Israel" Tablet (*Courtesy Cairo Museum.*)

1. Merneptah's "Israel" Tablet. In 1906 Sir Flinders Petrie found a slab of black syenite containing a record of Merneptah's victories, made in the 5th year of his reign. It is 10 feet high, 5 feet wide; now in the Cairo Museum. The word "Israel" occurs in the middle of the second line from the bottom. It says: "Plundered is Canaan. Israel is desolated; his seed is not. Palestine is become a widow for Egypt." This seems like a reference to the Exodus. "His seed is not" may be a reference to the destruction of the boy babies. Inasmuch as ancient kings never recorded anything but their victories, it may be that, although he did all he could to prevent the departure of Israel, yet recorded their departure from Egypt as a victory over them. Those scholars who hold to the earlier date for the Exodus consider this a reference to a raid of Merneptah's into Palestine some 200 years after Israel had settled in the land.

2. Rameses II's claim that he Built Pithom and Rameses, with Israelite labor (Exodus 1:11).

Naville (1883) identified the site of Pithom. He found an inscription of Rameses II, "I built Pithom at the mouth of the East."

He found a long rectangular building with unusually thick walls, whose bricks were stamped with the name of Rameses II.

Petrie (1905) identified the site of Raamses. Fisher, of the University Museum of Pennsylvania (1922), found, at Bethshan in Palestine, a stele of Rameses II, 8 feet high, 2½ feet wide, on which he says he "built Raamses with Asiatic Semitic (Hebrew) slaves."

These two inscriptions thus specify Rameses II as the Pharaoh for whom these cities were built, and the oppressor of Israel; and so point to his successor, Merneptah, as the Pharaoh of the Exodus. It is, however, known that Rameses II was a great plagiarist, taking to himself credit for some of the monuments of his predecessors, having his own name carved on their monuments. Those scholars who hold to the earlier date for the Exodus and Thothmes III as the builder of these cities take these inscriptions to mean that Rameses II rebuilt or repaired them with Hebrews who did not go out with Moses.

On the whole, we think that the evidence is more conclusive that Amenhotep II was the Pharaoh of the Exodus.

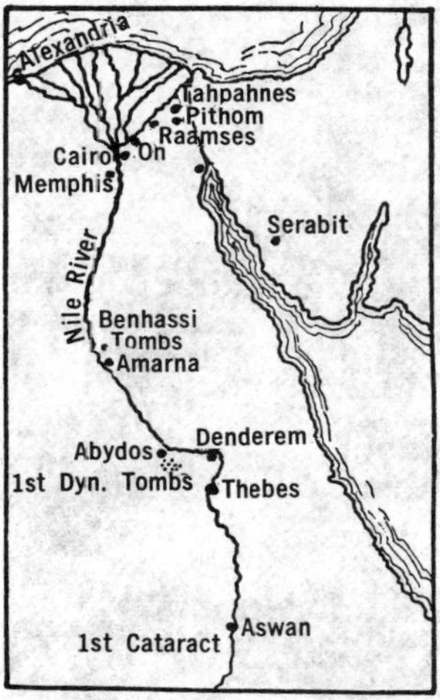

Map 29.

Fig. 30. Statue of Rameses II, Temple of Luxor. © *Matson Photo*

Chapter 1. Israel in Egypt

Ruins of Thebes

The Ruins of Thebes, which Israelites helped to build, are among the grandest in the world. Thebes was situated on both sides of the Nile, in an amphitheatre-like plain between the east and west cliffs. Its ruins cover an area about 5 miles wide east and west, and 3 miles north and south. No city had so many temples, palaces, and monuments of stone, inscribed in the most gorgeous and brilliant colors, and gleaming in gold. It became a great city in the 12th dynasty, 2000 B.C., time of Abraham. Was in its glory 1600 to 1300 B.C., the period of Israel's sojourn in Egypt; and many of its magnificent monuments, no doubt, represent the toil and sweat and blood of unnumbered thousands of Israelite slaves. It was destroyed by the Assyrians 661 B.C. Rebuilt. Destroyed by Persians 525 B.C.

At Karnak, in the east section of Thebes, was one of the largest buildings ever erected. Its central section was called Hypostyle Hall, a model of which, as it is thought to have appeared in its glory, is in Metropolitan Museum. Over the main entrance is one stone, 40 feet long, weighing 150 tons. There are 134 gigantic columns, the 12 central ones being, each 78 feet high, and 11½ feet in diameter. On the top of one column a hundred men could stand.

Fig. 31. Entrance, Ruins of Great Temple of Ammon at Karnak.
© *Matson Photo*

Two Obelisks of Queen Hatshepsut, one still standing, 97 feet high, weighing 150 tons, carry an inscription that they were towed on a barge of 30 galleys, by 960 oarsmen, from quarries 150 miles away. (See Figure 14.)

Chapter 2. Moses

His critics come and go. But Moses still stands out as the foremost man of the pre-Christian world. He took a race of slaves, and, under inconceivably trying circumstances, molded them into a powerful nation which has altered the whole course of history.

He was a Levite (1). The sister who engineered his rescue was Miriam (15:20). His father's name was Amram; his mother, Jochebed (6:20). And what a mother! She so thoroughly imbued him in childhood with the traditions of his people, that all the allurements of the heathen palace never eradicated those early impressions. He had the finest education Egypt afforded, but it did not turn his head, nor cause him to lose his simple childhood faith.

His 40 Years in the Palace

The "Pharaoh's Daughter" who adopted Moses is generally thought to have been the famous Queen Hatshepsut (see page 112). This may have made him a possible heir to the throne, so that, had he renounced his mother's training, he might have been king on the proudest throne on earth.

Fig. 32. Portal of Euergetes II in Karnak, typical of ancient Egyptian architecture. © *Matson Photo*

Fig. 33. Portion of Temple of Rameses III in Karnak, Egypt. © *Matson Photo*

Moses, as he grew to manhood, is thought to have been appointed to high office in the government of Egypt. Josephus says he commanded an army in the South. He must have attained considerable power and reputation; else he would scarcely have undertaken so gigantic a task as the deliverance of Israel, which, it is said, in Acts 7:25, he had in mind in intervening in the fight (11–15). But, though conscious of his power, he failed, because the people were not ready for his leadership.

His 40 Years in the Wilderness

This, in God's Providence, was part of Moses' training. The loneliness and roughness of the wilderness developed sturdy qualities hardly possible in the softness of the palace. It familiarized him with the region in which he was to lead Israel for 40 years.

Midian (15). The center of the Midianite country, where Moses sojourned, was on the east shore of the Gulf of Akaba, though they roamed far to the north and west. In Moses' day they controlled the rich pasture lands around Sinai.

Moses married a Midianite woman, named Zipporah (21), daughter of Jethro, also called Reuel (18; 3:1). Jethro, as priest of Midian, must have been a ruler. Midianites were descended from Abraham, through Keturah (Genesis 25:2); and must have had traditions of Abraham's God. Moses had two sons, Gershom and Eliezer (18:3, 4). Some traditions have it that Moses wrote the Book of Job during this 40 years in Midian.

Chapters 3,4. The Burning Bush

After a life of brooding over the sufferings of his people, and the age-old promises of God, at last, when Moses was 80, the call to deliver Israel came clear direct from God. But Moses was no longer self-confident, as in his younger years. He was reluctant to go, and made all manner of excuses. But assured of Divine Aid, and armed with Power to work Miracles, he went.

Chapter 5. Moses' First Demand on Pharaoh

Pharaoh was insolent; and ordered the taskmasters to lay heavier burdens on the Israelites, requiring them to make the same number of bricks, and yet gather their own straw (10–19).

ARCHAEOLOGICAL NOTE: Bricks of Pithom. Naville (1883) and Kyle (1908) found, at Pithom, the lower courses of brick filled with good chopped straw; the middle courses, with less straw, and that was stubble plucked up by the root; and the upper courses of brick were of pure clay, having no straw whatever. What an amazing confirmation of the Exodus account!

Fig. 34. The Famous Statue of Moses by Michelangelo in the Church of St. Peter at Rome. (*Photo courtesy Radio Times Hulton Picture Library, British Broadcasting Corporation, London.*)

Chapter 6. The Genealogy of Moses

This must be an abbreviated genealogy, mentioning only the more prominent ancestors. Apparently, Moses was grandson of Kohath, yet in his day there were 8,600 Kohathites (Numbers 3:28).

Chapter 7. First of the Ten Plagues

Waters of the Nile turned to Blood. The magicians imitated the miracle on a small scale. Their names were Jannes and Jambres (II Timothy 3:8). Whatever the nature of the Miracle, the fish died, and people could not drink the water.

The Nile was a god. The Ten Plagues were aimed at the gods of Egypt, and were designed to give proof of the power of the God of Israel over the gods of Egypt. Over and over it is repeated that by these Miracles both Israel and Egyptians would come to "know that the Lord is God" (6:7; 7:5, 17; 8:22; 10:2; 14:4, 18); as later, Manna and the Quails were designed to show (16:6, 12).

The Religion of Egypt

On page 111 some of the principal Animal gods are named. In the various temples the sacred animals were fed, groomed and cared for, in the most luxurious way, by great colleges of priests. Of all the animals, the Bull was the most sacred. Incense and sacrifice were offered before the Sacred Bull. The animal, on its death, was embalmed, and with pomp and ceremony befitting a king, buried in a magnificent sarcophagus. The Crocodile also was greatly honored: waited on, in his Temple at Tanis, by 50 or more priests. This was the religion of the people among whom the Hebrew nation was nurtured for 400 years.

Chapter 8. Plagues of Frogs, Lice, and Flies

The Frog was one of Egypt's gods. At the command of Moses frogs swarmed out of the Nile and filled houses. The magicians again imitated the miracle, but Pharaoh was convinced, and promised to let Israel go. However, he changed his mind.

Lice. Moses smote the dust, and it became lice, on both man and beast. The magicians tried to imitate this miracle, but failed; and they were convinced that it was of God. They ceased their efforts to withstand Moses, and advised Pharaoh to yield.

Flies. Swarms of flies covered the people, and filled the houses of the Egyptians. But there were none on the Israelites.

Hardening of Pharaoh's Heart (15, 32). Pharaoh hardened his heart. God hardened Pharaoh's heart (10:20). Both did. God's purpose was to make Pharaoh Repent. But when a man sets himself against God, even God's mercies result in further hardening.

Chapter 9. Plagues of Murrain, Boils, Hail

Murrain, a pestilence among cattle. A terrible blow at Egyptian gods. The Bull was their chief god. Again a distinction between Egyptians and Israelites: Egyptians' cattle died in vast quantities, but not one of those belonging to Israelites. "All" in verse 6 was not meant to be taken literally. Some cattle were left (19–21).

Boils. This plague was upon both man and beast, even on the magicians, from ashes which Moses sprinkled into the air.

Hail. Before the hail fell a merciful warning was extended to believing Egyptians to drive their cattle to cover. Again a distinction between Egyptians and Israelites: no hail in Goshen.

By this time the people of Egypt had become convinced (10:7). The sudden appearance and disappearance of the Plagues, on such a vast scale, at the word of Moses, were accepted as evident Miracles from God. But Pharaoh hesitated, because of the immense loss it would be to him in slave labor. Israelite labor had contributed greatly to Egypt's rise to power, and, with Israel's departure, Egypt's decline began.

It is not known how long a period the Ten Plagues covered. Some think, nearly a year. Pharaoh, no doubt, would have killed Moses, if he had dared. But, with the passing Plagues, Moses' prestige went up and up (11:3).

Chapter 10. Plagues of Locusts, Darkness

Locusts were one of the worst of the Plagues. They came in vast clouds, and would eat every green thing. Would repose at night on the ground in layers to a depth of 4 or 5 inches. When mashed, the smell would be unbearable. The mere threat of it caused Pharaoh's officials to beg him to yield (7).

Darkness. This was a direct blow at Ra, Egypt's sun-god. There was midnight darkness over Egypt for 3 days; but light where Israelites dwelt. Pharaoh yielded; but again changed his mind.

Chapters 11,12. Death of Egypt's First-Born

Nearly a year had passed. At last the crisis was at hand. The blow fell. Pharaoh yielded and Israel departed.

Except for the Ten Plagues, Israel would never have been delivered, and there would have been no Hebrew nation.

"Borrowed" Jewels (12:35). RV says "asked." They were not loans, but outright Gifts: payment of debts for accumulated generations of slave labor. God himself had commanded the people to ask these gifts (3:21, 22; 11:2, 3). Egyptians were glad to comply, for they feared the God of Moses (12:33). A large part of Egypt's wealth was thus transferred to Israel. Some of it was used in construction of the Tabernacle.

ARCHAEOLOGICAL NOTE: Death of Pharaoh's First-Born (12:29). Inscriptions have been found indicating that Thothmes IV, successor of Amenhotep II, was not his first-born nor heir apparent.

Also that Merneptah's first-born met death in peculiar circumstances, and his successor was not his first-born nor heir apparent.

So, whichever the Pharaoh, the Biblical statement is confirmed.

The Beginning of Passover

The Lamb, Blood on the doorpost, Death of the First-Born, Deliverance out of a Hostile Country, and the continuance of this Feast throughout Israel's history, all seem to have been intended of God to be a grand Historical Picture of Christ the Passover Lamb, and our Deliverance out of a Hostile World by His Blood.

Chapter 13. Unleavened Bread. Consecration of First-Born

Unleavened Bread was to be eaten in the Passover Feast as a perpetual reminder of the haste of their night of deliverance (12:34).

Their First-Born were to be consecrated to God perpetually, as a reminder of their redemption by the death of Egypt's First-Born.

The Route to Canaan (17). The direct route, by the Sea Coast, through the Philistine country, was garrisoned with Egyptian armies. And at that time there was a great wall from the Red Sea to the Mediterranean. The most feasible route was the roundabout way through the Wilderness.

The Pillar of Cloud by Day and Pillar of Fire by Night (21, 22). As they left Egypt, now to journey through hostile lands, GOD took them under His Own Care, with this visible sign of His Guidance and Protection. It never forsook them, till they reached the Promised Land, 40 years later (14:19, 24; 33:9, 10; 40:34–38; Numbers 9:15, 23; 10:11).

Chapter 14. They Cross the Red Sea

The place is thought to have been near the location of modern Suez. God used a "strong east wind" to dry up the sea (21). The waters "stood up as a heap," making a perpendicular "wall on either side" (15:8; 14:22). This, and the timing of the waters' return, so as to save Israelites and destroy Egyptians, could have been done Only by a Direct Miraculous Act of God. It alarmed neighbor nations (15:14–16).

ARCHAEOLOGICAL NOTE (EMB)

The language of the record is preserved without irreverence or violence to the story, by the theory that the heavy wind "divided" the sea. The tongue of the Suez gulf may have reached further north than it does today. "Raised beaches" in the area indicate the possibility of such variations of land and water levels. If such were the case, the sea would flow north into the depressions known today as the Bitter Lakes. If a steady wind (verse 21) lowered the level of the water, and that is a commonly observed phenomenon, a land bridge would appear, defended by waters on the north and south. The waters were a "wall" and that means no more than a "defence." There is no need to assume a perpendicular heap of water defying gravity. The "heap" was a vast tide driven down the gulf. The Egyptian pursuit implies that the enemy saw no more than a strange, but not completely unnatural phenomenon. They could not attack from either flank. The waters in the depression to the north and the gulf to the south, were a "wall." They followed through the exposed sea mud and were caught and tangled by the returning tide (verse 25) following the relaxed pressure of the wind.

Chapter 15. The Song of Moses

This deliverance out of Egypt was so similar to what the deliverance of the Church out of the world will be, at the time of the end, that one of the triumphant Songs of the Redeemed is called the "Song of Moses and the Lamb" (Revelation 15:3). This song seems to prefigure the mightier works for which the Redeemed will Sing Praises to God through Endless Ages of Eternity.

Chapter 16. Manna and Quails

One month out, and the hardships of wilderness life began to affect their dispositions. They began complaining, their eyes on the flesh-pots of Egypt, rather than the Promised Land (2, 3).

Manna was a small round flake, used for bread, tasting, it is said, like wafers made with honey (31). It was either a direct creation, or a natural product miraculously multiplied. It fell with the dew each night, looked like coriander seed. They ground it in mills, or beat it in mortars, and boiled it in pots, and make cakes of it. Each person was allowed an omer (7 pints) daily. There was enough on the 6th day to last over the Sabbath. It began one month after they left

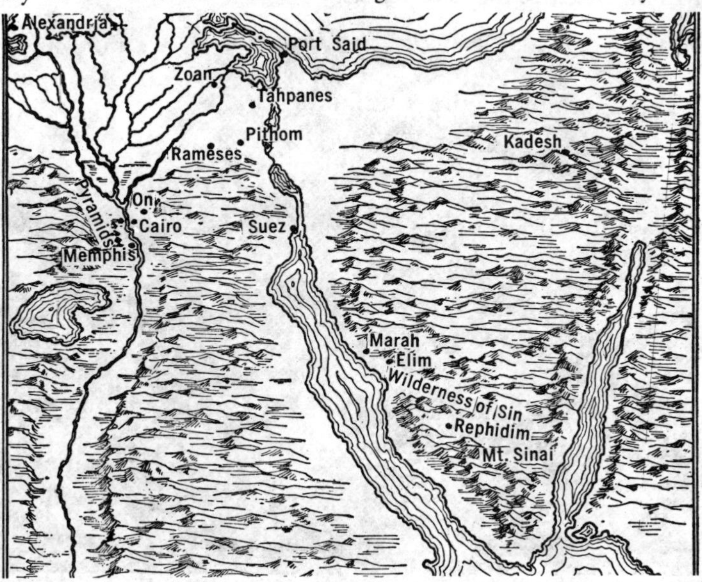

Map 30.

Egypt, and was given daily throughout the 40 years, till they crossed the Jordan, when it ceased as suddenly as it began (Numbers 11:6–9, Joshua 5:12). Jesus regarded Manna as a shadow of himself (John 6:31–58).

Quails (13) were sent, not continuously, as Manna was. Only twice are they mentioned, here and a year later after Israel had left Mt. Sinai (Numbers 11:31–34). The people had great herds of cattle (12: 38), but had to be sparing in their use as food. Their flesh-food in Egypt had been mostly fish.

Mount Sinai

Also called Horeb. The Peninsula of Sinai is triangular in shape, situated between two arms of the Red Sea. The west shore is about 180 miles long; the east shore about 130; and the north border line about 150. The north part of the peninsula is desert; the south part is a "great cluster of rugged chaotic mountains."

The region was named, probably, for the Babylonian moon god, Sin. It was early known for its mines of copper, iron, ochre and precious stones. Long before the days of Abraham, the kings of the East had made a road around the north and west fringes of the Arabian Desert to the Sinai region.

Fig. 35. Mt. Sinai. (*Photo copyright Matson Photo Service.*)

Mount Sinai, where Israel received the Law, is located toward the south point of the Peninsula. It is an "isolated mass of rock, rising abruptly, from the plain in awful grandeur." On the northwest side is a plain, 2 miles long, ½ mile wide, where Israel could have encamped.

40 miles to the northwest of Mt. Sinai, in the Valley of the Caves, there is a sculpture, 400 feet above the mines, which king Semerkhet, of the 1st Dynasty of Egyptian Pharaohs, had made of himself slaying the king of Sinai. There are 250 inscriptions of later kings. 10 miles north of the Valley of the Caves is Serabit-el-Khadem, where Sir Flinders Petrie found the Oldest Known Alphabetic Writing.

Chapter 17. Water from the Rock

Shortly before this, Moses had made the Waters of Marah sweet (15:25). Here, in Rephidim, he produces Water out of a Rock. Later, he performs a similar Miracle, at Meribah (Numbers 20:1–13).

Battle with Amalek (8–15). First attempt, outside of Egypt, to interfere with Israel's march to Canaan. As a result, God commanded that Amalekites be exterminated (14; Deuteronomy 25:17–19).

Chapter 18. Jethro's Advice

Through the counsel of this friendly Midianite prince, Moses' father-in-law, Moses, though inspired in a degree given to few men, was led to form a more efficient organization of the people.

Chapter 19. God's Voice on Mt. Sinai

They were at Mt. Sinai about 11 months (1; Numbers 10:11). In a terrific thunderstorm, accompanied by earthquakes and supernatural trumpet blasts, the mountain capped with terrifying flames, God Spoke out the Ten Commandments, and gave the Law.

500 years later, Elijah, at same mountain, was given a hint that God's Work would be accomplished, Not by Fire and Earthquake methods, but by the Still Small Voice of a Later Prophet (I Kings 19).

Chapter 20. The Ten Commandments

Thou shalt have No Other Gods besides Me.
Thou shalt not worship any Graven Image.
Thou shalt not take the Name of the Lord thy God in vain.
Remember the Sabbath Day, to keep it holy.
Honor thy Father and thy Mother.
Thou shalt not Kill.
Thou shalt not Commit Adultery.
Thou shalt not Steal.
Thou shalt not bear False Witness.
Thou shalt not Covet anything that is thy neighbor's.

These Commandments were afterward engraved on both sides of two tables of stone, "written with the finger of God." "The tables were the work of God, and the writing was the writing of God" (31:18; 32:15, 16). They were kept for centuries in the Ark. It is thought that possibly they were destroyed in the Captivity. What if some day they should be found?

The Ten Commandments were the basis of Hebrew Law. Four of them have to do with our attitude toward God; six, with our attitude toward our fellowman. Jesus condensed them into two: "Thou Shalt Love the Lord thy God with All thy Heart and Soul and Strength and Mind; and thy Neighbor as Thyself."

Reverence for God is the basis of the Ten Commandments. Jesus indicated that he considered it the elemental quality in man's approach to God, and made it the first petition in the Lord's Prayer. "Hallowed be Thy Name." It is surprising how many people, in their ordinary conversation, continually Blaspheme the Name of God, and use it in such a light and trivial way. Idolatry is Absolutely Forbidden.

Chapters 21,22,23,24. "The Book of the Covenant"

After the Ten Commandments, this was the first installment of Laws for the Hebrew Nation. They were written in a Book. Then the Covenant to Obey was sealed with blood (24:4, 7, 8).

Laws about: Slavery. Death for Murder, Kidnapping, or Cursing Parents. "Eye for Eye" Compensation. Stealing. Damage to Crops. Restitution. Seduction. Sorcery. Cohabitation with an Animal. Idolatry. Kindness to Widows and Orphans. Lending. Pledges. Curse not a Ruler. First-fruits and First-born. False Reports. Mobs. Justice. Consideration for Animals. Bribes. Strangers. Sabbath. Sabbatical Year. Passover. Feast of Harvest. Feast of Ingathering. A Kid not to be boiled in its mother's milk. No Covenant with Canaanites, Obedience to be Rewarded.

Chapters 25 to 31. Directions for the Tabernacle

God himself gave the pattern in detail (25:9). It is doubly recorded: here, "thus it shall be"; and in chapters 35 to 40, where the details are repeated verbatim, "thus it was built."

The Tabernacle was a "likeness" of something, a "copy and shadow" of heavenly things (Hebrews 8:5).

It had special meaning to the Hebrew nation; yet it was a "pattern of things to come" (Hebrews 9 and 10).

The Tabernacle, and Temple, which was later built after the pattern of the Tabernacle, were center of Jewish national life.

Of direct Divine Origin, it was an immensely important representation of certain Ideas which God wished to impress on mankind, foreshadowing many teachings of the Christian Faith.

Chapters 32,33. The Golden Calf

The Bull was principal god of Egypt. Later became god of the Ten Tribes (I Kings 12:28). This pitiful apostasy, so soon after God had thundered out from the mountain, "Thou shalt have No Other gods besides Me," and after the Marvelous Miracles in Egypt, indicates the depths to which Israelites had sunk in Egyptian Idolatry. It was a crisis, calling for immediate discipline, and punishment was swift and severe.

Moses' willingness to be "blotted out of God's book" (32:31, 32), for the people's sake, shows the grandeur of his character.

Chapter 34. Moses Again in the Mount

He had been in the Mount 40 days and nights, the first time (24:18). He now returned, for another 40 days and nights (34:2, 28). The first time, he had received the Two Tables and Specifications for the Tabernacle. Now the Two Tables are remade.

Moses' "face shone" (29–35): God was in him: as the face of Jesus "did shine as the sun," when he was Transfigured (Matthew 17:2).

Chapters 35 to 40. The Tabernacle Built

The Tabernacle and all its Furnishings, are now built, exactly according to the specifications already given in chapters 25 to 31.

45 feet long, 15 feet wide, 15 feet high. Made of Perpendicular Boards, covered with Curtains. It faced the East.

The Boards, 20 each for north and south sides, 6 for west end, were each 15 feet long, 2 feet 3 inches wide, were made of hard, acacia wood, and overlaid with gold. Each had 2 tenons at one end, to be stood upright on 2 sockets of silver; and held together with 5 bars run through golden rings on the boards.

The Curtains, 10 in number, each 42 feet long and 6 feet wide, were made of finest linen, blue, purple and scarlet, with cherubs exquisitely worked thereon; and were coupled together with clasps of gold in loops of blue, to make one whole. This One Whole Curtain, thus formed of the 10 Curtains, was 60 feet east and west, 42 feet north and south, the extra 15 feet to hang over the west end. This Curtain was spread over the enclosure made by the golden boards, forming the Tabernacle proper.

The gold and silver, used in the construction of the Tabernacle and its furniture, is estimated at about $1,250,000. This was supplied out of the treasures given by Egyptians (12:35).

The Tent

This covered the Tabernacle. It was made of goat's hair cloth:

Fig. 36. Dr. Schick's Model of the Tabernacle.
© *Matson Photo*

11 curtains, each 45 feet long, 6 feet wide: coupled together with clasps of brass, the whole being 66 feet east and west, 45 feet north and south. Over it a covering of Red Leather made of ram's skins. And over it a covering made of Badger (seal? or porpoise?) skins.

This Threefold Tent, of Goat's Hair Cloth, Red Leather, Badger Skin, was probably supported by a ridge-pole at the top.

The Most Holy Place, or Holy of Holies

West 15 feet of the Tabernacle, a perfect cube. Represented God's Dwelling Place. It contained only the Ark. Was entered by the High-Priest once a year. A "shadow of heaven" (Hebrews 9:24).

The Ark

A Chest, 3¾ feet long, 2¼ feet wide, 2¼ feet high. Made of acacia wood, overlaid with pure gold. It contained the Two Tables of the Ten Commandments, a Pot of Manna and Aaron's Rod.

The Mercy-Seat was the top of the Ark, a lid of solid gold. A Cherub at each end, of one piece with the lid, facing each other, their wings spread out, looking down toward the Mercy-Seat. The Mercy-Seat being just above the Two Tables of the Ten Commandments, represented the meeting place of Law and Mercy: thus, a "shadow" of Christ. The Cherubs presented a very vivid picture of the Interest of Heavenly Beings in Human Redemption. This seems to be what Peter had in mind when he said, "which things the Angels desire to look into" (I Peter 1:12).

The Ark was probably lost in the Babylonian Captivity. In Revelation 11:19, John saw the Ark "in the temple." But that was in a vision, certainly not meaning that the actual material Ark was there; for in heaven there will be "no temple" (Revelation 21:22).

The Holy Place

The east 30 feet of the Tabernacle. It contained the Table of Shewbread, on north side; the Candlestick, on south side; the Altar of Incense, just before the Veil. Perhaps a "shadow" of the Church.

The Veil

Made of the finest linen, blue, purple and scarlet, exquisitely embroidered with Cherubs. It separated the Holy from the Most Holy: or, so to speak, God's Throne Room from Man's Waiting Room. The Veil was rent in twain, at Christ's Death (Matthew 27:51), signifying that, at that moment, the door to God's presence was open to man.

There was another Veil, called the Screen, for the entrance at the east end of the Tabernacle: of fine linen, blue, purple, scarlet.

The Candlestick

Made of pure gold. A central shaft, with 3 branches on each side. Thought to have been about 5 feet high, and 3½ feet across the top. Fed with olive oil; and trimmed and lighted daily (30:7, 8).

The Candlesticks of Solomon's Temple, patterned after this, and may have included it, were, no doubt among the treasures taken to Babylon, and afterward returned (Ezekiel 1:7).

Fig. 37. The Candlestick as sculptured in the Arch of Titus. (*Courtesy Dr. S. H. Horn, Andrews University, Berrien Springs, Mich.*)

The Candlestick in Herod's Temple, in Jesus' day, may have been one of these. It was taken to Rome, A.D. 70; sculptured on the Arch of Titus; afterward "respectfully deposited in the Christian Church at Jerusalem" A.D. 533. Nothing further is known of it. The sculpture on the Arch of Titus may be a fair representation of the appearance of the original.

The Candlestick may have been a "shadow" of God's Word; though in Revelation 1:12, 20, Candlesticks represent Churches.

Table of Shewbread

3 feet long, 1½ feet wide, 2¼ feet high. Made of acacia wood; overlaid with pure gold. Was to hold 12 loaves of bread, replaced each Sabbath with new loaves. On north side of Holy Place. A symbol of gratitude to God for daily bread (Luke 11:3).

Laver

A Great Brass Bowl to hold water, for priests to wash their hands and feet, before ministering at Altar, or in Tent. Signified Cleanliness, literally, and from Sin. A "shadow" of Cleansing by the Blood of Christ, and perhaps of Christian Baptism.

Court

Fence around the Tabernacle. 150 feet long, 75 feet wide; facing the east. Hangings of fine twined linen, 7½ feet high, on pillars of brass 7½ feet apart, with fillets and hooks of silver, set in sockets of brass. The Gate, in east end, 30 feet wide, of linen, blue and scarlet.

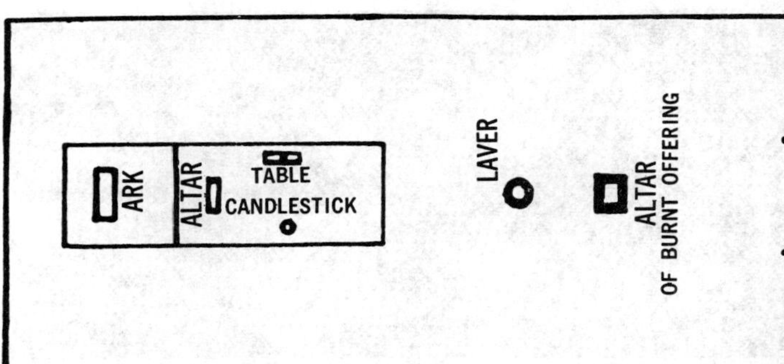

Map 31. Plan of the Tabernacle.

Altar of Incense

3 feet high, 1½ feet square. Made of acacia wood; overlaid with pure gold. In front of Veil. Incense to be burned thereon, morning and evening (30:8). Signifying perpetual Prayer (Revelation 8:3–5).

Altar of Burnt Offering

The Great Altar for the Sacrifice of Animals, 7½ feet square, 4½ feet high. Built of acacia boards, covered with brass; hollow, to be filled with earth. A ledge around it, about halfway up, for priests to stand on. It stood east of the Tabernacle, near the entrance to the Court. The Fire on it was miraculously kindled and never went out (Leviticus 9:24; 6:9). A symbol that man has no access to God, except as a Sinner atoned for by Blood. A "shadow" of the Death of Christ.

LEVITICUS

Sacrifices
The Priesthood
Holy Seasons
Various Laws

The word "Leviticus" means "pertaining to Levites"; that is, the book contains the System of Laws, administered by the Levitical Priesthood, under which the Hebrew nation lived. These laws were given mostly at Mt. Sinai, with additions, repetitions and explanations, throughout the Wilderness wanderings.

Levites, one tribe out of the Twelve, were set apart for the work of God. God took them, in lieu of First-Born sons. God claimed the First-Born, both of men and flocks. They were supported by Tithes; and had 48 cities (Numbers 35:7; Joshua 21:19).

One Family of Levites, Aaron and Sons, were set apart to be Priests. The Rest of the Levites were to be Assistants to the Priests. Their duties were the care of the Tabernacle, and, later, the care of the Temple; and to be Teachers, Scribes, Musicians, Officers and Judges. (See on I Chronicles 23.)

Chapters 1 to 5. Various Kinds of Offerings

Burnt-Offerings: of Bullocks, Rams, Goats, Doves, Pigeons: were wholly burned, signifying entire Self-Dedication to God.

Meal-Offerings: of Grain, Flour or Cakes, without leaven: a handful was burned: the rest was for priests.

Peace-Offerings: of Cattle, Sheep or Goats: the fat was burned: the rest, eaten, partly by priests, partly by offerers.

Sin-Offerings and Trespass-Offerings: different offerings for different sins: fat was burned: the rest, in some cases was burned without the camp, and in some cases eaten by the priests. Where wrong had been done to another, restitution, with a fifth added, had to be made before the offering.

Chapters 6,7. Further Directions about Offerings

Beside the offerings mentioned, there were Drink-Offerings, Wave-Offerings, Heave-Offerings: appendages to other Offerings.

Manner of Sacrifice: the animal was presented at the Tabernacle. The offerer laid his hands on it, making it his representative. Then it was slain. The blood was sprinkled on the Altar. Then the specified part was burned.

Frequency of Sacrifice: there were Daily Burnt-Offerings. On the first of each Month, additional Offerings; and at feasts of Passover, Pentecost and Tabernacles, and on Day of Atonement, and special offerings of various kinds.

Chapters 8,9. Consecration of Aaron

And his Sons to the Priesthood. Previous to the time of Moses, sacrifices were offered by Heads of Families. But now, the nation organized, a place set apart for sacrifice, and a ritual prescribed, a special Hereditary Order of men was created, in solemn ceremony, for the service. Aaron, and his First-Born Son, in succession, were High-Priests. The priesthood was maintained by tithes of Levites' tithes, and parts of some sacrifices. 13 cities were given to them (Joshua 21:13–19).

The High-Priest's Garments. Every detail was specified of God (Exodus 28). A Robe of blue, with bells at bottom.

An Ephod, which was a sort of cape, two pieces joined on the shoulders, hanging, one over front, one over back, with an onyx stone on each shoulder, each bearing six names of the tribes: made of gold, blue, purple, scarlet and fine linen.

A Breastplate, about 10 inches square, of gold, blue, purple, scarlet and fine linen, double, open at the top, fastened with gold chains to the Ephod, adorned with 12 precious stones, each stone bearing the name of a tribe; containing the Urim and Thummim, which were used to learn the will of God, but what they were is not known.

This Sacrificial System, of Divine Origin,

Was placed of God at the very center and heart of Jewish national life. Whatever its immediate applications and implications may have been to Jews, the unceasing sacrifice of animals, and the never-ending glow of altar fires, beyond doubt, were designed of God, to burn into the consciousness of men a sense of their deep Sinfulness, and to be an agelong picture of the Coming Sacrifice of Christ, toward Whom they pointed and in Whom they were fulfilled.

The Levitical Priesthood

Was divinely ordained as mediator between God and the Hebrew nation in the ministry of Animal Sacrifices. Those sacrifices were fulfilled in Christ. Animal Sacrifices are No Longer Necessary. Christ Himself is the Great High-Priest for Man: the Only Mediator between God and Man. Hebrews 8, 9, 10, makes this very clear.

Chapter 10. Nadab and Abihu

Their swift and terrible punishment was a warning against high-handed treatment of God's ordinances; even to Church Leaders who distort the Gospel of Christ with all kinds of Human Traditions.

Chapter 11. Clean and Unclean Animals

There was a distinction before the Flood between Clean and Unclean animals (Genesis 7:2). Moses enacted this distinction into law. It was based partly, on their wholesomeness as food; and, partly, on religious considerations, designed to serve as one of the marks of Separation of Israel from other nations. Jesus abrogated the distinction (Mark 7:19), "making all meats clean."

Chapter 12. Purification of Mothers after Childbirth

The period of separation, in case of boy babies, was 40 days; and, in case of girl babies, 80 days. The purpose of this is thought to have been to help hold the Balance of Sexes, as Men, by exigencies of war, were subject to greater fatalities than Women.

Chapters 13,14. Test of Leprosy

These regulations were for the purpose of controlling the spread of one of the most loathesome and dreaded diseases.

Chapter 15. Uncleanness

The elaborate system of specifications as to how a person could become ceremonially "unclean," and the requirements concerning it, were, it seems, designed to promote personal physical cleanliness, and continual Recognition of God in all the ways of life.

Chapter 16. Annual Atonement

This was on the 10th day of the 7th month (see page 148). Most solemn day of the year. The removal of sin was only for a year (Hebrews 10:3), but it pointed forward to eternal removal (Zechariah 3:4, 8, 9; 13:1; Hebrews 10:14).

"Scapegoat" (8) is translated in RV, "Azazel," which is thought to have been a name for Satan. After the sacrificial goat had been offered, then the High-Priest laid his hands on the head of the goat for Azazel, and confessed over him the sins of the people. Then the goat was led away into a solitary land, bearing away the sins of the people. This ceremony was one of God's historical fore-pictures of Coming Atonement for Human Sin by the Death of Christ. What else could it mean?

Chapter 17. Manner of Sacrifice

The law required presentation of animals at the door of the Tabernacle. Eating of Blood was strictly forbidden (3:17; 7:26, 27; 17:10–16; Genesis 9:4; Deuteronomy 12:16, 23–25); and still is (Acts 15:29).

Chapter 18. Canaanite Abominations

If we wonder that some of these things: Incest, Sodomy, Cohabitation with Animals: are even mentioned, it was because they were in common practice among Israel's neighbors.

Chapters 19,20. Miscellaneous Laws

About the Sabbath. Idolatry. Peace-Offerings. Gleanings. Stealing. Swearing. Wages. Courts. Tale-Bearing. Brotherly Love. Diverse Breeding and Planting. Adultery. Orchards. Augury. Marred Beards and Flesh Cuttings. Harlotry. Respect for the Aged. Kindness to Strangers. Just Weights and Measures. Moloch Worship. Sorcery. Parents. Incest. Sodomy. Animals. Clean and Unclean.

Thou Shalt Love Thy Neighbor as Thyself, 19:18

This was one of the highlights of Mosaic law. Great consideration was shown to the Poor. Wages were to be paid day by day. No usury was to be taken. Loans and gifts were to be made to the needy. Gleanings were to be left in harvest fields for the poor. All through the Old Testament, unceasing emphasis is placed on Kindness to widows, orphans and strangers.

Concubinage, Polygamy, Divorce, Slavery

Were allowed, but greatly restricted (19:20; Deuteronomy 21:15; 24:1–4; Exodus 21:2–11). Moses' law lifted Marriage to a far higher level than existed in surrounding nations. Slavery was hedged around with humane considerations; and it never existed on a large scale among the Jews, nor with such cruelties, as were prevalent in Egypt, Assyria, Greece, Rome and other nations.

Capital Punishment

Offenses punishable with Death were: Murder (Genesis 9:6; Exodus

21:12; Deuteronomy 19:11–13), Kidnapping (Exodus 21:16; Deuteronomy 24:7), Death by Negligence (Exodus 21:28, 29), Smiting or Cursing a Parent (Exodus 21:15–17; Leviticus 20:9; Deuteronomy 21:18–21), Idolatry (Leviticus 20:1–5; Deuteronomy 13; 17:2–5), Sorcery (Exodus 22:18), False Prophecy (Deuteronomy 18:10, 11, 20), Blasphemy (Leviticus 24:15, 16), Sabbath Profaning (Exodus 31:14), Adultery (Leviticus 21:10; Deuteronomy 22:22), Rape (Deuteronomy 22:23–27), Ante-Connubial Immorality (Deuteronomy 22:13–21), Sodomy (Leviticus 20:13), Animal Cohabitation (Leviticus 20:15, 16), Incestuous Marriages (Leviticus 20:11, 12, 14).

These Laws were the Laws of God

Some of them are similar to the Laws of Hammurabi, with which Moses no doubt, was well-acquainted. And, though Moses may have been influenced by his Egyptian training, and by Babylonian tradition, yet over and over he repeats, "Thus Saith the Lord," indicating that these Laws were the direct Enactment of GOD HIMSELF.

Some of them may seem severe to us. But, if we could transport ourselves back to Moses' world, they probably would not seem severe enough. On the whole, Moses' Law, "in its insistence on Personal Morality, and Personal Equality, and its consideration for the Old and Young, for Slave and for Enemy, for Animals, and its Health and Food regulations, was far Purer, more Rational, Humane, and Democratic than, and showed a wisdom far in advance of, Anything in Ancient Legislation, Babylonian, Egyptian or any other." The "Moral Miracle" of the pre-Christian world.

Moses' Law was designed of God as a "schoolmaster to bring us to Christ" (Galatians 3:24). Some of its provisions were accommodations to their "hardness of heart" (Matthew 19:8).

Chapters 21,22. Priests and Sacrifices

An expansion of the provisions of chapters 1 to 9. Priests must be without physical blemish, and may marry only a virgin. Sacrificial animals must be without blemish, and at least 8 days old.

Chapters 23,24. Feasts, Lamp, Shewbread, Blasphemy

Feasts (see on Deuteronomy 16). The Candlestick to be kept burning continually. The Shewbread to be changed each Sabbath. Blasphemy to be punished with death. The "eye for eye" legislation (24:19–21), was part of civil law, perfectly just (see on Matthew 5:38 and Luke 6:27).

Chapter 25. Sabbatic Year. Year of Jubilee

Sabbatic Year was every 7th year. The land was to lie fallow. No sowing, no reaping, no pruning of vineyards. Spontaneous produce was to be left for the poor and the sojourner. God promised enough in the 6th year to carry over. Debts of fellow Jews were to be cancelled.

Jubilee Year was every 50th year. It followed the 7th Sabbatic Year, making two rest years come together. It began on the Day of Atonement. All debts were cancelled, slaves set free, and lands that had been sold returned. Jesus seemed to regard it as a sort of picture of the Grand Jubilee which He came to proclaim (Leviticus 25:10; Luke 4:19).

Ownership of Land

The Land of Canaan was divided among the 12 tribes, and, in the tribes, among families. With certain exceptions, it could not be sold in perpetuity out of the families. A sale amounted to a Lease till Jubilee, when it would be returned to original family.

The Number SEVEN

Every 7th day a Sabbath.
Every 7th year a Sabbatic year.
Every 7th Sabbatic year was followed by a Jubilee year.
Every 7th month was especially holy, having 3 feasts.
There were 7 weeks between Passover and Pentecost.
Passover Feast lasted 7 days.
Tabernacles Feast lasted 7 days.
At Passover 14 lambs (twice 7) were offered daily.
At Tabernacles 14 lambs (twice 7), daily, and 70 bullocks.
At Pentecost 7 lambs were offered.

(*See further page 688.*)

Chapter 26. Obedience or Disobedience

This chapter, like Deuteronomy 28, of Magnificent Promises and Frightful Warnings, is one of the great chapters of the Bible.

Chapter 27. Vows and Tithes

Tithes (Genesis 14:20; 28:22; Leviticus 27:30–32; Numbers 18:21–28; Deuteronomy 12:5, 6, 11, 17, 18; 14:23, 28, 29; 26:12). One-Tenth of the land and of the increase of flocks and herds was to be given to God.

Three Tithes are mentioned: Levitical, Festival and for the Poor every 3rd year. Some think there was only One Tithe, and that it was used partly for festivals, and every 3rd year partly for the poor. Others think that the Festival Tithe was taken out of the 9/10 left after the Levitical Tithe had been paid.

The Tithe was in use long before the days of Moses. Abraham and Jacob paid Tithes. Among the Jews the Tithe was for the support of Levites; and Levites were used in civil government as well as in religious service (see on I Chronicles 23).

First-Fruits. God claimed as His Own, not only the Tithes, but also First-Born sons of all families (in lieu of whom he accepted the tribe of Levi), and First-Born of all Flocks and Herds, and First-Fruits of the field. The First-Fruits of the harvest were to be offered at Passover, and No Part of the New Crop could be used till this was done (Leviticus 23:14). The First Crop of a young orchard (the 4th year) was to be Given to God, and No Fruit of it could be used Till This Was Done. Lesson: Make God First in life.

NUMBERS

The Forty Years in the Wilderness
Israel's Journey to the Promised Land

Outline and Chronology of the Journey

Departure from Egypt:	1st month 15th day
Cross the Red Sea	
At Marah (Map 30); Elim; Wilderness of Sin;	
People Murmur	
Quails and Manna	2nd month 15th day
At Rephidim: Water from Rock;	
Battle with Amalek; Jethro	
At Sinai: Ten Commandments; Covenant;	3rd month (?) day
Book of Laws; Moses 40 days in Mt.	
Golden Calf; 2nd 40 days in Mt.	
Tabernacle Built; Census	2nd year 2nd month 1st day
Set forward from Sinai	2nd year 2nd month 20th day
Had been at Sinai about a year	
At Taberah: Fire; Quails; Plague	
At Hazeroth:	
Sedition of Miriam and Aaron	
At Kadesh-barnea: Spies Sent;	
People Rebel; Moses Intercedes;	
People Defeated; More Laws;	
Korah; 14,700 die; Aaron's Rod	
38 years in Surrounding Wilderness	
At Kadesh-barnea, second time:	40th year 1st month
Miriam's Death; Water from	
Rock; Moses' Sin	
Final Start for Canaan	
Edom Refuses Passage	
At Mt. Hor: Aaron's Death	40th year 5th month 1st day
Israel Defeats Canaanites	
South from Mt. Hor: Serpents	
East and North around Edom	
Then North along East Border of Moab	
Conquer Amorites and Bashan	
Camp on the Plains of Moab:	
Balaam; Sin of Peor;	

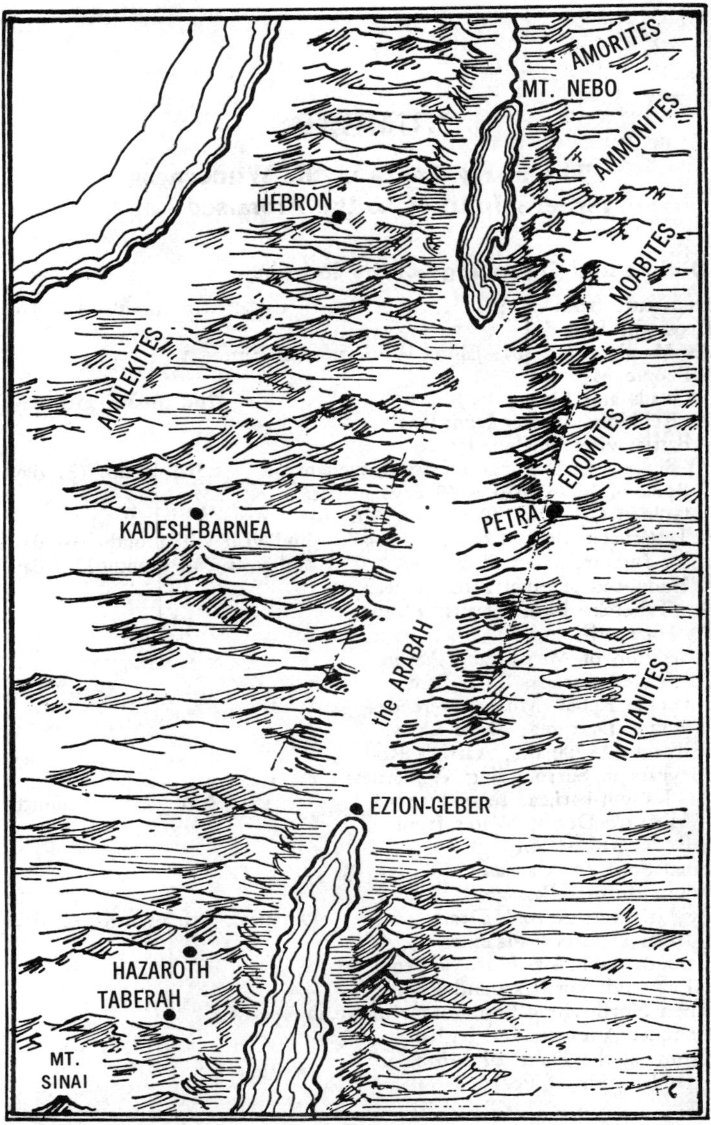
AMORITES
MT. NEBO
AMMONITES
HEBRON
MOABITES
AMALEKITES
EDOMITES
PETRA
KADESH-BARNEA
the ARABAH
MIDIANITES
EZION-GEBER
HAZAROTH
TABERAH
MT.
SINAI

Map 32.

24,000 Slain; Census; Destruction of Midianites; 2½ Tribes Settle East of Jordan; Moses' Farewell; His Death	40th year 11th month 1st day
They Cross the Jordan	41st year 1st month 10th day
Keep Passover; Manna Ceases	41st year 1st month 14th day

Chapter 1. The Census

This census, taken at Mt. Sinai, showed 603,550 males above the age of 20, exclusive of Levites (45–47). Another census, 38 years later, showed 601,730 (see on chapter 26).

Chapters 2,3,4. Organization of the Camp

Every detail was assigned with military precision. This was necessary in handling so vast a multitude. Arrangement of tribes was:

	Dan 62,700	Asher 41,500	Naphtali 53,400	
Benjamin 35,400		Merarites 6,200		Judah 74,600
Manasseh 32,200	Gershonites 7,500	TABERNACLE	Moses Aaron	Issachar 54,400
			W←——→E	
Ephraim 40,500		Kohathites 8,600		Zebulon 57,400
	Gad 45,650	Simeon 59,300	Reuben 46,500	

When they broke camp, Judah and eastern tribes led the march. In center, the Tabernacle was bulwarked with southern and western tribes; northern tribes bringing up the rear.

Chapters 5,6. A Group of Laws

About Lepers; Restitution; Women suspected of Adultery; Vows. The Beautiful Benediction (6:24–26).

Chapters 7,8,9. Preparation for the Journey

Offerings of the Princes. Dedication of the Tabernacle. Levites Consecrated. Passover Observed. Cloud (9:15–25, see on Exodus 13:21).

Chapters 10,11. They Set Forward to the Promised Land

At Mt. Sinai one year. The Cloud lifted. The Silver Trumpets sounded. Judah led the march. And they were on their way.

Within 3 days, at Taberah, they began Murmuring (10:33; 11:1–3). That was their specialty. They knew how to Complain. God sent them quails, but smote them with a plague. (See on Exodus 16.)

Chapter 12. Sedition of Miriam and Aaron

Poor Miriam, before it was over, wished she had never started the thing. Moses was "very meek" (3). What an admirable trait in one of the greatest men of the ages! Jesus, was "meek," and said, "Blessed are the meek" (Matthew 5:5; 11:29).

Chapters 13,14. The Twelve Spies Sent to Canaan

Moses planned to go directly from Sinai to Canaan. He went straight to Kadesh, 150 miles north of Sinai, 50 miles south of Beersheba, the south gateway to Canaan, intending to enter at once.

But the Spies brought a discouraging report, and the people refused to go forward, and would have stoned Moses except for the miraculous intervention of God. This was the crucial point of the journey. Within sight of the Promised Land, they turned back. For them the opportunity Never Returned. Caleb and Joshua, the two spies who wanted to go forward, were the only ones of the 600,000 men over 20 who lived to enter Canaan.

Chapters 15 to 19. Various Laws. Korah

Korah, jealous of Moses, sought to usurp his leadership. Moses went straight to God. And God settled the matter in no time. The earth opened, and the rebels went down.

Moses' Troubles

He sure had a lot of them. No sooner was he out of Egypt than trouble began. The Amalekites attacked immediately, and a year later at Kadesh. Edomites, Moabites, Ammonites, Amorites and Midianites, all joined hands to block Israel's path to Canaan.

And his own people, who had been delivered out of Egypt, and sustained, by Marvelous Miracles, murmured and murmured, and complained and complained and rebelled and rebelled. They began complaining in Egypt. Then at the Red Sea. Then at Marah. Then in the Wilderness of Sin. Then at Rephidim; at Taberah; Hazeroth; Meribah; and now at Kadesh, in sight of the Promised Land, they flatly refused to go further, which must have well-nigh broken Moses' heart.

Besides all this Moses had no end of trouble with his own trusted leaders. Aaron made the golden calf at Sinai. Miriam and Aaron tried to usurp his authority (chapter 12). 10 of the 12 Spies led the people in their refusal to enter Canaan. They were ready to stone Moses (14:10; Exodus 17:4).

And, last of all, Moses was not permitted to enter the Promised Land, the one lifetime dream of his heart.

Except for the Miraculous Grace of God, we do not see how he could have borne up under it all. But when, on the banks of the Jordan, God took him to the Upper Land, then he understood.

Chapter 20. Final Start for Canaan

There seems to be a gap of 38 years between the 19th and 20th chapters, covering the interval between the first arrival at Kadesh (13:26), and the final departure from Kadesh for Canaan. In the 33rd chapter there is a list of encampments, 40 in all, from Egypt to the Plains of Moab. Of these, 18 were between Rithmah and Kadesh. Rithmah may be another name for Kadesh.

We judge, from the expression, "many days at Kadesh" (Deuteronomy 1:46), and the mention of these 18 camping stations between the first and second arrivals at Kadesh, that, possibly, Kadesh may have been a sort of general headquarters, with these other encampments as God directed. Remaining for some time at one spot, with their flocks and herds on surrounding hills and valleys. Then moving on at signal from the Tent.

Moses' Sin, which cost him the Promised Land, seems to have been his failure to Give God Credit for the Miracle of Water (10:12).

Miriam, Aaron and Moses Died, all three, in the same year. Miriam, at Kadesh (1). Aaron, at Mt. Hor (28). Moses, in Mt. Nebo (Deuteronomy 32:50; 34:1, 5). Miriam, about 130. Aaron, 123. Moses, 120.

"Gathered to his people" (24), is a beautiful Old Testament expression for Death, hinting Reunion with Loved Ones beyond the grave.

ARCHAEOLOGICAL NOTE: Kadesh-barnea (20:1; Deuteronomy 1:19), is now generally identified as 'Ain Kadees, a "strangely beautiful" oasis, fed by Two springs flowing from beneath a Rock cliff. Alongside is a Dry spring. Cobern thinks that Moses must have struck the Rock above the Dry Spring. He struck "twice" (Numbers 20:11); and these Two new springs burst forth; and are still flowing. (See Cobern's "Recent Explorations in Palestine.")

Chapter 21. From Kadesh to the Jordan

Perhaps the coalition of Amalekites and Canaanites just to the north of Kadesh seemed too strong for Israel to attempt the direct route to Hebron. At any rate, God had other plans.

They started eastward, to go up the east shore of the Dead Sea, through Edom's territory. But Edom refused permission.

Then Moses turned southward, down the Araba, the desolate valley extending from Dead Sea to Red Sea, "a great and terrible wilderness," for the long, and circuitous, and hazardous route, around Edom and Moab, and then northward, along the borders of Arabia, as far as to Bashan, east of the Sea of Galilee, and then southwestward to the Plains of Moab, opposite Jericho. God commanded Moses not to molest the Edomites, Moabites or Ammonites, even though they tried to stop Israel.

The Fiery Serpent (6–9). An historical fore-picture of the Gospel. As those who were bitten by poisonous serpents looked to the Brazen Serpent, and were healed; so, if we, who have been wounded by Sin, Look to Jesus, we Live (John 3:14).

The Israelites afterward made an Idol of the Brazen Serpent, called it Nehushtan, and burned incense to it, till 700 years later, Hezekiah destroyed it (II Kings 18:4).

Conquest of Gilead and Bashan (21–35). The Amorites, who had crossed to the east of the Jordan, attacked Israel. Moses had refrained from attacking any of the nations through whose country he marched. But now that the Amorites attacked, he fought back, and took their country. Then Bashan attacked; and he defeated them; and the region east of the Jordan was his.

How Could the Wilderness Support 3,000,000 for 40 Years?

By the DIRECT MIRACULOUS HELP OF GOD. The Miracles were so Continuous and so Stupendous that the evident intention of the record is that it Could Not Have Been Done Except by the Hand of God. To those who find it difficult to believe these things, we answer: for some of us, it is easier to believe them, exactly as they are recorded, than it is to believe the Strange and Fanciful Theories invented to discredit them. They are in accord with the entire Bible story. The numbers recorded may be a misreading of the text. Perhaps the "thousands" were "clan groups." If so, it might be possible drastically to reduce the totals without doing despite to the text.

The Purpose of the Wilderness Miracles, we may think, was: 1. To Preserve the Nation. In God's plan a Messianic Nation had been devised to pave the way for a Coming Messiah. 2. To build in the nation, which had been nurtured in Egyptian Idolatry, Faith in GOD, the One True God; and to be an Example, for all time to come, that God can be Trusted in all the exigencies of life. 3. For effect on surrounding nations, particularly Canaanites; that they might understand that the movement of Israel toward Canaan was of God, and that it would be with GOD that they would have to reckon.

Aside from various accompanying miracles, the Transplanting of a Whole Great Nation, bodily, from one land to another, meanwhile maintaining it 40 years in a Desert, was in itself one of the most Stupendous Miracles of the ages.

ARCHAEOLOGICAL NOTE: Israel's Route. Recent excavations have revealed the ruins of hundreds of fortified cities that once covered the hills of Moab, Ammon and Gilead, indicating dense population, and powerful peoples, of the time of Moses.

Chapters 22 to 25. Balaam

His prophecies were a remarkable prediction of Israel's influential place in history, through a "Star," to arise out of Jacob (24:17). Though God used him to utter correct prophecy, yet, Balaam, for money, was instigator of Israel's shameful Sin with Moabite and Midianite Women, for which Balaam was slain, and 24,000 Israelites perished (31:8, 16; 25:9). And Balaam's name became a synonym (II Peter 2:15; Jude 11; Revelation 2:14).

Chapter 26. 2nd Census

Wilderness life must have been hard, for, of 600,000 above 20, at the first census (chapter 1), only 2 beyond 60 survived. The younger generation, inured to, and hardened by, the desert, were a different class of men from what their fathers had been as slaves freshly freed from the fleshpots of Egypt.

The book of NUMBERS is named from these Censuses.

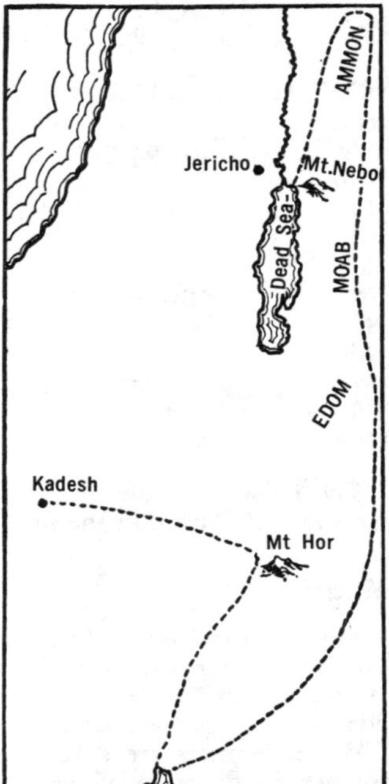

Map 33. Journey to Canaan.

Chapters 27 to 36. Various Regulations and Events

Brotherless Daughters (27). Feasts and Offerings (28, 29). Vows (30). Slaughter of Midianites (31). Two Tribes and a Half settled east of Jordan (32). Summarized Diary of the 40 Years (33). Directions for the Division of the Land (34; see on Joshua 13). Levitical Cities (35: see on Joshua 21). Brotherless Daughters (36, also 27).

The Jewish Calendar

There was a Sacred year, and a Civil year. The Sacred year began in the Spring. The Civil year began in the Fall. The 7th Sacred month was the 1st Civil month. The Year was divided into 12 Lunar Months, with a 13th Month 7 times in every 19 years.

The Natural Day was from sunrise to sunset. The Natural Night, from sunset to sunrise. The Civil Day was from sunset to sunset.

Hours were counted from 6 in the morning, and 6 in the evening. The First Watch, in the evening, was from 6 to 9; Second Watch, 9 to 12; Third Watch, 12 to 3; Fourth Watch, 3 to 6.

MONTH	NAME	APPROXIMATELY	FEASTS
1st	Abib, or Nisan	April	Passover
2nd	Ziv, or Iyar	May	
3rd	Sivan	June	Pentecost
4th	Tammuz	July	
5th	Ab	August	
6th	Elul	September	
7th	Ethanim, or Tishri	October	Tabernacles
8th	Bul, or Marcheshvan	November	
9th	Chislev	December	Dedication
10th	Tebeth	January	
11th	Shebat	February	
12th	Adar	March	Purim

The Feast of Dedication was instituted later in Maccabean times; the Feast of Purim, in the times of Esther.

Miracles

The Bible is God's Word. An integral part of the Bible record is MIRACLE, for the Specific Purpose of showing it to be God's Word. Except for Miracles, how could we know it to be a Revelation of God? No Miracle, No Evidence of Deity.

While Miracles are a very conspicuous feature of the Bible, they are not abundant in all parts of the Bible. Bible Miracles, not including Prophecies and their Fulfillment, are particularly noticeable in Four Great Periods, centuries apart:

At	Establishment of Nation: Moses and Joshua:	1400 B.C.
At	Crisis in Struggle with Idolatry: Elijah and Elisha:	850 B.C.
At	Captivity, when Idolatry was Victorious: Daniel:	600 B.C.
At	Introduction of Christianity: Jesus and the Apostles.	

The Miracles of Moses

Aside from Jesus, it has never been given to any man to be agent of so many stupendous manifestations of Divine Power:

The Plagues of Egypt. Waters of Red Sea Dried Up. Water Made Sweet at Marah. Quails Sent in Wilderness of Sin, and at Taberah. Manna Supplied Daily for 40 Years. Water from the Rock at Rephidim, and Meribah. Cataclysmic Scenes at Sinai. God's Voice from the Mountain. The Ten Commandments Written on Stone with God's Finger. Moses' Face Shone. Moses Talked Face to Face with God. Miriam's Leprosy Sent and Removed. Korah and his Rebels Swallowed by Earth. Punitive Plagues at Taberah, Kadesh and Peor. Aaron's Rod Buds. People Healed by Brazen Serpent. Balaam's Ass Speaks. Balaam Utters Amazing Prophecies. Israel Guided 40 Years by a Supernatural Cloud. Clothes Waxed Not Old, and Feet Swelled Not.

Moses could not have delivered Israel out of Egypt, and sustained them in the Wilderness 40 years, without the Direct Miraculous Help of God. This high privilege, as in case of Paul, was accompanied by almost unbelievable Suffering (see pages 144, 603).

DEUTERONOMY

Moses' Farewell Addresses
Recounting of History
Rehearsal of Principal Laws
Solemn Warnings

This book contains:
Prediction of Prophet like unto Moses (18:15–19).
What Christ called The Great Commandment (6:4).
Words Christ quoted to the Tempter (6:13, 16; 8:3).
Some of the world's Finest Eloquence

The word "Deuteronomy" means "Second Law," or "Repetition of the Law." In Exodus, Leviticus and Numbers, laws had been promulgated, at intervals. Now, their wanderings over, on the eve of entrance into Canaan, these laws were rehearsed and expounded, in anticipation of, and with applications to, settled life.

Some passages, for genuine eloquence, are unsurpassed in literature, even by Demosthenes, Cicero, Pitt or Webster.

Chapters 1,2,3. From Sinai to the Jordan

An epitome, in retrospect, of Numbers 1–33. After one of the noblest and most heroic accomplishments of the ages, Moses' final appeal to God to let him go over the Jordan, was denied (3:23–28), because God had something better for him, in a Better World.

Chapters 4,5. Cling to God's Word

Very earnest exhortations to Observe God's Commandments, to Teach them diligently to their Children, and to Shun Idolatry; with the ever-recurring reminder that their Safety and Prosperity would depend on their Loyalty and Obedience to God.

The Ten Commandments (chapter 5) are also given in Exodus 20.

Chapter 6. The Great Commandment

"Thou shalt Love the Lord thy God with All Thy Heart, with All Thy Soul, and with All Thy Might" (5). This is repeated over and over (10:12; 11:1, 13, 22). And it was re-emphasized by Jesus (Matthew 22:37), and given First Place in his teaching.

For the perpetuation of God's Ideas among the people, they were not to depend on Public Instruction alone; but were to teach them diligently at Home (6–9). Because books were few and scattered, the people were to write certain important parts of the Law on their doorposts, and bind them on their arms and foreheads, and talk of them constantly.

Chapter 7. Canaanites and Idols to be Destroyed

No covenants or marriages to be made with them. This was necessary in order to save Israel from Idolatry and its Abominations.

Chapter 8. Wonders of the Wilderness Recalled

For 40 years they had been "proved" and fed with manna; "their raiment waxed not old, and their feet swelled not"; that they might learn to Trust God, and Live by His Word (2–5).

Chapters 9,10. Israel's Persistent Rebellion

Three times over Israel is reminded that God's wondrous dealings with them was "not for their righteousness" (9:4, 5, 6). They had been a rebellious and stiffnecked people all the way.

Chapter 11. Blessings of Obedience

A great chapter. Like chapters 6 and 28, it is an appeal for Devotion to God's Word and Obedience to His Commandments as basis for National Prosperity, with wondrous Promises and ominous Warnings.

Chapters 12,13,14,15. Various Ordinances

All Idols to be Destroyed. Moses, reared in the hot-bed of Egyptian Idolatry, and surrounded all his life by Idol-Worshiping peoples, never compromised with Idolatry. And, as he repeatedly warned, Idolatry did turn out to be the Ruin of the nation.

"Rejoice": note how often the word is used (12:7, 12, 18; 14:26; 28:47). It is a favorite word in Psalms and Epistles.

Clean and Unclean Animals (14:1–21, see on Leviticus 11). Tithes (14:22–29, see on Leviticus 27). Sabbatic Year (15:1–11, see on Leviticus 25). Slavery (15:12–18, see on Leviticus 19). First-fruits (15:19–23, see on Leviticus 27).

Chapter 16. Set Feasts

Three times a year all males were required to appear before God: at the Feasts of Passover, Pentecost and Tabernacles. Besides these were the Feasts of Trumpets, and Day of Atonement. These Feasts were designed to Keep God in the thought of the people, and to promote National Unity.

Passover, also called the Feast of Unleavened Bread, was kept in the spring, on the 15th day of the 1st month, lasting 7 days, as a Memorial of their Deliverance out of Egypt.

Pentecost, also called the Feast of Weeks, of Harvest, or of First-Fruits, was kept on the 50th day after Passover, lasting 1 day.

Tabernacles, also called Feast of Ingathering, was kept on 15th day of 7th month, 5 days after Day of Atonement, lasting 7 days.

Feast of Trumpets, on the 1st day of the 7th month, ushered in the Civil Year (see on Numbers 28).

Day of Atonement, on 10th day of 7th month (see on Leviticus 16).

Chapter 17. Prediction of a King

God here prophesied it, with some instructions, and some warnings (14–20). The Kingdom came some 400 years later (see on I Samuel 8). Samuel told the people that, in asking for a king, they were rejecting God. This is not a contradiction. The fact that God foreknew they would want a king is not saying that He approved their action; but only that He foreknew they would do it, and wanted to be consulted in their choice. In rejecting the Form of Government which God had given them, they were rejecting God. Note the instruction about Kings being lifelong Readers of God's Word (18–20). What a suggestion to present-day Rulers! Note too that Kings began right away to do what God had said they should not do: multiply to themselves Wives, and Horses and Gold (16, 17; I Kings 10:14–29; 11:1–13).

Chapter 18. The Prophet Like unto Moses

This prediction (15–19) may have a secondary reference to the Prophetic order at large, that is, a succession of Prophets, to be raised up for emergencies in Israel's history. But its language unmistakably points to One Illustrious Individual, THE MESSIAH. It is one of the Old Testament's most specific predictions of Christ. Jesus himself so understood it (John 5:46). And so did Peter (Acts 3:22).

The Hebrew Nation was being founded of God as the medium through which one day All Nations would be Blessed. Here is an explicit statement that the System around which the Hebrew Nation was now being organized would Not be the System by which the Nation would Bless All Nations; but that it would be Superseded by Another System, given by Another Prophet, which would contain God's Message to All Nations. Judaism to be superseded by Christianity.

Chapter 19. Cities of Refuge

For protection of those causing accidental deaths. Moses had already set aside three such cities east of the Jordan: Bezer, Ramoth and Golan (4:41–43). Later, Joshua set aside three west of the Jordan: Kedesh, Shechem and Hebron. All six were Levitical cities, included in the Levites' 48 cities (Numbers 35:6).

Chapter 20. Rules of Warfare

Those who had built a new house, or planted a new vineyard, or were newly married, or faint-hearted, were to be excused from military service. Canaanites were to be destroyed; food-bearing trees to be spared.

Chapters 21 to 26. Various Laws

In case of Unknown Murderer. Slave Wives. Polygamous Children. Rebellious Sons. Death to be by Hanging. Stray Animals. Lost Articles. Clothes of Men and Women to be Different. Setting Birds to be Spared. House-roofs to have Railings. About Farming and Clothing. Harlotry. Adultery. Rape. Eunuchs. Bastards. Ammonites. Moabites, Edomites. Cleanliness in Camp. Treatment of Slave Refugees. Prostitutes. Sodomites. Harlots. Usury. Vows. Divorce. Marriage. Pledges. Kidnapping. Leprosy. Wages. Justice for the Poor. Gleanings. 40 Stripes to be limit. Levirate Marriages. Interference in Strife. Diverse Weights and Measures. Amalekites. First-Fruits and Tithes.

Chapter 27. The Law to be Recorded on Mt. Ebal

Joshua did this (Joshua 8:30–32). In an age when books were scarce it was a custom to record laws on stones, and set them up in various cities, so the people could know them. It was done in Egypt, and in Babylonia, as, for instance, the Code of Hammurabi (see page 50). Moses commanded Israel to do it first thing on arrival in Canaan. The stones were to be plastered with plaster, and the laws written thereon "very plainly."

Chapter 28. The Great Prophecy about the Jews

An amazing chapter. The Whole Future History of the Hebrew Nation is outlined. The Babylonian Captivity and Destruction by the Romans, is vividly pictured. The "eagle" (49), was the ensign of the Roman army. In both the Babylonian and Roman sieges of Jerusalem, men and women ate their own children for food (53–57). The

Jews' Dispersion, Wanderings, Unceasing Persecutions, Trembling of Heart and Pining of Soul, even unto the present time, are all graphically Foretold. This 28th Chapter of Deuteronomy, placed alongside the History of the Hebrew Nation, constitutes one of the Most Astounding and Indisputable Evidences of the Divine Inspiration of the Bible. How else account for it?

Chapters 29,30. The Covenant, and Final Warnings

Moses' last words, as he envisions the fearful consequences of Apostasy: serve God, the Way of Life; serve Idols, Certain Death.

Chapter 31. Moses Wrote This Law in a Book

Moses, 40 years before, had written God's Words in a Book (Exodus 17:14; 24:4, 7). He had written a Diary of his Journeys (Numbers 33:2). Now, his Book completed, he handed it over to the Priests and Levites, with instruction, that it be Read Periodically to the people. The Constant Teaching of God's Written Word to the people is the safest and most effective way to guard against the corruption of their religion. When Israel gave heed to God's Word, they prospered. When they neglected it, they suffered adversity.

Reading of God's Book brought Josiah's Great Reformation (II Kings 23). Likewise, Ezra's (Nehemiah 8). Likewise, Luther's. New Testament books were written to be Read in the Churches (I Thessalonians 5:27; Colossians 4:16). God's Word itself is the Power of God in the human heart. O that the Present-Day Pulpit would somehow learn to keep itself in the background, with God's Word in the Foreground!

ARCHAEOLOGICAL NOTE (EMB)

The Law had many historical roots:

(a) Many of the cult objects were in general use. The Tabernacle and the Ark have Egyptian antecedents in many details. Ras Shamra Tablets contain similar details.

(b) Much of the ritual was in earlier use. e.g. animal sacrifice. The trespass, peace, tribute, "wave" offerings, the first-fruits, shewbread, etc. are details from the Ras Shamra Tablets, which cannot be proved imitations of the Mosaic ritual. Rather they betray a common origin (cf. Creation and Flood Tablets).

(c) Much of the social legislation can be paralleled from the Codes of Hammurabi and the Hittites.

Thus, in a sense, much of the Law is pre-Mosaic, in the same sense that much of the Lord's Prayer is pre-Christian. No originality in the narrow sense of the word is claimed for either.

But:

(a) Moses' code is the divinely sanctioned order for a theocracy.
(b) Moses' code is more humane in its penology.
(c) Moses' code contains none of the paganism of the earlier codes (e.g. Ras Shamra provisions for "seething a kid in its mother's milk").
(d) Moses' code sets a higher value on human life and relates all to God, the love of God, and love for one's neighbor.

Chapter 32. The Song of Moses

After Moses had finished "writing the book," he composed a Song for the People to Sing. He had celebrated their deliverance from Egypt with a Song (Exodus 15). He had written another, which is known as the 90th Psalm. Popular Songs are among the best means of Writing Ideas on People's Hearts. Deborah and David poured out their souls to God in Song. The Church, from its inception till now, has used this same means of United Rhythmic Expression to perpetuate and spread the Ideas for which it stands.

Chapter 33. The Blessings of Moses

Wherein the Tribes are called by Name, with predictions about each; similar to Jacob's Blessing on his Sons (Genesis 49).

Chapter 34. Death of Moses

"At 120, his eye not dimmed, nor his natural force abated, the aged man climbed Mt. Pisgah, and, as he viewed the Promised Land, into which he longed to go, God gently lifted him into the Better Land. In a moment his soul had passed within the veil, and he was at home with God. God buried his body. Of his sepulchre no man knows. His remains were removed from all reach of idolatry."

Mt. Nebo

The loftiest peak of Mt. Pisgah, 8 miles east of the mouth of the Jordan. The end of Moses' earthly journey. From its summit could be seen the hills of Judea and Galilee; and Mt. Carmel, where, Elijah, 500 years later, called down fire from heaven, and from which Elijah went to Mt. Sinai, where Moses had given the Law, and then to Mt. Pisgah, where Moses had died, as if he wanted to be with Moses in death. And then, from where Moses had died the angels came down, and bore Elijah away to join Moses in Glory.

At the Transfiguration of Jesus

From the top of Mt. Pisgah, could be seen, on a clear day, far to the north, the snow-capped summit of Mt. Hermon, where Jesus was Transfigured; and where Moses was again seen by mortal eyes, he and Elijah, the two representatives of the Law and the Prophets, talking with Jesus of the work for which the Law and the Prophets had paved the way. And there Moses participated in the heavenly announcement that the time had come for the Dispensation which he had inaugurated to give place to that of the Greater Prophet whom he had foretold: that henceforth it would be, not the thunders of Sinai, but the "still small voice" of "Jesus only." Mt. Sinai, Mt. Pisgah, Mt. Hermon. Moses, Elijah, Jesus.

Moses

Here closes the first fourth of the Old Testament (almost as large as the entire New Testament), all written by one man, Moses. What a man Moses must have been! How intimate with God! What a work he did! What a benefactor to mankind! 40 years in the Palace of Pharaoh. 40 years a refugee in Midian. 40 years leader of Israel in the wilderness. Delivered a nation of some 3,000,000 from servitude; transplanted them from one land to another; organized for them a system of jurisprudence that has been a fountain source of much of the world's civilization.

Winston Churchill's Opinion of Moses

"We reject with scorn all those learned and labored myths that Moses was but a legendary figure upon whom the priesthood and the people hung their essential social, moral and religious ordinances. We believe that the most scientific view, the most up-to-date and rational conception, will find its fullest satisfaction in taking the Bible story literally. We may be sure that all these things happened just as they are set out according to Holy Writ. We may believe that they happened to people not so very different from ourselves, and that the impressions those people received were faithfully recorded, and have been transmitted across the centuries with far more accuracy than many of the telegraphed accounts we read of goings on of today. In the words of a forgotten work of Mr. Gladstone, we rest with assurance upon 'The Impregnable Rock of Holy Scripture.' Let men of science and learning expand their knowledge, and probe with their researches, every detail of the records which have been preserved to us from those dim ages. All they will do is to fortify the grand simplicity and essential accuracy of these recorded truths which have so far lighted the pilgrimage of man."

JOSHUA

The Conquest of Canaan
Crossing the Jordan
Fall of Jericho
Victories over Canaanites
Sun Made to Stand Still
Tribes Settled in the Land

The Man Joshua

He was of the tribe of Ephraim (Numbers 13:8). The Grecianized form of his name was "Jesus." In that he led his people into the Promised Land, he may have been a prototype of his Greater Successor, who is leading His own into the Promised Land of Heaven.

Joshua had been a personal attendant of Moses throughout the 40 years of wilderness wandering. Was with Moses in the Mount (Exodus 24:13). Was one of the Twelve Spies (Numbers 13:8, 16). Josephus says he was 85 when he succeeded Moses. Is thought to have been about 6 years subduing the land; and the rest of his life, settling and governing the twelve tribes; his rule over Israel, in all, covering about 25 years. He died at 110, and was buried in Timnath-serah, in Ephraim. He was a great warrior, disciplined his forces, sent spies, but prayed, and trusted in God.

ARCHAEOLOGICAL NOTE: Joshua's Name. In the Amarna Tablets, written, at that time, from Palestine, to Pharaoh in Egypt, about the rout of the king of Pella, these words occur: "Ask Benjamin. Ask Tadua. Ask Joshua."

Chapter 1. The Book

A grand chapter. Israel had a Book. It was only a fraction of what we now have in God's Word. But, O how important! God's solemn warning to Joshua, on the threshold of a gigantic task, was to be very careful to keep close to the words of that Book. Joshua gave heed, and God honored him with phenomenal success. What a lesson for Church Leaders!

Chapter 2. The Two Spies and Rahab

Rahab had heard of the miracles wrought on behalf of Israel, and had become convinced that Israel's God was the True God (10, 11). And when she met the spies, she decided, at the risk of her life, to cast her lot with Israel and their God.

She may not have been as bad as the word "harlot" now implies. She lived among people without morals. Priestesses of the Canaanite religion were public prostitutes. Her profession was considered by the people among whom she lived, as honorable, and not disgraceful, as it now is among us.

Rahab married an Israelite named Salmon (Matthew 1:5). Caleb had a son named Salmon (I Chronicles 2:51). It may have been the same Salmon. If so, then she married into a leading family of Israel. She, thus, became ancestress of Boaz, David and of Christ. She is named among the heroes of Faith (Hebrews 11:31).

ARCHAEOLOGICAL NOTE: Rahab's House on the Wall (2:15). In Jericho they did build houses on the wall (see next page).

Chapter 3. They Cross the Jordan

When the Ark of the Lord stood in the water's edge, the river rose

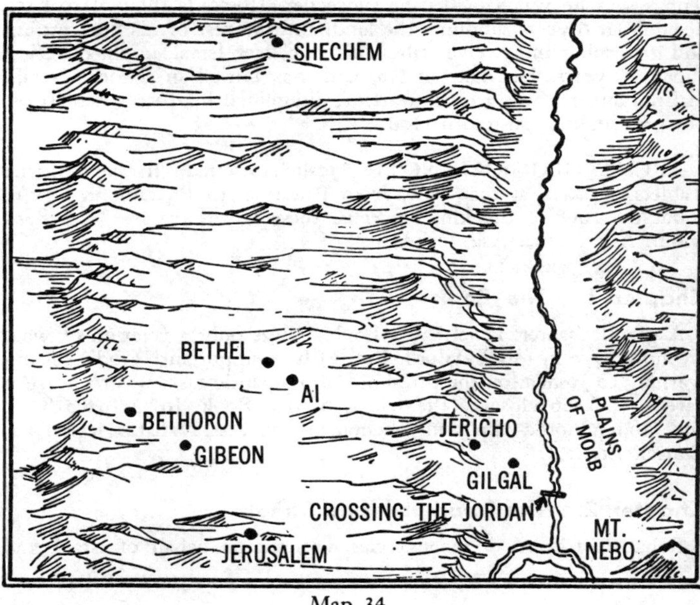

Map 34.

up in a great heap, at Adam (16). Adam was 16 miles to the north. Below that the water drained off, and left the pebbly river bottom dry enough to walk on. At Adam, the Jordan flows through clay banks 40 feet high, which are subject to landslides. In 1927 an earthquake caused these banks to collapse, so that no water flowed past them for 21 hours. God may have used some such means to make the waters "stand" for Joshua. At any rate, it was a mighty miracle, and terrified the already frightened Canaanites (5:1).

Jesus, 1400 years later, was baptized, in the Jordan, at the same place where Joshua crossed.

Chapter 4. The Memorial Stones

There were two piles of them: one where the Ark stood in the east edge of the river (9); the other, where they lodged on the west side, at Gilgal (4:20); placed there, so that generations to come would not forget the place of the gigantic miracle.

Chapter 5. They Keep the Passover

At long last, within the Promised Land, on the 4th day after they had crossed the Jordan, their first act was to keep the Passover (4:19; 5:10). Next day the Manna ceased (5:12). Then God sent His Invisible Army, to encourage Joshua for the task ahead (5:13–15).

Chapter 6. The Fall of Jericho

Jericho was taken by the direct help of God, to inspire the Israelites with confidence, in beginning their conquest of more powerful peoples. Led by the Ark of the Lord, with trumpets blowing, they compassed the city 7 days. Hovering above were the invisible hosts of the Lord (5:14), waiting for the appointed hour; and, on the 7th day, at the blast of the trumpets, the walls fell.

In an amazing prophecy a curse was pronounced on anyone who would attempt to rebuild the city (26, see on I Kings 16:34).

Jericho was about 6 miles from the Jordan; Gilgal, Joshua's headquarters, being about halfway between.

The wall of Jericho enclosed about 7 acres. It was an inner fortress city for the thick population roundabout.

New Testament Jericho was about a mile south of the ruins of Old Testament Jericho. The modern village of Jericho is about a mile to the southeast.

ARCHAEOLOGICAL NOTES: Dr. John Garstang, director of the British School of Archaeology in Jerusalem and of the Department of Antiquities of the Palestine Government, excavated the ruins of Jericho (1929–36). He found pottery and scarab evidence that the

Fig. 38. Ruins of ancient Jericho, showing old city wall.
© *Matson Photo*

Fig. 39. Airview of mound of ancient Jericho (foreground), and the Jericho Plain.
© *Matson Photo*

city had been destroyed about 1400 B.C., coinciding with Joshua's date, and, in a number of details, dug up evidence confirming the Biblical account in a most remarkable way.

"The wall fell down flat" (20). Dr. Garstang found that the wall did actually "fall down flat." The wall was double, the two walls being 15 feet apart; the outer wall, 6 feet thick; the inner wall, 12 feet thick; both being about 30 feet high. They were built, not very substantially, on faulty uneven foundations, of brick 4 inches thick and 1 to 2 feet long, laid in mud mortar. The two walls were linked together by houses built across the top, as Rahab's house "on the wall." Dr. Garstang found that the outer wall fell outward, and down the hillside, dragging the inner wall and houses with it, the streak of bricks gradually getting thinner down the slope. The foundation walls of the palace, 4 courses of stone high, remain, in situ, tilted outward. Dr. Garstang thinks there are indications that the wall was shaken down by an earthquake (of which traces may be seen), a method which God could have used as easily as any other.

"They burnt the city with fire" (24). Signs of the conflagration and destruction were very marked. Garstang found great layers of charcoal and ashes and wall ruins reddened by fire. The outer wall suffered most. Houses alongside the wall were burned to the ground. The stratum generally was covered with a deep layer of black burnt debris, under which there were pockets of white ash, overlaid with a layer of fallen reddish brick.

"Keep yourselves from the devoted thing" (18). Garstang found, under the ashes and fallen walls, in the ruins of storerooms, an abundance of food stuffs, wheat, barley, dates, lentils, and such, turned to charcoal by intense heat, untouched and uneaten: evidence that the conquerors refrained from appropriating the foods.

Chapters 7,8. Fall of Ai and Bethel

At Ai, Israel, at first, met with a dreadful reverse, due to Achan's trespass. Coming right after the miraculous crossing of the Jordan, and the miraculous fall of Jericho, it was a terrible shock to Israel. It was a disciplinary lesson. God was with them, but he meant them to understand that He expected Obedience.

ARCHAEOLOGICAL NOTE: Bethel. The statements in 8:9, 12, 17, indicate that it was a joint battle, both Ai and Bethel being included; 8:28; 12:9, 16, that both cities were destroyed. They were only 1½ miles apart.

The mound of Bethel (Beitan) was excavated by the Kyle Memorial Expedition under the joint auspices of the American School at Jerusalem and Xenia Theological Seminary of Pittsburgh (1934), under the leadership of W. F. Albright. They found that it had been

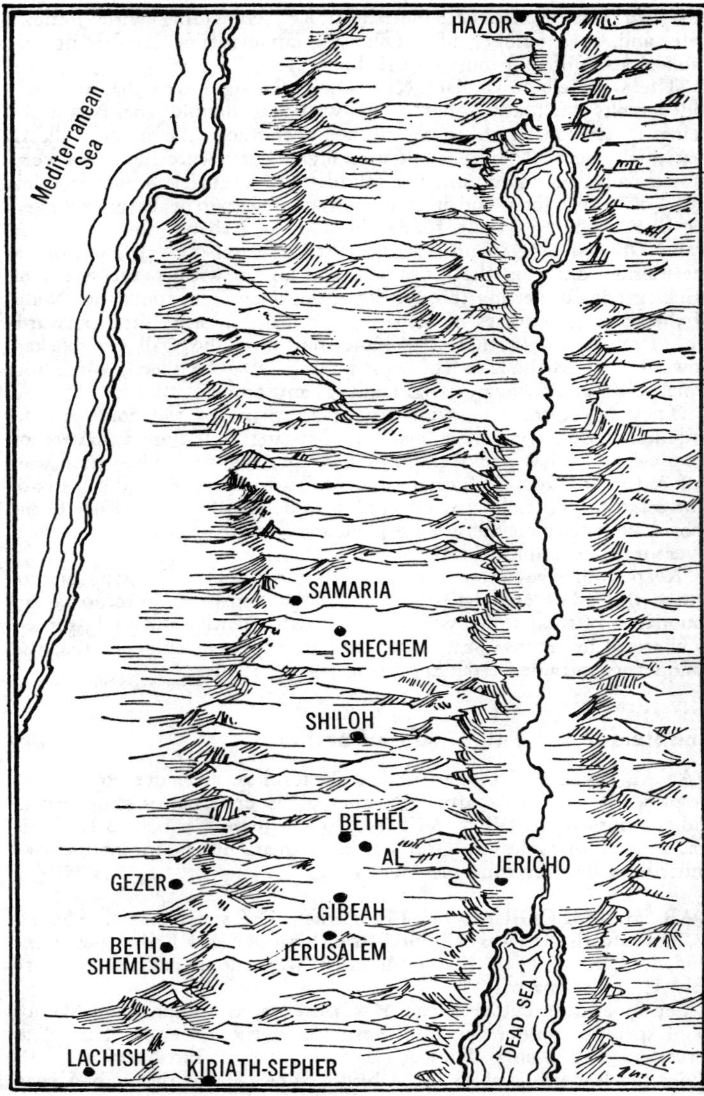
Mediterranean
Sea
HAZOR
SAMARIA
SHECHEM
SHILOH
BETHEL
AI
JERICHO
GEZER
GIBEAH
BETH
SHEMESH
JERUSALEM
DEAD SEA
LACHISH
KIRIATH-SEPHER

Map 35.

destroyed, at a time coinciding with Joshua's invasion, by a "tremendous conflagration," which "raged with peculiar violence." There was a solid mass, 5 feet thick, of "fallen brick, burned red, black ash-filled earth, and charred and splintered debris." Albright said he had seen nowhere in Palestine indications of a more destructive conflagration.

Chapter 8:30-35. The Law Recorded at Mt. Ebal

Moses had commanded that this be done (see on Deuteronomy 27). Shechem, in the center of the land, was between Mt. Ebal and Mt. Gerizim, in a vale of surpassing beauty. Here Abraham, 600 years before, had erected his first altar in the land. Here Joshua, in solemn ceremony, read the Book of the Law to the people.

Chapters 9,10. Battle where the Sun Stood Still

Gibeon, about 10 miles northwest of Jerusalem, was one of the land's greatest cities (10:2). The Gibeonites, frightened at the fall of Jericho and Ai, made haste to enslave themselves to Israel. This enraged the kings of Jerusalem, Hebron, Jarmuth, Lachish and Eglon; and they marched against Gibeon. Then Joshua came to the rescue of Gibeon. This led to the famous battle of Gibeon, Bethhoron and westward, where the Sun stood Still for a whole day. In what way the sun stood still we do not know. Some have calculated that the calendar lost a day about that time. At any rate, in some way or other, daylight was miraculously prolonged, so that Joshua's victory might be made complete.

ARCHAEOLOGICAL NOTES: Lachish, Debir are named among cities destroyed (10:32, 39).

Lachish. The Wellcome Archaeological Expedition (1931–), found there a great layer of ashes coinciding with Joshua's time.

Debir (Kiriath-sepher, Tel Beit Mirsim). Here, the Joint Expedition of Xenia Seminary and the American School at Jerusalem (1926–28), found a deep layer of ashes, charcoal and lime, with indications of a terrible fire, and cultural marks of Joshua's time; everything under it Canaanite; everything above it Israelite.

Chapter 11. Kings of the North Defeated

In the battle of Bethhoron, where the Sun Stood Still, Joshua had broken the power of the kings of the South. Now, his victory over the kings of the North, at Merom, gave him control of the whole land.

Three Stupendous Miracles, mainly, did the job: Jordan Divided; Jericho's Fall; and Staying of the Sun. GOD did it.

ARCHAEOLOGICAL NOTE: Hazor. Joshua "burnt Hazor with fire" (11:11). Garstang found the ashes of this fire, with pottery evidence that it had occurred about 1400 B.C.

Also: an Amarna Tablet, written to Pharaoh, 1380 B.C., by the Egyptian envoy in north Palestine, says, "Let my lord the king recall what Hazor and its king have already had to endure."

Thus, Joshua's conquest of Palestine is testified by great layers of ashes, bearing marks of Joshua's time, in Jericho, Bethel, Lachish, Debir and Hazor, exactly confirming Biblical statements.

Chapter 12. List of Destroyed Kings

31 are named. Generally speaking, the whole land was conquered (10:40; 11:23; 21:43). However, small groups of Canaanites remained (13:2–7; 15:63; 23:4; Judges 1:2, 21, 27, 29, 30, 31, 33, 35). After Joshua's death, these made trouble for Israel. Also, Philistine, Sidonian and Lebanon country was still unconquered.

Chapters 13 to 22. Division of the Land

Map on next page shows approximate location of Canaanite nations, and distribution of Twelve Tribes of Israel. There were 6 cities of Refuge (chapter 20, see on Deuteronomy 19); and 48 cities for Levites, including 13 for Priests (21:19, 14). The Altar, by the Jordan (chapter 22), was intended as a token of National Unity for a nation divided by a great river.

Chapters 23,24. Joshua's Farewell Address

Joshua had received from Moses the Written Law of God (1:8). He now added to it his own book (24:26). Joshua made good use of "books," as Moses had done (see on Deuteronomy 31). He had the land surveyed with a "book" (18:9). He read to the people the "book" of Moses (8:34). At Mt. Ebal he "wrote on stones" a copy of the Law (8:32).

The main urge of Joshua's final address was against Idolatry. Canaanite idolatry was such an aesthetic combination of religion with free indulgence of fleshy desire that only persons of exceptional strength of character could withstand its allurements.

The Canaanites

"Canaanites" was a general term for all the inhabitants of the land. In a more restricted sense, it applied to those dwelling in the plain of Esdraelon and adjoining plains. "Amorites" also was a general term sometimes applied to all the inhabitants, but more specifically to a

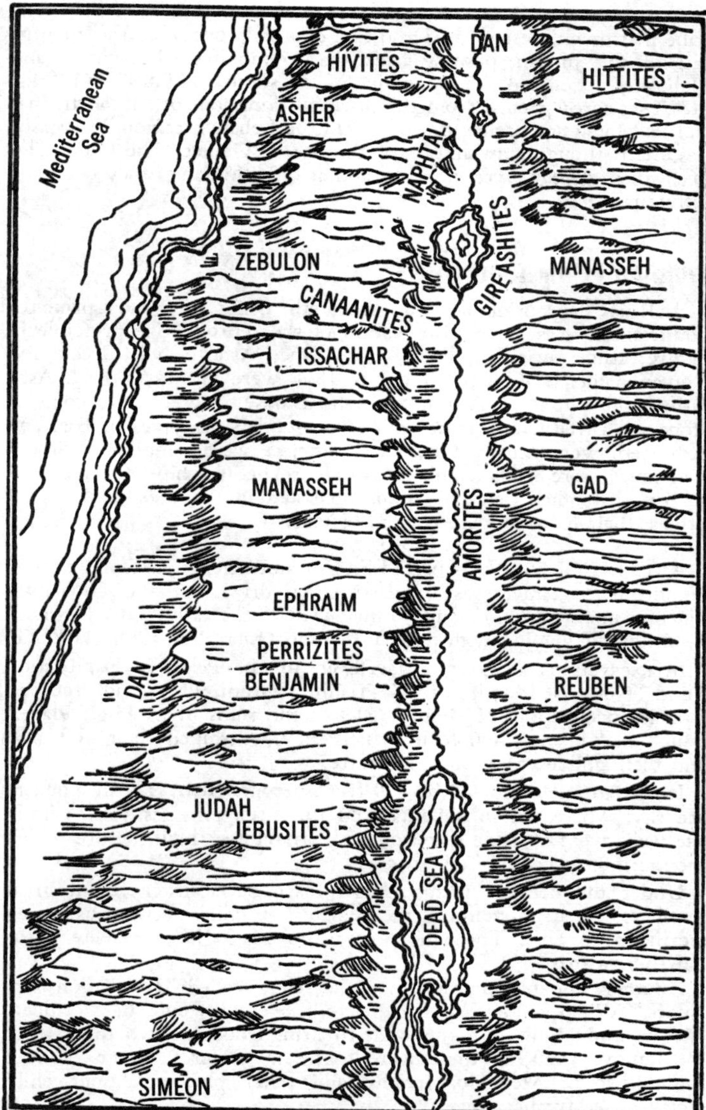

Map 36. Location of Tribes.

tribe that dwelt west of the Dead Sea, and had conquered the country east of the Jordan, pushing back the Ammonites. "Perizzites" and "Jebusites" occupied the mountains of the south. "Hivites" and "Hittites," scattered groups from the powerful kingdom of the north that had its capital at Carchemish, occupied the Lebanon region. "Girgashites," it is thought, dwelt east of the Sea of Galilee. The boundaries of all these people were movable, and at different times they occupied different places.

Religion of the Canaanites

Baal was their principal god; Ashtoreth, Baal's wife, their principal goddess. She was the personification of the reproductive principle in nature. Ishtar was her Babylonian name; Astarte her Greek and Roman name. Baalim, the plural of Baal, were images of Baal. Ashtaroth, the plural of Ashtoreth. Ashera was a sacred pole, cone of stone, or a tree trunk, representing the goddess. Temples of Baal and Ashtoreth were usually together. Priestesses were temple prostitutes. Sodomites were male temple prostitutes. The worship of Baal, Ashtoreth, and other Canaanite gods consisted in the most extravagant orgies; their temples were centers of vice.

ARCHAEOLOGICAL NOTES: Canaanite Religion. God's express command to Israel was to destroy or drive out the Canaanites (Deuteronomy 7:2, 3). And Joshua went at the task in dead earnest, God himself helping with mighty miracles. In reality, GOD DID IT.

In excavations at Gezer, Macalister, of the Palestine Exploration Fund (1904–09), found, in the Canaanite stratum, which had preceded Israelite occupation, of about 1500 B.C., the ruins of a "High Place," which had been a temple in which they worshiped their god Baal and their goddess Ashtoreth (Astarte).

It was an enclosure 150 by 120 feet, surrounded by a wall, open to the sky, where the inhabitants held their religious festivals. Within the walls were 10 rude stone pillars, 5 to 11 feet high, before which the sacrifices were offered.

Under the debris, in this "High Place," Macalister found great numbers of jars containing the remains of children who had been sacrificed to Baal. The whole area proved to be a cemetery for new-born babes.

Another horrible practice was that they called "foundation sacrifices." When a house was to be built, a child would be sacrificed, and its body built into the wall, to bring good luck to the rest of the family. Many of these were found in Gezer. They have been found also at Megiddo, Jericho and other places. (About child sacrifice, see further page 198.)

Also, in this "High Place," under the rubbish, Macalister found enormous quantities of images and plaques of Ashtoreth with rudely exaggerated sex organs, designed to foster sensual feelings.

So, Canaanites worshiped, by immoral indulgence, as a religious rite, in the presence of their gods; and then, by murdering their first-born children, as a sacrifice to these same gods.

It seems that, in large measure, the land of Canaan had become a sort of Sodom and Gomorrah on a national scale.

Do we wonder any longer why God commanded Israel to exterminate the Canaanites? Did a civilization of such abominable filth and brutality have any right longer to exist? It is one of history's examples of the Wrath of God against the Wickedness of Nations.

Archaeologists who dig in the ruins of Canaanite cities wonder that God did not destroy them sooner than He did.

God's object, in the command to exterminate the Canaanites, besides being a Judgment on the Canaanites, was to keep Israel from IDOLATRY and its shameful practices. God was founding the Israelite nation for the one grand specific purpose of paving the way for the Coming of Christ, by establishing in the world the IDEA that there is One True Living God. If Israel fell into Idolatry, then there ceased to be any reason for its existence as a nation. As a matter of precaution, it was needful to clean the land of the last vestige of Idolatrous Worship. In this matter Joshua gave Israel a good start. If only Israel had kept it up, what a different story there would have been to tell!

JUDGES

First 300 Years in the Promised Land
Alternate Oppressions and Deliverances
A Record of Great Exploits

The Hebrew Nation, after the death of Joshua, had no strong central government. They were a confederacy, of twelve independent tribes, with no unifying force, except their God. The form of government in the days of the Judges is spoken of as the "Theocracy"; that is, God himself was supposed to be the direct ruler of the nation. But the people did not take their God very seriously, and were continually falling away into Idolatry. Being in a state of anarchy, more or less, and harassed at times by civil war among themselves, and surrounded by enemies who made attempt after attempt to exterminate them, the Hebrew Nation was very slow in its National Development, and did not become a great nation till it was organized into a Kingdom in the days of Samuel and David.

The Exact Duration of the period of the Judges is uncertain. The years assigned to oppressions, 111 (see below), and to Judges, with the periods of rest, 299, total 410. But some of these figures may overlap. Jephthah, who lived near the end of the period, spoke of it as 300 years (11:26). And it is thought to have been, in round numbers, about 300 years; roughly, about 1400–1100 B.C. From Exodus to Solomon, which includes also the periods of the Wilderness, and of Eli, Samuel, Saul and David, is called, in I Kings 6:1, 480 years.

Oppressions by:		*Judges, or Periods of Rest:*	
Mesopotamians	8 years	Othniel, of Kiriath-sepher, in Judah	40 years
Moabites, Ammonites, Amalekites	18 years	Ehud, of Benjamin	80 years
Philistines		Shamgar	
Canaanites	20 years	Deborah, of Ephraim; Barak, of Naphtali	40 years
Midianites, Amalekites	7 years	Gideon, of Manasseh	40 years
		Abimelech (usurper), of Manasseh	3 years
		Tola, of Issachar	23 years
		Jair, of Gilead, in E Manasseh	22 years

Ammonites	18 years	Jephthah, of Gilead, in E Manasseh	6 years
		Ibzan, of Bethlehem, in Judah (?)	7 years
		Elon, of Zebulun	10 years
		Abdon, of Ephraim	8 years
Philistines	40 years	Samson, of Dan	20 years
Total Periods	111 years		299 years

There were also oppressions by Sidonians and Maonites (10:12).

"40 Years"

Othniel, Deborah and Barak, and Gideon, are each said to have judged Israel 40 years; and Ehud, twice 40. Later, Eli judged 40 years; and Saul, David and Solomon each reigned 40 years. "40 years" seems to have been a round number denoting a generation. Note how often 40 is used throughout the Bible: at the Flood it rained 40 days; Moses fled at 40; was in Midian 40 years; was in the mount 40 days. Israel wandered 40 years. The spies were 40 days in Canaan. Elijah fasted 40 days. 40 days' respite was given to Nineveh. Jesus fasted 40 days, and sojourned 40 days after resurrection.

Chapter 1. Canaanites that were Left in the Land

Joshua had destroyed the Canaanites in some sections of the land, and had kept others in subjection (Joshua 10:40, 43; 11:23; 13:2–7; 21:43–45; 23:4; 24:18). After his death, they remained in considerable numbers (Judges 1:28, 29, 30, 32, 33, 35).

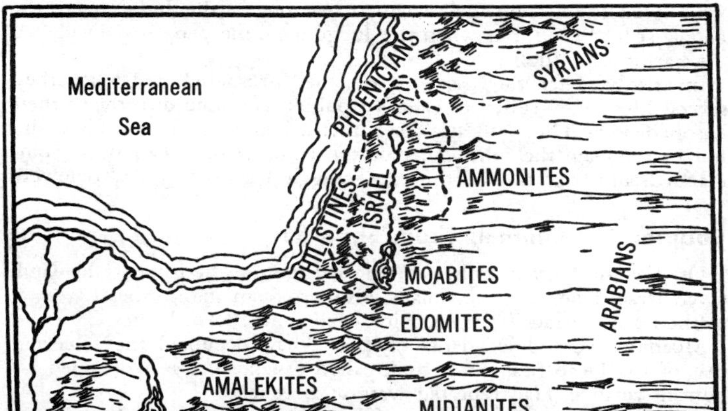

Map 37. Neighbor Nations.

God had commanded Israel to utterly destroy or drive out the Canaanites (Deuteronomy 7:2–4). If Israel had fully obeyed this command, it would have saved them a lot of trouble.

ARCHAEOLOGICAL NOTE: Iron in Palestine. The Bible states that Iron in possession of Canaanites and Philistines was the reason Israel could not drive them out (1:19; 4:3; Joshua 17:16–18; I Samuel 13:19–22). And that only after Saul and David broke the power of the Philistines did Iron come into use in Israel (II Samuel 12:31; I Chronicles 22:3; 29:7).

Excavations have revealed many Iron relics of 1100 B.C. in Philistia; but none in the hill country of Palestine till 1000 B.C.

Chapter 2. Apostasy after the Death of Joshua

As the hardy, wilderness-bred generation, who, under the powerful leadership of Joshua, had conquered the land, died off, the new generation, settled in a land of plenty, soon lapsed into the easy-going ways of their idolatrous neighbors.

The Refrain Running Through the Book

Every man did that which was right in his own eyes. They were ever and anon falling away from God into the worship of Idols. When they did this God delivered Israel into the hands of their oppressors. Then when Israel, in their suffering and distress, turned back, and cried to God, God had pity on Israel, and raised up Judges, who saved Israel from their enemies. As long as the Judge lived, the people served God. But when the Judge died, the people again played the harlot after Idols.

Invariably, when they served God, they prospered; and when they served Idols, they suffered. Israel's troubles were due directly to their Disobedience. They did not keep themselves from Idols. They did not exterminate the inhabitants of the land, as they had been commanded; and from time to time the struggle for mastery was renewed.

Chapter 3. Othniel, Ehud, Shamgar

Othniel, of Kiriath-sepher, in the extreme south part of the land, saved Israel from Mesopotamians, invaders from the northeast.

Ehud saved Israel from Moabites, Ammonites, Amalekites.

Moabites were descendants of Lot. They occupied the tableland east of the Dead Sea. Their god, called Chemosh, was worshiped by human sacrifice. Had repeated wars with Israel.

Ammonites were descendants of Lot. Their territory joined Moab, beginning about 30 miles east of the Jordan. Their god, called Moloch, was worshiped by the burning of little children.

Amalekites were descendants of Esau; a wandering tribe, centering mainly in north part of Sinai peninsula, but roaming in wide circles, even into Judah, and far to the east. First to attack Israel on departure from Egypt. Moses authorized their extinction (Exodus 17:8–16). They have disappeared from history.

Shamgar, of whom little is told, saved Israel from Philistines.

Philistines were descendants of Ham. They occupied the Coastal Plain on the southwest border of Canaan. The word "Palestine" is derived from them. Again oppressed Israel in Samson's days.

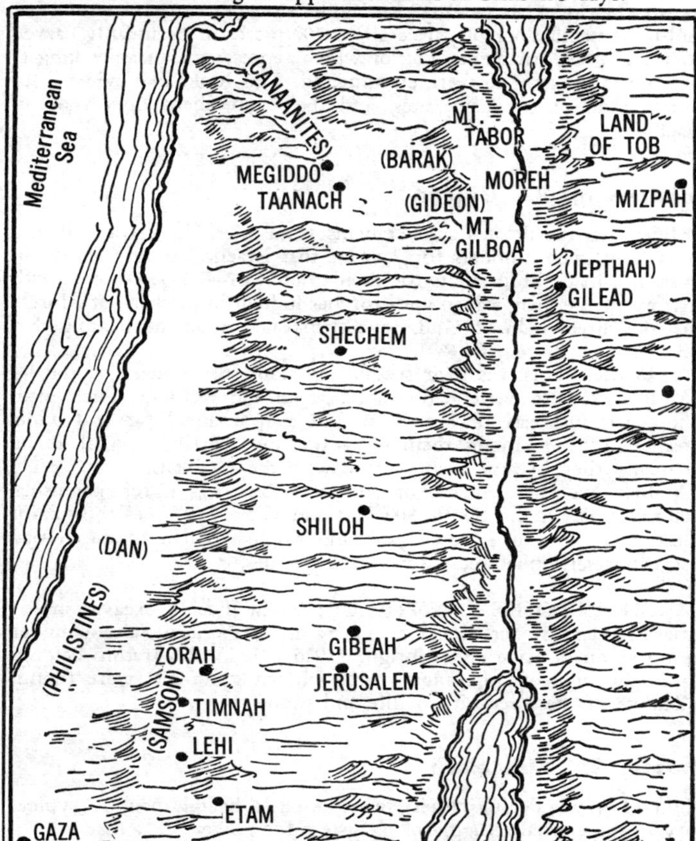

Map 38.

Chapters 4,5. Deborah and Barak

They saved Israel from the Canaanites, who had been subdued by Joshua, but had become powerful again, and with their chariots of iron were grinding out the life of Israel.

ARCHAEOLOGICAL NOTE: Canaanite Oppression (4:3). Israel's Victory at Megiddo (5:19)

The Oriental Institute, excavating at Megiddo, found (1937), in the stratum of 12th century B.C., indications of a tremendous fire. And underneath floor of palace about 200 pieces of beautifully carved ivory and gold ornaments, one of which represents Canaanite king as receiving captives who were circumcised. This looks like evidence of a terrific defeat for Canaanites, and their antecedent oppression of Israel.

Chapters 6,7,8. Gideon

Midianites, Amalekites and Arabians (6:3; 8:24), had swarmed into the land, in such numbers for 7 years, that Israelites sought refuge in caves, and made hidden pits for their grain (6:2–4, 11). Gideon, with an army of 300 men, armed with torches hidden in pitchers, at Moreh, with the direct help of God, gave them such a terrific beating that they came no more.

Amalekites. This was their second invasion. (See under chapter 3.)

Midianites were descendants of Abraham and Keturah. Their main center was just east of Mt. Sinai, but they roamed far and wide. Moses had lived among them 40 years, and married one of them. Gradually they became incorporated with the Arabians.

Arabians were descendants of Ishmael. Arabia was a great peninsula, 1500 miles North and South, 800 East and West. 150 times the size of Palestine. It was an elevated tableland sloping North to the Syrian desert. Sparsely inhabited by wandering tribes.

ARCHAEOLOGICAL NOTE: The Grain Pits. In excavations, at Kiriath-sepher, by the Xenia Seminary and American School, under the direction of Kyle and Albright (1926–28), in the stratum belonging to the time of the Judges, many hidden grain pits were found; indicative of the insecurity of life and property.

Chapter 9. Abimelech

Son of a wonderful father, but himself a brutal man. A typical story in the eternal struggle of gangsters for power.

ARCHAEOLOGICAL NOTE: Abimelech's Destruction of Shechem. With money from the temple of Baal (4), he hired men to murder his brothers, and "beat down the city, and sowed it with salt" (45).

Sellin (1913–14, 1926–28), identified a mound near the modern city of Shechem as the ruins of ancient Shechem. He found a stratum of Canaanite ruins of 1600 B.C.; and above that an Israelite layer, with indications that it had been destroyed and abandoned about 1100 B.C. He found the ruins of a temple of Baal, believed to be the temple mentioned in verse 4.

Chapters 10,11,12. Tola, Jair, Jephthah, Ibzan, Elon, Abdon

Tola, mentioned as a Judge. Jair, mentioned as a Judge.

Jephthah was of Mizpah, in Gilead, land of Job and Elijah, in east Manasseh. Ammonites, whose power had been broken by Ehud, one of the earlier Judges, had again become strong, and were plundering Israel. God gave Jephthah a great victory over the Ammonites, and delivered Israel. The pitiful thing in the story of Jephthah is the sacrifice of his daughter.

Ibzan, Elon and Abdon, are mentioned as Judges.

Chapters 13,14,15,16. Samson

Of the tribe of Dan, on the Philistine border, he was, before birth, appointed of God to be Israel's deliverer from the Philistines. God endowed him with superhuman strength and, under God, his exploits were amazing. He was the last of the Judges mentioned in the book of Judges. Soon followed the organization of the Kingdom.

Chapters 17,18. Migration of the Danites

Danites had been assigned territory that included the Philistine plain, which they had not been able to take, and, being cramped for room, part of the tribe, with a stolen god, migrated to the far north, and settled near the headwaters of the Jordan.

Chapters 19,20,21. The Benjamite Deed of Shame

A narrative of savage justice, for a crime unspeakably horrible, as a result of which the tribe of Benjamin was almost wiped out.

ARCHAEOLOGICAL NOTE: Albright (1922–23), found, in the ruins of Gibeah, a layer of ashes, from a fire that occurred about 1200 B.C. It must have been this very fire (20:40).

Heroes of Faith

Barak, Gideon, Jephthah and Samson, are included among the

Heroes of Faith in Hebrews 11:32. In spite of some things in their lives about which we wonder, they had Faith in God.

Miracles in the Book of Judges

Angel appearances to Gideon, and to Samson's parents. Dew on the Fleece sign. Gideon's defeat of Midianites, with 300. Samson born of a barren mother, and his superhuman strength. These show that God, in his mercy, still had his eye on his people, even though they had sunk into the lowest depths.

Archaeological Discoveries

Philistines had Iron, when Israel had none. At Migiddo, Canaanite Oppression of Israel, and Defeat by Israel. Hidden Grain Pits at Kiriath-sepher. Abimelech's Destruction of Shechem. Burning of Gibeah. These are evidences that the Book is real history.

Why Such a Book in the Bible?

Well, it is simple history. God had founded a nation, for the purpose of paving the way for the coming of a Redeemer for the human race. God was determined to maintain that nation. And in spite of its Idolatry, and its Wickedness, God did maintain it. Except for such leaders as the Judges, and except for God's Miraculous aid in times of crisis, Israel would have been exterminated.

RUTH

Great Grandmother of David
Beginning of Messianic Family

This lovely story of a lovely woman, following, like calm after a storm, the turbulent scenes of Judges, is a delightful and charming picture of domestic life in a time of anarchy and trouble.

A thousand years earlier, Abraham had been called of God to found a Nation for the purpose of one day bringing a Saviour to mankind. In this book of Ruth we have the founding of the Family within that Nation in which the Saviour would come. Ruth was the great grandmother of king David. From here on Old Testament interest centers mainly around the Family of David.

Chapter 1. The Sojourn in Moab

A Bethlehem family, Elimelech and Naomi and two sons, on account of famine, went to sojourn in Moab. Moabites were descendants of Lot (Genesis 19:37); thus distantly related to the Jews. But they were Idolaters. Their god, Chemosh, was worshiped by Child Sacrifice. The two Bethlehem boys married two Moabite girls. After ten years the father and both boys had died. Ruth, widow of one of

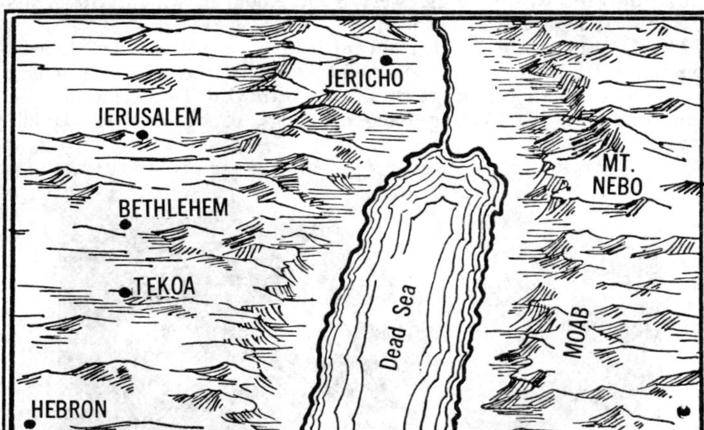

Map 39.

the boys, with a burst of devotion of superb beauty (1:16, 17), returned with Naomi to Bethlehem.

Chapter 2. Ruth Gleans in Field of Boaz

Boaz was son of Rahab, the Jericho Canaanitish harlot (Joshua 2:1; Matthew 1:5; see on Joshua 2). Thus David's great grandmother was Moabite, and his great grandfather half Canaanite: outside blood to form the Chosen Family within the Chosen Nation: foregleam of a Messiah for All nations.

About a mile east of Bethlehem is a field, called "Field of Boaz," where, tradition says, Ruth gleaned. Adjoining is "Shepherds' Field," where, tradition says, the angels announced the birth of Jesus. According to these traditions, the scene of Ruth's romance with Boaz, which led to the formation of the Family that was to produce Christ, was chosen of God, 1100 years later, as the place for the Heavenly Announcement of Christ's Arrival.

Chapters 3,4. Their Marriage

Under the Church of the Nativity, in Bethlehem, there is a room in which, it is said, Jesus was born. An old tradition says that this same room was part of the ancestral home of David, and before David, of Boaz and Ruth. Thus, according to this tradition, Boaz took Ruth to be his bride, and started the Family that was to bring Christ into the world, in the Very Same Room in which, 1100 years later, Christ himself was born.

The Genealogy (4:17–22), showing Ruth's son to be Obed, Obed's son to be Jesse, and Jesse's son to be David, is the thing for which the Book of Ruth was written. Thenceforth Old Testament thought centers around the Coming King of Kings, to be born in David's line.

Fig. 40. The Shepherds' Fields and Fields of Boaz, looking toward Bethlehem.
© *Matson Photo*

I SAMUEL

Organization of the Kingdom
Samuel Saul David

Samuel was connecting link between Judges and the Kingdom. Date, approximately 1100–1050 B.C.

Scene of Samuel's Ministry

Ramah, about 6 miles north of Jerusalem, was his birthplace, judicial residence, and place of burial (1:19; 7:17; 25:1).

Bethel, about 5 miles north of Ramah, was Samuel's northern office. It was one of the four highest points in the land, the others being Mt. Ebal, Hebron and Mizpah. The view over the land from Bethel is magnificent. Here, 800 years before, Jacob had seen the heavenly ladder.

Mizpah, 3 miles west of Ramah, on Mt. Neby Samwil, was Samuel's western office. Here Samuel set up the "Ebenezer" stone (7:12). On its northern slope was Gibeon, where Joshua had made the "sun stand still."

Gibeah (its modern name, Tell-el-Ful), about halfway between Ramah and Jerusalem, was Saul's home.

Bethlehem, David's birthplace, and, later, the birthplace of Jesus, was 12 miles south from Ramah.

Shiloh, about 15 miles north of Ramah, was abode of Tabernacle from Joshua to Samuel, where Samuel ministered as a child.

Kiriath-jearim, where Ark was kept after its return from Philistines, was about 8 miles southwest from Ramah.

Chapters 1-2:11. Birth of Samuel

He was of Levitical parents (I Chronicles 6:33–38). All honor to his mother, Hannah. A noble example of motherhood, her son turned out to be one of the noblest and purest characters in history.

ARCHAEOLOGICAL NOTE: Shiloh (1:3).

Joshua set up the Tabernacle in Shiloh (Joshua 18:1).

From year to year Israel went to Shiloh to sacrifice (I Samuel 1:3).

David brought the Ark to Jerusalem (II Samuel 6:15), about 1000 B.C.

Jeremiah (7:12–15), about 600 B.C., refers to Shiloh as destroyed. The implication of these passages is that Shiloh was an important

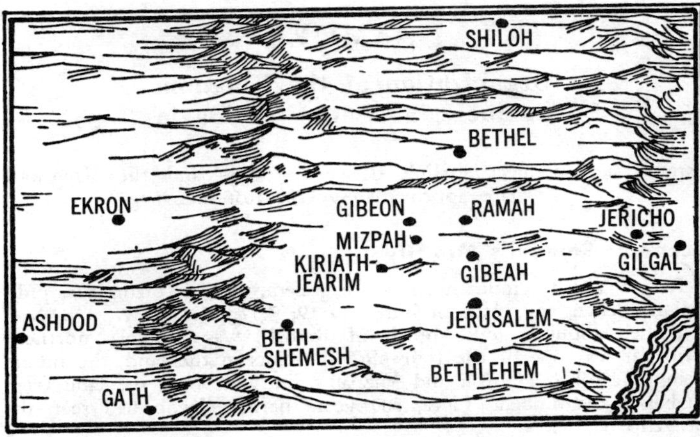

Map 40. Scene of Samuel's Ministry.

city from Joshua to David, and, after that, sometime before 600 B.C., it was destroyed, deserted and ceased to exist.

A Danish Expedition (1922–31), found in the ruins of Shiloh, potsherds of 1200–1050 B.C., bearing evidence of Israelite culture, with no evidence of previous occupation, or later occupation till about 300 B.C. Albright dates the destruction of Shiloh about 1050 B.C. Thus, excavations exactly parallel the Biblical record.

Chapter 2:12-36. Change in the Priesthood Announced

The words in 31–35 seem to have application to Samuel, who succeeded Eli as Judge, and also as acting Priest (7:9; 9:11–14); but also have reference to a priesthood that shall last "forever" (35).

They were fulfilled when Solomon displaced Abiathar of Eli's family with Zadok of another line (I Kings 2:27; I Chronicles 24:3, 6).

But their ultimate fulfillment was in the Eternal Priesthood of Christ. In chapters 8, 9, 10, we are told how Samuel initiated a change in the form of government, from Judges to the Kingdom. Under the kingdom, office of king and priest were kept separate.

As here, in verse 35, an Eternal Priesthood is promised, so in II Samuel 7:16 David is promised an Eternal Throne. Eternal Priesthood and the Eternal Throne looked forward to the Messiah, in whom they merged, Christ becoming man's Eternal Priest and Eternal King.

The temporary merging of the offices of Judge and Priest in the person of Samuel, during the passage period from Judges to the

Kingdom, seems to have been a sort of historical forepicture of the final fusing of the two offices in Christ.

Chapter 3. Samuel's Prophetic Call

Samuel was a "Prophet" (3:20). He served as a "Priest" offering sacrifice (7:9). And he "Judged" Israel (7:15–17), his circuit being Bethel, Gilgal and Mizpah, with his main office at Ramah. He was the last "Judge," the first "Prophet," and founder of the "Monarchy"; sole ruler between Eli and Saul. His main mission was the Organization of the Kingdom.

The form of government under the Judges had been a sort of failure (see introductory note to the book of Judges). So God raised up Samuel to unify the nation under a King. (See on Chapters 8, 9, 10.)

Prophets

The word "prophet" occurs occasionally before the time of Samuel, as in Genesis 20:7 and Exodus 7:1. But Samuel, it seems, was founder of a regular order of prophets, with schools, first at Ramah (I Samuel 19:20); and afterward at Bethel, Jericho, and Gilgal, (II Kings 2:3, 5; 4:38). The priesthood had become quite degenerate, and contemporaneous with the organization of the Kingdom. Samuel, it seems, initiated these schools as a sort of moral check on both priests and kings.

These Prophets functioned through a period of some 300 years before the time of the Prophets who wrote the closing 17 books of the Old Testament. They are called "Oral" Prophets, to distinguish them from the "Literary" Prophets who wrote the books.

The leading "Oral" Prophets were: Samuel, organizer of the Kingdom; Nathan, adviser to David; Ahijah, adviser to Jeroboam; Elijah and Elisha, who led in the grand fight against Baalism.

Chapters 4,5,6,7. Ark Captured by Philistines

The Ark, after its capture by the Philistines, was never taken back to Shiloh. Shiloh thenceforward ceased to be a place of importance. The Ark remained in Philistine cities for 7 months, in which time great plagues afflicted the Philistines.

It was taken to Beth-shemesh. Then to Kiriath-jearim, where it remained 20 years (7:2). Later it was taken to Jerusalem by David, who built a tabernacle for it (II Samuel 6:12; II Chronicles 1:4); which it occupied till Solomon built the Temple. Nothing is known of its history after the destruction of Jerusalem.

The Tabernacle, after the Ark was gone from Shiloh, was part time at Nob (21:1; Mark 2:26); and part time at Gibeon (I Chronicles 21:29); till Solomon laid it up in the Temple (I Kings 8:4).

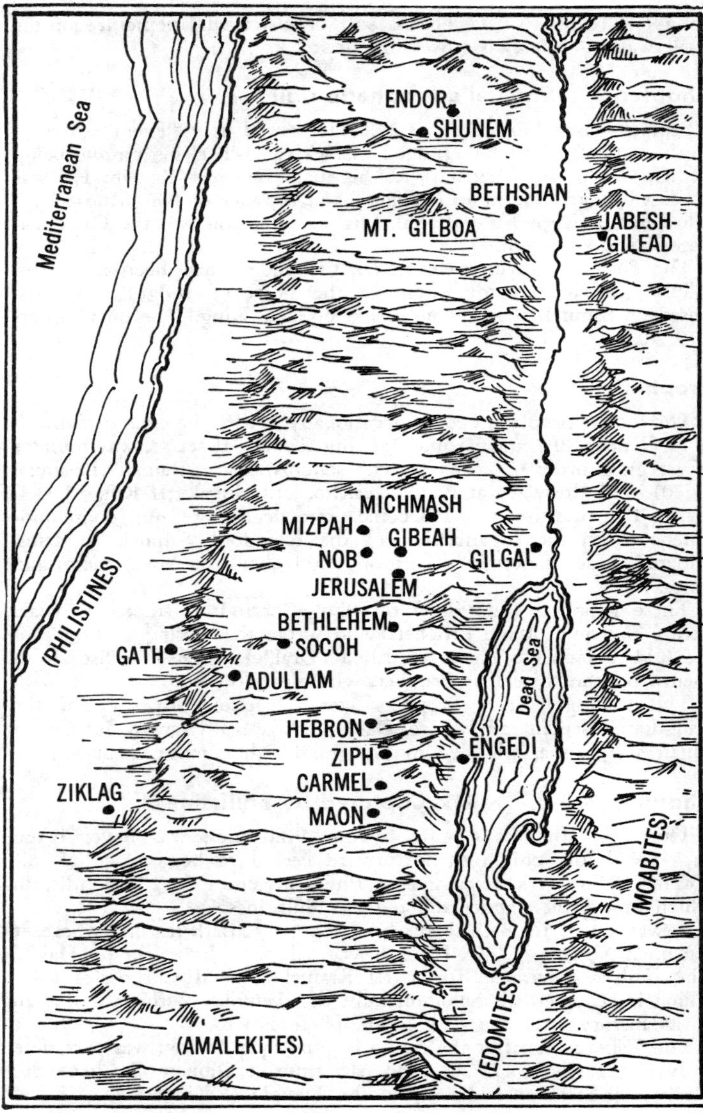
Mediterranean Sea
ENDOR
SHUNEM
BETHSHAN
MT. GILBOA
JABESH-GILEAD
MICHMASH
MIZPAH
GIBEAH
NOB
GILGAL
JERUSALEM
(PHILISTINES)
BETHLEHEM
GATH
SOCOH
ADULLAM
Dead Sea
HEBRON
ZIPH
ENGEDI
CARMEL
ZIKLAG
MAON
(MOABITES)
(EDOMITES)
(AMALEKITES)

Map 41.

After the return of the Ark from the Philistines, Samuel, with the aid of God, administered a terrific defeat to the Philistines at the place where they had captured the Ark (4:1; 7:12).

Chapters 8,9,10. Organization of the Kingdom

Up to this time the form of government had been the "Theocracy" (see top of page 168). In a predatory world, where only the law of the jungle was recognized, a nation, in order to survive, needed to be fairly strong. So, God, accommodating himself to human ways, permitted his nation to UNIFY, as other nations did, under a King. The first king, Saul, was a failure. But the second king, David, was a magnificent success.

ARCHAEOLOGICAL NOTE: Saul's House in Gibeah (10:26).
Albright (1922–23), found in Gibeah, in the stratum of 1000 B.C. the ruins of the fortress which Saul had built.

Chapters 11,12,13,14,15. Saul as King

Saul was of the tribe of Benjamin, which, in the days of the Judges, had almost been annihilated; and of the city of Gibeah, where the horrible catastrophe had started (see page 173).

Tall, handsome and humble, Saul began his reign with a brilliant victory over the Ammonites. Any misgivings about the new "Kingdom" disappeared.

Then followed Samuel's warning to nation and king, not to forget GOD, confirmed by a miraculous thunderstorm (chapter 12).

Saul's First Mistake (chapter 13). His successes rapidly went to his head. Humility gave place to pride. He offered sacrifice, which was the exclusive function of priests. This was the first sign of Saul's presumptive self-importance.

Saul's Second Mistake (chapter 14). His silly order for the army to abstain from food, and his senseless death sentence for Jonathan, showed the people what a fool they had for a king.

Saul's Third Mistake (chapter 15). Deliberate disobedience to God. For this he heard Samuel's ominous pronouncement, "Because you have rejected God, God has rejected you from being king."

Chapter 16. David Secretly Anointed to be King

It could not have been done openly, for then Saul would have killed David. Its purpose was to give David a chance to train himself for the office. God took David under His care (13).

David was short of stature, ruddy, of beautiful countenance, handsome, of immense physical strength, and great personal attractiveness, a man of war, prudent in speech, very brave, very musical and very religious.

His fame as a musician brought him to the notice of king Saul, who did not at the time know that he had been anointed to be his successor. He became Saul's armor-bearer. This threw David into association with the king and his counsellors.

Chapter 17. David and Goliath

It seems that David's first residence at the court was only temporary; that he returned to Bethlehem; that some years passed; and that, in the meantime, the boy David had so changed in appearance that Saul did not recognize him (55–58).

Socoh, where Goliath was encamped, was about 15 miles west of Bethlehem. Goliath was about 9 feet tall; his armor weighed about 150 pounds, and his spear-head about 20 pounds. David's offer, with only a staff and a sling, to take on Goliath, was an act of unheard-of bravery and Amazing Trust in God. His victory thrilled the nation. He became at once the king's son-in-law, commander of armies, and the nation's popular hero.

Chapters 18,19,20. Saul's Jealousy of David

David's popularity turned Saul against him. Saul tried to kill him. David fled, and for years was a fugitive in the mountains.

Jonathan's Friendship for David (chapter 20). Jonathan was heir to the throne. His brilliant victory over the Philistines (chapter 14), and his nobility of character, were good evidence that he would have made a worthy king. But he had learned that God had ordained David to be king, and his graceful effacement of himself from the succession, and his unselfish devotion to his rival, form one of the noblest stories of Friendship in history.

Chapters 21 to 27. David a Fugitive from Saul

David escaped to the Philistines, feigning insanity. Sensing danger, he fled to the Cave of Adullam in west Judah; then to Moab; then back to south Judah, in Keilah, Ziph and Maon. He had accumulated 600 followers, Saul hot after him, but David always escaping. Many of the Psalms he composed in this period.

At En-gedi, Saul was trapped; but David, refusing to come to the throne by blood, spared Saul's life. And again, at Ziph, Saul acknowledged being a "fool"; but kept on being one.

At Maon, Abigail, a wealthy, tactful and gracious woman, became David's wife. David finally found refuge among the Philistines again, and was there till the death of Saul.

Chapters 28,29,30,31. The Death of Saul

The Philistines invaded the land, and encamped at Mt. Gilboa. One of the Philistine princes had wanted David and his men to go along with them. But the other princes did not trust David. So, David remained behind, and, with his 600 men, guarded the South against the Amalekites.

Meantime, Saul, thoroughly frightened, sought, through a witch at Endor, an interview with the spirit of Samuel. The straightforward simplicity of the narrative seems to imply that the spirit of Samuel did actually appear. However, there is difference of opinion as to whether the apparition was real or fraudulent. At any rate, in the battle, Saul was slain. He had reigned 40 years (Acts 13:21).

ARCHAEOLOGICAL NOTE: Saul's Armor (31:10).

It is here stated that Saul's "armor was put in the house of Ashtaroth" in Bethshan, and, in I Chronicles 10:10, it is said that his "head was fastened in the house of Dagon."

Bethshan (Beisan) is just east of Mt. Gilboa, at the junction of the Jezreel and Jordan valleys. The University Museum of Pennsylvania (1921–30), uncovered, in Bethshan, in the stratum of 1000 B.C., the ruins of a temple of Astaroth, and also a temple of Dagon, the very same buildings in which Saul's armor and head were fastened: at least, it is proof that there were such temples in Bethshan in Saul's day.

II SAMUEL

The Reign of David
David the Head of an Eternal Dynasty of Kings

Chapters 1 to 6

David's Grief over the Death of Saul. David made King over Judah. Seven Years' War with Ish-bosheth, Saul's Son. David made King over all Israel. Jerusalem made Capital of the nation.

Chapter 7. God Promises David an Eternal Throne

The Old Testament is the story of God's dealing with the Hebrew Nation for the purpose of one day Blessing All Nations.

As the story unfolds, it is explained that the way the Hebrew Nation would Bless All Nations would be through the Family of David.

As the story further unfolds, it is further explained that the way the Family of David would bless the world would be through ONE GREAT KING who would one day be born in Family, who would himself personally LIVE FOREVER, and establish a KINGDOM of ENDLESS DURATION.

Here, in this 7th chapter of II Samuel, begins the long line of promises that DAVID'S FAMILY should reign FOREVER over God's people; that is, there should come from David an Eternal Family Line of Kings, culminating in ONE ETERNAL KING. Here are some of these promises:

"Thy throne shall be established forever" (7:16).

"If thy children take heed to their way, to walk before me in truth with all their heart and with all their soul, there shall not fail thee a man on the throne of Israel" (I Kings 2:4).

"A son shall be born to thee . . . His name shall be Solomon . . . I will establish the throne of his kingdom over Israel forever" (I Chronicles 22:8, 9, 10).

"If thou wilt walk before me, as David thy father walked . . . then I will establish the throne of thy kingdom, according as I have covenanted with David thy father, saying, There shall not fail thee a man to be ruler in Israel" (II Chronicles 7:17, 18).

"I have made a covenant with My Chosen. I have sworn unto David My Servant, Thy Seed will I Establish Forever, and build up Thy Throne unto all generations . . . I will make Him, my

First-born, higher than the kings of the earth . . . And my covenant shall stand fast with Him. His Seed will I make to endure Forever, and His Throne as the days of Heaven . . . My Covenant I will not break, nor alter the thing that has gone out from My Lips. Once I have sworn by My Holiness, I will not lie to David . . . His Throne shall be Established Forever" (Psalm 89:3, 4, 27–29, 34–37).

"The Lord hath sworn in truth unto David: he will not turn from it: Of the fruit of thy body will I set upon thy throne" (Psalm 132:11).

"In that day will I raise up the tabernacle of David that is fallen . . . that they may possess . . . all the nations, which are called by my name, saith the Lord" (Amos 9:11, 12).

"Unto us a Child is born, unto us a Son is given; and the government shall be upon his shoulders: and his name shall be called Wonderful Counsellor, Mighty God, Everlasting Father, Prince of Peace. Of the increase of his government and peace there shall be NO END, upon the throne of David" (Isaiah 9:6, 7).

"There shall come forth a rod out of the stem of Jesse, and a Branch shall grow out of his roots . . . which shall stand for an ensign of the people, and to him shall the nations seek" (Isaiah 11:1, 10).

"Thou, Bethlehem (city of David) . . . out of thee shall come forth One unto me who is to be ruler in Israel; whose goings forth are from of old, from everlasting . . . He shall be great unto the ends of the earth" (Micah 5:2, 4).

"O earth, earth, earth, hear the word of the Lord . . . Behold, the days come, saith the Lord, that I will raise up unto David a Righteous Branch, and a King shall reign . . . and this is his name whereby he shall be called, THE LORD OUR RIGHTEOUSNESS" (Jeremiah 22:29; 23:5, 6).

"If ye can break my covenant of the day, and my covenant of the night, so that there should not be day and night in their season; then may also my covenant be broken with David" (Jeremiah 33:20, 21).

"I will bring forth my servant the Branch . . . And I will remove the iniquity of the land in one day" (Zechariah 3:8, 9).

"The man whose name is The BRANCH . . . he shall build the temple of the Lord, and he shall bear the glory, and shall sit and rule upon his throne . . . and his dominion shall be from sea to sea, and from the river to the ends of the earth" (Zechariah 6:12, 13; 9:10).

"In that day . . . the house of David shall be as God . . . In that day there shall be a fountain opened to the house of David . . . for sin and for uncleanness" (Zechariah 12:8; 13:1).

Thus, the promise of an Eternal King, to arise in David's Family, was repeated over and over: to David himself, to Solomon, and again and again in the Psalms, and by the prophets Amos, Isaiah, Micah, Jeremiah and Zechariah, over a period of some 500 years.

By and by, in the fulness of time, the angel Gabriel was sent to Nazareth, to Mary, who was of the family of David, and he said: "Fear not, Mary; for thou hast found favor with God. And, behold, thou shalt conceive, and bring forth a son, and shalt call his name JESUS. He shall be great, and shall be called the Son of the Highest; and the Lord God shall give unto him the THRONE of his father DAVID; And he shall reign over the house of Jacob FOREVER; and of His Kingdom there shall be NO END" (Luke 1:30–33).

In THIS CHILD the Davidic promises found their fulfillment.

Chapters 8,9,10. David's Victories

After Saul's death David had been made king over Judah. 7 years later he was made king over all Israel. He was 30 when he became king. He reigned over Judah 7½ years, and over all Israel 33 years; 40 years in all (5:3–5). He died at 70.

Soon after becoming king over all Israel, David made Jerusalem his capital. Situated in an impregnable position, and with the tradition of Melchizedek, priest of God Most High, David thought it best suited to be the nation's capital. He took it, brought in the Ark of God, and planned the Temple (chapters 5, 6, 7).

David was very successful in his wars. He completely subdued the Philistines, Moabites, Syrians, Edomites, Ammonites, Amalekites, and all neighbor nations. "The Lord gave victory to David whithersoever he went" (8:6).

David took an insignificant nation, and, within a few years, built it into a mighty kingdom. In the southwest the Egyptian world empire had declined. Over in the east the Assyrian and Babylonian world empires had not yet arisen. And here, on the highway between, under David, the kingdom of Israel, almost overnight, became, not a world empire, but perhaps the most powerful single kingdom on earth at the time.

Chapters 11,12. David and Bathsheba

This was the blackest spot in David's life: adultery, and virtual murder to cover the adultery. His remorse made him a broken man. God forgave him; but pronounced the fearful sentence, "The sword shall never depart from thy house" (12:10), and it never did. David reaped exactly what he had sown, and more of it; a long and hard and bitter harvest. His daughter Tamar was raped by her brother Amnon, who in turn was murdered by their brother Absalom. Absalom led a rebellion against his father David, and was killed in the struggle. David's wives were violated in public, as he had secretly violated the wife of Uriah. Thus, David's glorious reign was clouded with unceasing troubles. What a lesson for those who think they can sin, and sin, and sin, and get away with it!

Yet this was the "man after God's own heart" (I Samuel 13:14; Acts 13:22). David's reaction showed him to be just that. Some of the Psalms, as 32 and 51, were born of this bitter experience.

Chapters 13 to 21. David's Troubles

Absalom probably knew that Solomon was slated to be David's successor as king. Hence this effort to steal the throne from his father David. Judging by the space given to the account of it, it must have been one of the most troublesome things in David's reign. It involved defection of some of David's advisers, and utterly broke his heart. But Absalom was finally killed, and David restored to his throne.

Then followed Sheba's Rebellion (chapter 20). Absalom's attempted usurpation probably weakened David's hold on the people. So Sheba tried his hand at it, but soon was crushed. Then the Philistines grew bold again (chapter 21); and again David was victorious.

Chapter 22. David's Song of Praise

Here, as in many Psalms, David exhibits his unfailing Trust in God, and his unbounded Gratitude to God for His constant care.

Chapter 23. David's Last Words

That is, his last Psalm. It shows what David's mind was on at the close of his glorious but troubled life: the Justice of his reign as king; his creation of the Psalms; his devotion to God's Word; God's covenant with him of an Eternal Dynasty.

Chapter 24. The People Numbered

It is difficult to see just wherein was the sin of taking a national census. God himself had ordered such a census both at the beginning and at the end of the 40 years of wilderness wanderings (Numbers 1:2; 26:2). Perhaps in this case, it may have indicated that David, who had so consistently, all his life long, relied implicitly on God, might have been beginning to slip, in a tendency to rely on the greatness of his kingdom. The census was Satan's idea (I Chronicles

21:1). Satan may have considered it an opportunity to move David away from his trust in God to trust in himself. At any rate, God regarded the act as a sin to be punished.

The census showed a population of about a million and a half of fighting men, exclusive of Levi and Benjamin (I Chronicles 21:5); or a total population of, probably, about six to eight million.

In punishment, God sent the angel of pestilence to destroy Jerusalem. In the place where the angel's hand was stayed, there David built an altar (25). Where David built the altar, there Solomon built the Temple (II Chronicles 3:1).

David

All in all, David was a grand character. He did some things that were very wrong, but, for an oriental king, he was a most remarkable man. He was, heart and soul, devoted to God and the ways of God. In a world of Idolatry, and in a nation that was continually falling away into Idolatry, David stood like a rock for God. In every circumstance of life he went directly to God, in Prayer, in Thanks or in Praise. His two great accomplishments were: the Kingdom and the Psalms.

I KINGS

The Reign of Solomon
The Temple
Splendor of Solomon's Court
Golden Age of Hebrew History
Division and Decay of the Kingdom
Apostasy of the Ten Tribes
Elijah

The two books, I and II Kings, in the Hebrew Old Testament, were one book (see page 26). It was divided by the Septuagint translators. Roughly, they narrate: 1. The Reign of Solomon. 2. Division of the Kingdom, and Parallel History of the Two Kingdoms. 3. Subsequent History of Judah to the Captivity.

I Kings opens with the Hebrew nation in its glory. II Kings closes with the nation in ruin. Together they cover a period of about 400 years, approximately, 1000–600 B.C.

Author

The author is not known. A Jewish tradition says it was Jeremiah. Whoever the author, he makes frequent reference to state annals and other historical records existent in his day: as, "The book of the acts of Solomon," "The book of the chronicles of the kings of Judah," "The book of the chronicles of the kings of Israel" (I Kings 11:41; 14:19, 29; 15:7, 23, 31; 16:5, 14, 27, etc.). Thus, it seems, there was an abundance of Written Records, to which the sacred writer had access, guided, of course, by the Spirit of God.

Chapters 1,2. Solomon Becomes King

Born of Bathsheba, to whom David had no right, and, though not in line for the succession, yet he was chosen by David, and approved of God, to be David's successor (1:30; I Chronicles 22:9, 10).

Adonijah, David's 4th son, it seems, was heir expectant to the throne (2:15, 22; II Samuel 3:3, 4); for Amnon, Absalom and probably Chiliab, were dead. So, while David was on his deathbed, and before Solomon was formally anointed king, Adonijah plotted to seize the kingdom. But the plot was thwarted by Nathan the prophet. Solomon was generous in his treatment of Adonijah. But Adonijah persisted in his effort to steal the throne, and it was not long till he suffered death.

Chapter 3. Solomon's Choice of Wisdom

This was at Gibeon (3:4), where the Tabernacle and Brazen Altar were at the time (I Chronicles 21:29), about 10 miles northwest of Jerusalem; although the Ark was at Jerusalem (3:15). God told Solomon to ask what he would. Solomon asked for wisdom to govern his people. That pleased God, and God richly rewarded him (10–12). "No fairer promise of true greatness, or more beautiful picture of youthful piety is known in history."

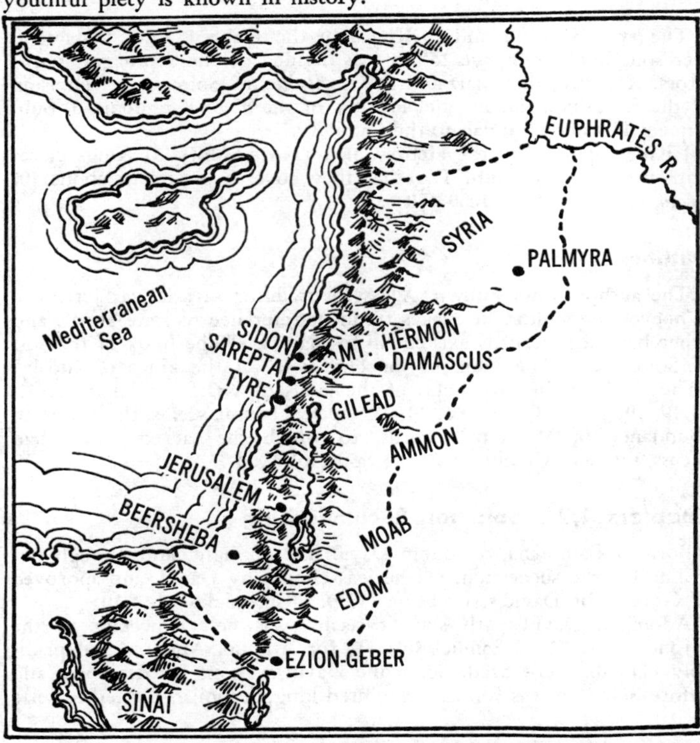

Map 42. Dotted line indicates extent of Solomon's kingdom.

Chapter 4. Solomon's Power, Wealth and Wisdom

He had inherited the throne of the most powerful kingdom then existent. It was an era of peace and prosperity. Solomon had vast business enterprises, and was famous for his literary attainments. He wrote 3000 proverbs, 1005 songs, and scientific works on botany and zoology (32, 33). He wrote three of the Bible books: Proverbs, Ecclesiastes, and Song of Solomon. Chapters 5, 6, 7, 8. Solomon Builds Temple. (See on II Chronicles 2 to 7.)

Chapters 9,10. Splendor of Solomon's Kingdom

These two chapters are an expansion of chapter 4. Solomon devoted himself to commerce and gigantic public works. He made a deal with the king of Tyre, to use his navy on the Mediterranean. He had a navy at Ezion-geber, and controlled the trade route South through Edom to the coasts of Arabia, India and Africa. He built his empire by peaceful commerce.

This era of David and Solomon was the Golden Age of Hebrew history. David was a warrior. Solomon was a builder. David made the Kingdom. Solomon built the Temple. In the outside world, this was the age of Homer, the beginning of Greek history. Egypt, and Assyria and Babylon, at the time, were weak. Israel was the most powerful kingdom in all the world; Jerusalem the most magnificent city, and the Temple the most splendid building, on earth. They came from the ends of the earth to hear Solomon's wisdom and see his glory. The famous Queen of Sheba exclaimed, "The half was not told me."

ARCHAEOLOGICAL NOTE: Solomon's Stables

The writer here speaks of Solomon's horses (10:26, 28). Megiddo is named as one of the cities where he kept his horses (9:15, 19).

The Oriental Institute has uncovered, in Megiddo (see page 206), ruins of stables. In the photograph, just below, may be seen the stone hitching poles, to which Solomon's horses were tied, and mangers out of which they ate.

Fig. 41. Ruins of Solomon's Stables, Megiddo.
(Courtesy Oriental Institute, University of Chicago)

ARCHAEOLOGICAL NOTE: Solomon's Gold

Solomon's annual income, and supply, in gold, is spoken of as enormous: shields of gold, bucklers of gold, all the vessels of his palace of gold, his throne of ivory overlaid with gold, gold as common in Jerusalem as stones (10:10–22; II Chronicles 1:15). Within 5 years after Solomon's death, Shishak, king of Egypt, came and took away all this gold (14:25, 26; II Chronicles 12:2, 9–11).

Amazing to be told, just recently (1939), the mummy of Shishak was found in Tanis, in Egypt, in a gold-covered sarcophagus, perhaps some of this very same gold which he had taken from Solomon.

ARCHAEOLOGICAL NOTE: Solomon's Navy at Ezion-geber

Solomon made a navy of ships in Ezion-geber (9:26). This was for his trade with Arabia, India and the east coast of Africa. Ezion-geber was situated at north end of the Gulf of Akaba, on Red Sea.

Its ruins have been identified, and were excavated (1938–39), by Dr. Nelson Glueck, of the American Schools of Oriental Research. He found ruins of Solomon's smelters, furnaces, crucibles and refineries; also, copper and iron ore deposits, in the vicinity; of which, dishes, nails, spearheads and fishhooks, were manufactured, and exported in exchange for ivory and gold.

ARCHAEOLOGICAL NOTE: Stones of Solomon's Wall

"Costly stones, great stones, stones of ten cubits," were used in Solomon's buildings, and the walls of Jerusalem (7:9–12; 9:15).

At the southeast corner of the Temple area the wall rises 77 feet. In 1868 a shaft was sunk 79 feet to native rock. The wall is thus 156 feet. Its corner stone is 14 feet long, 4 feet high. Solomon's repairs (11:27), are plainly indicated.

Barkley (1852) discovered the quarry from which Jerusalem's great stones were taken. It is now an immense cavern extending under a large part of the city. The entrance is a small hole near the Damascus gate. Partly cut stones are there, from which their methods of quarrying were learned. With long-handled picks they made incisions above, below and at the sides. Small holes were drilled, in rows, into which wooden wedges were driven, on which water was poured. The wedges swelled and split the stone. Little holes were cut in the rocks to hold candles by which the men worked in pitch darkness.

Chapter 11. Solomon's Wives and Apostasy

Solomon's glorious reign was clouded by a grand Mistake: his Marriage to Idolatrous women. He had 700 wives and 300 concubines (11:3), which, in itself, was an enormous crime, both against himself and his women. This wise man of the ages, in this respect at least, we think, was just a plain common fool. Many of these women were Idolaters, daughters of heathen princes, wedded for the sake of political alliance. For them, he, who had built God's Temple, built alongside of it Heathen Altars. Thus, Idolatry, which David had been so zealous to suppress, was re-established in the palace. This brought to a close the glorious era ushered in by David, and started the nation on its road to ruin: the Sunset of Israel's Golden Age. The besotted apostasy of Solomon's old age is one of the most pitiful spectacles in the Bible. Perhaps the account of it was intended of God to be an example of what luxury and ceaseless rounds of pleasure will do to even the best of men.

Chapter 12. Division of the Kingdom

The Kingdom had lasted 120 years: Saul, 40 years (Acts 13:21); David, 40 years (II Samuel 5:4); Solomon, 40 years (I Kings 11:42). After the death of Solomon the Kingdom was Divided: Ten Tribes forming the Northern Kingdom, called "Israel"; Judah and Benjamin forming the Southern Kingdom, called "Judah." The Northern Kingdom lasted a little over 200 years, and was destroyed by Assyria, 721 B.C. The Southern Kingdom lasted a little over 300 years, and was destroyed by Babylon, about 600 B.C.

The Secession of the Ten Tribes "was of God" (11:11, 31; 12:15); as punishment for apostasy of Solomon, and a lesson to Judah.

Religion of the Northern Kingdom

Jeroboam, founder of the Northern Kingdom, to keep the two kingdoms separate, adopted Calf Worship, the religion of Egypt, as State Religion of his newly formed kingdom. God Worship had become identified with Judah and the Family of David. The Calf came to stand as a symbol of Israel's Independence of Judah. Jeroboam rooted Calf Worship in the Northern Kingdom so deeply that it was not swept away till the fall of the kingdom.

Baal Worship, introduced by Jezebel, prevailed about 30 years, and was exterminated by Elijah, Elisha and Jehu, and never returned, though it did persist intermittently in Judah.

Every one of the 19 kings of the Northern Kingdom followed the worship of the Golden Calf. Some of them also served Baal. But not one ever attempted to bring the people back to God.

Religion of the Southern Kingdom

God-Worship: though most of the kings served Idols, and walked in the evil ways of the kings of Israel; some of Judah's kings served God, and at times there were great reformations in Judah. On the whole, however, in spite of the repeated warnings, Judah sank lower and lower in the horrible practices of Baal worship and other Canaanite religions, till there was no remedy.

Kings of Israel

Jeroboam	22 years	Bad
Nadab	2 years	Bad
Baasha	24 years	Bad
Elah	2 years	Bad
Zimri	7 days	Bad
Omri	12 years	Extra Bad
Ahab	22 years	The Worst
Ahaziah	2 years	Bad
Joram	12 years	Bad mostly
Jehu	28 years	Bad mostly
Jehoahaz	17 years	Bad
Joash	16 years	Bad
Jeroboam II	41 years	Bad
Zechariah	6 months	Bad
Shallum	1 month	Bad
Menahem	10 years	Bad
Pekahiah	2 years	Bad
Pekah	20 years	Bad
Hoshea	9 years	Bad

Kings of Judah

Rehoboam	17 years	Bad mostly
Abijah	3 years	Bad mostly
Asa	41 years	Good
Jehoshaphat	25 years	Good
Jehoram	8 years	Bad
Ahaziah	1 year	Bad
Athaliah	6 years	Devilish
Joash	40 years	Good mostly
Amaziah	29 years	Good mostly
Uzziah	52 years	Good
Jotham	16 years	Good
Ahaz	16 years	Wicked
Hezekiah	29 years	The Best
Manasseh	55 years	The Worst
Amon	2 years	The Worst
Josiah	31 years	The Best
Jehoahaz	3 months	Bad
Jehoiakim	11 years	Wicked
Jehoiachin	3 months	Bad
Zedekiah	11 years	Bad

Some of the reigns were, in part, concurrent.
All the kings of Israel served the Calf; the worst served Baal.
Most of the kings of Judah served Idols; a few served Jehovah.
Some bad kings were partly good; some good kings, partly bad.

Chronology of the Divided Kingdom

The date of the Division of the Kingdom is variously placed between 983 B.C. and 931 B.C. There are difficulties in the chronology of the period; and apparent discrepancies, which may, in part, be accounted for by "overlapping reigns," "associated sovereignty," "intervals of anarchy," and "parts of years as years." These dates are only approximate.

Kings of Israel

Jeroboam	933–911
Nadab	911–910
Baasha	910–887
Elah	887–886
Zimri	886
Omri	886–875

Kings of Judah

Rehoboam	933–916
Abijah	915–913
Asa	912–872

Ahab	875–854	Jehoshaphat	874–850
Ahaziah	855–854	Jehoram	850–843
Joram	854–843	Ahaziah	843
Jehu	843–816	Athaliah	843–837
Jehoahaz	820–804	Joash	843–803
Joash	806–790	Amaziah	803–775
Jeroboam II	790–749	Uzziah	787–735
Zechariah	748	Jotham	749–734
Shallum	748		
Menahem	748–738		
Pekahiah	738–736	Ahaz	741–726
Pekah	748–730		
Hoshea	730–721	Hezekiah	726–697
		Manasseh	697–642
		Amon	641–640
		Josiah	639–608
		Jehoahaz	608
		Jehoiakim	608–597
		Jehoiachin	597
		Zedekiah	597–586

Chapters 13,14. Jeroboam, king of Israel, 933-911 B.C.

Encouraged by the prophet Ahijah, and promised the throne of the Ten Tribes, and a sure house, if only he would walk in God's ways, he led a revolt against Solomon. Solomon sought to kill him. He fled to Egypt, to the court of Shishak king of Egypt; probably came to an understanding with Shishak, and made him lustful of Solomon's riches.

On Solomon's death he returned, and established the Ten Tribes as an independent kingdom. But disregarding Ahijah's warning, he instituted CALF worship. And God sent Ahijah to tell him that Israel should be rooted up out of the land, and scattered in the country beyond the Euphrates (14:10, 15).

The amazing prophecy, calling Josiah by name 300 years before he was born (13:2), was fulfilled (II Kings 23:15–18).

There was long continued War between Israel and Judah, after the Division of the Kingdom.

The Northern Kingdom, "Israel," 933-721 B.C.

1st	50 years:	Harassed by Judah and Syria.
Then	40 years:	Quite prosperous, under Omri's house.
Then	40 years:	Brought very low, under Jehu and Jehoahaz.
Then	50 years:	Reached its greatest extent, under Jeroboam II.
Last	30 years:	Anarchy, ruin and captivity.

The Southern Kingdom, "Judah," 933-606 B.C.

1st	80 years:	Quite prosperous, growing in power.
Then	70 years:	Considerable disaster; introduction of Baalism.
Then	50 years:	Under Uzziah, reached its greatest extent.
Then	15 years:	Under Ahaz, became tributary to Assyria.
Then	30 years:	Under Hezekiah, regained independence.
Last	100 years:	In the main, a vassal of Assyria.

Relation to Each Other

1st	80 years:	Continuous war between them.
2nd	80 years:	They were at peace with each other.
Last	50 years:	Intermittent war, to the end.

Dynasties

In the Northern Kingdom there were 9 Dynasties (family lines of kings): 1. Jeroboam, Nadab. 2. Baasha, Elah. 3. Zimri. 4. Omri, Ahab, Ahaziah, Jehoram. 5. Jehu, Jehoahaz, Joash, Jeroboam II, Zechariah. 6. Shallum. 7. Menahem, Pekahiah. 8. Pekah. 9. Hoshea. 19 kings in all. An average of about 11 years to a reign. 8 of these kings met death by violence.

In the Southern Kingdom there was only 1 Dynasty, that of David: except usurper Athaliah from the Northern Kingdom, who by marriage, broke into David's line, and interrupted the succession for 6 years. 20 kings in all. An average of about 16 years to a reign.

Chapter 14:21–31. Rehoboam, king of Judah. (See on II Chronicles 10.)

Chapter 15:1–8. Abijah, king of Judah. (See on II Chronicles 13.)

Chapter 15:9–24. Asa, king of Judah. (See on II Chronicles 14.)

Chapter 15:25-32. Nadab, king of Israel. 911-910 B.C.

Son of Jeroboam. "Walked in the sins of his father." Reigned 2 years. Assassinated by Baasha, who slew all the house of Jeroboam.

Chapters 15:33-16:7. Baasha, king of Israel. 910-887 B.C.

Got the throne by violence. Reigned 24 years. "Walked in sins of Jeroboam." Warred with Judah. Judah hired Assyria to attack him.

Chapter 16:8-14. Elah, king of Israel. 887-886 B.C.

Son of Baasha. Reigned 2 years. A debauchee. Assassinated, while he was drunk, by Zimri, who slew all the house of Elah.

Chapter 16:15-20. Zimri, king of Israel. 886 B.C.

Reigned 7 days. A military officer, whose only accomplishment was the extermination of the Baasha dynasty. Was burnt to death.

Chapter 16:21-28. Omri, king of Israel. 886-875 B.C.

Reigned 12 years. "Wicked above all who had been before him." Gained such prominence that for a long time after his day Israel was known as the "land of Omri." Made Samaria his capital. Tirzah had been the Northern capital till then (14:17; 15:33).

ARCHAEOLOGICAL NOTES: Omri
Moabite Stone (850 B.C.) mentions "Omri, king of Israel."
An inscription of Adadnirari (808–783 B.C.) mentions "Omri."
The Black Obelisk, of Shalmaneser III (860–825 B.C.) speaks of tribute from Jehu, "successor of Omri."
Samaria. In 16:24 it is said that Omri built Samaria. A Harvard University Expedition (see page 206), found in the ruins of Samaria the foundations of Omri's palace, but nothing older than Omri, evidence that he was founder of the city.

Chapters 16:29-22:40. Ahab, king of Israel. 875-854 B.C.

Reigned 22 years. Wickedest of all the kings of Israel. He married Jezebel, a Sidonian princess, an imperious, unscrupulous, vindictive, determined, devilish woman, a demon incarnate. A devotee of Baal worship, she built a temple for Baal in Samaria, maintained 850 prophets of Baal and Ashtoreth, slew the prophets of Jehovah, and abolished Jehovah worship (18:13, 19). She gave her name to later prophetesses who sought to fasten voluptuous practices of idol worship on the Church (Revelation 2:20).

ARCHAEOLOGICAL NOTE: Rebuilding of Jericho (16:34).
An amazing fulfillment of Joshua's prediction, 500 years before (Joshua 6:26). The ruins of Jericho show that it was inhabited continuously from pre-Abrahamic times to about 1400 B.C. with no signs of habitation from then to the 9th century B.C., time of Ahab, the ruins of which are very small. In this stratum a large house was uncovered, which may have been the house of Hiel (16:34). A jar with the remains of a child was found in the masonry of a gate, and two such jars in the walls of a house.

Elijah. I Kings 17 to II Kings 2

Six chapters are given to Ahab's reign, while most of the kings have only a part of one chapter. The reason: it is largely the story of Elijah. Elijah was God's answer to Ahab and Jezebel, who had substituted Baal for God. God sent Elijah to eradicate Baalism, a vile and cruel religion.

Elijah's "rare, sudden and brief appearances, his undaunted courage and fiery zeal, the brilliance of his triumphs, the pathos of his despondency, the glory of his departure, and the calm beauty of his reappearance on the Mt. of Transfiguration, make him one of the grandest characters Israel ever produced."

Chapter 17,18. The Drouth

Fig. 42. Jar burial, remains of an infant. (*Courtesy Oriental Institute, University of Chicago*)

God gave Elijah power to shut the heavens for 3½ years, during which time he was fed by ravens at Brook Cherith, and by the widow of Sarepta, whose jar of meal and cruse of oil failed not.

Elijah's venture of faith, on Mt. Carmel, was magnificent. God must have revealed to Elijah, some way or other, that he would send the fire and rain. But it all made no impression on Jezebel.

ARCHAEOLOGICAL NOTE: Baal Worship

The Oriental Institute, excavating at Megiddo (see page 206), which is near Samaria, found, in the stratum of Ahab's time, the ruins of a temple of Ashtoreth, goddess wife of Baal. Just a few steps from this temple was a cemetery, where many jars were found, containing remains of infants who had been sacrificed in this temple, one of which is shown in Figure 42. Prophets of Baal and Ashtoreth were official murderers of little children. This is a sidelight on Elijah's execution of the prophets of Baal (18:40), and helps us to understand why Jehu was so ruthless in his extermination of Baalism.

Chapter 19. The "Still Small Voice"

Utterly discouraged, Elijah fled to Mt. Horeb, where he asked God to let him die (19:4). And God taught him a wonderful lesson: God was not in the "wind," or "earthquake," or "fire," but "in a still small voice" (11, 12). Elijah's ministry had been a ministry of Miracles, Fire and the Sword. He had shut the heavens, had been sustained by ravens, and by a jar of meal and cruse of oil that failed not, had raised the dead, had called down fire from heaven, had slain the prophets of Baal with the sword, and had brought rain to the land.

It seems like God was aiming to tell Elijah that, while force and spectacular demonstrations of power are sometimes necessary, by reason of a crisis in God's plans, yet, after all, God' real work in the world is not accomplished by such methods: that God sometimes does, and sometimes calls men to do, things that are utterly contrary to God's nature to do.

Many centuries later Elijah again appeared to mortal view, in the Mount of Transfiguration, talking with Christ, of the work that now at last was being introduced into the earth, namely, the transforming of human lives into the image of God by the "still small voice" of Christ in the hearts of men.

Chapters 20,21,22. Ahab's Death

He closed his reign with a brutal crime against Naboth, and was slain in war with Syria, the end of a contemptible character.

ARCHAEOLOGICAL NOTES: Ahab

An inscription to Shalmaneser, 860–825 B.C. mentions Ahab: "I destroyed . . . 2,000 chariots and 10,000 men of Ahab king of Israel."

Ahab's Ivory House" (22:39). A Harvard University Expedition (see page 206) found, in Samaria, the ruins of this house. Its walls had been faced with Ivory. There were thousands of pieces of the most exquisitely carved and inlaid panels, plaques, cabinets and couches. It was just above the ruins of Omri's palace.

Chapter 22:41–50. Jehoshaphat, king of Judah. (See II Chronicles 17.)

Chapter 22:51–53. Ahaziah, king of Israel. (See II Kings 1.)

II KINGS

The Divided Kingdom
Elisha
Last 130 Years of Northern Kingdom
Last 250 Years of Southern Kingdom
Captivity of Israel by Assyria
Captivity of Judah by Babylon

II Kings is a continuation of I Kings, beginning about 80 years after the Division of the Kingdom, and carrying parallel accounts of the two kingdoms on for about 130 years, to the Fall of the Northern Kingdom; and then proceeding with the further history of the Southern Kingdom for another 120 years, to its Fall. The book covers the last 12 kings of the Northern Kingdom, and the last 16 kings of the Southern Kingdom (see under I Kings 12); a period, in all, of about 250 years, approximately 850–600 B.C.

The Northern Kingdom, called Israel, fell (721 B.C.) at the hands of the Assyrians, whose capital was Nineveh (see under chapter 17).

The Southern Kingdom, called Judah, fell, 600 B.C., at the hands of the Babylonians, whose capital was Babylon (see under chapter 25).

Elijah and Elisha were prophets sent of God, in an effort to save the Northern Kingdom. Their ministry together lasted about 75 years in the middle period of the Northern Kingdom, about 875–800 B.C., through the reigns of 6 kings, Ahab, Ahaziah, Joram, Jehu, Jehoahaz, Joash.

Chapter 1. Ahaziah, king of Israel. 855-854 B.C.

Account of his reign starts back in I Kings 22:51. Reigned 2 years. Co-regent with his father Ahab, and wicked like him. We have here another of Elijah's "fire" miracles (9–14).

Chapter 2. Elijah's Translation

Elijah was a native of Gilead, the land of Jephthah. A child of the wild loneliness of mountain ravines, he wore a cloak of sheep skin or coarse camel hair, with his own thick long hair hanging down his back. His mission was to drive Baalism out of Israel. His ministry may have lasted about 25 years through the reigns of the wicked

Ahab and Ahaziah. He had some hard and rough and very disagreeable work to do. He thought he had failed. And, though intimate with God in measure that has been given to few men, yet how utterly human he was, like us; and he asked God to take his life. But God did not think he had failed. His work done, God sent a deputation of Angelic chariots to bear him away in triumph to heaven.

Elijah had recently been in Mt. Horeb, where Moses had given the law. Now, conscious that the time of his departure had come, he headed straight for the land of Moses' burial, Mt. Nebo (Deuteronomy 34:1), as if he wanted to be with Moses in death. We surmise that he was not long in finding Moses, and that they straightway became heavenly pals, and that they found their greatest joy in looking forward to the coming of their Greater Pal, with whom they made a brief earthly appearance (Matthew 17:3).

Elijah had been a prophet of "fire." He had called down "fire" from heaven on Mt. Carmel, and he had called down "fire" to destroy the officers of Ahaziah. Now he is borne away to heaven in "chariots of fire." Only one other, Enoch, was taken to God without having to pass through the experience of death (Genesis 5:24). Possibly the translation of these two men may have been intended of God to be a sort of dim forecast of the Rapture of the Church, in that glad day when Angel chariots shall sweep in and swing low to gather us up to welcome the Returning Saviour.

Elisha. II Kings 2 to 13

Elijah, under instruction from God, had anointed Elisha to be his successor (I Kings 19:16–21); and had taken him in training. As Elijah went away to heaven, his mantle fell on Elisha, and Elisha began immediately to work miracles, as Elijah had done.

Waters of the Jordan were divided, for Elisha, as just before they had divided for Elijah (2:8, 14). The spring at Jericho was healed (2:21). 42 idolatrous lads at Bethel were torn by bears (2:24). God, not Elisha, sent the bears. Bethel was a seat of Baal worship. The lads' taunt, presumably, was at Elisha's God.

God had hinted to Elijah that fire and sword methods were not the methods by which God's real work would be accomplished (I Kings 19:12). Nevertheless the fire and sword work went on. Baalism could understand no other language. Elisha anointed Jehu to exterminate official Baalism (I Kings 19:16, 17; II Kings 9:1–10). And Jehu did, with a vengeance (chapters 9, 10).

Chapters 3 to 9. Jehoram (Joram), king of Israel. 854-843 B.C.

Reigned 12 years. He was killed by Jehu (9:24). In his reign, the king of Moab, who had paid tribute to Ahab, rebelled (3:4–6).

ARCHAEOLOGICAL NOTE: The Moabite Stone. Chapter 3 is an account of Jehoram's effort to re-subdue Moab. "Mesha, king of Moab," named in 3:4, made his own record of this rebellion. That record has been found. It is called the "Moabite Stone." Found (1868) in Moab, at Dibon, 20 miles east of the Dead Sea, by F. A. Klein, a German missionary. It is a bluish basalt stone, 4 feet high, 2 feet wide, 14 inches thick, with an inscription of Mesha. While the Berlin Museum was negotiating for it, the French Consulate at Jerusalem offered to pay a large sum for it.

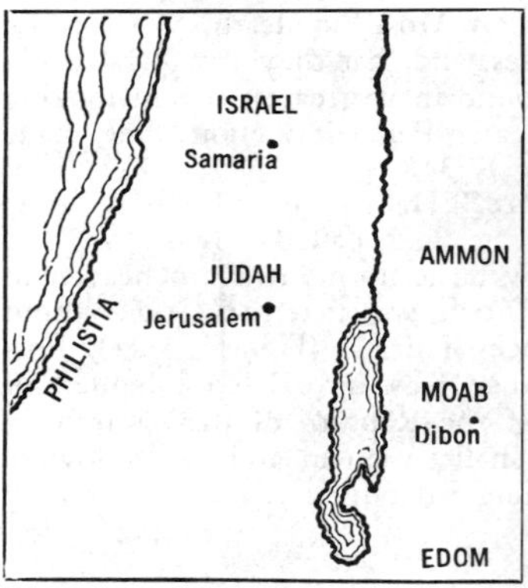

Map 43.

Fig. 43. Moabite Stone
© *Matson Photo*

The next year Arabs, by lighting a fire around it, and pouring cold water over it, broke it in pieces, to carry away as charms. Later the French secured the pieces, and, by putting them together, saved the inscription. It is now in the Louvre Museum.

It reads: "I, Mesha, king of Moab, made this monument to Chemosh (god of Moab), to commemorate deliverance from Israel. My father reigned over Moab 30 years, and I reigned after my father. Omri, king of Israel, oppressed Moab many days, and his son (Ahab) after him. But I warred against the king of Israel, and drove him out, and took his cities, Medeba, Ataroth, Nebo, and Jahaz, which he built while he waged war against me. I destroyed his cities, and devoted the spoil to Chemosh, and the women and girls to Ashtar. I built Qorhah with prisoners from Israel."

Chapters 4,5,6,7. Elisha's Miracles

Elisha had begun his ministry with miracles, as told in chapter 2.

Miracle upon miracle follows. Widow's Oil Increased. Shunammite's Son Raised from the Dead. Poisonous Pottage Healed. Loaves of Bread Multiplied. Naaman's Leprosy Healed. Axe Head Made to Swim. Samaria Delivered by Elisha's Invisible Chariots. Syrians Routed by Horses and Chariots of God (7:6). Nearly all that is recorded of Elisha is about his miracles. Most of Elisha's miracles were deeds of kindness and mercy.

Jesus took Elisha's healing of Naaman, as predictive that He himself would also be sent to Other nations (Luke 4:25–27).

Chapter 8:1-15. Elisha Anoints Hazael

To succeed Ben-hadad as king of Syria. A prophet of Israel anointed a foreign king to punish the prophet's own nation. God had instructed that this be done (I Kings 19:15); in punishing Israel for their frightful sins (10:32, 33).

ARCHAEOLOGICAL NOTE: Ben-hadad and Hazael (8:7–15). An inscription of Shalmaneser king of Assyria says: "I fought with Ben-hadad. I accomplished his defeat. Hazael, son of a nobody, seized his throne."

Elisha

Elisha began his ministry in the reign of Jehoram (3:1, 11), probably about 850 B.C., continuing through the reigns of Jehu and Jehoahaz, dying in the reign of Joash (13:14–20), about 800 B.C.

He was a farmer boy, of Abel-meholah, in the upper Jordan valley (I Kings 9:16, 19). He got his prophetic training from Elijah (I Kings 19:21; II Kings 3:11). He and Elijah were very different. Elijah was like the tempest and earthquake; Elisha, like the still small voice. Elijah was flint-like; Elisha, gentle, gracious, diplomatic. Elijah was a man of the wilderness, with a cloak of camel's hair; Elisha lived in cities, dressed like other people. Yet Elijah's mantle fell on Elisha (I Kings 19:19; II Kings 2:13).

Elisha's Miracles

They are enumerated in chapters 2, 4, 5, 6, 7. Among them was one of the Bible's Seven recorded Resurrections, the Seven being:
Elijah: the Widow's Son (I Kings 17). Elisha: Shunammite's Son (II Kings 4). Jesus: Jairus' Daughter (Mark 5); Widow of Nain's Son (Luke 7); Lazarus (John 11). Peter: Dorcas (Acts 9). Paul: Eutychus (Acts 20).

These seven do not include the Resurrection of Jesus, capstone of them all, and which was accomplished without human instrumentality; nor the strange incident of Elisha's bones (II Kings 13:21).

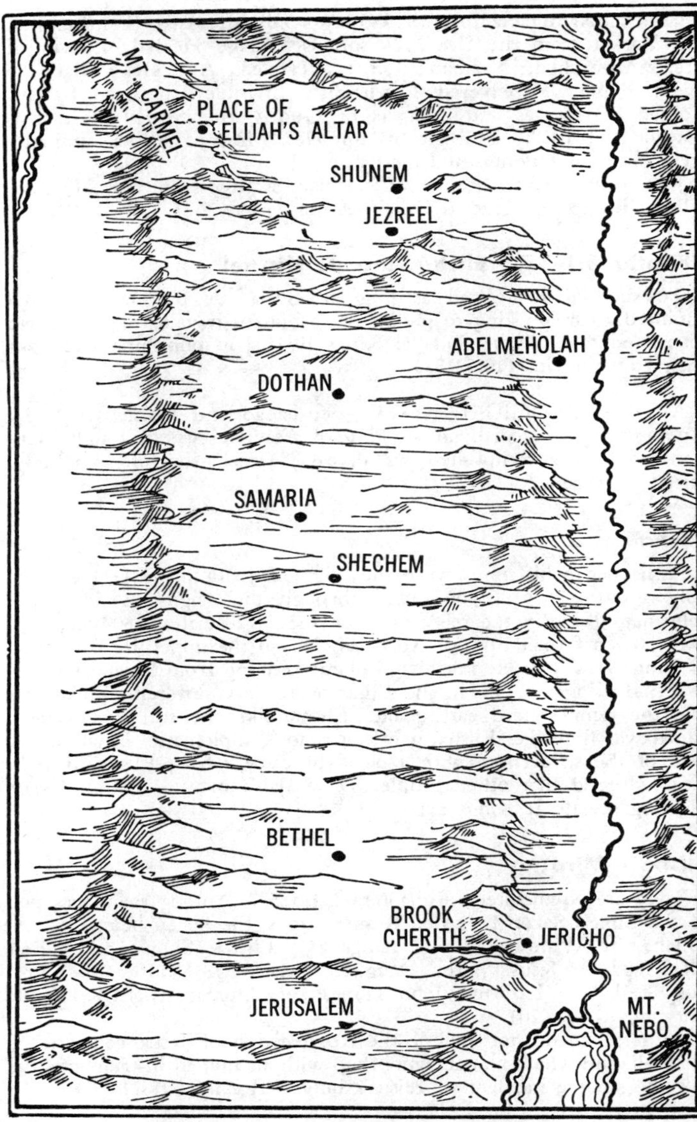
MT. CARMEL
PLACE OF ELIJAH'S ALTAR
SHUNEM
JEZREEL
ABELMEHOLAH
DOTHAN
SAMARIA
SHECHEM
BETHEL
BROOK CHERITH
JERICHO
JERUSALEM
MT. NEBO

Map 44.

Elisha's Seminary Work

Samuel, it seems from I Samuel 19:20, had started a school of prophets at Ramah. Elisha had such schools at Bethel, Jericho, Gilgal and other places (II Kings 2:3, 5; 4:38; 6:1). Beside these, he seems to have resided at Carmel, Shunem, Dothan and Samaria (II Kings 2:25; 4:10, 25; 6:13, 32). He must have been a sort of pastor-prophet-teacher. Also adviser to the king. His advice was always acted on. He did not approve all that the kings did, but in times of crisis he came to their rescue.

Elisha, in the Northern Kingdom, may have been contemporary with Joel, in the Southern Kingdom. He may have been teacher of Jonah and Amos, for they were boys at the time.

Elijah and Elisha, as a pair, in their personal lives and in public work, seem to have been a prototype, a fore-picture-in-action, of John the Baptist and Jesus, as a pair. John is called Elijah (Matthew 11:14); and Jesus' ministry of kindness was an extensive expansion of Elisha's ministry of the same nature. An illustration that men of utterly different types may work together for the same ends.

Chapter 8:16–24. Joram, king of Judah. (See on II Chronicles 21.)

Chapter 8:25–29. Ahaziah, king of Judah. (See on II Chronicles 22.)

Chapters 9,10. Jehu, king of Israel. 843-816 B.C.

Reigned 28 years. An officer of the bodyguard of Ahab. He was anointed by Elisha to be king, to cut off the house of Ahab, and to eradicate Baalism. He proceeded immediately and furiously to his bloody work. Jehu was fitted for it. He was intrepid, relentless, pitiless. Perhaps nothing else could have done it. He slew Joram king of Israel, Jezebel, Ahaziah king of Judah (son-in-law of Ahab), Ahab's 70 sons, the brothers of Ahaziah, all the friends and partisans of Ahab's house, all the priests of Baal, and all the worshipers of Baal; and destroyed the temple and pillars of Baal. Though Jehu eradicated Baal worship, he "departed not from the sins of Jereboam, and took no heed to walk in the law of God."

If we wonder at God's use of an agent like Jehu, let us remember that Baalism was unspeakably vile. God sometimes uses men and nations who are far from what they ought to be to execute His judgments on the wicked.

While Jehu was occupied with his bloody revolution within Israel, Hazael king of Syria took away Gilead and Bashan, Israel's realm east of the Jordan (10:32, 33). Jehu also had his troubles with Assyria, whose power was rising with ominous rapidity.

Fig. 44.
"Black Obelisk"

Bettmann Archive

ARCHAEOLOGICAL NOTE: Jehu. At Calah, near Nineveh, Layard (1845–49) found, in ruins of the palace of Shalmaneser, a block of black stone, 7 feet high, covered with reliefs and inscriptions, depicting his exploits. It is called the "Black Obelisk." Now in British Museum. In second line from top is a figure with marked Jewish features kneeling at the feet of the king, and above it this inscription:

"The tribute of Jehu, son (successor) of Omri, silver, gold, bowls of gold, chalices of gold, cups of gold, vases of gold, lead, sceptre for the king, and spear-shafts, I have received."

ARCHAEOLOGICAL NOTE: Jezebel. Jezebel "painted her eyes" (9:30). An Expedition sponsored by Harvard University, Hebrew University of Jerusalem, British School of Archaeology, and Palestine Exploration Fund (1908–10, 1931–), found, in Samaria, in the ruins of Ahab's "ivory house," saucers, small stone boxes, in which Jezebel mixed her cosmetics. They had a number of small holes to contain the various colors: kohl for black; turquoise for green; ochre for red; and a central depression for mixing. They still had traces of red.

ARCHAEOLOGICAL NOTE: Megiddo. In Megiddo, in the stratum of Ahab and Jezebel's time, jars were found containing remains of children that had been sacrificed to Baal (see page 198), illustrating the horrible nature of Baal worship.

Megiddo was the famous battlefield, Armageddon, which gives its name to the Great Final Battle of the Ages (Revelation 16:16). It was situated on the south side of the Plain of Esdraelon, 10 miles southwest of Nazareth, at the entrance to a pass across the Carmel mountain range, on the main highway between Asia and Africa, key position between the Euphrates and the Nile, meeting place of armies from the East and from the West. Thothmes III, who made Egypt a world-empire, said, "Megiddo is worth a thousand cities." It was at Megiddo, in the First World War, that General Allenby (1918) broke the power of the Turkish army. More blood has been shed around this hill than any other spot on earth, it is said.

The Oriental Institute of Chicago University, with aid of the Palestine Government (1924), acquired control of the hill, and from that time has been systematically removing layer after layer, recording and preserving everything historical. (See further page 198.)

Fig. 45. Hill of Megiddo.
© *Matson Photo*

Chapter 11. Athaliah, queen of Judah. (See on II Chronicles 22.)

Chapter 12. Jehoash, king of Judah. (See on II Chronicles 24.)

Chapter 13:1–9. Jehoahaz, king of Israel. 820–804 B.C. Reigned 17 years. Under him Israel was brought very low by the Syrians.

Chapter 13:10–25. Jehoash (Joash), king of Israel. 806–790 B.C. Reigned 16 years. Warred with Syria, and retook cities which his father had lost. Warred with Judah and plundered Jerusalem.

Chapter 14:1–22. Amaziah, king of Judah. (See on II Chronicles 25.)

Chapter 14:23-29. Jeroboam II, king of Israel. 790-749 B.C.

Reigned 41 years. Continued the wars of his father Joash against Syria, and, with the help of Jonah the prophet (25) brought the Northern Kingdom to its greatest extent. The idolatry and abominable social conditions of Jeroboam's reign called forth the ministry of the prophets Amos and Hosea.

ARCHAEOLOGICAL NOTE: A Seal of Jeroboam's Servant. At Megiddo, Schumacher (1903–05) found, in the layer of ruins belonging to Jeroboam's time, a beautiful jasper seal, bearing the inscription, "Belonging to Shema the Servant of Jeroboam." It was placed in the royal treasury of the Sultan of Turkey.

Chapter 15:1–7. Azariah, king of Judah. (See on II Chronicles 26.)

Chapter 15:8–12. Zechariah, king of Israel. 748 B.C. 6 months.

Chapter 15:13–15. Shallum, king of Israel. 748 B.C. 1 month.

Chapter 15:16–22. Menahem, king of Israel. 748–738 B.C. Reigned 10 years. Cold-blooded and brutal, he assassinated his predecessor.

ARCHAEOLOGICAL NOTE: Menahem. His Tribute to Pul, king of Assyria (19, 20). In one of Pul's inscriptions he says: "Tribute of Menahem of Samaria . . . I received." Pul's inscriptions name: "Uzziah," "Ahaz," "Pekah" and "Hoshea."

Chapter 15:23–26. Pekahiah, king of Israel 738–736 B.C. Reigned 2 years. Like Zechariah and Shallum, he was assassinated.

Chapter 15:27-31. Pekah, king of Israel. 748-730 B.C.

Reigned 20 years. A powerful military officer, who, it is thought, had been co-regent with Menahem and Pekahiah. In alliance with Syria, he attacked Judah. Judah appealed to Assyria for help. Then came the king of Assyria, and conquered both Israel and Syria, and carried away the inhabitants of North and East Israel. This was the Galilee Captivity (734 B.C.). Samaria alone was left, in the Northern Kingdom. Told more fully in II Chronicles and Isaiah 7.

ARCHAEOLOGICAL NOTE: Captivity of North Israel. By Tiglath-pileser (29). Tiglath-pileser's own inscription says: "The people of the land of Omri I deported to Assyria, with their property."

Chapter 15:32–38. Jotham, king of Judah. (See on II Chronicles 27.)
Chapter 16. Ahaz, king of Judah. (See on II Chronicles 28.)

Captivity of Israel, by Assyria, 721 B.C.

Chapter 17. Hoshea, 730–721 B.C., last king of Israel. Reigned 9 years. He paid tribute to the king of Assyria, but made a secret alliance with the king of Egypt. Then came the Assyrians, and administered the final death-blow to the Northern Kingdom. Samaria fell, and its people followed the rest of Israel into Captivity. The prophets at that time were Hosea, Isaiah and Micah. The Northern Kingdom had lasted about 200 years. Every one of its 19 kings had walked in the sins of Jeroboam its founder. God had sent prophet after prophet, and judgment after judgment, in an effort to turn the nation back from its sins. But in vain. Israel was joined to its idols. There was no remedy, and the wrath of God arose and removed Israel out of the land.

ARCHAEOLOGICAL NOTE: Hoshea. "Hoshea slew Pekah, and reigned in his stead" (15:30). "Hoshea brought tribute to the king of Assyria" (17:3).

An inscription of Tiglath-pileser says: "Pekah their king they had overthrown. I placed Hoshea over them. From him I received 10 talents of gold and 1000 talents of silver."

ARCHAEOLOGICAL NOTE: Captivity of Israel. "The king of Assyria besieged Samaria 3 years . . . and took it . . . and carried

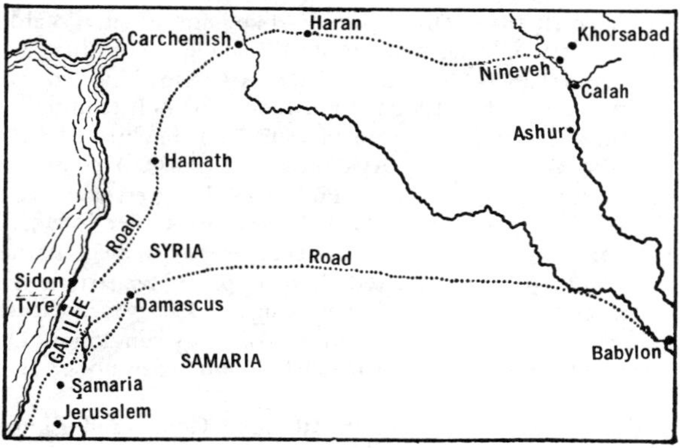

Map 45.

Israel away . . . and brought men from Babylon . . . and placed them in the cities of Samaria" (17:5, 6, 24).

An inscription of Sargon (see page 287) says: "In my first year I captured Samaria. I took captive 27,290 people. People of other lands, who never paid tribute, I settled in Samaria."

Assyria

It was by the Assyrian Empire that the Kingdom of Israel was destroyed. In recent years annals of Assyrian kings have been found in which they themselves had their own exploits recorded. In these annals names of ten Hebrew kings occur: Omri, Ahab, Jehu, Menahem, Pekah, Hoshea, Uzziah, Ahaz, Hezekiah, Manasseh. Many statements are found which confirm Biblical statements. Nineveh its capital (see pages 365, 369).

Assyrian policy was to deport conquered peoples to other lands, to destroy their sense of nationalism and make them more easily subject. Assyrians were great warriors. Most nations then were robber nations. Assyrians seem to have been about the worst of them all. They builded their state on the loot of other peoples. They practiced cruelty. They skinned their prisoners alive, or cut off their hands, feet, noses, ears, or put out their eyes, or pulled out their tongues, and made mounds of human skulls, all to inspire terror.

Assyria was founded, previous to 2000 B.C., by colonists from Babylon, and for many centuries was subject to, or in conflict with, Babylon. About 1300 B.C. Shalmaneser I, threw off the yoke of Babylon, and ruled the whole Euphrates Valley. Then Assyria declined. Tiglath-pileser I (1120–1100), made Assyria again a great kingdom. Then another period of decline. Then followed the brilliant epoch of 300 years in which Assyria was a World-Empire, under the following kings:

Assur-nasipal II (885–860 B.C.). Warlike and cruel. Welded Assyria into the best fighting machine of the ancient world.

Shalmaneser II (860–825 B.C.). First Assyrian king to come in conflict with Israel. Ahab fought him. Jehu paid him tribute.

Shansi-adad (825–808). Adad-nirari (808–783). Shalmaneser III (783–771). Assur-dayan (771–753). Assur-lush (753–747). Decline.

Tiglath-pileser III (747–727). "Pul" was his personal name. He carried North Israel into Captivity (734 B.C. See under Isaiah 7).

Shalmaneser IV (727–722). He besieged Samaria; died in the siege.

Sargon II (722–705). Completed destruction of Samaria and Israel's captivity. Sargon I was a Babylonian king of 2000 years earlier.

Sennacherib (705–681). Most famous of Assyrian kings. Defeated by an angel before Jerusalem. Burned Babylon. (See under II Chronicles 32.)

Esar-haddon (681–668). Rebuilt Babylon. Conquered Egypt. Was one of the greatest of Assyrian kings.

Assur-banipal (668–626). (Sardanopalus, Osnapper). Destroyed Thebes. Collected a great library. Powerful, cruel, literary.

Assur-etil-ilani, Sin-sar-iskun (Saracos) (626–607). Beset by Scythians, Medes and Babylonians, the brutal Empire fell.

Chapters 18 to 25 tell of the remaining 9 kings of Judah, Hezekiah to Zedekiah. (For notes on these kings see on II Chronicles 29 to 36).

Captivity of Judah, by Babylon, 606 B.C.

Chapter 25. Zedekiah (597–586 B.C.), last king of Judah. The Captivity of Judah was accomplished in four installments.

606 B.C. Nebuchadnezzar conquered Jehoiakim, and took temple treasures, and seed royal, including Daniel, to Babylon (II Chronicles 36:6–7. Daniel 1:1–3).

597 B.C. Nebuchadnezzar came again, and took the rest of the treasures, and king Jehoiachin, and 10,000 of the princes, officers and chief men, and carried them to Babylon (II Kings 24:14–16).

586 B.C. The Babylonians came again, and burned Jerusalem, broke down its walls, put out the eyes of king Zedekiah, and carried him in chains to Babylon, with 832 captives, leaving only a remnant of the poorest class of people in the land (II Kings 25:8–12; Jeremiah 52:28–30). The summary is less in Jeremiah than in Kings, probably including only the more important. It took the Babylonians a year and a half to subdue Jerusalem. They besieged it in the 9th year of Zedekiah, 10th month, 10th day. It fell in the 11th year, 4th month, 9th day. A month later, the city was burned, on the 7th day of the 5th month.

Thus Nebuchadnezzar was 20 years in destroying Jerusalem. He could have done it at first, if he had wished to. But he only wanted tribute. Then, too, Daniel, whom he took to Babylon at the beginning of the 20 years, soon became Nebuchadnezzar's friend and adviser; and may have had a restraining influence on him: till Judah's persistence in making alliance with Egypt forced Nebuchadnezzar to wipe Jerusalem off the map.

581 B.C. 5 years after the burning of Jerusalem, the Babylonians again came and took 745 more captives (Jeremiah 52:30), even after a considerable group, including Jeremiah, had fled to Egypt (Jeremiah 43). The Fall of Jerusalem brought forth the ministry of the three great prophets, Jeremiah, Ezekiel, Daniel.

The Captivity of Judah by Babylon had been predicted 100 years before by Isaiah and Micah (Isaiah 39:6; Micah 4:10). Now that it was accomplished Jeremiah predicted that it would last 70 years (Jeremiah 25:11, 12).

This was the end of David's earthly kingdom. It had lasted 400 years. It revived, in a spiritual sense, with the arrival of Christ, to be consummated in glory at His Return.

ARCHAEOLOGICAL NOTE: Nebuchadnezzar. His Burning of the Cities of Judah (25:9; Jeremiah 34:7). In Lachish, Bethel, Kiriath-sepher, and Beth-shemesh, there have been found layers of ashes from destructive fires that occurred about 600 B.C. These were Nebuchadnezzar's fires. In Lachish and at Beth-shemesh the fires had swept the cities so suddenly that underneath the great layers of debris and ashes and charcoal there were found: in Lachish, temple treasures, altar, censer, bowls, and bones of sacrifice; and in Beth-shemesh, stores of food supplies, lentils, raisins, olives.

Babylon

Assyria took ISRAEL away in Captivity (734–721 B.C.).
Babylon took JUDAH away in Captivity (606–586 B.C.).
Assyria was the North part of the Euphrates-Tigris valley.
Babylon was the South part of the Euphrates-Tigris valley.
Nineveh was the Capital of the Assyrian Empire.
Babylon was the Capital of the Babylonian Empire.
Nineveh and Babylon, 300 miles apart (see Map, page 209).

The Old Babylonian Empire

Babylonia was the cradle of the human race (see pages 42, 64, 65).
About 2000 B.C. Babylon was the dominating power of the world.
Then, 1000 years, intermittent struggle.
Then, 300 years of Assyrian Supremacy (885–607 B.C., see page 209).

The New Babylonian Empire

(606–536 B.C.). Sometimes called the Neo-Babylonian Empire. This was the Empire that broke the power of Assyria, and, in its westward sweep, destroyed JUDAH, and conquered Egypt. Its kings were:

Nabopolassar (625–604 B.C.) viceroy of Babylon. He threw off the yoke of Assyria (625 B.C.) and established the independence of Babylon. With the aid of Cyaxares the Mede, he conquered and destroyed Nineveh (607 B.C. [or 612], see page 368). His son Nebuchadnezzar (609 B.C.), became commander of his father's armies; and (606 B.C.), became co-regent with his father.

Nebuchadnezzar (606–561 B.C.), greatest of all Babylonian kings, one of the mightiest monarchs of all time. He reigned 45 years. The Babylonian Empire was largely his work. He extended the power of Babylon over most of the then known world, and beautified the city of Babylon almost beyond imagination (see pages 336, 341). He was the one that carried the Jews into captivity, including Daniel and Ezekiel. He took a great liking to Daniel, and made him one of his chief advisers. And Daniel's influence, no doubt, must have eased the lot of Jewish captives. (See further about Nebuchadnezzar, and Babylon, pages 336–344).

Evil-Merodach (561–560). Neriglissar (559–556). Labash-Marduk (556).

Nabonidus (555–536 B.C.). His son, Belshazzar, co-regent the last few years of his reign. Babylon fell. Supremacy passed to Persia. (For the story of the Handwriting on the Wall, and the Fall of Babylon, see page 344.)

The Babylonian Empire lasted 70 years. The 70 years of Judah's Captivity was exactly the same 70 years that Babylon ruled the world. The year that Cyrus, king of Persia, conquered Babylon (536 B.C.), that same year he authorized the Return of the Jews to their own land.

Babylon, oppressor of God's Old Testament people, gave its name to the Apostate Church (Revelation 17).

I CHRONICLES

Genealogies
The Reign of David

The Twelve preceding Books of the Bible ended with the Hebrew nation in Captivity. These two books of Chronicles retell the same story, and end at the same point. They are a Recapitulation of all that has gone before, with special attention to the reigns of David, Solomon and subsequent kings of Judah.

I Chronicles is, in part, the same as II Samuel. It has to do with the story of David, prefaced with 9 chapters of Genealogies. The Genealogies cover the period from Adam to the Jews' Return from Captivity; a sort of epitome of all previous sacred history.

Author

I and II Chronicles, Ezra and Nehemiah, were, originally, one series of works. Jewish tradition had it that Ezra was the author.

Frequent reference is made to other histories, annals and official archives: "The chronicles of King David" (I Chronicles 27:24); "The book of Samuel the seer, the book of Nathan the prophet, and the book of Gad the seer" (I Chronicles 29:29); "The book of Nathan the prophet, the prophecy of Ahijah the Shilonite and the visions of Iddo the seer" (II Chronicles 9:29); "The book of Shemaiah the prophet, and of Iddo the seer" (II Chronicles 12:15); "The story of the prophet Iddo" (II Chronicles 13:22); "The book of Jehu the son of Hanani, who is mentioned in the book of the kings of Israel" (II Chronicles 20:34); "The story of the book of the kings" (II Chronicles 24:27); "The acts of Uzziah, which Isaiah wrote" (II Chronicles 26:22); "The vision of Isaiah the prophet" (II Chronicles 32:32); "The book of the kings of Judah and Israel" (II Chronicles 32:32); "The sayings of the seers" (II Chronicles 33:19).

Thus, it is seen, the author had access to journals, diaries and public records that are not now known. He also had access to previous Old Testament books. Guided of God, he transcribed that which suited the purpose of his own writing. So, in this part of the Old Testament, we have a double narrative.

Significance of the Double Narrative

Believing, as we do, that the whole Bible is the Word of God, designed for Universal use, we wonder if God had some purpose other than Ezra's immediate need in resettling the land in thus repeating TWICE over this part of the sacred story.

Repetition means Importance. At least, it is a caution not to neglect this part of the Bible. Even though we think of Kings and Chronicles as rather dry reading, yet they contain the story of God's dealings with His people; and, now and then, in reading, we find therein some of the finest jewels of Scripture.

Difference between Kings and Chronicles

Kings gives a parallel account of the Northern and Southern Kingdoms, while Chronicles confines itself to the Southern Kingdom. Chronicles seems to be concerned primarily with the Kingdom of David, and bringing his line down to date.

Chapters 1 to 9. The Genealogies

These genealogies seem to have had for their immediate object the resettling of the land according to the public records. Those who had returned from the Captivity were entitled to lands formerly held in their own families. In the Old Testament land had been apportioned to families, and could not be sold in perpetuity out of the family (see under Leviticus 25).

So, the Priesthood was hereditary in families. A priest was to be succeeded by his son. This was the law of the land.

So, with the Kingly Line of David. The most important and precious of all promises was that the World's Saviour would come in David's family. The central interest of these genealogies is their tracing the descent of David's line. (See further on page 415.)

Most of the genealogies are incomplete, with many breaks in the lists. But the main line is there. They were probably compiled from many records which had been written on tablets, papyrus or vellum; partly copied from preceding Old Testament books.

These 9 chapters of genealogies form the generation-to-generation tie-up of all preceding Biblical history. They need not be read, for devotional purposes, as often as some other parts of Scripture. But in reality these, and similar genealogies, are the skeleton framework of the Old Testament, the thing that binds the whole Bible together, and gives it unity, and makes it look like real HISTORY, not legend.

Chapters 10,11,12. David Made King

The book of II Samuel, and the book of I Chronicles, except the genealogies, are both devoted entirely to the Reign of David. I Chronicles pays special attention to the Organization of Temple

Services. Being written after the Return from Captivity, it might not be out of the way to say that I Chronicles was a sort of historical sermon, based on II Samuel, designed to encourage the Returned Exiles in the work of Restoring Temple Worship to its proper place in their national life.

In II Samuel 2–4 it is told how David was made king over Judah, after death of Saul, his capital at Hebron; and reigned there 7½ years; in which time there was war with Saul's son, Ish-bosheth. After Ish-bosheth's death, David was made king over all Israel.

David's first act, as king over all Israel, was to take Jerusalem, and make it Capital of the nation. This is told more fully in II Samuel 5. Jerusalem was more central; and was impregnably located on a mountain with valleys on east, west and south sides. During the 400 years from Joshua to David Israel had been unable to take it. Jebusites were still there (Joshua 15:63; II Samuel 5:6–10; I Chronicles 11:4, 5).

ARCHAEOLOGICAL NOTE: The Watercourse. This Watercourse (II Samuel 5:8), by which David's men gained entrance to Jerusalem, was discovered (1866), by Warren, of the Palestine Exploration Fund. It is a sloping tunnel, with stairsteps, cut down through solid rock, from the top of the hill to Gihon Spring (see map page 39), which was at the east base of the hill, thus giving access, within the walls, to a water supply. The hill was surrounded by a wall 24 feet thick. It was impregnable till David discovered this secret passage from the spring into the city.

ARCHAEOLOGICAL NOTE: David's Wall. In 11:8 it is said that David "built the city round about." The remains of this wall have been uncovered for 400 feet. In places the old Jebusite foundations are still visible under David's masonry.

Chapters 13,14,15,16. The Ark Brought to Jerusalem

The Ark had been captured by the Philistines (I Samuel 4:11). It remained with them 7 months (I Samuel 6:1). Then was sent back to Israel, and was at Kiriath-jearim, 10 miles northwest from Jerusalem, for 20 years (I Samuel 7:2). David, having established Jerusalem as the national capital, assembled all Israel to bring the Ark, in a grand ceremonial procession, to Jerusalem.

But the unfortunate Uzzah incident (13:10), interrupted the procession. Uzzah's death, for his impulsive gesture to save the Ark (13:9), to us seems severe. However, only Levites were to carry the Ark (15:2, 13). Then, too, Uzzah's act was in direct violation of the law (Numbers 4:15); his death, a warning to be careful.

After 3 months at the house of Obed-edom (13:14), who was a Levite (15:17, 18, 21, 24), the Ark was brought into Jerusalem, amid great rejoicing, and placed in a Tent which David had made for it (15:1). The original Tent was at Gibeon (21:29).

David's Polygamy (14:3), was against the law of God. But it was the custom of ancient kings; one of the signs of prestige and royalty, which the people seemed to expect of their rulers; toward which, in Old Testament times, God seemed lenient. However, in family troubles, David reaped his harvest (see on II Samuel 13).

Chapter 17. David's Purpose to Build the Temple

It was David's idea. God was satisfied with a Tent (4–6). However, God gave in. But he would not let David build the Temple, because he had been a "man of war" and had "shed much blood" (22:8; 28:3); and assigned the task to Solomon (17:11–14; 28:6).

Chapters 18, 19, 20. David's Victories. (See on II Samuel 8.)

Chapter 21. The People Numbered. (See on II Samuel 24.)

Chapter 22. David's Preparations for the Temple

Though forbidden to actually build the Temple, David laid the plans for it, and devoted a large part of his reign to collecting vast stores of gold and silver, and all kinds of building material, estimated, variously, to value in our money between two and five billions of dollars. It was to be "exceeding magnificent, of fame and glory in all the earth" (22:5). It was to be the crowning glory of the kingdom. David's charge is expanded in chapter 28.

Chapter 23. Duties of Levites Designated

No more need to carry the Tabernacle (26), now that the Temple was to be permanently located in Jerusalem, the work of the Levites was respecified. Some of them were to oversee the work of the Temple (4). Some, to be doorkeepers (5). Some to be musicians (5; 15:16), a choir of 4000. Some were to be "officers and judges," "for the outward business over Israel," and "for the affairs of the king" (23:4; 26:29, 32). This last certainly looks as if the Levites had some work to do for the Civil Government.

Chapter 24. Priests Organized

Into 24 courses, for service in the Sanctuary. They were called "princes of the sanctuary," "princes of God" (5). They had charge of the Sacrifices. Their business ceased with the coming of Christ. Ironically enough, it was "Priests" who engineered the Crucifixion of

Christ (Matthew 27:1, 6, 20, 41). The Epistle to the Hebrews was written to show that "priests" were no longer necessary. The only places where the word is used with a Christian meaning is in Revelation 1:6; 5:10; 20:6; and there it applies to ALL Christians, and not solely to Christian Leaders.

Chapters 25,26,27. Further Organization

For efficiency in the Temple service, and in Government of the nation; specially the Musicians, whose business did not cease with the Coming of Christ, but rather took on new meaning. David was a great musician. With all his soul, he delighted in making the heavens ring with Songs of Praise to God (15:27, 28; 16:41, 42).

Chapters 28,29. David's Final Word and Prayer

Concerning the Temple. That is what his heart was on, as his soul took its flight to the "house not made with hands." The "man after God's own heart" had "served his generation" nobly. And what a joy it must have been when he met Him who later bore the name "Son of David."

II CHRONICLES

Reign of Solomon
The Temple
History of Judah after Secession of the Ten Tribes

II Chronicles covers the same ground as I and II Kings, except it omits the narratives about the kings of the seceded Ten Tribes.

Chapters 1 to 9. The Temple, and Glory of Solomon's Reign

(See also on I Kings 1 to 11)

Israel had gone for 400 years with only a Tent as God's dwelling place among them, and God, it seems, had been satisfied (II Samuel 7:5–7). Yet when it seemed expedient that they have a Temple, God wanted to have a say as to the kind of building it should be, and gave the plans for it, to David, in his "own handwriting" (I Chronicles 28:19; Exodus 25:9), that it be "exceeding magnificent, of fame and glory in all the earth" (I Chronicles 22:5).

David had wanted to build the Temple, but was forbidden, because he was a man of war (I Chronicles 22:8). God helped David in his wars. But, it appears, that God thought it not best for a man of war to be the builder of God's House; lest subdued nations feel bitter toward Israel's God; for, after all, God's purpose was, through His nation, to win other nations to Himself.

The Temple was built of great stones, cedar beams and boards, overlaid within with gold (I Kings 6:14–22; 7:9–12). The gold and silver, and other material, used in building the Temple (I Chronicles 22:14–16; 29:2–9), is variously estimated to equal, in our money, from 2 to 5 billions of dollars; no doubt, the most costly and resplendent building on earth at the time. The pomp and grandeur of the Temple may have served a purpose, but its gold became an object of cupidity to other kings.

It was built after the general plan of the Tabernacle (see page 132), every part twice the size: that is, figuring the cubit at a foot and a half, 90 feet long, 30 feet wide, and 45 feet high (I Kings 6:2).

It faced the east. The west 30 feet constituted the Most Holy Place, or Oracle. The east 60 feet was the Holy Place, or House (I Kings 6:16–20). They were separated by a Veil (II Chronicles 3:14).

In the Most Holy Place was the Ark, overshadowed by the two

Cherubim (I Kings 6:23–28). In the Holy Place, next to the Veil, in the center, was the Golden Altar of Incense; and, 5 Golden Candlesticks on North side, and 5 on South side; and 5 Tables of Showbread on North side, and 5 on South side (I Kings 7:48, 49; II Chronicles 4:8).

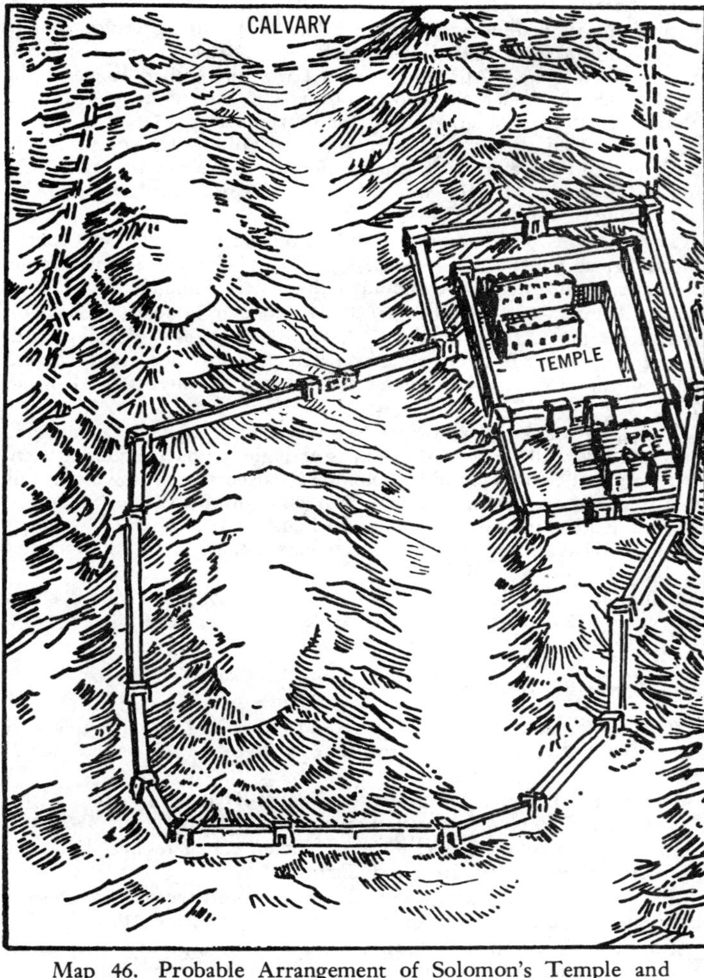

Map 46. Probable Arrangement of Solomon's Temple and Palace Buildings.

In front, on the east, was a Porch, width of the House, 15 feet deep. On the porch were two Pillars of brass, each about 6 feet in diameter, and 35 feet high, one on either side (I Kings 6:3; 7:15–21).

Against the wall of the Temple, on north, south, and west sides, were three stories of side-chambers, for priests (I Kings 6:5–10).

In front of Temple was Brazen Altar of Burnt Offering, 30 feet square and 15 feet high (II Chronicles 4:1); thought to have stood on the Rock Where Abraham offered Isaac, now called Rock of the Dome, directly under the center of present Mohammedan Mosque. Nearby, to the south, stood the great Brazen Laver, 15 feet in diameter, 8 feet deep, set on 12 brazen oxen, to hold water for priests to wash in. And there were 10 smaller portable Lavers, 5 on north side, and 5 on south side, for water for the sacrifices (I Kings 7:38,39; II Chronicles 4:1–6).

The Temple was surrounded by two Courts: an "inner court," and a "great court" (I Kings 6:36; 7:12). Their size is not known. The great court may have included the Palace buildings.

The Temple was built by 30,000 Israelites, and 150,000 Canaanites (I Kings 5:13–16; II Chronicles 2:17, 18; 8:7–9). Was 7 years in building (I Kings 6:38). Every part prepared at a distance from the site, and put in place without sound of hammer or any tool (I Kings 6:7).

Jerusalem was built on 5 hills (see page 39). David's Wall covered the Southeast hill. Solomon's Wall is thought to have included Central East and Southwest hills. Solomon's Palace stood, down the hill, just south of the Temple Court; and south of the Palace, Solomon's Throne Room; and south of that, the house of the forest of Lebanon, thought to have been an Armory (I Kings 7:2, 8). Roughly illustrated in Map on preceding page.

Solomon's Temple stood 400 years (970–589 B.C.). Zerubbabel's, 500 years (520–20 B.C.). Herod's, 90 years (20 B.C.–A.D. 70).

The Temples of God

The Tabernacle. Only a Tent. God's localized dwelling-place in Israel for 400 years. Most of the time at Shiloh. (See on Exodus 25 to 40.)

Solomon's Temple. Its glory was short-lived. Plundered within 5 years after Solomon's death. Destroyed by Babylonians 586 B.C.

Ezekiel's Temple (Ezekiel 40–43). Not an actual temple, but a vision of a Future Ideal Restored Temple.

Synagogs. Arose during the Captivity. Not temples, but small buildings, in scattered Jewish communities. (See page 410.)

Zerubbabel's Temple. Built after Return from Captivity. (See under Ezra and Nehemiah.) Stood 500 years.

Herod's Temple. This was the Temple to which Christ came. Built by Herod, of marble and gold. Magnificent beyond description. Destroyed by the Romans A.D. 70. (See under John 2:13.)

Christ's Body. Jesus called his body a Temple (John 2:19–21). In Him God tabernacled among men. Jesus said that earthly temples were not necessary to the worship of God (John 4:20–24).

The Church, collectively, is a Temple of God, God's dwelling-place in the world (I Corinthians 3:16–19).

Each Individual Christian is a Temple of God (I Corinthians 6:19), of which the grandeur of Solomon's Temple may have been a type.

Church Buildings are sometimes called Temples of God, but nowhere so designated in the Bible.

The Temple in Heaven. The Tabernacle was a pattern of something in Heaven (Hebrews 9:11, 24). John saw a Temple (Revelation 11:19). Later God and the Lamb had become the Temple (Revelation 21:22).

Chapters 10,11,12. Rehoboam, king of Judah. 933-916 B.C.

Son of Solomon. Reigned 17 years. (Told also in I Kings 12, 13, 14.) Under his reign the magnificent kingdom of Solmon took a plunge from its pinnacle of glory. Ten Tribes, out of the Twelve, seceded from his kingdom, and Shishak, king of Egypt, plundered Jerusalem (12:2–9).

ARCHAEOLOGICAL NOTE: Shishak's Invasion of Judah

Shishak's own record of this campaign is inscribed on the south wall of the great Temple of Amon at Karnak, in which he is depicted as presenting 156 cities of Palestine to his god Amon.

A layer of ashes from his burning of Kiriath-sepher has been uncovered.

Also a fragment of a monument he set up in Megiddo.

Shishak's Mummy was found (1939) at Tanis, in a sarcophagus of silver encased in solid gold, possibly some of Solomon's gold which he had taken from Jerusalem.

Fig. 46. Shishak's Relief, Karnak.
© *Matson Photo*

Chapter 13. Abijah (Abijam), king of Judah. 915-913 B.C.

Reigned 3 years. (Told also in I Kings 15:1–8.) Wicked, like his father. But, in battle with Jeroboam, he "relied upon the Lord," and defeated him, recovering some of the Northern cities.

Chapters 14,15,16. Asa, king of Judah. 912-872 B.C.

Reigned 41 years. (Told also in I Kings 15:9–24.) His long reign overlapped the reigns of 7 kings in the Northern kingdom. He was a good king, serving the Lord with great zeal. A great wave of reform swept the land. He broke down the foreign altars, high places, pillars, sun-images and asherim; he put away the sodomites (male prostitutes), and removed his mother from being queen because she worshiped an idol. Very prosperous.

Chapters 17,18,19,20. Jehoshaphat, king of Judah. 874-850 B.C.

Reigned 25 years. (Told also in I Kings 22:41–50.) Very religious: "sought the Lord in all things." Inaugurated a system of public instruction, sending priests and levites on regular circuits, with the "book of the law," to teach the people. He established courts of justice throughout the land. He maintained a vast army, and waxed exceeding great.

Chapter 21. Jehoram (Joram), king of Judah. 850-843 B.C.

Reigned 8 years. (Told also in II Kings 8:16–24.) Son of a good father and grandfather, made vile by marriage to a wicked woman, Athaliah, daughter of the infamous Jezebel. Under his reign Jerusalem was plundered by Arabians and Philistines. He died of a horrible disease. "His bowels fell out."

Chapter 22:1-9. Ahaziah (Jehoahaz), king of Judah. 843 B.C.

Reigned 1 year. (Told also in II Kings 8:25–29.) Son of Athaliah, grandson of Jezebel; a scion of the house of David in an awful tie-up. Very wicked. Was killed by Jehu.

Chapters 22:10-23:21. Athaliah, queen of Judah. 843-837 B.C.

Reigned 6 years. (Told also in II Kings 11.) She was daughter of the infamous Jezebel; and devilish, like her mother. She married

Jehoram, king of Judah; and was mother of Judah's next king, Ahaziah. Thus, she was queen eight years, queen mother 1 year, beside the 6 years she ruled in her own right; 15 years in all. Fanatically devoted to Baalism, she massacred her own grandchildren.

Chapter 24. Joash (Jehoash), king of Judah. 843-803 B.C.

Reigned 40 years (probably included Athaliah's 6 years). (Told also in II Kings 12.) Joash was grandson of Athaliah. While Athaliah was murdering the seed royal, Joash, son of Ahaziah, as a babe, was stolen away, and hid in the Temple, for 6 years. When Joash was 7 years old, Jehoiada, the high priest, his uncle, engineered the removal of Athaliah, and placed Joash on the throne. Jehoiada was the real ruler as long as he lived. Under his tutorship, Joash cleared the land of Baalism, repaired the Temple which Athaliah had broken down, and restored the worship of God.

Joash "did right all the days of Jehoiada." But after the death of Jehoiada, he apostatized, and set up idols. The princes who had known the licentious worship of Ashtoreth were the ruin of Joash. Joash even ordered Zechariah, son of Jehoiada who had placed him on the throne, to be stoned to death. And within a year after Zechariah's death, the Syrians came, and plundered Jerusalem, slew the princes, and "executed judgment on Joash."

Chapter 25. Amaziah, king of Judah. 803-775 B.C.

Reigned 29 years. (Told also in II Kings 14:1–22.) "Did right, but not with a perfect heart." Served the gods of Edom. Had war with Israel, and Jerusalem was plundered by Israel's king.

Chapter 26. Uzziah (Azariah), king of Judah. 787-735 B.C.

Reigned 52 years. (Told also in II Kings 15:1–7.) Thought to have been part time co-regent with his father Amaziah. "Did right. Set himself to seek God." "As long as he sought God, God made him to prosper." He had a huge army, with the best military equipment. Was victorious over Philistines, Arabians and Ammonites. Paid great attention to agriculture. Greatest extent of kingdom since the Secession of the Ten Tribes. But he became arrogant, and God smote him with leprosy.

ARCHAEOLOGICAL NOTE: Uzziah. An inscription of Tiglathpileser, Assyrian king (747–727 B.C.), who carried North Israel into captivity, mentions, four times, "Azariah (Uzziah) the Judean."

Uzziah's Gravestone has been discovered, in the Russian Archaeological Museum on the Mt. of Olives, by Dr. E. L. Sukenik, of the Hebrew University of Jerusalem. It is inscribed, in Aramaic script of the time of Christ, thus: "Hither were brought the bones of Uzziah, king of Judah—do not open." Uzziah had been buried in the city of David (II Kings 15:7); but, for some reason or other, it seems, the tomb site was later cleared, and his bones removed to another location.

Chapter 27. Jotham, king of Judah. 749-734 B.C.

Reigned 16 years, mostly co-eval with his father. (Told also in II Kings 15:32–38.) "He became mighty, because he ordered his ways before the Lord his God," as his father Uzziah had done.

ARCHAEOLOGICAL NOTE: Jotham. A Seal has been found in the excavations at Ezion-geber inscribed "Belonging to Jotham."

Chapter 28. Ahaz, king of Judah. 741-726 B.C.

Reigned 16 years. (Told also in II Kings 16.) Part time co-regent with his father, it seems; but utterly different. A wicked young king who set himself against the policies of his forefathers. He reintroduced Baal worship; revived Moloch worship; burnt his own sons in the fire. "But it helped him not." Syria and Israel attacked him from the north; Edomites from the east; and Philistines from the west. And Judah was brought very low because of Ahaz.

ARCHAEOLOGICAL NOTE: Ahaz. A Seal has been found inscribed an "Official of Ahaz."

Ahaz and his Tribute to Tiglath-pileser (16; II Kings 16:6–8). An inscription of Tiglath-pileser says, "The tribute of Ahaz the Judean I received, gold, silver, lead, tin, and linen. Damascus I destroyed. Rezin I took. His officers I impaled alive on stakes. I hewed down his orchards, nor did I leave a tree standing." This exactly parallels the accounts in II Kings 16 and Isaiah 7.

Chapters 29,30,31,32. Hezekiah, king of Judah. 726-697 B.C.

Reigned 29 years. (Told also in II Kings 18, 19, 20.) Inherited a disorganized realm and a heavy burden of tribute to Assyria. Began his reign with a great Reformation. Broke down the idols Ahaz had set up. Reopened and cleansed the Temple. Restored the service of God. "Trusted in God." "God was with him, and he prospered." Gained independence from Assyria. Isaiah was his trusted adviser.

In Hezekiah's 6th year (721 B.C.), the Northern Kingdom fell. In his 14th year (713 B.C.), it seems, Sennacherib, as leader of his father Sargon's armies, invaded Judah. Hezekiah paid him tribute. Then the visit of the Babylonian embassy (II Kings 20:12–15), which looked suspicious to Sennacherib, who again (701 B.C.) invaded Judah. Hezekiah strengthened the wall, built the conduit and made great military preparation. Then followed the Great Deliverance by the Angel (II Kings 19:35). This victory brought Hezekiah great prestige and power.

ARCHAEOLOGICAL NOTES: Hezekiah's Repairs in the Wall (32:5), hurriedly done, under pressure of the Assyrian siege, are distinctly indicated in the walls as they stand today. Foundations of the "outer wall" have been discovered, running parallel to David's wall, 30 feet apart.

Hezekiah's Tunnel (32:3, 4; II Kings 20:20), by which he brought water into the city. This Tunnel has been found. Gihon Spring was situated at the east foot of Ophel Hill (see Map 8), just outside the wall. Hezekiah's workmen cut a tunnel through solid rock, under the hill, running 1700 feet southwest from the Spring, to the Pool of Siloam, within the wall, thus diverting the water of the Spring from its natural flow into the Brook Kidron. The tunnel is an average height of about 6 feet, and average width of 2½ feet. Its fall is 7 feet. At its mouth the Siloam Inscription was found.

The Siloam Inscription. A truant school boy (1880), playing in the mouth of Hezekiah's Tunnel, noticed some marks cut on the rock wall, 19 feet from the opening, that looked like writing. He told his teacher, Dr. Schick, who found it to be an account, in the Hebrew language, of the building of the Tunnel. It was cut out of the wall, and sent to the Constantinople Museum, where it is now. It reads:

"The tunnel is completed. This is the story of the tunnel. While the stonecutters were lifting up the pick, each toward his neighbor (from opposite ends), and while they were yet 3 cubits apart, there was heard a voice of one calling to another; and after that pick struck against pick; and waters flowed from the Spring to the Pool, 1200 cubits, and 100 cubits was the height of the rock above."

Sennacherib's Invasion of Judah (32:1), in which he took "fortified cities" of Judah (II Kings 18:13); besieged Jerusalem (II Kings

Fig. 47.

18:17), and returned without taking Jerusalem (II Kings 19:35, 36).

Sennacherib's own account of this invasion has been found, on a clay prism which he himself had made (Figure 47). It is now in the Oriental Institute Museum in Chicago. It says: "As for Hezekiah, king of Judah, who had not submitted to my yoke, 46 of his fortified cities, and smaller cities without number, with my battering rams, engines, mines, breaches and axes, I besieged and captured. 200,150 people, small and great, male and female, and horses, mules, asses, camels, oxen, sheep, without number, I took as booty. Hezekiah himself I shut up like a caged bird in Jerusalem, his royal city. I built a line of forts against him, and turned back everyone who came forth out of his city gate. His cities which I captured I gave to the king of Ashdod, king of Ekron, and king of Gaza."

While no Assyrian king would ever record a defeat, such as Sennacherib's army received before the walls of Jerusalem (II Kings 19:35, 36), it is significant that he did not claim to have taken Jerusalem. It is indeed a most remarkable confirmation of Biblical History.

Sennacherib "Before Lachish" in "All his Power" (32:9). On walls of Sennacherib's palace at Nineveh, uncovered by Layard, a sculptured relief of his encampment at Lachish bore this inscription: "Sennacherib, king of the world, sat upon his throne, and caused the spoil of Lachish to pass before him."

The Tribute which Hezekiah sent to Sennacherib (II Kings 18:14–16). The inscription says: "Fear of my majesty overwhelmed Hezekiah. He sent tribute: 30 talents of gold, 800 talents of silver, precious stones, ivory, women of his palace, and all sorts of gifts."

Lachish and Gibeah (32:9; Isaiah 10:29), are named among the cities which suffered at the hands of Sennacherib. At Lachish, the Wellcome Archaeological Expedition found a layer of ashes from a fire of 700 B.C. And at Gibeah, Albright found a layer of ashes from a fire of 700 B.C.

Sennacherib's Assassination by his own sons (32:21; II Kings 19:36, 37). An Assyrian inscription says: "On the 20th day of Tebet, Sennacherib was killed by his sons in revolt. On the 18th day of Sivan, Esarhaddon, his son, ascended the throne."

Chapter 33:1-20. Manasseh, king of Judah. 697-642 B.C.

Reigned 55 years. (Told also in II Kings 21:1–18.) Wickedest of all Judah's kings; and the longest reign. Rebuilt the idols his father

Hezekiah had destroyed. Re-established Baal worship. Burnt his own children in the fire. He filled Jerusalem with blood. Tradition says that he had Isaiah sawn asunder.

ARCHAEOLOGICAL NOTE: Manasseh. An inscription of Esarhaddon, Assyrian king (681–668 B.C.) says: "I compelled 22 kings of the West Land to provide building material for my palace," and names "Manasseh king of Judah."

Chapter 33:21-25. Amon, king of Judah. 641-640 B.C.

Reigned 2 years. (Told also in II Kings 21:19–25.) Wicked.

Chapters 34,35. Josiah, king of Judah. 639-608 B.C.

Reigned 31 years. (Told also in II Kings 22, 23.) Began to reign when he was eight years old. When he was 16, he began to seek after the God of David. When he was 20, he began his reforms. When he was 26, the finding of the "Book of the Law" gave great impetus to his reforms, the most thoroughgoing reformation Judah had known. But the people were at heart idolaters; for the long and wicked reign of Manasseh had just about obliterated God from their thinking. Josiah's reforms delayed, but could not avert, the fast approaching doom of Judah.

In Josiah's day the Scythian Invasion (see page 310) swept over Western Asia, and greatly weakened Assyria. Pharaoh's march against Carchemish (35:20–24) was to give a final blow to the sinking Assyrian Empire. Josiah, as a vassal of Assyria, felt it his duty to attack Pharaoh, at Megiddo, and was killed.

Chapter 36:1-4. Jehoahaz, (Joahaz), king of Judah. 608 B.C.

Reigned 3 months. (Told also in II Kings 23:30–34.) Was deposed by Pharaoh, and taken to Egypt, where he died.

Chapter 36:5-8. Jehoiakim, king of Judah. 608-597 B.C.

Reigned 11 years. (Told also in II Kings 23:34–24:7.) Was placed on the throne by Pharaoh. After 3 years he was subdued by Babylon (Daniel 1:1). Then he served the king of Babylon 3 years. Then revolted. And the king of Babylon came, and bound him in chains to carry him to Babylon (II Chronicles 36:6). But ere he left the city, he died, or was killed, and buried as an ass (Jeremiah 22:18, 19; 36:30). He was conceited, hard-hearted, and wicked, exact opposite of his father Josiah. He sought repeatedly to kill Jeremiah (Jeremiah 26:21; 36:26).

Chapter 36:8-10. Jehoiachin (Jeconiah), king of Judah. 597 B.C.

Reigned 3 months. (Told also in II Kings 24:6–17.) He was taken to Babylon, where he lived at least 37 years (II Kings 24:15; 25:27).

ARCHAEOLOGICAL NOTES: Jehoiachin. Seal of Jehoiachin's Steward. At Kiriath-sepher (1928), Kyle and Albright found, in the layer of ashes left by Nebuchadnezzar's fire, two jar handles stamped, "Belonging to Eliakim Steward of Jehoiachin." One of these is now in the Pittsburgh-Xenia Seminary. Same impression was found (1930) at Beth-shemesh, by Grant.

Jehoiachin "Lifted Up," and "Given an Allowance" (II Kings 25:27, 30). Albright has reported a discovery by Weidner, in the ruins of the Hanging Gardens of Babylon, of tablets listing the names of those to whom regular allotments of oil and grain were made, among them, "Jehoiachin king of the land of Judah."

Fig. 48. Impression of Eliakim's Seal. (*Courtesy Dr. J. L. Kelso.*)

Fig. 49. Detail of Writing on Eliakim's Seal. (*Courtesy Dr. W. F. Albright.*)

Chapter 36. Zedekiah, king of Judah. 597-586 B.C.

Reigned 11 years. (Told also in II Kings 24, 25.) He was placed on the throne by Nebuchadnezzar. A weak king. In his 4th year he visited Babylon. But later he rebelled against Babylon. Then Nebuchadnezzar came, and destroyed Jerusalem, took Zedekiah, put out his eyes, and carried him in chains to Babylon, where he died in prison (Jeremiah 52:11). This was the apparent end of David's kingdom. (See further under II Kings 25.)

Gedaliah made Governor (II Kings 25:22. See on Jeremiah 40).
Remnant's Flight to Egypt (II Kings 25:26. See on Jeremiah 42).
Proclamation of Cyrus (36:22. See on Ezra I).

ARCHAEOLOGICAL NOTE: Zedekiah. Zedekiah's Flight "between the two walls" (II Kings 25:4). That "way between the two walls," on the southeast edge of Jerusalem, can now be seen for 150 feet.

EZRA—NEHEMIAH—ESTHER

Return from Captivity
Jerusalem Rebuilt

These three books form the closing section of Old Testament History. They tell the story of the Jews' Return from Babylon, the Rebuilding of the Temple and of Jerusalem, and the Reestablishment of the Jews' National Life in their Home Land. They cover about 100 years (536–432 B.C.).

The last three of the Prophets, Haggai, Zechariah, Malachi, lived and wrought in this era of the Jews' Restoration.

There were Two Distinct Periods:

536–516 B.C. 20 years, in which, under Zerubbabel the Governor and Joshua the Priest, the Temple was rebuilt (Ezra chapters 3 to 6). To this period belonged Haggai and Zechariah.

457–432 B.C. 25 years, in which, under Nehemiah the Governor and Ezra the Priest, the Wall was rebuilt, and Jerusalem restored as a fortified city. To this period belonged Malachi.

Ezra gives an account of both periods.

Nehemiah gives an account of the second period.

Esther comes in between the two periods.

There were Three Returns:

536 B.C. Zerubbabel, with 42,360 Jews, 7,337 servants, 200 singers, 736 horses, 245 mules, 435 camels, 6,720 asses, and 5,400 gold and silver vessels.

457 B.C. Ezra with 1754 males, 100 talents of gold, 750 talents of silver. Not stated whether women and children went. It took 4 months.

444 B.C. Nehemiah, as governor, with an army escort, went to rebuild and fortify Jerusalem, at government expense.

Chronology of the Restoration:

536 B.C. 49,897 return from Babylon to Jerusalem.
536 B.C. 7th month, they built the altar, and offered sacrifice.
535 B.C. Work on the Temple begun, and stopped.

520 B.C. Work renewed by Haggai, Zechariah.
516 B.C. Temple completed.
478 B.C. Esther becomes Queen of Persia.
457 B.C. Ezra goes from Babylon to Jerusalem.
444 B.C. Nehemiah rebuilds the Wall.
432 B.C. Nehemiah returns again from Babylon.

Israel had been taken captive by ASSYRIA, 721 B.C.
Judah had been taken captive by BABYLON, 606 B.C.
Return from the Captivity was permitted by PERSIA, 536 B.C.

The Persian Empire

As the policy of Assyrian and Babylonian kings had been to Deport conquered peoples, that is, take them away out of their own lands, and scatter them in other lands, so, the policy of Persian kings, exactly the opposite, was to Repatriate those peoples, that is send them back to their own lands. Persian kings were more humane than Assyrian and Babylonian kings.

One of the first acts of the first Persian king, Cyrus, who was a "singularly noble and just monarch," in his first year, was to authorize the Return of the Jews to their own land.

Persia was the mountainous plateau east of the lower end of the Euphrates-Tigris Valley. The Persian Empire was vaster in extent than its predecessors had been, extending eastward to India, and reaching westward to Greece. Its capitals were Persepolis and Susa, its kings sometimes residing at Babylon. As a world-empire, it lasted 200 years (536–331 B.C.). Its kings were:

Cyrus (538–529 B.C.). Conquered Babylon (536 B.C.). Made Persia a World-Empire. Permitted the Jews to return to their homeland, in fulfillment of Isaiah's prophecy (see pages 301, 302).

Cambyses (529–522 B.C.). He is thought to have been "Artaxerxes" mentioned in Ezra 4:7,11,23, who stopped work on Temple.

Darius I (Hystaspes) (521–485 B.C.). Authorized completion of Temple (Ezra 6). Made the "Behistun" inscription (see page 43).

Xerxes (Ahasuerus) (485–465 B.C.). Famous for wars with Greece. Esther was his wife (see page 237). Mordecai his prime-minister.

Artaxerxes I (Longimanus) (465–425 B.C). Very favorable to the Jews. Authorized Nehemiah, his cupbearer, to rebuild Jerusalem.

Xerxes II (424). Darius II (Nothius) (423–405). Artaxerxes II (Mnemon) (405–358). Artaxerxes III (Ochus) (358–338). Arses (338–335).

Darius III (Codomanus) (335–331). He was defeated by Alexander the Great (331 B.C.), at the famous battle of Arbela, near the site of Nineveh. This was the Fall of Persia, and the Rise of Greece. Empire passed from Asia to Europe.

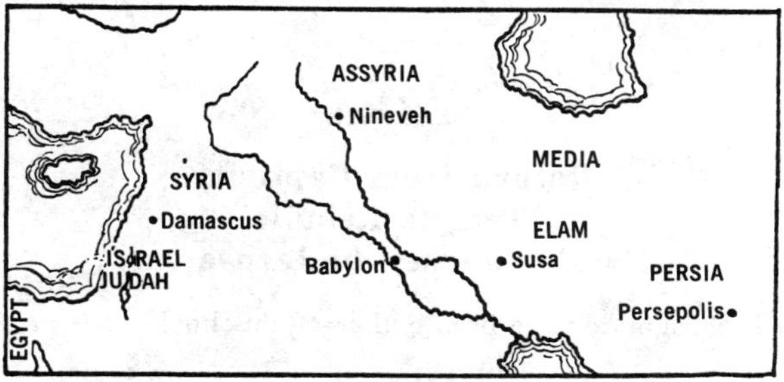
ASSYRIA
Nineveh
MEDIA
SYRIA
Damascus
ELAM
ISRAEL
Babylon
Susa
PERSIA
JUDAH
Persepolis
EGYPT

Map 47.

EZRA

Return from Captivity
Temple Rebuilt
Ezra's Journey to Jerusalem

Ezra is thought to have been author of this book. (See page 235.)

Chapter 1. Proclamation of Cyrus

The last two verses of II Chronicles are the same as the first two of Ezra, probably because Chronicles and Ezra were originally one book. This proclamation, permitting the Jews to return to Jerusalem, was issued shortly after Daniel had read the handwriting on the wall, in which it was declared that Babylon would fall to Persia; which came to pass the same night (Daniel 5:25–31). Probably Daniel showed to Cyrus the prophecies that were thus fulfilled (Jeremiah 25:11–12; 29:10); and also the prophecies of Isaiah, who 200 years before had called Cyrus by name, stating that under him the Jews would return and rebuild Jerusalem (Isaiah 44:26–28; 45:1,13). No wonder Cyrus had high regard for the Jews' God (3).

Chapter 2. Register of Those who Returned

42,360, besides servants (64, 65). The total of the itemized numbers fall about 11,000 short of this number. This surplus of 11,000 is thought to have been composed of exiles from tribes other than Judah. Ephraim and Manasseh are mentioned in I Chronicles 9:3. "Israel" is named in Ezra 10:25. The term "All Israel" is used of those that returned (2:70; 6:17; 8:35). 12 bullocks and 12 he-goats were offered for "all Israel." This looks as if the returning exiles of Judah, in their homeward journey, gathered in some from other Tribes. It helps us to understand how, in New Testament times, Jews were still spoken of as the "Twelve Tribes" (Luke 22:30; Acts 26–7; James 1:1).

Chapter 3. Foundation of the Temple is laid

In the 7th month of the 1st year of their Return, they built the Altar, and kept the Feast of Tabernacles, in joyous thanksgiving to God. In the 2nd month of the following year, when the foundation of the Temple was laid, they made the heavens ring with their glad hosannas. But the older men, who had seen the first Temple, wept aloud, so insignificant was this compared to that. "Zerubbabel" (2), governor (Haggai 1:1), was grandson of king Jehoiachin, who had been carried to Babylon (I Chronicles 3:17–19). He was the one who would have been king, if it had been a kingdom. With fine courtesy Cyrus appointed him to be Governor of Judah.

Chapter 4. The Work Stopped

As work on the Temple, and Wall (16), progressed, the peoples to whom the Jews' land had been given, and their neighbors, began to object; and, through bluff and intrigue, succeeded in stopping the work for 15 years, till the reign of Darius.

Chapters 5,6. The Temple Completed

Darius was friendly to the Jews; and, in his 2nd year (520 B.C.), 16 years after the Jews had been home, under the encouragement of the prophets Haggai and Zechariah, work on the Temple was resumed. Shortly came the decree from Darius for the Temple to be completed, with an order to draw on the royal treasury for the needed money. Within 4 years (520–516 B.C.), it was completed, and dedicated amid great rejoicing.

The famous Behistun Inscription, which supplied the key to the ancient Babylonian language (see page 43) was made the same year the Temple was completed, by this same Darius.

For some reason or other, after the Temple was completed, the work of restoring the city went on further for some 70 years.

Chapters 7,8. Ezra's Journey to Jerusalem

This was 457 B.C., in the reign of Artaxerxes, who was queen Esther's stepson, about 60 years after the Temple had been completed, 80 years after the Jews had first gone back to Jerusalem. Ezra was a priest. He went to teach Judah the Law of God, to beautify the Temple, and restore the Temple service.

Chapters 9,10. Mixed Marriages

When Ezra arrived in Jerusalem he found a situation that made him heartsick. The people, priests, Levites, princes and rulers had freely intermarried with their Idolatrous neighbors: a thing that God had again and again forbidden the Jews to do, the thing that had led the Jews into Idolatry, which had been the cause of their Captivity. God had sent prophet after prophet, and judgment after judgment, and at last had resorted to the Captivity, almost wiping the nation out of existence. Now a little remnant had come home cured. And very first thing they were up to their old tricks of intermarrying with Idolatrous peoples. Ezra's measures to rid them of their Idolatrous wives, to us, may seem severe. But it was effective. The Jews, who up to the Babylonian Captivity just would be Idolaters, were cured; and, from that day to this, generally speaking, have remained cured.

Ezra helped in further reforms, as noted in the book of Nehemiah. Tradition makes him originator of Synagog worship, and president of the "Great Synagog" (see next page, and page 410).

NEHEMIAH

The Wall of Jerusalem Rebuilt

According to persistent Jewish tradition, Ezra was author of the books of I and II Chronicles, Ezra and Nehemiah; the four books being originally one work (see page 213), though some think that Nehemiah himself may have written the book of Nehemiah.

Ezra was the great grandson of Hilkiah the priest, who, 160 years earlier, had directed king Josiah's reformation (Ezra 1:1; II Kings 22:8); a most worthy descendant of his famous ancestor. He went from Babylon to Jerusalem (457 B.C.); 80 years after the Jews had first returned, and 13 years before Nehemiah came.

Nehemiah went to Jerusalem (444 B.C.). Ezra had been there 13 years. But Ezra was a priest, teaching religion to the people. Nehemiah came as civil governor, with authority from the king of Persia to rebuild the Wall, and restore Jerusalem as a fortified city. The Jews had been home nearly 100 years, and had made little progress beyond rebuilding the Temple, a very insignificant Temple at that, because whenever they would start work on the Wall, their more powerful neighbors would either bluff them off by force, or through intrigue get orders from the Persian court for the work to stop.

Chapters 1,2. Nehemiah's Journey to Jerusalem

Parts of the book are in the first person, being direct quotations from Nehemiah's official reports.

Nehemiah was a man of Prayer, Patriotism, Action, Courage and Perseverance. His first impulse always was to pray (1:4; 2:4; 4:4, 9; 6:9, 14). He spent 4 months in prayer before he made his request to the king (1:1, 2:1).

Nehemiah was cupbearer to king Artaxerxes (1:11; 2:1), a trusted and important official. Artaxerxes was king of Persia (465–425 B.C.); son of Xerxes, and so, stepson of Queen Esther the Jewess. Esther became Queen of Persia about 60 years after the Jews had returned to Jerusalem. This must have given the Jews great prestige at the Persian court. Esther most probably was still alive, and an influential personage in the palace, when both Ezra and Nehemiah went to Jerusalem. Our guess is that we have Esther to thank for Artaxerxes' kindly feeling toward the Jews, and his interest in having Jerusalem rebuilt.

Chapter 3. The Gates Repaired

ARCHAEOLOGICAL NOTE: "stairs that go down from the city

of David" (15); "bend in the wall" (25); "tower that stands out" (26): the remains of these may now be clearly detected.

Chapters 4,5,6. The Wall Built

Old-time enemies of the Jews, who were now in possession of the land, Moabites, Ammonites, Ashdodites, Arabians, and the recently imported Samaritans, craftily and bitterly opposed the rebuilding of the Wall of Jerusalem. They mobilized their armies, and marched against Jerusalem. But Nehemiah, with faith in God, skillfully arming and arranging his men, drove straight ahead with the work, day and night; and, in spite of all obstacles, the Wall was finished in 52 days. And Jerusalem was again a fortified city, 142 years after its destruction in 586 B.C.

Chapters 7,8. Public Reading of the Book of Law

After the Wall was built, Nehemiah and Ezra gathered the people together to organize their national life. Chapter 7 is about the same as Ezra 2, giving the list of those who had returned to Jerusalem with Zerubbabel nearly 100 years before. There were certain genealogical matters that had to be attended to.

Then, for seven days, every day from early morning till midday, Ezra and his helpers, "opened the Book of the Law, and read in the Law of God, distinctly, and gave the sense, so that the people understood the reading." This public reading and exposition of God's Book brought a great wave of repentance among the people, a great "revival," and a solemn covenant to keep the Law, as noted in chapters 9, 10.

It was the finding of the Book of the Law that brought Josiah's great Reformation (II Kings 22). It was Martin Luther's finding of a Bible that made the Protestant Reformation, and brought religious liberty to our modern world. The weakness of present-day Protestantism is its Neglect of the Bible which it professes to follow. The grand need of today's pulpit is Simple Expository Preaching.

Chapters 9,10,11,12. Covenant. Dedication of Wall

In deep penitence and great earnestness, they "made a sure covenant, and wrote it, and sealed it, and entered into an oath and a curse, that they would walk in God's Law" (9:38; 10:29). The Wall completed, and dedicated, one-tenth of the population was brought into the city to live, and its government and Temple services organized.

Chapter 13. Close of Nehemiah's Work

Correction of laxities about Tithes, Sabbath, and Mixed Marriages. Nehemiah was Governor of Judah at least 12 years (5:14). Josephus says that he lived to great age, and governed Judah the rest of his life.

ESTHER

The Jews' Deliverance from Extermination

The Jews Returned from Babylon to Jerusalem 536 B.C.
The Temple was Rebuilt 536–516 B.C.

Esther, a Jewess, became Queen of Persia 478 B.C.
Esther saved the Jews from massacre 473 B.C.

Ezra went from Babylon to Jerusalem 457 B.C.
Nehemiah Rebuilt the Wall of Jerusalem 444 B.C.

Thus Esther appeared about 40 years After the Temple was Rebuilt, and about 30 years Before the Wall of Jerusalem was Rebuilt.

Chronologically, though this book comes after the book of Nehemiah, yet its events antedate Nehemiah by about 30 years. Esther, it seems, made possible the work of Nehemiah. Her marriage to the King must have given Jews great prestige. It is impossible to guess what might have happened to the Hebrew nation had there been no Esther. Except for her, Jerusalem might never have been rebuilt, and there might have been a different story to tell to all future ages.

This book of Esther is about a Very Important Historical Event, not just a story to point a moral: The Hebrew Nation's Deliverance from Annihilation in the days following the Babylonian Captivity. If the Hebrew Nation had been entirely wiped out of existence 500 years before it brought Christ into the world, that might have made some difference in the destiny of mankind; no Hebrew Nation, no Messiah: no Messiah, a lost world. This beautiful Jewish girl of the long ago, though she herself may not have known it, yet played her part in paving the way for the coming of the world's Saviour.

Chapter 1. Queen Vashti Deposed

"Ahasuerus" was another name for Xerxes, who ruled Persia 485–465 B.C., one of the most illustrious monarchs of the ancient world. The great feast described in this chapter, it has been learned from Persian inscriptions, was held in preparation for his famous expedition against Greece, in which he fought the battles of Thermopylae and Salamis, 480 B.C. It seems that he deposed Vashti (482 B.C.), before he left, and married Esther (478 B.C.), after he returned from his expedition against Greece (1:3; 2:16).

ARCHAEOLOGICAL NOTE: Shushan the Palace (2).

Shushan, or Susa, 200 miles east of Babylon, was the winter residence of Persian kings. Its site was identified by Loftus (1852), who found an inscription of Artaxerxes II (405–358 B.C.): "My ancestor Darius built this palace in former times. In the reign of my grandfather (Artaxerxes I) it was burned. I have restored it."

This palace was residence of Darius, who authorized rebuilding of the Temple; of Xerxes, Esther's husband; and Artaxerxes I, who authorized Nehemiah to rebuild Jerusalem.

A Frenchman, named Dieulafoy, continued excavations (1884–86); and definitely located, in the ruins, the "king's gate" (4:2); the "inner court" (5:1); the "outer court" (6:4); the "palace garden" (7:7); and even found one of the dice, "Pur" (3:7).

Chapter 2. Esther Becomes Queen

Ahasuerus died 13 years later. Esther, no doubt, lived far into the reign of her stepson Artaxerxes; and, as queen-mother, may have been a person of influence in the days of Ezra and Nehemiah.

Chapters 3,4,5,6,7. Haman's Decree

To kill all the Jews in all the provinces (3:12, 13). This was in the king's 12th year (3:7), after Esther had been Queen 5 years.

When Esther went in to intercede with the king on behalf of her people, his cordiality (5:3), showed that, even though she had been his wife for 5 years, he still adored her.

The outcome was that Haman was hanged, and his place was given to Mordecai, Esther's cousin.

The name of God is not mentioned in the book, probably because it may have been copied from Persian records. Yet God's Providential Care of his people is nowhere more evident.

Chapters 8,9. Deliverance. Feast of Purim

Since a Persian king's decree could not be changed (8:8; Daniel 6:15), the decree for the Jews' massacre could not be reversed. But Esther did persuade the king to make another decree authorizing the Jews to resist and slay all who would attack them, which they did. Thus Esther saved the Jewish race from annihilation.

Esther was not only beautiful, but wise. We admire her for her patriotism and bravery and tact.

This was origin of Feast of Purim, which Jews still observe.

Chapter 10. Mordecai's Greatness

Mordecai was great in the king's house, next unto the king; he waxed greater and greater; his fame went forth throughout all the provinces (9:4; 10:3). This was in the reign of Xerxes, the mighty monarch of the Persian Empire: Xerxes' prime minister, a Jew; his favorite wife, a Jewess: Mordecai and Esther, the brains and heart of the palace! This paved the way for the work of Ezra and Nehemiah. Like Joseph in Egypt, and Daniel in Babylon, so here Mordecai and Esther in Persia.

JOB

The Problem of Suffering
Poetic-Philosophic Meditations on the Ways of God

The Poetical Books

Job is the first of the so-called Poetical, or Wisdom, group of Old Testament books, the others being Psalms, Proverbs, Ecclesiastes and Song of Solomon. Many of the Wisdom sections are written in Poetry.

This group of books, mostly, but not altogether, belongs to the Golden Age of Hebrew history, the era of David and Solomon, except Job is generally assigned to an earlier date, and some of the Psalms are later. But many of the Psalms are assigned to David; and Proverbs, Ecclesiastes and Song are attributed to Solomon. So, as these five books stand grouped together in the Bible, and as they are largely the work of David and Solomon, it is not out of the way to speak of the group as, roughly, though not exclusively, being of the age of David and Solomon.

Hebrew Poetry did not have metre or rhyme, like the poetry of our language. It consisted rather of parallelisms, or thought rhythm, in synonymous or antithetical couplets, "The sentiment of one line echoed in the next." "Sometimes the couplets being doubled, or trebled, or quadrupled, making 2-liners, 4-liners, 6-liners, or 8-liners."

Literary Merit of the Book of Job

Victor Hugo said: "The Book of Job is perhaps the Greatest Masterpiece of the Human Mind."

Thomas Carlyle said: "I call this book, apart from all theories about it, one of the Grandest things ever written. Our first, oldest statement of the never-ending problem: Man's Destiny, and God's Ways with him in the earth. There is nothing written, I think, of equal literary merit."

Philip Schaff said: "The Book of Job rises like a pyramid in the history of literature, without a predecessor and without a rival."

Scene of the Book

The Land of Uz (1:1), is thought to have been along the border between Palestine and Arabia, extending from Edom northerly and easterly toward the Euphrates river, skirting the caravan route between Babylon and Egypt.

The particular section of the land of Uz which tradition has called the home of Job was Hauran, a region east of the Sea of Galilee, noted for its fertility of soil and its grain, once thickly populated, now dotted with the ruins of three hundred cities.

The Man Job

The Septuagint, in a postscript, following ancient tradition, Identified Job with Jobab, the second king of Edom (Genesis 36:33). Names and places mentioned in the book seem to give it a setting among the descendants of Esau (see under chapter 2). If this is correct, and if Hauran was Job's home, it would indicate that the early kings of Edom may, at times, have migrated from the rock cliffs of Edom northward to the more fertile plains of Hauran. At any rate the book has the atmosphere of very primitive times, and seems to have its setting among the early tribes descended from Abraham, along the northern border of Arabia, about contemporary with Israel's sojourn in Egypt.

Author of the Book

Ancient Jewish tradition ascribed the book to Moses. While Moses was in the wilderness of Midian (Exodus 2:15, see Map 32, page 142), which bordered on the Edomite country, he could easily have learned of the story of Job from Job's immediate descendants. Or, indeed, Job himself may have still been alive, and may have personally related the story to Moses, giving him a copy of his own family records. Job being a descendant of Abraham, naturally Moses could recognize him as being within the circle of God's revelation. Modern criticism, with its great show of scholarship, guesses at a much later date for the book of Job, but it is only a guess. We believe the traditional view is more likely to be correct.

Nature of the Book

It might be called an Historical Poem, that is, a Poem based on an event that actually occurred. Job was the greatest and most widely known man in his part of the world. All at once, in one day, he was crushed with a number of overwhelming calamities. His vast herds of camels were stolen, and their attending servants killed, by a band of Chaldean robbers. At the same time, his herds of oxen were stolen, and their attending servants killed, by a band of Sabean robbers. And, at the same time, his 7000 sheep, and their attending servants, were killed by a thunderstorm. And, at the same time, his family of ten children were all killed by a cyclone. And, a little later,

Job himself was smitten with the most hideous and painful disease known to the ancient world.

It became known far and wide, and was a subject of public conversation everywhere, for months (7:3). Some wrote their opinions (13:26). The book contains some of the things that Job, and his friends, and God, said, or wrote. They must have been brilliant men. Some of the language is grand, though, in places, somewhat obscure.

Subject of the Book

The Problem of Human Suffering. Very early in history men began to be troubled over the Awful Inequalities and Injustices of Life: how a Good God could make a world like this, where there is so much Suffering, and so much of the Suffering seems to fall on those who least deserve it.

And I don't know that we understand the problem one bit better than they did in Job's day. We come into life, having nothing whatever to do with bringing ourselves here. As we grow up, we open our eyes, and look around, and we are just a great big question mark: What's it all about? And the older we grow, and the more we see of the world's Inequalities and Injustices, the bigger grows the question mark, How a Good God could make a world like this.

But, even though we may not understand the problem any better than they did in Job's day, we have more reason to be reconciled to it. For, in the meantime, God Himself came down here, and, in the Person of Jesus, became a Partaker with us of our Suffering. The story of Jesus, the world's most Righteous man, and the world's Greatest Sufferer, is an illustration of God Suffering With His Creation. And we ought not to have any difficulty in believing it is all for some Good Purpose, even though we cannot now understand. And, one day, when all is come to fruition, we shall never cease our Hallelujahs of Praise to God for having given us such an existence.

Chapter 1. Job's Sudden Affliction

The book opens with an account of Job, a patriarchal Chieftain, a desert Prince, or what was in those times called a King, of immense wealth and influence, famous for his Integrity, his Piety and Benevolence: a Good man, who suffered fearful reverses that came so suddenly and overwhelmingly that it stunned all that part of the then known world.

Sabeans (15), were from the land of Sheba, in South Arabia, descendants of Shem (Genesis 10:28). Chaldeans (17), were from the East, land of Abraham.

Chapter 2. Satan's Hand In It

Satan accused Job of being Mercenary in his Goodness. Then God permitted Satan to test his accusation. Job stood the test, and in the end was blessed more than ever.

Job's Disease (7), is thought to have been a form of Leprosy, complicated with Elephantiasis, one of the most Loathesome and Painful Diseases known to the oriental world.

Job's Three Friends. Eliphaz the Temanite (11), was a descendant of Esau (Genesis 36:11), an Edomite. Bildad the Shuhite was a descendant of Abraham and Keturah (Genesis 25:2). Zophar the Naamathite was of unknown origin or locality. Nomad Princes.

Elihu the Buzite (32:2), was a descendant of Abraham's brother Nahor (Genesis 22:21).

Chapter 3. Job's Complaint

He wishes he had never been born, and longs for death. In the conversations that follow, Job speaks 9 times; Eliphaz, 3 times; Bildad, 3 times; Zophar, 2; Elihu, 1; God 1.

In the main, their discussions are dispassionate, but sometimes with great feeling. Sometimes it is not easy to see the point. In some of their passages we are tempted to wonder whether they themselves knew exactly what they were aiming to say, except to see which could use the finest rhetoric, and indeed many of their passages are simply superb. On many things they seem to be in harmony. Their main contentions may be detected to be these:

Job's Three Friends seemed to think that all Suffering is sent upon men as a Punishment for their Sins; and, if we are great Sufferers, that, on the face of it, is proof that we have been great Sinners; and, if our Sins have been Secret, then Suffering is evidence of our Hypocrisy.

Elihu's idea seemed to be that Suffering is sent upon men, not so much as a Punishment for Sin, but rather to Keep them from Sinning; Corrective rather than Punitive.

God's speech, at the end of the book, seems to indicate that God's idea is that men, with their finite minds, ought not expect to understand all the mysteries of God's Creation and Government of the Universe.

The grand lesson of the book, as a whole, seems to be that Job, out of the Patient Endurance of his Sufferings, in the end comes to See God, and is abundantly rewarded with greater Prosperity and Blessedness than he had at first (42:12–16).

Chapters 4 to 7

Chapters 4, 5. Reply of Eliphaz. His night vision of God is sublime (4:12–19). Advises Job to Turn to God (5:8); and suggests if Job would Repent his Troubles would Disappear (5:17–27).

Chapters 6, 7. Job's Second Speech. Job is disappointed in his friends. He longed for sympathy, not stinging reproof (6:14–30). He seems dazed. He knew full well that he was not a Wicked man. Yet his flesh was clothed with worms (7:5). He just could not understand. Even if he had sinned, it surely was not so heinous as to deserve such terrible punishment. He prays that he might die (6:9).

Chapters 8 to 21

Chapter 8. Bildad's First Speech. He insists that God is Just; and that Job's Troubles must be evidence of his Wickedness, and that if he would only Turn to God, all would be well again.

Chapters 9, 10. Job's Third Speech. He insists that he is Not Wicked (10:7); and that God sends Punishment on the Righteous as well as the Wicked (9:22). He complains bitterly, and wishes he had never been born (10:18–22).

Chapter 11. Zophar's First Speech. He brutally tells Job that his punishment is less than he deserves (6); and insists that, if Job will put away his Iniquity, his Sufferings will pass and be forgotten, and Security, Prosperity and Happiness will return (13–19).

Chapters 12, 13, 14. Job's Fourth Speech. He grows sarcastic at their cutting words (12:2); and asks them to let him alone (13:13). Insists that the Wicked Prosper, and that the Righteous Suffer. Seems doubtful about Life after Death (14:7, 14). Yet, later his Assurance was magnificent (see on chapter 19).

Chapter 15. Eliphaz' Second Speech. His sarcasm becomes bitter. They become excited and angry. Job's eyes flash (12). He tore himself in his anger (18:4). They shook their heads at him (16:4).

Chapters 16, 17. Job's Fifth Speech. If you were in my place, I could shake my head at you (16:4). Job continues his complaint. His eyes red with weeping (16:16). His friends scoff at him (16:20). He is a byword among the people, and they spit in his face (17:6).

Chapter 18. Bildad's Second Speech. In a fit of anger, he cries to Job, Why do you tear yourself in anger? (4); and, assuming Job's Wickedness, he tries to frighten Job into Repentance, by depicting the awful doom of the Wicked.

Chapter 19. Job's Sixth Speech. His friends abhor him (19); his wife a stranger to him (17); children despise him (18); broken on every side, he appeals for pity (21).

Then, suddenly, out of the depths of despair, as the sunlight breaks through a rift in the clouds, Job bursts forth into one of the Sublimest expressions of Faith ever uttered: I KNOW THAT MY REDEEMER LIVES, and at last He will Stand upon the Earth; and, after my body is destroyed, apart from my flesh, I SHALL SEE GOD, and that not as a stranger (25–27).

Chapter 20. Zopher's Second Speech. Assuming Job's Wickedness, he lays himself out to portray the deplorable fate in store for the Wicked.

Chapter 21. Job's Seventh Speech. Agreeing that, in the end, the Wicked Suffer, he insists that they are often prosperous.

Chapters 22 to 42

Chapter 22. Eliphaz' third Speech. He bears down haraer and harder on Job's Wickedness, especially naming his cruel treatment of the poor.

Chapters 23, 24. Job's Eighth Speech. He protests his Righteousness. The expression, "Words of God's Mouth" (23:12), indicates that in Job's day there were Writings which were recognized as God's Word.

Chapter 25. Bildad's Third Speech. A very short speech. Bildad was through.

Chapters 26 to 31. Job's Last Speech. He grows more confident in protesting his Innocence. "Till I die I will hold fast my Integrity" (27:5). He contrasts his past Prosperity, Happiness, Honor, Respect, Benignity, Kindness and Usefulness (chapter 29), with his present Cruel Sufferings (chapter 30); a "Song of the Rabble," a "By-word" (30:9, 12); they "Spit in his face" (10); he is a "Brother to Jackals" (30:29). Then he specifically denies that he had ever Oppressed the Poor, or had been Covetous, or had been Immoral, or had Covered his Sins (chapter 31).

Idolatry. The only hint of Idolatry in the book of Job is in 31:26–28, which seems like a reference to Sun-Worship. This is one of the indications of the Primitive Date of the book, written while the tradition of Primeval Monotheism was still widely held.

Chapters 32 to 37. Elihu's Speech. Job had silenced the three Friends. Elihu was angry at them, because they were too dumb to answer Job. And he was angry at Job because Job seemed to him to be righteous in his own eyes, and justified himself rather than God. And now it was Elihu's turn to tell them a thing or two. And was he conceited? Let all the earth keep silence: Elihu is about to Speak.

Much of his speech consisted in telling them what Wonderful Things he was going to say. But, like the others, his chief wisdom was in the use of words which concealed rather than made plain his meaning. His main contention seems to have been that Suffering is intended of God to be Corrective rather than Punitive.

Chapters 38 to 41. God's Speech. He spoke out of a Whirlwind, dwelling on the Ignorance, Impotence, Helplessness and Infinitesimal Smallness of Man compared to God, asking question after question, that awed Job into silence, and drove him to his knees. These are grand, sublime chapters.

Chapter 42. Job's Repentance and Restoration. God endorsed the ideas Job had expressed, rather than the ideas of the others (7). Job was not a Wicked man, as they had contended, but a genuinely Righteous man, who, when brought face to face with God, cried out "I abhor Myself, and Repent in Dust and Ashes."

Job stood his Trials Magnificently, and God Blessed his Old Age with Magnificent Rewards (42:12–17).

PSALMS

Songs of Trust
Hymns of Devotion
Israel's Hymn Book and Prayer Book
Called in Hebrew the "Book of Praises"
Best Loved Book in the Old Testament
150 Poems to be Set to Music for Worship
For Use in Private Life and in Public Worship
Most Glorious Accomplishment of Israel's Golden Age
Of 283 N.T. Quotations from O.T., 116 are from Psalms

Authorship of the Psalms

In the Titles, 73 Psalms are ascribed to David; 12 to Asaph; 11 to the sons of Korah; 2 to Solomon (72, 127); 1 to Moses (90); 1 to Ethan (89); 50 are Anonymous.

Some of the Anonymous Psalms may, it is thought, be ascribed to the Author of the Preceding Psalm. David, no doubt, was Author of some of the Anonymous Psalms.

The Titles are not a certain indication of Authorship; for "of," "to," and "for," are the same preposition in Hebrew. A Psalm "of" David may have been one that he himself wrote, or that was written "for" David, or dedicated "to" David.

However, the Titles are very Ancient, and the most natural presumption is that they indicate Authorship. The age-old, universal and unbroken tradition is that David was the Principal Author of the Psalms.

Some modern critics have made a desperate effort to read David out of the picture. But there is every reason to accept, and no substantial reason to question, the Book of Psalms as quite largely the work of David. The New Testament so recognizes it.

So, we speak of the Psalms as the Psalms of David, because he was the principal writer, or compiler. It is generally accepted that a few were in existence before David's time, forming the nucleus of a Hymnal for Worship. This was greatly enlarged by David, added to from generation to generation, and, it is thought, brought to completion in its present form by Ezra.

David was a Warrior of unprecedented Bravery, a Military Genius, and a Brilliant Statesman, who led his Nation to its Pinnacle of Power. He was also a Poet and a Musician, and with all his heart a Lover of God.

David's creation of the Psalms was in reality a far grander accomplishment than his creation of the Kingdom. The Book of Psalms is one of the Noblest Monuments of the Ages.

In the Psalms the real character of David is portrayed; and in them God's people generally see a pretty fair picture of themselves, their struggles, their sins, their sorrows, their aspirations, their joys, their failures and their victories.

For the Psalms, to Endless Ages, David will have the Undying Gratitude of millions upon millions of God's Redeemed People.

Jesus was Very Fond of the Psalms

So thoroughly they became a part of His Mental Nature, that He uttered His Dying Agonies on the Cross in quotation from them (22:1; 31:5; Matthew 27:46; Luke 23:46). He said that many things in the Psalms referred to Him (Luke 24:44).

W. E. Gladstone said of the Psalms:

"All the wonders of Greek Civilization heaped together are less Wonderful than is this simple Book of the Psalms."

Classification of the Psalms

They are arranged in Five Books: Psalms 1–41: Psalms 42–72: Psalms 73–89: Psalms 90–106: Psalms 107–150.

From very ancient times this subdivision has been indicated in both Hebrew and Septuagint, in imitation, it is thought, of the Five Books of the Pentateuch.

Within these Five Books there are further Sub-Groups: Psalms of Sons of Korah, 42–49: Psalms of Asaph, 73–83: Michtam Psalms, 56–60: Songs of Degrees, 120–134.

As to Structure and Subject Matter, some are Messianic: some, Historical: some, Penitential: some, Imprecatory: some, Acrostic: some, Theocratic: some, Hallel: some, Hallelujah.

119 is the Longest Psalm, also Longest Chapter in the Bible. 117 is Shortest Psalm, also Shortest, and Middle, Chapter of Bible. Psalm 118:8 is the Middle Verse of the Bible.

The Psalms were Written to be Sung

Moses Sang, and taught the People to Sing (Exodus 15; Deuteronomy 32).

Israel Sang along the Journey to the Promised Land (Numbers 21:17).

Deborah and Barak Sang praise to God (Judges 5).
David Sang with All His Heart (Psalm 104:33).
Hezekiah's Singers Sang the Words of David (II Chronicles 29:28–30).
Nehemiah's Singers Sang Loud (Nehemiah 12:42).
Jesus and the Disciples Sang at the Last Supper (Matthew 26:30).
Paul and Silas Sang in Prison (Acts 16:25).
At the dawn of Creation "The morning stars Sang Together, and all the Sons of God Shouted for Joy" (Job 38:7).
In Heaven 10,000 times 10,000 Angels Sing, and the Whole Redeemed Creation joins in the Chorus (Revelation 5:11–13). In Heaven Everybody will Sing, and Never Tire of Singing.

Liturgical and Musical Titles

The meaning of some of the Titles is not certain. They are very ancient, being prior to the Septuagint. Here is an alphabetic list of these Titles, with their possible meanings.
Aije-leth-Shahar (Psalm 22): Time Note? Or, Name of Melody?
Alamoth (Psalm 46): Chorus of Young Women?
Al-tash-hith (Psalms 57, 58, 59, 75): Destroy Not.
Gittith (Psalms 8, 81, 84): Musical Instrument, or Melody, of Gath.
Hig-gai-on (Psalm 9:16): A Meditation? Or, Interlude?
Je-du-thun (Psalms 39, 62, 77): One of David's Music Leaders.
Jonath-elem-rechokim (Psalm 56): Name of a Melody?
Ma-ha-lath (Psalm 53): A Melancholy Tune?
Ma-ha-lath-Lean-noth (Psalm 88): A Song for Sickness.
Mas-chil (Psalm 32), and other Psalms: Didactic or Reflective.
Mich-tam (Psalms 16, 56–60): A Jewel, or Golden Poem?
Muth-lab-ben (Psalm 9): Probably the Name of a Melody?
Negi-noth (Psalms 4, 6, 61): A Stringed Instrument.
Ne-hil-oth (Psalm 5): Probably a Flute?
Selah (Psalm 3:2): 71 times: Probably an Interlude?
Shem-in-ith (Psalms 6, 12): Probably a Male Choir?
Shig-gai-on (Psalm 7): Wild and Mournful Melody?
Sho-shan-nim (Psalms 45, 69, 80): Lilies: Bridal-Song?
Shu-shan-eduth (Psalms 60, 80): Lily of Testimony: A Melody?
For the Chief Musician: Heading of 55 Psalms.

Musical Instruments

They had Stringed Instruments, mainly the Harp and Psaltery: and Wind Instruments, Flute, Pipe, Horn, Trumpet: and Instruments to be Beaten, Timbrel and Cymbal. David had an Orchestra of 4,000, for which he made the Instruments (I Chronicles 23:5).

Leading Ideas in the Psalms

"Trust" is the foremost idea in all the book, repeated over and over. Whatever the occasion, joyous or terrifying, it drove David straight to God. Whatever his weaknesses, David literally LIVED IN GOD.

"Praise" was always on his lips. David was always Asking God for something, and always Thanking Him with his whole soul for the answers to his Prayers.

"Rejoice" is another favorite word. David's unceasing troubles could never dim his Joy in God. Over and over he cries, "Sing," "Shout for Joy." Psalms is a book of Devotion to God.

"Mercy" occurs hundreds of times. David often spoke of the Justice, Righteousness and Wrath of God. But God's Mercy was the thing in which he Gloried.

Messianic Psalms

Many Psalms, written a thousand years before Christ, contain references to Christ, that are wholly inapplicable to Any Other Person in history. Some references to David seem to point forward to the Coming King in David's Family. Besides passages that are clearly Messianic, there are many expressions which seem to be veiled Foreshadowings of the Messiah.

Psalms most obviously Messianic are:

Psalm 2: Deity and Universal Reign of the Messiah.
Psalm 8: Man through Messiah to become Lord of Creation.
Psalm 16: His Resurrection from the Dead.
Psalm 22: His Suffering: Psalm 69: His Suffering.
Psalm 45: His Royal Bride, and Eternal Throne.
Psalm 72: Glory and Eternity of His Reign.
Psalm 89: God's Oath for Endlessness of Messiah's Throne.
Psalm 110: Eternal King and Priest.
Psalm 118: To be Rejected by His Nation's Leaders.
Psalm 132: Eternal Inheritor of David's Throne.

Messianic Passages

Here are statements in the Psalms which the New Testament explicitly declares refer to Christ.

"They pierced my hands and feet" (22:16; John 20:25).
"Zeal for Thy House hath eaten Me up" (69:9; John 2:17).
"Lo, I am come to do Thy will, O God" (40:7, 8; Hebrews 10:7).
"Thy Throne, O God, is Forever and Ever" (45:6; Hebrews 1:8).
"He trusted in God; let God deliver Him" (22:8; Matthew 27:43).
"Thou hast put all things under His feet" (8:6; Hebrews 2:6–10).
"His office (the Betrayer) let another take" (109:8; Acts 1:20).

"My God, My God, why hast Thou forsaken Me?" (22:1; Matthew 27:46).

"Thou art My Son: this day have I begotten Thee" (2:7; Acts 13:33).

"Blessed is He that comes in the Name of the Lord" (118:26; Matthew 21:9).

"They gave Me gall, and in My Thirst they gave Me vinegar to drink" (69:21; Matthew 27:34, 48).

"My own familiar friend, who did eat My bread, lifted up his heel against Me" (41:9; John 13:18).

"They part My garments among them; and upon My vesture did they cast lots" (22:18; John 19:24).

"God has sworn, Thou art a Priest Forever after the order of Melchizedek" (110:4; Hebrews 7:17).

"The stone which the builders rejected is become the head of the corner" (118:22; Matthew 21:42).

"The Lord said unto My Lord, Sit on My right hand till I make Thine enemies Thy footstool" (110:1; Matthew 22:44).

"Thou wilt not leave My soul in Hades; neither wilt Thou suffer Thy Holy One to see corruption" (16:10; Acts 2:27).

See further under II Samuel 7 *and Matthew* 2:22.

Psalm 1. Delight in God's Word

Blessedness of those who derive their Ideas of Life from God's Word, rather than from their worldly neighbors. Happiness and Prosperity are theirs. Not so the Wicked. Over and over the Godly and the Wicked are contrasted.

Thus the Book of Psalms opens with an Exaltation of God's Word. If David so loved the Brief Writings that then constituted God's Word, how much more should we love that same Word, which has now been brought to completion, headed up around the Beautiful Story of Christ. Other Psalms of the Word are 19 and 119. Note too that Psalms' first word is Blessed: a Beatitude: like the Sermon on the Mount: as below.

Some of David's Beatitudes

Blessed is he that Fears the Lord (112:1).
Blessed is he that Considers the Poor (41:1).
Blessed is the nation whose God is the Lord (33:12).
Blessed is he whose Transgression is Forgiven (32:1).
Blessed are they that Dwell in the Lord's House (84:4).
Blessed is the man whom Thou Chastenest, O Lord (94:12).
Blessed are all they that put their Trust in Him (2:12).
Blessed is the man that takes Refuge in the Lord (34:8).
Blessed is the man whose Strength is in the Lord (84:5).

Blessed are they that Keep His Testimonies, that Seek Him with the Whole Heart (119:2).
Blessed is the man . . .
whose Delight is in the Law of the Lord (1:1, 2).

Psalm 2. A Hymn of the Coming Messiah

His Deity (7), and Universal Reign (8). First of the Messianic Psalms. (See page 250.)

Psalm 3. David's Trust in God

At the time of Absalom's Rebellion (II Samuel 15). A most remarkable example of Peaceful Trust at a very trying time. He could sleep because "God's Hand was his Pillow."

Psalm 4. An Evening Prayer

Another Hymn of Trust, as David retired, to sleep, so to speak, on the bosom of God. Trust in God (5). Gladness of Heart (7). Peace of Mind (8). Communion with God in our bed time Meditations (4). Confidence that God is watching (8).

Psalm 5. A Morning Prayer

Beset by treacherous enemies, David Prays, and shouts for Joy, in Confidence that God will Protect him. David must have had many enemies. He refers to them again and again. Many of the most magnificent Psalms were born of David's troubles.

Psalm 6. Cry of a Broken Heart

In time of Sickness, Bitter Grief, Tears, Humiliation, Shame, and Reproach by Enemies, possibly on account of David's Sin with Bathsheba. First of the Penitential Psalms (see on Psalm 32).

Psalm 7. Another Prayer for Protection

In grave danger, David protests his own righteousness (see on Psalm 32). Cush, in title, possibly may have been one of Saul's officers in pursuit of David (see on Psalm 54).

Psalm 8. Man the Crown of Creation

This to be brought to pass under the Messiah, in the day of His

Triumphant Reign (Hebrews 2:6–9). Jesus quoted verse 2 as referring to an incident in His own life (Matthew 21:16).

Psalm 9. Thanks for Victories

Over Enemies, National and Individual. God sits as King Forever. Let the Nations know themselves to be but men. Praise God. Trust God.

This Psalm, with Psalm 10, forms an Acrostic. Acrostic Psalms are those in which the Initial Letters of successive verses follow the order of the Hebrew Alphabet; a device, it is thought, to assist the memory. Other Acrostic Psalms are: 25, 34, 37, 111, 112, 119, 145.

Psalm 10. David's Prayer for Help

In contending with Wickedness, Oppression and Robbery, apparently within his own realm. Prevalence of Wickedness troubled David greatly, especially their Defiance of God. To David, as to other Bible writers, there are just two classes: the Righteous and the Wicked; though many try to be both.

Psalms 11,12,13. Prevalence of Wickedness

The Wicked walk on every side. David overwhelmed with Wicked Enemies, almost to death. But Trusts in God, and Sings for Joy. Such Psalms as these seem to belong to the period when David was hiding from Saul.

Psalm 14. Universal Sinfulness

About the same as Psalm 53. Quoted in Romans 3:10–12. Infidels are here called Fools. Prevalent Wickedness shows what Fools men are. For as sure as there is a God, there will be a Day of Judgment for the Wicked. But among them God has a people, for whom Judgment will be a Day of Joy.

Psalm 15. True Citizens of Zion

The Righteous, Truthful, Just, Honest. Thomas Jefferson called this Psalm the picture of a True Gentleman.

Psalm 16. Resurrection of the Messiah

David appears to be speaking of himself; yet mystic words of the Coming Davidic King find their way into David's mouth (10); quoted in New Testament as a prediction of Jesus' Resurrection (Acts 2:27). Two magnificent verses (8, 11). Michtam, in title, means a Golden Poem, which it is indeed.

Psalm 17. A Prayer for Protection

Overwhelmed by enemies, David looks to God. Protests his own Innocence, but Trusts in God. Surrounded by Lovers of This World, David set his Heart on the World Beyond (14, 15).

Psalm 18. David's Hymn of Thanksgiving

On his accession to the Throne, with the Kingdom firmly established in his hands, after years of flight from Saul. Repeated in II Samuel 22. He attributed it all to God, his Strength, Rock, Fortress, Deliverer, Stay, Refuge, Shield, Horn, High Tower, One of the best Psalms.

Head of the Nations (43–45), true of David only in a partial sense, it looked forward beyond the time of David to the Throne of David's Greater Son.

Psalm 19. Nature and the Word

Wonder and Glory of Creation, and Perfection and Power of God's Word. Spurgeon called it, World Book and Word Book. The God of Nature made known to man through God's Written Word. Thoughts about God's Word are greatly expanded in Psalm 119. One of the best Psalms. And its closing Prayer (13, 14), is one of the best Prayers in the whole Bible. God's Word is Perfect, Sure, True, Gives Joy, and is Sweeter than Honey.

Psalm 20. A Song of Trust

Seems like a Battle Hymn, sung in setting up their banners, with Prayer for Victory, as David entered battle, Trusting, not in chariots and horses (7), but in the Lord.

Psalm 21. Thanks for Victory

After the Battle, for which they had Prayed in Psalm 20 before the Battle. It seems to refer to David, but it seems also to have a Messianic hint in its reference to the Eternal Feature of the King's Reign (4).

Psalm 22. A Psalm of the Crucifixion

It seems like a cry of Anguish from David. But, though written a thousand years before the days of Jesus, it is so vivid a description of the Crucifixion of Jesus that one would think of the writer as being personally present at the Cross: Jesus' Dying Words (1),

Sneers of His Enemies (7, 8). His Hands and Feet Pierced (16), His Garments Parted (18). Some of these statements are not applicable to David, nor to any known event in history except the Crucifixion of Jesus.

Psalm 23. The Shepherd Psalm

Best loved chapter in the Old Testament. Beecher said something like this: "This Psalm has flown like a bird up and down the earth, Singing the Sweetest Song Ever Heard. It has charmed more griefs to rest than all the philosophies of the world. It will go on Singing to your children, and to my children, and to their children, till the end of time. And when its work is done, it will fly back to the bosom of God, fold its wings, and Sing On Forever in the happy chorus of those it had helped to bring there."

David may have composed this Psalm while he was yet a Shepherd boy, watching his father's flocks, on the very same Shepherd Field where, 1000 years later, the Angel Choir announced the Birth of Jesus.

Psalm 24. The King's Arrival in Zion

May have been written when the Ark was brought to Jerusalem (II Samuel 6:12–15). Maybe we will Sing it in that Glad Day when the King of Glory Comes Again.

Psalm 25. Prayer of a Sin-Oppressed Soul

David has his periods of Soul Depression, on account of his Sins and Troubles. There are many Petitions here which we may very profitably make our own. Read this Psalm often.

Psalm 26. David Protests his Integrity

In rather positive terms; very different from the preceding Psalm. (See on Psalm 32.)

Psalm 27. Devotion to God's House

And Fearless Trust in God. God the Strength of his life. David loved to Sing, and to Pray, and to Wait on the Lord.

Psalm 28. A Prayer

And Thanks for its Answer. David was Hopeless, except for God. He Depended on Him, and Rejoiced in Him.

Psalm 29. The Voice of God

In the Thunderstorm, sometimes frightening, suggestive of Terrifying Cataclysms at the End of the World.

Psalm 30. Dedication of David's Palace

After he had conquered Jerusalem, and made it his Capital (II Samuel 5:11; 7:2). Had often been near death, but God brought him through. He would Sing Praise to God Forever.

Psalm 31. A Song of Trust

David, in Constant Danger, Trouble, Grief or Humiliation, always Implicitly Trusted in God. Jesus quoted His dying word from this Psalm (5; Luke 23:46).

Psalm 32. A Psalm of Penitence

Occasioned, no doubt, by David's Sin with Bathsheba (II Samuel 11–12). He can find no words to express his Shame and Humiliation. Yet this is the same David who repeatedly avowed his Righteousness (Psalms 7:3, 8; 17:1–5; 18:20–24; 26:1–14).

How reconcile these paradoxical features of David's life? 1. The Righteousness statements may have been made before David made this dreadful mistake. 2. In most things David was Righteous. 3. There is a difference between a Sin of Weakness and Wilful Habitual Sin. A Good man may Sin, and yet be a Good man. David's Remorse showed him to be just that. That is quite different from Wicked Men who Purposely and Wilfully and Habitually flout all the laws of Decency. (See on II Samuel 11.)

Augustine is said to have had this Psalm written on the wall in front of his bed, where it was always in view, reading it incessantly, weeping as he read.

Other Penitential Psalms are: 6, 25, 38, 51, 102, 130, 143.

Psalm 33. A Psalm of Joy and Praise

It mentions a New Song (3), and in 40:3; 96:1; 98:1; 144:9. There are certain Old Songs that will Never Grow Old; but, to God's People, as they travel along life's road, there are ever and anon New Deliverances and New Joys that put New Meaning into Old Songs, to be climaxed at last with New Outbursts of Joy at the Dawn of Heaven's Glories (Revelation 5:9; 14:3).

Psalm 34. David's Thanks for Deliverance

In every trouble David went straight to God in Prayer. On every Deliverance he went instantly to God in Thanks and Praise. What a glorious thing to thus LIVE IN GOD. And how that must please God. Someone has said, Thank God for the Starlight, and He will give you the Moonlight. Thank Him for the Moonlight, and He will give you the Sunlight. Thank Him for the Sunlight, and by and by He will take you where He Himself is the Light.

Psalm 35. An Imprecatory Psalm

Others are 52, 58, 59, 69, 109, 137. They breathe vengeance on Enemies. They are not God's pronouncements of His wrath on the wicked, but are the prayers of a man for vengeance on his enemies, just the opposite of Jesus' teaching that we should Love our Enemies. How explain this?

In the Old Testament God's purpose was to maintain a Nation to pave the way for the Coming of Christ. He was working with Human Nature as it was, and did not necessarily endorse everything that even His most devoted servants did or said. Some of these Psalms are Battle Hymns, expressions of intense Patriotism, designed, in life and death struggles with powerful enemies, to help the Nation survive. With the Coming of Christ, God's Revelation of the meaning of human life, and its standards of conduct, were completed; and God shifted the direct emphasis of His Work from the Maintenance of a Nation to the Transformation of Individuals into the Kind of Persons He wants us to be; and God will not NOW excuse some things He overlooked THEN. In Old Testament times God, in measure, for expedience' sake, accommodated Himself to Men's Ideas. In New Testament times God began to deal with men according to His Own Ideas. (See on Luke 6:27.)

Psalms 36,37. Trust in God

Psalm 36. Wickedness of Men. Mercy and Faithfulness of God.

Psalm 37. This is one of the best loved Psalms. David, always puzzled by the Prevalence of Wickedness, here states his philosophy as to how to live in the midst of Wicked People: Do Good; Trust God; Don't Worry.

Psalm 38. A Psalm of Bitter Anguish

One of the Penitential Psalms (see on Psalm 32). It seems that David was suffering from a loathesome disease, caused by his sin, on account of which his closest friends and nearest relatives had become estranged, and enemies had multiplied and become very bold. It shows how the "man after God's own heart" sometimes went to the depths in Sorrow and Humiliation for his sin.

Psalm 39. Frailty and Vanity of Life

Jeduthun, in this, and titles of 62 and 77, was one of David's three Music leaders, the other two being Asaph and Heman (I Chronicles 16:37–42). Also he was the King's Seer (II Chronicles 35:15).

Psalm 40. Praise for a Great Deliverance

The Law of God was in his heart (8). Yet he was utterly crushed by his Iniquities (12). The last part of this Psalm is same as Psalm 70. Seems to have Messianic reference (7, 8; Hebrews 10:5–7).

Psalm 41. A Prayer for Deliverance

Thought to belong to the time of Absalom's Usurpation (II Samuel 15), when David's sickness (3–8), gave opportunity for the plot to mature. The Familiar Friend (9), must have been Ahithophel, the Old Testament Judas (II Samuel 15:12, John 13:18).

Psalms 42,43. Thirst for the House of God

On the part of an exile, in the Hermon region, east of the Jordan (6), among ungodly and hostile people. These two Psalms form one poem. Sons of Korah, in the title of Psalms 42–49, 84, 85, 87, 88, were a family of Poetic Levites, organized by David, into a Musical Guild (I Chronicles 6:31–48; 9:19, 22, 33).

Psalm 44. A Cry of Despair

In a time of National Disaster, when their Army, it seems, had been overwhelmingly defeated.

Psalm 45. Nupital Song of a King

Bearing the name of God, seated on an Eternal Throne. It may, in part, have reference to David or Solomon. But some of its statements are wholly inapplicable to either, or to any other human sovereign. It surely seems to be a Song of the Messiah, anticipating the Marriage of the Lamb (Revelation 19:7).

Psalm 46. Zion's Battle Song

Basis of Luther's famous hymn, "A Mighty Fortress is our God," Song of the Reformation.

Psalms 47,48. God Reigns

God is King. Zion is the City of God. This God is our God Forever. God is on the Throne. Let the Earth Rejoice.

Psalms 49,50. Vanity of Riches

God the owner of the Earth and all that is therein. In giving to God we merely return that which is His Own. Vanity of Life. Death comes to all. Similar to Psalm 39.

Psalm 51. Prayer for Mercy

Aftermath of David's Sin with Bathsheba (II Samuel 11, 12). A Penitential Psalm (see on Psalm 32). Create in me a Clean Heart (10), a prayer we all would do well to pray constantly.

Psalm 52. David's Trust in God

Contrasted with the Wicked Boastfulness of his enemy Doeg (I Samuel 21:7; 22:9), confident that he would be Delivered.

Psalm 53. Universal Sinfulness of Men

Similar to Psalm 14. Quoted in Romans 3:10–12. Mahalath, in title, a Melancholy Tune? Maschil, a Meditative Poem?

Psalm 54. David's Cry to God

When Ziphites told Saul where David was hiding (I Samuel 26). Other Psalms composed while David was in flight from Saul are: 7(?), 34, 52, 54, 56, 57, 59, 63(?), 142.

Psalm 55. Betrayed by Friends

Like Psalm 41, it seems to belong to the time of Absalom's Rebellion, and specifically to refer to Ahithophel (12–14; II Samuel 15:12, 13). Foregleam of Judas. David Trusts in God.

Psalm 56. Prayer for Deliverance

From Philistines, like Psalm 34, I Samuel 21:10–15. David used his own resources to the limit, even feigning himself to be Insane. Yet he Prayed and Trusted in God for the result. Psalm 34 is his Song of Thanks for Escape.

Psalm 57. David's Prayer

In the Cave of Adullam, while hiding from Saul (I Samuel 22:1; 24:1, 26:1). His heart was Fixed in Trusting God (7).

Psalm 58. Destruction of the Wicked

Their day of Retribution is Sure. David complained much about the Prevalence of Wickedness. And repeated over and over that it Does Not Pay. It is still so.

Psalm 59. Another of David's Prayers

When Saul sent soldiers to entrap David at home (I Samuel 19:10–17). But David Trusted in God. Another Golden Poem.

Psalm 60. A Psalm of Discouragement

At time of Reverses in war with Syrians and Edomites (II Samuel 8:3–14). Other Psalms in time of National Reverse are 44, 74, 79, 108. David's Prayer was answered (II Samuel 8:14).

Psalm 61. A Hymn of Confidence

While David, apparently, was away from home, on some distant expedition (2); or, possibly, at the time of Absalom's Rebellion.

Psalm 62. A Poem of Fervid Devotion

To God and Unwavering Trust in Him. David had a lot of Trouble. But he never failed to Trust in God.

Psalm 63. A Hymn of the Wilderness

David's Thirst for God. It seems to belong to the period when David was in the wilderness of Engedi (I Samuel 24), in flight from Absalom, confident of Restoration.

Psalm 64. Prayer for Protection

From plots of Secret Enemies. David is Confident that through God he will triumph.

Psalm 65. A Song of the Sea and the Harvest

God crowns the year with Goodness. The earth shouts for Joy, with its Abundant Crops.

Psalm 66. A Song of National Thanksgiving

Praise God. Fear God. Sing. Sing. Sing. Rejoice. Rejoice. Rejoice. God's eyes observe the Nations.

Psalm 67. A Missionary Psalm

Anticipatory of the Glad News of the Gospel encircling the Earth. Let the Nations Sing for Joy.

Psalm 68. A Battle March

Of God's Victorious Armies. This Psalm was a favorite of the Crusaders, the Huguenots, Savonarola, Oliver Cromwell.

Psalm 69. A Psalm of Suffering

Like Psalm 22. Glimpses of the Suffering Messiah. So quoted in the New Testament: 4, 9, 21, 22, 25: John 2:17; 15:25; 19:28–30; Acts 1:20; Romans 11:9; 15:3. (See further page 397.)

Psalm 70. An Urgent Cry for Help

God never failed David. The Believer's Joy in God in a time of Persecution. About the same as the latter part of Psalm 40.

Psalm 71. A Psalm of Old Age

Retrospect of a Life of Trust, beset by troubles and enemies all the way, with his Joy in God undimmed.

Psalm 72. Glory and Grandeur of Messiah's Reign

This is one of Solomon's Psalms, the other being 127. Solomon's kingdom was at the pinnacle of its Glory. We may think that this Psalm was, in part, a description of his own peaceful and glorious reign. But some of its statements, and its general tenor, can allude only to the Kingdom of ONE Greater than Solomon. (See further page 397.)

Psalm 73. Prosperity of the Wicked

Solution: Consider their Latter End. This is one of Asaph's Psalms: 50, 73–83. Asaph was David's Song Leader (I Chronicles 15:16–20; 16:5). Hezekiah's choirs sang Asaph's Psalms (II Chronicles 29:30).

Psalm 74. National Disaster

Jerusalem was in ruins (3, 6, 7). Possibly at time of Shishak's Invasion (I Kings 14:25); or Captivity by the Babylonians.

Psalm 75. God is Judge

Certain Destruction of the Wicked: Certain Triumph of the Righteous: in the day when the earth shall be dissolved.

Psalm 76. Thanks for a Great Victory

Seems to refer to the Destruction of Sennacherib's Army by the Angel of God at Jerusalem (II Kings 19:25).

Psalms 77,78. Historical Psalms

Review of God's Marvellous Works, in His dealings with Israel. Contrasting God's Mighty Works, and Israel's Habitual Unfaithfulness and Disobedience.

Psalms 79,80. National Disaster

Like Psalm 74, they belong to a time of Great Calamity, like the Invasion of Shishak, or the Fall of the Northern Kingdom, or the Babylonian Captivity.

Psalms 81,82. Israel's Waywardness

The Cause of her Troubles. If they had only hearkened to God, it would have been different. Unjust Judges share in the blame, forgetting their responsibility to Supreme Judge.

Psalm 83. A Prayer for Protection

From a Conspiracy of Federated Nations: Edomites, Arabians, Moabites, Ammonites, Amalekites, Philistines and others.

Psalm 84. God's House

Blessedness of Devotion to God's House. God Loves those who Love the Highways to Zion. This applies to the Church.

Psalms 85,86. Thanks, and a Cry for Mercy

Thanks for Return from Captivity, and a Prayer for Restoration of the Land, and a Better Future. And a Prayer for Mercy: even though Godly, yet in need of Forgiveness.

Psalm 87. Zion

God's Love for Zion. What is here said of Zion more truly applies to the Church. Our Birth in Zion recorded in Heaven (6).

Psalm 88. A Life-Long Sufferer

Prayer of a Shut-In, Suffering from a prolonged and terrible disease. One of the Saddest of the Psalms. Pitiful.

Psalm 89. God's Oath

For the Endlessness of David's Throne. A Magnificent Psalm. Ethan, in title, was one of David's Song Leaders (I Chronicles 15:17).

Psalm 90. Eternity of God

And Brevity of Human Life. Being a Psalm of Moses, who lived 400 years before David, it may have been the first Psalm to be written. Moses wrote other Songs (Exodus 15, Deuteronomy 32). Rabbinic tradition assigns the ten following Psalms, 91–100, to Moses.

Psalm 91. A Hymn of Trust

One of the Best Loved Psalms. Magnificent. Amazing Promises of Security to those who Trust God. Read It Often.

Psalm 92. A Sabbath Hymn of Praise

Seeming to look back to the Sabbath of Creation, and forward to the Age of Eternal Sabbath. Wicked Perish. Godly Flourish.

Psalms 93,94. Majesty of God

And Destruction of the Wicked. Power, Holiness and Eternity of God's Throne. From Everlasting God Reigns Forevermore. Prevalence of Wickedness in this world, but their doom is certain: one of the most frequent notes of Scripture.

Psalms 95-98. Reign of God

Continuing the idea of Psalm 93, these are called Theocratic Psalms, because they relate to the Sovereignty of God, with hints of the Kingly Reign of the Coming Messiah.

Psalm 95. Sing. Rejoice. God is King. Let us kneel before Him.

We are His people. Let us give heed to His voice. Verses 7–11 are quoted in Hebrews 3:7–11 as words of Holy Spirit.

Psalm 96. Sing. Sing. Sing. Be Joyful. Be Thankful. Praise God. It will be a day of Triumph for God's People when He comes to Judge the World. Let the Heavens be glad, and the Earth Rejoice. The Day of Judgment is on the way.

Psalm 97. The Lord Comes. The Earth is moved. A Coronation Anthem, referring, possibly, to both First and Second Advents.

Psalm 98. A Song of Crowning Day. Being a New Song (1), it may be one of those Sung in Heaven (Revelation 5:9–14).

Psalms 99,100. God. Praise

Psalm 99. God Reigns. God is Holy. Let the nations tremble. God loves Justice and Righteousness. He answers Prayer.

Psalm 100. Praise God. His Mercy endures Forever, and His Faithfulness to all generations.

Psalm 101. A Psalm for Rulers

Thought possibly to have been written when David ascended the Throne, enunciating principles of his Government.

Psalm 102. A Prayer of Penitence

In a time of terrible Affliction, Humiliation and Reproach (see on Psalm 32). The Eternity of God (25–27), is quoted in Hebrews 1:10–12 as applying to Christ.

Psalm 103. A Psalm of God's Mercy

Thought to have been written in David's old age, summarizing God's dealings with him. One of the best loved Psalms.

Psalm 104. A Nature Psalm

God the Creator, and Care-Taker in detail, over all the works of the world. Reminds us of Jesus' word, Not a sparrow falls to the ground without your Heavenly Father.

Psalms 105,106. Two Historical Psalms

A Poetic Summary of Israel's History. Dwells especially on their Miraculous Delivery out of Egypt.

Psalms 107,108,109. God's Mercy and Justice

Psalm 107. Wonders of God's Lovingkindness, in His dealings with

His People and management of the works of Nature.

Psalm 108. Seems to be one of David's Battle Songs. It is almost identical with parts of Psalms 57 and 60.

Psalm 109. Vengeance on God's Adversaries. One of the Imprecatory Psalms (see on Psalm 35). Judas is in the picture (8).

Psalm 110. Eternal Dominion of the Coming King

This Psalm cannot refer to any person in history except Christ; yet it was written 1000 years before Christ (1, 4). So quoted in the New Testament (Matthew 22:44; Acts 2:34; Hebrews 1:13; 5:6).

Psalms 111,112. Songs of Praise

Psalm 111. Majesty, Honor, Righteousness, Mercy, Justice, Faithfulness, Truth, Holiness, and Eternity of God. Verse 9 is the only place in the Bible where the word "Reverend" occurs, and it is applied to God, NOT to Ministers.

Psalm 112. Blessedness of the man who Fears God, and is Righteous, Merciful, Gracious, Kind to the Poor, and Loves the Ways and Word of God, and whose Heart is Fixed in God. Everlasting Blessedness is his.

Psalms 113-118. The Hallel Psalms

They were sung, in families, on the night of the Passover: 113 and 114 at the beginning of the meal: 115, 116, 117, 118, at the close of the meal. They must have been the hymns that Jesus and his disciples sang at the Last Supper (Matthew 26:30). Hallel means Praise.

Psalm 113. A Song of Praise. Begins and ends with Hallelujah, which means Praise. Praise God Forever.

Psalm 114. A Song of the Exodus, recalling the Wonders and Miracles of Israel's Deliverance out of Egypt, the Beginning of the Passover Feast. The Earth, Sea, Rivers, Mountains, Hills trembled at God's presence.

Psalm 115. The Lord the only God. Blessed are His People. Blessed are they who Trust in Him, and not in the gods of the Nations. God's Glory. Mercy. Truth. Trust. Our Help, Our Shield. Praise. Forevermore. Dumbness of Idols, like those who make them. Our God Is God. Where are the gods of the nations? Our God will Bless us, And we will Bless His Name Forevermore.

Psalm 116. A Song of Gratitude to God for Deliverance from Death, and from Temptation, and for Repeated Answers to Prayer. One of the best Psalms. Gracious. Merciful. Praise.

Psalm 117. A Summons to the nations to accept the Lord. So quoted in Romans 15:11. Middle chapter in the Bible, and shortest. Praise. Truth. Mercy. Forever.

Psalm 118. This was Jesus' Farewell Hymn with His disciples, as He left the Passover, on His way to Gethsemane and Calvary (Matthew 26:30). It embodied a prediction of His Rejection (22, 26; Matthew 21:9, 42). God, His Strength and His Song.

Psalm 119. The Glories of God's Word

Longest chapter in the Bible. Has 176 verses. Every verse mentions the Word of God under one or another of these names, Law, Testimony, Judgments, Statutes, Commandments, Precepts, Word, Ordinances, Ways, except 90, 121, 122, 132.

It is an Acrostic, or Alphabetic Psalm, having 22 stanzas. Each Stanza has 8 lines, each of the 8 lines beginning with the same letter (see on Psalm 9). It was Ruskin's favorite Psalm.

Psalms 120-134. Songs of Degrees

Also called Songs of Ascent, or Pilgrim Songs. Believed to have been designed for Vocal Music, to be sung by pilgrims on the road up to the Feasts at Jerusalem: or, as they went up the 15 steps to the Men's Court; or, Ascents may mean the Elevated Voice in which they were sung.

Psalm 120. A Prayer for Protection by one who lived among Deceitful and Treacherous people far away from Zion.

Psalm 121. Pilgrims may have sung this hymn as they first caught sight of the mountain surrounding Jerusalem.

Psalm 122. This may have been what the pilgrims sang as they neared the Temple Gate within the city walls.

Psalm 123. And this, within the Temple, as the pilgrims lifted their eyes to God in Prayer for His Mercy.

Psalm 124. A Hymn of Thanksgiving and Praise for repeated National Deliverances in times of fearful danger.

Psalm 125. A Hymn of Trust. As the mountains are round about Jerusalem, so God is round about His People.

Psalm 126. A Song of Thanksgiving for Return from Captivity. It seemed as if they were dreaming. (See Psalm 137.)

Psalm 127. Seems like a combination of two poems: Temple-Building and Family-Building. One of Solomon's Psalms.

Psalm 128. A Marriage-Song. Continuation of last half of Psalm 127. Godly Families are the basis of National Welfare.

Psalm 129. Israel's Prayer for Overthrow of her Enemies, who, generation after generation, had afflicted her.

Psalm 130. Keeping our eyes on God. A Cry for Mercy. One of the Penitential Psalms. (See on Psalm 32.)

Psalm 131. A Psalm of Humble Childlike Trust in God: Stilled and Quieted his soul in God, as a Child with his Mother.

Psalm 132. A Poetic Re-iteration of God's Unbreakable Promise to David of an Eternal Inheritor of his Throne.

Psalms 133, 134. A Psalm of Brother Love, and Life Forevermore. And a Psalm of the Temple-Night-Watchers.

Psalms 135-139. Psalms of Thanksgiving

Psalm 135. A Song of Praise for God's Wonderful Works, in Nature and in History: Vapors, Lightnings, Winds, Miracles in Egypt and in the Wilderness.

Psalm 136. Seems to be an expansion of Psalm 135, about God's mighty works of Creation, and in His dealings with Israel, arranged for antiphonal Singing. "His Mercy endures Forever" occurs in every verse. It is called a Hallel Psalm, was sung at the opening of Passover, and was a favorite Temple Song (I Chronicles 16:41; II Chronicles 7:3; 20:21; Ezra 3:11).

Psalm 137. A Psalm of the Captivity. Exiles in a foreign land longing for home. Sure retribution for those who took them captive. This is not a Psalm of Thanksgiving. But its counterpart, Psalm 126, written after they got back Home from Babylon, is full of Thanks.

Psalm 138. A Song of Thanks, seemingly on occasion of some Notable Answer to Prayer.

Psalm 139. God's Universal Presence and Infinite Knowledge. He knows our Every Thought, Word, Act, Nothing Hid from Him. Closing sentence is one of the most needed Prayers in the whole Bible.

Psalms 140-143. Prayers for Protection

Psalm 140. David had a host of Enemies. They drove him ever closer and closer to God. Ultimate Destruction of Wicked.

Psalm 141. Another of David's Prayers for Protection against being driven himself to Sin.

Psalm 142. One of David's Prayers in early life, while hiding in a cave from Saul (I Samuel 22:1; 24:3).

Psalm 143. David's Penitent Cry for Help and Guidance; possibly when he was being pursued by Absalom (II Samuel 17, 18).

Psalms 144,145. Songs of Praise

Psalm 144. One of David's Battle Songs. His army may have chanted such hymns as this as they moved into conflict.

Psalm 145. David may have had his army sing such a Hymn as this, after a battle, in thanks for Victory.

Psalms 146-150. Hallelujah Psalms

These are called "Hallelujah" Psalms, each beginning and ending with "Hallelujah," which means "Praise the Lord." The word appears often in other Psalms.

The grand outburst of Hallelujahs, with which the book of Psalms comes to a climactic close, is carried over to the end of the Bible itself, and is echoed in the heavenly choirs of the Redeemed (Revelation 19: 1, 3, 4, 6).

Psalm 146. God Reigns. While I live I will Praise God. I will Sing Praise to God while I have any being.

Psalm 147. Let All Creation Praise God. Sing unto God with Thanksgiving. Let Israel Praise God. Let Zion Praise God.

Psalm 148. Let the Angels Praise God. Let the Sun, Moon and Stars Praise God. Let the Heavens shout, Hallelujah!

Psalm 149. Hallelujah! Let the Saints Praise God. Let them Sing for Joy. Let Zion Rejoice. Hallelujah!

Psalm 150. Hallelujah! Praise God with Trumpet and Harp. Let everything that has breath Praise God. Hallelujah!

PROVERBS

Wise Sayings
Mostly by Solomon
About the Practical Affairs of Life
Specially Emphasizing Righteousness and Fear of God

This Book

Like Psalms and Pentateuch, this Book is divided, according to its Titles, into Five Parts: Proverbs of Solomon (1–9); Proverbs of Solomon (10–24); Proverbs of Solomon, which men of Hezekiah copied (25–29); Words of Agur (30); Words of Lemuel (31).

Thus, most of the Proverbs are ascribed to Solomon. Solomon seems to have borne about the same relation to Proverbs that David did to Psalms. Each was the Principal Writer. Psalms a Book of Devotion. Proverbs a Book of Practical Ethics.

Solomon

As a young man, he had a consuming passion for Knowledge and Wisdom (I Kings 3:9–12). He became the literary prodigy of the world of his day. His intellectual attainments were the wonder of the age. Kings came from the ends of the earth to hear him. He lectured on Botany and Zoology. He was a Scientist, a Political Ruler, a Business Man with Vast Enterprises, a Poet, Moralist and Preacher. (See on I Kings 4 and 9.)

A Proverb

Is a Short, Pithy, Axiomatic Saying, the life of which is Antithesis or Comparison. They are wholly Unconnected. Designed primarily for the Young: a form of Teaching: repetition of Practical Thoughts in form that would stick in mind.

Subjects

Wisdom. Righteousness. Fear of God. Knowledge. Morality. Chastity. Diligence. Self-Control. Trust in God. Tithes. Proper Use of Riches. Considerateness of the Poor. Control of the Tongue. Kindness to Enemies. Choice of Companions. Training of Children. Industry. Honesty. Idleness. Laziness. Justice. Helpfulness. Cheerfulness. Common Sense.

Technique of Treatment

This Book aims to inculcate Virtues that are insisted upon throughout the Bible. Over and over and over, in all the Bible, in multiform ways, and by diverse methods, God has supplied to man a great abundance of Instruction, line upon line, precept upon precept, here a little and there a little, as to How He Wants Men to Live, so that there be no excuse for our missing the mark. The Teachings of this Book of Proverbs are not expressed in a "Thus Saith the Lord," as in the Law of Moses, where the Same Things are taught as a direct Command of God; but rather are given as coming out of the Experience of a man who tried out and tested just about everything that men can engage in. Moses had said, These things are the Commandments of God. Solomon here says, The things which God has Commanded are proved by Experience to be Best for men, and the Essence of Human Wisdom is in the Keeping of God's Commandments.

God, in the long record of His Revelation of Himself and His Will to Man, it seems, resorted to every possible method, not only by Commandment, and by Precept, but by Example also, to convince men that God's Commandments are worth living by.

Solomon's fame was a sounding board that carried his voice to the ends of the earth, and made him an Example to All the World of the Wisdom of God's Ideas.

This Book of Proverbs has been called one of the "Best Guide Books to Success that a young man can follow."

Chapter 1. Object of the Book

To Promote Wisdom, Instruction, Understanding, Righteousness, Justice, Equity, Prudence, Knowledge, Discretion, Learning, Sound Counsels (2–7). What splendid words!

The starting point is the Fear of God (7). Next, giving heed to Parental Instruction (8–9). Then, Avoidance of Bad Companions (10–19). Wisdom cries aloud her Warnings (20–33).

Chapters 2 to 6

Chapter 2. Wisdom, to be had, must be sought Whole-Heartedly. The place to find it is God's Word (6). Then follows a warning against the Strange Woman, a warning often repeated.

Chapter 3. A superb and beautiful chapter. Kindness. Truth. Long Life. Peace. Trust in God. Honoring God with our Substance. Prosperity. Security. Happiness. Blessedness.

Chapter 4. Wisdom is the Principal Thing. Therefore Get Wisdom. The path of the Righteous grows Brighter and Brighter. The path of the Wicked grows Darker and Darker.

Chapter 5. Marital Joy and Loyalty. A warning against Unchaste Love. Solomon had Many Women, but advised against it. He seemed to think the One-Wife arrangement better (18–19).

Chapter 6. Warnings against: Questionable Business Obligations: Laziness: Cunning Hypocrisy: Haughtiness: Lying: Trouble-Making: Disregard of Parents: Illegitimate Love.

Chapters 7 to 14

Chapter 7. Warning against the Adulteress while her husband is away from home. Chapters 5, 6, 7, are about loose women. Judging from the space Solomon devotes to them, there must have been a good many such women then (Ecclesiastes 7:28).

Chapters 8, 9. Wisdom, personified as a woman, inviting all to her banquet of Best Things: in contrast to lustful women, calling to the simple, "Stolen waters are sweet" (9:13–18).

Chapter 10. Terse contrasts between Wise Men and Fools, Righteous and Wicked, Diligent and Lazy, Rich and Poor.

Chapter 11. A False Balance an Abomination to God. A Beautiful woman without discretion like a jewel in a swine's snout. A Liberal soul shall be made fat. He that Wins Souls is Wise.

Chapter 12. A Worthy Woman the Glory of her Husband. Lying Lips an Abomination to God. Precious Blessings to the Diligent. In the pathway of the Righteous there Is No Death.

Chapter 13. He that guards his Mouth guards his Life. Hope deferred makes the heart sick. The way of the Transgressor is Hard. Walk with Wise Men, and you shall be Wise.

Chapter 14. He that is soon Angry will deal Foolishly. He that is Slow to Anger is of Great Understanding. Fear of God is a Fountain of Life. Tranquility of Heart is the Life of the Flesh. He that Oppresses the Poor Reproaches his Maker.

Chapters 15 to 20

Chapter 15. A Soft Answer turns away Wrath. A Gentle Tongue is a Tree of Life. Prayer of the Upright is God's Delight. He that is of Cheerful Heart has a Continual Feast. A Wise Son makes a Glad Father.

Chapter 16. A Man's Heart Devises his way, but God Directs his Steps. Pride goes before Destruction. The Hoary Head is a Crown of Glory, if it be found in the way of Righteousness.

Chapter 17. He that begets a Fool does it to his Sorrow. A Cheerful Heart is a Good Medicine. Even a Fool, when he holds his Peace, is counted Wise.

Chapter 18. A Fool's Mouth is his Destruction. Death and life are in the power of the Tongue. Before Honor goes Humility. Whoso finds a Wife finds a Good Thing.

Chapter 19. A Prudent Wife is from God. He that has pity on the Poor lends to God; and his Good Deed will God Repay. Many devices in man's Heart: but Counsel of God Shall Stand.

Chapter 20. Wine is a Mocker. It is an honor for a man to hold aloof from Strife, but every Fool will be Quarreling. Lips of Knowledge are like Precious Jewels. Diverse Weights and a False Balance are an Abomination to God.

Chapters 21 to 25

Chapter 21. It is better to dwell in a desert than with a Contentious and Fretful woman in a wide house. Whoso stops his ear at the cry of the Poor, he also shall cry, and not be heard. Whoso keeps his Tongue keeps his soul from Trouble. The horse is prepared for battle, but Victory is of God.

Chapter 22. A Good Name is rather to be chosen than Great Riches. Train up a child in the way he should go, and when he is old he will not depart from it. He that has a Bountiful eye shall be Blessed. See a man Diligent in business? He shall stand before kings.

Chapter 23. Weary not yourself to be rich. Hearken to your Father and Mother: let them Rejoice in you when they are old. Who has Woe? They that tarry long at the wine. At last it bites like a Serpent, and stings like an Adder.

Chapter 24. In a multitude of counsellors there is safety. I went by the field of the Sluggard. It was overgrown with thorns. I saw, and received instruction; a little more folding the arms to Sleep: So shall come your Poverty.

Chapter 25. A Word Fitly Spoken is like apples of gold in baskets of silver. If your enemy hunger, feed him; if he thirst, give him to drink; and God will reward you.

This group of Solomon's Proverbs (chapters 25 to 29), are here said to have been copied by Men of Hezekiah (25:1). Hezekiah lived over 200 years after Solomon. Solomon's manuscript may have been worn out. A basic item in Hezekiah's Reform Movement was renewed interest in God's Word (II Kings 18).

Chapters 26 to 31

Chapter 26. See a man wise in his own conceit? There is more hope of a Fool than of him. A Lying Tongue hates those whom it has wounded.

Chapter 27. Boast not yourself of Tomorrow, for you know not what a day may bring forth. More Proverbs about Fools.

Chapters 28, 29. He that hides his eyes from the Poor shall have many a Curse. A Fool utters all his Anger, but a wise man keeps it back, and stills it. Further dissertations on Fools. Solomon did not like Fools: often paid his respects to them.

Chapter 30. It is not known who Agur was. Probably a friend of Solomon's. Solomon liked his Proverbs so well that he thought worthwhile to include them in his own book.

Chapter 31. A Mother's Counsel to a King. Lemuel is thought possibly to have been another name for Solomon. If so, then Bathsheba was the mother who taught him this beautiful poem.

Few mothers have raised finer boys. As a young man, Solomon's character was almost as splendid as any in history. In his old age, however, he did depart from it, contrary to his own Proverb (22:6). The chapter is about Mothers rather than Kings.

ECCLESIASTES

Vanity of Earthly Life Apart from the Sure Hope of Immortality Exemplified in the Experience of Solomon

Solomon, author of this book, was the most famous and most powerful king in all the world, in his day, noted for Wisdom, Riches and Literary Attainments (see on I Kings 4 and 9).

Vanity of Vanities: All is Vanity

This is the theme of the book. It embodies also an attempt to give a philosophic answer as to how best to live in a world where All is Vanity. The book contains many things of Superb Beauty and Transcendant Wisdom. But its predominant strain is one of Unutterable Melancholy: so different from the Psalms.

David, Solomon's father, in his long and hard struggle to build the kingdom, was forever shouting, Rejoice, Shout for Joy, Sing, Praise God. Solomon, sitting in peaceful security on the throne David had built, with Riches, Honor, Splendor, Power, and living in almost Fabled Luxury, was the one man in all the world whom men would have called Happy. Yet his unceasing refrain was, All is Vanity. And the book, a product of Solomon's old age, leaves us with the distinct impression that Solomon was not a happy man. The word "Vanity" occurs 37 times.

Eternity

"Eternity" (3:11), RV, a more correct translation than AV "World," may suggest the Key Thought of the book. Eternity in the Hearts of Men. In the inmost depths of his nature man has a longing for Things Eternal. But, at that time, God had not revealed very much about Things Eternal.

In various places in the Old Testament there are hints and glimpses of the Future Life; and Solomon seems to have had vague ideas of it. But it was Christ who Brought Life and Immortality to light (II Timothy 1:10). Christ, by Resurrection from the Dead, gave the world a mathematical demonstration of Certainty of Life beyond the Grave. And Solomon, who lived 1000 years before Christ, could not possibly have the same feeling of Sureness about Life Beyond that Christ later gave the world.

But Solomon saw earthly life at its best. Not a whim but what he could gratify whenever he wanted to. And he seems to have made it his chief business in life to see how good a time he could have. And this book, the result of Solomon's experience, has running through it a note of Unspeakable Pathos, All is Vanity and Vexation of Spirit.

How Can Such a Book be God's Word?

In that God Had the Record Made. Not that all of Solomon's Ideas were God's Ideas (see note on I Kings 11). But the general Self-Evident Lessons of the book are from God. God gave Solomon Wisdom and Unparalleled Opportunity to observe and to explore every avenue of earthly life. And, after much research and experiment, Solomon concluded that, on the whole, humanity found little solid Happiness in life; and in his own heart he found an Unutterable Yearning for something beyond himself. Thus the book, in a way, is Humanity's Cry for a SAVIOUR.

With the coming of Christ, the cry was answered. The Vanity of life disappeared. No longer Vanity. But Joy, Peace, Gladness. Jesus never used the word Vanity. But talked much of his Joy, even under the shadow of the Cross. Joy is one of the Key Words of the New Testament. In Christ humanity found the Desire of the Ages: Life; Full, Abundant, Joyous, Glorious Life.

Chapters 1,2,3,4. All is Vanity

In a world where everything passes away, and fails to satisfy, Solomon sets himself to answer the question, What is the solution to life in such a world? A World of Unending Monotony. Solomon's feeling of the vanity, Emptiness and Uselessness of his own vast works. Even Wisdom, which Solomon sought so diligently, and prized so highly, was Disappointing. Pursuits and Pleasures of mankind generally seemed to him to be merely a Striving after Wind. And it was all made worse by the prevalent Wickedness and Cruelties of men.

Chapters 5 to 10. Miscellaneous Proverbs

Interspersed with various observations, bearing on the general theme of the book. Solomon's favorite form of literature was Proverbs. In 7:27, 28, there may be a sidelight on Solomon's harem. He had a thousand women (I Kings 11:1–11). One would guess, from 7:26–28 that he had had some difficulty in holding the faithless ladies of his court in line.

Chapters 11,12. Solomon's Answer

To his theme question, What is it that it is good for men to do, in a world where All is Vanity. His answer, scattered through the book, is summed up at the close: Eat, Drink, Rejoice, Do Good, Live Joyfully with your Wife, Do with your Might what your hands find to do, and, above all, FEAR GOD, keeping your eyes on the Day of Final Judgment. With all his complaints about the nature of creation, Solomon had no doubt as to the Existence and Justice of the Creator. GOD is mentioned at least Forty times in this book.

SONG OF SOLOMON

Glorification of Wedded Love

A Love Song, set in blossoming Springtime, abounding in metaphors and a profusion of Oriental imagery, exhibiting Solomon's fondness for Nature, Gardens, Meadows, Vineyards, Orchards and Flocks (I Kings 4:33).

It is called, The Song of Songs, possibly indicating that Solomon considered it the choicest of all the 1005 Songs which he wrote (I Kings 4:32). Also called, Canticles. Thought to have been written to celebrate marriage to his favorite wife.

As a Poem

It is considered by scholars who are familiar with the structure of Hebrew Poetry to be a superb composition. But its sudden transition from speaker to speaker, and from place to place, with no explanation of its shifting scenes and actors, makes it difficult to understand. In Hebrew the change of speakers is indicated by gender: in some Bibles, by extra space.

The Speakers

It seems clear that the speakers are: a Bride, called the Shulammite (6:13): the King: and a Chorus of Palace Ladies called, Daughters of Jerusalem. Solomon's harem was as yet small, only 60 wives and 80 concubines, with innumerable virgins on the waiting list (6:8). It afterward grew to include 700 wives and 300 concubines (I Kings 11:3, where see note).

The Bride

A common opinion, and probably the best, is that the Shulammite was Abishag, of Shunem, the fairest maiden in all the land, who attended David in his last days (I Kings 1:1–4), and who, no doubt, became Solomon's wife, for her marriage to another might have endangered his throne (I Kings 2:17, 22).

Interpretations

On its face, the poem is a eulogy of the Joys of Wedded Life. Its essence is to be found in its tender and devoted expressions of the intimate delights of Wedded Love. Even if it is no more than that, it is worthy a place in God's Word; for Marriage was ordained of God (Genesis 2:24). And on proper Mutual Attitudes in the inner familiarities of Married Life depend, to a very large extent, Human Happiness and Welfare.

However, both Jews and Christians have seen deeper meanings in this poem. Jews read it at Passover as allegorically referring to the Exodus, where God espoused Israel to Himself as His Bride, His Love for Israel being here exemplified in the "Spontaneous Love of a Great King and an Humble Maid." In Old Testament Israel is called God's Wife (Jeremiah 3:1; Ezekiel 16 and 23).

Christians have, quite commonly, regarded it as a Pre-Nuptial Song of Christ and the Church; for, in the New Testament, the Church is called the Bride of Christ (Matthew 9:15; 25:1; John 3:29; II Corinthians 11:2; Ephesians 5:23; Revelation 19:7; 21:2; 22:17); indicating that Human Wedlock is a sort of Counterpart and Foretaste of the Rapturous Relation between Christ and His Church.

How could a Man with 1000 Women have a Love for any one of them that would be Fit to be Typical of Christ's Love for the Church? Well, a number of Old Testament saints were Polygamists. Even though God's Law was against it from the beginning, as Christ so plainly stated, yet in Old Testament times God seemed to have accommodated Himself, in measure, to prevailing customs. Kings generally had Many Wives. It was one of the signs of Royalty. And Solomon's devotion to this lovely girl did seem to be genuine and unmistakable. Then too he was King in the Family which was to produce the Messiah. And it seems not unfitting that his Marriage should, in a sense, prefigure the Messiah's Eternal Marriage to His Bride. The Joys of this Song, we think, will find their Climax in the Hallelujahs of the Lamb's Marriage Supper (Revelation 19:6–9).

Subjects of the Chapters

To appreciate the meaning, try to identify the speakers, which, in some passages, is not easy.

Chapter 1. The Bride's Love for the King. Mostly words of her own devotion, with brief replies by King and Chorus.

Chapter 2. The Bride's Delight in the King's Love. Mostly her own words, in soliloquy, about the King's embraces.

Chapter 3:1–5. The Bride's Dream of her Lover's Disappearance, and her Joy at finding him again.

Chapter 3:6–11. The Bridal Procession. Greetings, in the palace garden, of the Nuptial Chariot, by the palace ladies.

Chapter 4. The King Adores his Bride. She replies, inviting him to her garden of marital delights.

Chapter 5. Another Dream of her Lover's Disappearance, following their nuptial union; and her devotion to him.

Chapter 6. The Shulammite the Loveliest among the 140 beauties of the palace, and so recognized by them and the King.

Chapter 7. Their Mutual Devotion, told each to the other, in a profusion of Spring-song metaphors.

Chapter 8. Their Love Unquenchable, and their Union Indissoluble; words partly of Bride, and partly of Chorus.

THE PROPHETS

The Historical Books of the Old Testament, Genesis to Esther, are the story of the Rise and Fall of the Hebrew Nation.

The Poetical Books, Job to Song of Solomon, roughly, belong to the Golden Age of the Hebrew Nation.

The Prophetical Books, Isaiah to Malachi, belong to the days of the Fall of the Hebrew Nation.

There are 17 books of the Prophets; only 16 Prophets, for Jeremiah wrote two: the book called by his name, and Lamentations.

These books are ordinarily spoken of as "Major Prophets" and "Minor Prophets," as follows:

Major Prophets: Isaiah, Jeremiah, Ezekiel, Daniel.

Minor Prophets: Hosea, Joel, Amos, Obadiah, Jonah, Micah, Nahum, Habakkuk, Zephaniah, Haggai, Zechariah, Malachi.

This classification is based on the size of the books. Any one of the three books, Isaiah, Jeremiah or Ezekiel, is in itself alone larger than all 12 of the Minor Prophets combined together. Daniel is about the combined size of the two largest Minor Prophets, Hosea and Zechariah.

Every Bible reader should MEMORIZE the names of these Prophets, so as to be able to turn readily to any of the books.

Classified as to Time: 13 of the Prophets were connected with the Destruction of the Hebrew Nation; 3 with its Restoration.

The Destruction of the Nation was accomplished in two periods.

The Northern Kingdom fell, 734–721 B.C. Preceding, and during, this period were: Joel, Jonah, Amos, Hosea, Isaiah, Micah.

The Southern Kingdom fell, 606–586 B.C. In this period were: Jeremiah, Ezekiel, Daniel, Obadiah, Nahum, Habakkuk, Zephaniah.

The Restoration of the Nation occurred 536–444 B.C. Connected with this were: Haggai, Zechariah, Malachi.

Classified as to Message: addressed mainly as follows:

To Israel: Amos, Hosea.

To Nineveh: Jonah, Nahum.

To Babylon: Daniel.

To Captives in Babylon: Ezekiel.

To Edom: Obadiah.

To Judah: Joel, Isaiah, Micah, Jeremiah, Habakkuk, Zephaniah, Haggai, Zechariah, Malachi.

The Historical Event

That called forth the work of the Prophets was the Apostasy of the Ten Tribes at the close of Solomon's reign (see under I Kings 12). As a political measure, to keep the two kingdoms separate, the Northern Kingdom adopted as their national religion Calf-Worship, the religion of Egypt. Soon afterward they added Baal-Worship, which also got a hold on the Southern Kingdom. At this crisis, when God's name was disappearing from the minds of men, and God's plans for the ultimate redemption of the world were coming to naught, then it was that the Prophets appeared.

Prophets and Priests

Priests were the regularly appointed religious teachers of the nation. They were an hereditary class, and were often the wickedest men in the nation. Still they were religious teachers. Instead of crying out against the sins of the people, they fell in with them, and became leaders in iniquity. Prophets were not an hereditary class. Each one got his call directly from God. They were called from different vocations. Jeremiah and Ezekiel were priests; and perhaps also Zechariah. Isaiah, Daniel and Zephaniah, were of royal blood. Amos was a shepherd. What the rest were is not known.

Mission and Message of the Prophets

1. To try to save the nation from its Idolatry and Wickedness.
2. Failing in this, to announce the nation will be destroyed.
3. But not completely destroyed. A Remnant will be saved.
4. Out of this remnant will come a Person who will bring All Nations to God.
5. That Person will be a Great Man who will one day arise in the family of David. The Prophets called him "THE BRANCH." The family tree of David, once the most powerful family in the world, cut down, in the days of the Prophets, to rule a kingdom that was disappearing, the family would have a comeback. Out of the family stock would come a Branch who will become King of Kings.

The Whole Period of the Prophets

Roughly, covered about 400 years (800–400 B.C.). The Central Event of the period was the Destruction of Jerusalem, about the middle of the period chronologically. With this event, one way or another, Seven of the Prophets were connected, actually or chronologically: Jeremiah, Ezekiel, Daniel, Obadiah, Nahum, Habakkuk, Zephaniah. The Fall of Jerusalem was the time of the greatest

Prophetic activity, trying to prevent it, or explain it. Though God himself brought on the destruction of Jerusalem, humanly speaking, he did all he could to avert it. It seems that God would rather have an Institution that stands for the idea of God in the world, even though that Institution be shot through and through with wickedness and corruption, than not to have any institution at all. Perhaps that is why God permitted the Papacy to have a continuous existence through the Middle Ages. At any rate God sent a brilliant array of Prophets in an effort to save Jerusalem.

Failing to save the Unholy Holy City, the Prophets literally glow with Divine explanations and assurances that the collapse of God's nation does not mean the end of God's plans; that, after a period of punishment, there would be a Restoration, and, for God's people a Glorious Future.

Social Message of the Prophets

Modern books on the Prophets lay great emphasis on their social message, their denunciation of the political corruption, oppression and moral rottenness of the nation. However, the thing that bothered the prophets most was the IDOLATRY of the nation. It is surprising how largely this is overlooked by modern writers.

Predictive Element

Modern Scholarship is inclined to minimize the Predictive Element in the Bible. But the predictive element is there. The most persistent thought in the entire Old Testament is this: Jehovah, the God of the Hebrew nation, eventually is going to become the God of All Nations. The successive generations of Old Testament writers pass from the general to the particular in describing the detail and manner of that accomplishment. And in the Prophets, though they themselves may not have understood the full import of some of their words, and though some of their predictions are cloudily blurred with historic events of their own day, yet the whole Story of Christ and the Spread of Christianity over the earth is pictured beforehand, in outline and in detail, in language that cannot refer to anything else in history.

Message of Each Prophet, Expressed in One Line

Joel: a vision of the Gospel Age, Ingathering of the nations.
Jonah: interest of Israel's God in Israel's enemies.
Amos: David's House will yet rule the world.
Hosea: Jehovah will one day be God of all nations.
Isaiah: God has a Remnant, and for it a Glorious Future.

Micah: Coming Prince of Bethlehem, and his Universal Reign.
Nahum: impending judgment on Nineveh.
Zephaniah: coming of a New Revelation, called by a New Name.
Jeremiah: Jerusalem's sin, doom and future glory.
Ezekiel: the fall of Jerusalem, restoration and glorious future.
Obadiah: Edom shall utterly perish.
Daniel: the Four Kingdoms, and God's Everlasting Kingdom.
Habakkuk: ultimate triumph for Jehovah's people.
Haggai: the second Temple, and Coming Greater Temple.
Zechariah: the Coming King, his House and Kingdom.
Malachi: closing message of Messianic Nation.

Historical Setting and Approximate Dates of the Prophets

Division of the Kingdom (933 B.C.)

ISRAEL		JUDAH		PROPHETS	
Jeroboam	933–911	Rehoboam	933–916		
Nadab	911–910	Abijah	915–913		
Baasha	910–887	Asa	912–872		
Rise of Assyria to World Power (about 900 B.C.)					
Elah	887–886				
Zimri	886				
Omri	886–875				
Ahab	875–854	Jehoshaphat	874–850	Elijah	875–850
Ahaziah	855–854	Jehoram	850–843	Elisha	850–800
Joram	854–843	Ahaziah	843		
Jehu	843–816	Athaliah	843–837		
God began to "cut off" Israel (II Kings 10:32)					
Jehoahaz	820–804	Joash	843–803	Joel ?	840–830
Joash	806–790	Amaziah	803–775		
Jeroboam II	790–749	Uzziah	787–735	Jonah	790–770
Zechariah	748	Jotham	749–734	Amos	780–740
Shallum	748			Hosea	760–720
Menahem	748–738			Isaiah	745–695
Pekahiah	738–736				
Pekah	748–730	Ahaz	741–726	Micah	740–700
Captivity of North Israel (734 B.C.)					
Hoshea	730–721	Hezekiah	726–697		
End of Northern Kingdom (721 B.C.)					
		Manasseh	697–642		
		Amon	641–640		
		Josiah	639–608	Zephaniah	639–608

Jehoahaz	608	Nahum	630–610
Jehoiakim	608–597	Jeremiah	626–586

Fall of Assyria, 607 B.C. (Rise of Babylon)

Jehoiachin	597	Habakkuk	606–586
Zedekiah	597–586	Obadiah	586

Jerusalem conquered and burned (606–586)
The Captivity (606–536)

		Daniel	606–534
		Ezekiel	592–570

Fall of Babylon, 536 B.C. (Rise of Persia)
Return from the Captivity (536 B.C.)

Joshua	536–516	Haggai	520–516
Zerubbabel	536–516	Zechariah	520–516

Temple rebuilt (520–516)

Ezra	457–430		
Nehemiah	444-432	Malachi	450–400

ISAIAH

The Messianic Prophet

Called the Messianic Prophet because he was so thoroughly imbued with the idea that his nation was to be a Messianic Nation to the world; that is, a nation through whom one day a great and wonderful blessing would come from God to all nations; and he was continually dreaming of the day when that great and wonderful work would be done.

The New Testament says that Isaiah "saw the glory of Christ, and spoke of him" (John 12:41).

The Man Isaiah

He was a prophet of the Southern Kingdom, Judah, at the time the Northern Kingdom, Israel, was destroyed by the Assyrians.

Isaiah lived in the reigns of Uzziah, Jotham, Ahaz and Hezekiah. His call was in the year of Uzziah's death, but some of his visions may have been earlier (see on 6:1). He was slain, according to Jewish tradition, by Manasseh. Tentatively we may place his active ministry at about 745–695 B.C.

Rabbinic tradition has it that Isaiah's father, Amoz (not Amos the prophet), was a brother of king Amaziah. This would make Isaiah first cousin to king Uzziah, and grandson of king Joash, and thus of royal blood, a man of the palace.

His Literary Work. He wrote other books, which have not been preserved to us: a Life of Uzziah (II Chronicles 26:22); and a book of the Kings of Israel and Judah (II Chronicles 32:32). He is quoted in the New Testament more than any other prophet. What a mind he had! In some of his rhapsodies he reaches heights unequaled even by Shakespeare, Milton or Homer.

His Martyrdom. A tradition, in the Talmud, which was accepted as authentic by many early Church Fathers, states that Isaiah resisted Manasseh's idolatrous decrees, and was fastened between two planks, and "sawn asunder," thus suffering a most horrible death. This is thought to be referred to in Hebrews 11:37.

Assyrian Background of Isaiah's Ministry

For 150 years before the days of Isaiah the Assyrian Empire had been expanding. As early as 840 B.C. Israel, under Jehu, had begun to pay tribute to Assyria. While Isaiah was yet a young man (734 B.C.), Assyria carried away all of north Israel. 13 years later (721), Samaria fell, and the rest of Israel was carried away. Then, a few years later, the Assyrians came on into Judah, destroyed 46 walled cities, and carried away 200,000 captives. Finally (701 B.C.), when Isaiah was an old man, the Assyrians were stopped before the walls of Jerusalem by an angel of God. Thus, Isaiah's whole life was spent under the shadow of threatening Assyrian power, and he himself witnessed the ruin of his entire nation at their hands, except only Jerusalem.

ARCHAEOLOGICAL NOTE: The Isaiah Scroll

All original copies of Bible books, as far as is known, have been lost. Our Bible is made from copies of copies. Until the invention of Printing A.D. 1454, these copies were made by hand.

Old Testament books were written in Hebrew. New Testament books were written in Greek. The oldest known extant complete Bible manuscripts date from the 4th and 5th centuries A.D. They are in Greek, containing, for the Old Testament, the Septuagint, which was a Greek Translation of the Hebrew Old Testament made in 2nd century B.C. (See pages 402–412, 750–756.)

The oldest known existing Hebrew manuscripts of Old Testament books were made about A.D. 900. On these are based what is called the Massoretic Text of the Hebrew Old Testament, from which our English Translations of Old Testament books have been made. The Massoretic Text comes from a comparison of all available manuscripts, copied from previous copies by many different lines of scribes. In these manuscripts there is so little variation that Hebrew scholars are in general agreement that our present Bible text is essentially the same as that in the original books themselves.

And now, in 1947, at Ain Fashkha, about 7 miles south of Jericho, 1 mile west of the Dead Sea, some wandering Arab Bedouins, carrying goods from the Jordan Valley to Bethlehem, searching for a lost goat, in a wady that empties into the Dead Sea, came upon a partially collapsed cave, in which they found a number of crushed jars with protruding ends of scrolls. The Bedouins pulled out the scrolls, took them along, and passed them on to St. Mark's Syrian Orthodox Convent in Jerusalem who turned them over to American Schools of Oriental Research.

One of these scrolls was identified as the BOOK OF ISAIAH, Written 2000 Years Ago, a 1000 Years Older than any known manuscript of any Hebrew Old Testament book. An AMAZING DISCOVERY!

It is a roll, written on parchment, about 24 feet long, made up of sheets about 10 by 15 inches, sewed together, in script of ancient Hebrew, with evidence that it was made in 2nd century B.C.

This, and the other scrolls, had, originally, been carefully sealed in earthenware jars. Evidently they were part of a Jewish library, which had been hidden in this isolated cave, in time of danger, perhaps in the Roman Conquest of Judea.

Essentially it is the same as the Book of Isaiah in our Bible, a voice from 2000 years ago, preserved in the wondrous Providence of God, confirming the integrity of our Bible. W. F. Albright calls it, "The greatest manuscript discovery of modern times." (*See 1948 and 1949 issues of Bulletins of the American Schools of Oriental Research and The Biblical Archaeologist.*)

The Grand Achievement of Isaiah's Life

Was the deliverance of Jerusalem from the Assyrians. It was through his prayer, and by his advice to king Hezekiah, and by the direct miraculous intervention of God, that the dread Assyrian army was discomfited before the walls of Jerusalem. (See chapters 36, 37.) Sennacherib, king of Assyria, though he lived 20 years after this, never again came against Jerusalem.

Contemporary Kings of Judah

Uzziah,	787–735 B.C.	A good king. Long and successful reign.
Jotham,	749–734 B.C.	Good. Mostly co-regent with Uzziah.
Ahaz,	741–726 B.C.	Very wicked. (See under II Chronicles 28.)
Hezekiah,	726–697 B.C.	A good king. (See under II Chronicles 29.)
Manasseh,	697–642 B.C.	Very wicked. (See under II Chronicles 33.)

Contemporary Kings of Israel

Jeroboam II, 790–749 B.C.	A long, prosperous, idolatrous reign.
Zechariah, 748.	Assassinated, Shallum (748).
Menahem, 748–738 B.C.	Extremely brutal.
Pekahiah, 738–736 B.C.	Assassinated by Pekah.
Pekah, 748–730 B.C.	Captivity of North Israel (734 B.C.).
Hoshea, 730–721 B.C.	Samaria fell (721 B.C.). End Northern Kingdom.

ARCHAEOLOGICAL NOTE: Sargon. In Isaiah 20:1 it is said: "Sargon king of Assyria sent Tartan and fought against Ashdod and took it."

This is the only known mention of Sargon's name in extant ancient literature. Thus mentioning the name of a king, never known to have existed, the critics said, was one of the Bible's blunders.

But, amazing to be told, in 1842, Botta discovered the ruins of the Sargon's palace, in Khorsabad, on the north edge of Nineveh, with treasures and inscriptions showing him to have been one of Assyria's greatest kings. Yet his name had disappeared from history, save this lone mention in Isaiah, till Botta's discovery.

In recent years the ruins of Sargon's palace have been excavated by the Oriental Institute. On the next page are reproductions of photographs of the ruins of Sargon's throne room, his throne, and the great stone bull which guarded his doorway.

From inscriptions it is learned that Shalmaneser died while besieging Samaria, and that he was succeeded by Sargon, who completed the capture. Furthermore, verifying the statement above quoted from Isaiah 20:1, an inscription of Sargon says: "Azuri, king of Ashdod, planned in his heart not to pay tribute. In my anger I marched against Ashdod with my usual bodyguard. I conquered Ashdod, and Gath. I took their treasures and their people. I settled in them people from the lands of the east. I took tribute from Philistia, Judah, Edom and Moab."

Chapter 1. Appalling Wickedness of Judah

This frightful indictment seems to belong to the middle period of Hezekiah's reign, after the Fall of the Northern Kingdom, when the Assyrians had invaded Judah and had carried away a large part of its population, Jerusalem alone being left (7–9). Hezekiah's reforms had barely scratched the surface of the rotten life of the people. The dread Assyrian tornado was drawing ever closer and closer. But it made no difference. On with the dance. The diseased nation, instead of cleansing itself, only gave more meticulous attention to the camouflage of devotion to religious services. Isaiah's scathing denunciation of their hypocritical religiosity (10–17), reminds us of Jesus' merciless condemnation of the Scribes and Pharisees (Matthew 23). The point is that it is of no avail for "Sodom" (10), to make a show of religion. Only genuine repentance and obedience would save them (16–23). Then Isaiah turns from the sickening picture to the day of Zion's purification and redemption, the wicked to be left to their own eternal burnings (24–31).

Chapters 2,3,4. A Pre-Vision of the Christian Age

These three chapters seem to be an expansion of the closing thought of chapter 1: the Future Glory of Zion, in contrast with Judgment on the Wicked. The allusion (2:6–9), to idols and foreign customs may locate this vision in the reign of Ahaz.

Zion to be the Center of World Civilization; in an era of Universal and Endless Peace (2:2–4). This passage of magnificent optimism was uttered at a time when Jerusalem was a veritable cesspool of filth. Whatever, whenever, wherever that happy age is to be, it will be the inheritance of God's people, with the wicked left out. (See further under 11:6–9.)

Coming Judgment for Idol Worshippers (2:5–22). Suffering and Captivity ahead for Judah (3:1–15); including the fashionable ladies

Fig. 50. Throne-room in Sargon's palace, excavated. Base of throne is seen at far end. At left is the central doorway.
(*Courtesy Oriental Institute, University of Chicago*)

Fig. 51. Great Winged Human-Headed Bull, carved out of stone, 16 feet high, stood at the doorway of Sargon's Palace.
(*Courtesy Oriental Institute, University of Chicago*)

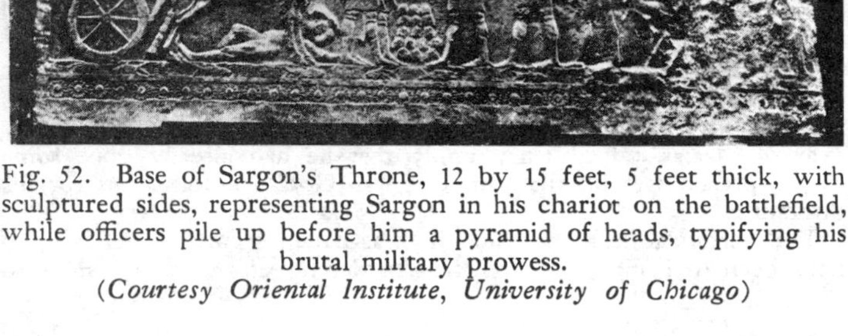

Fig. 52. Base of Sargon's Throne, 12 by 15 feet, 5 feet thick, with sculptured sides, representing Sargon in his chariot on the battlefield, while officers pile up before him a pyramid of heads, typifying his brutal military prowess.
(*Courtesy Oriental Institute, University of Chicago*)

of Jerusalem (3:16–26), like the ladies of luxury in Samaria (Amos 4:1–3). "Seven women to one man" (4:1), because the men will have been killed in war.

The Coming "Branch" (4:2–6). This is Isaiah's first mention of the Future Messiah. "THE BRANCH" reviving out of the stump of David's fallen family tree (11:1, 53:2, Jeremiah 23:5, 33:15, Zechariah 3:8, 6:12). HE would be the one to purge away the filth of Zion, and make her a blessing to the world.

Chapter 5. A Song of the Vineyard

A sort of funeral dirge. After centuries of most extraordinary care, God's vineyard, his nation, fruitless and disappointing, is now to be abandoned. Jesus' parable of the Vineyard (Matthew 21:33–45), seems to be an echo of this parable. The sins here specially denounced are Greed, Injustice, Drunkenness. The vast estates of the rich, accumulated by robbery of the poor, soon were to become waste land. "Gone into captivity" (13); like chapter 53, the future is so certain that it is spoken of as already past. Then, too, at that time, a large part of the nation already had gone into captivity. "Sin with a cart rope" (18); that is, excuse their depravity by scoffing at the idea that God would punish them. Invading Nations from far (25–30); Assyrians, in Isaiah's own time; Babylonians, who, a hundred years later, destroyed Jerusalem; Romans, who, A.D. 70, struck the death-blow to Jewish national existence.

"Bath" (10): that is, 9 gallons: "Homer," 11 bushels.

"Ephah" (10): 1 bushel: that is, the Harvest shall be much smaller than the Planting.

Chapter 6. Isaiah's Call

As to whether this vision antecedes the visions of the first five chapters there is difference of opinion. Dates mentioned in the book are in chronological sequence: 6:1 7:1 14:28 20:1 36:1. This indicates that the book follows a general chronological order, but not necessarily in all particulars. Isaiah, in later life, probably rearranged visions which he had written in various periods of his long ministry, being guided in part by sequence of thought, so that some chapters may antedate preceding chapters.

Also, opinion varies as to whether this was Isaiah's original call, or a summons to a special mission. The statement in 1:1 that some of his ministry was in the days of Uzziah, and that this call was in the year of Uzziah's death, may imply that he had already done some earlier preaching, and that this call was God's authorization for his utterances.

The particular task to which he was called seems, on its face, to have been to bring about the final hardening of the nation so as to insure its destruction (9–10). But, of course, God's purpose was not to harden the nation, but rather to bring it to repentance in order to save it from destruction. Isaiah's whole ministry, with its marvelous visions, climaxed with one of the most stupendous miracles of the ages, was, if we may so speak, as if God were frantically waving a red flag to halt the nation in its mad sweep toward the whirlpool. But when a nation sets itself against God even his wondrous mercies result only in further hardening.

"How long?" (11): that is, how long shall this hardening process go on? Answer: till the land be desolate, and the people gone (11–12). "Tenth" (13): a remnant shall be left, which, in its turn, shall be destroyed. This was uttered 735 B.C. Within a year North Israel was carried away by the Assyrians. Within 14 years all the rest of the Northern Kingdom had fallen (721 B.C.), and Judah (roughly, a "tenth," one tribe out of the twelve) alone was left. Another 100 years, and Judah was destroyed.

Chapter 7. The Child "Immanuel"

The occasion of this prophecy was the invasion of Judah by the kings of Syria and Israel. They attacked Judah separately (II Chronicles 28:5–6), then conjointly (II Kings 16:5). Their object was to displace Ahaz with another king (6). Ahaz appealed to the king of Assyria for help (II Kings 16:7). The king of Assyria responded with an invasion of Syria and North Israel, and carried their peoples away into captivity (II Kings 15:29; 16:9). This was the Galilee Captivity (734 B.C.).

In the early part of this Syro-Israelite attack on Jerusalem Isaiah ventured to assure Ahaz that the attack would fail, Syria and Israel be destroyed, and Judah be saved. The 65 years (8), is thought to cover the period from the first deportation of Israel (734 B.C.), to the settlement of foreigners in the land by Esar-haddon about 670 B.C. (II Kings 17:24, Ezra 4:2).

The "Virgin" and her son "Immanuel" (10–16). This is spoken of as a "sign" intended to give assurance to skeptical Ahaz of speedy deliverance. A "sign" is a miracle, wrought for evidential purposes. The "virgin" is not named, but the reference is to something very unusual, and not further explained, that was to happen forthwith in David's family (Ahaz' own household). It is a case of blending pictures in the near and far horizons, as is so frequent in the prophets. The Kingly character of the child is indicated in 8:8, and the context identifies him with the Wonderful Child of 9:6–7 who can be no other than the Future Messiah. It is so quoted in Matthew 1:23. Thus, as Isaiah was talking to Ahaz of signs in his own family, the House of David, God projects before his mind an image of one of the grander signs yet to occur in David's Family: the Virgin Birth of the Greater Son of David Himself.

Judah to be Desolated by Assyria (17–25); this same Assyria who was now helping Judah against Israel and Syria. It came to pass within Isaiah's lifetime, Jerusalem alone remaining.

Chapter 8. "Maher-shalal-hash-baz"

In connection with the Syro-Israel invasion of Judah, three children are mentioned: one in the family of David, "Immanuel" (7:13–14); and two in Isaiah's own family, "Shear-jashub" (7:3), and "Maher-shalal-hash-baz" (8:1–4).

"Shear-jashub" means "A remnant shall return." Isaiah, assuming, a hundred years before it came to pass, the Babylonian Captivity of Judah envisions a Rescued Remnant, and names his son for the idea. That Remnant, and its Glorious Future, is main theme of Isaiah's book.

"Maher-shalal-hash-baz" means "The spoil speeds, the prey hastens," that is, Syria and Israel shall speedily be despoiled. Thus naming his child for the idea of swift deliverance was Isaiah's way of emphasizing what he had already predicted in 7:4, 7, 16. It promptly occurred. The victorious Assyrians swept on into Judah (8), and were stopped by direct intervention of God (37:36).

Thus names of Isaiah's sons embodied ideas of his daily preaching: Present Deliverance, Coming Captivity, Future Glory.

The Distress and Gloom of the Captivity (9–22). Isaiah is bidden to write his prophecy, and preserve it for reference in the day of its fulfillment (16).

Chapter 9. The Wonderful Child

The setting for this sublime vision was the Fall of Israel, which Isaiah had just predicted in chapters 7 and 8. Zebulun and Naphtali (1), the Galilee region, was the first section to fall before the Assyrians (II Kings 15:29). But that same region would one day have the proud honor of giving to the world the Redeemer of Mankind, the King of the Ages. In 2:2–4 Isaiah had cast a glance at Zion's Future Universal Reign; in 4:2–6, at the King Himself (John 12:41); in 7:14 his Virgin-Birth is predicted; and here, in 9:6–7, in measured, majestic words, it is his Deity and Eternity of his Throne.

Samaria's Persistent Impenitence (9:8–10:4). Following his habit of sudden shiftings back and forth between his own times and the future, Isaiah abruptly turns his eyes toward Samaria. The most of Israel was carried away 734 B.C.; but Samaria held out till 721 B.C. These lines seem to belong to the 13 years intervening, when the people who were left, still persevered in their defiance both of God and the Assyrians. It is a poem of four stanzas, warning Samaria what is in store for them.

Chapter 10:5-34. The Advancing Assyrians

This was written after the Fall of Samaria (11), flinging defiance to the boastful Assyrians, as they marched on into Judah, up to the very gates of Jerusalem. The cities named in 28–32 were just north of Jerusalem. God had used the Assyrians to punish Israel, but here cautions them against over-estimating their power (15), and promises them a humiliating defeat (26), like that of the Midianites by Gideon (Judges 7:19–25), and that of the Egyptians in the Red Sea (Exodus 14). Sargon, one year after he had destroyed Samaria, turned southward, invaded Judah (720 B.C.), took certain Philistine cities, and defeated the Egyptian army. Again (713 B.C.), Sargon's army invaded Judah, Philistia, Edom and Moab. And again (701 B.C.), a vast army of Assyrians came into the land; at which time God made good his promise, and dealt the Assyrians such a sudden and violent blow that they came no more against Jerusalem (37:36).

Chapters 11,12. The "Branch" and His Kingdom

An expansion of 2:2–4, 4:2–6, 7:14, 9:1–7. Here, from predicting the overthrow of the Assyrian army, Isaiah again suddenly turns his eyes to the future, and gives us one of the most glorious pictures of the Coming World to be found in all Scripture. A Warless World, under the reign of a righteous and benevolent King of Davidic descent, formed of the redeemed of all nations together with the restored remnant of Judah. Whether this will ever be in our world of flesh and blood, or in an era beyond the veil, we do not know. But that it is to be is as sure as the morning. The subject is continued in 25:6. Chapter 12 is a song of praise for the day of glad triumph, which God put in Isaiah's mouth, one of the songs in the hymnbook of heaven, which we will all sing when we get there, where all discordant elements shall have disappeared.

Chapters 13,14:1-27. The Fall of Babylon

In Isaiah's time Assyria was the dominant power of the world. Babylon was a dependency of Assyria. Babylon rose to World-Power 606 B.C., and fell 536 B.C. Thus Isaiah sang of the Fall of Babylon a hundred years before its rise. Modern critics, therefore, opine that these cannot be the words of Isaiah, but of some later prophet. However, it is specifically stated that they are Isaiah's words (13:1).

The splendor to which Babylon rose a hundred years after Isaiah's day, as the Queen City of the Pre-Christian world, "the glory of kingdoms" (13:19), "the city of gold" (14:4), is here as clearly envisioned as if Isaiah had been right there. It is an astounding illumination of God's Spirit in Isaiah's mind. But the burden of the prophecy is the Fall of Babylon, pictured in detail that awes us into profound wonderment. Medes, who in Isaiah's day were an almost unknown people, are named as destroyers of Babylon (13:17–19).

The gist of the prophecy: Babylon shall supercede Assyria (14:25); Media shall supercede Babylon (13:17); and Babylon shall pass away forever (13:19–22, 14:22–23). For fulfillment of this astonishing prediction see under II Kings 25.

The point of special interest was that the Fall of Babylon would mean the release of the Captives (14:1–4). Within one year after Babylon fell, Cyrus, the Medo-Persian king, issued a decree for the Return of the Jews to their home-land (Ezra 1:1).

A hundred years after Isaiah, when Babylon had risen to power, and was demolishing Jerusalem, Jeremiah takes up Isaiah's cry for vengeance (see Jeremiah 50, 51).

Babylon, oppressor of the Jews, was counterpart and pattern of a New Testament Power which would enslave the Church (Revelation 17 to 19).

Chapter 14:28-32. Philistia

"Palestina" A.V., but in R.V. "Philistia" (from which the name "Palestine" is derived). The "serpent" (29), probably means Tiglath-pileser, who had taken certain Philistine cities, and who had died just a year ahead of Ahaz (28). The more poisonous serpent and his issue probably were Sargon and Sennacherib, who completed the desolation of Philistia. "Messengers" (32), probably were Philistine ambassadors asking Jerusalem for help against the Assyrians. Other denunciations of the Philistines are found in Jeremiah 47, Amos 1:6–8, Zephaniah 2:4–7, Zechariah 9:5–7.

Chapters 15,16. Moab

Moab was a rolling plateau of rich pasture lands lying east of the Dead Sea. Moabites were descendants of Lot (Genesis 19:37), and thus a kindred nation to the Jews. This was one of Isaiah's earlier predictions, now reiterated with a time limit of 3 years (16:14). The cities named were pillaged by Tiglath-pileser (734 B.C.); by Sargon (713 B.C.); and by Sennacherib (701 B.C.). It is not indicated to which of these Isaiah refers. However, Isaiah advises them that it would be to their advantage to renew their allegiance to the House of David (16:1–5), in the mention of which there comes into his vision an image of the Future Messiah (5). The Moabites had had a hand in the founding of the House of David in the person of Ruth. (For other prophecies about Moab see Jeremiah 48, Amos 2:1–3, Zephaniah 2:8–11.)

Chapter 17. Damascus

A continuation of the thought of chapter 7, probably written about the same time, during the Syro-Israelite attack on Judah (734 B.C.), and fulfilled shortly thereafter in the invasions of Tiglath-pileser and Sargon. It is directed against Israel also (3–4), because they were in alliance with Damascus. "Look to their Maker" (7): that the remnant left in the Northern Kingdom returned to Jehovah is indicated in II Chronicles 34:9. Closes with a vision of the overthrow of the Assyrians, following their victory over Syria and Israel (12–14), specially 14, which seems like a definite reference to 37:36.

Chapter 18. Ethiopia

Ethiopia was South Egypt, whose powerful king at that time had sway over all Egypt. This is not a prophecy of doom; but seems rather to refer to the excitement and call to arms among the Ethiopians at the advance of Sennacherib's army into Judah, whose fall would leave open the gateway for the Assyrian march on into Egypt (1–3); the miraculous deliverance of Jerusalem (4–6, 37:36); and Ethiopia's message of gratitude for the destruction of the Assyrian army (7, II Chronicles 32:23).

Chapter 19. Egypt

A Period of Anarchy and Internal Strife (1–4). This actually began about the time of Isaiah's death. "Cruel lord" (4); Esar-haddon, shortly after Isaiah's death, subdued Egypt, and split it into a number of petty governments, whose main duty was to "slay, plunder and spoil" their subjects.

Decline and Disintegration of Egypt Predicted (5–17). This all came to pass. (See Jeremiah 46, Ezekiel 29.)

Permeation of Egypt and Assyria with the Religion of Judah (18–25). After the Captivity many Jews remained in the Euphrates valley, and great numbers of them settled in Egypt. Alexandria, second city of the world in Jesus' day, was predominantly a Jewish city. There the Septuagint translation of the Old Testament was made. At Heliopolis, city of "the sun," a temple, modeled after that in Jerusalem, was erected (149 B.C.), as a center of worship for Egyptian Jews. At the time of Christ's appearance the Hebrew nation was composed of three main sections, with connecting highways (23): Palestinian, Egyptian and Mesopotamian: making Israel to be a sort of three-fold nation (24). These regions were among the first to accept Christianity. Thus this chapter is a very accurate pre-charting of one phase of Israel's history for the following six hundred years.

Chapter 20. Egypt and Ethiopia

Isaiah's warning of their defeat and captivity, intended to discourage Judah from looking to Egypt for aid against Assyria. This was 713 B.C. The prediction was fulfilled 12 years later. Sennacherib's annals for 701 B.C. says: "I fought with the kings of Egypt, accomplished their overthrow, and captured alive charioteers and sons of the king." Esar-haddon further desolated Egypt (see under 19:1–4). "Sargon" (1): this is the only known mention of Sargon's name, till archaeological excavations of the past century revealed him as one of the greatest of Assyrian monarchs (see page 287). "Tartan" (1:) this was not the name of a person, but an official title, equivalent to "commander-in-chief."

Chapter 21. Babylon, Edom, Arabia

Babylon (1–10), surrounded by a vast system of dykes and canals, was like a city in the sea. This is a graphic announcement of its fall. The mention of Elam and Media (2), point to its capture by Cyrus (536 B.C. See further under chapters 13, 14).

Dumah (11–12), was the name of a district south of Edom, and is here used for Edom, of which Seir was the central district.

Arabia (13–17), was the desert between Edom and Babylon. Dedan, Tema, and Kedar were leading Arabian tribes. This is a prediction that they will experience a terrific blow within a year. Sargon invaded Arabia 716 B.C.

Chapter 22. Jerusalem

Called "Valley of Vision," because the hill on which it was situated was surrounded by valleys, with higher hills beyond, and was the place where God revealed Himself. It is rebuked for giving itself to reckless indulgence while besieged by the Assyrian army. Their defense (9–11, II Chronicles 32:3–5) included everything except turning to God.

Demotion of Shebna (15–25). He, as officer of the House of David, may have been leader in the city's frivolous conduct in face of grave danger. In the elevation of Eliakim to the office there may be hints of Messianic implication (22–25).

Chapter 23. Tyre

Tyre had been for centuries the maritime center of the world's commerce. It had planted colonies ali around the Mediterranean. The grain of Egypt was one of the principal commodities in which it traded. It suffered terribly at the hands of the Assyrians, who had recently extended their sway over Babylon (13). Its overthrow, depression for 70 years, and restoration, are here predicted (14–18). This is thought to refer to its subjugation by Nebuchadnezzar. (See further under Ezekiel 26 to 28.)

Chapter 24. World Convulsions

This vision seems to relate to the same period that Jesus spoke of in Matthew 24. It delineates the fearful calamities under which the earth, with all its castes, occupations, and social distinctions, shall pass away. As Jeremiah said of Babylon that it would "sink and not rise" (Jeremiah 51:64), so here says Isaiah of the earth (20). Later he looks beyond to a "new heavens and new earth" (65:17–66:24.)

Chapter 25. The Abolition of Death

Here Isaiah has transported himself beyond the crash of worlds, into the age of the new heavens and new earth, and put into the mouth of the redeemed a song of praise to God for his wonderful works. Most wonderful of all is the Destruction of Death (8), "in this mountain" (6), of Jerusalem. This cannot refer to anything else than the Resurrection of Jesus from the Dead, the one and only thing that has nullified death and brought to mankind the guarantee of Eternal Life; the "feast of rich wines for all peoples" (6); the joy-shout of the ages; the event that "wipes away tears from off all faces." The mention of Moab in this connection (10), illustrates Isaiah's mental habit of abrupt transition back and forth between future glory and present local circumstance. The fate of Moab, constant rival and recurrent enemy of Judah, may be used here as typical of the fate of Zion's enemies generally.

Chapter 26. A Song of Trust and Triumph

A continuation of the song of the preceding chapter. "Strong city" (1), central rendezvous of God's people. "Lofty city" (5), idealized stronghold of the wicked. Verse 3 is a grand verse. The grandest verse in the chapter is 19: the Resurrection. In 25:8 it was the Resurrection of Christ. Here it is the General Resurrection of God's People. "Disclose her blood" (21): in Day of Judgment, when man's long reign of wickedness shall be ended.

Chapter 27. Revival of God's Vineyard

In 5:1–7 Isaiah sang the funeral dirge of God's Vineyard. Here it is a joy-song of the Vineyard coming to life again. What a beautiful figure of Christianity blossoming out of the remnant of desolated Judah and spreading its benign influences over the whole earth! "Leviathan," "serpent," "dragon" (1): possibly meaning Assyria,

Babylon, Egypt: or names of powers of evil. Corrective Judgments on Judah (7–11). Final Gathering of Israel into the Church Triumphant (12–13).

"In That Day" (1, 2, 12, 13). Notice how often the phrase is used in Isaiah: 4:2; 7:20, 23; 11:10,11; 12:1; 14:3; 17:4, 7, 9; 19:16, 18, 19, 23, 24; 22:12; 26:1; 28:5; 29:18; 30:23 etc. We might almost call "That Day" the subject of the book; all mixed up with references to Isaiah's own day.

Chapter 28. Denunciation of Samaria and Jerusalem

Back from visions of "that day," Isaiah sternly warns his own people, who were given over to sensual indulgence, of impending calamity, as in chapter 22. This evidently was before the Fall of Samaria 721 B.C. "Glorious beauty" (1): Samaria, capital of the North Kingdom, was situated on a well-rounded hill, in a rich and beautiful valley, crowned with luxurious palaces and gardens. "Strong one" (2): the Assyrian power, which, after a 3-year siege, took Samaria, but which was turned back "at the gate" of Jerusalem (6). The scoffing revelers called Isaiah's warnings childish (9–10). Isaiah's reply (11–13): they will find Assyrian bondage as monotonous as his warnings. Sneering rulers of Jerusalem (14–22); Hezekiah was a good king, but many of the powerful nobles in his government, scorning both Isaiah and Jehovah, were relying on their own power and Egypt. "Covenant with death" (15): their scornful boast of security. "Corner-stone" (16): God's promise to David, on which they should have relied. "Strange Act" (21): God's punishment of His own people by the sword of foreigners. Comfort to the Faithful (23–29): the import of these words seems to be that God's people need varied and seasonable treatment adapted to their condition.

Chapter 29. The Imminent Siege of Jerusalem

"Ariel" (1): a name for Jerusalem, meaning "The Lion of God," defiantly holding the Assyrian army at bay. The besieging army, composed of soldiers of many nations, to be suddenly overwhelmed (5–8), which shortly came to pass (37:36). Zion's blindness to her God, even though rendering lip service (9–16), while substituting commandments of men for the Word of God. Jesus quoted this as applicable to the Pharisees of his day. "Marvelous work" (14), the miraculous deliverance of Jerusalem (37:36). Field and Forest to Change Places (17–24); this difficult language may be a hint of the day when Gentiles would be grafted in with the people of God (Romans 11).

Chapter 30. Judah's Dependence on Egypt

Caravans laden with rich presents from Jerusalem make their way through the beast-infested desert of the south, to seek the aid of Egypt (6–7). Captivity of Judah (8–17). Egypt would be of no avail. Judah shall be broken. Write it down in a book, so that future generations may see that it was foretold. It came to pass 100 years later, at the hands of Babylon. Very shortly the Assyrian army was routed (37:36); and within 100 years the Assyrian Empire destroyed.

Chapter 31. God's Promise of Deliverance

Isaiah asserts his confidence in the triumphant outcome of Zion's Assyrian crisis (37:36), which coming event seems to be the background of almost every verse in this chapter.

Chapter 32. Messiah's Reign

As Isaiah is thinking of the joyous aftermath of Zion's deliverance from the Assyrian army, and the consequent vastly increased prestige of Hezekiah's kingdom, there comes in the distant line of his vision a picture of David's Future King, to whom all Old Testament prophecy pointed, and toward whom all Old Testament history moved, under whose righteous and blessed Reign persons and things will stand in their true light and be called by right names. It is difficult to see the connection in the digressive address to "careless women" (9–15). There must have been a group of influential godless women in the court who had set themselves against everything that Isaiah stood for (3:12, 16–26). His meaning here seems to be that a period of trouble is to intervene between the defeat of the Assyrian army and the Reign of the Messiah. The "forest" (19): Assyrian army. The "city" (19): Nineveh; or, the centralized forces of evil in the latter days. "Sow beside all waters" (20): patient continuance in paths of daily duty, as an expression of Trust in God, while waiting for the happy era of restored prosperity.

Chapter 33. Just Before the Battle

Chapters 28 to 33 belong to the terrifying days of the Assyrian siege of Jerusalem, as told in 36 and 37. Sennacherib's army was pillaging cities and ravaging the countryside (8–9). The people were panic-stricken (13–14). Through it all Isaiah goes about calmly assuring the people that God will smite the enemy with terror, and they shall flee leaving vast loot (3–4); God himself protecting Jerusalem like an encircling stream on which the enemy's disintegrating ships go down (21–23. See chapters 36, 37.)

Chapter 34. God's Wrath on the Nations

Like chapter 24, this chapter seems to be a vision of the End-Time.

Edom is used as a typical specimen of God's wrath. Once populous and fertile, it is now one of the most desolate lands on earth, inhabited mainly by noxious beasts, birds and reptiles (10–15. See under Obadiah, 16, 17): Isaiah's challenge to future ages to note his words about Edom.

Chapter 35. The Day of the Church Triumphant

One of the choicest chapters in the Bible. A poem of rare and superb beauty. A picture of the Last Times, when the Church, after long affliction, finally shines forth in all the radiance of its heavenly glory. Returning captives journeying along the highway (8–10), is a most exquisite representation of the redeemed traveling home to God.

Chapters 36,37. The Assyrian Army Overthrown

This is recorded three times: (here, II Kings 18, 19, and II Chronicles 32): one of the most astounding miracles of the Old Testament; in one night the Assyrian army is destroyed by a direct stroke from heaven (37:36). The grand climax of which Isaiah had given repeated assurance: (10:24–34; 17:12–14; 29:5–8, 14; 30:27–33; 31:4–9; 33:3–4, 21–23; 38:6). These passages seem to be a blended account of two invasions. Sennacherib, as leader of his father Sargon's armies, invaded Judah (713 B.C.), and took many cities. Hezekiah bought him off (II Kings 18:14–16). He came again (701 B.C.); at which time the Angel smote him. (See under II Kings 17.)

Chapters 38,39. Hezekiah's Sickness. Babylon's Heralds

Hezekiah's sickness was 15 years before his death (38:5), that is, 712 B.C. Deliverance from Assyria was still future (38:6). Hezekiah's miraculous recovery had excited interest in Babylon (II Chronicles 32:31; Isaiah 38:7–8). Babylon's embassy to Jerusalem, no doubt, looked suspicious to Sennacherib, and may have hastened his second invasion.

Chapters 40-66. Magnificent Rhapsodies of the Future

Isaiah spent his life under menace of the dread Assyrian Empire. The Assyrians had destroyed North Israel (734 B.C.); the rest of the Northern Kingdom (721 B.C.); had invaded Judah (713 B.C.); and by 701 B.C. had taken all Judah except Jerusalem. Through these years Isaiah had steadfastly predicted that Jerusalem would stand. It did stand. This was the grand achievement of Isaiah's life. He had saved his city when doom seemed certain. But now, the Assyrian crisis past, Isaiah, having prophesied that Jerusalem would later fall to Babylon (39:6–7), assumes the Babylon Captivity as an accomplished fact, and, in his mind's eye, takes his stand with the captives. So clear were some of his visions that in them he speaks of the future as already past.

Two Isaiah's?

Nowhere in the book itself, or in the Bible, or in Jewish or Christian tradition, is there mention, or even a hint, of two authors. A "second Isaiah" is a figment of modern criticism. The book of Isaiah, in our Bible, and in Jesus' day, was ONE book, not Two. It is not a patchwork, but, from beginning to end, it is characterized by a UNITY of thought, set forth in the sublimest of language, that makes it one of the grandest things ever written. There was just one Isaiah, and this is his book, the critics to the contrary notwithstanding.

Chapter 40. Voices of Comfort

Some of the sentences seem to be utterances of angels, crying to Isaiah, or to each other, in exultation over the wondrous things in store for God's people when the long night of affliction is past. The Advent of Christ is the subject of 1–11. Verses 3–5 are quoted in all four Gospels as referring to His arrival in the earth (Matthew 3:3; Mark 1:3; Luke 3:4–6; John 1:23). Mention, in this connection, of God's Word as eternally impregnable (6–8), means that God's prophetic promises cannot fail; Christ and Heaven are SURE. The Infinite Power of God, and the Eternal Youth of those who trust him, form the subject matter of 12–31. It is a grand chapter.

Chapter 41. The Rise of Cyrus

Cyrus is not here named, but is named in 44:28 and 45:1, and unmistakably is the "one from the east" (2), and the "one from the north" (25), (armies from the east always entered Palestine from the north). Isaiah died 150 years before the days of Cyrus; yet here is given a vision of his rapid conquest of the world, which is ascribed to the Providence of God (4). God promises protection for Israel (8–20); and then challenges the gods of the nations to show their ability to predict the future (21–29. See further under chapter 44).

Chapter 42. The Servant of the Lord

Another vision of the Coming Messiah and his work (1–17). It is so quoted in Matthew 12:17–21. But in verses 18–25 the Lord's servant is Israel the nation, who had to be chastised over and over for their perverseness.

Chapter 43. God's Care of Israel

God had formed the nation for Himself. The nation had been unceasingly disobedient. Still they were God's nation, and through all their sins and sufferings God would work to demonstrate to all the world that He, and He alone, is God.

Chapters 44,45. Cyrus

These two chapters are a forecast of Israel's Return from the Captivity under Cyrus, with special emphasis on God's unique power to PREDICT the future. Cyrus, king of Persia, reigned 538–529 B.C. He permitted the Jews to return to Jerusalem, and issued a decree authorizing the rebuilding of the Temple (II Chronicles 36:22–23; Ezra 1:1–4). Isaiah prophesied 745–695 B.C., over 150 years before the days of Cyrus. Yet he calls him by name, and predicts that he would rebuild the Temple, which in Isaiah's day had not yet fallen.

The main point of these two chapters is that God's superiority over idols is proved by his ability to Foretell the Future, an idea that recurs all through chapters 40 to 48 (41:21–24; 42:8–9; 43:9–13; 44:6–8; 45:20–21; 46:9–11; 48:3–7). The calling of Cyrus by name long before he was born is given as an example of God's power to "declare things yet to come" (45:4–6). If this is not a PREDICTION it does not even make sense in the connection in which it is used. Critics who assign these chapters to post-exilic authorship have strange ideas of contextual unity.

That Predictive Prophecy is an evidence of Deity was one of Isaiah's foremost theses. He was very fond of ridiculing idols and idol-worshippers, saying, These gods that the nations worship cannot even do what men can do, cannot see, nor speak, nor hear. But, says Isaiah, Our God whom we worship in our Hebrew nation, not only can do what men can do, but He can do some things that men cannot do: He can Foretell things to come. Then Isaiah invites a conference of nations, for comparison of gods, and asks if any nation has in its literature predictions from of old of things that afterward came to pass. We have, says he, in our national annals, from of old, a continuous stream of predictions of things that were afterward continually coming to pass. The author of this Handbook would like to ask the same question now: Is there, anywhere, in the literature of the whole wide world, predictions from of old of the whole unfolding story of man's religious history—anywhere except in the BIBLE?

Chapters 46,47,48. The Fall of Babylon

A continuation of chapters 13, 14. Babylon's multitude of idols, sorcerers, and enchanters would be of no avail against the armies of Cyrus (47:12–15). Instead, the golden images of her boasted gods, helpless to save, not only their city, but even themselves, would be hauled away as loot on beasts and in wagons (46:1–2). Reiteration of God's exclusive and unique power to predict and control the course of history. It is a solemn re-prediction of the Fall of Babylon at the hands of Cyrus, and the Jews' Deliverance. "He whom God loves" (48:14), that is, Cyrus, who was a singularly noble and just monarch.

Chapters 49,50. The Servant of Jehovah

In preceding chapters 40–48 a leading idea is: God's Predictions of the Future as evidence of His Deity.

In chapters 49–55 the thoughts revolve around The Servant of God. In some passages the Servant seems to be Israel the Nation, and in other passages, the Messiah, the ONE in whom Israel would be Personified. And the passages are pretty well blended, the context itself indicating which is meant.

It is a resumption of thoughts that have been accumulating (41:8; 42:1, 19; 43:10; 44:1, 2, 21; 49:3–6; 52:13; 53:11).

These chapters seem to be a sort of soliloquy of the Servant, with interspersed replies from God, having to do mainly with his work of bringing all nations to God.

Chapters 51,52. Zion's Redemption and Restoration

Israel's release from sufferings of the Captivity is as certain as God's wondrous works of the past. It is a part of God's eternal plan, building from one pair (51:2), through the ages, a redeemed world of endless glory (51:6). Chapter 52 is a song of the day of Zion's triumph.

Chapter 53. Jehovah's Servant a Man of Sorrows

One of the best loved chapters in all the Bible. A picture of the Suffering Savior. It begins at 52:13. So vivid in detail that one would almost think of Isaiah as standing at the foot of the cross. So clear in his mind that he speaks of it in the past tense, as if it had already come to pass. Yet it was written seven centuries before Calvary. It cannot possibly fit any person in history other than Christ.

Chapters 54,55. Zion's Vast Expansion

The Servant of God by virtue of his Suffering, would rejuvenate Zion, and lead her onward and upward to heights of endless glory. Chapter 55 is the Servant invitation to all the world to enter his kingdom and share his blessings.

Chapters 56,57,58,59. Sins of Isaiah's Day

Profaning the Sabbath; Gluttony of Israel's leaders; prevalence of Idolatry, with its vile practices; punctilious in fasting, yet practicing flagrant injustice; all to be surely avenged.

Chapters 60,61,62. Zion's Redeemer

A Song of the Messianic Age, beginning at 59:20, picturing an era of World Evangelization, blending into the Eternal Glory of Heaven. Chapter 60 is one of the grandest chapters of the Bible. Jesus quoted 61:1–3 as referring to himself (Luke 4:18). Zion's "New Name" (62:2): it is repeated in 65:15 that God's servants would be called by "Another Name." Up to the coming of Christ, God's people were known as "Jews," or "Hebrews." After that, they were called "Christians." "A Crown of Beauty" (62:3): that is what the Church is to God. Though the Visible Church has been corrupted at the hands of men, and has been anything but a "crown of beauty," yet it is true of the body of God's faithful saints. Throughout eternity they will be God's delight and joy (3–5).

Chapters 63,64. The Exiles' Prayer

It is a bit puzzling to see the reason for the mention of Edom at this place (63:1–6). These two chapters, except the first 6 verses, are of the nature of a prayer to God to liberate Captive Israel. Edomites, age-old enemies of Judah, had associated themselves with the Babylonians in destroying Jerusalem (see under Obadiah), and may here be meant to symbolize all the enemies of God's people. The blood-stained Warrior, "treading down" Edom in his wrath, "mighty to save" Zion, is identical with Zion's Redeemer of the preceding three chapters. The language seems to be the basis of the imagery of the Lord's Coming in Revelation 19:11–16.

Chapters 65,66. The New Heavens and New Earth

These two chapters are God's answer to the Exiles' Prayer of the previous two chapters. The prayer shall be answered. The faithful remnant shall be restored (65:8–10). New nations shall be brought into the fold (65:1; 66:8). All shall be called a New Name (65:15). They shall inherit a New Heavens and New Earth (65:17; 66:22). The faithful and the disobedient shall be forever separated, Eternal Blessedness for one, Eternal Punishment for the other (66:22–24). Jesus himself endorsed these words (Mark 9:48). Peter's closing message to Christians was to keep their eyes on the New Heavens and New Earth (II Peter 3:10–14). The Bible reaches its final climax in a magnificent vision of the New Heavens and New Earth (Revelation 21, 22); which vision is an expansion of Isaiah 66. No temple or sacrifice, it seems, will be needed in the new order (66:1–4; Revelation 21:22).

Summary of Isaiah's Predictions

Fulfilled in His Own Lifetime

Judah to be delivered from Syria and Israel (7:4–7, 16).
Syria and Israel to be destroyed by Assyria (8:4; 17:1–14).
Assyria to invade Judah (8:7–8).
Philistines to be subjugated (14:28–32).
Moab to be plundered (15 and 16).
Egypt and Ethiopia to be conquered by Assyria (20:4).
Arabia to be pillaged (21:13–17).
Tyre to be subdued (23:1–12).
Jerusalem to be delivered from Assyria (see under 36).
Hezekiah's life to be extended 15 years (38:5).

Fulfilled after Isaiah's Time

Babylonian Captivity (39:5–7).
Babylon to be overthrown by Cyrus (46:11).
And the Medes and Elamites (13:17; 21:2; 48:14).
Babylon's perpetual desolation (13:20–22).
Cyrus called by name (44:28; 45:1, 4).
Cyrus' conquest of the world (41:2–3).
Cyrus to liberate the captives (45:13).
Cyrus to rebuild Jerusalem (44:28; 45:13).
Israel to be restored (27:12–13; 48:20; 51:14).
Israel's religion to permeate Egypt and Assyria (19:18–25).
Israel's religion to spread over the whole world (27:2–6).
Tyre's captivity and restoration (23:13–18).
Edom's perpetual desolation (34:5–17).

About the Messiah

His Advent (40:3–5).
His Virgin Birth (7:14).
Galilee to be the scene of his ministry (9:1–2).
His Deity and Eternity of his throne (9:6–7).
His Sufferings (53).
To die with the wicked (53:9).
To be buried with the rich (53:9).
Might and gentleness of his reign (40:10–11).
Righteousness and beneficence of his reign (32:1–8; 61:1–3).
His justice and kindness (42:3–4, 7).
His rule over Gentiles (2:2–3; 42:1, 6; 49:6; 55:4–5; 56:6; 60:3–5).

His vast influence (49:7, 23).
Idols to disappear (2:18).
A warless world to be brought into being (2:4; 65:25).
The earth to be destroyed (24; 26:21; 34:1–4).
Death to be destroyed (25:8; 26:19).
God's people to be called by a New Name (62:2; 65:15).
A New Heaven and New Earth to be created (65:17; 66:22).
Righteous and wicked to be eternally separated (66:15, 22–24).

JEREMIAH

God's Final Effort to Save Jerusalem

Jeremiah lived about a hundred years after Isaiah.
Isaiah had saved Jerusalem from Assyria.
Jeremiah tried to save it from Babylon, but failed.

Jeremiah was called to the prophetic office (626 B.C.), Jerusalem was partly destroyed (606); further devastated (597); finally burned and desolated (586). Jeremiah lived through these terrible forty years, "the close of the monarchy," "the death agony of the nation"; a pathetic, lonely figure, God's last measure to the Holy City which had become hopelessly and fanatically attached to Idols; carelessly crying that if they would repent God would save them from Babylon.

Thus, as Assyria had been the background of Isaiah's ministry, so Babylon was the background of Jeremiah's ministry.

The Internal Situation

The Northern Kingdom had fallen, and much of Judah. They had suffered reverse after reverse, till Jerusalem alone was left. Still they ignored the continued warnings of the prophets, and grew harder and harder in their Idolatry and Wickedness. The hour of doom was about to strike.

The International Situation

A three-cornered contest for world supremacy was on: Assyria, Babylon and Egypt. For 300 years Assyria, the North Euphrates valley, Nineveh its capital, had ruled the world; but now was growing weak. Babylon, in the South Euphrates valley, was becoming powerful. Egypt, in the Nile valley, which 1000 years before had been a world-power, and had declined, was again becoming ambitious. Babylon won, about the middle of Jeremiah's ministry. It broke the power of Assyria (607 B.C.); and 2 years later crushed Egypt, in the battle of Carchemish (605 B.C.); and for 70 years ruled the world, same 70 years as Jews' Captivity.

Jeremiah's Message

From the outset, 20 years before the issue was settled, Jeremiah unceasingly insisted that Babylon would be the victor. All through his incessant and bitter complaints over Judah's wickedness these ideas are ever recurring:

1. Judah is going to be destroyed by victorious Babylon.
2. If Judah will turn from her wickedness, somehow God will save her from destruction at the hands of Babylon.
3. Later, when there seemed no longer any hope of Judah's repentance: if, only as a matter of political expedience, Judah will submit to Babylon, she shall be spared.
4. Judah, destroyed, shall recover, and yet dominate the world.
5. Babylon, destroyer of Judah, shall herself be destroyed, never to rise again.

Jeremiah's Boldness

Jeremiah unceasingly advised Jerusalem to surrender to the king of Babylon, so much that his enemies accused him of being a traitor. Nebuchadnezzar rewarded him for thus advising his people, not only by sparing his life, but by offering him any honor that he would accept, even a worthy place in the Babylonian court (39:12). Yet Jeremiah cried aloud, over and over, that the king of Babylon was committing a heinous crime in destroying the Lord's people, and for that, Babylon, in time, would be desolated, and lie forever so (see chapters 50, 51).

Contemporary Kings of Judah

Manasseh (697–642 B.C.). 55 years. Very wicked (see under II Chronicles 33). In his reign Jeremiah was born.

Amon (641–640 B.C.). 2 years. The long and wicked reign of his father Manasseh had sealed the doom of Judah.

Josiah (639–608 B.C.). 31 years. A good king. A great reformation. Jeremiah began his ministry in Josiah's 13th year. The reformation was only outward. At heart the people were still Idolaters.

Jehoahaz (608 B.C.). 3 months. Was carried to Egypt.

Jehoiakim (608–597 B.C.). 11 years. Openly for Idols, boldly defiant of God, a bitter enemy of Jeremiah.

Jehoiachin (597 B.C.). 3 months. Was carried to Babylon.

Zedekiah (597–586 B.C.). 11 years. Rather friendly to Jeremiah, but a weak king, a tool in the hands of the wicked princes.

Chronology of Jeremiah's Times

627 B.C. Josiah began his reforms. (See under II Chronicles 34.)
626 B.C. Jeremiah's Call.
626 B.C. Scythian Invasion. (See under Jeremiah 4.)

621 B.C. Book found. Josiah's Great Reformation. (II Kings 22, 23.)
608 B.C. Josiah slain at Megiddo, by Pharaoh.
607 B.C. Nineveh destroyed by Babylon. (Or 612 B.C.?)
606 B.C. Judah subdued by Babylon. First Captivity.
605 B.C. Battle of Carchemish: Babylon crushed Egypt.
597 B.C. Jehoiachin's Captivity.
593 B.C. Zedekiah's Visit to Babylon.
586 B.C. Jerusalem Burned. Temporary End of David's Kingdom.

Contemporary Prophets

Jeremiah was leader in the brilliant constellation of prophets clustered around the destruction of Jerusalem.

Ezekiel, a fellow priest, somewhat younger than Jeremiah, preaching in Babylon, among the captives, the same things that Jeremiah was preaching in Jerusalem.

Daniel, a man of royal blood, holding the line in the palace of Nebuchadnezzar.

Habakkuk and Zephaniah helping Jeremiah in Jerusalem.

Nahum, at same time, predicting the Fall of Nineveh.

Obadiah, at same time, predicting the Ruin of Edom.

Chronology of Jeremiah's Book

Some of Jeremiah's messages are dated. Some are not. Time notices which are indicated are: In Josiah's reign: 1:2; 3:6. In Jehoiakim's reign: 22:18; 25:1; 26:1; 35:1; 36:1; 45:1. In Zedekiah's reign: 21:1; 24:1, 8; 27:3, 12; 28:1; 29:3; 32:1; 34:2; 37:1; 38:5; 39:1; 49:34; 51:59. In Egypt: 43:7, 8; 44:1. Thus it will be seen that the book is not arranged in chronological order. Some late messages come early in the book, and some early messages come late in the book. These messages were delivered orally, and perhaps repeatedly, for years, possibly, before Jeremiah began to write them. The writing of such a book was a long and laborious task. Writing parchment, made of sheep or goat skins, was scarce and expensive. It was made into a long roll, and wound around a stick. This may, in part, account for the lack of order in Jeremiah's book. After writing an incident or discourse, some other utterance delivered previously would be suggested, and he would write it down, in some cases without dating it, thus filling up the parchment as he unrolled it.

Chapter 1. The Call of Jeremiah

It was to a hard and thankless task. Like Moses (Exodus 3:11; 4:10), he was reluctant to accept the responsibility. It came when he was only a "child," probably about 20. "Anathoth" (1), his home, was about 2½ miles northeast of Jerusalem. It is now called "Anata." The "boiling caldron" (13), meant the Babylonian army. Opening utterance: Destruction by Babylon (14).

Chapter 2. Israel's Apostasy

In a pathetic and impassioned rebuke for their shameless Idolatry, Israel is likened to an espoused wife who has forsaken her husband for promiscuous association with men, making of herself a common prostitute.

Chapter 3. Judah Worse than Israel

In chapter 2 "Israel" means the whole nation. In this chapter it means the Northern Kingdom, which 300 years before had split off from Judah, and 100 years before had been carried away captive by the Assyrians. Judah, blind to the significance of Israel's fall, not only did not repent, but under the wicked reign of Manasseh sunk to lower and lower depths of depravity. The re-union of Judah and Israel is predicted (17–18; also 50:4–5; Hosea 1:11). Metaphor of an Adulterous Wife (20).

Chapter 4. Approaching Desolation of Judah

This chapter describes the advance of the devastating Babylonian armies which destroyed Jerusalem (606–586 B.C.). It may also, in part, refer to the Scythian invasion, which shortly preceded that of the Babylonians.

The Scythian Invasion

The very same year in which Jeremiah was called (626 B.C.), immense swarms of Barbarians from the North struck terror to the nations of Southwest Asia. They dealt a terrific blow to the tottering Assyrian power. Rawlinson thus speaks of them: "Pouring through the passes of the Caucasus—whence coming or what intending none knew—horde after horde of the Scythians blackened the rich plains of the south. On they came like a flight of locusts, countless, irresistible, finding the land before them like a garden, leaving behind them a howling wilderness. Neither age nor sex would be spared. The inhabitants would be ruthlessly massacred by the invaders, or at best, forced to become slaves. The crops would be consumed, the herds swept off or destroyed, the villages or homesteads burned, the whole country made a scene of desolation." Their ravages resembled those of the Huns.

Chapter 5. Universal Depravity of Judah

Not one righteous man (1), promiscuous sexual indulgence, even among the married, like animals (7–8); scoffing at the prophet's warning (12); wholly given to deceit, oppression, and robbery (26–28); satisfied with rottenness in the government (30–31. For note on False Prophets [30], see under chapter 23.)

Chapter 6. Destruction from the North

A vivid prophetic description of the destruction of Jerusalem at the hands of Babylonian invaders (22–26), which later came to pass within Jeremiah's own lifetime. Over and over (16–19), he warns, with pathetic insistence, that Repentance would be their last possible chance to escape ruin.

Chapter 7. Repentance their Only Hope

This is one of Jeremiah's heart-rending appeals for repentance, based on God's amazing promise that if only the people would hearken to their God Jerusalem would never fall (5–7). With all their abominable practices (9, 31), and even though they had erected idols in the Temple (30), yet they had a superstitious regard for the Temple and its services, and seemed to think that, come what may, God would not let Jerusalem be destroyed because his Temple was there (4, 10). "Queen of heaven" (18), Ashtoreth, principal female Canaanite deity, whose worship was accompanied with the most degrading forms of immorality. "Hinnom" (31–32), the valley on the south side of Jerusalem, where children were burnt in sacrifice to Molech, afterward came to be used as the name of hell, "Gehenna."

Chapter 8. "The Harvest is Past"

Fully conscious of the futility of his appeals and rebukes, Jeremiah speaks of the impending desolation of Judah as if it were already accomplished (20). False prophets (10–11): their insistence that Jerusalem was in no danger constituted one of Jeremiah's most difficult problems (see under chapter 23).

Chapter 9. The Broken-Hearted Prophet

Jeremiah, a man of sorrows, in the midst of a people abandoned to everything vile (8:6; 9:2–9), weeping day and night at the thought of frightful impending retribution, moved about among them, begging, pleading, persuading, threatening, entreating, imploring that they turn from their wickedness. But in vain.

Chapter 10. Jehovah the True God

It seems that the threat of Babylonian invasion spurred the people of Judah to great activity in the manufacture of idols, as if idols could save them. This gave Jeremiah occasion to remind them that what they were doing was further aggravation of their already appalling sin against God.

Chapter 11. The Broken Covenant

This chapter seems to belong to the period of reaction, after Josiah's great reformation, as told in II Kings 23, when the people had restored their idols. For Jeremiah's rebuke they had plotted his death (9:21).

Chapter 12. Jeremiah's Complaint

Contrasting his own sufferings with the apparent prosperity of those against whom he was preaching, and who were ridiculing his threats (4), Jeremiah complains of the ways of God. Then the promise of future restoration (15–17).

Chapter 13. The Marred Girdle

Jeremiah made considerable use of symbols in his preaching (see on 19:1). The girdle was probably richly decorated, a conspicuous part of Jeremiah's dress, as he walked about the streets of Jerusalem. Later, rotted, ragged and dirty, it served to attract attention. As curious crowds gathered around the prophet it gave him occasion to explain that even so Judah, with whom Jehovah had clothed Himself to walk among men, once beautiful and glorious, would be marred and cast off.

Chapters 14,15. Jeremiah's Intercession

A prolonged drouth had stripped the land of food. Jeremiah, though hated, ridiculed and mocked, it made his heart ache to see them suffer. His intercession to God is as near an approach to the spirit of Christ as is to be found anywhere in the Old Testament. What is called "Jeremiah's Grotto," one of the retreats to which he was said to have retired to weep, was at the foot of the knoll on which, 600 years later, the cross of Jesus stood (see Figure 63).

Chapter 16. Jeremiah Forbidden to Marry

The domestic life of the prophets, in some cases, was used to reinforce the burden of their preaching. Isaiah and Hosea were married, and named their children for their principal ideas. Jeremiah was commanded to remain single, as a sort of symbolic background to his persistent predictions of impending bloody slaughter: "What's the use of raising a family just to be butchered in the frightful carnage about to be loosed upon the inhabitants of Judah"? Again the promise of Restoration (14–15).

Chapter 17. Judah's Sin Indelible

Their downfall inevitable. Yet the promise is flung out again and again that if only they would turn to God, Jerusalem would remain forever (24–25).

Chapter 18. The Potter's Clay

A very apt illustration of God's power to alter the destiny of a nation. Jeremiah used it as the basis for another appeal to the wicked nation to amend its ways. But in vain.

Chapter 19. The Earthen Bottle

It may have been a vase of exquisite workmanship. Being broken in the presence of Jerusalem's leaders was an impressive way of re-announcing impending ruin of the city.

Some other symbols which Jeremiah used to gain attention to his preaching were: the Marred Girdle (chapter 13); Abstinence from Marriage (chapter 16); the Potter's Clay (chapter 18); Bonds and Bars (chapter 27); Buying a Field (chapter 32).

Chapter 20. Jeremiah Imprisoned

Jeremiah went from his vase-breaking rendezvous with the leaders in the valley of Hinnom to the Temple, and began to proclaim there the same message to the people. For this, Pashhur, one of the chief officers of the Temple, put him in prison. "Stocks" (2), consisted of a wooden frame in which feet, neck and hands were fastened so as to hold the body in a distorted and painful position. It drew from Jeremiah an outburst of remonstrance with God (7–18).

Chapter 21. The Siege Begins

This chapter belongs to the last days of Jeremiah's life. King Zedekiah, frightened at the approach of the Babylonian army, appeals to Jeremiah to intercede with God. Jeremiah advises Zedekiah to yield the city to the Babylonians, in order to save the people from death.

Chapter 22. Warning to King Jehoiakim

This chapter belongs to the reign of Jehoiakim, a wicked and cruel king. "Shallum" (11), was Jehoahaz, who was carried to Egypt, and died there (II Kings 23:31–34). Jehoiakim's miserable death (18–19), is hinted in II Kings 24:6; II Chronicles 36:6. Coniah (Jeconiah, Jehoiachin) "childless" (30): he had children (I Chronicles 3:17; Matthew 1:12), out of whom came Christ, but he and his uncle Zedekiah were the last earthly kings to sit on David's throne. It was the end of the temporal kingdom of Judah.

Chapter 23. False Prophets

A bitter indictment of the leaders of God's people. Jeremiah's stinging arraignment of Davidic kings supplies a background for a pre-vision of the coming Davidic Messiah (23:5–8, see under chapter 33). As for the false prophets: they were the greatest hindrance to the acceptance of Jeremiah's preaching: in the name of God, delivering their own messages crying out, "Jeremiah is lying. We are prophets of God, and God has told us Jerusalem is safe."

Chapter 24. The Two Baskets of Figs

The good figs representing the best of the people, who had been carried to Babylon in Jehoiachin's captivity (597 B.C.), and earlier, including Ezekiel and Daniel; the bad figs, those who had remained in Jerusalem, minded, with Egypt's aid, to resist Babylon (II Kings 24:10–20).

Chapter 25. Seventy Years' Captivity Predicted

This was in the early part of Jehoiakim's reign (1), about 604 B.C. The remarkable thing is that the exact duration of Babylon's sway is foretold (11–14; 29:10; II Chronicles 36:21; Ezra 1:1; Daniel 9:2; Zechariah 7:5). An amazing prophecy. No possible way for Jeremiah to know that, except by direct revelation from God.

Chapter 26. Jeremiah's Trial before the Princes

His accusers were the priests and false prophets. But Jeremiah had friends among the princes, especially one Ahikam, who saved him from death. However, one of Jeremiah's fellow prophets, named Uriah, did not fare so well (20–24).

ARCHAEOLOGICAL NOTE: Uriah; Elnathan; Nedabiah; Shallum. Uriah fled to Egypt (20–24). King Jehoiakim sent "Elnathan," one of the princes (22; 36:12), to Egypt, to bring him back.

One of the "Lachish Letters" (see under chapter 34), makes reference to "The commander of the host, Chebariah, son of Elnathan, having passed by on his way to Egypt." This seems like a reference to the incident told in verses 20–24.

This Lachish Letter also speaks of "The letter of Nedabiah, servant of the king, which came to Shallum from the prophet." Nedabiah was grandson of king Jehoiakim (I Chronicles 3:18). Shallum (Jehoahaz) was brother of Jehoiakim (II Kings 23:30, 34; I Chronicles 3:15; Jeremiah 22:11), who had been taken to Egypt.

Chapters 27,28. Bonds and Bars

Jeremiah put a yoke, like that worn by oxen, on his neck, and went about the city, saying, Thus shall Babylon put a yoke on the necks of this people. One of the false prophets, Hananiah, with brazen impudence, broke the yoke (28:10); and, as a punishment died within two months (28:1, 17).

Chapter 29. Jeremiah's Letter to the Exiles

Written after Jehoiachin, and the best of the people, had been taken to Babylon, advising them to be peaceful and obedient captives, and promising return, after 70 years (10), to their homeland. But even in Babylon the false prophets kept up their fight against Jeremiah (21–32).

Chapters 30,31. A Song of Restoration

For both Israel and Judah, with Messianic foregleams, commanded of God to be written (2), so that it could be kept to compare with the events of after ages.

The New Covenant (31:31–34). The Old Testament is the story of God's dealings with the Hebrew nation on the basis of the Covenant given at Mt. Sinai. Here is a definite prediction that the Mosaic Covenant would be superceded by Another Covenant. Displacement of the Mosaic Covenant by the Christian Covenant is the main thesis of the Epistle to Hebrews.

Chapter 32. Jeremiah Buys a Field

This was the year before Jerusalem fell. The burning of the city and desolation of Judah was almost at hand. Amid the gloom and despair of the hour Jeremiah was commanded of God to buy a field, in public ceremony, and put away the deed for safe keeping, to emphasize his prediction that the captives would return, and the land again be cultivated.

Chapter 33. The "Branch"

Of the 20 Davidic kings who reigned over Judah during the 400 years between David and the Captivity, most of them were very bad. Only a few were worthy the name of David. In chapters 22 and 23 Jeremiah bitterly indicted this family line of kings to whom God had given the promise of an ETERNAL THRONE. Here, in chapter 33, he repeats with fuller explanation, the prophecy of ONE GREAT KING, called "The Branch," in whom the promise would be fulfilled.

Chapter 34. Zedekiah's Proclamation of Liberty

During the siege Zedekiah proclaimed freedom to all slaves, evidently to gain God's favor; but failed to enforce it.

ARCHAEOLOGICAL NOTE: The "Lachish Letters." In 34:7 Lachish and Azekah are mentioned as being besieged by the king of Babylon. Fragments of 21 Letters, written during this siege, from an outpost of Lachish, to the captain of the guard who was defending Lachish, were found (1935), by the Wellcome Archaeological Expedition, under the direction of J. L. Starkey and Sir Charles Marston.

These letters were written just before Nebuchadnezzar launched his final attack, by kindling fires against its walls.

They were found in a deposit of ash and charcoal on the floor of the guard room.

In one of the letters the outpost says that he was "watching for signals from Lachish," and that "he could see no signals from Azekah" (perhaps already fallen).

These letters refer to and mention by name certain persons whose names appear in the Biblical narrative, "Gemariah," an officer of king Zedekiah (Jeremiah 29:3). "Jaazaniah," a military captain of Nebuchadnezzar (II Kings 25:23). "Mattaniah," original name of king Zedekiah (II Kings 24:17). "Neriah," father of Baruch, Jeremiah's scribe (Jeremiah 43:3). They were written in Hebrew, by a contemporary of Jeremiah. Like a voice from the dead, they confirm the reality of Jeremiah's story.

Chapter 35. The Example of the Rechabites

Rechabites were a tribe, descended from the time of Moses (I Chronicles 2:55; Numbers 10:29–32; Judges 1:16; II Kings 10:15, 23), who, through the centuries, had adhered to their ascetic life.

Chapter 36. The King Burns Jeremiah's Book

Jeremiah, at this time, had been prophesying for 23 years, from the 13th year of Josiah to the 4th year of Jehoiakim. He is now commanded to gather these prophecies into a book, so that they could be read to the people, for, at the time, Jeremiah himself was not free to speak to the people (5). It took a year or so to write the book (1, 9). The reading of the book made a profound impression on some of the princes, but the king brazenly and defiantly burned the book. Then Jeremiah wrote it all over again.

Chapters 37,38. Jeremiah's Imprisonment

During the siege, when the Babylonians had temporarily withdrawn, Jeremiah, probably because of the scarcity of food in Jerusalem, attempted to leave the city to go to his home in Anathoth. This, because of his persistent advice to yield to the king of Babylon, looked, to his enemies, as if it might be an effort to join the Babylonians. Thus, on suspicion that Jeremiah was a traitor, working in the interest of the Babylonians, he was imprisoned. Zedekiah was friendly to Jeremiah, but he was a weak king.

Chapter 39. Jerusalem Burned

This is told also in chapter 52, and in II Kings 25, where see note, and II Chronicles 36. Nebuchadnezzar, knowing of Jeremiah's lifelong admonition to Jerusalem to submit to him, now offered to confer on Jeremiah any honor that he would accept, even a worthy place in the Babylonian court (11–14; 40:1–6).

Chapters 40,41. Gedaliah Made Governor

Gedaliah, whom Nebuchadnezzar appointed governor over Judah, was son of Ahikam, Jeremiah's friend (40:5; 26:24). But within 3 months he was assassinated (39:2; 41:1).

ARCHAEOLOGICAL NOTE: Gedaliah's Seal. At Lachish (1935), Starkey, of the Wellcome Archaeological Expedition, found, in the lay of ashes left by Nebuchadnezzar's fire, among the "Lachish Letters," a seal bearing this inscription, "Belonging to Gedaliah, the one who is over the house."

Also, Jaazaniah's (Jezaniah) Seal (Jeremiah 40:8; II Kings 25:23). He was one of Gedaliah's army captains. In 1932 W. F. Bade, of the Pacific School of Religion, found in the ruins of Mizpah, seat of Gedaliah's government (Jeremiah 40:6), an exquisite agate seal inscribed, "Belonging to Jaazaniah, servant of the king."

Chapters 42,43. Departure for Egypt

The remnant, fearing reprisal by Nebuchadnezzar, for the slaying of Gedaliah, fled to Egypt, though explicitly warned of God that it would mean extinction. They took Jeremiah along.

ARCHAEOLOGICAL NOTE: Tahpahnes (43:8–13). Its site has been identified about 10 miles west of the Suez Canal. In 1886 Sir Flinders Petrie uncovered the ruins of a large castle, in front of which was a "great open platform of brick work," the very place, Petrie believed, where Jeremiah hid the stones (43:8).

Also, Nebuchadnezzar's annals state that he did invade Egypt in 568 B.C., which was 18 years after Jeremiah uttered the prophecy that he would (43:10). Three of Nebuchadnezzar's inscriptions have been found near Tahpahnes.

Chapter 44. Jeremiah's Final Appeal

This last effort to induce them to abandon their idolatry failed. They were defiant. The "queen of heaven" (17), was Ashtoreth, whose worship was with acts of immorality, in this case with their husband's consent (15, 19).

The place and manner of Jeremiah's death are not known. One tradition is that he was stoned to death in Egypt. Another is that he was taken from Egypt by Nebuchadnezzar, with Baruch, to Babylon, and died there.

Chapter 45. Baruch

Baruch, Jeremiah's scribe, was a man of prominence, with high ambitions (5). He was recognized as having great influence with Jeremiah (43:3).

Chapter 46. Egypt

A description of the defeat of the Egyptian army at Carchemish (605 B.C.), in the middle period of Jeremiah's life (1–12); and a later prophecy that Nebuchadnezzar would invade Egypt (13–26), which is an expansion of 43:8–13, which see. Over 100 years earlier Isaiah had prophesied Assyrian invasions of Egypt (see under Isaiah 18 to 20). Ezekiel also had something to say about Egypt (Ezekiel 19 to 32).

Chapter 47. The Philistines

This prophecy, foretelling the desolation of Philistia by Babylon, was fulfilled 20 years later when Nebuchadnezzar took Judah. Other prophets who paid their respects to the Philistines were: Isaiah (14:28–32); Amos (1:6–8); Ezekiel (25:15–17); Zephaniah (2:4–7); Zechariah (9:1–7).

Chapter 48. Moab

A picture of impending desolation of Moab. Moab helped Nebuchadnezzar against Judah, but later was devastated at his hands (582 B.C.). For centuries the land has lain desolate and sparsely inhabited, the ruins of its many cities testifying to its ancient populousness. Its restoration (47), and that of Ammon (49:6), may have been fulfilled in their absorption into the general Arab race, some of whom were present at Pentecost when the Gospel was first proclaimed to the world (Acts 2:11). Or, it may mean that the land will yet again be prosperous. Other prophecies about Moab are: Isaiah 15, 16; Ezekiel 25:8–11; Amos 2:1–3; Zephaniah 2:8–11.

Chapter 49. Ammon. Edom. Syria. Hazor. Elam

A prediction that Nebuchadnezzar would conquer these nations, which he did. Ammon (see under Ezekiel 25:1–11). Edom (see under Obadiah).

Chapters 50,51. Prediction of the Fall of Babylon

The fall and perpetual desolation of Babylon is here predicted, in language matching the grandeur of the theme (51:37–43), as Isaiah had done earlier (Isaiah 13:17–22). The Medes, leading a great company of nations, are named as the conquerors (50:9; 51:11, 27, 28). These two chapters, pronouncing the doom of Babylon, were copied in a separate book, and sent to Babylon, in a deputation headed by king Zedekiah, seven years before Nebuchadnezzar burned Jerusalem (51:59–64). The book was to be read publicly, and then, in solemn ceremony, sunk in the Euphrates, with these words, "Thus shall Babylon sink, and not rise."

Chapter 52. Captivity of Judah. (See on II Kings 24, 25.)

LAMENTATIONS

A Funeral Dirge Over the Desolation of Jerusalem

Jeremiah's Sorrow over the city he had done his best to save; not without faith that the city would rise again from its ruins (3:21, 31, 32). Jerusalem did rise, and gave its name to the capital of a Redeemed World of Eternal Glory (Hebrews 12:22; Revelation 21:2).

An Appendage to Jeremiah

The last chapter of Jeremiah should be read as an introduction to this book. The Septuagint gives this prefix: "And it came to pass, after Israel was led into captivity and Jerusalem was laid waste, that Jeremiah sat weeping, and lamented this lamentation over Jerusalem, and said:"

However, in the Hebrew Old Testament this book does not follow Jeremiah, as in our Bible, but is in the group called "Hagiographa," or "Writings": Song, Ruth, Lamentations, Ecclesiastes, Esther. These were on separate rolls, because they were read at different feasts. This book of Lamentations, to this day, throughout the world, wherever there are Jews, is read in the synagogs, on the 9th day of the 4th month (Jeremiah 52:6).

"Jeremiah's Grotto"

Is the name of the place, just outside the north wall of Jerusalem, where tradition says, Jeremiah wept bitter tears and composed this sorrowful elegy. This grotto is under the knoll that is now called "Golgotha," the self-same hill on which the cross of Jesus stood. Thus the suffering prophet wept where later the suffering Saviour died.

An Alphabetic Acrostic

The book consists of five poems, four of which are acrostic, that is, each verse begins with a letter of the Hebrew alphabet, in alphabetic sequence. This was a favorite form of Hebrew poetry, adopted to help the memory. In chapters 1, 2, 4, there are 22 verses in each, 1 verse to a letter. In chapter 3 there were 3 verses to each letter, making 66 in all. Chapter 5 has 22 verses, but not in alphabetic order.

Its Immediate Use

The book must have been composed in the 3 months between the burning of Jerusalem and the departure of the remnant to Egypt (Jeremiah 39:2; 41:1, 18; 43:7), during which the seat of government was at Mizpah (Jeremiah 40:8). Probably a number of copies were made: some taken to Egypt; others sent to Babylon, for the captives to memorize and sing.

Chapter 1. Zion Desolate

It is not easy to give a subject to each chapter. The same ideas, in different wording, run through all the chapters: horrors of the siege; desolate ruins; all due to Zion's sins. Jeremiah, stunned, dazed, heartbroken, weeps with grief inconsolable. Special emphasis of this chapter is that the people brought the catastrophe upon themselves by their sins (5, 8, 9, 14, 18, 20, 22).

Chapter 2. God's Anger

The devastation of Jerusalem is attributed to the Anger of God (1, 2, 3, 4, 6, 21, 22). Jerusalem, situated on a mountain, surrounded by mountains, was, for physical situation, the most beautiful city then known, "the perfection of beauty" (15), even when compared to Babylon, Nineveh, Thebes and Memphis, which were built on river plains. Moreover, it was the city of God's special care, chosen of Him for a unique mission, the main channel for God's dealings with men, most favored and highly privileged city in all the world, beloved of God in an exceptional way, and under His special protection. Moreover, it was so well fortified that it was generally believed to be impregnable (4:12). But this City of God had become worse than Sodom (4:6). That the God of Love is also a God of Wrath is a teaching that is stated and illustrated again and again throughout the Bible.

Chapter 3. Jeremiah's Grief

In this chapter Jeremiah seems to be complaining that God had ignored him and his prayers (8); God "had covered himself with a cloud that no prayer could pass through" (44). Though complaining, he justifies God, acknowledging that they deserved worse (22). The high point of the book is 21–39.

Chapters 4,5. Sufferings of the Siege

Enumerated and summarized. Jeremiah could not keep his mind

off the horrors of the siege, cries of starving children (2:11, 12, 19; 4:4), women boiling their babies for food (2:20; 4:10).

Howbeit, in spite of its horrible sufferings, Jerusalem failed to learn its lesson. After the Captivity it was rebuilt, and in Jesus' day had again become a great and powerful city, and climaxed its sin by crucifying the Son of God. Then followed its eradication by the armies of Rome (A.D. 70. See under Hebrews 13).

EZEKIEL

The Fall of Jerusalem
Judgments on Surrounding Nations
The Restoration of Israel
"They shall Know that I am God"

Ezekiel was a prophet of the Captivity. He was carried to Babylon 597 B.C., 11 years before Jerusalem was destroyed.

The Assyrian Captivity of Israel had been 120 years earlier:
734 B.C. Galilee and North and East Israel, by Tiglath-pileser.
721 B.C. Samaria and the rest of Israel, by Sargon.
701 B.C. 200,000 of the inhabitants of Judah, by Sennacherib.

The Babylonian Captivity of Judah was accomplished:
606 B.C. Some captives taken to Babylon, including Daniel.
597 B.C. More captives taken to Babylon, including Ezekiel.
586 B.C. Jerusalem burned. (See further page 211.)

The Captivity lasted 70 years. 606–536 B.C. Ezekiel was there from 597 B.C. to at least 570 B.C.

Ezekiel and Daniel

Daniel had been in Babylon 9 years when Ezekiel arrived; and had already attained to great fame (14:14, 20). Daniel in the palace; Ezekiel in the country. They may have met often.

Ezekiel and Jeremiah

Jeremiah was the older. Ezekiel may have been his pupil. Ezekiel preached among the exiles the same things that Jeremiah was preaching in Jerusalem: certainty of Judah's punishment for her sins.

Ezekiel and John

Some of Ezekiel's visions seem to be extended into the book of Revelation: Cherubim (Ezekiel 1, Revelation 4); Gog and Magog (Ezekiel 38, Revelation 20); Eating the book (Ezekiel 3, Revelation 10); New Jerusalem (Ezekiel 40–48, Revelation 21); River of Water of Life (Ezekiel 47, Revelation 22).

"They Shall Know that I am God"

This is a dominant note of the book. We have counted 62 places in which it occurs, in 27 of the 48 chapters, as follows: 6:7, 10, 13, 14; 7:4, 9, 27; 11:10, 12; 12:15, 16, 20; 13:9, 14, 21; 14:8; 15:7; 16:62; 17:21, 24; 20:12, 20, 28, 38, 42, 44; 21:5; 22:16, 22; 23:49; 24:24, 27; 25:5, 7, 11, 17; 26:6; 28:22, 23, 24, 26; 29:6, 9, 16, 21; 30:8, 19, 25, 26; 32:15; 33:29; 34:27, 30; 35:4, 9, 12, 15; 36:11, 23, 36, 38; 37:6, 13, 14, 28; 38:16, 23; 39:6, 7, 22, 23, 28.

Ezekiel's mission seems to have been to explain the action of God in causing or permitting Israel's captivity. It was because of the unspeakable abominations of which they had been guilty; abominations for which other nations had been blotted out. But for Israel it was punitive. By their punishment they would come to KNOW THAT GOD IS GOD. They did. The Babylonian Captivity CURED the Jews of Idolatry. Up to that time they just would be Idolaters. From that day to this, whatever other sins the Jews have been guilty of, they have not been Idolaters.

Chronology of Ezekiel's Book

The pivot around which the book centers is the Destruction of Jerusalem, which occurred 586 B.C. Ezekiel's prophecies began 6 years before that, and continued 16 years thereafter, covering a period of 22 years. Until Jerusalem fell, Ezekiel was unceasingly predicting its certainty (chapters 1–24). After that his prophecies deal with the Overthrow of surrounding Heathen Nations (chapters 25–32); and the Re-establishment and Glorious Future of Israel (chapters 33–48).

His visions, with minor exceptions, are given in chronological sequence. The years are dated from king Jehoiachin's Captivity, which was 597 B.C. The "30th year" (1:1), which was the equivalent of the "5th year" of Jehoiachin's captivity (1:2), is thought to have been the 30th year of Ezekiel's life (age at which Levites began their service [Numbers 4:3]: Jesus and John the Baptist began their work at 30). Or, it may have been the 30th year in the Babylonian calendar of Babylon's independence of Assyria, won by Nebopolasar 625 B.C.

Dates of Ezekiel's visions are as follows:

Chapter 1:2	5th year	4th month (July)	5th day	592 B.C.
Chapter 8:1	6th year	6th month (September)	5th day	591 B.C.
Chapter 20:1	7th year	5th month (August)	10th day	590 B.C.
Chapter 24:1	9th year	10th month (January)	10th day	587 B.C.
Siege of Jerusalem began 9th year 10th month 10th day				
Chapter 26:1	11th year	5th (?) month (August)	1st day	586 B.C.

Chapter 29:1	10th year 10th month (January)	12th day	586 B.C.
Chapter 29:17	27th year 1st month (April)	1st day	570 B.C.
Chapter 30:20	11th year 1st month (April)	7th day	586 B.C.
Chapter 32:1	12th year 12th month (March)	1st day	584 B.C.
	Jerusalem Fell 11th year 4th month 9th day		
Chapter 32:1	12th year 12th month (March)	1st day	584 B.C.
Chapter 32:17	12th year 12th (?) month (March)	15th day	584 B.C.
Chapter 33:21	12th year 10th month (January)	5th day	584 B.C.
Chapter 40:1	25th year 1st (?) month (April)	10th day	572 B.C.

Since Ezekiel was so meticulous in dating his visions, even to the exact day, it is assumed that all that follows a given date belongs to that date, till the next date is mentioned.

Chapter 1:1-3. Ezekiel's Abode and Date

He was carried captive with king Jehoiachin (597 B.C.), "our" captivity (33:21; 40:1). He had a wife (24:15–18); a home (8:1). He lived by the river Chebar, the great ship canal branching off from the Euphrates above Babylon and running through Nippur to the Tigris. Nippur, about 50 miles Southeast of Babylon, was Calneh, one of the cities Nimrod had built (Genesis 10:10). Telabib seems to have been Ezekiel's home town (3:15, 24). It is thought to have been near Nippur (see map page 65). There is in the region a village called "Kilfil," the Arabian for "Ezekiel," which, tradition says, was his residence. About 40 miles away was Fara, traditional home of Noah. This may have suggested the use of Noah's name (14:14, 20). Eridu, traditional site of the Garden of Eden, was only 100 miles away. Maybe this is what suggested to Ezekiel frequent mention of the Garden of Eden (28:13; 31:8, 9, 16, 18; 36:35).

"Son of Man": Ezekiel is thus addressed 90 times. In Daniel 7:13 it is used of the Messiah. It was the title by which Jesus commonly spoke of himself (see under John 1:14).

Visions and symbolic actions are characteristic of Ezekiel's book. Some of his symbolic actions were accompanied by most painful personal sufferings. He had to remain dumb for a long period (3:26; 24:27; 33:22). Had to lie on his side in one position for over a year (4:5, 6). And eat loathsome food (4:15). His wife, whom he dearly loved, was suddenly taken (24:16–18).

Chapter 1:4-28. Ezekiel's Vision of God

The "Living Creatures" are identified as "Cherubim" (10:20). They stood, one in the middle of each side of a square, their outspread wings touching at the corners of the square. Each cherub had four faces: the face of a man, looking outward from the square; on his right, the face of a lion; on his left, the face of an ox; in the rear, looking toward the center of the square, the face of an eagle. There were four immense whirling (10:6) wheels, one beside each cherub. The wheels appeared to be of beryl, green precious stone; their rims full of eyes. This Fourfold Living Creature moved like flashes of lightning from place to place, with noise like the roar of the ocean.

Above the Living Creature was a crystal platform. On the platform, a throne of blue sapphire. On the throne, the likeness of a Man, enswathed in the glow of incandescent light, encircled in a rainbow. It was all set within a vast storm cloud, with whirling flashes of fire. This was the form in which God appeared to Ezekiel. It signified His Glory, Power, Omniscience, Omnipresence, Omnipotence, Sovereignty, Majesty and Holiness.

Cherubim guarded the entrance to the Tree of Life (Genesis 3:24). Likenesses of Cherubim were placed on the Ark of the Covenant (Exodus 25:18–20), and embroidered on the Veil of the Tabernacle (Exodus 26:31). They were reproduced in the Temple (I Kings 6:23, 29; II Chronicles 3:14). They had been interwoven in Biblical thought from the beginning as angelic attendants of God. In Revelation 4:6, 7; 5:6; 6:1, 6; 7:11; 14:3; 15:7; 19:4, they are intimately connected with the unfolding destiny of the Church.

Chapters 2,3. Ezekiel's Commission

Ezekiel is warned at the outset that he is being called to a life of hardship and persecution. His message is delivered to him from God in the form of a book, which he is commanded to eat, as was John (Revelation 10:9). In his mouth the book was sweet, which seems to mean that he found joy in being God's messenger, though the message was a message of woe. Eating the book, whether literally, or only in vision, signified thoroughly digesting its contents, so that its message would become a part of himself. In 3:17–21 God seemed to lay upon Ezekiel responsibility for the doom of his nation, which he could escape only by a faithful declaration of God's message. He is also warned that God would, at times, impose silence upon him (3:26; 24:27; 33:22), this being a caution to Ezekiel to speak, not his own ideas, but only as God commanded.

Chapters 4,5,6,7. Symbolic Siege of Jerusalem

Ezekiel's opening message to the exiles, who were hoping for a speedy return to Jerusalem, was this graphic warning that Jerusalem was about to be destroyed, and that they would soon be joined by other captives, and that their captivity would last at least 40 years. The 40 years may be meant as a round number denoting a generation. At this time, 592 B.C., some of the captives had already been there 14 years. In 6 more years Jerusalem was burned. From that time on the captivity lasted 50 years, 586–536 B.C.

As for the 390 years for Israel's iniquity (4:5), the Septuagint has 190, which was the approximate period from 721 to 536 B.C. If 390 is the correct reading, the 200 additional years would extend the time to the Greek period of Alexander the Great, who in his conquests of those lands showed a great consideration to all Jews. Some think the 430 years (390 plus 40), duration of the Sojourn in Egypt (Exodus 12:40), is meant as a symbol of a second similar captivity.

As a sign of famine, Ezekiel lived on loathsome bread. Throughout the siege he lay on one side, either continuously or for the greater part of each day, which with famine diet, meant great discomfort.

Chapter 5. When the siege is finished he is commanded, as a further symbol of the fate of Jerusalem's inhabitants, to shave off his hair, burn part of it and scatter rest to the winds.

Chapters 6, 7. A sort of Dirge over the Destruction and Desolation of the Land of Israel, the main point being that the Jews would, by this terrible punishment, come to know that God is God.

Chapters 8,9,10,11. Ezekiel's Vision-Journey to Jerusalem

September (591 B.C.), a year and two months after his call. He was transported, in rapture, to Jerusalem, where God showed him the abhorrent idolatries being practiced in the Temple. The "image of jealousy" (8:3), probably was Astarte (Syrian Venus). Secret animal worship (8:10), probably an Egyptian cult. It was led by Jaazaniah II, whose father Shaphan had been leader in Josiah's reformation (II Kings 22:8); and whose brothers Ahikam and Gemariah were Jeremiah's close friends (Jeremiah 26:24; 36:10, 25), even while Jeremiah himself was crying out in horror at the sacrilege. Tammuz (14), was the Babylonian Adonis, consort of Syrian Venus, whose worship was celebrated in wild orgies of immoral indulgence. Thus, in spite of warning after warning, and punishment after punishment, the once powerful kingdom of Judah, reduced now almost to the point of extinction, was still sinking lower and lower in the depths of idolatrous infamy–a stench no longer to be endured in the nostrils of God.

Chapter 9. A Vision of the Slaughter of Jerusalem's idolaters, except the faithful who bore the mark of the angel-scribe (3, 4).

Chapter 10. Re-appearance of the Cherubim of chapter 1, superintending the destruction and slaughter of Jerusalem.

Chapter 11. A Vision of the Future Restoration of the Exiles, humbled, purified, and cured of idolatry (10, 12).

The mission ended, Ezekiel was borne, on the cherub chariot, back to his exile home; and reported to the elders (8:1; 11:25).

Chapter 12. Ezekiel Moves his Household Goods

Another symbolic action to emphasize Jerusalem's impending captivity. It contains an amazing detailed prophecy of Zedekiah's fate; his secret flight, capture, and removal to Babylon without seeing it (10, 12, 13). 5 years later it came to pass; Zedekiah attempted a secret escape, was captured, his eyes put out, and he was taken to Babylon (Jeremiah 52:7–11).

Chapter 13. False Prophets

These were very numerous both in Jerusalem and among the captives. The "pillows" (18), and "kerchiefs" (21), must have been used in some sort of magical rite.

Chapter 14. Hypocritical Inquirers

To a delegation of Idol lovers God's answer is not words, but the swift and terrible destruction of Idolatrous Israel. It may be that for Daniel's sake (14), Nebuchadnezzar had spared Jerusalem thus far, now to be spared no longer.

Chapter 15. Parable of the Vine-Tree

Useless for fruit, or as wood. Fit only for fuel. So, Jerusalem was no longer fit for anything but burning.

Chapter 16. Allegory of the Unfaithful Wife

This chapter is a very graphic and vivid portrayal of Israel's Idolatry under the imagery of a Bride, beloved of her husband, who made her a queen, and lavished upon her silks and sealskins and every beautiful thing; who then made herself a prostitute to every man that passed by, shaming even Sodom and Samaria.

Chapter 17. Parable of the Two Eagles

The first eagle (3), was the king of Babylon. The "topmost twig" (4), was Jehoiachin, who was carried to Babylon (II Kings 24:11–16), six years before this parable was uttered. The "seed of the land" (5:13), who was planted was Zedekiah (II Kings 24:17). The other eagle (7), was the king of Egypt, toward whom Zedekiah leaned. For his treachery Zedekiah shall be brought to Babylon, to be punished, and to die there (13–21). This came to pass 5 years later (II Kings 25:6, 7), a repetition of what Ezekiel had previously prophesied (12:10–16). The "tender twig" (22–24), which God would later plant, in the Restored Royal Family of David, had its fulfillment in the Messiah.

Chapter 18. "The Soul that Sins, It shall Die"

Much is said in the prophets to the effect that Israel's Captivity was due to the cumulative sins of preceding generations. The Captivity generation, overlooking the fact that they were "worse than their fathers," were now trying to lay the blame on their fathers. The burden of this chapter is that God judges every man on his own individual and personal conduct. It is an impassioned appeal to the wicked to repent (30–32).

Chapter 19. A Dirge over the Fall of David's Throne

Under the imagery of a Lioness. David's Family, once great and powerful, now overthrown. The first whelp (3), was Jehoahaz (Shallum), who was taken to Egypt (II Kings 23:31–34). The second whelp (5), was either Jehoiachin or Zedekiah, both of whom were taken to Babylon (I Kings 24:8–25:7).

Chapter 20. Rehearsal of Israel's Idolatries

Generation after generation they had wallowed in the filth of Idol-worship. Note the prophecy of Restoration (see chapter 37).

Chapter 21. "A Song of the Sword"

About to be unsheathed against Jerusalem and Ammon. "The south" (20:46), was the land of Judah. "Until he come whose right it is" (21:27): that is, the overturning of Zedekiah's throne (25–27), would be the end of David's kingdom till the coming of the Messiah (34:23–24; 37:24; Jeremiah 23:5, 6).

Chapter 22. The Sins of Jerusalem

Over and over Ezekiel names the sins of Jerusalem: defiles herself with Idols, sheds blood, profanes the Sabbath, practices robbery, promiscuous adultery; and the princes, priests and prophets are ravening wolves after dishonest gain.

Chapter 23. Oholah and Oholibah

Two sisters, insatiable in their lewdness. A parable of Israel's Idolatry. Oholah, Samaria; Oholibah, Jerusalem. Both grown old in their Adulteries. Again and again the relation between husband and wife is used to represent the relation between God and his people (see under chapter 16). Promiscuous adultery must have been very widespread (16:32; 18:6, 11, 15; 22:11; 23:43; Jeremiah 5:7, 8; 7:9; 9:2; 23:10, 14; 29:23).

Chapter 24. The Boiling Caldron

Symbolic of the destruction of Jerusalem, now at hand. The rust on the pot represented the bloodshed and immorality of the city.

Death of Ezekiel's Wife (15–24). This was on the day that the siege of Jerusalem began (1, 18; II Kings 25:1): a heart-rending sign to the exiles that their beloved Jerusalem, was now to be taken from them. Silence was imposed on Ezekiel till news came of the fallen city, 3 years later (27; 33:21, 22).

Chapter 25. Ammon, Moab, Edom, Philistia

These four nations were Judah's closest neighbors, who rejoiced at Judah's destruction by Babylon. Ezekiel here predicts for them the same fate, as did Jeremiah (Jeremiah 27:1–7). Nebuchadnezzar subdued the Philistines when he took Judah, and four years later invaded Ammon, Moab and Edom.

Chapters 26,27,28. Tyre. Visions of 586 B.C.

These visions of the doom of Tyre were given to Ezekiel in the same year that Jerusalem fell, that is, the 11th year (26:1).

Chapter 26. A prophecy of Nebuchadnezzar's Siege, and Tyre's Permanent Desolation. Next year (585 B.C.) Nebuchadnezzar laid siege to Tyre. It took 13 years to conquer the city (585–573 B.C.).

Tyre, located 60 miles northwest of Nazareth, was a double city, one part on an island, the other on the mainland in a fertile and well-watered plain at the western foot of the Lebanon mountain range. It was the great maritime power of the ancient world, at its zenith from the 12th to the 6th centuries B.C., with colonies on the north and west coasts of Africa, in Spain, and Britain, controlling the commerce of the Mediterranean, with the wares of all nations passing through its port. A city renowned for its splendor and fabulous wealth. With its subjugation by Nebuchadnezzar it ceased to be an independent power. It was later subdued by the Persians; and again by Alexander the Great (332 B.C.). It never recovered its former glory, and has for centuries been a "bare rock" where fishermen "spread their nets" (26:4, 5, 14), an amazing fulfillment of Ezekiel's prophecy that it "nevermore should have any being" (26:14, 21; 27:36; 28:29).

Chapter 27. Tyre, Mistress of the Mediterranean, pictured under imagery of a Majestic Ship, of incomparable beauty, bearing the wares and treasures of the nations, about to be submerged.

Chapter 28:1–19. Overthrow of Tyre's Proud King, who, in his inaccessible and impregnable island throne, made sport of any threat to his security.

Chapter 28:20–24. Overthrow of Sidon, 20 miles north of Tyre. It was taken by Nebuchadnezzar when he took Tyre.

Chapter 28:25–26. Restoration of Israel, after enemy neighbor nations shall have disappeared.

Chapters 29,30,31,32. Egypt. Six Visions

Predicting Nebuchadnezzar's invasion of Egypt, and Egypt's reduction to a place of minor importance for all future time.

Nebuchadnezzar invaded and plundered Egypt 572 and 568 B.C. Egypt never recovered its former glory, and ever since has played a very minor part in world history, fulfilling in a very real sense Ezekiel's prophecy that it would be "the basest of kingdoms" (29:15).

29:1–16. January, 586 B.C. 6 months before Jerusalem fell. 15 years before Nebuchadnezzar invaded Egypt. In this vision Egypt is pictured as a Crocodile, as Tyre has been pictured as a Ship in chapter 27. The Crocodile, monarch of the Nile, was one of the gods of Egypt. The "40 years" of Egypt's captivity and desolation (11, 12): it was nearly 40 years from Nebuchadnezzar's subjugation of Egypt to the Rise of Persia (536 B.C.), which permitted all captive peoples to return to their native lands.

29:17—30:19. April, 570 B.C.: 16 years after the Fall of Jerusalem. This vision, given many years after the other five visions, and on the eve of Nebuchadnezzar's march into Egypt, is inserted here for unity of subject. "No wages for his army" (29:18): Nebuchadnezzar, God's servant in punishing the nations, had besieged Tyre for 13 years (585–573 B.C.). In proportion to the time expended, the booty had been disappointing, because so many inhabitants fled with their wealth. But now he will make up for it in Egypt (20). "No more a prince" (30:13), that is, native ruler of importance.

30:20–26. April, 586 B.C. 3 months before Jerusalem fell. "Have broken" (21), probably refers to the defeat of Pharaoh's army (Jeremiah 37:5–9).

Chapter 31. June, 586 B.C. 1 month before Jerusalem fell. Egypt warned to take heed to the fate of Assyria, which was more powerful than Egypt, yet it had fallen to Babylon.

32:1–16. March, 584 B.C. 1 year 8 months after Jerusalem fell. A lamentation over Egypt, to be crushed at the hands of Babylon.

32:17–32. March, 584 B.C. 1 year 8 months after Jerusalem fell. A picture of Egypt and her companions in realm of the dead.

Chapter 33. News of the Fall of Jerusalem

A year and a half after the city had fallen (see Chronology page 324). Ezekiel had been silent since the day the siege had begun, a period of 3 years (24:1, 26, 27; 32:22). The visions of chapters 26 to 31, most of which came within that 3 years, directed against Tyre and Egypt, must have been written, not spoken.

Ezekiel's first utterance, after receiving the news, was that the wicked left in Judah would be exterminated (23–29). 5 years later Nebuchadnezzar took 745 more captives (Jeremiah 52:30).

Then follows a note about Ezekiel's popularity with exiles (30–33), charmed with his speech, but continued unrepentant.

Chapter 34. An Indictment of the Shepherds of Israel

Responsibility for the captivity of Israel is here laid directly at the door of the greedy and cruel kings and priests who had exploited and led astray the people. Against this background Ezekiel sees a vision of the Future Shepherd of God's People in the Coming Messiah (15, 23, 24), under whom they shall never more suffer, and "there shall be showers of blessing" (26).

Chapter 35. The Doom of Edom

The inhabitants of Judah now carried away, Edom thought here was a chance to take possession of their land (10; 36:2, 5). But three years later the same fate befell Edom. (See under Obadiah.)

Chapter 36. The Land of Israel to be Re-Inhabited

Now desolate, it will one day become like the garden of Eden (35); peopled with a penitent Judah and Israel (10, 31). This will be for the glory of God's own name (22, 32).

Chapter 37. Vision of the Dry Bones

A prediction of the national resurrection of scattered Israel, their return to their own land, the re-union of Judah and Israel, under the reign of an everlasting king called "David" (24–26). It is a plain forecast of the Conversion of the Jews to Christ; as Paul also foretold in Romans 11:15, 25, 26.

The vision is of the "whole house of Israel" (11–22), both Judah and Israel. The Return of Judah is told in Ezra and Nehemiah, where there is no mention of returned captives of Israel. Yet those returned are called "Israel" (Ezra 9:1; 10:5; Nehemiah 9:2; 11:3).

As to how much of the language is to be interpreted literally of the Jews and what may be a "shadow" of the Christian Covenant in its universal aspect (26–28), there is difference of opinion. It is not always easy to draw a clear line of demarkation between what is to be taken literally and what figuratively. For instance, the great battle of Gog and Magog of chapters 38, 39, yet future, it does not seem can be fought with literal "bows and arrows and handstaves and spears" (39:9). "David" (37:24) is not literal David, but the Messiah. The term "Israel" in the New Testament, while usually used of Jews, is sometimes applied to Christians (Galatians 6:16), and it is indicated that Gentiles were included in the meaning (Galatians 3:7–9, 29; Romans 2:28–29; 4:13–16; Philippians 3:3). So, this vision of a re-inhabited land and a revived and glorified nation, making all due allowance for its evident literal meaning, may, in a sense be also a symbolic picture of a regenerated earth; as the book of Revelation depicts Heaven under the imagery of a magnificent earthly city (Revelation 21). Biblical prophecies of the future were often pictured in terms of what was then present. We think that in such passages as this there may be both a literal and a figurative meaning, just as in Matthew 24 some of Jesus' words seem to refer both to the Destruction of Jerusalem and the End of the World, one typical of the other.

The Messiah is central in Ezekiel's visions of Israel's future. He calls Him "The Prince" (34:23, 24; 37:24, 25; 44:3; 45:7; 46:16, 17, 18; 48:21).

Chapters 38,39. Gog and Magog

Gog was ruler of the land of Magog. In Genesis 10:2 Magog, Meshech, Tubal, and Gomer are named the sons of Japheth and founders of the northern group of nations. In Ezekiel 27:13 Meshech and Tubal are mentioned as being sellers of slaves to Tyre; and in 32:26 as being ancient bandit nations. Rosh is thought by some to mean Russia; by others the identification is regarded as uncertain. Meshech is thought to mean Moscow; or Muscovy, an ancient Russian name; or a people called Moschi spoken of in the Assyrian inscriptions as dwelling in the Caucasus. Tubal is thought to be Tobolsk, a Siberian city; or, a people called Tibareni on the Southeast shores of the Black Sea. Gomer is thought to have been the Cimmerians, who poured in from the north through the Caucasus in the days of the Assyrian Empire, and occupied parts of Asia Minor, but were driven back. Togarmah is thought to be Armenia.

Whatever may be the exact identification of these peoples, Ezekiel speaks of them as dwelling in "the uttermost parts of the north" (38:6, 15; 39:2), and there can be little doubt but that he means nations beyond the Caucasus. A glance at the map makes it plain that he has in mind that part of the world known as Russia.

These peoples were barbarous, and were in a general way spoken of in ancient literature as Scythians. Just about the time Ezekiel was born Southwest Asia was terrorized by vast hordes of them pouring in from the north (see "Scythian Invasion" under Jeremiah 4). Its horrors were still alive in the memories of Ezekiel's older associates.

In these two chapters Ezekiel predicts Another Scythian invasion, on a far more stupendous scale, confederate with peoples from the East (38:5), into the Holy Land, against Restored Israel, "in the latter years" (38:8), apparently during the Messianic Age; and that with the help of God, they will be so overwhelmingly defeated that their weapons will supply fuel for 7 years (39:9), and it will take 7 months to bury their dead (39:14).

In the book of Revelation the same words, Gog and Magog, are used as representing all nations in Satan's final furious attack on the people of God (Revelation 20:7–10).

Chapters 40 to 48. The Rebuilt Temple

April, 572 B.C. Passover time. 14 years after the destruction of Jerusalem. Ezekiel's second vision-journey to Jerusalem, the first having been 19 years earlier (8:1, 3), on a mission of doom for the city. This, to give specifications for its reconstruction, dealing largely with Temple details.

This vision was not fulfilled in the Return from Babylon. Very evidently it is a prediction of the Messianic Age.

Some interpret it literally, as meaning that the Twelve Tribes will one day again inhabit the land, and be distributed as here indicated, that the Temple will be rebuilt literally in all particulars as here specified, and that there will be literal animal sacrifices. They call it "The Millennial Temple."

Others interpret it figuratively, taking the vision to be a metamorphical preview of the Whole Christian Era, under the imagery of a Revived, Restored and Glorified Nation.

This Temple of Ezekiel's vision, with its courts, arrangements and furnishings, roughly, though with many variations, follows the general plan of Solomon's Temple.

God was to "dwell in this Temple forever" (43:7). This language can scarcely be predicated of a literal material Temple. It must be a figurative representation of something; for Jesus, in John 4:21–24, abrogated Temple worship; and in Heaven there will be no Temple (Revelation 21:22).

Offerings and Sacrifices (45:9–46:24). One wonders why there should be Sacrifices under the reign of the "Prince." The Epistle to the Hebrews explicitly states that these were fulfilled and done away in the death of Christ, "once for all." Those who think that this

Temple is a literal "Millennial Temple" consider that these animal sacrifices are to be offered by the Jewish nation while it is still unconverted, or that the sacrifices are commemorative of the death of Christ.

The Life-Giving Stream (47:1–12). This is one of Ezekiel's grandest passages. Joel and Zechariah also spoke of this stream (Joel 3:18, Zechariah 14:8). It seems to be a picture of Heaven's "river of water of life" (Revelation 22:1–2). Whatever specific or literal application these waters might have, certainly, without any straining whatever, they can, in a general way, be taken as a beautiful picture of the benign influences of Christ, coming out of Jerusalem, and flowing forth, in an ever-widening, ever-deepening stream, to the whole wide world, blessing the nations with their life-giving qualities, on into the eternities of Heaven.

Eastern Gate of the Temple to be closed, except to the "Prince" (44:1–3).

The Sacred Area, for the City, Temple, Priests and Levites, was to be in the approximate center of the land, with the lands of the "Prince" on either side (45:1–8).

Boundaries of the Land and Location of the Tribes (47:13–48:29). The land was not quite as large as the domain of David. Roughly, it was the south half of the eastern shore of the Mediterranean, about 400 miles North and South averaging about 100 miles East and West. The Tribes were not in their original arrangement, but as here indicated.

The City (48:30–35). 7½ miles square. Pattern, in part, of the New Jerusalem (Revelation 21). Home of God (35).

Dan
Asher
Naphtali
Manasseh
Ephraim
Reuben
Judah

Temple

Prince City Prince

Benjamin
Simeon
Issachar
Zebulun
Gad

DANIEL

The Hebrew Statesman-Prophet at Babylon

While yet a mere youth Daniel was carried to Babylon where he lived during the whole period of the Captivity, at times occupying high office in the Babylonian and Persian Empires.

The City of Babylon

Babylon, scene of Daniel's ministry, was the wonder city of the ancient world. Situated in the cradle of the human race, near the Garden of Eden region, built around the Tower of Babel (see page 83), first seat of empire, a favorite residence of Babylonian, Assyrian and Persian kings, even of Alexander the Great, a commanding city through the whole pre-Christian era, Babylon was brought to the zenith of its power and glory in the days of DANIEL, by Nebuchadnezzar, who was Daniel's friend, and who, during his 45 years reign, never wearied of building and beautifying its palaces and temples.

The Size of Babylon. Ancient historians said that its wall was 60 miles around, 15 miles on each side, 300 feet high, 80 feet thick, extending 35 feet below the ground so that enemies could not tunnel under; built of brick 1 foot square and 3 or 4 inches thick; ¼ mile of clear space between the city and the wall all the way around; the wall protected by wide and deep moats (canals) filled with water; 250 towers on the wall, guard rooms for soldiers; 100 gates of brass. The city was divided by the Euphrates into two almost equal parts; both banks guarded by brick walls all the way, with 25 gates connecting streets, and ferry boats; one bridge, on stone piers, ½ mile long, 30 feet wide, with drawbridges which were removed at night. A tunnel under the river, 15 feet wide, 12 feet high. Excavations of recent years have, to large extent, verified the seemingly fabulous accounts of ancient historians.

The Great Temple of Marduk (Bel), adjoining the Tower of Babylon (Babel?), was the most renowned sanctuary in all the Euphrates valley. It contained a golden image of Bel and a golden table which together weighed not less than 50,000 pounds. At the top were golden images of Bel and Ishtar, 2 golden lions, a golden table 40 feet long and 15 feet wide, and a human figure of solid gold 18 feet high. Truly Babylon was a "city of gold," (Isaiah 14:4). The city was very religious: It had 53 temples; and 180 altars to Ishtar.

It may have been in the plain between Tower of Babylon and Palace of Nebuchadnezzar that the "image of gold" was set up (3:1).

Nebuchadnezzar's Palace, into which Daniel often went, was one of the most magnificent buildings ever erected on earth. Its vast ruins were uncovered by Koldewey (1899–1912). The south walls of the Throne Room were 20 feet thick (see Figure 56, page 345). The north side of the palace was protected by three walls. Just north of them were more walls 50 feet thick. A little further on still more massive walls. And about a mile further out was the Inner Wall of the city, which consisted of two parallel walls of brick, each about 20 feet thick, 40 feet apart, the space between filled with rubble, making a total thickness of 80 feet, with a deep and wide moat (canal) on the outside. Further on was the Outer Wall, built in the same manner. In the days of ancient warfare the city was simply impregnable.

The Hanging Gardens of Babylon were one of the Seven Wonders of the ancient world; built by Nebuchadnezzar for his Median Queen, beautiful daughter of Cyaxeres who had helped his father conquer Nineveh; on several tiers of arches, one over another, each bearing a solid platform; 400 feet square; terraces and top covered with flowers, shrubs and trees, garden on the roof; watered from reservoir at top to which water was raised from the river by hydraulic pumps. Underneath, in the arches, were luxurious apartments, the pleasure ground of the palace. Built while Daniel was chief governor of the wise men of Babylon. Koldeway uncovered arches in the Northeast corner of the palace which he thought were the Hanging Gardens.

Fig. 53. Ruins of the "Hanging Gardens" of Babylon.
(*Courtesy Oriental Institute, University of Chicago.*)

Processional Street, the great royal and sacred road, entered at the North, gradually ascended, passed into the palace grounds at the Northeast corner, through Ishtar gate, and high over the center of the city, gradually descending to the Southeast corner of the Tower of Babylon wall, where it turned directly West to the river bridge. On both sides were highly defensive walls 20 feet thick, adorned with brilliant, many-colored glazed reliefs of lions. The street was paved with stone slabs, 3 feet square. Near the entrance to the palace the blocks are still in their place, just as they were when Daniel walked over them.

The City of Babylon

Destruction Prophesied. "Babylon, the glory of kingdoms, the beauty of the Chaldeans pride, shall become a wilderness, a dry land, a desert wholly desolate. It shall no more be inhabited. Neither shall it be dwelt in from generation to generation. The wild beasts of the desert shall lie there. Their houses shall be full of doleful creatures. Wolves shall cry in their castles, and jackals in their pleasant palaces. And Babylon shall be desolate forever. They shall sleep a perpetual sleep and not wake" (Isaiah 13:17–22; Jeremiah 51:37–43).

It remained an important city through the Persian period. Alexander the Great would have restored its glory, but his plans were cut short by death. After him, it declined. By the time of Christ its political and commercial supremacy had gone, and in the first century

Fig. 54. Among the Ruins of Babylon. © *Matson Photo*

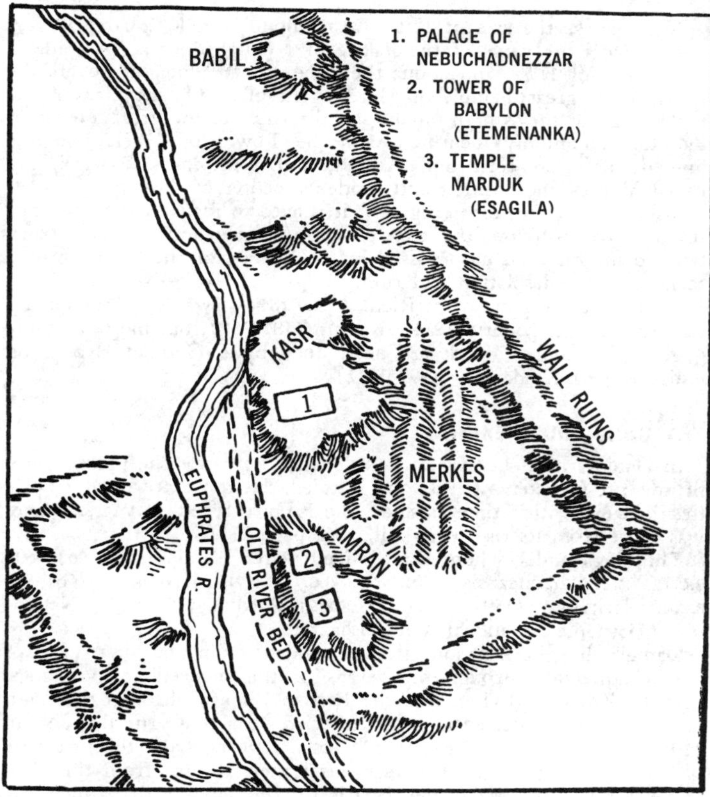

Map 48. Ruins of Babylon.

A.D. the greater part was in ruins. Its bricks have been used in building Baghdad and repairing canals. For centuries it has been a desolate heap of mounds, a place for the beasts of the desert; a remarkable fulfillment of prophecy; still uninhabited except for a little village at the Southwest corner.

The Ruins. The present day mounds are the remains of the great buildings which occupied the central part of the city. They are mostly on the East side of the river, and cover an area about 3½ by 3 miles. The three principal mounds, as may be noted on the map, are Babil, the North mound; Kasr, the central mound; and Amran, the South mound. Babil was the fortress guarding the North entrance to the city, about 1½ miles between it and Kasr; 130 feet high, but only about ⅓ the size of Kasr. Kasr, about ½ mile square, 70 feet high, covers the ruins of the Palace of Nebuchadnezzar. Amran, ½ mile south of Kasr, and about the same size and height, covers the ruins of the great Temple of Marduk (Esagila). On the plain at the north edge of the Amran mound are the ruins of the great Tower of Babylon, commonly identified with the Tower of Babel. The low mounds between Kasr and Amran, and somewhat eastward, are called Merkes, the business and residence center of the city.

In looking at the ruins (Fig. 54), it is hard to realize that here once stood Great Babylon, the city of extravagance and wicked luxury beyond imagination, unsurpassed in the history of the world, now a scene of utter desolation and ruin.

Excavations began with Rich (A.D. 1811); were continued by Layard (1850); Oppert (1854); Rassam (1878–89); but the most thorough and complete work has been done by a German Expedition under Robert Koldeway (1899–1912).

The Babylonian Empire

In Daniel's day, the city of Babylon not only was the premier city of the pre-Christian world, but it ruled the most powerful empire that had up to that time existed. The Empire lasted 70 years. Daniel was there from its rise to its fall. (See page 212).

The kings under whom Daniel lived were: Nabopolassar (625–604 B.C.); Nebuchadnezzar (606–561 B.C.); Evil-Merodach (561–560 B.C.); Neriglissar (559–556 B.C.); Labash-Marduk (556 B.C.); Nabonidas (555–536 B.C.), and his son Belshazzar.

Daniel's life in Babylon, thus, extended from the first year of Nebuchadnezzar, through the reigns of the succeeding five kings, past the Fall of Babylon, into the Persian Empire, through the reign of Darius the Mede, even unto the third year of Cyrus the Persian (10:1); in all, from 606 B.C. to 534 B.C., 72 years, from the first year of the Jews' Captivity till 2 years after their Return from the Captivity–God's witness in the palace of the empire that ruled the world.

Nebuchadnezzar

Daniel was friend and adviser to Nebuchadnezzar. Nebuchadnezzar was the genius and real builder of the Babylonian Empire. Of its 70 years' existence, he ruled 45 years.

Nabopolassar, father of Nebuchadnezzar, viceroy of Babylon, threw off Assyrian yoke (625 B.C.) and ruled city (625–604 B.C.).

In 609 B.C. Nebuchadnezzar was placed at the head of his father's armies. Invading the Western countries, he wrested control of Palestine from Egypt (606 B.C.), and took some Jewish captives to Babylon, among them DANIEL.

That same year (606 B.C.), he became co-regent with his father; and sole ruler (604 B.C.). He proved to be one of the mightiest monarchs of all time.

The following year (605 B.C.), he broke the power of Egypt, in the famous battle of Carchemish.

In 597 B.C. he crushed a new rebellion in Palestine, and took king Jehoiachin and many captives to Babylon, among them EZEKIEL.

In 586 B.C. he burned Jerusalem, and took more captives. Then for 13 years his army besieged Tyre (585–573 B.C.).

In 582 B.C. he invaded and plundered Moab, Ammon, Edom and Lebanon; and in 581 B.C. he again took captives from Judah. In 572 B.C. he invaded and plundered Egypt. Died 561 B.C.

Daniel exerted a powerful influence over him; and three times he called the God of Daniel God (2:47; 3:29; 4:34).

Fig. 55. Nebuchadnezzar's Cameo. (*Reproduced from Schaff's Bible Dictionary. Courtesy of American Sunday-School Union*)

ARCHAEOLOGICAL NOTE: Nebuchadnezzar's Cameo. It is stated in Schaff's Bible Dictionary that "in the Berlin Museum there is a black cameo, with Nebuchadnezzar's head upon it, cut by his order, with the inscription, 'In honor of Merodach, his lord, Nebuchadnezzar, king of Babylon, in his life-time had this made.'" Above is a photographic reproduction of this cameo.

The Book of Daniel

The book itself represents Daniel as its author (7:1, 28; 8:2; 9:2; 10:1, 2; 12:4, 5). Its genuineness was sanctioned by Christ (Matthew 24:15). It was so accepted by Jews and Early Christians. Porphyry, an infidel of the 3rd century A.D. propounded the theory that the book was a forgery of the period of the Maccabean revolt (168–164 B.C.). However, the traditional view that the book is a true historical document dating from the days of Daniel himself persisted unanimously among Christian and Jewish scholars, till the rise of modern criticism. And now the critics, in the name of "modern scholarship," have revived the theory of Porphyry, and put it forth as a settled fact, that the book was written by an unknown author, who, living 400 years after the days of Daniel, assumed Daniel's name, and palmed off on his own generation his own spurious work as the genuine work of a hero long dead. If the book is not exactly what it professes to be, how can we think that God could be a party to the deception? For writers to put forth their own ideas in the names of heroes who lived long before is not even common honesty. We suspect that the real crux of the attempt to discredit the book of Daniel is the unwillingness of intellectual pride to accept the marvelous miracles and amazing prophecies recorded in the book.

The language of the book is Aramaic, or Chaldee, from 2:4 to 7:28, which was the commercial and diplomatic language of the time. The rest is in Hebrew. This is what might be expected in a book written for Jews living among Babylonians, containing copies of official Babylonian documents in their original Babylonian language.

Chapter 1. The Man Daniel

Daniel was in the first group of captives taken from Jerusalem to Babylon (606 B.C.). He was of royal or noble blood (3). Josephus says that Daniel and his three friends were kin to king Zedekiah. That gave them easier entree to the palace of Babylon. Handsome, brilliant young men, who were under the special care of God, and trained of Him to bear witness to His name in the heathen court that then ruled the world. The "king's dainties" (8), which they refused to eat, probably were foods that had been offered in sacrifice to Babylonian idols. Daniel's meteoric rise to world-wide fame is indicated in Ezekiel 14:14, 20; 28:3, written only 15 years later, while Daniel was still a very young man. What a remarkable man! Absolutely unswerving in his own religious convictions, yet so loyal to his idolatrous king that he was trusted with the affairs of the Empire.

Chapter 2. The Dream-Image

This was in the 2nd year of Nebuchadnezzar's reign as sole ruler. Daniel was still a mere lad, having been in Babylon only 3 years.

The Four World Empires here predicted are generally understood to have been the Babylonian, Persian, Greek and Roman. From the days of Daniel to the coming of Christ the world was ruled by these Four Empires, exactly as Daniel had predicted. In the days of the Roman Empire Christ appeared, and set up a kingdom which, starting as a grain of mustard seed, and passing through many vicissitudes, is now giving every evidence that it will become a Universal and Everlasting Kingdom, blossoming into full glory at the Lord's Return.

Critics who assign a Maccabean date to the book of Daniel, in order to explain it as referring to past events instead of being a prediction of the future, find it necessary to place all four empires prior to the date of composition, and so call the Persian Empire two Empires, Median and Persian, in order to make the Greek Empire the

Fourth. But as a matter of fact there was not a Median Empire and a Persian Empire following the Fall of Babylon. To make it appear so is only an effort to distort the facts of history to substantiate a theory. Medes and Persians constituted One Empire under the rule of Persian kings. Darius the Mede was only a sub-king, ruling for a little while, under Cyrus the Persian, till Cyrus arrived.

Moreover, nothing happened in the Maccabean period that answers to the "Stone cut out of the mountains."

This prophecy of the Four Kingdoms is further expanded in chapter 7, the Four Beasts; chapter 8, the Ram and the He-Goat; chapter 9, the Seventy Weeks; and chapter 11, the Struggles between the Kings of the North and Kings of the South.

Chapter 3. The Fiery Furnace

According to the Septuagint this incident occurred in the 18th year of Nebuchadnezzar's reign, after Daniel and his three friends had been in Babylon about 20 years. That was the same year that Nebuchadnezzar had burned Jerusalem (586 B.C.).

Just as God had revealed to Daniel the dream of Nebuchadnezzar, and its interpretation, years before, so now He puts into the hearts of these three men the firm determination to be true; and then He goes with them into the fire, not only to honor their faith, but to demonstrate before the assembled dignitaries of the far-flung empire, the Power of the God of Jerusalem over the boasted gods of Babylon. Thus a second time God manifested himself in the palace of the mighty empire, and a second time the mighty Nebuchadnezzar bowed before God, and proclaimed Him to be the True God to the utmost bounds of his empire.

The Apocryphal book called the "Song of the Three Holy Children" purports to be the song of praise of these three men for their deliverance. Inserted after 3:23. It embodied a popular tradition, but was never regarded as a part of the Hebrew Bible.

Oppert, who excavated in the ruins of Babylon (1854), found a pedestal of a colossal statue that may have been remains of Nebuchadnezzar's golden image.

Chapter 4. Nebuchadnezzar's Insanity and Recovery

This is the story of another Dream of Nebuchadnezzar's which Daniel interpreted, and which came true. Nebuchadnezzar was smitten with a mental disease, in which he fancied himself a beast and tried to act like one, roaming among the animals in the parks of the palace grounds. A third time Nebuchadnezzar bowed before God, and proclaimed His power to all the world. "Seven times" (32): the word means "seasons." Rendal Harris says that in Babylonia "summer and winter were the only seasons counted," according to which it would be 3½ years.

In one of Nebuchadnezzar's inscriptions giving an account of his buildings and accomplishments occurs this as read by Sir Henry Rawlinson: "For four years the residence of my kingdom did not delight my heart. In no one of my possessions did I erect any important building by my might. I did not put up buildings in Babylon for myself and the honor of my name. In the worship of Merodach my god I did not sing his praise, nor did I provide his altar with sacrifices, nor clean the canals." This is thought by some possibly, to be a euphemistic reference to his insanity, though ancient kings in having their inscriptions made avoided recording such things.

Lenormant states that Chaldeans had a tradition that Nebuchadnezzar ascended the roof of his palace, and cried, "O Babylonians, there shall come a Persian to impose servitude upon you. A Mede shall be his associate." This, if true, looks like Nebuchadnezzar had absorbed some of Daniel's ideas.

Chapter 5. Belshazzar's Feast

This was on the night of the Fall of Babylon. Daniel had been in Babylon 70 years. He was now a very old man.

ARCHAEOLOGICAL NOTE: Belshazzar. Until 1853 no mention of Belshazzar was found in Babylonian records; and Nabonidas (555–538 B.C.), was known to have been the last king of Babylon. To the critics this was one of the evidences that the book of Daniel was not historical. But in 1853 an inscription was found in a cornerstone of a temple built by Nabonidas in Ur to a god, which read: "May I, Nabonidas, king of Babylon, not sin against thee. And may reverence for thee dwell in the heart of Belshazzar, my first-born, favorite son."

From other inscriptions it has been learned that Nabonidas, much of the time, was in retirement outside of Babylon, and that Belshazzar was in control of the army and the government, co-regent with his father, and that it was he who surrendered to Cyrus. This explains how Daniel could be "third ruler" in the kingdom (16, 29).

ARCHAEOLOGICAL NOTE: Handwriting on the Wall (25–28). The foundation of this very wall has been uncovered. (See next page.)

The Fall of Babylon is thus related by Xenophon, Herodotus and Berosus: "Cyrus diverted the Euphrates into a new channel, and, guided by two deserters, marched by the dry bed into the city, while the Babylonians were carousing at a feast of their gods."

Inscriptions, found in recent years, state that the Persian army, under Gobryas, took Babylon without a battle, that he killed the son of the king; that Cyrus entered later.

Darius (31), who reigned in Babylon till Cyrus took over (6:28; 9:1), is not mentioned in the inscriptions.

He is thought to have been either Gobryas who was named in

Fig. 56. Ruins of Nebuchadnezzar's Palace, Babylon.
(Courtesy Oriental Institute, University of Chicago.)

Babylonian tablets as conqueror of Babylon, or, as Josephus says, Cyaxares the Median father-in-law of Cyrus. To have a Babylonian name and a native name was common: as Daniel and his three friends were given new names (1:7). But whether Darius was father-in-law of Cyrus, or one of his generals, he led the army that conquered Babylon, while Cyrus was busy with his northern and western wars; and, until the personal arrival of Cyrus, reigned as king of Babylon, probably for about two years (538–536 B.C.).

Chapter 6. Daniel in the Lions Den

Daniel had been a high officer of the Babylonian Empire throughout its whole 70 years, and, though now a very old man, probably over 90, Darius the conqueror of Babylon immediately placed Daniel in charge of the Babylonian government. This probably was because Daniel had just foretold the victory of the Medes (5:28). What a compliment to his wisdom, integrity and fairness. Yet he was unswerving in his personal devotion to his own God (10). What faith! And what courage! And what a doughty old man!

The Miracles of this Book

Wonderful things are told in this book. To those who find it difficult to believe these things we say: let us remember that for a thousand years God had been nurturing the Hebrew Nation for the purpose of through that nation establishing in a world of Idol-worshipping nations THE IDEA that GOD IS GOD. Now God's nation had been destroyed by a nation that worshiped Idols. That was plain evidence to all the world that the gods of Babylon were more powerful than the God of the Jews. It was a crisis in God's struggle with Idolatry. If ever there was a time when God needed to do something to SHOW WHO IS GOD it was during the Babylonian Captivity. Strange indeed would it have been had nothing unusual happened. Something would have been lacking in the Biblical story had not these stupendous Miracles been wrought. Hard as it seems to believe them, it would be harder to believe the rest of the story without them.

At least the Jews, who had, from the beginning, been always falling into Idolatry, were now at last, in the Babylonian Captivity, convinced that their own God was the True God; and they have never since relapsed into Idolatry. No doubt these Miracles had something to do with convincing them. These Miracles had a powerful influence on both Nebuchadnezzar and Darius (3:29; 6:26).

Chapter 7. The Four Beasts

This is a continuation of the prophecy of chapter 2, which was uttered 60 years earlier: "two aspects of one grand scheme of history": Four World Empires, and then the Kingdom of God. In chapter 2 these are represented by an Image with a Head of Gold, a Breast of Silver, Thighs of Brass, and Feet of Iron, broken in pieces by a Stone. In this chapter these same Four World Empires are represented as a Lion, a Bear, a Leopard and a Terrible Beast.

These Four World Empires are commonly taken to be Babylon, Persia, Greece and Rome (see under chapter 2), representing the period from Daniel to Christ. These Beasts seem to form the basis of the imagery of the Seven-Headed, Ten-Horned Beast of Revelation 13.

The "Ten Horns" of the Fourth Beast (24), are taken to be the ten kingdoms into which the Roman Empire was resolved. The "Other Horn" (8, 20, 24, 25), which should arise among the Ten Horns, is a combination of the Leopard Beast and Lamb Beast of Revelation 13. The "three kings" which he displaced (8, 24), are thought to refer to Lombards, Ravenna and Rome, which were handed over to the Popes as the beginning of their Temporal Kingdom, (A.D. 754).

On this interpretation we have a birds-eye view of World History: Egypt, Assyria, Babylon, Persia, Greece, Rome, Papal Rome. Rome was followed by "ten kingdoms," a round number we think denoting control of the world by a number of nations. A sort of ten-fold continuation of the Roman Empire till the End. There never has been a world empire since. Napoleon tried it; he failed. The Kaiser tried it; he failed. So did Hitler, but in vain.

The "other horn" (8, 20, 24, 25), possibly refers to Antichrist.

Time periods of the Book of Daniel

"A time, times, and a half" (7:25), denotes the duration of the Other Horn of the Fourth Beast.

"A time, times, and a half" (12:7), denotes the period from Daniel to the time of the end (12:6).

"A time, times, and a half" is used in Revelation 12:14 as identical with 42 months and 1260 days (Revelation 11:2, 3; 12:6, 14; 13:5), which expressions denote the period the Holy City was Trodden Down, the Two Witnesses Prophesied, the Woman was in the Wilderness, and the Re-Vived Beast was on the Throne.

"2300 evenings and mornings" (8:14), the time the sanctuary was trodden under foot by the Little Horn of the Third Beast. It means either 2300 days; or 2300 half-days, that is, 1150 days; which is slightly short of 3½ years, or almost double it.

"1290 days" (12:11), is the duration of the abomination of desolation, from its beginning to the time of the end.

"1335 days" (12:12), apparently is an extension of 45 days beyond the 1290 day period, culminating in final blessedness.

"70 weeks" (9:24), is the period from the decree to rebuild Jerusalem to the coming of the Messiah. It includes a "seven weeks" of troublous times (9:25), and a "one week" in which the anointed one was to be cut off (9:26, 27).

The word "time," in the phrase "a time, times, and a half," is generally taken to mean "year," the phrase thus meaning 3½ years; which is 42 months, which is 1260 days.

By some it is taken to mean a literal 3½ years. Others, on the year-day interpretation (Numbers 14:34; Ezekiel 4:6), take it to be a period of 1260 years. Still others look upon the figures, not as defining time limits or periods, but as being symbolical: 7 being the symbol of completeness, 3½, which is ½ of 7, represents incompleteness, that is, the reign of evil shall be only temporary.

These time periods are used in close connection with the phrase "abomination of desolation" wrought by the Little Horn of the Third Beast (8:13; 11:31); which "abomination" also follows the cutting off of the Messiah (9:27); and is the point from which the 1290 days run (12:11). Jesus quotes this expression, "abomination of desolation," as referring to the impending Destruction of Jerusalem by the Roman army (Matthew 24:15), in a discourse of blended words involving the End of the World.

"Troublous times" as spoken of for the 7 weeks at the beginning and 1 week at the end of the 70 week period (9:25, 27). A "time of trouble such as never was" (12:1), is predicted for the "time of the end" (12:4, 9, 13); and Jesus quotes the expression as doubly referring to the Destruction of Jerusalem and the End of the World (Matthew 24:21).

Desecration of the Temple by Antiochus lasted 3½ years (168–165 B.C.). The Roman war against Jerusalem lasted 3½ years (A.D. 67–70). The Papacy dominated the world for approximately 1260 years, 6th to 18th centuries A.D. Mohammedanism got control of Palestine (A.D. 637), and it was approximately 1260 years before it passed to control of Christendom (A.D. 1917).

We think that no one interpretation can exhaust the meaning of these time marks of Daniel. Possibly they may be taken both literally, figuratively and symbolically. Possibly they may have primary fulfillment in an event of history, secondary fulfillment in another event, and ultimate fulfillment at the time of the end. The desecration of the Temple by Antiochus, the Destruction of Jerusalem by Titus, Papal Usurpation in the Church, may all be forerunners and symbols of the Great Tribulation in the days of Antichrist. We should not be too disappointed if we fail to feel sure that we understand, for Daniel himself felt sick in not understanding (8:27).

Chapter 8. The Ram and the He-Goat

This chapter contains further predictions about the Second and Third World-Empires spoken of in chapters 2 and 7, that is, the Persian and Greek Empires.

The Persian Empire, represented in 7:5 as a devouring Bear, is here presented as a Two-Horned Ram (3–4), it being a coalition of the Medes and Persians.

The Greek Empire, pictured in 7:6 as a Four-Headed Leopard, is here portrayed as a swift He-Goat bounding furiously from the west, having One great horn, which, when broken, was replaced by Four horns.

The Great Horn was Alexander the Great, who broke the Persian Empire 331 B.C. This prophecy was written 539 B.C., 200 years before its fulfillment. It is a most remarkable prediction of a clash, and the outcome, between two world-empires, neither of which had, at the time of the prediction, yet arisen.

Four Horns (8, 21–22), and Four Heads of 7:6, were Four Kingdoms into which Alexander's Empire was divided (see on chapter 11).

The Little Horn (9), which arose out of the Four, is generally agreed to mean Antiochus Epiphanes (175–164 B.C.), of the Syrian branch of the Greek Empire, who made a determined effort to stamp out the Jewish religion (see under 11:21–35). Yet the repeated phrase "time of the end" (17, 19), may mean that along with the near view of Antiochus there may have been in the distant background of the vision the ominous outline of a far more terrible Destroyer (26), to mar the closing days of history, of whom Antiochus was a symbolic forerunner.

Chapter 9. The Seventy Weeks

The Captivity, which was then drawing to a close, had lasted 70 years. Daniel is here told by the angel that it would yet be "70 weeks" till the coming of the Messiah (24).

The "70 weeks" is generally understood to mean 70 weeks of years, that is, 70 sevens of years, or seven times 70 years, that is 490 years. As if the angel were saying, The Captivity has been 70 years; the period between the Captivity and the Coming of the Messiah will be seven times that long.

Seven, and cycles of seven, sometimes have symbolic meanings; yet the actual facts of this prophecy are most amazing, as follows:

The date from which the 70 weeks was to be counted was the decree to rebuild Jerusalem (25). There were three decrees issued by Persian kings for this purpose (536 B.C., 457 B.C., 444 B.C., see under Ezra). The principal one of these was 457 B.C.

The 70 weeks is subdivided into 7 weeks, 62 weeks, and 1 week (25, 27). It is difficult to see the application of the "7 weeks"; but the 69 weeks (including the 7) equal 483 days, that is, on the year-day theory (Ezekiel 4:6), which is the commonly accepted interpretation, 483 years.

This 483 years is the period between the decree to rebuild Jerusalem and the coming of the "Anointed One" (25). The decree to rebuild Jerusalem, as noted above, was 457 B.C. Adding 483 years to 457 B.C. brings us to A.D. 26, the very year that Jesus was baptized and began his public ministry. A most remarkable fulfillment of Daniel's prophecy, even to the year.

Further, within 3½ years Jesus was crucified, that is, "in the midst of the one week" "the Anointed One" was "cut off," "purged away sin and brought in everlasting righteousness" (24, 26, 27).

Thus Daniel foretold not only the Time at which the Messiah would appear, but also the Duration of his Public Ministry, and his Atoning Death for Human Sin.

Some think that God's chronology was suspended at the death of Christ, to remain so while Israel is scattered, and that the last half of the "one week" belongs to the time of the End.

Summary of Daniel's Prophecies

The Four Kingdoms, and then God's Everlasting Kingdom (chapter 2).

Nebuchadnezzar's Insanity, and Recovery (chapter 4).
Fall of Babylon, and Rise of Persian Empire (chapter 5).
"Fourth" Empire, its "Ten Horns," and "Other Horn" (chapter 7).
Greek Empire, and its "Four Horns" (chapter 8).
The Seventy Weeks, time from Daniel to Messiah (chapter 9).
Troubles of Holy Land in Inter-Testament period (chapter 11).
Signs of the Time of the End (chapter 12).

Chapter 10. Angels of the Nations

This last vision (chapters 10, 11, 12), was given two years after the Jews had returned to Palestine (534 B.C.), God lifted the veil and showed Daniel some realities of the unseen world—conflicts going on between superhuman intelligences, good and bad, in an effort to control the movements of nations, some of them seeking to protect God's people. Michael was the guardian angel of Israel (13:21). An unnamed angel talked with Daniel. Greece had her angel (20), and so did Persia (13, 20). It seems that God was showing Daniel some of his secret agencies in operation to bring about the Return of Israel. One of them helped Darius (11:1). In this chapter they are represented as being interested in the destiny of Israel; in Revelation, the destiny of the Church. In Revelation 12:7–9 Michael and his angels are in war with Satan and his angels. In Ephesians 6:12 powers of the unseen world are the chief enemies against which Christians have to fight. There was great angelic activity when Jesus was born. Jesus believed in angels (see under Matthew 4:11).

Chapter 11. Kings of the North and Kings of the South

Chapters 2, 7, 8, 9, 11 contain predictions about Four Empires, and events, from Daniel to Christ, and seem to have references to later world powers and events onward from Christ to the End. Here is a general outline of world history thus covered:
Babylonian Empire (606–536 B.C.).
Persian Empire (536–332 B.C.).
Greek Empire, with its Four Divisions (331–146 B.C.).
Wars of Syrian and Egyptian Greek Kings (323–146 B.C.).
Antiochus Epiphanes, Desecration of Jerusalem (175–164 B.C.).
Roman Empire (146 B.C.–A.D. 400).
Public Ministry of Christ (A.D. 26–30).
Destruction of Jerusalem by Roman Army (A.D. 70).
The Papacy as a World-Power, 6th to 18th centuries.
Mohammedan Control of Holy Land, 7th to 20th centuries.
World Troubles, and the Resurrection, at "time of the End."

These predictions are progressive in their explanations of details. In chapter 2 a general statement that from the days of Daniel to the days of the Messiah there would be Four World Empires. In chapter 7 details of Fourth Empire. In chapter 8 details of Second and Third Empires. In chapter 11 more details of Third Empire.

The Third Empire was the Greek Empire founded by Alexander the Great (331 B.C.). On his death it was divided among his generals as follows: Greece, Asia Minor, Syria, Egypt. In this chapter the kings of Syria are called "kings of the north." Kings of Egypt are called "kings of the south." Daniel's predictions of the movements of these kings were uttered 200 years before there was a Greek Empire and nearly 400 years before these kings existed. His minute description of their movements is a most extraordinary parallel between prediction and subsequent history. Chapter 11 is pre-written Inter-Testament history. Here is an outline of events answering to the verses in which they were predicted:

"Three kings in Persia" (2): Cyrus, Cambyses, Darius Hystaspes. The "fourth": Xerxes, the richest and most powerful of Persian kings, invaded Greece, but was defeated at Salamis (480 B.C.).

"A mighty king" (3): Alexander the Great. "Fourfold" division of his kingdom (4): Greece, Asia Minor, Syria, Egypt.

"King of the south" (5): Ptolemy I of Egypt. "One of his princes": Seleucus Nicator, originally an officer under Ptolemy I, became king of Syria, most powerful of Alexander's successors.

"Daughter" (6): Berenice, daughter of Ptolemy II, was given in marriage to Antiochus II, and was murdered.

"A shoot from her roots" (7): Ptolemy III, brother of Berenice, in retaliation, invaded Syria, and won a great victory (8).

"Two sons" (10): Seleucus III and Antiochus III (11–12): Ptolemy IV defeated Antiochus III with great loss in the battle of Raphia, near Egypt (217 B.C.) (13): Antiochus III, after 14 years, returned with a great army against Egypt. (14): Jews helped Antiochus. (15): he defeated the forces of Egypt. (16): Antiochus conquered Palestine. (17): Antiochus gave his daughter Cleopatra in treacherous marriage alliance to Ptolemy V, hoping through her to get control of Egypt. But she stood with her husband (18–19): Antiochus then invaded Asia Minor and Greece, and was defeated by the Roman army at Magnesia (190 B.C.). Returned to own land and was slain.

"A contemptible person" (21–35): Antiochus Epiphanes. (21): Not the rightful heir, he got the throne by treachery. (22–25): He made himself master of Egypt, partly by force and partly by cunning deceit. (26): Ptolemy VI, son of Cleopatra, nephew of Antiochus, was defeated by treachery of his subjects. (27): Under guise of friendship Antiochus and Ptolemy vied with each other in treachery. (28): Returning from Egypt Antiochus attacked Jerusalem, slew 80,000, took 40,000 and sold 40,000 Jews into slavery. (29): Antiochus again invaded Egypt. But the Roman fleet compelled him to retire. (30, 31): He vented his anger on Jerusalem and desecrated the

Temple. (32): He was helped by apostate Jews. (32–35): Exploits of the heroic Maccabean brothers.

As to verses 36–45: Antiochus Epiphanes? Or Mohammedan Possession of Holy Land? Or Antichrist? Or all three?

Chapter 12. The Time of the End

Daniel closes his sketches of the epochs and events of world history with a sweep forward to the End (4, 9, 13); when there shall be trouble such as never was (1), followed by Resurrection of the dead, and the Everlasting Glory of the Saints (2, 3).

"A time of trouble, such as never was" (1), is not inapplicable to our own generation: torture, suffering and death, of whole populations, by demon dictators, no more intense perhaps than the atrocities perpetrated by Antiochus, Titus, the Roman Emperors, and the Popes of the Inquisition, but on a scale unparalleled in all previous history.

"Many shall run to and fro, and knowledge shall be increased" (4), is to be a characteristic of the time of the End. This, too, applies to our own generation, as it has to no other: trains, automobiles, ships, airplanes, books, newspapers and radios; as a means of travel and dissemination of knowledge, on a scale never before dreamed of.

And now, on top of all this, has come the nuclear bomb, which has struck terror to the hearts of men to such a degree, that it makes us wonder if we may be living in the period which Jesus spoke of as a setting for His Return, "on the earth distress of nations, in perplexity for the roaring of the sea, men fainting for fear, and expectation of the things that are coming on the world" (Luke 21:25, 26).

HOSEA

Apostate Israel to be Cast Off
Other Nations to be Called In

Hosea was a prophet of the Northern Kingdom: he speaks of its king as "our" king (7:5). His message was to the Northern Kingdom, with occasional reference to Judah.

Hosea's Date

About the last 40 years of the Northern Kingdom. He began his ministry when Israel, under Jeroboam II, was at the zenith of its power. He was a younger contemporary of Amos; an older contemporary of Isaiah and Micah. As a child he may possibly have known Jonah. The kings in whose reigns he prophesied were Uzziah, Jotham, Ahaz, Hezekiah, kings of Judah, and Jeroboam II king of Israel. The approximate dates of these kings were as follows:

Kings of Israel, the Northern Kingdom

Jeroboam II (790–749). A reign of great prosperity.
Zechariah (748). Reigned 6 months. Was killed by Shallum.
Shallum (748). Reigned 1 month. Was killed by Menahem.
Menahem (748–738). Unspeakably cruel. Was a puppet of Assyria.
Pekahiah (738–736). Was killed by Pekah.
Pekah (748–730). Was killed by Hoshea. Galilee captivity (734).
Hoshea (730–721). Fall of Samaria (721). End of kingdom.

Kings of Judah, the Southern Kingdom

Uzziah (787–735). A good king.
Jotham (749–734). A good king.
Ahaz (741–726). Very wicked. Galilee captivity (734).
Hezekiah (726–697). A good king. Fall of Samaria (721).

Some of these dates overlap, and are confusing. The maximum period, thus, in which Hosea could have prophesied would be 790-697 B.C., and the minimum period about 750–725. Assuming that his ministry extended into some considerable part of the reigns of both Jeroboam and Hezekiah, it would be safe, perhaps, to place him at about 760–720.

The Situation

Some 200 years before Hosea's time the Ten Tribes had seceded, and set up an independent kingdom, with the Golden Calf as its official national god. Meantime God had sent the prophets Elijah, Elisha, Jonah, Amos and now Hosea.

Chapters 1,2,3. Hosea's Wife and Children

Hosea was commanded of God to take a wife of "whoredom" (1:2). Israel, as God's "bride" (Ezekiel 16:8–15), had forsaken God, giving herself to the worship of other gods, as a married woman yielding herself to another man. Thus "whoredom" was a fitting name for the nation as a whole in its spiritual adultery, and may not necessarily imply that Gomer herself personally was a lewd woman.

However, the simple, natural implication of the language is that it was an actual experience in Hosea's life; and a generally accepted interpretation is that Hosea, a prophet of God, was in reality commanded of God to marry an unchaste woman, as a symbol of God's love for wayward Israel; or a woman who, if she was chaste at first, afterward proved unfaithful, left him, and became the paramour of a man who could better satisfy her fondness for luxury (2:5), and whom Hosea still loved, and bought back (3:1–2). The idolatrous worship of the land was so universally accompanied with immoral practices (4:11–14), that it was hard for a woman to be chaste, and "whoredom" in its literal sense was probably true of most of the women of the times. For Hosea, possibly, it was that kind of woman, or none at all.

Some of the language applies to Hosea's family literally, some to the nation figuratively, some to both, the literal and figurative alternating. "His sentences fall like the throbs of a broken heart."

Hosea's Recovery of his Wife (3:1–5). He bought her back, but required her to remain for a while without conjugal privilege, as a picture prophecy of Israel remaining "many days without king and without sacrifice," before their eventual return to their God and David their king (3, 4).

The Children. Not only was Hosea's marriage an illustration of the thing he was preaching, but he named his children for the main messages of his life. "Jezreel" (1:4, 5), his first-born. Jezreel was the city of Jehu's bloody brutality (II Kings 10:1–14). The valley of Jezreel was the age-old battle field on which the kingdom was about to collapse. By naming his child Jezreel, Hosea was saying to the king and to the nation: Retribution; the hour of punishment is come.

"Lo-ruhamah" (1:6), was the name of the second child, meaning "No more mercy," for Israel, though there would be a respite for Judah (7). "Lo-ammi" (1:9), name of the third child, meaning "No longer my people." Hosea then repeats the two names without the "Lo" (not) (2:1), of the time when they would again be God's people; and in a play on the words predicts the day when Other Nations would be called the People of God (1:10), a passage which Paul quotes as meaning the extension of the Gospel to Gentiles (Romans 9:25).

Chapter 4. "Ephraim is Joined to Idols"

Idolatry is the source of their horrible crimes (1–3). Priests feed on the sins of the people (4–10). The young women are harlots; married women entertain other men; the men go apart with prostitutes (11–14). Judah (15), had not sunk as deep into Idolatry as Israel had, and was spared for about 100 years after Israel was destroyed. Ephraim (17), being the largest and most central of the Northern Tribes, became a name for the whole Northern Kingdom. "The wind" (19), had already wrapped the sinful nation in its wings to bear it away to another land, a most striking metaphor. "Beth-aven" (15), another name for Bethel the main Idol sanctuary of the Northern Kingdom.

Chapter 5. "Ephraim shall Become a Desolation"

Priests, king and people are "revolters" against God (1–3). Steeped in sin, and proud of it, "their doings would not suffer them to turn to God" (4–5). "Strange children" (7), that is, by men other than husbands. "Content to walk after man's command" (11), referring to the ordinances which Jeroboam I had "devised out of his own heart," when he first established the Northern Kingdom.

Chapter 6. "Priests Murder and Commit Lewdness"

"The third day" (2), probably meaning that after a short period Israel would be restored, and generally understood to be a forehint of the Messiah's resurrection on the third day. "Gilead" (8), and "Shechem" (9), two of the principal cities of the land, were particularly horrible as centers of vice and violence.

Chapter 7. "They are All Adulterers"

"Hot as an oven, devouring their kings" (4, 7), probably refers to the period of passionate indulgence and violence in which four of their kings were assassinated in quick succession, even while Hosea was speaking. "A cake not turned" (8), burnt on one side, raw on the other, therefore unfit for use. "Gray hairs" (9), symptoms of the approaching end.

Chapter 8. "Have Sown the Wind: Shall Reap the Whirlwind"

"Set up kings, but not by me" (4). God had appointed David's family to rule his people. The Ten Tribes had rebelled, and set up a different line of kings for themselves. "Hired lovers" (9): flirting with Assyria, by paying tribute.

Chapter 9. "Abominable Like the Idols they Love"

"Return to Egypt" (3), not literally, but to Egypt-like bondage in Assyria, though after the captivity many Jews did settle in Egypt. "The prophet is a fool" (7): either Hosea's opinion of false prophets; or, more probably, the people's opinion of Hosea. "Deeply corrupted themselves" (9), as in the days of Gibeah where one woman was ravished all night long by beastly men (Judges 19:24–26). "Wanderers among the nations" (17): it began in Hosea's life-time, and has continued with relentless persistence to this day, for Jews, as with no other nation.

Chapter 10. "The Glory of Bethel is Departed"

"Calves of Bethel" (5), shall be broken in pieces (8:6), and thorns and thistles shall grow over their altars (7). "Shalman" (14), is probably Shalmaneser.

Chapter 11. "How Shall I Give You Up"

"Out of Egypt" (1): this is quoted in Matthew 2:15 as referring to the flight of Jesus' parents to Egypt: as the Messianic Nation was called out of Egypt in its childhood, so the Messiah himself in his childhood was called out of Egypt. "Bent on backsliding from God" (7), but God's heart was yearning over them.

Chapter 12. "Jacob Found God at Bethel"

"Assyria" and "Egypt" (2): Israel's lying diplomacy, making secret agreements with Assyria and Egypt, each against the other, would bring disaster. "Bethel" (4): the center of their abominable idolatry was on the very spot where their father Jacob had dedicated his life to God (Genesis 28:13–15).

Chapter 13. "They Sin More and More"

"Offended in Baal" (1): the addition of Baal worship to Calf worship, under Ahab brought national death.

Chapter 14. "Israel Shall Return to God"

Jehovah's wayward bride shall return to her husband, and again respond to his love, as in the days of her youth (2:14–20).

Hosea's book is about four things: Israel's Idolatry, her Wickedness, her Captivity and her Restoration.

Hosea had as filthy a mess as is found anywhere in the Bible. The beastly degradation of the people was simply unbelievable. Yet Hosea labored unceasingly to make them see that GOD STILL LOVED THEM. An amazing book.

JOEL

A Plague of Locusts
The Coming Day of God
Prediction of Gospel Age
And Outpouring of Holy Spirit

Like Zephaniah, it is a book of Coming Judgment. Like Revelation, it forecasts the Earth's Harvest (3:13, 14; Revelation 14:15, 16).

Joel's Date

Is not indicated in the book itself. Usually considered one of the earliest of the prophets of Judah, in the time of Joash (about 830 B.C.); or possibly in the reign of Uzziah (about 750 B.C.).

Chapters 1:1-2:27. The Plague of Locusts

An appalling famine, caused by an unprecedented plague of locusts, followed by prolonged drouth, had devastated the land. The locust is an insect, resembling a large grasshopper. The four different names used in 1:4 indicate different species of locusts, or different stages of growth. Vast clouds of locusts, darkening the sun, swarming upon the earth, devouring every green thing, brought the people to their knees. God heard their cry, removed the locusts, and promised an era of prosperity. These locusts suggest, and may be typical of, those in Revelation 9:1–11.

Chapters 2:38-3:21. The Coming Day of God

In Acts 2:17–21 Peter quotes Joel 2:28–32 as a prediction of "the day" he was inaugurating. This means that God intended the passage to be a forecast of the Gospel era. It would be a day of judgment for the nations (3:1–12). To Joel himself that meant enemy nations of his own times, Sidonians, Philistines, Egyptians and Edomites (3:4, 19). But more. The great battle in the valley of Jehoshaphat (valley of Kidron on the east side of Jerusalem, 3:9–12), is spoken of in connection with the "harvest" (13), the "valley of decision" (14), God "uttering his voice from Jerusalem" (16), the "heavens and earth being shaken" (16), and the "fountain flowing from the house of God" (18)—all of which is a continuation of the thought about the Holy Spirit era of 2:28–32. So, as a whole, the passage seems to be a picture of the Christian age, in which God's Word, embodied in the Gospel of Christ, and borne by the gracious influences of the Holy Spirit to all mankind, would be the sickle, in a grand harvest of souls.

AMOS

Apostasy and Wickedness of Israel
Certain Doom
Restoration
Future Glory of David's Kingdom

This prophecy seems to have been delivered on a visit to Bethel (7:10–14), about 30 years before the Fall of Israel.

Amos was a prophet of Judah, the Southern Kingdom, with a message to Israel, the Northern Kingdom, in the reigns of Uzziah king of Judah (787–735 B.C.), and Jeroboam II king of Israel (790–749, 1:1). The "earthquake" (1:1), Josephus says, was co-incident with the imposition of Uzziah's leprosy (II Chronicles 26:16–21), according to which, Amos' prophecy was about 751 B.C.

Jeroboam's reign had been very successful. The kingdom had been considerably enlarged (II Kings 14:23–29). Israel was in the high tide of prosperity; but brazen in its Idolatry, and reeking in moral rottenness; a land of Swearing, Stealing, Injustice, Oppression, Robbery, Adultery and Murder.

It had been some 200 years since the Ten Tribes had set up the Northern Kingdom, with Calf-Worship as its religion (I Kings 12:25–33). During part of this time Baal-Worship also had been adopted, and many of the abominable practices of Canaanite Idolatry were still rampant. Meantime God had sent Elijah, and Elisha and Jonah. But to no avail. Israel, hardened in its Idolatry and Wickedness, was now speeding on to its ruin, when God sent Amos and Hosea in a final effort to stay the nation in its mad dash for death.

Amos' Contemporaries

Amos, as a boy, probably had known Jonah, and may have heard him tell of his visit to Nineveh. Possibly, too, he may have known Elisha, and may have heard him tell of his association with Elijah. Jonah and Elisha were passing off the stage as Amos was coming on. Joel also may have been his contemporary, or near predecessor. It may have been Joel's plague of locusts to which he referred (4:9). Hosea was a co-worker with Amos. He may have been in Bethel at the time of Amos' visit. They, no doubt, knew each other well, and may often have compared notes on the messages God had given them. Hosea was the younger, and continued his work after Amos was gone. Then, too, just as Amos was closing his work, Isaiah and Micah were beginning theirs.

Chapters 1,2. Doom of Israel and Neighbor Nations

Amos starts with a general impeachment of the whole region, eight nations, Syria, Philistia, Phoenicia, Edom, Ammon, Moab, Judah and Israel. Then centers his attention on Israel. He arraigns each under the same formula, "for three transgressions, yea, for four," specifying their particular transgressions. "Captivity," is one of the key words of the book (1:5, 15; 5:5, 27; 6:7; 7:9, 17). Within 50 years these predictions were fulfilled.

Tekoa (1:1), the home of Amos, was 10 miles south of Jerusalem, 5 miles from Bethlehem, on an elevation of 2700 feet, in the bleak pasture lands overlooking the wilderness of Judea, in the same region where, it is thought, John the Baptist, 8 centuries later, grew to manhood. Amos would now be called a layman, for he was not a priest or professional prophet (7:14), but a herdsman and dresser of sycamore trees. The sycamore was a species of fig of poor quality, a cross between fig and mulberry.

The "earthquake" (1:1), must have been very severe, for it was remembered for 200 years (Zechariah 14:5), and likened ominously unto Judgment Day.

Chapter 3. The Luxurious Palaces of Samaria

Samaria, capital of the Northern Kingdom, was situated on a hill 300 feet high, in a vale of surpassing beauty, surrounded on three sides by mountains, as impregnable as it was beautiful. Its palatial residences had been built out of the blood of the poor (2:6, 7; 3:10; 5:11; 8:4–7)—with a heartlessness that would shock even heathen Egyptians and Philistines (9–10).

Bethel (14), where Amos was speaking (7:13), was the religious center of the Northern Kingdom, 12 miles north of Jerusalem, where Jeroboam I set up a Golden Calf ((I Kings 12:25–33),, which was still there (Hosea 13:2). To this degenerate center of Idolatry came Amos with final warning.

Chapter 4. "Prepare to Meet Your God"

Pampered Ladies of Samaria (1–3), were living in sumptuous indulgence on gains squeezed out of the poor. "Cows of Bashan" (1), fatted animals, waiting for slaughter. Within a few years they were taken away "with hooks" (2). Assyrians literally lead their captives with hooks through the lip.

Israel's Religiosity (4–5). Pitiless in their cruelty, yet intensely religious. What a satire on religion!

God's Repeated Efforts (6–13), to save them, had been in vain. Time for the nation to meet its God had come.

Chapter 5. The Day of God

A lament over the fall of Israel (1–3); another appeal to turn to God (4–9): another denunciation of their evil ways (10–27). Verses 18–26 seem to indicate that they were willing to turn and offer sacrifices to God instead of to the Calf. But what Amos wanted was, not sacrifices, but a Reformation in their Manner of Life. Turn, O Sinner, Turn. Why will you Die?

Chapter 6. The Captivity

Over and over Amos contrasts the voluptuous ease, palatial luxury, and feeling of security, of the leaders and the rich, with the intolerable sufferings about to befall them.

Chapter 7. Three Visions of Destruction

The Locusts (Grasshoppers, AV) (1–3), symbolizing destruction of the land. Amos interceded. God relented.

The Fire (4–6). Another symbol of coming destruction. Again Amos interceded. Again God relented.

The Plumb-Line (7–9). The city measured for destruction. Twice God had relented. But no more. He had punished and punished, and forgiven and forgiven. Their case was hopeless.

The Bethel Priest (10–17). How long Amos was at Bethel is not known. But his repeated denunciations and warnings were shaking the land (10). The priest reported it to Jeroboam. But Amos grew bolder and bolder, telling the priest that he himself would be a captive.

Chapter 8. The Basket of Summer Fruit

Another symbol that the sinful kingdom was ripe for ruin. And a reiteration of the causes: Greed, Dishonesty and Merciless brutality toward the poor. Over and over, under many figures, the Bible makes it plain that there is no possible way to escape the consequences of persistent sin.

Chapter 9. Future Glory of David's Kingdom

Further Prediction of Captivity (1–8). Within 30 years it came to pass, and the apostate kingdom ceased to exist.

The restored Throne of David (8–15). An ever-recurrent prophetic vision of radiant days beyond the gloom. Amos lived near Bethlehem, the city of David. He took it to heart that the Ten Tribes had renounced the Davidic Throne, which God had ordained for his people, and for 200 years had obstinately declined to return to its fold. His last word: In coming days David's Kingdom, which they had despised, will recover, and rule, not over one nation only, but over a World of Nations, in Eternal Glory.

OBADIAH

The Doom of Edom

Edomites

Edom was the rocky range of mountains east of the Arabah (see page 142), stretching about 100 miles north and south, and about 20 miles east and west. It was well watered, with abundant pasturage. Sela (Petra), carved high in a perpendicular cliff, overlooking a valley of marvellous beauty, far back in the mountain canyons, was the capital. Edomites would go out on raiding expeditions, and then retreat to their impregnable strongholds high up in the rocky gorges.

Edomites were descendants of Esau; but were always bitter enemies of the Jews, perpetuating the enmity of Esau and Jacob (Genesis 25:23; 27:41). They refused passage to Moses (Numbers 20:14–21); and were always ready to aid an attacking army.

Date of This Prophecy

It was called forth by a plunder of Jerusalem, in which the Edomites participated. There were four such plunderings:

1. In reign of Jehoram, 850–843 B.C. (II Chronicles 21:8, 16, 17; Amos 1:6).
2. In reign of Amaziah, 803–775 B.C. (II Chronicles 25:11, 12, 23, 24).
3. In reign of Ahaz, 741–726 B.C. (II Chronicles 28:16–21).
4. In reign of Zedekiah, 597–586 B.C. (II Chronicles 36:11–21; Psalm 137:7).

There are various opinions as to which of these Obadiah belongs. Inasmuch as the "destruction" of Judah is mentioned (11–12), the prophecy is generally assigned to reign of Zedekiah, when Jerusalem was burnt by the Babylonians (586 B.C.).

Other Scriptures which foretell Edom's doom are: Isaiah 34:5–15; Jeremiah 19:7–22; Ezekiel 25:12–14; 35:1–15; Amos 1:11–12.

Fulfillment of the Prophecy

Obadiah predicted that the Edomites would be "cut off forever," and "be as though they had not been" (10, 16, 18); and that a remnant of Judah would be saved, and that the kingdom of Judah's God would yet prevail (17, 19, 21).

Within 4 years after Jerusalem was burned, Edom was raided and desolated (582 B.C.), by the very same Babylonians whom they had aided against Jerusalem. Nabathaeans took over Edom. The few Edomites that were left were confined to a region in south Judea, where for four centuries they continued to exist, as active enemies of the Jews. In 126 B.C. they were subdued by John Hyrcanus, one of the Maccabean rulers, and were absorbed into the Jewish state. When Palestine was conquered by Romans (63 B.C.), the Herods, an Edomite (Idumean) family, were placed in control of Judah. This was the last of the Edomites. With the destruction of Jerusalem (A.D. 70), they disappeared from history.

Fig. 57. Yunas Mound, "Tomb of Jonah," near Nineveh.
© *Matson Photo*

JONAH

An Errand of Mercy to Nineveh

Nineveh was capital of the Assyrian Empire. The Assyrian Empire was a World-Empire for about 300 years (900–607 B.C.). It began its rise to world power about the time of the Division of the Hebrew Kingdom at the close of Solomon's reign. It gradually absorbed and destroyed the Northern Kingdom of Israel. Assyrian kings who had to do with Israel and Judah were:

Shalmaneser II (860–825 B.C.). Began to "cut off Israel."
Adad-Nirari (808–783). Took tribute from Israel. Jonah's visit?
Tiglath-pileser III (747–727). Deported most of Israel.
Shalmaneser IV (727–722). Besieged Samaria.
Sargon II (722–705). Carried rest of Israel captive. Isaiah.
Sennacherib (705–681). Invaded Judah. Isaiah.
Esar-haddon (681–668). Very powerful.
Assur-banipal (668–626). Most powerful and brutal, Nahum?
Two weak kings (626–607). The giant empire fell (607 B.C.).

Thus Jonah was called of God to prolong the life of the enemy nation which was already in the process of exterminating his own nation. No wonder he fled in the opposite direction, in patriotic dread of a brutal and relentless military machine which was closing in on God's people.

Jonah was a native of Gath-hepher. He lived in the reign of Jeroboam II (790–749), and helped to recover some of Israel's lost territory (II Kings 14:25). Thus Jonah was a famous Statesman, as well as Prophet.

Is the Book Historical?

Naturally, because of the fish story, the unbelieving mind rebels at accepting it as factual. They call it fiction, or allegory, or parable, or prose poem, etc., etc. Jesus unmistakably regarded it as an historical fact (Matthew 12:39–41). It takes considerable straining to make anything else out of his language. He called it a "sign" of his own resurrection. He put the fish, the repentance of the Ninevites, his resurrection, and the judgment day in the same category. He surely was talking of REALITY when he spoke of his resurrection and the judgment day. Thus Jesus accepted the Jonah story. For us that settles it. We believe that it actually occurred just as recorded; and that Jonah himself, under the direction of God's Spirit, wrote the book, with no attempt to excuse his own unworthy showing; and that the book, under the direction of God's Spirit, was placed among the Sacred Writings in the Temple as a part of God's unfolding revelation of Himself.

The Fish. The word, wrongly translated "whale," means "great fish," or "sea-monster." Many sea-monsters have been found large enough to swallow a man. However, the point of the story is that it was a MIRACLE, a divine attestation of Jonah's mission to Nineveh. Except for some such astounding miracle the Ninevites would have given little heed to Jonah (Luke 11:30).

Archaeological Confirmation. As far as we know, there is no record of Nineveh's repentance in the Assyrian inscriptions. There are, however, traces that Adad-Nirari made reforms similar to those of Amenophis IV in Egypt. And, under the reigns of the three kings following Adad-Nirari there was a let-up in Assyrian conquests. In this period Israel recovered lost territory (II Kings 14:25). There are hints that Jonah's influence on Nineveh was profound, in this Old Testament Suggestion of World Missions.

God's Purpose in It

For one thing, it may have postponed the captivity of Israel, for lust of conquest was one of the things repented of (3:8).

Mainly, it seems to have been intended of God as a hint to His Own Nation that He was also interested in Other Nations.

Further, Jonah's home was Gath-hepher (II Kings 14:25), near Nazareth the home of Jesus, of whom Jonah was a "sign."

Further, Joppa, where Jonah embarked, to avoid preaching to Another Nation, was the very place which God chose, 800 years later, to tell Peter to receive men of Other Nations (Acts 10).

Further, Jesus quoted it as a prophetic picture of his own resurrection on the "third" day (Matthew 12:40).

So, all in all, the Story of Jonah is a grand historical picture of the Messiah's Resurrection and Mission to All Nations.

Chapter 1. Jonah's Flight

"Tarshish" (3), is thought to have been Tartessus, in Spain. Jonah was making for the utmost bounds of the then known world.

Chapter 2. Jonah's Prayer

He must have been used to praying in the words of the Psalms, so like this beautiful prayer. His return landing may have been near Joppa, and may have been witnessed by many.

Chapter 3. Nineveh's Repentance

Jonah, in his preaching, no doubt told his experience with the fish, with witnesses along to verify his story. Speaking in the name of the God of the nation whom the Ninevites had begun to plunder, they took him seriously, and became terrified.

Chapter 4. Jonah's Disappointment

He had come, not to seek their repentance, but to announce their doom. But God was pleased at their repentance, and deferred punishment, much to Jonah's chagrin. (See further under Nahum.)

We think the most beautiful touch in the book is in its last verse: God's compassion for little children. God was influenced to stay the destruction of the city because His own heart rebelled at the thought of the slaughter of innocent babes. Jesus was very fond of children, and child-like dispositions in adults.

Nineveh

Nineveh proper was 3 miles long and 1½ miles wide. Greater Nineveh included Calah 20 miles to south, and Khorsabad 10 miles to north. The triangle formed by the Tigris and the Zab was included in the fortifications of Nineveh. (See page 369.)

Calah, south outpost of Nineveh, covered 1000 acres. Here Layard and Loftus uncovered palaces of Assurnasipal, Shalmaneser and his Black Obelisk, Tiglath-pileser and Esarhaddon.

Khorsabad, north outpost of Nineveh, was built by Sargon, who destroyed Israel (721 B.C.), and whose palace, second to that of Sennacherib, was most magnificent of all (see pages 287, 370).

The "Jonah" Mound. The second largest mound in the ruins of Nineveh is called "Yunas." "Yunas" is the native word for "Jonah." The mound covers 40 acres, and is 100 feet high. It contains the reputed tomb of Jonah. This was one of the indications to Rich that these were the ruins of Nineveh, and led to their identification (see page 42). This tomb is so sacred to the natives that no large scale excavation has been permitted in the mound. Layard uncovered the ruins of the palace of Esarhaddon. It is hoped that some day the secrets of this palace may be explored. (For further notes on Nineveh, see pages 369–371.)

MICAH

Impending Fall of Israel and Judah
The Messiah to be Born at Bethlehem

Micah prophesied in the reigns of Jotham, Ahaz and Hezekiah. Jotham and Hezekiah were good kings, Ahaz was extremely wicked. Thus Micah witnessed the apostasy of the government and its recovery. His home was Moresheth, on the Philistine border, near Gath, about 30 miles SW of Jerusalem. He was contemporary with Isaiah and Hosea.

Micah's message was to both Israel and Judah, addressed primarily to their two respective capitals, Samaria and Jerusalem. Its three main ideas were: their Sins; their Destruction; and their Restoration. These ideas, in the book, are mixed up, with abrupt transitions between Present Desolation and Future Glory.

Chapter 1. Samaria Doomed

Samaria was the capital of the Northern Kingdom. Its rulers were directly responsible for prevalent national corruption (5). Since their apostasy from God, 200 years before, they had adopted Calf worship, Baal worship, and other Canaanite, Syrian, and Assyrian Idols and Idol practices. God had sent Elijah, Elisha and Amos, to turn them back from idols. But in vain. They were about ripe for the death blow. Micah lived to see his words come true (6). In 734 B.C. the Assyrians carried away all of north Israel, and in 721 Samaria itself became a "heap."

Places named in 10–15 were in west Judah, in Micah's home territory. They were devastated by the Assyrians, along with the overthrow of the Northern Kingdom.

Chapters 2,3. Brutality of the Rulers

In addition to their Idolatry (1:5–7), the ruling classes were merciless in their treatment of the poor, seizing their fields, even their clothes, and ejecting women with little children from their homes, and, on top of it all, heaping to themselves false prophets who condoned their unjust and cruel practices (6:11). Micah, having mentioned the captivity (1:16), now abruptly pictures their restoration, God marching at their head (2:12–13).

Continued arraignment of the wanton and inhuman cruelty of the ruling classes, with special reference to Jerusalem (10), and in particular to the religious leaders (5–7, 11). Then Micah pronounces the doom of Jerusalem (12), as he had, in 1:6, of Samaria.

Chapter 4. Zion's Universal Reign

Vision of a Warless, Happy, Prosperous, God-Fearing world, with Zion at its head. What a contrast! 4:1–3 is the same as Isaiah 2:2–4; sublime, grand words, abundantly worthy of repetition. Suddenly, in the midst of this rhapsody of the future, the prophet reverts to his own troublous times and the doom of Jerusalem, which he had just mentioned (3:12), announcing that the people would be carried away captive to Babylon (4:10). It is an amazing prophecy. At the time Assyria was sweeping everything before it. This was 100 years before the rise of the Babylonian empire. Yet Jerusalem survived the Assyrian onslaught, and lived on till Assyria was overthrown by Babylon, at whose hands Jerusalem fell (606 B.C.); and its people were carried away to Babylon.

Chapter 5. Zion's Coming King

Ruler from Bethlehem at the head of Zion. In 4:1–8, the Glorious Future. In 4:9–10, back to the Captivity. In 4:11–12, further back to the prophet's own times, the siege of Jerusalem by the Assyrians. In 4:13, a forward sweep to the future. Then, in 5:1, a return to the siege of Jerusalem. This is the setting for the appearance of the DELIVERER from BETHLEHEM (2–5). In Micah's horizon it was a deliverance from Assyria (5–6). But beyond the horizon, in the dim distance, loomed the majestic figure of the coming MESSIANIC KING, making his advent, out of Eternity (2), by way of Bethlehem. Zion's deliverance from Assyria by the Angel of God was, in some respects, a picture forecast of a coming Greater Deliverance by the Saviour of men. Many Old Testament predictions of Christ were cloudily blurred with historic situations of the prophet's own times, yet too clear to be mistaken. Unquestionably the Eternal Ruler from Bethlehem (2), is to be identified with the Wonderful Child of Isaiah 9:6–7. This is the only place in the Old Testament it is specifically stated that the Christ would be born in Bethlehem (see under Matthew 2:22).

Chapter 6. Jehovah's Controversy with His People

Again, the sins of Micah's times: Ingratitude to God; Religious Pretense; Dishonesty; Idolatry; Certain Punishment.

Chapter 7. Zion's Final Triumph

Micah laments prevailing Treachery, Violence and Blood-Thirstiness. Promises Punishment. Closes with a vision of the future when God and His people shall be supreme, and the promise to Abraham be fully accomplished.

NAHUM

The Doom of Nineveh

Two of the Prophets had to do with Nineveh: Jonah, about 785 B.C., and Nahum, about 630 B.C.; about 150 years apart. Jonah's was a message of Mercy; Nahum's, a message of Doom. Together they illustrate God's way of dealing with nations: prolonging the day of grace, in the end visiting punishment for sins.

The Man Nahum

Little is known of Nahum. He is called the "Elkoshite" (1:1). His name is in the word "Capernaum," which means "village of Nahum." This may indicate that he was a resident, or founder, of Capernaum, which was later made famous as the center of Jesus' ministry. Elkosh, his birthplace, was probably nearby. There is said to have been an Elkosh on the Tigris, 20 miles north of Nineveh, and that Nahum may have been among the Israelite captives. If Capernaum were his home then Nahum was of the same locality as Jonah and Jesus.

Nahum's Date. The book itself indicates the limits within which it belongs. Thebes (No-Amon) had fallen (3:8–10, 663 B.C.). The fall of Nineveh is represented as impending. It took place 607 B.C. Thus Nahum was between 663 and 607. As Nineveh is pictured in the full swing of its glory, and as its troubles began with the Scythian invasion (626 B.C.), it may be a good guess to place this prophecy shortly before the Scythian invasion, say about 630 B.C.—which would make Nahum a contemporary of Zephaniah, who also predicted the ruin of Nineveh in language of amazing vividness (Zephaniah 2:13–15).

Chapters 1,2,3. Nineveh's Utter Ruin

Throughout these three chapters, in language spoken partly of Nineveh and partly to Nineveh, Nineveh's destruction is foretold in astonishing and graphic detail.

God's "slowness to anger" (1:3), may have been mentioned as a reminder of Jonah's visit to Nineveh years before. God's wrath (1:2–8), throughout the Bible, stands opposite his mercy.

The fall of the bloody city (3:1), would be news of untold joy to the world it had so pitilessly crushed, especially to Judah. (For note on Assyrian brutality see page 209).

"Like a pool of water" (2:8), the great number of protecting canals along the edges of the walls gave Nineveh this appearance.

Zephaniah also predicted the Fall of Nineveh, in these words: "Nineveh, the joyous city that dwells carelessly, and says in her heart, I am, and there is none besides me, shall become a desolation, a place for beasts to lie down in, a wilderness; the pelican and the porcupine shall lodge in the capitals thereof; and every one that passes by shall hiss" (Zephaniah 2:13–15).

Nineveh

Nineveh was capital of the Assyrian Empire, which had destroyed Israel (see page 209). Founded by Nimrod, shortly after the Flood (Genesis 10:11–12), it had, from the beginning, been a rival of Babylon: Babylon in the south part of the Euphrates valley, Nineveh in the north part of the Euphrates valley; the two cities about 300 miles apart (see map page 49). Nineveh rose to world power about 900 B.C. Soon thereafter it began to "cut off" Israel. About 785 B.C. God had sent Jonah to Nineveh in an effort to turn it aside from its path of brutal conquest. Within the following 60 years (by 721 B.C.), the Assyrian armies had completed the destruction of the Northern Kingdom of Israel. For still another 100 years Nineveh continued to grow more and more powerful and arrogant.

At the time of Nahum's prophecy, Nineveh was queen city of the earth, mighty and brutal beyond imagination, head of a warrior state built on the loot of nations. Limitless wealth from the ends of the earth poured into its coffers. Nahum likens it to a den of ravaging lions, feeding on the blood of nations (2:11–13).

The term Nineveh refers to the whole complex of associated villages served by one great irrigation system, and protected by the one network of fortifications based on the river defenses. The city proper is also called Nineveh. It is the great palace area in the heart of the greater system.

Greater Nineveh was about 30 miles long and about 10 miles wide (see page 365). It was protected by 5 walls and 3 moats (canals) built by the forced labor of unnumbered thousands of foreign captives, Jonah's mention of 120,000 babes (Jonah 4:11), suggests it might have had a population of near a million. The inner city of Nineveh proper, about 3 miles long, and 1½ miles wide, built at the junction of the Tigris and Khoser rivers, was protected by walls 100 feet high, and broad enough at the top to hold 4 chariots driven abreast, 8 miles in circuit.

At the height of Nineveh's power, on the eve of its sudden overthrow, Nahum appeared with this prophecy, called by some, "Nineveh's Death-Song," a "Cry of Humanity for Justice."

The Fall of Nineveh

The Fall of Nineveh, 607 B.C. (or 612?). Within about 20 years after Nahum's prediction an army of Babylonians and Medes closed in on Nineveh. After 2 years of siege a sudden rise of the river washed away part of the walls. Nahum had predicted that the "river gates would be opened" for the destroying army (2:6). Through the breach thus made the attacking Babylonians and Medes swept in to their work of destruction. Prancing horses, cracking whips, rattling wheels, bounding, raging chariots, flashing swords, great heaps of dead bodies (2:3–4; 3:1–7). It all came to pass exactly as Nahum had pictured it; and the bloody vile city passed into oblivion.

Its destruction was so complete that even its site was forgotten. When Xenophon and his 10,000 passed by 200 years later he thought the mounds were the ruins of some Parthian city. When Alexander the Great fought the famous battle of Arbela (331 B.C.), near the site of Nineveh, he did not know there had ever been a city there.

Discovery of the Ruins of Nineveh. So completely had all traces of the glory of the Assyrian Empire disappeared that many scholars had come to think that the references to it in the Bible and other ancient histories were mythical; that in reality such a city and such an empire never existed. In 1820 an Englishman, Claude James Rich, spent 4 months sketching the mounds across the Tigris from Mosul, which he suspected were the ruins of Nineveh. In 1845 Layard definitely identified the site; and he and his successors uncovered the ruins of the magnificent palaces of the Assyrian kings, whose names have now become household words, and hundreds of thousands of inscriptions in which we read the history of Assyria as the Assyrians themselves wrote it, and which to a remarkable degree confirm the Bible.

Koyunjik is the name of the principal mound. East of the Tigris, just across from the modern city Mosul. It covers about 100 acres,

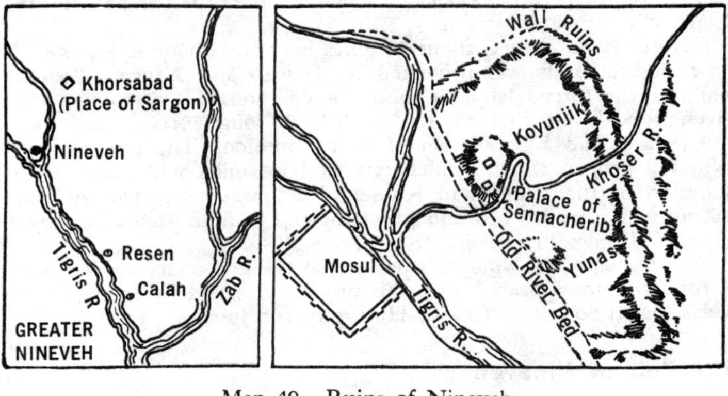

Map 49. Ruins of Nineveh

Fig. 58. Ruins of ancient Nineveh (in Iraq).
Looking Northwest from the Yunas Mound
(*Courtesy Oriental Institute, University of Chicago.*)

and is on an average about 90 feet high. It contains the palaces of Sennacherib and Assurbanipal. Sennacherib was the king who raided Judah. His palace was the grandest of them all. It was uncovered by Layard (1849–50). About the size of three large city blocks.

Library of Assur-banipal. Perhaps the most epochal archaeological discovery ever made. Uncovered by Layard, Rassam, and Rawlinson (1852–54), in the palace of Sennacherib. Originally contained 100,000 volumes. About a third of it has been recovered and is in the British Museum. Assurbanipal was something of an archaeologist; had his scribes search and copy the libraries of ancient Babylon, of an age 2000 years before his day. Thus to him we are indebted for preserving knowledge of primitive Babylonian literature.

HABAKKUK

Invasion of Judah
Doom of the Chaldeans
"The Just Shall Live by Faith"

This prophecy belongs to period between 625 and 606 B.C., probably about 607 B.C., early in Jehoiakim's reign. The Chaldeans (Babylonians) were sweeping westward (1:6), but had not yet reached Judah (3:16). Chronology of the period was:

639–608 B.C. Josiah. Great Reformation. Zephaniah.
626 B.C. Assyria greatly weakened by Scythian Invasion.
625 B.C. Babylon declared its Independence of Assyria.
608 B.C. Jehoahaz reigned 3 months. Taken to Egypt.
608–597 B.C. Jehoiakim. A very wicked reign. Habakkuk?
607 B.C. (or 612?). Babylonians destroyed Nineveh.
606 B.C. Babylonians invaded Judah. Took captives.
605 B.C. Babylonians defeated Egypt at Carchemish.
597 B.C. Jehoiachin reigned 3 months. Taken to Babylon.
597–586 B.C. Zedekiah. A weak, wicked king. Taken to Babylon.
586 B.C. Jerusalem burned. Land desolated.

Chapter 1:1-11. Habakkuk's Complaint

The prophecy is a complaint to God that his own nation should be destroyed, for its wickedness, by a nation that was more wicked. Habakkuk could not see the justice of such a thing.

God's Answer. God replied that He Himself had a purpose in the terrorizing conquests of the Chaldean armies.

Chapters 1:12-2:20. Habakkuk's Second Complaint

Acknowledging that Judah deserved punishment for her Sins, and correction, Habakkuk seeks further enlightenment.

God's Answer. The Chaldean power, drunk with the blood of nations, shall, in her turn, be destroyed; and God's People shall yet fill the earth.

Chapter 3. Habakkuk's Prayer

A cry to God to do again his wonders, as of old; yet with sublime resignation, and confidence in the eternal security of God's people (16–19). The lesson of the book is, Man shall live by Faith (2:2–4).

Faith is the ability to feel so sure of God, that, no matter how dark the day, there is no doubt as to the outcome. For God's people there is a GLORIOUS FUTURE. It may be a long way off. But it is absolutely Sure. Thus, in the midst of his gloom and despair, Habakkuk was an optimist of the first magnitude.

ZEPHANIAH

The Great Day of God at Hand
The Coming of a "Pure Language"

Zephaniah prophesied in the days of Josiah (1:1). He was a great-great grandson of Hezekiah (1:1), thus of royal blood, and kin to Josiah. Josiah (639–608 B.C.), preceded by the long wicked reign of Manasseh, wrought a great reformation (see under II Chronicles 34), in which Zephaniah was a prime mover. Thus this prophecy was uttered only a few years before Judah's Day of Doom struck.

Chapters 1:1-2:3. An Impending Day of Wrath for Judah

It is called The Great Day of God, mentioned over and over (1:7, 8, 9, 10, 14, 15, 16, 18; 2:2, 3; 3:8). A day of terror, about to break on Judah and surrounding nations: having partial reference, perhaps, to the Scythian Invasion (see under Jeremiah 4); but very definite, unmistakable reference to the Babylonian invasion and Judah's captivity, which followed 20 years later; possibly, also, being a sort of symbolic delineation of catastrophes to happen at the time of the end. "Chemarim" (1:4), idolatrous priests. "Host of heaven" (1:5), sun and star worship, Assyrian idolatry. "Malcam" (1:5), Milcom, or Moloch, the Ammonite god. "Maktesh" (1:11), probably a business district of Jerusalem.

Chapter 2:4-3:8. A Day of Wrath for the Nations

Gaza, Ashkelon, Ashdod, Ekron: (4), cities of Philistines. "Cherethites" (5), another name for Philistines. Ethiopia (12), was south Egypt, whose rulers at that time controlled all Egypt. Assyria (15), with Nineveh, its proud capital, terror of the world. Within 20 years these lands all lay desolate under the heel of Babylon.

Chapter 3:9-20. The Coming of a "Pure Language"

The calm after the storm. Three times the prophet speaks of a remnant being saved (2:3, 7; 3:12–13), and twice of their return from captivity (2:7; 3:20), with the introduction into the earth of a "pure language" (9), that is, a Correct System of Thought about God.

Language is the vehicle and expression of Truth. It is the prediction of a complete and perfect revelation of God to man (obviously meaning the Gospel of Christ), as a result of which converts from among all nations would be brought to God, joyful with glad songs of redemption, all the earth resounding with the praise of God's people.

HAGGAI

Rebuilding the Temple
Forecast of the More Glorious Temple Yet to Be

The first step, after returning from the Captivity, for the Jews, in the restoration of their national life in their homeland, was the rebuilding of the Temple.

Haggai, Zechariah, Malachi

These three Prophets belonged to the period after Return from Captivity, the period told about in the books of Ezra, Nehemiah and Esther. (See under Ezra.)

Haggai and Zechariah aided in building the Temple (520–516 B.C.). Malachi is thought to have been associated with Nehemiah nearly 100 years later, in rebuilding the Wall of Jerusalem.

Chronology of the Period

536 B.C.:	50,000 Jews, under Zerubbabel, return to Jerusalem.
536 B.C.:	7th month, they build the Altar, and offer sacrifice.
535 B.C.:	2nd month, work on Temple begins, and is stopped.
520 B.C.:	6th month (September), 1st day, Haggai's Call to Build.
	6th month, 24th day, Building Begins.
	7th month (October), 21st day, Haggai's 2nd Appeal.
	8th month (November), Zechariah's Opening Address.
	9th month (December), 24th day, Haggai's 3rd and 4th.
	11th month (February), 24th day, Zechariah's Visions.
518 B.C.:	9th month (December), 4th day, Zechariah's Visions.
516 B.C.:	12th month (March), 3rd day, the Temple is completed.
515 B.C.:	1st month (April), 14th–21st days, Joyful Passover.
457 B.C.:	Ezra comes to Jerusalem, and makes certain reforms.
444 B.C.:	Nehemiah Rebuilds the Wall. Period of Malachi.

Haggai and His Book

Haggai may have been an old man who had seen the first Temple (2:3)?. His book is composed of four brief discourses.

The Situation

Judah had been conquered, Jerusalem burned, the Temple demolished, and the people carried away to Babylon (606–586 B.C., as told in II Kings 24, 25). After 70 years' Captivity, about 50,000 Jews, by the edict of king Cyrus, had returned to their own land (536 B.C.), and had begun to rebuild the Temple. But ere they had laid the foundation the work was stopped by their enemy neighbors.

Nothing further was done for 15 years. Meantime a new king, Darius, had ascended the Persian throne. He was kindly disposed toward the Jews. And, under the direct preaching of Haggai and Zechariah, work was resumed and the Temple completed in four years (520–516 B.C.). The Wall of Jerusalem was built about 70 years later by Nehemiah.

Chapter 1. Work on the Temple Begins

15 years earlier the foundation of the Temple had been laid (Ezra 3:10). But meantime nothing more had been done. The people had lost interest. God, speaking through Haggai, informs them that this was the reason for their poor crops. One of the most insistent Old Testament teachings is that National Adversity is due to National Disobedience to God.

Haggai's message had immediate effect. People accepted it as God's word, and within 24 days work was under way.

Chapter 2. Future Glory of God's House

Within another 27 days the old foundations had been cleared and reared sufficiently to reveal the outline of the building. Then Haggai came forward with his vision of the Temple's Future beside whose Glory Solomon's Temple itself would pale into insignificance.

This is distinctly a Messianic vision. Haggai's mind was on that Temple, which he was helping Zerubbabel to build. But his words were God's words; and God's mind, in a sense deeper perhaps than even Haggai himself realized, was on Another Temple, yet to be, of which Solomon's Temple and Zerubbabel's Temple were but dim pictures: the Church, built not of stones, but of Souls of the Redeemed. The Church, of Fadeless, Endless, Ineffable Glory, the Consummation of all God's wondrous works, is the Temple of God (I Corinthians 3:16–17; II Corinthians 6:16; Ephesians 2:21), of which Haggai here dreamed.

"Shake the heavens and the earth" (6, 7). Though this may have had immediate reference to political convulsions, it is quoted in Hebrews 12:26 as the fading of earthly things in the dawn of Heaven's Eternal Kingdom.

"The desire of all nations" (7), may refer to the Messiah. Or, more likely, as RV, "precious things of all nations," which would go into the construction of God's House, that is, precious Souls saved by the Messiah.

It was mid-winter (10). The earth had not yet had time to bear its crops. But the people had stirred themselves, and had put their hands to the task of building God's House; and God promises that henceforth their crops would be sure.

Haggai closes with a vision of Zerubbabel's crowning day. Zerubbabel represented David's Family (see under Zechariah 4).

ZECHARIAH

Rebuilding the Temple
Forecasts of the Grander Future Temple
Visions of the Coming Messiah
And His Universal Kingdom

Zechariah was contemporary with Haggai. While Haggai seems to have been an old man, it seems that Zechariah was a young man, for he was grandson of Iddo who had returned to Jerusalem 16 years previously (Nehemiah 12:4, 16). Haggai had been preaching 2 months, and the Temple work had already started, when Zechariah began. Haggai's total recorded ministry lasted a little less than 4 months; Zechariah's, about 2 years. But, no doubt, they were on hand the whole 4 years, exhorting and helping.

The book of Zechariah is considerably larger than that of Haggai. It teems with Messianic flashes, mentioning literally, many details of the life and work of Christ.

Chapter 1:1-6. The Captivity Due to Disobedience

This opening message of Zechariah came between Haggai's 2nd and 3rd message, between verses 9 and 10 of Haggai 2, when work on the Temple was a little over a month along, and its manifest insignificance was disheartening the people. Zechariah warns against their evident rising tendency to return to the ways of their disobedient fathers which had brought them to their present pitiful condition. He then proceeds to encourage them with visions which God had given him of the Magnificent Future.

Chapter 1:7-17. Vision of the Horses

The only time notice of the visions from here to the end of the 6th chapter is in 1:7, when work on the Temple was about 5 months along. So we assume the visions came, one following another; written down at the time.

God's messages through the prophets generally came by the direct moving of God's Spirit upon the prophet's mind. But here they are given through an angel who talks back and forth with the prophet. (For note on Angels see under Matthew 4:11.)

This Vision of the Horses means that the whole world was at rest under the iron hand of the Persian Empire, whose king, Darius, was favorably disposed toward the Jews, and had decreed that the Temple should be built. This vision concludes asserting that Jerusalem shall once again be a great and prosperous city (see under chapter 2).

Chapter 1:18-21. Vision of the Horns and Smiths

The Four Horns represented the Nations that had destroyed Judah and Israel. The Four Smiths ("carpenters" AV) represented God's Destroyers of those nations. It was a figurative way of saying that prevailing World-Powers would be broken, and Judah again be exalted. God is on the throne, even when His people are temporarily vanquished.

Chapter 2. Vision of the Measuring Line

A grand chapter. It is a forecast of a Jerusalem so populous and prosperous and secure that it will overflow its walls, God himself being its protection. Work on the Temple, 5 months along, was going nicely, and the people no doubt were making plans to rebuild the Wall of Jerusalem, which, however, was not built till 75 years later. But their plans were the setting for this vision of the day when "many nations out of all the languages of the earth" shall come to the God of the Jews, based on this call for captives still in Babylonian lands to return.

Chapter 3. Vision of Joshua the High Priest

A prevision of the Atonement of Christ. Joshua the High Priest is clothed in filthy garments, symbolizing the sinfulness of the people. Joshua's filthy garments are removed, meaning that the people's sins are forgiven and they are accepted of God. It was a picture of the time when the sins of mankind would be removed "in one day" (9), as the coming "Branch" in David's House (the Messiah) is "pierced" (12:10), and "a fountain for sin be opened" (13:1. See further under 13:1–9).

Chapter 4. A Candlestick and the Two Olive-Trees

What is here said is meant directly for Zerubbabel and the House he was building. But there is unmistakable reference to a Later More Glorious House, to be built by a Descendant of Zerubbabel, called The Branch. It is an exhortation to take courage, in the day of small beginnings, by keeping our eyes on the grandeur of the end. The Candlestick was a symbolic representation of God's House, or the Light-Bearing qualities of God's House. It was in the Tabernacle, and in the Temple. In Revelation 1:20 it represents the Church. The Two Olive Trees seem to have represented Joshua and Zerubbabel. In chapter 3 the vision was specially for Joshua. Here it is specially for Zerubbabel. The imagery here is carried over into the vision of the Two Witnesses in Revelation 11.

Chapter 5:1-4. The Flying Roll

A sheet, like an unrolled wall-map, 30 feet long, 15 feet wide, inscribed with curses against stealing and swearing, soaring over the land, removing sin by destroying the sinners.

Chapter 5:5-10. The Flying Ephah

Another representation of the Removal of Sin. A large basket, having the appearance of an ephah, containing a Woman, is borne away, by two Women, out of the land. While Sin is here represented by a Woman, it is also by Women that she is removed (9). Might this possibly be a prophetical hint that the Coming Branch who would remove man's sin in one day (3:8–9), would be brought into the world by Woman without the agency of man? The imagery here is somewhat similar to that of the "Scapegoat" of Leviticus 16, on whose head the sins of the people were placed and borne away into the wilderness. An "Ephah" was a measuring basket, slightly larger than a bushel.

Chapter 6:1-8. The Four War Chariots

Messengers of God's Judgments, patrolling the earth, executing the decrees of God on Israel's enemies. An expansion of the thought in the vision of Horns and Smiths (1:18–21).

Chapter 6:9-15. The Coronation of Joshua

This is a prophetic symbolical act, amplifying the vision of the "Branch" (3:8–9), and vision about Zerubbabel (4:6–9).

The "Branch" (12), was the name of the Coming Messiah in David's family, to be called the "Nazarene" (Isaiah 4:2; 11:1, 10; Jeremiah 23:5–6; 33:15–17; Revelation 5:5; 22:16).

Zerubbabel, the governor, was grandson of king Jehoiachin who had been carried to Babylon, and was heir to David's throne. What is said of Zerubbabel refers in part to himself personally, and in part to his Family, that is, David's Family, more particularly to the One Great Representative of David's Family, the Coming Messiah.

To David's Family God had, among other things, assigned the

task of Building God's House. To David himself God gave, in His own handwriting, the plans and specifications of the Temple (I Chronicles 28:11, 19). Solomon, David's son, built the Temple, according to those specifications (II Chronicles 2–7), the most magnificent building in all the world at that time. Zerubbabel, a descendant of David, was now (520–516 B.C.), engaged in rebuilding the Temple. He was assured that he would bring it to completion (4:6–9), with mystic hints of yet Another Temple to be built by the "Branch," with help of "many from afar" (6:12–15).

The "Branch" was to be of Zerubbabel's (David's) family, the kingly line. But here Joshua, the Priest, is crowned, and is represented as the "Branch," sitting on the throne of David (6:12–13); a symbolic merging of the two offices of King and Priest in the Coming Messiah.

Chapters 7,8. Questions about Fasting

For 70 years the people had been fasting in the 4th, 5th, 7th and 10th months (8:19), mourning the destruction of the Temple. Now that it looked as if they were soon to have a Temple again, the question arose as to whether these fasts should be continued. In reply Zechariah reminds them that there had been good reason for their fasts, in penitence for their disobedience and consequent affliction; but that now their fasts had become a mere outward pretense of exhibiting their own holiness, and their religious feasts were for their own pleasure.

Then, following prophetic custom of alternating scenes of present distress and future glory, Zechariah draws a picture of the age when fasts shall be joyful feasts (8:19).

The Jews, once a mighty nation, with traditions from of old that they had been designed of their God to be the leading people of all the world, now a remnant insignificant and despised, were existing in their own land only by the permission of Persian kings. Zechariah tried hard to encourage them by repeating over and over that it would not be forever thus; that by and by the mighty empire that then ruled would be broken, and God's people yet come into their own.

Zechariah's picture of a prosperous and peaceful Zion, its streets full of happy boys and girls and old men and old women (8:3–5), center of the world's civilization, all the nations of the earth coming to the Jews to learn of their God (8:22–23), is also found in other passages (1:17; 2:4, 11; 14:8, 16). Whatever may have been the original intent of these passages, the language is certainly a remarkable picture of what has been going on for twenty centuries: influences emanating from Jerusalem, in the name of Christianity, molding the course of history, bringing the nations of the world to the God of the Jews.

Chapters 9,10,11. God's Judgments on Neighbor Nations

Chapters 9–14 contain things that have evident reference to the Greek Wars, which came 200 years after Zechariah.

Chapter 9 seems to be a forecast of Judah's struggle with Greece. Alexander the Great, on his invasion of Palestine (332 B.C.), devastated the cities named in verses 1–7, in the order in which they are named, and yet spared Jerusalem (8). Verses 13–17 seem to refer to the continuation of Judah's struggle against the Greek Ptolemies and Seleucids into the Maccabean period.

A Picture of Zion's Coming King (9:9–10), is here set amid scenes of Judah's fierce struggle with Greece. Verse 9 is quoted in the New Testament as referring to the Triumphal Entry of Christ into Jerusalem (Matthew 21:5; John 12:15). In the same breath (10), the prophet sweeps forward to the day of Final Triumph. A glimpse at the Beginning of Messiah's Kingdom; then a glimpse at the End.

Chapter 10 is a forecast of the Restoration of God's Scattered People. At that time only a small remnant had returned.

Chapter 11 is a Parable of Shepherds. God's flock had been scattered and slaughtered because their shepherds had been false. In the arraignment of false shepherds is a picture of their rejection of the Good Shepherd (12–13). We might not, from the context, connect this passage with the betrayal of Christ by Judas Iscariot, except that it is so quoted in the New Testament (Matthew 26:15; 27:9–10). The fact that it is so quoted is a key to God's meaning in the passage. The rejection of their True Shepherd was accompanied by the breaking of the staves Beauty and Bands, that is, the covenant of God's protecting care, and postponement of their reunion in the land.

Then they are delivered over to the Worthless Shepherd ("Idol" Shepherd, AV, 15–17). This is thought to refer to the Destruction of Jerusalem by the Romans, shortly after the Death of Christ, and consequent Re-Dispersion of the Jews; or, possibly, it may be an impersonation of the whole list of the Jews' persecutors from the Maccabean period to the time of the Beast of Revelation 13.

Chapters 12,13,14. Vision of Israel's Future

As chapters 9, 10, 11 are called the "burden" concerning Neighbor Nations (9:1), so chapters 12, 13, 14 are called the "burden" concerning Israel (12:1). The two sections are quite similar. Both are an enlarging continuation of ideas in the visions of the first 8 chapters, the same ideas ever recurring in different dress.

12:1–6. Judah's Coming Struggle with All Nations. Description of this struggle is continued in 14:1–8. Some consider the language to be a figurative representation of God's struggle with the nations through the whole Christian era. Others apply it more literally to the time of the End.

12:7–13:9. Mourning in the House of David. The thoughts here are evidently centered around the House of David. Though the language is difficult, yet there is clearly depicted a tragedy of some kind or other as occurring in the family of David, an occasion for great sorrow, when some leading personage of the family would be smitten (13:7), his hands be pierced (12:10; 13:6), and a fountain for sin be opened (13:1). It was to happen in the day when "the House of David shall be as God" (12:8). Only one member of David's family was God. That one was Jesus. This identifies the person here referred to as the "Branch" of 3:8, who would "remove the sin of the earth in one day" (3:9), and who would "build the house of God" (6:12), and rule from sea to sea (see under 6:9–15). It is an amazing forecast in detail of the Death of Jesus, in nowise applicable to any other known person. Thus the death of the Branch in David's family would be the source of God's power against the nations (12:2–4) and its efficiency would be shown in the eventual removal of idols and false prophets from the earth (13:2–5).

14:1–2. Judah's Struggle with the Nations. (See on 12:1–6.)

14:3–21. God's Victory and Universal Reign. The grand consummation of prophetic dreams, the day of the Lord's Return, and the inauguration of his Everlasting Kingdom. Some Biblical scholars think that verses 4–8 mean that Jesus, when he Returns, will literally make his throne on the Mount of Olives, that the mountain will literally be cleft, that waters literally will flow eastward and westward from Jerusalem, and that Jerusalem literally will be the center of pilgrimages from nations outlined in verses 10–21. Others take the language to be a figurative representation of the New Heavens and New Earth, under the imagery of a benign, prosperous, and all-powerful earthly kingdom, as Revelation 21 describes Heaven under the imagery of a magnificent earthly city. The "two thirds" (13:8), may mean the larger part of the nation that fell in the destruction of Jerusalem (A.D. 70), following their Rejection of Christ.

Summary of Zechariah's Fore-Glimpses of Christ

His Atoning Death for the Removal of Sin (3:8–9; 13:1).
As Builder of the House of God (6:12).
His Universal Reign as King and Priest (6:13; 9:10).
Triumphal Entry (9:9, quoted in Matthew 21:5; John 12:15).
Betrayal for 30 pieces of silver (11:12, quoted in Matthew 27:9,10).
His Deity (12:8).
His Hands Pierced (12:10; 13:6, quoted in John 19:37).
A Smitten Shepherd (13:7, quoted in Matthew 26:31, Mark 14:27).

Here are plain statements which forecast, in specific language, not only the great doctrines of the Coming Messiah's Atoning Death for human sin, his Deity, and his Universal Kingdom, but also mention detailed incidents in his life, such as his Entry into Jerusalem Riding on a Colt, his Betrayal for 30 pieces of silver, etc.

MALACHI

Final Old Testament Message to a Disobedient Nation

Malachi's exact date is not known. It is generally accepted that he lived nearly 100 years after Haggai and Zechariah; and that he was associated with Ezra and Nehemiah in their reforms. His date is placed approximately at 450–400 B.C.

A Remnant had returned from Captivity (536 B.C.). Under leadership of Haggai and Zechariah they had rebuilt the Temple (520–516 B.C.). Then 60 years later (457 B.C.), Ezra came to help reestablish the nation. Then, 13 years later (444 B.C.), Nehemiah came, and rebuilt the wall.

Thus, in Malachi's time, the Jews had been home from Babylon about 100 years, cured, by the Captivity, of their Idolatry, but prone to neglect the House of God. The priests had become lax and degenerate, Sacrifices were inferior. Tithes were neglected. The people had reverted to their old practice of intermarrying with idolatrous neighbors (see on Ezra 9).

So, the Jews, favored of God above all nations, discouraged by their weakness, and wedded to their sins, had settled down, in a lethargic state of mind, to await the coming of the Promised Messiah. Malachi assured them that the Messiah would come, but that it would mean judgment for such as they.

Chapter 1. Contempt for Temple Sacrifices

Verses 2–3 are quoted in Romans 9:10–13 as applying to God's choice of Jacob instead of Esau (Genesis 25:22–34). Malachi uses the language as referring to the two nations that sprang from Jacob and Esau, Israelites and Edomites. Both had been destroyed by the Babylonians. Israel had been restored, but Edom was still a desolation.

Their offering of diseased and blemished animals, which they would not have dared to offer to their governor (8), was in reality an insult to God. Against this Malachi envisions the day when the God whom his own nation thus despises will become the beloved God of the whole earth (11).

Chapter 2. Marriages with Heathen Neighbors

Priests, who had been ordained of God to lead the people in

righteousness (5–7), were responsible for the deplorable situation. They had become so debased, mercenary and corrupt that the name "priest" had become a word of contempt among the people.

Loose Marriage Morals (10–16). Jews were divorcing their wives to marry heathen women. This was a double sin, which was disastrous to proper rearing of children.

Skepticism was at the root of their religious indifference and their low morals. Noticing that wicked nations were more prosperous, the people were commonly saying, What is the use of serving God? (See under 3:13–18.)

Chapter 3:1-6. The Coming Day of the Lord

Malachi's reply to their skepticism: the Coming Day of Judgment will answer their taunts, and show whether it pays to serve God (5. See further under 3:13–18).

Chapter 3:7-12. Tithes

Another abrupt change of subject. Withholding tithes is called "robbing God"; for by the Mosaic constitution the tithe was God's property, to which the donor had no more right than he had to another man's property. Note God's promise of prosperity to faithful tithers, and the challenge to test Him on the promise.

Chapter 3:13-18. National Skepticism Again

They did not believe God's promise about tithes. They considered that money and effort offered to God were wasted. Malachi's answer: Wait and see; the end will show (16–17). This beautiful passage pictures the faithful few, in a time of general apostasy, and God recording their names for recognition in "that day."

Chapter 4. The Coming Day of the Lord

Four times Malachi sweeps forward to "The Day of the Lord" (1:11; 3:1–6, 16–18; 4:1–6). He calls it "The Day" (3:2, 17; 4:1, 3, 5). It seems to mean the whole Christian era, with special application to the time of the end.

Closing Old Testament admonition: Remember the Law of Moses (4).

Its closing prediction: Elijah will usher in the "Day of the Lord" (5). He did, 400 years later, in the person of John the Baptist (Matthew 3:1–12; 11:14).

Its last-mentioned virtue: Parental and filial love (6), including, as quoted in Luke 1:17, regard for ideals of forefathers.

Its last word: "Curse," meaning that the plight of mankind would be hopeless should the Lord fail to come.

Thus closes the Old Testament. 400 years elapsed. Then came the Messiah, whom the Hebrew nation had been born to bring forth. As through the centuries they had rejected the prophets of God, so when the Messiah arrived, they rejected Him. Since which time Jews have been homeless wanderers over the earth, the tragedy and miracle of the ages.

MESSIANIC STRAIN OF THE OLD TESTAMENT

Fore-Shadows and Predictions of the Coming Messiah

The Old Testament was written to create an anticipation of, and pave the way for, the Coming of Christ. It is the Story of the Hebrew Nation, dealing largely with events and exigencies of its own times. But all through the Story there runs unceasing Expectancy and Prevision of the Coming of ONE MAJESTIC PERSON, who will Rule and Bless the Whole World. This Person, long before He arrived, came to be known as the MESSIAH.

The Predictions and Foregleams of His Coming constitute the Messianic Strain of the Old Testament. They form the Golden Thread extending through, and binding together, its many and diverse books, into One Amazing Unity.

Starting with Vague Hints, there soon begin to appear Specific Definite Predictions, which, as the story sweeps onward, become more Specific, more Definite and more Abundant.

And, as Definite Predictions multiply, accompanying Symbols, Pictures, Types and indirect Foregleams, also increase.

So that, by the time we come to the end of the Old Testament, the entire Story of Christ has been Pre-Written and Pre-Figured in Language and Symbol, which, taken as a whole, Cannot Refer to Any Other Person in History.

In addition to Predictions and Types which are most evident, there may be many Hidden Messianic Intimations which are not clearly visible on the surface.

And some incidents or passages may have meaning or bearing on later developments, not noticeable till after the later developments came to pass.

However, we think it best not to overdo the matter of Types, except they are so explained in the Scripture, or are so apparent as to be unmistakable.

Our purpose here is to give, in their own order, a brief outline of Old Testament passages which most plainly point forward to the Coming of Christ.

Genesis 3:15. Seed of the Woman

Seed of the WOMAN shall bruise the Serpent's Head. Serpent shall bruise HIS heel.

This seems to say that God is determined, in spite of Man's Sin, to bring His creation of Man to a successful issue. As through Woman Man Fell, so through Woman shall Man be Redeemed. It will be by a Man, "His," who will be of the Seed of the Woman, that is, born of Woman without the agency of Man. It seems like a primeval hint of the Virgin Birth of Christ. For there has been only ONE descendant of Eve who was born of Woman without being begotten by Man.

Genesis 4:3-5. Abel's Offering

"Cain brought of the fruit of the ground an offering to the Lord. And Abel brought of the Firstlings of his Flock. . . . And the Lord had respect unto Abel and his Offering. But unto Cain and his Offering he had not respect."

This looks like the institution of Blood Sacrifice, right at the start, as the condition of man's Acceptance with God—a primal Hint, and the beginning of a long line of Pictures and Predictions of Christ's Atoning Death for Human Sin.

Genesis 12:3; 18:18; 22:18. Call of Abraham

"In Thee shall All the Nations of the earth be Blessed."

Here is a clear definite statement, repeated three times, to Abraham, that in him God was founding a Nation for the express purpose of, through the Nation, Blessing All Nations. (See page 94.) By and by it came to be called The Messianic Nation.

Genesis 14:18-20. Melchizedek

Melchizedek, King of Salem, Priest of God, brought Bread and Wine, and Blessed Abraham. And Abraham gave Tithes to Melchizedek. In Psalm 110:4 it is said of the Coming Messiah, "Thou art a Priest Forever after the order of Melchizedek." In Hebrews 7 Melchizedek, as a King-Priest, is called a type of Jesus.

So, here we have a sort of Historical Shadow-Picture of the Coming Super-Human PERSON Whom Abraham's Nation was being formed to bring into the world as Saviour of Mankind. And it was in Salem, that is, Jerusalem, same city where Jesus was Crucified. And the Bread and Wine: what a Beautiful Primeval Picture of the Lord's Supper and all that it means!

Genesis 22:1-19. Abraham Offers Isaac

A Father Offering His Son: the Son, for Three Days, in the Father's Mind, as good as Dead (22:4): a Substitutionary Sacrifice (22:13): and it was on Mount Moriah (22:2), same mount on which

Jesus was Crucified, same place where Abraham had paid tithes to Melchizedek (14:18), Salem being on Mount Moriah.

As Melchizedek seems to have been a primeval Shadow, in Abraham's Life, of the PERSON Abraham's Nation would bring into the world, so here seems to be a Shadow of the EVENT in the Coming Person's Life by which He would do His work. What an apt Picture of the Death and Resurrection of Christ!

Genesis 26:4; 28:14. The Promise Repeated

Made three times to Abraham, it is here repeated to Isaac, and then to Jacob, that their seed would be a Blessing.

Genesis 49:10,11. Shiloh

The Sceptre shall not depart from Judah till Shiloh Come. And unto Him shall the gathering of the people be. He Washed His Garments in the Blood of Grapes.

Here is the first Clear, Definite Prediction that ONE PERSON would arise in Abraham's Nation to Rule All Nations, Shiloh, He Whose Right It Is. He must be the One of Whom Melchizedek was a Shadow. He would appear in the tribe of Judah. His Garments Washed in the Blood of Grapes may be a metaphorical Fore-Hint of His Crucifixion.

Exodus 12. Institution of the Passover

Israel's Deliverance out of Egypt. Death of Egypt's First-Born. Israel's Houses marked with the Blood of a Lamb. The Lord Passed Over those so marked. The Feast to be Kept Annually throughout all their generations. It became Israel's principal Feast. Observed in Memory of Deliverance from Egypt.

Kept for 1400 years, as the Very Heart of the Hebrew Nation. Unmistakably it was designed of God to be a Gigantic Historical Fore-Picture of the Basic Event of Human Redemption, the Death of Christ, the LAMB OF GOD, who Expired on the Cross, at a Passover Feast, bringing Eternal Deliverance from Sin, for those marked with His Blood, even as the First Passover brought deliverance from Egypt for Israel. It shows how much God's Mind was on the Coming of Christ long before He Came.

Leviticus 16. The Day of Atonement

Once a Year. 10th Day of 7th Month. Two Goats. One Killed as a Sin-Offering. High Priest Laid Hands on Head of Other, called Scapegoat, Confessing over him the People's Sin. Then Scapegoat was Led Away, and Let Go in the Wilderness.

This, and the whole system of Levitical Sacrifices, as continuing Features of Hebrew Life, are Clear Historical Fore-Pictures of the Atoning Death of the Coming Messiah.

Numbers 21:6-9. The Fiery Serpent

In the Wilderness, Serpents Bit the People. Many Died. Moses made a Serpent of Brass. Whoever Looked at it Lived.

Jesus took this to be a Picture of Himself being Lifted up on the Cross (John 3:14). Mankind, bitten with Sin in the Garden of Eden, may Look to Him, and Live.

Numbers 24:17,19. The Star

There shall come a Star out of Jacob. A Sceptre shall rise out of Israel. He shall Have Dominion.

Here is another definite Prediction of a PERSON, a Brilliant Ruler: evidently meaning the Same Person as the Shiloh of Genesis 49:10, who is to Rule the Nations.

Deuteronomy 18:15-19. A Prophet Like unto Moses

God would raise up a Prophet like unto Moses, through Whom God would Speak to Mankind. Evidently another characterization of the Shiloh and the Star aforementioned.

Thus, in the first five books of the Old Testament, there is specific prediction, repeated five times, that the Hebrew Nation was being launched into the world for the one express purpose of Blessing All Nations.

And also specific predictions that there would arise in the Nation ONE PERSON, called Shiloh, a Star, a Prophet, with rather plain intimations that it would be through this ONE PERSON that the Nation would fulfill its mission.

Also, there are various hints about the nature of this PERSON'S work, especially featuring His Sacrificial Death. Thus early, 1400 years before Christ came, there were drawn, in fairly distinct lines, some leading characteristics of Christ's Life.

Joshua

This book seems to have no direct prediction of the Messiah, though Joshua himself is thought, in a sense, to have been Typical of Jesus. The Names are the same, "Jesus" being the Greek form of the Hebrew "Joshua." As Joshua led Israel into the Promised Land, so Jesus will lead His People into Heaven.

Ruth

Ruth was the Great Grandmother of David: beginning of the Family in which the Messiah would come. (See page 175.)

Boaz was of Bethlehem. Jesus was born in Bethlehem. An old tradition has it that Boaz took Ruth to be his bride, and started the Family which was to bring Christ into the world, in the Very Same Room in which, 1100 years later, Christ was born.

I Samuel 16. David

David anointed King over Israel. From here on David is the Central Figure of Old Testament History. The most specific and most abundant of all Messianic Prophecies cluster around his Name. Abraham founder of the Messianic Nation. David founder of the Messianic Family within the Nation.

II Samuel 7:16. David Promised an Eternal Throne

"Thy Throne Shall Be Established FOREVER." Here begins a long line of Promises that DAVID'S FAMILY should Reign FOREVER over God's People. (See page 184.)

This Promise is Repeated over and over, throughout the rest of the Old Testament, with an ever increasing mass of Detail, and Specific Explanations, that the Promise will find its Ultimate Fulfillment in ONE GREAT KING, who will Himself Personally Live Forever, and establish a Kingdom of Endless Duration.

This Eternal King, evidently, is the Same Person previously spoken of as Priest after the order of Melchizedek, Shiloh, Star, and Prophet Like unto Moses.

I Kings 9:5. The Promise Repeated to Solomon

"I will Establish the Throne of Thy Kingdom Forever." Repeated over and over to David and Solomon.

However, the books of Kings and Chronicles relate the story of the Fall of David's Kingdom and Captivity of the Hebrew Nation, apparently bringing to naught God's Promise to David's Family of an Eternal Throne.

But in the period covered by these books many Prophets arose, crying out that the Promise would yet be fulfilled.

The books of Ezra, Nehemiah, and Esther relate the story of the Return of the Fallen and Scattered Hebrew Nation, without direct Messianic Predictions. However, the Re-Establishment of the Nation in its Own Land was a necessary antecedent to the Fulfillment of Promises about David's Throne.

Job 19:25-27

The book is a discussion of the problem of Suffering, without much direct bearing, as far as we can see, on the Messianic Mission of the Hebrew Nation, except it be in Job's Exultant Outburst of Faith, "I Know that my Redeemer Lives, and that He Shall Stand at the Latter Day upon the Earth."

Psalms

The book of Psalms, written mostly by David himself, is brim full of Predictions and Fore-Shadowings of the Eternal King to arise in David's Family. Some of them, in a limited and secondary sense, may refer to David himself. But, in the main, they are inapplicable to any person in history, other than Christ: written 1000 years Before Christ Came.

Psalm 2. The Lord's Anointed

"The Lord's Anointed (2) . . . I have set My King upon My Holy Hill of Zion (6) . . . Thou art My Son (7) . . . I shall give Thee the Nations for Thine Inheritance (8) . . . Kiss the Son (12) . . . Blessed are all they that Put their Trust in Him."

Evidently meaning the Eternal King to arise in David's Family. A very positive statement as to His Deity, His Universal Reign, and the Blessedness of those who Trust Him.

Psalm 16:10. His Resurrection

"Thou wilt not . . . suffer Thy Holy One to See Corruption." This is quoted in Acts 2:27, 31 as referring to the Resurrection of Christ. There had been many hints of the Coming Messiah's Death. Here is a clear-cut Prediction of His Victory over Death. And Life Forevermore.

Psalm 22. A Fore-Picture of the Crucifixion

"My God, My God, why hast Thou Forsaken Me?" (1). Even His Dying Words Foretold (Matthew 27:46).

"All that see Me laugh Me to scorn, saying . . . He Trusted in God, let God deliver Him" (7, 8). Sneers of His Enemies, in their exact words (Matthew 27:43).

"They Pierced My Hands and Feet" (16). This indicates Crucifixion as the manner of His Death (John 20:20, 25).

"They part my Garments among them, and cast lots upon My Vesture" (18). Even this detail is Forecast (Matthew 27:35).

What can all this refer to except the Crucifixion of Jesus? Yet it was Written a Thousand Years Before it happened.

Psalm 41:9. To be Betrayed by a Friend

"My own familiar Friend, in whom I Trusted, who did eat my bread, lifted up his heel against me."

Apparently, David is referring to his own friend, Ahithophel (II Samuel 15:12). But Jesus quoted it as a Picture-Prophecy of His own Betrayal by Judas (John 13:18–27; Luke 22:47, 48).

Psalm 45. Reign of God's Anointed

"Thy God hath Anointed Thee with the oil of gladness above thy fellows" (7). "Thy Throne, O God, is Forever and Ever" (6). "In Majesty Ride on Prosperously" (4). "All Generations . . . shall Praise Thee Forever and Ever" (17).

Here is depicted the Glorious Reign of a King, bearing the Name of God, seated on an Eternal Throne. It can refer to no other than the Eternal King to arise in David's Family. A Nuptial Song of Christ and His Bride, the Church.

Psalm 69:21. Gall and Vinegar

"They gave me Gall for my food; and in my thirst they gave me Vinegar to drink."

Another incident in the Fore-Picture of the Coming Messiah's Sufferings (Matthew 27:34, 48).

Psalm 72. His Glorious Reign

"In His days the Righteous shall flourish" (7). "He shall have Dominion from sea to sea, and from the River to the Ends of the Earth" (8). "All Kings shall fall down before Him: All Nations shall serve Him" (11). "Blessed be His Glorious Name Forever. Let the Whole Earth be Filled with His Glory" (19).

This Psalm seems, in part, to have been a description of the Reign of Solomon. But some of its statements, and its general tenor, surely refer to ONE Greater than Solomon.

Psalm 78:2. To Speak in Parables

"I will open my mouth in Parables." Another detail of the Messiah's Life: His Method of Teaching in Parables. (Quoted in Matthew 13:34, 35, as fulfilling this verse.)

Psalm 89. Endlessness of David's Throne

"I have made a Covenant with David" (3). "I will build up Thy

Throne unto All Generations" (4). "I will make Him, My First-Born, Higher than the Kings of the Earth" (27). "And My Covenant Shall Stand" (28). "By My Holiness I have Sworn . . . David's Throne . . . Shall Endure Forever" (35–37).

God's Oath, Repeated Over and Over, for the Endlessness of David's Throne, under God's First-Born.

Psalm 110. Messiah to be King and Priest

"The Lord said to my Lord, Sit Thou at My Right Hand, till I make thine enemies thy Footstool" (1). "Thou art a Priest Forever after the order of Melchizedek" (4).

Eternal Dominion and Eternal Priesthood of the Coming King. Jesus quoted this as referring to Himself (Matthew 2:42–44).

Psalm 118:22. Messiah to be Rejected by Rulers

"The Stone the Builders Rejected is become Head of Corner." Jesus quoted this as referring to Himself (Matthew 21:42–44).

Isaiah 2:2-4. Magnificent Pre-Vision of Messianic Age

"In the last days, the mountain of the Lord's House shall be established in the top of the mountains . . . And All Nations shall flow unto it. And Many Peoples shall say, Come, let us go up to . . . the House of the God of Jacob. He will Teach us His Ways, and we will Walk in His Paths.

"The Word of the Lord shall go forth from Jerusalem . . . and the Nations . . . shall beat their Swords into Plowshares, and their Spears into Pruninghooks. Nation shall not lift up Sword against Nation, neither shall they learn War any more."

Isaiah, pre-eminently, the Old Testament book of Messianic Prophecy, in language unsurpassed in all literature, goes into ecstacy over the Glories of the Reign of the Coming Messiah.

Isaiah 4:2-6. The Branch of the Lord

"In that day shall the Branch of the Lord be Beautiful and Glorious" (2). "A Cloud by day . . . and a Fire by night" (5) . . . "A Tabernacle . . . and a Place of Refuge" (6).

The Messiah is here represented as a Branch growing up out of the Stump of the Family Tree of David, becoming a Guide and Refuge for His People. (Explained more fully in Isaiah 11:1–10.)

Isaiah 7:13,14. Immanuel

"O house of David . . . a Virgin shall conceive, and shall bear a Son, and shall call His Name Immanuel."

This seems to say that Some One, to be called Immanuel, will be born in David's Family, of a Virgin: evidently meaning the same Person as the Branch of 4:2 and 11:1, and the Wonderful Child of 9:6. The Deity of the Child is implied in the name Immanuel, which means God With Us. Thus the Virgin Birth and Deity of the Messiah are here Foretold. It is quoted in Matthew 1:23 as referring to Jesus. (See page 291.)

Isaiah 9:1,2,6,7. The Wonderful Child

"In Galilee . . . the people have seen a Great Light" (1, 2). "For unto us a Child is born, unto us a Son is given: and the Government shall be upon His shoulder: and His Name shall be called Wonderful, Counsellor, Mighty God, Everlasting Father, Prince of Peace. Of the increase of His Government and Peace there shall be No End, upon the Throne of David, and upon His Kingdom, from henceforth even Forever" (6, 7).

This Child, unmistakably, is the ETERNAL KING promised to David's Family (II Samuel 7:16): the same Person spoken of centuries earlier as Shiloh, the Star, and the Prophet like unto Moses. His Deity is here emphasized. His ministry to be in Galilee. A very accurate Fore-Cast of Jesus.

Isaiah 11:1-10. Reign of the Branch

"There shall come forth a Rod out of the Stem of Jesse, a Branch shall grow out of his roots" (1).

That is, a Shoot out of the Stump of David's Family Tree, meaning the Messiah.

"And the Spirit of the Lord shall rest upon Him, the spirit of Wisdom and Understanding" (2) . . . "He shall stand for an Ensign to the Peoples, and to Him shall the Nations Gather" (10).

"He shall smite the earth with the Rod of His Mouth" (4). And the wolf shall dwell with the lamb. The leopard shall lie down with the kid: and the calf and the young lion and the fatling together. And a little child shall lead them.

"The cow and the bear shall feed: their young ones shall lie down together: and the lion shall eat straw like the ox . . .

"They shall not Hurt nor Destroy in all my holy mountain: for the earth shall be full of the Knowledge of the Lord as the waters cover the sea" (6–9).

A Magnificent Description of Universal Peace in the World-To-Be under the Reign of the Coming Messiah.

Isaiah 25:6-9; 26:1,19. Resurrection of the Dead

"In this mountain the Lord . . . will swallow up Death in Victory, and Wipe away Tears from off all faces" (6, 8) . . . "In that day . . . thy Dead shall Live, my Dead Body shall Rise . . . and the Earth shall Cast Forth the Dead" (26:1, 19).

A Fore-Cast of the Resurrection of Jesus in Mt. Zion, and also of a General Resurrection.

Isaiah 32:1,2. Again the Reign of the Coming King

"A King shall Reign in Righteousness . . . A Man (The Man) shall be as a Hiding Place from the Wind, a Covert from the Tempest, as Streams of Water in a Dry Place, and as the Shade of a Great Rock in a Weary Land."

In Isaiah 9:6 the Deity of the Coming King was predicted. Here it is His Humanity, a Man (2). A Man who is a Personal Refuge to Each One of His People from Every Trouble.

Isaiah 35:5,6. Messiah's Miracles

"Eyes of the Blind shall be Opened; Ears of the Deaf shall be Unstopped . . . the Lame shall Leap . . . the Tongue of the Dumb shall Sing" (5, 6).

An exact description of Jesus' Ministry of Miracles.

Isaiah 35:8-10. Messiah's Highway

"A Highway shall be there. . . . called the Way of Holiness" (8). "The Ransomed of the Lord shall return and come to Zion with Singing and Everlasting Joy upon their heads: they shall obtain Joy and Gladness: Sorrow and Sighing shall flee away" (10).

Holiness, Happiness, SINGING, Joy, No More Sorrow, Tears Forever Gone, for the Coming Messiah's People.

Isaiah 40:5,10,11. Messiah's Tenderness

"The Glory of the Lord shall be revealed, and All Flesh shall see it together"(5). "The Lord God will Come with a Strong Hand, and His Arm shall Rule for Him" (10). "He shall Feed His Flock like a Shepherd: He shall gather the Lambs with His Arms, and carry them in His bosom, and shall Gently Lead those that are with young" (11).

Another Pre-View of the Glory of Jesus, His Power and His Gentleness toward the weak of His flock.

Isaiah 42:1-11. Gentiles

"Behold, My Servant (1) . . . I give Him for a Light to Gentiles (6) . . . The Isles shall wait for His Law (4) . . . And from the End of the Earth they Sing unto the Lord a New Song" (10).

Israel's Coming King will Rule over Gentiles also, and Cover the Whole Earth with Songs of Praise and Joy.

Isaiah 53. The Messiah's Sufferings

"He is Despised and Rejected of men; a Man of Sorrows and acquainted with Grief . . . He hath borne our Griefs and carried our Sorrows . . . He was Wounded for Our Transgressions, and Bruised for Our Iniquities . . . With His Stripes We are Healed.

"The Lord hath laid on Him the Iniquity of Us All . . . He was Oppressed, He was Afflicted, yet He opened not his mouth. He is brought as a Lamb to the Slaughter . . . He poured out His soul unto Death . . . and Bore the Sin of Many . . .

"It pleased the Lord to Bruise Him . . . to make His Soul an Offering for Sin . . . And the Pleasure of the Lord shall Prosper in His Hand . . . By Knowledge of Him shall Many be Justified."

The most conspicuous feature in the Prophecies about the Coming King is that He would be a Sufferer. It was hinted in Abel's Sacrifice, and in Abraham's Offering of Isaac, and vividly fore-pictured in the Institution of the Passover Feast, and in the Annual Day of Atonement, and some of its details described in Psalm 22. And here, in Isaiah 53, detail upon detail is added, making the picture more complete. And in chapters 54, 55, 60, 61, the Suffering King Fills the Earth with Songs of Joy. Marvelous Forecasts of the Christian Era.

Isaiah 60. To be Light of the World

"Darkness shall Cover the Earth" (2). "Arise, Shine; for thy Light is Come, and the Glory of the Lord is Risen upon thee" (1). "The Lord shall be thine Everlasting Light, and the days of thy Mourning shall be Ended" (20).

In the New Testament, Jesus is repeatedly called The Light of the World.

Isaiah 62:2; 65:15. A New Name

"Thou shalt be called by a New Name" (62:2). "The Lord will call His Servants by Another Name" (65:15).

In Old Testament times God's People were called Israelites. Since the days of Christ they have been called Christians.

Jeremiah 23:5,6. The Branch

"The days come, saith the Lord, that I will raise up unto David a Righteous Branch . . . a King . . . This is His Name whereby He shall be called, THE LORD OUR RIGHTEOUSNESS."

As Isaiah, chapters 4 and 11, speaks of the Coming King as a Branch out of the Family of David, so, here, Jeremiah repeats the Name, and asserts His Deity.

Ezekiel 34. The Prince of the House of David

"My servant David . . . shall be . . . Shepherd . . . of my Flock . . . King over them . . . and be their Prince Forever" (34:22–24; 37:24, 25).

In describing the Reign of the Prince, there is given a transcendantly beautiful picture of the Blessed Influences arising out of Jerusalem, under the imagery of the Life-Giving Stream issuing from the Temple and flowing out to the Whole World, as recorded below, in Ezekiel 47:1–12. (See page 335.)

Ezekiel 47:1-12. The Life-Giving Stream

"In visions of God . . . waters issued from under the Temple eastward. A man who had a measuring line . . . measured a thousand cubits, and caused me to pass through the waters, waters that were up to the ankle.

"Again he measured a thousand . . . and waters were up to the knees . . . Another thousand, and waters were up to the loins.

"Afterward he measured a thousand, and it was a River that Could Not Be Passed Through. And he said to me, Son of man, these waters shall go on and on to the sea. Whithersoever the waters come Everything shall Live."

Daniel 2. The Four Kingdoms

"In the days of these kings . . . of the Fourth Kingdom . . . the God of Heaven shall set up a Kingdom . . . which shall Stand Forever" (2:40, 44).

In the 600 years from Daniel to Christ there were Four World Empires: Babylon, Persia, Greece and Rome. They are exactly described in the imagery of this 2nd chapter of Daniel. In the 7th chapter of Daniel the same Four World Empires are more fully described. It was in the days of the Roman Empire that Christ appeared. (See more fully pages 342, 346.)

Daniel 9:24-27. The Time More Exactly

"From the going forth of the commandment to restore and build Jerusalem unto the Messiah, the Prince, shall be Seven Weeks and Three Score and Two Weeks . . . And after the Three Score and Two Weeks . . . in the midst of the One Week . . . shall Messiah be Cut Off . . . to make Reconciliation for Iniquity, and bring in Everlasting Righteousness" (24–27).

Here Daniel set the Exact Date for the Coming of the Messiah. (See pages 349, 350.) And further said, 600 years before the Messiah came, that the Messiah, after a Three and half year public ministry, would be Cut Off in Atonement for Sin. An Amazing Prediction!

Hosea 1:10. Gentiles to be Included

"In the place where it was said, Ye are Not My People, it shall be said unto them, Ye are Sons of the Living God."

Here Hosea repeats what has already been said time and again, that the Messiah's Kingdom will Include All Nations.

"I called My Son out of Egypt" (11:1). A way of saying, Part of Messiah's Childhood would be spent in Egypt (Matthew 2:15).

Joel 2:28,32; 3:13,14. The Gospel Era

"I will pour out My Spirit upon All Flesh . . . Whosoever shall Call on the Name of the Lord shall be Delivered . . . Put in the sickle. The harvest is Ripe . . . Multitudes, Multitudes in the Valley of Decision."

The Messiah to institute an Era of World Evangelization, under leadership of the Holy Spirit (Acts 2:16–21).

Amos 9:11,12,14. David's Fallen Throne to Rise

"I will bring back the captivity of My people . . . and I will plant them in their own land . . . And in that day I will Raise up the Tabernacle of David that is fallen . . . to possess All the Nations that are called by My Name."

Jonah 1:17. A Sign to Nineveh

"Jonah was in the fish Three Days and Nights." Jesus took it to be a Three-Day Picture Miracle of His Own Resurrection from the Tomb, as a Sign to the World (Matthew 12:40).

Micah 5:2-5. Bethlehem to be Messiah's Birthplace

"Thou, Bethlehem . . . out of thee shall He come forth that is to be Ruler in Israel; whose goings forth have been . . . from Everlasting . . . He shall be great unto the Ends of the Earth. And This Man shall be our Peace."

Evidently meaning The KING so often mentioned before.

Zephaniah 3:9. A New Language

"Then will I turn unto the Nations a Pure Language, that they may all call upon the Name of the Lord, to Serve Him with One Consent." That is, a Correct System of Thought about God, evidently meaning the Gospel of Christ.

Haggai 2:6,7. The Desire of All Nations

"Yet a little while . . . and the Desire of All Nations shall Come, and . . . Fill this House with Glory." That will be Crowning Day for David's Son, here typified in Zerubbabel (2:23).

Zechariah

"I will bring forth My Servant The BRANCH" (3:8). "O Jerusalem, thy King cometh to thee . . . Lowly, Riding upon a Colt" (9:9). "In that day the House of David shall be as God" (12:8). "I will Remove the Iniquity of the Land in One Day" (3:9). "They weighed for my price Thirty Pieces of Silver . . . and Cast them to the Potter" (11:12, 13). "They shall look upon Me Whom they have Pierced" (12:10). "In that day a Fountain shall be Opened . . . for Sin and Uncleanness" (13:1. See further page 383).

Malachi 3:1; 4:5. A Forecast of John the Baptist

"Behold, I will send My Messenger . . . Elijah the Prophet before the great day of the Lord . . . and He shall Prepare the way before Me." Jesus, in speaking of John the Baptist, in Matthew 11:7–14, quotes this passage from Malachi, and expressly states that it referred to John the Baptist.

Summary

Near the beginning of the Old Testament it is stated that the Hebrew Nation was being founded for the purpose of Blessing All Nations. Then there begins to loom the figure of ONE PERSON through Whom the Nation will accomplish its mission.

First He is called Shiloh, to arise in the Tribe of Judah, and Rule the Nations. Then He is called a Star, Who will have Dominion. And next, a Prophet like unto Moses, through Whom God will Speak to Mankind.

And then, over and over, He is spoken of as a King, to arise in David's Family, to be called The Branch, The Prince, The Anointed One, God's First-Born, Wonderful, Mighty God, Everlasting Father, Prince of Peace.

. The Exact Time of His Coming was Foretold. He was to be born of a Virgin. At Bethlehem. Part of His Childhood to be spent in Egypt. He would be brought up at Nazareth.

He would be Introduced to His Nation by an Elijah-like forerunner. Galilee to be the scene of His Ministry. He would work Miracles of Healing. And Speak in Parables. Be Rejected by the leaders of His Own Nation. Be a Smitten Shepherd, a Sufferer, a Man of Sorrows. He would enter Jerusalem riding on a Colt. He would be Betrayed by a Friend, for thirty pieces of silver, the thirty pieces of silver to be spent for a Potter's field. He would be led as a Lamb to the Slaughter.

He would Die with the Wicked, opening a Fountain for Sin, Removing Sin in One Day. Even His Dying Words Foretold. He would be given Gall and Vinegar in His Agony. His Hands and Feet would be Pierced. Not a Bone to be Broken. Lots to be cast for His Garments. To be Buried with the Rich. To be in the Tomb Three Days. To Rise from the Dead, and Ascend to Heaven at God's Right Hand.

It was foretold that He would introduce a New Language into the earth, that is, a New Idea, Salvation. That He would offer a New Covenant to mankind, and give God's People a New Name. That He would introduce an Era of the Holy Spirit. That His Kingdom would include Gentiles, and be Universal and Endless.

This Pre-Written Story of Jesus, recorded Centuries Before Jesus came, is so Astonishing in Detail that it reads like an Eye-Witness Account of His Life and Work.

Suppose a number of men of Different Countries, who had never seen, nor in any way communicated with, one another, would walk into a room, and each lay down a piece of Carved Marble, which pieces, when Fitted Together, would make a Perfect statue—how account for it in any other way than that Some One Person had drawn the Specifications, and had sent to each man his part? And how can this Amazing Composite of Jesus' Life and Work, put together by Different Writers of Different Centuries, Ages Before Jesus Came, be explained on any other basis than that ONE SUPER-HUMAN MIND supervised the Writing? The Miracle of the Ages!

BETWEEN THE TESTAMENTS

Approximately 400 Years

Persian Period, 430-332 B.C.

At close of Old Testament, about 430 B.C., Judea was a Persian province. Persia had been a World-Power for about 100 years. It remained so for another 100 years, during which period not much is known of Jewish history. Persian rule was, for the most part, mild and tolerant. (For Persian Kings of this period see page 230.)

Greek Period, 331-167 B.C.

Up to this time the great powers of the world had been in Asia and Africa. But looming ominously on the western horizon was the rising power of Greece. The beginnings of Greek history are veiled in myth. It is thought to have commenced about the 12th century B.C., the time of the Biblical Judges. Then came the Trojan War, and Homer, about 1,000 B.C., the age of David and Solomon. The beginning of authentic Greek history has usually been reckoned from the First Olympiad, 776 B.C. Then came the Formation of Hellenic States, 776–500 B.C. Then the Persian Wars, 500–331 B.C. And the famous battles: Marathon, 490; Thermopalyae and Salamis, 480. Then the brilliant era of Pericles, 465–429, and Socrates, 469–399, contemporaneous with Ezra and Nehemiah.

Alexander the Great, 336 B.C., at the age of 20, assumed command of the Greek army, and, like a meteor, swept eastward over the lands that had been under the dominion of Egypt, Assyria, Babylon, and Persia. By 331 B.C. the whole world lay at his feet. On his invasion of Palestine, 332 B.C., he showed great consideration to the Jews, spared Jerusalem, and offered immunities to the Jews to settle in Alexandria. He established Greek cities all over his conquered domains, and along with them Greek culture and the Greek language. After a brief reign he died, 323 B.C.

On Alexander's death his empire fell to four of his generals, the two eastern sections going, Syria to Seleucus, and Egypt to Ptolemy. Palestine, lying between Syria and Egypt, went first to Syria, but shortly passed to Egypt (301 B.C.), and remained under control of Egypt till 198 B.C.

Under the kings of Egypt, called the "Ptolemies," the condition

The seafront of modern Alexandria, Egypt's second city. This city was one of those originally founded by Alexander.
© *Matson Photo Service.*

of the Jews was mainly peaceful and happy. Those that were in Egypt built synagogs in all their settlements. Alexandria became an influential center of Judaism.

Antiochus the Great re-conquered Palestine (198 B.C.), and it passed back to the kings of Syria, called the "Seleucids."

Antiochus Epiphanes (175–164 B.C.), was violently bitter against the Jews, and he made a furious and determined effort to exterminate them and their religion. He devastated Jerusalem (168 B.C.), defiled the Temple, offered a sow on its altar, erected an altar to Jupiter, prohibited Temple worship, forbade circumcision on pain of death, sold thousands of Jewish families into slavery, destroyed all copies of Scripture that could be found, and slaughtered everyone discovered in possession of such copies, and resorted to every conceivable torture to force Jews to renounce their religion. This led to the Maccabean revolt, one of the most heroic feats in history.

The Ptolemies, Greek Kings of Egypt, were: Ptolemy I (323–285 B.C.). Ptolemy II (285–247). Ptolemy III (247–222). Ptolemy IV (222–205). Ptolemy V (205–182). Ptolemy VI (182–146). Ptolemy VII (146–117).

The Seleucids, Greek Kings of Syria, were: Seleucus Nicator (312–280 B.C.). Antiochus I (280–261). Antiochus II (261–246). Seleucus II (246–226). Seleucus III (226–223). Antiochus III (222–187). Seleucus IV (187–175). Antiochus IV Epiphanes (175–164). Antiochus V (163–161). Alexander Balas (161–146). Antiochus VI (146–143). Tryphon (143–139). Antiochus VII (139–130).

Period of Independence, 167-63 B.C.

Also called the Maccabean, or Asmonean, or Hasmonaean, period. Mattathias, a priest, of intense patriotism and unbounded courage, infuriated at the attempt of Antiochus Epiphanes to destroy the Jews and their religion, gathered a band of loyal Jews and raised the standard of revolt. He had five heroic and warlike sons; Judas, Jonathan, Simon, John and Eleazar. Mattathias died (166 B.C.). His mantle fell on his son Judas, a warrior of amazing military genius. He won battle after battle against unbelievable and impossible odds. He re-conquered Jerusalem (165 B.C.); and purified and re-dedicated the Temple. This was the origin of the Feast of Dedication. Judas united the priestly and civil authority in himself, and thus established the line of Asmonean priest-rulers who for the following 100 years governed an independent Judea. They were: Mattathias (167–166 B.C.). Judas (166–161). Jonathan (161–144). Simon (144–135). John Hyrcanus (135–106), son of Jonathan. Aristobulus and sons (160–63), unworthy the Maccabean name.

Roman Period, 63 B.C. to the time of Christ

In the year 63 B.C. Palestine was conquered by the Romans under Pompey. Antipater, an Idumean (Edomite, descendant of Esau), was appointed ruler of Judea. He was succeeded by his son Herod the Great who was king of Judea (37–3 B.C.). Herod, to obtain favor of the Jews, rebuilt the Temple with great splendor. But he was a brutal, cruel man. This is the Herod who ruled Judah when Jesus was born, and he it was who slew the children of Bethlehem.

The Old Testament Canon

The word "Canon," literally meaning "cane," or "measuring rod," came to be used as the name of the list of books which were recognized as the genuine, original inspired, authoritative WORD OF GOD, the "rule" of Faith.

Early in history God began the formation of the Book which was to be the medium of His revelation of Himself to man:
Ten Commandments, written on stone (Deuteronomy 10:4, 5).
Moses' Laws, written in a book (Deuteronomy 31:24–26).
Copies of this book were made (Deuteronomy 17:18).

Joshua added to the book (Joshua 24:26).
Samuel wrote in a book, and laid it up before God (I Samuel 10:25).
This book was well known 400 years later (II Kings 22:8–20).
Prophets wrote in a book (Jeremiah 36:32; Zechariah 1:4; 7:7–12).
Ezra read this book of God publicly (Ezra 7:6; Nehemiah 8:5).

In Jesus' day this book was called "The Scriptures," and was taught regularly and read publicly in synagogs. It was commonly regarded among the people as the "Word of God." Jesus himself repeatedly called it the "Word of God."

In the New Testament there are about 300 quotations from these "Scriptures"; and no book outside these "Scriptures" is thus quoted in the New Testament, with the single exception of words of Enoch in the book of Jude. Many of these quotations are from the Septuagint version of the Old Testament, which was in common use in New Testament times; and even though the Septuagint contained the "Apocryphal" books there is not one quotation from the Apocryphal books. This is evidence that neither Jesus nor the Apostles recognized the Apocryphal books as part of "The Scriptures."

These "Scriptures" were composed of the 39 books which constitute our Old Testament, though under a different arrangement. They were spoken of as the "Law," 5 books; the "Prophets," 8 books; and the "Writings," 11 books; thus:

Law: Genesis, Exodus, Leviticus, Numbers, Deuteronomy.
Prophets: Joshua, Judges, Samuel, Kings, Isaiah, Jeremiah, Ezekiel, The Twelve.
Writings: Psalms, Proverbs, Job, Song, Ruth, Lamentations, Ecclesiastes, Esther, Daniel, Ezra-Nehemiah, Chronicles.

Thus combining the 2 books each of Samuel, Kings and Chronicles into 1; and Ezra and Nehemiah into 1; and the 12 Minor Prophets (which were written on one roll) into 1; these 24 books are exactly the same as the 39 books of our Old Testament.

Just when this group of books was completed, and set apart as the definitely recognized Word of God, is involved in obscurity. The Jews' tradition was that it was done by Ezra. We believe that, as these books were written, beginning with Moses, they were, at the time, recognized as Inspired of God, and placed in the Tabernacle or Temple along with the accumulating group of Sacred Writings. Copies were made as needed. In the Babylonian Captivity they were scattered, and many copies destroyed. Ezra, after Return from the Captivity, re-assembled scattered copies, and restored them as a complete group to their place in the Temple. From Temple copies, other copies were made for synagogs.

Josephus considered the Old Testament Canon as fixed from the days of Artaxerxes, time of Ezra. Here are his words:

"We have but 22 books, containing the history of all time, books that are believed to be divine. Of these, 5 belong to Moses, containing his laws and the traditions of the origin of mankind down to the time of his death. From the death of Moses to the reign of Artaxerxes the prophets who succeeded Moses wrote the history of the events that occurred in their own time, in 13 books. The remaining 4 books comprise hymns to God and precepts for the conduct of human life. From the days of Artaxerxes to our own times every event has indeed been recorded; but these recent records have not been deemed worthy of equal credit with those which preceded them, on account of the failure of the exact succession of prophets. There is practical proof of the spirit in which we treat our Scriptures; for, although so great an interval of time has now passed, not a soul has ventured to add or to remove or to alter a syllable; and it is the instinct of every Jew, from the day of his birth, to consider these Scriptures as the teaching of God, and to abide by them, and, if need be, cheerfully to lay down his life in their behalf."

This testimony is of no small value. Josephus was born A.D. 37 in Jerusalem, of priestly aristocracy. He received an extensive education in Jewish and Greek culture. He was governor of Galilee and military commander in the wars with Rome, and was present at the destruction of Jerusalem.

These words of Josephus are unquestionable testimony to the belief of the Jewish nation of Jesus' day as to what books comprised the Hebrew Scriptures, and that that collection of books had been completed and fixed for 400 years preceding his time.

(As to the "22" books of Josephus see page 26.)

As to arrangement: the Septuagint translators re-classified them according to subject matter, which re-classification has been followed by Latin and English translators. The books of our Old Testament, though in different order, are identical with the books of the Hebrew Scriptures. They were not called the "Old Testament" till after completion of the "Christian Scriptures," to differentiate the two.

The Apocrypha

This is the name usually given to the 14 books contained in some Bibles between the Old and New Testaments. They originated in the 1st to 3rd centuries B.C., mostly of uncertain authorship, and were added to the Septuagint, which was a Greek translation of the Old Testament made in that period. They were not in the Hebrew Old Testament. They were written after Old Testament prophecy, oracles and direct revelation had ceased. Josephus rejected them as a whole. They were never recognized by the Jews as part of the Hebrew Scriptures. They were never quoted by Jesus, nor anywhere in the New Testament. They were not recognized by the Early Church as of canonical authority, nor as of divine inspiration. When the Bible was translated into Latin in the 2nd century A.D., its Old Testament was translated, not from the Hebrew Old Testament, but from the Greek Septuagint version of the Old Testament. From the Septuagint these Apocryphal books were carried over into the Latin translation; and from thence into the Latin Vulgate, which became the common version in Western Europe till the time of the Reformation. Protestants, basing their movement on the Divine Authority of God's Word, at once rejected these Apocryphal books as being no part of God's Word, as the Early Church and ancient Hebrews had done. Then the Roman Catholic Church, in the council of Trent, A.D. 1546, which was held to stop the Protestant movement, declared these books to be canonical, and they are still in the Douay Version (Roman Catholic Bible). These Apocryphal books are as follows:

I Esdras. Esdras is the Greek form of Ezra. This book is a compilation of passages from Ezra, II Chronicles and Nehemiah, with added legends about Zerubbabel. Its object was to picture the liberality of Cyrus and Darius toward the Jews as a pattern for the Ptolemies.

II Esdras. Sometimes called "IV Ezra." It purports to contain visions given to Ezra, dealing with God's government of the world, a coming new age, and the restoration of certain lost Scriptures.

Tobit. A romance, entirely devoid of historical value, of a rich young Israelite captive in Nineveh, who was led by an angel to wed a "virgin-widow" who had lost seven husbands.

Judith. An historical romance of a rich, beautiful and devout Jewish widow who, in the days of the Babylonian invasion of Judah, adroitly went to the tent of the Babylonian general, and under guise of offering herself to him, cut off his head, and thus saved her city.

Rest of Esther. Interpolated passages in the Septuagint version of the Old Testament book of Esther, mainly to show the hand of God in the story. These fragments were gathered, and grouped together by Jerome.

Wisdom of Solomon. Very similar to parts of Job, Proverbs and Ecclesiastes. A sort of fusion of Hebrew thought and Greek philosophy. Written by an Alexandrian Jew who impersonates himself as Solomon.

Ecclesiasticus. Also called the "Wisdom of Jesus, the son of Sirach." Resembles the book of Proverbs. Written by a widely traveled Jewish philosopher. Gives rules for conduct in all details of civil, religious, and domestic life. Extols a long list of Old Testament heroes.

Baruch. This book purports to come from Baruch, the scribe of Jeremiah, who is represented as spending the last portion of his life in Babylon. It is addressed to the exiles. It consists mostly of paraphrases from Jeremiah, Daniel and other Prophets.

Song of the Three Holy Children. An unauthentic addition to the book of Daniel, inserted after 3:23, purporting to give their prayer while in the fiery furnace, and their triumphal song of praise for deliverance.

History of Susanna. Another unauthentic amplification of the book of Daniel, relating how the godly wife of a wealthy Jew in Babylon, falsely accused of adultery, was cleared by the wisdom of Daniel.

Bel and the Dragon. Another unauthentic addition to the book of Daniel. Two stories, in both of which Daniel proves that the idols Bel and the Dragon are not gods, one of which is based on the story of the lions' den.

Prayer of Manasses. Purports to be the prayer of Manasses, king of Judah, when he was held captive in Babylon, which is spoken of in II Chronicles 33:12–13. Author unknown. Date probably 1st century B.C.

I Maccabees. An historical work of great value on the Maccabean period, relating events of the Jews' heroic struggle for liberty (175–135 B.C.). Written about 100 B.C., by a Palestinian Jew.

II Maccabees. This is also an account of the Maccabean struggle, confining itself to the period of 175–161 B.C. It professes to be an abridgment of a work written by a certain Jason of Cyrene, of whom nothing is known. Supplements I Maccabees, but is inferior to it.

Other Writings

Besides the Apocrypha, described on the preceding two pages, there were other Jewish writings, originating in the period between the 2nd century B.C. and the 1st century A.D., much of which was "Apocalyptic" in nature, in which the writer "assumed the name of a hero long since dead, and rewrote history in terms of prophecy." They are composed quite largely of visions purporting to come from ancient personages of Scripture, some of them containing the wildest of fantasies. They are occupied, to a considerable extent, with the Coming Messiah. The sufferings of the Maccabean period intensified Jewish expectation that the time was drawing near. Based partly on uncertain traditions, and partly on imagination. Some of the better known are:

Books of Enoch. A group of fragments, of various unknown authorship, written in the 1st and 2nd centuries B.C., containing revelations reputed to have been given to Enoch and Noah. They speak of the Coming Messiah and the Day of Judgment. (See further under Jude 14.)

Assumption of Moses. Written by a Pharisee, about the time of the birth of Christ. Contains prophecies attributed to Moses, when he was about to die, which he entrusted to Joshua.

Ascension of Isaiah. Relates a legendary account of the martyrdom of Isaiah, and certain of his purported visions. Thought to have been written in Rome, by a Christian Jew, during the Neronian persecution of the Jews.

Book of Jubilees. A commentary on Genesis. Written, probably, in the Maccabean period, or a little later. Named from its system of time reckoning, based on the Jubilee periods of 50 years.

Psalms of Solomon. A group of songs, by an unknown Pharisee, of the coming Messiah, written probably soon after the Maccabean period.

Testament of the Twelve Patriarchs. A product of the 2nd century B.C., purporting to give the dying instructions of the Twelve Sons of Jacob to their children, each reporting the story of his own life and its lessons.

Sibylline Oracles. Written in Maccabean times, with later additions, in imitation of Greek and Roman Oracles, dealing with the downfall of oppressing empires and the dawn of the Messianic age.

The Septuagint

This was a translation of the Hebrew Old Testament into Greek. It was made in Alexandria, where there were many Greek speaking Jews. Tradition has it that, at the request of Ptolemy Philadelphus (285–247 B.C.), 70 Jews, skillful linguists, were sent from Jerusalem to Egypt. The Pentateuch was first translated. Later the rest of the Old Testament books were added to the translation. It was called the "Septuagint" from the 70 translators who were reputed to have begun it. Greek was the language of the world at that time. This version was in common use in the days of Christ. The New Testament was written in Greek. Many of its quotations from the Old Testament are from the Septuagint.

The Text of the Old Testament

It is believed that the Old Testament books were written originally on skins. They were copied by hand. Hebrew was in square characters, from right to left with small dots or signs, variously attached for vowels (the vowel system was not introduced till the 6th century A.D.). Though copied with the greatest care, it was easily productive of various readings. Until the Captivity official copies were kept in the Temple. Afterward many copies were made for Synagogs. Apparently, in some cases, marginal notes made by copyists, were, by later copyists, incorporated into the body of the text. The invention of printing removed danger of errors in the text; and now, as a result of the work of scholars in comparing the various manuscripts, there is a recognized Hebrew text known as Massoretic.

The Aramaic Language

This was the common language of Palestine in Jesus' day. After the Return from Babylonian Captivity it had gradually displaced Hebrew as the ordinary speech of the people. It was the ancient language of Syria, very similar to Hebrew.

The Targums

These were translations of the Hebrew Old Testament books into Aramaic, oral translations, paraphrases, and interpretations reduced to writings. They became necessary as the use of Aramaic became prevalent in Palestine.

The Talmud

A collection of various Jewish traditions and oral explanations of the Old Testament which were committed to writing in the 2nd century A.D., with a later commentary thereon.

The Great Synagog

This is the name of the council, consisting of 120 members, said to have been organized by Nehemiah, about 410 B.C., under the presidency of Ezra, for the purpose of re-constructing the religious life of the returned captives. It is thought to have been a continuing body, governing the returned Jews till about 275 B.C. It is said to have had an important part in gathering, grouping, and restoring the Canonical books of the Old Testament.

The Sanhedrin

The recognized headship of the Jewish people, in the days of Christ. It is thought to have originated in the 3rd century B.C. It was composed of 70 members, mostly priests and Sadducean nobles, some Pharisees, scribes, and elders (tribal or family heads), presided over by the high priest.

Synagogs

Synagogs arose in the days of the Captivity. The Temple destroyed, and the nation scattered, there was need for places of instruction and worship wherever there were Jewish communities. After the Return synagogs were continued both in the homeland and in Jewish centers in other lands. All larger towns had one or more. In Jerusalem, even though the Temple was there, there were many synagogs. They were presided over by a board of elders, or rulers. Early Christian meetings were modeled in part after the pattern of synagogs.

The Dispersion

This is the name of the Jews living outside of Palestine. Very many of them chose to remain in the lands of the Captivity. In the Inter-Testament period Jews outside Palestine came to be far more numerous than those in Palestine. There grew to be strong colonies of Jews in every land and in all the chief cities of the civilized world: Babylon, Assyria, Syria, Phoenicia, Asia Minor, Greece, Egypt, North Africa and Rome. The three main divisions of the Dispersion were Babylonian, Syrian and Egyptian. In the time of Christ the number of Jews in Egypt was estimated at a million. And there were strong populations in Damascus and Antioch. So, in the Providence of God, captivities turned out to be for the benefit of the nations among whom they were scattered. They influenced the thought of the nations, and also were influenced by thought of the nations.

Pharisees

The sect of Pharisees is thought to have originated in the 3rd century B.C., in days preceding the Maccabean wars, when under Greek domination and the Greek effort to Hellenize the Jews, there was a strong tendency among the Jews to accept Greek culture with its pagan religious customs. The rise of the Pharisees was a reaction and protest against this tendency among their fellow-countrymen. Their aim was to preserve their national integrity and strict conformity to Mosaic law. They later developed into self-righteous and hypocritical formalists. (See under Matthew 23.)

Sadducees

The Sadducees as a sect are thought to have originated about the same time as the Pharisees. Being guided by secular considerations, they were in favor of adopting Greek customs. They took no part in the Maccabean struggle for their nation's liberty. They were a priestly clique, and though they were the religious officials of their nation, they were avowedly irreligious. They were not numerous, but were wealthy and influential. To a great extent they controlled the Sanhedrin, even though they were rationalistic and worldly-minded.

Scribes

Scribes were copyists of the Scripture. It was a calling of very early origin. Their business was to study and interpret, as well as copy, the Scriptures. Because of their minute acquaintance with the law they were also called lawyers, and were recognized authorities. The decisions of leading scribes became oral law, or "tradition." They were quite numerous in the Maccabean period, and became very influential among the people. A vocation of great importance before the days of printing.

Preparation for Christ

The Old Testament is the story of God's dealing with the Hebrew nation for the purpose of bringing into the world a Messiah for ALL nations. The Old Testament is a sort of paean of the Coming Messiah. Starting with low, scattered notes, it expands, as time passes, with enlarging crescendo, into clear, loud trumpet tones of the approaching King. Meantime God, in His Providence, was making ready the nations. Greece united the civilizations of Asia, Europe and Africa, and established one universal language. Rome made one empire of the whole world, and Roman roads made all parts of it accessible. The Dispersion of the Jews among the nations, thus paved the way for the propagation of the Gospel of Christ in their Synagogs and their Scriptures.

MATTHEW

Jesus the Messiah

The special emphasis of Matthew is that Jesus is the Messiah foretold by Old Testament Prophets. He quotes from the Old Testament repeatedly. He seems to have had Jewish readers particularly in mind.

Such frequent use of the term "Kingdom of Heaven" occurs that this Gospel is commonly called the Gospel of the Kingdom.

While, in the main, it follows a general chronological order, its material is grouped rather by Subjects.

It gives Jesus' Discourses quite fully, specially the Sermon on the Mount, and about His Coming and End of the World.

Matthew

This Gospel does not name its author. However, from Early Church Fathers, beginning with Papias, a pupil of John, onward, it has been accepted as the work of Matthew.

We know almost nothing of Matthew, also called Levi. He is mentioned in the four lists of the Twelve: (Matthew 10:3; Mark 3:18; Luke 6:15; Acts 1:13). The only other mention is his call to follow Jesus (Matthew 9:9–13; Mark 2:14–17; Luke 5:27–32).

The only word that Matthew has about himself is that he was a Publican. Publicans were collectors of Roman taxes, ordinarily extortioners, and generally despised. Luke tells us that Matthew made a Great Feast for Jesus, and Forsook All to follow Him. But Matthew does not even give himself credit for that. He loses sight of himself utterly in Adoration of his Master. We love him for his self-effacing Humility.

And we marvel at the Grace of God in choosing such a man to be the author of what is said to be "the most Widely Read Book in all the world," first book in New Testament.

Tradition says that Matthew preached in Palestine for some years, and then traveled to foreign countries; that he wrote his Gospel originally in Hebrew, and some years later, probably about A.D. 60, issued a more complete edition in Greek. What a service to mankind is the production of this Book!

His business as a tax-collector accustomed him to keeping records. He was a Personal Companion of Jesus through most of Jesus'

Public Ministry. The widely-held, but unsubstantiated, present-day hypothesis that Matthew copied from Mark's Gospel is, on the face of it, absurd. It is not at all certain that Mark even knew Jesus. Why should Matthew have to copy from one who had Not been an Eye-witness of things that he himself had seen with his own eyes and heard with his own ears over and over and over?

The Four Gospels

The Four Gospels are, by all odds, the Most Important part of the Bible: more important than all the rest of the Bible put together: more important than all the rest of the books in the whole world put together: for we could better afford to be without the knowledge of everything else than to be without the knowledge of Christ.

Bible books that precede are Anticipatory, and those that follow are Explanatory, of the Hero of the Four Gospels.

Why Four?

There were many more than four to start with (Luke 1:1). It was a period of great Literary Activity, the age of Caesar, Cicero, Sallust, Virgil, Horace, Seneca, Livy, Tacitus, Plutarch and Pliny. Within a generation the Story of Jesus had spread over the whole known world, and had enlisted countless thousands of devoted followers. Naturally there arose a great demand for Written Narratives of His Life.

God Himself, we believe, took a hand in the Preparation and Preservation of These Four, as containing that which He wanted to be Known about Christ. In the Old Testament there are some Double Narratives. But only here are Four of the Bible books about the Same Person. It must mean Superlative Importance.

The Authors

Matthew was a Publican. Luke, a Physician. John, a Fisherman. It is not stated what Mark was. Matthew and John were Companions of Jesus. Mark was a companion of Peter. His Gospel contains what he had heard Peter tell times without number. Luke was a companion of Paul. His Gospel contains what he had heard Paul preach from one end of the Roman Empire to the other, verified by his own investigation. They all told the Same Story. They traveled far and wide. They often went together. John and Peter were intimate companions. Mark was associated with both Peter and Paul, Luke and Mark were in Rome together between A.D. 61 and 63 (Colossians 4:10, 14).

It may be that they wrote many copies, in part or complete, of these same Gospels, for different churches or individuals. It may be that all of the Apostles and their helpers, at times, put in Writing that which they had told about Jesus, for churches which they had founded or visited.

But whatever Writings there may have been perished, mostly, no doubt, in the Imperial Persecutions of the first three centuries, except those which we have in the New Testament, which God, in His Providence, watched over and preserved as being sufficient to convey His Word to all future generations. (See further under Mark 1, Luke 1, John 1.)

Chapter 1:1-17. Genealogy of Jesus

This is given also in Luke 3:23–38. The Coming of Christ to the earth had been anticipated from the beginning. In the early days of human history God had chosen One Family Line, that of Abraham, and, later on, another Family within the Abrahamic Family, that of David, to be the Family through which His Son would make entrance into the world.

The Hebrew Nation was founded, and nurtured, of God, through the ages, to bulwark that Family Line of descent.

The Genealogy, as given in Matthew, is abridged. Some names are omitted. But that does not invalidate the line of descent.

42 generations, 3 groups of 14 each, cover 2000 years: the 1st group, 1000 years; 2nd group, 400 years; 3rd, 600 years.

The 3rd group, however, names only 13 generations, the 14th evidently being intended for Mary.

The Genealogy as given in Luke is somewhat different. Matthew goes back to Abraham; Luke to Adam. One is descending, "begat"; the other is ascending, "was son of." From David they are separate lines, touching in Shealtiel and Zerubbabel.

The commonly accepted view is that Matthew gives Joseph's line, showing Jesus to be Legal Heir to the Promises given Abraham and David; and that Luke gives Mary's line, showing Jesus' blood descent, "Son of David according to the flesh" (Romans 1:3).

Mary's genealogy, in accord with Jewish usage, was in her husband's name. Joseph was the "son of Heli" (Luke 3:23), that is, "son-in-law" of Heli. Jacob was Joseph's father (Matthew 1:16).

These genealogies, given more fully in I Chronicles 1–9, form the backbone of Old Testament annals. Carefully guarded through long centuries of epochal vicissitudes, they contain a "family line through which a Promise was transmitted 4000 years, a fact unexampled in history."

The Four Gospels Compared

The Four Gospels narrate, largely, the same things, but with some differences. Only Matthew and Luke tell of the Birth and Childhood of Jesus. Matthew and Mark dwell on the Galilean Ministry: Luke, the Perean: John, the Judean. John omits most of the Galilean Ministry, and records visits to Jerusalem which the others omit. The others omit the Judean Ministry, except the Last Week, which all four give rather fully.

The Last Week occupies one-third of Matthew, about, one-third of Mark, one-quarter of Luke, and one-half of John. John devotes 7 chapters, about one-third of his book, to Crucifixion Day, sunset to sunset.

Matthew has 28 chapters. Mark, 16. Luke, 24. John, 21. Luke has the most pages, and is the longest. Mark is the shortest.

Chapter 1:18-25. The Birth of Jesus

Only Matthew and Luke tell of the Birth and Childhood of Jesus, each narrating different incidents. (See under Luke 1:5–80.)

Mary, for the first three months following her visit by the heavenly messenger, was away at Elisabeth's (Luke 1:36). When she returned to Nazareth, and Joseph learned of her condition, it must have filled him with "strange and agonized perplexity." But he was a good man, and disposed to protect Mary's name from what he supposed would be public disgrace or worse. Then the angel appeared to him, and explained. He still had to keep the family secret, to avoid scandal, for nobody would have believed Mary's story. Later, when Jesus' Divine Nature became certified by his Miracles and his Resurrection from the dead, then Mary could speak freely of her heavenly secret and the Supernatural Conception of her child. (For note on the Virgin Birth see under Luke 1:26–38.)

Joseph

Very little is told of Joseph. He went with Mary to Bethlehem, and was with her when Jesus was born (Luke 2:4, 16). He was with Mary when Jesus was presented in the Temple (Luke 2:33). He conducted their flight to Egypt, and the return to Nazareth (Matthew 2:13, 19–23). And took Jesus up to Jerusalem at the age of 12 (Luke 2:43, 51). The only further reference to him is that he was a carpenter, and the head of a family of at least seven children (Matthew 13:55, 56). He surely must have been a good and exemplary man, to have been thus chosen of God to be the foster-father of God's Own Son. He may have died before Jesus began his public ministry, though the language of Matthew 13:55 and John 6:42 may imply that he was still alive. At any rate he must have died before Jesus' crucifixion, else why did Jesus commit the care of his mother to John (John 19:26–27)?

Comparative View of the Four Gospels

	MATTHEW	MARK	LUKE	JOHN
Pre-Incarnation Existence of Jesus				1:1–3
Jesus' Birth and Childhood	1, 2		1, 2	
John the Baptist	3:1–12	1:1–8	3:1–20	1:6–42
Jesus' Baptism	3:13–17	1:9–11	3:21–22	
The Temptation	4:1–11	1:12–13	4:1–13	
Preliminary Miracle				2:1–11
Early Judean Ministry (about 8 months)				2:13 to 4:3
Visit to Samaria				4:4–42
Galilean Ministry (about 2 years)	4:12 to 19:1	1:14 to 10:1	4:14 to 9:51	4:43–54 6:1–7:1
Visit to Jerusalem				5:1–47
Perean and Later Judean Ministry (about 4 months)	19, 20	10	9:51 to 19:28	7:2 to 11:57
The Last Week	21 to 27	11 to 15	19:29 to 24:1	12 to 19
Post-Resurrection Ministry	28	16	24	20 to 21

Mary

After the story of the Birth of Jesus, and his visit to Jerusalem at the age of 12, very little is said of Mary. According to Matthew 13:55–56, she was the mother of at least six children besides Jesus. At her suggestion Jesus turned water into wine at Cana, his first miracle (John 2:1–11). Later, she is mentioned as trying to get to him in the crowd (Matthew 12:46; Mark 3:31; Luke 8:19), where Jesus' words plainly indicate that her family relation to him gave her no special spiritual advantage. She was present at the crucifixion, and was committed by Jesus to the care of John (John 19:25–27). There is no record of Jesus appearing to her after his resurrection, though he did appear to Mary Magdalene. The last mention of Mary is in Acts 1:14, as being with the disciples in prayer. This is all the Scripture has to say about Mary. Of the women who figured in Jesus' public life Mary Magdalene seems to have played a much more prominent part than Jesus' mother (Matthew 27:56, 61; 28:1; Mark 15:40, 47; 16:9; Luke 8:2; 24:10; John 19:25; 20:1–18, see note under Luke 8:1–3).

Mary was a quiet, meditative, devoted, wise woman, most honored of women, queen of mothers, sharing the cares common to motherhood. We admire her, we honor her, and we love her because she was the mother of our Savior.

Who were the "brothers" and "sisters" of Jesus, mentioned in Matthew 13:55–56 and Mark 6:3? Mary's own children? Or children of Joseph by a former marriage? The plain, simple, natural meaning of these passages is that they were Mary's own children. This is the opinion commonly held among Bible commentators. And it is substantiated by the statement in Luke 2:7 that Mary "brought forth her FIRST-BORN son." Why "first-born," if there were no others?

Chapter 2:1-12. Visit of the Wise-Men

This must have occurred in the period when Jesus was between 40 days old and 2 years old (Matthew 2:16; Luke 2:22, 39). The 2 years seem to denote the time when the star first appeared (7), to start them on their journey, a journey of many months, and not necessarily to signalize the exact time of the child's birth. But Herod, in order to be sure, took the outside limit. At least, the child was not still in the manger, as is sometimes pictured, but in the "house" (11. See on Luke 2:6–7).

These Wise-Men came from Babylon, or the country beyond, the land where the human race had its origin, the land of Abraham, land of the Jewish Captivity, where many Jews still lived. They belonged to the learned class, advisers of kings. Perhaps they were familiar with the Jewish Scriptures, and knew of the expectation of a coming Messianic King. It was the land of Daniel, and no doubt they knew of Daniel's 70 weeks' prophecy; and also Balaam's prophecy about "A Star out of Jacob" (Numbers 24:17). They were men of high standing, for they had access to Herod. They are commonly spoken of as the "Three Wise-Men." But the Scripture does not say how many. There were probably more, or at least they were with an entourage of scores or hundreds, for it would not be safe for a small group to travel a thousand miles over desert wastes that were infested with bandits. Their arrival in Jerusalem was of sufficient show of importance to stir the whole city.

Aside from symbolizing the homage of wisdom, and of distant lands, to the new-born KING, and of calling to the attention of Jerusalem that He had arrived, one of the objects of their visit, which they themselves knew not, was to supply money for the child's flight to Egypt. The parents were poor, and, except for the gold brought by the Wise-Men, escape from Herod may not have been possible. Return of the Wise-Men may have paved the way, in their own country, for later preaching of the Gospel.

The Star

It has been calculated that there was a conjunction of Jupiter and Saturn (6 B.C.). But that can scarcely explain how "the star went before them till it came and stood over where the child was." Some think that possibly it was a "nova," that is, a star that explodes and burns brightly for a while. But how could that fit the case?

The star that the Wise-Men saw was, no doubt, a distinct phenomenon, a Supernatural Light, which by a direct Act of God, went before them, and pointed out the exact spot; a Supernatural Announcement of a Supernatural Birth.

Chapter 2:13-15. Flight to Egypt

Even this incident did not escape God's unfailing eye in the long line of prophecies anticipatory of the Messiah (15, Hosea 11:1). The angel (13), who directed their flight to Egypt probably was Gabriel, to whom God had entrusted the care of the Infant Child (see under Luke 2:8–20). The stay in Egypt was short, probably only a year or two, for Herod soon died, and it was safe to return. (See Chronology of Jesus' Childhood, under Luke 2:39.)

The place in Egypt at which Joseph and Mary and the child resided is not named. Tradition says it was On, also called Heliopolis; same place from which another Joseph had ruled Egypt long centuries before (Genesis 41:45). An Obelisk, erected in the days of Abraham, still standing, marks the ruins.

Chapter 2:16-18. Slaughter of the Children

Strange that one who believed in the coming of the Christ (4), could have been conceited enough and stupid enough to think that he could thwart His Coming.

Herod

The Herods were an Edomite line of kings, who, under Rome, got control of Judea shortly before Christ. Herod the Great (37–3 B.C.), got his throne, and kept it, by crimes of unspeakable brutality, murdering even his wife and two sons. He was cruel, cunning, cold-blooded. It was he who slew the children of Bethlehem in an effort to kill Christ.

His son, Herod Antipas, some 33 years later, killed John the Baptist (Mark 6:14–29), and mocked Christ (Luke 23:7–12).

His grandson, Herod Agrippa I, 14 years still later, killed James the Apostle (Acts 12:1–2).

His great grandson, Herod Agrippa II, 16 years still later, was the king before whom Paul was tried (Acts 25:13–26:32).

Chapter 2:19-21. Return from Egypt

This, too, was directed by the angel. It seems, from verse 22, that Joseph was planning to return to Bethlehem, to make that, the ancestral city of David, their permanent residence, as the proper place in which to rear the child Messiah. But God planned differently, and sent them back to their Galilean home.

Jesus' Names

Jesus had been named long before he appeared, "THE MESSIAH" (Hebrew), or "THE CHRIST" (Greek). Both words mean the same, "Anointed": the "One Anointed" of God to Redeem and Rule the world. "Jesus" was his personal name. "The Messiah," or "The Christ," his official name.

Chapter 2:22-23. Return to Nazareth

Matthew makes no mention of Nazareth having been the home of Joseph and Mary. We learn that from Luke. The thing that Matthew specially points out is that it was in Fulfillment of Prophecy.

The Prophecy that Matthew here refers to is thought to be Isaiah 11:1; Jeremiah 23:5; Zechariah 3:8, where the Messiah is spoken of as the "Branch." The Hebrew form of the word Nazareth means "Branch." So Jesus was a Nazarene in a double sense: He lived at Nazareth, and He was the Branch foretold in Prophecy.

Old Testament Prophecies of Christ Quoted in the Gospels

Since Matthew used Old Testament quotations so abundantly, exhibiting his inclination to dovetail the incidents and features of Christ's Life into Prophetic Forecasts, here is a good place to give a list of Old Testament Prophecies which are quoted in the Four Gospels, particularly Matthew, as referring to Christ. Most of them are quite clear as referring to the Messiah. A few of them we might not so construe, except they are so quoted by the Inspired New Testament writers. For ourselves, we are entirely satisfied with New Testament interpretations of Old Testament passages. They register God's intended meaning in those passages. Here are the Prophecies.

That He was to be of David's Family,
(Matthew 22:44; Mark 12:36; Luke 1:69, 70; 20:42–44; John 7:42; II Samuel 7:12–16; Psalms 89:3–4; 110:1; 132:11; Isaiah 9:6, 7; 11:1).

That He would be Born of a Virgin (Matthew 1:23; Isaiah 7:14).

That He would be Born in Bethlehem (Matthew 2:6; John 7:42; Micah 5:2).

That He would Sojourn in Egypt (Matthew 2:15; Hosea 11:1).

That He would Live in Galilee (Matthew 4:15; Isaiah 9:1, 2).

At Nazareth (Matthew 2:23; Isaiah 11:1).

That His Coming would be Announced by an Elijah-like Herald
(Matthew 3:3; 11:10–14; Mark 1:2–3; Luke 3:4–6; 7:27; John 1:23; Isaiah 40:3–5; Malachi 3:1; 4:5).

His Coming would occasion Massacre of Bethlehem's Children
(Matthew 2:18; Genesis 35:19–20; 48:7; Jeremiah 31:15).

That He would proclaim a Jubilee to the World
(Luke 4:18–19; Isaiah 58:6; 61:1).

That His mission would include Gentiles (Matthew 12:18–21; Isaiah 42:1–4).

That His Ministry would be one of Healing (Matthew 8:17; Isaiah 53:4).

That He would Teach by Parables
(Matthew 13:14, 15, 35; Isaiah 6:9–10; Psalm 78:2).

That He would be Disbelieved and Rejected by the Rulers
(Matthew 15:8, 9; 21:42; Mark 7:6, 7; 12:10, 11; Luke 20:17; John 12:38–40; 15:25; Psalms 69:4; 118:22; Isaiah 6:10; 29:13; 53:1).

That He would make a Triumphal Entry into Jerusalem
(Matthew 21:5; John 12:13–15; Isaiah 62:11; Zechariah 9:9; Psalm 118:26).

That He would be like a Smitten Shepherd
(Matthew 26:31; Mark 14:27; Zechariah 13:7).

Betrayed by a Friend for 30 Pieces of Silver
(Matthew 27:9–10; John 13:18; Zechariah 11:12–13; Psalm 41:9).

That He would Die with Malefactors (Luke 22:37; Isaiah 53:9, 12).

That He would be Buried by a Rich Man
(Isaiah 53:9; Matthew 27:57–60; Fact stated, Prophecy not quoted).

That He would be given Vinegar and Gall
(Matthew 27:34; John 19:29; Psalm 69:21).
They would Cast Lots for His Garments (John 19:24; Psalm 22:18).
Even His Dying Words were Foretold
(Matthew 27:46; Mark 15:34; Luke 23:46; Psalms 22:1, 31:5).
Not a Bone would be Broken
(John 19:36; Exodus 12:46; Numbers 9:12; Psalm 34:20).
His Side would be Pierced (John 19:37; Zechariah 12:10; Psalm 22:16).
He would Rise from the Dead the Third Day (Matthew 12:40; Luke 24:46). No particular passage is quoted from the Old Testament for this. That He would Rise from the Dead is definitely quoted in Acts 2:25–32, 13:33–35, from Psalm 16:10–11. Jesus said it was Written that He would Rise the Third Day (Luke 24:46). He must have had in mind Hosea 6:2 and Jonah 1:7, and Isaac being released from Death the Third Day (Genesis 22:4).
And that His Rejection would be followed by the Destruction of Jerusalem and Great Tribulation
(Matthew 24:15; Mark 13:14; Luke 21:20; Daniel 9:27; 11:31; 12:1, 11).
Jesus Himself realized that in His Death
He was Fulfilling the Scripture (Matthew 26:54, 56).
Here is an Amazing thing: The Complete Story of Jesus' Life, its Main Features, Events, and Accompanying Incidents, even in Minutest Detail, is Plainly Foretold in the Old Testament Scriptures. Is it not Overwhelming Evidence of the Existence and Working of a MIND that Transcends the Human Mind to a degree that Awes us into Wonderment?

Chapter 3. Baptism of Jesus

Told also in Mark 1:1–11 and Luke 3:1–22. (For note on John the Baptist see on Luke 3:1–20). In all three accounts, and in John 1:31–33, the things specifically featured are the descent of the Holy Spirit and the Voice from Heaven. It seems, from John 1:31–33, that John did not know Jesus, but Matthew 3:14 implies that he did know him. Undoubtedly as boys Jesus and John had known each other, for their families were kin (Luke 1:36), and their mothers were together for three months just preceding their births (Luke 1:39, 56). And it seems certain that the boys must have been told by their parents of the heavenly announcements concerning their respective missions. But from the time that John withdrew to become a hermit of the desert (Luke 1:80)., he may not again have seen Jesus till the day of his Baptism. Naturally he would not recognize the man whom he had not seen since boyhood days, till God pointed him out. Then, under direct heavenly endorsement, Jesus was publicly anointed as the Son of God, the nation's Messiah and the Saviour of the world.

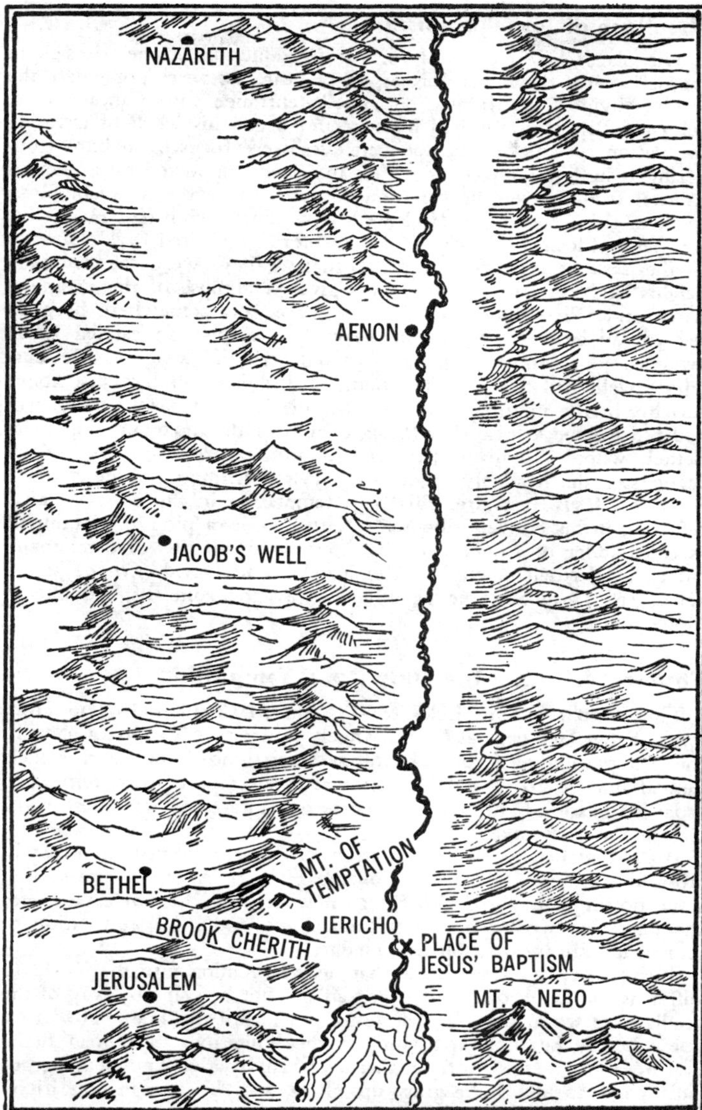
NAZARETH
AENON
JACOB'S WELL
MT. OF TEMPTATION
BETHEL
JERICHO
BROOK CHERITH
PLACE OF JESUS' BAPTISM
JERUSALEM
MT. NEBO

Map 50.

The Place of Jesus' Baptism

The place chosen of God for the introduction of the Messiah to the nation was the lower Jordan, at, or near, the very spot where the waters divided for Joshua on Israel's entrance into Canaan. Here John the Baptist established himself, and began his work of arousing the nation to expectancy. Soon all eyes were focused on him, wondering if he himself were the Messiah. Then, supported by a demonstration from heaven, he pronounced Jesus to be the Messiah. Here, soon, in this same region, followed Jesus' Early Ministry. Here, too, was Jesus' Closing Ministry. What memories clustered here! Directly to the east, at the edge of the Jordan Valley, were the towering heights of Nebo, where Moses was given a glimpse of the Promised Land, and where God buried him. There, too, somewhere between the Jordan and Mt. Nebo, the heavenly chariots had carried Elijah away to join Moses in glory. Five miles to the west, was Jericho, whose walls had fallen at the sound of Joshua's trumpet. Just above Jericho, in the mountain fastnesses of the Brook Cherith, the ravens had fed Elijah. A little further up, on top of the mountain ridge, was Bethel, where Abraham had erected an altar to God and where Jacob saw the heavenly ladder of angels ascending and descending, to which Jesus, just after His own temptation in the same vicinity, referred, in his conversation with Nathaniel, as a picture of Himself as the Ladder of Angels. Nearby, southward, on the same mountain ridge, lay Jerusalem, city of Melchizedek and David. To the south, across the Dead Sea, the plain where lay the ruins of Sodom and Gomorrah.

Chapter 4:1-10. The Forty Days' Temptation

This is told also in Luke 4:1–13, and Mark 1:12–13. The Holy Spirit, Satan (see page 497) and Angels (see page 426) took a hand in the Temptation of Jesus. The Holy Spirit guided him, and Angels helped him, as Satan made attempt after attempt to turn him aside from his mission. The whole universe was interested. The destiny of Creation was at stake.

We wonder why the Temptation of Jesus followed immediately after his Baptism. The descent of the Holy Spirit upon him at that time, possibly, involved two things new in Jesus' human experience: the Power to work Miracles without limit; and a full restoration to him of his Pre-Incarnation Knowledge.

Back in eternity Jesus knew that he was coming into the world to suffer as the Lamb of God for human sin. But he came by way of the cradle. Are we to suppose that Jesus as a little baby knew all that he knew before he took upon himself the limitations of human flesh? Is it not more natural to think that his preincarnation knowledge gradually came to him as he grew up, along with his human education?

Fig. 59. The Traditional Mount of Temptation.
© *Matson Photo*

Of course his mother had told him of the circumstances of his birth. He knew he was the Son of God and the Messiah. No doubt he and his mother had often talked over the plans and methods by which he would do his work as the world's Messiah. But when the Holy Spirit came down upon him, at his baptism, "without measure," then there came to him fully and clearly, for the first time as a Man, some of the things he had known before he became a Man: among them, the CROSS as the way by which he was to accomplish his mission. It stunned him; took from him the desire for food; drove him from the haunts of men; and for 40 days he wondered about it.

What was the nature of his temptation? It may have included the ordinary temptations of men in their struggle for bread and their desire for fame and power. But more. Jesus was too great for us to think that such motives could weigh strongly with him. From his antecedents and background we must believe that he had already formed a consuming passion to save the world. He knew that was his mission. The question was, How to do it. By using the miraculous powers which had just been bestowed upon him—powers which no mortal man had ever before known—to give men bread without their having to work, and to overcome the ordinary forces of nature, he could have raised himself to the rulership of the world, and by FORCE made men do his will. That was Satan's suggestion. But Jesus' mission was, not to compel obedience, but to Change the Hearts of Men.

Was the devil actually present? Or was it just an inner struggle? We are not told in what form the devil appeared to Jesus. But unmistakably Jesus recognized the suggestions as coming from Satan, who was there, determined to thwart Jesus' mission. (See note on Satan under Luke 4:1–13.)

The place of Jesus' Temptation is thought to have been in the barren heights of the mountain region overlooking Jericho, above the brook Cherith where the ravens had fed Elijah, in distant view, possibly, of Golgotha where he was to meet the final test. (See Map 50 under Matthew 3:13–17.)

Jesus fasted for 40 days (2). Moses had fasted for 40 days in Mt. Sinai, when the Ten Commandments were given (Exodus 34:28). Elijah had fasted for 40 days, on the way to the same mountain (I Kings 19:8). Moses represented the Law. Elijah, the Prophets. Jesus was the Messiah to whom the Law and the Prophets pointed. From the mountain top where Jesus was fasting looking eastward across the Jordan, he could see the mountain ranges of Nebo where Moses and Elijah, centuries before, had ascended to God.

Some three years later these three men had a rendezvous, amid glories of the Transfiguration, on Mt. Hermon (Map 53, under Mark 10), 100 miles to the north, whose snow-capped summit was in plain view of the Mt. of Temptation: companions in Suffering, then companions in Glory.

After the Temptation Jesus went back to the Jordan where John was baptizing. (See note on John 1:19–34.)

Chapter 4:11. Angels

Angels Figured Largely in the Life of Jesus

An Angel announced the Birth of John (Luke 1:11–17).
And named him (Luke 1:13).
An Angel foretold to Mary the Birth of Jesus (Luke 1:26–37).
An Angel foretold to Joseph the Birth of Jesus (Matthew 1:20–21).
And named Him (Matthew 1:21).
Angels announced to Shepherds the Birth of Jesus (Luke 2:8–15).
And Sang Hallelujahs (Luke 2:13–14).
An Angel directed the Child's Flight to Egypt (Matthew 2:13, 20).
Angels ministered to Jesus at His Temptation (Matthew 4:11).
An Angel came to Jesus in Gethsemane (Luke 22:43).
An Angel rolled away the stone at His Tomb (Matthew 28:2).
And announced to the women His Resurrection (Matthew 28:5–7).
Two Angels presented Him to Mary Magdalene (John 20:11–14).

Jesus Said a Good Deal about Angels

Angels ascending and descending upon Himself (John 1:51).
Could have 12 Legions of Angels Deliver Him (Matthew 26:53).
Angels will Come with Him (Matthew 25:31; 16:27; Mark 8:38; Luke 9:26).
Angels will be the Reapers (Matthew 13:39).
Angels will Gather the Elect (Matthew 24:31).
Angels will Sever the Wicked from the Righteous (Matthew 13:41, 49).
Angels carried the Beggar to Abraham's Bosom (Luke 16:22).
Angels Rejoice over the Repentance of Sinners (Luke 15:10).
Little Children have Guardian Angels (Matthew 18:10).
Jesus will Confess His People before the Angels (Luke 12:8).
Angels have No Sex, Cannot Die (Luke 20:35–36; Matthew 22:30).
The Devil has Evil Angels (Matthew 25:41).

Jesus Himself Said These Things. His statements about Angels are so Specific, so Varied, and so Abundant that to explain them on the theory that Jesus was merely accommodating Himself to current beliefs would undermine the validity of any of Jesus' Words as Truth.

Angels in the Book of Acts

An Angel Opened Prison Doors for the Apostles (Acts 5:19).
An Angel Directed Philip to the Ethiopian (Acts 8:26).
An Angel Released Peter from Prison (Acts 12:7, 8, 9).
And was called "His" Angel (Acts 12:15), Peter's Angel.
An Angel Struck Herod Dead (Acts 12:23).
An Angel Directed Cornelius to Send for Peter (Acts 10:3).
An Angel Stood by Paul during the Storm (Acts 27:23).

Angels in the Old Testament

An Angel rescued Hagar (Genesis 16:7–12).
Angels announced the Birth of Isaac (Genesis 18:1–15).
Angels announced the Destruction of Sodom (Genesis 18:16–33).
Angels Destroyed Sodom, and Rescued Lot (Genesis 19:1–29).
An Angel intercepted the slaying of Isaac (Genesis 22:11–12).
Angels Guarded Jacob (Genesis 28:12; 31:11; 32:1; 48:16).
An Angel Commissioned Moses (Exodus 3:2).
An Angel Led Israel (Exodus 14:19; 23:20–23; 32:34).
An Angel arranged the Marriage of Isaac and Rebecca (Genesis 24:7).
Angels gave the Law (Acts 7:38, 53; Galatians 3:19; Hebrews 2:2).
An Angel rebuked Balaam (Numbers 22:31–35).
A Prince of God's Host appeared to Joshua (Joshua 5:13–15).
An Angel rebuked the Israelites for Idolatry (Judges 2:1–5).

An Angel commissioned Gideon (Judges 6:11–40).
An Angel announced the Birth of Samson (Judges 13).
An Angel smote Israel with Pestilence (II Samuel 24:16–17).
An Angel rescued Elijah (I Kings 19:5–8).
Elisha was surrounded by Invisible Angels (II Kings 6:14–17).
An Angel Saved Daniel from the Lions (Daniel 6:22).
An Angel Smote the Assyrian Army (II Kings 19:35; Isaiah 37:36).
Angels Camp round about God's People (Psalms 34:7; 91:11).
Angels aided in Writing of Zechariah (Zechariah 1:9; 2:3; 4:5, etc.).

Angels in the Epistles and Revelation

There are Elect Angels (I Timothy 5:21).
Angels are Innumerable (Hebrews 12:22; Revelation 5:11).
Angels Minister to Heirs of Salvation (Hebrews 1:13–14).
Angels will Come with Jesus in Flaming Fire (II Thessalonians 1:7).
We are Not to Worship Angels (Colossians 2:18; Revelation 22:8, 9).
An Angel directed the Writing of Revelation (Revelation 1:1).
Churches have Guardian Angels (Revelation 1:20; 2:8, 12, 18; 3:1, 7, 14).
Revelation is largely a Drama of Angels (see page 692).

There are different Orders of Angels, organized into Principalities, Powers, Thrones and Dominions (Romans 8:38; Ephesians 1:21; 3:10; Colossians 1:16; 2:15; I Peter 3:22).

Michael is the name of the Archangel. He was the Patron Angel of Judah (Daniel 10:13, 1; 12:1). He contended with the Devil about the Body of Moses (Jude 9). He struggles with Satan in behalf of the Church (Revelation 12:7). He will be with Christ at Second Coming; his Voice will Raise the Dead (I Thessalonians 4:16).

Gabriel is one of the Angel Princes (see page 491).

Occasionally the word "Angel" seems to refer to the inanimate forces of nature. But generally it unmistakably means Personalities of the Unseen World.

Chapter 4:12. Jesus Begins Galilean Ministry

Between verses 11 and 12 about a year elapses, including Jesus' Early Judean Ministry, covering the events of John 1:19 to 4:54 and Luke 4:16–30 (See note under Mark 1:14–15).

To the Galilean Ministry

Matthew devotes one-half his book, 14 chapters (4:12 to 19:1).
Mark devotes one-half his book, 8 chapters (1:14 to 10:1).
Luke devotes less than 6 chapters (4:14 to 9:51).
John almost omits it.

The Galilean Ministry

Comparative View of the Four Accounts

MATTHEW

Call of Simon, Andrew, James, John (4:18–22).
Journeys, Preaching, Healing, Multitudes, Fame (4:23–25).
Sermon on the Mount (5, 6, 7).
A Leper, and the Centurion's Servant, Healed (8:1–13).
Peter's Mother-in-law, and Many Others, Healed (8:14–17).
Tempest Stilled (8:23–27). Gadarene Demoniacs (8:28–34).
A Paralytic Healed (9:1–8).
Call of Matthew, and his Feast (9:9–13). "Fasting" (9:14–17).
Jairus' Daughter, and the Woman with Hemorrhage (9:18–26).
Two Blind Men, and a Dumb Demoniac, Healed (9:27–38).
The Twelve Sent Forth (10).
Messengers from John the Baptist (11:1–19).
Cities Upbraided (11:20–24). "Come unto Me" (11:25–30).
Eating Grain, and Healing, on the Sabbath (12:1–14).
A Blind and Dumb Demoniac Healed (12:15–23).
Jesus Accused of being in League with Beelzebub (12:24–45).
Jesus' Mother and Brothers (12:46–50).
Parables: Sower, Tares, Mustard, Leaven, Treasure, Pearl, Net (13).
Visit to Nazareth (13:54–58).
John the Baptist Beheaded (14:1–12).
The 5,000 Fed, Jesus Walks on the Water (14:13–33).
Multitudes Healed in Gennesaret (14:34–36).
Pharisees, Tradition, and Defilement (15:1–20).
The Canaanitish Woman (15:21–28).
The 4,000 Fed (15:29–39).
"Leaven of the Pharisees" (16:1–12).
Peter's Confession, Passion Foretold (16:13–28).
The Transfiguration, Passion again Foretold (17:1–13).
The Epileptic Boy, Passion again Foretold (17:14–23).
The Temple Tax (17:24–27). "Little Children." "Forgiveness" (18).

MARK

Call of Simon, Andrew, James, John (1:14–20).
Demoniac, Peter's Mother-in-law, Many Others, Healed (1:21–34).
Journeys, Miracles; a Leper, a Paralytic, Healed (1:40–2:12).
Call of Levi, and the Feast (2:13–17). "Fasting" (2:18–22).
Eating Grain, and Healing, on the Sabbath (2:23–3:6).
Multitudes, Fame, Miracles (3:7–12).
The Twelve Chosen (3:13–19).

Jesus Accused of being in League with Beelzebub (3:20–30).
Jesus' Mother and Brothers (3:31–35).
Parables: Sower, Growing Seed, Mustard Seed (4:1–34).
The Tempest Stilled (4:35–41). The Gerasene Demoniac (5:1–20).
Jairus' Daughter, Woman with Hemorrhage (5:21–43).
Visit to Nazareth (6:1–6).
The Twelve Sent Forth (6:7–13).
John the Baptist Beheaded (6:14–29).
The 5,000 Fed, Jesus Walks on the Water (6:30–52).
Multitudes Healed in Gennesaret (6:53–56).
Pharisees, Tradition, and Defilement (7:1–23).
The Syrophoenician Woman, a Deaf Mute (7:24–37).
The 4,000 Fed, "Leaven of the Pharisees" (8:1–21).
Blind Man at Bethsaida given his Sight (8:22–26).
Peter's Confession, Passion Foretold (8:27–9:1).
Transfiguration, Passion again Foretold (9:2–13).
The Epileptic Boy, Passion again Foretold (9:14–32).
"Who is Greatest?", Unknown Wonder Worker (9:33–50).

LUKE

Visit to Nazareth (4:14–30).
Demoniac, Peter's Mother-in-Law, Many Others, Healed (4:31–44).
Call of Peter, James, John (5:1–11).
A Leper, and a Paralytic Healed (5:12–26).
Call of Levi, and the Feast (5:27–32). "Fasting" (5:33–39).
Eating Grain, and Healing, on the Sabbath (6:1–11).
The Twelve Chosen (6:12–19).
Sermon on the Mount (6:20–49).
Centurion's Servant, Widow's Son, Messengers from John (7:1–35).
The Sinful Woman, The Women, Parable of the Sower (7:36–8:18).
Jesus' Mother, Brothers, Storm, Gerasene Demoniac (8:19–39).
Jairus' Daughter, Woman with Hemorrhage (8:40–48).
The Twelve Sent Forth (9:1–6).
John the Baptist Beheaded (9:7–9). The 5,000 Fed (9:10–17).
Peter's Confession, Passion Foretold (9:18–27).
The Transfiguration (9:28–36).
The Epileptic Boy, Passion again Foretold (9:28–43).
"Who is Greatest?", Unknown Wonder Worker (9:46–50).

JOHN

Preliminary Miracle at Cana, Sojourn in Capernaum (2:1–12).
Nobleman's Son Healed (4:43–54). The 5,000 Fed (6:1–7:1).

Chapter 4:13–17. Residence in Capernaum. This is one of the things foretold of the Messiah. (See under Matthew 2:22–23.)

Chapter 4:18–22. Call of Simon, Andrew, James, John. (See under Mark 1:16–20. Also under Matthew 10.)

Chapter 4:23–25. Journeys, Fame, Multitudes, Miracles. (See under Mark 1:38–39.)

Duration and Chronology of the Galilean Ministry

The Galilean Ministry started "four months before harvest" (December) (John 4:35, 43).

It closed just before the Feast of Tabernacles (October), or just before the Feast of Dedication (December) (Luke 9:51; John 7:2; 10:22).

It covered a Passover (John 6:4); and another Passover, if, as is generally thought, the Feast of John 5:1 was a Passover.

Thus starting in December, and extending past the second Passover to the following October or December, it lasted about 2 years; or, only one year, if the Feast of John 5:1 was not a Passover.

Matthew, Mark and Luke, in a general way, seem to follow a chronological order, though not in detail; for they differ as to the order of many of the incidents. As to which of the three is more strictly chronological there is difference of opinion among Bible scholars. Inasmuch as the Gospel writers seem to have been guided by other considerations in grouping their material, and inasmuch as notices of time and place are so largely ignored, it is not possible to classify in exact chronological arrangement all of the material that is recorded.

However, there are some well-marked events and periods in the Galilean Ministry around which others may be grouped.

The 5,000 were fed at Passover time (John 6:4). John the Baptist was beheaded just before that (Matthew 14:12–13). At the same time the Twelve returned from their preaching tour (Luke 9:10).

All three writers place the Transfiguration shortly before the Final Departure from Galilee.

The Final Departure from Galilee was either just before the Feast of Tabernacles (October) or the Feast of Dedication (December) (Luke 9:51; John 7:1–10; 10:22): most likely the latter; for the earlier was in secret (John 7:10); the latter in publicity (Luke 10:1).

This makes a period of five or eight months between the Feeding of the 5,000 and the Transfiguration, part of which time Jesus spent in regions north of Galilee, of which not much is told.

The main part of the story of the Galilean Ministry is concerned with the sixteen months preceding the Feeding of the 5,000, a period of intense activity and great popularity.

The following table gives a general outline view of the Galilean Ministry, the chronological place of some of the incidents being only conjectural.

The Galilean Ministry

Tentative Chronological Arrangement

December:	Begins Galilean Ministry
A.D. 27	From Cana Heals Nobleman's Son at Capernaum
	Visits Nazareth, and is rejected
	Makes Capernaum his Headquarters
	Calls Simon, Andrew, James and John
	Heals Demoniac, Peter's Mother-in-law, Many others
	Journeys about, Heals a Leper, and a Paralytic
	Calls Matthew
	Questions about Fasting, and the Sabbath
A.D. 28	
Passover?:	Visits Jerusalem
	Heals on Sabbath, Arouses Opposition of Rulers
	Asserts his Deity, Returns to Galilee
Midsummer:	Journeys, Multitudes, Miracles, Fame
	The Twelve Chosen
	Sermon on the Mount
	Journeys about, Speaks Many Parables
	Stills the Tempest, Heals the Gerasene Demoniacs
	Raises Jairus' daughter from the Dead
	Is Accused of being in League with Beelzebub
	Raises the Widow of Nain's Son from the Dead
	Receives Messengers from John the Baptist
	Visits Nazareth again
	Heals Centurion's Servant, Forgives Sinful Woman
A.D. 29	
February?:	The Twelve Sent Forth
Passover:	The Twelve Return, John the Baptist Beheaded
	The 5,000 Fed, Jesus Walks on the Water
	Discourses on the Bread of Life
	Refuses Popular Demand to be King
	Heals Many, Discourses on Defilement
	Upbraids Cities, "Come unto Me"
	Retires to North, Syrophoenician Woman
	Returns to Galilee, Deaf Mute Cured, 4,000 Fed
	At Magdala, "Sign of Jonah," Blind Man Healed
October?:	
	Visits Jerusalem, Discourses, Woman Taken in Adultery
	Blind Man Healed, Open Conflict with Rulers
November:	Returns to Galilee
	Retires to Caesarea-Philippi, Peter's Confession
	The Transfiguration, the Epileptic Boy

	Passion Foretold Three Times
	In Galilee again, Tax Money, "Who is Greatest?"
	"Children," "Unknown Wonder Worker,"
December?:	Final Departure from Galilee (or October?)

Chapters 5,6,7. The Sermon on the Mount

Matthew places the Sermon on the Mount in the forefront of his story of the Galilean Ministry, although it seems to have come some months later at the time of Choosing the Twelve (Luke 6:12–20), if indeed Luke is reporting the same sermon. It must have been that Matthew regarded the Sermon on the Mount as an epitome of Jesus' Teaching, of which His whole ministry was an illustration.

Containing, as it does, the very Heart of Jesus' Teaching, we may think of the Sermon on the Mount as being to the New Testament what the Ten Commandments were to the Old Testament. Every Christian ought to Memorize the Sermon on the Mount, and strive earnestly to Live according to its Teachings.

The Mountain on which this Sermon was delivered is not named. Tradition says it was Horns of Hattin (see Map page 473).

(For note on comparison with Luke's record, see on Luke 6:20–49.)

Chapter 5:1-12. The Beatitudes

Blessed, Happy, are the Discouraged, the Sorrowful, the Lowly, the Spiritually-Depressed, the Merciful, the Pure in Heart, the Peaceful, and the Persecuted. In part, the exact opposite of the world's standards. But the Blessing is not in the Unfortunate Condition in itself, but in the Glorious Rewards to come. Heaven, to Jesus, who knew, was so Infinitely Superior to Earthly Life, that He regarded anything that increased the Longing for Heaven a Blessing.

Chapter 5:13-16. Salt and Light of the World

That is, Preserver and Guide. Jesus Himself is the Light of the World (John 8:12). His followers reflect His Light and Glory. The grandest motive that a person can have is that, by his, or her, Manner of Life, others may be constrained to Glorify God.

Chapter 5:17-48. Jesus and the Law

He came not to Destroy the Law, but to Fulfill it. There is no contradiction here between Jesus' Teaching and the Teaching of Romans, Galatians and Hebrews, that we are Saved by Faith in Christ rather than by Works of the Law. Jesus' meaning is that God's Moral Law is the expression of God's Own Holiness, and is of Eternal

Obligation on God's People. And that, in reality, He came to give the Law's former declaration a deeper meaning, and to enforce it, not merely in Outward Acts, but in the inner depths of the Human Heart. He then proceeds to illustrate in five particulars: Murder, Adultery, Swearing, Revenge and Hatred of Enemy.

Murder (5:21–26). The law against Murder was one of the Ten Commandments (Exodus 20:13). Jesus forbids our cherishing in the Heart the Anger that leads to the Act.

Adultery (5:27–32). The law against Adultery also was one of the Ten Commandments (Exodus 20:14). Jesus forbids our cherishing the Lust that leads to the Act. Notice that in connection with both Anger and Lust Jesus warns of Hell Fire (22, 29, 30). He not only warns us to watch our Inner Feelings, but goes much further than Moses in restricting Divorce (32).

Swearing (5:33–37). This probably applies to Judicial Oaths, and Common Blasphemy, and even the Light-Hearted use of God's Name in ordinary conversation.

Revenge (5:38–42). The Eye for Eye legislation was part of the Civil Law, administered by Judges (Exodus 21:22–25). Jesus is not here legislating for Courts of Justice. Civil Government is ordained of God (Romans 13:1–7), to save human society from its Criminal Elements. The sterner the Courts deal out Justice, the better for society. But Jesus is here teaching principles by which Individuals as Individuals should deal with other Individuals. (See on Luke 6:27–38.)

Hatred of Enemies (5:43–48), was not enjoined in the Old Testament. It may have been implied in some Old Testament dealings with Israel's enemies. However that may be, Jesus Forbids it. (See on Luke 6:27–38.)

Chapters 6 and 7. Heavenly Teachings

Secret Motives of Life (6:1–18. See on Luke 12:1–12). Here illustrated in three particulars: Alms, Prayer, Fasting.

Alms (6:2–4), as unto God: Not to make a Show. (See on Matthew 23.)

Prayer (6:5–15). (See on Luke 11 and 18.)

Fasting (6:16–18). (See on Mark 2:18–22.)

Treasures in Heaven (6:19–34). (See on Luke 12:13–34.)

Judge Not Your Brother (7:1–5). (See on Luke 6:39–45.)

Pearls before Swine (7:6). This means we should use Common Sense and Tact in talking about our religion. Else we may do our cause more harm than good.

Persistent Prayer (7:7–11). (See on Luke 18:1–8.)

The Golden Rule (7:12). (See on Luke 6:27–38.)

The Narrow Way (7:13–14). Many Lost. Few Saved: Few, in comparison to the number of the Lost: but still, in the end, a Great Multitude which no man can number (Revelation 7:9).

False Teachers (7:15–23). Jesus warned, and prophesied, of False Teachers (Matthew 24:11, 24). So did New Testament writers, again and again. The Most Devastating Obstacle to the Progress of Christianity among men has been its Ruthless Corruption at the hands of its own promoters—besmirched almost beyond recognition.

Building on the Rock (7:24–27). A very plain statement that it is useless to call ourselves Christians unless we Practice the things that Jesus taught in this Sermon on the Mount.

Chapter 8:1–4.	A Leper Cleansed. (See on Mark 1:40–44.)
Chapter 8:5–13.	The Centurion's Servant. (See on Luke 7:1–10.)
Chapter 8:14–15.	Peter's Mother-in-law. (See on Mark 1:29–31.)
Chapter 8:16–17.	Multitudes Healed. (See on Mark 1:32–34.)
Chapter 8:18–22.	"Foxes Have Holes." (See on Luke 9:57–62.)
Chapter 8:23–27.	The Tempest Stilled. (See on Mark 4:36–41.)
Chapter 8:28–34.	The Gadarene Demoniacs. (See on Mark 5:1–20.)
Chapter 9:1–8.	A Paralytic Healed. (See on Mark 2:1–12.)
Chapter 9:9–13.	Call of Matthew. (See on Mark 2:13–17.)
Chapter 9:14–17.	Question about Fasting. (See on Mark 2:18–22.)
Chapter 9:18–26.	Jairus' Daughter. (See on Luke 8:40–56.)
Chapter 9:27–31.	Two Blind Men. (See on Mark 8:22–26.)
Chapter 9:32–34.	A Dumb Demoniac. (See on Mark 7:31–37.)
Chapter 9:35–38.	Journeying About. (See on Mark 1:39.)

Chapter 10. The Twelve Sent Forth

Told also, more briefly, in Mark 6:7–13 and Luke 9:1–6. It must have been shortly before Passover, for they returned at Passover time, just before the feeding of the 5,000 (Luke 9:10–17, John 6:4).

These instructions of Jesus to the Twelve contain some wonderful advice for Christians: to be wise as serpents and harmless as doves; to expect hardship; to trust in God's unfailing care of His own; and to keep our eyes fixed on the eternal goal.

Some of Jesus' instructions were of only temporary application; for instance, to take no money. With the power to heal there would be no difficulty about their lodging and meals being supplied. But afterward they were told to take money (Luke 22:35–38).

The Call of the Twelve

Jesus took about a year and a half to complete his choice. Then they were with him about two years.

A.D. 26, November? John, Andrew, Simon, Philip, Nathanael believed on him at John's baptizing (John 1:35–51); accompanied him to Cana; then went back to their occupations till a later call.

A.D. 28, January? After he had finished his Early Judean Ministry, and as he began his Galilean Ministry, he called Simon, Andrew,

James and John to leave their fishing business, and definitely associate themselves with him (Mark 1:16–20).
Shortly thereafter Matthew was asked to join the group (Matthew 9:9).
A.D. 28, May? The Twelve were formally chosen (Luke 6:12–16).
A.D. 29, March? They were given power to heal, and sent out in pairs, on a tour of possibly a month or so (Matthew 10).
A.D. 30, May. Their final commission to carry the Gospel to the ends of the earth (Matthew 28:16–20).

The Training of the Twelve

The choosing and training of the men to whom he was to entrust his work was an extremely important part of Jesus' earthly mission. Jesus' primary purpose in coming into the world was to die as the Lamb of God in expiation for human sin and to rise from the dead to bring eternal life to mankind. But his Life, Death and Resurrection would be useless to the world unless the world knows about it. If the men to whom he entrusted his work should fail him, then his coming to earth would have been in vain.

The first sending out of the Twelve was a part of their training, intended possibly to give them practice work, and was a part of Jesus' method of advertising to the nation that the Messiah had arrived. There were no newspapers. The only means of spreading the news was by word of mouth. Later the Seventy were sent out for the same purpose. These men authenticated their message by special miracles, not only to attract attention, but to indicate to the nation the extraordinary nature of the ONE whom they proclaimed.

Their training was not an easy task, for they were being trained for a work utterly different from what they thought they were being trained for. They began to follow him as politicians, with no thought whatever of becoming preachers, as they turned out to be. They were expecting, that, as the Messiah, he would establish a political world empire, of which they would be the administrators. (See further, under Matthew 13.)

His method of changing their minds about the work that he and they were to do was, first, to present himself to them in all the fulness of his divine glory, so that, no matter how differently he talked and acted from the way they expected the Messiah to talk and act, they would still believe that he was the one. That is one of the reasons he wrought miracles, and that he was transfigured.

Then, along with that, he spoke in parables, veiled sayings, to give them the impression that he did not always mean exactly what he appeared to mean. Kept them for a while in a state of wonderment. If he had told them plainly at the start, they might not have been interested in following him at all.

When at last he told them that he was going to be crucified, instead of erecting a throne, it stunned them. But they still persisted in thinking it was only a parable. Even at the Last Supper, their minds were still on which one of them was to have the greatest office.

Not till after his Resurrection and the descent of the Holy Spirit did they at last come to understand that it was to be a kingdom in which Jesus would reign in the Hearts of men, and that their part would be simply TELLING THE STORY OF JESUS. That is all. The Story would do its own work. If men know about Jesus they will love him.

Chapter 11:1-19. Messengers from John the Baptist

This was while John was in prison. Jesus was at the height of his popularity. John evidently was looking for a political Messiah (see on Luke 3:1–20), and could not understand why Jesus was not taking proper action toward that end.

Jesus' answer indicated that he considered his miracles as sufficient evidence of his Messiahship.

Notice that John's doubt did not lower him in Jesus' estimation. There had not arisen a greater, said Jesus.

Yet the lowliest in Christ's kingdom are greater than John, that is, in point of privilege. What a comment on the privilege of being a Christian!

"Suffers violence" (12), that is, the followers both of John and Jesus were making every effort to force Jesus into the leadership of a political movement of military and worldly nature.

Jesus, in contrasting his own manner of life with that of John, said that both were from God and had their place in God's effort to appeal to that generation.

Chapter 11:20-24. The "Mighty Works" of Jesus

Three cities, at the north end of the Sea of Galilee, are named as the principal scene of Jesus' miracles (see Map 52, page 473). Capernaum, Bethsaida, Chorazin. Most favored of all cities on earth. Jesus' pronouncement of their doom shows that Jesus regarded his miracles as having evidential value that it was dangerous to ignore.

Chapter 11:25-30. "Come unto Me"

Dearest, sweetest words ever heard by mortal ears. Jesus seemed glad that it was the simple-minded common people who received him. Paul said the same thing (I Corinthians 1:26). It seems hard for intellectuals, in their mental pride, to humble themselves enough to acknowledge their need of a Saviour.

Chapter 12:1–8. Eating on the Sabbath. (See on Mark 2:23–27.)
Chapter 12:9–14. Healing on the Sabbath. (See on Mark 3:1–6.)

Chapter 12:15-21. Many Miracles

In Mark 3:7–12 it is stated that the multitudes, besides those from Galilee, had assembled from Judea, Jerusalem, Idumea, beyond the Jordan, and the region of Tyre and Sidon. Thus, for a hundred miles around, north, south and east, in days when travel was by foot, great throngs, hearing of his miracles, came, bringing their sick, and he healed them all (15).

Chapter 12:22-23. A Blind and Dumb Demoniac Healed

Told also in Luke 11:14–15. A great miracle, for the people, though they had become accustomed to miracles, were "amazed." "Son of David" (23), was the commonly accepted title of the expected Messiah (Matthew 1:1; 9:27; 15:22; 20:30; 21:9; 22:42; John 7:42).

Chapter 12:24-37. The Unpardonable Sin

This is told also in Mark 3:22–30; Luke 11:14–26; 12:8–10. Note that the Pharisees, as heartily as they hated Jesus, did not deny his miracles, which were too numerous and too well-known to deny. Though the miracles were entirely benevolent in their nature, yet so hardened and hypocritical were the Pharisees that they attributed them to Satanic origin. Such vile and devilish accusations were evidence of a nature almost beyond redemption. This may be the import of Jesus' words, a condition of heart to which they were perilously near. In Luke 12:10 the unpardonable sin is connected with the denial of Christ. Jesus seems to make a distinction between sin against himself, and sin against the Holy Spirit (32). Quite commonly the Unpardonable Sin is understood thus: rejecting Christ, while as yet he was in the flesh, his work unfinished, when even his disciples did not understand him, was forgivable. But after his work was completed, and the Holy Spirit was come, then, in full knowledge, deliberate final rejection of the Holy Spirit's offer of Christ would constitute the "eternal sin which hath never forgiveness." Similar sin is spoken of in Hebrews 6:6; 10:26 and I John 5:16. (See notes on those passages.)

"Idle Words" (36), are here mentioned in connection with the unpardonable sin. Our words show our character (34). Our every word, as well as every secret act, is being recorded for reproduction in the Day of Judgment.

Chapter 12:38-45. The Sign of Jonah

Told also in Luke 11:29–32. It was brazen impudence to ask Jesus for a sign just after they had been accusing him of working signs by the aid of Beelzebub. Jesus promised them a sign even more astounding, which he called "the sign of Jonah"–his own resurrection from the dead, the GRAND SIGN OF ALL THE AGES. The habits of demons (43–45, see on Mark 5:1–20).

Chapter 12:46-50. His Mother and Brothers

Told also in Mark 3:31–35; Luke 8:19–21. Jesus' reply teaches that spiritual ties are stronger than fleshly ties, and implies that his mother was no closer to him than any who do the will of God.

Chapter 13:1-53. Parables of the Kingdom

A Parable is a sort of "extended metaphor"; a comparison; illustrating spiritual things by ordinary. Roughly speaking, parables are stories to illustrate certain truths.

Jesus used parables, in part, as dark sayings, with apparent double meanings, "to conceal for a time what he had to reveal." The Kingdom that Jesus intended to establish was so utterly different from what was commonly expected of the Messiah that it was necessary for him to be very tactful. So he used these stories, to illustrate the "origin, development, mixed character and consummation" of the Kingdom, which to us seem very plain, but were enigmas to his immediate hearers.

In interpreting the parables, the problem is to know which details are significant, and which are incidents necessary to the story. Ordinarily a parable was meant to show ONE point, and should not be pressed for lessons in every detail.

The number of parables is variously given from 27 to 50. What some call parables others call metaphors. Ordinarily the number of parables is reckoned as about 30. Some of them are quite similar. Jesus used different stories to illustrate the same point, and sometimes the same story to illustrate different points.

Chapter 13:1-23. Parable of the Sower

Told also in Mark 4:1–25; Luke 8:4–16. The seed is God's Word (Luke 8:11). Souls are born of God's Word (I Peter 1:23). This parable is a prophecy of the Gospel's reception. Some will not even listen. Some will accept it, but soon fall away. Some will hold on longer, but gradually lose interest. And some will hold on, in varying degrees, to final fruition.

Chapter 13:24-30; 36-43; 47-53. The Tares and the Net

Two illustrations, with slightly different shades of emphasis, that, though the earth shall be leavened by the Gospel, yet the bad shall persist along with the good till the end of the world, when there will be a final separation, the wicked going to their unhappy destiny, and the righteous into the kingdom of eternal glory. Jesus had no illusions about this world becoming a Utopia. He knew full well that to the end his Gospel would be rejected by a large part of the world. He recognized only two classes, the saved and the lost. Again and again he spoke of the miseries of the lost, their "weeping and gnashing of teeth." He surely knew what he was talking about.

Chapter 13:31-33. The Mustard Seed and the Leaven

Told also in Mark 4:30–32; Luke 13:18–20. Two similar parables, illustrating the small beginning of Christ's kingdom, its gradual and imperceptible growth, both in the individual and in the world at large, ultimately reaching vast proportions, leavening all institutions, philosophies and governments.

Chapter 13:44-46. The Hid Treasure and the Goodly Pearl

A double illustration of the same thing: the priceless value of Christ to the human soul. What Christ offers is worth giving up everything, even life itself, to obtain.

The Kingdom

Notice how frequently the word "Kingdom" occurs in Matthew: 3:2; 4:17, 23; 5:3, 10, 19, 20; 6:10, 33; 7:21; 8:11; 9:35; 10:7; 11:11, 12; 12:28; 13:11, 24, 31, 33, 43, 44, 45, 47, 52; 16:19, 28; 18:23; 19:12, 14, 23, 24; 20:1; 21:31, 43; 22:2; 23:13; 24:14; 25:1, 34; 26:29.

A political Kingdom, in which the Jewish nation, under their Messiah, would rule the world, is what they were expecting. Herod shared that notion, and tried to destroy Jesus in childhood, because he thought the Christ's kingdom would be a rival political kingdom to his own. John the Baptist shared that notion, and when Jesus gave no indication of being that kind of king John began to doubt whether after all Jesus was the Messiah (Matthew 11:3). The Twelve Apostles shared the notion till after the resurrection. The last question they asked Jesus was, "Lord, will you now restore the kingdom to Israel?" (Acts 1:6). Their minds were on political independence for their country, rather than personal eternal salvation.

What was the Kingdom that Jesus came to found? Not a political kingdom, but to REIGN IN THE HEARTS OF MEN, and through their hearts control and transform their lives. The human heart is the realm in which Jesus came to reign. To make all mankind LOVE HIM. And why Love Him? To Change us over into His Own Image. Out of an Affection for Him, a Devotion to Him, an Adoration of Him, will grow all the beauty and comfort of life, the transformation of character, the regeneration of the soul.

The Word "Kingdom," as used in the New Testament, is pliable. Sometimes it seems to mean the reign of God in the individual. Sometimes, the general reign of righteousness among men. Sometimes, the church. Sometimes, Christendom. Sometimes, the millennial reign. Sometimes, heaven. The basic idea of the word implies Jesus' dominion in the hearts of his people through all dispensations, onward into eternity, with special reference, at times, to one or another of its various aspects or stages.

Chapter 13:54–58. Visit to Nazareth. (See on Mark 6:1–6.)
Chapter 14:1–12. John Beheaded. (See on Luke 3:1–20.)
Chapter 14:13–21. The 5,000 Fed. (See on John 6:1–15.)
Chapter 14:22–33. Jesus Walks on Water. (See on John 6:16–21.)

Period from Feeding 5,000 to Transfiguration

Chapters 14:34 *to* 16:12. (*See on Mark* 6:53.)

Chapter 14:34–36. Multitudes in Gennesaret. (See on Mark 6:53.)
Chapter 15:1–20. Pharisees and Defilement. (See on Mark 7:1–23.)
Chapter 15:21–28. The Canaanite Woman. (See on Mark 7:24–30.)
Chapter 15:29–39. The 4,000 Fed. (See on Mark 8:1–9.)
Chapter 16:1–12. Leaven of Pharisees. (See on Mark 8:10–21.)

Chapter 16:13-20. Peter's Confession

This is told also in Mark 8:27–29 and Luke 9:18–20. It had been some three years since Peter had first accepted Jesus as the Messiah (John 1:41, 42). Called him "Lord," a year later (Luke 5:8.) Half a year later he called him "The Holy One of God" (John 6:68, 69). Now after two and a half years of association with Jesus he expresses his conviction in the Deity of Jesus.

The "Rock" (18), on which Christ would build his Church, is not Peter, but the Truth to which Peter confessed, that Jesus is the Son of God. The Deity of Jesus is the foundation on which the Church rests, the fundamental creed of Christendom. This is the unmistakable meaning of the language.

ARCHAEOLOGICAL NOTE (EMB)

Verse 18 is the theme of a famous controversy. Perhaps the imagery is derived from the rocky terrain of the lofty view of Mount Hermon above. The Greek text runs literally, "Thou art Petros and upon this 'petra' I will build my church." The word "petros" means a small stone. In Liddell and Scott's Greek lexicon the word is quoted as applied to sling-stones and boundary-stones among other contexts. Even boundary stones are not too big for one man to lift and move. On the other hand the lexicon quotes "petra" as applied to Mt. Olympus and the Caucasus. Remember, further, that both Greek and Latin often use "and" for "but" (e.g. "Be angry and sin not") and the meaning of the passage is clear. The Lord says, "You are Peter, and any man can move you, but the faith you have expressed in My deity is a rock immovable as the mountains. On it I will build My church."

"The Keys of the Kingdom", 19

The ordinary interpretation of this is that Peter opened the door of salvation, on the day of Pentecost, to the Jews (Acts 2), and later to the Gentiles (Acts 10). Not that he was given the power to Forgive Sins, but to proclaim the terms of forgiveness. Whatever authority it gave to Peter was also given to the other Apostles (Matthew 18:18; John 20:23). And that, only in a Declarative sense. Christ forgives. His apostles were inspired by the Holy Spirit to proclaim the terms of that forgiveness.

Chapter 16:21–28. Passion Foretold. (See on Mark 9:30–32.)

Chapter 17:1–13. Jesus is Transfigured. (See on Mark 9:2–13.)

Chapter 17:14–20. The Epileptic Boy. (See on Mark 9:14–29.)

Chapter 17:22–23. Passion again Foretold. (See on Mark 9:30–32.)

Chapter 17:24–27. The Tax Money. This was a sort of poll tax for the sanctuary, required of every male over 20 (Exodus 30:11–15). It was equivalent to about 16 cents. Jesus, as Lord of the Sanctuary, was exempt. Yet, lest his attitude toward the Temple be misunderstood, he paid it.

Chapter 18:1–6. "Who is Greatest?" (See on Luke 9:46–48.)

Chapter 18:7–14. "Occasions of Stumbling." (See Mark 9:41–50.)

Chapter 18:15–35. Forgiveness. A talent (24), was about $1000. A pence, or shilling (28), was about 17 cents. The man was forgiven $10,000,000, but was unwilling to forgive $17.00. That is Jesus' comparison of our own sins against God to those sinned against us. Notice Jesus' statement that there is no hope of forgiveness unless we forgive (35).

The Perean Ministry

Chapters 19 *and* 20. (*See Luke* 9:51.)

Chapter 19:1–2. Departure from Galilee. (See on Luke 9:51.)

Chapter 19:3–12. Question about Divorce. Jesus' teaching about divorce is recorded here and in Matthew 5:31; Mark 10:2–12; Luke 16:18; and Paul discusses the subject in I Corinthians 7. One man and one woman married for life is God's will for the human race. Christ seems to allow only one cause for divorce (9).

Chapter 19:13–15. Little Children. (See on Luke 18:15–17.)

Chapter 19:16–30. Rich Young Ruler. (See on Luke 18:18–30.)

Chapter 20:1–16. Parable of Laborers in the Vineyard. This does not mean that all will be treated alike in heaven, or that there will be no rewards. The parable of the Talents (Matthew 25:14–30), seems to teach that there will be rewards. And Paul taught it (I Corinthians 3:14–15). Jesus here meant to teach just one thing: that some who think they are first in this world are going to find themselves last in heaven. He said that a number of times (Matthew 19:30; 20:16; Mark 10:31; Luke 13:30). Heavenly standards and earthly standards are so utterly different that many of earth's humblest Christians, slaves and servants, will have the highest places in heaven; and many of the great church dignitaries, if there at all, will be under those who were here their servants. (See further under Luke 16:19–31.)

Chapter 20:17–19. Passion again Foretold. (See on Mark 9:30–32.)

Chapter 20:20–28. Request of James and John. The pathos of this is that it was their reaction to Jesus' announcement that he was on his way to the cross. (See on Luke 9:46–48.)

Chapter 20:29–34. Blind man at Jericho. (See on Luke 18:35–43.)

Jesus' Last Week

Chapters 21 *to* 28.

Chapter 21:1-11. The Triumphal Entry

Told also in Mark 11:1–10; Luke 19:29–38; John 12:12–19. It was on the Sunday before his death. Jesus had come as the long-foretold Messiah. For three years he had proclaimed himself to the nation by unceasing journeys and miracles, and the journeys and miracles of the Twelve, and of the Seventy. He knew that his death had been determined upon by the rulers. He was ready for it. In a grand public demonstration, as final notice to the Holy City, he entered amid the hallelujahs and hosannas of the expectant multitudes. The people were jubilant. They thought the hour of deliverance was at hand.

Jesus rode on a colt, because it was foretold (Zechariah 9:9), that Messiah would come that way.

Chapter 21:12-17. Jesus Cleanses the Temple

Told also in Mark 11:15–18; Luke 19:45–47. This was Monday. He had done the same thing three years before at the opening of his public ministry (see note on John 2:13–22). The enormous profits from the market booths inside the Temple area, went to enrich the family of the high priest. Jesus burned with indignation at such a perversion of the uses of God's House. (See further under John 2:13–22.)

Chapter 21:18-22. Jesus Withers the Fig Tree

Told also in Mark 11:12–14; 20–24. This was Monday morning, as he went from Bethany into Jerusalem, along the road over Mount of Olives. The disciples noticed it next morning, as they came into the city. Evidently they had gone out to Bethany Monday evening along the road around the south foot of the Mount.

Chapter 21:23-27. "By What Authority?"

Told also in Mark 11:27–33; Luke 20:1–8. The rulers were bitter, and they made every conceivable effort to trap Jesus. But he was a master dialectician, and parried every question to their own discomfiture.

Chapter 21:28-32. Parable of the Two Sons

This parable is aimed directly at religious leaders; chief priests, elders, scribes and Pharisees. They rejected Jesus. But the common people accepted Him joyfully.

Chapter 21:33-46 Parable of the Vineyard

Told also in Mark 12:1–12; Luke 20:9–19. Parable of Two Sons, just preceding, had been aimed primarily at the leaders of the Jewish nation. This parable is aimed at the Nation itself.

Chapter 22:1-14. Parable of the Marriage Feast

Another illustration of the same thing: that God's Elect nation, for its shameful treatment of God's messengers, was now to be cast off, and other nations called in. Also, it is a sort of double parable:

having a warning for the newcomers, that they be careful, lest they meet the same fate.

Chapter 22:15–22. Tribute to Caesar. (See on Mark 12:13–17.)

Chapter 22:23–33. The Resurrection. (See on Mark 12:18–27.)

Chapter 22:34–40. The Great Commandment. (See on Mark 12:28–34.)

Chapter 22:41–46. "The Son of David." (See on Mark 12:35–37.)

Chapter 23. Woe to Scribes and Pharisees

Pharisees were the most numerous and influential of the religious sects of Jesus' day. They were strict legalists. They stood for the rigid observance of the letter and forms of the Law, and also for the Traditions. There were some good men among them. But in the main they were known for their covetousness, self-righteousness and hypocrisy.

Scribes were copyists of the Scriptures. Because of their minute acquaintance with the Law they became recognized authorities. They were sometimes called "lawyers." Scribes and Pharisees were the religious leaders of the nation.

These words of Jesus, constitute the most bitter denunciation that ever fell from his lips. Jesus never talked that way to sinners, publicans and the common people. Jesus himself was the most genuinely religious man that ever lived. But how his soul loathed religious pretense!

Those fellows did not all die in that generation. Through all the centuries the Church has been cursed with leaders exactly described in the 23rd chapter of Matthew, irreligious professional religionists, parading themselves in holy garments, pompous fellows, self-important, strutting around like lords, preaching religion, yet having none.

Farewell to the Temple

On Monday Jesus had cleansed the Temple. Tuesday, after final warnings that the Kingdom of God would now be taken from the Jews and given to other nations, he left the Temple, nevermore to enter, abandoning it to its ruin. His departure from the Temple ended his public ministry, to await in quiet his death three days later.

Great Discourse on the End

Chapters 24, 25. (Told also in Mark 13 and Luke 21.)

This discourse was delivered after Jesus had left the Temple for the last time. It was about the Destruction of Jerusalem, his Coming, and the End of the World. Some of his words are so mixed up that it is difficult to know to which event they refer. Perhaps it was intentional. It seems plain that he had in mind two distinct events, separated by an interval of time; indicated by "these" in 24:34, and "that day" in 24:36. Some would explain "this generation" (Matthew 24:34), to mean this nation, that is, the Jewish race shall not pass away till the Lord comes. The more common view is that he meant Jerusalem would be destroyed within the lifetime of those then living. To one looking at two distant mountain peaks, one behind the other, they seem close together, though they may be far apart. So in Jesus' perspective, these two events, one in some respects typical of the other, stood in close proximity, though there is a long interval between. What he said in a sentence may be of an age. What happened in one case may be a "begun fulfillment" of what will happen in the other.

His words concerning Jerusalem were fulfilled literally, within 40 years. The magnificent buildings of marble and gold, were so completely demolished, by the Roman army, (A.D. 70) that Josephus said it looked like a site that had never been inhabited. (See further under Hebrews 13.)

His Second Coming

By far the larger part of this great discourse is devoted to the subject of Jesus' Coming Again. With his death only three days away, and knowing that his disciples would be stunned almost out of their faith he takes a good deal of pains to explain that they would yet realize their hopes in a far grander way than they had yet ever dreamed.

Jesus' thoughts dwelt a great deal on his Second Advent:

"When the Son of Man shall come in his glory, and all the angels with him" (Matthew 25:31).

"The Son of Man shall come in the glory of his Father, with his angels" (Matthew 16:27).

"As the lightning comes out of the east and is seen even to the west, so shall the coming of the Son of Man be" (Matthew 24:27).

"As it was in the days of Noah, so shall the coming of the Son of Man be" (Matthew 24:37).

"As it was in the days of Lot: . . . so shall it be in the day that the Son of Man is revealed" (Luke 17:28–30).

"They shall see the Son of Man coming in a cloud with power and great glory" (Luke 21:27).

"Whosoever shall be ashamed of me, . . . of him shall the Son of Man be ashamed when he comes in the glory of his Father with the holy angels" (Mark 8:38).

"I am going to prepare a place for you, and I will come again to receive you unto myself" (John 14:2–3).

His Coming will be heralded with "a great sound of a trumpet" (Matthew 24:31), as of old the nation was gathered together (Exodus 19:13, 16, 19). The fact that Paul repeated this expression, "the trumpet shall sound," in connection with the resurrection (I Corinthians 15:52), and in I Thessalonians 4:16 says, "The Lord himself shall descend from heaven with a shout, with the voice of the archangel, and with the trump of God," indicates that it may be more than a mere figure of speech. An actual, sudden, grand historical event, in which He assembles to himself his own from among the living and the dead, on a vast and mighty scale.

Neither his coming to Jerusalem in judgment (A.D. 70); nor the coming of the Holy Spirit on the day of Pentecost; nor our going to him in death; none of these can exhaust the meaning of Jesus' words as to his Coming again.

It is best not to be too dogmatic as to certain concomitant events connected with his Coming. But if language is a vehicle of thought at all, certainly it takes a good deal of explaining and interpreting to make anything else out of Jesus' words than that he himself looked forward to his Coming Again as a definite historical event in which He Himself personally and literally will appear to gather to Himself and to Eternal Glory those who have been redeemed by his blood.

And it is best not to cloud the hope of his Coming with too detailed a theory as to what is going to happen when he Comes. Some people, we suspect, will be disappointed if Jesus does not follow the schedule they have mapped out for him.

It is related that Queen Victoria, deeply touched by a sermon of F. W. Farrar on the Lord's Second Coming, said to him: "Dean Farrar, I should like to be living when Jesus comes, so that I could lay the crown of England at his feet."

Chapter 24:45–51. Faithful and Wise Servants. From here on Jesus' Discourse is an exhortation to Watchfulness. His Second Advent was uppermost in his thoughts. So it should be in ours.

Chapter 25:1–13. Parable of the Ten Virgins. This parable means just one thing: that we should keep our minds on the Lord, and be ready when he Comes.

Chapter 25:14–30. Parable of the Talents. This means that we are in training for a larger service in an order yet to be, and that our place and standing there will depend on the faithfulness of our stewardship here.

Chapter 25:31–46. Final Judgment Scene. One of the most magnificent passages in the Bible, a picture of how Common Kindness will affect our standing in the Eternal World.

Chapter 26:1–5. Plot to Kill Jesus. (See on Mark 14:1–2.)
Chapter 26:6–13. Anointing at Bethany. (See on Mark 14:3–9.)
Chapter 26:14–16. Bargain of Judas. (See on Mark 14:10–11.)

Chapter 26:17-29. The Last Supper

Told also in Mark 14:12–25; Luke 22:7–38; John 13 and 14. This was the night before his death. There were two suppers: Passover Supper and Lord's Supper. Lord's Supper was instituted at close of Passover Supper. Luke mentions two cups (22:17–20). Matthew, Mark and Luke mention both suppers. John mentions only Passover.

For 14 centuries the Passover had been pointing forward to the coming of the Paschal Lamb. Jesus ate the Passover, substituted in its place His Own Supper, and then was himself slain as the Paschal Lamb. Jesus expired on the cross in the same day in which paschal lambs were being slain in the Temple.

The Passover had served its purpose, and had now given place to the New Memorial Supper which was to be kept in loving remembrance of Jesus till He Comes again (I Corinthians 11:26).

As the Passover pointed back to deliverance out of Egypt, and forward to His Coming; so the new Memorial points back to his death, and forward to His Coming in Glory.

The order of incidents at the Supper is somewhat confusing. Matthew and Mark seem to place the Lord's Supper after Judas had gone out. Luke seems to say that Judas was there. John gives the contention first. Luke gives it after the supper. The writers evidently were guided by other considerations than the order in which the incidents occurred. Here is the probable order:

1. Their contention. Jesus washes their feet.
2. Jesus announces the betrayal, All answer, "Is it I?"
3. Sop given to Judas. He says, "Is it I?" and goes out.
4. The Lord's Supper instituted.
5. The "new commandment," and tender words of John 14.

The Cup

In 1910 there was found, in the ruins of a cathedral on the site of Antioch, a cup, containing an inner cup, that is thought by able scholars possibly to have been the actual cup that Jesus used on that holy night. The inner cup is a plain silver cup. The outer cup, of silver, is exquisitely carved with twelve figures, representing Christ and the Apostles. The outer cup was evidently made to hold the inner, as a sacred, precious object older than itself. The art and workmanship is considered to be of the first century. The Last Supper is thought probably to have been in the home of Mark's mother. Mark frequently visited Antioch.

Fig. 60. The Chalice of Antioch. Front view showing Christ in center, Peter and Paul below.
(Courtesy of Mr. Fahim Kouchakji.)

After fall of Jerusalem, Antioch became chief center of Christianity. What more natural than that this object, precious beyond measure to Christians, would be kept in a church in Antioch, where, when the church was destroyed, it was buried in the ruins, till recently found. It is owned by Mr. Fahim Kouchakji, New York, through whose courtesy a photo is here shown.

Chapter 26:30–46. Agony in Gethsemane. (See on Luke 22:39–46.)
Chapter 26:47–56. Betrayal and Arrest. (See on John 18:1–12.)
Chapter 26:57–68. Before the High Priest. (See on Mark 14:53.)
Chapter 26:69–75. Peter's Denial. (See on John 18:15–27.)
Chapter 27:1–2. Officially Condemned. (See on Mark 14:53.)
Chapter 27:3–10. Suicide of Judas. (See on Mark 14:10–11.)

Chapter 27:11-25. Trial before Pilate

For note on the Successive Steps in the Trial of Jesus see under Mark 14:53ff.

Pilate was Roman governor of Judea, 26–37 A.D. He assumed office about the time that Jesus began his public ministry. His official residence was at Caesarea. He came to Jerusalem at time of Feasts to keep order. He was merciless, cruel, noted for his habitual brutality. Like the Roman emperors of his day, he rather enjoyed the spectacle of the torture and death of a man. At one time he had mingled the blood of Galileans with their sacrifices, Luke 13:1.

One of the strangest pictures in history is the impression that Jesus made on this hard-hearted Roman governor. Whether Jesus was erect and handsome, as one tradition has it, or stoop-shouldered and ugly, as another tradition has it, there must have been something about his countenance and bearing so divine, so commanding, that although he was dressed in the robes of mock royalty, with the crown of thorns on his head, and the blood streaming down his face, Pilate could not keep his eyes off him.

Pilate's effort to get out of crucifying Jesus is a pitiful story. He did not want to do it. He appealed from the Jewish rulers to Herod. Then from Herod back to the rulers. Then from the rulers to the multitudes. Then when the multitudes turned against Jesus, Pilate tried to appeal to their pity, by having Jesus scourged, in hope that they would be satisfied with partial punishment, and not require him to go all the way to crucifixion. Failing in that, he did not finally make up his mind to crucify Jesus till the Jews threatened to report him to Caesar. Not till it began to look as if it might cost him his position as Governor of Judea did he at last give his consent to the death of Jesus.

Pilate is said to have committed suicide.

Pilate's wife, Procula, tradition says, became a Christian.

"His blood be on us, and on our children," 25. How fearfully this has been fulfilled!

An artist's restoration of the Ecce Homo Arch and the Gabbatha (pavement) at the Tower of Antonia in Jerusalem, the traditional site of Pilate's famous declaration, "Behold, the man!"
© *Matson Photo Service*

Chapter 27:26. Jesus is Scourged

Scourging usually preceded capital punishment. In this case Pilate seems to have hoped that the multitudes would consider it to be sufficient punishment. Scourging was done with a whip which was made of a number of leather thongs weighted with pieces of lead or sharp metal. The victim was stripped to the waist, then bound, in a bent-over position, to a post, and beaten on the bare back with the scourge till the flesh was all torn open. Sometimes death resulted.

Chapter 27:27-31. Jesus is Mocked

The Jews, in their trial, had mocked him (Luke 22:63–65). Herod and his soldiers had mocked him (Luke 23:11). Now Pilate's soldiers mock him. And, a little later, on the cross, priests, elders and scribes mock him (27:29–43). To their brutal minds it was great sport to see one who claimed to be the Son of God having to submit to such humiliation and torture.

Chapter 27:32. Simon of Cyrene

In John 19:17 it is said that Jesus went out bearing his own cross. Exhausted by his night of agony, and the scourging, he had not gone far, till he became too weak to carry it further. Then Simon was pressed into service. Little is known of Simon. But how proud, in heaven, throughout all eternity will Simon be, to think he helped Jesus to bear his cross!

Chapter 27:33–56. Jesus is Crucified. (See also on Mark 15:21–41; Luke 23:32–43 and John 19:17–30.)

The Darkness

For three hours (45), inanimate nature hid her face in shame at the unspeakable wickedness of men. God may have meant the darkness to be creation's symbolic mourning for Jesus while he was suffering the expiatory pains of the lost.

The Earthquake

The earthquake, the rocks rent, and the tombs opened (51–55), were God's salute to the Conquering Saviour. The rending of the veil in the temple (51), was God's own proclamation that in the death of Christ the barrier between God and man disappeared (Hebrews 9:8). The risen saints (52–53), were God's evidence and guaranty that the power of death had been broken. Note that even the centurion, officer of the Roman soldiers who crucified Jesus, was convinced that Jesus was indeed the Son of God (54).

Chapter 27:57–61. Burial. (See on John 19:38–42.)

Chapter 27:62–66. The Tomb Sealed. (See on Matthew 28:11–15.)

The "Third Day"

"The Third Day" (64), is here used as being identical with "after three days" (63). In Hebrew usage parts of days at the beginning and end of a period were counted as days (Esther 4:16; 5:1). "Three days and three nights" (Matthew 12:40) (a long way of saying "three days," I Samuel 30:12–13); "after three days" (Mark 8:31; 10:34; John 2:19); and "the third day" (Matthew 16:21; 17:23; 20:19; Luke 9:22; 24:7, 21, 46) are interchangeable phrases for the period Jesus was in the tomb, Friday afternoon till Sunday morning.

Chapter 28:1-8. The Women Visit the Tomb

This is told in all four Gospels (Mark 16:1–8; Luke 24:1–11; John 20:1–3). Mary Magdalene is named in all four. Mary, mother of James and Joses, called also "the other Mary" (Matthew, Mark, Luke). Salome, mother of James and John (Mark). Joanna, wife of Herod's steward (Luke). And "other women" (Luke). In all, half a dozen, or possibly a dozen or more. They had spices to complete the embalming of his body for permanent burial, with no thought whatever that he would be risen.

"As it began to dawn" (Matthew). "Very early," "when the sun was risen" (Mark). "At early dawn" (Luke). "While it was yet dark" (John). These variant notes as to the time mean, evidently, that they started while it was yet dark, and reached the tomb about sunrise. Their various lodging-places, in Bethany or Jerusalem, ranged, probably, from 1 mile to two miles or more distant.

"An angel," sitting upon the stone (Matthew). "A young man," sitting in the tomb (Mark). "Two men" stood by them (Luke). "Two angels," sitting in the tomb (John). These different expressions simply mean that the angels, in human form, were waiting outside the tomb to greet the women, then led them inside, and explained that Jesus had risen. Part time two were visible, and part time only one was visible. Probably there were myriads of angels hovering over the tomb that morning, waiting to welcome the risen Saviour, for it was a triumphant moment in the annals of heaven. Angels will have charge of the general resurrection (Matthew 24:31, see note on "Angels" under Matthew 4:11).

"Late on the Sabbath" (1). The Sabbath, strictly speaking, was from sunset to sunset. But in common usage, as here, it extended into the night, indicated by the expression "as it began to dawn toward the first day of the week."

"A great earthquake" (2). There had also been an earthquake as Jesus expired on the cross (Matthew 27:51). And at the giving of the law on Mt. Sinai (Exodus 19:16, 18). It is one of God's ways of calling attention to momentous events.

Chapter 28:9-10. Jesus Appears to the Women

Between verses 8 and 9, we gather from the Gospel records, the women had told the disciples, and were returning again to the tomb; in which interval Peter and John had run to the tomb, and gone away, and Mary Magdalene, ahead of the others, was at the tomb alone, and Jesus appeared to her. Then a little later to the other women. (See under Mark 16 on "Order of Events.") Thus Jesus' first two appearances were to women.

Through Woman, without the aid of Man, came the Saviour, and now to Women first the Glorious News of His Resurrection.

Chapter 28:11-15. The Guards Bribed

They had been put there at the request of the Sanhedrin, as a precaution against the possibility of Jesus' body being stolen. Terrified at the earthquake, the angel, and the absence of Jesus' body from the tomb, they fled to report to the Sanhedrin. The Sanhedrin bribed them to say that they had fallen asleep. This inside knowledge of what took place at the tomb no doubt had something to do with the conversion of a multitude of priests a little later (Acts 6:7).

That afternoon, Jesus appeared to the Two (Luke 24:13–32).

And, about the same time, to Peter (Luke 24:34).

And in the evening, to the Ten (John 20:19–25).

A week later, to the Eleven, in Jerusalem (John 20:26–29).

Sometime later, to the Seven, by the Sea of Galilee (John 21).

And to James, at a time and place unknown (I Corinthians 15:7).

Chapter 28:16-20. Jesus Appears to the Eleven

In a mountain in Galilee, by his own appointment (26:32; 28:7). It is thought to have been the time when "above 500" were present (I Corinthians 15:6). The "Great Commission" (18:20), is recorded, in substance, four times (see on Mark 16:14–18).

"I am with you always" (20). This is our favorite verse in all the Bible. Jesus rose, nevermore to die. He is ALIVE now, and is with his people, in guiding and protecting power, all the time.

Not merely the commander-in-chief of some vast organization of angels and arch-angels. He is that. But more. The Commander-in-chief of the hosts of heaven is himself personally interested in and personally with each one of his people all the time.

We cannot understand how One Person can be with millions and billions of persons at the same time. But it is Deity. And Jesus said it in the plainest possible language, "I AM WITH YOU ALL THE

TIME." Jesus said that. And Jesus did not use idle words. He did not talk just to hear himself talk. He meant something when he said that, and we believe that, in some real sense, beyond our comprehension, mystic, but real, HE is with each one of us all the time.

No matter how weak, or humble, or unimportant, HE is our friend, our companion. Invisible, but there. Now, right now. Tonight, while we are asleep. Tomorrow, while we are at work. Next week. Next year. Shadowing us through life. Walking by our side. Watching with kindly interest every detail of life's pitiful struggle, trying so patiently to lead us up to a place of immortal happiness in His Father's home. This all seems like just a beautiful dream. But it is a FACT, the one fundamental fact of our existence.

After this, Jesus appeared once more (Luke 24:44–51).

ARCHAEOLOGICAL NOTE: *The Nazareth Decree.* (EMB)

The Nazareth Decree is an inscription cut on a slab of white marble, sent in 1878 from Nazareth for the private collection of a German antiquarian named Froehner. It was not until 1930, when, on Froehner's death, the inscription found a place in the Cabinet de Medaillés of the Louvre, that the historian Michel Rostovtzeff noticed its significance. The Abbé Cumont published the first description in 1932.

The decree runs: "Ordinance of Caesar. It is my pleasure that graves and tombs remain undisturbed in perpetuity for those who have made them for the cult of their ancestors, or children, or members of their house. If, however, any man lay information that another has either demolished them, or has in any other way extracted the buried, or has maliciously transferred them to other places in order to wrong them, or has displaced the sealing or other stones, against such a one I order that a trial be instituted, as in respect of the gods, so in regard to the cult of mortals. For it shall be much more obligatory to honor the buried. Let it be absolutely forbidden for anyone to disturb them. In the case of contravention I desire that the offender be sentenced to capital punishment on the charge of violation of sepulture."

Evidence suggests that the inscription falls within the decade which closed with A.D. 50. The central Roman government did not take over the administration of Galilee until the death of Agrippa in A.D. 44. This limits the date, in the opinion of competent scholarship, to five years under Claudius (e.g. vid. A. Momigliano, *The Emperor Claudius and His Achievement*, 1932). It is possible to date the inscription rather more precisely. The *Acts of the Apostles*, confirmed by Orosius and Suetonius, the Roman historians, says that Claudius expelled the Jews from Rome (18:2). This was in A.D. 49. Suetonius adds that this was done "at the instigation of one Chrestos." The reference is obviously to Christ, and Suetonius' garbled account confuses two Greek words *christos* and *chrestos*.

Claudius was a learned man, misjudged by his contemporaries because of physical defects, probably due to the effects of what may possibly have been Parkinson's disease. His interest in continuing Augustus' religious policy led to a wide knowledge of the religions of the Empire, and would prompt investigation in the courts of any case involving cults or religious beliefs. Suetonius' phrase, and the act of expulsion, probably reflect the first impact of Christianity in Rome, disturbance in the ghetto, proceedings in the courts, and a review of the rabbis' complaints with a Christian apologia in reply, before the court with the Emperor on the bench. He hears the Pharisaic explanation of the empty tomb (Matthew 28:13), and Nazareth having recently fallen under central control he proceeds to deal with the trouble on the spot. Inquiries are made in Palestine, and the local authority asks for directions. The result is a "rescript" or imperial ruling. Claudius wrote more than one long letter on religious matters (e.g. a notable letter to the Jews of Alexandria in A.D. 41). The decree set up at Nazareth was a quotation from such a communication, verbatim or adapted from a larger text.

MARK

Jesus the Wonderful

The special emphasis of Mark is the Superhuman Power of Jesus, demonstrating His Deity by His Miracles. Omits most of Jesus' Discourses. Narrates things Jesus Did rather than things Jesus Said. Seems to have had Gentile readers in mind.

Mark

From the beginning, and by unbroken tradition, this Gospel has been regarded as the work of Mark, containing, substantially, the Story of Jesus as told by Peter.

John Mark was son of a Mary, whose home in Jerusalem was a meeting place for the disciples of Jesus (Acts 12:12). Being a cousin of Barnabas (Colossians 4:10), he may have been a Levite (Acts 4:36). It has been surmised that he was the young man who fled naked on the night of Jesus' arrest (Mark 14:51–52). The language of I Peter 5:13 may mean that he was a convert of Peter's.

Mark's Mother must have been quite an influential leader in the Jerusalem Church. It was to her home that Peter went when the Angel released him from prison (Acts 12:12).

About A.D. 44 Mark went with Paul and Barnabas to Antioch (Acts 12:25), and started with them on their First Missionary Journey, but turned back (Acts 13:13).

Later, about A.D. 50, Mark wanted to go with Paul on his Second Missionary Journey, but Paul refused to take him. This occasioned the separation of Paul and Barnabas (Acts 15:36–39). Then Mark went with Barnabas to Cyprus.

Some 12 years later, about A.D. 62, Mark appears in Rome with Paul (Colossians 4:10; Philemon 24). 4 or 5 years still later, Paul, just before martyrdom, is asking for Mark to come to him (II Timothy 4:11). Thus, it seems that Mark, in his later years, became one of Paul's intimate and beloved helpers.

Early Christian tradition has it that Mark was, in the main, a companion of Peter. He was with Peter in "Babylon" (Rome? see page 663) when Peter wrote his First Epistle (I Peter 5:13). Mark's Gospel is thought to have been written and published in Rome between A.D. 60 and 70.

What Papias Said about Mark

Papias, A.D. 70–155, a pupil of the Apostle John (see page 763), wrote, in his "Explanation of the Lord's Discourses," that he had made it his business to inquire of the Elders and followers of the Elders, and "The Elder said this also: Mark, having become the Interpreter of Peter, wrote down accurately all that he remembered—not, however, in order—of the Words and Deeds of Christ. For neither did he hear the Lord, nor was he a follower of His, but later on, as I said, he attached himself to Peter, who would adapt his instruction to the need of the occasion, but not teach as though he were composing a connected account of the Lord's Oracles; so that Mark made no mistake in thus writing down some things as he remembered them. For one object was in his thoughts—to omit nothing that he had heard, and to make no false statements."

The Four Gospels

For Whom Written. The Four Gospels, ultimately intended for All Mankind, originally were written for, or addressed to, certain Churches or individuals. Matthew's original, it is thought, may have been made for the Church at Jerusalem. From it other Churches secured copies. Mark, it is thought, may have intended his book for the Church in Rome. Copies, no doubt, were sent to other Churches. Luke wrote his Gospel for an individual named Theophilus, a high official in the Roman Government. John's Gospel is thought to have been intended originally for the Church in Ephesus. While God inspired these men to write Exactly what He wanted them to write, for the use of All Mankind of all generations, yet they themselves must have had in mind the background of their immediate readers; which may have influenced their choice of material.

The Writers' Individualities. While they had their Readers in mind, yet each, in his writing, must have reflected his own personality. They had the Same Story to tell, the Story of a MAN. How He Lived, and What He Did and Said. But each told the Story in his own way, mentioning that which especially appealed to himself; which accounts for differences in the books.

"Contradictions" in the Gospels. It is surprising with what utter abandon the statement is made in many present-day scholarly works that the Four Gospels are "full of contradictions." Then when we see what the things are that they call "contradictions," we are almost tempted to lose respect for some of the so-called "scholarship." The fact that there are different details and slight variations in describing the same incident makes the testimony of the various writers all the more trustworthy, for it precludes the possibility of pre-arranged collusion among them.

Time of Writing. Present-day tendency is to regard Mark as the first to be written. However, the universal early tradition was that

Matthew wrote first. In the early codices the Four Gospels, generally, stood in the same order in which they now stand, which indicates the early tradition as to the order in which they were written. Occasionally John stood first, but never Mark.

Chapter 1:1-8. Preaching of John the Baptist

This is told in all Four Gospels. (See note under Luke 3:1–20.) Mark starts his book with a quotation from the Old Testament. Passing over the story of Jesus' Birth, he launches at once into the crowded memoirs of his public life.

Chapter 1:9–11. Jesus is Baptized. (See on Matthew 3:13–17.)

Chapter 1:12–13. Forty Days' Temptation. (See on Matthew 4:1–10.)

Duration and Chronology of Jesus' Public Life

Jesus was about 30 years old in the 15th year of Tiberius Caesar (Luke 3:1, 23). He was still a young child at the death of Herod (Matthew 2:19–20). This fixes Jesus' place in the Roman calendar, which was later replaced by the Christian calendar (see under Luke 2:39. See page 491).

Shortly after his baptism he visited Jerusalem at Passover time (John 2:13). Passover, most of the time, was in April.

Intervening between his Baptism and this visit to Jerusalem are the events of John 1:29–2:12, and the Forty Days' Temptation (Matthew 4:1–11).

The Temptation was immediately after his Baptism, and lasted forty days (Mark 1:12–13).

After the Temptation he re-appeared at the Jordan where John was preaching (John 1:26), and was there for three successive "morrows" (John 1:29, 35, 43). The "third day" thereafter he arrived in Cana, where he turned the water into wine (John 2:1).

Then he went to Capernaum, for "not many days" (John 2:12), before he went to Jerusalem to Cleanse the Temple.

Thus, the 40 days, the three "morrows," the "third day" thereafter, and the "not many days," constitute the time between his Baptism and Passover, which, in all, probably, was somewhere between three and five months.

So, his Baptism, which marks the beginning of his Public Life, must have been in the fall or early winter.

As for the Duration of his Public Life: three Passovers are mentioned: when he Cleansed the Temple (John 2:13); when he Fed the 5,000 (John 6:4); and when he was Crucified (Luke 22:15).

If the "Feast" in John 5:1 was a Passover, as is commonly supposed, that would make four Passovers, with three full years between the first and fourth. If it was some other feast, coming in between Passovers, then there were only three Passovers, with two years between the first and third.

Thus the duration of Jesus' Public Ministry was either about 3½ years or about 2½ years. Prevailing opinion favors 3½ years.

Outline of Jesus' Public Life

With its probable chronology

Fall A.D. 26: or Early Winter	Baptism, in the Lower Jordan Temptation, in nearby Wilderness First Disciples, in Lower Jordan First Miracle, in Cana
A.D. 27 Passover:	Cleanses Temple, in Jerusalem Early Judean Ministry, in Lower Jordan (8 months. See on John 3:22–36)
	Return through Samaria
December:	Begins Galilean Ministry (2 years. See page 431)
A.D. 28	
Passover?:	Visits Jerusalem (John 5:1)
Summer:	The Twelve Chosen Sermon on the Mount
A.D. 29	
February?:	The Twelve Sent Forth John the Baptist Beheaded The Twelve Return
Passover:	The 5,000 Fed
October:	Visits Jerusalem (John 7:2, 10)
November?:	The Transfiguration
December?:	Close of Galilean Ministry (See on Luke 9:51)
December:	Again in Jerusalem (John 10:22) Later Judean and Perean Ministry (about 4 months)
A.D. 30	
Passover:	Crucifixion and Resurrection

The Galilean Ministry. 1:14 to 10:1

The Galilean Ministry occupies about one-half of Mark.
For outline see Comparative Table under Matthew 4:12.
For Chronological Table see under Matthew 4:13–25.

Chapter 1:14-15. Jesus Begins Galilean Ministry

Between verses 13 and 14, that is, between Jesus' Temptation and the Beginning of his Galilean Ministry, are to be placed the events of John 1:19 to 4:54, covering about a year:

First Disciples, at John's Baptizing.
Water Turned to Wine, at Cana.
Cleansing of Temple. Conversation with Nicodemus.
Preaching in the Lower Jordan, about 8 months.
Conversation with Samaritan Woman.
Healing of Nobleman's Son, from Cana.
Rejection at Nazareth (Luke 4:16–30).

Jesus had been preaching in the Lower Jordan (John 3:22–24; 4:1–3). But growing hostility of Pharisees (John 4:1–3), and Herod's imprisonment of John (Matthew 4:12), made it look dangerous. Having some work to do before his death, he thought best to get further away from Jerusalem.

Chapter 1:16-20. Call of Simon, Andrew, James, John

This is told also in Matthew 4:18–22; Luke 5:1–11. Three of these had believed on Jesus a year before, at John's baptism (John 1:35–42). They are now called to become his companions in travel. (See further under Matthew 10 and Mark 3:13–19.)

Chapter 1:21-28. The Demoniac Healed

Told also in Luke 4:31–37. This is Jesus' first recorded miracle in Capernaum, after making it his headquarters. Shortly before he had healed the Nobleman's Son in Capernaum merely by an act of will from Cana, 15 miles distant (John 4:46–54. For note on the nature of Demon possession see under Mark 5:1–20).

Capernaum

On his arrival in Galilee, after an 8 months' absence in his Early Judean Ministry (John 2:13 to 4:43), Jesus came to Cana, where, nearly a year before, he had turned Water into Wine. Then, after healing the Nobleman's Son, he went to Nazareth, but they rejected him (see on Luke 4:16–30). Then he established himself in Capernaum as the center from which to carry on his ministry of Preaching, Teaching and Healing.

From Capernaum he made many journeys around over Galilee, occasionally going to Jerusalem, and occasionally to the regions north of Galilee. He traveled on foot, usually with a group of his disciples, often accompanied by great multitudes.

Capernaum is now identified with the ruins called Tel Hum, 3 miles southwest from the Jordan entrance to the Sea of Galilee. (See further under Luke 7:1–10, and Map under Mark 6:45–52.)

Chapter 1:29-31. Peter's Mother-in-law Cured

Told also in Matthew 8:14–15; Luke 4:38–39. So Peter had a wife. Jesus' first miracle was a Blessing on Marriage. Here he heals the mother-in-law of his leading Apostle.

Chapter 1:32-34. Multitudes Healed

Told also in Matthew 8:16–17; Luke 4:40–41. This was after sunset, because sunset marked the close of Sabbath. The news about the demoniac and Peter's mother-in-law had spread all over the city, and great crowds, with their sick, gathered around the house. And Jesus healed them. It was his Miracles that attracted the multitudes. The light of Divine Compassion for Suffering Humanity had begun to shine. It was a great day in Capernaum.

Chapter 1:35-37. Retirement to Pray

Told also in Luke 4:42–43. It had been a busy day. Jesus had healed, possibly, hundreds of people. He was now in the full swing of his public work. He often slipped away from the multitudes, seeking, in solitude, to keep in touch with God. (See note on his prayer life under Luke 11:1–13.)

Chapter 1:38-39. Journeying about in Galilee

Jesus made many journeys, returning ever and anon to Capernaum (Matthew 4:23–25; 9:35–38; Luke 4:44). Galilee was crossed by famous international highways between the Euphrates and the Nile. And there were many side roads. (See map under Mark 3:7–12.)

Chapter 1:40-45. A Leper Cleansed

Told also in Matthew 8:2–4; Luke 5:12–16. Leprosy was a loathsome and pitiful disease. Jesus told him to show himself to the priest, because that was requirement of the Law (Leviticus 13, 14). He told him to say nothing about it, lest the popular movement to make Jesus king might get beyond control.

Chapter 2:1-12. A Paralytic Healed

Told also in Matthew 9:2–8 and Luke 5:18–26. The paralytic was lying on a bed carried by four men. Their Faith in Jesus' Power to Heal, and their Determination to get to Him pleased Jesus.

Jesus' fame had spread so widely that Pharisees and Scribes from Jerusalem and all over the land (Luke 5:17), had come to investigate. Before their critical, hostile eyes Jesus boldly asserted his Deity by offering to forgive the man's sins, and worked the miracle to prove it. This is one miracle that Jesus himself said he wrought expressly to demonstrate his Deity. It had an amazing effect on the people, but only further irritated the Pharisees and Scribes, religious custodians of the nation.

Chapter 2:13-17. Call of Levi (Matthew)

Jesus had recently chosen four Fishermen to be his associates in the establishment of his kingdom. Now he adds a Publican. (For note on Matthew see Introduction to Matthew, and on Matthew 10.)

Chapter 2:18-22. Question about Fasting

Narrated also in Matthew 9:14–17; Luke 5:33–38. It was probably occasioned by Jesus' participation in Matthew's feast, which greatly surprised John's disciples, and the Pharisees, and probably also some of Jesus' own disciples. Feasting was so different from the way John the Baptist had lived. There may be times of crisis when Fasting may be a proper expression of humility and penitence and religious devotion. There was special significance in it in the case of John the Baptist (see under Luke 3:1–20). But the religionists of Jesus' day greatly overdid it. Jesus did not attach a great deal of importance to Fasting, as generally practiced (Matthew 6:16–18). Moses, Elijah and Jesus, each, fasted forty days. But it was in a period of great strain. The three metaphors, the bridegroom, the rent garment, the old wine-skins (bottles made from goat skins), seem to mean that there are occasions when Fasting is proper, but that it is out of place in ordinary life, specially as a regular practice to advertise one's holiness (Matthew 6:16–18), just to make a show of religion.

Chapter 2:23-27. Eating Grain on the Sabbath

This incident is mentioned also in Matthew 12:1–8; Luke 6:1–5. The Old Testament had strict laws about Sabbath observance, but Jewish tradition had added restrictions to such extremes that it had voided God's original intent. Jesus' assertion that he was Lord of the Sabbath was equivalent to a claim of Deity.

Chapter 3:1-6. Healing on the Sabbath

This incident is mentioned also in Matthew 12:9–14; Luke 6:6–11. The healing of the man who had a withered hand on the Sabbath so irritated the Pharisees and Herodians that they laid plans to kill Jesus. To these hard-hearted, depraved professional religionists a common deed of kindness on the Sabbath was a terrible crime. There are seven recorded healings by Jesus on the Sabbath (see under John 5).

Chapter 3:7-12. Multitudes and Miracles

The multitudes that came to Jesus were motivated by two reasons: one, to have their sick healed; the other, the popular expectation that he was the Messiah.

Jesus' Public Life

Was spent mostly in Galilee. He made five recorded visits to Jerusalem. Three recorded retirements from publicity: to the region of Tyre and Sidon; to Caesarea-Philippi; and to the wilderness of Ephraim to await his death.

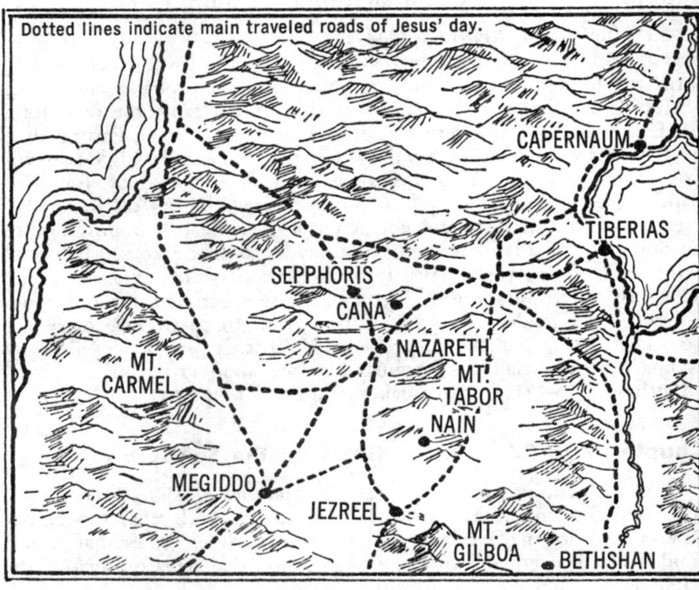

Map 51.
Dotted lines indicate main traveled roads of Jesus' day.

Chapter 3:13-19. The Twelve Chosen

Their names are listed in four places (see below). Some of them had two names; either a surname, or a name given otherwise. Why Jesus chose Twelve we do not know. Of these, three were an inner group. Besides the 12, he sent 70 on a special errand. 3, 12 and 70 figure largely in Scripture symbolism. 12 tribes of Israel were the foundation of the Hebrew nation. 12 Apostles laid the foundation of the Church (Revelation 21:12–14). Moses had 70 elders. Sanhedrin had 70 members. These numbers may have some mystic meaning unknown to us.

Of the Twelve four were fishermen. One a publican. One a zealot. We do not know what the others were. All were Galileans, except Judas the betrayer. There was not one professional religionist in the group, not one who advertised his piety by the kind of clothes he wore.

Matthew 10:2–4	Mark 3:16–19	Luke 6:12–19	Acts 1:13
Simon	Simon	Simon	Peter
Andrew	James	Andrew	James
James	John	James	John
John	Andrew	John	Andrew
Philip	Philip	Philip	Philip
Bartholomew	Bartholomew	Bartholomew	Thomas
Thomas	Matthew	Matthew	Bartholomew
Matthew	Thomas	Thomas	Matthew
James son Al-	James son Al-	James son Al-	James son Al-
Thaddaeus	Thaddaeus	Simon Zealot	Simon Zealot
Simon Zealot	Simon Zealot	Judas son James	Judas son James
Judas Iscariot	Judas Iscariot	Judas Iscariot	Matthias

Peter. First mentioned at John's Baptism (John 1:40–42). At this first recorded meeting with Jesus, Jesus re-named him, as if Jesus had already decided to make him an Apostle. "Simon" was his natural name. His new name was "Peter" (Greek), "Cephas" (Aramaic), both meaning "Rock." It was reaffirmed three years later, at his confession (Matthew 16:18).

Peter had a wife (Matthew 8:14; Mark 1:30; Luke 4:38). She went about with him in his work as an Apostle (I Corinthians 9:5). He was a native of Bethsaida (John 1:44). Had a home in Capernaum (Mark 1:29). Either he had two homes, or had moved from Bethsaida to Capernaum.

He was a partner in the fishing business with James and John (Luke 5:10). Evidently a very well-to-do business man.

He was energetic, enthusiastic, impulsive, impetuous, a natural born leader, with a good deal of human nature. Generally the spokesman of the Twelve.

The name which Jesus gave him, "Rock," was indicative of his real character, which Jesus well understood: strength of conviction, courage, boldness, though he did once deny his Master, and once "dissimulated" at Antioch. He was absolutely fearless under persecution. He laid the foundations of the Judean Church, and led it onward with such momentum that the rulers stood aghast. (See further under Introduction to I Peter.)

John. (See Introductory Note to John.)

Matthew. (See Introductory Note to Matthew.)

James. Older brother of John. Jesus named the two, "Boanerges," Sons of Thunder. Doesn't it indicate that possibly Jesus had a playful sense of humor? Not much is known of James. He was the first of the Twelve to die; killed by Herod, A.D. 44. Traditions are that most of the Twelve died as martyrs.

Two families were partners in the fishing business: brothers James and John, with Zebedee their father; and brothers Simon and Andrew. They had hired servants. It must have been a fairly large business. All four became apostles. Three of them, the inner circle friends of Jesus. The Twelve as a whole must have been men of the very highest grade, for Jesus knew men. These three, What magnificent men they must have been!

Andrew. Of Bethsaida. He and John were Jesus' first converts. He brought his brother Peter to Christ. Tradition says he preached in Asia Minor, Greece and Scythia (Russia).

Philip. Of Bethsaida. Fellow-townsman of Peter and Andrew. Brought Nathaniel to Christ. Matter-of-fact turn of mind. According to tradition, he preached in Phrygia, and in Hierapolis.

Bartholomew. Thought to be the surname of Nathaniel, who was of Cana. Perhaps it was through him that Jesus came to the wedding feast. Tradition: he preached in Parthia.

Thomas. A twin. Cautious, thoughtful, skeptical, gloomy. The traditions make him labor in Syria, Parthia, Persia and India.

James. Son of Alphaeus. Called "The Little," probably because of his stature. Tradition: he preached in Palestine and Egypt.

Thaddaeus. Thought to be same as Judas son of James: also called Lebbaeus. Tradition: he was sent to Abgarus, king of Edessa; and to Syria, Arabia and Mesopotamia.

Simon. The Zealot (Greek), or Cananaean (Aramaic). Nothing is known of him. The Zealots were an intensely nationalistic sect, the direct opposite of the Publicans. Jesus chose a Zealot and a Publican, from bitterly rival factions.

Judas Iscariot. The betrayer. Of Kerioth, a town of Judah. The only non-Galilean apostle. Avaricious, dishonest. Expected rich reward when his Master was seated on the throne of David. Disappointed when he saw his worldly dream fade. After his hideous crime, hanged himself, fell from the scaffold, and burst asunder.

Chapter 3:20–30. The Unpardonable Sin. (See on Matthew 12:24–37.)
Chapter 3:31–35. His Mother and Brothers. (See on Matthew 12:46–50.)
Chapter 4:1–25. Parable of the Sower. (See on Matthew 13:1–23.)
Chapter 4:30–34. The Mustard Seed. (See on Matthew 13:31–32.)

Chapter 4:26-29. Parable of the Growing Seed

It was generally expected that the Messianic Kingdom would be inaugurated in a flare of glory and power that would shake the world. This parable means that it would be a matter of a very small beginning, and slow long growth, quietly, secretly, imperceptibly, and irresistibly moving on to the day of harvest.

Chapter 4:35-41. The Tempest Stilled

Told also in Matthew 8:23–27; Luke 8:22–25. In the tossing boat, the disciples were frightened, but Jesus was calmly sleeping. How we would love to know the inner processes and powers by which his word stilled the raging waters! What a rebuke to the disciples. "Why are you afraid? Where is your faith?"

Chapter 5:1-20. The Gerasene Demoniac

Told also in Matthew 8:28–34; Luke 8:26–37. Matthew says Gadarenes. Mark and Luke, Gerasenes. Gerasa is identified with the ruins now called "Kerza" (Kersa, Gergesa) (see Map under Mark 6:45–52). It is about five miles from the Jordan entrance. Just south of it is the only place where the steep hills come close to the water (Matthew 8:32).

Matthew says there were two demoniacs. Mark and Luke mention only one, probably because he was the more violent of the two, and spokesman. A dangerous, wild lunatic, of immense muscular strength, dwelling naked among the tombs and in the desert, mutilating himself, and screaming in pain.

There were many demons, "legion," in the two men, probably most of them in the more violent man. There were 2,000 swine, probably at least that many demons.

They recognized the authority of Jesus immediately.

Notice that the demons would rather live in swine than go to their own place. But they soon went anyhow.

They could control the men, but not the swine. They did not drive the swine into the sea. Neither the swine nor the demons wanted to go into the sea. The swine got panic-stricken, with the demons inside, and lost control of themselves on the precipitous hillside. Once on the move they could not stop.

Notice, too, that the natives wanted Jesus to get out of their country, for, though he had healed their insane, he had, in the act, destroyed their swine. They thought more of their swine than they did of their people. Such folks are not all dead yet.

Jesus told the man to go out and tell about his cure (19). He had commanded the leper to say nothing about his (Matthew 8:4). The reason for the difference was that in Gerasa he was not as yet widely known, whereas in Galilee his publicity was already out of hand with movements budding to proclaim him a political king.

Demons

A considerable number of those whom Jesus healed were "possessed with demons" (or "devils," AV: Matthew 4:24; 8:16, 9:32; 12:24, 26, 43; Mark 1:24, 32, 34; 3:11, 12; Luke 4:41; 6:18; etc).

What were demons? Were they a reality? Or did Jesus and the New Testament writers speak that way because it was commonly believed that the afflicted were under the control of evil spirits, making no effort to correct the popular error?

In the Gospels, demons are represented as knowing that Jesus was the Son of God, as belonging to the kingdom of Satan, as passing through waterless places, awaiting torment in the abyss, as preferring to dwell in swine rather than go to their own place. Many could dwell in one person. They spoke, recognizing that they had a separate personality and consciousness from the person in whom they dwelt, plainly distinct from the person. They looked forward with trembling to the judgment. Jesus was not interested in them, but only those who suffer by them.

Only in some cases were the diseases attributed to demon possession. In one case they made the man crazy; another dumb; another blind and dumb; another, epileptic. These were the effects of demon possession, but not identical with it.

It seems that there are "evil spirits," "unclean spirits," "seducing spirits," "fallen angels," "the devil's angels"; and that they are organized as "principalities," "powers," "rulers of darkness," "spiritual hosts of wickedness"; against whom humans have to struggle (Matthew 12:43, 45; 25:41; II Peter 2:4; Ephesians 6:12).

The rather plain implication of Scripture is that "demoniacs" were not mere lunatics, but cases of "invaded personality"; and that demons, whatever their origin or nature, were evil spirits that did actually enter and afflict, one way or another, certain persons.

It is thought to have been a special exhibition of the devil against Jesus, permitted of God, during Jesus' stay on earth, to demonstrate that Jesus' power extended even into the unseen realm. Faith in Him is protection from whatever evil they might be able to do.

From what sometimes goes on in the world, one could almost think that even now men are actually demon-possessed.

Paul says the Christian's struggle is against evil personalities of the unseen world (Ephesians 6:12). But Jesus is our strength in the struggle. Satan and his evil spirits are helpless against the Name and Power of Jesus.

Chapter 5:21–43. Jairus' Daughter Raised. (See on Luke 8:40–56.)

The Miracles of Jesus

Aside from supernatural manifestations, such as angelic announcements, virgin birth, the star that guided the wise-men, Jesus passing through hostile mobs, cleansing the temple, his transfiguration, soldiers falling, darkness at the crucifixion, the veil rent, the tombs opened, the earthquake, Jesus' resurrection, angel appearances, there are recorded 35 miracles which Jesus wrought.

17 BODILY CURES

Nobleman's Son Healed (John 4:46–54), Capernaum.
Infirm Man Healed (John 5:1–9), Jerusalem.
Peter's Mother-in-law (Matthew 8:14–17; Mark 1:29–31; Luke 4:38, 39).
A Leper (Matthew 8:2–4; Mark 1:40–45; Luke 5:12–15).
A Paralytic (Matthew 9:2–8; Mark 2:3–12; Luke 5:17–26).
Man with Withered Hand (Matthew 12:9–14; Mark 3:1–6; Luke 6:6–11).
Centurion's Servant (Matthew 8:5–13; Luke 7:1–10).
Two Blind Men (Matthew 9:27–31).
Deaf and Dumb Man Healed (Mark 7:31–37).
Blind Man at Bethsaida (Mark 8:22–26).
Blind Man in Jerusalem (John 9).
Woman of 18 Years Infirmity (Luke 13:10–17).
Woman with Hemorrhage (Matthew 9:20–22; Mark 5:25–34; Luke 8:43–48).
Man with Dropsy (Luke 14:1–6).
Ten Lepers (Luke 17:11–19).
Blind Bartimaeus (Matthew 20:29–34; Mark 10:46–52; Luke 18:35–43).
Malchus' Ear (Luke 22:50–51).

9 MIRACLES OVER FORCES OF NATURE

Water Turned to Wine (John 2:1–11), Cana.
Draught of Fishes (Luke 5:1–11), near Capernaum.
Another Draught of Fishes (John 21:6).

Tempest Stilled (Matthew 8:23–27; Mark 4:35–41; Luke 8:22–25).
5,000 Fed (Matthew 14:13–21; Mark 6:34–44; Luke 9:11–17; John 6:1–14).
Jesus Walked on the Water (Matthew 14:22–33; Mark 6:45–52; John 6:19).
4,000 Fed (Matthew 15:32–39; Mark 8:1–9).
Tax Money (Matthew 17:24–27).
Fig Tree Withered (Matthew 21:18–22; Mark 11:12–14, 20–26).

6 CURES OF DEMONIACS

A Demoniac in the Synagog (Mark 1:21–28; Luke 4:31–37), Capernaum.
A Blind and Dumb Demoniac (Matthew 12:22; Luke 11:14).
Gerasene Demoniacs (Matthew 8:28–34; Mark 5:1–20; Luke 8:26–39).
A Dumb Demoniac (Matthew 9:32–34).
The Syro-phoenician's Daughter (Matthew 15:21–28; Mark 7:24–30).
The Epileptic Boy (Matthew 17:14–21; Mark 9:14–29; Luke 9:37–43).

3 RAISED FROM THE DEAD

Jairus' Daughter (Matthew 9:18–26; Mark 5:22–43; Luke 8:41–56).
Widow's Son, at Nain (Luke 7:11–15).
Lazarus, at Bethany (John 11:1–44).

OTHER MIRACLES

Beside the 35 that are named and described, Jesus did innumerable other miracles, indicated thus:

"Many believed on his name, beholding the signs which he did," in Jerusalem (John 2:23).

"Jesus went about healing all manner of diseases" (Matthew 4:23, 9:35).

"They brought unto him all that were sick, holden with divers diseases and torments, possessed with demons, epileptic, and palsied, and he healed them" (Matthew 4:24).

"All that had any sick brought them to him; and he laid his hands on every one of them and healed them" (Luke 4:40).

"There came great multitudes, having the lame, blind, dumb, maimed, and many others, and cast them down at his feet; and he healed them; insomuch that the multitude wondered, when they saw the dumb speaking, the maimed whole, the lame walking, and the blind seeing" (Matthew 15:30–31).

"Wheresoever he entered, into villages, or cities, or into the country, they laid the sick in the market-places, and besought him that they might touch the border of his garments; and as many as touched were made whole" (Mark 6:53–56).

"He came into borders of Judea beyond Jordan, and great multitudes followed and he healed them there" (Matthew 19:1–2).

"A great multitude from Judea and Jerusalem, and the region of Tyre and Sidon, came to hear him, and to be healed of their diseases, and he healed them all" (Luke 6:17–19).

"All the city was gathered at the door, with their sick and those possessed with demons, and he healed them" (Mark 1:32–34).

"Many other things Jesus did, the which, if they should be written every one, I suppose that even the world itself would not contain the books" (John 21:25).

METHOD OF THE MIRACLES

They were usually wrought by the act of Jesus' will, or by his word; sometimes by his touch, or the laying on of his hands. Occasionally he used saliva.

PURPOSE OF THE MIRACLES

Jesus' miracles imply an exercise of creative power. They were a part of God's way of authenticating Jesus' mission. Jesus said that if he had not done works that no other ever did, they would not have had sin (John 15:24), thus indicating that he regarded his miracles as proofs that he was from God. Then, too, his miracles were the natural expression of his sympathy for suffering humanity.

Chapter 6:1-6. Visit to Nazareth

Told also in Matthew 13:54–58. This seems to have been his second visit to Nazareth after he began his public ministry, about a year after the visit recorded in Luke 4:16–30. Note that Jesus had four brothers, and "sisters" (more than one). They did not at that time believe on him (John 7:5). They did afterward, and, according to common opinion, two of them, James and Jude, were authors of the two Epistles called by their names. The other two were Joseph and Simon.

Chapter 6:7–13. The Twelve Sent Out. (See on Matthew 10.)
Chapter 6:14–29. John Beheaded. (See on Luke 3:1–20.)
Chapter 6:30–44. The 5,000 Fed. (See on John 6:1–14.)
Chapter 6:45–52. Jesus Walks on the Water. (See on John 6:15–21.)

Fig. 61. The Sea of Galilee. Capernaum across the lake. Mt. Hermon in distance.

The Sea of Galilee. 13 miles long, 7 wide. 680 feet below sea level. Surrounded by hills averaging about 300 feet in height. The coast averaging about half a mile in width, except on the northwest where the Plain of Gennesaret is about 4 miles wide, and at the north

Fig. 62. Looking from Capernaum eastward.
© *Matson Photos*

where the Jordan enters and the south where it leaves. The hills are now bare, but in Jesus' day were heavily wooded, according to Josephus. Its shores teemed with population. 10 cities of not less than 15,000 each. Surrounded by an almost unbroken line of buildings. The western shore extremely fertile. Mild winter climate. Tropical crops of all kinds. Yielded its products every month. Its industries consisted principally of agriculture, fruit growing and fishing. Its waters abounded in fish, which were exported throughout the Roman Empire. The north end was the principal scene of Jesus' earthly ministry hallowed forever as the place where God, clothed in human form, walked among men; the story of which is the most beautiful thing in the annals of mankind.

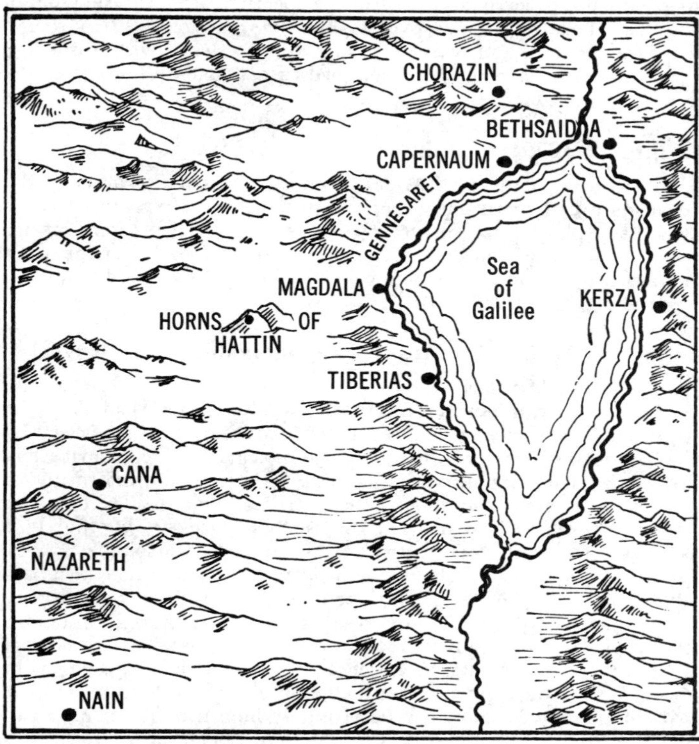

Map 52.

Period from Feeding 5,000 to Transfiguration

Mark 6:53 *to* 8:26 *Matthew* 14:34 *to* 16:12

This was a period in Jesus' life, of probably, about eight months, April to November, of which we have only slight knowledge. It is told only by Matthew and Mark, Luke passes directly from the Feeding of the 5,000 to the Transfiguration incidents (Luke 9:17, 18). John goes immediately from the Feeding of the 5,000 to Jesus' Tabernacle Visit to Jerusalem, six months later (John 6:71; 7:1).

Part of this eight months was spent in the regions of Tyre and Sidon, Decapolis, and Caesarea-Philippi, largely Gentile populations. Decapolis was the region east of the Sea of Galilee extending northward to Damascus. It was under the rule of Philip, who was a very good and just ruler, and who had no special reason for antagonism to Jesus. Herod was ruler over Galilee. He had recently murdered John the Baptist, and was beginning to eye Jesus with suspicion, especially since some of the people had turned against Jesus after the feeding of the 5,000.

Chapter 6:53-56. Multitudes in Gennesaret

Told also in Matthew 14:34–36. Gennesaret was the plain along the shore south of Capernaum. It appears that the day after Jesus fed the 5,000 he explained to the crowd in Capernaum the nature of his mission, and many fell away from him (John 6:66). Then he went southward to Gennesaret, where great crowds gathered, and he healed multitudes.

Chapter 7:1-23. Pharisees and Defilement

Told also in Matthew 15:1–20. The rulers at Jerusalem had already determined to kill Jesus (John 5:18). No doubt they had heard of his waning popularity in Galilee (John 6:66), and sent this delegation of Pharisees to push their propaganda campaign, hoping to make him more unpopular with his own disciples, for it is likely that many of them held the same traditions as the Pharisees. The washing of hands that is here referred to was not for sanitary purposes, but purely a religious ceremonial, not of the Law, but an invention of the Scribes. Jesus told them that such ceremonials were of no value, that real defilement is of the heart, and then denounced them roundly for voiding the Word of God by some of their Traditions of human origin. His words apply directly to many of the practices that through the centuries have crept into the Church. It is amazing with what cunning and ingenuity many church leaders strive to make their forms and practices, known to be of purely human origin, conform to God's Word. Slavish bondage to Tradition. Slight regard for God's word.

Chapter 7:24-30. The Syro-phoenician Woman

Told also in Matthew 15:21–28. In Matthew she is called a "Canaanitish" woman. Phoenicians were of Canaanite descent. This was about 50 miles north of Capernaum, outside of Jewish territory, in a region of Gentiles, same section in which Elijah had been sent to the woman of Serepta (I Kings 17:9). Jesus did not mean to call her a "dog" (27). He was only echoing what was in the disciples' minds. Her persistence, humility and faith won her request.

Chapter 7:31-37. Healing of a Deaf and Dumb Man

Jesus returned from the region of Tyre and Sidon, whither he had gone for a temporary retirement from publicity, eastward and southward through Decapolis to the east side of the Sea of Galilee. He was now back in the region where a few weeks before they had tried to make him king. So he cautioned the man to keep quiet, to avoid publicity.

Chapter 8:1-9. Feeding of the 4,000

Told also in Matthew 15:29–39. This probably was near where he had fed the 5,000 a few weeks before. Matthew adds that it was at a time when he was healing great multitudes. The people in Galilee must have heard that Jesus had returned to their borders.

Chapter 8:10-21. "Leaven of the Pharisees"

Told also in Matthew 16:1–12. This incident was in Dalmanutha (10). Matthew 15:39 says Magdala, or Magadan (RV), the home of Mary Magdalene, which was a city in a region called Dalmanutha, on the central west coast of the lake (see Map 52 under Mark 6:45–52). No sooner had Jesus arrived back in Galilee than his enemies were on hand resorting to every conceivable scheme to discredit him in the eyes of the people. They wanted a "sign." For two years he had been healing vast multitudes of people sick with every kind of disease, in uninterrupted succession. And had fed the 5,000 and the 4,000. Still they wanted a "sign." And Jesus was troubled by the slowness of the disciples to understand the significance of his Miracles, and rebuked them for their Worry about Food while they were With Him (7–12).

Chapter 8:22-26. A Blind Man Healed

This was at Bethsaida, where Jesus had done many miracles (Matthew 11:21), and near which he had fed the 5,000. Hence his caution to the man to avoid any unnecessary publicity.

Chapter 8:27–30. Peter's Confession. (See on Matthew 16:13–20.)
Chapter 8:31–33. Passion Foretold. (See on Mark 9:30–32.)
Chapter 8:34–9:1. Cost of Discipleship. (See on Luke 14:25–35.)

Chapter 9:2-13. Jesus is Transfigured

Told also in Matthew 17:1–13 and Luke 9:28–36. Thought to have occurred in Mt. Hermon, shortly before Jesus' Final Departure from Galilee, about four months before his death. One of the purposes of the Transfiguration was to confirm the Faith of the disciples in the Divine Nature of Christ's Person against the shock of the troublous days ahead. Peter never forgot it. It gave him a sense of Surety as he was facing his own martyrdom (II Peter 1:14–18). Also, it was a sort of grand climactic testimony direct from heaven that Jesus was THE ONE in whom all Old Testament prophecies converged and found their fulfillment.

Chapter 9:14-29. The Epileptic Boy

Told also in Matthew 17:14–19; Luke 9:37–42. It was a bad case of demon possession, that baffled the disciples. (See on Mark 5:1–20.)

Chapter 9:30-32. Passion Again Foretold

Up to this time Jesus had not talked much about His coming Crucifixion. But from here on He wanted them to understand plainly what was going to happen to Him. Between Peter's confession, and their arrival in Jerusalem, He told them five recorded times that He would be Killed and Rise from the Dead:

1st: after Peter's Confession (Matthew 16:21; Mark 8:31; Luke 9:22).
2nd: after Transfiguration (Matthew 17:9, 12; Mark 9:9, 12).
3rd: after Healing of the Epileptic (Luke 9:44).
4th: while passing through Galilee (Matthew 17:22–23; Mark 9:31).
5th: near Jerusalem (Matthew 20:17–19; Mark 10:32–34; Luke 18:31–34).

Chapter 9:33–37. Who is the Greatest? (See on Luke 9:46–48.)

Chapter 9:38–40. Unknown Wonder Worker. (See on Luke 9:49–50.)

Chapter 9:41–50. Occasions of Stumbling. A supreme Christian motive is that we conduct ourselves that no one else may be lost on account of our example. Jesus said this a number of times, in different connections (Matthew 18:7–14; Luke 17:1–10).

The Perean Ministry. Chapter 10. (See on Luke 9:51)

Chapter 10:1. Departure from Galilee. (See on Luke 9:51.)
Chapter 10:2–12. Question about Divorce. (See on Matthew 19:3–12.)

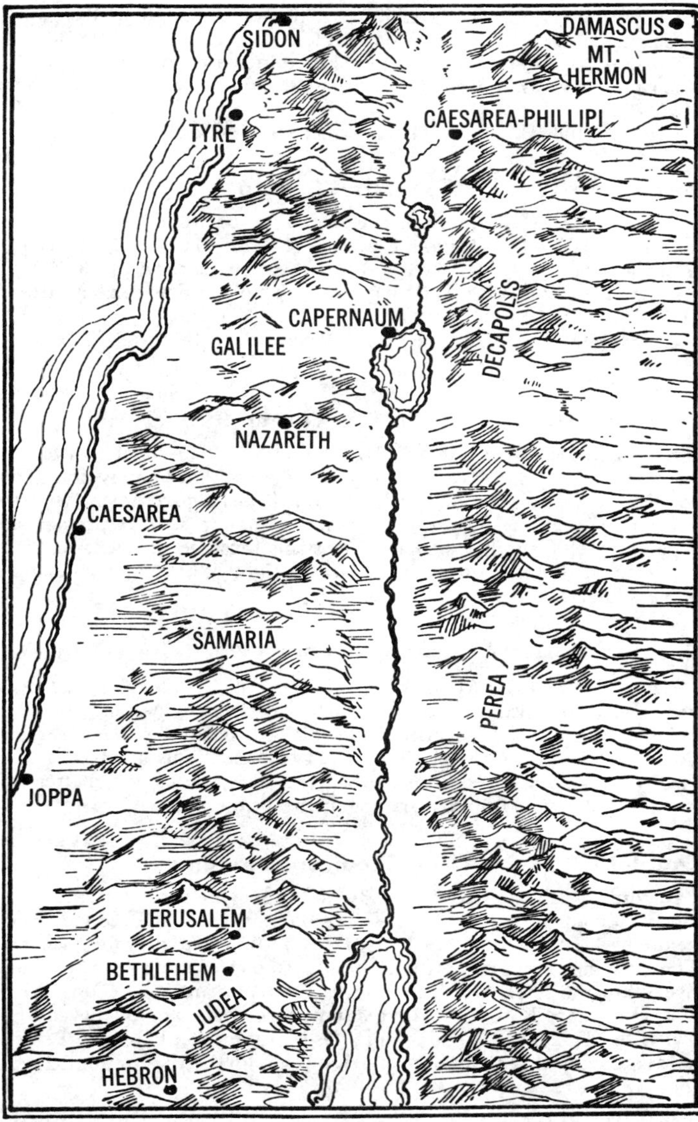
SIDON
DAMASCUS
MT.
HERMON
TYRE
CAESAREA-PHILLIPI
CAPERNAUM
GALILEE
DECAPOLIS
NAZARETH
CAESAREA
SAMARIA
PEREA
JOPPA
JERUSALEM
BETHLEHEM
JUDEA
HEBRON

Map 53

Chapter 10:13–16. Little Children. (See on Luke 18:15–17.)
Chapter 10:17–31. Rich Young Ruler. (See on Luke 18:18–30.)
Chapter 10:32–34. Passion again Foretold. (See on Mark 9:30–32.)
Chapter 10:35–45. Request of James, John. (See on Matthew 20:20–28.)
Chapter 10:46–52. Blind Bartimaeus. (See on Luke 18:35–43.)

Jesus' Last Week. Chapters 11 to 16

Chapter 11:1–11. Triumphal Entry. (See on Matthew 21:1–11.)
Chapter 11:15–18. Temple Cleansed. (See on Matthew 21:12–17.)
Chapter 11:12–14; 19–25. Fig Tree. (See on Matthew 21:18–22.)
Chapter 11:27–33. "By What Authority"? (See on Matthew 21:23–27.)
Chapter 12:1–12. Parable of Vineyard. (See on Matthew 21:33–46.)

Chapter 12:13-17. Tribute to Caesar

Recorded also in Matthew 22:15–22; Luke 20:20–26. This was an effort to trap Jesus into a statement of some kind on which they could base a charge of disloyalty to the Roman government, and so hand him over to Pilate. Jesus, with a master stroke, proclaimed Separation of Church and State. Christians must be obedient to their government. But the government has no right to dictate the religion of its subjects.

Chapter 12:18-27. Question about the Resurrection

Recorded also in Matthew 22:23–33; Luke 20:27–40. Sadducees were the materialists of that day. They were not numerous, but educated, wealthy and influential. They did not believe in the resurrection. The question by which they tried to baffle Jesus involved a case that would require polygamy in heaven. Jesus settled the matter instantly: there will be no marrying in heaven.

Chapter 12:28-34. The Great Commandment

Recorded also in Matthew 22:34–40. What Jesus gave as the First commandment he quoted from Deuteronomy 6:4–5; the second, from Leviticus 19:18. Notice that Jesus put God first, our neighbor second. The one most important thing in life is our attitude toward God. Everything depends on that. Jesus is God incarnate. The one thing that He wants is that we love Him more than we love even our own life. The one last thing that Jesus wanted to know of Peter—he asked him three times over—"Do you love ME?" (John 21:15, 16, 17).

Chapter 12:35-37. "The Son of David"

Recorded also in Matthew 22:41–46; Luke 20:41–44. The point in the question is, How could a man call his own son Lord? Simple as the answer seems to us, it silenced them (Matthew 22:46).

Chapter 12:38–40. Scribes Denounced. (See on Matthew 23.)

Chapter 12:41-44. The Widow's Mites

Recorded also in Luke 21:1–4. This was just after his denunciation of the Scribes and Pharisees. It was his last act in the Temple, after a day of controversy. He took time to pay this glowing tribute to the dear old widow who gave all she had. Then he left the Temple, never again to enter.

Chapter 13. Discourse on His Coming. (See on Matthew 24.)

Chapter 14:1-2. Plot to Kill Jesus

Recorded also in Matthew 26:1–5; Luke 22:1–2. This was on Tuesday evening. About a month before this, after Jesus had raised Lazarus from the dead, the Sanhedrin had definitely decided that Jesus must be put to death (John 11:53). But Jesus' popularity made it difficult (Luke 22:2). Even in Jerusalem the multitudes hung upon him (Mark 12:37; Luke 19:48). The opportunity came, the second night after this, through the treachery of Judas, who, in a surprise move, delivered Jesus to them in the night, while the city was asleep. They hurried to get him condemned before day, and in the morning, ere the city's multitudes were awake, they had him on the cross.

Chapter 14:3-9. The Anointing at Bethany

Recorded also in Matthew 26:6–13; John 12:1–8. This seems to have occurred on Saturday evening before the Triumphal Entry (John 12:2, 12). But Matthew and Mark narrate it in connection with the plot of the priests as a setting for Judas' bargain. (See further under John 12:1–8.)

Chapter 14:10-11. Bargain of Judas

Recorded also in Matthew 26:14–16; Luke 22:3–6. His part was to deliver Jesus to them in the absence of the multitudes. They did not dare arrest him openly, lest they be stoned by the people. Judas led them to Him after the city had gone to sleep.

Jesus "knew from the beginning" that Judas would betray him. Why he was chosen is one of the mysteries of God's ways. Judas may have thought that Jesus would use his miraculous power to deliver himself. Yet, in God's eyes his deed was dastardly, for Jesus said it would have been better for him if he had never been born (Matthew 26:24). The whole performance was amazingly forecast (Zechariah 11:12–13). "Jeremiah" (Matthew 27:9–10), is either a copyist's error, or because the whole group of Prophetical books was sometimes called by Jeremiah's name.

Chapter 14:12–25. Last Supper. (See on Matthew 26:17–29.)
Chapter 14:26–31, 66–72. Peter's Denial. (See on John 18:15–27.)
Chapter 14:32–42. Agony in Gethsemane. (See on Luke 22:39–46.)
Chapter 14:43–52. Betrayal and Arrest. (See on John 18:1–12.)

Chapter 14:53-15:20. The Trial of Jesus

Told also in Matthew 26:57–27:31; Luke 22:54–23:25; John 18:12–19:16. There were two trials: before the Sanhedrin, and before Pilate the Roman governor. Judea was subject to Rome. The Sanhedrin could not execute a death sentence without the Roman governor's consent. There were three stages in each trial, six in all.

1. Before Annas (John 18:12–24). About midnight. Caiaphas was high priest. But his father-in-law, Annas, who had been deposed A.D. 16, still retained the influence of the office. The family had grown immensely wealthy through the trading booths in the Temple. On the High Priest of the Hebrew nation rests primary responsibility for the death of Jesus.

2. Before the Sanhedrin, in the house of Caiaphas (Matthew 26:57; Mark 14:53; Luke 22:54; John 18:24). Between midnight and daybreak. This was the main Jewish trial. They condemned him on the charge of blasphemy, from his own acknowledgement that he was the Son of God (Mark 14:61–62). Then, while waiting for daylight, they mocked him. This was when Peter denied him. This session, being in the night, was, by their own law, illegal.

3. At Daylight, the Sanhedrin officially ratified its midnight decision (Matthew 27:1; Mark 15:1; Luke 22:66–71), to give it appearance of Legality. The charge was "blasphemy." But with Pilate that would have little weight. So, for him, they concocted the charge of sedition against the Roman government. Their real reason was their envy of Jesus' popularity (Matthew 27:18).

4. Before Pilate (Matthew 27:2, 11–14; Mark 15:1–5; Luke 23:1–5; John 18:28–38), shortly after daylight. Jesus made no reply to their accusations. Then Pilate took him within the palace, for a private interview, which further satisfied him of Jesus' innocence. Learning that Jesus was from Galilee, Pilate sent him to Herod, who had jurisdiction over Galilee. (See on Matthew 27:11–25.)

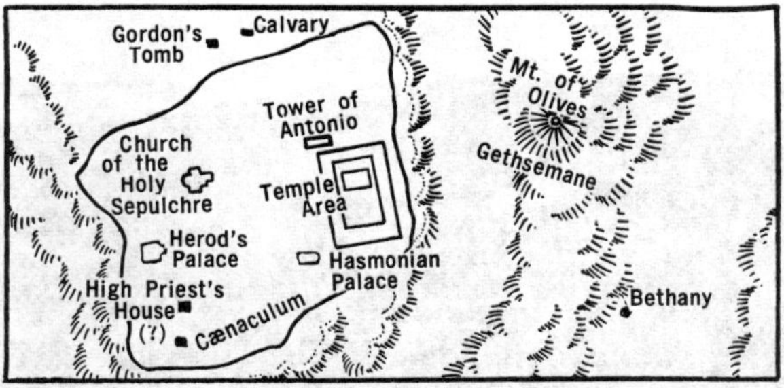

Map 54.

5. Before Herod (Luke 23:6–12). This was the Herod who had killed John the Baptist, and whose father had murdered the children of Bethlehem. Jesus refused to answer any of his questions. Herod mocked Jesus, and sent him back to Pilate.

6. Before Pilate again (Matthew 27:15–26; Mark 15:6–15; Luke 23:13–25; John 18:39–19:16). Pilate attempted to go over the head of the rulers to the people. But the packed court chose Barabbas. Then Pilate ordered Jesus to be scourged, hoping that would satisfy the multitude. His wife sends words of her dream. Pilate is amazed at the calm majesty of Jesus under the crown of thorns. But there are rumblings of a rising riot, and threats to report to Caesar, and Pilate gives sentence.

Chapter 15:21-41. The Crucifixion

(See on Matthew 27:32–60; Luke 23:26–49 and John 19:17–30.) Chapter 15:42–47. Burial of Jesus. (See on John 19:38–42.)

The Site of the Crucifixion

Jesus was crucified "outside the city" (John 19:17, 20; Hebrews 13:12). At a place called "The Skull" (Mattthew 27:33; Mark 15:22; Luke 23:33; John 19:17). "Calvary" is Latin, "Golgotha" is Hebrew, for "skull." There is only one place around Jerusalem which has borne, and still bears, the name "Skull Hill." It is just outside the North wall, near the Damascus gate. (See map 54.) It is a rock ledge, some 30 feet high, just above "Jeremiah's Grotto," with a striking resemblance to a human skull.

The traditional place of the Crucifixion is the Church of the Holy Sepulchre. It is inside the wall. Prevailing archaeological opinion is that the wall is now just where it was in Jesus' day, and that the actual place of Jesus' Crucifixion was the "Skull Hill."

Fig. 63. Calvary: where, it is thought, the Cross stood.
© *Matson Photo*

Chapter 16:1-8. The Women Visit the Tomb

(See note on Matthew 28:1–8.) "And Peter" (7). Peter, in bitter humiliation over his denial of the Lord, no doubt felt that he had been disowned, and needed this special message. How gracious of Jesus to send it to him. Later in the day Jesus appeared to Peter (Luke 24:34). What took place at that meeting we can only imagine. Hot tears, burning shame, loving forgiveness. It sealed a devotion that never again was broken, even unto Peter's martyrdom. (See further on John 21:15–19.)

The women run to tell the disciples. Peter and John run to the Tomb (John 20:3–10.)

Chapter 16:9-20. The Last 12 Verses of Mark

These are not in the Sinaitic and Vatican manuscripts, but were early accepted as a genuine part of Mark's Gospel. It is thought likely that the last page of the original copy was lost, and added later. It does not seem that verse 8 could have been a proper ending for the book.

Chapter 16:9-11. Appears to Mary Magdalene

(See John 20:11–18.) And to the Other Women (Matthew 28:9–10). And to the Two (Mark 16:12–13. See on Luke 24:13–32).

Chapter 16:14-18. Jesus Appears to the Eleven

Told also in Luke 24:33–43 and John 20:19–25. (See on these

passages.) The final commission to go into all the world (15–16), seems to have been uttered at this appearance. It may, however, have been a summary of final instructions which Jesus repeated over and over during his 40-days post-resurrection ministry. In substance it is recorded four times.

Here, in connection with his first appearance to the Eleven.
Again, at his Galilean appearance (Matthew 28:18–20).
Again, at his final appearance in Jerusalem (Luke 24:47).
And, at his Ascension (Acts 1:8. See on those passages).

The power to work miracles (17–18), was a divine attestation to their mission in founding the Church. (See on Acts 3.)

Between verses 18 and 19 there elapses 40 days, in which
Jesus Appears to the Eleven, a week later (John 20:26–31).
And to the Seven, by the Sea of Galilee (John 21).
And to the Eleven, in Galilee, with 500? (Matthew 28:16–20).
And to James (I Corinthians 15:7). Time and Place unknown. It is not known which James, but it is commonly supposed to have been James the Lord's brother, who afterwards became the main leader in the Judean Church, and wrote the Epistle of James.

And the Final Appearance in Jerusalem (Luke 24:44–49; Acts 1:3–8).

Chapter 16:19–20. Jesus' Ascension. (See on Luke 24:44–53.)

Order of Events of the Resurrection Morning

It is not easy to harmonize into a connected consecutive story the fragmentary records of the four Gospels about the Resurrection of Jesus. In a few sentences there are generalizations of many details. We are not told all the incidents in the precise order of their occurrence.

Let it be remembered that there were different groups of disciples, lodging at various places, going to the tomb, in different companies, and that they were not expecting Jesus to rise, (see page 554), but were visiting the tomb to complete the embalming of his body for permanent burial.

The first sight of the empty tomb, and the angel announcement that Jesus had risen, threw them into wild excitement.

They ran to tell the others, hurrying back and forth in alternate joy, fear, anxiety, wonder and bewilderment.

Many things happened that are not recorded. Of what is recorded, one writer tells one thing; another, another thing. One gives in a sentence what another describes in detail. Some, in a general statement, cover various incidents. No one gives a complete account.

There are a number of ways in which the accounts may be harmonized. The following, only provisional, is generally accepted.

1. At the first break of dawn, two or more groups of women, from their abodes in Jerusalem or Bethany, probably a mile or two distant, start groping their way toward the tomb.

2. It was probably about that time that Jesus was emerging from the tomb, accompanied by angels who rolled away the stone and neatly folded the shroud.

3. The guards, meantime, frightened and dazed, fled to tell the priests who had placed them there.

4. About sunrise, as the women approach the tomb, Mary Magdalene, ahead of her group, seeing the tomb empty, but not seeing the angel, nor hearing his announcement that Jesus had risen (John 20:13, 15), turns and runs to tell Peter and John.

5. The other women draw near. See and hear the angels. Hurry away, by another route, to tell the main group of disciples.

6. By this time, Peter and John reach the tomb. Go in. See the empty shroud. Depart, John believing, Peter wondering.

7. Mary Magdalene, meantime, following hard after Peter and John, returns to the tomb, and remains, alone, weeping. Then she sees the angels. And Jesus Himself appears to her.

8. Shortly thereafter, Jesus appears to the other women, as they were on their way to tell the disciples, or, as, having told the disciples, they were returning to the tomb.

This all happened in probably less than an hour's time.

LUKE

Jesus the Son of Man

The special emphasis of Luke is the Humanity of Jesus. Representing Jesus as the Son of God, Luke features His Kindness toward the Weak, the Suffering and the Outcast.

While each of the Gospels was intended ultimately for All Mankind, Matthew seems to have had in immediate view the Jews; Mark, the Romans; and Luke, the Greeks.

Jewish civilization had been built around their Scriptures. Therefore Matthew appeals to their Scriptures.

Roman civilization gloried in the idea of Government, Power. Therefore Mark calls particular attention to the Miracles of Jesus as exhibiting His Superhuman Power.

Greek civilization represented Culture, Philosophy, Wisdom, Reason, Beauty, Education. Therefore, to appeal to the Thoughtful, Cultured, Philosophic Greek Mind, Luke, in a complete, orderly, and classical story, which has been called the "Most Beautiful Book Ever Written," depicts the Glorious Beauty and Perfection of Jesus, the Ideal, Universal Man.

Then, to these three Gospels, John added his, to make it clear and unmistakable that Jesus was GOD in Human Form.

Luke

His name is mentioned only three times in the New Testament: Colossians 4:14, where he is called the "Beloved Physician," Philemon 24, where he is called Paul's "Fellow-Worker"; and II Timothy 4:11, indicating that he was with Paul in the dark hours of approaching martyrdom. In all three passages mention is made also of Mark, indicating that Mark and Luke were companion workers.

In the latter part of the book of Acts, the varying use of the pronouns "they" and "we" indicate that Luke was with Paul from Troas to Philippi, in the early part of Paul's Second Missionary Journey, and that, about 6 years later he re-joined Paul at Philippi at the close of Paul's Third Missionary Journey, and was with him, through his Imprisonment in Caesarea and Rome, to the end (see further page 559).

Date

Quite commonly it is thought that Luke wrote his Gospel about the year A.D. 60, while Paul was in prison in Caesarea; and followed it with the Book of Acts during Paul's imprisonment in Rome the next two years; for the two books, addressed to the same person, are, in a sense, two volumes of one work.

Luke's two year sojourn in Caesarea, A.D. 58–60, afforded him abundant opportunity to get, firsthand, from original companions of Jesus, and first founders of the Church, accurate information concerning all details.

Caesarea was only a few miles from Jerusalem. Jesus' Mother may have been still alive, at John's home in Jerusalem. Luke may have spent many precious hours with her, listening to her reminiscences of her Wondrous Son. And James, Bishop of Jerusalem, Jesus' own Brother, could have supplied Luke with full details of the whole story of Jesus' Life.

The "Synoptic Problem"

Matthew, Mark and Luke are called the Synoptic Gospels, because they give the same general view of Christ's Life, recording, to some extent, the same things. "Their authorship, mutual relations, and possible connection with a common original" is called the "Synoptic Problem."

By some it is thought that Mark's was the earliest of the Gospels, and that Matthew enlarged Mark's, and that Luke made use of both. Others think that Matthew wrote first, and that Mark made an abridged edition of Matthew's Gospel.

It is not necessary to think that Matthew, Mark or Luke quoted from or in any way made use of the others. The events of Jesus' Life and His Sayings were repeated orally for years by the Apostles and others, and were in common circulation among Christians. They were the substance of the daily preaching of the Apostles.

It is likely that, from the beginning, many of these things were written down, some perhaps in a mere fragmentary way, others in more complete form. And when Matthew, Mark and Luke wrote their Gospels, they chose that which suited their purpose from the fund of knowledge oral or written which was the common possession of and in general circulation among Christians, to much of which Matthew had been an eyewitness, and which they themselves had told times without number.

Chapter 1:1-4. Introduction

Many Narratives (1), were already in existence, about Jesus. Luke carefully and painstakingly examined all Authentic Records, and consulted all available Eyewitnesses and original Companions of Jesus, that he might sift out the Exact Facts.

Theophilus (3), to whom this Gospel and the book of Acts are addressed, or dedicated, was a Roman Official of high rank, as indicated by the title Most Excellent. It is not known who he was. Possibly, he may have been one of Luke's converts, in Philippi or Antioch. It may be that he bore the expense of publication of Luke's two books, in having copies made for many Churches.

Chapter 1:5-80. Birth of John the Baptist

Only Matthew and Luke tell of the Birth and Childhood of Jesus, Luke more fully than Matthew, each narrating different incidents.

Matthew	Luke
The Genealogy (1:1–17).	Notice to Zacharias (1:5–25).
Notice to Joseph (1:18–25).	Notice to Mary (1:26–38).
Visit to Wise-Men (2:1–12).	Mary and Elisabeth (1:39–56).
Flight to Egypt (2:13–15).	Birth of John (1:57–80).
Murder of Children (2:16–18).	Birth of Jesus (2:1–7).
Return from Egypt (2:19–23).	The Shepherds (2:8–20).
	Presentation (2:21–38).
	Return to Nazareth (2:39).

(For chronological arrangement of these incidents woven together see under Luke 2:39.)

Chapter 1:5-25. Announcement to Zacharias

The EVENT on which Old Testament prophecy converged was at hand, arrival of Messiah. The closing Old Testament utterance was that Elijah would re-appear as his harbinger (Malachi 4:5–6). An angel now notifies the saintly old priest that his child, yet to be born, is the one to whom that prophecy pointed (17). Jesus so interpreted the passage (Matthew 11:14). John another Elijah.

General Expectation of the Messiah

Josephus, Tacitus and Suetonius state that there was general expectancy over the East that the time for the Messiah to appear was at hand. It was based, partly at least, on Daniel's "70 Weeks' Prophecy" (Daniel 9:24–27). By the popular interpretation, the 70 weeks was understood to mean 70 sevens of years, that is, 490. The decree to rebuild Jerusalem, from which they were to be reckoned (Daniel 9:25), was issued 457 B.C. Hence the time was about up. The Son of God was about to appear.

The Glow of the Supernatural

It was the evident intention of the writers to show that Christianity had a supernatural origin. Long foretold, it did not take place without heavenly evidence that the Event of the Ages was at hand. He was born of a Virgin. His forerunner was born of a barren woman who was past the age for child-bearing. Angels announced it to Zacharias, to Mary, to Joseph, and to the shepherds; and saved the child from being murdered. Wise-Men were supernaturally guided from distant lands to pay their homage, and to provide means for the child's flight from Herod.

Chapter 1:26-38. Announcement to Mary

This is commonly called the Annunciation. The Messiah was to be born in David's family. It had been a thousand years since David, and there had come to be thousands of families of Davidic descent. God, in looking them over, to choose the one through whom His Son should come into the world, passed up the ruling families around Jerusalem, as His eye rested on a humble woman, in a lowly home, in an obscure village of the distant hills of Galilee. What a woman she must have been, to be thus chosen of God to impart and mold the human nature of His Son! And how her heart must have thrilled at the angelic message that she was to be the mother of the Divine King of the Ages!

The Virgin Birth

Luke is thought to have gotten his story of Jesus' birth directly from Mary herself. Matthew probably got his from Joseph. Both state plainly, explicitly, unmistakably and unequivocally that Jesus was born of a Virgin. From the beginning, in unbroken sequence, it has been held as a tenet of the Church, till the rise of modern criticism. If we believe in the Deity of Jesus and his Resurrection from the dead, what is gained by discrediting the Virgin Birth? The Resurrection is the greatest of miracles. If we do not believe that, why concern ourselves with Christ at all? If we do believe it, then why carp at the other parts of the miraculous story? His supernatural exit from the world pre-supposes a supernatural entrance into the world. To call Jesus an illegitimate child is nothing less than blasphemy.

Chapter 1:39-56. Mary's Visit to Elisabeth

Mary and Elisabeth were kin (1:36), "cousins" (AV), "kinswoman" (RV). Elisabeth's home city is not named, except that it was in the hill country of Judah (39). As she was of the tribe of Levi (1:5), it may have been Hebron, which was a Levitical city (Joshua 21:11). Mary's Song of Thanksgiving (46–55), called the "Magnificat," is similar to Hannah's Song at the birth of Samuel (I Samuel 2:1–10).

In her meditations she, probably, had uttered these thoughts over and over till they took the beautiful poetic form in which they here appear as her personal liturgy. Mary was with Elisabeth for three months (56), time for John's birth (36). Then she returned to Nazareth. (See on Matthew 1:18–24.)

Chapter 1:57-80. Birth of John the Baptist

The naming of the child, and his father's prophecy, filled the countryside with expectancy. (See further under Luke 3:1–20.)

Chapter 2:1-38. The Birth of Jesus

What is here told in chapters 1 and 2 is omitted in the other Gospels, except the statement in Matthew 1:25–2:1 that Jesus was born in Bethlehem, and the return to Galilee (Matthew 2:22–23).

Bethlehem

The birthplace of Jesus was a center of historic associations. The city of David. Rachel's burying place. The home of Ruth. 15 miles to the south was Hebron, the home of Abraham, Isaac and Jacob. 10 miles northwest was Gibeon, where Joshua made the sun stand still. 12 miles west was Socoh, where David had slain Goliath. 6 miles north was Jerusalem, where Abraham paid tithes to Melchizedek, the magnificent capital of David and Solomon, the scene of the ministry of Isaiah and Jeremiah, the center of God's age-long effort to reveal Himself to mankind.

The Church of the Nativity in Bethlehem, oldest church building in Christendom, was built originally by Helena, mother of Constantine the first Christian Emperor of the Roman Empire, A.D. 330. There is a cave-like room underneath the church that is said to be the actual manager room in which Jesus was born. There is a tradition that this same room was a part of the ancestral home of David and Boaz and Ruth. In this room Jerome the Latin scholar spent 30 years, making his Translation of the Bible into Latin.

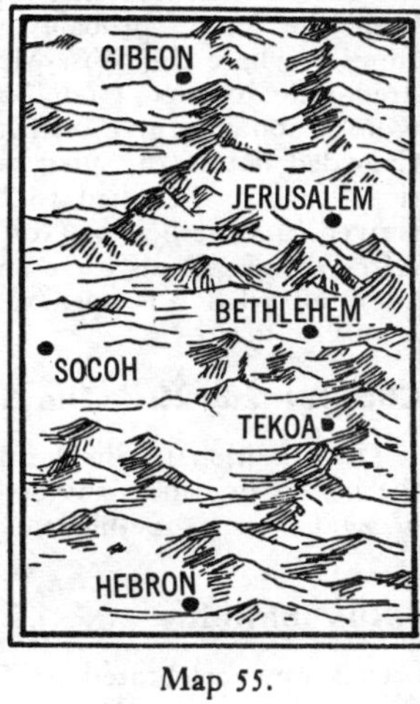

Map 55.

Chapter 2:1-5. The Enrolment of Quirinius

This was a census of the Roman Empire. Roman historical records place the Enrolment of Quirinius in A.D. 7, which was 10 or 12 years after Jesus was born. This historical discrepancy was for a long time troublesome to Biblical students. But in recent years ancient papyri have been found from which it is learned that Quirinius was TWICE governor of Syria. Luke expressly says it was "the first" enrolment. It has been found also that people were required to go to their ancestral homes for the census. Thus, the spade of the archaeologist goes on, confirming, one by one, even to minutest detail, the historical accuracy of Bible statements.

The Amazing Providence of God

The Messiah was to be of the family of David, and to be born in Bethlehem (Micah 5:2–5). But the chosen parents lived at Nazareth, 100 miles from Bethlehem. A decree of Rome requires them to go to Bethlehem, just as the child is to be born. Thus God makes the decree of a pagan empire to be the instrument of fulfilling his prophecies.

Chapter 2:6-7. Born in a Manger

The word translated "inn" may mean a public lodging place, or the guest room adjoining a private home. Here it is thought to have been the latter, probably the home of their Davidic kin, same "house" where the Wise-Men later came (Matthew 2:11). The hundred mile journey from Nazareth, by foot or on a donkey, for a woman about to give birth to a child, must have been long and hard. Crowded out of the guest room, temporarily, by others who had arrived earlier, they had to lodge in the stable. The sacred moment arrived, and the Son of God had an animal feed-trough for his cradle. After the shepherds came and told their story, no doubt the best the home afforded was open to Joseph and Mary.

Chapter 2:8-20. The Shepherds

The traditional "Shepherds' Field," where the angelic choirs sang the birth-day hallelujahs of earth's new King, is about three-quarters of a mile east of Bethlehem. (See pages 175, 176.)

Jesus' Birthday

It is now celebrated on December 25th. There is nothing in the

Bible to indicate it. This date first appears as Jesus' birthday in the 4th century, in the West. The Eastern church date is January 6th.

Gabriel

Gabriel was the name of the Angelic prince sent from heaven to direct arrangements for the Son of God's arrival (Luke 1:19, 26). We presume he was the angel who appeared to the shepherds (2:9, 13). And also, the one sent to Joseph (Matthew 1:24); and directed the flight to Egypt (Matthew 2:13, 19). He had given to Daniel the Seventy Weeks' Prophecy (Daniel 9:21). How interested was he in human redemption! And how we will love to make his acquaintance when we get to Heaven.

Chapter 2:21-38. Jesus' Circumcision and Presentation

That they offered two pigeons instead of a lamb and a pigeon is an indication that Joseph and Mary were poor (Leviticus 12:8).

Chapter 2:39. Return to Nazareth

Luke here proceeds directly from the Presentation in the Temple to the Return to Nazareth, omitting events recorded in Matthew 2:1–21, Visit of Wise-Men, Flight to Egypt, Slaughter of Children, and Return from Egypt.

Chronology of Jesus' Birth and Childhood

Mark and John say nothing about the Birth and Childhood of Jesus. Matthew and Luke record different incidents (see under Luke 1:5–80). To harmonize these into exact chronological sequence is not easy. Here are approximate probable dates:

5 B.C.	Announcement to Zacharias	Luke 1:5–25
6 months later	Announcement to Mary	Luke 1:26–38
	Mary's Visit to Elisabeth	Luke 1:39–56
3 months later	Mary's Return to Nazareth	Luke 1:56
	Announcement to Joseph	Matthew 1:18–24
	Birth of John the Baptist	Luke 1:57–80
4 B.C.	Birth of Jesus Matthew 1:25	Luke 2:1–7
	Announcement to Shepherds	Luke 2:8–20
8 days later	Jesus' Circumcision	Luke 2:21
32 days later	Jesus' Presentation	Luke 2:22–38
3 B.C.	Visit of Wise-Men	Matthew 2:1–12
	Flight to Egypt	Matthew 2:13–15
	Slaughter of Children	Matthew 2:16–18
2 B.C.	Return to Nazareth Luke 2:39	Matthew 2:19–23

Why Christ was born 4 years "Before Christ"

When Christ was born time was reckoned in the Roman Empire from the founding of the city of Rome. When Christianity became the universal religion over what had been the Roman world, a monk named Dionysius Exiguus, at the request of the Emperor Justinian, made a calendar A.D. 526, reckoning time from the Birth of Christ, to supersede the Roman calendar. Long after the Christian Calendar had replaced the Roman Calendar it was found that Dionysius had made a mistake in placing the birth of Christ in 753 from the founding of Rome. It should have been about 749, or a year or two earlier.

Chapter 2:40. Jesus' Childhood

The first few months as a babe at Bethlehem. Then a year or two in Egypt. Then at Nazareth. The incident in the Temple indicates that he was a remarkably precocious boy. But of his childhood the Bible says little. Jesus was eldest of a family of seven children. They were poor. So we infer that Jesus early learned responsibility. How we wish we had a glimpse of his home life—how the Son of God as a growing boy bore himself under the daily round of irritations usual in such a situation.

The Apocryphal Gospels are full of ridiculous fables about Jesus' childhood miracles. They are totally unauthentic. The Bible says the Cana miracle was his first (John 2:11).

Jesus' Education

Jesus had a devout and sensible mother, who from earliest childhood had taught him Old Testament stories and precepts. Then there were schools connected with the synagogs. After he was 12 he must have visited Jerusalem regularly at least three times a year at the great festivals; and, no doubt, at an early age, the wicked splendor, glaring corruption and utter godlessness of the hierarchy that ruled in the name of God, burned into his soul, and filled him with a holy zeal to stop it. Then, too, along with his human education, there must have come to him gradually his pre-incarnation knowledge.

Chapter 2:41-50. His Visit to Jerusalem

At the age of 12. This is thought to have been his first trip to Jerusalem. So interested, and utterly engrossed in the discourses of the teachers, he failed to miss his parents for three days after they were gone. And they failed to notice his absence from the caravan group for a whole day, till they came to the evening resting place. It must have been a rather large company, extending a long distance over the road. The parents felt sure that their self-reliant boy was somewhere along the line, and that he was abundantly able to take care of himself, till the evening round-up.

Jesus' Knowledge of the Old Testament (47). At that time the Old Testament constituted the written Word of God. Jesus loved it. His familiarity with it at the age of 12 astounded the great theologians of the Temple. He lived by it. Used it to resist the tempter (Matthew 4:4, 7, 10). Went to the cross to fulfill it (Matthew 26:54). Uttered his dying agonies in quotation from it (Matthew 27:46). To the Old Testament writings there has been added another group of writings, called the New Testament, centered around the life of Jesus himself. If what Jesus had of our Bible was dear to him, it seems like a thousandfold dearer ought what we have be to us.

"In my Father's House" (49, RV), "About my Father's business" (AV). Literally, "In the things of my Father." This saying rather puzzled his mother. Probably she had not yet told him of the nature of his birth. She had just spoken of Joseph as his "father" (48). In his reply, his speaking of God as "my Father," possibly, conveyed to her a hint that he knew her secret.

Chapter 2:51-52. The 18 Years' Silence

How we would love to know something of Jesus' life from 12 to 30. But God, in his wisdom, has drawn a veil over it.

The Language of Galilee

Aramaic was the common language of the people. This was the language Jesus used. He was instructed in Hebrew, the language of the Old Testament Scriptures. He must have known Greek, for it was the language of a large part of the population, and the universal language of the time. Jesus was familiar with both the Hebrew and Septuagint Old Testament. His own language is superb.

Nazareth

Situated in a basin in the south side of a hill 1150 feet above sea level. From the top of the hill, ten minutes climb, a view unrivalled in Galilee. To the north a beautiful panorama of fertile hills and valleys, dotted with prosperous cities, snow-capped Hermon in the distance. Nearby, 3 miles distant, was Gath-hepher, the ancient home of Jonah. To the south the Plain of Esdraelon extending from the Jordan to the Mediterranean, the principal scene of Israel's age-old struggle for existence. Ten miles to the west of Nazareth, in full view, Mt. Carmel, where Elijah, in his contest with Baal, had called

Fig. 64. Nazareth, seen from the east. © *Matson Photo*

down fire from heaven. To the Southwest, about the same distance, the pass of Armageddon, famous battlefield of the nations, which suggested to Jesus the name of the great final battle of the ages in which he himself will lead his own to victory. To the South from Nazareth, only eight miles, Shunem, where Elisha raised the Shunammite's son to life. Nearby the spring of Harod, where Gideon with his 300 had put the Midianites to route. And Jezreel, where the infamous Jezebel had met her unhappy fate. And Mt. Gilboa, where king Saul was slain by the Philistines. And Endor, where the witch had called back Samuel's spirit. The river Kishon, where Deborah and Barak subdued the Canaanites. All this in full view from the top of the hill of Nazareth. What a center of historic associations. We can imagine that Jesus often climbed the hill, and meditated deeply on history that had been made to bring him into the world.

Chapter 3:1-20. John the Baptist

The preaching of John is told by all Four Gospels (Matthew 3:1–12; Mark 1:1–8; John 1:6–8; 19–28). Luke's account is fullest.

The story of John's childhood and youth is passed over in one sentence (1:80). He shunned the habitations of men, and lived in the solitude of the wild and bleak region west of the Dead Sea.

He had known from childhood that the Event of the Ages was at hand, and that he had been born to herald its arrival.

Reared in daily view of Mt. Nebo, from whose heights Moses had viewed with longing eyes the Promised Land and spoke of the Promised Messiah; overlooking the Jordan where Joshua had crossed, and Jericho whose walls had fallen at Joshua's blast; living in the same region where Amos had pastured his flocks and had dreamed of a Coming Davidic King who would rule all nations; often visiting the brook Cherith where Elijah had been fed by the ravens; he medi-

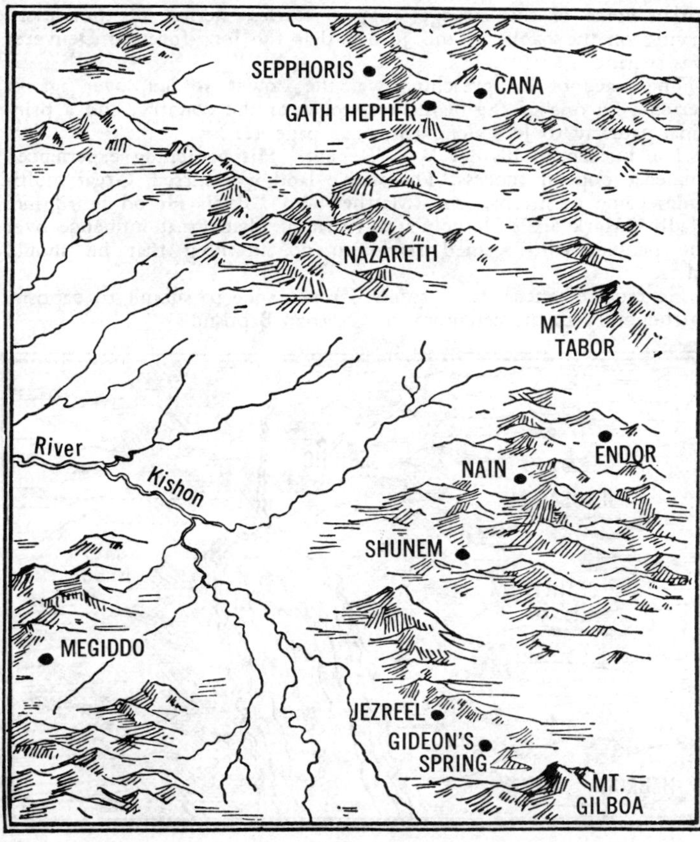

Map 56.

tated deeply on the history that was now heading to its climax, and waited for the call of God.

Knowing he was to be the Elijah of prophecy (1:17; Matthew 11:14; 17:10–13; Malachi 4:5, not Elijah in person, John 1:21), intentionally, perhaps, he copied the habits and dress of Elijah.

He lived on locusts and wild honey (Matthew 3:4). Locusts had been used as food from earliest times. They were roasted, or sundried, and eaten like parched grain. Are said to taste like shrimp.

When John was 30 years old his call came. The nation, groaning under the cruelties of Roman bondage, was electrified by the stentorian voice of this strange, rugged, fearless hermit of the desert, crying on the banks of the Jordan that the long-foretold Deliverer was at hand.

The place of his preaching was the Lower Jordan, over against Jericho, on one of the main cross-roads of the country, and a principal gateway to Jerusalem. (See map page 423.)

The burden of his cry was "Repent." His preaching experienced immense popular success. The whole land was stirred. Great multitudes came to his baptism (Matthew 3:5). Even Herod heard him gladly (Mark 6:20). Josephus says that he "had great influence over the people, who seemed ready to do anything that he should advise."

He required those who professed repentance to submit to baptism, introductory to the ceremony of Christian Baptism.

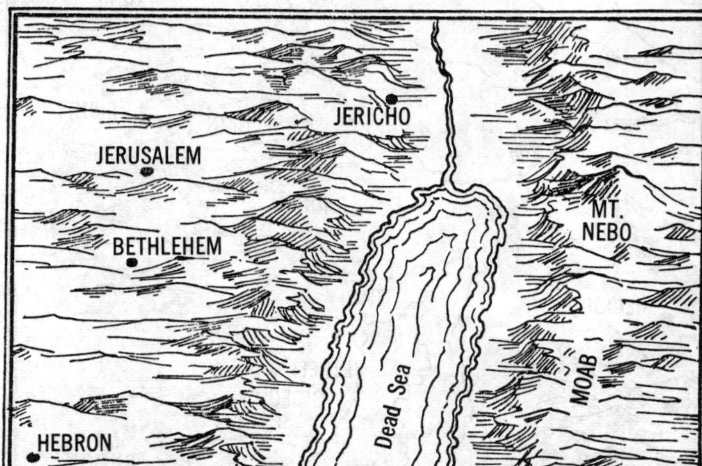

Map 57.

At the height of his popularity he baptized Jesus, and proclaimed him the Messiah. Then, his mission accomplished, he passes off the stage. He had roused the nation, and presented the Son of God. His work was done.

However, he continued preaching and baptizing for a few months, moving northward to Aenon (John 3:23. See map page 423).

About a year after he had baptized Jesus, he was imprisoned by Herod, to satisfy the whim of a wicked woman (Matthew 14:1–5). This was at the close of Jesus' Early Judean Ministry (December, Matthew 4:12; John 3:22; 4:35).

The place of his imprisonment is not named. It is thought to have been at Machaerus, east of Dead Sea, or at Tiberias, on west shore of Sea of Galilee, at both of which places Herod had a residence. He was beheaded about the time of the second following Passover (Matthew 14:12–13; John 6:4).

We wonder about John's doubt (Matthew 11:3). He had borne such confident and positive testimony that Jesus was the Lamb of God and the Son of God (John 1:29–34). But now, as he mused behind dungeon walls, he was puzzled. Jesus was not doing what he thought the Messiah would do. He evidently shared the popular notion of a Political Messianic Kingdom. God did not reveal to him everything as to the nature of the Kingdom. Even the Twelve were slow in learning it. (See on Matthew 10.)

Assuming that John began his ministry shortly before he baptized Jesus, it lasted about a year and a half. 30 years in seclusion. A year and a half of public preaching. A year and 4 months in prison. Then the curtain. This is the brief epitome of the man who ushered in the Saviour of the World, and of whom Jesus said there had not been born a greater (Matthew 11:11). John did no miracles (John 10:41).

Chapter 3:21–22. Jesus is Baptized. (See on Matthew 3:13–17.)
Chapter 3:23–28. Genealogy of Jesus. (See on Matthew 1:1–17.)

Chapter 4:1-13. The Forty Days' Temptation

See note on Matthew 4:1–11. In all three accounts, Matthew, Mark, Luke, it is stated that it was Satan who tempted Jesus.

Satan

Jesus said a good deal about Satan.

Called him "the enemy" (Matthew 13:39).
"The evil one" (Matthew 13:38).
"The prince of this world" (John 12:31; 14:30).
"A liar," and "the father of lies" (John 8:44).
"A murderer" (John 8:44).

Said that he "saw him fallen from heaven" (Luke 10:18).
That he has a "kingdom" (Matthew 12:26).
That "evil men are his sons" (Matthew 13:28).
That he "sowed tares among the wheat" (Matthew 13:38, 39).
He "snatches Word from hearers" (Matthew 13:19; Mark 4:15; Luke 8:12).
That he "bound a woman for 18 years" (Luke 13:16).
That he "desired to have Peter" (Luke 22:31).
That he has "angels" (Matthew 25:41).
That "eternal fire is prepared for him" (Matthew 25:41).

The Bible represents Satan as:

"The tempter" (Matthew 4:3).
"The prince of demons" (Matthew 12:24; Mark 3:22; Luke 11:15).
"Source of demoniacal possession" (Matthew 12:22–29; Luke 11:14–23).
That he put the betrayal into the heart of Judas (John 13:2, 27).
That he perverts the Scripture (Matthew 4:4; Luke 4:10, 11).
That he is "the god of this world" (II Corinthians 4:4).
That he is "the prince of the power of the air" (Ephesians 2:2).
That he "fashions himself into an angel of light" (II Corinthians 11:14).
That he is our "adversary" (I Peter 5:8).
He is "the deceiver of the whole world" (Revelation 12:9; 20:3, 8, 10).
Calls him "the great dragon," "the old serpent" (Revelation 12:9; 20:2).
The "seducer of Adam and Eve" (Genesis 3:1–20).
That he will "flee if resisted" (James 4:7).
That he caused "Paul's thorn in the flesh" (II Corinthians 12:7).
Hindered Paul's missionary plans (I Thessalonians 2:18).
Caused Ananias to lie (Acts 5:3).
That Gentiles are under his power (Acts 26:18).
That he blinds the minds of unbelievers (II Corinthians 4:4).
False teachers are "a synagog of Satan" (Revelation 2:9; 3:9).
Can produce false miracles (II Thessalonians 2:9).
Is the moving spirit of the "Apostasy" (II Thessalonians 2:9).
As a roaring lion seeks to devour Christians (I Peter 5:8).
Is overcome by faith (I Peter 5:9).
Is wiley (Ephesians 6:11).
Is the spirit that works in the disobedient (Ephesians 2:2).
Moved David to Sin (I Chronicles 21:1).
Caused Job's Troubles (Job 1:7–2:10).
Was the Adversary of Joshua (Zechariah 3:1–9).
Gets the advantage of Christians (II Corinthians 2:11).
Evil men are his children (I John 3:8, 10).

Is there really a devil? The language of Jesus certainly indicates his own belief in the existence of a personal devil. Jesus knew what he was talking about. If Jesus was merely accommodating himself to popular error, his words are no revelation of truth at all, for who, then, can discern between the actual truth that he is aiming to teach and the error that he speaks of as if it were truth?

The Galilean Ministry. 4:14 to 9:51

Luke gives nothing like as much space to the Galilean Ministry as do Matthew and Mark. (See notes under Matthew 4:12 and Mark 1:14).

Chapter 4:14-15. Jesus Begins Galilean Ministry

Luke, like Matthew and Mark, passes entirely over events of the year between Jesus' Temptation and beginning of his Galilean Ministry, as told in John 1:19 to 4:54. (See on Mark 1:14–15).

Chapter 4:16-30. Rejection at Nazareth

This seems to have been his first return to Nazareth since his baptism over a year before. As fas as we know he had spent the intervening time in the Wilderness, at Cana, in Capernaum, and in Judea (John 2:1, 12; 4:46). They marveled at his gracious, magnetic and evident powerful personality in speaking, and were amazed. They could hardly believe that it was their own humble townsman. Even in that small town Jesus had lived so quiet a life, and was from such a lowly family, that the synagog congregation scarcely recognized him (22). The point in his reference to Elijah and Elisha is that they were sent to Gentiles, not Israelites—a hint of his own mission. This, and the performance of miracles in other towns than his own, so offended their narrow provincialism that they flew into a frenzy and attempted to kill him. The brow of the hill from which they attempted to dash him down may be seen at the right of the photo under Luke 2:51–52.

Chapter 4:31–37. Demoniac Healed. (See on Mark 1:21–28.)

Chapter 4:38–39. Peter's Mother-in-law. (See on Mark 1:29–31.)

Chapter 4:40–41. Multitudes Healed. (See on Mark 1:32–34.)

Chapter 4:42. Retirement to Pray. (See on Mark 1:35–37.)

Chapter 4:43–44. Journeying about. (See on Mark 1:38–39.)

Chapter 5:1–11. Call of Peter, James, John. (See on Mark 1:16–20.)

Chapter 5:12–16. A Leper Cleansed. (See on Mark 1:40–45.)

Chapter 5:17–26. A Paralytic Healed. (See on Mark 2:1–12.)
Chapter 5:27–32. Call of Levi (Matthew). (See on Matthew 1:1.)
Chapter 5:33–39. Question about Fasting. (See on Mark 2:18–22.)
Chapter 6:1–11. Eating, Healing, on Sabbath. (See on Mark 2:23.)

Chapter 6:12-19. The Twelve Chosen

To these men He was entrusting the issue of his life's work. Of course he knew that He Himself, from heaven, through his Spirit, would guide and direct and help them. Nevertheless their natural traits and talents had to be considered. And before making final choice Jesus spent all night long in prayer to God.

After two years of training (see under Matthew 10) he sent them forth to be his "witnesses to the uttermost parts of the earth." The New Testament tells only a little of their work—that in Palestine, Asia Minor, Greece and Rome.

Perhaps the Twelve agreed among themselves to go in different directions. Or, each may have been guided to go wherever he thought best. They went, part time, in pairs. No doubt each visited the work of others.

Paul, about A.D. 62, said, in Colossians 1:23, that "the gospel had been preached in all creation under heaven." Thus, within 30 years the Story of Christ had been told over the known world.

Traditions, variant and uncertain, are that most of the Twelve sealed their testimony to Christ with their martyrdom.

So, all in all, allowing for one traitor in the group, Jesus' choice and training of the Twelve was a grand success.

Chapter 6:20-49. The Sermon on the Mount

This is commonly taken to be an abbreviated form of the same sermon as that recorded in Matthew 5, 6, 7. In Matthew 5:1 he "went up into the mountain and sat down." In Luke 6:17 he "came down and stood on a level place," that is, from a higher location. He could have done both, seeing the transactions involved considerable time.

The two records are somewhat different. We cannot be sure whether they are different reports of the same sermon, or substantially the same sermon delivered on different occasions. Jesus was teaching continually, and it is likely that he uttered some of these words, in varying forms, hundreds of times. This may be a collection of his representative sayings, a sort of summary of his main teachings. Their literary beauty, as well as their matchless teaching, is unexcelled in literature.

Chapter 6:20–26. The Beatitudes. (See on Matthew 5:1–12.)

Chapter 6:27-38. The Golden Rule

Here is a sort of condensation of Matthew 5 and 7. Some of Jesus' teachings, such as loving our neighbor as ourself, loving our enemies, and doing unto others as we would that they should do unto us, are so high above our selfish human nature that we are in the habit of excusing ourselves from even trying to live up to them by saying to ourselves that Jesus surely knew that he was setting before us impossible ideals.

However, Jesus himself lived up to them, and taught unequivocally that we must keep our hearts free from resentment, no matter how we may be mistreated; and not only that, but that we should actually seek the welfare of those who seek our hurt. Not possible? Yes, it is, in some measure, by the strictest self-discipline, and by the gracious help of God, possible to love those who hate us.

To practice the Golden Rule, even in small measure, makes us happy, helps us in our business, and in every relation of life. It is the most practical thing in this world. In serving others we serve ourselves. People like to deal with those who believe in and practice the Golden Rule. Try it, and see.

The Golden Rule is not a sufficient basis for exemption from military service. Jesus was speaking to INDIVIDUALS, not Governments. Governments are ordained of God (Romans 13:1–7; I Peter 2:13–17). Criminal elements have to be suppressed by force. Jesus expressly stated that his kingdom could exist within the kingdom of Caesar (Matthew 22:21). The first Gentile to be admitted into the Church was a Roman soldier (Acts 10:1). He was not required to renounce military service. A judge, a police officer, or a military man, may, in his own heart and life, practice the principles of the Golden Rule, so far as he can as an individual, while as an officer of the law or the government he must follow strictly the rules of justice. Governments may, in certain respects, and in certain limited measure, follow the Golden Rule. But if force were abandoned, it would mean anarchy, with a free hand for murderers, robbers, rapists and every vile criminal. Let us have clear thinking on this point. As much as we abhor war, a Christian is not at all to be commended for making the Golden Rule an excuse for letting others do the fighting to preserve his liberty.

Chapter 6:39-49. Building on the Rock

Such words as these, and there are plenty of them, make it very plain that Jesus intends to be taken seriously. There is going to be a day of sad disillusionment for many who make glib profession of his name (Matthew 7:22–23). DOING the things Jesus taught, PRACTICING them in our LIVES, is what will count in the final round up.

Chapter 7:1-10. The Centurion's Servant

This is told also in Matthew 8:5–13. A Centurion was a Roman officer in charge of a hundred soldiers. At that time Palestine had been under Roman control about a hundred years. Roman officers, all too generally, were brutal and despised men. But some of them, influenced by the Jewish religion, were good men. The first Gentile to be received into the Church was a Centurion, named Cornelius (Acts 10).

This Centurion had built the Jews their synagog in Capernaum (5). In this same synagog Jesus had often taught, and had healed the demoniac (Mark 1:21–23). In 1905 a German expedition uncovered the remains of a synagog which appeared to have been built in the 4th century A.D. and under it the floor of a still older synagog which is thought to have been the actual synagog in which Jesus taught (Mark 1:21; Luke 7:5). On the West wall are the stone seats where the Scribes and Pharisees sat. The pulpit was at the north end. One may see almost the exact spot where the Lord stood.

Fig. 65. Ruins of Synagog in Capernaum. © *Matson Photo*

Chapter 7:11-17. Widow of Nain's Son Raised

This is one of the three resurrections. (See Mark 5:22 and John 11:1.) Jesus may have raised others (Luke 7:22). He commissioned the Twelve to raise the dead (Matthew 10:8).

Chapter 7:18–35. Messengers from John. (See on Matthew 11:1–19.)

Chapter 7:36-50. The Sinful Woman

There is not the slightest basis for identifying this woman with Mary Magdalene, or with Mary of Bethany. This anointing is NOT the same as the anointing at Bethany (John 12:1–8). An oriental banquet was a sort of public affair. Jesus half reclining on a couch, his face toward the table, his knees bent back, it was easy for the woman to approach. Weeping, kissing his feet, bathing them with the costly perfume, and wiping away the falling tears with her hair—how she puts us respectable people to shame in thus bowing low in abject humility and devoted adoration at the feet of her Lord.

Jesus was very tender in his attitude toward women who had made a mis-step (John 4:18; 8:1–11). Yet no one ever attributed to him questionable motives (John 4:27).

Chapter 8:1-3. The Women

Three are named, beside "many others." Nothing further is known of Susanna. Joanna was wife of Herod's steward, from the king's palace. She belonged to the group of Jesus' closest friends. She was among those at the tomb (Luke 24:10).

Mary Magdalene

Mary Magdalene was the most prominent and outstanding leader among the women. She is named more than any of the others, and usually first (Matthew 27:56, 61; 28:1; Mark 15:40, 47; 16:1, 9; Luke 8:2; 24:10; John 19:25; 20:1, 18). She was the first to whom Jesus appeared after his resurrection. That she was named among those who "ministered of their substance" (3), suggests that she was a woman of some wealth. That she had been healed of "seven demons" (2), is no indication that she was unchaste. Demons caused sickness and disease of various kinds (see under Mark 5:1–20), but are nowhere connected with human immorality. Unquestionably she was a woman of unblemished character. She was NOT the sinful woman of the preceding chapter. It is simply unthinkable that Jesus would accept a common prostitute as the leading woman of his group.

It may be a good thing that we humans among ourselves make a distinction between respectable sins and gross sins, and put a sort of disgrace upon those who are guilty of certain forms of gross sin. The fact that we do may help to save our human society from utter ruin. But to God sin is sin. And it is, no doubt, just as hard for God to forgive our respectable sins as it is for him to forgive those who have brought upon themselves the disgrace of society. For a prostitute to have her sins forgiven and be accepted in the fellowship of the saved, is one thing, but it would be quite a different thing to immediately place such an one at the head of religious work.

Chapter 8:4–18. Parable of the Sower. (See on Matthew 13:1–23.)
Chapter 8:19–21. Jesus' Mother, Brothers. (See on Matthew 12:46–50.)
Chapter 8:22–25. The Storm Calmed. (See on Mark 4:35–41.)
Chapter 8:26–39. The Gerasene Demoniac. (See on Mark 5:1–20.)
Chapter 8:40–56. Jairus' Daughter Raised. (Told also in Matthew 9:18–26; Mark 5:22–43.) Three times Jesus raised the dead. (See on Luke 7:11–17 and John 11.)
Chapter 9:1–6. The Twelve Sent Forth. (See on Matthew 10.)
Chapter 9:7–9. Herod's Perplexity. (See on Luke 3:1–20.)
Chapter 9:10–17. The 5,000 Fed. (See on John 6.)
Between verses 17 and 18, about 8 months intervene.
Chapter 9:18–20. Peter's Confession. (See on Matthew 16:13–20.)
Chapter 9:21–27. The Passion Foretold. (See on Mark 9:30–32.)
Chapter 9:28–36. The Transfiguration. (See on Mark 9:2–13.)
Chapter 9:37–43. The Epileptic Boy. (See on Mark 9:14–29.)
Chapter 9:43–45. Passion Again Foretold. (See on Mark 9:30–32.)

Chapter 9:46-48. Who is Greatest?

The pathos of this incident is that it was while they were fresh from the Transfiguration. And the further pity was that it was in response to Jesus' announcement of his approaching crucifixion. Worse still, they repeated the performance when they got to Capernaum (Matthew 18:1–5; Mark 9:33–37). And again, as they neared his crucifixion (see on Matthew 20:20–28). What infinite patience Jesus must have had! And what a master-workman with men!

Chapter 9:49-50. The Unknown Wonder Worker

Told also in Mark 9:38–40. Another rebuke of John, for wanting to monopolize the privilege of working miracles. And another immediately following, for anger (52–56). Three rebukes in a row.

Chapters 9:51-19:28. Perean and Later Judean Ministry

The period between Jesus' Final Departure from Galilee and his Last Week is usually spoken of as the Perean, or Later Judean, Ministry—partly in Perea and partly Judea: Perea east of Jordan (Map page 477), in Herod's jurisdiction; Judea west of Jordan, under Pilate's jurisdiction.

Chapter 9:51. Final Departure from Galilee

Mentioned also in Matthew 19:1; Mark 10:1. This is thought to be identical with Jesus' visit to Jerusalem at the Feast of Dedication (December), John 10:22. Thus, the Perean and Later Judean Ministry covered a period of about four months.

The Four Accounts of the Perean-Judean Ministry

Matthew 19 and 20

Divorce (19:1–12)
Little Children (19:13–15)
Rich Young Ruler (19:16–30)
Laborers in Vineyard (20:1–16)
Passion Foretold (20:17–19)
James and John's Request (20:20–28)
Blind Men at Jericho (20:29–34)

Mark 10

Divorce (10:1–12)
Little Children (10:13–16)
Rich Young Ruler (10:17–31)
Passion Foretold (10:32–34)
Request James and John (10:35–)
Blind Bartimaeus (10:46–52)

Luke 9:51–19:29

Inhospitable Samaritans (9:51–56)
"Foxes have holes" (9:57–62)
70 Sent forth (10:1–16)
70 Return (10:17–24)
The Good Samaritan (10:25–37)
Mary and Martha (10:38–42)
The "Lord's Prayer" (11:1–4)
Importunity in Prayer (11:5–13)
"By Beelzebub" (11:14–26)
The Word of God (11:27–28)
The Sign of Jonah (11:29–32)
The Lighted Lamp (11:33–36)
Pharisees Denounced (11:37–54)
The Unpardonable Sin (12:1–12)
The Rich Fool (12:13–21)
Treasures in Heaven (12:22–34)
Watchfulness (12:35–40)
The Faithful Steward (12:41–48)
"Fire upon the earth" (12:49–53)
Signs of the times (12:54–59)
The Galileans' Blood (13:1–5)
The Barren Fig Tree (13:6–9)
Woman Bowed together (13:10–)
Mustard Seed, Leaven (13:18–21)
"Few Saved"? (13:22–30)
"Tell that fox" (13:31–35)
Man with Dropsy (14:1–6)
"Chief Seats" (14:7–11)
"Feasts for poor" (14:12–14)
Excuses (14:15–24)
Cross Bearing (14:25–35)
Lost Sheep, Lost Coin (15:1–10)
The Prodigal Son (15:11–32)
The Unjust Steward (16:1–17)
Divorce (16:18)
Rich Man and Lazarus (16:19–31)

John 7 to 11
At Tabernacles (7:1–52)
Adulterous Woman (8:1–11)
Jesus' Discourse (8:12–59)
A Blind Man Healed (9:1–41)
The Good Shepherd (10:1–21)
At Dedication (10:22–39)
In Lower Jordan (10:40–42)
Raising of Lazarus (11:1–53)
In Ephraim (11:54–57)

Forgiveness (17:1–4)
Power of Faith (17:5–10)
Ten Lepers (17:11–19)
Coming of the Lord (17:20–37)
The Importunate Widow (18:1–8)
Pharisee and Publican (18:9–14)
Little Children (18:15–17)
Rich Young Ruler (18:18–30)
Passion Foretold (18:31–34)
Blind Man at Jericho (18:35–43)
Zacchaeus (19:1–10)
Parable of Pounds (19:11–28)

Chapter 9:52-56. Samaritans Reject Jesus

Their rejection of Jesus infuriated James and John, who then and there gave an exhibition of why Jesus had nicknamed them "Sons of Thunder" (Mark 3:17). Jesus, without resentment, changed his route, on his way toward Jerusalem.

Chapter 9:57-62. "Foxes Have Holes"

More than a year before Jesus had said that same thing to a scribe who offered to follow him across the lake (Matthew 8:19–22). Probably he had made that answer many times to those whom he knew were looking for a kind of preferment which he did not have to offer. Jesus' replies to the second and third men did not, of course, mean that we should ignore the tender ministries of earthly life. The Bible teaches over and over that one of the truest marks of a Christian is to be thoughtful and considerate in all the relations of family life, especially in times of sorrow. Jesus means that the things of God are of infinitely greater importance, and in case of conflict there should not be a moment's hesitation. God first always.

Chapter 10:1-16. The Seventy Sent Forth

This seems to have been on his final departure from Galilee. His purpose was to complete the advertisement to the nation that the Messiah was there. Probably, they were sent ahead of him down the Jordan valley, 4 or 5 months before his death.

How Did Jesus Finance His Work?

Jesus was a poor man, "had not where to lay his head." For some three years he traveled about, much of the time with a considerable entourage; and at least twice organized large preaching expeditions.

In part they lived on the hospitality of the people (Matthew 10:11). He received offerings from the well-to-do, and others (Luke 8:3). From the multitudes of followers, and of the sick that he had healed, he could have amassed a fortune and lived like a king, if he had so chosen. But he lived and died in poverty.

Chapter 10:17-24. Return of the Seventy

The extent of their journey is not stated. Probably it was all the way down to the Jericho region, Jesus following more slowly. Their success, to Jesus, was a foregleam of Satan's overthrow. But notice that Jesus warned them not to be too exultant even over their good works. The real cause of joy is Heaven (20).

Chapter 10:25-37. The Good Samaritan

This is one of the most superb classics on the subject of Human Kindness in all literature. Luke had just told about Jesus being rejected by Samaritans (9:52). Here is Jesus' reaction: to exalt a Samaritan to the love of all future ages.

Kindness

Jesus himself was the Kindest man who ever lived. It is said of him, and it is said of no other in history, that if all the deeds of Kindness that he did in three short years were written, the world would not contain the books (John 21:25).

Jesus talked a great deal about Kindness, just the plain, old-fashioned every-day habit of common Kindness.

Judging by what he said, he would rather see that in his followers than any other trait of character. Not that our kindness will save us. If we are ever saved, HE saves us. But there are things in us that please or displease him.

Jesus put so much stress on this thing of Kindness that he identifies himself with those who need it, and in effect tells us that we cannot be friends with him and at the same time be indifferent to the suffering (Matthew 25:40, 45).

He intimates that heaven will be inhabited exclusively by those who have learned how to be Kind and only Kind and always Kind. Jesus came to build a world of beings like himself, and when completed no others will be there (Matthew 25:34, 41).

He further intimates that there are going to be some surprises in the Day of Judgment. Some who have been accustomed to think of themselves as very religious are going to find out, after it is too late, that they have been altogether overlooking the things the recording angels have been taking down (Matthew 25:44).

Jesus further makes the remarkable statement that not one single act of kindness, no matter how small, will, in the economy of God's government of the universe, ever go unrewarded (Matthew 10:42).

However, we must remember that Jesus does not mean that we should give encouragement to able-bodied lazy men. Laziness is one of the greatest of sins. The Bible nowhere excuses it. "If any man will not work neither let him eat" (II Thessalonians 3:10).

Chapter 10:38-42. Mary and Martha

This is thought to have been at the end of his great publicity campaign down the Jordan valley, heralded by the Seventy. He was now approaching Jerusalem for the Feast of Dedication (?) (John 10:22). Mary and Martha lived at Bethany, which was on the eastern slope of the Mount of Olives, about two miles from Jerusalem. This incident is recorded to show that Jesus thought that listening to the Word of the Lord is of great importance.

Chapter 11:1. Jesus Praying

Jesus, although he was the Son of God, and claimed to have been in some respects equal with God, yet, in the days of his flesh, he seems to have felt himself utterly dependent on a Power higher than himself; and he prayed a great deal.

Here are some of the recorded instances:

Jesus' Prayers

At his baptism (Luke 3:21).
In a solitary place (Mark 1:35).
In the wilderness (Luke 5:16).
All night, before choosing the Twelve (Luke 6:12).
Before his invitation, "Come unto Me" (Matthew 11:25–27).
At the Feeding of the 5,000 (John 6:11).
After the Feeding of the 5,000 (Matthew 14:23).
When he gave the Lord's Prayer (Luke 11:1–4).
At Caesarea-Philippi (Luke 9:18).
Before his Transfiguration (Luke 9:28–29).
For Little Children (Matthew 19:13).
Before the Raising of Lazarus (John 11:41–42).
In the Temple (John 12:27–28).
At the Supper (Matthew 26:26–27).
For Peter (Luke 22:32).
For the Disciples (John 17).
In Gethsemane (Matthew 26:36, 39, 42, 44).
On the Cross (Luke 23:34).
At Emmaus (Luke 24:30).

In every recorded prayer Jesus addressed God as "Father" (Matthew 6:9; 11:25; 26:39, 42; Luke 11:2; 23:34; John 11:41; 12:27, 28; 17:1, 5, 11, 21, 24, 25): so different from the bombastic, labored, lofty and ponderous openings of many "pastoral" prayers.

Chapter 11:2-4. The Lord's Prayer

Given in longer form in Matthew 6:9–13. We doubt that Jesus intended this as a form to be repeated in unison in religious services. We rather think they were meant to be a sort of norm, to guide us in our approach to God, and on the subject matter of our petitions.

And above all things, why say "Our Father 'which' "? "Which" is neuter gender. God is a Person, not a Thing. Why not say "Our Father 'who' ", as in the RV?

Secret Prayer

Jesus put considerable emphasis on Secret Prayer (Matthew 6:6). This does not rule out attendance upon, and participation in, public prayer. We should never be ashamed to pray, or to give our testimony to our faith in prayer, as occasion may demand. But we should be on guard lest our thought is what impression we are making on the people. Prayer is the expression of ourself to God. It is a matter between ourselves and God; not something to talk about. By far the larger part of our Prayer Life should be absolutely SECRET, so as to give ourselves no chance to fool ourselves on our motives. If, before and after every important act or decision, we will lift our heart to God, for guidance, or strength, or in thanksgiving, and never say anything about it to anybody, not even our most intimate friend, not even our husband or wife, but let it be strictly a matter between ourselves and God–if we will do this often, and keep it positively to ourselves, there is no other one habit that will do so much to give us joy in life and strength for every emergency–as thus to go through life hand in hand with an All-Powerful Friend whom we take into our confidence and consult about everything with which we have to do, even to the smallest detail.

Chapter 11:5–13. Persistence in Prayer. (See on Luke 18:1–8.)

Chapter 11:14–26. Casting out Demons. (See on Matthew 12:34–37.)

Chapter 11:27-28. The Word of God

A woman called out to Jesus, "Blessed is the mother that bore you." Jesus answered, "Rather blessed are they that hear the Word of God, and keep it."

In Jesus' day there was in the literature of his nation a group of writings, which we now call the Old Testament, which the people then commonly regarded as having come from God. Jesus shared that popular notion. He loved those writings. To him they were not just "Hebrew Thought," but the actual Word of God. Jesus himself had had a part in their writing. They were the main item in his education (see on Luke 2:40).

In Bethany, Mary sat at his feet listening to his Word. Jesus called it "the one good thing" (Luke 10:42).

There came one and said, "Your mother and brothers stand without, desiring to see you." Jesus answered, "My mother and my brothers are they that hear the Word of God, and do it" (Luke 8:19–21).

Again Jesus said, "The SEED of the kingdom is the Word of God" (Luke 8:11). A soul can be born into the kingdom of God only through the seed of the kingdom, the Word of God (I Peter 1:23).

"Man shall not live by bread alone, but by every word that proceeds out of the mouth of God" (Matthew 4:4).

"If a man believe not the Scriptures, neither will he believe though one rose from the dead" (Luke 16:31). "Heaven and earth shall pass away, but my Word shall not pass away" (Matthew 24:35).

Chapter 11:29–32. Signs. (See on Matthew 12:39–42.)
Chapter 11:33–36. The Lighted Lamp. (See on Matthew 5:13–16.)
Chapter 11:37–54. Pharisees Denounced. (See on Matthew 23.)

Chapter 12:1-12. The Secret Motives of Life

Jesus dealt a good deal with Motive, that is, the thing within ourselves that makes us do what we do, and guides our conduct. In his sight our Motive is ourself. Our one grand Motive should be the desire for God's approval and the fear of God's disapproval. The religious people of Jesus' day performed many of their religious practices for man's approbation (Matthew 6:1–18). It is still a part of our nature with which we have a constant struggle. When we are with irreligious people we are tempted to be ashamed of our religion; but when we are with religious people we desire to be considered religious, and this desire sometimes leads us to pretend to be more religious than we really are, and leads to hypocrisy. The desire for man's approbation, within proper bounds, is legitimate and laudable. But the one grand fact of existence is GOD. The one thing that really matters is our relation to HIM. Let us ever keep HIM in mind, and how our thoughts, motives and deeds stack up in HIS sight.

Many of the things in this chapter are contained in the Sermon on the Mount (Matthew 5, 6, 7). Jesus had favorite sayings which he uttered again and again. One of them was about God's unfailing Care and Guidance of His People (6–12).

Notice especially Jesus' warning of hell (5). He appealed repeatedly to the fear of hell as a motive of life. (See on Luke 16:19–31.)

Notice, too, his saying that one day every secret thing about our hypocritical selves shall be known (2–3). God's unerring phonographic plates are recording our every inner thought and secret act, to be played aloud one day before our startled selves, and the assembled universe, when we shall be recognized for what we really are, "Unpardonable sin" (10, see on Matthew 12:24–37).

Chapter 12:13-21. Parable of the Rich Fool

Notice that Jesus declined to enter into this man's family dispute. He did not attempt to run everybody else's business.

The rich fool had gotten his money honestly—through the productiveness of his land. Nevertheless in God's eyes he was a "fool" (20), because he had his heart on this world and not on the world to come. Rich in this world, a pauper in the other. This world lasts only a little while, the other world lasts Forever.

Chapter 12:22-34. Treasures in Heaven

This is a part of the Sermon on the Mount (Matthew 6:19–34), which Jesus repeated. Jesus was right at home when he was talking about heaven. His language here is superb. And the sentiments are among the most important he ever uttered.

Christians are citizens of heaven, sojourners here awhile, cumbered with daily earthly cares, but their eyes ever fixed on the eternal home-land. An estate there which we build while here. Only that which we give to God is ours forever. Said one man to another, of an acquaintance who had just died, "How much did he leave?" Answered the other, "He left it ALL." Even so. Shortly we must, every one of us, quit our earthly tent, and leave to others that which we called ours. Fortunate for us if we have sent on ahead for a Reservation in the Eternal Mansions of God.

Chapter 12:35-48. Watchfulness

Jesus' thoughts pass from heaven to the glorious day of his Second Coming, and warn that it might be to a sleeping world in the dead of night (38). Blessed are the faithful who are ready to welcome their returning Lord.

This parable (41–48) is meant for every Christian. But degrees in talent and position entail corresponding degrees in responsibility. Fearful is the warning here for faithless pastors.

Chapter 12:49-59. Spiritual Stupidity

Though Jesus came to bring Peace, he knew he would be the occasion of Strife. It reminded him of the world's hostility to himself, and how he wished it were over.

They were well versed in things that were of no great matter, but woefully stupid in their attitude toward him.

Chapter 13. Various Lessons

The two recent disasters, which had horrified the nation, reminded Jesus of the horrors of Judgment Day (1–5).

The Barren Fig Tree (6–9), was used by Jesus to illustrate the Patience of God with Jerusalem, whose day of doom was fast approaching, and with individuals generally.

The Woman Bowed Together (10–17). Jesus, moved with pity, did not wait for the woman to ask to be healed. He welcomed the opportunity to shame the Pharisees.

Mustard Seed and Leaven (18–21. See on Matthew 13:31–33).

"Are There Few Saved?" (22–30). Jesus, here, answered that many who expect to be saved are going to be sadly disappointed. But in Matthew 7:14 he answered the question plainly.

"Herod Would Fain Kill You" (31–35). Jesus evidently was in Perea, Herod's domain. He was safer there than in Judea. His answer: "You, not Herod, are my murderers. Jerusalem, not Perea, the place for it."

Chapter 14. Various Teachings

A Sabbath Healing (1–6). He had just healed a woman in the synagog on the Sabbath (13:10–17). This was in a Pharisee's home at a Sabbath feast. The Pharisees had no compunctions about feasting on the Sabbath. But to heal the sick was simply unforgivable. (See on Mark 3:1–6.)

Advice to Guests (7–11). Jesus insisted that self-seeking assertiveness defeats its own aim. The way of humility is better, and leads to real advancement. It is the "meek" that shall inherit the earth (Matthew 5:5). It is the lowly publican, and not the proud Pharisee, that pleases God (Luke 18:9–14). It is the humble who shall receive final exaltation (11). Jesus said that a number of times (Luke 18:14; Matthew 23:12).

Kindness to the Unfortunate (12–14). There is no virtue in entertaining those whom you expect to return the favor. Rather spend the effort on those who can do nothing for you, with your eye on the heavenly reward. How often Jesus advised us to keep our eyes on heaven. (See on Luke 10:25–37.)

Excuses (15–24). Jesus had no illusions as to the general reception of his Kingdom. He knew that many, from the religious leaders of his own nation, and the nation itself, to the distant Gentiles, would flout him and his offer of eternal redemption, giving the most trivial excuses, preferring for themselves the husks of the world.

Cost of Discipleship (25–35). These are stern words. Following Jesus was a far more serious business than the multitudes imagined. He knew that they were following him with slight conception of his kingdom. That is the reason he used such strong statements. Jesus did not mean that we should hate our parents or our children (26). Faithful devotion to those who are our own flesh and blood is one of the unfailing teachings of Scripture. But Jesus here means that if it is necessary to make a choice between Him and Them, there must not be the slightest hesitancy.

The Severity of Jesus. Jesus said some things that sound so hard and impossible that in themselves, apart from other sayings (see on His Tenderness, next page), they might discourage anyone from even trying to follow him. He came to bring us the priceless gift of Everlasting Life. But he will not force it on us. The prime condition on which it may be obtained is that we want it more than we want anything else, and that we LOVE HIM more than we love anything else. Jesus requires, and must have, the FIRST place in our hearts. If he has that, his mercy is infinite. But if we make him secondary to our every whim, and treat him as such, he will spew us out of his mouth.

Chapter 15. Lost Sheep. Lost Coin. Prodigal Son

This chapter, following the exacting words of the 14th, is like the calm after the storm. So different that one would scarcely attribute them to the same person. However, they are not contradictory, but only supplementary.

The starting point is that we give ourselves unreservedly to Him. There can be no divided loyalties. Once we enthrone him as the Lord of our life his compassion is boundless. We may stumble and stumble and stumble. But as long as we keep our face toward him he will forgive and forgive and forgive, till at last, by his grace and power, everything that is displeasing to him shall be banished from our lives.

This is illustrated by the three parables in this beautiful chapter: Joy over finding the Lost Sheep, Recovery of the Lost Coin, and Return of the Prodigal Son. It is a companion chapter to the story of the Sinful Woman of Luke 7:36–50 and of the Adulterous Woman of John 8:1–11.

It is a glorious picture of the Heavenly Father and his angels welcoming home returning souls. When we grow discouraged over our sinfulness this is a good chapter to read.

The Tenderness of Jesus

Jesus was not only the kindest man who ever lived. He was the tenderest. He loved to forgive. He himself was without sin. But how his heart ached in sympathy for those who were having a hard time with their sins.

One of the most beautiful pictures in all the Bible is that of Jesus and his tenderness toward the sinful woman weeping at his feet (Luke 7:36–50).

The fact that he was tender and forgiving toward that outcast wayward woman is a sort of guarantee that he will be tender and forgiving toward his Church.

Even if we have not sinned the way the woman had, we have sinned, And to God, sin is sin.

And it is, no doubt, just as hard, perhaps harder, for God to forgive our respectable, refined, polite, selfish, snobbish sins, as it is for Him to forgive the grosser sins of the poor souls that have lost in the battle of life.

It is no small consolation to know that the ONE before whom we ourselves shall stand to be judged is that kind of Person. He was merciful to that broken woman in the thing in which she needed his mercy. We may therefore feel that He will be merciful to us in the things in which we need his mercy.

Is this tenderness of Jesus toward the weak and wayward an encouragement to keep on sinning? No. It is the very thing that produces in us a determination to overcome.

And the closer our walk with Him, paradoxical as it may seem, the more we realize our sinfulness, and need of his mercy.

Chapter 16:1-13. The Unjust Steward

Jesus commends his foresight, not his dishonesty; his providing for his future, not his crooked method of doing it.

A. "measure" of oil was about 9 gallons. A "measure" of wheat was about 11 bushels.

As the steward made friends by the use of his master's goods, so, we should make friends by the use of our own means. It is a beautiful picture (9): those whom we have befriended will be at the door to welcome us home to heaven.

Jesus said hard things about money, or rather love of money. Covetousness is one of the most ruinous of sins, the cause of many crimes.

We have to have money to supply our daily needs. But the struggle is in our hearts, as to whom we really serve, and depend on, the money itself or Him who gives the money.

Chapter 16:14-18. The Pharisees Scoff

They ridiculed Jesus' teachings about money, because they were lovers of money, worldly-minded professional religionists.

It is difficult to see the connection in the verses about the Law and Divorce. Perhaps Jesus meant that since the Gospel was so profoundly influencing the people it was harder for Pharisees to justify their hypocritical teachings. While they professed to be guardians of the law, they ignored the teachings of the law about divorce, allowing it for any trivial cause.

Chapter 16:19-31. The Rich Man and Lazarus

"Abraham's bosom" (22), is Paradise, the intermediate state in which souls of the just await resurrection. "Hades" is the intermediate state of the lost, awaiting judgment.

Jesus here gives a conversation between Abraham and Lazarus after death. To what extent it is imaginary we do not know. But its implications are rather plain:

For one thing, angels are on hand at the death of saints to bear them away to glory.

For another, the lost are in torment (23).

And, there is an impassable gulf between Paradise and Hades, implying that death ends our opportunity for salvation.

And, the Scriptures are entirely sufficient to bring men to repentance (31).

And, the standards of this world are not to persist in heaven: Many of those who are first here will be last there. Those who occupy high places here may be in the lowest there. And many of those whom high church dignitaries here ignore may be their masters there (Matthew 19:30; 20:1–16; Mark 10:31).

Heaven and Hell

The story of the Rich Man and Lazarus is one of the many, many side-lights on the hereafter to be found in Jesus' teachings. He talked much about the future life. He appealed to the hope of heaven and the fear of hell. He spoke often of the unhappy fate of the lost as well as the blessedness of the redeemed, setting them over against each other. Run through these passages and see (Matthew 5:12, 22, 29, 30; 6:20; 7:21–27; 10:28; 13:39–43, 49–50; 18:8–9; 22:13, 23:33; 25:23, 30, 34, 41, 46; Mark 9:43–48; Luke 12:4–5; 16:22–28; John 3:15–16, 36; 5:24, 28–29, 39; 6:27, 39–40, 44, 47, 49, 50, 51, 54; 17:2). Note how often the words "heaven," "hell," "eternal life" occur.

It is a pity that the present day pulpit so generally deprecates the very motives that Jesus himself appealed to. One of the most powerful stimulants to good and deterrents from evil in this life is a profound conviction as to the reality of the future life, and that our estate there will depend on our behavior here. A heart firmly fixed in heaven will surely mean a more careful walk in this world. This one has an end. That one lasts forever.

Chapter 17:1-10. Forgiveness

Jesus here seems to imply that unwillingness to forgive is the cause of many losing their souls.

In Matthew 18:21–35 Peter asks Jesus how often must we forgive, and Jesus answered "seventy times seven."

Then the disciples cried out, "Lord, increase our faith." If we have to be that forgiving, we need more Faith.

Then, to help their faith, Jesus speaks of the Unlimited Power of Faith, and then by the parable of the obedient servant shows them that Humility is the groundwork of Faith.

Chapter 17:11-19. The Ten Lepers

This seems to be told, not only as one of Jesus' miracles, but to show that he gladly used his power to heal for those who would not even thank him for it, illustrating the kindly unresentful heart which he had just been talking about. Also, it shows up the Samaritan in a good light compared to those of Jesus' own race. Those nine Jewish lepers surely must have been hardened characters not even to thank Jesus.

Chapter 17:20-37. The Coming Kingdom

To the Pharisees Jesus said "The Kingdom of God is within you," a matter of the heart. Then his thoughts passed to the future, and he discoursed to the disciples about the glorious day when He would come in power with the redeemed of all ages. (See on Matthew 24.)

Chapter 18:1-8. The Importunate Widow

This, like the story of the Friend at Midnight in Luke 11:5–13, was told for the one specific purpose of teaching that God will honor Patient, Persistent, Persevering Prayer. In Matthew 6:7 Jesus warned of "vain repetitions," and added "Your Father knows what things you need before you ask Him." How reconcile this with the persistence of the widow and the importunity of the friend at midnight (Luke 11:8), which Jesus commended? Well, it is not always easy to reconcile two sides of any truth. Our own desires must be tempered by the calm submission to the Will of God. Yet God does want us to present our desires to Him, without allowing ourselves to become discouraged if there is delay in the answers. To learn how to pray successfully is a matter of life-time study and severe self-discipline. For one thing, we must learn how to Forgive (Mark 11:25). And in Matthew 7:12 prayer is directly connected with the practice of the "golden rule." The one prime requirement, however, is FAITH. Assuming that we ourselves do all in our power to answer our own prayers, God's promises for those who have FAITH are simply amazing. Note below the emphasis on Faith in the statements of Jesus.

The Power of Faith

Jesus prayed a great deal, (see on Luke 11:1). And he talked a great deal about Prayer. Here are some of the things he said about FAITH as a part of the act of prayer:

In Nazareth, "He did not many mighty works because of their Unbelief" (Matthew 13:58).

To the disciples, in the storm, "Why are you afraid? Where is your Faith?" (Mark 4:40; Luke 8:25).

To Jairus, "Only Believe, and she shall live" (Luke 8:50).

To the woman with a blood issue, "Your Faith has made you whole" (Mark 5:34).

Centurion to Jesus, "Only say the word, and my servant shall be healed." Jesus, "I have not found so great Faith, even in Israel." And the servant was healed. (Matthew 8:8, 10, 13.)

To the blind men, "Do you believe that I am able to do this? Be it unto you according to your Faith" (Matthew 9:28, 29).

To the disciples, "If you have Faith, and doubt not, you shall do what is done to this fig tree" (Matthew 21:21).

To the Syro-phoenician woman, "O woman, great is your Faith. Be it unto you even as you desire" (Matthew 15:28).

To Peter, sinking in the water, "O you of little Faith, why did you doubt?" (Matthew 14:31).

To the disciples, "O Faithless generation, how long shall I bear with you?" (Mark 9:19).

The disciples to Jesus, "Why could not we cast it out?" Jesus, "Because of your little Faith" (Matthew 17:19, 20).

To the disciples, "If you have Faith, even as a grain of mustard seed, and doubt not in your heart, but believe that it shall come to pass, you shall say to this mountain, Remove from hence to yonder, it shall be done; and nothing shall be impossible unto you. All things, whatsoever you shall ask in prayer, Believing, you shall receive. All things are possible to him that Believes" (Matthew 17:20; 21:22; Mark 9:23; 11:22–25).

To Martha, at the grave of Lazarus, "If you Believe, you shall see the glory of God" (John 11:40).

To the multitudes at Capernaum, "This is the work of God, that you BELIEVE on him whom He has sent" (John 6:29).

Some of these statements seem like oriental hyperbole. Nevertheless the emphasis that Jesus put on FAITH is just simply astounding. We are not sure that it can be explained away by calling it "hyperbole." Nor by interpreting these strange, strong words to mean only that

Jesus was conferring upon the Apostles special miraculous powers as a divine attestation to their mission in founding the Church. We know that Jesus did give the Apostles power to work miracles that it would be foolish for us to claim. We know also that the Apostles could not use those powers at will. Sometimes they could work miracles. Sometimes they could not. In Ephesus multitudes were healed by handkerchiefs that had touched Paul's body (Acts 19:12). Yet at another time Paul could not heal even his own beloved co-worker, and wrote, "Trophimus I left at Miletus sick" (II Timothy 4:20). So it seems that God used his own judgment as to when to let the Apostles work miracles.

When Jesus talked about Prayer and Faith, strange as some of his words may sound to us, he knew what he was talking about. He came out of the unseen world, and he was perfectly familiar with forces and powers that play behind the veil that we know nothing about. We ought not to be too determined to explain everything that Jesus said about Prayer so as to bring it within range of our finite understanding. It might be, if only we would apply ourselves with enough Patience and Persistence and Perseverance to the practice of Prayer, that we could reach attainments that we do not ordinarily dream are possible.

Jesus certainly meant something by these words. He did not talk just to hear himself talk. We think he was aiming to teach some of the most fundamental lessons of human existence for all mankind of all generations. God holds in His hands the workings and inter-workings of the forces of the universe, and is able to bring into play powers that we know nothing about to supplement and control those that we do know about. Jesus said that God may be induced to do this through our FAITH in HIM.

Chapter 18:9-14. The Pharisee and the Publican

Pharisees were so generally self-righteous and hypocritical in their haughty attitude toward their fellow-men that the word has almost become a synonym for "sham." They bore that same self-complacency in their attitude toward God, as if they thought that God would feel honored to have their homage. Jesus, in his soul, loathed religious pretense. The bitterest words he ever uttered were against the hypocrisy of the Pharisees (Matthew 23). He did not condone the sins of publicans and harlots. He came to save them. Being acknowledged sinners, it was easier for them to take the first step and confess it. This parable is aimed to show that the fundamental basis of approach to God is a realization of our sinfulness and the need of His mercy.

Chapter 18:15-17. Little Children

This incident is related also in Matthew 19:13 and Mark 10:13–16.

Jesus had just spoken of the publican being on his way to salvation because he was depressed with his sinfulness. Here he indicates that heaven will be exclusively occupied by child-like people. No pompous fellows in heaven, strutting around as if they owned the universe. There are plenty of them in the Church here. But not so up there. Jesus said flatly, "Except you become as little children, you shall in no wise enter into the kingdom of heaven" (Matthew 18:3). A little child is teachable, trustful, free from mental pride, unsophisticated and loving. Jesus loved children. The disciples did not think children were important enough to bother with. That made Jesus "indignant" (Mark 10:13–14).

Chapter 18:18-30. The Rich Young Ruler

Also told in Matthew 19:16–30; Mark 10:17–31. Jesus told him to give all. Jesus did not mean that everybody should give up all their money to follow him. Zachaeus offered to give half, and Jesus bestowed upon him salvation (Luke 19:9).

But this young ruler was too much in love with his riches to be of any use in the kingdom of Christ.

A "needle's eye" (25), is thought by some to be the small gate for foot passengers situated in or by the large city gate, through which a camel, by kneeling and with great difficulty, could pass. More generally it is thought to be an actual needle. At any rate, Jesus meant an "impossible" thing (27). Then modified it by saying that the impossible for men is possible for God.

Note the wonderful promise to those who give up all to follow Jesus (28–30). It is amplified in Mark 10:28–31. A hundredfold in this life, and in the world to come, Life Eternal.

Social Standing of the Disciples

They were mostly from the humbler classes. But some of them were wealthy and influential. Peter, James, John and Andrew were well-to-do business men. Matthew, being a tax renter or collector, probably was financially well-to-do. Among the women who went about with Jesus was Joanna the wife of Herod's steward, a woman from the palace of the king. Martha, Mary and Lazarus were among the wealthy families around Jerusalem (see on John 12:1–8). Joseph of Arimathea, and Nicodemus, were members of the Sanhedrin. The Nobleman of Capernaum (John 4:46), was probably an officer of Herod's court. The Centurion of Capernaum, who built their synagog (Luke 7:1–10), was an officer of the Roman army. Zacchaeus the publican was a rich man (Luke 19:2).

Chapter 18:31-43. A Blind Man at Jericho

Told also in Matthew 20:29–34 and Mark 10:46–52. Matthew says there were two blind men. Mark and Luke mention only one. Luke says Jesus was entering Jericho. Matthew and Mark say it was as he went out. Mark calls him Bartimaeus. Possibly one was healed as Jesus entered the city, and the other as he left. Probably, as Jesus entered, they followed along, and after Jesus was through at the house of Zacchaeus, placed themselves by the road where they knew he would pass. Just before he healed the blind man, Jesus had told his disciples, for the fifth time, that he was on his way to Crucifixion (31–34). But they did not understand (34).

Chapter 19:1-10. Zacchaeus

Zacchaeus was a chief publican, head of a large office of tax collectors. Publicans were classed with harlots (7, Matthew 21:31–32). They were hated generally, because the taxes were for a foreign power. Jericho was a city of priests. Jesus chose a publican rather than a priest to abide with. Zacchaeus was converted immediately, and gave genuine evidence of it. Jesus had told the rich young ruler to give "all" (Luke 18:22). Zacchaeus gave "half" (8), and Jesus pronounced him an heir of salvation.

Chapter 19:11-28. Parable of the Pounds

This differs in some points from the Parable of the Talents (Matthew 25:14–30), but it illustrates the same general truths: that we are accountable to the Lord for the way we use our means and time; that there will be rewards and punishments when Jesus comes; that we are in training here for life there. It is a parable of the Second Advent. "A far country" (12), in this parable, and "after a long time" in the parable of the Talents (Matthew 25:19), hint a long interval between his First and Second Coming. The "wise" virgins prepared for it. (See further under II Thessalonians and II Peter 3.)

Chapter 19:29 to chapter 24. Jesus' Last Week

Chapter 19:29–44.	The Triumphal Entry. (See on Matthew 21:1–11.)
Chapter 19:45–48.	The Temple Cleansed. (See on Matthew 21:12–17.)
Chapter 20:1–8.	"By What Authority?" (See on Matthew 21:23–27.)
Chapter 20:9–20.	Parable of Vineyard. (See on Matthew 21:33–46.)
Chapter 20:21–26.	Tribute to Caesar. (See on Mark 12:13–17.)
Chapter 20:27–40.	"The Resurrection." (See on Mark 12:18–27.)
Chapter 20:41–44.	"David's Son." (See on Mark 12:35–37.)
Chapter 20:45–47.	Scribes Denounced. (See on Matthew 23.)

Chapter 21:1–4. The Widow's Mites. (See on Mark 12:41–44.)
Chapter 21:5–36. Discourse on the End. (See on Matthew 24.)
Chapter 21:37–22:2. Plot to Kill Jesus. (See on Mark 14:1–2.)
Chapter 22:3–6. Bargain of Judas. (See on Mark 14:10–11.)
Chapter 22:7–38. The Last Supper. (See on Matthew 26:17–29.)

Chronological Outline of Jesus' Last Week

Saturday:	Arrives at Bethany (John 12:1).
	Evening: the Supper.
Sunday:	The Triumphal Entry. Weeps over Jerusalem.
Monday:	Withers the Fig Tree. Cleanses the Temple.
Tuesday:	His Last Day in the Temple.
	His "Authority" challenged by the Sanhedrin.
	Parable of the Two Sons.
	Parable of the Vineyard.
	Parable of the Marriage Feast.
	Question about Tribute to Caesar.
	Question about the Resurrection.
	Which is the Great Commandment?
	How could David's Son be his Lord?
	Certain Greeks Desire to See Jesus (or Monday?).
	Fearful Denunciation of Scribes and Pharisees.
	Jesus Observes the Widow's Mites.
	Final Departure from the Temple.
	On the Mount of Olives: His Great Discourse:
	Destruction of Jerusalem and His Coming.
	Parable of the Ten Virgins, and of the Talents.
	Final Judgment Scene.
	Judas' Bargain with the Priests? (or next day?).
Wednesday:	Day of Quiet at Bethany.
Thursday:	Evening: the Last Supper. (See note under Matthew 26.)
	Night: the Agony in Gethsemane.
Friday:	Trial and Crucifixion. (See under Mark 15 and Luke 23.)
Sunday:	Jesus Rises from the Dead. (See under John 20 and 21.)

Chapter 22:39-46. The Agony in Gethsemane

(Told also in Matthew 26:36–46; Mark 14:32–42; John 18:1.) Gethsemane was a garden near the foot of the western slope of the Mount of Olives. The traditional site (see Map page 547) cannot be far from the actual site.

The human race started in a garden. Jesus suffered his agony in a garden. He was crucified in a garden, and buried in a garden (John 19:41). Paradise will be a garden.

The most pitiful incident in the whole sorrowful story of Jesus' suffering was that night in Gethsemane.

We wonder why he dreaded his death. We read of martyrs being burned at the stake with songs of joy on their lips. But Jesus, whom we think of as stronger than ordinary men, when he was brought face to face with his death, acted as if he just could not go through with it, and cried out in anguish that, if possible, it might not be.

We wonder why. It must be that Jesus knew that he was going to suffer something that men do not ordinarily suffer in death, or at least that they do not know beforehand that they are to suffer.

Jesus died for the sins of the world. Whatever theory of the atonement we may hold, Jesus, in some sense or other, died to save us from being lost. He must, therefore, have suffered something of what we will suffer if we are lost. Else how could his death save us from being lost?

Jesus had come out of eternity knowing that the Cross was at the end of the road, for he knew that he was coming as the Lamb of God to take away the sin of the world. As a man, he left Galilee, and set his face steadfastly to go to Jerusalem, walking with steady tread, never wavering, never faltering, knowing that the Cross was at the end of the road.

But now he had come to the end of the road, and there stood that ghastly thing. It made even Jesus the Son of God temporarily entertain the thought of turning back. The language of his three prayers shows that the "possibility" of not going to the cross was in his mind.

Then, as the two or three or four hours of wavering passed, and he put out of his mind all thought of escape, and set his face like steel to go to it, what it meant to him made him sweat drops of blood, and so weak that God sent an angel to strengthen him.

We can never in this world understand the awful mystery of the atonement—why it had to be. Only this—it was to save us. The simple story of Jesus' suffering, whatever else it may mean, has been the most blessed influence that has ever been in the world.

Chapter 22:47–53 Jesus is Arrested. (See on John 18:1–12.)
Chapter 22:54–62 Peter's Denial. (See on John 18:15–18.)
Chapter 22:54—23:25 Trial of Jesus. (See on Mark 14:53.)
Chapter 23:26 Simon of Cyrene. (See on Matthew 27:32.)

Chapter 23:27-31. The Weeping Multitude

On the way to Calvary. "Weep not for me, but for yourselves and your children" (28), seems to be an echo of the murderous words they had just heard, "his blood be on us and on our children" (Matthew 27:25). And, Oh, how His Blood has been on them through all these centuries!

Chapter 23:32–49. The Crucifixion. (See also on Matthew 27:26–56; Mark 15:21–41; and John 19:17–37.)

Chapter 23:32-43. The Penitent Robber

Both robbers at first joined in the mockery (Matthew 27:44). But one changed his mind. And, in one respect, he put the disciples to shame. For two years or more Jesus had tried so hard to teach them that his kingdom was not to be a kingdom of this world. Now he was dying. To them that was the end of his kingdom. No thought that he would come to life again to reign in glory (see page 554). But to the robber not so. Perhaps, from the outskirts of a crowd, he had heard Jesus talk of his kingdom. And, though Jesus was now dying, the robber still believed that he had a kingdom beyond the grave (42). Amazing! A robber understood Jesus better than Jesus' own intimate friends. Blessed Jesus! He surely loved sinners. As he returned to God, he bore in his arms the soul of a robber, first-fruits of his mission to redeem a world.

Crucifixion

Crucifixion was Rome's punishment for slaves, foreigners, and criminals who were not Roman citizens. It was the most agonizing and ignominious death a cruel age could devise. Nails were driven through the hands and feet, and the victim was left hanging there in agony, starvation, insufferable thirst and excruciating convulsions of pain. Death usually followed in four to six days. In Jesus' case it was over in six hours. (See under John 19:33–34.)

The "True Cross"

There is a tradition that the actual cross on which Jesus was crucified was found, A.D. 325, under the site of the present Church of the Holy Sepulchre, identified by a miracle of healing on one who touched it. Tiny fragments were sold. There was such demand for it that there was invented the miracle of the "multiplication of the cross," so that pieces could be removed, and yet leave the cross intact.

Chapter 23:50–56. Burial. (See on John 19:38–42.)

Outline Story of the Crucifixion

Arranged in order from the four accounts

9 A.M. they arrive at Golgotha. As they are about to drive the

nails in his hands and feet, they offer him wine mixed with gall, to stupefy him, and deaden the sense of pain. But he refused it.

"Father, forgive them: they know not what they do," as they nailed him to the cross. It is hard for us to control our anger for his murderers even as we read about it. But he was absolutely without resentment. Amazing self-control!

His garments are parted among the soldiers. The superscription, "King of the Jews," is placed above his head, in three languages, Hebrew, Latin and Greek, so that all might read and understand what crime he was accused of.

He is mocked, scoffed at, railed on, jeered, by the chief priests, elders, scribes and soldiers. What a hard-hearted, inhuman, brutal, contemptible crowd it was!

"Today thou shalt be with me in Paradise," to the penitent robber, possibly after an hour or two. (See on Luke 23:32–43.)

"Woman, behold thy son." To John, "Behold thy mother." Probably as it drew on toward noon, after the jeering mob had gone. What a glorious death! Prayed for his murderers; promised Paradise to the robber; and provided a home for his mother, which was his last earthly act.

The Darkness, from noon till 3. His first three hours on the cross marked by words of mercy and kindness. Now he enters the final stage of expiation for human sin. Perhaps the darkness symbolizes God's withdrawal, so that it might be an act of complete atonement. What Jesus suffered in that last awful three hours we can never know in this world. (See on John 19:33–34.)

His last four utterances came just as he was expiring.

"My God, my God, why hast thou forsaken me?" Alone, in the pains of hell, to keep us from going there.

"I thirst." Burning fever and excruciating thirst were the accompaniments of crucifixion. It may have meant more (see Luke 16:24). They offered him vinegar. His sufferings over, he took it.

"It is finished." A cry of triumphant relief and joy. The long reign of human sin and death is broken.

"Father, into thy hands I commend my spirit." To Paradise.

The Earthquake, veil rent, tombs opened. God's salute.

The centurion believes. The multitudes grief-stricken.

"Blood and water" from his side. (See on John 19:34.)

Joseph and Nicodemus ask for his body, for burial.

Night settles on the blackest, foulest crime in history.

Chapter 24:1–10 The Women at the Tomb. (See on Matthew 28:1–8.)

Chapter 24:11–12 Peter Runs to Tomb. (See on John 20:3–10.)

Chapter 24:13-32. Jesus Appears to the Two

This is mentioned also in Mark 16:12–13. This was on the way to Emmaus. Emmaus is thought to have been on the road to Joppa, about 7 miles northwest of Jerusalem. It may have been the home of these two disciples. The two disciples were Cleopas and an unnamed companion.

It was in the afternoon. Jesus had in the early morning already appeared to Mary Magdalene (Mark 16:9–11; John 20:11–18); and also to the other women (Matthew 28:9–10). But these two disciples had only heard the report that the tomb was empty, and that angels had announced that Jesus was risen (22–24).

Chapter 24:33-35. Jesus Appears to Peter

The time is not stated. It was probably just before or just after he had appeared to the Two, in the afternoon. In the early morning he had sent a special message by the angels and the women to Peter (Mark 16:7. See note there).

Chapter 24:36-43. Jesus Appears to the Eleven

See also on Mark 16:14–18 and John 20:19–23. "The Eleven" (33), was the name of the group as a group. In this instance it was only ten, for Thomas was absent (John 20:24). Note their joyous belief (34), and yet their "disbelief" (41), even after he had showed them his hands and feet. Faith and Doubt alternating.

A week later, he appears to the Eleven, in Jerusalem (John 20:26–29).

Afterward, to Seven, by the Sea of Galilee (John 21).

Again, to the Eleven, in a Mountain in Galilee (Matthew 28:16–20).

And, to James, time and place unknown (I Corinthians 15:7).

Chapter 24:44-53. Final Appearance and Ascension

This is told also in Mark 16:19 and in Acts 1:3–12. Verses 44–49 seem to belong to his final appearance rather than to the appearance just mentioned in verses 36–43; for that evidently was on the first Sunday evening, and in this he tells them to "tarry at Jerusalem" (49), which must have been after they had gone to Galilee and returned to Jerusalem. Then he led them out of Jerusalem to his beloved Bethany. His forty days of post-resurrection ministry finished, his earthly mission accomplished, waiting Angel Chariots bore the Triumphant Saviour away to the throne of God.

The Four Resurrection Accounts Compared

Matthew	The Women Visit the Tomb
	Jesus Appears to the Women
	The Guards Bribed
	Jesus Appears to the Eleven, in Galilee
Mark	The Women Visit the Tomb
	Jesus Appears to Mary Magdalene
	To the Two, on the way to Emmaus
	To the Eleven, in Jerusalem, first evening
	The Ascension
Luke	The Women Visit the Tomb
	Peter Runs to the Tomb
	Jesus Appears to the Two; and to Peter
	To the Eleven, in Jerusalem, first evening
	Final Appearance, 40 days later
	The Ascension
John	Mary Magdalene Visits the Tomb
	Peter and John Run to the Tomb
	Jesus Appears to Mary Magdalene
	To the Eleven, first evening, Thomas absent
	To the Eleven, a week later, Thomas present
	To the Seven, beside the Sea of Galilee

Jesus' Appearances After His Resurrection

1. To Mary Magdalene (Mark 16:9–10), early morning
2. To the Other Women (Matthew 28:9–10), early morning
3. To Two, on way to Emmaus (Mark 16:12–13; Luke 24:13–32)
4. To Peter (Luke 24:34), sometime that day
5. To the Eleven (Mark 16:14, Luke 24:36–; John 20:19–), that night
6. To the Eleven (John 20:26–31), a week later, Thomas present
7. To the Seven, beside the Sea of Galilee (John 21)
8. To Eleven (and 500?), in Galilee (Matthew 28:16–20)
9. To James (I Corinthians 15:7). Time and place unknown
10. Final Appearance, Ascension (Mark 16:19; Luke 24:44–; Acts 1:3–)

Later, Jesus made a special appearance to Paul.

In I Corinthians 15:5–8, 27 years after the Resurrection, Paul lists the appearance thus: "He appeared to Cephas, then to the twelve, then to above 500 brethren at once, then to James, then to all the apostles, last of all to me."

The statement in Acts 1:3, "showed himself alive by many proofs by the space of 40 days, speaking things concerning the kingdom of God," along with similar statements in Acts 10:41 and 13:31, implies the possibility that he may have made many appearances beside those recorded, and that his post-resurrection ministry may have been more extensive than we know.

JOHN

Jesus the Son of God

The special emphasis of John is the Deity of Jesus. Consists chiefly of Jesus' Discourses and Conversations. Gives things Jesus Said rather than things He Did. Schaff calls this Gospel the "Most Important literary production ever composed."

Author

The Author does not identify himself till he comes to the end of the book (21:20, 24), where he states that he is the "disciple whom Jesus loved" (13:23; 20:2), that is, John the Apostle, most intimate earthly friend of Jesus.

Ancient tradition and unbroken subsequent opinion have recognized his authorship, till the rise of modern criticism. The same class of critics who deny the Virgin Birth of Jesus, His Deity, and His Bodily Resurrection, basing their hypothesis on an ancient vague mention of a certain John the Presbyter of Ephesus, have inferred that the author was not John the Apostle, but another John of Ephesus. This would undermine the value of the book as a testimony to the Deity of Jesus. The theory is based on such flimsy evidence and such obvious desire to discredit the book that it is not even entitled to serious consideration by Christian believers, and is mentioned here only because it is one of the pet propaganda of a certain school of present-day "scholarship."

John

His father's name was Zebedee (Matthew 4:21). His mother seems to have been Salome (Matthew 27:56; Mark 15:40), who, by comparing John 19:25, seems to have been a sister of Mary the mother of Jesus. If so, John was a cousin of Jesus, and, being about the same age, must have known Him from childhood.

John was a business man of some means. He was one of five partners in a fishing business that employed "hired servants" (Mark 1:16–20). Besides his fishing business in Capernaum, he had a house in Jerusalem (John 19:27), and was a personal acquaintance of the high-priest (John 18:15,16).

He was a disciple of John the Baptist (John 1:35, 40). If he was a cousin of Jesus, as seems implied in passages above cited, then he was kin to John the Baptist (Luke 1:36), and must have known of the Angelic announcements about John and Jesus (Luke 1:17, 32). So when John the Baptist appeared, crying that the Kingdom of Heaven was at hand, John the son of Zebedee was ready to take his stand with him.

On the Baptist's testimony he became an immediate disciple of Jesus (John 1:35–51), one of the first five disciples, and returned with Jesus to Galilee (John 2:2, 11). Then, it seems, he went back to his fishing business. Later, probably about a year, Jesus called him to leave his business, and go about with Him. He was thenceforth with Jesus continually, and thus was an eyewitness of what is written in his Gospel.

Jesus nicknamed him "Son of Thunder" (Mark 3:17), which seems to imply that he had a vehement, violent temper. But this he brought under control. The incident of forbidding the stranger to use the name of Christ in casting out demons (Mark 9:38), and the desire to call down fire on the Samaritans (Luke 9:54), are interesting side-lights on his nature.

He was one of the three inner circle disciples. And was recognized as the one closest to Jesus. Five times he is spoken of as the disciple "Whom Jesus Loved" (John 13:23; 19:26; 20:2; 21:7, 20). He must have been a man of rare qualities of character to thus attract the Companionship of Jesus.

He and Peter became the recognized leaders of the Twelve, and, though utterly different in disposition, were generally together (John 20:2; Acts 3:1, 11; 4:13; 8:14).

For a number of years Jerusalem seems to have been his chief residence. According to well-established tradition, his later years were spent at Ephesus. Nothing is known of his activities or whereabouts in the interim. At Ephesus he lived to great age, and wrote his Gospel, three Epistles and Revelation.

The Date of his Gospel is usually assigned to about A.D. 90. Some think that John originally wrote this Gospel much earlier, while he was still in Jerusalem, soon after the Resurrection, in Hebrew, and in later years, issued, in Greek, the Ephesian edition, which was the parent of all extant manuscripts.

Chapter 1:1-3. Eternity and Deity of Jesus

Reminds us of the opening words of Genesis. Jesus is called GOD and CREATOR. John is very positive that Jesus was a Personality existing from Eternity, and that He had a hand in the Creation of the Universe. In John 17:5 Jesus is quoted as referring to the "Glory He had with the Father before the World Was." Jesus is here called THE WORD. That is, Jesus was God's Expression of Himself to Mankind. Jesus was God. Jesus was Like God. Jesus is God's Message to Mankind.

Chapter 1:4-13. Jesus the Light of the World

Jesus said this again and again (8:12; 9:5; 12:46). It is one of the keynotes in John's Thought about Jesus (I John 1:5–7). It means that Jesus, as Light of the World, is the One who makes clear the Meaning and Destiny of Human Existence.

Chapter 1:14-18. The Incarnation

God became a Man in order to win man to himself. God could have made man with an instinct to do His will; but he chose rather to give man the power to decide for himself his attitude toward his Creator. But God is a spirit; and man is hedged in by the limitations of a material body, and has scant conception of what a Spirit is. So, the Creator came to his creatures in the form of one of them to give them an idea of the kind of being He is. God is like Jesus. Jesus is like God.

"Son of Man"

This was Jesus' favorite name for himself. It occurs about 70 times in the Gospels: Matthew, 30 times, Mark, 5, Luke, 25, John, 10.

It was used in Daniel 7:13, 14, 27 as a name of the Coming Messiah. Jesus' adoption of it is thought to have been equivalent to a claim of Messiahship.

Also, it suggests that Jesus rejoiced in his experience as God in human form, sharing the life of mankind. He carried the title with him to heaven (Acts 7:56; Revelation 1:13; 14:14).

Ezekiel was thus addressed about 90 times (Ezekiel 2:1, 3, 6, 8 etc), implying the lowliness of man compared to God.

Jesus' World

Although a citizen of the universe, familiar with the infinite depths of stellar space, yet his earthly life was spent in a very limited circle, howbeit a strategically important circle. Palestine was the junction of three continents, lying between the Mediterranean Sea and the Great Arabian Desert, meeting place of the world's highways. In Jesus' day, it consisted of four divisions, all under the control of Rome:

Judea, the south part, stronghold of Jewish conservatism.
Galilee, the north part, with large admixture of Greek population.
Samaria, in between, a hybrid race, partly of Jewish blood.
Perea, east of lower Jordan, with many prosperous Roman cities.
Herod ruled Galilee and Perea. Pilate ruled Judea and Samaria.

Alexandria, second city of the Roman Empire, was 300 miles to the southwest. Antioch, third city of the Roman Empire, was 300 miles to the north. Along the Palestinian coast, and through Galilee, passed

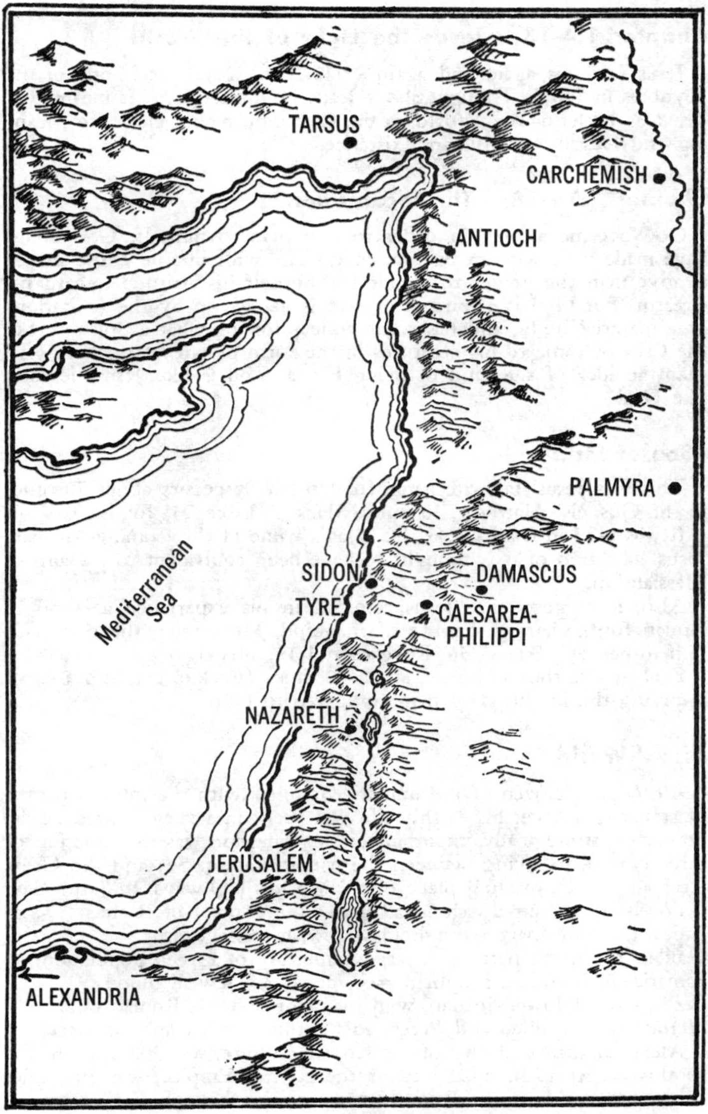
TARSUS
CARCHEMISH
ANTIOCH
PALMYRA
Mediterranean Sea
SIDON
DAMASCUS
TYRE
CAESAREA-PHILIPPI
NAZARETH
JERUSALEM
ALEXANDRIA

Map 58.

the commerce and armies of the world. Aside from his childhood flight to Egypt, there is no record of his going more than 70 miles away from Nazareth. Jerusalem on the south, Sidon on the north, Decapolis and Perea on the east, were the limits of his known travels.

Galilee. Its population was estimated by Josephus at 3,000,000. It was covered with rich Greek cities. It was a center of world culture. Its Roman capital, and royal residence of Herod, was Sepphoris, only 4 miles from Nazareth.

Chapter 1:19-34. John's Testimony

After brief statements about the Deity of Jesus, his Pre-Existence and Incarnation, John's Gospel, passing over Jesus' Birth, Childhood, Baptism and Temptation, starts with this testimony of John the Baptist before the Committee from the Sanhedrin as to the Deity of Jesus.

This was at the close of the Forty Days' Temptation. It is nowhere stated that Jesus returned from the Wilderness Temptation to the Jordan where John was baptizing. The three Synoptics pass directly from the Temptation to the Galilean Ministry (Matthew 4:11–12; Mark 1:13–14; Luke 4:13–14). But the three successive "morrow's" (29, 35, 43), followed by the "third day" (2:1), for his arrival in Galilee, make it evident that Jesus went back from the wilderness to the place where John was preaching before departing for Galilee.

"The Prophet" (21), a prophetic name of the Messiah, and so generally understood by the people in Jesus' day (John 6:14).

Note John's profound humility in his devotion to Christ (27)—not worthy even to untie his shoe latch. This is so noteworthy that it is recorded in all four Gospels (Matthew 3:11; Mark 1:7; Luke 3:16). What a boon to the world if all preachers could exhibit the same humble adoration of the Lord whom they preach!

Chapter 1:35-51. First Disciples

There were five of them: John, Andrew, Simon, Philip and Nathanael. They had been prepared by the preaching of John the Baptist, and all five later became Apostles. This was one of the contributions of the Baptist's ministry to the work of Christ. Temporarily, however, they went back to their regular occupations. About a year later they were called to follow Christ continuously. (See note under Matthew 10.)

John the Apostle is assumed to be the unnamed disciple (40). If he was a cousin of Jesus (see introductory note to this Gospel), then he must already have known Jesus before this.

The "tenth hour" (39), was 10 A.M. John uses Roman time, like ours, counted from midnight or noon (4:6; 19:14).

Simon, being a business partner of John, may already have known

Jesus personally, but not that he was the Messiah till now at John the Baptist's public proclamation. The fact that Jesus gave Simon a new name at this, their first recorded meeting, seems to indicate that Jesus already had him in mind for the Apostleship.

Nathanael was converted by the majesty of Jesus' person (46–49). Jesus' statement about angels (51), marks HIM as the connecting highway between earth and heaven (Genesis 28:12).

Personal Appearance of Jesus

There was something in Jesus' bearing that had an instant effect on Nathanael (1:49). No hint of Jesus' personal appearance is given in the New Testament. The earliest legendary description dates from the 4th century. It is an apocryphal letter ascribed to Publius Lentulus, a friend of Pilate, written to the Roman Senate. It is not authentic. In part it is as follows:

"In this time appeared a man endowed with great powers. His name is Jesus. His disciples call him the Son of God. He is of noble and well-proportioned stature, with a face full of kindness, and yet firmness, so that beholders both love him and fear him. His hair is the color of wine, straight and without lustre, but from the level of the ears curling and glossy. His forehead is even and smooth, his face without blemish, and enhanced by a tempered bloom, his countenance ingenuous and kind. Nose and mouth are in no way faulty. His beard is full, of the same color as his hair; his eyes blue and extremely brilliant. In reproof and rebuke he is formidable; in exhortation and teaching, gentle and amiable of tongue. None have seen him to laugh, but many, on the contrary, to weep. His person is tall, his hands beautiful and straight. In speaking, deliberate, grave, little given to loquacity; in beauty surpassing most men."

There are other traditions. One, that he was erect and handsome. Another, that he was stoop-shouldered and ugly. Whatever his personal appearance, there must have been something about his countenance and bearing that was Majestic, Commanding, Divine. The fore-gleam in the 53rd chapter of Isaiah hints an unattractive appearance, but it probably refers to his lowly manner of life for one who was to be a King, rather than his personal appearance.

Being a carpenter, he must have had considerable physical strength. Speaking so effectively to vast multitudes in the open air, we imagine he must have had a powerful voice. From his discourses, conversations and teachings, we think of him as being always under control, never in a hurry, in perfect poise, slow and majestic in all his movements. There are hints that he had a sense of humor.

Periods in Jesus' Life

There are certain periods in Jesus' life into which may be grouped all that is told of him:

His Birth and Childhood

His Baptism, Temptation, and Beginning of Public Work

His Early Judean Ministry, 8 months

His Galilean Ministry, about 2 years?

His Perean and Later Judean Ministry, about 4 months?

His last Week

His Post-Resurrection Ministry

Chapter 2:1-11. Water Made Wine

Cana was about 4 miles northeast of Nazareth. Nathanael was of Cana (21:2). He did not have a very high opinion of his neighbor town Nazareth (1:46). The marriage, evidently, was in the home of some friend or relative of either Jesus or Nathanael.

"Woman" (4), was a title of respect in the usage of that day. Jesus used it again, on the cross, at a time when there could have been no possible savor of disrespect (19:26). The point of his remark seems to be: "Suppose the wine is gone, what have I to do with it? It is not my affair. My time to work miracles has not yet come." Probably he had just told her of the new miraculous powers bestowed upon him by the descent of the Holy Spirit at baptism. See note on his Temptation, Matthew 4:1–10. She saw in the situation an opportunity for him. While he did this miracle at her suggestion, his "hour" (4), for the general use of his miraculous powers came about four months later, at the official beginning of his public ministry in Jerusalem at Passover time (13).

"Two or three firkins" (6). A firkin was about 8 gallons. The stone jars were about the size of half a barrel.

Significance of this miracle: Jesus had just submitted himself, for forty days, to every suggestion Satan was capable of offering, as to how he should use his miraculous powers, and had steadfastly refused to use them for his own personal need. Then from the wilderness directly to the wedding. And though his subsequent miracles were wrought largely to relieve suffering, this first miracle was done at a wedding feast, on a festive occasion, ministering to human joy, making people happy, as if Jesus wanted to announce, right at the start, that the religion which he was now introducing into the world was no religion of asceticism, but a religion of natural joy. It was Jesus' blessing on marriage.

"Beginning of miracles" (11). This was Jesus' first miracle. The fabulous and silly tales, in the Apocryphal writings, about his childhood miracles are sheer fabrications.

"Manifested his glory" (11), as Creator (1:3, 14). The miracle involved a speeding up process which required actual creative power. (See note on Jesus' Miracles, Mark 5:21–43.)

Chapter 2:12. Brief Sojourn in Capernaum

This was a sort of family visit, including his mother and brothers, probably to the home of John or Peter to lay plans for his future work. About a year later Capernaum became his main residence. He did no more miracles in Galilee till after his return from the Judean Ministry (4:54).

The Early Judean Ministry, 2:13 to 4:3

This is told only in John's Gospel. It lasted 8 months, beginning at Passover time (2:13), April, and ending "four months" before harvest (4:3, 35), December. It includes Cleansing of Temple, Visit of Nicodemus, and Ministry by the Jordan.

Chapter 2:13-25. Jesus Cleanses the Temple

Evidently there were two Cleansings, three years apart: this, at the beginning of his public ministry (note the word "after," 3:22); the other, at the close, during his Last Week (Matthew 21:12–16; Mark 11:15–18; Luke 19:45–46). In this, he drove out the cattle; in the other, he drove out the traders. In this, he called the Temple "a house of merchandise"; in the other, "a den of robbers."

From his previous visits to Jerusalem, like Luther in Rome, he had, no doubt, already become appalled at the unspeakable godlessness of the hierarchy that ruled in the name of God. The formal opening act of his public work, which he intended as a sign to the nation that he was the Messiah, (for so it was expected, Malachi 3:1–3), was in open and utter defiance of the ruling clique, whose antagonism was immediately aroused, and which Jesus seemed never to care to pacify. Thus he began his ministry, and thus he closed it.

There must have been something very majestic in Jesus' personal appearance, or, more likely, it may have been through his miraculous power, that a lone stranger, with only a scourge in his hand, could have cleared and held control of the Temple area, so that (the second time) not even a vessel could be carried through (Mark 11:16). Even the police were cowed into silence.

What was it that was so displeasing to Jesus in the Temple? They were profiteering to such an extent that the whole service of God had been Commercialized and Scandalized, inside the sacred area which had been dedicated to other purposes. (See further under Matthew 21:12–17.)

The Temple, built by the Herods, of marble and gold, was magnificent beyond imagination. Surrounded by four courts, on lower successive levels: for priests, Israel, women, Gentiles. Bordered by covered colonnades, with pillars of whitest marble, each 40 feet high and made of a single stone. That on the east was called Solomon's Porch, where the traders were. The whole area surrounded by a massive wall, 1000 feet on each side, about the size of four average city blocks.

Miracles (23). Jesus had done only one miracle in Galilee, up to this time (2:11; 4:54). But now, along with the opening of his campaign by the spectacular demonstration in the Temple, he wrought such an abuandance of miracles, that many were ready to accept him as Messiah, But he knew too well what they expected of the Messiah.

Chapter 3:1-21. Nicodemus

The Cleansing of the Temple, and accompanying miracles, had made a deep impression on the city. Nicodemus, a Pharisee and one of the Sanhedrin, influential, cautiously seeks a private interview with Jesus. He is interested, but desires to satisfy himself as to Jesus' claims. To what extent he believed we do not know. Two years later he took Jesus' part in the council (7:50–52). Later, he and Joseph, another member of the Council, buried Jesus (19:39). He was a secret disciple in the formative days of his faith, but later he was willing openly to share with Jesus the shame of his cross. His coming out of the shadows in the hour of Jesus' humiliation, when even the Twelve had fled to cover, risking his own life in that tender final ministry, is one of the noblest incidents of Scripture. He surely atoned for his original inclination to secrecy, especially considering he was a member of the Sanhedrin, right in the very heart of the enemies' camp.

The "New Birth" that Jesus was talking about is not merely a metaphor, but an actual reality, resulting from the impregnation of the human heart by the Spirit of God (see Romans on 8:1–11). Nicodemus, no doubt, shared the common notion that the Messiah's kingdom was to be a political kingdom in which his nation would be freed from Roman domination. Jesus tries to tell him of its personal spiritual nature, so different from what was in Nicodemus' mind, that Nicodemus did not know what Jesus was talking about. He just could not see how he, a good man, a genuine Pharisee, one of the rulers of the Messianic nation, would not be welcomed into the Messianic Kingdom with open arms, just as he was. He just could not take it in that, instead, he would have to entirely re-construct his ideas and himself.

"Be lifted up" (14). This is an announcement, at the opening of Jesus' ministry, that the Cross would be his Messianic throne. It is a reference to the brazen serpent to which those who had been bitten looked and lived (Numbers 21:9), meaning that the "new birth," of which he had just been speaking, into eternal life, would come by virtue of his death. It suggested the beloved John 3:16.

Chapter 3:22-36. Jesus' Ministry in the Lower Jordan

This was in the same region where he had been baptized. Meantime, John had moved further up the Jordan, about 40 miles, to a place called Aenon (see map page 423). Both men were preaching the same thing: The long-foretold kingdom of Heaven is at hand. Soon Jesus had a wider following than John, because of His Miracles, and because He was the Messiah whom John proclaimed, and had a more Commanding Personality.

After 8 months John was imprisoned (Matthew 4:12); the rulers at Jerusalem were taking notice (John 4:1); it began to look as if it might be dangerous for Jesus to continue in that region; and, lest he be cut off prematurely, before his work was completed, he withdrew to Galilee.

That this period was 8 months is indicated thus: it began about Passover time (April, John 2:13; 3:22); it closed "four months to harvest" (December, John 4:35).

Chapter 4:1-42. The Samaritan Woman

Jesus returned to Galilee through Samaria, instead of the more common route up the Jordan valley, possibly for prudential reasons. Samaria was outside Herod's jurisdiction, who had just imprisoned John. Jesus was only passing through. His conversation with the Samaritan woman was only incidental. It is one of the most beautiful, delightful and helpful things in the story of Jesus' life.

Samaritans of an alien race, had been planted there by the Assyrians, 700 years before (II Kings 17:6, 24, 26, 29; Ezra 5:1, 9, 10), and had accepted the Pentateuch. They were expecting the Messiah to make Samaria, not Jerusalem, his seat of government.

Jesus was being eyed with suspicion by the rulers of his own nation. But here the despised Samaritans received him gladly. One of the ever-recurring contrasts of the Gospels is the repudiation of Jesus by the religious custodians of his nation, and his acceptance by the outcast, sinners and common people.

Jacob's Well is still there, 100 feet deep, 9 feet in diameter. It is one of the few places where an exact spot connected with the story of Jesus can be identified.

"Sixth hour," Roman time, like ours, 6 P.M.

This visit of Jesus laid the groundwork for the hearty reception of the Gospel by Samaritans a few years later (Acts 8:4–8).

Chapter 4:43-54. The Nobleman's Son

Cana was 4 miles northeast of Nazareth. It was the home of Nathanael, and the place where, a year earlier, Jesus had wrought his first miracle (John 2:1–11).

The Nobleman was one of Herod's officials, in Capernaum. Capernaum was 15 miles northeast of Cana. This miracle was performed by word of mouth on a person 15 miles distant. "Second sign" (54), means second in Galilee. He had done miracles in the meantime in Jerusalem (John 2:23).

Following this miracle, seems to have been the time when Jesus went back to Nazareth (Luke 4:16–30). The healing of the nobleman's son in Capernaum was what the inhabitants of Nazareth had heard of and wanted Jesus to repeat in his own city (Luke 4:23).

Chapter 5. A Sabbath Miracle at Jerusalem

This was during a Feast (1). It is not stated which Feast. The Feasts which the Jews observed in Jesus' day, and which Jesus, no doubt, attended regularly, were:

Passover. (April). Celebrating Exodus 1,400 years before.
Pentecost. (June). 50 days later. Celebrating Giving of Law.
Tabernacles. (October). Celebrating ingathering of harvests.
Dedication. (December). Started by Judas Maccabaeus.
Purim. (Shortly before Passover). No mention of it in Gospels.

Jesus had returned to Galilee in December, about the time of the Feast of Dedication. The Feast next following would be Purim. Next was Passover, which is quite generally accepted as the time of this visit.

A year before Jesus had cleansed the Temple, as an introductory sign that he was the Messiah. This time he works a Sabbath miracle, for the purpose, it would seem, of violating their ideas of the Sabbath, in order to get attention of the rulers, so as to give his claims of Deity the fullest possible publicity in the nation's capital. It gave him a hearing for a detailed explanation of his claims, and resulted in the Sanhedrin's determination to kill him (18), which it took them two years to bring about.

The Pool of Bethesda, traditionally, was located just north of the Temple. But some scholars identify it with what is now called the Virgin's Pool, just south of the Temple, which is still an intermittent spring.

Jesus referred to this miracle, and their determination to kill him, a year and a half later. It was one of the main contentions of his enemies (John 9:14; Luke 13:14). For healing the man with the withered hand on the Sabbath they planned to kill him (Mark 3:6). Jesus called them inconsistent in circumcising on the Sabbath while objecting to his healing on the Sabbath.

The only recorded instance of Jesus' "anger" is at their objecting to his healing on the Sabbath (Mark 3:5), except that it is recorded that he was "moved with indignation" at the disciples trying to keep children from him (Mark 10:14).

Healings on the Sabbath

Seven are recorded, as follows:

A Demoniac, in Capernaum (Mark 1:21–27).
Peter's Mother-in-law, in Capernaum (Mark 1:29–31).
An Impotent Man, in Jerusalem (John 5:1–9).
Man with Withered Hand (Mark 3:1–6).
Woman Bowed Together (Luke 13:10–17).
Man with Dropsy (Luke 14:1–6).
Man Born Blind (John 9:1–14).

Chapter 6. The Feeding of the 5,000

This is the only one of Jesus' miracles told in all four Gospels (Matthew 14:13–33; Mark 6:32–52; Luke 9:10–17).

The place was on the northeast shore of the Sea of Galilee. A spot two miles southeast of the Jordan entrance fits the description.

The time was Passover (6:4), one year before Jesus' death, when the passing multitudes were on their way to Jerusalem. Jesus himself did not go to Jerusalem this Passover, because on his previous visit they had formed a plot to kill him (John 5:1, 18). It was probably the first Passover he had missed going to Jerusalem since he was 12. He celebrated it by working one of his most marvelous miracles for the Passover-bound multitudes.

Notice Jesus' love of order; he made the people sit down in companies of 50's and 100's (Mark 6:39–40), probably arranged around him in a circle or semi-circle.

Notice, too, that he was not wasteful. He commanded that the left-overs be gathered up (12–13).

The miracle made a telling impression. The people wanted to enthrone him as king immediately (14–15).

Jesus Walks on the Water (16–21). This was in the "fourth watch" (Mark 6:48), after three in the morning. Jesus had spent most of the night alone in the mountain (Mark 6:46).

The disciples were rowing to Capernaum (John 6:17), by way of Bethsaida (Mark 6:45). Bethsaida was at the Jordan entrance. Capernaum was about five miles southwest of the Jordan entrance (see Map page 473). They were hugging the shore, because of the storm. When Jesus appeared they were "25 or 30 furlongs" out, that is, about 3 or 4 miles, half way across.

When Peter saw Jesus walking on the water he wanted to do it too. Dear, lovable, impetuous Peter! But he began to sink. Then Jesus chided him for his lack of faith. To us it seems that Peter had a good deal of faith, to even try it—a good deal according to man's way of looking at things, but in Jesus' eyes so little.

Jesus' Discourse on the Bread of Life (22–71). Jesus had worked this mighty miracle as a setting for a plain talk on his true mission in the world.

While he had spent much time ministering to men's bodily needs, the real purpose of his coming into the world was to save men's Souls. When he told them that they began to lose interest. As long as he fed their bodies they thought he was great. They wanted him to be their king.

It seems that the people generally were expecting the Messiah to bring in a social order in which men could get their bread without working. It would have been just wonderful if they could have had a king who would every day feed them miraculously, as he had done the day before, as Moses had given the daily manna.

Chapter 7. Jesus again at Jerusalem

This was at the Feast of Tabernacles (October), a year and a half since he had been there, six months before his death.

On his previous visit he had healed a man on the Sabbath, and announced to the rulers that he was the Son of God (John 5:18), for which they laid plans to kill him. He remained away during the intervening Passover (John 6:4).

But now his work was drawing toward a close, and he again went to the capital of his nation to further present his claim that he was sent from God. However, the time for his death was not yet fully come. Knowing their plan to kill him (for it was generally known, 7:25), he made the journey incognito, till he appeared in the midst of the Temple multitudes. Then he opened his address by referring to their plot to kill him (7:19–23).

When the rulers heard it they sent officers to take him. But the officers somehow were awed by his presence. And he went ahead with his message from God.

The Deity of Jesus

Jesus is called "The Son of God" in all four Gospels:
Matthew 3:17; 4:3, 6; 8:29; 14:33; 16:16; 17:5; 26:63; 27:54.
Mark 1:1; 1:11; 3:11; 5:7; 9:7; 14:61, 62.
Luke 1:32, 35; 3:22; 4:41; 9:35; 22:70.
John 1:34; 1:49; 3:16, 18; 5:25; 9:35; 10:36; 19:7; 20:31.

Jesus called himself "The Son of God" (John 5:25); "making himself equal with God" (John 5:18). Three times Jesus categorically said "I am THE SON OF GOD" (Mark 14:61–62; John 9:35–37; 10:36).

Jesus repeatedly used expressions about himself that can be predicated only of Deity:

"I am the Truth" (John 14:6).

"I am the Way" (to God) (John 14:6).

"I am the door; by Me if any man enter in he shall be saved, and shall go in and out, and shall find pasture" (John 10:9).

"No one can come unto the Father but by Me" (John 14:6).

"I am the Bread of Life" (John 6:35, 38).

"I am the Life" (John 11:25; 14:6).

"I am the Resurrection" (John 11:25).

"He that believes on Me shall Never Die" (John 11:26).

"I am the Messiah" (John 4:25–26).

"Before Abraham was I am" (John 8:58). This is an amazing statement, beyond the reach of finite conception, eliminating the passage of time, and resolving the past and future into one Eternal Now.

"Father, glorify Me with the glory I had with Thee before the world was" (John 17:5). A clear recollection of his pre-incarnation existence.

"He that has seen Me has seen the Father" (John 14:9).

"I and the Father are one" (John 10:30).

"All Power on earth and in heaven had been given unto me" (Matthew 28:18).

"I am with you always, even to the end of the world" (Matthew 28:20).

Who else could have said such things about himself? Of whom else could we say them?

Mark called Jesus "The Son of God" (Mark 1:1).
John called Jesus "The Son of God" (John 3:16, 18; 20:31).
John the Baptist called Jesus "The Son of God" (John 1:34).
Nathanael called Jesus "The Son of God" (John 1:49).
Peter called Jesus "The Son of God" (Matthew 16:16).
Martha called Jesus "The Son of God" (John 11:27).
The Disciples called Jesus "The Son of God" (Matthew 14:33).
Gabriel called Jesus "The Son of God" (Luke 1:32, 35).

GOD HIMSELF called Jesus His Own "BELOVED SON" (Matthew 3:17; 17:5; Mark 1:11; 9:7; Luke 3:22; 9:35).

Evil Spirits called Jesus "The Son of God" (Matthew 8:29; Mark 3:11; 5:7, Luke 4:41, see on Demons, page 468).

It was commonly recognized that he made the claim:
"If you are the Son of God" (Matthew 4:3, 6).
"Of a truth you are the Son of God" (Matthew 14:33).
"If you are Son of God come down from cross" (Matthew 27:40).
"He said 'I am the Son of God'" (Matthew 27:43).
"Truly this was the Son of God" (Matthew 27:54).
"He made himself the Son of God" (John 19:7).

The Old Testament prophets foretold his Deity: "His name shall be called Mighty God, Everlasting Father" (Isaiah 9:6). "This is the name whereby He shall be called, God our Righteousness" (Jeremiah 23:6; 33:16), "In that day the house of David shall be as God" (Zechariah 12:8).

The "Rock" on which Jesus said He would build his church (Matthew 16:18), was the truth that He is the Son of God.

Jesus is Himself called "God" (John 1:1; 10:33; 20:28; Romans 9:5; Colossians 1:16; 2:9; I Timothy 1:17; Hebrews 1:8; I John 5:20; Jude 25).

Thus, neither Jesus himself, nor the Scriptures, leave any possible doubt as to the nature of Jesus' Person. Why not accept the record just as it is? If he was only a good man, he can do nothing for us, except to set us an example. If he was really God, he can be to us a Saviour as well as an example.

Chapter 8:1-11. The Woman Taken in Adultery

There are three instances of Jesus' dealings with women who had made a misstep: This one; the sinful woman of Luke 7:36–50; and the Samaritan Woman (John 4:18). In all three Jesus was exceedingly considerate. (See under Luke 15.)

The language of verse 7 may imply that Jesus knew that the men who were accusing the woman were themselves guilty of the very thing of which they accused her.

Chapter 8:12-59. Jesus Continues Discourse on His Deity

His categoric and amazing statements about Himself infuriated the rulers, and they attempted to mob him (59). Aside from the statements on the preceding two pages, Jesus made other claims for himself approximating Deity.

"I am the Light of the world" (John 8:12).
"I am the good Shepherd" (John 10:11).
"You are of this world. I am not of this world. You are from beneath. I am from Above" (John 8:23).

"Your father Abraham rejoiced to see my day, and he saw it, and was glad" (John 8:56).

"Moses wrote of Me" (John 5:46).

"Search the Scriptures; you think that in them you have eternal life, and they bear witness of me" (John 5:39).

"The Father, he has borne witness of me" (John 5:37).

"The works which the Father has given me to do, the very works that I do, bear witness of me" (John 5:36).

"If I had not done among them the works which none other did, they had not sin" (John 15:24).

"Except you believe that I am he, you shall die in your sins" (John 8:24).

"Blessed are your eyes, for I say unto you many kings and prophets desired to see the things that you see, but did not see them, and to hear the things you hear, but did not hear them" (Luke 10:23–24).

"The queen of Sheba came from the ends of the earth to hear the wisdom of Solomon. A greater than Solomon is here. The Ninevites repented at the preaching of Jonah. Here is a greater than Jonah" (Matthew 12:41–42).

Names and Titles Applied by the Scripture to Christ

"The Christ" "The Messiah" "Saviour" "Redeemer" "Wonderful Counsellor" "Faithful Witness" "The Word of God" "The Truth" "The Light of the World" "The Way" "The Good Shepherd" "Mediator" "Deliverer" "The Great High Priest" "The Author and Perfector of our Faith" "The Captain of our Salvation" "Our Advocate" "The Son of God" "The Son of Man" "God" "The Holy One of God" "Only Begotten Son" "Mighty God" "The Image of God" "Everlasting Father" "Lord" "Lord of All" "Lord of Glory" "Lord of Lords" "Blessed and Only Potentate" "King of Israel" "King of Kings" "Ruler of the Kings of the Earth" "Prince of Life" "Prince of Peace" "The Son of David" "The Branch" "David" "Root and Offspring of David" "The Bright and Morning Star" "Immanuel" "The Second Adam" "The Lamb of God" "The Lion of the Tribe of Judah" "The Alpha and the Omega" "The First and the Last" "The Beginning and the End" "The Beginning of the Creation of God" "The First-Born of All Creation" "The Amen."

What Napoleon Said about Christ

Generally accepted as a genuine word of Napoleon. Some doubt its authenticity. "I know men, and I tell you, Jesus is not a man. He commands us to believe, and gives no other reason than his awful word, I AM GOD. Philosophers try to solve the mysteries of the universe by their empty dissertations: fools: they are like the infant that cries to have the moon for a plaything. Christ never hesitates. He speaks with authority. His religion is a mystery; but it subsists by its own force. He seeks, and absolutely requires, the love of men, the most difficult thing in the world to obtain. Alexander, Caesar, Hannibal conquered the world, but had no friends. I myself am perhaps the only person of my day who loves Alexander, Caesar, Hannibal. Alexander, Caesar, Charlemagne and myself founded empires; but upon what? Force. Jesus founded his empire on Love; and at this hour millions would die for him. I myself have inspired multitudes with such affection that they would die for me. But my presence was necessary. Now that I am in St. Helena, where are my friends? I am forgotten, soon to return to the earth, and become food for worms. What an abyss between my misery and the eternal kingdom of Christ, who is proclaimed, loved, adored, and which is extending over all the earth. Is this death? I tell you, the death of Christ is the death of a God. I tell you, JESUS CHRIST IS GOD."

What Josephus Said about Christ

Considered authentic by many scholars, but some think it may have been an interpolation. Josephus was a Jewish historian, A.D. 37–100, born and educated in Jerusalem, a general in the Jewish army.

"There was about this time Jesus, a wise man, if it be lawful to call him a man, for he was a doer of wonderful works. He was Christ. Pilate, at the suggestion of the principal men among us, condemned him to the cross. He appeared to his followers alive again the third day."

Chapter 9. Jesus Heals a Man Born Blind

On a previous visit to Jerusalem (5:9), Jesus had healed an impotent man on the Sabbath, for which, and his claim that he was the Son of God, they attempted to stone him (John 8:52–59). He now proceeds to work a still more notable Sabbath miracle (9:14).

Chapter 10:1-21. Jesus the Good Shepherd

Jesus declares himself to be the Shepherd of mankind, that is, of as many of mankind as will accept him as their Shepherd. It is a beautiful metaphor, ever cherished by Christians, of Jesus' tender and devoted care of his people.

Chapter 10:22-39. At the Feast of Dedication

There is an interval of two months between verses 21 and 22. The Feast of Tabernacles was in October. Jesus' visit to that Feast is covered by John 7:2 to 10:21. Now it is the Feast of Dedication (December). In the interval, it seems, Jesus had gone back to Galilee, and North, and was Transfigured.

Chapter 10:40-42. Beyond the Jordan

Where Jesus had spent eight months at the opening of his public ministry (John 3:22). He was there probably about two months. It was a thickly populated region, with many prosperous Roman cities, under Herod's rule, out of reach of the Jerusalem authorities. (Covered by Luke 11 to 18 inclusive.)

Chapter 11. Jesus Raises Lazarus from the Dead

Probably about a month before his own death. It was his third raising of the dead: Jairus daughter (Mark 5:21–43), the widow of Nain's son (Luke 7:11–17); and Lazarus, climaxed by His own, nevermore to die. The miracle brought the Sanhedrin to a final decision to kill Jesus (53). Jesus therefore retired to the wilderness of Ephraim, about 12 miles north of Jerusalem, to await, in quiet with the Twelve, the Passover.

Chapter 12:1-8. The Supper at Bethany

John places this supper on the day before the Triumphal Entry (12), which could be Saturday evening (see further on Mark 14:3–9). It was probably about a month after he had raised Lazarus from the dead. They were a rich family. 300 pence, or shillings, in our money is about $50. Only wealthy people can afford $50 bottles of perfume. Jesus probably had spoken of his coming Crucifixion. Mary, kind-hearted, compassionate, thoughtful, lovely Mary, perhaps, noticing a look of pain in his eyes, said to herself, "This is no parable. He means it." And she went and got the rarest treasure of her household, and poured it on his head and feet, and wiped them with her hair. Perhaps not a word was said. But he understood. He knew that she was trying to tell him how her heart ached. Jesus appreciated it so much that he said that what she had done would be told of her wherever his name would be carried to the ends of the earth and to the end of time.

Bethany is about two miles from Jerusalem, on the east slope of the Mount of Olives. It was Jesus' abiding place when he visited Jerusalem. From the hills of Bethany Jesus ascended to heaven.

Chapter 12:9–19. The Triumphal Entry. (See on Matthew 21:1–11.)

Chapter 12:20–36. The Greek's Desire to See Jesus. It is not stated when, but is thought possibly to have been on Tuesday, in the

Fig. 66. Village of Bethany. Tomb of Lazarus, center. House of Simon the Leper, right. © *Matson Photo*

Temple, as the determined hostility of the rulers was becoming manifest. Peoples from distant lands brought him their homage. It occasioned a sort of soliloquy-prayer-conversation on the necessity of his death. How he dreaded it!

Chapter 12:37–43. Their Unbelief. Why, in spite of the overwhelming evidence of Jesus' miracles, the rulers of the Jewish nation would not believe on Jesus, is one of the knottiest of Scripture problems. John's answer is that it was in fulfillment of Scripture.

Chapter 12:44–50. Jesus' Final Temple Message. Probably as he left at the close of Tuesday, never again to enter.

Chapters 13,14. The Last Supper

(See more fully on Matthew 26:17–29)

Jesus Washes their Feet (13:1–20). This was occasioned by their contention among themselves as to which of them were to have the chief offices in the Kingdom. That had been one of their standing problems (see on Luke 9:46–48). In spite of Jesus' repeated statements that he was going to be crucified (see on Mark 9:30–32), which they somehow, even to the last, took to be parables, they seemed to think that the Triumphal Entry, five days before, portended that it was about time for him to erect the throne of a world empire in Jerusalem. Jesus finally had to get down on his hands and knees and wash their feet, the menial service of a slave, to burn into their minds that he had called them to Serve, and not to Rule. Oh, how the Church has suffered through all the centuries because so many of its leaders have been consumed by the passion to be great! Powerful organizations and high offices have been created to satisfy men's worldly and selfish ambitions. Great churchmen, instead of humbly serving Christ, have used the name of Christ to serve themselves.

Jesus Points out the Betrayer (21–30). So shrewdly had Judas kept his secret that no one of them suspected him. (See on Mark 14:10–11). Judas knew that Jesus knew his secret. But with a heart of steel he went forward with his dastardly crime.

Jesus' Final Farewell to the Twelve (13:31 to 17:26), Judas gone. These four chapters are the tenderest words in the Bible. Chapter 14 was uttered while yet at Supper. 15, 16 and 17, while on the way to Gethsemane.

He knew the end had come. He was ready for it. Instead of calling it "crucified" he called it "glorified" (13:31). He dreaded the pain, but kept his eye on the joy beyond the pain.

They were mystified at his statement that he was leaving them. What could he mean? Had he not told them over and over? We think his heart must have ached for them more than it did at the thought of his own suffering.

Peter, suspecting that Jesus meant he was going on a dangerous mission, offered to follow even at the cost of his own life. Jesus reminded Peter that he did not realize what he said.

Chapter 14. The House of Many Mansions

The best loved chapter in all the Bible, the one that goes with us as we near the valley of the shadow. Jesus, as a master workman, is preparing the heavenly palace for the glorious day when he will receive his Bride, the Elect of all the Ages, unto himself. But the Bride also needs to be made ready. The Church must be gathered, nurtured and perfected, to be made fit for the mansions of God. The people, as well as the place must be prepared. As Jesus departs to make ready the Eternal Home, he promises to send the Holy Spirit to train, comfort, and lead the saints on the homeward way.

1. "Coenaculum," name of traditional place of Last Supper, possibly the home of Mary the mother of Mark. From here, about 8 or 9 in the evening, he went to Gethsemane, a mile distant, indicated by dotted lines.
2. Gethsemane. Here he was in agony for 2 or 3 or 4 hours. Then he was arrested, and taken to the High Priest's House, in the same vicinity where he had eaten the Last Supper.
3. High Priest's House. Here Jesus was kept from midnight to day-

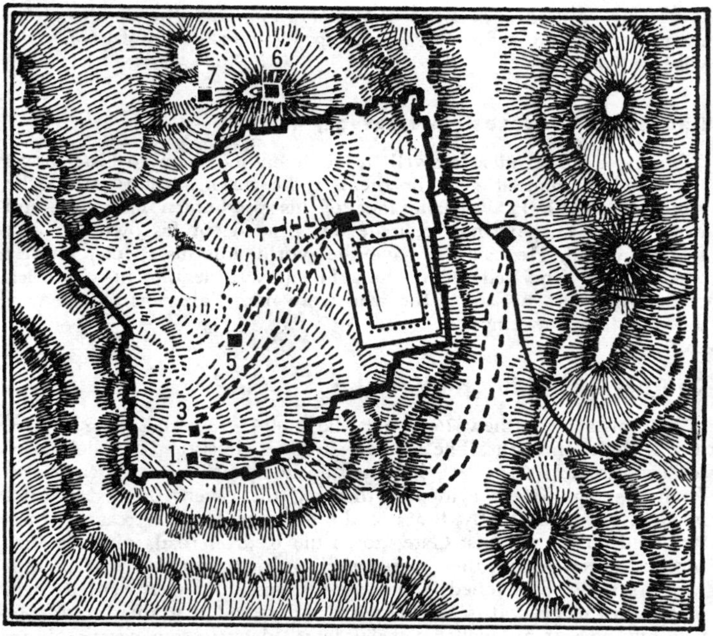

Map 59. Illustrating Jesus' Movements the Last Night.

light. Condemned, mocked, spit upon, denied by Peter, and at daylight, officially sentenced and sent to Pilate.

4. Pilate's Judgment Hall, called the "Tower of Antonio." Pilate tried to escape responsibility, and sent Jesus to Herod.
5. Herod's Palace. Here he was mocked. Sent back to Pilate.
4. Again at Pilate's. Scourged, and sentenced to Crucifixion.
6. Calvary, just outside north wall, where he was crucified (Figure 64).
7. Garden Tomb, where he was buried. (See Figures 68–70.)

Chapters 15,16,17. On the Way to Gethsemane

The ideas ever and anon appearing in these precious chapters are that the disciples Love One Another, that they Keep Christ's Commandments, that they Abide in Him, that they must expect Pruning and Persecution, that it was necessary for him to go away, that the Holy Spirit would take his place, that their sorrow would be turned to Joy, and that in his absence Wondrous Answers to their Prayers would be granted. The Blessed Master going into the depths of his own sorrow and suffering was doing his best to comfort his bewildered disciples.

Chapter 17. Jesus' Intercessory Prayer

He closes his tender farewell by commending them to God, praying both for himself and for them, as he turns away to tread the winepress ALONE. Remembrance of his pre-human existence, and its "glory" (5), gave him courage. He prayed for his own (9), not for the world. He came to save the world, but his special interest was in those who believed on him. He drew a definite line between those who were his and those who were not. This runs all the way through John's writings.

Chapter 18:1-12. His Arrest

Told also in Matthew 26:47–56; Mark 14:43–50 and Luke 22:47–53. It was about midnight. The Roman garrison, consisting of a cohort of soldiers, about 500 or 600, led by the chief captain, with emissaries from the high priest evidently thinking they were on a dangerous mission, were guided by Judas to the place of Jesus' retreat. As they streamed out of the East Gate, down the Kedron road, with lanterns, torches and weapons, they were visible from the garden where Jesus was. As they approached, Jesus, by his unseen power, caused them to fall to the ground, to make them understand that they could not take him against his will. To make Jesus' identification certain, Judas pointed him out by kissing him.

Chapter 18:12 to 19:16. Trial of Jesus. (See on Mark 14:53).

Chapter 18:15-27. Peter's Denial

It occurred in the court of the high priest, as Jesus was being condemned. Peter had just been willing to fight the whole Roman garrison alone. He was not a coward by any means. He deserves some credit. We can never know the whirl of emotions that tore at Peter's soul that night. As Peter was vehemently denying that he knew Jesus, Jesus turned and looked at him. That look broke Peter's heart.

Chapter 19:17-37. Jesus is Crucified

See also notes on Matthew 27:33–56; Mark 15:21–41 and Luke 23:32–49. The legs of the robbers were broken (32) to hasten death, which otherwise might not have occurred for four or five days.

Chapter 19:33-34. The "Blood and Water"

Jesus was already dead when the spear pierced his side, after being on the cross six hours. Some medical authorities have said that in the case of heart rupture, and in that case only, the blood collects in the pericardium, the lining around the wall of the heart, and divides into a sort of bloody clot and a watery serum. If this is a fact, then the actual immediate physical cause of Jesus' death was heart rupture. Under intense pain, and the pressure of his wildly raging blood, his heart burst open. It may be that Jesus, literally, died of a heart broken over the sin of the world. It may be that suffering for human sin is more than the human constitution can stand.

Possibly there may here be a mystic parallel to Genesis 2:21–22. As God took from Adam's side, in sleep, that from which He made a bride for Adam, so He took from Jesus' side, in sleep on the cross, that from which He made the Church, the bride of Jesus.

The courtyard of Caiaphas, where a monk looks at a plaque representing a cock crowing, in remembrance of Peter's denial of his Lord.
© *Matson Photo Service*

Chapter 19:38-42. Burial

(For note on the place of burial see next page.) Joseph and Nicodemus, both members of the Sanhedrin, secret disciples—secret in the hour of Jesus' popularity—now, in the hour of his humiliation, came out boldly to share with Jesus the shame of his cross. All hail, Joseph! All hail, Nicodemus!

The "Holy Shroud." The Scientific American of March, 1937, contained an article by a French scientist about a sheet of linen cloth that was in a Roman Catholic church at Turin, Italy, which he believed to have been the actual winding sheet of Jesus' body. He

Fig. 67. The Garden Tomb enclosure. Entrance at lower left.
© *Matson Photo*

Fig. 68. Tomb Entrance.
© *Matson Photo*

described it as being 14 feet long, 3 feet 7 inches wide, with negative images of the front and back of a full-grown human body, indicating that the man was laid on one half, and the other half was folded over lengthwise. The figures, he claimed, are not paintings, but images produced by ammoniac vapors, given off in great abundance in sweat produced by intense suffering. The scourge marks, the wound in the hands, on the head, and in the side, are plainly visible, with evidence that serum and blood flowed from the wound. It is unmistakably the image of a man crucified, with every detail dovetailing with the Scripture account, and with the countenance of a man of noble appearance. It first appeared in France in 1355, with notices that it had been seen in Constantinople 1204. However, we do not know for sure whether it is a fake or the real shroud of Jesus.

Chapter 19:41-42. The Tomb of Jesus

"In the place where Jesus was crucified there was a garden; and in the garden a new tomb wherein was never man yet laid." This means that the tomb in which Jesus was buried was very close to the place where he was crucified. (See under Mark 15:21–41.)

General Christian Gordon, 1881, found at the west foot of the "Skull Hill" a "Garden." He set a gang of men to digging, and, under 5 feet of rubbish, he found a tomb of Roman times, cut in a wall of solid rock, with a trench in front where the stone rolled to the door.

The tomb is a room 14 feet wide, 10 feet deep, 7½ feet high. As you enter, there are, at the right, two graves, one next to the front wall, and one next to the back wall, as illustrated in Map 60. They are slightly lower than the floor of the room, with a low dividing wall between. The front grave seems never to have been completed. Indications were that only the rear grave had ever been occupied, and that with no marks of mortal corruption. The tomb is sufficiently large for a company of women and two angels to stand inside, with room at the head and feet where an angel could sit (Mark 16:5; John 20:12). A window where, at dawn, the sunlight would fall on the occupied grave, seen at the right of the door in Figure 69. Every item fits the Scripture account.

Further, according to Eusebius, the Roman Emperor Hadrian, in his persecution of the Christians, A.D. 135, built a temple of Venus over the tomb where Jesus had been buried. Constantine, the first Christian Emperor, A.D. 330, destroyed this temple of Venus. General Gordon, in the debris which he cleared away from the tomb, found a shrine-stone of Venus. He found traces of a building that had been erected over the tomb. Above the tomb entrance, two recesses characteristic of Venus temples.

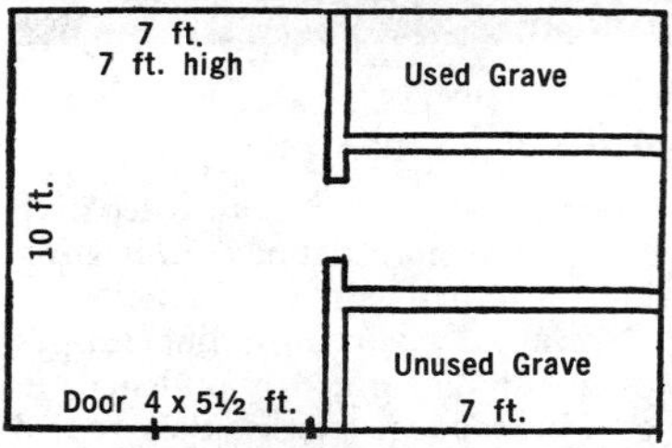

Map 60. Floor Plan of Tomb.

Further, in a vault adjoining the tomb, a tombstone was found, inscribed, "Buried near his Lord."

So, all in all, there seems to be a very good basis for the opinion that this "Garden Tomb" was the actual spot where Jesus was buried. and from which He came forth ALIVE. Therefore, to Christians, it is the holiest spot on earth, the place whence came Assurance of Life that Shall Never End.

Chapter 20:1-2. Mary Magdalene Goes to the Tomb

Other women were with her. (See on Matthew 28:1–8, and note on "Order of Events" under Mark 16.)

Chapter 20:3-10. Peter and John Run to the Tomb

Told also in Luke 24:12. They may have been lodging nearer than the other disciples, probably at John's home, where Jesus' mother also was staying (19:27).

Fig. 69. Interior of the Garden Tomb
© *Matson Photo*

Chapter 20:11-18. Jesus Appears to Mary Magdalene

This was his first appearance (Mark 16:9–11). The other women had gone. Peter and John had gone. Mary is there alone, weeping as if her heart would break. No thought that Jesus had risen. She had not heard the angel announcement that he was alive. Jesus himself had repeatedly said that he would rise the third day. Somehow she had not understood him. But, oh, how she loved him! And now he was dead. Even his body was gone. In that moment of grief Jesus stood by her, and called her name. She recognized his voice, and cried out in ecstatic joy. Jesus not dead, but alive!

A little later he appeared to the Other Women (Matthew 28:9–10).
That afternoon he appeared to the Two (Luke 24:13–32).
And to Peter (Luke 24:33–35).

Chapter 20:19-25. Jesus Appears to the Eleven

That evening, in Jerusalem, Thomas absent (24). This appearance is recorded three times: here, and in Mark 16:14 and Luke 24:33–43. (See notes on those passages.) Jesus was in the same body, with the wound marks in his hands, feet and side; and he ate food. Yet he had power to pass through walls, to appear and disappear at will. "Whose soever sins you forgive" (23. See on Matthew 16:19).

Chapter 20:26-29. Again Appears to the Eleven

A week later, in Jerusalem, Thomas present. No modern critic could possibly be more "scientific" than Thomas.

Chapter 20:30-31. Purpose of the Book

Here is the author's unequivocal statement that his purpose was to demonstrate and illustrate the Godhood of Jesus.

Their Slowness to Believe that Jesus had Risen

They were not expecting it, although Jesus had repeatedly and plainly told them that he would rise on the third day (Matthew 16:21; 17:9, 23; 20:19; 26:32; 27:63; Mark 8:31; 9:31; Luke 18:33; 24:7). They must have taken his words to be a parable with some mysterious meaning. When the women went to the tomb it was, not to see if he had risen, but to prepare his body for permanent burial.

John alone, of all the disciples, believed at the sight of the empty tomb (John 20:8).

Mary Magdalene had only one thought, that some one had removed the body (John 20:13, 15).

The report of the women that Jesus had risen appeared to the disciples as "idle talk" (Luke 24:11).

When the Two from Emmaus told the Eleven that Jesus had appeared to them, "neither believed they them" (Mark 16:13).

Peter reported that Jesus had appeared to him (Luke 24:34). But still they believed not (Mark 16:14).

Thus, Jesus had repeatedly foretold it. Angels announced it. The tomb was empty. His body was gone. Mary Magdalene had seen him. The other women had seen him. Cleopas and his companion had seen him. Peter had seen him. Still the group as a whole did not believe. It just seemed to them incredible.

Then, when Jesus appeared to the Ten that night he upbraided them for their hard-hearted unwillingness to believe those that had seen him (Mark 16:14). Still they thought he was only a ghost, and he invited them to look closely at his hands, side and feet, and to "handle" him. Then he asked for food, and "did eat before them" (Luke 24:38–43; John 20:20).

After all that, Thomas, gloomy, doubting Thomas, was sure that there was a mistake somewhere, and did not believe till he personally saw Jesus a week later (John 20:24–29).

Thus, those who first proclaimed the story of Jesus' Resurrection were themselves totally unprepared to believe it, determined not to believe it, and came to believe it in spite of themselves. This renders untenable any possibility that the story was born of an excited and expectant imagination. There is no conceivable way to account for the origin of the story except that it was an ACTUAL FACT. We, too, one day, by His Grace, shall Rise.

DeWette: "Although a mystery which cannot be dissipated rests on the manner of the Resurrection, the Fact of the resurrection can no more be brought into doubt by honest historic evidence than the assassination of Caesar."

Edersheim: "The Resurrection of Christ may unhesitatingly be pronounced the Best Established Fact in history."

Ewald: "Nothing is more historically certain than that Jesus Rose from the Dead and appeared again to his followers."

John A. Broadus: "If we do not know that Jesus of Nazareth Rose from the Dead, we do not know anything historical whatever."

Chapter 21. Jesus Appears to the Seven

The disciples had now returned to Galilee, which Jesus had told them to do (Matthew 28:7, 10; Mark 16:7). He had appointed a certain mountain (Matthew 28:16), and probably had set the time. While waiting, they resume their old business. It may have been at, or near, the same spot where two or three years before he had first called them to become fishers of men (Luke 5:1–11). This time, as at first, he gave them a miraculous haul of fish. He may have intended it as a symbolic hint of the great success of the redemptive movement among men which they were about to initiate.

"The third time" (14), that is, to the assembled disciples, the other two being those of 20:19, 26. Counting the individuals to whom he had appeared, Mary Magdalene, the Women, the Two, Peter, it was his seventh appearance.

"More than these" (15). These things? Or, these men? The masculine and neuter forms of the Greek word for "these" are the same. There is no way to tell in which sense it is here used. "Do you love me more than these other disciples love me?" Or, "do you love me more than you love this fishing business?" Was Jesus twitting Peter for his three-fold denial? Or, was he gently chiding him for returning to the fishing business? We are inclined to think the latter.

"Lovest thou me?" (15, 16, 17). Jesus uses "agapan." Peter uses "philein." Two Greek words for "love." "Agapan" expresses a higher type of devotion. Peter refuses to use it. The third time Jesus comes down to Peter's word.

"Feed my sheep" (15, 16, 17), three times in variant forms. The idea seems to be something like this: "Peter, do you love ME more than you love this fishing business? Then you better be giving your time to the care of my flock; to my business, Peter, rather than to yours."

Jesus' Prophecy of Peter's Martyrdom (18–19). It had come to pass long before John wrote this. (See note on I Peter.)

The Author's Identification (24). A specific statement that John the Beloved Apostle was the author of this book.

Many Other Things (25). An hyperbole, but certainly a forceful description of the good deeds of the Saviour's earthly life.

Later he appeared to the Eleven, in Galilee (Matthew 28:16–20).

At a time and place unknown he appeared to James (I Corinthians 15:7).

Final appearance and Ascension, at Bethany (Luke 24:44–51).

The Five Most Important Chapters in the entire Bible we consider to be Matthew 28, Mark 16, Luke 24, John 20 and 21, because they tell of the Most Important Event in human history, the Resurrection of Christ from the Dead, capstone of the whole Bible.

The Resurrection

The Resurrection of Christ from the Dead is the ONE MOST IMPORTANT item in the whole fund of human knowledge: the grand event of the ages, toward which all previous history moved, and in which all subsequent history finds its meaning. The story of it has plowed through the centuries, and changed the face of the earth. (See note on I Corinthians 15.)

Is It a Fact? Did he really rise from the dead? If he did not, what became of his body? If enemies stole it, they surely would have produced it, for they stopped short of nothing to discredit the story, even to the murdering of those who told it. If friends stole it, they would have known they were believing a lie; but men do not become martyrs to what they know to be false.

One Thing Is Certain: those who first published the story that Jesus had risen from the dead BELIEVED it to be a fact. They rested their faith, not only on the empty tomb, but on the fact that they themselves had SEEN Jesus ALIVE after his burial; not once, nor twice, but at least ten recorded times; and not singly, nor alone, but in groups of two, seven, ten, eleven, five hundred.

An Hallucination? Could it not have been an ecstasy? a dream? a fantasy of an excited imagination? an apparition? Different groups of people do not keep on seeing the same hallucination. 500 people in a crowd would not all dream the same dream at the same time. Moreover, they were not expecting it. Considered it an "idle tale" at first (Luke 24:11). Did not believe it till they had to.

Only in a Swoon? Could it not be that Jesus was not really dead when they buried him, and that he came to again? In that case, weak and exhausted, he could scarcely have removed the heavy stone door and gotten out of the tomb. Besides he had new powers that he had never manifested before—to appear and disappear through locked doors. The eleven (or 120?), in a group, personally saw him slowly rise from the earth, and disappear behind the clouds.

The Records Tampered With? Could it not be that the resurrection was a later addition to the story of Christ, invented years later to glorify a dead hero? It is known, from historical records outside the Scripture, that the sect known as Christians came into existence in the reign of Tiberius, and that the thing that brought them into existence was their belief that Jesus had risen from the dead. The resurrection was not a later addition to the Christian faith, but the very cause and start of it. They rested their faith, not on records, but on what they had seen with their own eyes. The records were the result of their faith, not the cause of it. Had there been no resurrection, there would have been no New Testament, and no Church.

What a Halo of Glory this simple belief sheds on human life. Our hope of resurrection and life everlasting is based, not on a philosophic guess about immortality, but an historic fact.

ACTS

Formation and Spread of the Church
Extension of the Gospel to Gentiles
Life and Work of Paul

Within the Apostolic generation the Gospel of Christ expanded in all directions till it reached every nation of the then known world (Colossians 1:23).

The book of Acts, however, confines itself to the story of the expansion of the Gospel over Palestine, northward to Antioch, and thence westward, through Asia Minor and Greece, to Rome, covering the region that then constituted the backbone of the Roman Empire.

This book, called the Acts of the Apostles, is, mainly, the Acts of Peter and Paul, mostly Paul. Paul was the Apostle to Gentiles, that is, Nationalities other than Jewish. One of the leading subjects of the book, if not the leading subject, in its relation to the general scheme of Bible books, is the Extension of the Gospel to Gentiles.

The Old Testament is the story of God's age-long dealing with the Hebrew Nation for the specific purpose of, through the Hebrew Nation, Blessing All Nations.

The Hebrew Messiah, long foretold by the Prophets, at last had come. And in this book of Acts the Great and Wonderful Work among the Nations Begins. And the Household of God, in this book, passes from being a National Set-Up, and becomes an International World Institution.

Author

Unlike Paul's Epistles, the Author of Acts does not name himself. The use of the personal pronoun, "I," in the opening sentence, seems to indicate that the book's first recipients must have known who the writer was. From the beginning, this book and the Third Gospel have been accepted as from Luke.

Date

The book closes with Paul being in prison in Rome Two Whole Years (28:30). It is quite generally thought that this indicates that the book must have been written at that time, about A.D. 63; for, after giving so much space to the narration of Paul's imprisonment (chapters 21–28), it seems incredible that the writer would have omitted to mention the Outcome of Paul's Trial, if the book had been written later.

Luke

Little is known of Luke (see page 485). In Colossians 4:11, 14 he seems to be classed as a Gentile; which, if so, would make him, as far as is known, the only Gentile writer of the Bible.

Eusebius says Luke was a native of Antioch: Ramsey, one of the greatest modern Pauline scholars, thinks he was of Philippi.

He is recognized as a man of culture and scientific education, a master of Hebraic and classical Greek. By profession, a Physician.

He first appears as the one who brought Paul from Troas to Philippi; was a leader in the Philippian Church for its first 6 years; then rejoined Paul (Acts 16:10; 16:40; 20:6). We, They, We; and was with him to the end.

Chronology of Acts

There are not enough data given to form an exact Chronology, but sufficient to approximate most of the dates. It is known that Herod's death (Acts 12:23), was in A.D. 44. Mention of Paul's arrival in Jerusalem about the time that Herod killed James (11:30–12:2); and Paul's departure from Jerusalem right after the death of Herod (12:23, 25), makes it look like this was the visit referred to in Galatians 2:1, "14 years" after Paul's conversion.

If so, considering Hebrew usage of counting parts of years at the beginning and end of a period as years, the "14 years" may actually have been only about 13 years, or even less; which would place Paul's conversion about A.D. 31 or 32.

This, with A.D. 30 as a starting point, and A.D. 60 as the known date of Festus' appointment as Governor at Caesarea (24:27), the following dates may be regarded as probably approximately correct.

Formation of Church in Jerusalem, chapter 2 .... A.D. 30
Stoning of Stephen, Dispersion of Church, chapters 7, 8 .. A.D. 31 or 32
Conversion of Saul, chapter 9 .... A.D. 31 or 32
Paul's First Visit to Jerusalem after Conversion .... A.D. 34 or 35
Conversion of Cornelius, the Gentile .... between A.D. 35 and 40
Reception of Gentiles at Antioch, chapter 11 .... About A.D. 42
Paul's Second Visit to Jerusalem (11:27–30) .... A.D. 44
Paul's First Missionary Journey, Galatia, chapters 13, 14 .... A.D. 45–48
Council at Jerusaelm, chapter 15 .... About A.D. 50
Paul's Second Missionary Journey, Greece,
chapters 16, 17, 18 .... A.D. 50–53

Paul's Third Missionary Journey, Ephesus, chapters 19, 20. . A.D. 54–57
Paul Reached Ephesus, chapter 19. . . . . A.D. 54
Paul Left Ephesus in June (I Corinthians 16:8) . . . . A.D. 57
Paul in Macedonia, Summer and Fall (I Corinthians 16:5–8) . . A.D. 57
Paul in Corinth Three Months, Winter (Acts 20:2–3) . . . . . . A.D. 57–58
Paul Left Philippi in April (Acts 20:6) . . . . A.D. 58
Paul Reached Jerusalem in June (Acts 20:16) . . . . A.D. 58
Paul in Caesarea, chapters 24, 25, 26. . . . Summer A.D. 58 to Fall A.D. 60
Paul's Voyage to Rome, chapters 27, 28. . . . . Winter A.D. 60–61
Paul in Rome 2 years. . . . . A.D. 61–63

Chapter 1:1-5. The Forty Days

In the 40 days between His Resurrection and Ascension, Jesus made 10 or 11 recorded appearances to the disciples (see page 526), to banish forever from their minds any doubt as to His Continued Existence as a Living Person. What a wonderful experience, in those 40 days, to have thus seen, talked with, eaten with, and felt with their hands, Jesus in His actual Crucified and Glorified Body, as He appeared, and disappeared, through closed doors, out of the nowhere, and back into the nowhere, all climaxed, as, with the blessing of His uplifted hands, He rose, gradually, up and up, and disappeared in the Clouds.

Former Treatise (1:1): Gospel of Luke (1:3).

Theophilus (1:1): A Roman Official of high rank, (see page 485).

Jesus Began (1:1): Implies that what is recorded in the book of Acts was Still the Doing of Jesus.

Chapter 1:6-11. The Ascension of Christ

This last meeting with the disciples was in Jerusalem (1:4); from whence He led them out to Bethany (Luke 24:50, see page 544).

Restore the Kingdom to Israel? (1:6): their minds still on Political Independence for their nation. They understood better after the Day of Pentecost.

Uttermost Part of the Earth (1:8): this was Jesus' last word, as He Passed behind the Clouds. They did not forget it. Most of them, tradition says, died as Martyrs in Distant Lands.

Come in Like Manner (1:9, 11). From the hill tops above Bethany He passed into the Clouds. He will Return, in the Clouds, Visible to All the World (Matthew 24:27, 30; Revelation 1:7).

Chapter 1:12-14. The Upper Room

This may have been the same room where Jesus had instituted the Lord's Supper (Luke 22:12); and, possibly, the room where Jesus had twice appeared to them (John 20:19, 26); and, possibly, the place where the Holy Spirit came upon them (2:1). It was large enough to accommodate 120 persons (1:15).

Mary the Mother of Jesus (1:14). This is the New Testament's last mention of her. Esteemed and honored as she was as Mother of the Saviour, the Apostles gave not the slightest indication of feeling the need of her mediation between them and Christ.

Chapter 1:15-26. Choice of Judas' Successor

Judas, after betraying Jesus, hanged himself (Matthew 27:5). Then his body fell, and burst open (Acts 1:18). Then his money was used to buy a potter's field (Matthew 27:7). It is, to this day, known as Aceldama, the Field of Blood.

Matthias was chosen to take Judas' place, to keep the number at 12. Nothing further is known of Matthias. There must be symbolic meaning in the number 12 beyond our knowledge. The foundations of the New Jerusalem bear the names of the 12 Apostles (see page 738).

Chapter 2:1-13. Pentecost

A.D. 30. Birth-Day of the Church. 50th Day after Jesus' Resurrection. 10th Day after His Ascension to Heaven. Beginning of Gospel Era. That particular Pentecost was on Sunday.

Pentecost was also called Feast of First-Fruits, and Feast of Harvest

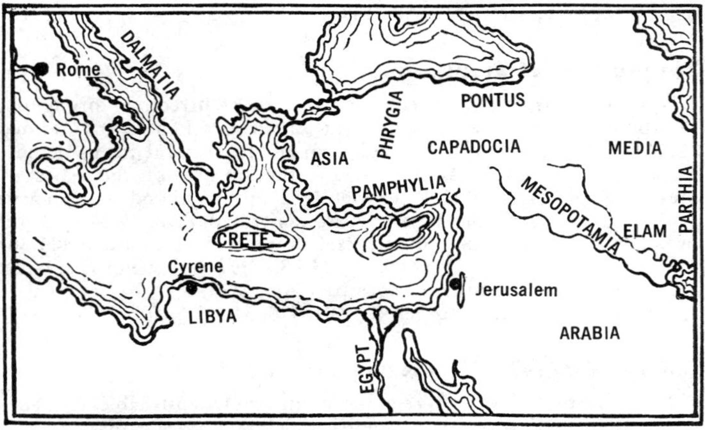

Map 61. Nations represented at Pentecost.

(see page 152). How fitting then to have been chosen as the Day for First-Fruits of the World Gospel Harvest.

Jesus, in John 16:7–14, had spoken of the Coming of the Holy Spirit Era. It is now inaugurated in a Mighty Miraculous Manifestation of the Holy Spirit, with sound as of a Roaring Wind, and with Tongues as of Fire parting asunder, upon each of the Apostles—the opening Public Proclamation to the World of the Resurrection of Jesus, to Jews and Jewish Proselytes assembled at Jerusalem, for Pentecost, from all the countries of the then known world—15 nations are named (2:9–11)—the Galilean Apostles speaking to them in their own language.

Chapter 2:14-26. Peter's Sermon

The amazing spectacle of the Apostles speaking under Tongues of Fire, in languages of all nations there represented, Peter explains (15–21), was in fulfillment of Prophecy from Joel 2:28–32.

What happened that day may not have been a complete fulfillment, but only the beginning of a great and notable era, of which, thus ushered in, some prophecies may refer to the end.

Fulfillment of Prophecy

Note the repeated statement that what was happening had been Foretold: Betrayal by Judas (1:16, 20): Crucifixion (3:18): Resurrection (2:25–28): Ascension of Jesus (2:33–35): Coming of the Holy Spirit (2:17). "All the Prophets" (3:18, 24): for an outline of Messianic Prophecy, see pages 387–401.

Resurrection of Jesus

Note, too, the unceasing emphasis on the Resurrection throughout this book. It was the pivotal point of Peter's Pentecostal sermon (2:24, 31, 32). And in his second sermon (3:15). And in his defense before the council (4:2, 10). It was the burden of the Apostles' preaching (4:33). It was Peter's defense in his second arraignment (5:30). A vision of the Risen Christ converted Paul (9:3–6). Peter preached it to Cornelius (10:40). Paul preached it in Antioch (13:30–37). Thessalonica (17:3). Athens (17:18, 31). Jerusalem (22:6–11). Felix (24:15, 21). Festus and Agrippa (26:8, 23).

(On Resurrection, see pages 483–484, 526, 554, 556, 598–599.

Chapter 2:37-47. The New-Born Church

3,000 the first day (2:41): a testimony to Unmistakable Evidence of the Resurrection of Jesus. "Baptized" (2:38, see page 568).

"Had All Things Common" (2:44, 45). This Community Life of

the Church was an accompaniment of the Miraculous Introduction of Christianity into the world, intended, we think, to be an example extraordinary of what the Spirit of Christ could do for mankind, but no more intended to be a permanent normal arrangement than the daily Apostolic Miracles. It was voluntary, temporary and limited. Only those gave who felt so inclined. There is no mention of its practice in other New Testament churches. Philip, one of the Seven, who ministered these tables, later lived in his own home in Caesarea (Acts 21:8).

There were many poor in Jerusalem. Paul, years later, took great offerings to the Mother Church (Acts 11:29; 24:17).

Miracles in Book of Acts

Miracles form a very conspicuous part of the Book of Acts. The book starts with Visible Appearances of Jesus, after His Death, to His disciples (1:3).

Then, before their eyes, His Ascension to Heaven (1:9).

Then, on Pentecost, a Miraculous Visible Manifestation of the Holy Spirit in Tongues as of Fire (2:3).

Then, Wonders and Signs were done by the Apostles (2:43).

The Healing of the Lame Man, at the Temple Gate (3:7–11), made a deep impression on the whole City (4:16, 17).

God answered Prayer by an Earthquake (4:31).

Ananias and Sapphira died by a Stroke from the Lord (5:5–10).

Signs and Wonders, by the Apostles, continued (5:12).

Multitudes from surrounding cities were Healed by Peter's Shadow (5:15, 16). It reads like the days of Jesus in Galilee.

Prison Doors were Opened by an Angel (5:19).

Stephen wrought great Wonders and Signs (6:8).

In Samaria, Philip did great Miracles and Signs (8:6, 7, 13); and Multitudes Believed.

Saul was Converted by a Direct Voice from Heaven (9:3–9).

At the word of Ananias, scales fell from Saul's eyes (9:17, 18).

In Lydda, Peter Healed Aeneas, and the whole region was converted to Christ (9:32–35).

In Joppa, Peter raised Dorcas from the Dead, and many Believed on the Lord (9:40–42).

Cornelius was converted by the Appearance of an Angel, and the Speaking in Tongues (10:3, 46).

A Voice from God sent Peter to Cornelius (10:9–22); and convinced the Jews that Peter was right (11:15, 18).

A Prison Gate Opened of its own accord (12:10).

The Blinding of a Sorcerer led the Proconsul of Cyprus to Believe (13:11, 12).

Paul did Signs and Wonders in Iconium, and a multitude Believed

(14:3, 4). At Lystra, the Healing of a Cripple made the multitudes think that Paul was a god (14:8–18).

Narration of Signs and Wonders convinced Jewish Christians that Paul's work among Gentiles was of God (15:12, 19).

In Philippi, Paul Healed a Soothsayer, and an Earthquake Converted the Jailor (16:16–34). In Ephesus, 12 men Spoke in Tongues (19:6), and Special Miracles done by Paul (19:11, 12), made the Word of the Lord to prevail mightily (19:20).

In Troas, Paul Raised a young man from the Dead (20:8–12).

In Melita, the Healing of Paul's Hand from the viper's bite (28:3–6), made the natives think Paul was a god; and Paul Healed all in the island that had Diseases (28:8, 9).

Take Miracles out of the book of Acts, and there is little left. However much critics may disparage the Evidential Value of Miracles, the fact remains that God made abundant use of Miracles in giving Christianity a start in the world.

Chapter 3. Peter's Second Sermon

On the day of Pentecost the Fiery Tongues and Roaring as of a Mighty Wind brought together the astonished multitudes. That gave Peter a vast audience for his first Public Proclamation of the Gospel. Apparently, some days had passed (2:46, 47). Pentecost crowds had returned home. The city had quieted down. The Apostles kept busy instructing the believers and working signs (2:42–47). And now a notable miracle, the Healing of a Lame man, right in the Temple Gate, a familiar sight to the whole city, again set the city all astir. And to the amazed multitudes, Peter attributed the Healing to the Power of the Risen Christ. And this brought the number of believers to five thousand men (4:4), as he told again the beloved Gospel Story.

Chapter 4:1-31. Peter and John Imprisoned

The rulers, who had crucified Jesus, now alarmed at the spreading report of His Resurrection from the Dead, and the growing popularity of His Name, arrested Peter and John, and ordered them to stop speaking in the Name of Jesus. Note the boldness of Peter (4:9–12, 19, 20). This is the same Peter who, a few weeks before, in the same place, and before the same people, had cowed at the sneer of a girl and denied his Master. Now, in utter fearlessness, he defies his Master's murderers.

After one night in prison (4:5, 21), Peter and John were released. And, by an earthquake, God approved their boldness (4:29, 31).

Chapter 4:32-35. Continued Growth of the Church

The threat of the rulers made little impression on the Church. The Church kept right on in its brotherly spirit; and kept right on growing by leaps and bounds. 3,000 the first day (2:41). Then, 5,000 men (4:4). Then multitudes both of men and women (5:14). Then "multiplied exceedingly," including a great company of priests (6:7), from inside the opposition ranks.

Chapter 4:36,37. Barnabas

A Levite, of Cyprus. A cousin of John Mark (Colossians 4:10), whose mother's home was a meeting place for Christians (Acts 12:12). A man of commanding appearance (14:12). A good man and full of the Holy Spirit (Acts 11:24). He persuaded the Jerusalem disciples to receive Paul (9:27). Was sent to receive the Gentiles at Antioch (11:19–24). Brought Paul from Tarsus to Antioch (11:25, 26). Accompanied Paul on his First Missionary Journey.

Chapter 5:1-11. Ananias and Sapphira

Their lie was in pretending to give all, when they had given only a part. Their death was an act of God, not of Peter: evidently intended to be an example for all time of God's displeasure at the sin of Covetousness and Religious Hypocrisy. God does not strike us dead every time we are guilty of it. If He did, people would be falling down dead in the churches all the time. But the incident indicates God's attitude toward a Wrong Heart: a warning, right in the beginning days of the Church, against using, or misusing, the Church as a means of Self-Glorification. The incident, as a disciplinary example, did have an immediate salutary effect on the Church (5:11).

Chapter 5:12-42. Second Imprisonment of the Apostles

In their first imprisonment, after the healing of the lame man, Peter and John had been warned to speak no more in the name of Jesus (4:17–21). But they kept right on proclaiming the Resurrection of Jesus. God kept on doing Mighty Miracles (5:12–16). And believers kept on increasing (5:14).

The rulers stood aghast at the expanding power of the Nazarene whom they had crucified. They re-arrested the Apostles, and, except for fear of the people, and restraining influence of Gamaliel, would have stoned them.

Note Peter's undaunted defiance of the rulers (5:29–32); and the Apostles, though they were Scourged (40), kept right on Proclaiming Jesus, and Rejoicing in Suffering for Him (41, 42).

Gamaliel, who saved the day, temporarily, for the Apostles (34–40), was the most famous rabbi of his day. It was he at whose feet Paul had been brought up (22:3). Young Saul may have been present in this council meeting: for he was a member (26:10), and, just a little later, when the council stoned Stephen, Saul was a participant (7:58).

Chapter 6:1-7. Appointment of the Seven

Up to this time, the Apostles, it seems, administered the business affairs of the Church (4:37). In the few months, or year or two, the Church had grown enormously. And tables were absorbing too much of the Apostles' time.

The Apostles were the ones who had first-hand knowledge of the precious story of Jesus. The one means of making it known was by word of mouth. Their one business, from morning till night, in public and in private, to their last ounce of energy, was to keep on telling the story to the multitudes coming and going. So these Seven Assistants were appointed. The arrangement worked well: it was followed by an enormous increase of believers (7), under the Apostles' preaching.

Chapter 6:8-15. Stephen

Of the Seven, two were great preachers: Stephen and Philip. Stephen had the honor of being the Church's first Martyr. Philip carried the Gospel to Samaria and west Judea.

Stephen's particular sphere of labor seems to have been among the Greek Jews. At that time there were about 460 synagogs in Jerusalem, some of which were built by Jews of various countries for their own use. Five of these were for sojourners from Cyrene, Alexandria, Cilicia, Asia and Rome (6:9). Tarsus being in Cilicia, Saul may have been in this very group. Some of these foreign-born Jews, brought up in centers of Greek culture, felt themselves to be superior to the Jews of the home-land. But they met their match in Stephen. Unable to withstand him in argument, they hired false witnesses, and brought him before the council. Stephen must have been a very brilliant man. Then God was there helping with Miracles (6:8).

Chapter 7. Stephen's Martyrdom

He was before the same council that had Crucified Jesus, and that had just recently attempted to stop the Apostles speaking in the name of Jesus (4:18)—the same Annas and Caiaphas were there (4:6).

Stephen's address before the council was mainly a recital of Old Testament history, climaxing in a stinging rebuke for their murder of Jesus (7:51–53). As he spoke, his face shone as the face of an Angel

(6:15). They rushed upon him like wild beasts. As the stones began to fly, he looked steadfastly up into heaven, and saw the Glory of God, and Jesus standing at the right hand of God, as if Heaven were reaching its hand across the border to welcome him home. He died as Christ had died, without a trace of resentment toward his contemptible murderers, saying, Lord, lay not this sin to their charge (7:60).

"A Young Man Named Saul", 7:58

Here is one of the TURNING POINTS OF HISTORY. Young Saul seems already to have been a member of the Sanhedrin (26:10). He may have been present at one, or both, of the Sanhedrin meetings in which they tried to stop the Apostles from preaching Christ (4:1–22; 5:17–40), and may himself have witnessed Peter's bold and defiant refusal. But now, in all his life, he had never seen a death like that of Stephen. Though its immediate effect was to start Saul on his rampage of Persecuting the disciples, yet it may be that Stephen's dying words went straight to the mark, and lodged deep in Saul's mind, there quietly working to make him ready and receptive for the Great Vision on the road to Damascus (26:14). It may be, in part at least, that Stephen's Martyrdom was the price paid for Saul's soul. And what a soul! Next to Jesus, the Greatest Man of All the Ages. The One Man, who, more than any other, Established Christianity in the Main Centers of the then known world, and Altered the Course of History, Saul of Tarsus (see page 582).

Chapter 8:1-4. Dispersion of the Church

This was the Church's first Persecution. The Church was, probably, a year or two old. The Persecution lasted, probably, a few months. Paul was leader in the Persecution. He had two kinsmen who were already Christians (Romans 16:7). But the Persecution, set off by the Stoning of Stephen, was Furious and Severe. Saul, breathing Threatening and Slaughter (9:1), laid waste the Church, dragging men and women into prison (8:3), beating them that believed (22:19, 20), putting many to death (26:10–11), making havoc of the Church beyond measure (Galatians 1:13).

This persecution resulted in the Dispersion of the Church. In Jerusalem the Church had become a formidable and mighty movement pressing irresistibly on. Jesus' last command to the disciples was to Proclaim the Gospel to All the World (Matthew 28:19; Acts 1:8). Now, in the Providence of God, this Persecution started the Missionary Work of the Church. They had listened to the Apostles long enough to have fully learned the whole story of Jesus and His Death and Resurrection. And wherever they went they carried the

Precious News. The Apostles, however, too popular and too powerful to be persecuted, remained, temporarily, in Jerusalem, to care for Church Headquarters. Later they traveled about.

Chapter 8:4-40. Philip in Samaria and Judea

God authenticated Philip's message with Miracles (6, 7, 13). But Peter and John were sent to impart the Holy Spirit (15).

Then God directed Philip southward, to the Treasurer of Ethiopia, to relay the Gospel on to the heart of Africa.

Then Philip told the Gospel Story in all the cities from Azotus to Caesarea. Caeserea was his home (21:8, 9).

Baptism, 36-39

Initial rite in becoming a Christian. Its mention here is quite conspicuous. Jesus commanded it (Matthew 28:19). 3000 at Pentecost were Baptized (2:38). Samaritans (8:12). Saul (9:18; 22:16). Cornelius (10:47, 48). Lydia (16:15). Philippian Jailer (16:33). Corinthians (18:8). Ephesians (19:5. See also Romans 6:4; Colossians 2:12).

Chapter 9:1-30. Conversion of Saul

He was of the tribe of Benjamin (Philippians 3:5), a Pharisee; a native of Tarsus, third university center of the world, being surpassed, at the time, only by Athens and Alexandria; born a Roman citizen (Acts 22:28), of influential family; thus of Jewish, Greek and Roman background.

He evidently had determined to Destroy the Church. Having crushed and scattered the Jerusalem Church, he set out for Damascus to ferret out Christians who had fled there.

On the way, as by a stroke from heaven, the Lord appeared to him. His conversion is told three times, here, and in 22:5–16 and 26:12–18. It was a real vision, not just a dream. He was actually blinded (8, 9, 18). His attendants heard the voice (7). Henceforth he served the Christ he had sought to destroy with a devotion unmatched in history.

He spent "many days" in Damascus, preaching Christ (23). Then the Jews sought to kill him. He went away into Arabia. Returned to Damascus. Was in Damascus and Arabia 3 years. Then returned to Jerusalem (Galatians 1:18). Was there 15 days. They sought to kill him (9:29). And he returned to Tarsus (9:30). Some years later, Barnabas brought him to Antioch (11:25).

Chapter 9:31-43. Peter in Joppa

In Lydda, Peter healed Aeneas. In Joppa, he raised Dorcas from the dead: miracles that led many to believe (35, 42).

Peter abode in Joppa many days (43). Thus, in the Providence of

God, Peter was nearby when God was ready for the Gospel door to be opened to Gentiles, in Caesarea, 30 miles to the north.

Chapter 10. Extension of Gospel to Gentiles

Cornelius was the First Gentile Christian. Hitherto the Gospel had been preached only to Jews and Jewish Proselytes, and Samaritans, who observed the Law of Moses.

The Apostles must have understood from Jesus' Final Commission (Matthew 28:19), that they were to preach the Gospel to All Nations. But it had not yet been revealed to them that Gentiles were to be received as Gentiles. They seemed to have thought that Gentiles must first be circumsized, become Jewish Proselytes, and Keep the Law of Moses, before they could be accepted into the household of God as Christians.

Jews were scattered among all nations, and the Apostles, till God led them out of the notion, may have thought their mission was to them. For a while, they preached only to Jews (11:19).

But now, Judea, Samaria and Galilee, having been evangelized, the time had come, to offer the Gospel to Gentiles.

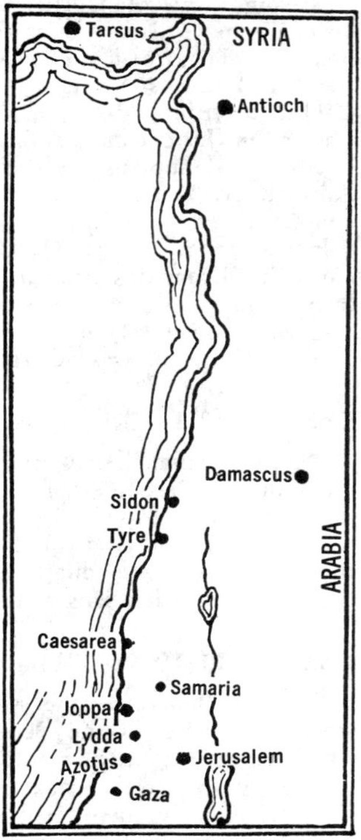

Map 62.

Cornelius

The first Gentile, chosen of God, to be offered the Gospel, was an officer of the Roman Army in Caesarea, named Cornelius.

Caesarea, on the sea coast, about 50 miles northwest of Jerusalem, was the Roman Capital of Palestine, residence of the Roman Governor, and Military Headquarters of the Province. The band of which Cornelius was Centurion is thought to have been bodyguard to the Governor. Thus, next to the Governor, Cornelius must have been one of the most important and best known men in the whole region.

Cornelius was a good and devout man. He must have known something of the God of the Jews and of the Christians. Caesarea was

Philip's home (8:40; 21:8). But, though Cornelius prayed to the God of the Jews, he was still a Gentile.

It was of God that Cornelius was chosen to be the First Gentile to whom the Gospel Door was opened. God Himself directed the whole proceedings. He told Cornelius to send for Peter (5). It took a special vision from God to induce Peter to go (9–23). And God put His own seal of approval on the reception of Cornelius into the Church (44–48), The First-Fruits of the Gentile World.

This, probably, was about 5 to 10 years after the founding of the Church in Jerusalem, possibly about A.D. 40. Knowledge of it, no doubt, gave impetus to the founding of the Gentile Church in Antioch (11:20). But it was hard for some Jews to accept (see next chapter).

It was from Joppa (5), that God sent Jewish Peter to Gentile Cornelius. From this same Joppa, 800 years before, God had to use a little extra persuasion on Jewish Jonah to get him to go to Gentile Nineveh (Jonah 1:3).

Note: Cornelius was not required to quit his army work.

Chapter 11:1-18. Apostles' Approval

Peter's acceptance of Cornelius, the Gentile, into the Church, without requiring Circumcision, was approved by the rest of the Apostles only after Peter explained it was all God's doing: God told Cornelius to send for Peter; God told Peter to go to Cornelius; and God sealed the transaction by sending the Holy Spirit (12–15). But there arose a sect of Jewish Christians who refused to acquiesce (15:5).

Chapter 11:19-26. The Church at Antioch

Founded soon after the stoning of Stephen, by those who were scattered abroad in the Persecution that followed, probably about A.D. 32, consisting at first only of Jewish Christians (19).

Some years later, probably about A.D. 42, certain Christians of Cyprus and Cyrene, possibly having heard of the reception of Cornelius into the Church, came to Antioch and began to preach to the Gentiles that they could be Christians without becoming Jewish Proselytes, God Himself, in some way showing His approval (21).

The Jerusalem Church heard of it. Convinced by Peter's story of Cornelius that the work was of God, they sent Barnabas to carry the Blessing of the Mother Church. And multitudes of Gentiles came in (24).

Barnabas went to Tarsus, about 100 miles northwest from Antioch, and found Saul, and brought him to Antioch. This seems to have been some 10 years after Saul's Conversion, 3 years of which he had spent in Damascus and Arabia, and the rest, as far as is known, in Tarsus. God had called Saul to carry the Gospel "far hence to the

Gentiles" (22:21). No doubt, he had spent his time, wherever he may have been, unceasingly telling the story of Jesus. Now he becomes an active leader in this new-born Center of Gentile Christianity.

Antioch

Third City of the Roman Empire. Population, 500,000. Surpassed only by Rome and Alexandria. Mediterranean Doorway to the Great Eastern Highways. 300 miles north of Jerusalem. Called "Queen of the East," and "Antioch the Beautiful." Embellished with everything that "Roman Wealth, Greek Aestheticism and Oriental Luxury could produce."

Its worship of Ashtaroth was accompanied with immoral indulgence and unbelievable indecency. Yet multitudes of its people accepted Christ. It became birthplace of the name "Christian," and Center of Organized Effort to Christianize the World.

Chapter 11:27-30. Antioch Sends Relief to Jerusalem

By Barnabas and Saul. This seems to have been Saul's second return to Jerusalem after his Conversion (Galatians 2:1). On his first, they had attempted to kill him (Acts 9:26–30). His arrival in Jerusalem (11:30), just before mention of Herod's killing of James and imprisonment of Peter (12:1–4), and mention of his return to Antioch (12:25), just after the death of Herod (12:23), and the death of Herod being known to have been in A.D. 44, would seem to place this visit in A.D. 44.

Chapter 12. James Killed. Peter Imprisoned.

This James, brother of John, one of the three inner circle friends of Jesus, was first of the Twelve to die, A.D. 44. Another James, brother of Jesus, came to be recognized as leading bishop of Jerusalem.

When Herod imprisoned Peter, God Himself took a hand, and delivered Peter (7), and smote Herod (23). This Herod was son of the Herod who had killed John the Baptist and mocked Christ. (See page 420.)

Chapters 13,14. Paul's First Missionary Journey

Galatia, About A.D. 45–48

Antioch rapidly became the leading center of Gentile Christianity. One of its teachers was foster-brother of Herod (13:1); from which we judge the Church had considerable prestige. It became Paul's headquarters for his Missionary work. From Antioch he started on his Missionary Journeys, and to Antioch he returned to report.

Paul had been a Christian now for some 12 or 14 years. He had become a leader in the Antioch Church. The time had come for him to set forth on the work of bearing the Name of Christ far hence to the Gentile world (22:21).

The Galatian region, in central Asia Minor, to which he went, was about 300 miles northwest from Antioch. It was a rather long journey. In those days there were no railroads, automobiles or airplanes: only horses, donkeys, camels or on foot; or sail and oar boats.

Cyprus, 13:4-12

The route would have been more direct by land, going through Tarsus, the southeastern gateway to Asia Minor. But Paul had already been in Tarsus some 7 or 8 years. So they went through the Island of Cyprus; then from west end of Cyprus north into central Asia Minor.

In Cyprus, the Roman Governor was a convert. A miracle did the work (11, 12). The blinding of the sorcerer was an act of God, not of Paul. From here on, Saul is called Paul (9). Paul was the Roman form of the Hebrew name Saul.

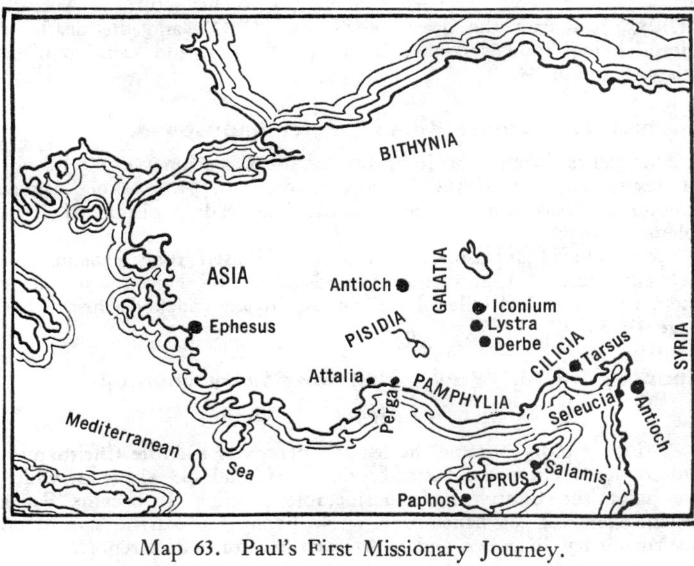

Map 63. Paul's First Missionary Journey.

Up to here, it is Barnabas and Paul. From here on, it is Paul and Barnabas. Henceforth Paul is leader.

Antioch, Iconium, Lystra, Derbe

In Antioch, of Pisidia, Paul, as his custom was, started his work in the Jewish synagog. Some Jews believed, and many Gentiles, in all the region round about (13:43, 48, 49). But the unbelieving Jews stirred up a persecution, and drove Paul and Barnabas out of the city.

In Iconium, about 100 miles east of Pisidian Antioch, they stayed a long time (14:3); wrought signs and wonders; and a great multitude believed (14:1). Then the unbelievers drove them out of the city.

In Lystra, about 20 miles south of Iconium, Paul healed a cripple; and the multitudes thought he was a god. Later they stoned him, and left him for dead. Lystra was the home of Timothy (16:1). Perhaps Timothy saw the occurrence (II Timothy 3:11).

In Derbe about 30 miles southeast of Lystra, they made many disciples. And then returned through Lystra, Iconium and Antioch.

Paul's Thorn in the Flesh (II Corinthians 12:2, 7), came upon him 14 years before he wrote II Corinthians. That was about the time he entered Galatia (Galatians 4:13. See further page 606).

Chapter 15:1-35. Council at Jerusalem

Question of Circumcizing Gentile Converts

About A.D. 50. 20 years after founding of the Church. Probably about 10 years after reception of Gentiles into the Church.

Although God had expressly revealed to Peter that Gentiles should be received without circumcision (chapter 10), and the Apostles and Elders were convinced (11:18), yet a sect of Pharisee believers persisted in teaching that it was necessary. And the Church was rent with discord over the question.

In this Council, God (28), led the Apostles to give unanimous and formal expression to the judgment that Circumcision was not necessary for Gentiles; and they sent a tolerant letter to that effect to Antioch, insisting though that Gentile Christians abstain from Idolatry and Immorality, which was so commonly practiced among Gentiles. Abstention from Blood, ante-dating Moses (Genesis 9:4) was for all the race.

This is the last mention of Peter in the book of Acts, (7). Up to chapter 12, Peter is the leading figure. (For his earlier life, see page 465. For his later life, see page 662.)

Chapters 15:36 to 18:22. Paul's Second Missionary Journey

His Work in Greece. About A.D. 50–53

Silas was Paul's companion on this journey (15:40). Little is known of Silas. He first appears as one of the leaders of the Judean Church (15:22, 27, 32). Like Paul, he was a Jew and a Roman citizen (16:21, 37). Sent with the Jerusalem Letter to Gentiles (15:27). Also called Sylvanus. Later, he joined in Paul's Letters to the Thessalonians (I Thessalonians 1:1, II Thessalonians 1:1). And carried I Peter to its first readers (I Peter 5:12).

Paul and Barnabas separated over John Mark. But later they worked together again (I Corinthians 9:6; Colossians 4:10. For Barnabas, see page 565.)

Mark, also called John Mark, turned back from Paul's First Journey (13:13), possibly through timidity, or fear, or maybe not fully convinced on Gentile evangelization. But now he wanted to go. But Paul thought it not best. (For note on Mark, see page 457.)

Re-Visits Galatian Churches, 16:1-7

At Lystra, Paul finds Timothy, and takes him along (16:1). Timothy ever afterward was Paul's unfailing companion. (See page 631.)

It seems that Paul was making his way toward Ephesus, "Asia" (6), but God stopped him. Then he started northward into Bithynia, and again God stopped him (7). Then he turned northwest, and came to Troas. Even Paul, intimate as he was with the Spirit of God, was in some cases a little slow in finding out the will of God for himself.

Troas, Philippi

At Troas (not ancient Troy which stands on an escarpment twenty miles away), Luke joined the party, "they" (8), "we" (10), and went with them to Philippi, and remained there, "they" (17:1), after Paul left; and rejoined Paul six years later, "we" (20:6).

God, who had steered Paul away from Ephesus and Bithynia (6, 7), now beckons him to Philippi (10). In prison, Paul and Silas Sang Hymns, God sent an earthquake (25, 26), and the Church they founded turned out to be one of the best in all the New Testament. (See page 617.)

Thessalonica, Berea, Athens

Philippi, at the northeast corner of Greece, was Paul's first European Church. Thessalonica, about 100 miles west of Philippi, was the

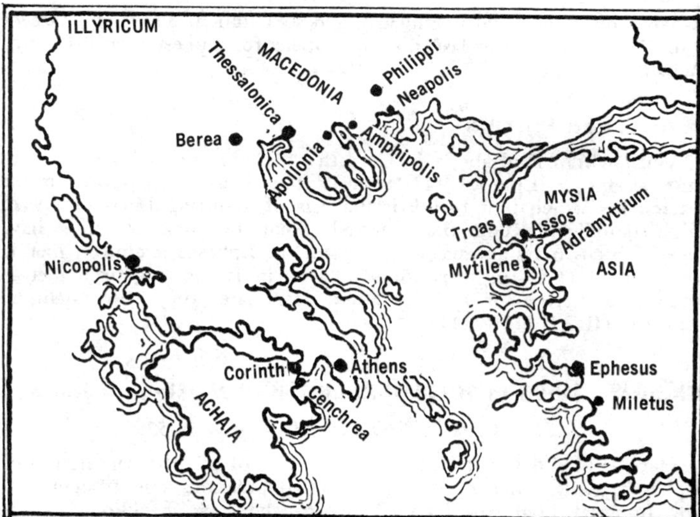

Map 64. Paul's Second Missionary Journey.

largest city of Macedonia. They were there only a short time, but made a great multitude of converts (17:1–9. See page 625.)

In Berea (17:10–14), they made many believers.

In Athens (17:15–34), the home of Pericles, Socrates, Demosthenes and Plato; center of Philosophy, Literature, Science and Art; seat of greatest university of the ancient world; meeting place of world's intelligentsia; wholly given to Idolatry. This was Paul's poorest reception but it was also his most exacting task to date. It revealed how truly at home he was with Greek thought. It was not a failure as some, misreading the first letter to Corinth, have maintained, but a brilliant translation of his message into Hellenic thought and language. Nor was the address without notable results.

At Corinth, 18:1-22

A principal city of the Roman Empire (see page 593). Here Paul stayed a year and a half, and established a great church (10, 11).

And then returned to Jerusalem and Antioch, stopping, en route, at Ephesus, on which his mind had so long been set. He may have been headed toward Ephesus, on his First Journey, when, at Pisidian Antioch, on the western border of Galatia, he was turned back eastward by his thorn in the flesh (Galatians 4:13, II Corinthians 12:2, 7). On his Second Journey, he was definitely headed toward Ephesus, when God turned him northward, and sent him to Troas and Greece (16:6, 7). And now at last, the door opens for Ephesus, on his Third Missionary Journey.

Aquila and Priscilla

With whom Paul abode in Corinth (18:2, 3), and who went with him as far as Ephesus (18:18, 19). There are inscriptions in the catacombs which hint that Priscilla was of a distinguished family of high standing in Rome. She is usually mentioned first. She must have been a woman of unusual talent. Later, in Ephesus a church met in their house (I Corinthians 16:19). Later, in Rome, a church met in their house (Romans 16:3–5). Some years later they were again in Ephesus (II Timothy 4:19).

Chapters 18:23 to 20:38. Paul's Third Missionary Journey

His Work in Ephesus. About A.D. 54–57

Here Paul did the most marvelous work of all his marvelous life. Ephesus, a magnificent city of 225,000 population, was at center of the Imperial Highway from Rome to the East, backbone of the Roman Empire. (See pages 687, 700.)

Vast multitudes of Diana worshipers became Christians. Churches were founded for a hundred miles around (19:10, 26). Ephesus rapidly became leading center of the Christian world.

The Temple at Diana

One of the Seven Wonders of the World. 220 years in building. Built of purest marble. Diana worship was "a perpetual festival of vice." Her influence later got into the churches (see page 694).

Apollos, 18:24-28

An eloquent Jew. Became a powerful leader in Corinthian Church (I Corinthians 3:6); and in Ephesus (I Corinthians 16:12). Some years later he was still helping Paul (Titus 3:13). Apollos, Aquila and Priscilla, helpers of Paul in Ephesus and Corinth.

Special Miracles in Ephesus, 19:11

With a school room as his headquarters (19:9), speaking publicly, and from house to house (20:20), day and night, for three years (20:31), maintaining himself by working at his own trade (20:34), with the aid, at times, of Special Miracles (19:11, 12), Paul shook the mighty city of Ephesus to its foundations. Magicians, who pretended to work miracles, were so over-awed that they made a great bonfire of their books (19:19).

It was only at times that Paul could work Miracles. He did Miracles in Cyprus, Iconium, Lystra, Philippi, Ephesus and Melita (see page 563), and, apparently, in Corinth (I Corinthians 2:4), and Thessalonica (I Thessalonians 1:5). But none are mentioned for Paul in Damascus, Jerusalem, Tarsus, Antioch, Pisidian Antioch, Derbe, Athens or Rome. Nor could Paul heal his own beloved fellow-worker Trophimus (II Timothy 4:20).

Paul's Plan to Go to Rome, 19:21

Having begun his work at Antioch, East end of the Backbone of the Roman Empire, now having done his greatest work at Ephesus, center of the Empire's Backbone, and having made known the Story of Christ all over Asia Minor and Greece, he now plans to journey on to the West end of the Empire.

Paul Re-Visits Greece, 20:1-5

He left Ephesus in June, A.D. 57 (I Corinthians 16:18). Was in Macedonia, summer and fall (I Corinthians 16:5–8). In Corinth the three winter months (I Corinthians 16:6). Returned through Macedonia (Acts 20:3). And sailed away from Philippi, April, A.D. 58 (20:6). Making nearly a year in Greece. This may have been the time he went to Illyricum (Romans 15:19).

Paul's Four Great Epistles were written in this period: I Corinthians, from Ephesus: II Corinthians, from Macedonia: Galatians, about same time, it is thought: and Romans, from Corinth.

Farewell to the Ephesian Elders, 20:17-38

They were tender words. He never expected to see them again (25). But his plans changed, and he did come back (see page 583).

This was the close of Three Missionary Journeys, covering about 12 years, A.D. 45 to 57. Powerful Christian centers planted in almost every city of Asia Minor and Greece, in the very heart of the then known world.

Chapter 21:1-16. Paul's Journey to Jerusalem

One purpose of the journey was to deliver the Offering of Money which he had gathered from Gentile Churches in Greece and Asia Minor for the poor saints in Jerusalem (Acts 24:17; Romans 15:25, 26; I Corinthians 16:1–4; II Corinthians 8:10; 9:1–15). It was a great offering. He had spent over a year gathering it. A crowning demonstration of the spirit of Brotherly Kindness, to encourage a feeling of Christian Love between Jew and Gentile.

Another purpose of the journey was to keep a Vow (21:24). A Vow had brought him to Jerusalem at the close of his Second Journey (18:18). These Vows he had made to show to the Jews that, while he taught Gentiles that they could be Christians without keeping the Law of Moses, he himself, as a Jew, was zealous to observe all Jewish Laws.

From the start of the Journey, he was warned not to go. The Holy Spirit, in every city, warned him (20:23). In Tyre (21:4). In Caesarea, while he was at Philip's house, the warning was repeated with graphic emphasis (21:10, 11). Even Luke begged him not to go (21:12).

But it was settled in Paul's mind, even if it meant death (21:13). Why these warnings from God? Could it be that Paul was mistaken, and God was trying to tell him so? Or could it be that God was testing him? Or preparing him? Could it be that Paul may have thought his own martyrdom at Jerusalem would have been a fitting climax, in the same city where he himself had martyred many Christians?

Chapters 21:17 to 23:30. Paul in Jerusalem

He arrived there about June, A.D. 58 (20:16). It was his 5th recorded visit to Jerusalem after his conversion. In intervening years he had won vast multitudes of Gentiles to the Christian Faith, for which unbelieving Jews hated him.

After he had been there nearly a week, fulfilling his vow, in the Temple, certain Jews recognized him. They began to yell, and in no time the mob was on him like a pack of wild dogs. Roman soldiers appeared on the scene in time to save him from being beaten to death.

On the stairway to the Roman castle, same castle where Pilate had condemned Jesus to death 28 years before, Paul, with the consent of the soldiers, made a speech to the mob, in which he told the story of Christ's appearance to him on the way to Damascus. They listened till he mentioned the word Gentiles, at which the mob broke loose again.

Next day Roman officers brought Paul before the Jews' Council to try to find out what was wrong. It was the same Council that had crucified Jesus; the same Council of which Paul had once been a member; the same Council that had stoned Stephen, and had made repeated efforts to crush the Church. Paul was about to be torn to pieces, and the soldiers took him back to the castle.

That night, in the castle, the Lord stood by Paul, and assured him that He would see him to Rome (23:11). Paul had often hoped to get to Rome (Romans 1:13). In Ephesus, the plan took definite shape (19:21), to follow this visit to Jerusalem, not sure, however, that he would get away from Jerusalem alive (Romans 15:31, 32). But from now on, Sure, SURE. For GOD Had Said It.

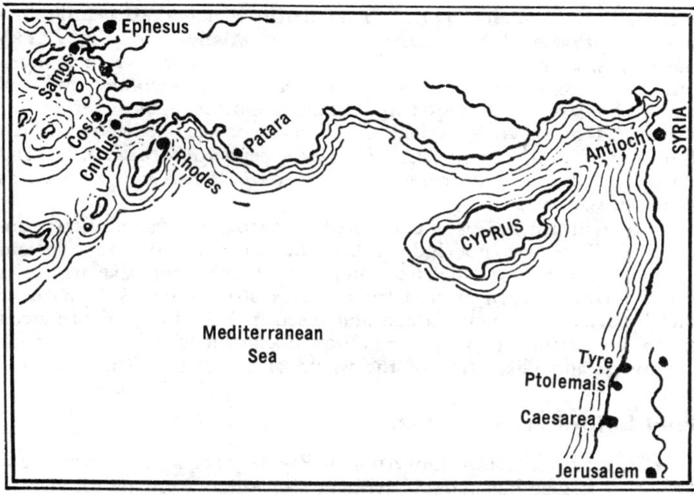

Map 65.

Next day the Jews renewed their plot to waylay Paul. Public frenzy was at the boiling point. It took 70 horsemen, 200 soldiers, and 200 spearmen to get him out of the city, and that under cover of darkness.

Chapters 23:31 to 26:32. Paul in Caesarea

Two Years, from Summer of A.D. 58 *to Fall of A.D.* 60

Paul had just been in Caesarea a week before, in Philip's house, on his way to Jerusalem, where a prophet, named Agabus, had come from Jerusalem to warn him (21:8–14).

Caesarea was Roman Capital of Judea, chosen of God, for the reception of the First Gentile into the Church, Cornelius, an Officer of the Roman Army, some 20 years before.

Here, in this most important Roman city of Palestine, Paul spent two years, as a prisoner in the Palace of the Roman Governor (23:35), with privilege of visitors. What an opportunity to make Christ known!

ARCHAEOLOGICAL NOTE: Caesarea

Modern Israel, conscious of its nation-hood, has a care for monuments of the historic past, and Caesarea is receiving the archaeologists' attentions. The harbor works have been surveyed by skin-divers, and interesting information gained. The theatre is under excavation, and one surprising find has been the name of Pontius Pilate in a fragmentary inscription. The garrison town, of course, was his headquarters as procurator, and the scene of a famous contest between him and a Jewish deputation in Jerusalem. Obstinate and overbearing, Pilate had hung votive shield on Herod's palace, dedicated to the Emperor. The Jews won their point by a deputation to Tiberius, and Pilate's symbols of his clumsy loyalty were transferred to Rome's shrine in Caesarea.

More will emerge as the covered remnants of the city are uncovered. They are not hidden like the relics of so many ancient towns under the accumulated building of the ages. Caesarea is a barren site, and open ground for the excavator. A city so typical of the three worlds which clashed and fused in Palestine, and produced the New Testament as their common document, should yield much of interest and illustration of the world of Christ and Paul.

Paul before Felix, 24:1-27

Felix had been Roman Governor of Palestine for a number of years. He knew something about Christians, for there were multitudes of them under his jurisdiction. Now he was to sit in judgment on the most noted of all Christian teachers. Paul made a deep impression on Felix. Felix sent for him often. But his covetousness kept him from accepting Christ or releasing Paul (26). Drusilla was sister of Agrippa (25:13).

Paul before Festus, 25:1-12

Festus succeeded Felix as Governor, A.D. 60. The Jews were still plotting to murder Paul. Festus, though convinced of Paul's innocence, was disposed to turn him over to the Jews; which Paul knew would mean death. So Paul appealed to Caesar (11), which, as a Roman Citizen, he had a right to do, and which appeal Festus had to honor.

Paul's Roman Citizenship, probably conferred on his father for some service to the State, more than once saved his life.

Paul before Agrippa, 25:13 to 26:32

This Agrippa was Herod Agrippa II, son of Herod Agrippa I who 16 years before had killed James (12:2), grandson of Herod Antipas who had killed John the Baptist and mocked Christ, great grandson of Herod the Great who had murdered the children of Bethlehem. Scion of this murderous family, king over the Province on northeast border of Palestine, he is now asked to aid Festus.

Bernice was his Sister, living with him as his wife. A woman of rare beauty, she had already been married to two kings, and had come back to be her own brother's wife. Later she became mistress to Emperor Vespasian and to Emperor Titus.

Think of Paul making his defense before a pair like that.

Even so, Agrippa was profoundly impressed (26:28). But to Festus the idea of a Resurrection from the Dead was so unthinkable that he cried out that Paul must be crazy (26:24).

They all agreed that Paul was innocent of any wrong (26:31).

Luke

Luke, though not in prison, was with Paul in Caesarea, "we" (21:17, 18; 27:1). It is thought that this was when Luke wrote his Gospel (Luke 1:1–3). His two years' sojourn in Caesarea gave him opportunity to spend time in Jerusalem, and perhaps Galilee, talking with apostles and original companions of Jesus, gathering first-hand information. Mary, the mother of Jesus, may have been still living, from whose lips Luke could have learned her own story of Jesus' Birth and Childhood and many incidents of His Life.

Chapters 27:1 to 28:15. Paul's Voyage to Rome

Begun in early Fall of A.D. 60. Three winter months in Melita. Arrived in Rome in early Spring of A.D. 61.

Made in three different ships: one from Caesarea to Myra; another from Myra to Melita; and the third from Melita to Puteoli.

Soon after leaving Myra they ran into fierce adverse winds, were driven off course, and, after many days, when all hope was gone, God, who, two years before, back in Jerusalem, had told Paul that He would see him to Rome (23:11), now again appears to Paul to assure him that He would make good His word (27:24). And He did.

Chapter 28:16-31. Paul in Rome

Rome, Queen City of the Earth. Center of History. For two millenniums, 2nd century B.C. to 18th century A.D. dominating power of the world. Still called the "Eternal City." Population, then, 1,500,000, half slaves. Capital of an Empire extending 3,000 miles east and west, 2,000 miles north and south, with population of 120,000,000.

Paul was there at least two years (28:30). Though a prisoner, he was allowed to live in his own hired house, with his guard (28:16), with freedom to receive visitors, and to teach Christ. There were already many Christians there (see his greetings in Romans 16 written three years before). Paul's two years in Rome were very fruitful, reaching even into the Palace (Philippians 4:23). While there he wrote the Epistles to the Ephesians, Philippians, Colossians, Philemon and possibly Hebrews.

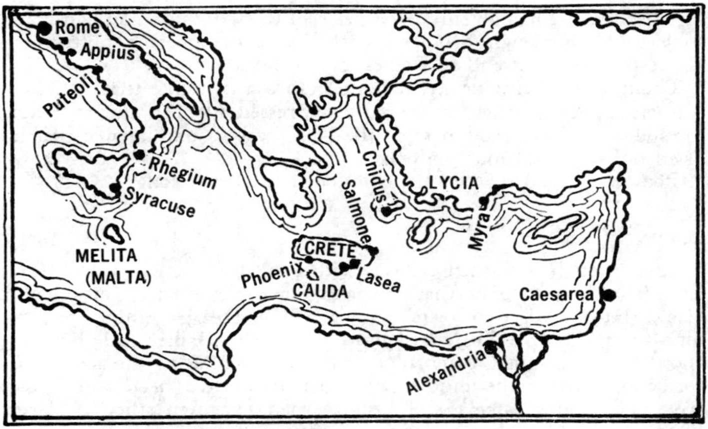

Map 66. Paul's Voyage to Rome.

Paul's Later Life

It is generally accepted that Paul was acquitted, about A.D. 63 or 64. Whether he went on to Spain, as he had planned (Romans 15:28), is not known. Tradition intimates that he did. But if he did, he did not remain long. It seems fairly certain that he was back in Greece and Asia Minor about A.D. 65 to 67, in which period he wrote the Epistles to Timothy and Titus. Then, rearrested, he was taken back to Rome, and beheaded about A.D. 67. (See further page 635.)

Summary of Paul's Life

With Tentative Approximate Dates

Paul first appears as a persecutor of Christians, resolutely determined to blot out the name of Jesus. No doubt he thought the Resurrection of Jesus from the Dead was a fixed up story.

Then, on the road to Damascus, as by a stroke from heaven, he was smitten down. Jesus Himself spoke to him, about A.D. 32.

From that moment he was a Changed Man. With zeal and devotion unparalleled in history, he went up and down the highways of the Roman Empire crying out, Jesus Did Rise from the Dead, It is True, It is True, IT IS TRUE, He is Risen, He is Risen, HE IS RISEN.

In Damascus they tried to kill him. He went into Arabia. Then back to Damascus. Then returned to Jerusalem, about A.D. 35. They tried to kill him. Then he went to Tarsus.

In Antioch, about A.D. 42 to 44. Went up to Jerusalem, about A.D. 44 with an offering of money for the poor.

First Missionary Journey, about A.D. 45 to 48. Galatia: Pisidian Antioch, Iconium, Lystra, Derbe. Returned to Antioch.

Conference at Jerusalem about Gentile Circumcision, about A.D. 50.

Second Missionary Journey, about A.D. 50–53; Greece: Philippi, Thessalonica, Berea, Athens, Corinth: return to Jerusalem, Antioch.

Third Missionary Journey, about A.D. 54–57: Ephesus, Greece.

To Jerusalem, A.D. 58, with great offering of money.

In Caesarea, A.D. 58–60, a prisoner in the governor's castle.

In Rome, A.D. 61–63, a prisoner. Here the book of Acts ends.

Back in Greece and Asia Minor, about A.D. 65–66.

Beheaded in Rome, about A.D. 67.

His ministry lasted about 35 years. In those 35 years he won vast multitudes to Christ.

At times God helped him with Miracles. In almost every city he was persecuted. Again and again they mobbed him, and tried to kill him. He was beaten, scourged, imprisoned, stoned, driven from city to city. On top of all this, his "thorn in the flesh" (II Corinthians 12). His sufferings are almost unbelievable. He must have had a constitution like iron. God must have used supernatural power to keep him alive.

ROMANS

Fundamental Nature of Christ's Work
Basis of Man's Standing before his Creator

Paul was chosen of God to be the chief expounder of the Gospel to the world, and his Epistle to the Romans is Paul's completest explanation of his understanding of the Gospel. Coleridge calls it, "The most profound work in existence."

Date and Occasion of the Epistle

Winter of A.D. 57–58. Paul was in Corinth, at the close of his Third Missionary Journey, on the eve of his departure to Jerusalem with the offering of money for the poor saints (15:22–27). A woman named Phoebe, of Cenchreae, a suburb of Corinth, was sailing for Rome (16:1, 2). Paul availed himself of the opportunity to send this letter by her. There was no postal service in the Roman Empire except for official business. Public Postal Service as we know it is of modern origin. Then personal letters had to be carried by friends or chance travelers.

Purpose of the Epistle

To let the Roman Christians know that he was on his way to Rome. Then, too, this was before God had told Paul that He would see him to Rome (Acts 23:11), and Paul did not as yet feel sure that he would get away from Jerusalem alive (Romans 15:31): in which case, it seemed proper that he, the Apostle to Gentiles, should leave on file, in the Capital of the World, a Written explanation of the Nature of the Gospel of Christ.

The Church in Rome

Paul had not yet been there. He reached Rome three years after he wrote this Epistle. The nucleus of the Roman Church probably had been formed by the Romans who were at Jerusalem on the Day of Pentecost (Acts 2:10).

In the intervening 28 years many Christians, from various parts of the East, for one cause or another, had migrated to the Capital City, some of them Paul's own converts and intimate friends (see chapter 16).

Paul's martyrdom, and probably Peter's, occurred in Rome, about 8 years after this Epistle was written.

Background of the Epistle

Common Jewish Belief in the Finality of Mosaic Law as the expression of the Will of God, and of Universal Obligation, and Jewish insistence that Gentiles who would be Christians must be Circumcized and keep the Law of Moses. Thus the question whether a Gentile could be a Christian without becoming a Jewish Proselyte was one of the great problems of the time. Christianity started as a Jewish Religion, and certain powerful Jewish leaders were determined it should remain so. Circumcision was a physical rite which stood as the initial ceremony in Jewish naturalization of Gentiles.

Paul's Main Insistence

In this Epistle is that Man's Justification before God rests fundamentally, not on the Law of Moses, but on the Mercy of Christ. It is not a matter of Law at all, because Man, on account of his Sinful Nature, cannot fully live up to God's Law, which is an expression of God's Holiness. But it is wholly because Christ, out of the Goodness of His Heart, Forgives Men's Sins. In the last analysis, Man's Standing before God depends, not so much on what Man has done, or can do, for himself, as on what Christ has done for him. And therefore Christ is entitled to the Absolute and Whole-Hearted Allegiance and Loyalty and Devotion and Obedience of Every Human Being.

Chapters 1,2. Universal Need of the Gospel

Universal Sinfulness of Mankind (1:1–32). The first sentence is a long one (1–7), summarizing Paul's life: Jesus, Foretold in Prophecy, Risen from the Dead, commissioned Paul to Preach Him to All Nations.

Paul's long time desire to come to Rome (9–15), hindered by unevangelized fields elsewhere (15:20).

Not ashamed of the Gospel (16), even in Rome, the gilded and haughty cesspool of every foul thing. The terrible Depravity of Man, pictured in 18–32, had reached its depths in Rome, specially the sexual practices of 26, 27.

Jews Included (2:1–29). Paul's frightful picture of Man's Sinfulness is true of the Jews also, even though they were God's own nation, for they practice the sins common to mankind.

Whosoever (1), includes every one of us. Not that every one does All the things mentioned in 1:29–31. That is a picture of the race as a whole. But each one of us is guilty of some of the things there mentioned.

The Day when God shall Judge the Secrets of Men (2:16). In That Day, the test will be, not race, not whether one is a Jew or a Gentile, but the Inner Nature of the Heart and its attitude toward the Practices of Life.

Chapter 3. Christ a Propitiation for Man's Sin

Why the Jews? (1–20). If Jews, in the matter of Sinfulness, are on the same standing before God as other nations, why then the necessity of there being a Jewish Nation at all?

The answer: to be entrusted with the Oracles of God, and Pave the Way for the Coming of Christ. Under God, the Hebrew Nation was founded to serve a special purpose in the working out of God's age-long Plan for Human Redemption. But that does not mean that intrinsically within themselves they are any better in God's sight than other nations.

One of the purposes of the Law was to make Man understand that he is a Sinner (20), in need of a Saviour.

Christ our Propitiation (21–31). In the Eternal Nature of things, as Sin is Sin, and Right is Right, and God is Just, there can be No Mercy apart from Justice. Sin must be Punished. God Himself took upon Himself the Punishment of Man's Sin, in the Person of Christ.

Therefore He can Forgive Man's Sin, and regard those who, in gratitude, accept the Saviour's Sacrifice, as possessed of the Saviour's Own Righteousness.

Chapter 4. The Case of Abraham

This is taken up because those who were teaching that Gentiles must become Jewish Proselytes in order to be Christians were basing their claims for Circumcision on the Promise made to Abraham, that it was to his seed; that, if one was not of the seed of Abraham by nature, he would have to become so by Circumcision. Paul explains that the Promise was given on Abraham's Faith, while he was still Uncircumcized; and that Abraham's Heirs are those who have the same Faith, rather than those who are Circumcized. The grand thing in Abraham's life was his Faith, Not his Circumcision.

Chapter 5. Christ and Adam

Paul bases the Efficacy of Christ's Death as an Atonement for Human Sin on the Unity of the Race in Adam.

How could One die for Many? One might die as a Substitute for another One—some justice in that. But for One to Die for Millions—how could it be?

Paul's answer is that Men are not to blame for being Sinners. They are born that way, brought into Life without being asked if they wanted Existence. Just woke up in this world to find themselves in a Body with a Sinful Nature. But, says Paul, the Founder of our Race, Adam, did not start with a Sinful Nature.

Paul explains the doctrine of Christ's Atonement for our Sin, not by setting Him over against each one of us singly, but by setting Him over against the Head of our Race.

Adam the Natural Head of the Human Race. Christ the Spiritual Head. What One Head Did, the Other Head Undid. One Man's Sin brought Death to our race. Therefore One Man's Death is sufficient to bring Life to those who will accept it.

Chapter 6. What Motive, then, to Right Living?

If we are no longer under the Law, and Christ Forgives our Sins, then why not continue to Sin? Keep on Sinning, and Christ keep on Forgiving.

Paul answers that such a thing is unthinkable. Christ died to Save us from our Sins. His Forgiveness is for the purpose of making us Hate our Sins.

We cannot be servants of Sin, and servants of Christ. We must choose one or the other. It is not possible to please Christ, and continue at the same time to live in Sin.

This does not mean that we can entirely overcome All our Sins, and place ourselves beyond the need of His Mercy. But it does mean that there are two essentially different Ways of Life: the Way of Christ and the Way of Sin. In heart we belong to one or the other, but not both.

Christ, the perfect embodiment of the Law of God, furnishes us with the Motive, and supplies us with the Power, to struggle on unto the attainment for ourselves of that Perfect Holiness which, by His Grace, ultimately shall be ours.

Chapter 7. Why the Law?

If we are no longer under the Law, why then was the Law given? It was not given as a scheme of Salvation, but as a preparatory measure, to educate Man to see his Need of a Saviour: to make us know the difference between Right and Wrong. Not until we realize our Helplessness is there desire for, and appreciation of, a Saviour.

Struggle between our Carnal and Spiritual Natures (14–25). We wonder if this is a picture of Paul's own inner struggle. In I Corinthians 4:4 he says He Knew Nothing Against Himself. Yet he must have felt powerful impulses within his nature against which he had a continuous desperate struggle. Else he could never have written these words. His unspeakable Gratitude to Christ for Deliverance from that against which he felt himself powerless reminds one of Luther's Unbounded Joy when he realized all at once that Christ could do for him what he had vainly struggled to do for himself. It is an illustration of the power of the Law on an earnest soul depressed by inability to live up to it, and the Relief found in Christ.

Chapter 8. The Law of the Spirit

This is one of the Best Loved Chapters in the Bible

The Indwelling Spirit (1–11). In Christ, we not only have our Sins Forgiven, but there is also an Impartation of a New Life. A New Birth. Our natural life, so to speak, is Impregnated by the Spirit of God, and a Baby Spirit, a Divine Nature, is born within us, in a manner somewhat similar to that in which our physical life, our Adam Nature, was started by our parents.

Our Natural Life from Adam. A New Divine Life from Christ. This is a Reality within ourselves. We may not feel it, nor be conscious of it. But it is there. We accept it as a matter of Faith. There is within ourselves, beyond the realm of our Conscious Knowledge, a Divine Life, the child of God's Spirit, under His loving care, working in stillness, ever unwearied, never exhausted, to gain control of our Whole Being, and Transform us into the Image of God. This is the Life that will blossom into Immortal Glory in the day of Resurrection.

Our Obligation to the Spirit (12–17). Walking after the Spirit means that, while depending wholly and implicitly on Christ for our Salvation, we still struggle to the utmost to Live up to His Law. Paul is explicitly explicit that the Grace of Christ does not release us from doing everything in our power to Live Right. Walking after the Flesh means giving ourselves to the gratification of our Fleshly Desires.

Our body is Flesh. Some Fleshly Desires are perfectly natural and necessary. Some are Wrong. Those that are Wrong we must abstain from altogether. The others we may enjoy, but be careful to Keep our Affection Above the Border Line.

Suffering Creation (18–25). The whole natural creation, including ourselves, is groaning for a Better Order of Existence, to be revealed in the day of God's Completed Redemption, when the Body of This Death (7:24), shall receive the Freedom of Heaven's Glory, now in the various processes of creation. It is a grand conception of the work of Christ.

Intercession of the Spirit (26–30). Not only is the in-dwelling Spirit our pledge of Resurrection and Future Glory, but through His prayers in our behalf we are assured that God will make Everything that might happen to us Work Together for Our Good. We may forget to Pray. The Spirit Never Does. God will see us through. Let us never forget to Trust Him.

The Inviolable Love of Christ (31–39). He Died for us. Has Forgiven us. Has given Himself to us in the person of His Spirit. If we are His, no power on earth or in heaven or in hell can prevent His bringing us to Himself in the Eternal Bosom of God. This is one of the most magnificent passages in all the Bible.

Chapters 9,10,11. Problem of Jewish Unbelief

One of the greatest stumbling-blocks to the general acceptance of the Gospel of Christ was Jewish Unbelief. While considerable numbers of Jews, especially in Judea, had become Christians, yet the Nation as a whole was not only Unbelieving but bitterly Antagonistic.

The Jewish rulers had Crucified Christ. At every opportunity they had persecuted the Church. It was Jewish Unbelievers that made trouble for Paul in almost every place he went.

If Jesus was really the Messiah of their own Scripture Prophecy, how did it happen that God's own nation thus Rejected Him? In these three chapters is Paul's answer.

Paul's Sorrow for Israel (9:1–5). A very expressive way of saying it: would almost be willing to give his own soul.

Sovereignty of God, 9:6-24

In this passage Paul is not discussing the Predestination of Individuals to Salvation or Condemnation, but is asserting God's Absolute Sovereignty in the choice and management of Nations for World Functions so as to bring all at last in subjection to Him. The strong statement (16), may include Individuals. Other similar passages certainly do: Acts 2:23; 4:28; 13:48; Romans 8:28–30.

How to reconcile the Sovereignty of God and the Freedom of the Human Will we do not know. Both doctrines are plainly taught in the Bible. We believe them both. But to explain how both can be true we shall have to leave to others, for the present. Some things we now see in a glass darkly. But some day we shall Know, even as we are Known.

Foretold by the Scriptures (9:25–33): Israel's Rejection, and the Adoption of Gentile peoples. So, instead of stumbling at it, we should have expected it.

Jews Themselves to Blame (10:1–21). God did not make the Jews Reject Christ. They did it of their own accord. It was simply a matter of Hearing (8–17). The Jews Heard, and were wilfully Disobedient (18–21). How to reconcile this with 9:16 we do not know. Maybe we will Understand better by and by.

Israel's Future Salvation, 11:1-36

Israel's Rejection of Christ is temporary. The days will come when all Israel shall be Saved (26). When or how that will be is not here stated. Nor is it stated whether it will be in connection with their Return to Palestine, but merely the bare fact that it will be. One of the darkest spots in the panorama of human history is the age-long Suffering of this Sorrowful, Disobedient people. But one day it will end. Israel shall turn in penitence to the Lord. And all creation shall give thanks to God for the Unsearchable Wisdom of His Providence.

Chapter 12. The Transformed Life

A Magnificent Chapter. In tone, it reminds us of Jesus' Sermon on the Mount. Paul invariably closed any theological discussion with an earnest exhortation to a Christian Manner of Life. And so here. In previous chapters he has been insisting that our standing before God depends wholly on the Mercy of Christ, and not on our own Good Works. Here he is equally insistent that that Mercy, which so graciously Forgives, is the very thing that supplies us with a powerful and irresistible Urge to Good Works, and Transforms our Whole Outlook on Life.

Humility of Spirit (3–8). This is specially for Church Leaders. So often position of Leadership, which should make us Humble, puffs us up. And so often a person with a certain Talent is inclined to disparage the value of different Talents possessed by others. (See more fully on I Corinthians 12–14.)

Heavenly Qualities (9–21). Brotherly Love, Hatred of Evil, specially within ourselves. Diligence, Joyfulness, Patience. Prayerfulness. Hospitality. Sympathy. Concern for that which is Honorable. Peaceable. Without Resentment.

Chapter 13. Obedience to Civil Law

Civil Governments are ordained of God (1), even though often run by evil men, to restrain the criminal elements of human society. Christians should be law-abiding citizens of the Government under which they live, in all their attitudes and relations of life, governing themselves by the principles of the Golden Rule (8–10), making special effort to be Honorable in all things, and always Considerate of others.

Approaching Dawn (11–14). The Night is Far Spent, and the Day is At Hand. This refers to Individuals who have been Christians for some time, or to the Christian Era moving on toward its consummation, or both. The Lord's Coming in Glory, or our Going to Him, in Death.

Chapter 14. Judging One Another

In such things as the eating of Meats and the observing of Days. The Meats referred to, though it is not so specified, must be Meat that had been offered in sacrifice to Idols (see on I Corinthians 8). As for Days, reference must be to Jewish insistence that Gentiles observe the Sabbath and other Jewish Festival Days. The Lord's Day, first day of the week, was the Christian's Day. If, in addition, a Gentile Christian wanted to observe a Jewish Sabbath, it was his privilege. But he must not insist on others doing it.

Chapter 15:1-14. Brotherly Unity

A continuation of the exhortations of the previous chapter. We rather suspect, from 16:17, and the discussion about Days and Meats in chapter 14, that Paul had learned, some way or other, that some of the Jewish Christians in Rome were determined to enforce Jewish habits on Gentile Christians.

Chapter 15:15-33. Paul's Plan to Come to Rome

If Paul had been like some people, as soon as he received his commission from Christ as Special Apostle to the Gentiles, he would have immediately set out for Rome, Capital of the Gentile World, and made it his headquarters for the Evangelization of the Roman Empire. One reason he did not, probably, was because from the day of Pentecost (Acts 2:10), a Church had been in Rome. And Paul's mission was to carry the Name of Christ to regions where Christ was not yet known. His plan was to take the territory as it came, working his way gradually westward. And now, after 25 years, having firmly planted the Gospel in Asia Minor and Greece, he is ready to press on to Spain, stopping at Rome on the way (24), He got to Rome about 3 years after he wrote this. (Whether he got to Spain, see on Acts 28.)

Chapter 16. Personal Matters

This is a chapter of personal greetings. 26 names of church leaders who were Paul's personal friends.

Phoebe (1–2), was bearer of the Epistle, probably on a business errand to Rome. Cenchreae was the east port of Corinth.

Prisca and Aquila (3–5), had formerly lived in Rome (Acts 18:2), had been with Paul in Corinth and Ephesus, and had now returned to Rome. A church met in their house.

Epaenetus (5), first convert of Asia, now in Rome.

Mary (6). Note how many of them are women.

Andronicus, Junias (7) Paul's kinsmen, now old men, for they had been Christians longer than Paul, and in prison with him.

Ampliatus, Urbanus, Stachys, Apelles (8–10), Paul's friends.

Household of Aristobulus (10), and of Narcissus (11), probably churches in their homes. Herodian, another of Paul's kinsmen.

Tryphaena, Tryphosa, Persis (12), names of women.

Rufus (13), probably the son of Simon who bore Jesus' cross (Mark 15:21), whose mother had taken a motherly interest in Paul.

Asyncritus (14), and brethren with them, their congregation.

Philologus (15), and the saints with them, their congregation.

Tertius (22), wrote what Paul dictated, his amanuensis.

Gaius (23), in whose home Paul was living at the time, and which was a general meeting place for Corinthian Christians.

Erastus (23), must have been a man of considerable influence being treasurer of the city of Corinth.

I CORINTHIANS

Mainly about Certain Church Disorders

Factions. Immorality. Lawsuits. Meat Offered to Idols. Abuses of the Lord's Supper. False Apostles. Problems about Marriage. Disorderly Conduct of Assemblies. Woman's Part in the Church. Heresies about the Resurrection.

Corinth

Commercial metropolis of Greece. Situated on the Isthmus of Greece, about 50 miles west of Athens (see Map page 575). One of the largest, richest, and most important cities of the Roman Empire. Population, 400,000, surpassed only by Rome, Alexandria and Antioch. On the principal trade route of the Roman Empire. Through its harbors flowed the commerce of the world. "A renowned and voluptuous city, where the vices of East and West met." Here Paul stayed a year and a half, on his Second Missionary Journey, about A.D. 52–53, and founded one of his greatest churches, right in the shadow of Athenian Philosophy.

Occasion of the Letter

About three years after Paul had left Corinth, while he was in Ephesus, some 200 miles to the east, across the Agean Sea, doing the most marvelous work of all his marvelous life, a delegation of leaders of the Corinthian Church was sent to Ephesus to consult Paul about some very serious problems and disorders that had arisen in the Church. Then it was that Paul wrote this Letter. He had written a previous Letter, now lost (5:9), possibly many of them. The two cities were on a busy trade route, with ships plying between constantly.

Date. Spring of A.D. 57, before Pentecost (16:8). He was planning to spend the following winter in Corinth (16:5–8), which he did (Acts 20:2, 3).

Chapter 1. Church Factions

In Corinth, as everywhere, except Jerusalem, Christians had no one great central meeting place. Church Buildings did not begin to be erected till 200 years later, when the age of Persecution began to ease. They met in Homes, or Halls, or wherever they could. There were multitudes of Christians in Corinth. Not one great congregation, but many small congregations, each under its own leadership. These, it seems, were developing into rival, competing units, rather than cooperating units, in the general cause of Christ, in the wicked city.

Some of the Greeks, in the fondness for Intellectual Speculation, and their Pride of Knowledge, were very boastful of their Philosophic interpretations of Christianity. And, in addition to this grouping of themselves around one Doctrine or another, they were rallying as partisans around one Leader or another. Thus the Church was split into Factions, each trying to stamp Christ with its own little trademark, a practice which still prevails in frightful proportions.

Chapter 2. The Wisdom of God

The Knowledge Party came in for the brunt of Paul's scathing rebuke. Corinth was close to Athens, where the atmosphere was dominated by egotists who paraded themselves as Philosophers. The spirit of Athens had penetrated the Church in Corinth.

Paul was a University man, the Outstanding Scholar of his generation. But Paul despised Pedantic Show of Learning. True Learning and True Scholarship should make us Humble, and more Broad-minded toward the ignorant.

Chapter 3. Bigness of the Church

Their Philosophic Pretense was a sign of their Spiritual Infancy, produced Faction, tended to Destroy the Church (17), and resulted in nothing of Permanent Value (12–15). The Church is too big to become the Exclusive Nest of one group of such Partisans (21–23). Why not be big enough to see this?

Chapter 4. Paul's Self-Vindication

There must have been a very considerable group of Church Leaders, Paul's own converts, who, in Paul's absence, had become influential and self-important, and were trying to run away with the Church. They had become Haughty, Overbearing, and Boastful in their attitude toward Paul. Hence Paul's vindication of himself.

Chapter 5. The Case of Incest

One of them was openly co-habiting with his father's wife. And the Church, instead of administering discipline, was proud of their Liberality in harboring such a person. Paul directed that he be delivered to Satan (5) that is, formally excommunicated from the Church: for two purposes: one, to serve as an example, to keep the practice from spreading: the other, in hope of bringing the guilty party to Repentance. The case is referred to again in II Corinthians 2.

Chapter 6:1-8. Lawsuits

Very unbecoming in followers of a religion of Brotherly Love to air their difficulties in Heathen Courts. Christians will be associated with God in the Final Judgment of the World; yet they were unable to settle their own quarrels (2–7). Why not be willing to Suffer Wrong?

Chapter 6:9-20. Immorality

Venus was the principal Deity of Corinth. Her Temple was one of the most magnificent buildings in the city. In it a thousand Priestesses, Public Prostitutes, were kept, at public expense, there always, always ready for Immoral Indulgence, as worship to their Goddess. Some of the Corinthian Christians, having been used to a religion that Encouraged Immoral Living, were finding it a little hard to adapt themselves to their new religion which Prohibited Immoral Living. Paul had said, in discussing certain things, that All Things are Lawful (12). Some of them evidently were quoting this to justify their Promiscuous Sexual Indulgence. Paul positively states that it does not so apply; and positively, in unmistakable language, prohibits Christians from such Indulgences.

Chapter 7. Marriage

They had written asking if it was Legitimate for Christians to Marry. Strange, they were puffed up over the case of Incest (5:2), yet had scruples about Lawful Marriage. Paul advises Marriage for those who desire it. Paul himself was not married (8). Some think he may have been a Widower, and lost his wife while yet young: for two reasons: one, he Voted in the Sanhedrin (Acts 26:10), for which, it is said, Marriage was a necessary prerequisite: the other reason, this chapter seems to have been written by one who knew something of the intimacies of Married Life.

Chapter 8. Meat Sacrificed to Idols

There were many Gods in Greece, and much of the Meat offered for sale in public market places had first been offered in sacrifice to some Idol. The question at issue involved not only the eating of the meat, but the matter of participating in social functions of their Heathen friends, many of which functions were often accompanied with Shameful Licentiousness. The matter is further discussed in 10:14–33.

Chapter 9. Pay for the Ministry

One of the objections which Paul's critics had brought against him was that he had taken no pay for his work in Corinth (II Corinthians 12:13), which, to their covetous minds, looked suspicious. Paul explains that he had a right to be supported at the expense of the Church (4–7). The Lord had definitely ordained that the Ministry should be so supported (14). But, so far as is recorded, Paul took pay from no Church except Philippi. In Corinth, Ephesus, Thessalonica, he supported himself by working at his trade. It was his life principle, so far as he could, to Preach without pay (16–18). It gave Paul great personal satisfaction to think that he was doing more than he had been commanded to do. Then, too, he did not want his example to be abused by false teachers whose main concern would be their Salary (II Corinthians 11:9–13).

Chapter 10:1-13. Danger of Falling

Paul had just spoken of exerting himself to the utmost, lest he should be a Castaway. That reminded him of the same danger to Christians generally. They had better take their Religion seriously. Most of those who were delivered out of Egypt never got to the Promised Land. The Temptations that caused them to Fall by the wayside were very much the Same Temptations that the Corinthians were facing (7–8), Lustful Indulgence. If they would strive wholeheartedly, with resolute determination, to overcome, as he was doing (9:25–27), God's promise of protection is sure against any temptation (13).

Chapter 10:14-33. Meat Sacrificed to Idols

Continued from chapter 8. There he had stated the general principle of governing our conduct in such matters by the law of Brotherly Love. There are some things more important than meat. Here Paul forbids Christians to participate in Heathen Temple Festivals; but explains that, in buying Meat in the markets, it is not necessary to ask whether it had been sacrificed to an Idol (25), nor at a feast in a private home (27), but, if someone tells him it is Idol meat, to refrain.

Chapter 11:2-16. Woman's Part in Church

It was customary in Greek and Eastern cities for women to cover their heads in public, except women of immoral character. Corinth was full of temple prostitutes. Some of the Christian women, taking advantage of their new-found liberty in Christ, were making bold to lay aside their veils in Church meetings, which horrified those of more modest type. They are here told not to defy public opinion as to what was considered proper in feminine decorum.

Men and women are of equal value in God's sight. But there are certain natural distinctions between women and men without which human society could not exist. Christian women, living in heathen society, should be cautious in their innovations, lest they bring reproach on their religion. It is bad generally when women become too much like men.

Angels (10), are onlookers in Christian worship.

Chapter 11:17-34. The Lord's Supper

It seems that after the Pentecostal Community of Goods (Acts 2:44–45), ceased, the wealthier members of a Church would bring food to certain services, for a Love-Feast (Jude 12), to be held after the Communion, in which rich and poor joined.

This, in Corinth, is seems, had overshadowed the Lord's Supper. Those that brought the food ate it in their own clique, without waiting for the whole congregation to assemble.

Imitating the drunken revels of heathen peoples in their Idol Temples, Christians were thus making their Love-Feasts occasions for gluttony, losing sight entirely of the true significance of the Lord's Supper.

Chapter 12. Spiritual Gifts

Before the New Testament was completed, while it was in the process of being written, in certain places, and at certain times, God gave special Miraculous Manifestations of the Holy Spirit to help the Churches guide themselves in the Truth.

This was necessary, because the Apostles were few, the Churches far apart, the means of transportation and communication slow, no railroads, telegraphs or radios. Ideas could travel no faster than people could travel, the Churches everywhere overrun with false teachers making all kinds of false claims, and Churches had no written records as to actual facts.

Apparently there had recently been a brilliant display of Gifts of the Holy Spirit in Corinth. One of these gifts was that of Speaking in Tongues, that is, in a Foreign Language, probably, as the Apostles did on the day of Pentecost (Acts 2:8). This gift, whatever it was, was very popular with the Corinthians. They all wanted it. If a brother could get up in meeting, and speak right out in a language that his neighbors knew he had never studied, that would be plain evidence that he was under direct control of the Holy Spirit. And they would look up to him. Then, as now, some people went to Church for the honor they could get out of it for themselves.

The various gifts of the Spirit, some natural, some supernatural, as enumerated in 8–10, were Wisdom, Knowledge, Faith, Healings, Miracles, Prophecy, Tongues, Interpreting of Tongues.

It is in a discussion of the Relative Value of these various gifts that the Love chapter is set.

Chapter 13. Love

The Premier Teaching of Christianity. An undying expression of Jesus' doctrine of Heavenly Love. More potent for the building of the Church than any, or all, of the various manifestations of God's Power. Love, the Church's most effective weapon. Love, without which all the various Gifts of the Spirit are of no avail. Love, the Essence of God's Nature. Love, the Perfection of Human Character, Love, the most Powerful Ultimate Force in the Universe.

Even if I bestow all my goods to Feed the Poor, even if I give my body to be burned, if I Have Not Love, it Profits me Nothing (3). What a Thought-Provoking passage! The Gift of Speaking like an Angel, of Prophesying, of having All Knowledge, of Faith that Moves Mountains, of Charity to the last dollar, even Martyrdom, all of no use unless we have the Spirit of Christian LOVE. What a call to Self-Examination!

Chapter 14. Tongues and Prophesying

This chapter is a discussion of the Relative Value of Tongues and Prophesying, which seem to have been the two gifts most sought after.

"Prophecy" was teaching on a lofty plane. It is not "foretelling" so much as Prophesying, which ordinarily meant Predicting Future Events, here seems to mean Teaching by special aid of the Spirit. Ordinarily it was far more valuable than Speaking in Tongues, because everybody understood it.

Woman's Part in Church (33–40), continued from 11:2–16. Paul here forbids (34, 35), what he seems to allow in 11:5. There must have been some local circumstance, unknown to us, that gave point to these instructions–possibly some bold women unbecomingly putting themselves forward.

Chapter 15. The Resurrection

The fact that some of the Corinthian Church Leaders were already Denying the Resurrection (12), is an indication of the extent to which False Teaching, of the very Worst Kind, had crept into the Church.

Paul insists, in the strongest language of which he is capable, that

Except for the Hope of Resurrection there is no excuse for the Existence of Christianity (13–19).

The Resurrection of Jesus from the Dead was the one unvarying refrain of the Apostles (see page 562). This 15th chapter of I Corinthians is the fullest discussion of it in the New Testament. In the meaning it gives to Human Life it is the most significant and grandest single chapter in the Bible.

The Resurrection of Jesus from the Dead was a Fact attested by Actual Witnesses who had Seen Jesus Alive after His Resurrection (see pages 554, 556). Paul himself personally had seen Him. There is no other explanation to the phenomenon of Paul's life. The occurrence on the road to Damascus was no hallucination. Jesus Himself was actually there.

Besides a number of Appearances to the Apostles, singly, or in groups, Jesus had Appeared to a Crowd of 500 People at one time. It had been 27 years, and more than half of these 500 were still living (6). It must have been a Reality. A crowd of People would not just Imagine the same thing.

The disciples at first were Slow to Believe that Jesus had Risen from the Dead (see page 554). But when they were finally convinced that it was a Fact that Jesus had Actually Burst the Bonds of Death, and had Come Out of the Grave Alive, it put such a New Meaning into Life that nothing else seemed worthwhile. They Knew the Resurrection of Jesus to be a Fact. Believed it even Unto Death. And they went up and down the highways of the Roman Empire telling the Story of it with such Earnestness and Sincerity that Unnumbered Thousands Believed It even Unto Death.

The Resurrection of Jesus from the Dead is the One Most Important and Best Established Fact in All History.

And the story of it has come down to us through the centuries Beautifying Human Life with the Halo of Immortality: making us to Feel Sure that because He Lived Again We Too Shall Live: making our hearts to thrill with the thought that we are Immortal: that we have begun an Existence that Shall Never End: that nothing can harm us: that Death is merely an incident in passing from one phase of existence to another: that whether Here or There we are His, doing the thing He has for us to do: that millions of ages after the sun has grown cold we ourselves shall still be Young in the Eternities of God.

The one most exhilarating thing in the whole range of Human Experience is the Thought that we are Immortal, that we Cannot Die, that whatever may happen to the body, We Ourselves shall Live on and on and on and on. And we have this feeling made Sure in our Hearts because Jesus Rose from the Dead.

If this story of Jesus is True, life is Beautiful, life is Glorious, looking down a vista that Shall Never End.

If this story of Jesus should turn out to be a Myth, then the mystery of existence is an unsolved riddle, and for humanity there is nothing left but the blankness and blackness of Eternal Despair.

But by all the laws of Historic Evidence it is a True Story. Christ was. Christ Is. A Living Person. With His People, in Guiding and Protecting Power, leading them on to the day of their Own Glorious Resurrection.

Christ's Mediatorial Reign (23–28). Here is a glimpse through successive Future Ages into the Endless End of things, when Christ's Mediatorial work shall have been finished, and God's Created Universe shall have entered its final stage.

Baptized for the Dead (29). This seems to mean Vicarious Baptism, that is, Baptism for a dead friend. But there is no other Bible reference to such a practice, and no evidence that it existed in the Apostolic Church. Perhaps a better translation would be "Baptized in Hope of Resurrection."

Resurrection of the Body (35–58). Our hope is not merely Immortality of the Spirit, but actual Resurrection of the Body. New Testament teaching is very plain on this (Romans 8:23; I Thessalonians 5:23; II Corinthians 5:4). It will not be the same corrupt earthy Body, but a Spiritual Body partaking of the nature of God's own Heavenly Glory.

Chapter 16. Personal Matters

The Collection (1–4). This was for poor saints in Jerusalem (II Corinthians 8:10). Order of Galatia (1), is not mentioned in Galatian Epistle. He must have written them another Letter, not preserved. First Day of the Week (2), was the established Day for Christian Worship (Acts 20:7).

Paul's Plans (5–9). This was Spring A.D. 57, before Pentecost (8). He spent Summer in Macedonia, from whence he wrote II Corinthians. Got to Corinth in the Fall. Wintered there. Wrote Romans. Following Spring set out for Jerusalem.

Apollos (12). Probably they had asked him to come to Corinth, but he refused to go at the time, no doubt, because certain Corinthians were determined to make him a Party Leader.

My Own Hand (21). Sosthenes, a Corinthian, who had gone to Ephesus, probably wrote this Epistle, at Paul's dictation (1:1; Acts 18:17). Then Paul signed it with his own hand (21), and added "Maranatha" (22), which means "O Lord, Come."

II CORINTHIANS

Paul's Vindication of his Apostleship The Glory of his Ministry And the Long Martydom of his Life

Date and Occasion of Writing

Paul had spent a year and a half, about A.D. 52–53, in the latter part of his Second Missionary Journey, in Corinth, and made a multitude of disciples (Acts 18:10, 11). Then, on his Third Misionary Journey, he had spent three years at Ephesus, A.D. 54–57. In the Spring of A.D. 57, while still at Ephesus, Paul wrote I Corinthians (I Corinthians 16:8). Soon afterward the great Riot occurred, in which Paul nearly lost his life (Acts 19).

Leaving Ephesus, he went into Macedonia, on his way to Corinth (see Map page 575). While in Macedonia, in the Summer and Fall of A.D. 57, visiting churches in the region of Philippi and Thessalonica, in the midst of many anxieties and sufferings, after long waiting to hear from Corinth, he met Titus, returning from Corinth with the word that Paul's Letter had accomplished much good (II Corinthians 7:6); but that there were still some of the Leaders in the Corinthian Church who were denying that Paul was a Genuine Apostle of Christ.

Then it was that Paul wrote this Letter, and sent it on ahead by Titus (8:6, 17), expecting soon himself to reach Corinth.

Its purpose seems mainly to have been Paul's Vindication of himself as an Apostle of Christ, and to remind them that, inasmuch as he himself had founded the Church in Corinth, he did have a right to have a say in its management.

A little later Paul reached Corinth, and spent the winter there (Acts 20:2, 3), as he had planned (I Corinthians 16:5, 6). While in Corinth he wrote his great Epistle to the Romans.

Chapter 1. Paul's Comfort in his Suffering

The Comfort (3, 4), to which Paul refers in starting the Letter, was occasioned by his meeting Titus (7:6, 7), who, returning from Corinth, brought him the glad news of the Corinthians' Loyalty. This, with his Thankfulness for escape from Death in Ephesus (8, 9;

Acts 19:23–41), accounts for Paul's note of joy in the midst of his Sufferings.

Ephesus and Corinth were only about 200 miles apart, with ships plying between constantly. And, it seems, from 2:1; 12:14; 13:1–2, that Paul had paid a visit from Ephesus to Corinth, with Sorrow (2:1), occasioned by a very grave crisis that had arisen in Paul's relation to the Corinthian Church, probably shortly after he had written the First Epistle. This may, in part, account for Paul's anxiety to meet Titus.

Chapter 2. The Case of Discipline

This seems to be the Incestuous Person, whom, in his First Epistle (I Corinthians 5:3–5), Paul had ordered to be Delivered to Satan; on account of which a revolt of considerable proportions against Paul had spread in the Church.

So serious was it, that Paul personally went from Ephesus to Corinth (1), but was rebuffed to such an extent that he here speaks of it as a Sorrowful Visit.

Then, it is thought, from 2:3, 9; 7:8, 12; 10:10, which passages imply things not found in I Corinthians, that Paul wrote another Letter, now lost, between the two which we have. It must have been quite stern, for it changed the tide in Corinth, to such an extent that those who had been upholding the disciplined person turned furiously against him (7:11). But Paul did not know it till he met Titus (7:6, 7).

The Affliction, Anguish and Many Tears (4), were caused, not only by the terrible experience he had just passed through in Ephesus (1:8, 9), but by his bitter Anxiety over the Corinth Situation. So distressed was he in not meeting Titus in Troas, according to plan (2:12, 13), that he passed up a grand opportunity for the Gospel in Troas, to hurry on to Macedonia, in hope of finding Titus whom he knew was on his way with the news from Corinth.

Savour unto Life and Death (14–16), is a figure of speech based on the incense-scented triumphal processions with which conquering emperors returned to Rome with long lines of captives, of whom some were to be put to death and others permitted to live. So, Paul bore along the Fragrance of God, which, according to one's reaction, meant Death or Life. Paul, so to speak, regarded his ministry as a march of triumph.

Chapter 3. The Glory of His Ministry

Epistles of Commendation (1). This expression was probably suggested by the fact that the Judaizing teachers carried Letters of Introduction from Jerusalem. They were always edging in on Paul's work, and were among his chief trouble-makers, and availed themselves of every possible excuse or opportunity to fight him. They were now asking, Who is Paul? Can he show Letters from anybody of standing in Jerusalem? Which, on the face of it, was absurd. Letters commending Paul to a Church which Paul himself had founded? The Church Itself was Paul's Letter.

This led to a Contrast of His ministry with Theirs: the Gospel with the Law. One written on Stone, the other on Hearts. One of the Letter, the other of the Spirit. One unto Death, the other unto Life. One Veiled, the other Unveiled. One unto Condemnation, the other unto Righteousness. One Passes, the other Remains. Beholding Christ, we are Changed, from Glory to Glory, into His Own Image.

Chapter 4. Paul's Living Martyrdom

In this Epistle Paul speaks much of his Sufferings, especially in chapters 4, 6, 11. At his conversion the Lord had said, I will show him how many things he must Suffer for My Name's sake (Acts 9:16). The Sufferings began immediately, and continued in unbroken succession for over thirty years.

They plotted to Kill him in Damascus (Acts 9:24). And in Jerusalem (Acts 9:29). Drove him out of Antioch (Acts 13:50). Attempted to Stone him in Iconium (Acts 14:5). Did Stone him, and leave him for Dead, in Lystra (Acts 14:19). In Philippi they Beat him with Rods, and put him in Stocks (Acts 16:23, 24). In Thessalonica the Jews and rabble tried to Mob him (Acts 17:5). They drove him out of Berea (Acts 17:13, 14). Plotted against him in Corinth (Acts 18:12). In Ephesus they almost Killed him (Acts 19:29; II Corinthians 1:8, 9). In Corinth again, shortly after he had written this Epistle, they plotted his Death (Acts 20:3). In Jerusalem again they would have made a quick end of him, except for the Roman soldiers (Acts 22). Then he was imprisoned in Caesarea for two years, and two more in Rome.

And besides all this, there were unrecorded Beatings, Imprisonments, Shipwrecks, and unceasing Privations of every kind (II Corinthians 11:23–27). Then finally he was taken to Rome to be executed as a Criminal (II Timothy 2:9).

He must have had Amazing Endurance, for he Sang as he Suffered (Acts 16:25). None but an iron constitution could have lived through it. Even that would not have been sufficient, except for the Marvelous Grace of God. By the Lord's help, Paul must have felt himself Immortal until his work was done.

Chapter 5. After Death What?

This chapter is a continuation of his reason for Joy in his Sufferings. He had just said that the greater the Suffering in this present world the greater will be the Glory in Eternity. Paul's mind was on the Future World.

What is the teaching here? Is the New Body put on at the moment of Death? Death is spoken of as, not an Unclothing, but as Being Clothed Upon (4), To be Absent from the Body is to be At Home with the Lord (8). In Philippians 1:23 Death is regarded as a Departure to be With Christ, which is Very Far Better.

But in I Corinthians 15 and I Thessalonians 4 the Resurrection Body is connected with the Coming of Christ. Evidently, the teaching is that those who Die before the Lord's Coming enter immediately a state of Conscious Blessedness with the Lord, which is very far Better than Life in the Flesh, but which is still short of the Glorious Existence following the Resurrection.

Chapter 6. Paul's Sufferings Again

Paul continues with his vindication of his own ministry. The disaffection in the Corinthian Church against him must have been considerable (12). Else he surely would not have devoted so much of this Epistle to a Defense of Himself. In 14–18 he seems to blame the trouble, partly at least, on the Heathen atmosphere in which they lived. Corinthians were very lax in morals.

Chapter 7. The Report of Titus

Timothy had been sent earlier (I Corinthians 4:17; 16:10). Timothy was timid by nature, and not exactly suited for stern disciplinary measures required by the Corinthian situation.

Then Paul sent Titus (II Corinthians 2:13; 7:6, 13; 12:18), who, for such situations, was probably the most capable helper Paul had. He probably went after Paul's second visit, and carried the Letter referred to in 2:3. His mission was successful.

The person over whom the trouble had arisen (I Corinthians 5:1–5), was probably very influential. It seems that he persisted in his sin, and led an open revolt against Paul, carrying some of the leaders with him. But under the influence of Paul's second Letter, and the presence of Titus, the Church as a whole was brought back into line, resulting in the Humiliation of the Offender. This was the Good News that Titus reported (7–16).

Chapters 8,9. Offering for the Mother-Church

These two chapters contain instructions about the Offering for the Poor Saints in Jerusalem, which Paul took at the close of his Third Missionary Journey. It was probably gathered in all the Churches of Asia Minor and Greece, although only those of Macedonia, Achaia and Galatia are named. It had been started a year before (8:10). The

Macedonian Churches had entered into it Whole-Heartedly. Even the very poor were giving generously. Paul was there at the time he wrote this.

Philippi, the leading Macedonian Church, was the only Church from which Paul had accepted Pay for his work, and that after he had gone away.

In these two chapters we have the most complete instructions about Church Giving which the New Testament contains. Though it is an offering for Charity, we presume the Principles here stated should be the Guide for Churches in the taking of all their Offerings, both those for Self-Support and those for Missionary and Benevolent enterprises. Voluntary. Proportionate. Systematic. Above Reproach in its Business Administration (8:19–21). That God will abundantly Reward those who Give Liberally is specially emphasized. The spirit of Brotherly Kindness thus manifested is called the Unspeakable Gift (9:15).

Chapter 10. Paul's Personal Appearance

Some things in this chapter seem to have been suggested by the charge of his enemies that Paul was Weak in Personal Appearance (1, 10). There is no hint in the New Testament as to what Paul looked like. A legend, dating from the 2nd century, says he was a man of Moderate Stature, Curly Hair, Scanty Crooked Legs, Blue Eyes, Large Knit Brows, Long Nose, and was full of the Grace and Pity of the Lord, sometimes having the Appearance of a Man, sometimes looking like an Angel.

Another tradition has it that he was Small in Stature, Baldheaded, Bow-legged, Stout, Close-browed, with a slightly prominent Nose, and full of Grace.

There are New Testament hints that he had Eye Trouble which, at times, made him repulsive in appearance (see next page). But the charge of his enemies that he was a Weak Personality (10), certainly was without basis. It is just not possible to think that of a man who turned city after city upside down, as Paul did. Unquestionably Paul was as Powerful and Dominating a Personality, and, all in all, as Great a Man as has ever lived on this earth, except only Jesus.

In reply to the charge that he was Weak, he tells them, that, at least, he Founded His Own Churches, and did not go around Troubling Churches founded by others, as they were doing.

Chapter 11. Paul's Apology for Boasting

In parts of the Epistle Paul is addressing the Loyal Majority, in other parts the Disloyal Minority. The latter seem to be in his mind in the last four chapters. He realizes the unseemliness of Boasting about himself, but they forced him to it.

They had been making capital out of the fact that he had Refused Pay for his work in Corinth (7–9). He explains that, while as an Apostle of Christ, he had the right (I Corinthians 9), yet he had purposely Refused Pay, lest his example be abused by False Teachers who were seeking to Make Merchandise of the Church. From the beginning of his work in Corinth Paul must have noticed tendencies to Covetous Leadership in some of his converts, and so governed himself accordingly.

One of the things of which Paul could boast was that they could not accuse him of Covetousness.

Then, in a passage of dramatic power (22–33), he challenges his critics to compare themselves with him by every standard: as a Loyal Hebrew: and as an Effective Worker for Christ—he had done more than all of them put together: and as a Sufferer for Christ—his whole career as a Christian Apostle had been an unbroken story of Living Martyrdom.

Chapter 12. Paul's Thorn in the Flesh

His Vision of Paradise (1–7). He was caught up "into" Paradise (4), "even to" the Third Heaven (2); as if Paradise and the Third Heaven are two separate parts of the Future World.

Jesus went into Paradise immediately at Death (Luke 23:43). As to the Third Heaven, there is no other passage in which the term is used, which might throw light on its meaning.

Some think Paradise and Third Heaven are synonymous terms for the Abode of God. But Into one, Even To the other, make it appear that they are two distinct places.

Inasmuch as Jesus passed Immediately into Paradise, Paradise is thought to be the abode of disembodied spirits Between Death and Resurrection. The Third Heaven is thought to be the Final Abode of the redeemed in their Resurrection Bodies: an existence more glorious than Paradise, as Paradise is more glorious than earthly existence. That there is an Intermediate state between Death and the Resurrection seems to be plainly implied in New Testament teaching (see note under chapter 5).

What Paul saw and heard in his Vision of Paradise, it was not Lawful for him to utter (4). This may mean that, to strengthen Paul for his special mission and the exceptional suffering he was to endure, God gave him a special vision of Future Glory, part of which he was forbidden to reveal to others. But probably "possible" would be a better translation than "lawful," the meaning being that there is no human language adequate to describe the Glory of Heaven: as the idea of Color could not be conveyed to a person who had been born blind.

Paul's Thorn in the Flesh (7). There are various opinions as to what this was. The view quite generally held, and which, to us, seems most likely to be correct, is that it was Chronic Ophthalmia, a disease of the Eyes, which was not extremely Painful, but, at times, made him Repulsive in Appearance.

This seems to be borne out by the language of the Epistles. It came upon Paul 14 years before he wrote this Epistle (2, 7), which was about the time of his entrance into Galatia, on his First Missionary Journey.

His entrance into Galatia was occasioned by some sort of Physical Infirmity, Galatians 4:13, so offensive in appearance that it constituted a sore trial to anyone in his presence, Galatians 4:14.

They would have given their own Eyes, Galatians 4:15. Why Eyes, unless that was his particular need?

Paul's customary "large" handwriting, Galatians 6:11, may have been due to poor eye-sight. This may have been the reason Paul Dictated his Epistles to some of his helpers.

Chapter 13. Paul's Intended Visit to Corinth

Paul wrote this Epistle in the Summer of A.D. 57. He got to Corinth in the Fall. Spent the Winter there. And, in the following Spring departed for Jerusalem.

GALATIANS

By Grace, Not by Law
Finality of the Gospel

Galatia

In Central Asia Minor (see Map page 572). Region of Paul's First Missionary Journey. Its borders at times varied. It included the cities of Iconium, Lystra, Derbe, and probably Pisidian Antioch. (Read Acts 13 and 14.)

Galatians were a branch of Gauls, originally from north of the Black Sea, split off from the main migration westward to France, and settled in Asia Minor, 3rd century B.C.

Occasion of This Epistle

Paul's work in Galatia had been extremely successful. Great multitudes, mostly Gentiles, had enthusiastically accepted Christ. Sometime after Paul had left Galatia, certain Jewish teachers came along insisting that Gentiles could not be Christians without keeping the Law of Moses. And the Galatians gave heed to their teaching with the same whole-heartedness with which they had at first received Paul's message; and there was a general epidemic of Circumcision among these Gentile Christians. Circumcision is the name of the Initiatory Rite into Judaism. Paul heard of the movement.

And then it was that Paul wrote this Epistle to explain to them that Circumcision, while it had been a necessary part of Jewish National Life, was not a part of the Gospel of Christ and had nothing whatever to do with Salvation.

Date

Paul had founded these Galatian Churches about A.D. 45–48. He had re-visited them, as he was setting out on his Second Journey about A.D. 50 (Acts 16:1–6); and again, as he was starting on his Third Journey, about A.D. 54 (Acts 18:23).

The commonly accepted traditional date of the writing of this Epistle is about A.D. 57, at the close of Paul's Third Missionary Journey, while he was in Ephesus, or Macedonia, or Corinth, shortly before he wrote the Epistle to the Romans.

Some think it more probably was written about A.D. 49, from Antioch, soon after Paul's first return from Galatia, before the Jerusalem Council of A.D. 50, whose Letter stating that Circumcision was Not Necessary was carried without delay to the Galatian Churches (Acts 15:1–16:4); for, if written after that, it seems like Paul would have referred to the Jerusalem Letter. But "first" (4:13), favors the later date.

The Judaizers

Judaizers were a sect of Jewish Christians who, not willing to accept the teaching of the Apostles on the question (Acts 15), continued to insist that Christians must come to God through Judaism, that a Gentile, in order to be a Christian, must become a Jewish Proselyte, and keep the Jewish Law.

They made it their business to visit and unsettle and trouble Gentile Churches. They were simply determined to stamp Christ with the Jewish Trademark.

Against this Paul stood adamant. "Had the observance of the Law been imposed on Gentile converts Paul's whole lifework would have been wrecked."

"The expansion of Christianity from a Jewish sect into a World Religion was Paul's consuming passion, in pursuit of which he broke every hindering tie, and strained every faculty of mind and body for upwards of thirty years."

The effort to Judaize the Gentile Churches was brought to an end by the Fall of Jerusalem, A.D. 70, which "Severed all relation between Judaism and Christianity. Up to this time Christianity was regarded as a Sect or Branch of Judaism. But from then on Jews and Christians were apart. A small sect of Jewish Christians, the Ebionites, remained, in decreasing numbers, for two centuries, hardly recognized by the general Church, and regarded as Apostates by their own race."

Circumcision was the name of the initiatory physical rite of Judaism. If a male, not born a Jew, wished to become a Jewish Proselyte, he could do so by being Circumcized, and observing the ceremonial law of the Jews; in some respects, as a foreigner may become a citizen of our country.

Chapter 1. Paul's Gospel Direct from God

To discredit Paul in the eyes of the Galatians the Judaizers, it seems, were saying that Paul was not an original Apostle, and that he derived his teaching from the Twelve. This may supply the background for his passionate vindication of himself as an independent Apostle. He got his Gospel direct from God, and there is no other Gospel.

"Arabia" (17). There is no mention of this in the account in Acts. The three years (18), includes the time he was in Damascus and in Arabia (Acts 9:23). According to Jewish usage of reckoning part years at the beginning and end of a period as years the three years may have been only one full year and parts of two years. Arabia is the desert country east of Palestine, extending southeastward from Damascus. Paul was so stunned by the stroke from heaven, and the instant realization that his whole life had been wrong, that he felt he had better think is over, and sought solitude to get himself reconstructed. It was in Arabia that some of his revelations came (16).

Chapter 2. Paul's Relation to the Other Apostles

The Visit to Jerusalem (1–10). Paul waited three years after his conversion before he returned to Jerusalem, where he had laid waste the Church. Was there only 15 days, talking things over with Peter (18). Compare the account in Acts 9:26–30. Then after 14 years he went again to Jerusalem. This must have been the visit recorded in Acts 11:27–30, which was in A.D. 44, for the context, along with the implication of "again" in 1, appears to mean his second visit to Jerusalem after his conversion. He took Titus, one of his Gentile converts, along as a test case, in the moot question of Gentile circumcision. He stood his ground, and won the complete endorsement of the other Apostles (9).

Peter's Dissimulation at Antioch (11–21). It is not stated when this visit took place. Probably it was soon after Paul's return to Antioch from the visit referred to in 1, and before Paul set out on his First Missionary Journey. To get the setting and significance of the incident our tentative chronology would be something like this: Peter received the first Gentile convert without circumcision, Cornelius (Acts 10), probably about A.D. 40, which action was approved by the other Apostles (Acts 11). Then, about A.D. 42 the Gentile church at Antioch came into being, with the approval of Barnabas as emissary from Jerusalem (Acts 11:22–24). Then, A.D. 44, this trip of Paul, with Titus, to Jerusalem, at which Peter joined in the endorsement of Paul's reception of Gentiles without circumcision. Then, soon thereafter, about A.D. 44 or 45, this trip of Peter's to Antioch, at which he separated himself from the uncircumcised Gentiles, and drew the scathing rebuke from Paul (11). But five or six years later, at the Jerusalem Council, A.D. 50, Peter was the first to speak out in favor of Paul's work (Acts 15:7–11).

What does this vascillation on the part of Peter, and this disagreement over so fundamental a teaching between the two leading Apostles, mean? In this particular incident either Peter or Paul was wrong. How can we know which it was? If either of them was mistaken in one thing, how do we know but what they may have been mistaken in other things? Does not the doctrine that the Apostles were Inspired of God break down under this incident? Not at all; for the simple fact that God did not reveal the full complete truth about His Kingdom to the Apostles all at once, Jesus had told them that he still had many things to teach them that they could not then bear (John 16:12). Jesus dealt very patiently with human prejudice, allowing them to hold to their old notions of the Messianic Kingdom, till, as need arose, he led them, step by step, into the newer phases of the Kingdom. He did not bother them with the Gentile problem till the problem arose. Then, after the Gospel had been fully proclaimed among the Jews over their Palestinian homeland, God, by direct and special revelation, undertook to instruct Peter on the Gentile matter (Acts 10), which was probably about ten years after the Pentecostal birthday of the Church. It took a few years for the Apostles to get readjusted to the new teaching. Paul came out of the old notion more readily than Peter did. The Galatian incident happened after Paul had come all the way out, and while Peter was on the way out. But Peter came all the way out before any of the New Testament books were written, and there is not an iota of difference between the teachings of Paul and Peter in the New Testament.

Chapters 3,4. Bondage Under the Law

These Gentile Galatians had swallowed the Judaizers' message so completely that they had instituted Jewish Festival Days and Ceremonies (4:8–11), evidently trying to combine the Gospel with Mosaic Law. But Paul tells them that the two systems do not combine. Did the Judaizers work any miracles among them, as he had done? (3:5). Did not that mean anything to them? Abraham figures largely in these two chapters, because the Jewish message which they had accepted was based largely on the promise to Abraham. They were misinterpreting the promise, as was shown plainly in the Abraham narrative itself (4:21–31). Their early love for Paul was in sad contrast with their present coolness (4:12–20. For note on his "infirmity," 4:13, see under II Corinthians 12).

Chapters 5,6. Freedom in Christ

How any human being would deliberately choose to risk his salvation on his own works rather than on the gracious mercy of Christ, Paul could not see. Christ saves us. We do not save ourselves. It is the difference between freedom and slavery. But freedom in Christ does not mean license to continue in sin. Paul never fails to lay special stress on that. Those who follow fleshly lusts cannot be saved (5:19–

21). One of the "spiritual laws of the natural world" is that a man shall "reap what he sows" (6:7), inevitable in its working, whether the seed be wheat or tares. "Large letters" (6:11), evidence of the genuineness of his own handwriting (see note on his "thorn in the flesh" under II Corinthians 12). "Branded with the marks of Jesus" (6:17). His enemies claimed that Paul was not a genuine Apostle of Christ. His battered, bruised, and scarred body was his testimony. (See II Corinthians 4, 6, 11.)

EPHESIANS

Unity of the Church
Jews and Gentiles One in Christ

Paul spent his life teaching Gentiles that they could be Christians without becoming Jewish Proselytes. This was very displeasing to Jews generally, for they thought of the Mosaic Law as binding upon All, and were bitterly prejudiced against Uncircumcised Gentiles who presumed to call themselves disciples of the Jewish Messiah.

While Paul taught Gentile Christians to stand like a rock for their Liberty in Christ, as he did in Galatians and Romans, yet he did not want them to be Prejudiced against their Jewish fellow-Christians, but to regard them as Brothers in Christ.

Paul did not want to see Two Churches: a Jewish Church and a Gentile Church: but ONE CHURCH: Jews and Gentiles One in Christ. His gesture, in behalf of Unity, to Jewish elements in the Church, was the Great Offering of Money which he took from Gentile Churches, at the close of his Third Missionary Journey, to the Poor in the Mother-Church at Jerusalem (Acts 21). His hope was that this demonstration of Christian Love might bring Jewish Christians to feel more kindly toward Gentiles.

Paul's gesture, in behalf of Unity, to Gentile elements in the Church, was This Epistle, written to the leading center of his own Gentile Converts, exalting the ONENESS, UNIVERSALITY and UNSPEAKABLE GRANDEUR of the Body of Christ.

To Paul, Christ was a Great Big Something, in Whom there is room, not only for people of different Races, Viewpoints and Prejudices, but He is One who has Power to solve all the problems of mankind, and bring into unity and harmony with God all earthly Social and Family life (5:22–6:9), and even the Myriads of Beings in the Infinite Unseen Universe (3:10).

This is one of the four "Prison Epistles," written from Paul's Roman imprisonment, A.D. 61–63, the others being Philippians, Colossians, Philemon. Three of these were written at the same time, and carried by the same messengers (6:21; Colossians 4:7–9; Philemon 10–12: Ephesians, Colossians, Philemon). There was another, not now extant (Colossians 4:16).

Chapter 1. Spiritual Blessings

"At Ephesus" (1), is not in some of the most ancient manuscripts. It is thought that, probably, it was intended as a Circular Letter to the Asian Churches, Tychicus bearing a number of copies, with space for each city to insert its own name. This would account for its lack of personal greetings, with which most of Paul's Letters abound.

Paul had spent three years in Ephesus, and had there many devoted friends. But if this was a circular Letter to Ephesus and neighboring cities that would account for its more formal tenor. The Laodicean Letter (Colossians 4:16), possibly, may have been one of the copies.

God's Eternal Purpose (3–14). A magnificent epitome of God's plans: the redemption, adoption, forgiveness, and sealing of a people for God's own possession, determined from eternity, now being brought to pass through the effective exercise of God's will.

"Heavenly places" (3), is a key phrase of this book (10, 20; 2:6; 3:10; 6:12). It means the unseen sphere above this world of sense, which is the Christian's ultimate home, and with which we now, in a measure, have communication.

Paul's Prayer for Them (16–23). That is the way Paul usually begins his Letters. Four such prayers are especially beautiful: This, and those in 3:14–19; Philippians 1:9–11; and Colossians 1:9–12.

Chapters 2,3. The Church Universal

Saved by Grace (1–10). The Body of Christ is being built up out of unworthy sinful men, to be an everlasting demonstration of the Kindness of God. When God's work in us is completed we will be creatures of Unutterable Bliss in a state of heavenly glory beyond anything we can now imagine. It will be God's work, not ours; and through the ages heaven will never cease to resound with the glad hallelujahs from grateful hearts of the redeemed.

Once One Nation, Now All Nations (2:11–22). "Circumcision" as a term came to be used as a name of the Jews, as distinct from other nations which were spoken of as the "Uncircumcision" (11). For a while the Jews constituted the body of God's people, of which circumcision was the fleshly sign, and from which other nations were excluded. But now the Call from God rings out clear and strong to ALL, from every tribe and nation, to come and join His household.

The "Mystery" of Christ (3:3–9), hid for ages in God (9), in this passage plainly means that the Nations are heirs to the promises which God gave to the Jews, but which the Jews hitherto had thought belonged to them exclusively. That phase of God's plan had been hid, though He had purposed it from the beginning (1:5), till the coming of Christ, but now is fully revealed: namely: that God's future world of glory will be builded, not out of the Jewish nation, but from All Mankind.

Grandeur of the Church (3:8–11). Through the Church God unites the hostile elements of the human race into One Body, and demonstrates His wisdom to the superhuman orders of heavenly beings, actually summing up all things in Christ.

Chapter 4. Oneness of the Church

ONE BODY (1–16). A complex organism, with many functions, each in its own place, working in harmony, its basic principle love (16), Christ himself its head and directive force.

Being composed of many members of diverse talents and tempers, the fundamental requisite to its proper functioning is a spirit of humility and mutual forbearance on the part of the members one toward another (2).

Its object is to nurture each of its members into the perfect image of Christ (12–15). The idea of growth, as expressed in these verses, seems to apply both to individuals and to the Church as a whole. The childhood of the Church will pass. Its maturity will come. (Compare the companion passage, I Corinthians 12, 13.)

The Church is nearly 2,000 years old, and, in this respect, is still in its childhood state. It has not yet, in its visible manifestation as a whole, known Unity. Paul's unceasing fight was against factional elements in local churches and the Jew-Gentile dissension. Then came the bitter controversies of the 2nd to 4th centuries. Then the Imperial Church, with its outward semblance of Unity under State authority, but poisonous blight of its spiritual life. Then the Papal Hierarchy with its Unity of Authority that robbed men of their rights of conscience and drove the Bible out of circulation.

Then, 400 years ago, the Protestant break for freedom. Naturally, when men began again to think for themselves, after the long night of Papal bondage, they would see things somewhat differently; and it was inevitable that the Protestant Movement would go down the years in different streams. So we still have a Divided Christendom. Whether there will ever, in this world, be an outward organic Unity of the Visible Church, we do not know. The selfishness and pride of men are against it. But there always has been, and still is, a Unity in the Invisible Church, of God's true saints, which, somehow, sometime, somewhere, will come to full fruition, in answer to Christ's own prayer (John 17), and manifest itself as the fullgrown body of Christ.

New obligations (25–32). Seeing the Church is a brotherhood, it is necessary that its members be very considerate of one another. "Anger" (26): perhaps Paul thought it was a little too much to tell them not to get angry at all; so he cautions them to be careful not to hold it. "Stole" (28): some of them evidently had been tough characters; but now they must respect the rights of others. (See note on II Thessalonians 3:6–15.)

Chapters 5,6. New Obligations

In these two chapters Paul continues with what he began in 4:17: their obligation to Live differently.

Fornication (5:3–14), that is, immorality, promiscuous sexual indulgence. It was a very common sin in Paul's day, in many places a part of heathen worship. Paul warns against it again and again. (See notes on I Corinthians 7 and I Thessalonians 4:1–8.)

Singing (5:18–21). The joyful praise of Christian meetings is here put in contrast with the riotous indulgence of noisy drunken revels (18, 19). Hymn singing is by far the most natural, simplest, best loved, and by all odds the most spiritually stimulating of all the exercises of religious meetings.

Husbands and Wives (5:22–33). If we are Christians, we must show it in all the relations of life: business, social and domestic. The relation between husband and wife is here represented as being a counterpart of the relation between Christ and the Church (25, 32). The exhortation is to mutual love and devotion, and in no way suggests that a man has a right to make a slave of his wife. Each is dependent on the other, because of the different functions that each has in human society. Each, in serving the other, best serves self (28). "He that loves his wife loves himself": husbands, take note.

Parents and Children (6:1–4). It was one of the Ten Commandments that we honor those who gave us life. So doing would prolong that life. This was the promise of God, and is a fact of nature. Fathers are cautioned against being too severe with their children, both here and in Colossians 3:21. Parental authority was generally too austere then, as it is now generally too lax. Fathers are named, because mothers are naturally more lenient. We suspect that it was easier then for parents to raise children after their old mold than it is now, for they were not exposed to so many influences outside the home so early and so continuously as today.

Servants and Masters (6:5–9). Half the population of Rome, and a large proportion of the population of the Empire, were slaves. Many of the Christians were slaves. They are here told that faithful service to their master is a prime requisite of their Christian faith. It is a remarkable teaching: that, in the performance of our earthly tasks, however menial, we are always under the watchful eye of Christ, for His approval or disapproval, as we may deserve. So are masters in their treatment of slaves.

The Christian's Armor (6:10–20). This passage certainly means that the Christian's warfare is against more than the natural temptations of his flesh. There are powers in the unseen world against which we are powerless except through the aid of Christ. Truth, Righteousness, Peace, Faith, Salvation, the Word, Prayer, are weapons that ward off the darts of the unseen enemy.

PHILIPPIANS

A Missionary Letter

It is not easy to give a Subject to this Epistle. It is, letter-like, about a number of things. However, as it was occasioned by the reception of an Offering of Money from one of Paul's Churches, to help support him in his Foreign Missionary work, we call it a Missionary Letter.

As a rule, Paul would not take pay for Preaching, but maintained himself by working at his trade, as a Tent-Maker (I Corinthians 9:12; Acts 18:3), because there were many false teachers who would make wrong use of his example or put a wrong construction on it. However, he did accept offerings from the Philippian Church, while he was in Thessalonica (4:16), and also while he was in Corinth (II Corinthians 11:9).

Philippi

At the southeast corner of Europe, in Macedonia, the north part of what we know as Greece (see Map page 575). A strategic city. On the Great Northern Highway between the East and the West. Noted for its gold mines. It was on the plains of Philippi (42 B.C.), that the battle was fought, in which, with the defeat of Brutus and Cassius, the Roman Republic fell, and the Roman Empire was born. Augustus made it a Roman Colony.

The Church in Philippi

This was Paul's first European Church. Founded about A.D. 51, in the early part of Paul's Second Missionary Journey (Acts 16). Lydia and the Jailor were among the converts. Luke, the beloved physician, was its pastor the first six years.

It may have been Luke's home, where he practiced medicine. Luke must have had a hand in the development of the unspotted character of the Church. As far as we know, the Philippian Church was one of the purest of New Testament Churches.

Occasion of the Letter

Paul was in prison in Rome, A.D. 61–63, about ten years after he had founded the Church in Philippi, and about three or four years after he had last visited there. Apparently (4:10), he had begun to wonder if they had forgotten him. Then Epaphroditus arrived from far away Philippi with an offering of money. Paul was deeply touched. Epaphroditus had nearly lost his life, in the journey. When he recovered (2:25–30; 4:18), Paul sent him to Philippi with this beautiful Letter.

Chapter 1. The Gospel in Rome

Timothy (1), probably wrote the Letter, at Paul's dictation. He had helped Paul found the Philippian church. So Paul had him join in the salutation. Timothy had also helped in the writing of II Corinthians, Colossians, I & II Thessalonians, and Philemon.

Paul's Prayer for Them (3–11). Thus he nearly always starts his Letters. Compare the beautiful prayers of Ephesians 1:16:23; 3:14–19; Colossians 1:9–12. "Fellowship in the furtherance of the Gospel" (5): this refers to the offerings of money which they had sent him. This made them sharers in his work. (See further under 4:17.) "Bowels" (8; 2:1): this is one of the instances where the Revised Version, "tender mercies;" is a better translation than the King James' Version.

The Gospel Growing in Rome (12–18). His coming to Rome as a prisoner had turned out to be a help rather than a hindrance in making Christ known in the Imperial City. Had given access to official circles, so that he had some converts in Nero's court (4:22). As he had rejoiced that night in the Philippian jail (Acts 16:25), so now he was rejoicing in his Roman chains (18).

Paul's Desire for Death (19–26). No doubt there were ever present pains in his scarred and broken body from repeated stonings and beatings. An old man. He knew the churches needed him. But he longed to go home. Still it was no great matter. In prison or in Paradise Christ was his Life and Joy. Whether he was to depart or remain was in God's hands. He was hoping to return to Philippi (26; 2:24).

The Sufferings of the Philippians (27–30). It had been ten years, and they were still being persecuted. Paul kept his eye on the day of vindication, when tables would be turned, and persecutors would reap what they had sown (28; II Thessalonians 1:5–10).

Chapter 2. The Humility of Christ

An Example of Humility (1–11). There is less of rebuke in this Epistle than in most New Testament books. But we wonder, from the connection in which this charming exhortation to humility is set, if perhaps Epaphroditus had brought Paul hints that there were seeds of faction in the pride of certain Philippian leaders, as, possibly, Euodia and Syntyche (4:2). "A thing to be grasped" (6): here is another instance where the RV translation is better than the AV "robbery." The Humility and Suffering of Christ are often set over against his Exaltation and Glory, as in 8–11. (See Hebrews 2:9–10; I Peter 1:11.)

His Joy in the Day of Christ (2:12–18). Paul conceived of earthly friendships as continuing on into eternity. He expected his happiness to come to rapturous climax in greeting his beloved friends in the upper kingdom, at the feet of Jesus, his own offering to the Lord, saved forever, because he himself had brought them to Jesus (16).

His Plan to Return to Philippi (19–30). This reads as if he were expecting his trial to come to a speedy end, especially in 24. There is no hint here of going on to Spain, as he had planned originally (Romans 15:24). His long imprisonment seems to have changed his plans. The commonly received view is that he was acquitted, and did re-visit Philippi and other churches in the East (I Timothy 1:3). Was later rearrested, brought back to Rome, and executed, some five years later.

Chapter 3. The Heavenly Goal

This One thing (1–21). The background of the picture in this chapter seems to have been the appearance in Philippi of the Judaizers, though they had not made much headway, emphasizing the observance of the Law, quarreling over un-essential matters, with dispositions like dogs (2). Paul himself had possessed the righteousness of the Law, which they were preaching, in a marked degree (4–6). But he now counted it as "refuse" (8 RV is better than the AV "dung"). His whole dependence was on Christ. His one aim was to know Him.

Paul pictures himself as in a race, straining every nerve and muscle, and exerting every ounce of strength, like a runner, with bulging veins, lest he come short of the goal. That goal was that he might attain unto the resurrection from the dead (11). This was the secret of Paul's life. He had had a glimpse of the glory of Heaven (II Corinthians 12:4), and was determined that for himself he would, by the grace of Christ, get there, with as many others as he could possibly persuade to come along. This chapter is one of the fullest of Paul's statements of his own personal hope of heaven. "Citizenship" (20), RV is better than AV "conversation." Strangers here, our homeland is there. Our walk here, our hearts there.

Chapter 4. Joy

Euodia and Syntyche (2–3). Two women leaders, either of social rank, or deaconesses, or those whose homes were used as churches, who were allowing their personal differences to become an annoyance to the church.

Rejoice, Rejoice, Rejoice (4–7). Joy is the predominant note of this Epistle. Written by a man in prison, who for thirty years had been mobbed, beaten, stoned, and cuffed about, enough to make the angels gasp. Yet he is overflowing with JOY. The very things which would naturally tend to make him sour only added to his happiness. It is simply amazing what Christ can do in one's life. "The Lord is at hand" (5): Paul had said, ten years earlier, in II Thessalonians 2, that the Lord would not come till after the Apostasy; but that apostasy was working fast in some of Paul's churches, and he never got his mind completely off the approaching nearness of the Lord's Coming. This was one of the secrets of his perennial joy. Another was his unceasing prayer with thanksgiving (6). Gratitude to God for what He does give us will surely incline Him to grant what we do not have.

The Coming of Epaphroditus (10–20). He had brought the offering of money to Paul (18). Paul was profoundly grateful, for as a prisoner he had no means of sustenance except what the prison allowed. The most beautiful and exquisitely delicate touch in this entire Epistle is in 17, where, in thanking them for the money, he tells them that he appreciated it, not so much because he needed it, though he did need it sorely (2:25), but because it gave them a share in the rewards for his work, "fruit credited to their account." Because they supported him, his work was theirs. In the Final Day they would be rewarded for the multitudes of souls they had helped him to save. The lesson holds for us, in our missionary offerings, of the modern world. Each offering, just a mite of an offering, does not amount to much. But even as the tiny raindrops that fall all over the central part of the North American continent make possible the torrent that rolls over Niagara Falls, so these mites of offerings from hundreds of thousands of Christians all over the land together constitute the stream of funds which is supporting the vast army of foreign missionaries out on the far-flung battle lines of the Cross, enduring hardships for Christ we would not think of enduring here at home, the noblest army of men and women the sun ever shone on. Those who, by their offerings to Missions, make themselves a part of this mightiest movement of all the ages, will, in the day of final reckoning, be entitled to share in its rewards.

Social Standing of New Testament Christians (22), "they of Caesar's household," from the palace of Nero. Most of the early Christians were of the humbler classes. Many of them slaves. But there were some prominent people among the converts, as these from Caesar's palace. The treasurer of Ethiopia (Acts 8:27). Cornelius the centurion (Acts 10:1). A foster-brother of Herod (Acts 13:1). Proconsul of Cyprus (Acts 13:12). Chief women not a few of Thessalonica (Acts 17:4). Greek women of honorable estate in Berea (Acts 17:12). City treasurer of Corinth (Romans 16:23). Joanna the wife of Herod's steward (Luke 8:3).

COLOSSIANS

The Godhood and All-Sufficiency of Christ

The Church at Colossae. Colossae was a city of Phrygia, from which country some were present at Jerusalem on the Day of Pentecost (Acts 2:10), and through which country Paul had gone on both his second and third missionary journeys (Acts 16:6; 18:23). It may be that on one of these journeys Paul had visited Colossae, though the language of 2:1 may, but not necessarily, imply that Paul had not been there. Another possibility is that the church may have been the result of Paul's work in Ephesus (Acts 19:10), for Colossae was near the border of "Asia," about 100 miles east of Ephesus. Epaphras (1:7; 4:12–13), may have been its founder.

Occasion and Date of the Epistle. Paul was in prison in Rome, A.D. 61–63. He had written a previous Letter concerning Mark (4:10). Meantime Epaphras, one of the Colossians, had come to Rome with the word that a dangerous heresy was making headway in the church. He was imprisoned, it seems (Philemon 23). Then Paul wrote this Letter, and sent it by Tychicus and Onesimus (4:7–9), who also bore the Letter to the Ephesians and the one to Philemon (Ephesians 6:21).

The Colossian Heresy. It seems to have been an admixture of Greek, Jewish and Oriental religions, a sort of "higher thought" cult, parading itself under the name of "philosophy" (2:8), calling for the worship of angels as intermediaries between God and man (2:18), and insisting on the strict observance of certain Jewish requirements almost to the point of asceticism (2:16, 21), put forth in high-sounding phrases of an assumed superiority: all as a part of the Gospel of Christ.

Similarity to Ephesians. Colossians and Ephesians were written at the same time. They are both carefully wrought out statements of the great doctrines of the Gospel, to be read aloud in the churches, and are very similar in many of their passages. But their main themes are entirely different: Ephesians, the Unity and Grandeur of the Church; Colossians, the Deity and All-Sufficiency of Christ.

Chapter 1. The Deity of Christ

Paul's Thanksgiving for Them (3–8). "We give thanks" (3). How often Paul starts his Letters that way: Romans 1:8; I Corinthians 1:4;

Ephesians 1:16; Philippians 1:3; I Thessalonians 1:2; II Thessalonians 1:3; II Timothy 1:3; Philemon 4. Good news from the scattered brethren filled his soul with joyful gratitude. "Faith," "Love," "Hope" (4–5), are his favorite words: Faith in Christ, Love toward the saints, Hope of heaven. Notice that it is their Hope that is the motive that produces their Love, "because of" (5. See I Corinthians 13; I Thessalonians 1:3). "Heard of" (4), does not necessarily mean he had not been to Colossae, for he uses it in Ephesians 1:15. We know he had been in Ephesus. But had been away some years. "All the world" (6), and "all creation" (23), mean that the Gospel had, by that time, 32 years after the death of Jesus, been preached to the whole known world. Within the first generation the Church became an established world-wide fact.

Paul's Prayer for Them (9–12). One of the four most beautiful of Paul's prayers for his churches, the other three being Ephesians 1:16–19; 3:14–19; Philippians 1:9–11. "Spiritual wisdom" (9), means knowing how to live a Christ-like life. "Strengthened with all power" (11), so as to be joyfully patient under all circumstances.

The Godhood of Christ (13–20). Epithets applied to Christ in this Epistle are: "Image of the invisible God," "First-born of all creation," "All things created through Him," "He is before all things," "In Him all things hold together," "Head of the Church," "The beginning," "The first-born from the dead," "In Him all fulness dwells," "Through Him all things are reconciled," "Christ in you is the hope of glory," "In Him are all the treasures of wisdom and knowledge," "In Him dwells all the fulness of Godhood bodily," "In Him you are made full" (brought to perfection), "The head of all principality and power." "First-born of all creation" (15), does not mean that He was created, but has the Old Testament meaning that He is "heir" to the created universe.

Thrones, Dominions, Principalities, Powers (1:16). This, and such passages as Ephesians 6:12, are a Biblical intimation that there are in the unseen world numerous varieties of persons and governments of which our visible world is a tiny counterpart, and that Christ's death not only made possible man's redemption, but became the means of restoring the broken harmony of the whole vast universe.

Suffering for the Church (24–29), to fill up that which is lacking. Not that the suffering of Christ is insufficient for our salvation, but the Church as a whole cannot arrive at perfection till it has gone through suffering. Paul was anxious to bear his share. (See I Peter 4.) "The mystery" (26, 27, see note on Ephesians 3:3).

"Christ in You, the Hope of Glory" (27). The essence of Paul's message in this Epistle is this: Christ is the Head of the Universe. We approach Him directly, not through intermediary angels. He, not this or that philosophy, or this or that set of rules, but Christ Himself is our Wisdom, our Life, our Hope of Glory. Being a

Christian, essentially, is Loving HIM, Living in HIM, a Person, a Glorious, Divine Person, through whom the universe was created, and in whom is entire sufficiency for Man's Redemption and Eternal Perfection.

Chapter 2. Christ All-Sufficient

Paul's Personal Interest in Them (1–5). "As many as have not seen my face in the flesh" (1), is taken by some to mean that Paul had not been in Colossae. But there is no way of knowing whether it includes, or is in addition to, the "you" preceding. The personal greetings of 4:7–18 certainly indicate that Paul was well acquainted in Colossae. He was hoping soon to come there (Philemon 22), (Philemon was one of them). "Laodicea" (1), was a nearby city, about ten miles away. Paul had written them a Letter also, along with this one to the Colossians (4:16). Some think it may have been a copy of the Ephesian Letter.

"The Mystery" (2). This may have been one of the pet words of the "philosophers" of Colossae. It is used a number of times (1:26, 27; 4:3), of certain phases of God's purpose, hitherto unrevealed. (See note on Ephesians 3:3–9.)

The Philosophers of Colossae (4, 8). A philosopher is a man who spends his life trying to understand what he knows before he starts that he cannot understand. Christ is the center of a whole system of truth, some of it very easy to understand, and some not so easy, stretching out to things "beyond the reaches of our souls." A philosopher sees in Christian teaching certain things that fit in with his philosophy. He accepts Christ, and calls himself a Christian. But in his thinking certain of his philosophic abstractions are central, and Christ himself personally is just a sort of shadow in the background. We know people like that: militant proponents of some pet theory or doctrine, but you would never suspect them of having much love or admiration for Christ personally.

Legalists (16; 20–22). Unlike the philosopher, a man with a more practical turn of mind does not bother much about things he cannot understand, but wants to know what to do to be a Christian. He sees certain plain commandments, or what appear to him to be plain commandments, and he obeys them. And to him those commandments are central, and Christ himself personally is just a sort of shadow in the background. We know people like that too.

Who are Legalists? They are those who rest their salvation on themselves rather than on Christ. Of course we want to believe all the doctrines correctly, and to our utmost obey all the commandments. But, if, in our thinking, we put too much stress on what we believe or what we do, are we not perilously near to resting our salvation on ourselves? Christ, not a doctrine, not a commandment, is our Saviour. He, not ourselves, is the basis of our hope. We must not minimize the necessity of believing right doctrines. But after all, being a Christian is, essentially, Loving Christ, a Person, rather than believing this or that doctrine, or obeying this or that commandment. We believe doctrines or obey commandments as unto Christ. We must not love them more than we love Him. If we love a doctrine overmuch we are apt to grow cross and hard and sour toward those who do not agree with our doctrine. If we love a Person, Christ a Person, we grow like Him. Paul, in this Epistle, was aiming to correct the false doctrines of the Judaizers on the one hand and the Greek philosophers on the other, and resultant compromise doctrines. But even if our beliefs are Scripturally sound there is such a thing as exalting some truth about Christ above Christ Himself. And when we thus top the balance of our partnership with Christ to our own side we are Legalists. It is possible to be a legalist over a doctrine of Grace.

Worship of Angels (18). Some were teaching that man is too unworthy to approach Christ directly: he needs the mediation of angels. And they were proud of their humility. We do not know of any such teaching today. But its counterpart remains in the worship of the Virgin Mary as an intermediary.

Asceticism (20–23). The practices referred to are not specified. Self-imposed austerities and self-chosen humiliations in certain directions are of no value in offsetting unrestrained sensual indulgence in other directions.

Chapter 3. Life in Christ

The Person to Person Relation with Christ is the emphasis of this Epistle: Christ in you the hope of glory (1:27). Walk in Him, Rooted in Him, Builded up in Him (2:6, 7). In Him brought to perfection (2:10). Died with Him (2:20). Raised with Him (3:1). Your life is hid with Him in God (3:3).

The Word and Singing (16), are mentioned together. This refers to Christian assemblies, where the teaching of the Word and the singing of hymns are the main means of promoting the growth of Christian life. O for more of it in the churches!

Chapter 4. Personal Matters

Churches Met in Houses. Several are mentioned. Nymphas in Laodicea (Colossians 4:15). Philemon in Colossae (Philemon 2). Gaius in Corinth (Romans 16:23). Aquila and Priscilla in Ephesus (I Corinthians 16:19); and later in Rome (Romans 16:5). They had to meet where they could. It was not until the third century that church buildings came into general use. Yet the church made marvelous growth. Many small congregations are better than a few large ones.

I THESSALONIANS

The Lord's Second Coming

The Church in Thessalonica was founded about A.D. 51, on Paul's Second Missionary Journey (Acts 17:1–9).

It seems, from Acts 17:2, that Paul was there only three weeks. But Philippians 4:16; I Thessalonians 2:9; II Thessalonians 3:8 imply that he was there longer. It may be that he preached in the synagog three sabbaths, and later in some other place. But, at most, he was not there long enough to fully instruct the church.

Driven out of Thessalonica, he went to Berea, about 50 miles to the west. But soon was driven from Berea, leaving Silas and Timothy there. When he got to Athens, 200 miles to the south, lonesome, he sent word back to Berea for Silas and Timothy to come to him with all possible speed (Acts 17:14, 15). When they reached Athens, Paul, filled with anxiety about the young church in Thessalonica, immediately sent Timothy back. By the time Timothy returned Paul had gone from Athens to Corinth. Timothy brought word that the Thessalonian Christians were enduring their persecutions bravely; but some had died, and the others were puzzled to know how those who had died would get any benefit of the Lord's Coming, a doctrine that Paul evidently had specially stressed in Thessalonica.

Then it was that Paul wrote this Letter, to tell them, mainly, that those who had died would be at no disadvantage when the Lord Comes.

Thessalonica. Modern "Saloniki." Situated at the northwest corner of the Aegean Sea, facing a fine harbor, on a rich and well-watered plain, on the great Northern Military Highway from Rome to the East. Within sight of Mt. Olympus, home of the Greek gods. Leading city of Macedonia in Paul's day. Still a prosperous city.

Paul's Work in Thessalonica. Though there only a short time, Paul created a great stir. His enemies accused him of "turning the world upside down" (Acts 17:6). A "great multitude of Greeks and chief women" believed (Acts 17:4). It was heralded all over Greece (I Thessalonians 1:8, 9).

Chapter 1. Fame of the Church

"In power" (5), must refer to miracles which accompanied and attested Paul's preaching, though none are mentioned in Acts. "An example" (7), to all Greece, of fortitude under persecution, and of a genuinely Christian manner of life. "Wait for his Son" (10), thus

Paul closes every chapter with a reference to the Lord's Coming (2:19; 3:13; 4:16–18; 5:23).

Chapter 2. Paul's Conduct Among Them

This chapter is given mainly to Paul's vindication of his conduct in Thessalonica. The language rather conveys the impression that the enemies who were so bitterly persecuting the Thessalonian Christians were militantly engaged in a campaign to blacken Paul's character.

He reminds them that he had taken no pay from them, which was in itself evidence that he could not have been actuated by motives of covetousness, as some travelling philosophers were.

And reminds them also of his unselfish and tender devotion to them, and that he was, in every way, an example to them of the things which he preached.

Their Suffering (13-16). It seems that the unbelieving Jews and "certain vile fellows of the rabble" (Acts 17:5), who had driven Paul out of Thessalonica, were still, with relentless fury, venting their wrath against Jason and the rest of the Christians there. Paul tries to comfort them by reminding them that the mother churches in Judea had been persecuted in the same manner. So had Christ. So had he himself. But "wrath to the uttermost" (16), is their lot: those who killed the Lord and persecute the Church. There is no hope of their repentance, and no escape from their doom: the impending destruction of Jerusalem, and their eternal doom in the Day of Judgment.

Paul's Plan to Return to Thessalonica (17–20). "Once and again" (18), means that at least twice he had made an effort to get back to Thessalonica, but "Satan hindered" him. In the early part of this same Missionary Journey Paul had made certain plans, and the Holy Spirit hindered him (Acts 16:6, 7). Then it was God who was interfering with his plans. Now it is Satan. We wonder how Paul knew that in one case it was God, and in the other case Satan. How did Satan hinder him? Possibly, by illness, or by opposition of the civil authorities. At any rate, Paul knew that it was the arch enemy of the Church who was keeping him away from his beloved Thessalonian brethren. He was still praying "night and day" (3:10–11), that he might return. He felt that one of the brightest stars in his crown in the day of the Lord's Coming would be the Thessalonian Church, his "hope, joy, crown and glory" (19–20).

Chapter 3. Timothy's Report

Paul, in deepest anxiety for the new-born Thessalonian Church, had sent Timothy back to encourage them under their bitter persecution. (See Introductory Note, and Acts 17:15; 18:1, 5; I Thessalonians 3:1, 2, 6.) Timothy's return with the news of their steadfastness and devotion filled Paul with unbounded joy.

Chapter 4. Immorality. Love. The Lord's Coming

Immorality (1–8), was common among heathen peoples. It may be that, in his report of the general steadfastness of the Thessalonian Christians, Timothy had mentioned some cases of moral laxness—which occasioned this exhortation. "Sanctification" (3), as here used, means sexual purity. "Vessel" (4), seems to mean "body," though some think it means "wife," that is, fidelity to the marriage vow, or, that in order to avoid immorality, each should have his own wife. "Wrong his brother" (6), that is, invade the rights of another's home, of which some may have been guilty.

Brotherly Love (9–12). It seems that those who had means, of whom there were many (Acts 17:4), were taking the doctrine of Christian charity seriously, and were dispersing their means to the poorer brethren of all the Macedonian churches. This was an opportunity for those who were inclined to be lazy, and they were making the most of it. As Paul commended the charitable, he rebuked the lazy. To be willing to live off of their neighbors was contrary to every principle of brotherly love. Able-bodied beggars, they were glad for others to practice brotherly love, while they themselves exhibited the essence of self-love. It looked bad to those outside the Church.

The Lord's Second Coming (13–18). Here we come to the main topic of the Epistle. Its mention in every chapter implies that Paul must have given it particular emphasis in his preaching at Thessalonica.

Though it is commonly spoken of as the Lord's "Coming" or "Appearing," it is specifically called "Second" coming in Hebrews 9:28. Jesus' word, "again," in John 14:3, means a second time. So it is perfectly proper and Scriptural to speak of it as the "Second Coming."

It is mentioned or referred to in almost every New Testament book. The chapters in which it is explained most fully are Matthew 24, 25; Luke 21; I Thessalonians 4, 5; II Peter 3.

The Thessalonian Epistles are commonly regarded as the earliest written New Testament books. They are about the Lord's Coming again. The last of the New Testament books is Revelation, of which the final word is, "I come quickly," "Even so, come, Lord Jesus" (Revelation 22:20). Thus the New Testament begins, and thus it ends.

"Fallen asleep" (14), is a Scriptural expression for the Christian's death (Matthew 27:52; John 11:11; Acts 7:60; 13:36; I Corinthians 15:6, 18, 20, 51; II Peter 3:4). It is found often in Christian epitaphs in the catacombs. Jesus taught it. It must be true. Only asleep. One day we shall awake. Glorious morn! This does not mean lapse into a state of unconsciousness till the day of resurrection. There is an intermediate state of conscious bliss (Philippians 1:23).

"With a shout, the voice of the archangel, and the trump of God" (16). This is similar to Jesus' words (Matthew 24:30–31). It may be literal. "The clouds" (17), will be his triumphal chariot. He went away in the "clouds" (Acts 1:9), and so will return (Revelation 1:7). The angels will be with him, in all the glory of heaven (Matthew 25:31). The saints of past ages will be raised, those still in the flesh will be changed, and, as Enoch and Elijah were translated, the whole Church will rise in joyful welcome to the Returning Savior, to be with Him forevermore. It thrills us through and through to think of it.

Chapter 5. The Lord's Coming

Its Suddenness (1–11). There is nothing here to indicate when it will be. Only that, whenever it is, it will be with unexpected suddenness. "Signs" will precede the Coming, so that patient believers may feel that it is near, while the world generally scoffs at the idea. But even those who are watching are warned lest they be caught off guard. It will be as a "thief in the night" (2). Jesus had said that over and over (Matthew 24:36, 42; 25:13; Mark 13:32–37; Luke 12:39, 46; 21:25–35), and with solemn earnestness warned his disciples to "watch." (For note as to the time of His Coming see under II Thessalonians 2 and II Peter 3.)

Honor Pastors (12–13). Seeing it was a very young church, the pastors must have been, quite largely, novices. Yet the people were urged to love and esteem them. When church members love their pastor, and are at peace among themselves, other things being equal, the church is sure to grow.

Fifteen Exhortations (14–22). Beautiful. So characteristic of Paul. Thus he closes most of his Epistles, however abstract, argumentative, or abstruse, with exhortations to peace, longsuffering, joy, prayer, thankfulness and every good.

"Spirit and Soul and Body" (23). "Spirit" and "soul" are often used synonymously, but here there seems to be a distinction. "Soul," the principle of life. "Spirit," the organ of communion with God. Christ redeems the entire human personality. The language certainly contemplates the resurrection of the body.

"Holy Kiss" (26). The kiss, between persons of the same sex, on the cheek, was a common mode of salutation in many ancient countries. It became a custom in the churches. As its use as a salutation passed its use in the churches ceased.

"Read to All the Brethren" (27). This shows that Paul intended his Epistles to be read in the churches. That is what the New Testament books were written for (Colossians 4:16; I Timothy 4:13; Revelation 1:3).

II THESSALONIANS

Further Instruction about the Lord's Coming

Written, probably about A.D. 52, only a few weeks, or months, after the First Epistle. In that Paul had spoken of the Lord's Coming as being sudden and unexpected. In this he explains that it will not be till after the Apostasy.

Chapter 1. The Day of the Lord

The particular feature of the Lord's Coming emphasized in this chapter is that it will be a day of terror for the disobedient.

In I Thessalonians 4 Paul had said that He would descend from heaven, and, at the shout of the archangel, the Church would be caught up to be forever with the Lord.

Here he adds that the Lord will be accompanied with "the angels of his power in flaming fire" (7), rendering vengeance to the disobedient. Jesus had spoken of "eternal fire" (Matthew 25:41), and "unquenchable fire" (Mark 9:43). In Hebrews 10:27 "devouring fire" is connected with the day of judgment. In II Peter 3:7, 10 it is stated that the destiny of the earth is to be burned with "fire" (see note on that passage).

Chapter 2. The Apostasy

The express purpose of this Epistle was to caution the Thessalonians that the Lord's Coming was not immediately at hand; that it would not be till after the Apostasy.

What is the Apostasy? It is called the "falling away," in which a person called the "man of sin," in the temple of God professes himself to be God, and exalts himself against God (3, 4). A False Church headed by an Impostor.

The early fathers unanimously looked for a Personal Antichrist, to be manifested after the fall of the Roman Empire.

The Protestant Reformers, being directly in touch with the awful corruption of the Church of the Middle Ages, believed the Papacy, an institution headed up in a person, usurping to itself authority that belongs only to Christ and being itself responsible for the prevailing corruption, to have been a manifestation of the man of sin.

In our own times, after 2,000 years of church history, there is still wide difference of opinion. There are many who think it refers to a period immediately before the Lord's Coming.

The spirit of the thing was already at work in Paul's day (7). The story of the Church as a whole, even to this day, makes a sorry looking picture. Taking a broad general view of the visible Church, as it has existed from the first century to the present time, it is not inaccurate to call it an Apostate Church. What the final culmination is to be is yet to be seen.

"That which restrains" (6), was generally understood by the early fathers to have been the Roman Empire. Some take it to mean the Holy Spirit.

Paul's Ideas of the Second Coming. It is quite common among a certain class of critics to say that Paul "had to reconstruct his ideas about the Lord's Second Coming," that his "earlier and cruder view" contradicts his later view. This is absolutely not true. Paul's earlier view was his only view, first, last and always. The Thessalonian Epistles are his earliest extant writings. In them he specifically states that he did NOT expect the immediate appearance of the Lord, and that it would not be till after the Apostasy, which in his day was only beginning to work. It may not have been revealed to Paul what the Apostasy would be. But whatever his idea of it, it did not preclude the possibility that the Lord would come in his own lifetime, evidenced by the expression "we that are alive" (I Thessalonians 4:15; I Corinthians 15:52). First and last Paul looked for the Lord's Coming as a glorious consummation, meanwhile anticipating the eventuality of, in death, "departing to be with Christ" (Philippians 1:23); it not being any great matter whether he was in the body or out of it at the time of the Coming. In his last written word (II Timothy 4:6, 8), at the time of his "departure," his mind was on the "appearing" of the Lord.

Chapter 3. The Disorderly

"Pray for Us" (1–2), that we may be delivered from "unreasonable and evil men." At that very time Paul was in trouble in Corinth. Their prayer was answered (Acts 18:9–10).

The Disorderly (6–15), were lazy people who, taking advantage of the charitable disposition of the church (I Thessalonians 4:9–10), and, making their expectation of the immediate appearance of the Lord an excuse for abandoning their ordinary occupations, were claiming the right to be supported by the brethren who had means.

Paul, though he was an ardent advocate of charity toward those who were really in need, and though he spent a good deal of time gathering offerings of money for the poor, yet he spared no words in condemning the able-bodied who could but would not work. In these verses he positively forbids the brethren to support such people; even commands the church to withdraw fellowship from them.

There is nothing in the teaching of Paul, or of Christ, or anywhere in the Bible, to encourage charity to able-bodied lazy men whose profession is begging.

I TIMOTHY

Care of the Church at Ephesus

The Pastoral Epistles

I and II Timothy and Titus are commonly called the "Pastoral Epistles." Prevailing opinion is that they were written between Paul's first and second imprisonment, between A.D. 64 and 67. Some rationalistic modern critics have advanced the theory that they are the work of some unknown author, who, thirty to fifty years after Paul's death, wrote in Paul's name, to promote certain doctrines. For this opinion there is no historical basis. These Epistles have, from the very beginning, been regarded as the genuine writings of Paul. If they are not the genuine writings of Paul, but the false writings of some pretender-Paul, how can any man with any sense of honesty regard them as a part of God's Word? To the average mind such a thing is forgery.

Timothy

A native of Lystra (Acts 16:1). His mother a Jewess, his father a Greek. Mother's name Eunice, grandmother Lois (II Timothy 1:5). Paul's convert (I Timothy 1:2). Joined Paul on his second Journey, about A.D. 51 (Acts 16:3). His choice indicated of God (I Timothy 1:18). Set apart by the Elders and Paul (I Timothy 4:14; II Timothy 1:6). Accompanied Paul to Troas, Philippi, Thessalonica, Berea. Tarried at Berea till Paul sent for him to come to Athens (Acts 17:14–15). Then Paul sent him back to Thessalonica (I Thessalonians 3:1–2). By the time he returned Paul had gone to Corinth (Acts 18:5; I Thessalonians 3:6). Joined in writing the Thessalonian Letters (I Thessalonians 1:1; II Thessalonians 1:1). Later Paul sent him from Ephesus to Corinth (I Corinthians 4:17). Paul joined him in Macedonia, and he joined in the writing of II Corinthians; Acts 19:22; II Corinthians 1:1. Went part way on Paul's journey to Jerusalem (Acts 20:4). Whether he accompanied Paul all the way to Jerusalem and Rome is not stated, but he appears with Paul in Rome (Philippians 1:1; 2:19–22; Colossians 1:1; Philemon 1). Later he is in Ephesus, where this Epistle is addressed to him. Is urged to come to Rome (II Timothy 4:9). Whether he reached Rome before Paul's death is not known. Is mentioned in Hebrews 13:23 as having been released from prison. He was timid and retiring by nature, not as well fitted as Titus for handling trouble-makers. Was not in the best of health (I Timothy 5:23). He and Luke were Paul's two most constant companions. Paul loved him devotedly, and was lonesome without him. Tradition says that after Paul's death his work was the care of the Ephesian church, and that he suffered martyrdom under Nerva or Domitian. This would make him a co-worker with the Apostle John.

Ephesus

This was where Paul had done his greatest work, about A.D. 54–57 (Acts 19). Some four years after he had left Ephesus, from his Roman imprisonment, he had written the Epistle to the Church at Ephesus, about A.D. 62. Now, a little later, probably about A.D. 65, he addressed this Epistle to Timothy about the work in Ephesus. Later Ephesus became the home of John, where he wrote his Gospel, his Epistles, and the book of Revelation.

Occasion of the Epistle. When Paul bade the Ephesian elders farewell he told them that they would not see his face again (Acts 20:25). But, it seems, his long imprisonment changed his plans, and, some six or seven years later, after release from the Roman prison, he did re-visit Ephesus. Passing on to Macedonia, he left Timothy at Ephesus, expecting himself soon to return (I Timothy 1:3; 3:14). Being detained in Macedonia longer than he had planned (3:15), he wrote this Letter of instruction about the work that Timothy was to do.

The Church at Ephesus. From the narrative in Acts 19, it appears that Paul had made a vast multitude of Christian converts. In the intervening years the number of converts had continued to grow. Within the following fifty years Christians in Asia Minor had become so numerous that the heathen temples were almost forsaken. Within the Apostolic generation Ephesus became the numerical, as well as geographical, center of Christendom, the region where Christianity won its quickest laurels.

The Church Situation. There were no church buildings. Houses for Christian worship did not begin to be built till two hundred years after the days of Paul, and were not general till Constantine put an end to the persecutions of Christians. In Paul's day churches met, mostly, in the homes of the Christian people. Thus, the scores of thousands of Christians, in and around Ephesus, met, not in one, or a few, great central congregations, but in hundreds of small groups in various homes, each congregation under its own pastoral leadership.

The Pastors. There must have been hundreds of them. In Acts 20:17 they are called "elders." In this Epistle they are called "bishops" (3:1): different names for same office.

Timothy's work was primarily with these pastors, or congregational leaders. There were no seminaries to supply Paul with trained pastors. He had to develop his pastors out of his converts. Sometimes he got brilliant men; but probably most of his pastors were from the ordinary walks of life. He had to do the best he could with available material. Without seminaries, without church buildings, and in spite of persecution, the church made more rapid progress than at any time since, because it had to keep its mind on the essentials rather than the superficials of Christianity.

Chapter 1. False Teachers

The False Teachers (3–11). Paul had forewarned, when he left Ephesus, seven years before, that grievous wolves would ravage the Ephesian flock of Christians (Acts 20:29–30). Now they had appeared in full force, and constituted Timothy's main problem. They appear to have been the same brand as those in Crete with whom Titus had to deal, basing strange teachings on apocryphal Jewish legends connected with Old Testament genealogies.

Paul's Sinfulness (12–17). The one man who had done more for Christ, possibly, than all others combined, yet bowed to the depths with feelings of unworthiness. The closer the walk with Christ, the deeper the sense of humility. He regarded his conversion as intended of God to be an everlasting example of God's longsuffering to wayward men.

Hymenaeus and Alexander (19–20), two ring-leaders of the false teachers, from whom, in his Apostolic authority, Paul had withdrawn church membership ("delivered to Satan," 20): probably the same Alexander (II Timothy 4:14), who later went to Rome to testify against Paul, and possibly the one who earlier had been Paul's devoted friend.

Chapter 2. Prayer. The Place of Women

Prayer for Rulers (1–8). Nero was at that time ruler of the Roman Empire, under whom Paul had been imprisoned and was soon to be executed. This shows that prayers and intercessions should be made for bad rulers as well as good.

The Place of Women in Church (9–15. See on I Corinthians 11:5–15; 14:34–35). The caution here is against the overdoing of display of dress, specially in Christian worship; and also against becoming too much like men. In heaven there will be no sex (Matthew 22:30); but in this world there is a natural difference between the sexes which it is best not to override. "Saved through her childbearing" (15), probably refers to the birth of Jesus, who was born of a woman without the agency of man. Even if sin did come into the world through woman (14), so did the Saviour.

Chapter 3. Bishops and Deacons

Their Qualifications (1–16). Probably intended as an ideal, not a legal enactment. "One wife" (2), probably meant to exclude, not single men, but polygamists. Paul was a single man (I Corinthians 7:8). "Women" (11), probably meaning deaconesses. "Pillar of the truth" (15): except for the Church Christ's name would disappear. Verse 16 is thought to have been a fragment of a Christian hymn.

Chapter 4. Coming Apostasy. A Minister's Work

Apostasy (1–5). This passage seems to say that, though the Church is the pillar of the Truth, there shall arise within the Church gross systems of error, of demoniacal origin, teaching abstinence from meat foods and conjugal intercourse. This was one of the forms of Gnosticism, even then developing, which later grew to vast proportions: a heresy that is now almost extinct, except as its remains are found in the pretended celibacy of the Roman priesthood and their periodical fasts from animal food.

A Good Minister (6–16). The best way to combat incipient or prevailing error is by unceasing reiteration of simple Gospel truth. "Reading, exhortation, teaching" (13). The Bible itself will do the job, if only given a chance. Studying it in private, reading and expounding it in public. If ministers today would only give heed to Paul's advice, the Church would take on new life, and grow by leaps and bounds. Why, why, why, O why, cannot ministers understand that the simple exposition of God's Word is more desired by the people, and more powerful by far, than their finely worked out sermonic platitudes?

Chapter 5. Widows. Elders

Widows (1–16). The church in Ephesus was something like ten years old, and had its charity work very well developed and carefully administered. A Christian who would not support his own dependents is worse than an unbeliever (8). The church in Ephesus had to be extremely careful with its women servants, for the women servants of the temple of Diana were prostitutes.

Elders (17–25). Called "bishops" in 3:1–7. There it was their qualifications. Here it is their treatment. Then as now busybodies were whispering against their church leaders (19). "Wine" (23): it was "little," and for medicinal purposes.

Chapter 6. Slaves. Riches

Slaves (1–2. Compare I Corinthians 7:20–24). No great matter whether slave or free. Become free if you can. But if not, be a good slave. Slaves are thus frequently exhorted (Ephesians 6:5–9; Colossians 3:22–25; Titus 2:9–10). Christianity abolished slavery, not by denouncing it, but by teaching the doctrine of human brotherhood.

The Desire for Riches (3–21), was the motive back of much false teaching (5). Through the ages church doctrines have been corrupted to produce income for church coffers. "A root of all kinds of evils" (10, RV), is more accurate than AV, "the root of all evil." O man of God, flee covetousness (11); turn away from profane babblings of "scholarship" falsely so called (20).

II TIMOTHY

Paul's Final Word
His Dying Shout of Triumph

The book of Acts closes with Paul in prison in Rome about the year A.D. 63. The common belief is that he was acquitted, returned to Greece and Asia Minor, was later re-arrested, taken back to Rome, and executed about A.D. 66 or 67. This Epistle was written while he was awaiting martyrdom.

Background of the Epistle

The Neronian Persecution. The Great Fire in Rome occurred A.D. 64. Nero himself burned the city. Though an inhuman brute, he was a great builder. It was in order to build a new and grander Rome that he set fire to the city, and fiddled in glee at the sight of it. The people suspected him; and historians have commonly regarded it as a fact that he was the perpetrator of the crime. In order to divert suspicion from himself he accused the Christians of burning Rome.

The Bible makes no mention of Nero's persecution of Christians, though it happened in Bible times, and is the direct background of at least two N T books, I Peter and II Timothy, and was the persecution that brought Paul to his martyrdom, and, according to some traditions, Peter also. Our source of information is the Roman historian Tacitus. He knew that the Christians did not burn Rome. But somebody had to be made the scapegoat for the Emperor's crime. Here was a new and despised sect of people, mostly from the humbler walks of life, without prestige or influence, many of them slaves. Nero accused them of burning Rome, and ordered their punishment.

In and around Rome multitudes of Christians were arrested and put to death in the most cruel ways. Crucified. Or tied in skins of animals, and thrown into the arena to be worried to death by dogs, for the entertainment of the people. Or thrown to the wild beasts. Or tied to stakes in Nero's gardens, pitch poured over their bodies, and their burning bodies used as torches to light Nero's gardens at night, while he drove around in his chariot, naked, indulging himself in his midnight revels, gloating over the dying agonies of his victims.

A bust of Nero.

It was in the wake of this persecution that Paul was re-arrested, in Greece or Asia Minor, possibly at Troas (II Timothy 4:13), and brought back to Rome. This time by the agents of Rome, not as at first by the Jews. This time as a criminal (2:9), not as at first on some technical violation of Jewish law. For all we know, it may have been in connection with the burning of Rome. For was not Paul the world leader of the people who were being punished for that crime? And had not Paul been in Rome for two years just preceding the fire? Very easy to lay this crime at Paul's door. But whether that was the charge we do not know. The Christian religion, somewhere before this time, had been officially proscribed. It was one of the consequences of Nero's personal persecution and a face-saving device. Paul, at any rate, was indicted. His trial had proceeded far enough that he knew there was no hope of escape. While waiting in the Roman dungeon for the "time of his departure" he wrote this last Letter to Timothy, his bosom friend and trusted co-worker, begging him to be faithful, in spite of everything, to his trust as a minister of Christ, and to hurry on to Rome before winter (4:21).

Paul's Note of Triumphant Faith

In that dark hour is one of the noblest passages of Scripture. Being executed for a crime of which he was not guilty. His friends forsaking him, and leaving him to suffer alone. The cause for which he had given his life being blotted out in the West by persecution, and in the East going into apostasy. Yet no hint of regret that he had given his life to the service of Christ and the Church. No hint of doubt but that the Church, though now apparently being defeated, would eventually be triumphant. And no hint of doubt but that the moment his head would be cut from his body he would go straight to the arms of HIM whom he had loved and served so devotedly. This Epistle is the exultant cry of a dying conqueror.

General Note on the Persecutions Under the Empire (EMB)

Persecution, in its most common sense, signifies a particular course or period of systematic infliction of punishment or penalty for adherence to a particular religious belief. Oppression is to be distinguished from it. Pharaoh oppressed the Hebrews; so did Nebuchadnezzar. Daniel and Jeremiah were persecuted. Systematic persecution began with the Roman imperial government. Notably tolerant toward alien religious beliefs in general, the Romans clashed with the Christians over the formalities of Caesar-worship. In that fact, according to W. M. Ramsay, lies the prime significance of the persecutions. Persecution began as a social reaction, and became political later, a process which can be detected in the surviving documents (Acts of the Apostles; Tacitus' *Annals;* Pliny, *Epistles* X). The state's policy of repression was intermittent, and as the evidence of Tertullian shows, was visibly daunted by the growing numbers of the Christians. A considerable body of literature has gathered round the difficult theme of the legal basis on which the authorities pursued their policy, and on the incidence and severity of the persecutions themselves. Disregarding Claudius' anti-semitism of A.D. 49 (Acts 18:2), in which the Christians were not distinguished from Jews, Nero must be regarded as the first persecutor. In A.D. 64 (Tacitus, *Annals* 15:38–44) this emperor used the small Christian community as scapegoats for a disastrous fire in Rome and the charge of incendiarism which was popularly leveled against him. Domitian's execution of Glabrio and Flavius Clemens in A.D. 95, and the exile of Domitilla for "atheism," and "going astray after the customs of the Jews" (Dio Cassius 67:44), was probably anti-Christian action, an incident which strikingly reveals the vertical spread of Christianity by the end of the first century. Pliny's famous correspondence with Trajan in A.D. 112 (Pliny, *Epistles* 10:96, 97) reveals the state more moderately but quite uncompromisingly in action. Trajan's policy, laid down for Pliny in Bithynia, was followed by Hadrian and

Antoninus Pius (A.D. 117–161). Marcus Aurelius was guilty of a sharp persecution at Lyons (A.D. 117). At the close of the second century, with the death of Septimius Severus, a long period of peace followed, broken by Maximinus Thrax, Decius, and Valerian, but without widespread action or much determination. Diocletian continued a now established policy of toleration until A.D. 303 when, under the influence of Galerius, he initiated the last short but savage period of persecution, described by Lactantius and Eusebius. (The historical questions involved are dealt with in W. M. Ramsay, *The Church in the Roman Empire before A.D. 170;* E. G. Hardy, *Christianity and the Roman Government.* More briefly, the social background and historical significance are dealt with in Tyndale Lectures 1951 and 1959 by E. M. Blaiklock: *The Christian in Pagan Society* and *Rome in the New Testament*).

The Zondervan Pictorial Bible Dictionary

Chapter 1. "I Know Him"

His Prayers for Timothy (3–5). Paul opens almost every Epistle thus: prayers and thanks: Romans 1:9–10; I Corinthians 1:4–8; II Corinthians 1:3–4; Ephesians 1:3; Philippians 1:3, 9–11; Colossians 1:3–10; I Thessalonians 1:2–3; II Thessalonians 1:3; "Thy tears" (4): probably at their separation at Troas (4:13). When Paul wrote I Timothy he was in Macedonia and Timothy was in Ephesus. Possibly they later met at Troas, and possibly it was here that the Roman soldiers seized Paul and hustled him off to Rome on the humiliating charge of setting fire to the city.

Paul's Assurance (6–14). He had seen Christ. He had suffered for Him. Christ, though unseen, was the one unquestioned reality of Paul's life, his intimate actual companion, and he "knew him" (12), as one knows his best friend. "Preacher, apostle, teacher" (11): "preacher," proclaimer of the Gospel to those who never heard it, foreign missionaries; "apostle," with direct personal authority from Christ; "teacher," instructor of settled Christian communities, our pastors.

The Disaffection at Ephesus (15–18). This was one of the saddest things in Paul's life. In Ephesus, where he had done his greatest work, and almost turned the whole city to Christ, the false teachers had so gotten the upper hand that they were able to make capital of Paul's arrest to turn the church against him, at the time of all times when he needed their love and sympathy.

Chapter 2. Advice to Timothy

Avoid Business Entanglements (1–7). Paul advises Timothy to take pay for his work as a minister, the very thing which Paul for the most part had refused to do, before the churches had become established. Possibly Timothy had been of a well-to-do family, and had by now lost his money in persecutions. Being reticent about the matter, he may have needed this advice.

Endure Suffering (8–12). Paul, at that time, was enduring the cruelest of all suffering for a good man, the charge of being a criminal (9). But notice, his mind is on "eternal glory" (10). The quotation (11–13), may have been from a hymn.

Handle the Word Aright (14–21). Do not distort its natural meaning to bolster pet doctrines. The Church will depart from the teachings of the Word. But within the historical visible Church God will have a remnant of true believers (19).

Be Gentle (22–26). God's Word, in the hands of a ministry possessed of true Christian gentility will break down opposition and hold the Church in its true course.

Chapter 3. Grievous Times

Coming Apostasy (1–14). The determined effort of mankind to corrupt the Gospel and thwart the work of Christ is one of the burdens of the New Testament. It is spoken of again and again (Matthew 7:15–23; II Thessalonians 2; I Timothy 4; II Peter 2; Jude; Revelation 17). The terrible picture (2–5), with the exception of temporary periods of reform, is a fairly correct picture of the Visible Church as a whole to this present time. "Jannes and Jambres" (8), traditional names of the magicians of Pharaoh (Exodus 7:11–22). "Lystra" (11), was where Paul was stoned, the home of Timothy, which stoning Timothy may have witnessed. "All shall suffer persecution" (12): we are told that over and over (Matthew 5:10–12; John 15:20; Acts 14:22; I Thessalonians 3:4); so that when it comes we may be prepared for it.

The Bible (14–17), is the one antidote against Apostasy and Church Corruption. The Roman Church pushed the Bible aside, and brought on the Dark Ages. The Protestant Church rediscovered the Bible, but now neglects it. Widespread disregard of the Bible by the present day Church is simply appalling. Many prominent church leaders not only neglect the Bible, but with great intellectual pride, in the name of "modern scholarship," resort to every conceivable means to undermine its Divine Origin, and toss it aside as a patchwork of "Hebrew Thought."

Chapter 4. Paul's Last Words

Solemn Farewell Charge (1–5). Paul knew the day of his execution was approaching. Not sure that he would ever see Timothy again, or even have the opportunity to write him another letter. He begs him to keep his mind on the day of the Lord's appearing, and to preach Jesus with unceasing diligence. Again false teachers (3, 4): O how that bothered Paul! The perverse determination of men to corrupt the Gospel of Christ.

Paul's Valedictory (6–8). Grandest utterance of the grandest mortal man that ever lived. The battle-scarred old warrior of the cross, looking back over a long and hard and bitter fight, cries out in exultation, "I have won." Not long afterward the executioner's ax released Paul's soul from his worn and broken body to be borne away by flights of angels to the bosom of his beloved Lord. We imagine his welcome home to heaven surpassed any triumphal procession he had ever witnessed in Rome to returning conquerors. Our guess is that when he got to heaven, his very first act, after a rendezvous with the Lord, was to hunt up Stephen to beg his forgiveness.

Personal Matters (9–22). Whether Timothy got to Rome before Paul's martyrdom (9), we do not know. The first stage of Paul's trial had already passed (16). Things looked so bad for him that even three of his four companions in travel fled, and Luke alone remained (10–11). Whether Titus went to Dalmatia (10), of his own accord, or was sent by Paul, as he and Paul may have planned in Nicopolis (Titus 3:12), is not stated. Those were dark days in Rome. Known Christians had been murdered. Now they had the great Christian leader himself on trial. It was dangerous to be seen with him. "Mark" (11): Paul wanted him. They had separated years before (Acts 15:36–41), but he had been with Paul in his first Roman imprisonment (Colossians 4:10). Mark and Peter worked together, and if Mark got to Rome, possibly Peter did also. One of the traditions is that Peter was martyred in Rome about the same time as Paul or soon after. The "cloak" (13): winter was coming on (21), and Paul needed it. The "books" (13), probably were parts of the Scripture. "Alexander" (14), was no doubt the same Alexander whom Paul had "delivered to Satan" (I Timothy 1:20), who now had his opportunity to get even. And he did. He had journeyed all the way from Ephesus to Rome to testify against Paul, which he did with considerable success. The "lion" (17), may be a veiled reference to Nero, or it may refer to Satan (I Peter 5:8). "Trophimus" (20): this is a very interesting side-light on Paul's power to work miracles. He had in various places healed multitudes. But here was one of his own beloved friends he could not heal.

TITUS

Concerning the Churches of Crete

Titus

He was a Greek, who accompanied Paul to Jerusalem, whose circumcision Paul steadfastly resisted (Galatians 2:3–5). One of Paul's converts (Titus 1:4).

Some years later he appears with Paul in Ephesus, and is sent to Corinth to look after certain disorders, and to initiate the offering for the poor saints in Jerusalem (II Corinthians 8:6, 10). Returning from Corinth, he meets Paul in Macedonia, and, after explaining the situation to Paul, he is then sent back to Corinth, ahead of Paul, bearing the Second Epistle to the Corinthians, to pave the way for Paul's coming, and to complete the offering (II Corinthians 2:3, 12, 13; 7:5, 6, 13, 14; 8:16, 17, 18, 23; 12:14, 18). The fact that Titus was chosen to look after the troublous situation in Corinth indicates that Paul must have considered him a very capable, wise and tactful Christian leader.

The next we hear of him, some 7 or 8 years later, is in this Epistle to Titus, about A.D. 65. He is in Crete. The expression "left in Crete" (Titus 1:5) shows that Paul had been there with him. Paul's ship, in his voyage to Rome (Acts 27) touched on the south shore of Crete, but it is scarcely likely that that could have been the time when he left Titus there. The prevailing opinion is that, after Paul's release from his first imprisonment in Rome, about A.D. 63, he returned east, including Crete in his intinerary. After setting the Cretan churches in order, Titus is to be replaced by Artemas or Tychicus, and is asked to rejoin Paul in Nicopolis, in western Greece (Titus 3:12).

The last notice of Titus is in II Timothy 4:10, where it is said that he had gone from Rome to Dalmatia. Evidently he had rejoined Paul, and was with him when arrested, accompanying him to Rome. Whether he forsook Paul in that dark and lonely hour because of threatening dangers or Paul sent him to finish the evangelization of the coast northwest of Greece, we do not know. Let us hope the latter, for he was a good and great man. Tradition says that Titus became bishop of Crete, and died peaceably at an advanced age.

Crete

An island, also known as Candia, southeast of Greece, on the border between the Aegean and Mediterranean seas, about 150 miles long, and 7 to 30 wide. Mountainous, but its valleys were fertile and populous and rich; the "island of a hundred cities." The seat of an ancient and powerful civilization that had already become lengendary at the dawn of Greek history. The work of Sir Arthur Evans and his successors gave the knowledge of the Cretan civilization to the world early in this century. The script was deciphered in 1953 by Michael Ventris and found to be in primitive Greek.

The highest mountain in Crete, Mt. Ida, was famous as the legendary birth-place of the Greek god Zeus. Home of the half-mythical lawgiver Minos, son of Zeus, and of the fabulous Minotaur. The people were akin to the Philistines, thought to have been identical with the Cherethites (I Samuel 30:14). Daring sailors and famous bowmen, with a very bad moral reputation.

The nucleus of the Church in Crete, probably, was started by the "Cretans" who were at Jerusalem on the Day of Pentecost (Acts 2:11). There is no New Testament mention of an Apostolic visit to Crete other than by Paul on his voyage to Rome (Acts 27), and that implied in the Epistle to Titus. Inasmuch as Paul was inclined to avoid building on other men's foundations, it seems likely that the Cretan churches, in the main, were Paul's work. Else he would not have assumed the authority over them indicated in this Epistle. Possibly they may have been the fruit of his work in Corinth or Ephesus, both of which cities were nearby.

Similarity to I Timothy. Titus and I Timothy, it is thought, were written about the same time, around A.D. 65. They deal with the same general subject: the appointment of proper leaders. Titus in Crete, Timothy in Ephesus; the problem in both places very much the same.

Chapter 1. Elders

In Hope of Eternal Life (2). Paul, like Peter (I Peter 1:3–5), as he neared the end of his earthly road, kept his eyes steadfastly fixed on heaven. It had been the unceasing burden of his preaching and the one grand motive of his life: the Glories of Existence when the body shall have been redeemed (Romans 8:18, 23); the Ecstasy of the day when the mortal shall have put on Immortality (I Corinthians 15:51–55); his longing for the House not made with hands (II Corinthians 5:1–2); his Citizenship in Heaven with a body like the Saviour's (Philippians 3:20–21); his Joy at the thought of being caught up to be Forever with the Lord (I Thessalonians 4:13–18); the Crown of Righteousness which he would receive in "that day" (II Timothy 4:6–8).

Qualifications of an Elder (1:5–9). "Elder" (5), and "Bishop" (7), are here used as identical terms for the same office. Their qualifications, as here enumerated, are practically the same as those given in I Timothy 3:1–7, which see.

The False Teachers (1:10–16). The Cretan churches were beset with false teachers who, like those spoken of in II Peter 2 and Jude, while professing to be Christian teachers, were "abominable" and "reprobate" (16). The quotation from the Cretan poet (12), is from Epimenides 600 B.C. The "mouths" of the false teachers were to be stopped, not by force, but by vigorous proclamation of the truth (11). "Whole houses" probably means whole congregations, for churches then met in family homes.

Chapters 2 and 3. Good Works

The grand emphasis of this Epistle is "Good Works." Not that we are saved by good works, but by His Mercy (3:5), and justified by His Grace (3:7). But because of this we are under strict obligation to be "zealous of good works" (2:14); "an example of good works" (2:7); "ready unto every good work" (3:1); "be careful to maintain good works" (3:8); "maintain good works for necessary uses" (3:14). One of the indictments of the false teachers was that they were "unto every good work reprobate" (1:16).

The Power of Beautiful Lives (2:1–14). Aged men, aged women, young women, mothers, young men, and slaves are exhorted to be so faithful to the natural obligations of their own station in life that critics of their religion would be silenced (2:8).

Slaves, of whom there were many in the early Church, are exhorted to be so obedient, diligent, and faithful that their lives would "adorn" their religious profession (2:10), and their heathen masters would be constrained to think, "If that is what the Christian religion does for slaves, there must be something to it."

The Blessed Hope (2:11–14). The Lord's Coming Again supplies the motive to godly living in this present world. It is mentioned in almost every one of the New Testament books.

Obedience to Civil Authorities (3:1–2), is a prime Christian virtue. Citizens of heaven should be good citizens of the earthly government under which they live (Romans 13:1–7; I Peter 2:13–17).

The Genealogies (3:9), referred to here and in I Timothy 1:4, seem to have figured quite prominently in the doctrine of the false teachers who were at that time infesting the churches of Crete and Ephesus. Possibly they were basing their claims for their teaching on Davidic ancestry and kinship to Jesus, with inside information on the Gospel. Or teaching strange doctrines grounded on abstruse interpretations of passages in genealogies.

"Heretic" (3:10, RV "factious man"). After a reasonable effort to set a false teacher right, avoid him. "Artemas" (3:12), is nowhere else mentioned. Tradition says he became bishop of Lystra. "Tychicus" (12), was of Asia (Acts 20:4). Either he or Artemas was to take Titus' position in Crete. "Nicopolis" (12), in Greece, about 100 miles northwest of Corinth. (See note on Paul's Later Movements under Acts 28:31.) "Zenas" (13), mentioned nowhere else. Either a Jewish scribe or a Greek civil lawyer. "Apollos" (13, see on Acts 18). It seems that he and Zenas, on a journey to some unknown destination, bore this letter to Titus.

PHILEMON

Concerning a Runaway Slave

Philemon

Was a Christian of Colossae, a convert of Paul's, a very well-to-do man. A church met in his house. He and Paul, it seems, were intimate friends. It is likely, though not recorded, that Paul visited Colossae during his 3-year stay at Ephesus (Acts 19).

Onesimus was the name of a slave who belonged to Philemon. He may have been a very talented young man. The Roman army, in its excursions, often took the brightest and best young men and women, and brought them home to be sold into slavery.

Occasion of This Letter. Some four or five years after Paul had left that part of the world, and was way to the west in prison in Rome. Onesimus, it seems, stole some money from his master Philemon and ran away to Rome. While there, perhaps the stolen money gone, he managed to find Paul. Possibly he had learned to love him in his master's home years before. It is not likely that he could have just met him by accident in a city of 1,500,000. Paul persuaded him to be a Christian, and sent him back to his master, bearing this beautiful little Letter.

The Object of the Letter was to intercede with Philemon to forgive the runaway slave, and receive him as a Christian brother, Paul himself offering to repay the stolen money. The Letter is a perfect gem for its Courtesy, Tact, Delicacy and Generosity, climaxing with its tender appeal to Philemon to receive Onesimus "as you would receive me" (17).

The Slave's Reception. The Bible gives no hint as to how the master received his returning slave. But there is a tradition that says his master did receive him, and took Paul's veiled hint and gave the slave his liberty. That is the way the Gospel works. Christ in the heart of the slave made the slave recognize the social usages of his day, and go back to his master determined to be a good slave and live out his natural life as a slave. Christ in the heart of the master made the master recognize the slave as a Christian brother and give him his liberty. There is a tradition that Onesimus afterward became a bishop in Berea.

"Apphia" (2), was, probably, Philemon's wife. "Archippus" (2), probably pastor of the congregation. "Onesimus" (10), means "profitable." Notice the play on the word. "Forever" (15), is a hint of the persistence into eternity of earthly friendships. "Epaphras" (23), was a Colossian imprisoned in Rome. The salutations (24), indicate personal friends of Philemon.

HEBREWS

God's Final Message to Judaism
Christ the Author of a New Covenant
The Glorious Destiny of Man

To Whom Addressed

This Epistle does not name the Persons to whom it is addressed. Its unmistakable tenor is to Jews, inasmuch as it is a discussion of the Relation of Christ to the Levitical Priesthood and the Temple Sacrifices. It continually quotes the Old Testament to confirm its affirmations. The traditional, and commonly accepted, view is that it was addressed to the Jewish Christians of Palestine, specially those in Jerusalem.

Author

In the King James Version it is called, in the title, The Epistle of Paul. In the American Revised Version it is anonymous, because in the oldest manuscripts, found since the King James Translation was made, its Author is not named.

The Eastern Church accepted its Pauline Authorship from the beginning. Not until the 4th century did the Western Church accept it as the work of Paul. Eusebius considered Paul the author. Tertullian called it the Epistle of Barnabas. Clement of Alexandria thought that Paul wrote it in Hebrew, and that Luke translated it into Greek (it is written in most excellent Greek). Origen considered Paul as the probable author. Luther guessed Apollos, for which opinion there is no ancient evidence. Ramsey suggests Phillip. Harnack and Rendel Harris suggest Prisca. Ferrar Fenton thinks nobody but Paul could have written it, and that he wrote it originally in Hebrew, and had it translated by one of his helpers into Greek.

On the whole, the traditional view, held through the centuries, and still widely held, is that Paul was the Author.

Date

Unmistakably it was written before the Destruction of Jerusalem, which occurred A.D. 70. If Paul wrote it, it seems likely that it must have been written from Rome, A.D. 61–63.

The natural, though not necessary, meaning of "They of Italy salute you" (13:24), is that it was written from Italy.

Timothy was with the writer (13:23). He had gone with Paul to Jerusalem (Acts 20:4), from whence he had accompanied Paul to Rome (Colossians 1:1). He had just been released, and Paul was sending him back east (Philippians 2:19, 24); and hoping soon to come himself. And it looks as if he and Timothy were planning to return to Jerusalem (13:23, 19).

It happens that that was just about the time that James the Overseer of the Jerusalem Church was killed, A.D. 62 (see page 657). Paul and James were beloved friends. Paul, some three years before, had been in Jerusalem. It is thought, possibly, that, on hearing of the Death of James, Paul wrote this Epistle to the Leaders of the now pastorless Judean Church, to help them steady their flock for the terrible times ahead.

If this is correct, then there was reason for the Epistle being sent without Paul's name; for Paul was not very popular in Jerusalem. While the Leaders knew who wrote it, the Epistle would have more weight if it were read in the Churches without Paul's Name. New Testament Epistles were written to be READ IN THE CHURCHES, a practice now generally overlooked.

Purpose

One of the objects of this Epistle was, we think, to Prepare Jewish Christians for the approaching Fall of Jerusalem. After accepting Jesus as their Messiah, they continued to be zealous for the Temple Rites and Sacrifices, thinking, we suppose, that their Beloved City, under their Messiah's Reign, was about to become Capital of the World. Instead, they were to receive the shock of their lives. By one stroke of the Roman Army the Holy City was to be wiped out, and the Temple Rites cease.

This Epistle was written to explain to them that Animal Sacrifices, to which they were so zealously attached, were no longer of any use, that the killing of a bullock or a lamb could never take away sin; that those Sacrifices had never been intended to be Perpetual; that they had been planned to be a sort of Age-Long Picture of the Coming Sacrifice of Christ; and now that Christ had come, they had served their purpose.

A Counterpart to the Epistle to Romans

Romans was addressed to the Capital of the Gentile World; Hebrews, to the Capital of the Jewish Nation. God had founded, and nourished the Jewish Nation through long centuries, for the purpose of through the One Nation Blessing All Nations, through a Great King who would arise in the One Nation, and Rule over All Nations. But now the King had come. ROMANS has to do with the relation of the King to His Universal Kingdom, the Basis of their Allegiance to Him. HEBREWS has to do with the relation of the King to the One Nation out of which He came.

Its Literary Excellence

Whoever the Author, as a Literary Gem, it is superb; orderly and logical; "in balanced and resonant sentences of remarkable precision, rising to wonderful heights of eloquence."

Chapter 1:1-4. Deity of Jesus

This opening sentence is one of the most magnificent passages in the Bible, for grandeur taking its place alongside the opening sentences of Genesis and John's Gospel. Jesus, His Deity, His Ineffable Glory, Creator, Preserver and Heir of the Universe. By an Eternal Act of God, ONCE FOR ALL, Jesus made Purification of Man's Sin, and brought him Eternal Salvation.

Chapter 1:4-14. Jesus Compared to Angels

The main argument of the Epistle is that Christ is the Fulfilment, rather than the Administrator, of the Mosaic System. Christ is compared to Angels, through whom the Law was given (Acts 7:53); and to Moses, the Law-Giver; and to the Levitical Priesthood, through whom the Law was Administered.

The language seems to indicate that Human Beings are a Higher order of Creation than Angels. Human Spirits and Angels are not the same. We do not become Angels when we die. Angels are now, and in Heaven will be, our Servants (14). Angels Worship Christ, as we do (6).

Chapter 2:1-8. Man, Not Angels, Lord of Future World

In verse 7 Man is spoken of as a little Lower than Angels, although in 1:14 Angels are called Servants of Heirs of Salvation. In II Peter 2:11 Angels are spoken of as Greater in Might and Power. In verse 9 Jesus was made a Little Lower than Angels. The marginal rendering in RV, in verse 7 and verse 9, is, For a Little While Lower than Angels. Whatever the nature of Angels, by way of comparison with Man, the passage is a side-light on the Ultimate Grandeur of God's Redeemed Human Creation.

Note the Fearful Warning, in verses 2, 3, that if Disobedience to the Word of Angels was Dangerous, How Much More Dangerous to be Neglectful of Words Spoken by Jesus.

Chapter 2:9-18. Christ's Unity with Man

God Created Man to have Lordship Over All Things (6–8). But

Not Yet. Meantime Christ has become One with Man, sharing with Man his Temptations, and Sufferings, even Death itself, that He might Enable Man to Become One With Him, to Share With Him His Nature and His Dominion. And because of this, Christ has now been Crowned with Glory and Honor.

And now Man, in his effort to become One With Christ, and thus Qualify for his Glorious Inheritance, yet to be, has Assurance that Christ is Gracious, and Kindly, and Understanding, and will be Helpful to those who Love Him (17, 18).

Chapter 3:1-6. Christ Compared to Moses

Many Jewish Christians, in their infantile state (5:11–13), had not yet fully learned the Relation of Christ to Moses. It seems that they still thought of Moses as the Law-Giver, and of Christ as an Executive to Enforce the Law of Moses on All Other Nations: Moses First, Christ under him. But they had it just backward. Christ is as far Above Moses, as the Heir and Owner of a house is Above the Servants in the house.

Chapter 3:7-19. Warning against Unbelief

We become Partakers of Christ IF we Hold Fast unto the End; Be on Guard against Falling into Unbelief and Disobedience. This Warning is one of the keynotes of the Epistle, repeated with increasing earnestness in 6:4–6 and 10:26–29.

The example is cited of the Israelites, who, after being delivered out of Egypt with Mighty Signs and Wonders, yet, because of Unbelief and Disobedience, Perished in the Wilderness, and Never Reached the Promised Land (16–19). If they Failed because they were Disobedient to the Word of Moses, what hope can there be for those who are Disobedient to Christ?

The danger of Apostasy among the Jewish Christians must have been Imminent and Serious. The writer may have had in mind the approaching Fall of Jerusalem, most awful calamity in Jewish history, which would tempt Jews to Lose Faith in Jesus.

Chapter 4:1-11. Canaan a Type of Heaven

Those that entered the Promised Land under Joshua found an Earthly Haven, a land of Liberty and Plenty. An Earthly Picture of the Heavenly Homeland in the Eternal Beyond.

Chapter 4:12-13. Power of God's Word

God's Word, Living and Active, has Power to Penetrate the Inmost Depths of the Human Heart, to Separate and View Every

Motive and Desire and Purpose and Will, and Evaluate them at their Intrinsic Value, when we ourselves scarcely know our own motives. Israelites of the Wilderness missed the Promised Land through Disregard of God's Word (3:17; 4:11). Our Best Hope of Reaching Our Promised Land is in Obedience to God's Word. If only our Churches could realize what Power they would gain by giving God's Word its proper place in the services! But Alas! Alas! Everything else but God's Word!

Chapter 4:14-16. Christ Our High Priest

Here begins the Main Theme of the Epistle, Comparison of Christ with the Levitical Priesthood, continuing into chapter 10.

Chapter 5:1-10. Christ Compared to Levitical Priests

They were of the Tribe of Levi: Christ was of the Tribe of Judah. They were Many: He was One. They offered Animal Sacrifices: He offered Himself. They Died: He Lives.

Chapter 5:11-14. Dull of Hearing

Here is a personal message to the original recipients of this Epistle. In former time they had been notably zealous in Ministering to the Saints (6:10). But now they had Forgotten even the First Principles of the Gospel (5:12).

If the traditional view that this Epistle was addressed to the Judean Church is correct, then this passage evidently refers to the Decline from the Spiritual and Brotherly quality of the Jerusalem Church described in Acts 4:32–35. The Epistle of James, written shortly before, implies a Worldly, Selfish Church.

As time passed, many thousands of Jews had accepted Jesus as their Messiah (Acts 21:20), still holding to the old Materialistic idea of the Messianic Kingdom, that it would be a Political Kingdom in which the Jewish Nation, under their Messiah, would Rule the World. So that their Christian Faith was largely of the nature of a Political Slogan.

After the death of James this Idea seems to have so largely Dominated the Jerusalem Church, that the writer tells them that, instead of being Teachers of the Christian World, as the Mother Church should have been, they, like little children, needed to be instructed over again in the First Principles of the Gospel of Christ (12).

Chapter 6. Warning Against Apostasy

The language seems to imply that the Jerusalem Church quite

largely had Fallen from the High Standards of Christian Living that had once been theirs, and were Headed away from the Goals toward which they should be Earnestly Struggling.

The Fall of a Christian, spoken of in verse 6, may be Partial or Total; as a person may fall from the top of a building to a projecting ledge, or all the way to the bottom. As long as the Apostasy is Partial, there may be Hope. When it becomes Total, Recovery may be Impossible.

The Sin here spoken of may be similar to the Unpardonable Sin mentioned by Jesus (Matthew 12:31, 32, and Mark 3:28–30), where the implication is that that Sin consisted in attributing the Miracles of Jesus to Satan, and which, in Luke 12:9–10, is connected with Denial of Jesus. It could be committed by a person Outside the Church. The Sin here referred to is the Fall of a Christian. The Essence of the Fatal Sin, whether by a Christian or by One Outside, is the Deliberate and Final Rejection of Christ. It is as if a person in the bottom of a well, to whom a rope is let down, slashes the rope above his reach, thus cutting off his only hope of escape. For those who Reject Christ, there will Never Be Another Sacrifice for Sin (10:26–31). They will have to suffer for their own sin.

Over against this Fearful Warning against Falling Away from Christ, the writer is very positive that, for those who remain Faithful and True to Christ, the Hope of Eternal Salvation is Absolutely Sure and Stedfast, based on the Immutability of God's Promises to those who Trust Him (9–20).

Chapter 7:1-10. Melchizedek

Christ a Priest after the Order of Melchizedek. That is, Jesus was not a Levitical Priest, but His Priesthood rather was similar to that of Melchizedek, a Personage of the Dim Past, ante-dating the Levitical Priesthood by some 600 years: a Priest far Greater than the Levitical Priests, Greater even than Abraham: to whom Abraham, and the as yet unborn Levitical Priests, still in the loins of Abraham, paid tithes.

The account of Melchizedek is in Genesis 14:18–20. He was King of Salem, and Priest of God Most High. A King and a Priest.

Previous to the time of Moses Sacrifices were offered by the Heads of Families. Thus the Priest of each Family was the Father, or Grandfather or Great Grandfather, Oldest living man in the paternal line. As the Family grew to be a Tribe, the Head came to be King of the Tribe, as well as Priest; and thus he was a King-Priest, or Priest-King.

In the days of Moses, when the aggregate of Families of God's Chosen People had grown to be a Nation, the Nation was Organized, a Place set apart for Sacrifice, a Ritual prescribed, and a Special

Hereditary Order of Men was created to act as Priests, of the Family of Levi.

Later another Family was set apart to supply the Kings, the Family of David. A King ruled the people. A Priest, as mediator between God and Man, offered Sacrifices. One Family supplied the Kings; another, the Priests. But Christ was Both, combining office of King and Priest, like Melchizedek.

What is the meaning of "without father, without mother, without genealogy, having neither beginning of days nor end of life"? Not that it was actually so, but that it appeared so in the Old Testament Records. Levitical Priests were Priests Because of their Genealogy. But Melchizedek, Without Genealogy, was the Recognized Priest of the Human Race at that time. Hebrew tradition is that Shem, who was still alive in the days of Abraham, and, as far as is known, Oldest Living Man at the time, was Melchizedek. A mysterious, solitary picture and type, in the dim past, of the Coming Eternal Priest-King.

Chapter 7:11-12. Levitical Priesthood Temporary

It was Imperfect, those Sacrifices being insufficient to take away Sin (10:4). It was Carnal (16), that is, they were Priests solely because they were of a certain Family, without regard to spiritual qualifications. And the Covenant under which they operated has been superceded by Another Covenant (8:8).

Chapter 7:13-28. Christ's Priesthood Eternal

Levitical Priests offered Sacrifices Every Year. Christ Died Once for All. Theirs were Unavailing. His Removed Sin Forever. Christ Lives on, Mediator of an Eternal Covenant and an Endless Life.

Eternal is one of the favorite words of the Epistle. Eternal Salvation (5:9). Eternal Judgment (6:2). Eternal Redemption (9:12). Eternal Spirit (9:14). Eternal Inheritance (9:15). Eternal Covenant (13:20). It is also a favorite word in John's Gospel.

Chapter 8. The New Covenant

Christ brought to mankind a New Covenant. The First Covenant, centered around the Tabernacle Services and the Ten Commandments, had served its purpose (9:1–5). Its Laws were written on tables of stone (9:4). Christ's Laws would be written on our Hearts (8:10). The First Covenant was Temporal. Christ's Covenant would be Everlasting (13:20). The First Covenant was sealed with the blood of Animals. Christ's Covenant was sealed with His Own Blood (10:29). It was a Better Covenant, with Better Promises, based on the Immutability of God's Word (6:18).

"Better" is one of this Epistle's favorite words. Better Covenant (8:6). Better Promises (8:6). Better Hope (7:19). Better Possession in Heaven (10:34). Blood that Speaks Better than Abel (12:24). Better Country, Heaven, not Canaan (11:16). Better Resurrection, Never to Die again (11:35).

Chapter 9:1-14. Christ and the Tabernacle

The Tabernacle was a Sanctuary of This World: the True Tabernacle, not made with hands, is Heaven (9:1, 11, 24). The High Priest entered Once a Year; Christ entered Once for All (7, 12). The High Priest obtained Annual Redemption; Christ obtained Eternal Redemption (10:3; 9:12). The High Priest offered the Blood of Animals; Christ offered His Own Blood (9:12). The High Priest's sacrifices cleansed the Flesh; Christ's sacrifice cleanses the Conscience (9:13, 14).

Chapter 9:15-28. The New Testament

The New Covenant is here called "The New Testament." A Testament is a Will, a bequeathment to heirs, effective only after the Death of the maker. The New Covenant is the Will which Christ made for His Heirs, which could not become effective till, by His Death, He had Atoned for their Sins.

This is where we get the Names of the Two Divisions of the Bible: Old Testament and New Testament. The Old Testament is the story of the Covenant of the Law. The New Testament is the story of the Covenant of Christ. The abundant use of Blood in the rites of the Old Covenant prefigured the urgent necessity of some Great Sacrifice for Human Sin (19–22).

Once for All (26–28). Christ Offered Himself Once for All (7:27). Once for All He Entered the Holy Place (9:12). Once for All put away Sin at the end of the ages (9:26). Men appointed Once to Die (9:27). Christians Sanctified Once for All by the Offering of Christ (10:10). Christ Once Offered shall Appear a Second Time for His Waiting Heirs (9:28). Here the Lord's Coming Again is called His Second Coming.

Chapter 10:1-25. Sin Removed Forever

No need for further Sacrifice. Christ's Death is entirely sufficient to take care of all previous Sins, and those that in weakness we may in daily life commit. God can now Forgive, and will Forgive, those who place their Trust in Christ.

Let us therefore Hold Fast to Christ (23). He, and He alone, is our Hope and our Saviour.

Chapter 10:26-39. Rejection of Christ

Another Fearful Warning against Falling Away from Christ, similar to that in 6:1–8. Addressed to Christians who had once been a gazingstock in their Sufferings for the Name of Christ, and who had given their all in their compassion for their fellow-sufferers (32–34); some of whom were now losing interest in the things of Christ (25).

The point is that there has been ONE SACRIFICE for Sin. There will Never be another. Whoever will not avail himself of what Christ has done for him on the Cross may as well make up his mind to say Goodby to God Forever, and go his own way, and suffer for his own sin (27–31).

Chapter 11. Heroes of Faith

Abel's Faith: First Sacrifice for Sin (4; Genesis 4:1–15).

Enoch's Faith: Walked with God; Translated (5, 6; Genesis 5:22, 24).

Noah's Faith: Kept on building the Ark when nobody thought there would be any use for it (7; Genesis 6:14–22).

Abraham's Faith: Started, he knew not where, to find the City of God: was willing to offer his son, in Confidence that God would bring him back to Life (8:10; 17–19; Genesis 12:1–7; 22).

Sarah's Faith: Came to Believe what she at first had laughed at as impossible (11, 12; Genesis 17:19; 18:11–14).

Isaac's Faith: Foretold the Future (20; Genesis 27:27–29).

Jacob's Faith: God would fulfill His Promises (21; Genesis 49).

Joseph's Faith: Bones to rest in Canaan (22; Genesis 50:25).

Moses' Faith: Chose to suffer with Israel: Forsook Egypt: Kept the Passover: Crossed the Red Sea: Saw Him who is Invisible (23–29; Exodus 2:2–11; 12:21, 50; 14:22–29).

Joshua's Faith: Walls of Jericho Fell (30; Joshua 6:20).

Rahab's Faith: Cast her lot with Israel (31; Joshua 2:9; 6:23).

Gideon's Faith: Waxed Mighty in War (32; Judges 7:21).

Barak's Faith: Subdued Kingdoms (32; Judges 4).

Samson's Faith: From Weakness Made Strong (32, 34; Judges 16:28).

Jepthah's Faith: Defeated Armies (32, 34; Judges 11).

David's Faith: Obtained Promises (32, 33; II Samuel 7:11–13).

Daniel's Faith: Stopped Mouths of Lions (32, 33; Daniel 6:22).

Jeremiah's Faith: Was Tortured (32, 35; Jeremiah 20:2).

Elijah's Faith: Raised the Dead (32, 35; I Kings 17:17–24).

Elisha's Faith: Raised the Dead (32, 35; II Kings 4:8–37).

Zechariah's Faith: Was Stoned (32, 37; II Chronicles 24:20, 21).

Isaiah's Faith: Sawn Asunder? (32, 37; Tradition).

Chapter 12. Keep Your Eyes Upon Jesus

Surrounded by a vast crowd of those who, in former ages, had run their race for God victoriously, and who were now gazing with breathless interest at the initial struggle of the New-Born Church, the runners are urged to Keep their Eyes on the Goal, and Strain Every Nerve and Muscle to Win (1, 2).

And Be Not Discouraged by their Sufferings; for Chastening is one of the means by which God's Saints are Perfected (3–13).

And be Very Careful to Guard against Defiling themselves in any way, lest they Sell their Birthright (14–17).

Sinai and Zion (18–29). The terrifying demonstrations of the inauguration of the Old Covenant are contrasted with the Heavenly Fellowships of the Church: One Vast Brotherhood, in which Saints on Earth, and Spirits of the Redeemed, and Infinite Hosts of Angels, are in Sweet and Mystic Communion around the Throne of God, Forever and Ever and Ever (22–24).

Chapter 13. Gracious Exhortations

This Epistle, though argumentative in nature, closes with tender appeals to its readers to be Loyal to Christ, and to Follow Him in all the Ways of Life, especially in Brotherly Love and Kindness and Purity and Goodness, and with Unceasing Prayer and Unwavering Faith in God.

As Malachi was the Old Testament's final message to the Nation founded to bring the Messiah into the world, so the Epistle to the Hebrews is the New Testament's final message to the Nation after the Messiah had come. Written shortly before the Jewish State was swept away by the Fall of Jerusalem, "One of the most appalling events in all history."

Destruction of Jerusalem

Jewish Wars, in revolt against Rome, began A.D. 66. Titus with his Roman Army arrived before the walls of Jerusalem on the day of Passover, A.D. 70. Banks of earthwork were built, battering rams were placed, and the siege began.

The Roman Army numbered 30,000; the Jewish Army, 24,000. The city was crowded with 600,000 visitors, according to Tacitus. After 5 months the walls were battered down, the Temple burned, and the city left ruined and desolate, except Herod's three great towers at the northwest corner, which were left standing as a memorial of the massive strength of the fortifications which Titus had demolished.

The Roman Army moved down to Caesarea. Over 1,000,000 Jews were killed. 95,000 captives were taken, among them Josephus.

Eusebius says that Christians, on the appearance of the Roman Army, through Prophetic warning, fled to Pella.

Later History of Jerusalem

For the 50 years following, Jerusalem disappeared from history. In A.D. 135, Barcocheba, a pretended Messiah, led a revolt, got possession of the city, and attempted to rebuild the Temple. The revolt was suppressed by the Roman Army. 580,000 Jews were killed, and Judah desolated. Jews were forbidden to reenter Jerusalem, on pain of death. A temple to Jupiter was erected where the Temple of God had stood.

Under Constantine, A.D. 326, the temple of Astarte was torn away from the site of the present Holy Sepulchre; and the city again became a leading Christian center.

In the 5th century it became the seat of one of the Five Patriarchs who quite largely dominated Christendom, the other cities being Rome, Constantinople, Antioch, Alexandria.

In the year A.D. 637 Jerusalem fell to Mohammedans, and remained a Mohammedan city, except for about 100 years in the Crusade Period, till 1917 it returned to control of Christendom.

JAMES

Christian Wisdom
Good Works
Pure Religion

James

Two Apostles were named James: one the brother of John, the other the son of Alphaeus (Matthew 10:2, 3. See page 466).

The oldest brother of Jesus was named James (Matthew 13:55). This James was early recognized as leading Overseer of the Judean Church (Acts 12:17, Galatians 1:19), and is commonly regarded as the writer of this Epistle.

He was known as an unusually good man. Was surnamed "the Just" by his countrymen. It is said that he spent so much time on his knees in Prayer that they became hard and callous like a camel's knees. He is thought to have been married (I Corinthians 9:5). He was very influential both among the Jews and in the Church. Peter reported to him on his release from prison (Acts 12:17). Paul acted on his advice (Acts 21:18–26). He was a very strict Jew himself, but was author of the tolerant letter to Gentile Christians (Acts 15:13–29). He endorsed Paul's Gentile work, but was himself mainly concerned with Jews. His life work was to win Jews, and "smooth their passage to Christianity."

Story of His Martyrdom

According to Josephus; and Hegesippus, a Christian historian of the second century, whose narrative Eusebius accepts:

Shortly before Jerusalem was destroyed by the Roman army, A.D. 70 (see page 655), when Jews were, in large numbers, embracing Christianity, Ananus, the High-Priest, and the Scribes and Pharisees, about the year A.D. 62 or A.D. 66, assembled the Sanhedrin, and commanded James, "the brother of Jesus who was called Christ," to proclaim from one of the galleries of the Temple that Jesus Was Not the Messiah. But, instead, James cried out that Jesus Was the Son of God and Judge of the World.

Then his enraged enemies hurled him to the ground, and stoned him till a charitable fuller ended his sufferings with a club, while he was on his knees praying, "Father, forgive them, they know not what they do."

The Epistle

Addressed to Christian Jews (2:1), scattered abroad (1:1), it seems like a book of Christian Proverbs, about a number of subjects, bearing on the Practical Phases of Christian Life.

Written, probably, about A.D. 60, near the close of James' life, after a 30 year pastorate of the Judean Church.

Chapter 1:1-8. Trials. Patience. Wisdom. Faith

Rejoice in Trials (2), Persecutions, Afflictions, Sufferings, of one kind or another, endurance of which Proves our Faith, and helps build us into the kind of person that Christ came to make of us. Peter calls Trials Precious (I Peter 1:7).

Trials work Patience (3, 4). Patience, in time of Suffering, is the ability to Wait calmly and in Joy for that glad day when God shall wipe away all tears.

Patience works Perfection (4). We are just poor sinners, saved by Grace. But Perfection is our ultimate goal. Some day we shall be Perfect, Like Him (I John 3:2).

Wisdom (5). Sound Judgment about the Practical things of Daily Life, in all its phases, so as to live, in all things, as a Christian should.

Prayer (5), will help attain such Wisdom. The Epistle begins, and ends (5:13–18), with an exhortation to Prayer.

Faith (6–8). Unwavering Faith, that stands Sure and Undisturbed, in all the storms of life, is the condition of Prevailing Prayer. All Things are possible to him that Believeth (Mark 9:23).

Chapter 1:9-18. Riches. Temptation. New Birth

Riches (9–11). A solemn reminder that our status, not here, but in Eternity, should be our main concern. Even the poor may Rejoice in their Glorious Destiny. (See further 2:1–13.)

Temptation (12–15), same word as in verse 2. There it seems to mean being Proved by Suffering. Here it means Enticement to Sin. And Sin, born in Lust, gives birth to Death.

The Christian's New-Born Soul (16–18). As Lust brings forth Sin, and Sin brings forth Death, so God, through His Word, and in the Name of Christ, begets and brings forth New-Born Souls in those who are destined to constitute His Inheritance through the Endless Ages of Eternity. Peter also speaks of the Word of God as being the Seed of Impregnation that brings forth the New-Born Soul of a Christian (I Peter 1:23).

Chapter 1:19-27. Tongue. The Word. Pure Religion

Watch your Tongue (19–21). Control your Temper. Be a good Listener. Abstain from Filthy Talk.

Doers of the Word (21–25). In verse 18 the Word is called the instrument of the Soul's Birth. In verse 21 it is the agent of the Soul's Salvation. In verse 23 it is represented as a Mirror, showing us ourselves in our true light.

Pure Religion (26, 27). A magnificent passage. The Tongue again. An Uncontrolled Tongue in a religious person indicates his religion is useless. A life of Charity and Kindness, free from over-much attachment to earthly things, is religion's Glory. (Compare Jesus' eulogy on Kindness, Matthew 25:31–46.)

Chapter 2:1-13. Respect of Persons

There must have been a decidedly worldly element in the Judean Church, to call forth such words as these. So different from the way the Church had started (Acts 2:45; 4:34).

Christ taught that the Glory of His Church would be in its Kindness to the Poor. But very evidently some of the congregations were developing into social circles where the Poor were given to understand they were not wanted. But God loves the Poor. And the Rich ought to love them too.

Chapter 2:14-26. Faith and Works

Paul's doctrine of Justification by Faith, and James' doctrine of Justification by Works, are supplementary, not contradictory. Neither was opposing the teaching of the other. They were devoted friends and co-workers. James fully endorsed Paul's work (Acts 15:13–29; 21:17–26).

Paul preached Faith as the basis of justification before God, but insisted that it must issue in the right kind of Life. James was writing to those who had accepted the doctrine of Justification by Faith but were not Living Right, telling them that such Faith was No Faith at all.

Chapter 3:1-12. The Tongue

Sins of the Tongue: not only Harsh and Angry Words, but False and Foolish Doctrines. From the general tone of this chapter we suspect there must have been many presumptuous, quarrelsome, worldly-minded men, of uncontrolled temper, putting themselves forward as leaders and teachers.

Power of the Tongue. The Tongue is the main expression of our Personality, and usually calls forth an immediate reaction, of one kind or another, in others. Mean words have wrecked many a home, divided many a church, and sent unnumbered millions to despair and ruin. Yet we know many very Religious people who seem never to make even the slightest effort to control their Tongue.

Chapter 3:13-18. Wisdom

This passage seems to be aimed at certain loquacious teachers, who, bigoted over some pet doctrine, with little personal affection for Christ, and ambitious to be considered brilliant in argument, were producing only jealousy and faction. James calls such Wisdom "devilish," and suggests that the best way to show Real Wisdom is by a Good Life.

Chapter 4. Worldly-Mindedness

Origin of Wars: Covetousness (1, 2). The desire to get that which belongs to others. This has been the cause of most wars.

Reason for Unanswered Prayer: because they are for the gratification of our worldly pleasures (3).

Double-Mindedness (4–10). An expansion of Jesus' statement that a person cannot serve God and Mammon (Matthew 6:24), and similar to John's warning against Love of the World (I John 2:15–17). Such passages suggest the need of unceasing Self-Examination; for, having to live in the world, and worldly things being needful to our daily subsistence, it requires great watchfulness to keep our affection above the border line. We need constantly to Draw Nigh to God, to Cleanse our Hands, to Purify our Heart and to Humble ourselves.

The Tongue, again (11, 12). This time on the utter absurdity of one sinner setting himself up as judge of another sinner.

If the Lord Will (13–17). One of the most amazing doctrines of Scripture is that God, with the infinite universe on His hands, yet has a definite Plan for each of His people (Acts 18:21; Romans 1:10; 15:32; I Corinthians 4:19; I Peter 3:17).

Chapter 5. Riches. Patience. Tongue. Prayer

The Rich (1–6). James's fourth and strongest blast at them, the others being 1:9–11; 2:1–13; 4:1–10. There must have been a good many rich men in the Judean Church who were thoroughly Un-Christian bent on Worldly Pleasure. Rare Christian souls are to be found among the rich; but, quite largely, James' picture of them still holds; and his warning to them of coming retribution is frightful.

Patience under Suffering (7–11). One day the Lord will Come, and all Suffering will be over. Keep your eyes and your heart fixed on That Glad Day. The greater the Suffering here the greater will be the Glory there.

The Tongue, again (12). Our Sinful Tongue. The cause of so much trouble. This time, Swearing. A very serious Sin, very displeasing to God. Yet how many professed Christians, in their ordinary conversation, profane God's Name. A better use of the Tongue is to Sing (13).

Prayer, again (13–18). Believing Prayer will surely be answered. Elijah's closing and opening of the heavens was a rare and mighty miracle (I Kings 18). Yet it is quoted to us as an incentive to Pray.

Anointing with Oil (14), was a recognized medical treatment (Isaiah 1:6; Luke 10:34), to be re-inforced by Prayer, not to be used for magical purposes.

To win a Soul for Christ (19, 20), pleases God immensely for which He loves us, and overlooks our weaknesses. For it, we shall shine as the stars forever (Daniel 12:3).

I PETER

To a Persecuted Church

Peter

For his early life, see note on page 465. Of his later life there are no Scriptural notices other than his two Epistles. From Jesus' word in John 21:18 we judge he must have died a martyr's death. As leader of the Twelve it seems likely that he visited leading Church centers of the Roman World.

Some church historians think there is not sufficient evidence that Peter was ever in Rome. Most of them, however, agree that it is probable that, about the last year of his life, Peter did go to Rome, either by order of Nero, or, of his own accord to help steady the Christians under the teriffic blows of Nero's Persecutions.

The "Quo Vadis" tradition has it that Peter, being overcome by the solicitation of friends to save himself, was fleeing from Rome, and in the night, out on the Appian Way, in a vision, he met Jesus, and said, "Lord, whither goest thou?" Jesus answered, "I am going to Rome to be Crucified again." Peter, utterly ashamed and humiliated, returned to the city, and was Crucified head downward, feeling not worthy to be Crucified as his Lord was. This is only a tradition, and we do not know how much of historical fact it may contain.

Tradition also has it that Peter's wife, named Concordia, or Perpetua, suffered martyrdom, as Peter encouraged her to be brave, saying, "Remember, dear, our Lord."

To Whom Written

To Churches in Asia Minor (1:1), which, in the main, had been founded by Paul. Though it is not so stated, we presume that Peter had sometime or other visited these Churches. To some of them Paul had written Galatians, Ephesians and Colossians. I Peter has some striking similarities to Ephesians. Later, to some of these Churches John addressed the book of Revelation.

From Whence Written

"Babylon" (5:13). Some take this to be the literal Babylon of the Euphrates. But quite generally it is thought to mean Rome, figuratively called Babylon. In Revelation 17:5, 18 Rome is called Babylon. In those times of persecution, Christians, for prudence' sake, had to be careful how they spoke of the ruling power, and had a name for it that they, among themselves, but not an outsider, would understand.

Mark was with Peter at the time (5:13); and from II Timothy 4:11, we judge that Mark may have been in Rome about the time this Epistle was written.

Occasion of Writing

Nero's Persecution of Christians, A.D. 64–67, was very severe in and around Rome, but not general over the Empire. However, the example of the Emperor encouraged the enemies of Christians everywhere to take advantage of the slightest pretext to Persecute. It was a trying time. The Church was about 35 years old. It had suffered Persecutions in various localities at the hands of local authorities. But now Imperial Rome, which had hitherto been indifferent, even in some cases friendly, had accused the Church of a terrible crime, and was undertaking to punish it (see page 635).

The Church was undergoing a world trial (5:9). It seemed as if the end had come. It was literally a "fiery trial" (4:12). Christians were being burned nightly in Nero's gardens. It did look as if the Devil, as a "roaring lion" (5:8), was about to devour the Church.

It is thought, possibly, that Peter may have written this Letter immediately after Paul's martyrdom, about A.D. 66, and sent it by Silas (5:12), who had been one of Paul's helpers, to these Churches which Paul had founded, to encourage them to bear up under their Suffering, Silas personally carrying the news of Paul's martyrdom to Paul's Churches.

Thus the Epistle was born in the atmosphere of Suffering, shortly before Peter's own martyrdom, exhorting Christians not to think it strange that they had to Suffer, reminding them that Christ did His work by Suffering.

Chapter 1. The Christian's Glorious Inheritance

A Magnificent chapter. Almost every word fraught with precious meaning.

"Strangers" (1:1), seems to mean Scattered Jewish Christians. But 2:10 indicates they were, mainly, Gentiles. Peter addresses them as Sojourners, Pilgrims, Citizens of Another World, living for a little while in This World, away from Home, Journeying along toward their Home Land.

Suffering and Glory (1:7). The greater our Suffering in This World the greater will be our Glory in the Next World. Trials here, Glory at the Coming of the Lord (1:7). Again and again Suffering and Glory are paired. The Sufferings of Christ, and the

Glory that should follow (1:11). Partakers of Christ's Sufferings will Rejoice with Exceeding Joy at the Revelation of His Glory (4:13). Peter, a witness of Christ's Suffering, will be a partaker of His Glory (5:1). After you have Suffered a while, Eternal Glory (5:10). This was also Paul's comfort: Our Light Affliction works for us a far more exceeding and Eternal Weight of Glory (II Corinthians 4:17).

"Precious," a favorite word with Peter. Trial of Faith more Precious than gold (1:7). Redeemed with the Precious Blood of Christ (2:19). Precious Lord (2:4, 7). Precious Faith (II Peter 1:1). Great and Precious Promises (II Peter 1:4).

Christ, Himself, Personally, Whom, not having seen, you Love (1:8), in Whom you Rejoice with Joy Unspeakable and Full of Glory (1:8), by Whose Power you are Kept for Final Salvation (1:5)—Christ Himself is the Center of Heaven's Glory (1:3–9). Set your Hope perfectly on HIM and His Coming (1:13).

Chapters 2,3. The Christian's Earthly Pilgrimage

Christians, Born into a Glorious Inheritance, by the Word of God (1:23), in Journeying along through this world toward their Heavenly Home Land, still, for Nourishment, Guidance, and Strength, need constantly to Feed on God's Word (2:2); thus, along the way, Tasting and Experiencing that their precious Lord, by their side, is Gracious, Kind, Loving and Helpful, as He leads them onward (2:2, 3).

Pilgrims (2:11), Elect, Holy (2:9), a people of Good Works (2:12; 3:13), who, by their Manner of Life, Glorify God (3:16). It reminds us of Jesus' word (in Matthew 5:14–16), that the Light of the World is the Good Works of His Disciples.

Be a Good Citizen, or Subject, as far as possible, of the Earthly Government under which you live, Law-Abiding and Obedient, to promote the good name of your religion, even though the Government be headed by a Nero (2:13–17).

Christian Servants (2:18–25). There were many Slaves in the first century Church. They are exhorted to be Good Slaves, even to brutal masters, and to endure, without resentment, any suffering wrongfully administered.

Christian Wives (3:1–6). "Calling him Lord" (6), surely is not to be construed as meaning abject slavery to her husband, but rather unselfish devotion, so as to win his admiration and affection, and, if he is an unbeliever, by her loving tact, win him to Christ. We do not understand verses 3–4 to prohibit a woman's desire to be attractive in personal appearance, but rather a caution against overdoing it, remembering that no amount of finery can be a substitute for gracious Christian Personality. (See further on Ephesians 5:22–33.)

Christian Husbands (3–7). It is Manly to be Tender toward the gentler sex. God's plan is that Marital Love be Mutual, each considerate of the other. If either has a mean disposition or tongue, that makes it all the harder for the other to be considerate. "That your Prayers be not hindered" (7). Nothing extinguishes the flame of Prayer like marital friction.

Christ Preached to Spirits in Prison (3:18–22). This passage seems to say that Jesus, in the interval between His death and resurrection, preached to the imprisoned spirits of the disobedient of Noah's day. Or, it may mean that the Spirit of Christ was in Noah preaching to the antediluvians.

Chapters 4,5. The Fiery Trial

Be Armed for Suffering (4:1–6). It was a time of Persecution. The special exhortation of this Epistle was for Christians to be ready for it. But there is comfort here for Christians who live in normal times; for very few people get through life without a good deal of Suffering of one kind or another: physical suffering, mental suffering, heart suffering. One of the strange ways of Providence is that many people have to suffer in the very way in which they would rather not have to suffer, have to go through life denied the one thing that most of all they would rather not be denied. Such people may very properly comfort themselves in the assurance that when God is bearing down extra hard in His grinding it is that the finished diamond may be extra bright and beautiful.

Christian Love (4:7–11), the Supreme Virtue of Life. Peter's exhortations to Love are beautiful. Love one another from the Heart Fervently (1:22). Honor all men; Love the Brotherhood (2:17). Loving as Brothers, Tenderhearted (3:8). Above all things being Fervent in your Love among yourselves (4:8). Brothers in a common Glorious Hope, be real Brothers to one another in time of Suffering.

The Fiery Trial (4:12–19). Nero's Persecution of Christians was the direct work of the Devil (5:8). Nevertheless, in the mysterious Providence of God, it would turn out for the good of the Church, a Trial more Precious than gold (1:7). There have been many Persecutions since, many of them more brutal and widespread than Nero's, in which unnumbered millions of Christians have endured every conceivable kind of torture. When we think of this we ought to be ashamed of ourselves for our fretfulness over our petty troubles.

Peter's Humility (5:1–7) is discernable in this section.

Mark (13), was with Peter at the time. He is thought to have written his Gospel under Peter's direction, possibly about the time Peter wrote this Epistle.

II PETER

Prediction of Apostasy

Author

The Epistle specifically claims to be the work of Simon Peter (1:1). The writer represents himself as having been present at the Transfiguration of Christ (1:16–18); and of having been warned by Christ of his impending death (1:14). This means that the Epistle is a genuine writing of Peter, or that it was the work of some one who professed himself to be Peter.

Though it was slow in being received into the New Testament Canon (see page 747), it was recognized by the early Church as a genuine writing of Peter, and has, through the centuries been revered as a part of Holy Scripture.

Some modern critics regard it as a pseudonymous work of the late second century, written by some unkown person who assumed Peter's name, a hundred years after Peter's death. To the average mind this would be just plain common forgery, an offence against civil and moral law and ordinary decency. The critics, however, over and over aver that there is nothing at all unethical in thus counterfeiting another's name.

To Whom Addressed

Unlike most of the Epistles, no locality is mentioned. It was, however, Peter's "second epistle" to the same persons (3:1). While Peter may have written many epistles which have not been preserved to us, yet the assumption is that this language refers to that which is commonly known as his "First Epistle," which was addressed to churches of Asia Minor (I Peter 1:1), churches to whom Paul also had written (II Peter 3:15).

Date

If I Peter was written during Nero's Persecution (see page 663), and if Peter was martyred in that Persecution (see page 662), then this Epistle must have been written shortly before Peter's death, probably about A.D. 67, or within a year or two, one way or the other.

II Peter and Jude

In some passages are so similar that some scholars think one must have copied from the other. It is not necessary to think that. The Apostles, constantly hearing one another talk, certain expressions and Scripture illustrations became part of the common Christian vocabulary.

Chapter 1:1-11. Making Sure of Salvation

Knowledge of Christ, the foundation of our Precious Faith (1:1), is here emphasized as the medium of Grace and Peace (2), and of all things that pertain to Life and Godliness (3), and one of the means by which we may make our Calling and Election Sure (5), and by which the Defilements of the World are Overcome (2:20). It is the closing exhortation of the Epistle (3:18). Original, Authentic Knowledge about Christ is contained in God's Word. So Peter's farewell warning was, Don't Neglect God's Word.

The Precious Promises (4), include not only the External Glories of the Eternal Kingdom (11), but a Changed, Divine Nature within ourselves, which God will, of His own Grace, bestow upon us, which we, on our part, must do our best to attain (5–11).

Seven Divine Qualities (5–11). Virtue. Knowledge. Self-Control. Patience. Godliness. Brotherly Kindness. Love. These are the Fruits (8), of the Precious Faith (1), which we are to Add (5), to the Blessings which God has Multiplied (2), to us. They are Steps from Earth to Heaven, starting in Faith, and culminating in Love in the Eternal Home of God.

Chapter 1:12-15. Peter's Martyrdom Near

This seems like a reference to what Jesus had told him some 37 years before (John 21:18, 19). Or, it may be that Jesus had recently appeared to him (14); possibly the Quo Vadis appearance (see page 662). At any rate, he had a premonition that Martyrdom was at hand (14). Reminds us of Paul's dying shout of Triumph (II Timothy 4:6–8). "The Putting Off of my Tabernacle" (14), is a Beautiful Scripture name for Death.

Chapter 1:16-21. Gospel Testimony Sure

It seems that, in Peter's day, there were precursors of our modern critics, who were calling the Story of Jesus and His Mighty Works a set of Cunningly Devised Fables (16). But Peter had Seen With His Own Eyes, and he KNEW that what he told about Jesus was TRUE. Over a period of three years he had seen Jesus, with a word, Heal Multitudes of Sick People. He had seen Him Walk on Water, and with a word Still the Storm. He had seen Him Transfigured. Three times he saw Him Raise the Dead. He Saw Jesus Alive after Crucifixion. And, after Pentecost, Peter himself, In Jesus' Name, did multitudes of Mighty Miracles (Acts 5:15), and even Raised Dorcas from the Dead (Acts 9:40).

All this, confirmed in marvelous detail in Old Testament prophecies of the coming Messiah (1:19–21, see also pages 387–401), gave Peter Full Assurance, and Made him Ready for approaching Martyrdom. He Knew that, for him, the Door of Glory was about to open into the immediate presence of his Beloved Lord, nevermore to leave.

Chapter 2. Church Apostasy

The Coming of False Teachers is spoken of again and again in the New Testament. Jesus warned of Ravening Wolves who would come to the Church in Sheep's Clothing (Matthew 7:15), and Lead Many Astray (Matthew 24:11). Paul warned of Grievous Wolves who would arise in the Church, Speaking Perverse Things (Acts 20:29, 30). Again Paul Predicted that, before the Second Coming of the Lord, there would be, in the Church, a Falling Away of Appalling Magnitude and Satanic Nature (II Thessalonians 2:1–12). Again Paul Foretold the rise to Church Leadership of Ungodly Men, Traitors and Hypocrites, who, with a Form of Godliness, would fill the Church with Doctrines of Devils (I Timothy 4:1–3; II Timothy 3:1–9). Jude seems to have been written mainly to Warn of an Ominous and Deadly Trend toward Apostasy which, in his own day, he saw rising in the Church (Jude 4–19). And, in Revelation 17, John gives a detailed description of the Full-Grown Harlot Church.

Peter, in his First Epistle, wrote to encourage the Church to bear up under Persecution from Without. Here, in this Second Epistle, it is to Caution the Church to Guard against Corruption from Within.

He warns of Coming Apostasy, when Leaders in the Church, for money considerations, would permit Licentiousness and general Wrong-Doing. He speaks of it as being in the future (2:1). Yet some of the language implies that False Teachers were already at work within the Church.

He speaks of their Destructive Heresies (1), their Pernicious Ways (2), their Covetousness (3), their Walking in Lust (10), Brute Beasts (12), Eyes full of Adultery (14), Servants of Corruption (19). Note: these expressions are used as referring, not to the World, but to Leaders Within the Church.

It is a sorry picture. Even within the Apostolic generation the World and the Devil had succeeded in making heavy onslaughts on the Purity of the Church. Then followed the long centuries of Papal Corruption. And, even now, in our own enlightened age, the Gospel of Christ, in its original beauty and simplicity and Purity, in many sections of the Church, still is buried and hid from view by the rubbish of forms and doctrines heaped upon the Church, through the ages, by the World and the Devil.

It is a terrible Sin to Corrupt the Church. All the Ungodly shall be Destroyed. This is an unceasing note of Scripture. But One of the worst of Sins is, in the Name of Christ, to Foist Lies upon the Church in substitution for Christian Truth. Let those who do it take warning from what happened to the Fallen Angels (4), and to the world of Noah's time (5), and to Sodom and Gomorrah (6).

Chapter 3. Delay of the Lord's Coming

Jesus had said things which might have been construed to imply His Return in that generation (Matthew 16:28; 24:34). The Apostles used expressions which indicated His Near Appearance (Romans 13:12; Hebrews 10:25; James 5:8; Revelation 1:3).

Yet Jesus hinted that His Return might be After a Long Time (Matthew 25:19); and suggested that it would be Wise to prepare for a Delay (Matthew 25:4). Paul expressly stated that it would not be till After the Apostasy (II Thessalonians 2:2–3). Peter, in the present chapter, hints that it might, in human expectation, be in the proportion of thousand years to a day (8). God does not count time as man does. With God a thousand years are as yesterday (Psalm 90:4). He will keep His promise according to His Own chronology. These passages put together seem to indicate that God designed that each successive generation should live in constant expectation of the Lord's Coming.

What bearing should all this, after 2000 years of Delay, have on our thought about the Lord's Coming? Should we abandon hope? NEVER. At least, His Coming is 2000 years nearer than it was. The night is far spent. Day may be nearer than we think. Who knows but what the Lord's Train, at long last, may, even now, be whistling for the Grand Central Station, with Angels ready to shout, All Aboard? Or Air-Planes? maybe.

One of the subjects ridiculed by False Teachers mentioned in chapter 2 is the Lord's Second Coming (3:3, 4). But the Lord Will Come (3:10). And it will be a day of Destruction for the Ungodly (3:7), like the Flood in the days of Noah. Next time it will be by Fire. This is very plainly stated (3:10). Whether by Explosion, or by Collision with some other heavenly body, we do not know. Both of these things, astronomers tell us, do happen. There are such things as "Novae," new stars, which appear suddenly, grow rapidly brighter, then slowly wane, then disappear. The Earth is now one of these, or rather a fragment of one, once thrown off from the sun a burning mass. When God's plans are ready, it may, by explosion from within, or by collision with some other heavenly body, again flare into a seething mass of flame.

But, from it all, God's People will be delivered, and for them there will be a New Heavens and New Earth (3:13, 14).

In closing, Peter mentions Epistles of Paul (15), and classes them as Scripture (16). And, as in his First Epistle Peter spoke of the Word of God as being the Source of Birth (I Peter 1:23), and the Means of Growth (I Peter 2:2), for the Christian, so, in this Epistle foretelling Apostasy in the Church, Peter insists that Knowledge of Christ through His Word will help us make our calling and election Sure (1:2, 4, 10); and that the way for the Church to combat Apostasy, and Keep itself Pure and Free from Worldly Corruption, is to Hold Fast to the Word of God as given by the Prophets and Apostles (1:19; 3:2).

I JOHN

Jesus is the Son of God
Those who Follow Him Must Live Righteously
If We are His We Will Love One Another

This Epistle, like the Epistle to the Hebrews, names neither its Author, nor the Persons to whom it is addressed, though it is very personal, as appears from the frequent use of "I" and "You." From the beginning it has been recognized as a Circular Letter of the Apostle John to the Churches around Ephesus, to emphasize the Main Essentials of the Gospel, and to warn against incipient Heresies which later produced a Corrupt and Paganized Form of Christianity.

John

According to long received tradition, John made Jerusalem his headquarters, caring for Jesus' Mother till her death, and, after the destruction of Jerusalem, made his residence at Ephesus, which by the close of the Apostolic generation had become the Geographic and Numerical Center of Christian Population. Here John lived to great age, and wrote his Gospel, his Three Epistles and Book of Revelation. Among his pupils were Polycarp, Papias, and Ignatius, who became, respectively, bishops of Smyrna, Hierapolis and Antioch.

Background of the Epistle

Christianity had been in the world some sixty or seventy years, and in many parts of the Roman Empire had become an important religion and a powerful influence. Naturally there came to be all sorts of efforts to amalgamate the Gospel with prevailing philosophies and systems of thought.

A form of Gnosticism which was disrupting the Churches in John's day taught that there is in human nature an irreconcilable principle of Dualism: that Spirit and Body are two separate entities: that Sin resided in the Flesh only: that the Spirit could have its raptures, and the Body could do as it pleased: that lofty mental mystical Piety was entirely consistent with voluptuous sensual life. They denied the Incarnation, that God had in Christ actually become Flesh, and maintained that Christ was a Phantom, a Man in Appearance Only.

In Ephesus a man named Cerinthus was leader of this cult. He claimed for himself inner mystic experiences and exalted knowledge of God, but was a Voluptuary. Throughout this Epistle it seems that John must have had these heretics in mind, in insisting that Jesus was the Actual, Material, Authentic Manifestation of God in the Flesh, and that Genuine Knowledge of God must result in Moral Transformation.

Chapter 1:1-4. The Incarnation

God became Flesh, in Human Form. 21 times in this Epistle Jesus is called The Son of God. 12 times God is spoken of as The Father. Thus the Deity of Jesus, the Father and Son relation of God and Jesus, is a special emphasis of the Epistle.

John was Jesus' most intimate earthly Friend. For three years John accompanied Jesus in His journeys over Palestine, ministering to Him day and night, as Jesus wrought His Mighty Miracles. At the Last Supper, John leaned on Jesus' bosom, as Jesus talked of His approaching Crucifixion.

To John, Jesus was no Phantom, or Dream, or mere Vision; but a Real Person, the Embodiment of Life, Eternal Life (2).

And John wrote this Epistle that others might share his feeling of Fellowship, Companionship and Joy, in Christ and in the Father, and with one another (3, 4).

Chapter 1:5-10. God is Light

That is the way John's Gospel starts: the Word of God . . . the Light of Men (John 1:1, 4). Jesus had said, I am the Light of the world (John 8:12).

Light stands for God's Realm of Truth, Righteousness, Purity, Joy, Ineffable Glory. Darkness stands for this World of Error, Evil, Ignorance, Wickedness and Abode of the Lost.

In a more real and literal sense, Light may be an attribute of God beyond the understanding of fleshly eyes. God Clothes Himself with Light (Psalm 104:2). God dwells in Light Unapproachable (I Timothy 6:16). Father of Lights is one of God's names (James 1:17). Jesus' Garments, at His Transfiguration, became glistering White (Mark 9:3). The Angel at Jesus' Resurrection was White as Snow (Matthew 28:3). The two who accompanied Jesus in His Ascension were in White (Acts 1:10). In the vision in Revelation 1:14–16, Jesus' Head and Hair were White as Snow. (See further on Revelation 3:4.)

Chapter 2:1-17. Walking in the Light

Walking with God does not mean that we are Without Sin. We have Sinned in the past, and we still have Sin in our nature. It is by virtue, Not of our Sinlessness, but of Christ's Death for our Sin, that we have our Companionship with God. The moment we are conscious of any Sinful Act, if that moment, in genuine penitence and humility, we confess it, our Companionship with God may remain unbroken. The Saintliest of men invariably have been deeply conscious of their own Sinfulness.

One of the conditions of having our Sins Forgiven is that we Keep His Commandments (1–6). Yet Sin is itself the Failure to Keep His Commandments. This is one of John's paradoxes. (See further on 3:1–12.)

Chapter 2:18-29. Antichrist

The word "Antichrist" is mentioned in 2:18, 22; 4:3; II John 7. It occurs nowhere else in the Bible. It is commonly identified with the Man of Sin (II Thessalonians 2), and the Beast of Revelation 13. But the Bible itself does not make the identification. The language implies that John's readers had been taught to expect an Anti-Christ in connection with the closing days of the Christian Era (18). However, John applies the word, not to One Person, but to the whole group of Anti-Christian Teachers (2:18; 4:3). The New Testament idea seems to be that the Spirit of Antichrist would arise in Christendom, manifesting itself in many ways, both Within the Church and Without, finally culminating in One Person, or an Institution, or Both.

Chapter 3:1-12. Righteousness

Here are some very strong statements about Sin. Whoever Sins Knows Not Christ (6). He that does Sin is of the Devil (8). Whoever is Begotten of God Cannot Sin (9). Yet, John had just said, If we say that we have No Sin we deceive ourselves (1:8). If we say that we have Not Sinned we make God a Liar (1:10).

How explain these paradoxical statements? There is a difference between Sins of Weakness and Wilfull Habitual Sin. It is largely a matter of the Inner Nature. An Eagle may dip its wings in the mud, and yet be an Eagle. A Righteous man may have Sins of Weakness, and yet Be a Righteous Man. John may have had in mind certain heretic teachers, like Jezebel (Revelation 2:20), who, while claiming superior Fellowship with God, were at the same time wallowing in the Filth of Immorality.

Chapter 3:13-24. Love

The dominant note of this Epistle is Love. We should Love One Another (3:11). He that Loveth Not his Brother is Not of God (3:10). We know that we have passed out of Death into Life because we Love the Brethren (3:14). He that Loves Not abides in Death (3:14). Whoever Hates his Brother is a Murderer (3:15). Let us Love One Another (4:7). Everyone that Loves is begotten of God, and Knows God (4:7). Love is of God (4:7). We ought to Love One Another (4:11). God is Love (4:16). He that Abides in Love Abides in God (4:17). If we Love One Another God Abides in us (4:12). Perfect Love Casts Out Fear (4:18). We Love because He first Loved Us (4:19). If a man say, I Love God, and Hates his Brother, He Is a Liar (4:20). He that Loves Not his Brother whom he has seen, How can he Love God Whom he has Not Seen? (4:20).

Chapter 4:1-6. False Prophets

Apparently, Churches were beset by False Teachers, claiming Inspiration of the Holy Spirit for their Doctrines. Generally, says John, their trustworthiness could be tested by their Loyalty to the Deity of Jesus (2).

Chapter 4:7-21. Love

John returns to his favorite theme, Love, the keynote of the Epistle. He is very insistent that being Saved by the Grace of Christ Does Not Release us from the necessity of Obeying Christ's Commandments. And Christ's Chief Commandment is Love. We Know Christ if We Keep His Commandments (2:3). He that says I Know Him, and Keeps Not His Commandments, Is a Liar (2:4). Whatsoever we Ask, we receive, because we Keep His Commandments (3:22). This is His Commandment, that we Love One Another (3:23). He that Keeps His Commandments Abides in Him (3:24). This Commandment we have from God, that he who Loves God Love his Brother also (4:21). This is the Love of God, that we Keep His Commandments (5:3). It is told of John that, when he was old and too feeble to walk, he would be carried into the Church, and, in speaking, would always say, "Little children, Love One Another. It is the Lord's Commandment."

Chapter 5. Assurance of Eternal Life

"Know" is one of the key words of this Epistle. We Know that we Know God (2:3). We Know that we are in Him (2:5). We Know that when He shall Appear we shall be Like Him (3:2). We Know that we have Passed from Death to Life, because we Love the Brethren (3:14). We Know that we are of the Truth (3:19). We Know that God Abideth in us (3:24). We Know that we Abide in God (4:13). These things have I written that you may Know that you have Eternal Life (5:13). We Know that God hears us (5:15). We Know that we are of God (5:19).

Many Christians are discouraged because they do not feel Sure that they are Saved. Sometimes we hear it said that if we do not Know we are Saved, that is a sign that we are Not Saved. We think this is an extreme assertion. It is a mistake to identify Assurance with Salvation. A new-born babe scarcely Knows it has been born, but it has. Assurance comes with Growth. We believe it is possible for a Christian's Faith to get stronger and stronger till, to himself, at least, it reaches the Full Assurance of Knowledge.

Eternal Life (13), begins when a person becomes a Christian, and Never Ends. It is a Life of Divine Quality and Endless Duration. Assurance of it is the object of this Epistle.

The Sin unto Death (16), probably, refers to the unpardonable Sin spoken of by Jesus (Matthew 12:31–32. See note on Hebrews 6:4–6).

II JOHN

Caution against False Teachers

This and III John were Personal Little Notes to Friends whom John expected soon to visit. He wrote other letters (I John 2:14; III John 9), possibly many of them. Personal Letters, such as these, on account of their brevity and private nature, would be less generally read in Christian Assemblies than Church Letters, and consequently be less widely known. These Two Little Epistles, under the guidance of God's Spirit, were rescued from oblivion, and preserved for the Church, possibly, by being attached to a copy of I John in the particular Church or Churches where they had been received.

The Elder, 1

The other Apostles had all passed on, years before. John alone was left, the Primate of all Christendom, the last surviving Companion of Jesus. How appropriate the title.

The Elect Lady, 1

She may have been, literally, a Person, a well-known and prominent Woman, somewhere near Ephesus, in whose Home a Church met. Or, she may have been a Church symbolically called by a Woman's Name. Her Elect Sister (13), another prominent Christian Woman Leader, in the Congregation in which John was resident, or the Congregation itself.

Truth, 1-4

The word "Truth" is used 5 times in the first 4 verses. Love in Truth (1). Know the Truth (1). Truth Dwells in us (2). Grace, Mercy, and Peace, in Truth (3). Walking in Truth (4). Truth is the True Doctrine of Christ (9), that He is the Son of God, and that Following Him means Walking in His Commandments (6), and His Chief Commandment is that We Love One Another (5).

False Teachers, 7-11

These already had been referred to in I John 2:18–29: going from

Church to Church, Teaching, in the Name of Christ, Doctrines that were utterly subversive of the Christian Faith. This Letter seems to have been written to caution the Elect Lady to be on her guard, and refuse Hospitality to such Teachers. The warning is prefaced with an exhortation to Love (5, 6), as if to indicate that the Practice of Christian Love does not mean that we should give encouragement to Enemies of the Truth.

III JOHN

Rejection of John's Helpers

Gaius, 1

There was a Gaius in Corinth, a convert of Paul's (I Corinthians 1:14; Romans 16:23), in whose home, in Paul's day, a Church met. A tradition says that he later became John's scribe. But verse 4 calls Gaius one of John's Children, that is, Converts. But, whoever he was, he was a Greatly Beloved Christian Leader. John Loved him and four times called him Beloved (1, 2, 5, 11).

Prosper in All Things, 2

Here is a prayer, from one who was very close to Christ, that a Christian might have Temporal as well as Spiritual Blessings: an indication that it is not wrong, in the sight of Christ, for one to possess This World's Goods and Benefits. John himself, in early life, had been a man of means. But this same John warns against Loving Things of This World (I John 2:15–17).

Truth, 1

A Favorite Word with John. Used over 20 times in John's Gospel. 9 times in I John. 5 times in II John. And 5 times in III John. Love in Truth (1). Walk in Truth (2, 3). Help the Truth (8). Witness of the Truth (12).

John's Helpers, 5-8

Paul, some forty years earlier, had established Churches in and around Ephesus, with no Seminaries to supply Pastors. He had to develop his Pastors out of his converts. Later, John, assuming the pastoral care of these Churches, it seems, gathered round himself, and trained great numbers of teachers and preachers to aid him, and sent them out among the Churches.

Diotrephes, 9

One of the domineering False Teachers, who would have nothing to do with John. It seems that he and Gaius were pastors of different congregations in the same city. Apparently, some of John's evangelists, on one of their recent tours, had been refused admission to the congregation over which Diotrephes presided, but Gaius had taken them in. On returning to Ephesus, they told the story of it in John's home church. John was now sending another delegation to the same city, with this little Epistle addressed to Gaius. Demetrius (12), it is thought, may have been the bearer of the Epistle.

JUDE

Imminent Apostasy
The Faith Once For All Delivered to the Saints

Jude

In the New Testament Church there were two Judes: Judas, one of the Twelve Apostles (Luke 6:16, see page 466), and Judas, the brother of Jesus (Matthew 13:55). The latter is commonly regarded as the writer of this Epistle.

Eusebius relates that Domitian, in his Persecution of Christians, A.D. 96, looking up the heirs of the Kingdom of David, ordered the arrest of the Grandsons of Jude the Brother of Jesus. They told the Emperor that they were farmers, and lived by the toil of their hands, and that Christ's Kingdom was Not a Kingdom of This World, but would be manifested when He Comes in Glory at the End of the World to Judge the Living and Dead.

Place and Date

The similarity of the situation to that mentioned in II Peter suggests the possibility that this Epistle may have been addressed to the same Churches, which, it seems from II Peter 3:1, were the same as those to whom I Peter was addressed, which were in Asia Minor (I Peter 1:1). Probably about A.D. 67.

Occasion of Writing

Evidently Jude had been planning to write a more general statement about the Gospel to this group of Churches, when news of the sudden appearance of a Devastating Heresy prompted him to dispatch this stern warning (3, 4).

The False Teachers, 4-19

Jude minces no words as to their nature. The frightful epithets which he uses refer to certain Leaders Within the Church. Ungodly Men (4). Turn the Grace of God into Lasciviousness (4). Deny Christ (4). Like Sodom, given to Fornication (7). In their Dreamings Defile the Flesh (8). As Brute Beasts Corrupt Themselves (10). Spots in your Lovefeasts (12). Shepherds that Feed Themselves (12). Clouds without Water (12). Trees Without Fruit (12). Raging

Waves of the Sea Foaming out their own Shame (13). Wandering Stars for whom the Blackness of Darkness has been Reserved Forever (13). Murmurers (16). Complainers (16). Speaking Great Swelling Words (16). Mockers Walking after their Own Ungodly Lusts (18). Sensual (19). Not Having the Spirit (19). Show Respect of Persons for the sake of their Own Advantage (16). And Make Separations (19).

These false teachers had already crept in (4), yet were spoken of as appearing in "the last time." While primarily referring to some particular class of men that belonged to Jude's day, it may possibly be a general characterization of the whole body of false teachers who, through the centuries, would, from within, corrupt the Church, and thus thwart the redemptive work of Christ. Those who are acquainted with Church History know well how the Church has suffered from such men.

The Fallen Angels, 6

Here and in II Peter 2:4 are the only Scripture references to the Fall of the Angels (Revelation 12:9 seems to refer to their later defeat). Some think this is an allusion to Genesis 6:1–5, where the "sons of God" intermarried with the "daughters of men." More probably it refers to an earlier event when Satan led certain of the angels in rebellion against God.

Michael's Contention with the Devil, 9

Michael is mentioned in Daniel 10:13, 21 as a "chief prince," and in Revelation 12:7 as leader of angels, but only in this passage is he called "the archangel." Moses' burial is told in Deuteronomy 34:5–7. But Michael's dispute with Satan about Moses' body is not there mentioned. Origen says that Jude's statement is a reference to a passage in the apocryphal book, "The Assumption of Moses" which was written about the time of the birth of Christ, only a part of which book is now extant, and which extant part has no such passage. Jude may have had knowledge of the incident from other sources. Josephus says God hid Moses' body lest it be made an idol. Possibly Satan wanted it to tempt Israel into idolatry. Jude's use of the incident seems to sanction its historicity. It served as an example against the sin of "railing": even the Archangel, highest of creatures, did not rail at the Devil, the most degraded of creatures.

The Prophecy of Enoch, 14, 15

This is the only Scripture allusion to the prophecy of Enoch. The brief story of his life is told in Genesis 5:18–24, but there is no mention of any of his words. Jude's quotation is from the apocryphal Book of Enoch, which was written about 100 B.C. He evidently regards it as a genuine word of Enoch. Thus while Adam, founder of the race, was yet alive, Enoch (contemporary with Adam for 300 years) prophesied of the eventual Coming of the Lord, with his angels, to execute judgment upon the disobedient race. Jude's Sanction of one passage in the book does not Sanction the whole book.

REVELATION

Grand Finale of the Bible Story
A Paean of Victory
Ultimate Triumph of Christ
The New Heavens and New Earth

The Book of Revelation is based on, or is a fuller explanation of, Christ's Discourse on Things to Come (Matthew 24, Mark 13, and Luke 21). It abounds in expressions used by Jesus. Some of its imagery seems to be drawn from Ezekiel and Daniel.

Author

God Himself. That is the Book's first statement. God Himself dictated it, through Christ, by an Angel, to John, who wrote it down, and sent the completed book to the Seven Churches (1:1, 4). Certain modern rationalistic critics see in the book no inspired prophecy at all, but only the "unbridled play of religious phantasy, clothing itself in unreal visual form." Such an opinion we abhor.

We believe absolutely that the book is Exactly What It Itself Says It Is: that it Bears the Stamp of its Author: that some of its passages are among the Most Superb and Most Precious in all the Bible: that its Climactic Grandeur makes it a fitting close to the Bible Story: and that its Glorious Visions of the Completed Work of Christ make it a veritable roadway of God into the Human Soul.

Human Author

By well-established tradition, from the days of the Apostolic Fathers, and in the judgment of the great body of Christian Believers, the Apostle John, the "Beloved Disciple," most intimate Earthly Friend of Jesus, writer of the Gospel of John, was the writer of this book (1:1, 4, 9; 22:8; John 21:20, 24). The suggestion, evidently born of a desire to discredit the book, that it was some other John, is without foundation.

Date

John had been banished to the Isle of Patmos (1:9). This, according to Apostolic tradition, was in the Persecution of Domitian, about

A.D. 95. The next year, A.D. 96, John was released, and permitted to return to Ephesus. The use of the past tense, "was," in Patmos, seems to indicate that, while he saw the Visions in Patmos, it was after his release, and return to Ephesus, that he wrote the book, about A.D. 96.

Books about Revelation

A thing that strikes one who browses around in the vast literature that has grown up about the book of Revelation is the UTTER DOGMATISM with which so many put forth their opinions, not as opinions, but in categorical statements, as to the meaning of even the most mysterious passages, as if they know all about it, and their say so settles the matter. We think a spirit of reverent humility, and openness of mind, would be more becoming in those seeking to interpret a book like this.

Interpretations

There are many interpretations of the book of Revelation. And every one has its difficulties. Whatever interpretation is accepted, some details require straining to fit.

Roughly speaking, there are four kinds of interpretation, each varying greatly within itself: commonly spoken of as "Preterist," "Historical," "Futurist" and "Spiritualist."

Preterist Interpretation regards the book as referring to its own day: Christianity's Struggle with the Roman Empire.

Historical Interpretation is that the book was designed to Forecast a General View of the Whole Period of Church History, from John's time on to the End of the World: a sort of Panorama, a series of Pictures, delineating the Successive Steps and Outstanding Features of the Church's Struggle to Final Victory: "A Vision of the Ages"; "Pictures of the Great Epochs and Crises of the Church."

Futurist Interpretation centers the book largely around the time of the Lord's Coming and End of the World.

Spiritualist Interpretation separates the imagery of the book entirely from any reference to Historical Events—those of John's day, or those at the time of the End, or those intervening—and deems it to be a Pictorial Representation, in highly figurative language, of the Great Principles of Divine Government applicable to all times.

To us, it seems, taking the language in its most apparent meaning, that the simplest, most obvious, most natural, most evident, and most reasonable interpretation is a sort of combination of the Historical and Futurist interpretations: some of the Visions picturing Epochal Events and Features of Church History; some Forecasting the Momentous Upheavals of the Last Days; and some, possibly, referring to Both, the Earlier, perhaps, being Typical and Predictive of the Later.

There is such an Amazing Parallel between some of the Imagery of the book and the Course of Church History that it seems that one of the objects of the book must have been to Foretell it.

And there is much in the book that so evidently refers to the Time of the End that it must be taken into account whatever our interpretation of the book.

The Book is in Two Parts

Chapters 1 to 3: "Things which Are" (1): that is, Things which Were in John's day: Seven Letters to Seven Churches, dealing with the situation as it then was. This, in a sense, is Introductory to the main body of the book, which follows:

Chapters 4 to 22: "Things which Shall Be Hereafter" (1:19; 4:1); covering the time from Then on to the End.

Chapter 1:1-3. A "Revelation" of Things to Come

That is what the book calls itself: a Revealing, Unveiling, Explaining, Making Known, of Things to Come (1:1, 19; 4:1). Thus, in its first word, the book is avowedly Predictive. That is what it was written for: to Unfold the Future: to Chart the Course and Destiny of the Church.

It is a Very Practical Book

Even though it is a book of Mystery, with many things we do not understand, it also has Many Things we Do Understand.

Imbedded in its Mysterious Imagery are some of the most Salutary Warnings and most Precious Promises of all Scripture.

Very likely John himself did not understand some of the things he saw and wrote. No doubt, God had meaning in some of the Visions that were to be revealed only with the unfolding story of the passing ages. Nevertheless John's soul thrilled with exultation, as his mind dwelt on what he saw.

Alternating simplest truth with mystical symbolism, it is a book of undiluted Optimism for God's people, assuring us again and again that we are under God's protection, with, come what may, a Life of Everlasting Blessedness ahead.

And, alternating scenes between earth and heaven, it is also a book of the "Wrath of God," ever and anon contrasting the Joys of the Redeemed with the Agonies of the Lost. And O how we need to be reminded of that in this careless and godless generation!

Attitude toward the Book

Some writers, and preachers, and others, greatly overdo Revelation, or rather their pet ideas of it. And, on that account, in part, at least, others stay away from it altogether. Both attitudes are wrong. The book should neither be neglected, nor over exalted above other Bible books. But surely it is entitled to, and will greatly reward, a reasonable share of a Christian's study and devotion.

Background of the Book

These visions were given, and the book written, in the lurid light of burning martyrs. The Church was 66 years old. It had made enormous growth. It had suffered, and was suffering, terrific Persecutions.

The First Imperial Persecution of Christians, 30 years before this book was written, was that of Nero, A.D. 64–67. In that Persecution multitudes of Christians were crucified, or thrown to wild beasts, or wrapped in combustible garments and burned to death while Nero laughed at the pitiful shrieks of burning men and women. In Nero's Persecution Paul and Peter suffered martyrdom.

The Second Imperial Persecution was instituted by Emperor Domitian (A.D. 95). It was short, but extremely severe. Over 40,000 Christians were tortured and slain. This was the Persecution in which John was banished to the Isle of Patmos (1:9).

The Third Imperial Persecution, that of Trajan, was soon to begin (A.D. 98). John had lived through the first two, and was now about to enter the third, of Rome's Imperial efforts to blot out the Christian Faith. Those were Dark Days for the Church. And still darker days were coming (see pages 761, 762).

And not only Persecution from Without, but the Church itself, from Within, was beginning to show signs of Corruption and Apostasy.

God gave these visions, evidently, to help steady the Church for the awful days ahead.

"Blessed is He that Reads", 1:3

And they that Hear, and Keep, the Words of this Book. Thus the book opens. And thus it closes (22:7). God Himself said it.

This includes both reading it for ourselves, and listening to its reading in Church. In those days books had to be written by hand, and were scarce and expensive; and the public, for their knowledge of Scripture, had to depend, in large measure, on the Reading and Teaching in Church. The invention of Printing, in modern times, and the wide possession of Printed Bibles among the people, do not void the need and value of Regular Exposition of God's Word in Church Services.

God's Word was intended to have the Central Place in Church

Services, Then, and Now and Always. It is the one thing designed of God to hold the Church True to its Mission.

If only Church Leaders, from the beginning, had given heed to this initial warning, the Church might have been saved from the Appalling Corruption it has suffered through the ages. And we never cease to wonder that present day Church Leadership still, to quite an extent, gives God's Word only nominal recognition in Church Services, of which God's Word ought to be the Very Heart.

Chapter 1:4-8. Greeting to the Seven Churches

Ephesus, Smyrna, Pergamum, Thyatira, Sardis, Philadelphia, Laodicea.

These Seven Cities, connected by a great triangular highway, are named in their geographical order, beginning with Ephesus, thence north about 100 miles to Pergamum, and thence southeast to Laodicea, which was about 100 miles east of Ephesus.

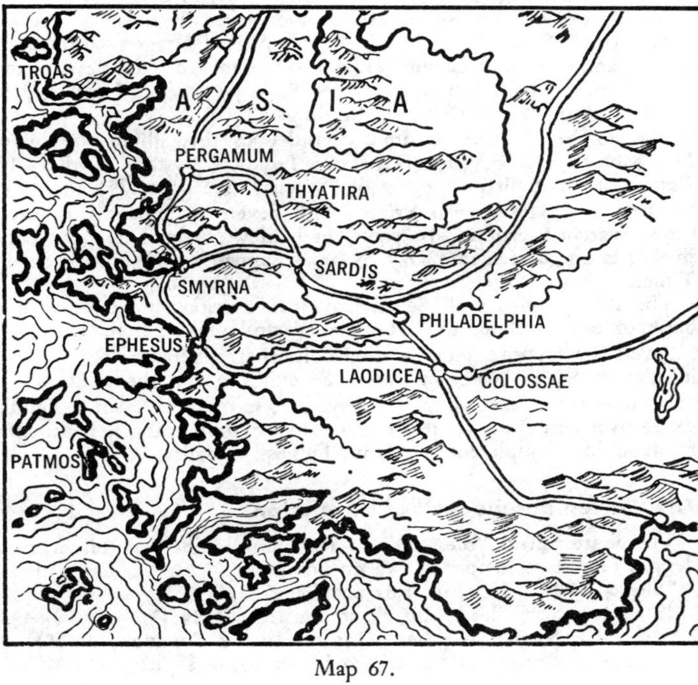

Map 67.

"Asia" (1:4), was a Roman Province in the west part of what we know as Asia Minor, now a part of Turkey. Ephesus was its chief city. Pergamum was its Political Capital.

There were many churches in "Asia." These, called "The Seven Churches," must have been main centers in their respective districts, key cities in John's pastoral care of the region.

Only Ephesus figures elsewhere in New Testament history. Thyatira is mentioned as the home of Lydia (Acts 16:14). Laodicea had had a letter from Paul (Colossians 4:13–16), now lost. The other four churches, not elsewhere mentioned in New Testament, were probably offshoots from Paul's work in Ephesus.

The Number "Seven"

The book is built around a system of "Sevens." Seven Letters to Seven Churches (chapters 1–3). Seven Seals and Seven Trumpets (chapters 4–11). Seven Vials (chapters 15, 16). Seven Candlesticks (1:12, 20). Seven Stars (1:16, 20). Seven Angels (1:20). Seven Spirits (1:4). A Lamb with Seven Horns and Seven Eyes (5:6). Seven Lamps (4:5). Seven Thunders (10:3, 4). A Red Dragon with Seven Heads and Seven Crowns (12:1). A Leopard-like Beast with Seven Heads (13:1). A Scarlet-colored Beast with Seven Heads (17:3, 7). Seven Mountains (17:9). Seven Kings (17:10).

The number "Seven" is quite conspicuous throughout the Bible. The Sabbath was Seventh Day. The Levitical System of the Old Testament was built on a cycle of "Sevens" (see page 139).

Jericho fell after Seven Priests, with Seven Trumpets, for Seven Days, marched around its walls, and blew their Trumpets Seven Times on the Seventh Day. Naaman dipped in the Jordan Seven Times.

The Bible begins with Seven Days of Creation, and ends with a book of Sevens about the Ultimate Destiny of Creation.

Seven is a favorite letter in God's alphabet. There are Seven Days in a week. Seven Notes in Music. Seven Colors in the rainbow.

Used as often as it is, in the way it is, it must have some significance over and above its numerical value. Symbolically, it is thought to stand for Completeness, a Unit, Fulness, Totality.

The "Seven Beatitudes" of Revelation

There are Seven "Blessed's" in the book. Whether this was of design, or just so happened, we do not know.

"Blessed is he that reads this prophecy" (1:3).
"Blessed are the dead who die in the Lord" (14:13).
"Blessed is he that watches" (for the Lord's Coming) (16:15).
"Blessed are those bidden to Lamb's marriage supper" (19:9).

"Blessed is he that has part in the first resurrection" (20:6).
"Blessed is he that keeps the words of this book" (22:7).
"Blessed are they that wash their robes" (22:14).

Significance of Other Numbers

Certain other numbers are used in such a way that they are thought to be in themselves a sort of language, with meanings beyond their numerical value. Here are some of them:

3: the numerical signature of God.
4: the numerical signature of Nature, Creation.
7: 3 plus 4: the signature of Totality.
12: 3 times 4: signature of God's People. (See page 738.)
10: signature of Wordly Power. (See page 730.)

"Him Who Is, and Who Was, and Who Is To Come", 1:4

Eternity of God's Nature: one of the emphases of the book.

"Him that Liveth Forever and Ever" (4:10).

"Lord God, Who Was, and Who Is, and Who Is To Come" (4:8).

"I am the Alpha and the Omega, the First and the Last, the Beginning and the End" (21:6; 22:13).

"I am the Alpha and the Omega, saith the Lord God, Who Is, and Who Was, and Who Is To Come, the Almighty" (1:8).

"I am the First and the Last, the Living One: I was dead, and, behold, I am Alive Forevermore; and I have the keys of Death and Hades" (1:17, 18).

In a world where empires rise and fall, where all things die and pass away, we are reminded that God is Changeless, Timeless and Eternal, and promised by Him that His Nature may be imparted to us, and that we, like Him, and by His Grace, unhurt by Death, may Live On and On. Alive Forevermore! Immortal Youth! What a meaning it gives to Life! And what a comfort to saints then facing Martyrdom!

"Christ the Ruler of Kings", 1:5

This affirms His unconditional supremacy over the world. It does not always seem that it is so. Kings have defied and continue to defy, Christ, with blatant, brazen boldness. Even today Monsters of Hell walk the earth as rulers of men. But their Doom is certain.

The Kingdom which Satan once offered, and Christ refused, Christ will yet have, in His Own, not Satan's, way. The redeemed of all ages, souls in Paradise, and saints now living, are longing for that Glad Day. As sure as the morning, It Will Come. Christ Is On The Throne, even when things look darkest. Let us never forget this.

"Washed from our Sins in His Blood", 1:5

Saved by the Blood of Christ: another emphasis of this book.
"Thou hast redeemed us to God by Thy Blood" (5:9).
"They overcame him (Satan) by the Blood of the Lamb" (12:11).
"These are they who . . . have Washed their Robes, and made them white in the Blood of the Lamb" (7:14).
"Blessed are they that Wash their Robes, that they may have the right to the Tree of Life" (22:14).

There are fastidious intellectuals who rebel at the thought of it. But it is an unbroken Biblical teaching, emphasized again and again in the New Testament. And how it touches our hearts! And how we Love and Adore Him for it, and will, through endless aeons of Eternity!

"To Him be Glory and Dominion Forever", 1:6

The book is filled with Doxologies of Praise to God.
"Worthy art Thou to receive Glory and Honor and Power" (4:11).
"Worthy is the Lamb . . . to receive Power . . . and Honor and Glory and Blessing" (5:12).
"Blessing and Honor and Glory and Power be to Him that sitteth on the Throne, and to the Lamb Forever" (5:13; 7:10, 12).
"Great and Marvellous are Thy works . . . Just and True are Thy Ways, Thou King of the Ages" (15:2, 3).
"Hallelujah! Salvation and Glory and Honor and Power to the Lord our God . . . Hallelujah! . . . Hallelujah! . . . Hallelujah! . . . The Lord God Omnipotent Reigns. Let us . . . Rejoice, and give Honor to Him" (19:1–7).

The Four Living Creatures, the Four and Twenty Elders, a Hundred Million Angels, and vast Multitudes of Redeemed from All Nations, in voices like the ocean's roar, make Heaven Resound with Praise to God. Why not have it in our Churches? Why not have the People SING?

"He Cometh with the Clouds", 1:7

The Lord's Coming: another Key-note of the book.
"Every eye shall see Him, and they that pierced Him" (1:7).
"Hold fast till I Come" (2:25).
"I will Come as a thief" (3:3).
"I Come quickly: hold fast that which you have" (3:11).
"Behold, I Come as a thief: blessed is he that Watcheth" (16:15).
"Behold, I Come quickly" (22:7).
"Behold, I Come quickly; and My reward is with Me" (22:12).
"Surely I Come quickly" (22:20).

"Even so, Come, Lord Jesus" (22:20).

The Lord's Coming is one of the first words in the book. And the last word is John's prayer that it may be "quickly."

Christ is Coming Again. The Grand Consummation of Human History. It will be On the Clouds, in Power and Glory. Visible to All the World. A day of Distress and Terror for those who have Rejected Him. A day of Unspeakable Joy for those who are His.

Jesus Himself had said these same things over and over (Matthew 13:42, 50; 24:30, 51; 25:30; 26:64; Luke 21:25–28). And, in Acts 1:9, 11, Jesus Ascended in a Cloud, and "Will Come Again in Like Manner."

Nearly two thousand years have passed, and He has Not Come yet. But against the background of Eternity a thousand years is as a day. One day He will Come with catastrophic Suddenness. Jesus first Came at the Appointed Time. He Will Come Again on Schedule Time.

"The Time is at hand" (1:3). So the book opens. And so it closes (22:10). It may be Nearer than we think.

Chapter 1:9-20. Christ in the Midst of the Churches

"Patmos" (1:9), the island to which John was banished in the persecution of Domitian, and in which these visions were given, is in the Aegean Sea, about 60 miles southwest of Ephesus, about 150 miles east of Athens. It is 10 miles long, 6 miles wide; treeless and rocky.

"The Lord's Day" (1:10), evidently was the "First Day of the Week" (Acts 20:7; I Corinthians 16:2): the Day on which Christians met for worship, in commemoration of the Lord's Resurrection. As the Seventh Day had been kept in commemoration of Creation, the First Day was set aside to keep forever fresh in men's minds the Story of Jesus' Resurrection from the Dead: the Most Momentous Day of All History: the One Event that Gives Meaning to human life.

"In the Spirit" (1:10; 4:2; 17:3; 21:10), seems to mean that his faculties were wholly taken over by the Spirit of God.

"Write", 1:11

Commands the Voice from Heaven

"What thou seest, Write in a book" (1:11).

"Write the things which thou hast seen" (1:19).

"To Ephesus . . . Write." "To Smyrna . . . Write." "To Pergamum . . . Write." "To Thyatira . . . Write." "To Sardis . . . Write." "To Philadelphia . . . Write." "To Laodicea . . . Write." (2:1, 8, 12, 18; 3:1, 7, 14).

"Write, Blessed are the dead who die in the Lord" (14:15).

"Write, Blessed are those bidden to the Marriage Supper" (19:9).

Thus, it is emphasized, again and again, in the strongest possible manner, that God Himself Commanded that the Book be Written, and that He Himself Told John Exactly What to Write.

The Vision of Christ, 1:13-18

Holding the Angels of the Churches in His Hand.
His Hair as White as Snow. His Eyes like a flame of Fire.
His Countenance like the Sun. His Feet like Burnished Brass.
His Voice as the Voice of Many Waters.
Out of His Mouth proceeding a Sharp Two-Edged Sword.

This is the aspect in which the Gentle Saviour of the Gospels now presents Himself to His Church, and with His Church, Girded for Battle, a Warrior, a Conqueror, with desperate and powerful Enemies to encounter. It is a bid to His Church for Confidence in His Leadership. Also, it is a stern and earnest Warning to His Church, with its growing Signs of Corruption and Apostasy, that He Will Not Tolerate Half-Heartedness or Disloyalty.

Angels, 1:20

Angels play a large part in directing the panorama and scenery of the visions, and in the writing of the book.

An Angel dictated the book to John (1:2; 22:16).
Each of the Seven Churches had an Angel (1:20; 2:1, etc.).
An Angel was interested in the Sealed Book (5:2).
100,000,000 Angels sang praise to the Lamb (5:11).
Four Angels were given power to hurt the earth (7:1–4).
An Angel sealed the Elect (7:1–4).
The Angels fell down on their faces before God (7:11).
An Angel was used in answering prayers of the saints (8:3–5).
Seven Angels sounded the Seven Trumpets (8:6, 7, etc.).
An Angel of the abyss was king of the locust army (9:11).
Four Angels loosed 200,000,000 Euphratean Horsemen (9:15, 16).
An Angel had the Open Book, announcing the End (10:1, 2, 6).
Michael and his Angels warred with Dragon and his Angels (12:7).
A flying Angel proclaimed the Gospel to the nations (14:6).
Another flying Angel proclaimed the Fall of Babylon (14:8).
An Angel pronounced doom of the Beast's followers (14:9, 10).
An Angel announced the Harvest of the Earth (14:15).
An Angel announced the Vintage of the Earth (14:18, 19).
Seven Angels had the Seven Last Plagues (15:1).
An Angel announced Judgment on Babylon (17:1, 5).
An Angel again announced the Fall of Babylon (18:2).
An Angel had part in dealing Babylon its Death-Blow (18:21).
An Angel presided over the Destruction of the Beast (19:17).
An Angel bound Satan (20:12).

An Angel showed John the New Jerusalem (21:9).
12 Angels guarded the 12 gates of the New Jerusalem (21:19)
An Angel forbade John to worship him (22:9).

Thus, here, in the book of Revelation, are twenty-seven different references to the activities of Angels.

The word "Angel," literally, means "Messenger." As used in the Bible, it applies, mostly, to Supernatural Personalities of the Unseen World, employed as messengers in the service of God or Satan.

Angels figured largely in the life of Jesus. Throughout the Bible a good deal is said about Angels (see pages 426, 427).

The "Angels" of the Churches (2:1, etc.), are thought, by some, to have been messengers sent by the Churches to visit John in Patmos; or, the Pastors of the Churches; or, the Guardian Angels of the Churches; or, Heavenly Representatives of the Churches.

John, in the Seven Letters, was portraying under divine direction, Heavenly Appraisals of Earthly Churches.

Chapters 2,3. Letters to the Seven Churches

Each Letter consisted of the whole book, with a brief special message to Each Church. We presume that seven copies of the book were made, and one sent to each city. Each Church could thus read the Lord's estimate, not only of itself, but also of the other Churches. Even today Churches may appraise themselves by these Letters.

Fig. 70. Ephesus. Marble Street showing ruins of theater.
© *Matson Photo.*

Character of the Churches

Two were very good: Smyrna and Philadelphia.
Two were very bad: Sardis and Laodicea.
Three were part good, and part bad: Ephesus, Pergamum, Thyatira.
The two Good churches, Smyrna and Philadelphia, were composed of the humbler classes of people, and were facing persecution.
The two Bad churches, Sardis and Laodicea, seem to have included the ruling classes, nominally Christian, but pagan in life.
Ephesus was orthodox in teaching, but losing their first love.
Pergamum was heretic, but faithful to the Name of Christ.
Thyatira was heretic, tolerating Jezebel, but growing in zeal.

The Heresy

It related to "fornication" and the "eating of things sacrificed to idols." Sexual vice was actually a part of heathen worship, and recognized as a proper thing in heathen festivals. Priestesses of Diana and kindred deities were public prostitutes.

The thing had been a troublesome question for Gentile churches from the start. The circular Letter from the Apostles at Jerusalem, nearly 50 years earlier (Acts 15), to Gentile churches, while tolerant in nature, yet definitely insisted that Christians must keep themselves from the licentious practices connected with idol worship.

Meantime great multitudes of heathen had become Christians, and had carried some of their old ideas into their new religion.

The voluptuous allurements of Diana worship had a tremendous appeal to human nature; and it was no easy thing for those who had been used to it to give it up. Naturally there were all sorts of attempts to harmonize these heathen practices with the Christian religion. Many professedly Christian teachers, claiming inspiration from God, were advocating the right to free participation in heathen immoralities.

In Ephesus, the Christian pastors, as a body, excluded such teachers. But in Pergamum and Thyatira, while we are not to think that the main body of pastors held such teachings, yet they tolerated within their ranks those who did.

General Note on the Churches (EMB)

Ephesus was an old Ionian foundation at the mouth of the Cayster. Greek colonies which surround the Mediterranean and Black Sea were primarily trading-posts. Migrant communities of Greeks did not seek to dominate the hinterlands, but to secure an *emporion* or "way in," a bridgehead for commerce, and enough surrounding coast and territory to support the community. Great cities grew from such foundations from Marseilles to Alexandria, some of them royal capitals. And in all cases colonies became centers or outposts of Hellenism, distinctive, and civilizing.

Ephesus displaced Miletus as a trading port, but when its harbor, like that of Miletus, in turn silted up, Smyrna replaced both as the outlet and *emporion* of the Maeander valley trade-route. In the heyday of Asia Minor 230 separate communities, each proud of its individuality and wealth, issued their own coinage and managed their own affairs. The dominance of Persian despotism, wide deforestation, and the ravage of war in a natural bridge and highway between the continents slowly sapped this prosperity, but in early Roman times as in the days of its Ionian independence, Ephesus was a proud, rich, busy port, the rival of Alexandria and Syrian Antioch.

Built near the shrine of an old Anatolian fertility goddess, Ephesus became the seat of an oriental cult. The Anatolian deity had been taken over by the Greeks under the name of Artemis, the Diana of the Romans. Grotesquely represented with turreted head and many breasts, the goddess and her cult found expression in the famous temple, served like that of Aphrodite at Corinth, by a host of priestess courtesans.

Round the cult clustered much trade. Ephesus became a place of pilgrimage for tourist-worshipers, all eager to carry away talisman and souvenir, hence the prosperous guild of the silversmiths whose livelihood was the manufacture of silver shrines and images of the meteoric stone which was said to be Diana's image "fallen from heaven." Ephesus leaned more and more on the trade which followed the cult as commerce declined in her silting harbor. Twenty miles of reedy marshland now separate the old harbor works from the sea and even in Paul's day the process was under way. Tacitus tells us that an attempt was made to improve the seaway in A.D. 65, but the task proved too great. Ephesus in the first century was a dying city, given to parasite pursuits, living, like Athens, on a reputation, a curious meeting place of old and new religions, of East and West. Acts 19 gives a peculiarly vivid picture of her unnatural life. The "lampstand" has gone from its place, for Ephesus' decline was mortal sickness, and it is possible to detect in the letter to Ephesus in the Apocalypse a touch of the lassitude which was abroad in the effete and declining community. The temple and part of the city have been extensively excavated.

Smyrna was a port on the west coast of Asia Minor at the head of the gulf into which the Hermus debouches, a well protected harbor, and the natural terminal of a great inland trade-route up the Hermus valley. Smyrna's early history was checkered. It was destroyed by the Lydians in 627 B.C., and for three centuries was little more than a village. It was refounded in the middle of the fourth century before Christ, after Alexander's capture of Sardis, and rapidly became the chief city of Asia. Smyrna was shrewd enough to mark the rising star of Rome. A common danger, the aggression of Antiochus the Great of Syria, had united the two states at the end of the third century before Christ, and the bond formed in the face of the eastern peril remained unbroken. Smyrna was, indeed, the handiest of bridgeheads, a useful Roman counterpoise in Aegean waters to the naval power of Rhodes. It was to this ancient alliance, which Smyrna referred in A.D. 26, when the city petitioned Tiberius to allow the community to build a temple to his deity (Tac. *Ann.* 4.56). The permission was granted, and Smyrna built the second Asian temple to the Emperor. The city had worshiped Rome as a spiritual power since 195 B.C.; hence Smyrna's historical pride in her Caesar-cult. Smyrna was famous for science, medicine, and the majesty of its buildings. Apollonius of Tyana refers to her "crown of porticoes," a circle of beautiful public buildings which ringed the summit of Mount Pagos like a diadem; hence John's reference (Revelation 2:10). Polycarp, Smyrna's martyred bishop of A.D. 155, had been a disciple of John.

Pergamum, Pergamos, was a city of Mysia in the Caicus valley, 15 miles inland; in KJV, Pergamos. Royally situated in a commanding position, Pergamum was the capital until the last of the Pergamenian kings bequeathed his realm to Rome in 133 B.C. Pergamum became the chief town of the new province of Asia, and the site of the first temple of the Caesar-cult, erected to Rome and Augustus in 29 B.C. A second shrine was later dedicated to Trajan, and the multiplication of such honor marks the prestige of Pergamum in pagan Asia. The worship of Asklepios and Zeus were also endemic. The symbol of the former was a serpent, and Pausanias describes his cult image "with a staff in one hand and the other on the head of a serpent." Pergamenian coins illustrate the importance which the community attached to this cult. Caracalla is shown on one coin, saluting a serpent twined round a bending sapling. On the crag above Pergamum was a throne-like altar to Zeus now in the Berlin Museum (Revelation 2:13?). It commemorated a defeat of a Gallic inroad, and was decorated with a representation of the conflict of the gods and the giants, the latter shown as monsters with snake-like tails. Zeus, to deepen Christian horror at Pergamum's obsession with the serpent-image, was called in this connection, "Zeus the Saviour." It is natural that "Nicolaitanism" should flourish in a place where politics and paganism were so closely allied, and where pressure on Christians to compromise must have been heavy. Pergamum was an ancient seat of culture and possessed a library which rivaled Alexandria's. Parchment (*charta Pergamena*) was invented at Pergamum to free the library from Egypt's jealous ban on the export of papyrus.

Fig. 71. Two Views of Smyrna, on the coast of Asia Minor. Above: standing pillars of the ancient Forum; below, a view over the city.
Dr. S. H. Horn, Andrews University, Berrien Springs, Mich.

Thyatira was a city in the province of Asia, on the boundary of Lydia and Mysia. Thyatira has no illustrious history, and is scarcely mentioned by ancient writers. Coinage suggests that, lying as it did on a great highway linking two river valleys, Thyatira was a garrison town over long centuries. Its ancient Anatolian deity was a warlike figure armed with a battle-axe and mounted on a charger. An odd coin or two shows a female deity wearing a battlemented crown. The city was a center of commerce, and the records preserve references to more trade-guilds than those listed for any other Asian city. Lydia, whom Paul met in Philippi, was a Thyatiran seller of "turkey red," the product of the madder-root (Acts 16:14). It is curious to find another woman, nicknamed after the princess who sealed Ahab's trading partnership with the Phoenicians, leading a party of compromise in the Thyatiran church (Revelation 2:20, 21). Necessity for guild membership in a trading community must have strengthened temptation to compromise. Thyatira played no significant part in the later history of the Church.

Sardis was the chief city of Lydia, under a fortified spur of Mount Tmolus in the Hermus valley, near the junction of the roads from central Asia Minor, Ephesus, Smyrna, and Pergamum, capital of Lydia under Croesus, and seat of the governor after the Persian conquest. Sardis was famous for arts and crafts, and was the first center to mint gold and silver coinage. So wealthy were the Lydian kings, that Croesus became a legend for riches, and it was said that the sands of the Pactolus were golden. Croesus also became a legend for pride and presumptuous arrogance, when his attack on Persia led to the fall of Sardis and the eclipse of his kingdom. The capture of the great citadel by surprise attack by Cyrus and his Persians in 549 B.C., and three centuries later by the Romans, may have provided the imagery for John's warning in Revelation 3:3. The great earthquake of A.D. 17 ruined Sardis physically and financially. The Romans contributed 10,000,000 sesterces in relief, an indication of the damage done, but the city never recovered.

Philadelphia was a Lydian city founded by Attalus II Philadelphus (159–138 B.C.). The king was so named from his devotion to his brother Eumenes, and the city perpetuated his title. Philadelphia was an outpost of Hellenism in native Anatolia. It lies under Mount Tmolus, in a wide vale which opens into the Hermus Valley, and along which the post-road ran. It is on a broad, low, easily defended hill, which explains Philadelphia's long stand against the Turks. The district is disastrously seismic, and the great earthquake of A.D. 17 ruined it completely. Placed right above the fault, Philadelphia was tormented by 20 years of recurrent quakes after the disaster of 17. Hence, says Ramsay, is derived the imagery of Revelation 3:12 ("a pillar," "go no more out," "a new name"). The "new name" is certainly a reference to the proposal to rename the city *Neocaesarea* in gratitude for Tiberius' generous earthquake relief. The district was vine-growing, and a center, in consequence, of Dionysiac worship. A Christian witness, in spite of Moslem invasion and pressure, was maintained in Philadelphia through medieval and into modern times.

Laodicea was a wealthy city in Asia Minor founded by Antiochus II (261–246 B.C.), and head of the "circuit" of "the Seven Churches of Asia." The city lay on one of the great Asian trade routes, and this ensured its great commercial prosperity. Laodicea was a leading banking center. In 51 B.C. Cicero, en route for his Cilician province, cashed drafts there. It was no doubt the rich banking firms which, in A.D. 60, financed the reconstruction of the city after the great earthquake which prostrated it. Laodicea refused the Senate's earthquake relief. She was "rich and increased with goods" and had "need of nothing" (Revelation 3:17). The Lycus valley produced a glossy black wool, the source of black cloaks and carpets, for which the city was famous. Laodicea was also the home of a medical school, and the manufacture of collyrium, a famous eye-salve. The scornful imagery of the apocalyptic letter to Laodicea is obviously based on these activities. It also has reference to the emetic qualities of the soda-laden warm water from nearby Hierapolis, whose thermal springs ran into the Maeander. Laodicea's water supply also came from Hierapolis, and Sir William Ramsay suggests that its vulnerability, together with the city's exposed position, and its easy wealth caused the growth in the community of that spirit of compromise and worldly-mindedness castigated in the Revelation. Under Diocletian, Laodicea, still prosperous, was made the chief city of the Province of Phrygia.

The Zondervan Pictorial Bible Dictionary

The Seven Letters follow the same pattern:
Beginning: "These things saith He–" and "I know thy works–."
Closing: "He that Overcometh–" "He that hath an ear let him hear–."

"These Things Saith He—"

Naming the aspect of His Nature pertinent to each Church.

To Ephesus, a Great and Powerful Church, but Losing Zeal:
"These things saith He that Holdeth Seven Stars in His Hand."

To Smyrna, a Poor, Suffering Church, facing Martyrdom:
"These things saith He that was Dead, and Lived Again."

To Pergamum, Tolerating Teachers of Immorality:
"These things saith He that hath Sharp Two-edged Sword."

To Thyatira, Growing in Zeal, but Tolerating Jezebel:
"These things saith the Son of God, who hath Eyes like Fire."

To Sardis, with a Name that it Lived, but was Dead:
"These things saith He that hath the Seven Spirits of God."
To Philadelphia, a Nobody in the city, but Faithful:
"These things saith He that Openeth and None Shall Shut."
To Laodicea, the Lukewarm Church:
"These things saith the Faithful and True Witness."

"I Know Thy Works"

To Ephesus: "I know thy works, thy labor, and patience."
To Smyrna: "I know thy works, and tribulation, and poverty."
To Pergamum: "I know where thou dwellest, where Satan's throne is."
To Thyatira: "I know thy works, thy love and faith and patience."
To Sardis: "I know thy works . . . a name thou livest, and art dead."
To Philadelphia: "I know thy works, thou hast kept My Word."
To Laodicea: "I know thy works, . . . neither cold nor hot."

"To Him that Overcometh"

In Ephesus: "He that Overcometh . . . Eat of Tree of Life."
In Smyrna: "He that Overcometh, not hurt of Second Death."
In Pergamum: "He that Overcometh, to Eat of Hidden Manna."
In Thyatira: "He that Overcometh, will I give Morning Star."
In Sardis: "He that Overcometh, not blot name from Book of Life."
In Philadelphia: "He that Overcometh, pillar in Temple of God."
In Laodicea: "He that Overcometh, to sit with Me in My Throne."

"He that Hath an Ear Let Him Hear"

Thus closes each Letter, as if the Lord were warning the Churches that they had better Take Seriously what He was Saying to Them.

Chapter 2:1-7. The Letter to Ephesus

Ephesus, mother of Asian Churches, a city of 225,000 population, was metropolis and commercial center of "Asia." Its Temple of Diana was one of the Seven Wonders of the World.

There, 40 years before, Paul had done his most successful work (A.D. 54–57); such a multitude of converts to Christ that, almost overnight, the Church became one of the most powerful influences in the city, and, soon, one of the most famous churches in the world.

After the death of Paul, Timothy, it is said, spent most of his time in Ephesus, and there suffered martyrdom under Domitian, same persecution that sent John to Patmos.

In Ephesus John spent his old age; and, if not an active pastor, on account of his age, as last surviving Apostle of Christ, he must have been a dominating influence among pastors.

In a sense, it was John's own Church. There John wrote his Gospel, three Epistles and Revelation.

Three of Paul's Epistles related to Ephesus: Ephesians, and I and II Timothy. And, in that region, it is thought, possibly, the two Epistles of Peter and that of Jude were first issued.

Ephesus, about halfway between Jerusalem and Rome, was the approximate geographic center of the Roman Empire; and it had, in John's own lifetime, become the approximate geographic and numerical center of the Christian population of the world.

About ten years after the death of John, the Emperor Trajan sent Pliny into the Asian region to investigate whether to persecute Christians. Pliny wrote back to Trajan that Christians had become so numerous that Heathen Temples were almost deserted.

Christian Churches in many cities of the region included large and influential elements of the population; with Ephesus as the Queen Church of them all.

It had been 66 years since Pentecost, birthday of the Church, at Jerusalem. The Church everywhere had made phenomenal growth. But signs of Corruption were beginning to appear. And that, we think, is one of the things that called forth the book of Revelation.

"The Church in Ephesus", 2:1

It was before the days of church buildings. They had to meet in halls, or homes, or wherever they could. Not one great central temple; but many, perhaps hundreds, of small congregations, each under its own pastoral leadership. Yet the Letter is addressed to "The Church in Ephesus." Hundreds of congregations: yet One Church.

"He that Holdeth the Seven Stars in His Hand", 2:1

Emblem of His Power. Perhaps intended as a suggestive warning that the Church was becoming too proud of its prestige: glorying in what was of little use to its real mission.

The "False Apostles", 2:2

These, evidently, were men who claimed to have known Christ, with authority from Him for their teaching, in their effort to harmonize the immoral indulgences of Idol worship with the Christian faith.

The "Nicolaitans" (2:6), it is thought, were a sect who advocated licentiousness as the proper way of life.

These False Teachers had caused great trouble in the Church. The Ephesian pastors, as a body, it seems, had stood patiently and solidly against their teaching; for which they were commended (2:2, 3).

"Fallen from their First Love", 2:4,5

This was their offense. Their Zeal for Christ was cooling off. They no longer Loved Him as they once did. They were becoming Indifferent, Half-Hearted: not yet Lukewarm, like the Laodicean Church (3:16), but headed in that direction. This hurt Christ. For it they received a stinging rebuke, and were warned to Repent (2:5). Else their "Candlestick would be removed." It has. The site of Ephesus is deserted.

"The Tree of Life", 2:7

Promised to those who Overcome allurements of false teaching and natural temptations to fleshly indulgence and worldly ease.

While the Ephesian Church, as a Church, has perished, the promise of the Tree of Life still holds good to Individuals, in any Church, who Overcome.

Archaeology and Ephesus

Ephesus was excavated by J. T. Wood (1869–1874); British Museum (1904–5); and an Austrian expedition (1894– and 1930).

Ruins of the Temple of Diana were uncovered; also ruins of the Theatre in which the great Riot was held (Acts 19:29).

Also they found remains of a Roman Bath, constructed of marble, with many rooms: steam rooms, cold rooms, lounge rooms: an evidence of the luxury of the city.

They also found a Temple which contained a statue of Domitian, the Emperor who called himself "God," who had banished John to the Isle of Patmos, and who was Persecuting Christians while these Visions of the book of Revelation were being given to John.

Chapter 2:8-11. The Letter to Smyrna

The Suffering Church. No word of fault, but only loving comfort.

Smyrna, about 50 miles north of Ephesus, was a splendid city, of rare beauty, on a fine bay, rival of Ephesus, with the proud tradition that it had been the birthplace of Homer.

Its bishop, at the time, was the beloved Polycarp. Iranaeus, who had talked with Polycarp, said that Polycarp was appointed bishop of Smyrna by John. (See page 763.)

The Church was composed of poor people, with nothing like the number or prestige that the Church in Ephesus had. They were "poor, but rich" (2:9).

"Who was Dead, and Is Alive", 2:8

This, to those facing Martyrdom: reminding them that He had already Suffered what they were about to Suffer: and that they too, shortly, like Him, would be ALIVE FOREVERMORE.

"Tribulation Ten Days", 2:10

This may mean a Persecution of brief duration. Or, it may refer to the Persecution of Trajan, which was about to begin, in which Ignatius was martyred, and which may have hit Smyrna extra hard. Or, the "ten days" may prefigure the Ten Imperial Persecutions (see page 761).

"The Crown of Life", 2:10

In Ephesus promise was "Tree of Life" (2:7). In Sardis, "Name in the Book of Life" (3:5). Here, in Smyrna, "Crown of Life" (2:10), and "Not hurt of the Second Death" (2:11; 21:8).

While these promises were intended for Individuals who "Overcome," in another sense, Smyrna, as a city, has been given a Crown of Life: it has Survived through all the centuries, and is now the largest city in Asia Minor, 200,000 population, its modern name, Iz-mir.

Chapter 2:12-17. The Letter to Pergamum

A Church, faithful to the Name of Christ, even unto Martyrdom

Fig. 72. Acropolis at Pergamum.
Radio Times Hulton Picture Library, B.B.C. London

(2:13), but Tolerant of False Teachers: probably the same class of False Teachers as those in Ephesus. But, it seems, that, while in Ephesus the pastors, as a body, stood solidly against the False Teachers, here, in Pergamum, the pastors, though not themselves holding to the False Teaching, Tolerated within their ranks those who did. The False Teaching: right of Christians to indulge in heathen immoralities.

To such a Church, the Lord, while commending their faithfulness to His Name, yet presented Himself as "He who hath the Sharp Two-Edged Sword." Better look out. The Lord is not pleased with His Church tolerating Sinful Indulgence.

"Satan's Throne" (RV), 2:13

Pergamum was a seat of Emperor Worship, where incense was offered before the statue of the Emperor as to God. Refusal of Christians to do this often meant death. Also, an Altar to Jupiter. And a Temple of Esculapius, a healing god, worshiped in the form of a Serpent, one of the names of Satan. Beside these, it was also a stronghold of Balaamite and Nicolaitan Teachers. Thus, as a notorious center of heathenism and wickedness, it was called "Satan's Throne."

Then, too, Satan, who was about to Persecute Christians in Smyrna (2:10), had already begun in Pergamum (2:13).

"The Teaching of Balaam", 2:14

In Numbers 25, it is related how the Israelites played the harlot with Midianite women, and, in Numbers 31:16, it is said that they did this on the advice of Balaam. So, in Pergamum, devotees of heathen practices, who had infiltrated the ranks of Christians, and were advising them to participate in the sexual vices of heathen worship, were nicknamed Balaam. Evidently, they had quite a following.

"The Hidden Manna", 2:17

The promise to those who Overcome temptations to sinful pleasure: "Hidden Manna" and a "White Stone" with a "New Name" known only to its owner. The Hidden Manna may be the Fruit of the Tree of Life (22:2). The New Name may stand for a form of existence that will be satisfying beyond anything we have ever known or dreamed of in this life (see page 707). "White" (see page 706).

Chapter 2:18-29. The Letter to Thyatira

The Church of Compromise. They had some good qualities. They were noted for their "love and service and faith and patience." They were growing in zeal, "their last works more than their first"

(2:19)—just the opposite of Ephesus, which had "lost its first love" (2:4).

But, like Pergamum, they were tolerant of False Teachers, only worse—they suffered Jezebel in their midst.

Who Was Jezebel? 2:20-24

Thyatira was famous for its magnificent Temple of Artemis, another name for Diana. Jezebel, it is thought, may have been a prominent woman devotee of Diana, with a gift for leadership, who had a following of influential people in the city, and who, attracted to the growing cause of Christianity, attached herself to the Church, militantly insisting, however, on the right to teach and practice licentious indulgence, claiming inspiration for her teaching.

She was called "Jezebel" because, like Jezebel the devilish wife of Ahab who had introduced the abominations of Astarte worship into Israel (I Kings 16), she was introducing the same vile practices into the Christian Church.

Not all of the Thyatira pastors accepted her teaching. But, trying to be Liberal, and thinking that she might be a help in winning the whole city to the Name of Christ, they accepted her as a fellow pastor.

With that the Lord was greatly displeased. And, in a stinging rebuke, He presented Himself "with Eyes like Fire and Feet like Brass" (2:18). No trifling with such a Church!

"The Deep Things of Satan", 2:24

This is the third mention of Satan in the Seven Letters. In Smyrna he cast Christians into prison (2:9, 10). In Pergamum, Satan's "throne," he was persecuting the Church, and corrupting it with False Teachings (2:13, 14). Here, in Thyatira, Jezebel's teachings were known as the "deep things of Satan" (2:24). Again, he is mentioned as the enemy of the Church in Philadelphia (3:9).

"The Morninq Star", 2:28

Promised to those who "Overcome." Jesus Himself is the Morning Star (22:16). One of the earliest prophecies of the Messiah calls Him a "Star" (Numbers 24:17). By Faithfulness, not by Compromise, will the Church attain True Leadership.

Chapter 3:1-6. The Letter to Sardis

The "Dead" Church. Alive in Name only. But "a few had not defiled their garments" (3:4). In Heaven, the Church, except the "few," about to be erased from the books (3:5).

To such a Church, Christ presented Himself as One Empowered, having the "Seven Spirits" (3:1), to blot them off Heaven's roll.

Sardis, in the 6th century B.C., under Croesus, had been one of the richest and most powerful cities in the world. And, in Roman times, it was still a famous city. Its conversion to Christ, though largely nominal, seems to have made a profound impression on the region.

"The Seven Spirits", 3:1

"Seven Spirits" shared in the greeting to the Churches (1:4).
Christ Himself dictated the Seven Letters (1:19).
Yet each Letter was what the Spirit said (2:7).
"Seven Spirits" were before the throne (4:5).
The Lamb's Seven Eyes were the Seven Spirits (5:6).

The Seven Spirits seem to represent the Seven-Fold, or Complete operation of the Holy Spirit, the Spirit of Christ, the Spirit of God, all One and the Same Spirit, in the Fulness of His Power: the form in which Christ works in His Churches and with His Churches, in the Age between His First Coming and His Second Coming.

"They Shall Walk with Me in White", 3:4

Jesus' head, in the vision (1:14), was "White" as snow.
He that Overcomes shall be arrayed in "White" garments (3:5).
Heaven's citizens will be clothed in "White" (3:18).
The 24 Elders were arrayed in "White" (4:4).
The Martyrs wore "White" robes (6:11).
Redeemed multitudes were arrayed in "White" robes (7:9).
Robes made "White" in the blood of the Lamb (7:14).
The Lord will Come on a "White" horse (19:11).
His armies, clothed in "White," will be on "White" horses (18:14).

All this may be more than a figure of speech. It may suggest the nature of our Glorified Bodies. God dwells in Light unapproachable (I Timothy 6:16). Jesus' garments, in Transfiguration, were White (Mark 9:3).

"The Book of Life"

"I will in nowise blot his name out of the Book of Life" (3:5).
The Beast's followers are Not in the Book of Life (13:8; 17:8).
Those Not in Book of Life cast into Lake of Fire (20:12, 15).
Heaven inhabited only by those written in Book of Life (21:27).
Daniel, 12:1, Malachi, 3:16, spoke of Heaven's Book of Records.

Chapter 3:7-13. The Letter to Philadelphia

An Humble but Faithful Church. Content to exemplify the Life of Jesus in the midst of a pagan and corrupt society. Lovers of

God's Word, and intent on Keeping it. Greatly beloved of the Lord. Not a word of reproof.

"An Open Door, which None Can Shut", 3:8

God had warned the churches of Ephesus and Sardis against boasting of their influential standing. Here, He cautions the Church in Philadelphia not to be discouraged because they are a nobody; for God is not dependent on worldly prestige.

"Kept from Trial", 3:10

The Church in Smyrna had been told that they were to Suffer Persecution (2:10). Here, to the Church in Philadelphia, the promise is to Keep them from Suffering (3:10). Both Faithful Churches. God does not deal with all in the same way, but with each as He Himself knows best, beyond our understanding till we reach the other shore.

"The New Name", 3:12

A "New Name," in 2:17, seems to refer to mysterious joys to be realized in Heaven. Here, he that Overcomes is to be labeled with the Saviour's Own New Name (3:12). It is a sign of ownership, and a mark of citizenship. So, followers of the Beast are tagged with the Mark of their Master (13:16, 17). Each of us belongs to the Lord or to the Beast.

Philadelphia is still a prosperous town, of about 15,000, with a Christian population.

Chapter 3:14-22. The Letter to Laodicea

The Lukewarm Church. Laodicea was a banking center, proud of its wealth. Beautified with resplendent temples and theatres. Noted for its manufacture of rich garments of black glossy wool; and a medical school that made powder for treatment of eye troubles. This may have suggested the "riches," "garments" and "eye salve" (3:17, 18).

"Spew Thee out of My Mouth", 3:16

A pretty strong expression of Indignant Disapproval. From this one would think that Christ prefers Outright Opposition to Lukewarmness. Laodicea has been spewed out of His mouth.

"I Stand at the Door and Knock", 3:20

Strange picture. A Church of Christ, with Christ Himself on the

OUTSIDE, asking to be let in to one of His Own Churches. In measure, it is quite true of many churches of the present time, operating in the Name of Christ, but all too evidently for the benefit and glorification of the ecclesiastics in control, with Christ Himself little in evidence.

"Sit with Me in My Throne", 3:21

That is, share with Christ the Glory of His Kingdom. The unfailing repetition in every Letter that Final Blessedness is only for those who OVERCOME seems to imply that many who had started in the Christian way were, one way or another, falling by the wayside.

Smyrna and Philadelphia, the two cities with good churches, are still flourishing cities. Sardis and Laodicea, the two cities with bad churches, are now deserted and uninhabited sites.

Typical Significance of the Seven Churches

The Seven Churches may have been chosen as representing a fair cross section of Churches of that generation; typical, perhaps, in varying degrees, of Churches in All Generations, in varying stages of Truth and Apostasy, in varying measure humanized with Worldly Traditions, each Church largely the product of its Leadership, with varying proportions of Faithful Leaders and Faithful Saints, many congregations being a pitiful admixture of Church and World, of True and False.

Chapter 4. A Vision of the Throne of God

Here begins the Predictive part of the book.

"Things which Are" (1:19), were pictured in the Seven Letters, dealing with the Church situation as it then was.

"Things which must be Hereafter" (4:1), is the theme from here on, relating to the History and Destiny of the Church.

Some think that, at this point, the Rapture of the Church takes place. It may be. But the book itself nowhere says so. It is only an Opinion, and should be stated as an Opinion, and not as an unequivocal teaching of Scripture.

The Throne of God, 4:2,3

First thing, in lifting the veil of the Future, is this vision of GOD, to assure the Church that, no matter how Disheartening some of the revelations may be, GOD IS STILL ON THE THRONE.

God's form is not described, except that He had the appearance of Jasper and Sardius in a Rainbow of Emerald. Jasper is thought to have been diamond. Sardius was Red. Emerald, Green. Thus God shows himself to earthly eyes as One enswathed in a halo of clear dazzling White, shaded with Red and Green. (See further, "White," page 706.)

The Twenty-Four Elders, 4:4,5

Seated on 24 thrones, around the Throne of God, clothed in White, with crowns of Gold, they are thought, by some, to represent the Glorified Church: union of the 12 Old Testament Tribes and the 12 New Testament Apostles: symbol of God's People.

Or, they may represent a distinct class of heavenly intelligences, princes of Heaven, or various classes of Angels. Notice, the number 12 figures in the framework of God's Throne, even as it does in the framework of the New Jerusalem (see page 738).

"Lightnings and Thunders" (5): Majesty and Power of God.

"Seven Burning Lamps" (5): Holy Spirit in His Complete Working.

"Sea of Glass" (6): Calmness of God's Rule.

The Four Living Creatures, 4:6-11

"Beasts" (AV) (6), is a mistranslation. It should be "Living Creatures" (RV). These are Heavenly Beings. It is a different word from that translated "Beast" in 13:1, the Horrible Monster that figures so largely in the latter part of the book. They are thought to be Cherubim, spoken of in Genesis 3:24 and Ezekiel 1:10; 10:14. Here they join in Songs of Praise for Man's Redemption.

Chapter 5. The Sealed Book

In chapter 4 the vision is of God the Creator. In this chapter, it is of Christ the Redeemer. The Sealed Book held the Secrets of the Future. It was Christ who opened it.

Out of the Seventh Seal came the Seven Trumpets. The Seven Seals and the Seven Trumpets (a double 7), form the central framework of the book, chapters 6 to 11. At the sounding of the Seventh Trumpet, the Kingdoms of the World become the Kingdom of Christ (11:15).

Then the writer, following a common literary method of Scripture, returns and proceeds anew with additional or explanatory details.

"Seven Horns, Seven Eyes, Seven Spirits of God" (5:6), belonging to the Lamb, meant All-Conquering Might, All Knowledge, and All Power. He Knows the Future, and is Able to Control it.

The Lamb

Christ, in the vision to the Seven Churches (1:13–16), appeared as a Warrior. Here He is called the "Lion" (5:5). The Lion, when seen, is a "Lamb" (5:6). "Lion" represents Power. "Lamb" represents Sacrifice. The secret of Christ's Power is His Suffering.

"Lamb" is Revelation's favorite name for Christ:

The "Lamb" took the Sealed Book, and opened it (5:6, 7; 6:1).
The Living Creatures and Elders worship the "Lamb" (5:8, 14).
100,000,000 Angels worship the "Lamb" (5:11–13).
The great day of the "Lamb's" Wrath is come (6:16, 17).
Multitudes from all nations worship the "Lamb" (7:9, 10).
Their robes were washed in the blood of the "Lamb" (7:14).
The "Lamb" leads them to fountains of living waters (7:17).
They overcame Satan by the blood of the "Lamb" (12:11).
The 144,000 follow the "Lamb" (14:1, 4).
They sing the song of Moses and the "Lamb" (15:3).
The "Lamb" is Lord of Lords and King of Kings (17:14).
Marriage of the "Lamb" to His Bride is come (19:7, 9; 21:9).
12 foundations of City are 12 Apostles of the "Lamb" (21:14).
The "Lamb" is the Temple and Light of the City (21:22, 23).
Only those in "Lamb's" Book of Life shall enter (21:27).
Water of Life from Throne of the "Lamb" (22:1, 3).

Thus, in the panorama outline of the struggle between the Kingdom of the World and the Kingdom of God, from 6:1 to 11:15, it is the Suffering LAMB of God that is Victor. Foreshadowed 1400 years in the Jewish Passover, commemorated now for nearly 2000 years in the Lord's Supper, the Sacrificial LAMB OF GOD in Eternity will Himself be the Center of the Redeemed World that He Himself will have brought into being.

The Songs of Praise, 5:8-14

In 4:8–11 the praise is to God the Creator. Here the first two songs are to the Lamb (9, 12), the third to Creator and Lamb (13).

"A New Song" (9): that is, the song of Redemption is New as related to the song of Creation.

It is a scene of transcendant grandeur. The 4 Living Creatures, the 24 Elders, a Hundred Million Angels, the Whole universe, join in thanksgiving over the Redemption of Men.

In Heaven EVERYBODY Sings. It is just too bad that our churches, in their regular services, neglect it so.

"Prayers of the Saints" (5:8), both here, and in 8:4, are weighed by the Divine Arbiter, as He charts the course of history. What a light this sheds on Prayer!

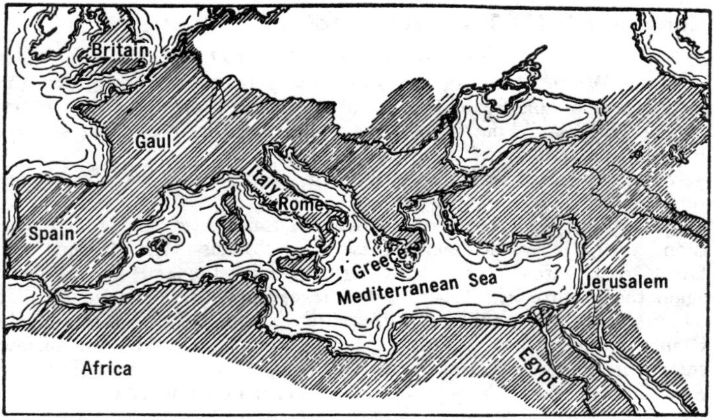

Map 68. The Roman Empire.

Chapter 6:1,2. The First Seal

The White Horse: Its Rider a Conquering King

This may symbolize Christ setting out to Conquer the World. Near the end of the book (19:11), another White Horse appears whose Rider is plainly stated to be Christ. They may be the same: the One Starting, the Other Finishing, His Conquest.

Or, this Horseman may symbolize, not Christ, but the World-Power under which Christ was Starting His work. The statement, at the end of the Seven Seals and Seven Trumpets (11:15), "The Kingdom of the World is become the Kingdom of our Lord and His Christ," may imply that the "Kingdom of the World" was in the saddle at the Start.

Or, this Horseman may symbolize the beginning of the reign of Antichrist at the time of the End. Or, possibly, Both, the World-Power under which Christ Started His work, and the Final World-Power under which He will Finish it; one, typical of the other.

If this Horseman represents the World-Power under which Christ was starting His work, it is indeed a very accurate picture of that Power. The Roman Empire, mightiest Government that had thus far been in the world, most of the known world under its control, was, at the time, just entering its Golden Age. The historian Gibbon calls the reigns of the five Emperors, Nerva, Trajan, Hadrian, Antoninus Pius and Marcus Aurelius A.D. 96 to A.D. 180, "the happiest and most prosperous period in the entire history of the human race."

Chapter 6:3,4. The Second Seal

The Red Horse: Civil War

If the White Horse of the First Seal represents Christ, then this Red Horse of this Second Seal and the Black Horse and Pale Horse of the Third and Fourth Seals may represent the Woes that scourge mankind on account of their Rejection of Christ.

If the First Seal refers to Antichrist, then these Three Seals must refer to his Terrifying Wars.

If the First Seal refers to the Roman Empire, in its Golden Age, then, again, it would seem, these Three Seals—War, Famine and Death—must refer to the following period in the same Empire. And again the Picture Fits Exactly: In the century between A.D. 200 and A.D. 300 over Fifty Different Pretenders claimed the Throne of the Roman Empire. And, instead of having strong rulers on the throne, they were Fighting among themselves as to Who should be Emperor. And through their Wars—a Hundred Years of Civil War, and what always follows Prolonged War—Famine, Pestilence and Death—the Roman Empire, in that century, Lost more than Half its Population, and was started on its road to ruin.

Chapter 6:5,6. The Third Seal

The Black Horse: Famine: Result of War

"Balance" meant scales. Food would be scarce, sold by weight.

"Penny," not our penny, was then an ordinary day's wages.

"Measure" of wheat was about a quart. Ordinarily, then, 15 to 20 measures could be had for a penny.

"Oil and wine hurt not" seems to indicate a situation where luxuries were abundant while necessities were at famine prices, possibly meaning that rulers had plenty while common people were in want: result of the Prolonged Wars of the Second Seal.

Chapter 6:7,8. The Fourth Seal

The Pale Horse: Death: Result of War and Famine

"Fourth Part of Earth Killed," in which "Wild Beasts" aided (6:8). The Roman Empire, in its century of Civil War, A.D. 200 to A.D. 300, referred to under the Second Seal, suffered Colossal Loss in Population, followed by an Enormous Increase of Wild Animals.

Chapter 6:9-11. The Fifth Seal

A Vision of the Souls of Martyrs

This seems to symbolize Persecution for the Church. Already there had been many thousands of Martyrs from the Persecutions of Nero and Domitian. And unnumbered thousands more were to come. There were Ten Imperial Persecutions of the Church, from Nero, A.D. 64, to Diocletian, A.D. 305. The vision may also be a prophetic hint of the Papal Persecutions of the Middle Ages, and perhaps also of the Persecutions of the Tribulation Period of the Last Days.

Chapter 6:12-17. The Sixth Seal

The Day of Wrath at Hand

Revolution. Upheaval. Convulsion. Consternation. Sun Darkened. Stars Falling. Heavens Rolled Up. Mountains and Islands Removed. Kings and Peoples Frightened.

In some respects, similar to description of the Battle of Armageddon (16:12–21), of which it may be a preliminary hint.

Jesus had used similar language, in speaking of the Time of His Coming Again (Matthew 24:29, 30; Luke 21:26).

So had Isaiah, in predicting the Fall of Babylon (Isaiah 13:10). And Ezekiel, in predicting the Fall of Egypt (Ezekiel 32:7). Similar language appears in Isaiah 34:4; Joel 2:30, 31; Acts 2:20; seeming to refer to God's Judgments on Nations, or the Final Day of Judgment.

Whatever else this Seal may refer to, it seems like a prediction of 4th century Upheavals in the Roman Empire. The Empire Ceased its Persecution of the Church. Emperor Constantine became a Christian (A.D. 312). Issued an Edict of Toleration (A.D. 313). Made Christianity the religion of his court. In A.D. 325 he issued a general exhortation to all to embrace Christianity. Moved his Capital to Con-

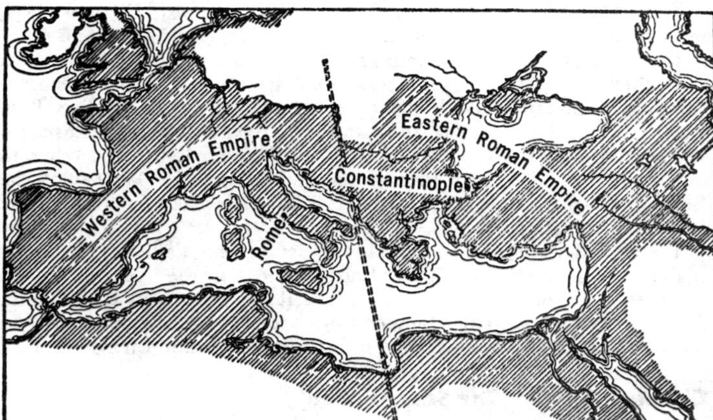

Map 69. Division of the Roman Empire.

stantinople. Theodosius (A.D. 378–395) made Christianity the State Religion of the Empire, and Church Membership Compulsory. A.D. 395 the Empire was Divided: the West with Rome its Capital; the East with Constantinople its Capital. This was the beginning of the break-up of the Mighty World Empire that had for 300 years tried so hard to destroy Christianity.

Chapter 7:1-8. The 144,000

Sealed out of the Twelve Tribes

This chapter, coming between the Sixth and Seventh Seals, seems to be a part of the Sixth Seal, contrasting the Happy Lot of the Elect with the Fearful Doom of the World out of which they were called, as just described in the closing verses of chapter 6.

144,000 is the square of 12, multiplied a thousandfold, and is thought to be understood, not numerically, but symbolically, representing the Sum Total of the Elect of Israel, the Firstfruits of the Gospel, or, the Sum Total of Christians.

"The Four Winds" (7:1–3), seem to be the agencies of the Lamb's Wrath, just mentioned in 6:16, and identical with the Seven Trumpets soon to follow, held back till the Sealing of the Elect is finished.

"The Sealing of God's Servants" (7:3), seems to refer to the process of Evangelization going on, in the Roman Empire, before it fell, or, in the Whole World, throughout the Whole Course of History, before the Final Day of the Lamb's Wrath.

Chapter 7:9-17. The Great Multitude in Heaven

The "144,000," of verse 4, and the "Great Multitude," of verse 9, seem to be two separate groups. One is the Elect of Israel. The other is from All Nations. With one group the scene was on Earth. With the other the scene is in Heaven. One group was sealed against a Coming Tribulation. With the other group, the Tribulation is Past. Yet they may be One and the Same group, under different aspects.

One relates to the Call, or "Sealing" period, on Earth; the other to the period of Victorious Blessedness in Heaven: the 144,000 of the Elect of Israel, turning out, in full fruition, to be the Great Multitude from Every Nation.

The blood-washed throng, safe at last in the Father's Home, as against the Day of Wrath on Earth (6:16), is the Answer to the Martyrs' Cry (6:10). Arrayed in white Robes. Palms in their hands. Songs on their lips. They hunger no more. All tears wiped away. In the Land where Fountains are Forever flowing with Living Waters.

Chapter 8:1-6. The Seventh Seal

Out of the Seventh Seal came the Seven Trumpets. The Double Seven is thought to emphasize the idea of Totality. Thus in the Two

Sevens, chapters 6 to 11, are outlined the Struggle, and the Complete, Final, Everlasting Victory of Christ over the "Kingdoms of the World" (11:15).

"Prayers of the Saints" (8:3, 4). God about to Answer the Cries of the Martyrs of 6:9, 10. Answer, the Awful Judgments of the Seven Trumpets. It seems to indicate that Prayer has some influence with God in shaping the course of history.

"The Half Hour's Silence" and "Thunders, Lightnings, Earthquake" (8:1, 5), may imply Momentous Events in the making.

Chapters 8:7-13. The First Four Trumpets

The sounding of these Four Trumpets seem to announce the releasing of the "Four Winds of the Lamb's Wrath" (6:16–17:3), held back while the Elect were being Sealed.

1st Trumpet: Hail, Fire, Blood, Cast upon the Earth.

2nd Trumpet: Great Burning Mountain, Cast into the Sea.

3rd Trumpet: Great Burning Star, Fell upon the Rivers.

4th Trumpet: Sun, Moon, Stars, Darkened.

"The Third Part" of the Earth, Sea, Rivers and Heavenly Bodies, was smitten, as if destruction was only partial.

These Four Trumpets may refer to God's Judgments on Roman Empire; or on World at time of End; or Both.

Fall of the Roman Empire

If they refer to the Roman Empire, then here again, as in previous visions, the imagery seems to be a very good symbolic predictive portrayal of Actual History. The parallel with the facts of the Breakup of the Roman Empire, fit so exactly, it seems it must have been envisioned in these Four Trumpets.

In the 1st and 2nd centuries A.D., Rome reached her zenith.

In 3rd century A.D., Empire began to crack with Civil War.

In all three centuries, Rome Persecuted the Church.

In 4th century A.D., in a colossal Government Upheaval, Christianity was accepted, and made State Religion of Empire.

In the same 4th century, the mighty Empire was Divided, and became: Eastern Roman Empire and Western Roman Empire. (See map, page 713.)

For 800 years no foreign enemy had set foot on Italian soil. But in the 5th century A.D., Barbarians from the North began to pour in.

"Hail, Fire, and Blood," of First Trumpet, Burned the Earth (8:7). The Goths (A.D. 409), descended upon Italy in savage fury, and left behind Burning Cities, and Scorched, Bloody and Desolated Lands.

"Great Burning Mountain," of Second Trumpet, cast into Sea (8:8, 9). The Vandals (A.D. 422), swept across Gaul and Spain into Africa.

They built a Navy, and, for 30 years, fought the Roman Navy, which for 600 years had controlled the Mediterranean, and Drove it from the Sea.

"Great Burning Star," Third Trumpet, fell upon the Rivers (8:10, 11). Attila the Hun, from the depth of Central Asia, appeared (A.D. 440), on the banks of the Danube, at the head of 800,000 fighting men. Pushing westward, he met the Roman armies, and defeated them with awful slaughter, successively, on the River Marne, the River Rhone, and the River Po, so that these rivers actually ran with Blood. Loaded with spoil, he returned to the Danube. When he died, the River was turned aside, and his body buried beneath its bed. The waters still flow over his grave. He was indeed a scourge of the Rivers.

"Sun, Moon, and Stars," Darkened, Fourth Trumpet (8:12). Another horde of Barbarians, from the Rhine country, headed by Odeacer (A.D. 476), besieged and took the city of Rome.

Four successive blows: Gothic Invasion of Italy (A.D. 409); Vandals' Destruction of Roman Navy (A.D. 422–452); Attila's Awful Slaughters on River systems of Central Europe; Odeacer's Seizure of Rome.

Under these Appalling Disasters, the Mighty Roman Empire, which, for more than half a millenium had ruled the world, went down, the light of Roman civilization went out, and the Dark Ages of the world began.

"Third Part" (8:7, 8, 10, 12). The Roman Empire fell in Three sections. The Western Part, Rome its capital, by all odds the most powerful part of the original Empire, fell A.D. 476. The Asiatic and African Parts of the Empire were overrun by Mohammedans in 7th century A.D. The Eastern European Empire, split off from Rome (A.D. 395), with Constantinople as its capital, fell to the Mohammedans (A.D. 1453).

Chapter 9:1-11. The Fifth Trumpet

The Army of Demon Locusts

This host of Horrible Monsters, with complex appearance of Locusts, Horses, Scorpions, Lions and Humans, came out of the Abyss (9:1, 2, 11), ("Bottomless Pit," AV), led by Abaddon, or Apollyon, who was the Devil, or one of his Angels. This indicates the Hellish Origin of the Woes to follow. Satan has already been mentioned as Persecuting and Corrupting the Churches in Smyrna, Pergamum and Thyatira (2:9, 10, 13, 14, 24); and is named as instigator of Rome's Imperial Persecutions of the Church (12:13–16). Of what he is now about to do in the Locust Plague, we are warned, "Woe, woe, woe," hinting its Frightfulness.

These Demon Locusts are thought, by many commentators, to be a predictive picture of the Rise and Spread of Mohammedanism; or, of the Tribulation Period of the Last Days; or, Both.

Mohammedanism

In the Seventh century A.D., Mohammedanism swept the Eastern World like a tidal wave, and Blotted out Christianity in Southwest Asia and North Africa: the Euphrates and Nile Valleys: the Eastern and Southern Borders of the Mediterranean: lands of the Bible Story: lands in which the Bible originated and grew: lands in which God's Revelation of Himself to Mankind was nurtured and brought to completion: lands in which God formed and trained the nation Israel, for two thousand years, to pave the way for the coming of Christ; lands hallowed forever as the scene of Christ's Life and Death and Resurrection and His Redemptive Work for Mankind; lands which were the Cradle of Christianity, and which were for 600 years Christian; the Original Christian World; in these lands, by one fell blow of the Mohammedan Sword, CHRISTIANITY WAS BLOTTED OUT, and Mohammedanism was Established. And they HAVE BEEN MOHAMMEDAN EVER SINCE.

600 years Christian. Now, for 1300 years, Mohammedan. More Mohammedans now in the world than Protestant Christians.

Mohammed (A.D. 570–632), in Mecca, Arabia, declared himself to be The Prophet of God, and set out, at the head of an army, to propagate his religion by the Sword. Soon the whole of Arabia was conquered. Mohammedan armies, under successive leaders, swept on in their conquest. Syria fell (A.D. 634), Jerusalem (A.D. 637), Egypt (A.D. 638), Persia (A.D. 640), North Africa (A.D. 689).

Asian and African Christianity, thus swept away, Mohammedans moved into Europe. Spain fell (A.D. 711). Then they headed on into France, where, at Tours, the Mohammedan Army was met and defeated (A.D. 732), by Charles Martel, grandfather of Charlemagne. That was one of the Decisive Battles of the Ages. EXCEPT FOR THAT VICTORY, CHRISTIANITY MIGHT HAVE BEEN ENTIRELY EXTERMINATED FROM THE EARTH.

Here are some of the things that make it look like this Fifth Trumpet might refer to Mohammedanism.

"Locusts" (9:3). Arabia, pre-eminently, was a land of Locusts. It was in Arabia that Mohammedanism originated.

"Shapes of Locusts like War-Horses, with Scorpion-like Tails, Crowns like Gold, Faces like Men's Faces, Hair like Women's Hair, Teeth like Lion's Teeth, Breastplates as of Iron, and Wings that sounded like Chariots and Horses rushing to War" (9:7–10).

This is indeed a very good description of Mohammedan Armies, composed of Fierce, Relentless Horsemen, famous for their Beards, with Long Hair like Women's Hair, with Yellow Turbans on their Heads that looked like Gold, and they had Iron Coats of Armor.

"Smoke from the Abyss" (9:2, 3). It was out of this Smoke that

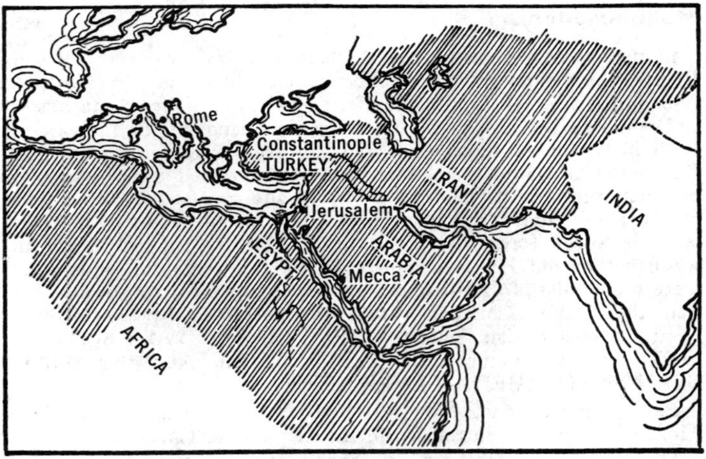

Map 70. Present Day Mohammedan World (shaded area).

the Locusts came. The Smoke had Darkened the Sun and the Air. This may refer to the False Teachings, which had Clouded and Corrupted the Church of Mohammed's day, in its Worship of Images, Relics and Saints. It was the IDOLATRY of a Degenerate and Apostate Church that gave Mohammed his chance. Destruction of Idols was his slogan.

"Hurt Not the Grass, nor any Green thing" (9:4). Mohammedans spared Trees, Grass and All Vegetation, because Mohammed had so commanded; for, to those living in the wastes of Arabian deserts, Trees and Vegetation were blessings.

"Torment Men Five Months" (9:5). 5 months, the normal stay of Locusts, May to September, is about 150 days; which, on the Year-Day interpretation (Ezekiel 4:6), would be 150 Years. That was, approximately, the period (A.D. 630 to A.D. 786), in which Mohammedanism continued its effort at World Conquest. With Haroun-Al-Raschid (A.D. 786–809), at the height of Mohammedan Power and Glory, they abandoned the idea of Conquest, and began to cultivate peaceful relations with other nations.

Chapter 9:12-21. The Sixth Trumpet

The Army of 200,000,000 *Euphratean Horsemen*

Horrible looking Monsters, of complex appearance of Men, Horses, Lions and Serpents, belching Fire, Smoke and Brimstone.

They also may be a predictive picture of Mohammedanism, with a possible more literal fulfillment in things yet to be.

ARABIANS ruled Mohammedan World 400 years (A.D. 630–1058).
TURKS then took over, and have been in control almost till now. This Trumpet seems to point to Turkish Mohammedanism.

"Euphrates" (9–14), from whence the Sixth Trumpet Armies of Horsemen were loosed. In A.D. 1057 a vast horde of Turks, from central Asia, appeared on the banks of the Euphrates. In their westward march they replaced the Arabians as rulers of Mohammedan lands.

The Turks were more cruel and intolerant than the Arabians had been. Their barbarous treatment of Christians in Palestine led to the Crusades (A.D. 1095–1272), almost 300 years of intermittent War in which European Christians tried to regain the Holy Land from Mohammedans.

"Out of the Horses' Mouths proceeded Fire, Smoke, Brimstone" (9:17). The Eastern Roman Empire (A.D. 395–1453), its capital, Constantinople, had, for centuries (A.D. 630–1453) been the bulwark of Europe against Mohammedanism. But in A.D. 1453 it fell to the Turks.

It was at the battle of Constantinople (A.D. 1453), that Artillery with GUNPOWDER was First Used; which gave victory to the Turks; the "Fire, Smoke and Brimstone," of 9:17.

Then followed another threat to European Christianity. The victorious Turks marched on in toward central Europe. But met their defeat in Vienna (A.D. 1683), at the hands of a Polish army under John Sobieski. As in the Battle of Tours (A.D. 732), so here, a second time, after almost 1000 years, Europe was again saved from Mohammedans.

"Hour, Day, Month, Year" (9:15), may mean at an exact appointed time. Or, on the Year-Day interpretation (Ezekiel 4:6), 365 plus 30 plus 1, 396 days, that is 396 years. From A.D. 1057, when the Turks crossed the Euphrates, to the Fall of Constantinople (A.D. 1453), was 396 years.

"Third Part of Men Killed" (9:18). This may refer to the Fall of the Eastern Roman Empire (A.D. 1453), the last remaining "Third" of the original Roman Empire, at the hands of the Turks. (See page 716.)

Antichrist

The word "Antichrist" is nowhere used in the book of Revelation; which is rather surprising, in view of its very abundant use in books about Revelation. It occurs in I John 2:18, 22; 4:3; and II John 7; where it is said that there were already many Antichrists.

Even though some commentators overdo "Antichrist," and read it into passages where it may not have been intended, yet there are many passages of Scripture, which, without calling it by the name "Antichrist," rather plainly indicate that this Gospel Age is to end in a Terrible Outbreak of Evil just preceding the Coming of the Lord.

Jesus said that His Coming would be preceded by "Great Tribulation" (Matthew 24:21, 29); that it will be a time of "Mourning" for all nations (Matthew 24:29, 30); and men will be "Fainting for Fear and Expectation of things coming on the world" (Luke 21:24–26); and implied that there will be little Faith at the time (Luke 18:8).

Daniel spoke of a "Time of Trouble such as never was" to be at the "Time of the End" (Daniel 12:1, 4, 9, 13). In II Thessalonians 2:3–10 it is said that there would rise to power a blasphemous "Man of Sin" who will be destroyed by the Lord's Coming.

In trying to interpret the prophetic imagery of the book of Revelation, it is easier to trace its parallel with what has so far transpired than it is to feel sure of its exact bearing on what is still in the future.

While the Seven Seals and Seven Trumpets seem to have portrayed an exact outline of Great Features of World History thus far, a more complete fulfillment may be in the making.

May it not be that the Roman Empire, in its furious persecution of the Church, was a manifestation of Antichrist? and Mohammedanism, another? And, now, the rise to world power, right before our own eyes, of Atheistic Russian Communism—may it not be the renewed growlings of Antichrist? May it not be that the Night IS Far Spent, and THE DAY IS At Hand?

Chapter 10. The Little Book Open

In chapter 5 it was a Sealed Book. Here it is an Open Book. The Open Book is one of the messages of the Sealed Book, for it appears under the Sixth Trumpet, which came out of the Seventh Seal.

It seems to be an announcement, in a setting of awful majesty, that the End is near (10:7); but that, before the End comes, there is yet another prophetic period to cover (10:8–11), as told in next chapter.

"Time no longer" (10:6), may mean that in Eternity our earthly concept of Time will have been abolished; and, like Jesus, we can say, "Before Abraham was I am." But "Delay" is thought to be a more accurate translation than "Time"; in which case the meaning would be, The Great Day of God is Come; the Hour of Doom is about to strike.

The particular message of the Open Book seems to be the prophecy about the Temple being Measured and the Two Witnesses (chapter 11); a prophecy that made John sick at heart (10:10).

But, in addition to this, may it not be that the "Little Book OPEN," itself, in its very phraseology, coming, as it does, just before the

Seventh Trumpet, may have been a symbolic hint that there would be an Era of The OPEN BOOK just preceding the End of the World?

If so, it exactly fits in with the course of History. Strange as it may seem, the Church, in the Middle Ages, TOOK THE BIBLE FROM THE PEOPLE.

But the Protestant Reformation, under the leadership of Martin Luther, RESTORED THE BIBLE TO THE PEOPLE. And the Invention of Printing, about that time, contributed greatly toward making it a Book of the People. And Modern History has been an Era of the OPEN BOOK, in a sense never before known. Every Blessing of Modern Civilization is a Direct Product of the Open Bible: Civil and Religious Liberty, Popular Education, Social Reform, Liberty of Conscience and Freedom of Speech.

Chapter 11. The Temple Measured

The Temple is measured, but the Court and the Holy City are left to be trodden under foot by the nations 42 months. This appears to draw a distinction between the True Inner Church and the External Visible Professing Church: the one to be Preserved and Protected of God, the other to be Corrupted, Desecrated and Exploited, by the World.

It seems to predict Large-Scale Apostasy in the Church; which, later, is more fully depicted, in chapter 13, under the form of Leopard-Lamb-Beast, and, in chapter 17, under the form of Babylon the Great Harlot. The vision of it made John sick at heart (10:10).

The Two Witnesses, prophesying in sackcloth 1260 days (11:3), seem to be identical with the Inner Temple of 11:1, as the Outer Holy City is trodden under foot by the nations 42 months. It is the same period for both: 42 months, at 30 days to a month, is 1260 days.

And, even as the Outer Holy City, or Apostate Church, takes the form of Leopard-Lamb-Beast in chapter 13, so the Inner Temple, or True Inner Church, here taking the form of the Two Witnesses, is more fully described in chapter 14, as the 144,000, the Lamb's True Followers.

"Two Olive Trees and Two Candlesticks" (11:4), is an obvious reference to Zechariah 4:1–14, where it is explained that the Candlestick represents the House of God, and the Olive Trees the Spirit of God, as if to include the Spirit in the Testimony of the Church. Or, since this is the message of the "Open Book" (10:2, 10, 11), and since the Spirit works through the Word, the Two Witnesses may thus be the True Church and the Word of God, faithfully bearing their Testimony while the Apostate Church is on the Throne of the Leopard-Lamb-Beast, as told in chapter 13.

If this is a correct interpretation, then the Killing of the Two Witnesses by the Beast (11:7), may be a symbolic picture of the

Bloody Persecution of Saints by Papal Rome (see page 776); and the Witnesses Coming to Life and being Exalted to Heaven (11:11, 12), may be a picture of a Purified Church and God's Word again becoming Free and Prominent in the World, under the leadership of the Lutheran Reformation. It is not possible to overestimate the influence of the Lutheran Movement in Restoring God's Word to the People. It was indeed like a Resurrection from the Dead of God's Witnesses to the World (11:11, 12).

However, this vision may have meanings yet to be revealed in events of the Final Struggle with Antichrist.

"Beast" (11:7, see page 724). "Great City" (11:8, see page 730).

Final Victory. Kingdoms of World Become Kingdom of Christ.

"Third Woe" (11:14). Final Judgment on Wicked (11:18).

The Seven Seals and Seven Trumpets, thus in outline seem to have given a Bird's Eye View of the Course of History.

Chapter 12:1-6. The Woman, the Child, and Dragon

Up to this point, in the Seven Seals and Seven Trumpets, the story has been carried forward to the Day of Final Judgment (11:15, 18), dealing largely with the fate of the WORLD.

Here, in chapter 12, the writer returns to the starting place, and, in another series of visions, begins portrayal of things previously omitted, relating largely to the fate of the CHURCH.

The Woman

The Woman, about to give birth to a Child, seems, up to verse 5, to represent Israel; and, from verse 6 onward, to represent the Church.

The Hebrew Nation, nurtured of God, through long centuries, for the purpose of bringing Christ into the world, is here personified as a Queen, in Heavenly Glory, giving birth to the Child of the Ages.

The Child

The Child was Christ, the Messiah. Satan was waiting to devour Him at birth (12:4). This seems like a reference to Herod's effort to kill Christ as a babe. If he could have succeeded, he may thus have thwarted Christ's Redemptive Work; for surely a new-born babe could not die for the sins of the world.

Satan did, however, through Judas (John 13:2, 27), succeed in having Jesus as a grown man put to death. But that boomeranged against Satan; for it supplied God's people with the one weapon against which Satan is powerless, the "Blood of the Lamb."

The Dragon

The Dragon is identified as the Devil, Satan, the Old Serpent (12:9). He had already been mentioned as Persecuting the Churches in Smyrna and Pergamum (2:10, 13); and he, or one of his angels, from the abyss, as king of the army of Demon Locusts (9:11), and murderer of the Two Witnesses (11:7). "Red" (12:3), may symbolize his Murderous Nature.

"Seven Crowned Heads and Ten Horns" (12:3), evidently, symbolizes his dominion as Prince of this World, permitted, in the wisdom of God, for some reason beyond human understanding, to make trouble for a while. But he is Not God. There are Not Two Gods. Satan is Not All-Powerful. He is Not Everywhere. Nor does he Know Everything. He fears the name of Christ. And his doom is inevitable.

"Stars of Heaven" (12:4), which he cast to earth, may symbolize his power to marshall hosts of the unseen world against saints, or, to influence Church Leaders to Apostasy, or, both.

Chapter 12:7-12. The War in Heaven

This may mean that Satan, infuriated at his failure to destroy Christ by Crucifying Him, followed Him in His Ascension, and made bold to storm the bulwarks of heaven, where he met a crushing defeat at the hands of Michael and his Angels, and lost forever any further power to harm Christ or the souls of the redeemed.

Then Satan, henceforth, gave attention to devising ways and methods of hindering the work of the Church on Earth.

"Michael" (12:7), was the Archangel, Prince of Angels, who had had some previous experience in contending with the Devil (Jude 9). He was Guardian Angel of Israel (Daniel 10:13, 21). He will be on hand at the time of the End, in the Great Tribulation (Daniel 8:17; 12:1, 9, 13); and at the Coming of the Lord (I Thessalonians 4:16).

Michael and his Angels may, even now, be fighting our battles, here on earth, in a more real sense than we know. Our struggle is not entirely against flesh and blood (Ephesians 6:12). The outcome may depend, far more than we realize, on the armies of the invisible world.

Chapter 12:13-17. The Woman's Flight to the Wilderness

In the "Wilderness" (12:14), the Woman sought refuge from the Dragon. This seems to symbolize the True Church as being Driven Underground by Persecution. It was in the "Wilderness" that Babylon, the Harlot Church developed (17:3). But, one day, for the True Church, it will be, Not a "Wilderness," but a Mountain with the Glory of God (Revelation 21:10, 11).

"The Flood of Water" (12:15), which the Dragon cast after the Woman, may refer to Persecutions of the Church by Roman Empire.

"The Earth Helped the Woman" (12:16), may allude to Conversion of Emperor Constantine and Christianization of Roman Empire, which put an end to the Persecutions. (See page 759.)

The 1260 Days

The Woman was in the Wilderness 1260 Days (12:6).
She was in the Wilderness "a time, times, and half a time" (12:14).
The Two Witnesses Prophesied in Sackcloth 1260 Days (11:3).
While the Holy City was Trodden Down 42 Months (11:2).
Beast Reigned after Death-Stroke was Healed, 42 Months (13:5).

42 months, 1260 days, and a time, times, and a half (a year, years, and a half: 3½ years), denote the same period. 3½ years are 42 months, which, at 30 days to a month, are 1260 days. (See page 347.)

Thus, Four Things are represented as being Co-Eval and Co-Terminous: Woman in the Wilderness: Holy City Trodden Down by the Nations: the Two Witnesses prophesying in Sackcloth: and the Beast's Reign after his Death-Stroke: all Four at Same Time. (See on chapters 13 and 17.)

Chapter 13:1-10. The Leopard-Beast

This seems to be the Beast which killed the Two Witnesses (11:7); and which is still more fully described in chapter 17.

The Dragon, that is the Devil, having failed to destroy the Church by Persecution, now installs himself in this Beast, to continue his War against the Saints (12:13–13:1).

The Beast had appearance of a Leopard, a Bear and a Lion (13:2); symbols which Daniel had used for World Power (Daniel 7:3–6).

Chapter 13:11-18. The Lamb-Beast

This Beast looked like a Lamb (13:11). The first Beast looked like a Leopard. But they were Allies. Leopard-Beast had been killed (13:3). Lamb-Beast brought him to life (13:15): the Dragon working in them both (13:2, 4, 11).

The Lamb-Beast was the Revived Leopard-Beast. While looking like a Lamb, he spoke like a Dragon (13:11). He had power to kill whoever would not wear his mark (13:15). He blasphemed the name of God, and made war on the Saints (13:6, 7).

His identification card was the number 666 (13:18).

This Lamb-Beast is afterward called "False Prophet" (16:13; 19:20; 20:10); that is, Pretender-Lamb. The Dragon, having failed in his attack on the Church from Without, now attacks from Within, himself Pretending to be the Lamb.

Coalition of Leopard-Beast and Lamb-Beast

This Coalition continued as a World-Government for 42 months (13:5). It seems to be another symbol of the Holy City being exploited by the World for 42 months (11:2).

A Beast, looking like a Lamb, and ruling in the Name of the Lamb, and the Holy City being trodden under foot by the Nations—these two symbols seem to mean a World-Government operating in the Name, and by the Aid, of an Apostate Church. What else can they mean?

Leopard-Beast represents Secular Power. Lamb-Beast represents Pretended Christian Power. The Dragon uniting them into One World-Power.

This Coalition is later called "Babylon," and is more fully described in chapters 17 and 18.

While it was on the throne of World-Power, the Two Witnesses were Prophesying in Sackcloth (11:3).

This Leopard-Lamb-Beast is thought by some to be the Antichrist. By others, to symbolize certain features of World History. To say the least, its parallel with the Course of the Church through History to the present time is most amazing, as noted on the next page.

The Seven Heads and Ten Horns

The Dragon had them (12:3). The Leopard-Beast had them (13:1). The Scarlet-Colored Beast of "Babylon" had them (17:3).

Seven, as a symbol for Completeness, and Ten, as a symbol for World Power, the Seven Heads and Ten Horns seem to represent World Power as a Whole: or, the Concentration and Personification of World Power continuing as One Entity through the Whole Period of History, manifesting itself under various forms and to various degrees in various ages, with many and diverse modifications.

Previous to the rise of our Modern Era, Seven World Powers have towered above, and very largely Dominated, the course of History. Egypt was a World Power about 400 years (1600–1200 B.C.). Then Assyria, about 300 years (900–600 B.C.). Then Babylon, 70 years (606–536 B.C.). Persia, 200 years (536–330 B.C.). Greece, about 200 years (330–146 B.C.). Rome, 600 years (200 B.C.–A.D. 400). Papal Rome, 1200 years (A.D. 600–1800).

The Death-Wound of One of the Seven Heads, 13:3

At the time the book was written, Five of the World Powers had fallen. One Was evidently Rome, and One was Yet to Come (17:10): evidently, Rome wounded, and brought to life again by the Lamb-Beast (13:3, 12).

Rome fell A.D. 476. But, in the Name of Christ, and by the aid of the Church, Rome Came to Life Again. And Papal Rome Ruled the World on a Vaster Extent, and for a Longer Time, and with a more Despotic Hand, than ever Pagan Rome had done, or any World Power before it.

"42 Months" (13:5), on year-day interpretation, 1260 years, duration of Papacy as a World Power, 6th to 18th centuries.

"Speaking Blasphemies" (13:6), exactly fits claims of Popes to Infallibility, to Forgive Sins, to hold the place of God on earth.

"War on the Saints" (13:7). Historians estimate that, in the Middle Ages and Early Reformation Era, more than 50,000,000 Martyrs perished.

"666", the Number of the Beast, 13:18

Called a "Man": meaning, possibly, a set of Men; or, an Institution headed by a Man or set of Men. It seems to mean a Name, the letters of which, when regarded as numerals, total 666.

Irenaeus, a pupil of Polycarp, who was a pupil of John, understood the 666 to be the Greek word "Lateinos": L,30: A,1: T,300: E,5: I,10: N,50: O,70: S,200. These total 666.

"Lateinos" means "Latin Kingdom." Papal Rome made Latin its official language. And it still is. Rome's canons, missals, prayers, decrees, bulls, blessings, cursings, are in LATIN.

Chapter 14:1-5. The Lamb and His 144,000

John had just seen a vision of a Beast Pretending to be the Lamb (13:11). Here it is a vision of THE LAMB Himself (14:1).

The 144,000, the Lamb's Faithful Followers, were marked with the Lamb's Name (14:1), even as followers of the Pretender Lamb were marked with his Name (13:16): the Lamb's True Church, in contrast to the False Church of the Pretender-Lamb: the Faithful Wife in the Wilderness (12:14), while the Unfaithful Wife was revelling in her Adultery with the World (chapter 17).

They were free from Falsehood (14:5), in contrast to the Lying wonders and False Teachings of the Pretender-Lamb (13:14).

They were "Virgins" (14:4). True to Christ, in contrast to the "Harlotry" of the False Church (17:5). We are not to understand that they were literal celibates, for the New Testament nowhere regards Marriage as sinful, but rather as a shadow of the union of Christ and His Bride.

They were "First-Fruits" (14:4), possibly the same as the 144,000 of 7:4, in contrast to the general harvest (14:15, 16).

The "New Song" of the 144,000 (14:2, 3), breaking on the ear like an ocean's roar, was one that only the Redeemed know. An unsaved person cannot know the joys of the redeemed. And the redeemed themselves, when they reach Heaven, will experience rapture beyond anything they had previously imagined. In Heaven EVERYBODY will SING. Why not here in our Churches? Why not have the PEOPLE SING?

Chapter 14:6,7. The Angel with the Everlasting Gospel

This seems to symbolize General Evangelization of the Whole World in the Whole Gospel Era. Yet, coming just before the announcement of the Fall of "Babylon" (14:8), may it not be a picture of our Modern Era of World-Wide Missions?

Note, while the Pretender-Lamb's method of conquest was to Kill those who would not worship him (13:15), the weapon of the Lamb is the Simple Preaching of the Gospel (14:6).

Chapter 14:8. The Fall of Babylon

This is the book's first mention of "Babylon." And the first thing mentioned about Babylon is that it has FALLEN. Its Fall announced before its Rise has even been hinted. It was such a horrible thing that the writer thought best to assure his readers that it would have only Temporary Existence before he undertook to tell them about it.

Fully described in chapters 17, 18, "Babylon" turns out to be another name for the Leopard-Lamb-Beast of chapter 13.

Chapter 14:9,11. Doom of Beast's Followers

Here the unhappy lot of the Beast's followers is in sad contrast to the Unspeakable Joy of those who belong to the Lamb (14:3). Their doom is more fully described in chapters 19, 20. The contrasting of the fate of the redeemed and the lost, so noticeable in this book, was also a characteristic of Jesus' teachings in the Gospels.

Chapter 14:12,13. The Blessed Dead

This is, again, in contrast to the Torment of the Wicked, just mentioned. The suffering of the martyrs is over. The time prayed for in 6:9–11, at long last, is come. Saved, and Happy, Forever.

Chapter 14:14-16. Earth's Harvest Reaped

This chapter began with a vision of the "First-Fruits" (14:4), of the Gospel; then an Era of World-Wide Gospel Preaching (14:6); and here closes with visions of the Final Harvest.

The Harvest of the human race had been spoken of long centuries before, in Joel 3:13, 14, "Multitudes, multitudes in the valley of decision. Put in the sickle. The harvest is ripe."

"Earth's Harvest Ripe" (14:15): waiting for this may be one of the reasons why the Lord Delays His Coming.

Chapter 14:17-20. Earth's Vintage Gathered

The "Harvest" seems to be of the Saved. The "Vintage," of the Lost. The "Winepress" is of the Wrath of God on the Wicked.

"1600 Furlongs" (14:20), is 200 miles in our measure. Its meaning must be in the number 1600, rather than in the actual distance. 1600 is 4 x 4 x 100: thought to be a symbol of Complete Destruction.

"Without the City" (14:20): probably the City of God: meaning that God's People are safe from the Wrath visited on the Wicked.

"The Horses" (14:20): they seem to be the same, and the event also the same, more fully described in 19:14–21.

Summary of Chapters 12-14

The Seals and Trumpets, in chapters 6–11, carried the panorama forward to Final Victory, dwelling mostly on Early part of the story.

Chapters 12–14, returning to the start, contain another series of pictures running to the End, dwelling more at length on the Middle part of the story, and detailing more fully some scenes of the End-Time. The visions seem to portray the Rise of an Apostate Church, seated on the Throne of a World-Empire; the True Church, meantime, faithfully bearing its Witness to All the World, and then The Harvest.

Chapters 15 and 16. The Seven Vials of God's Wrath

Judgments of God by which the Power of the Beast is Broken (15:2; 16:2, 10, 13): evidently, the Leopard-Lamb-Beast of chapter 13, identified as "Babylon" in 16:19, and detailed in chapters 17 and 18.

Chapter 15:1-8. Song of the Victors

Before describing the Judgments, we are given a glimpse of the Redeemed's unstinted Praise to God for the way He has managed the course of history (15:3, 4). It is similar to the "New Song" of 5:8–14—the outburst of Unutterable Joy at first sight of their Heavenly Surroundings and their first Unclouded Vision of God.

Then, in solemn ceremony, Seven Angels are given the Seven Vials of God's Wrath.

Chapter 16:1-9. The First Four Vials

The Seven Vials, as a whole, seem to portray the terrifying catastrophes that are to befall the world in the Last Days, climaxing in the Battle of Armageddon (16:14–16).

The First Five Vials, may, also, have specific reference to the Fall of Papal Rome, which was the form of World-Government, existing, and to exist, between the Fall of the Roman Empire and the Final Government of AntiChrist.

The First Four Vials, like the plagues of the First Four Trumpets (8:7–12), fell, successively, on Earth, Sea, Rivers and Sun.

"The Rivers" upon which the Third Vial was poured (16:4), were the same rivers where the Blood of Martyrs had been shed (16:6), by the Beast (13:15), and by Babylon (17:6; 18:24). This Vial may represent God's Avenging Judgments on the Papacy in the Very Same River Valleys where Millions of the Papacy's victims had been Martyred.

Chapter 16:10,11. The Fifth Vial

Poured out on the Throne of the Beast, whose Realm had already suffered terribly from the First Four Vials. These Five Vials, while they may have other meanings, seem, prophetically, to parallel the colossal convulsions of the 18th century by which the Papacy Ceased to be a World-Government.

The Papacy was the Dominating Power of the World from the 6th to the 18th centuries, the Most Despotic Power in history.

Its Growth was gradual, gaining from 6th to 9th centuries.

From 9th to 13th centuries it Dominated the Kings of Europe.

From the 13th century its Decline has been gradual.

Its power was tremendously shaken by the Protestant Reformation of the 16th century; and by the French Revolution and the Wars of Napoleon in the late 18th and early 19th centuries. At the hands of Napoleon, the Papacy received its crowning humiliation, and loss of prestige, from which it has never recovered. He just about ended the Pope's Political Power in Europe. Since then Papal Power in World-Government has been a mere shadow of what it was in the Middle Ages. In the Middle Ages, Popes spoke, and Kings trembled.

"Blasphemed the Name of God" (16:9). Perhaps a reference to the Pope's decree of his own Infallibility (A.D. 1870), the dying gasp of a World Power, the Crowning Blasphemy of the Ages. (See page 781.)

Chapter 16:12-16. The Sixth Vial

Battle lines being drawn for Armageddon. The Dragon, Beast, and False Prophet muster their Demon Army for One Last Desperate Attack on the Church (16:13, 14): the Dragon, Satan: the Beast, World Government: False Prophet, the Apostate Church: all in Alliance.

The "Euphrates" (16:12). The Vials, still paralleling the Trumpets; as, under the Sixth Trumpet, a Demon Army, from the Euphrates, had delivered a frightful blow against the Church (9:14–16), so, here, under the Sixth Vial, the Euphrates is the assembling place of the Hosts of Wickedness for a Final Effort to Destroy the Church.

The Garden of Eden, where the human race originated, and Babel, where earthly Government began its rebellion against God, were in the Euphrates Valley. Thus human history will come to an end where it began.

"Behold, I Come" (16:15). Note the caution that with the approach of Armageddon the Lord's Coming is at hand.

Chapter 16:17-21. The Seventh Vial

This seems to be the Battle of Armageddon. "Hailstones" from the "Air" (16:17, 21), each the weight of a talent, that is, about 100 pounds. Seems like a prophecy of Air-Planes and A-Bombs.

"Three Parts" (16:19). As the Roman Empire fell in Three parts (8:7–12; 9:18), so in Three stages will the Final Anti-Christian World Government go down: Babylon; Beast; False Prophet.

"Mighty Earthquake" (16:18). The Two Recent World Wars, threatening clouds of a Third, the present uneasy, disturbed, chaotic condition of nations and government, half the world already under control of Atheistic Communism avowedly Determined to Destroy Christianity—these things make us wonder, sometimes with anxious forebodings, if perchance we may even now be in the initial stages of Armageddon.

Chapter 17. Babylon, the Great Harlot

The Church, in Ephesians 5:25, 32, is spoken of as the Bride of Christ. Jesus likened His Coming to a Marriage Feast (Matthew 25:10). The Glorified Church is called the Lamb's Wife (Revelation 19:7; 21:2, 9). But here the Church is seen as a "Harlot," even as Israel, the Lord's Bride, in her Idolatry (Ezekiel 16:14–18), was playing the Harlot.

"The Great Harlot" (17:1), in Illegitimate Relation with Kings (17:2), Sitting upon a Scarlet-Colored Beast, full of names of Blasphemy, having Seven Heads and Ten Horns (17:3), the Harlot arrayed in Purple and Scarlet, Revelling in her Luxury and Filth (17:4), her Name, Babylon the Great (17:5), Drunk with the Blood of Martyrs (17:6).

The Woman is a City, 17:18

The Harlot Woman, in alliance with the Beast, called Babylon, is on a Throne of World-Government, reigning over kings of the earth.

The True Church, Bride of Christ, Wife of the Lamb, is also called a City, the New Jerusalem, the Holy City (19:7; 21:2, 9).

Two Women: the Harlot and the True Bride of Christ. Two Cities: Babylon and the New Jerusalem. The Harlot Church and the True Church, thus, in antithesis, are set the one over against the other. The One seated, in Power, on a Throne of Worldly Splendor, driving the Other Underground by Persecution. This all seems to identify Babylon the Harlot, of this chapter, with the Leopard-Lamb-Beast of chapter 13.

Seven Heads and Ten Horns, 17:3

The Dragon had them (12:3). The Leopard-Lamb-Beast had them (13:1). And here the Harlot-Beast, Babylon, has them. They are understood to symbolize World-Government.

"Babylon" is stated to be the great city reigning over the kings of the earth (17:18), which, at the time, was Rome. Rome is further identified in the expression, "The Seven Heads are Seven Mountains on which the Woman sits" (17:9): for Rome, literally, was built on Seven Mountains, and was known as the "Seven-Hilled City."

"Seven Kings: Five are Fallen: One Is: One Yet to Come" (17:10). This, further, indicates Rome. At the time this was written, Five World-Empires had Fallen: Egypt, Assyria, Babylon, Persia, Greece. One Is: Rome. One Yet To Come: Babylon the Harlot.

"An Eighth is of the Seven" (17:11). This looks like a Revival of the Beast, after the Seven Heads and Ten Horns have passed, perhaps pointing to the Final Form Antichrist will assume.

An Apostate Church on the Throne of a World-Empire

This description of Babylon the Great Harlot, Seated on the Seven-Headed Ten-Horned Beast, while it may have ultimate reference to a situation yet to appear, Exactly fits Papal Rome. Nothing else in World History does fit.

The desire for Worldly Power began to manifest itself in the Church, on a broad scale, in the 4th century, when the Roman Empire ceased its Persecutions, and made Christianity its State Religion. The spirit of Imperial Rome passed into the Church. The Church gradually developed itself into the pattern of the Empire it had conquered.

Rome fell. But Rome came to life again, as a World-Power, in the Name of the Church. The Popes of Rome were the heirs and successors of the Caesars of Rome. The Vatican is where the Palace of the Caesars was. The Popes have claimed all the authority the Caesars claimed, and more. The Papal Palace, throughout the centuries, has been among the most luxurious in all the world. Popes have lived in Pomp and Splendor unsurpassed by earthly kings. In no place on earth is there more ostentatious pageantry and show of magnificence than at the coronation of a Pope. The City of Rome, first Pagan, then Papal, has been the Dominating Power of the World for Two Thousand Years, 200 B.C. to A.D. 1800.

"Full of names of Blasphemy" (17:3). Popes claim to hold on earth the place of God, to have Supreme Authority over the Human Conscience, to Forgive Sin, to Grant Indulgences, and that Obedience to Them is necessary to Salvation. How could anything be more Blasphemous?

"Scarlet" (17:3, 4), color of the Beast and the Harlot, and also of the Dragon (12:3), is the Color of the Papacy. The Papal Throne is Scarlet. It is borne by twelve men clad in Scarlet. The Cardinals' hats and robes are Scarlet. Originally the Devil's color (12:3), it has now become the Color of Atheistic Communism: they are commonly spoken of as Reds, Red Army, Red Territory, the Red Square in Moscow, the Devil again marshalling his hosts from Without.

"Filthiness of her Fornication" (17:4). Appalling Immoralities of Popes of the Middle Ages are well known.

"Drunk with the Blood of Martyrs" (17:6). The Horrors of the Inquisition, ordered and maintained by the Popes, over a period of 500 years, in which unnumbered millions were Tortured and Burned, constitute the MOST BRUTAL, BEASTLY and DEVELISH PICTURE in all history.

It is not pleasant to write these things. It is inconceivable that any Ecclesiastical Organization, in its mania for Power, could have distorted and desecrated and corrupted, for its own exaltation, the beautiful and holy religion of Jesus, as the Papacy has done.

But Facts are Facts. And History is History. And, most amazing of all, it seems exactly pre-figured in Revelation. No wonder John's vision made him sick at heart (10:10).

Chapter 18. The Fall of Babylon

Old Testament Babylon, originally called Babel, where Human Government began its rebellion against God (Genesis 11:1–9), later became the wonder city of the ancient world (see pages 336–339), and enslaved Israel. Its name is here given to the World-Power which would enslave the Church. This chapter sounds like Jeremiah's Dirge over Babylon (Jeremiah 51).

"Come Out of Her, My People" (18:4). If "Babylon" is the prophetic name of the Papacy, as we think it may be, this seems like a forecast of the Protestant Reformation. In the Middle Ages, corrupt and diabolical as the Papal System had grown to be, yet God had His people in the Papal Domain. And, at the sound of Luther's clarion call, in the 16th century, a Mighty Exodus and Break-away from the Papal Eold began. It spread over Germany, Scandinavia, England, Scotland, United States and Canada. Out of it came our Modern Era of the Open Bible, Liberty of Conscience, Freedom of Speech, Popular Education, and Government of the People by the People and for the People. To Martin Luther, More Than to Any Other One Man, we owe the Blessings of Modern Civilization.

"Utterly Burned in One Day" (18:8). This seems to mean that Babylon's Destruction will be Sudden and Complete. It may refer to some feature of the Final Conflict with Antichrist, not yet come to pass.

"Babylon the Great Harlot" may be Heaven's Name for Apostate Christendom as a Whole.

Even in our own country, where we think we have the Purest Form of Christianity known since the days of Primitive Persecutions, while there are vast multitudes of Devoted Saints, and countless True and Faithful Churches, Seminaries, Organizations and Movements, headed by Pastors and Leaders of Unwavering Loyalty and Unquestioned Faith, YET, on the other hand, our Churches so generally are so thoroughly Humanized, so full of Worldliness, Indifference, Half-Heartedness, Pleasure-Seeking, all kinds of Evil Indulgence, so much Unbelief in Pulpits and in Seminaries, so little of God's Word in the Preaching, so little of Christ in the Services, so much Lifeless Formalism, so much Professionalism and Ecclesiastical Pomp, so little of the real spirit of Christ, so much Ignorance of God's Word, and such Indifference to it in the Pulpit—All This makes it look as if the Church as a Whole HAS NOT YET COME ENTIRELY OUT OF ITS GREAT APOSTASY.

The Ten Kings, 17:11,12

Interims between World-Powers, when the nations are ruled by a number of Governments, in round numbers, "Ten." As the Ten Horns of Daniel 7:7 seem to have predicted the Kingdoms into which the Roman Empire broke up, so these words in 17:12 may picture another Interim before the Rise of the Final Antichrist. There has been no One Power Dominating the World. Napoleon tried it. The Kaiser tried it. Hitler tried it. And now the Atheistic Russian Communists are trying it.

Chapter 19:1-10. Marriage Supper of the Lamb

Two Hallelujah Choruses. The first Chorus (1-5), expresses Heaven's Joyous Celebration over the Destruction of Babylon the Harlot Church.

The second Chorus (6-8), in a swell of voices like the ocean's roar and the roll of distant thunder, announces the Marriage of the Lamb to His True Bride.

At the Marriage Supper, Individuals are spoken of as Guests (9); but Collectively they are called the Bride (7).

Chapter 19:11-16. The White Horse and Armies of Heaven

If this White Horse is the same as that of the First Seal (6:2), then this is the final triumph of which that was the beginning.

If that White Horse represented the Kingdom of the World, then this White Horse has become victor over that one.

The vision seems to be a representation of the Lord's Coming in Glory, as KING OF KINGS AND LORD OF LORDS: Glory for those who are His: Wrath for the Wicked (12, 15); as also expressed in II Thessalonians 1:7–10.

Chapter 19:17-21. Final Doom of Beast and False Prophet

The Four Enemies of the Lamb were the Dragon, the Beast, the False Prophet and Babylon.

In chapter 18 Babylon, the Working Alliance of Beast and False Prophet, fell. Then the Beast and the False Prophet, Government and Apostate Church, their alliance dissolved, continued for a while, each in his own field. Now, in this chapter, their Destruction is foretold. And in chapter 20 the Dragon, Satan, the Evil Spirit that prompted it all, goes to his Final Doom.

The Beast, the False Prophet and Babylon, appear to be personifications of Institutions. The Dragon in a Person.

Not only are the Institutions destroyed, but also those who had the "Mark" of the Institutions (14:9–11; 19:20).

Chapter 20:1-10. The Millennium

The "Thousand Years," occurring six times in verses 2–7, is the only actual Biblical mention of the Millennium. The Lord's Second Coming is said to be mentioned over three hundred times in the New Testament; but the Millennium only here, in this most mysterious part of this most mysterious book in the Bible.

To live in the blessed hope and continual Expectation of the Lord's Coming is one thing: to have a theory about the Millennium is quite another. Some think the Millennium will be an Age of Blessedness in this present world; others, that it will be one of the Ages of Eternity after the flesh and blood order of existence has passed. And some talk as if they knew all about it.

Satan Bound, 1-3

Satan's expulsion from heaven (chapter 12), was connected with the Birth and Ascension of Christ (12:5). Here, Satan's binding is connected with the Second Advent of Christ.

Some think the two passages refer to the same event. But there Satan made trouble for the earth (12:12). Here he is kept from making trouble (20:3).

The "Bottomless Pit" (20:3), Satan's domain, presided over by Satan himself, or one of his archangels (9:11), now becomes his prison.

The Millennial Reign, 4-6

It will last 1000 years. By some, this is thought to be a literal 1000 years, foreshadowed as a Sabbath Rest after 6000 years of man's history. By others, to mean an indefinitely long time, as, in God's chronology, "One day is with the Lord as a 1000 years, and a 1000 years as one day" (II Peter 3:8).

"First Resurrection" (5). A Second resurrection is not mentioned. But the expression, "The rest of the dead lived not till the 1000 years should be finished," seems to imply that there will be Two resurrections, one before, and one after, the Millennium.

New Testament teaching generally links together the Lord's Coming, the Resurrection and Judgment Day, all in one perspective: as, when looking at distant mountain peaks, nearly in line, one behind the other, they seem to be close together, when in reality, they may be separated by immense distances.

However, Jesus, in using the phrase, "The resurrection of the just" (Luke 14:14), may have intended it as a hint that the resurrection of all would not take place at the same time.

Paul, speaking of the resurrection (I Corinthians 15:23), says, "Each in its own order: Christ the firstfruits; then they that are Christ's at His Coming; then comes the end"; as if the end might be some time after the resurrection of His people, as theirs will have been sometime after His.

Satan's Final Doom, 7-10

Babylon, the Beast and the False Prophet, the agencies through which Satan had done his deadly work, having been destroyed (chapters 17, 18, 19), Satan's own time has at last come. He makes a furious but brief and futile effort to regain his hold on the earth.

"Magog" (8), is the general name of the northern nations of Japheth's posterity (Genesis 10:2). "Gog" (8), is their prince (Ezekiel 38:2). Probably used here as general names for the wicked of all nations from the "four corners of the earth," in one last attack on the saints of God.

We wonder how Satan could muster such a vast following, when he had been bound for 1000 years. It has been suggested that, being the time of the general resurrection, the vast multitudes of vile and wicked men and women, of all centuries and all nations, who would be coming to life, would furnish Satan a fertile field for his work.

The "Lake of Fire and Brimstone" (10, 15), is the final destination of Satan, the Beast, the False Prophet and the Wicked.

If the "Beast" and "False Prophet" were Institutions, rather than Persons, they were, to say the least, created and managed by Persons, of whose spirit they were expressions.

If being cast into fire meant annihilation for Institutions, even so, Persons lived on and on in torment, "day and night forever" (10), a strong expression, meaning absolute endlessness.

Chapter 20:11-15. The Final Judgment

Babylon, Beast, False Prophet, Satan and evil influences, now being out of the way, the time has at last come for the assignment of each and every Human Individual to his Final Habitation.

"Flight of the earth" from presence of Him who "sat upon the Great White Throne," (11), may be by Fire (II Peter 3:10–12).

Those who had already been judged as worthy of the First Resurrection will here have their judgment confirmed in the presence of the assembled universe.

The Judgment will be complete. Every person from every age and nation will be there. Every deed and motive will have been recorded. It will be the "Day when God shall Judge the Secrets of men," spoken of by Paul in Romans 2:16.

There will be only two classes: the Saved and the Lost. The "Books" will have the records of men's lives. The "Book of Life" will have the roll of the Saved. There are many of such mixed character that we would not know where to place them. But God knows.

The "Second Death" (14), is the final doom, at the end, as distinguished from physical death which is the lot of all humanity. It is here called the "Lake of Fire."

Jesus talked about it: the place where the "Fire is not quenched"; "Eternal Fire prepared for the Devil and his angels."

Literal Fire? Who knows? It may be more painful to the soul than literal fire is to the body.

Even Death Itself was cast into the Lake of Fire (14). For those outside the "Lake," Death, the nightmare of earthly existence, will Never Again rear its hideous head (21:4).

Chapter 21:1-8. The New Heaven and New Earth

This chapter describes, not a new social order in this present world, but the Eternal Home of the Redeemed, the "Father's House of Many Mansions." One of the most precious chapters in all the Bible. How we love to read it!

The First Heaven and Earth had passed away (as said in II Peter 3:10), the Heavens with a great noise (explosion?), and the Earth and its works burned up. What amount of change in the physical universe, we do not know. Or, whether it will be this earth made over and renewed by fire, or an entirely different earth.

Nor can we now comprehend to what extent, with our glorified, incorruptible, spiritual bodies, we may be confined to any material planet or star, or be free to roam in the limitless spheres of space. How we would love to know. Some day we shall.

"The Sea is No More", 1

But there is a "River" (22:1). So we wonder if it is to be understood literally. Perhaps the "Fire" by which the Earth will have been consumed left no Sea. Or, perhaps the "River of the Water of Life" is not literal earthly water; but rather a beautiful symbol of the Life which is in Christ, as He said to the Samaritan woman, "Whosoever drinks of the Water that I shall give him shall Never Thirst" (John 4): and, "Whosoever will, let him take of the Water freely" (22:17).

"The Tabernacle of God is with Men", 3

In the Garden of Eden man was driven from the actual immediate, conscious presence of God. Here it is restored. In this world we walk by Faith. Up there we shall actually See God, and be With Him in loving fellowship through ceaseless cycles of never-ending ages.

No more Death, no Tears, no Pain, no Heartaches or Sorrow. A new universe come into being. How wonderful it will be to be there! Especially for those who have known little else but Suffering here: the greater the Suffering here, the greater the Glory up there.

"Without are the Abominable", 8

Many Christians are guilty of some of the things here mentioned. To us, it seems that there are gradations of character, and we would not know where to draw the line. But God knows. To God there are only two classes: those who are His, and those who are Not His.

Chapter 21:9-27. The New Jerusalem

The Bible begins with a Garden, and ends with a City. The Holy City, New Jerusalem, Bride of Christ, Wife of the Lamb (2, 9, 10), trodden under foot in 11:2, here shines forth in all its Glory. "Holy City" is the antithesis of "Babylon." Babylon, the Adulterous Church. Holy City, the True Church, Bride of Christ. The Adulteress has disappeared. The True Wife, Glorified.

A City of Gold, 18,21

Shown to John by one of the same angels who had showed him Babylon (9; 17:1). Ancient Babylon, which had given its name to the Adulterous Church, was known as a "City of Gold" (Isaiah 14:4), wonder city of the ancient world (see pages 336–340). Now the Real City of Gold appears in its Infinite Splendor and Magnificence.

Measurements of the City, 16

12,000 furlongs (1500 miles): the length of each side, or the entire distance around. Foursquare. A Cube, of which the Holy of Holies in the Tabernacle, a cube 15 feet each way, and the Holy of Holies in Solomon's Temple, a cube 30 feet each way, were types.

The Wall, 144 cubits (216 feet). Its height? Or thickness? If height, then the City within would tower above the Wall.

The measurements are in multiples of 12, which seems to be a symbol and signature of God's People. 1000 times 12 representing the Glorified Capital of God's Redeemed Universe. 12 times 12 (144), its Wall. 12 Gates inscribed with names of the 12 Tribes. 12 Foundations inscribed with names of the 12 Apostles. As if to say, the Glory of the City is the result of Foundation Work done by Israel and the Apostles in bygone ages. The Tree of Life has 12 kinds of fruit for 12 months.

The general pattern of the City, Foursquare, with its Walls, and River of Life, may have been suggested by the pattern of Ancient Babylon, which was Foursquare, its Walls 60 miles around, 300 feet high, its 100 Gates of brass, and Divided in the midst by the Euphrates River.

Its Precious Stones, 19-21

Each Gate was a Pearl. The 12 Foundations were each built of a Precious Stone: Jasper, Sapphire, Chalcedony, Emerald, Sardonyx, Sardius, Chrysolite, Beryl, Topaz, Chrysoprase, Jacinth, Amethyst.

They are similar to names of the 12 Stones on the Breastplate of the High Priest with names of the 12 Tribes (Exodus 28:15–30), which must have been intended as a sort of dim photograph, given in the distant past, of what God was working toward.

Some of these stones may not have been the same as those that now bear their names. Here are the colors they are thought to represent. Jasper, diamond. Sapphire, blue. Chalcedony, sky blue. Emerald, green. Sardonyx, red and white. Sardius, fiery red. Chrysolite, golden. Beryl, sea green. Topaz, transparent green. Chrysoprase, purple. Jacinth, red. Amethyst, violet.

City of Gold. Walls of Diamond. Gates of Pearl. Foundation of Precious Stones. Whether literal, or symbolic of something more glorious, Resplendent Beyond Imagination.

Chapter 22:1-5. The Tree of Life

The Tree of Life, beside the River of Water of Life (22:1, 2), flowing forever from the throne of God. First pictured in Eden's Tree of Life and River (Genesis 2:9, 10). Later, in Ezekiel's vision of Healing Waters (Ezekiel 47: 1–12). Still later, Jesus said, "Whosoever shall drink of the Water that I shall give him shall Never Thirst" (John 4:14); and, "I am the Bread of Life . . . If any man eat of This Bread he shall Live Forever" (John 6:35, 51). Here, the final fulfillment of it all, for citizens of the Lamb's World.

Chapter 22:6-10. Importance of the Book

A re-affirmation that it IS THE WORD OF GOD (22:6). As the book began by pronouncing blessing on those who read and keep its words (1:3), so it closes (22:7).

Chapter 22:11-15. End of the Day of Grace

"He that is filthy, Let Him Be Filthy Still; and he that is holy, Let Him Be Holy Still" (22:11), is a solemn commitment of the Lost to their fate, and of the Saved to theirs. Character, in this world, while the day of grace lasts, may become better or worse. But the time comes when it is fixed for eternity, as fruit issues from the bud.

Notice again the absolute separation of those who have Washed Their Robes and those who have Not (22:14, 15), as in 21:6–8. Over and over it is asserted in Scripture that there are only Two classes of people, and only Two destinies.

Chapter 22:16,17. Final Invitation

"I am the root and offspring of David, the bright and morning Star" (22:16; Numbers 24:17), means that Jesus is The ONE toward Whom all prophecy pointed and in Whom all prophecy is fulfilled. He alone is Saviour. Apart from Him there is no hope.

To all who will, He says, Come, and take of the Water of Life freely. His Spirit says, Come. His Church says, Come. Every one may join in the invitation. A Glorious World ahead. Come, before it is too late.

Chapter 22:18-21. Final Warning

Against any mutilation of the Book. It would mean forfeiture of the Book's Glorious Promises. Rationalistic critics do not like this passage, because it condemns them for assuming to themselves the liberty to eliminate whatever portions of Scripture they do not like (Deuteronomy 4:2; 12:32). Better accept God's Word, just as it is, and beware of treating any part of it too lightly.

"I Come Quickly," repeated three times in this chapter (7, 12, 20). It is Jesus' Last Recorded Word, His Parting Message to His Waiting Bride, as He passes out of sight. EVEN SO, COME, LORD JESUS.

Revelation and Genesis

The Bible is all One Story. The last Part of the Last Book in the Bible reads like the Close of the Story begun in the First Part of the First Book in the Bible.

The First word in Genesis:
"In the beginning God created the Heavens and Earth" (Genesis 1:1).

Almost the Last word in Revelation:
"I saw a New Heaven and a New Earth" (Revelation 21:1).

"The gathering together of waters He called the Sea" (Genesis 1:10).
"And the Sea is No More (Revelation 21:1).

"The Darkness He called Night" (Genesis 1:5).
"There shall be No Night there" (Revelation 21:25).

"God made the Two Great Lights (Sun and Moon)" (Genesis 1:16).
"The city has No Need of the Sun nor the Moon" (Revelation 21:23).

"In the day you eat thereof you shall surely Die" (Genesis 2:17).
"Death shall be No More" (Revelation 21:4).

"I will greatly multiply your Pain" (Genesis 3:16).
"Neither shall there be Pain any more" (Revelation 21:4).

"Cursed is the ground for your sake" (Genesis 3:17).
"There shall be No More Curse" (Revelation 22:3).

Satan appears as deceiver of mankind (Genesis 3:1, 4).
Satan Disappears Forever (Revelation 20:10).

They were driven from the Tree of Life (Genesis 3:22–24).
The Tree of Life re-appears (Revelation 22:2).

They were driven from God's Presence (Genesis 3:24).
"They shall See His Face" (Revelation 22:4).

Man's primeval Home was by a River (Genesis 2:10).
Man's Eternal Home will be beside a River (Revelation 22:1).

HOW WE GOT THE BIBLE

Formation of the New Testament

The New Testament "Canon." The word "Canon" literally means "Cane," or "Rod of Measurement." In Christian use it came to mean the "Written Rule of Faith," that is, the list of Original and Authoritative Books that composed God's Inspired Word The Canonical New Testament Books were those which came to be generally recognized by the Churches as the Genuine and Authentic Writings of Apostolic Authority.

In the days of Christ there was in the literature of the Jewish nation a group of Writings called "The Scriptures," now called the Old Testament, which the people commonly regarded as having come from God (see page 404). They called it THE WORD OF GOD. Jesus Himself so recognized it. It was Read Publicly and Taught Regularly in the synagogs.

Christian Churches, from the very first, accepted these Jewish Scriptures as God's Word, and gave them, in their assemblies, the same place they had had in the synagogs.

As the Writings of the Apostles appeared, they were added to these Jewish Scriptures, and were held in the same sacred regard. Each Church wanted, not only what had been addressed to itself, but copies of Writings addressed to other Churches.

New Testament Beginnings of the Canon

There are hints in the New Testament itself that, while the Apostles were yet living, and under their own supervision, collections of their Writings began to be made for the Churches, and placed with the Old Testament as the Word of God.

Paul claimed for his Teaching the Inspiration of God (I Corinthians 2:7–13; 14:37; I Thessalonians 2:13).

So did John for the Book of Revelation (Revelation 1:2).

Paul intended that his Epistles should be Read in the Churches (Colossians 4:16; I Thessalonians 5:27; II Thessalonians 2:15).

Peter wrote that "These Things" might remain in the Churches "after his departure" (II Peter 1:15; 3:1–2).

Paul quoted as "Scripture" (I Timothy 5:18): "The laborer is worthy of his hire." This sentence is found nowhere in the Bible except Matthew 10:10 and Luke 10:7: evidence that Matthew or Luke was then in existence, and regarded as "Scripture."

Peter classes Paul's Epistles with "Other Scriptures" (II Peter 3:15–16).

The Apostles, it seems, wrote many Letters, having in mind the immediate needs of the Churches. As to which Letters were to be preserved for future ages, we believe that God Himself watched over the matter, and made His Own choice.

The New Testament Books First Appeared: Matthew, James, Hebrews (?), in Palestine; John, Galatians, Ephesians, Colossians, I & II Timothy, Philemon, I & II Peter, I & II & III John, Jude, Revelation, in Asia Minor; I & II Corinthians, Philippians, I & II Thessalonians, Luke (?), in Greece; Titus, in Crete; Mark, Acts, Romans, in Rome.

Palestine, Asia Minor, Greece and Rome were far apart. The Old Testament books had originated within the compass of one small country; but the New Testament books in widely separated countries.

Earliest Collections Incomplete. It was not a world of railroads, airplanes and radios, like the world we live in today. Travel and communication were slow and dangerous. What is now a trip of a few hours would then have required months or years. Printing was then unknown, and the making of copies by hand was slow and laborious work. Morever, it was an age of persecution, when precious Christian writings had to be kept hid. And, there were no church councils or conferences, where Christians from distant parts could come together and compare notes on what writings they had, till the days of Constantine. So, naturally, the earliest collections of New Testament books would vary, in different regions; and the process of reaching unanimity as to what books properly belonged in the New Testament was slow.

"Spurious" New Testament Books. Beside the "canonical" New Testament books there were many others, both good and fraudulent, as noted in pages that follow: some so fine and valuable that they were for a while, in some sections, regarded as Scripture; others, that were unadulterated forgeries. The one criterion by which a book was judged before acceptance was whether it was of genuine Apostolic origin. Such investigation was not, in every case easy; especially of less known books of a distant region.

Primitive Testimony to New Testament Books. Extant writings of Christians whose lives overlapped the lives of the Apostles are few; because of the perishable nature of the writing material, and because it was a period of persecution in which Christian writings were destroyed. But, though few, they bear their unimpeachable testimony to the existence, in their day, of a group of authoritative writings which Christians regarded as "Scripture"; and they abound in quotations from, or references to, those writings.

Clement of Rome, in his Epistle to the Corinthians (A.D. 95), quotes from, or refers to, Matthew, Luke, Romans, Corinthians, Hebrews, I Timothy, I Peter.

Polycarp, in his Letter to the Philippians (about A.D. 110), quotes Philippians, and reproduces phrases from nine other of Paul's Epistles and I Peter. He says, "I have letters from you, and from Ignatius. I shall send yours to Syria, as you request; and I am sending the letter of Ignatius to you, with others, and the present one of my own." This indicates that, in Polycarp's day, churches had already begun to gather copies of Christian writings.

Formation of the New Testament

Ignatius, in his Seven Letters, written about A.D. 110, during his journey from Antioch to Rome for his martyrdom, quotes from Matthew, I Peter, I John, cites nine of Paul's Epistles, and his letters bear the impress of the other three Gospels.

Papias, (A.D. 70–155), a pupil of John, wrote "An Explanation of the Lord's Discourses," in which he quotes from John, and records traditions about the origin of Matthew and Mark.

The Didache, written between A.D. 80 and 120, makes 22 quotations from Matthew with references to Luke, John, Acts, Romans, Thessalonians, I Peter; and speaks of "The Gospel" as a written document.

The Epistle of Barnabas, written between A.D. 90 and 120, quotes from Matthew, John, Acts, II Peter; and uses the expression, "It is written," a formula commonly applied only to Scripture.

The Shepherd of Hermas, written about A.D. 100 or 140, the "Pilgrim's Progress" of the ancient church, made use of James, with abundant echoes of other New Testament books.

Tatian, about A.D. 160, made a "Harmony of the Four Gospels," called the "Diatessaron," an evidence that Four Gospels, and only Four, were generally recognized among the churches.

Justin Martyr, born about the year that John died, in his "Apologies," written about A.D. 140, mentions Revelation, and shows knowledge of Acts and eight Epistles. He calls the Gospels the "Memoirs of the Apostles," and says that they were read in Christian assemblies alternately with the "Prophets."

Basilides, a Gnostic heretic who taught in Alexandria in the reign of Hadrian (117–138), and who claimed to have knowledge of secret traditions handed down from the Apostles, in his written efforts to distort accepted Christian teachings, quotes from Matthew, Luke, John, Romans, I Corinthians, Ephesians, Colossians, as accepted Christian Scriptures.

Marcion, another heretic (about A.D. 140), in the interest of his heresy, made a canon of his own, consisting of Luke, Romans, I & II

Corinthians, Galatians, Ephesians, Philippians, Colossians, I & II Thessalonians, Philemon.

Irenaeus (A.D. 130–200), a pupil of Polycarp, quotes most of the New Testament books as "Scripture," which, in his time, had come to be known as "The Gospel and the Apostles," as the Old Testament books were called "The Law and the Prophets."

Tertullian (A.D. 160–220), of Carthage, living while the original manuscripts of the Epistles were still in existence, speaks of the Christian Scriptures as the "New Testament" (which title first appears in the writing of an unknown author about A.D. 193). In Tertullian's extant writings there are 1800 quotations from New Testament books. In his work "Against Heretics" he says:

"If you are willing to exercise your curiosity profitably in the business of your salvation, visit the Apostlic churches in which the very chairs of the Apostles still preside in their places; in which their very authentic Epistles are read, sounding forth the voice and representing the countenance of each of them. Is Achaia near you? You have Corinth. If you are not far from Macedonia, you have Philippi and Thessalonica. If you can go to Asia, you have Ephesus. If you are near Italy, you have Rome."

The Muratorian Fragment, made in Rome, about A.D. 170, contains a list of the Christian Scriptures. It omits Hebrews, I & II Peter, and James; but includes the Book of Wisdom and Apocalypse of Peter.

The Old Syriac Version, made about the middle of the second century A.D. omits James, I & II Peter, I, II, & III John, Jude, Revelation.

The Old Latin Version, made about the middle of the second century A.D. omits Hebrews, James, II Peter.

Origen (185–254), of Alexandria, a Christian scholar of extensive travel and great learning, devoted his life to the study of the Scripture. He wrote so extensively that at times he employed as many as twenty copyists. In his extant writings Two-Thirds of the entire New Testament can be found in quotations. He accepted the 27 books of the New Testament as we have them, though not sure of the authorship of Hebrews, and expressed doubt as to James, II Peter, II & III John.

What Books Constituted the New Testament? From the above citations, and that of Eusebius (on the page following), it will be seen that, for a while, there was slight variation as to what books were regarded as canonical. This was due simply to the fact that, on account of slow means of communication over the vast expanse of the Roman Empire, and on account of three hundred years of incessant and unrelenting persecution, there was not one single chance for the churches to make a fair and open and reasonable effort to come to general unanimity as to what books were of genuine Apostolic Authority, till Constantine, at the beginning of the 4th Century, issued his Edict of Toleration.

What about the "Doubtful" Books? They were not "doubtful" in regions where they first appeared. The exigencies of the times hindered their becoming widely known for a while. The fact that they were slow in being generally received is a testimony to the carefulness of the churches against impostors.

Formation of the New Testament

Eusebius (A.D. 264–340), bishop of Caesarea, Church Historian, lived through, and was imprisoned during Diocletian's persecution of Christians, which was Rome's final effort to blot out the Christian Name. One of its special objects was the destruction of all Christian Scriptures. For ten years Bibles were hunted by the agents of Rome, and burned in public market places. To Christians, the question of just what books composed their Scriptures was no idle matter.

Eusebius lived into the reign of Constantine, who accepted Christianity. Eusebius became Constantine's chief religious adviser. One of Constantine's first acts on ascending the throne was to order, for the churches of Constantinople, FIFTY BIBLES, to be prepared, under the direction of Eusebius, by skillful copyists, on the finest of vellum, and to be delivered by royal carriages from Caesarea to Constantinople. He wrote, in his order to Eusebius:

"I have thought it expedient to instruct your Prudence to order fifty copies of the Sacred Scriptures, the provision and use of which you know to be most needful for the instruction of the church, to be written on prepared parchment, in a legible manner, and in a commodious and portable form, by transcribers thoroughly practiced in their art. * * You have authority also, by virtue of this letter, to use two of the public carriages for their conveyance; by which arrangement, the copies, when fairly written, will most easily be forwarded for my personal inspection. One of the deacons of your church may be entrusted with this service, who, on his arrival here, shall experience my liberality. God preserve you, beloved brother."

What books constituted the New Testament of Eusebius? Exactly the same books that now constitute the New Testament.

Eusebius, by extensive research, made himself informed as to what books had been generally accepted by the churches. In his Church History he speaks of four classes of books:

1. Those universally accepted.
2. The "disputed" books: James, II Peter, Jude, II & III John, which, though included in his own Bibles, were doubted by some.
3. The "spurious" books: among which he mentions the "Acts of Paul," "Shepherd of Hermas," "Apocalypse of Peter," "Epistle of Barnabas" and "Didache."

4. "Forgeries of heretics"; "Gospel of Peter," "Gospel of Thomas," "Gospel of Matthias," "Acts of Andrew," "Acts of John."

The Council of Carthage (A.D. 397), gave its formal ratification to the 27 books of the New Testament as we know them, expressing what had already become the unanimous judgment of the churches, and accepted for itself THE BOOK that was destined to become MAN'S MOST PRECIOUS HERITAGE.

Modern Criticism

The Bible, with its 27-book New Testament canon, as accepted by the Early Christian Fathers, and finally ratified by the Council of Carthage, became, without further questioning, the recognized Bible of Christendom for a thousand years.

With the rise of the modern critical spirit came a renewed investigation into the origin and authenticity of the Bible books, as well as of all ancient books.

"Criticism," as applied to the Bible, is a rather unfortunate term, although with many irreverent wiseacres it has been exactly that, insomuch that the word is quite commonly regarded as being the name of the modern intellectual effort to undermine the Divine Authority of the Bible. So far as the word means critical and fair examination of facts, or alleged facts, in an honest search for historical truth, it is natural, reasonable and legitimate, and enlarges our knowledge of the Scripture.

Historical Criticism. This has to do with the genuineness and authenticity of the Bible books: that is, Who wrote each book, and When, and whether the book is Historical or otherwise.

In relation to the New Testament books, it is merely the re-opening of the question settled by, and to the satisfaction of, the First Generations of Christian fathers. Modern critics have made no more determined nor scholarly effort to ascertain the genuineness of the New Testament books than was made by the generations in which the books were first published. Indeed they were in far better position to determine the nature of those books than later critics. It is not easy to wreck a train long after it has gone by. Literary forgeries are soon detected. Whether a book is historical or fictional is recognized on publication. If I were to write a history of the American Revolutionary War, and sign George Washington's name to it, could I make anybody believe that Washington wrote it?

One of the unfortunate things about the critics who have discarded the traditional view of the origins of the Bible books is their presumption to themselves of a monopoly of "scholarship." Their opinion is the "unanimous opinion of scholarship." Are they so narrow-minded as to think that only those who hold to their theories are scholars? Viewpoint is not an indication of scholarship, but only of type of mind. The dear Old Book has worn out many anvils, and long after the critics have been forgotten will go marching on loved and honored by unnumbered millions. Precious Book!

Textual Criticism. This is the comparison of various manuscripts to ascertain the exact original text from which they are copied. It has resulted in the Old Testament Massoretic Hebrew and New Testament Westcott and Hort Greek texts, which, in the main, are the exact original Bible words. Printing removed the danger of textual errors.

Apocryphal New Testament Books

These are legendary and spurious Gospels, Acts of the Apostles and Epistles, which began to appear in the 2nd Century. They were mostly forgeries, and were so recognized from the first. "They are so full of nonsensical stories of Christ and the Apostles, that they have never been regarded as divine, nor bound in our Bible." "Deliberate attempts to fill the gaps of the New Testament story of Jesus, in order to further heretical ideas by false claims."

There are known to have been about 50 of the spurious "Gospels," besides many "Acts" and "Epistles." The great mass of these forged writings made it very important for the Early Church to distinguish between the false and the true.

It is said that Mohammed got his ideas of Christianity largely from these books. They are the origin of some of the dogmas of the Roman Catholic Church.

They are not to be confused with the writings of the "Apostolic Fathers," mentioned on the second page following.

Here is a list of some of the best known:

Gospel of Nicodemus. Embodies "Acts of Pilate," an alleged official report of the trial of Jesus to Emperor Tiberius. Produced in the 2nd or 5th century. Purely imaginary.

Protevangelium of James. Narrative from the birth of Mary to the slaughter of the Innocents. Stories that had begun to circulate in the 2nd century. Completed in the 5th century.

Passing of Mary. Abounds in silly miracles, and culminates in the removal of "her spotless and precious body" to Paradise. Written in the 4th century, with the rise of Virgin worship.

Gospel according to the Hebrews. Additions to the canonical Gospels, with some alleged sayings of Jesus. About A.D. 100.

Gospel of the Ebionites. Compiled from the synoptic Gospels, in interest of Ebionite doctrine. Between 2nd and 4th centuries.

Gospel of the Egyptians. Imaginary conversations between Jesus and Salome. Between A.D. 130 and 150. Used by the Sabellians.

Gospel of Peter. Middle of 2nd century. Based on canonical Gospels. Written in interest of Anti-Jewish, Docetic doctrines.

Gospel of Pseudo-Matthew. A 5th century forged translation of Matthew, abounding with the childhood miracles of Jesus.

Gospel of Thomas. 2nd century. Jesus' life from 5th to 12th year. Makes him a miracle worker to satisfy boyish whims.

Nativity of Mary. A deliberate forgery of 6th century, to further worship of Virgin Mary. Stories about daily visits of angels to Mary. With Papal growth it became immensely popular.

Arabic Gospel of the Childhood. 7th century. Stories of miracles during the sojourn in Egypt. Extremely fantastic.

Gospel of Joseph the Carpenter. 4th century. Originated in Egypt. Devoted to the glorification of Joseph.

Apocalypse of Peter. Purported visions of heaven and hell, granted to Peter. Called "spurious" by Eusebius.

Acts of Paul. Middle of 2nd century. A romance inculcating continence. Contains the supposed lost Epistle to the Corinthians.

Acts of Peter. End of 2nd century. A love affair of Peter's daughter. Conflict with Simon Magus. Contains "Quo vadis" story.

Acts of John. End of 2nd century. Story of a visit to Rome. Purely imaginary. Contains a revolting picture of sensuality.

Acts of Andrew. Story of Andrew persuading Maximilla to refrain from intercourse with her husband, resulting in his martyrdom.

Acts of Thomas. End of 2nd century. Like Acts of Andrew, a travel-romance, in interest of abstinence from sexual intercourse.

Letter of Peter to James. End of 2nd century. A violent attack on Paul. A pure fabrication in interest of the Ebionites.

The Epistle from Laodicea. Professes to be the one referred to in Colossians 4:16. A lot of Paul's phrases strung together.

Letters of Paul to Seneca, with Letters from Seneca to Paul. A 4th century forgery. Object: either to commend Christianity to the followers of Seneca, or to commend Seneca to Christians.

The main characteristic of these writings is that they are Fiction representing itself as History, but for the most part they are so utterly absurd that their falsity is self-evident.

The Abgarus Letters. These may have some basis of fact. Eusebius thought so. He relates that Abgarus, king of Edessa, sick, heard of Jesus' power, and wrote a letter begging Jesus to come and heal him; to which Jesus wrote answer: "It is necessary that those things for which I was sent should be completed, after which I shall be received up to Him who sent me. When, therefore, I shall be received into heaven, I will send one of my disciples who shall heal you." Accordingly, Thaddeus is said to have been sent, and was shown the Letters in the archives of Edessa. Possibly Jesus may have sent such a message verbally, which they recorded.

Writings of the Apostolic Fathers

These should not be confused with the false books, enumerated on the two preceding pages, in which the authors assumed names of Apostles to give credence to legendary tales.

The Apostolic Fathers (more exactly, the "Sub-Apostolic Fathers") were those whose lives overlapped the Apostolic generation. Their extant writings are few (how we wish there were more of them!), due to the perishable nature of their writing material, and to the persecutions of their day.

But they are extremely valuable, as they form the connecting link between the Apostles and later Church History. Some of them were so highly regarded that, in some localities, they were temporarily regarded as Scripture.

Epistle of Clement to the Corinthians. A.D. 95. Clement was a bishop of Rome (A.D. 91–100). A companion of Paul and Peter. He must have been acquainted with John. Wrote this Epistle the year that John was banished to Patmos. Said to have been condemned to the mines, and suffered martyrdom in the 3rd year of Trajan. Thought, possibly, to have been the Clement mentioned in Philippians 4:3.

This Epistle was occasioned by a division in the Corinthian church in which some Elders were excluded by younger worldly men. It was written in the name of the Roman church, is full of beautiful exhortations to humility, and dwells much on the resurrection. It was so highly esteemed that it was read publicly in many churches down to the 4th century. It was found, at the end of the New Testament in the Alexandrian manuscript of the Bible.

Epistle of Polycarp to the Philippians. About A.D. 110. Polycarp, pupil of John, bishop of Smyrna, wrote a number of letters, but this only is extant. It was in reply to a letter from the Philippians asking his advice. It reads very much like Paul's Epistles, which he commends to their careful study.

Epistles of Ignatius. About A.D. 110. Ignatius was a pupil of John, and bishop of Antioch. He suffered martyrdom in Rome A.D. 110. On his way from Antioch to Rome, passing through Asia Minor, he wrote Seven Epistles: To the Ephesians, Magnesians, Trallians, Philadelphians, Smyrnaeans, Romans and Polycarp. These Epistles of Ignatius abound in tender exhortations, and breathe a spirit of rejoicing at the prospect of his impending martyrdom. They emphasize the evil of heresy and division, and counsel submission to the elders of the church.

Epistle of Barnabas. Written between A.D. 90 and 120. Some think it was the New Testament Barnabas, but others question it. The Epistle is a General Epistle, addressed to all Christians, containing a sort of outline interpretation of Scripture. It was found in the Sinaitic manuscript of the Bible, at the end of New Testament, which indicates the high regard in which it was held.

The Papias' Fragments. Papias was a pupil of John, bishop of Hierapolis. Martyred about same time as Polycarp. He wrote an "Explanation of the Lord's Discourses," which was extant down to the 13th century. But now only fragments remain in quotations in Irenaeus, Eusebius and others.

The Didache, or Teaching of the Twelve. Written between 80 and 120, probably about A.D. 100. Not a genuine composition of the Apostles, but only a statement, by some unknown author, of what he understood those teachings to be. Resembles the Epistle of James. Early writers denied its canonicity, but held it in high regard. It abounds in quotations from New Testament books.

Shepherd of Hermas. Written about A.D. 100 or 140. Earliest example of Christian Allegory, the "Pilgrim's Progress" of the primitive Church. The writer was intensely religious, and saw visions which he wrote in this book, emphasizing repentance, spiritual life and the near Advent of the Lord. The book was read in many churches down to the time of Jerome. It is contained in the Sinaitic manuscript of the Bible, at close of New Testament. That the author was the Hermas of Romans 16:14 is only a guess.

Apology of Aristides. A philosopher of Athens. He wrote a "Defense of Christianity," to Hadrian, A.D. 125, and to Antonius, A.D. 137, appealing for protection of Christians against persecution. He said, "Blessed is the race of Christians above all men, because of their true and noble creed, and their pure and benevolent lives." Earliest known literary tribute of a philosopher to Christianity. From Athens, the home of philosophy.

Justin Martyr (A.D. 100–167). A philosopher, who, after trying Stoic, Peripatetic, Pythagorean, and Platonic philosophies, found satisfaction in Christianity. He wrote "Apologies," addressed to the Emperor Antoninus, in defense of Christianity. He also wrote a "Dialogue with Trypho," which was an argument with a Jew over the Messiahship of Jesus.

II Epistle of Clement. Between A.D. 120 and 140. A sermon. Uncertain whether it was the same Clement.

Epistle of Diognetus. A vindication of Christianity, by an unknown author who claimed he was "a disciple of the Apostles."

Manuscripts

The original manuscripts of all the New Testament books, as far as is known, have been lost.

Copies of these precious writings began to be made from the very first, for other churches; and copies of copies, generation after generation, as the older ones wore out.

The writing material in common use was Papyrus, made of slices of the water plant that grew in Egypt. Two slices, one vertical, the other horizontal, were pressed together and polished. Ink was made of charcoal, gum and water.

Single sheets were used for short compositions. For longer, sheets were fastened, side to side, to form rolls. A roll was usually about 30 feet long, and 9 or 10 inches high.

In the 2nd century A.D. the New Testament books began to be made up in "Codex" form, that is, modern book form, in which any number of leaves could be put into one volume, with numbered pages.

Papyrus was not very durable. It became brittle with age, or rotted with dampness, and soon wore out; except in Egypt, where the dry climate and shifting sands have preserved for discovery in our own times an amazing collection of ancient documents.

In 4th century A.D. Papyrus was superseded by Vellum as the main writing material. Vellum was parchment made from skins; much more durable; and made up in book form.

Until the recent discovery of the Egyptian Papyri, all known extant manuscripts of the Bible were on Vellum.

With the invention of Printing in the 15th century the making of manuscript Bibles ceased.

There are now in existence about 4000 known manuscripts of the Bible, or parts of the Bible, made between the 2nd and 15th centuries. This seems few to us, but it is far more than the manuscripts of any other ancient writings. There is not a complete known copy of Homer earlier than A.D. 1300; nor of Herodotus earlier than A.D. 1000.

The Vellum manuscripts now known are called "Uncials" and "Cursives." The Uncials were written in large capital letters. There are about 160 of them, made between the 4th and 10th centuries. The Cursives were written in small running letters linked together, and were made between the 10th and 15th centuries. The Uncials, being more ancient, are far more valuable.

The three oldest, completest, best known and most valuable manuscripts are: the Sinaitic, Vatican and Alexandrian, which were originally complete Bibles.

The Sinaitic Manuscript, or "Codex Sinaiticus," was found by a German scholar named Tischendorf (1844), at the Monastery of St. Catherine on Mt. Sinai. He noticed, in a waste basket of leaves set aside to be burned, vellum pages with Greek writing. On closer examination they proved to be parts of an ancient manuscript of the Septuagint Old Testament. There were 43 leaves. He searched, and searched, but could find no more. In 1853 he returned to the Monastery to continue the search, but found nothing. Again, in 1859, he returned. As he talked with the steward about the Septuagint, the steward remarked that he had an ancient copy of it, and he brought it forth wrapped in a paper napkin. It was the rest of the manuscript of which Tischendorf had seen the 43 leaves 15 years before. As he looked through its pages he realized that he held in his hand the most precious writing in existence. After long international negotiations it was finally secured for the Imperial Library in St. Petersburg, where it remained till 1933, when it was sold to the British Museum at the price of half a million dollars. It contains 199 leaves of the Old Testament, and the entire New Testament with the Epistle of Barnabas and part of the Shepherd of Hermas, on 148 leaves, making 347 leaves in all, written in beautiful hand on the finest of vellum, the leaves 15 by 13½ inches. It was made in the first half of the 4th century. It is the only ancient manuscript that contains the entire New Testament. The 43 leaves which Tischendorf secured on his first visit are in the University Library at Leipzig.

The Vatican Manuscript. Made in 4th century. In the Vatican Library since 1481. Some fragments of New Testament missing.

The Alexandrian. Made in 5th century, at Alexandria. In the British Museum since 1627. Entire Bible, with some fragments missing, and Epistles of Clement and Psalms of Solomon.

Others. The "Ephraem," 5th century, now in Paris, about half New Testament. The "Beza," 5th century, now in University of Cambridge, Gospels and Acts. The "Washington," 4th century, found in Egypt 1906, now in Smithsonian Library at Washington, the Gospels.

Printed Bibles

The Invention of Printing, from movable type, by John Gutenberg (A.D. 1454), made Bibles cheap and abundant, and greatly promoted the circulation and influence of the Bible among the people. Previously the price of a Bible was a year's wages. Gutenberg's first printed book was the Bible. One of them is in the Library of Congress at Washington, for which $350,000 was paid.

The Papyri

Their Discovery. Flinders Petrie, in excavations in central Egypt, noticed old sheets of papyrus appearing in rubbish heaps that had been buried beneath the sand, and suggested that they might be valuable. Two of his pupils, Grenfell and Hunt, Oxford students, began, in 1895, a systematic search for these papyri. In the following ten years, at Oxyrhynchus, and nearby places, they found 10,000 manuscripts and parts of manuscripts. Other excavators, also, found great quantities of similar manuscripts. They were dug out of sand-covered rubbish heaps, stuffings in mummy cases, and embalmed crocodile bodies. They consisted mostly of letters, bills, receipts, diaries, certificates, almanacs, etc. Some of them were valuable historical documents dating as far back as 2000 B.C. Most of them, however, dated from 300 B.C. to A.D. 300. Among them were some early Christian writings, which is the thing that makes them of interest to the Bible student.

Fragment of John's Gospel. A tiny scrap of Papyrus, 3½ by 2½ inches, containing on one side John 18:31–33, and on the other side John 18:37–38. It is a part of one leaf of a manuscript that had been originally 130 pages 8¼ by 8 inches. Comparing the shape of the letters and the style of writing with certain dated manuscripts, scholars assign it to the first part of the 2nd century. It is the oldest known Bible manuscript, and is evidence that the Gospel of John was in existence, and was in circulation in Egypt, in the years immediately following the death of John. It was found in 1920; is now in the Rylands Library, Manchester, England.

Gospels and Acts. Among the papyri are 30 imperfect leaves, containing parts of Matthew, Mark, Luke, John, and Acts, made in the early part of the 3rd century. It is a part of what is known as the Chester Beatty collection.

Paul's Epistles, consisting of 86 leaves, out of what had been 104, contains Romans, Hebrews, I & II Corinthians, Ephesians, Galatians, Philippians, Colossians, I & II Thessalanians. It was written about A.D. 200. Belongs to the Chester Beatty Collection of Papyri.

The Chester Beatty Collection also contains some manuscripts of Genesis, Numbers, Deuteronomy, Isaiah, Jeremiah, Ezekiel, Daniel, Esther, and about one-third of Revelation. It was published in 1931. Is owned partly by the University of Michigan. It is considered the most important discovery bearing on the text of the Bible since the discovery of the Sinaitic manuscript, and is valuable evidence for the authenticity and integrity of the New Testament books.

The Logia. Besides the many fragments of papyrus leaves containing parts of Bible books, there were some that contained hitherto unrecorded Sayings of Jesus, current in the 3rd century. And some with portions of an unknown Gospel, with parallels to the canonical Gospels; and many fragments containing similar incidents from Jesus' life.

The Language of the Papyri. Adolph Deissman, a German scholar, noticed that the Greek of the Papyri was the same as New Testament Greek, and not the classic Greek of the age of Pericles. There are 500 words in the Greek New Testament not found in classic Greek at all. This discovery that the New Testament was thus written in the every day language of the common people gave impulse to the modern speech translations of the New Testament that have recently appeared.

Ancient Translations

The Old Testament was written in Hebrew. The New Testament

was written in Greek. A Greek translation of the Old Testament called "The Septuagint," made in the 3rd century B.C. was in common use in Jesus' day. Greek was the language in general use throughout the Roman world.

The Old Syriac. Made in the 2nd century A.D. for use among the Syrians. No complete manuscripts extant.

The Peshito Syriac. Made in the 4th century. Based on the Old Syriac, which it completely superceded. "Peshito" means "simple." There were other later Syriac versions.

The Old Latin. Made in the 2nd century. Its Old Testament was translated, not from the Hebrew, but the Septuagint.

The Vulgate. A revision of the old Latin, by Jerome, A.D. 382–404. Its Old Testament, except the Psalms, was direct from the Hebrew. It became the Bible of the West for a thousand years.

The Coptic. The vernacular language of Egypt. Made in 2nd century A.D. A number of versions followed.

Other Translations. In the 4th century, Ethiopic and Gothic. In the 5th century, Armenian. 9th century, Arabic and Slavic.

With the growth of the Papacy the Bible fell into general disuse, being supplanted by the decrees and dogmas of councils and Popes.

With the Protestant Reformation came a renewed interest in the Bible, until now the Bible, or parts of it, is translated into more than a thousand languages and dialects. It is estimated that nine-tenths of the whole world's population, at the present time, may read or hear the Bible in their own language.

English Translations

Caedmon (A.D. 676), Bede (672–735), Alfred the Great (849–901), translated short parts of the Bible into Anglo-Saxon, followed by a few later fragmentary attempts.

Wyclif's Bible (A.D. 1382). First English Bible. Translated from the Vulgate. In manuscript only, because it was before the invention of printing. Not widely circulated, but reached the people, and was one of the main factors in paving the way for the Reformation. The Pope was against him. He was excommunicated, and, after death, his bones burned and cast into the river.

Tyndale's Bible (1525). Translated from the original Greek and Hebrew. More accurate than Wyclif's. Tyndale, persecuted, fled from England to Hamburg, then to Cologne and Worms, where his New Testament was printed, and smuggled into England in bales of merchandise. For translating the Bible into the language of the people, by order of the priesthood, he was burned, Oct. 6, 1536.

Coverdale's Bible (1535). From Dutch and Latin sources. This was followed by Roger's Bible (1537), which was almost wholly copied from Tyndale's. And by "The Great Bible" (1539), which was a compilation from Tyndale, Rogers and Coverdale.

Geneva Bible (1560). By a group of Protestant scholars, who had fled to Geneva. Based mainly on Tyndale's with strongly Calvinistic notes. Became very popular. Followed by the "Bishop's Bible" (1568), authorized for the Church of England.

King James' Version (1611). Ordered by King James, for the sake of uniform service in Presbyterian Scotland and Episcopal England. A revision of versions based on Tyndale's. For 300 years it has been the household Bible of the English-speaking world.

Anglo-American Revision (1881–1885). The work of 51 English and 32 American scholars. Became necessary because of changes in the meaning of some English words, and a purer text. It follows the King James Version, except where a word needed to be changed. In 1901 an American Edition was issued, embodying slight changes preferred by the American Revision Committee. In 1952 a further Revision was issued, known as the "Revised Standard Version."

Italics, in our Bibles, indicate that the word is lacking in the original text, and filled in to complete the sense.

Chapters and Verses, not in the original text, were added by Cardinal Caro (A.D. 1236), and Robert Stephens (A.D. 1551).

Modern Speech Translations

Many and diverse have been the efforts to reproduce in our own language the exact thought of the original. Below is a list of those best known:

The Amplified New Testament. Published 1958 by Zondervan Publishing House, Grand Rapids, Mich. Already has become one of the most popular New Testament translations. Contains brief explanatory notes which are very helpful.

The Amplified Old Testament. Part I. Genesis–Esther. Part II. Job–Malachi. Published by Zondervan Publishing House, Grand Rapids, Mich. Following in the footsteps of its popular predecessor. Includes brief, informative footnotes.

Twentieth Century New Testament. First of the popular modern speech translations. Published 1898. Made by about twenty English scholars. Considered a very good translation.

Weymouth's New Testament. A Baptist layman of England. Published 1903, after his death. Revised, by others, 1924, 1933.

Fenton's Complete Bible in Modern English. Ferrar Fenton, a wealthy Englishman, for years avoided reading the Bible in any but the original languages, that his own translation might not be influenced by other translations. Published 1903.

Moffat's Translation. Moffatt is a Scotchman, who was a Professor in Union Theological Seminary, New York. His New Testament was published in 1913. His Old Testament, 1924. His Bible, 1926.

Ballantine's Riverside New Testament. A Congregational minister, President of Oberlin Theological Seminary. Published 1923.

Smith and Goodspeed. Goodspeed, of Chicago University, published his New Testament in 1923. J. M. Powis Smith, of Chicago University, in collaboration with Gordon of McGill University, Meek of University of Toronto, and Waterman of University of Michigan, published an Old Testament translation in 1923.

Montgomery's Centenary New Testament. Published 1924. Mrs. Montgomery, of Rochester, N.Y., was President of the Northern Baptist Convention in 1921. Her New Testament was a centennial publication of the American Baptist Publication Society.

The New Testament in Basic English. Published 1941. Prepared by S. H. Hooke, of the University of London, with the assistance of eight other eminent scholars. Put into a 1000-word vocabulary of the simplest words in the English language. It has received very general praise in notices in the religious press.

Berkeley Version of the Bible. Published 1959 by Zondervan Publishing House, Grand Rapids, Michigan. Beautifully printed. Easy to read. Said by scholars to be a faithful conveyance of original meanings into modern English. Has brief footnotes which help create interest in Bible reading.

Norlie's New Testament. Published by Zondervan Publishing House. A new translation in easy-to-understand language.

The New English Bible; New Testament. Published in England, 1961, by Oxford and Cambridge university presses.

The Amplified Bible. Published by Zondervan Publishing House, Grand Rapids, Mich. The entire text of the amplified translation for the first time within one cover.

CHURCH HISTORY

The Bible Contains the Story of Christ
The Church Exists to Tell the Story of Christ
Church History is a Continuation of Bible History

To Show Our Connection with the Bible Story, and believing that Church people ought to be familiar with at least the elementary Facts of Church History, we give here a Brief Outline of its main Features, Events and Persons.

It is impossible to understand the Present Condition of Christendom except in the Light of History. But, alas, Ignorance of Church History is more widespread even than Ignorance of the Bible. We believe it is the Duty of Ministers to Teach their people the Facts of Church History.

World History is Thought of in Three Periods:

ANCIENT: Egypt, Assyria, Babylon, Persia, Greece, Rome.
MEDIEVAL: From Fall of Rome to Discovery of America.
MODERN: From 15th Century to Present Time.

Church History is Thought of in Three Periods

ROMAN EMPIRE PERIOD: Persecutions, Martyrs, Church Fathers, Controversies, Christianization of the Roman Empire.

MEDIEVAL PERIOD: Growth and Power of the Papacy, the Inquisition, Monasticism, Mohammedanism, the Crusades.

MODERN PERIOD: Protestant Reformation, Great Growth of Protestant Church, Wide Circulation of Open Bible, Growing Freedom of Civil Governments from Church and Priestly Control, World-Wide Missions, Social Reform, Growing Brotherhood.

The Three Great Divisions of Christendom

PROTESTANT: prevailing in Western Europe and North America.

ROMAN CATHOLIC: prevailing in Southern Europe and South America.

GREEK CATHOLIC: prevailing in Eastern and Southeastern Europe.

These are the result of Two Great Cleavages in the Church. One in the 9th century, when the Eastern Church separated itself from the Western Church.

The Other, in the 16th century, under the leadership of Martin Luther, Greatest man of Modern History.

Harnack said, "The Greek Church is Primitive Christianity, plus Greek and Oriental Paganism. The Roman Catholic Church is Primitive Christianity plus Greek and Roman Paganism."

The Protestant Church is an effort to Restore Primitive Christianity Free from All Paganism.

The Roman Empire

The Church was founded in the Roman Empire.
Rome was founded 753 B.C. Subdued Italy, 343–272 B.C.
Subdued Carthage, 264–146 B.C.
Subdued Greece and Asia Minor, 215–146 B.C.
Subdued Spain, Gaul, Briton, Teutons, 133–31 B.C.

ZENITH OF ROMAN POWER, 46 B.C.–A.D. 180

Extended from the Atlantic to the Euphrates, and from the North Sea to the African Desert. Population, 120,000,000.
Julius Caesar, 46–44 B.C. Lord of the Roman World.
Augustus, 31 B.C.–A.D. 14. In his reign CHRIST was born.
Tiberius, A.D. 12–37. In his reign CHRIST was Crucified.
Caligula, A.D. 37–41. Claudius, A.D. 41–54.
Nero, A.D. 54–68. Persecuted Christians. Executed Paul.
Galba, A.D. 68–69. Otho, Vitelius, A.D. 69.
Vespasian, A.D. 69–79. Destroyed Jerusalem. Titus, A.D. 79–81.
Domitian, A.D. 81–96. Persecuted Christians. Banished John.
Antoninus Pius, A.D. 138–161. Persecuted Christians.
Hadrian, A.D. 117–138. Persecuted Christians.
Antoninus Pius, A.D. 138–161. Persecuted Christians.
Marcus Aurelius, A.D. 161–180. Persecuted Christians.

DECLINE AND FALL OF ROMAN EMPIRE, A.D. 180–476

Commodus, A.D. 180–192.
Barrack Emperors, A.D. 192–284. Appointed by Army. Civil War.
Septimius Severus, A.D. 193–211. Persecuted Christians.
Caracalla, A.D. 218–222. Tolerated Christianity.
Elagabalus, A.D. 218–222. Tolerated Christianity.
Alexander Severus, A.D. 222–235. Favorable to Christianity.
Maximin, A.D. 235–238. Persecuted Christians.
Phillips, A.D. 244–249. Very favorable to Christianity.
Decius, A.D. 249–251. Persecuted Christians Furiously.
Valerian, A.D. 253–260. Persecuted Christians.
Galienus, A.D. 260–268. Favored Christians.
Aurelian, A.D. 270–275. Persecuted Christians.
Diocletian, A.D. 284–305. Persecuted Christians Furiously.

Constantine, A.D. 306–337. Became a Christian Himself.
Julian, A.D. 361–363. The Apostate. Sought to Restore Paganism.
Jovian, A.D. 363–364. Re-Established the Christian Faith.
Theodosius, A.D. 378–395. Made Christianity the State Religion.

THE EMPIRE DIVIDED, A.D. 395

West	*East*
Honorius, A.D. 395–423	Arcadius, A.D. 395–408
Valentinian III, A.D. 423–455	Theodosius II, A.D. 408–450
Western Empire Fell, A.D. 476	Anastasius, A.D. 491–518
at the hands of Barbarians,	Justinian, A.D. 527–565
ushering in the Dark Ages.	Eastern Empire Fell, A.D. 1453

Out of the ruins of the Western Empire arose the Papal Empire, and Rome still Ruled the World for 1000 years.

Christianization of the Roman Empire

Rapid Spread of Christianity. Tertullian (A.D. 160–220), wrote, "We are of yesterday. Yet we have filled your Empire, your Cities, your Towns, your Islands, your Tribes, your Camps, Castles, Palaces, Assemblies and Senate."

By the end of the Imperial Persecutions (A.D. 313), Christians numbered about One-Half the Population of the Roman Empire.

Constantine

His Conversion. In the course of his wars with competitors, to establish himself on the throne, on the eve of the battle of Milvain Bridge, just outside Rome (October 27, A.D. 312), he saw in the sky, just above the setting sun, a vision of the Cross, and above it the words, "In This Sign Conquer." He decided to fight under the banner of Christ, and he Won the Battle, a Turning Point in the history of Christianity.

His Edict of Toleration (A.D. 313). By this Edict, Constantine granted to "Christians and to all others Full Liberty of following that Religion which each may choose," the first edict of its kind in history. He went further. He favored Christians in every way: filled chief offices with them: exempted Christian ministers from taxes and military service; encouraged and helped in building Churches: made Christianity the Religion of his Court: issued a general exhortation (A.D. 325), to all his subjects, to embrace Christianity: and, because the Roman Aristocracy persisted in adhering to their Pagan Religions, Constantine moved his Capitol to Byzantium, and called it Constantinople, "New Rome," Capital of the New Christian Empire.

Constantine and the Bible. He ordered, for the Churches of Constantinople, 50 Bibles, to be prepared under the direction of Eusebius, on the finest vellum, by skillful artists; and he commissioned two Public Carriages for their speedy conveyance to the Emperor. It is possible that the Sinaitic and Vatican Manuscripts are of this group.

Constantine and Sunday. He made the Christians' day of Assembly, Sunday, a Rest Day; forbidding ordinary work; permitting Christian soldiers to attend Church services. This Rest for One Day a week meant much for slaves.

Houses of Worship. The First Church Building was erected in the reign of Alexander Severus (A.D. 222–235). After the edict of Constantine they began to be built everywhere.

Reforms. Slavery, Gladiatorial Fights, Killing of Unwelcome Children, and Crucifixion as a form of execution, were abolished with the Christianization of the Roman Empire.

Paganization of the Church

Emperor Constantine (A.D. 306–337), when he became a Christian, issued an Edict granting Everybody the right to choose his own Religion.

Emperor Theodosius (A.D. 378–398), made Christianity the State Religion of the Roman Empire, and made Church Membership Compulsory. This was the Worst Calamity that has ever befallen the Church. This Forced Conversion filled the Churches with Unregenerate People.

Not only so, Theodosius undertook the Forcible Suppression of all other Religions, and Prohibited Idol Worship. Under his decrees, Heathen Temples were torn down by mobs of Christians, and there was much bloodshed.

Christ had designed to conquer by purely Spiritual and Moral Means. Up to this time Conversion was Voluntary, a Genuine Change in Heart and Life.

But now the Military Spirit of Imperial Rome had entered the Church. The Church had Conquered the Roman Empire. But in reality the Roman Empire had Conquered the Church, by Making the Church over into the Image of the Roman Empire.

The Church had Changed its Nature, had entered its Great Apostasy, had become a Political Organization in the Spirit and Pattern of Imperial Rome, and took its Nose-Dive into the millennium of Papal Abominations.

The Imperial Church of the 4th and 5th centuries had become an entirely different institution from the persecuted church of the first three centuries. In its ambition to Rule it lost and forgot the spirit of Christ.

Worship, at first very simple, was developed into elaborate, stately, imposing ceremonies having all the outward splendor that had belonged to heathen temples.

Ministers became Priests. The term "priest" was not applied to Christian ministers before A.D. 200. It was borrowed from the Jewish system, and from the example of heathen priesthood. Leo I (440–61) prohibited priests from marrying, and Celibacy of priests became a law of the Roman Church.

Conversion of the Barbarians. The Goths, Vandals and Huns who overthrew the Roman Empire accepted Christianity; but to a large extent their conversion was nominal and this further filled the Church with Pagan practices.

Conflicts with Heathen Philosophies. Even as every generation seeks to interpret Christ in terms of its own thinking, so, no sooner had Christianity made its appearance than it began its process of amalgamation with Greek and Oriental Philosophies; and there arose many Sects: Gnosticism, Manichaeism, Montanism, Monarchianism, Arianism, Appolinarianism, Nestorianism, Eutychianism, Monophysites. From the 2nd to the 6th centuries the Church was rent with controversies over these and similar Isms, and almost lost sight of its true mission.

Persecutions

For the Neronic persecution see note under II Timothy, Background of the Epistle, page 635.

Domitian (A.D. 95). Domitian instituted a persecution against Christians. It was short, but extremely violent. Many thousands were slain in Rome and Italy, among them Flavius Clemens, a cousin of the Emperor, and his wife, Flavia Domitilla banished. The Apostle John was banished to Patmos.

Trajan (A.D. 98–117). One of the best Emperors, but felt he should uphold the laws of the Empire; and Christianity was regarded as an illegal religion, because Christians refused to take part in Emperor-worship, and the church was regarded as a secret society, which was forbidden. Christians were not sought out, but when accused were punished. Among those who perished in this reign were Simeon, the brother of Jesus, Bishop of Jerusalem, crucified A.D. 107, and Ignatius, second Bishop of Antioch, who was taken to Rome and thrown to the wild beasts (A.D. 110). Pliny, who was sent by the Emperor to Asia Minor, where Christians had become so numerous that the heathen temples were almost forsaken, to punish Christians, wrote to the Emperor Trajan: "They affirmed that the sum of their crime or their error, whichever it was, was this: they used to meet on a stated day before light, and to sing among themselves, in turn, a hymn to Christ, as to a god, and to bind themselves by an oath, not to any wickedness, but that they would never commit theft, or robbery, nor adultery; that they would never break their word; that they would never deny a trust when called to give it up; and after these performances, their way was to separate, and then meet again to partake of ordinary food."

Hadrian (117–138), persecuted the Christians, but in moderation. Telephorus, pastor of the Roman church, and many others suffered martyrdom. However, in this reign, Christianity made marked progress in numbers, wealth, learning and social influence.

Antonius Pius (138–161). This emperor rather favored the Christians, but felt he had to uphold the law; and there were many martyrs, among them Polycarp.

Marcus Aurelius (161–180). Like Hadrian he regarded the maintenance of the state religion a political necessity; but unlike Hadrian he encouraged persecution of Christians. It was cruel and barbarous, the severest since Nero. Many thousands were beheaded or thrown to wild beasts, among them Justin Martyr. Very ferocious in South Gaul. The tortures of the victims, endured without flinching, almost surpasses belief. Tortured from morning till night, Blandina, a female slave, would only exclaim, "I am a Christian; among us no evil is done."

Septimius Severus (193–211). This persecution was very severe, but not general. Egypt and North Africa suffered most. In Alexandria "many martyrs were daily burned, crucified or beheaded," among them Leonidas, the father of Origen. In Carthage, Perpetua, a noble lady, and her faithful slave, Felicitas, torn to pieces by wild beasts.

Maximin (235–238). In this reign many prominent Christian leaders were put to death. Origen escaped by hiding.

Decius (249–251), resolutely determined to exterminate Christianity. His persecution was coextensive with the Empire, and very violent; multitudes perished under the most cruel tortures, in Rome, North Africa, Egypt, Asia Minor. Cyprian said, "The whole world is devastated."

Valerian (253–260). More severe than Decius; he aimed at the utter destruction of Christianity. Many leaders were executed, among them Cyprian, Bishop of Carthage.

Diocletian (284–305). The last Imperial persecution, and the most severe; coextensive with the Empire. For ten years Christians were hunted in cave and forest; they were burned, thrown to wild beasts, put to death by every torture cruelty could devise. It was a resolute, determined, systematic effort to abolish the Christian Name.

The Catacombs of Rome

Vast subterranean galleries, commonly 8 to 10 feet wide, 4 to 6 feet high, extending for hundreds of miles beneath the city. Used by Christians as places for refuge, worship and burial in the Imperial persecutions. Christian graves are variously estimated at between 2,000,000 and 7,000,000. More than 4000 inscriptions have been found belonging to the period between Tiberius and Constantine.

Church Fathers

Polycarp (A.D. 69–156). Pupil of the Apostle John, Bishop of Smyrna. In the persecution ordered by the Emperor he was arrested and brought before the Governor, and, when offered his freedom if he would curse Christ, he replied "Eighty and six years have I served Christ and He has done me nothing but good; how then could I curse Him, my Lord and Savior?" He was burned alive.

Ignatius (A.D. 67–110). A pupil of John; bishop of Antioch. The Emperor Trajan, on a visit to Antioch, ordered Ignatius to be arrested; himself presided at the trial, and sentenced him to be thrown to the wild beasts at Rome. En route to Rome, he wrote a letter to the Roman Christians begging them not to try to procure his pardon; that he longed for the honor of dying for his Lord; saying, "May the wild beasts be eager to rush upon me. If they be unwilling I will compel them. Come, crowds of wild beasts; come, tearings and manglings, wracking of bones and hacking of limbs; come, cruel tortures of the devil; only let me attain unto Christ."

Papias (About A.D. 70–155). Another pupil of the Apostle John; bishop of Hierapolis, about 100 miles east of Ephesus. He may have known Philip, whom tradition says died in Hierapolis. He wrote a book, "Explanation of the Lord's Discourses," in which he says he made it a point to inquire of the Elders the exact words of Jesus. He suffered martyrdom at Pergamum, about same time as Polycarp. Polycarp, Ignatius, Papias, form the connecting link between the apostolic age and later.

Justin Martyr (A.D. 100–167). Born at Neapolis, ancient Shechem, about the time John died. Studied philosophy. In youth saw a good deal of persecution of Christians. Became a convert. Traveled in a philosopher's robe, seeking to win men to Christ. Wrote a Defense of Christianity addressed to the Emperor. One of the ablest men of his time. Died a martyr at Rome. Showing the growth of Christianity, he said that already, in his day, "there is no race of men where prayers are not offered up in the name of Jesus."

Here is Justin Martyr's picture of early Christian worship: "On Sunday a meeting is held of all who live in the cities and villages, and a section is read from the Memoirs of the Apostles and the writings of the Prophets, as long as time permits. When the reading is finished, the president, in a discourse, gives the admonition and exhortation to imitate these noble things. After this we all arise and offer a common prayer. At the close of the prayer, as we have before described, bread and wine and thanks for them according to his ability, and the congregation answers, 'Amen.' Then the consecrated elements are distributed to each one and partaken of, and are carried by the deacons to the houses of the absent. The wealthy and the willing then give contributions according to their freewill; and this collection is deposited with the president, who therewith supplies orphans, widows, prisoners, strangers, and all who are in want."

Iranaeus (A.D. 130–200). Brought up in Smyrna. Pupil of Polycarp and Papias. Traveled widely. Became bishop of Lyons, in Gaul. Noted chiefly for his books against the Gnostics. Died a martyr. Here in his reminiscence of Polycarp: "I remember well the place in which the holy Polycarp sat and spoke. I remember the discourses he delivered to the people, and how he described his relations with John, the apostle, and others who had been with the Lord; how he recited the sayings of Christ and the miracles he wrought; how he received his teachings from eyewitnesses who had seen the Word of Life, agreeing in every way with the Scriptures."

Origen. (185–254). The most learned man of the ancient church. A great traveler; and a voluminous writer, employing at times as many as twenty copyists. Two-thirds of the New Testament is quoted in his writings. He lived in Alexandria, where his father Leonidas, suffered martyrdom; later, in Palestine, where he died as a result of imprisonment and torture under Decius.

Tertullian. (160–220), of Carthage; "The father of Latin Christianity," a Roman lawyer, a pagan, after conversion, became a distinguished defender of Christianity.

Eusebius (264–340), "Father of Church History"; Bishop of Caesarea at the time of Constantine's conversion; had great influence with Constantine; wrote an "Ecclesiastical History"—from Christ to the Council of Nicaea.

John Chrysostom (345–407), "the Golden-mouthed," a matchless orator; greatest preacher of his day, an expository preacher, born at Antioch, became Patriarch of Constantinople, preached to great multitudes, in church of St. Sophia, a reformer, he displeased the king, was banished and died in exile.

Jerome (340–420), "most learned of the Latin Fathers," educated at Rome, lived many years at Bethlehem, translated the Bible into the Latin language, called the Vulgate.

Augustine. (354–430). Bishop of Hippo, North Africa. The great theologian of the early church. More than any other he molded the doctrines of the church of the Middle Ages.

Early Infidels

Celsus (A.D. 180), most famous early literary opponent of Christianity. No argument advanced since but what can be found in his writings. Many ideas now parading as "modern" are old as Celsus.

Porphyry (A.D. 233–300), also exerted a powerful influence against Christianity.

Ecumenical Councils

Nicaea. (A.D. 325). Condemned Arianism.
Constantinople. (381). Called to settle Apollinarianism.
Ephesus. (431). Called to settle the Nestorian Controversy.
Chalcedon. (451). Called to settle the Eutychian Controversy.
Constantinople. (553). To settle Monophysites Controversy.
Constantinople. (680). Doctrine of Two Wills in Christ.
Nicaea. (787). Sanctioned Image Worship.
Constantinople. (869). Final Schism between East and West.
Rome. (1123). Decided Bishops be appointed by Popes.
Rome. (1139). An effort to heal Schism of East and West.
Rome. (1179). To enforce ecclesiastical discipline.
Rome. (1215). To do the bidding of Innocent III.
Lyons. (1245). To settle quarrel of Pope and Emperor.
Lyons. (1274). A new effort for union of East and West.
Vienne. (1311). Suppressed the Templars.
Constance. (1414–18). To heal Papal Schism. Burned Huss.
Basel. (1431–49). To reform Church.
Rome. (1512–18). Another effort to reform.
Trent. (1545–63). To counteract the Reformation.
Vatican. (1869–70). Declared the Infallibility of the Pope.
Vatican. (October 11, 1962–). An effort to bring Christendom into one church. Largest ever.

Monasticism

Started in Egypt with Anthony (A.D. 250–350) who retired to the desert and lived in solitude. Multitudes followed his example. The movement spread to Palestine, Syria, Asia Minor and Europe. In the East each lived in his own cave or hut or on his pillar. In Europe they lived in communities called Monasteries, dividing their time between work and religious exercises. They became very numerous, and there arose many orders of monks and nuns. The Monasteries of Europe did the best work of the church of the Middle Ages in Christian philanthropy, literature, education and agriculture. But when they grew rich they became grossly immoral. In the Reformation in Protestant countries they soon disappeared, and are dying out in Catholic countries.

The Crusades

The effort of Christendom to regain the Holy Land from the Mohammedans. There were seven:
First (1095–1099); Captured Jerusalem.
Second (1147–1149); postponed the fall of Jerusalem.
Third (1189–1191); army failed to reach Jerusalem.
Fourth (1201–1204); captured and plundered Constantinople.
Fifth (1228–1229); took Jerusalem, but soon lost it.
Sixth (1248–1254); a failure.
Seventh (1270–1272); came to naught.

The Crusades were of influence in saving Europe from the Turks, and in opening up intercourse between Europe and the East, paving the way for the Revival of Learning.

Mohammedanism

Mohammed. Born at Mecca (A.D. 570), grandson of Governor. In youth he visited Syria, came in contact with Christians and Jews, became filled with horror of Idolatry. In 610 he declared himself a Prophet, was rejected at Mecca, 622 fled to Medina, was received, became a warrior, and began to propagate his faith by the Sword, 630 reentered Mecca at the head of an army, destroyed 360 Idols and became filled with enthusiasm for the destruction of Idolatry. Died 632. His successors were called Caliphs.

Rapid Growth. By 634 Syria was conquered; 637, Jerusalem; 638, Egypt; 640, Persia; 689, North Africa; 711, Spain. Thus within a short time the whole of Western Asia and North Africa, the cradle of Christianity, became Mohammedan. Mohammed appeared at a time when the Church had become Paganized with the worship of Images, Relics, Martyrs, Mary and the Saints. In a sense Mohammedanism was a revolt against the Idolatry of the "Christian world"; a judgment on a corrupt and degenerate Church. It itself, however, has proved a worse blight to the nations it conquered. It is a religion of Hate; was propagated by the Sword; has encouraged Slavery, Polygamy and the Degradation of Womanhood.

Battle of Tours, France (A.D. 732), one of the decisive battles of the world. Charles Martel defeated the Moslem army, and saved Europe from Mohammedanism which was sweeping the world like a tidal wave. But for that victory Christianity may have been completely submerged.

Arabians dominated the Mohammedan world (622–1058). The capital was moved to Damascus (661); to Bagdad in 750, where it remained till 1258.

Turks have ruled the Mohammedan world from 1058 to modern times. They were far more intolerant and cruel than the Arabians

Their barbarous treatment of Christians in Palestine led to the Crusades.

Mongols, from central Asia, arrested Turkish Rule under Genghis Khan (1206–1227), who, at the head of vast armies, traversed with sword and torch a great part of Asia; 50,000 cities and towns were burned; 5,000,000 people murdered; in Asia Minor 630,000 Christians were butchered; Under Tamerlane (1336–1402), a similar hurricane of destruction, route everywhere marked with ruined fields and burned villages and blood. At gate of every city his custom was to build piles of thousands of heads: at Bagdad, 90,000.

Fall of Constantinople (1453), to the Turks, brought to an end the Eastern Roman Empire, and jarred Europe with a second threat of Mohammedan control, which, later was stopped by John Sobieski in the battle of Vienna (1683).

The Papacy was a Gradual Development,
First appearing as a World Power in the 6th century A.D.,
Reaching the Height of its Power in 13th century A.D.,
Declining in Power from 13th century to present time.

Original Mission of the Church

The Church was founded, not as an institution of Authority to Force the Name and Teaching of Christ upon the world, but only as a Witness-Bearing institution to Christ, to hold Him before the people. Christ Himself, not the Church, is the Transforming Power in Human Life. But the Church was founded in the Roman Empire, and gradually developed a form of Government like the Political World in which it existed, becoming a vast Autocratic organization, ruled from the top.

Original Form of Church Government

At the close of the Apostolic age Churches were independent one of another, each being shepherded by a board of Pastors. The main leader came to be called Bishop. The others, later, were called Presbyters. Gradually the jurisdiction of Bishop came to include neighboring towns.

The First Pope

The word "Pope" means "Papa," "Father." At first it was applied to all Western Bishops. About A.D. 500 it began to be restricted to the Bishop of Rome, and soon, in common use, came to mean Universal Bishop. The Roman Catholic list of Popes includes the Bishops of Rome from the 1st century onward. But for 500 years Bishops of Rome were NOT Popes. The idea that the Bishop of Rome should have Authority over the Whole Church was a slow growth, bitterly contested at every step, and Never Has, at any time, Been Universally Recognized.

Peter

The Roman Catholic tradition that Peter was the First Pope is Fiction pure and simple. There is no New Testament hint, and no historical evidence whatever, that Peter was at any time Bishop of Rome. Nor did he ever claim for himself such Authority as the Popes have claimed for themselves. It seems that Peter had a divine foreboding that his "Successors" would be mainly concerned with "Lording it over God's flock, rather than showing themselves Examples to the flock" (I Peter 5:3).

Early Roman Bishops

Linus (A.D. 67–79)? Cletus (79–91)?

Clement (91–100), wrote a letter to the Corinthian Church, in the name of the Roman Church, Not in His Own Name, with no hint of Papal Authority such as Popes later assumed.

Evaristus (100–109). Alexander I (109–119). Sixtus I (119–128).

Telesphorus (128–139). Hyginus (139–142). Pius I (142–154).

Beginning of Rome's Domineering Policy

Anicetus, Bishop of Rome (154–168), tried to influence Polycarp, Bishop of Smyrna, to change the date of Easter observance; but Polycarp refused to yield.

Soter (168–176). Eleutherus (177–190).

Victor I (190–202), threatened to excommunicate the Eastern Churches for celebrating Easter on the 14th of Nisan. Polycrates, Bishop of Ephesus, replied that he was not afraid of Victor's threats, and asserted his independent authority. Iranaeus, of Lyons, though a Western Bishop, and in sympathy with the Western viewpoint on Easter Observance, that is, the week-day rather than the month-day, rebuked Victor for trying to Dictate to Eastern Churches.

Growing Influence of Rome

Zephyrinus (202–218). Calixtus I (218–223), was the first to base his claim on Matthew 16:18. Tertullian, of Carthage, called him a Usurper in speaking as if Bishop of Bishops.

Urban I (223–230). Pontianus (230–235). Anterus (235–236).

Fabian (236–250). Cornelius (251–252). Lucius I (252–253).

Stephen I (253–257), objected to certain baptismal practices in the

North African Church. Cyprian, Bishop of Carthage, in North Africa, answered that each Bishop was supreme in his own diocese, and refused to yield to Stephen. Nevertheless, the feeling grew that Rome, the Capital City, should be Head of the Church, even as it was Head of the Empire.

Sixtus II (257–258). Dionysius (259–269). Felix I (269–274). Eutychianus (275–283). Caius (283–296). Marcellinus (296–304). Marcellus (308–309). Eusebius (309–310). Miltiades (311–314).

Union of Church and State

Silvester I (314–335), was Bishop of Rome when, under Constantine, Christianity was virtually made the State Religion of the Roman Empire. The Church immediately became an institution of vast importance in World Politics. Constantine regarded himself as Head of the Church. He called the Council of Nicaea (A.D. 325), and presided over it, the First World Council of the Church. This Council accorded the Bishops of Alexandria and Antioch full jurisdiction over their Provinces, as the Roman Bishop had over his, with NOT EVEN A HINT that they were subject to Rome.

Marcus (A.D. 336–337)

Julius I (337–352). The Council of Sardica (A.D. 343), composed of Western churchmen only, Not an Ecumenical Council, was the First Council to recognize the authority of the Roman Bishop.

The Five Patriarchs

By the end of the 4th century the Churches and Bishops of Christendom had come to be largely dominated from FIVE great centers, Rome, Constantinople, Antioch, Jerusalem and Alexandria, whose Bishops had come to be called PATRIARCHS, of equal authority one with another, each having full control in his own Province. After the Division of the Empire (A.D. 395), into the East and the West, the Patriarchs of Antioch, Jerusalem and Alexandria, gradually came to acknowledge the Leadership of Constantinople; and henceforth the struggle for the Leadership of Christendom was between Rome and Constantinople.

Liberius (352–366). Damascus (366–384).

Division of the Roman Empire

Siricius (385–398), Bishop of Rome, in his Lust for Worldly Power, claimed Universal Jurisdiction over the Church. But, unfortunately for him, in his day the Empire Divided (A.D. 395), into two separate Empires, East and West, which made it all the more difficult for the Roman Bishop to get the East to recognize his authority.

(Anastasius, 398–402).

Augustine's "City of God"

Innocent I (402–417), called himself "Ruler of the Church of God," and claimed the right to settle the more important matters of controversy in the Whole Church.

Zosimus (417–418). Boniface (418–422). Coelestine I (422–432).

Sixtus III (432–440). The Western Empire was now rapidly dissolving amid the storms of the Barbarian Migration and, in the distress and anxiety of the times, Augustine wrote his monumental work, "The City of God," in which he envisioned a Universal Christian Empire. This book had vast influence in molding opinion favorable to a Universal Church Hierarchy under One Head. This promoted Rome's claim for Lordship.

Thus the Church was Changing its Nature, making itself over into the Image of the Roman Empire.

Imperial Recognition of the Pope's Claim

Leo I (A.D. 440–461), called by some historians the First Pope. The misfortunes of the Empire were his opportunity. The East was rent with controversies. The West, under weak Emperors, was breaking up before the Barbarians. Leo was the one strong man of the hour. He claimed that he was, by divine appointment, Primate of All Bishops; and (A.D. 445), he obtained from Emperor Valentinian III Imperial Recognition for his claim.

In A.D. 452 he persuaded Attila the Hun to spare the city of Rome. Later (455), he induced Genseric the Vandal to have mercy on the city. This greatly enhanced his reputation.

He proclaimed himself Lord of the Whole Church; advocated Exclusive Universal Papacy; said that Resistance to his authority was a Sure Way to Hell; advocated Death Penalty for heresy.

However, the Ecumenical Council of Chalcedon (451), composed of assembled Bishops from all the world, in spite of the Emperor's Act, and Leo's Claim, gave the Patriarch of Constantinople Equal Prerogatives with the Bishop of Rome.

Hilarus (A.D. 461–468). Continued the policy of predecessor.

Fall of Rome

Simplicius (468–483), was Roman Pope when the Western Empire came to an end (A.D. 476). This left the Popes free from Civil Authority. The various new small Kingdoms of the Barbarians into which the West was now broken furnished the Popes opportunity for advantageous Alliances, and gradually the Pope became the most commanding figure in the West.

Felix III (483–492). Gelasius I (492–496). Anastasius II (496–498). Symmachus (498–514). Hormisdas (514–523). John I (523–525). Felix

IV (526–530). Boniface II (530–532). John II (532–535). Agapetus I (535–536). Silverius (536–540). Vigilius (540–554). Pelagius I (555–560). John III (560–573). Benedict I (574–578). Pelagius II (578–590).

The First Real Pope

Gregory I (A.D. 590–604), generally regarded as the First Pope. He appeared at a time of Political Anarchy and great Public Distress throughout Europe. Italy, after the Fall of Rome (A.D. 476), had become a Gothic kingdom; later a Byzantine Province under control of the Eastern Emperor; and now was being pillaged by the Lombards. Gregory's influence over the various kings had a stabilizing effect. He established for himself complete control over the churches of Italy, Spain, Gaul and England whose Conversion to Christianity was the great event of Gregory's times. Gregory labored untiringly for the Purification of the Church; deposed neglectful or unworthy Bishops; and opposed with great zeal the practice of Simony, the Sale of Office. He exerted great influence in the East, although he did not claim jurisdiction over the Eastern Church. The Patriarch of Constantinople called himself "Universal Bishop." This greatly irritated Gregory, who rejected the title as Vicious and Haughty, and refused to allow it to be applied to himself. Yet he practically exercised all the authority the title stood for. In his personal life he was a good man, one of the purest and best of the Popes, untiring in his efforts for Justice to the Oppressed, and unbounded in his Charities to the Poor. If all Popes had been such as he, what a different estimate the world would have of the Papacy!

Sabinianus (604–606). Boniface III (607). Boniface IV (609–614). Deusdedit (615–618). Boniface V (619–625). Honorius I (625–638). Severinus (640). John IV (640–642). Theodore I (642–649). Martin I (649–653). Eugenius I (654–657). Vitalianus (657–672). Adeodatus (672–676). Donus I (676–678). Agatho (678–682).

Leo II (682–683), pronounced Honorius I a Heretic.

Benedict II (684–685). John V (685–686). Cono (686–687). Theodorus (687). Sergius I (687–701). John VI (701–705). John VII (705–707). Sisinnius (708). Constantine (708–715). Gregory II (715–731). Gregory III (731–741).

The Pope Becomes an Earthly King

Zacharias (741–752), was instrumental in making Pepin, father of Charlemagne, King of the Franks, a Germanic people occupying western Germany and northern France.

Stephen II (752–757). At his request, Pepin led his army to Italy, conquered the Lombards, and gave their lands, a large part of Central Italy, to the Pope.

This was the beginning of the PAPAL STATES, or TEMPORAL DOMINION of the Popes. Civil Control of Rome and Central Italy by the Popes, thus established by Popes Zacharias and Stephen, and recognized by Pepin (754), was later confirmed by Charlemagne (774). Thus, Central Italy, once the Head of the Roman Empire, later a Gothic Kingdom ruled by the "Head" of the Church. This TEMPORAL KINGDOM of the Church lasted 1100 years, till 1870, when, on the outbreak of the war between France and Germany, king Victor Immanuel of Italy took possession of Rome, and added the Papal States to the Kingdom of Italy.

Paul I (757–767). Stephen III (768–772). Adrian I (772–795).

Papal Power Greatly Promoted by Charlemagne

Leo III (A.D. 795–816), in return for Charlemagne's recognition (774) of the Pope's Temporal Power over the Papal States, conferred on Charlemagne (800) the title of Roman Emperor, thus combining the Roman and Frank realms into the HOLY ROMAN EMPIRE.

Charlemagne (742–814), King of the Franks, grandson of Charles Martel, who had saved Europe from the Mohammedans (see page 766), was one of the greatest rulers of all time. He reigned 46 years, and made many wars and conquests of vast magnitude. His realm included what is modern Germany, France, Switzerland, Austria, Hungary, Belgium, and parts of Spain and Italy. He helped the Pope, and the Pope helped him. He was one of the Greatest Influences in bringing the Papacy to a position of World Power. Soon after his death, by the treaty of Verdun (843), his Empire was divided into what became the foundations of modern Germany, France and Italy; and henceforth, for centuries, there was ceaseless struggle between Popes and German and French Kings for Supremacy.

"The Holy Roman Empire"

Thus established by Charlemagne and Leo III, was, in a sense, the re-establishment of the Western Roman Empire, with German kings on the throne bearing the title of "Caesar," which was conferred by the Popes, purporting to be a continuation of the Old Roman Empire, under the Joint Control of Popes and German Emperors, the Emperors having control in Temporal matters and the Popes in Spiritual matters. But inasmuch as the Church was a State institution jurisdiction was not always easy to define, and the arrangement resulted in many Bitter Struggles between Emperors and Popes.

The Holy Roman Empire, a "name rather than an accomplished fact," lived a thousand years, and was brought to an end by Napoleon (1806). It served a purpose in blending the Roman and German civilizations, out of which the life of the modern world arose.

Stephen IV (816–817). Pascal I (817–824). Eugene II (824–827). Valentine (827). Gregory IV (827–844). Sergius II (844–847). Leo IV (847–855). Benedict III (855–858).

Pseudo-Isidorian Decretals Help Papacy

Nicolas I (858–867). First Pope to wear a Crown. To promote his claim of Universal Authority he used with great effect the "PSEUDO-ISIDORIAN DECRETALS," a book that appeared about 857, containing documents that purported to be Letters and Decrees of Bishops and Councils of the 2nd and 3rd centuries, all tending to exalt the power of the Pope. They were Deliberate Forgeries and Corruptions of Ancient Historical Documents, but their Spurious Character was not discovered till some centuries later. Whether Nicolas knew them to be Forgeries, at least he Lied in stating that they had been kept in the archives of the Roman Church from ancient times. But they served their purpose, in "stamping the Claims of the Medieval Priesthood with the Authority of Antiquity." "The Papacy, which was the Growth of Several Centuries, was made to appear as something Complete and Unchangeable from the very Beginning." "The object was to Ante-Date by Five Centuries the Pope's Temporal Power." "The Most Colossal Literary Fraud in History."

"Yet it Strengthened the Papacy more than any other one agency, and forms to large extent the Basis of the Canon Law of the Roman Church."

The Great Cleavage of Christendom

Nicolas undertook to interfere in the affairs of the Eastern Church. He excommunicated Photius, Patriarch of Constantinople, who in turn excommunicated him. The Division of Christendom followed, 869 (completed 1054).

Although the Empire had been Divided since 395, and although there had been a long and bitter struggle between the Popes of Rome and the Patriarchs of Constantinople for supremacy, yet the CHURCH had remained ONE. The Councils had been attended by representatives of both the East and the West.

Up to 869 all Ecumenical Councils had been held in or near Constantinople, and in the Greek language. But now at last the Pope's insistent claim of being Lord of Christendom had become unbearable, and the East definitely separated itself. The Council of Constantinople (869), was the Last Ecumenical Council. Henceforth the Greek Church had its Councils, and the Roman Church had its Councils. And the Breach grew wider with the centuries. The brutal treatment of Constantinople by the armies of Pope Innocent III during the Crusades embittered the East all the more. And the creation of the dogma of Papal Infallibility in 1870 further deepened the chasm.

The Darkest Period of the Papacy

Adrian II (867–872). John VIII (872–882). Marinus (882–884). With these Popes began the Darkest Period of the Papacy (870–1050). The 200 years between Nicolas I and Gregory VII is called by historians the MIDNIGHT OF THE DARK AGES. Bribery, Corruption, Immorality and Bloodshed, make it just about the Blackest Chapter in the Whole History of the Church.

Adrian III (884–885). Stephen V (885–891). Formosus (891–896). Boniface VI (896). Stephen VI (896–897). Romanus (897). Theodore II (898). John IX (898–900). Benedict IV (900–903). Leo V (903). Christopher (903–904).

"Rule of the Harlots"

Sergius III (A.D. 904–911). Said to have had a mistress, Marozia. She, her mother Theodora, and her sister, "filled the Papal chair with their paramours and bastard sons, and turned the Papal Palace into a den of robbers." Called in history The Rule of the Harlots (904–963).

Anastasius III (911–913). Lando (913–914). John X (914–928), "was brought from Ravenna to Rome and made Pope by Theodora for the more convenient gratification of her passion." He was smothered to death by Marozia, who, then, in succession, raised to the Papacy Leo VI (928–929), and Stephen VII (929–931), and John XI (931–936), her own illegitimate son. Another of her sons appointed the four following Popes, Leo VII (936–939), Stephen VIII (939–942), Martin III (942–946), and Agapetus II (946–955). John XII (955–963), a grandson of Marozia, was "guilty of almost every crime; violated virgins and widows, high and low; lived with his father's mistress; made the Papal Palace a brothel; was killed while in the act of adultery by the woman's enraged husband."

Depths of Papal Degradation

Leo VIII (963–965). John XIII (965–972). Benedict VI (972–974). Donus II (974). Benedict VII (975–983). John XIV (983–984).

Boniface VII (984–985), murdered Pope John XIV, and "maintained himself on the blood-stained Papal Throne by a lavish distribution of stolen money." The Bishop of Orleans, referring to John XII, Leo VIII and Boniface VII, called them "monsters of guilt, reeking in blood and filth; Antichrist sitting in the Temple of God."

John XV (985–996). Gregory V (996–999). Sylvester II (999–1003). John XVII (1003). John XVIII (1003–1008). Sergius IV (1009–1012). Benedict VIII (1012–1024), bought the Office of Pope with open bribery. This was called SIMONY, that is, the purchase or sale of Church Office with money.

John XIX (1024–1033), Bought the Papacy. He passed through all the necessary clerical degrees in one day.

Benedict IX (1033–1045), was made Pope as a boy 12 years old, through a money bargain with the powerful families that ruled Rome. "Surpassed John XII in wickedness; committed murders and adulteries in broad daylight; robbed pilgrims on the graves of martyrs; a hideous criminal, the people drove him out of Rome." Some call him the Worst of all the Popes.

Gregory VI (1045–1046), Bought the Papacy. Three rival Popes: Benedict IX, Gregory VI, Sylvester III. "Rome swarmed with hired assassins; virtue of pilgrims was violated."

Clement II (1046–1047), was appointed Pope by Emperor Henry III of Germany "because no Roman clergyman could be found who was free of the pollution of Simony and Fornication."

Damascus II (1048). Loud protests against Papal Infamy, and a Cry for Reform found answer in Hildebrand.

Golden Age of Papal Power

Hildebrand, small of stature, ungainly in appearance, feeble in voice, yet great in intellect, fiery in spirit, determined, and a zealous advocate of Papal Absolutism, associated himself with the Reform Party, and led the Papacy into its Golden Age (1049–1294). He controlled the five successive Papal administrations immediately preceding his own: Leo IX (1049–1054); Victor II (1055–1057); Stephen IX (1057–1058); Nicolas II (1059–1061); Alexander II (1061–1073).

Hildebrand, Pope Gregory VII (1073–1085). His great object was to Reform the Clergy. The two prevailing Sins of the Clergy were Immorality and Simony. Simony was the Purchase of Church Office with Money. The Church owned a large share of all property, and had rich incomes. Practically all Bishops and Priests had paid for their office, for it gave them a chance to live in luxury. Kings habitually sold Church Offices to the highest bidder, regardless of fitness or character.

This brought Pope Gregory VII into bitter contest with Henry IV, Emperor of Germany. He deposed Gregory. Gregory, in turn, excommunicated and deposed Henry. War followed. For years Italy was devastated by the opposing armies. Gregory, in the end, was driven from Rome, and died in exile. But he had, in great measure, made the Papacy independent of Imperial Power. Repeatedly Gregory had called himself "Overlord of Kings and Princes," and made good his claim.

Victor III (1086–1087). Urban II (1088–1099), continued war with the German Emperor. Became leader in the Crusade Movement, which added to Papacy's Leadership.

Pascal II (1099–1118), continued War with German Emperor.

Gelasius II (1118–1119). Calixtus II, (1119–1124). Honorius II (1124–1130). Innocent II (1130–1143), maintained his office by armed force against Anti-Pope Anacletus II, who had been chosen by certain powerful families in Rome.

Celestin II (1143–1144). Lucius II (1144–1145). Eugene III (1145–1153). Anastasius IV (1153–1154).

Adrian IV (1154–1159). Only English Pope. Gave Ireland to the King of England, and authorized him to take possession. This authorization was renewed by the next Pope, Alexander III, and carried out in 1171.

Alexander III (1159–1181). In conflict with four Anti-Popes. Renewed war with the German Emperor for supremacy. Many campaigns and pitched battles between the Papal Armies and German Armies, with terrible slaughter. Alexander was finally driven from Rome by the people, and died in exile.

Lucius III (1181–1185). Urban III (1185–1187). Gregory VIII (1187). Clement III (1187–1191). Celestine II (1191–1198).

Summit of Papal Power

Innocent III (1198–1216). Most Powerful of all the Popes. Claimed to be "Vicar of Christ," "Vicar of God," "Supreme Sovereign over the Church and the World." Claimed the right to Depose Kings and Princes; and that "All things on earth and in heaven and in hell are subject to the Vicar of Christ."

He brought the Church into Supreme Control of the State. The Kings of Germany, France, England, and practically all the Monarchs of Europe obeyed his will. He even brought the Byzantine Empire under his control. Never in history has any one man exerted more power.

He ordered Two Crusades. Decreed Transubstantiation. Confirmed Auricular Confession. Declared that Peter's successor "can never in any way depart from the Catholic faith," Papal Infallibility. Condemned the Magna Charta. Forbade the Reading of the Bible in vernacular. Ordered the Extermination of Heretics. Instituted the Inquisition. Ordered the Massacre of the Albigenses. More Blood was Shed under his direction, and that of his immediate successors, than in any other period of Church History, except in the Papacy's effort to Crush the Reformation in the 16th and 17th centuries. One would think Nero, the Beast, had come to life in Name of the Lamb.

Papal Power Maintained by the Inquisition

The Inquisition, called the "Holy Office," was instituted by Pope Innocent III, and perfected under the second following Pope, Gregory IX. It was the Church Court for Detection and Punishment of

Heretics. Under it everyone was required to inform against Heretics. Anyone suspected was liable to Torture, without knowing the name of his accuser. The proceedings were secret. The Inquisitor pronounced sentence, and the victim was turned over to Civil Authorities to be Imprisoned for Life, or to be Burned. The victim's property was confiscated, and divided between the Church and the State.

In the period immediately following Pope Innocent III the Inquisition did its most deadly work against the Albigenses (see page 785), but also claimed vast multitudes of victims in Spain, Italy, Germany and the Netherlands.

Later on the Inquisition was the main agency in the Papacy's effort to Crush the Reformation. It is stated that in the 30 years between 1540 and 1570 no fewer than 900,000 Protestants were put to death in the Pope's war for the extermination of the Waldenses (see page 785).

Think of Monks and Priests, in holy garments, directing, with Heartless Cruelty and Inhuman Brutality, the work of Torturing and Burning alive Innocent Men and Women, and doing it in the Name of Christ, by the direct order of the "Vicar of Christ."

The Inquisition was the Most Infamous and Devilish Thing in Human History. It was devised by Popes, and used by them for 500 years, to Maintain their Power. For its record none of the subsequent line of "Holy" and "Infallible" Popes have ever apologized.

Continued War with German Emperor

Honorius III (1216–1227). Gregory IX (1227–1241). Innocent IV (1241–1254), gave Papal Sanction to the use of Torture in extracting confessions from suspected heretics. Under these three Popes, Emperor Frederick II of Germany led his Empire in its last great struggle with Papacy. After repeated wars, the Papacy emerged supreme.

Alexander IV (1254–1261). Urban IV (1261–1264). Clement IV (1265–1268). Gregory X (1271–1276). Innocent V (1276). John XXI (1276–1277). Nicolas III (1277–1280). Martin IV (1281–1285). Honorius IV (1285–1287). Nicolas IV (1288–1292). Celestine V (1294).

Beginning of Papal Decline

Boniface VIII (1294–1303), in his famous bull, "Unam Sanctam," said, "We declare, affirm, define, and pronounce that it is altogether necessary for Salvation that every creature be subject to the Roman Pontiff." However, he himself was so Corrupt that Dante, who visited Rome during his pontificate, called the Vatican a "Sewer of Corruption," and assigned him, along with Nicolas III and Clement V, to the lowest parts of hell.

The Papacy had been victorious in its 200-year struggle with the German Empire.

Boniface received the Papacy at its height; but he met his match in Philip the Fair, King of France, at whose feet the Papacy was humbled to the dust, and began its Era of Decline.

French Control of the Papacy

Benedict XI (1303–1304). In his day, Philip the Fair, King of France, had become the leading Monarch of Europe.

Among the French People, a feeling of Nationalism and a spirit of Independence was developing, an outgrowth, no doubt, in part, of the Papacy's Brutal Massacre of the French Albigenses in the preceding century (see page 785). And Philip the Fair, with whom the history of Modern France begins, took up the struggle with the Papacy. His conflict started with Pope Boniface VIII over taxation of the French Clergy. The Papacy was brought into complete submission to the State. And, after the death of Pope Benedict XI, the Papal Palace was removed from Rome to Avignon on the south border of France, and for 70 years the Papacy was a mere tool of the French Court.

"Babylonian Captivity" of the Papacy

70 years (1305–1377), in which Papal Palace was at Avignon. Clement V (1305–1314). John XXII (1316–1334). Richest man in Europe. Benedict XII (1334–1342). Clement VI (1342–1352). Innocent VI (1352–1362). Urban V (1362–1370). Gregory XI (1370–1378).

The Avarice of the Avignon Popes knew no bounds. Burdensome taxes were imposed. Every Church Office was sold for money, and many new offices were created to be sold, to fill the coffers of Popes and support the Luxurious and Immoral Court. Petrarch accused the Papal Household of Rape, Adultery, and all manner of Fornication. In many parishes men insisted on priests keeping concubines as a protection for their own families. The "Captivity" was a blow to Papal Prestige.

The Papal Schism

40 years (1377–1417), in which there were two sets of Popes, one at Rome, and one at Avignon, each claiming to be "Vicar of Christ," hurling anathemas and curses at each other.

Urban VI (1378–1389), under whom the Papal Palace was reestablished at Rome. Boniface IX (1389–1404). Innocent VII (1404–1406). Gregory XII (1406–1409). Alexander V (1409–1410).

John XXIII (1410–1415), called by some the most depraved criminal who ever sat on the Papal Throne; guilty of almost every crime; as cardinal in Bologna, 200 maidens, nuns and married women fell victims to his amours; as Pope he violated virgins and nuns; lived in adultery with his brother's wife; was guilty of sodomy and other nameless vices; bought the Papal Office; sold Cardinalates to children of wealthy families; and openly denied the future life.

Martin V (1417–1431). Healed the Papal Schism. But the Schism had been regarded by Europe as a Scandal. By it the Papacy suffered great loss of prestige. Eugene IV (1431–1447).

Renaissance Popes

Nicolas V (1447–1455), authorized the King of Portugal to war on African peoples, take their property and enslave people.

Calixtus III (1455–1458), a Pope of blameless life.

Pius II (1458–1464), was said to have been the father of many illegitimate children, spoke openly of the methods he used to seduce women, encouraged young men to, and even offered to instruct them in methods of self-indulgence.

Paul II (1464–1471), "filled his house with concubines."

Sixtus IV (1471–1484). Sanctioned the Spanish Inquisition. Decreed that money would deliver souls from Purgatory. Was implicated in a plot to murder Lorenzo de Medici, and others who opposed his policies. Used the Papacy to enrich himself and his relatives. Made eight of his nephews Cardinals, while as yet some of them were mere boys. In luxurious and lavish entertainment he rivaled the Caesars. In wealth and pomp he and his relatives surpassed the old Roman Families.

Innocent VIII (1484–1492). Had 16 children by various married women. Multiplied Church Offices, and sold them for vast sums of money. Decreed the extermination of the Waldenses, and sent an army against them. Appointed the brutal Thomas of Torquemada Inquisitor General of Spain, and ordered all rulers to deliver up Heretics to him. Permitted bull fights on St. Peter's Square. Was Background for Savonarola's cry against Papal Corruption.

Alexander VI (1492–1503), called the most corrupt of the Renaissance Popes, licentious, avaricious, depraved; bought the Papacy; made many new cardinals, for money; had a number of illegitimate children, whom he openly acknowledged and appointed to high church office while they were yet children, who, with their father, murdered cardinals and others who stood in their way. Had for a mistress a sister of a Cardinal, who became next Pope, Pius III (1503).

Popes in Luther's Day

Julius II (1503–1513), as richest of the Cardinals, with vast income from numerous bishoprics and church estates, bought the Papacy. As a Cardinal he had made sport of Celibacy. Involved in endless quarrels over the possession of cities and principalities, he maintained and personally led vast armies. Called the Warrior Pope. Issued Indulgences for money. Luther visited Rome, in his day, and was Appalled at what he saw.

Leo X (1513–1521), was Pope when Martin Luther started the Protestant Reformation. Was made an Archbishop at 8; a Cardinal at 13. Was appointed to 27 different church offices, which meant vast income, before he was 13. Was taught to regard ecclesiastical office purely as a source of revenue. Bargained for the Papal chair. Sold church honors. All ecclesiastical offices were for sale, and many new ones were created. He appointed Cardinals as young as 7. He was in endless negotiations with kings and princes, jockeying for secular power, utterly indifferent to the Religious welfare of the Church. He maintained the most Luxurious and Licentious Court in Europe. His Cardinals vied with kings and princes in Gorgeous Palaces and Voluptuous Entertainment, attended by trains of servants. Yet this Voluptuary re-affirmed the Unam Sanctam, in which it is declared that Every Human Being must be Subject to the Roman Pontiff for Salvation. He issued Indulgences for stipulated fees; and declared Burning of Heretics a Divine Appointment.

Adrian VI (1522–1523). Clement VII (1523–1534). Paul III (1534–1549). Had many illegitimate children. He was a determined enemy of the Protestants; offered Charles V an army to exterminate them.

Enter the Jesuits

Rome's answer to the Lutheran Secession: the INQUISITION under the leadership of the JESUITS, an order founded by Ignatius Loyola, a Spaniard, on the principle of Absolute and Unconditional OBEDIENCE to the Pope, having for its object the Recovery of territory lost to Protestants and Mohammedans, and the Conquest of the entire Heathen World for the Roman Catholic Church. Their supreme aim, the Destruction of Heresy, that is, thinking anything different from what the Pope said think; for the accomplishment of which Anything was Justifiable, Deception, Immorality, Vice, even Murder. Their motto, "For the Greater Glory of God." Their methods; Schools, seeking especially the children of ruling classes, aiming in all schools to gain absolute mastery over the pupil: the Confessional, especially with Kings, Princes and Civil Rulers, Indulging them in all kinds of Vice and Crime, for the sake of gaining their favor: Force, persuading rulers to execute Inquisition sentences.

In France they were responsible for St. Bartholomew's Massacre, Persecution of the Hugenots, Revocation of the Toleration Edict of Nantes, and the French Revolution. In Spain, Netherlands, South Germany, Bohemia, Austria, Poland and other countries, they led in the Massacre of Untold Multitudes. By these methods they stopped the Reformation in Southern Europe, and virtually saved the Papacy from ruin.

Julius III (1550–5): Marcellus II (1555). Paul IV (1555–9). Pius IV (1559–65). Pius V (1566–72). Gregory XIII (1572–85), celebrated, in solemn mass, with Thanksgiving and Joy, the news of St. Bartholomew's Massacre (see page 789). Sixtus V (1585–90). Urban VII (1590). Gregory XIV (1590–1). Innocent IX (1591).

Modern Popes

Clement VIII (1592–1605). Leo XI (1605). Paul V (1605–21). Gregory XV (1621–3). Urban VIII (1623–44), with aid of Jesuits, blotted out Protestants in Bohemia. Innocent X (1644–55). Alexander (1655–67). Clement IX (1667–9). Clement X (1670–6). Innocent XI (1676–89). Alexander VIII (1689–91). Innocent XII (1691–1700). Clement XI (1700–21), declared that Kings Reign Only with His Sanction; issued a Bull against Bible Reading. Innocent XIII (1721–4). Benedict XIII (1724–30). Clement XII (1730–40). Benedict XIV (1740–58). Clement XIII, (1758–69). Clement XIV (1769–74), suppressed the Society of Jesuits in Spain, France and Portugal. Pius VI (1775–99). Pius VII (1800–20), issued a Bull against Bible Societies. Restored the Jesuits: one ''infallible'' Pope restoring for all time what another ''Infallible'' Pope just before him had suppressed.

Leo XII (1821–9), condemned All Religious Freedom, Tolerance, Bible Societies and Bible Translations; and declared that "Everyone separated from the Roman Catholic Church, however unblameable in other respects, has No Part in Eternal Life."

Pius VIII (1829–30), Denounced Liberty of Conscience, Bible Societies and Freemasonry. Gregory XVI (1831–46), an ardent advocate of Papal Infallibility. Condemned Bible Societies.

Pius IX (1846–78), lost the Papal States; decreed PAPAL INFALLIBILITY; proclaimed the Right to Suppress Heresy by Force; Condemned Separation of Church and State; commanded Catholics to Obey the Head of the Church rather than Civil Rulers; Denounced Liberty of Conscience, Liberty of Worship, Freedom of Speech and Freedom of the Press; decreed the Immaculate Conception and Deity of Mary; Condemned Bible Societies; declared that Protestantism is "No Form of the Christian Religion"; and that "Every dogma of the Roman Catholic Church has been dictated by Christ through His Viceregents on earth."

Papal Infallibility

The idea that the Pope is Infallible found no expression in Christian literature for 600 years. It arose with the appearance of the False

Decretals (see page 773), and grew with Papal assertion in the Crusades and conflicts of Popes and Emperors.

Many Popes from Innocent III (1198–1216), onward, advocated it. But the Councils of Pisa (1409), Constance (1414), and Basel (1431), expressly decreed that Popes are subject to Councils.

Pius IX (1854), "Of his own Sovereign Authority, and without the cooperation of a Council," proclaimed the doctrine of the Immaculate Conception of Mary, as a sort of feeler to the Roman Catholic World, on the question. Its reception emboldened him to call the Vatican Council (1870), for the express purpose of having Himself declared Infallible, which, under his skillful manipulation, they did. The decree reads that it is "divinely revealed" that the Pope, when he speaks "ex cathedra," is "possessed of Infallibility in defining doctrines of faith and morals," and that "such definitions are irreformable."

And so the Pope now claims Infallibility, because the Vatican Council, at his bidding, so voted. The Eastern Church considered this the Papacy's Crowning Blasphemy.

Loss of Temporal Power

Since 754 the Popes had been Civil Rulers of a Kingdom called "The Papal States," which included a large part of Italy, with Rome as its Capital. Many Popes had been more concerned with extending the boundaries and wealth and power of this Kingdom than in the Spiritual Welfare of the Church. And Papal Corruption was just as glaring in their Secular Kingdom as in their Spiritual Kingdom. Papal Misrule of Rome became a byword: Venality of Officials, Frequency of Crime, Unwholesome Streets, Exactions upon Visitors, Falsified Coinage, Lotteries.

Pius IX ruled Rome with the help of 10,000 French troops. On the outbreak of the War between France and Germany (1870), these troops were recalled. And then Victor Immanuel, King of Italy, took possession of Rome, and added the Papal States to the Kingdom of Italy. The vote of the people transferring Rome from the Pope to the Government of Italy was 133,648 to 1,507.

Thus, the Pope not only lost his earthly Kingdom, but He Himself became a Subject of another King, which was deeply humiliating to him who claimed to be Ruler of All Kings.

His Temporal Power was restored on a miniature scale (1929), by Mussolini; and, though Vatican City comprises only 100 acres, the Pope is again a Sovereign in his own little Kingdom.

Present-Day Popes

Leo XIII (1878–1903), claimed that he was appointed to be Head of All Rulers, and that he holds on this earth the Place of Almighty God. Emphasized Papal Infallibility. Pronounced Protestants "enemies of the Christian Name." Proclaimed the only method of cooperation Complete Submission to the Roman Pontiff. Denounced "Americanism," and the Masonic Order.

Pius X (1903–1914), denounced leaders of the Reformation as "enemies of the Cross of Christ." Benedict XV (1914–1922).

Pius XI (1922–1939), in 1928 re-affirmed the Roman Catholic Church to be the Only Church of Christ, and the Re-Union of Christendom Impossible Except by Submission to Rome.

Pius XII (1939–1958). John XXIII (1958–1963). Paul VI (1963–).

Summary

The Papacy is an Italian Institution. It arose on the ruins of the Roman Empire, in the name of Christ occupying the throne of the Caesars; a Revival of the Image of the Roman Empire inheriting the Spirit thereof; "the Ghost of the Roman Empire come to life in the garb of Christianity." The Popes mostly have been Italians.

The Papacy's Methods. It brought itself to power through the prestige of Rome, and the Name of Christ, and by shrewd political alliances, and by deception, and by armed force; and by Armed Force and Bloodshed has maintained itself in power.

Papal Revenues. Through a large part of its history the Papacy, by the sale of ecclesiastical office, and its shameless traffic in Indulgences, has received vast revenues that enabled it to maintain, for much of the time the most luxurious Court in Europe.

Personal character of the Popes. Some of the Popes have been good men; some of them unspeakably vile; the most of them have been absorbed in the pursuit of Secular Power.

Papal Claims. Yet, in spite of the Character of the general run of Popes, their Methods, and the Secular and Bloody record of the Papacy, these "Holy Fathers" claim that they are the "Vicars of Christ," "Infallible," and that they "hold on this earth the place of Almighty God," and that Obedience to Them is necessary to salvation.

The Papacy and the Bible. Hildebrand ordered Bohemians not to read the Bible. Innocent III forbade the people reading the Bible in their own language. Gregory IX forbade laymen possessing the Bible, and suppressed translations. Translations among the Albigenses and Waldenses were burned, and people burned for having them. Paul IV prohibited the possession of translations without permission of the Inquisition. The Jesuits induced Clement XI to condemn the reading of the Bible by the laity. Leo XII, Pius VIII, Gregory XVI and Pius IX all condemned Bible Societies. In Catholic countries the Bible is an unknown book.

The Papacy and the State. Hildebrand called himself "Overlord of Kings and Princes." Innocent III called himself "Supreme Sovereign of the world." Pius IX condemned Separation of Church and State, and commanded all true Catholics to obey the Head of the Church rather than Civil Rulers. Leo XIII claimed that he was the "Head of All Rulers." At the coronation of the Popes, the Papal Crown is placed on their head with the words: "Thou art Father of Princes and Kings, Ruler of the World, and Vicar of Christ."

The Papacy and the Church. The Papacy is not the Church, but a Political Machine that got Control of the Church, and, by assumed prerogatives, interposed itself between God and God's people.

The Papacy and Tolerance. Pope Clement VIII declared that the Toleration Edict of Nantes whereby "liberty of conscience is granted to everybody is the most cursed thing in the world." Innocent X and his successors have condemned, rejected, annulled and protested against the Toleration articles of the 1648 Treaty of Westphalia. Leo XII condemned religious freedom. Pius VIII denounced liberty of conscience. Pius IX expressly condemned religious toleration and liberty. Leo XIII endorsed the decree of Pius IX. However much Roman priests in our own country may cry "Tolerance," the Official "Infallible" Law of the System to which they belong is Against it. Romanists are in favor of Tolerance ONLY in countries where they are in the Minority. The Papacy has FOUGHT Religious Freedom at every step.

Providential Purpose in the Papacy? It may be that, in the Providence of God, the Papacy served a purpose, in the Middle Ages, in saving Western Europe from chaos and in Blending the Roman and German civilizations. But just suppose that the Church had NEVER been made a STATE institution, and that it had entirely avoided the pursuit of Secular Power, and confined itself exclusively to its ORIGINAL policy of winning Converts to Christ and training them in His ways—then there might have been the MILLENNIUM instead of the DARK AGES.

This Story of the Papacy has been written as a background to the Reformation, in the belief that we ought to be familiar with the Wherefore of the Protestant Movement and the Historical Foundations of our Protestant Faith. Some of the things told herein seem Unbelievable. It seems inconceivable that men could take the Religion of Christ and develop it into an Unscrupulous Political Machine on which to ride to World Power. However, all statements made herein may be verified by reference to any of the completer Church Histories.

Forerunners of the Reformation

Albigenses or Carthari. In Southern France, Northern Spain and Northern Italy. Preached against the immoralities of the priesthood, pilgrimages, worship of saints and images; completely rejected the clergy and its claims; criticized church conditions; opposed the claims of the Church of Rome; made great use of the Scriptures; lived self denying lives and had great zeal for moral purity. By 1167 they embraced possibly a majority of the population of South France; by 1200 very numerous in North Italy. In 1208 a crusade was ordered by Pope Innocent III; a bloody war of extermination followed; scarcely paralleled in history; town after town was put to the sword and the inhabitants murdered without distinction of age or sex; in 1229 the Inquisition was established and within a hundred years the Albigenses were utterly rooted out.

Waldenses. Southern France and Northern Italy. Similar to Albigenses, but not identical. Waldo, a rich merchant of Lyons, South France (1176), gave his property to the poor and went about preaching; opposed clerical usurpation and profligacy; denied the exclusive right of the clergy to teach the Gospel; rejected masses, prayers for the dead and purgatory; taught the Bible as the sole rule of belief and life; their preaching kindled a great desire among the people to read the Bible. They were gradually repressed by the Inquisition except in the Alpine Valleys southwest of Turin where they still are found, the only medieval sect still surviving, a story of heroic endurance of persecutions. Now the leading Protestant body in Italy.

John Wyclif (1324–1384). A teacher at Oxford, England. Preached against the spiritual domination of the priesthood, the authority of the Pope; opposed the existence of Popes, cardinals, patriarchs, monks; attacked transubstantiation, and auricular confession. Advocated the people's right to read the Bible. Translated it into English language. His followers were called Lollards.

John Huss (1369–1415). Rector of the University of Prague, Bohemia. He was a student of Wyclif, whose writings had penetrated Bohemia. He became a fearless preacher; attacked the vices of the clergy and the corruptions of the church; with impassioned vehemence condemned the sale of indulgences; rejected purgatory, worship of saints and worship in a foreign language; exalted the Scriptures above the dogmas and ordinances of the church. He was burned alive at the stake, and his followers, a large part of the Bohemian population, were almost extirpated by a crusade ordered by the Pope.

Savonarola (1452–1498). Florence, Italy. Preached, like a Hebrew prophet, to vast crowds who thronged his cathedral, against the sensuality and sin of the city, and against Papal vice. The penitent city reformed. But Pope Alexander VI sought in every way to silence the righteous preacher; even tried to bribe him with a cardinal's hat; but in vain. He was hanged and burned in the great square in Florence 19 years before Luther posted his 95 theses.

Anabaptists appeared through the Middle Ages, in various European countries, under different names, in independent groups, representing a variety of doctrines, but usually strongly Anti-Clerical, rejecting Infant Baptism, devoted to the Scriptures, and standing for Absolute Separation of Church and State; very numerous in Germany, Holland, and Switzerland at the time of the Reformation, perpetuating ideas that had come down from preceeding generations; as a rule, a quiet and genuinely pious people, but bitterly persecuted, especially in the Netherlands.

The Renaissance, or Revival of Learning, occasioned, in part, as a result of the Crusades, helped along the Reformation movement. There arose a passion for the ancient classics. Vast sums of money were spent in the collection of manuscripts and the founding of libraries. Just at that time printing was invented. And there followed an abundance of dictionaries, grammars, versions and commentaries. There was study of the Scriptures in their original languages. "Renewed knowledge of the sources of Christian doctrine revealed the vast difference between the native simplicity of the Gospel and the ecclesiastical fabric that professed to be founded upon it." "THE REFORMATION OWED ITS BEING TO THE DIRECT CONTACT OF THE MIND WITH THE SCRIPTURES," and it resulted in the emancipation of the human mind from priestly and Papal authority.

Erasmus (1466–1536), greatest scholar of the Reformation. His great ambition was to free men from false ideas about religion; and thought the best way to do it was to return to the Scriptures. A relentless critic of the Roman Catholic Church; delighted especially to ridicule "unholy men in holy orders." Greatly helped the Reformation, but never joined it.

Conditions. There was widespread discontent with the corruption of the Church and the clergy. The people had grown restive under the cruelties of the Inquisition. Civil rulers had grown tired of Papal interference in governmental matters. And "at the blast of Luther's trumpet Germany, England, Scotland and other countries startled, like giants out of their sleep."

The Reformation

MARTIN LUTHER (A.D. 1483–1546), next to Jesus and Paul, the Greatest Man of all the ages. He led the world in its break for Freedom from the most Despotic Institution in history. Born of poor parents at Eisleben (1483). Entered University of Erfurt (1501), to study law. "A fine student, great talker and debater, very sociable and very musical," he took his degrees in an unusually short time. 1505 he suddenly decided to enter a monastery. An exemplary monk, and very religious, he practiced all the forms of fastings and scourgings, and invented new ones, and for two years endured, he said, "such anguish as no pen can describe." One day, in 1508, while reading Romans, his enlightenment and peace came suddenly: "the just shall live by faith." He saw, at last, that salvation was to be gained by Trust in God through Christ, and not by the rituals and sacraments and penances of the Church. It changed his whole life, and the WHOLE COURSE OF HISTORY. 1508 he became a teacher in the University of Wittenberg, which position he held till his death in 1546. 1511 he went to Rome, and was appalled at the Corruption and Vice of the Papal Court. Returned to Wittenberg. His sermons on the Bible began to attract students from all parts of Germany.

INDULGENCES. Tetzel's sale of Indulgences was the occasion of Luther's break with Rome. According to Romanist teaching, Purgatory is very much the same as Hell, only it does not last as long; but all have to pass through it. But the Pope claimed to have the power to lessen, or altogether remit, these sufferings; and this prerogative belonged exclusively to the Pope. It began with Popes Pascal I (817–24) and John VIII (872–82). Papal Indulgences were found to be exceedingly profitable, and soon came into general use. They were offered as inducement to go on Crusades, or Wars against Heretics, or against some King whom the Pope wished to punish, or to Inquisitors, or to those who brought faggots for the burning of a heretic, or SOLD for MONEY. Pope Sixtus IV (1476), was the first to apply them to souls already in Purgatory. Indulgences were farmed out, to be retailed. Thus "selling the privilege to sin" became one of the main sources of Papal Revenue. In 1517 John Tetzel came through Germany selling certificates, signed by the Pope, offering pardon of all sins, to buyers and their friends, without confession, repentance, penance, or absolution by the priest. He said to the people, "as soon as your coin clinks in the chest the souls of your friends will rise out of Purgatory into Heaven." This horrified Luther.

THE 95 THESES. On October 31, 1517, Luther posted on the church door in Wittenberg 95 theses, nearly all of which related to Indulgences, but which in substance struck at the authority of the

Pope. It was merely a notice that he was willing to discuss these things in the University. But printed copies were eagerly sought all over Germany. It proved to be "the spark that set Europe aflame." By 1520 he had become the most popular man in Germany.

Luther's Ex-Communication. In 1520 the Pope issued a Bull ex-communicating Luther, and declaring that, unless he would retract within 60 days, he should receive the "penalty due for heresy" (which meant death). When Luther received the Bull he Burned it Publicly (Dec. 10, 1520). "A New Age in History began That Day." (Nichols)

The Diet of Worms. 1521 Luther was summoned by Charles V, Emperor of the Holy Roman Empire (which at that time included Germany, Spain, Netherlands and Austria), to appear before the Diet of Worms, and in the presence of the assembled dignitaries of the Empire and the Church, ordered to retract. He replied that he could retract nothing except what was disproved by Scripture or reason: "Here I stand; I can do naught else; so help me God." He was condemned; but he had too many friends among the German Princes for the Edict to be carried out. He was hid by a friend for about a year, and then returned to Wittenberg to continue his work of speaking and writing. Among other things he translated the Bible into German; it "spiritualized Germany and made the German language."

THE POPE'S WAR ON THE GERMAN PROTESTANTS. Germany was made up of a great many small States. Many Princes, with their whole States, had been won to Luther's cause. By 1540 all North Germany had become Lutheran. Pope Paul III urged the Emperor Charles V to proceed against them, and offered him an army. The Pope declared the war a Crusade, and offered Indulgences to all who would take part. The war lasted from 1546 to 1555, ending with the Peace of Augsburg, by which the Lutherans won legal recognition of their religion.

The Name "Protestant." The Diet of Spires (A.D. 1529) at which Roman Catholics were in the majority ruled that Catholics could teach their religion in Lutheran States, but forbade Lutheran teaching in Catholic States, in Germany. Against this the Lutheran Princes made formal protest, and henceforth were known as "Protestants." The name, originally applied to Lutherans, has now come to be applied in popular use, to those protesting against Papal Usurpation—including all Evangelical Christian Bodies.

IN SWITZERLAND, the historic land of freedom, reform was started by Zwingli, and carried on by Calvin, the union of their followers (1549), constituting the "Reformed Church." Their reforms were more sweeping than Luther's.

Zwingli (A.D. 1484–1531), Zurich, became convinced, about 1516, that the Bible was the means by which to purify the church. 1525 Zurich officially accepted his teaching; and the churches gradually abolished Indulgences, Mass, Celibacy, Images, using the Bible as Sole Authority.

John Calvin (A.D. 1509–64), a Frenchman, accepted Reformation teachings 1533. Driven out of France 1534. Went to Geneva 1536. There his Academy became a pivotal center of Protestantism, attracting scholars from many lands.

IN THE NETHERLANDS the Reformation was received early; Lutheranism, and then Calvinism; and Anabaptists were already numerous. Between 1513 and 1531 there were issued 25 different translations of the Bible in Dutch, Flemish and French. The Netherlands were a part of the dominion of Charles V. In 1522 he established the Inquisition, and ordered all Lutheran writings to be burned. In 1525 prohibited religious meetings in which the Bible would be read. 1546 prohibited the printing or possession of the Bible, either vulgate or translation. 1535 decreed "death by fire" for Anabaptists. Philip II (1566–98), successor to Charles V, re-issued the edicts of his father, and with Jesuit help carried on the persecution with still greater fury. By one sentence of the Inquisition the whole population was condemned to death, and under Charles V and Philip II more than 100,000 were massacred with unbelievable brutality. Some were chained to a stake near the fire and slowly roasted to death; some were thrown into dungeons, scourged, tortured on the rack, before being burned. Women were buried alive, pressed into coffins too small, trampled down with the feet of the executioner. Protestants of Netherlands, after incredible suffering, in 1609, won their independence; Holland, on the North became Protestant; Belgium, on the South, Roman Catholic. Holland was the first country to adopt public schools supported by taxation, and to legalize principles of religious toleration and freedom of the press.

IN SCANDINAVIA Lutheranism was early introduced, and was made the State Religion, in Denmark (1536), Sweden (1539), Norway (1540). A hundred years later Gustavus Adolphus (1611–32), King of Sweden, rendered signal service in defeating Rome's effort to crush Protestant Germany.

IN FRANCE. By 1520 Luther's teachings had penetrated France. By 1559 there were about 400,000 Protestants. They were called "Huguenots." Their earnest piety and pure lives were in striking contrast to the scandalous lives of the Roman clergy. In 1557 Pope Pius urged their extermination. The king issued a decree for their massacre, and ordered all loyal subjects to help in hunting them out.

St. Bartholomew's Massacre. Catherine de Medici, mother of the King, an ardent Romanist and willing tool of the Pope, gave the order, and on the night of August 24, 1572, 70,000 Huguenots, including most of their leaders, were Massacred. There was great rejoicing in Rome. The Pope and his College of Cardinals went, in solemn procession, to the Church of San Marco, and ordered the Te Deum to be sung in thanksgiving. The Pope struck a medal in commemoration of the Massacre; and sent a Cardinal to Paris to bear the King and Queen-Mother the Congratulations of Pope and Cardinals.

The Huguenot Wars. Following St. Bartholomew's Massacre the Huguenots united and armed for resistance; till finally, in 1598, by the Edict of Nantes, they were granted freedom of conscience and worship. Pope Clement VIII called the Toleration Edict of Nantes a "cursed thing"; and, after years of underground work by the Jesuits, the Edict was Revoked, (1685); and 500,000 Huguenots fled to Protestant Countries.

The French Revolution, a hundred years later, (1789), one of the most frightful convulsions in history. The people, in a frenzy against the tyrannies of the ruling class (among whom were the Clergy, owners of one-third of all land, wealthy, lazy, immoral, and heartless in their treatment of the poor), rose up in a Reign of Terror and Blood, abolished the government, closed the churches, confiscated their property, suppressed Christianity and Sunday. Napoleon restored the church, but not the property; 1802 granted Toleration to all; and almost ended the Political Power of the Popes in every country.

In Bohemia, by 1600, in a population of 4,000,000, 80 per cent were Protestant. When the Hapsburgs and Jesuits had done their work, 800,000 were left, all Catholics.

In Austria and Hungary half the population Protestant, but under the Hapsburgs and Jesuits they were slaughtered.

In Poland, by the end of the 16th century, it seemed as if Romanism was about to be entirely swept away, but here, too, the Jesuits, by persecution, killed Reform.

In Italy, the Pope's own country, the Reformation was getting a real hold; but the Inquisition got busy, and hardly a trace of Protestantism was left.

IN SPAIN the Reformation never made much headway, because the Inquisition was already there. Every effort for freedom or independent thinking was crushed with a ruthless hand. Torquemada (1420–98), a Dominican monk, arch-inquisitor, in 18 years burned 10,200 and condemned to perpetual imprisonment 97,000. Victims were usually burned alive in the public square; made the occasion of religious festivities. From 1481 to 1808 there were at least 100,000 martyrs and 1,500,000 banished. "In the 16th and 17th centuries the Inquisition extinguished the literary life of Spain, and put the nation almost outside the circle of European civilization." When the Reformation began Spain was the Most Powerful country in the world.

The Spanish Armada (1588). One of the features of Jesuit strategy was to seek the overthrow of Protestant countries. Pope Gregory XIII "left nothing undone to impel Philip II, Emperor, and King of Spain, to proceed in war against Protestant England." Sixtus V, who became Pope as the enterprise was maturing, made it a Crusade (that is offered Indulgences to those who would take part). At that time Spain had the most powerful Navy that had ever sailed the seas; but the proud Armada met defeat in the English Channel. "England's victory was the final turning point in the great duel between Protestantism and Romanism; not only assured England and Scotland, but Holland, North Germany, Denmark, Sweden and Norway, to the Protestant cause." (Jacobs.)

IN ENGLAND it was Revolt, and then Reform. From the days of William the Conqueror (1066), there had been repeated protests against Papal Control of England. Henry VIII (1509–47) believed, as his predecessors had, that the English Church should be independent of the Pope. His Divorce was not the Cause, but the Occasion, of his break with Rome. Henry was no saint; but neither was the contemporary Pope, Paul III, who had many illegitimate children. In 1534 the Church of England definitely repudiated Papal authority, and settled down to an independent life under the spiritual direction of the Archbishop of Canterbury, Thomas Cranmer was Archbishop of Canterbury, and under him Reform began; monasteries were abolished on the grounds of immorality; an English Bible was put in the churches and a Prayer-Book for services in English, and the churches were stripped of many Romanist practices. Out of the English Church came the Puritans and Methodists.

IN SCOTLAND. The story of the Scotch Reformation is the story of John Knox.

John Knox (1515–72), a Scotch priest, about 1540 began teaching Reformation ideas. On the accession of Bloody Mary (1553), he went to Geneva, where he thoroughly absorbed Calvin's teaching. 1559 he was recalled to Scotland by the Parliament of Scotch Lords to become leader of the National Reform movement. The Political situation made Church Reform and National Independence ONE movement. Mary, Queen of Scots, had married Francis II, King of France, who was son of Catherine de Medici (of St. Bartholomew's Massacre fame). Scotland and France were thus in alliance, their crowns united by marriage. France was bent on the destruction of Protestantism. Philip II, King of Spain, with other Romanists, plotted the assassination of Queen Elizabeth, to put Mary queen of Scots on the English throne. Pope Pius V aided the scheme by issuing a Bull excommunicating Elizabeth and releasing her subjects from allegiance (which, by Jesuit teaching, meant that the assassin would be doing an act of service to God). Thus there was no chance for Reform of the Scotch Church as long as it was under French control. John

Knox believed that the future of Protestantism was bound up in an alliance between Protestant England and Protestant Scotland. He proved to be a magnificent leader. The Reformed Church was established 1560; and, with the help of England, by 1567, the French were driven out; and Romanism was more completely swept away than in any other country. John Knox, largely, made Scotland what it still is.

THE COUNTER-REFORMATION. In 50 years the Reformation had swept Europe, with most of Germany, Switzerland, Netherlands, Scandinavia, England, Scotland, Bohemia, Austria, Hungary, Poland in its grasp; and making headway in France. This was a terrific blow to the Roman Church, which, in turn, organized the Counter-Reformation; and by means of the Council of Trent (in session 18 years, 1545–63) and the Jesuits and the Inquisition some of the moral abuses of the Papacy were abolished, and by the close of the century Rome was organized for an aggressive onslaught on Protestantism; and under the brilliant and brutal leadership of the Jesuits regained much of the lost territory; South Germany, Bohemia, Austria, Hungary, Poland, Belgium, and crushed the Reformation in France. Within a hundred years, by 1689, the Counter-Reformation had spent its force. The principal Kulers who fought the Pope's Wars were: Charles V (1519–56) of Spain, against German Protestants; Philip II (1556–98), of Spain, against Holland, England; Ferdinand II (1619–37), of Austria, against Bohemians; Catherine de Medici, mother of three kings of France, Francis II (1559–60), Charles IX (1560–74), Henry III (1574–89), in the wars for the extermination of French Huguenots.

RELIGIOUS WARS. The Reformation movement was followed by a hundred years of religious war: 1. War on the German Protestants (1546–55); 2. War on the Protestants of the Netherlands (1566–1609); 3. Huguenot Wars in France (1572–98); 4. Philip's attempt against England (1588); 5. Thirty Years War (1618–48). In these wars political and national rivalries were involved, as well as questions of property, for the Church in most countries owned one-third to one-fifth of all lands. But every one of these wars was STARTED by Roman Catholic Kings, urged on by Pope and Jesuit, for the purpose of crushing Protestantism. They were the Aggressors. The Protestants were on the Defensive. Dutch, German nor French Protestants became Political Parties till after years of persecution.

THE THIRTY YEARS WAR (1618–48). In Bohemia and Hungary, by 1580, Protestants were in the majority, including most of the land-owning nobles. Emperor Ferdinand II, of the House of Hapsburg, had been educated by the Jesuits; and with their help undertook to suppress Protestantism. The Protestants united for defense. The first part of the war (1618–29), was a Catholic victory; they succeeded in driving Protestantism out of all Catholic States. Then they determined to re-Catholicize the Protestant States of Germany. Gustavus Adolphus, King of Sweden, realized that the fall of Protestant Germany would mean the fall of Sweden, and perhaps the end of Protestantism. He entered the war, and his army was victorious (1630–32). He saved the day for the Protestant cause. The rest of the war (1632–48), was mainly a struggle between France and the House of Hapsburg, ending with France the leading power in Europe. It ended with the Peace of Westphalia (1648), which fixed the lines between Romanist and Protestant States.

PAPAL PERSECUTIONS. The number of Martyrs under Papal Persecutions far outnumbered the Early Christian Martyrs under Pagan Rome: hundreds of thousands among the Albigenses, Waldenses, and Protestants of Germany, Netherlands, Bohemia and other countries. It is common to excuse the Popes in this matter by saying that it was the "spirit of the age." Whose age was it? and who made it so? The Popes. It was their world. For 1000 years they had been training the world to be in subjection to them. If the Popes had not taken the Bible from the people, the people would have known better, and it would NOT have been "the spirit of the age." It was NOT the spirit of Christ, and "Vicars of Christ" should have known better. Persecution is the spirit of the DEVIL, even though carried on in the name of Christ.

PROTESTANT PERSECUTIONS. Calvin consented to the death of Servetus. In Holland Calvinists executed an Arminian. In Germany Lutherans put to death a few Anabaptists. In England Protestant Edward VI executed 2 Roman Catholics in 6 years (Romanist Mary in the 5 following years burned 282 Protestants). Elizabeth executed, in 45 years 187 Romanists, most of them for treason, not heresy. In Massachusetts, 1659, 3 Quakers were hanged by Puritans, and, in 1692, 20 were executed for witchcraft. All told a few hundred martyrs may be charged against Protestants, at most not over a few thousand; but to Rome, untold millions. While the Reformation was a grand struggle for Religious Freedom, the Reformers were slow in granting to others what they sought for themselves. In Protestant countries Persecution ceased by 1700.

Protestantism

ITS DIVISIONS. The Protestant Movement was an effort of a part of the Western Church to free itself from the authority of Rome, and to gain for every man the right to worship God according to the dictates of his own conscience. Inevitably, in the breakaway, the struggle for freedom resolved itself into different streams with different emphasis carrying over some of Rome's errors. The

Movement, now about 400 years old, has made enormous growth and remarkable improvement. There is a growing spirit of unity, and a clearer understanding of Christianity. The Protestant Church, though it is a long way from perfection, in spite of its cross-currents and its weaknesses, beyond any doubt whatever, represents the Purest Form of Christianity in the world today; and probably the purest the church has known since the first three centuries. On the whole, there is no nobler set of men in the world than the Protestant Ministers.

NATIONAL CHURCHES. Wherever Protestantism triumphed a National Church arose: Lutheran in Germany; Episcopal in England; Presbyterian in Scotland; etc. Worship conducted in the language of the country, as against the universal use of Latin in Romanist churches. Invariably when the church in any country gained its freedom from the Pope it began to make progress in self-purification.

THE UNITED STATES was colonized: 1607, by Anglican Puritans, in Virginia: 1615, by Dutch Reformed, in New York; 1620, by Puritans, in Massachusetts; 1634, by English Catholics, in Baltimore, who could obtain their charter only by allowing freedom to all religions; 1639, by Baptists, in Rhode Island, under Roger Williams pioneer in advocating unlimited toleration for all religions; 1681, by Quakers, in Pennsylvania; lured to our shores in search of Religious Liberty. Thus our country came into being on the principles of Religious Toleration for all, and of absolute Separation of Church and State; principles that are now permeating all the Governments of the world, so that, in recent years, very many countries, even Roman Catholic countries, have decreed Separation of Church and State (though there seems to be a setback just now).

THE FUTURE OF THE PROTESTANT MOVEMENT is bound up in its attitude toward the Bible. "With the traditional form of Christianity there was handed down, in the Sacred Text itself, a source of divine knowledge, not exposed in like manner to corruption, from which the Church might learn how to distinguish Primitive Christianity from all subsequent additions, and so carry forward the work of keeping the Church pure till its completion."

THE SUNDAY SCHOOL. Founded by Robert Raikes, an editor of Gloucester, England (1780), to give Christian training to poor and unschooled children. Founded as a missionary branch of the church, it has grown enormously, and has now become a normal part of church life. Its great value is its promotion of the Bible, and its development of layman leadership.

MODERN WORLD-WIDE MISSIONS. The Most Important movement in history. Supplies some of the most thrilling stories in all literature, vibrant with life and heroism and helpfulness. Neither preachers nor Sunday School teachers pay enough attention to the lives of missionaries. Every congregation ought to hear over and over the story of Livingstone, unmatched among the world's heroes; and Carey, Morrison, Judson, Moffat, Martin, Paton and others, who have borne the tidings of Christ to distant lands and founded systems of preaching and Christian education and philanthropy which are transforming the world. When history is finished, and the whole story of mankind can be seen in its broad general perspective, it will probably be found that the World-Wide Missionary Movement of the past century, in its total influence on the nations, will have constituted THE MOST GLORIOUS CHAPTER IN THE ANNALS OF MAN.

The Greek, or Eastern Orthodox, Catholic Church

Christianity was first established in the Eastern, or Greek part of the Roman Empire. For two hundred years Greek was the language of Christianity.

In A.D. 330 Constantine made Constantinople Capital of the Roman Empire; henceforth, there was rivalry with Rome.

In 395 the Roman Empire was divided into Eastern and Western; Constantinople, the seat of Eastern, and Rome, Western.

In 632–638 the three Eastern centers of Christianity, Syria, Palestine and Egypt gave way to Mohammedanism; and Constantinople alone was left.

At the eighth Ecumenical Council (869), occurred the final schism between the Greek and Latin Churches. From the first the East refused to recognize the primacy of Rome.

At times there have been attempts to reunite the churches; but they have been futile, because the East would not acknowledge the authority of the Pope.

The Greek Church, now the church of southeastern Europe and Russia, is one of the three great divisions of Christendom, numbering 150,000,000 as against 340,000,000 Roman Catholics and 210,000,000 Protestants; or approximately one-fifth of Christian population of the world.

The Greek Church, in many of its practices, is very similar to the Roman Catholic Church. They do not require celibacy of their priests. They have no Popes.

Chronological View of the Protestant Movement in England and the United States

Edward II	1307–1327	
Edward III	1327–1377	Wyclif 1324–1384
Richard II	1377–1399	
Henry IV	1399–1413	
Henry V	1413–1422	
Henry VI	1422–1461	Invention of Printing 1450
Edward IV	1461–1483	
Richard III	1483–1485	
Henry VII	1485–1509	
		Discovery America 1492
Henry VIII	1509–1547	Luther 1483–1546
		Calvin 1509–1564
Edward VI	1547–1553	Knox 1515–1572
Mary	1553–1558	
Elizabeth	1558–1603	Rise of Puritanism
James I	1603–1625	
Charles I	1625–1649	Roger Williams 1604–1684
Cromwell	1653–1658	
Charles II	1660–1685	
James II	1685–1688	
Wm & Mary	1689–1702	
Anne	1702–1714	
George I	1714–1727	
George II	1727–1760	Wesley 1703–1791
		American Revolution 1775
George III	1760–1820	French Revolution 1789
George IV	1820–1830	
William IV	1830–1837	
Victoria	1837–1901	
Edward VII	1901–1910	
George V	1910–1936	
Edward VIII	1936 (Abdicated)	
George VI	1936–1952	
Elizabeth II	1952–	

Wyclif

14th century, the "morning star of the Reformation," translated the Bible into English, and paved the way for the Reformation in England.

Luther, Calvin, Knox

16th century, were the leaders in the Protestant Revolution that freed Western Europe from bondage to the Papacy.

Puritanism

Early half of the 17th century, arose in the latter part of the reign of Queen Elizabeth. It was produced by a popular interest in the Bible. It was a reform movement within the Church of England, protesting against the lifeless formalism of the times, and aiming at general purity and righteousness of life. Because they were persecuted by the ecclesiastical authorities, they separated themselves into Independent Churches, mostly Baptist, Congregational and Presbyterian. It was from among these Puritans that New England was colonized, lured to the shores of the New World, in search of liberty.

Roger Williams

17th century, an Episcopal clergyman, was driven out of Massachusetts (1636), and founded the colony of Rhode Island, where he affiliated himself with the Baptists. The Puritans had been very zealous in demanding liberty of conscience for themselves. But Williams insisted on it for ALL. His great passion was for the ABSOLUTE SEPARATION OF CHURCH AND STATE. All honor to the Baptists for their unceasing emphasis on it, for there are still mighty forces at work that would rob us of this precious heritage if they could.

John Wesley

18th century, a hundred years after the rise of Puritanism, and a product of it, for his mother was of Puritan stock. At a time when the Church had again fallen into lifeless formalism, he preached the doctrine of the witness of the Spirit and of a holy life. He was a rector in the Church of England, but they would not let him preach his doctrines in the churches. So he preached in the fields, mining camps and street corners. Organized societies of holy living, and spent his long life looking after them. Like the Puritan movement of the preceding century, he changed the whole moral tone of England. His movement is generally credited with saving England from a French Revolution. One of earth's greatest.

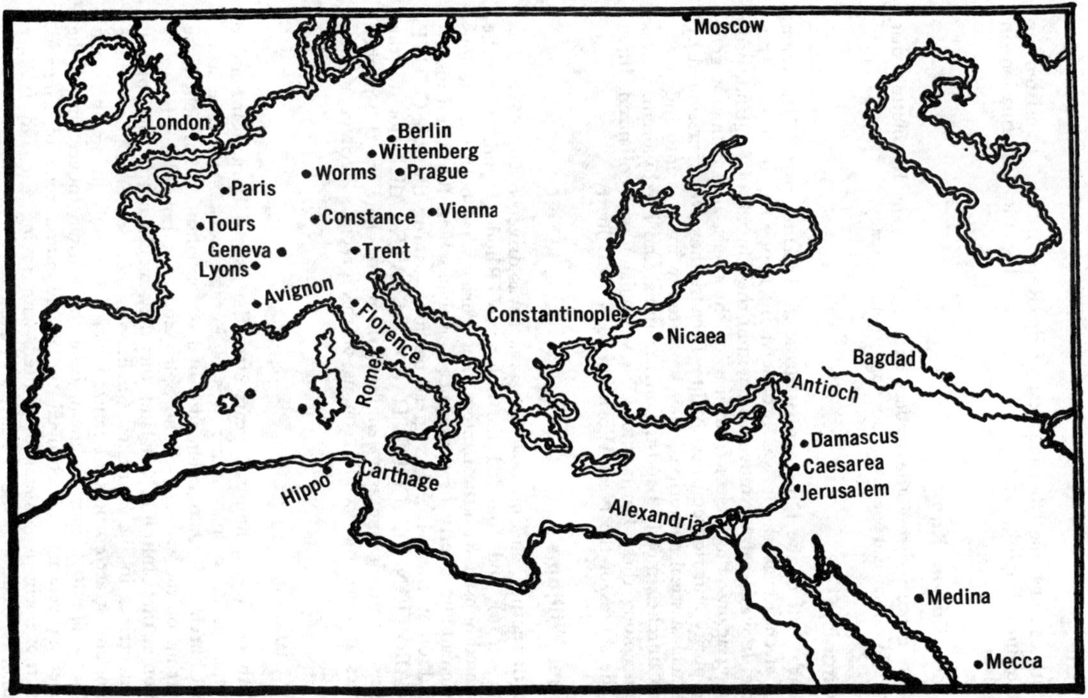
Moscow
London
Berlin
Wittenberg
Worms
Prague
Paris
Vienna
Tours
Constance
Geneva
Trent
Lyons
Avignon
Florence
Constantinople
Nicaea
Rome
Bagdad
Antioch
Damascus
Caesarea
Jerusalem
Carthage
Hippo
Alexandria
Medina
Mecca

Map 71.

The Mediterranean Basin, extending across the middle of the Eastern Hemisphere, between the Indian and Atlantic Oceans, bounded on the North by Europe, on the East by Asia, on the South by Africa, has been, until modern times, the area within which flowed the course of civilization. The Roman Empire, in the days of Christ, controlled the entire basin, under the sway of the Caesars.

Constantinople (Byzantium). Made Capital of Roman Empire by Constantine. Continued Capital of Eastern Empire, head of the Greek Church, and second city of the world during the middle ages. Home of Chrysostom. Fell to the Turks (1453).

Rome, where the spirit of the Caesars passed into the bishops of the Church, who became self-appointed Lords of Christendom, a claim which they have had trouble getting recognized, and which more than half of Christendom still refuses to recognize. However, the Papal Empire which arose on the ruins of the Pagan Empire has been a mighty factor in history, making Rome, till recently, on the whole, the world's most influential city.

Jerusalem, Antioch, Ephesus, Corinth, Rome, principal centers of Christianity in the first century.

Rome, Alexandria, Carthage, in 2nd and 3rd centuries.

Alexandria, in 3rd century became Intellectual Head of Christendom, Home of Origen.

Rome, Constantinople, Antioch, Jerusalem, Alexandria, seats of the five Patriarchs, or Metropolitans, who governed the church while the Papacy was developing.

Tours, Battle (A.D. 732), where Charles Martel stopped the onward rush of Mohammedans, and saved Europe.

Vienna, where John Sobieski (1683), defeated the Turks, and stopped the second Mohammedan menace to Europe.

North Africa, Western Asia, once Christian, in the 7th century, by the sword, became Mohammedan; and still are.

Jerusalem, Mother of Christianity.

Antioch. Center from which Empire was Christianized.

Mecca, Birthplace of Mohammed.

Medina, Capital of Mohammedanism till A.D. 661.

Damascus, Mohammedan Capital A.D. 661–750.

Bagdad, Mohammedan Captial A.D. 750–1258.

Lyons, Home of Iranaeus. Center of Gallic Christianity.

Caesarea, Home of Eusebius, Father of Church History.

Carthage, Home of Tertullian and Cyprian.

Hippo, Home of Augustine, famous theologian.

Prague, Home of John Huss.

Florence, where Savonarola was burned.

Constance, Council which ordered Huss burnt.

Wittenberg, Home of Luther, Liberator of Europe.

Worms, Famous Diet where Luther was tried.

Geneva, Home of Calvin; a center of Reformation.
Trent, Papal Council to stop Reformation.

Present World Situation

The figures on this and the following pages are only approximate, and in round numbers. Some are merely rough estimates. Statistical tables and estimates vary greatly.

Protestant figures, in these tables, indicate actual church membership. Roman Catholic and Eastern Orthodox figures count membership from birth and, in some cases, by families regardless of actual relationship with the church. So, Protestantism may, comparatively, be relatively stronger than the figures would indicate.

In Communist dominated lands the Church is suffering tremendous reverses. To what extent the Soviet has succeeded in crushing the Russian Church is not known.

To what extent present world convulsions may alter the religious status of the various countries is yet to be seen.

Religions of the World, Roughly, as of 1961

Total World Population	2,500,000,000
Protestant Christianity	240,000,000
Roman Catholic Christianity	400,000,000
Eastern Orthodox Christianity	150,000,000
Coptic Christianity (East Central Africa)	10,000,000
Mohammedan	300,000,000
Confucianist	300,000,000
Hindu	250,000,000
Buddhist	150,000,000
Animist	120,000,000
Jews	11,000,000
Under Atheistic Communist Domination	800,000,000

Confucianism is an ethical and philosophic system based on ancestor-worship.

Buddhism is an ascetic religion whose main tenet is the annihilation of desire.

Hinduism, the native religion of India, is an admixture of Buddhism, Brahminism, and many deities residing in objects and animals.

Animism is the belief that all inanimate objects are inhabited by spirits.

Figures above mentioned indicate about one-third of the world's population have professed Christianity in some of its forms, a large part of the third being a grossly corrupted Christianity.

Jewish population is distributed over the world, approximately, as follows: United States, 5,000,000; South America, 500,000; Europe, 3,500,000; Africa, 500,000; Israel, 1,500,000.

Religious Situation, by Continents, Roughly, as of 1961

North America

Population	220,000,000
Protestant Christianity	75,000,000
Roman Catholic Christianity	50,000,000

Predominantly Protestant

South America

Population	110,000,000
Roman Catholic Christianity	60,000,000
Protestant Christianity	10,000,000

Predominantly Roman Catholic

Europe

Population	500,000,000
Roman Catholic Christianity	240,000,000
Protestant Christianity	120,000,000
Eastern Orthodox Christianity	120,000,000

Southwest Europe, Roman Catholic
Northwest Europe, Protestant
East Europe, Eastern Orthodox

Asia

Population	1,300,000,000
Confucianist, Hindu, Buddhist	750,000,000
Mohammedan	250,000,000
Eastern Orthodox Christianity	20,000,000
Protestant Christianity	10,000,000
Roman Catholic Christianity	10,000,000

East Asia, Confucianist, Hindu, Buddhist
West Asia, Mohammedan

Africa

Population	200,000,000
Animist	100,000,000
Mohammedan	50,000,000
Coptic Christianity	10,000,000

Protestant Christianity 10,000,000
Roman Catholic Christianity 10,000,000
North Africa, Mohammedan
South Africa, Animist

Hinduism has made India what it is.
Confucianism and Buddhism have made China what it is.
Mohammedanism has made southwest Asia and north Africa what they are.
Roman Catholicism has made Italy, Spain and Latin America.
Protestantism has made Britain, United States and Canada.
THESE FACTS SPEAK FOR THEMSELVES, and SPEAK LOUDLY.

Present World Situation

By Countries, as of 1961

	Approximate Population	*Prevailing Religion*
Arabia	10,000,000	Mohammedan
Argentina	18,000,000	Roman Catholic
Australia	9,000,000	Protestant
Austria	7,000,000	Roman Catholic
Belgium	9,000,000	Roman Catholic
Brazil	55,000,000	Roman Catholic
Bulgaria	7,000,000	Eastern Orthodox
Burma	19,000,000	Buddhist
Canada	14,000,000	Protestant
Chile	6,000,000	Roman Catholic
China	470,000,000	Buddhist and Confucianist
Colombia	11,000,000	Roman Catholic
Czechoslovakia	12,000,000	Roman Catholic
Denmark	4,000,000	Lutheran
Egypt	20,000,000	Mohammedan
England	41,000,000	Protestant
Ethiopia	18,000,000	Coptic and Mohammedan
France	43,000,000	Roman Catholic
Germany	67,000,000	Lutheran
Greece	7,600,000	Eastern Orthodox
Holland	10,000,000	Protestant
Hungary	9,000,000	Roman Catholic and Protestant
India	360,000,000	Hindu and Mohammedan
Indo-China	27,000,000	Mohammedan
Indonesia	78,000,000	Mohammedan
Iran (Persia)	19,000,000	Mohammedan
Iraq (Mesopotamia)	5,000,000	Mohammedan

Ireland, Eire	3,000,000	Roman Catholic
Ireland, North	1,400,000	Protestant
Israel	1,500,000	Jewish
Italy	47,000,000	Roman Catholic
Japan	85,000,000	Shintoist and Buddhist
Korea	30,000,000	Buddhist, Confucianist, Christian
Mexico	27,000,000	Roman Catholic
Norway	3,000,000	Lutheran
Peru	9,000,000	Roman Catholic
Philippines	20,000,000	Roman Catholic
Poland	25,000,000	Roman Catholic
Portugal	8,000,000	Roman Catholic
Rumania	16,000,000	Eastern Orthodox
Russia	200,000,000	Eastern Orthodox and Atheist
Scotland	5,000,000	Presbyterian
Spain	28,000,000	Roman Catholic
Sudan	9,000,000	Mohammedan
Sweden	7,000,000	Lutheran
Switzerland	5,000,000	Protestant
Syria	3,400,000	Mohammedan
Thailand (Siam)	19,000,000	Buddhist
Turkey	21,000,000	Mohammedan
United States	160,000,000	Protestant
Venezuela	5,000,000	Roman Catholic
Yugoslavia	17,000,000	Eastern Orthodox and Roman Catholic

Religious Bodies in the United States

There are about 253 Religious Bodies in the United States. The figures given below cover, approximately, in round numbers, most of those reporting a membership of 100,000 or more, as of 1963.

Population	180,000,000
Protestant	66,854,200
Sunday School Enrollment	45,000,000
Roman Catholic	44,874,000
Jews	5,585,000
Baptists (28 bodies) in all	21,400,000
Southern Baptists	10,393,039
American Baptist Convention	1,559,103
Free Will Baptists	293,000
American Baptist Association	650,000
Methodist (21 bodies) in all	12,632,000
The Methodist Church	10,234,986

Lutheran (15 bodies) in all	8,340,000
Missouri-Synod Lutheran	2,591,762
American Lutheran	2,468,407
Augustana Lutheran	619,000
Wisconsin Synod Lutheran	354,840
Presbyterian (10 bodies) in all	4,327,000
Southern Presbyterian	957,558
United Presbyterian in U.S.A.	3,279,240
Protestant Episcopal	3,336,728
Eastern Orthodox	3,094,140
Disciples of Christ	1,834,206
United Church of Christ	2,023,611
Churches of Christ	2,250,000
Latter Day Saints (Mormon)	1,787,896
Evangelical United Brethren	757,719
Evangelical and Reformed	818,000
Assemblies of God	543,003
Churches of God	470,000
Church of God in Christ	413,000
Pentecostal Assemblies	430,000
Polish National Catholic	282,411
Seventh Day Adventists	366,000
Church of the Nazarene	342,032
Salvation Army	261,014
Reformed Church	230,000
Church of the Brethren	201,000
Christian Reformed	262,088
Reorganized Latter Day Saints	158,000
Friends	128,000

THE HABIT OF BIBLE READING

Everybody ought to Love the Bible. Everybody ought to Read the Bible. Everybody. It is God's Word. It holds the Solution of Life. It tells about the Best Friend mankind ever had, the Noblest, Kindest, Truest Man that ever trod this earth.

It is the Most Beautiful Story ever told. It is the Best Guide to human conduct ever known. It gives a Meaning, and a Glow, and a Joy, and a Victory, and a Destiny, and a Glory, to Life elsewhere unknown.

There is nothing in history, or in literature, that in any wise compares with the simple annals of the Man of Galilee, who spent his days and nights ministering to the Suffering, teaching Human Kindness, Dying for Human Sin, Rising to Life that Shall Never End, and promising Eternal Security and Eternal Happiness to all who will Come to Him.

Most people, in their serious moods, must have some wonderment in their minds as to how things are going to stack up when the End comes. Laugh it off, toss it aside, as we may, THAT DAY WILL COME. And THEN WHAT? Well, it is the Bible that has the answer. And an unmistakable answer it is. There Is a God. There is a Heaven. There is a Hell. There is a Saviour. There Will be a Day of Judgment. Happy the man, who, in the days of his flesh, makes his peace with the Christ of the Bible, and gets himself ready for the Final Take-Off.

How can any thoughtful person keep his heart from warming up to Christ, and to the Book that tells about Him? Everybody ought to love the Bible. Everybody. EVERYBODY.

Yet Widespread Neglect of the Bible by churches and by church people is just simply appalling. Oh, we talk about the Bible, and defend the Bible, and praise the Bible, and exalt the Bible. Yes indeed! But many church members Seldom Ever Even Look Into a Bible—indeed would be Ashamed to be seen Reading the Bible. And Church Leadership generally seems to be making no serious effort to get people to be Bible Readers.

Present-day Protestantism seems to Care So Little for the Book it So Loudly Professes. And Roman Catholicism avowedly prefers its own decrees above the Bible.

We are intelligent about everything else in the world. Why not be intelligent about our religion? We read newspapers, magazines, novels, and all kinds of books, and listen to the radio by the hour. Yet most of us do not even know the names of the Bible books. Shame on us! Shame on us! Worse still, the Pulpit, which could easily remedy the situation, seems, with rare exceptions, Not to Care.

Individual Direct Contact with God's Word is the principal means of Christian Growth. All leaders of Spiritual Power in Christian History have been devoted Readers of the Bible.

The Bible is the Book we Live by. Bible Reading is the means by which we Learn, and Keep Fresh in our Minds, the IDEAS that mold our Lives. Our Lives are the product of our Thoughts. To Live Right, we need to Think Right.

Thoughts have Power over our Lives by being OFTEN in our minds. We read the Bible Frequently and Regularly, so that God's Thoughts may be Frequently and Regularly in our Minds; that His Thoughts may become Our Thoughts; that Our Ideas may become Conformed to God's Ideas; so that we may be Transformed into God's Own Image, and be Made Fit for Eternal Companionship with our Creator.

We May, Indeed, Absorb Christian Truth, in some measure, by attending religious services, listening to sermons, Bible lessons, testimonies, and reading Christian literature.

But, in these things, however good and helpful they may be, we are receiving God's Truth SECOND-HAND, diluted through human channels, and, to quite an extent, glossed over with human ideas and traditions.

Such things cannot possibly take the place of our Reading for Ourselves the BIBLE ITSELF, and grounding, for Ourselves, our Faith and Hope and Life, Directly on God's Word, rather than on what men say about God's Word.

God's Word Itself is the Weapon of the Spirit of God for the Redemption and Perfection of the human soul. It is not enough to listen to others talk and teach and preach about the Bible. We need to keep ourselves, Every One of us, in Direct Touch with God's Word. It is the Power of God in our hearts.

Bible Reading is a Basic Christian Habit. We do not mean that we should worship the Bible as a fetish; but we do worship the God and the Saviour that the Bible tells us about. And because we Love our God and our Saviour, we Love Dearly and Devotedly the Book that is from Him and about Him.

Nor do we mean that the Habit of Bible Reading is in itself a virtue; for it is possible to read the Bible without applying its teachings to one's own life; and there are those who read the Bible, and yet are mean and crooked and un-Christian. But they are the exception.

As a rule, Bible Reading, if done in the right spirit, is a Habit out of which All Christian Virtues Grow, the Most Effective Character-Forming Power known to men.

As an Act of Religious Devotion. Our attitude toward the Bible is a pretty sure indication of our attitude toward Christ. If we Love a person, we love to Read about him, do we not?

If we could only bring ourselves to think of our Bible Reading as an act of devotion to Christ, we might be inclined to treat the matter less lightly.

It is a Glorious thing to be a Christian. The Most Exalted Privilege any mortal man can have is to Walk Through Life Hand in Hand with Christ as Saviour and Guide; or, to put it more correctly, to toddle along at His side, and, though always stumbling, Never Letting Go of His Hand.

This personal relation of each of us to Christ is one of the intimate things of life, and we do not talk much about it, probably because we realize that we are so pitifully unworthy to wear His Name. But deep down in our hearts, in our serious moods, we know that, in spite of our weakness, our worldliness, our frivolity, our selfishness, and our sins, we love Him more than we love anything else in the world; and, in our saner moments, we feel we would not willingly offend or hurt Him for anything. But we are thoughtless.

Well, now, the Bible is the Book that tells about Christ. Is it possible to Love Christ, and at the same time be complacently indifferent to His Word? IS IT POSSIBLE?

The Bible is the Best Devotional Book. Booklets for daily devotions, now advertised so abundantly by various denominational publishing houses, may have their place. But they are No Substitute for the Bible. The Bible is God's Own Word. And no other book can take its place. Every Christian, young and old, should be a Faithful Reader of the Bible.

George Muller, who, in his Orphanages in Bristol, England, did, by Prayer and Trust, one of the most remarkable things in Christian history, attributed his success, on the human side, to his love for the Bible. He said:

"I believe that the one chief reason that I have been kept in happy useful service is that I have been a lover of Holy Scripture. It has been my habit to read the Bible through four times a year; in a prayerful spirit, to apply it to my heart, and practice what I find there. I have been for sixty-nine years a happy man; happy, happy, happy."

Helps to Bible Study. The Bible is a big book, in reality a library of books, of the far distant past. And we need all the help we can get in trying to understand it. A Bible Dictionary, of the right kind, is the best of helps. A Commentary, of the right kind, is most valuable. And every one should have a Concordance.

But even so, it is surprising how largely the Bible is Self-Interpretive when we know what is in it. There are difficulties a plenty in the Bible, even beyond the comprehension of the most erudite. But, for all that, the Main Teachings of the Bible are unmistakable, so plain that "wayfaring men, though fools, need not err therein."

Accept the Bible Just As It Is, for Exactly What It Claims To Be. Don't worry about the theories of the critics. The ingenious and impudent effort of modern criticism to undermine the historical reliability of the Bible will pass; and the BIBLE ITSELF will still Stand as the Light of the Human Race to the End of Time. Pin your faith to the Bible. It is God's Word. It will never let you down. For men, it is the Rock of Ages. Trust its teachings; and be happy forever.

Read the Bible with an Open Mind. Don't try to straightjacket all its passages into the mold of a few pet doctrines. And don't read into its passages ideas that are not there, not even for a sermon. But try to search out fairly and honestly the main teachings and lessons of each passage. Thus we will come to believe what we ought to believe; for the Bible is abundantly able to take care of itself, if given a chance.

Read the Bible Thoughtfully. In Bible reading, we need to watch ourselves very closely, lest our thoughts wander, and our reading become perfunctory and meaningless. We must determine resolutely to keep our minds on what we are reading, doing our best to form an intelligent conception of it, and being on the lookout for lessons for ourselves.

Keep a Pencil at Hand. It is a good thing, as we read, to mark passages we like; and, now and then, run through the pages, and review, and re-read, passages thus marked. In time a well-marked Bible will become very dear to us, as the day draws near for us to meet the Author.

Habitual, Systematic Reading of the Bible is what counts. Occasional, or Spasmodic, reading does not mean much. Unless we have some sort of System to follow, and hold to it with Resolute Determination, the chances are that we will not read the Bible any too much. Our Inner Life, like our fleshy body, needs its Daily Food.

A Certain Time Each Day, whatever our plan of reading, should be set aside for it. Otherwise we are apt to neglect it.

First thing in the morning is good, if our routine of work permits. Or, in the evening, at the close of the day's work, we might find ourselves freer from the strain of hurry.

Or, maybe, both morning and evening. For some, a period in the middle of the day might be more suitable.

The particular time of day does not greatly matter. The important thing is that we choose a time that best fits in with our daily round of work; and that we try to hold ourselves to it, and not be discouraged if now and then our routine is broken into by things beyond our control.

On Sundays, we might do a good part of our Bible Reading, as it is the Lord's Day, set aside for the Lord's Work.

Memorize the Names of the Bible Books. Do this very first thing. The Bible is composed of sixty-six books. Each of these books is about Something. The starting point for any sort of intelligent conception of the Bible is, first of all, to know what those books are, and the order in which they are arranged, and, in a general way, what each one is about.

Memorize Favorite Verses. Thoroughly memorize them, and often repeat them to ourselves, verses that we live on: sometimes when we are alone; or, in the night, to help put ourselves to sleep on the Everlasting Arms.

To run God's thoughts through our mind often will make our mind grow like God's mind; and as our mind grows like God's mind, our whole life will be transformed into His image. It is one of the very best spiritual helps we can have.

Plans of Bible Reading. Many plans are suggested. One plan will appeal to one person; another plan, to another person. The same person may, at different times, like different plans. The particular plan does not greatly matter. The essential thing is that we Read the Bible with some degree of Regularity.

Our Plan of Reading Should Cover the Whole Bible with reasonable Frequency; for it is All God's Word, all One Story, a literary structure of profound and marvelous Unity, centered around Christ. CHRIST is the Heart and Climax of the Bible. All that goes before is, one way or another, anticipatory of HIM. All that comes after is interpretive of HIM. The whole Bible may very properly be called The Story of Christ. The Old Testament paves the way for His Coming. The Four Gospels tell the Story of His Earthly Life. The Epistles explain His Teachings. And Revelation, His Triumph.

However, Some Parts of the Bible are More Important than other parts, and should be read more often. The New Testament, of course, is more important than the Old Testament. In each Testament, some books, and in each book, some chapters, have special value. The Four Gospels are most important of all.

A Well-Balanced Plan of Bible Reading, we think, might be something like this: for every time we read the Bible through, let us read the New Testament an Extra Time or Two, with frequent Re-Reading of Favorite Chapters in both Testaments.

How Often? Once a Year, we think, through the Old Testament, and Twice through the New Testament, would be a good MINIMUM plan for the average person to follow. And it would simplify matters to make it co-terminous with the calendar year, beginning with January, and ending in December.

Such a Plan would mean an average of 4 or 5 chapters a day, and would require something like an average of 15 or 20 minutes a day. Can't find time? Well, it is important enough to take time. 1 minute a day, or 3 minutes a day, for religious devotion, is child's play. If we are Christians, why not take our religion seriously? Why play at it? Let us not fool ourselves. We CAN find time for the things we WANT to find time for.

How Go About It? First, let us choose our plan, and map out our year's schedule, assigning a certain number of chapters for each day, or a certain book, or part of book, or group of books, for each week, or for each month, as we may prefer.

More Particularly, the Old Testament has 39 books, 929 chapters. The New Testament has 27 books, 260 chapters. Total, 66 books, 1189 chapters. Both books and chapters vary greatly in length. Some are very short, some quite long. In an average size Bible, of average print, an average chapter is about equal in length to a page.

Some chapters, and some books, on account of the nature of their subject matter, may be read more rapidly than others. And some chapters are worthy of being Read Over and Over and Over, and Again and Again and Again.

Consecutive Reading. This is reading the books just as they come, from Genesis to Revelation. And then doing it over again. In this plan, unless one reads the Bible through very often, he goes too long without reading in the New Testament.

Alternating Between the Testaments. That is, going through both Testaments concurrently; reading some each day, or each week, in both Testaments; or, one week in the Old Testament, and next week in the New; or, a book in the Old, and then a book in the New.

A Chapter a Day. Many do this. And it is a wonderful habit. But it would be so much better if we could make it two, or three, or four chapters, a day.

Reading the Bible by Books: that is, a whole book, or large part of a book, at a time, or as continuously as possible. As a rule, it is better to think of our Bible Reading tasks in terms of Whole Books than piece-meal chapter selections.

Reading One Book Over and Over: that is, making a special study of some particular book, reading it over and over and over, day after day. This is exceedingly helpful. But should not be carried far enough to cause too-long neglect of the rest of the Bible.

Group Reading. What a wonderful thing it would be, if a Bible class, under the leadership of its teacher, or a congregation, under the leadership of its pastor, would Read the Bible TOGETHER, the teacher, or pastor, on Sundays, teaching, or preaching, from Scriptures read the past week. Why not? WHY NOT? How better could a pastor and his people walk together with God through life than thus in fellowship around God's Word?

Following is a suggested plan for such Group Reading.

Fig. 73. Studying the Bible.
Photo courtesy Harold M. Lambert

A Suggested Plan for Group Reading. For such a purpose, inasmuch as the Week is the unit of our religious life, probably as good a schedule as any to follow would be that of Alternating by Weeks between the Testaments, having a Book, or group of the smaller Books, for each Week, covering the Old Testament ONCE, and the New Testament TWICE, each year, something like that below.

Such a Plan, we think, would be a simple and sensible plan for any class or congregation to follow year after year. For anyone could

Weeks	
1st	Genesis
3rd	Exodus
5th	Leviticus
7th	Numbers
9th	Deuteronomy
11th	Joshua, Judges
13th	Ruth, I Samuel
15th	II Samuel
17th	I Kings
19th	II Kings
21st	I Chronicles
23rd	II Chronicles
25th	Ezra, Nehemiah, Esther
27th	Job
29th	Psalms
31st	Psalms
33rd	Psalms
35th	Proverbs, Ecclesiastes, Song
37th	Isaiah
39th	Isaiah
41st	Jeremiah
43rd	Jeremiah, Lamentations
45th	Ezekiel
47th	Daniel
49th	Hosea, Joel, Amos, Obadiah, Jonah, Micah
51st	Nahum, Habakkuk, Zephaniah, Haggai, Zechariah, Malachi

adjust himself to it. Those who would like to spend more time on the Bible than the plan calls for could read each book an extra time or two, as they go along. On the other hand, those who are too busy, or too lazy, or too indifferent, to give as much time as the plan calls for, could, at least, glance through the assigned books, and read some of the best chapters, and thus, in measure, follow along with the group, till, by and by, they might find themselves becoming more interested.

This plan is only a suggestion. Any pastor or teacher who would try out the plan should make his own schedule; for its success, in the last analysis, will depend on the conviction and earnestness with which the leader pushes it.

Weeks	
2nd	Matthew
4th	Mark
6th	Luke
8th	Luke
10th	John
12th	Acts
14th	Romans
16th	I & II Corinthians
18th	Galatians, Ephesians, Philippians, Colossians
20th	I & II Thessalonians, I & II Timothy, Titus, Philemon
22nd	Hebrew, James
24th	I & II Peter, I & II & III John, Jude
26th	Revelation
28th	Matthew
30th	Matthew, or John
32nd	Mark
34th	Luke
36th	John
38th	Acts
40th	Romans
42nd	I & II Corinthians
44th	Galatians, Ephesians, Philippians, Colossians
46th	I & II Thessalonians, I & II Timothy, Titus, Philemon
48th	Hebrews, James
50th	I & II Peter, I & II & III John, Jude
52nd	Revelation

THE MOST IMPORTANT THING IN THIS BOOK

IS

This Simple Suggestion:

THAT EACH CHURCH HAVE

A CONGREGATIONAL PLAN OF BIBLE READING

and

THAT THE PASTOR'S SERMON BE FROM

THE PART OF THE BIBLE READ THE PAST WEEK

Thus connecting

The Pastor's Preaching with the People's Bible Reading.

This suggestion, if followed, would, beyond any doubt whatever, produce a Re-Vitalized Church: PROVIDED the Pastor himself thoroughly Believes in the Bible as God's Word, and puts His Heart into the effort.

The Church and the Bible go together. The Church exists to proclaim and exalt the Christ of the Bible, and for Nothing Else. A Church that does not Enthrone the Bible in the Lives of its people is False to its Mission.

The Bible is not just a sort of text, or pretext, book for preachers and teachers. It is a book For the People, All the People. And preachers and teachers who build on any other foundation must not be surprised if their work in the end proves to be very superficial.

With all our facilities for propagating Christian truth, our well-organized churches and Bible schools, our seminaries, our highly trained ministers and church leaders, with the last word in up-to-date religious education methods, an endless amount of Christian literature, and an ever-increasing number of meetings and organizations where we talk and teach and preach in the name of the Bible, even quoting chapter and verse—Yet the Great Body of our Church Members Treat the Bible as if it were a Mere Side-Issue in their Lives.

They are willing, provided enough promotional pressure is put on them, to listen to preachers and leaders talk of Bible things; but, as for Reading it Themselves, only a Few do it. Of a hundred average church members, perhaps One may even know the names of the Bible books, or have any idea of what each book is about. Probably more than three-fourths of our American Protestant Church Members could not, off-hand, tell where to find the Sermon on the Mount, or the Ten Commandments.

And, on top of this Ignorance of the Bible, and Indifference to it, and Neglect of it, they have no great sense of Loyalty to the Church, or Conscience about it. On an average, less than one-third, or one-fourth, of a congregation's enrolled professed membership, attend its Sunday services with any degree of regularity.

What a fearful indictment of prevailing techniques of doing church work! Is not something sadly lacking in methods that are producing churches that are so largely of the Laodicean type, indifferent, half-hearted, lukewarm, disloyal and worldly-minded; or, the Sardis type, in which there are only a FEW who have not defiled their garments?

I marvel that Church People are so Indifferent to, and Neglectful of, the Book that tells them about their Saviour. But I marvel more that Church LEADERS are doing so little about it. Unquestionably the most fatal weakness of the present day Church is the Lack of Leadership in the Pulpit on this One Point of Guiding and Leading its people into the ONE HABIT that is the Source and Basis of Everything that the Church exists to accomplish in its people.

Congregational Bible Reading and the Pulpit

I do not wonder that so-called "modernist" preachers, holding the view of the Bible which they hold, show no interest in getting their people to be Bible Readers. Rather, like fifth-columnists, undermining the Christian Faith from within, their delight seems to be in blue-penciling the Scripture. These words are not addressed to them.

But what puzzles me is that our "conservative" preachers, who proclaim with militant vehemence their faith in the Bible as God's Word, and exhaust their vocabulary in exalting and glorifying the Bible, show so little concern about their people Reading the Bible for Themselves. That puzzles me.

Preachers preach their sermons, teachers teach their lessons, seminary professors diligently train young ministers how to develop their alliterative firstlies, secondlies and thirdlies—all from the Bible to be sure. But where are the churches, ministers, teachers or seminary professors, who, save for an occasional exhortation, are setting themselves to establish Bible Reading Habits among those who are under their pastoral care?

The whole set-up and technique of present day church organization and activity seem designed to give the impression that everything depends on Sermons. To be sure, Preaching is ordained of God, that is, New Testament Preaching. It may be a distortion of the New Testament word "preach" to apply it to the present prevalent type of pulpit effusions. Certainly the New Testament never intended that Preaching Should Be So Utterly Devoid of Instruction in the Word of God as are the common run of Text Sermons that church-going people now have to listen to. But be that as it may, Preaching, even in its truest sense, and at its best, was never designed of God to be a complete and sufficient Substitute for the People Themselves Reading for Themselves the Word of God Itself.

EVERY CHRISTIAN Ought to be a Bible Reader. It is the One Habit, which, if done in the right spirit, more than any other one habit, will make a Christian what he ought to be in every way. If any church could get its people as a whole to be devoted Readers of God's Word, it would Revolutionize the church. If the churches of any community, as a whole, could get their people, as a whole, to be Regular Readers of the Bible, it would Not Only Revolutionize the churches, but it would Purge and Purify the Community as nothing else could do.

Example of the Dark Ages. During the Dark Ages, the Church, under the domination of the Popes, for five hundred years, tenth to fifteenth centuries, Ruled the World with as Despotic a hand as any earthly empire had ever done. Strange, is it not, that Church Supremacy and the Dark Ages were CO-EVAL? The Church, the "Light" of the world, brought to the world Midnight Darkness. Why? Because the Papacy suppressed all liberty, and prohibited the circulation of the Bible among the people, even put people to death for reading the Bible (see page 776, 783); and in their infinite presumption, substituted Papal Decrees in place of God's Word. That is what made the Dark Ages—Man's Devilish Impudence in Exalting Himself above God's Word. If the Church had submitted itself to God's Word, and taught it to the people, and encouraged its circulation among the people, it MIGHT HAVE BEEN THE MILLENNIUM instead of the DARK AGES.

Example of the Reformation. It was the discovery of a Bible by Martin Luther, and its Release to the People, backed by Luther's own matchless invincible soul, that Brought Forth the Protestant Reformation, and Proclaimed Liberty to the Modern World—mightiest step forward in human progress ever known in history. Those who read history know full well how directly we owe our Freedom and All That is Dear to us to the Bible.

Example of Elizabethan England. In Green's Short History of the English People it is stated that "No Greater Moral Change ever passed over a nation than passed over England in the latter part of the reign of Queen Elizabeth. England became the people of a Book, and That Book Was The Bible. It was Read by Every Class of People. And the Effect was Amazing. The Whole Moral Tone of the Nation was Changed."

And Now, Today, The One Best Thing that the Church could do would be to Set Itself to Enthrone God's Word in the Lives of its People. The Rest Would Follow. That One Thing in itself would go further in solving all problems, individual, social and national, than anything else the Church could do. God's Word Is The Best Weapon the Church has.

Is Such a Thing Possible? or Practical? Could a Congregation as a Whole be made a Bible Reading People? It Most Certainly Could, and Within a Very Short Time. All that is needed is a Pastor who Believes in the Idea, and will Put His Heart Into It.

It will not be enough to preach sermons on Bible Reading, even though that be done ever so frequently. To such some would respond. But should a pastor wish to enlist his Whole Congregation, the best way to do it would be to make out some sort of a reasonably worthwhile Plan of Bible Reading, and Set it before them, and give them to understand that He Expects Them To Make It a Part of Their Church Life, and Lead them in it, and Hold them to it, and, from Sunday to Sunday, one way or another, Keep it before them, year after year, as if he really meant business; all the while making it the Basis of his Sermons.

As for the Sermons: merely to choose a Text from the section of Scripture the people have read, and then branch off into a typical text sermon devoid of any semblance of instruction—that is no stimulant to the Peoples' Own Bible Reading. Rather, the Sermon should be a Study of, or in, the section read, as a whole, or a worthwhile part of it, calling their attention to some of its best features, and most interesting facts, and worthwhile lessons, as if he were Teaching a Bible Class.

There Is Not The Slightest Doubt but that any average congregation would respond Gladly and Whole-Heartedly to such an effort on the part of their pastor.

But, says someone, to make the Sunday Church Service like a Bible Class would be entirely too Prosaic and Uninteresting. A Bible Study more uninteresting than the prevalent type of Text Sermon? Are we to assume that the average congregation of church people have too little intelligence to desire any Solid Instruction from their pastor? or from God's Word?

On the contrary, we are sure that the average congregation would LOVE such a plan. And they would never tire of it. Never. NEVER. And they would Love and Honor their pastor for thus leading and encouraging and helping them in the formation of a Habit they know they ought to follow.

And what wonders it would work! In Church Loyalty. Crowded Churches. Interest in the Sermons. Intelligence about God's Word. Christian Growth. Spiritual Power. Family Religion. Family Unity. And what better medicine for Half-Hearted, Indifferent, Pleasure-Loving, Worldly-Minded church members? What one thing could a pastor do that would be more worthwhile?

And what better Evangelistic technique? What easier, surer, and sounder way to lead a person to Christ than through Christ's Own Word? What more effective way to reach the unsaved? What better foundation for a Revival?

What better task could a Church set for itself than the task of Turning its Community into a Bible Reading Community? Suppose a church would have such a Plan of Combined Congregational Bible Reading and Sunday Preaching as here suggested; and suppose the Church would foster Bible Reading, not only among its own members, but throughout its community generally; periodically covering the community with leaflets containing its Plan of Bible Reading, with incidental invitations to the Church Services—what better evangelistic method could a Church have? If this isn't the CHURCH'S business, whose business is it? If it isn't the pulpit's business, then just what is the pulpit's business?

THE HABIT OF GOING TO CHURCH EVERY SUNDAY AS AN ACT OF WORSHIP TO GOD

All Christian People Ought to
Go to Church Every Sunday,
Unless Hindered by Sickness,
Or Necessary Work,
Or Necessity of Some Kind.
It Ought to be a Matter of Conscience,
And an Act of Worship.

The Churches are
The Most Important institutions
In any community.
The Sunday Services are
The church's Principal Way of doing its work;
It is THE EVENT of the community life.

Nothing ever happens in any community
As important to the life of the community
As the regular Sunday Worship Services.
Every community ought to love its churches,
And, at this appointed time, turn out, en masse,
To honor HIM in whose name the church exists.

What it Would Mean

Assuming the Pulpit to be Faithful,
And the Services what they Ought to be,
If the churches were Filled Every Sunday
The community would Take Notice,
Evangelistic work of the church would be done,
Financial problems would be solved,
Missionary problems would be solved.
The whole church program would be advanced.
It is the One Thing
That would make the churches Strong;
The one thing on which depends the
Solution of the Problems facing Christianity.

If all Christian Church people
Would stir themselves up to be Faithful
In this one Fundamental Christian Duty
It would set forward the Influence of the Church,
And the Christ for whom the church stands,
MORE THAN ALL THE REST OF
THE THINGS THE CHURCHES ARE DOING
PUT TOGETHER.

What the Church is For. To HOLD CHRIST before the people. The Church was not invented by men. Men have used it and misused it. But the Church was founded by Christ. Christ is the Heart of the Church, and its Lord. The Church exists to Bear Witness to Christ. Christ himself, not the Church, is the transforming power in men's lives. The mission of the Church is to exalt Christ, so that He Himself may do his own blessed work on the hearts of men.

The Church's Method. MEETING TOGETHER in the name of Christ. The word "Church" means a "Called Out Assembly," a "Congregation," those who "Come Together." In order to do his work on men's hearts Christ must be Often in their minds. So, church meetings need to be Frequent.

How Frequent? Weekly: First Day of the Week: The Lord's Day: Sunday. The Lord himself so ordained. It seems, from Acts 20:6, 7, that even Paul had to wait, in Troas, for the "first day of the week" to get the disciples together. God instituted the Church, and God appointed the First Day of the week as Church Day. All Christendom has so recognized it, and has made this day a day of cessation from the ordinary activities of life.

Other Meetings. A well-organized church has many meetings, for various groups and purposes. The Sunday School is its most valuable adjunct. The Sunday Evening service, very definitely, has an important place in church life. But what we are here saying is, that all Christendom unites in recognizing Sunday Morning as Church Time; the one grand central meeting of them all, in a class all by itself, with a pre-eminence all its own, for the whole Christian public, the center around which all church machinery should revolve; and, however many other meetings one may or may not attend, Habitual, Faithful, Conscientious, Life-Long Attendance on this ONE MOST IMPORTANT of all religious meetings is a UNIVERSAL CHRISTIAN DUTY, except for those hindered by sickness or necessity.

The Method will Never be Changed. The invention of Printing, making Bibles and Christian Literature cheap and abundant, so that the people may read for themselves about Christ; the coming of the Radio, so that we may sit at home and listen to sermons and church services; these will never do away with the need for the Church. It is God's plan that his people, in every community, throughout the whole world, at this appointed time, MEET TOGETHER, in this public way, to thus publicly honor Christ.

The Present Pitiful Situation. Normally, Sunday morning attendance should be nearly a hundred per cent of church membership. But, on the whole, taking the churches as they come, if their Sunday morning congregations were counted and averaged, for every Sunday in the year, winter and summer, good weather and bad, it would probably be found that the average Sunday morning congregation of the average Protestant church in our land would range between One-Third and One-Sixth of what the church calls its membership. THIS IS THE FUNDAMENTAL WEAKNESS OF PROTESTANTISM. Indifference to the Institution that stands for Christ, in its one principal way of functioning, is, without doubt, the very greatest hindrance to the progress of Christ's work.

The Sunday Morning Congregation is a fair measure of the people's interest in their church. Their interest in their church is a fair measure of their interest in Christ. Whether we will or no, our attitude toward Sunday morning church indicates our attitude toward Christ's influence in our community. If we are faithful, we are helping Him. If we are indifferent, we are hurting Him.

"Going As an Act of Worship." By this we mean the Motive that prompts it; the thing in our mind before we go that makes us start; doing it as a matter of common Christian principle, as an act of Conscience toward God, an obligation to Christ; not caring especially whom we may see, or what we may hear; going, if need be, in spite of what we expect to hear; finding our chief satisfaction in the thought that we are doing our duty to our God.

And, of course, it implies that we will try to be On Time; that we will leave the Back Seat for late-comers; that we will not settle ourselves in the end of the pew, so that others will have to climb over us; that we will be Quiet, Courteous, Reverent, Attentive and Sympathetic.

"So Little of Christ in the services," says some one, "services so poor, so little religion in the music, so little in the preaching worth listening to, so many things people do not go to church to hear, so little Bible teaching, so little spiritual help—how can we think of ourselves as going to church FOR CHRIST, when, so often, there is so little of Christ in the service?" Well, we are sorry to say, this is all too true. Nevertheless, IT IS Christ's work, even tho it is in human hands that are all too human, and pitifully unworthy and inefficient. With all its shortcomings, the average service in the average Protestant church, is helpful; and, if we can keep ourselves in the right spirit, it will do us good.

The Sunday School and the Church. The Sunday School is by far the most valuable branch of Church work. It is a fearful mistake for a church to neglect the children of its community. What a glorious thing it is to be a good Sunday School teacher, and help shepherd the children! But the Sunday School is a Feeder to, not a Substitute for, the Church. Religious Education that does not tie the child to the Church is not worthy the name. Unless children form the habit of going to Church while they are in Sunday School the chances are they never will.

Auxiliary Groups and Meetings. Churches, to be efficient, need to be well-organized. Much Christian work can best be accomplished in smaller groups. But Group Loyalty must not be allowed to supplant Church Loyalty. Attendance at a Group meeting should not be regarded as a substitute for attendance at the main Church service. Sunday Morning is Church Time; and activity in any form of Christian work cannot properly be regarded as a sufficient excuse for absence from the Sunday Morning Service, except necessity so requires.

Radio. Is it not better to stay at home and hear a good sermon over the radio than go to church and hear a poor sermon? NOT on Sunday Morning. We go to Church, not to hear sermons, but as an Act of Worship to God, and while there we are exposed to sermons, sometimes endure them. Radio provides no excuse for escape from this Christian Duty. Moreover, radio sermons are no better than church sermons.

Is it not Enough to be Fairly Regular? NO. The great body of church people who are just Fairly Regular hold the key to the present pitiful situation. If they would become Altogether Regular, then our churches would overflow every Sunday. It would mean Power for the Church. Every Sunday belongs to Christ; EVERY SUNDAY. The grand need of Protestantism is that our people make this thing a matter of Conscience rather than of Convenience.

The Excuses and Reasons that church members give for not attending church regularly are simply lamentable. "Don't feel like it." "Don't feel the need of it." "I would rather sleep." "I would rather lie around and read the newspaper." "Would rather go out riding." "Would rather go visiting." "Would rather have company." "Would rather play golf at church time." "I am a poetic soul, and at church time I would rather go out in the woods and commune with the birds and the brooks and the flowers." Etc. and etc. and etc. All of which adds up to one word, INDIFFERENCE, the kind of church members that Christ will "spew out of his mouth."

Sunday Work. Some people have to work at Church time. For such, we think, God will accept attendance on some other service as a substitute for the Sunday morning service.

How To Get The People To Do It

Put it on a WORSHIP basis, and WORK at it. Teach insistently and constantly, in the Pulpit, and in the Sunday School, that it is a Christian's DUTY to GOD, from childhood to old age, to be at Church, if possible, on Sunday Morning. It is simply a matter of teaching, Teaching, TEACHING.

Then conduct the service as if it were a WORSHIP service. The Church is GOD'S house. God Himself is there. Give GOD'S WORD its proper place. Let the Congregation have part. Let the Congregation SING Praise to God.

This Handbook Has Two Profound Convictions:

1. Every Christian ought to have a Conscience about REGULAR BIBLE READING and REGULAR CHURCH ATTENDANCE.

2. Regular Church Services should consist mainly of BIBLE TEACHING and CONGREGATIONAL SINGING.

A Suggested Resolution

which each one might make in his own heart

BELIEVING THAT

Christ founded the Church;
That the Church exists
To propagate Christ's Influence;
That the Church's method of doing this
Is Meeting Together frequently in Christ's name;
That God himself planned the frequency, Weekly;
And gave us a Day for it,
Sunday, the Lord's Day;
And, inasmuch as Common Usage recognizes
Sunday Morning as Church Time;

I HEREBY PLEDGE MYSELF, THAT

As long as I live, wherever I may be,
Unless hindered by sickness or necessity,

ON SUNDAY MORNING I WILL GO TO CHURCH,

Trying to do it with One Motive only: for Christ

I WILL TRY TO GO ON TIME,
AND, I WILL BE REVERENT IN CHURCH

And

All My Life I Will Be a READER OF GOD'S WORD

THE SUNDAY MORNING CHURCH SERVICE

The Sunday Morning Church Service is generally recognized as the Church's chief expression of itself to its community. Faithfully Attended, and Properly Conducted, it should be an entirely efficient and sufficient means of accomplishing most of that which the Church exists to accomplish.

A Regularly Good Sunday Morning Church Service is unquestionably THE VERY GREATEST BLESSING A COMMUNITY CAN HAVE. It is not possible to exaggerate its importance.

We attend it as an Act of Worship to God. However, it is incumbent on those who conduct it to make it the most Helpful and Interesting and Beautiful that it is possible to make it.

Its two most important features are Congregational Singing and Instruction in God's Word.

The Scripture Lesson, as commonly conducted, is given a very minor place, while the whole service is built around the Sermon. What a mistake! The Sermon the big thing! The Scripture Lesson very insignificant! Usually, just a few verses, read as a sort of lifeless form, in the opening part of the service, with the droning close, "May the Lord add his blessing to the reading of his Word." The effrontery of it! Asking the Lord to bless what the preacher himself treats as being of such petty importance! So often one is tempted to think of the Church, not as God's house, but the Preacher's house.

It would be so much better, if, instead of being a brief isolated ritual, in the opening part of the service, the Scripture Lesson would be combined with the Sermon, forming the Basis, Framework, Structure and Heart of the Sermon; with God's Word thus in the foreground, and the preacher himself, more or less, in the background.

A Responsive Reading is no adequate substitute for a Scripture Lesson. Nor is it of any great value, other than being a means of congregational participation in the service. The same Scripture could be read with far more effect by the minister. As for congregational participation in the service, the best way for that, is, by far, Congregational Singing.

The Prayers. The Sunday Morning Church Service is for Worship, Prayer, Thanksgiving and Praise to God. We should keep that in mind, and go in the Spirit of Prayer, and try, during the service, to keep ourselves in the Spirit of Prayer.

Long prayers are not necessary. They tend to put the congregation out of the spirit of prayer. A number of short prayers, interspersed in other parts of the service, are better.

Many hymns are prayers, and most effective prayers too. Soft organ strains of prayer hymns may be thought of as an expression of congregational prayer.

A minister's prayer should never be a paraphrase of the preceding hymn; it looks like he has run out of ideas. Neither should it be a sermon at the people over God's shoulders.

A prayer should be uttered in a spirit of humble petition. We have heard prayers, uttered by pompous fellows, not in a spirit of humility, but in a tone of command that sounded, not like prayer, but rather like army orders telling God where to get off at.

Whether prayers are read or uttered extempore is no great matter. Certainly a good prayer well read is better than one where an ill-prepared minister appears to be wondering what to say.

One Hour. Now and then services of a special nature may require more time. But for the regular church services, where the same people attend week after week and year after year, and listen to the same preacher, One Hour is long enough; all the more so because many of these same people attend other services the same day. Twenty Minutes for Congregational Singing; Twenty Minutes for Sermon; and Twenty Minutes for Prayers, Offering, Announcements, etc.

If every item of the service is thoroughly prepared, and all waste time and useless talk and all valueless features eliminated, and Singing and Bible Teaching be given the right of way, it can be made a beautiful and helpful service, a precious hour in the lives of the people.

The Music

Congregational Singing, next to Bible Teaching, is the BEST FEATURE of a religious service, the most effective way to preach the Gospel. A Singing church is always well attended. People love it. A SINGING church and a TEACHING pulpit.

Moses sang, and led the people in singing. Miriam sang. Deborah and Barak sang. David sang, and wrote the Psalms to be sung. Jesus and the Twelve sang. Paul and Silas sang. The angels sing. In heaven EVERYBODY will sing.

Power of Popular Singing. It was the Public Singing of Luther's hymns that bore his preaching over central Europe, and shook the world into the Reformation. It was Singing that made the great Welsh revival. Was there ever a revival without it? The very best way now to rejuvenate dead churches would be to SING them into life.

More Congregational Singing. Its dearth of Singing is the greatest lack in the average Sunday Morning Church Service. There ought to be TEN times as much as there is. No time for it? Well, shorten the sermon, omit some of the show-off stuff in the choir loft, and make time for it. It is no substitute to announce a "Hymn-Sing" for some odd hour when most people cannot attend. CONGREGATIONAL SINGING has a Rightful Place in the Regular Sunday Morning Church Service, and should not be shoved aside by an ambitious choir or long-winded preacher. It is entitled to ONE-THIRD or ONE-HALF of the whole service.

A Continuous Song Service is better than one that is continuously Interrupted with remarks by the leader, or the reading of a stanza, or by other parts of the service. That ruins the effect. Do nothing but Sing, for twenty or thirty minutes, so as to give it a chance to make its impression. People like the Singing so much better than they like the wise-cracks of the leader. It is the SINGING that counts, not the everlasting interrupting TALK by the song leader.

Sing the Same Hymns Often. Only as they are sung Often can the people become familiar with them. It is the hymns that we know that are the ones we love. And we never tire of the hymns that we love, Never. Sing the Old Hymns. Sing them over and over. A church that would do this would not have to beg people to come to church. It could not keep them away.

Memorize Hymns. A congregation should be taught to Memorize the hymns they sing most often, at least some of the verses. They will sing better, and feel deeper, the spirit and power of what they sing. It will give power to the service.

Train children to Sing Hymns, and to Memorize them. It is the Best Religious Education. It will develop their spiritual growth, and tend to tie them to the church for life.

Song Leaders. Churches generally have so little Congregational Singing that they appoint no Leader for the one or two verses of the one or two hymns that they announce. Result: Congregational Singing, the one part of the service that people Love Most, the one thing that is a church's Chief Expression of its Praise to God, so often, is little more than a farce.

Every congregation ought to have a Song LEADER: NOT one who imitates the silly antics of a certain prevalent type of revival song evangelists, who seem to treat a service mainly as an occasion to show-off their monkey-shines and wise-cracks, and as a preliminary setting for their own solos: But one who BELIEVES in CONGREGATIONAL SINGING. It is possible to be a Song Leader, and yet retain something of the dignity and pulpit decorum proper to the profession.

Choirs. What a good choir can mean to a service is beyond computation. But It Depends On What They Sing. How often have we heard choir performances that added Nothing Whatever to the RELIGIOUS value of the service!

But, even at best, it is better that The People SING than that they Listen to Singing.

WHY NOT TURN THE WHOLE CONGREGATION INTO A CHOIR? Under proper leadership, the hymns of a vast congregation could be made to rise like the swell of an ocean's roar, and cause angels in heaven to lean over and listen.

The Preaching

Preaching is the Most Important Ministry of the Church. The Spoken Word will never be superseded as the main agency in extending the Gospel of Christ. But Preaching should be TEACHING, not ranting. The PULPIT is the TEACHING AGENCY of the Church. In popular parlance there is too much "Preach," and not enough "Teach."

Text Sermons. Allegorizing, metaphorizing, devising a fanciful subject for a Scripture verse or phrase, repeating it over and over, playing around with it, ringing the changes on it, using it as a Pretext to give semblance of Biblical Authority to the preacher's build-up of His Own Ideas of Christian truth. This is the type of preaching so prevalent in our churches. People sit for life under such preaching, and remain in Abysmal Ignorance of the Bible. We sometimes wonder if preachers assume that their audiences are entirely devoid of Intelligence.

Expository Sermons, as a method, or technique, of proclaiming the truth of God's Word, is far superior to the Text Sermon technique. An Expository Sermon, usually, has for its subject a worthwhile portion of Scripture, a chapter, or part of a chapter, or a group of chapters, or a book, or section of a book, and sets forth the Leading Facts and Lessons of the chosen passage. This is Real Preaching. At least it has the appearance of Giving God's Word the Place of Authority.

We once were told by a minister who had heard Spurgeon, Beecher, Phillips Brooks, Joseph Parker, and all the noted preachers of the past generation, that the one most powerful sermon he had ever heard in all his life was preached by Alexander Whyte, the great Scotch preacher, who, for his sermon, simply read the Epistle to the Philippians, with here and there a comment. What a lesson for our present day pulpiteers! But let any preacher who would now dare try such a thing be sure to Spend a Lot of Time in Preparation.

One of the best sermons that we ourselves have ever heard was on a Chapter in the Epistle to the Ephesians. The minister who preached it, afterward told us that, in preparation for that sermon, he had read that chapter over a HUNDRED TIMES, studying out its great thoughts, writing them down, arranging, re-arranging, condensing, re-writing, to get them into final form for delivery. No wonder his audience was delighted.

The Sunday Morning Service a Great Bible Class. Why not? What better could it be? If a pastor had a congregation of Bible Readers, as suggested on pages 805–813, and if the congregation had a pastor who, in his sermons, would co-perate with them, in loving instruction in God's Word, as they went along, what a blessed thing it would be!

Twenty Minutes. There are special occasions, now and then, when longer sermons are justifiable. But in the regular services of the church, where, mostly, the same people come together, and have to listen to the same preacher, week after week, month after month, and year after year, Twenty Minutes is long enough for the sermon.

Over-Exercise in the Pulpit. Much preaching is ill-prepared, and delivered with an effort of over-emphasis, yelling, pounding, jumping, gyrating, raving, waving the arms, pawing the air, as if in a boxing match. This is not at all necessary. A spirit of simple humility is so much more becoming in a preacher than a spirit of fiery invective. No amount of gesture can atone for lack of IDEAS.

Writing Sermons. If a minister cannot learn to speak without continually halting, hesitating and repeating, it would be far better for him to write his sermons and read them. A sermon well-written and well-read may be delivered with as much force as if spoken off hand. It is surprising how much can be condensed into small space when the subject is worked over and over, and written, and re-written, and re-written again and again and again and again.

APPENDIX

SUMMARY OF ARCHAEOLOGICAL DISCOVERIES

Mentioned in this Handbook

Arranged, not topically, but in the order of the Biblical passages on which they bear, in the Biblical sequence of those passages.

Writing. Modern criticism developed the theory that writing was unknown in the days of Moses, and that the early Old Testament books could not have been written till long after the events they record, and that they thus embody only legends that had been handed down by oral tradition. This clever theory, widely accepted in certain intellectual circles, has been one of the most insidious onslaughts ever made on the Historical Reliability of the Bible. But now, thanks be to God, within the past century, hundreds of thousands of books, written on clay and stone tablets, antedating Moses by centuries and even by millenniums, have been uncovered by the spade of the archaeologist, showing that even the very earliest of Biblical events could have been recorded by contemporary writers. See pages 42–57.

Pre-Flood Writings have been found in the ruins of Ur, Kish and Fara. (See page 44.)

Vast Pre-Abrahamic Libraries have been found in the ruins of Ur, Nippur, Lagash and Sippar. (See pages 46–49.)

The Oldest Known "Historical Document" (record of a contemporaneous event), written soon after the Flood, was found (1923), by Woolley, at Obeid, near Ur. (See page 46.)

The Weld Dynastic Prism, oldest known Outline of World History, written 100 years before Abraham, was found (1922), at Larsa, by the Weld-Blundell Expedition. (See page 49.)

Accad, one of Nimrod's cities (Genesis 10:10), was also called "Sippar," which means "Book Town," indicating that it was known as a famous library center. (See page 48.)

Hammurabi's Code of Laws, carved in Abraham's day, on a great block of stone, and set up originally in Babylon, was found (1902), in Susa, by a French Expedition. (See pages 50, 51.)

A School Room, of Abraham's day, in Ur, with quantities of exercise tablets in mathematics, grammar, history and medicine, possibly the very school that Abraham attended, has been uncovered. (See pages 50, 51.)

Note that the places mentioned, where these primeval writings were found, Ur, Kish, Fara, Nippur, Lagash, Sippar, Larsa, Accad and Susa, were all in the Garden of Eden region. (See pages 64, 65.)

In Egypt thousands of inscriptions have been found antedating Moses by a thousand years. (See pages 52, 53.)

The Tell-el-Amarna Tablets, 400 of them, letters, written about the time of Moses, by various kings in Palestine and Syria, to the Pharaohs of Egypt, were found (1888). (See page 53.)

Alphabetic Writing, made about 1800 B.C., 400 years before Moses, was found (1905), by Petrie, at Serabit in Sinai. (See page 54.)

Alphabetic Writings in Palestine, of the period between Abraham and Moses have been found in the ruins of Shechem, Gezer, Beth-shemesh, Lachish, and Hittite cities north of Palestine. (See pages 54, 55.)

The Name "Kiriath-sepher," a city near Hebron, means "Scribe Town," indicating that it was a literary center. (See page 51.)

The Behistun Rock, key to the ancient Babylonian language, was discovered (1835), by Sir Henry Rawlinson. (See page 43.)

The Rosetta Stone, key to the ancient Egyptian language, was discovered (1799), by Boussard. (See page 52.)

Thus, while learned men were loudly proclaiming that there was no such thing as WRITING till long after the days of Moses, God, in his Providence, used the spade of the archaeologist to bring to light hundreds of thousands of books that were written long before the days of Moses. And not only so, but these same books, in many things, confirm Biblical records.

Creation, (Genesis 1). Babylonian Creation Stories, quite similar to the Genesis account, have been found on primitive tablets in the ruins of Babylon, Nippur, Ashur and Nineveh, showing that the Genesis ideas had become quite deeply fixed in the thought of earth's earliest inhabitants. (See page 62.)

Original Monotheism (Genesis 1). The Genesis idea that man started with a belief in One God, and that polytheistic idolatry was a later development, has been verified in inscriptions found by Langdon, in Pre-Flood layers, at Jemdet Nasr, near Babylon. In Egypt, Petrie found indications that Egypt's first religion was Monotheistic. (See page 62.)

The Garden of Eden (Genesis 2). Hall and Thompson, of the British Museum, found (1918), indications that Eridu, the traditional site of Eden, possibly may have been the first city ever built. (See pages 63, 64.)

The Fall of Man (Genesis 3). "The Temptation Seal." An ancient Babylonian tablet has been found, portraying in picture exactly what Genesis says in words. In the center is a tree, on one side a man, on the other side a woman plucking fruit, and behind the woman a serpent standing erect seeming to be whispering to her. (See page 68.)

"The Adam and Eve Seal." This was found by Speiser (1932), in Tepe Gawra, near Nineveh. He dated it at about 3500 B.C. It depicts a naked man and a naked woman, walking, bent over, as if brokenhearted, followed by a serpent. (See page 68.)

Early Use of Metals (Genesis 4:21, 22). It is here stated that copper and iron instruments were invented while Adam was yet living. Until recently the earliest known use of iron was 1200 B.C. But in 1933 Frankfort discovered, in the ruins of Asmar, near Babylon, an iron blade made about 2700 B.C., thus pushing back the known use of iron much nearer to the beginning. Copper instruments have been found in the ruins of Pre-Flood cities. (See pages 70, 72.)

Primeval Longevity (Genesis 5.) In this chapter ten names are listed as living to great age, and covering the period from Adam to the Flood. Early Babylonian tablets have been found naming ten Pre-Flood kings, and stating how long each reigned. While their figures are fabulous, it shows, at least, that there were ancient traditions that earth's earliest inhabitants did live long. (See pages 71, 72.)

The Flood (Genesis 6–9). Babylonian Flood Stories, very similar to the Genesis record, have been found on many tablets that were made soon after the Flood; and there repeatedly occurs in these tablets such expressions as "the age before the Flood," and "the writings of the time before the Flood." How account for this unless there was a Flood? (See pages 75, 76.)

Moreover, The Flood Deposit has actually been found, in four different places. At Ur, in 1929, Woolley found an 8-foot bed of water-laid clay, with the ruins of an earlier city buried beneath it. At Kish (1928–29), Langdon found a similar bed of water-laid clay, and underneath it a very well-preserved pre-flood chariot, with four wheels, made of wood and copper nails. At Fara, traditional home of Noah, Schmidt found (1931), a layer of clean water-laid clay, and underneath it relics of its pre-flood inhabitants. At Nineveh (1932–33), Mallowan found layers of viscous mud and riverine sand near the bottom of the Great Mound, which must have been put there by water, with a distinct difference between the pottery under the wet layer and that above it. This all looks like very tangible evidence that there really was such an event as the Biblical Flood. (See pages 77, 78.)

The Tower of Babel (Genesis 11:1–9). Inscriptions have been found which seem to identify the location of this Tower. (See page 83.)

Ur, the City of Abraham (Genesis 11:28–31). Its ruins have been pretty thoroughly excavated by Woolley (1922–34). In Abraham's day it was the most magnificent city in all the world. Much of the ruins of layer belonging to Abraham's time has been uncovered, so that the actual streets on which Abraham walked may now be seen. The whole story of the civilization and religion in which Abraham was reared has been brought to light. (See pages 87–89, 95.)

Abraham's Visit to Egypt (Genesis 12:10–20), is thought, possibly, to have been depicted on the tomb of one of the Pharaohs. (See page 96.) The whole amazing story of Egypt's early civilization, and its bearing on Biblical history, has been disclosed in the thousands of inscriptions made then, and discovered and deciphered in modern times. (See pages 89–93.)

Hammurabi's Battle with Abraham (Genesis 14:1–16). "Amraphel" (1), is commonly identified by archaeologists as Hammurabi, the discovery of whose famous Code of Laws has made his name a household word. It must have added greatly to Abraham's prestige that he met in battle and defeated the most famous king then living. (See page 97.)

The "Way of the Kings" (Genesis 14:5, 6). Albright, who once considered the cities here named to have been legendary, because they were so far east of the known trade routes, in 1929 discovered a line of great mound ruins of cities that flourished about 2000 B.C., indicating that it was a well settled region in Abraham's time, and on the direct trade route between Damascus and Sinai. (See page 97.)

Patriarchal Cities, mentioned in Genesis in connection with Abraham: Shechem, Bethel, Ai, Gerar. Critics who denied the historical existence of Abraham denied also the existence of these cities that early. But Albright and Garstang found sherds of about 2000 B.C. in the bottom levels of their ruins, showing that they were existent at that time. (See page 100.)

Destruction of Sodom and Gomorrah (Genesis 18, 19). Albright and Kyle (1924), found, at the southeast corner of the Dead Sea, great quantities of relics of a period dating between 2500 B.C. and 2000 B.C., with evidence of a dense population, a region "like the garden of God" (Genesis 13:10); and that the population ceased abruptly about 2000 B.C., and that the region has been desolate ever since, indicating that it was destroyed by some great cataclysm. This is indeed a most striking and overwhelming evidence of the historical truth of the Genesis story of these two cities. (See pages 98, 99.)

Joseph and Potiphar's Wife (Genesis 39). A story called the "Tale of Two Brothers," written in the reign of Seti (11), is so similar to this that the editor of the English edition of Brugsch's "History of Egypt" surmised that it was worked up from the annals of Joseph which must have been in the archives of the Egyptian court. (See page 106.)

Joseph's Palace in On (Genesis 41:45). Sir Flinders Petrie (1912), discovered the ruins of this palace. (See page 107.)

The Seven Years' Famine (Genesis 41:46–57). Brugsch, in his "Egypt under the Pharaohs," tells of a contemporary inscription which he calls a "very remarkable and luminous confirmation" of the Biblical account of the Seven Years' Famine. (See page 107.)

Moses and Pharaoh (Exodus 1–12). There is some difference of opinion as to which Pharaoh it was with whom Moses had to do. But whichever it was, his mummified body has been found, so that one may now look on the actual face of the Pharaoh whom Moses defied. This certainly adds a touch of reality to the story of Moses. (See pages 113–116.)

Pharaoh's Daughter (Exodus 2:1–10), who brought up Moses, is now quite commonly thought to have been the famous Queen Hatshepsut, who was one of Egypt's greatest rulers. Her statue and the ruins of many of her mighty works have been found, the building of some of which Moses himself may have superintended. (See pages 111, 114, 117.)

Bricks With and Without Straw (Exodus 1:11; 5:7–19). Naville (1883), and Kyle (1908), found, at Pithom, the lower courses of brick filled with good chopped straw, the middle course with less straw, and the upper course with no straw whatever. What an amazing confirmation of Exodus 5:7–19. (See page 120.)

Death of Pharaoh's First-Born (Exodus 12:29). Whichever the Pharaoh, Amenhotep II or Merneptah, one or the other of which must have been the Pharaoh of the Exodus, inscriptions have been found that neither was succeeded by his First-Born son, which seems like evidence that something must have happened to the first-born. (See page 124.)

Joshua's Name (Joshua 1:1), occurs in an Amarna tablet written from Palestine to Pharaoh. Referring to the rout of the king of Pella, it says, "Ask Benjamin. Ask Tadua. Ask Joshua." (See page 157.)

Rahab's House on the Wall (Joshua 2:15). Garstang found in Jericho the ruins of double walls, 15 feet apart, linked together by houses built across the top, showing that there were houses built "on the wall." (See page 159.)

Jericho's Wall "Fell Down Flat" (Joshua 6:20). Garstang found evidence that Jericho was destroyed about 1400 B.C., Joshua's date; and that the walls had fallen flat, outward, down the hillside. Joshua "burnt the city with fire" (Joshua 6:24). Garstang found the layer of ashes left by Joshua's fire. Israel was commanded to "keep themselves from the devoted thing" (Joshua 6:18). Garstang found underneath the layer of ashes an abundance of foodstuffs, wheat, barley, dates and such, turned to charcoal, evidence that the conquerors did refrain from appropriating the food. (See page 159.)

Ai and Bethel Destroyed (Joshua 8:1–29). Albright found in the Bethel mound, and Garstang in the Ai mound, evidences that they had been destroyed by fire at a time coinciding with Joshua's invasion. (See page 161.)

Lachish (Joshua 10:32), is named among the cities Joshua destroyed. The Wellcome Archaeological Expedition found (1934–), a great layer of ashes left by a fire of Joshua's time. (See page 163.)

Debir (Joshua 10:39), is also named among the cities Joshua destroyed. Here an expedition of Xenia Seminary and the American School at Jerusalem found a deep layer of ashes and charcoal with evidence that the fire was of Joshua's time. (See page 163.)

Hazor (Joshua 11:10, 11), too, is named among the cities which Joshua burned. Garstang found the ashes of this fire, with pottery evidences that it had occurred in Joshua's time. Also: an Amarna tablet, written to Pharaoh (1380 B.C.), from north Palestine, says, "Let my lord recall what Hazor and its king have already had to endure." (See page 164.)

Destruction of the Canaanites (Deuteronomy 7:2; 20:17). God commanded Israel to utterly destroy the Canaanites. Excavations in the ruins of Gezer, Kiriath-sepher, and other Canaanite cities, showing the shameful and loathsome degradation of the Canaanite religion and civilization, have caused archaeologists to wonder why God did not destroy them sooner than he did. (See page 166.)

Iron in Palestine (Judges 1:19). It seems from this and similar passages that the Canaanites and Philistines had iron in the period of the Judges. But iron did not appear among the Israelites till the time of David (II Samuel 12:31; I Chronicles 29:7). Excavations have revealed many iron relics of 1100 B.C. in Philistia, but none in the hill country of Palestine previous to 1000 B.C. (See page 170.)

Canaanite Oppression of Israel (Judges 4:3). A plaque of the 12th century B.C. has been found in the ruins of Megiddo representing the Canaanite king receiving Israelite captives. (See page 172.)

Deborah's Victory over the Canaanites (Judges 4:23, 24; 5:19), at Megiddo. The Oriental Institute found (1937), in the ruins of Megiddo, in the stratum belonging to the 12th century B.C., indications of a tremendous conflagration, on top of the layer of Canaanite relics, evidence of a terrific defeat for the Canaanites at that time, which was the time of Deborah and Barak. (See page 172.)

Hidden Grain Pits in Time of Gideon (Judges 6:2–4, 11). Some of these grain pits were found (1926–28), at Kiriath-sepher, by Albright and Kyle. (See page 172.)

Abimelech's Destruction of Shechem (Judges 9:45). Sellin (1913–14, 1926–28), found, in the ruins of ancient Shechem, evidence of Israelite occupation that had been destroyed about the 12th century B.C.; and in this layer he found the ruins of a temple of Baal, believed to have been the very same temple mentioned in Judges 9:4. (See page 172.)

The Burning of Gibeah (Judges 20:40). Albright found (1922–23), in the ruins of Gibeah, a layer of ashes of a fire of the 12th century B.C. It must have been this same fire. (See page 173.)

Shiloh (I Samuel 1:3; II Samuel 6:15; Joshua 18:1; Jeremiah 7:12–15), is indicated by these passages to have been an important city from Joshua to David (1400–1000 B.C.), and then to have been destroyed. A Danish expedition (1922–26), found sherds of 1200–1000 B.C., with indications of Israelite culture, and no evidence of later occupation till about 300 B.C. (See page 177.)

Saul's House in Gibeah (I Samuel 10:26). Albright (1922–23), found, in Gibeah, in the stratum of 1000 B.C., the ruins of a fortress that must have been this same house. (See page 181.)

Temples of Ashtoreth and Dagon (I Samuel 31:10; I Chronicles 10:10), in which Saul's head and armor were put, in Bethshan. The University Museum of Pennsylvania found (1921–30), in Bethshan, in the stratum of 1000 B.C., the ruins of a temple of Ashtoreth, and one of Dagon, which must have been these same temples. (See page 183.)

The Watercourse (II Samuel 5:8), by which David's men gained entrance to Jerusalem. This tunnel, cut through solid rock, was discovered (1866), by Warren, of the Palestine Exploration Fund. (See page 215.)

Solomon's Gold (I Kings 14:25, 26), which Shishak took away. Shishak's mummy was found (1939), in a gold covered sarcophagus, possibly some of the same gold he had taken from Solomon. (See page 192.)

Solomon's Stables. His horses are mentioned in I Kings 9:19 and 10:26–29. Megiddo is named as one of Solomon's cities (I Kings 9:15). The Oriental Institute has uncovered, in Megiddo, the ruins of Solomon's stables, with their stone hitching-poles and mangers. Nearby was a foundation stone of a house occupied by one of Solomon's army officers inscribed "Shield of David." (See page 191.)

Solomon's Navy at Ezion-geber (I Kings 9:26). Glueck (1938–39), identified the ruins of Ezion-geber, and found smelters, furnaces, crucibles and refineries, of Solomon's time, where iron and copper were manufactured into metal products that were exported to India, Arabia and Africa, in exchange for gold and ivory. (See page 192.)

Solomon's Building Stones (I Kings 7:9–12). Many of these enormous stones are still in place. In 1852 Barkley discovered the quarry from which they came. (See page 192.)

Omri Built Samaria (I Kings 16:24). A Harvard University Expedition has uncovered the ruins of Omri's palace in Samaria, with no relics older than the time of Omri, evidence that he was founder of the city. (See page 197.)

Re-Building of Jericho (I Kings 16:34; Joshua 6:26). Jericho was destroyed by Joshua, about 1400 B.C. Joshua predicted that whoever attempted to rebuild it would, in the effort, lose his first-born and youngest sons. 500 years later Hiel rebuilt it, losing his first-born and youngest sons (I Kings 16:34). Its ruins show that it was uninhabited from 14th to 9th centuries B.C. A jar with the remains of a child was found in the masonry of a gate; and two such jars in the walls of a house. (See page 197.)

Elijah and the Prophets of Baal (I Kings 18:40). The Oriental Institute found, in the ruins of Megiddo, in the stratum of Elijah's time, many jars containing the remains of infants who had been slain in sacrifice to Baal. Prophets of Baal were official legalized murderers of little children. This helps us to understand why Elijah slew these prophets. (See page 198.)

Ahab's Sudden Peace with Benhadad (I Kings 20:34). After an overwhelming victory, Ahab suddenly seemed to throw away his advantage. A rock inscription, telling of the approach of the Assyrian army, may explain what the Bible leaves unexplained. (See page 199.)

Ahab's House of Ivory (I Kings 22:39). A Harvard University Expedition found in Samaria the ruins of this "ivory" palace, with thousands of pieces of the most exquisitely carved ivory, just above the ruins of Omri's palace. (See page 199.)

Moab's Rebellion against Israel (II Kings 3:4, 5). The Moabite king's own account of this rebellion was found (1868), at Dibon, in Moab. It is called the "Moabite Stone." (See pages 201, 202.)

Hazael's Succession to Benhadad's Throne (II Kings 8:15). An Assyrian inscription tells the same thing. (See page 203.)

Jehu's Tribute to Assyria (II Kings 10:32–34). Additional information is supplied by the "Black Obelisk." It depicts Jehu paying tribute to the Assyrian king. (See page 205.)

Jezebel "Painted Her Eyes" (II Kings 9:30). The actual saucers in which Jezebel mixed her cosmetics have been found, in Samaria, in the ruins of Ahab's "ivory house": small stone boxes, with a number of holes for various colors: kohl for black, turquoise for green, ochre for red: with a central depression for mixing. They still had traces of red. (See page 206.)

A Seal of Jeroboam's Servant (II Kings 14:23–29), has been found in the ruins of Megiddo, inscribed, "Belonging to Shema the servant of Jeroboam." (See page 207.)

Menahem Paid Tribute to Pul, king of Assyria (II Kings 15:19, 20). One of Pul's inscriptions says, "Tribute of Menahem of Samaria, Rezin of Damascus, Hiram of Tyre, I received." (See page 208.)

Uzziah, Ahaz, Menahem, Pekah, Hoshea. These five Hebrew kings are named in the inscriptions of Pul, king of Assyria. (See page 208.)

North Israel was Carried away Captive (II Kings 15:29), by Tiglath-pileser. Tiglath-pileser's own inscription says, "The people of the land of Omri I deported to Assyria." (See page 208.)

Hoshea Slew Pekah, and Reigned in his stead, and Paid Tribute to the King of Assyria (II Kings 15:30; 17:3). An inscription of Tiglath-pileser says, "Pekah their king they had overthrown. I placed Hoshea over them. From him I received 10 talents of gold and 1000 talents of silver." (See page 208.)

Captivity of Israel. In II Kings 17:5, 6, 24 it is said: "The king of Assyria besieged Samaria 3 years . . . and took it . . . and carried Israel away . . . and brought men from Babylon . . . and placed them in the cities of Samaria." An inscription of Sargon says: "In my first year I captured Samaria. I took captive 27,290 people. People of other lands, who never paid tribute, I settled in Samaria." (See page 208.)

Jehoiachin, king of Judah (597 B.C., II Kings 24:6–17). Two impressions of his Steward's Seal have been found: one at Kiriath-sepher, the other at Beth-shemesh. (See page 228.)

Jehoiachin "Lifted Up," and "Given an Allowance" (II Kings 25:27, 30). Tablets have been found in the ruins of the Hanging Gardens of Babylon listing the names of those to whom regular allotments of grain and oil were made, among them "Jehoiachin king of the land of Judah." (See page 228.)

Nebuchadnezzar's Burning of the Cities of Judah (II Kings 25:9; Jeremiah 34:7). In four of these cities have the ash layers of Nebuchadnezzar's fires been found: Lachish, Bethel, Kiriath-sepher and Beth-shemesh. (See page 211.)

David's Wall (I Chronicles 11:8), which he "built from Millo round about." Remains of this wall have been uncovered for 400 feet. (See page 215.)

Shishak's Invasion of Judah (II Chronicles 12:9, 10). Shishak's own record of this invasion is inscribed on the wall of the Great Temple at Karnak. It left traces in Judah. (See page 221.)

Uzziah, king of Judah (787–735 B.C., II Chronicles 26). His name is mentioned four times in an inscription of Tiglath-pileser. (See page 223.)

Uzziah's Gravestone (II Chronicles 26:23), has been found, by Dr. Sukenik, of the Hebrew University of Jerusalem. (See page 224.)

Jotham, king of Judah (749–734 B.C., II Chronicles 27). His Seal, inscribed, "Belonging to Jotham," has been found in the excavations at Ezion-geber. (See page 224.)

Ahaz, king of Judah (741–726 B.C., II Chronicles 28). A Seal inscribed, "Belonging to an Official of Ahaz," has been found. (See page 224.)

Ahaz Sent Tribute to Tiglath-pileser (II Kings 16:7, 8). An inscription of Tiglath-pileser says, "The tribute of Ahaz the Judean I received, gold, silver, lead, tin and linen." (See page 224.)

Hezekiah's Repairs in the Wall of Jerusalem (II Chronicles 32:5). These repairs may be distinctly seen today. (See page 225.)

Hezekiah's Tunnel (II Kings 20:20; II Chronicles 32:3, 4). This tunnel, running 1700 feet through solid rock, has been found. (See page 225.)

The Siloam Inscription, telling how Hezekiah's Tunnel was built, was found in the tunnel's mouth. (See page 225.)

Sennacherib's Invasion of Judah (II Chronicles 32:1). Sennacherib's own account of this invasion has been found, on a clay prism which he himself had made. (See page 225.)

Hezekiah Paid Tribute to Sennacherib (II Kings 18:14–16). One of Sennacherib's inscriptions says, "The fear of my majesty overwhelmed Hezekiah. He sent tribute." (See page 226.)

Sennacherib Before Lachish in All his Power (II Chronicles 32:9). On the walls of Sennacherib's palace in Nineveh was found a sculptured relief of this encampment. (See page 226.)

Sennacherib's Destruction of Lachish and Gibeah (II Chronicles 32:9;

Isaiah 10:29). The Wellcome Archaeological Expedition found at Lachish, and Albright at Gibeah, layers of ashes left by Sennacherib's fires. (See page 226.)

Sennacherib's Assassination by his Sons, and Succession by Esarhaddon (II Kings 19:37). An Assyrian inscription says, "Sennacherib was killed by his sons . . . Esarhaddon ascended the throne." (Page 226.)

Manasseh, king of Judah (II Chronicles 33) is mentioned in an inscription of Esarhaddon as one of the "Western kings who supplied him with building material for his palace." (See page 227.)

Zedekiah's Flight "Between the Two Walls" (II Kings 25:4). This "way between the walls" can now be seen for 150 feet. (See page 228.)

Esther's Palace (Esther 1:2), has been excavated. The "king's gate" (4:2); the "inner court" (5:1); the "outer court" (6:4); the "palace garden" (7:7); have all been located in the ruins; and even one of the "Pur" dice (3:7), has been found. (See page 237.)

"Sargon" (Isaiah 20:1). This is the only known mention of Sargon's name in extant ancient literature. In 1842 Botta discovered the ruins of his palace, with inscriptions showing him to have been one of the greatest of Assyrian kings. (See page 287.)

Nebuchadnezzar's Attack on Lachish (Jeremiah 34:7). Fragments of 21 letters, written during his siege, have been found in the ashes of Lachish. They mention certain persons named in Jeremiah: Uriah, Elnathan, Gemariah, Neriah and others. (See page 316.)

Gedaliah, Governor of Judah (Jeremiah 40:5). His Seal, inscribed, "Belonging to Gedaliah . . . who is over the house," has been found. (See page 317.)

Jaazaniah (Jeremiah 40:8; II Kings 25:23). His Seal has been found, inscribed, "Belonging to Jaazaniah servant of the king." (See page 317.)

Tahpahnes (Jeremiah 43:9). Petrie uncovered the ruins of the brick work where Jeremiah hid the stones. (See page 318.)

Nebuchadnezzar (Daniel 1:1). A cameo of Nebuchadnezzar's head, carved by his own order, has been found. (See page 340.)

Babylon (Daniel 1:1), where Daniel walked with world rulers, dream city of ancient times, has been uncovered, and the ruins of its grandeur laid bare. (See pages 338–340.)

Belshazzar (Daniel 5). No mention of Belshazzar was found in Babylonian records till 1853. Since then inscriptions have been found showing him to have been co-regent of the last king of Babylon, and throwing light on Daniel 5. (See page 344.)

The Handwriting on the Wall (Daniel 5:5). The foundations of this same wall have been uncovered. (See page 344.)

Jonah and Nineveh (Jonah 1–4). One of Nineveh's mounds is called the "Jonah" mound. (See page 365. For note on the ruins of Nineveh see pages 369–371.)

Nineveh's Repentance (Jonah 8:5–10. For what archaeological evidence there is of this, see page 365).

The Enrolment of Quirinius (Luke 2:2). Papyri have been found, verifying Luke's statement that there was a "first" enrollment, clearing what seemed like an historical discrepancy. (See page 490.)

Synagog of Capernaum (Mark 1:21; Luke 7:1, 5). The ruins of a synagog have been uncovered which is thought to have been the actual synagog in which Jesus taught. (See page 502.)

The Last Supper (Matthew 26:17–29). The Chalice of Antioch, thought by many to have been the actual cup Jesus used at the Last Supper, has been found. (See pages 448, 449.)

Site of the Crucifixion (Mark 15:22), is thought by many to have been definitely located. (See page 481.)

The Tomb of Jesus (John 19:41). A Tomb answering all Scriptural details has been found. (See pages 551–553.)

The Seven Churches of Revelation (Revelation 2, 3). Excavations throw light on some of the statements. (See page 700.)

The Dead Sea Scrolls (WSLS)

The Dead Sea Scrolls, discovered, probably in 1947, by Arabic Bedouin and brought to the attention of the scholarly world late that year and early in 1948. The discoveries were made in caves located in the marly cliffs, a mile or so W of the northwestern corner of the Dead Sea, at a place known by the modern Arabic name of Qumran, which is near a copious spring of fresh water known as Ain Feshkha. This location is at the eastern edge of the Wilderness of Judah. Accordingly, alternate names for the discoveries including "Qumran," "Ain Feshkha," or "Wilderness of Judah" are sometimes used.

The scrolls were seen by several scholars in the latter part of 1947, some of whom have admitted that they passed them up as forgeries. One of the scholars who recognized the antiquity of the scrolls was the late Professor Eleazar L. Sukenik of Hebrew University, who was subsequently successful in purchasing some of them. Other scrolls were taken to the American School of Oriental Research in Jerusalem, where the Acting Director *pro tempore*, Dr. John C. Trever, convinced of their value, arranged to photograph the portions which were brought to him. One of his photographs was sent to Professor William F. Albright, who promptly declared that this was "*the most important discovery ever made* in Old Testament manuscripts."

The scrolls which were purchased by the Hebrew University included *the Hebrew University Isaiah Scroll* (lQIs[b]), which is a partial scroll of the book, the *Order of Warfare*, also known as the *War of the Sons of Light against the Sons of Darkness* (lQM), and the *Thanksgiving Hymns* or *Hodayot* (lQH). The scrolls purchased by the Syrian archbishop and published by the American Schools of Oriental Research included the *St. Mark's Isaiah Scroll* (lQIs[a]) which is a complete scroll of the book, the *Habakkuk Commentary* (lQpHab) which contains the text of chapters one and two of Habakkuk with a running commentary, and the *Manual of Discipline* (lQS), which contains the rules for the members of the Qumran community. These all have subsequently come into the possession of the State of Israel and are housed in a shrine in the Hebrew University, Jerusalem, Israel. They have been published in numerous editions and translated into many languages, and are readily available for anyone who wishes to study them either in translation or in facsimile.

Following the discovery of these important scrolls, which are now all but unanimously accepted as having come from the last century B.C. and the first century A.D., the region from which they came was systematically explored. Numerous caves were found, and so far eleven caves have yielded materials from the same period as the original scrolls. Most of these materials have come from the fourth cave explored (known as Cave Four or 4Q); others of significance come from Cave Two, Five, and Six. According to recent reports the most significant discoveries are those from Cave Eleven (11Q).

A least 382 manuscripts are represented by the fragments of Cave Four alone, about 100 of which are Biblical manuscripts. These include fragments of every book of the Hebrew Bible except Esther. Some of the books are represented in many copies: e.g., 14 different manuscripts of Deuteronomy, 12 manuscripts of Isaiah, and 10 manuscripts of Psalms are represented in Cave Four; other fragments of these same books have been found in other caves. Almost complete scrolls of Psalms and Leviticus have been found in Cave Eleven, but these have not yet been published. One of the significant finds, which may turn out to have important bearing on the theories of date and authorship, concerns the Book of Daniel, fragments of which have been found with the change from Hebrew to Aramaic in Daniel 2:4 and from Aramaic to Hebrew in 7:28–8:1, exactly as in our modern texts of Daniel.

In addition to Biblical books, fragments of Deuterocanonical writings have been found, specifically Tobit and Ecclesiasticus, as well as fragments of several noncanonical writings. Some of these latter were already known, such as Jubilees, Enoch, the Testament of Levi, etc.; others were not previously known, such as the peculiarly Qumranian documents: the Thanksgiving Psalms, the Book of Warfare, the commentaries on portions of Scripture, etc. These last give us insights into the nature and beliefs of the community of Qumran.

Near the cliffs on an alluvial plateau overlooking the shore of the Dead Sea is the site of an ancient building complex often referred to as the "Monastery." This was thoroughly excavated over several seasons, and has yielded important data about the nature, size, and date of the Qumran community. From coins found there, together with other remains, the community has been dated within the limits of 140 B.C. and A.D. 67. The members were almost all male, although the literature contains provisions for the admission of women and children. The number of living there at any one time was in the neighborhood of two to four hundred. A mile or so S at Ain Feshkha were found the remains of other buildings, the nature of which is not exactly clear. The fresh water of the spring probably was used for the growing of crops and other needs of the community.

From the sect's literature we know that the people of Qumran were Jews who had split off from the Jerusalem or main stream of Judaism, and indeed were quite critical of and even hostile toward the priests at Jerusalem. The fact that they used the name, "The Sons of Zadok" has suggested to some scholars that they should be connected with the Zadokites or Sadducees; other scholars believe that they are rather to be identified with the Essenes, a third sect of Judaism described by Josephus and Philo. It is not impossible that elements of truth are to be found in both of these theories and that there was originally a split in the priestly or Sadducean line which first joined the movement known as the Hasidim, the forerunners of the Pharisees, ultimately to split again and form a narrow separatist group part of which located at Qumran. We must await further discoveries before we attempt to give a final answer to this entire problem.

The community devoted itself to the study of the Bible. The life of the community was largely ascetic, and their practices included ritual bathing, sometimes referred to as baptism. This has been understood by some to be the origin of the baptism of John the Baptist. A study of John's baptism alongside that of the Qumranians shows, however, that the two practices were quite distinct; hence, if John did come from this community (which is not yet proven and may never be), he must have developed important distinctions in his own doctrine and practice of baptism.

Some scholars believe that Zoroastrian elements are to be found in the Qumran writings, particularly with reference to dualism and angelology. The problem is extremely complex. Zoroastrian dualism developed greatly in post-Christian times, and therefore it is precarious to assume that the Zoroastrian beliefs as we know them represent the beliefs a century or two before the time of Christ.

The discoveries at Qumran are important for Biblical studies in general. The matter of the canon is not necessarily affected, since the group at Qumran was a schismatic group in the first place, and, moreover, the absence of Esther does not necessarily imply that they rejected this book from the canon. In the matter of the text of the Old Testament, however, the Dead Sea Scrolls are of great importance. The text of the Greek Old Testament (or the Septuagint), as well as the quotations of the Old Testament in the New, indicate that there were other texts beside the one that has come down to us (the Masoretic Text). The study of the Dead Sea Scrolls makes it clear that at the time of their production, which would be about the time of the production of the Scriptures used by the New Testament authors, there were at least three texts in existence: one we might call the ancestor of the Masoretic Text; the second was a text closely related to that used by the translators of the Septuagint; the third was a text differing from both of these other texts. The differences are not great and at no point do they involve doctrinal matters; but for careful textual study of the Old Testament it is important that we free ourselves from the notion that the Masoretic Text is the only authentic text. As a matter of fact, the quotations of the Old found in the New Testament rather imply that it was not the Masoretic Text which was most commonly in use by New Testament authors. These statements should be qualified by pointing out that the quality of the text varies from book to book in the Old Testament, and that there is much more uniformity in the text of the Pentateuch than in some of the other portions of the Hebrew Bible.

The Dead Sea Scrolls have particularly made great contributions to the study of the text of Samuel.

In relation to the New Testament, the Dead Sea Scrolls are likewise of importance. There are no New Testament texts in the discoveries at Qumran, obviously, since the earliest book of the New Testament had been written only very shortly before the destruction of the Qumran community. Moreover, there was no reason why any of the New Testament writings should have reached Qumran. On the other hand, there are certain references and presuppositions found in the New Testament, particularly in the preaching of John the Baptist and Jesus Christ, and in the writings of Paul and John, which are placed against a background now recognizably similar to that furnished by the documents from Qumran. Thus, for example, the Gnostic background found in certain Pauline writings and formerly thought to be second century Greek Gnosticism—thus requiring a late date for the composition of Colossians—is now recognized as a Jewish Gnosticism of the first century or earlier. Similarly the Fourth Gospel is shown to be Palestinian and not Hellenistic.

A great deal has been written concerning the relationship of Jesus Christ to the Qumran community. There is no evidence in the Qumran documents that Jesus was a member of the sect, and nothing in the New Testament requires such a position. Rather, the outlook of Jesus with reference to the world and particularly toward His own people is diametrically opposite that of Qumran, and it can be safely asserted that He was not a member of that group at any time. He may have had some disciples who had come out of that background, particularly those who were formerly disciples of John the Baptist—though this is far from proven. The attempt to show that the Qumran Teacher of Righteousness was the pattern for the Gospel portrayal of Jesus cannot be established on the basis of the Dead Sea Scrolls. The Teacher of Righteousness was a fine young man with high ideals who died untimely; there is, however, no clear statement that he was put to death, certainly no indication that he was crucified or rose from the dead or that the Qumranians expected him to return. The difference between Jesus and the Teacher of Righteousness stands out clearly at several points: the Teacher of Righteousness was never referred to as the Son of God or God Incarnate; his death was not sacrificial in its nature; the sacramental meal (if such it was indeed) was not viewed as a memorial of his death or a pledge of his return in any way connected with the forgiveness of sin. Obviously in the case of Jesus Christ, all of these things are clearly asserted, not once but repeatedly in the New Testament, and indeed form a necessary basis without which there is no Christian faith.

The Zondervan Pictorial Bible Dictionary

APPENDIX II

SUMMARY OF PLACES

Where Important Archaeological Discoveries Have Been Made Alphabetically Arranged

Accad, also called Sippar, which means "Book Town," 30 miles north of Babylon. Excavated, by Rassam (1881); and by Scheil (1894). Vast quantities of primitive tablets were found. (See page 48.)

Ai, and Bethel, 12 miles north of Jerusalem, 1½ miles apart, were destroyed by Joshua, in a joint battle; (Joshua 8:28; 12:9, 16). Albright (1934), at Bethel, found the ruins left by Joshua's fire. (See page 161.)

'Ain Fashkha, 7 miles south of Jericho, 1 mile west of the Dead Sea. Here, in a cave, on the rocky mountain side (1947), was found the now famous Isaiah Scroll, written 2000 years ago. (See page 286.)

Amarna, or Tell-el-Amarna, in Egypt, about halfway between Memphis and Thebes. Here (1888), there were found 400 Letters on Clay Tablets, written, about the time of Moses, by various kings of Palestine and Syria, to the Pharaohs of Egypt. (See page 53.)

Antioch, at northeast corner of Mediterranean Sea. Here the "Chalice of Antioch" was found (1910), with evidence that it may possibly have been the actual cup used by Jesus at the Last Supper. (See page 448.)

Asmar, also called Eshnunna, 100 miles northeast of Babylon. Henri Frankfort (1933), in the layer of 2700 B.C., found an Iron Blade, thus pushing back the known use of Iron 1500 years.

Asshur, now known as Kalah-Sherghat, about 60 miles south of Nineveh. Excavated, by Andrae (1902–1914). Quantities of Inscriptions found.

Bab-ed-Dra, at southeast corner of Dead Sea. Excavated (1924), by Albright and Kyle, who found remains of a place of worship in the vicinity of Sodom and Gomorrah, with evidence of a dense population that ceased abruptly about the time of Abraham. (See pages 98, 99.)

Babylon. Wonder city of ancient world. Its vast ruins excavated by Koldewey (1899–1912); Rich (1811); Layard (1850); Rassam (1878–1889) Oppert (1854). Ruins of the Tower of Babel; Nebuchadnezzar's Palace; Hanging Gardens; Wall where Daniel read Handwriting uncovered; evidence of Jehoiachin's residence in Babylon. (See pages 83, 228, 336–344.)

Behistun, 200 miles northeast of Babylon. Sir Henry Rawlinson (1835), found the famous Behistun Inscription, which had been made by Darius the Great, and which proved to be Key to Babylonian Language. (Page 43.)

Benihassen, in Egypt, about halfway between Memphis and Thebes. An inscription has been found, on the tomb of one of the Pharaohs, which may have been a record of Abraham's visit to Egypt. (Page 96.)

Bethel, 12 miles north of Jerusalem. Layer of ashes left by Joshua's fire; also that left by Nebuchadnezzar's fire. (See pages 161, 211.)

Bethshan, also called Beisan. At junction of Jezreel and Jordan valleys. Excavated by University Museum (1921–30). Uncovered ruins of temples where Saul's armor was hung up. (See pages 116, 183.)

Bethshemesh, about 15 miles west of Jerusalem. Excavated by Elihu Grant (1930). Found Alphabetic Writing of 1800 B.C.; Ashes of Nebuchadnezzar's Fire; Seal of Jehoiachin's Steward. (See pages 54, 210, 228.)

Boghaz-keui, in eastern Asia Minor. An ancient Hittite center. A great library of inscriptions in many languages was found. (Page 55.)

Borsippa, southwest edge of Babylon. Rawlinson found an inscription that seemed like a tradition of the unfinished Tower of Babel. (Page 83.)

Calah, also called Nimrud, about 20 miles south of Nineveh. Excavated by Layard (1845–50). Ruins of Palaces of a number of Assyrian Kings; and the famous "Black Obelisk." (See pages 42, 206, 365.)

Calvary, also called Golgotha. Site of Jesus' Crucifixion, and nearby Garden Tomb where He was Buried. (Pages 482, 551–552.)

Capernaum. The floor of the Synagog, in which Jesus taught, was uncovered, by a German expedition (1905). (See page 502.)

Dibon, in Moab, about 20 miles east of Dead Sea. Place where the Moabite Stone was found (1868), by F. A. Klein. (See page 202.)

Dothan, just north of Schechem, where sherds of 2000 B.C. have been found, showing that it was in existence in Abraham's day. (Page 100.)

Elephantine, in Egypt, south of Thebes, where the Elephantine Papyri were discovered, 1904 and 1907.

El-Kab, in Egypt, south of Thebes, where there is a tomb with an inscription which seems to refer to the Seven Years' Famine. (Page 107.)

Ephesus, where Paul did his most marvelous work. Ruins of the Temple of Diana, and the Theatre, have been uncovered. (See page 702.)

Erech, also called Uruk, or Warka. 50 miles northwest of Eridu. Excavated (1913), by Koldewey; 1928–33, by Noldeke and Jordan. One of earth's oldest cities, with 18 distinct Pre-Historic layers. (Page 87.)

Eridu. Traditional Garden of Eden. 12 miles south of Ur. Excavated by Hall and Thompson, of the British Museum (1918–19), who found indications that possibly it was the first city ever built. Ancient tablets call it home of first two kings in history. (See pages 64–70.)

Ezion-geber, about 75 miles south of Dead Sea, at head of the Gulf of Akaba. Excavated by Nelson Glueck (1838–39). Found ruins of Solomon's smelters, furnaces, crucibles and refineries. (See pages 192, 224.)

Fara, also called Shurruppak, or Sukkurru. Traditional home of Noah. Halfway between Eridu and Babylon. Excavated by Eric Schmidt (1931), who found the Flood Deposit. (See pages 44, 72, 78.)

Gebal, a few miles north of Sidon. Montet (1922), and Dussard (1930), found inscriptions bearing on the history of the Alphabet.

Gezer, about 20 miles west of Jerusalem. Garstang (1929), found a jar handle of 2000–1600 B.C. with Alphabetic script. (See page 54.)

Gibeah, also called Tell-el-Ful. Home of Saul, 3 miles north of Jerusalem. Albright (1922–23), found the ruins of Saul's house; and also the layer of ashes from burning mentioned in Judges 20:40. (Pages 173, 181.)

Gilead. Albright (1929), discovered ruins of cities of 2000 B.C., as implied by Genesis 14:5, 6. (See page 97.)

Halaf, in the Euphrates valley, between Nineveh and Haran, where one of the earliest known cultures has been found.

Hauran, east of the Sea of Galilee, traditional home of Job. Albright found evidence of dense population of 2000 B.C. (See pages 97, 241.)

Hazor, north end of Palestine. Garstang found the layer of ashes left by Joshua's fire. (See page 164.)

Jemdet Nasr, 25 miles northeast of Babylon. Dr. Langdon, of Oxford University (1926), found here indications of Original Monotheism. (Page 49.)

Jericho. Garstang (1929–36), found, in its ruins, many evidences of the Biblical story of its destruction by Joshua; Burnt with fire; Walls fell down flat; Foodstuffs turned to charcoal. (Pages 159–161, 197.)

Jerusalem. David's Wall; Bend in the Wall; David's Stairs; Tower; David's Watercourse. Solomon's Quarries. Hezekiah's Wall Repairs; Hezekiah's Tunnel; Siloam Inscription. Walls between which Zedekiah fled. (See pages 192, 215, 224, 228, 233.)

Karnak, part of Thebes. Ruins among the grandest in the world. Many discoveries of great interest. (See pages 118, 119, 221.)

Karkar, about 100 miles north of Damascus. An inscription of Shalmaneser, king of Assyria (860–825 B.C.), was found here, telling of his wars with Ahab king of Israel. (See page 199.)

Khorsabad, on north edge of Nineveh. Here Botta (1842–52), laid bare the ruins of the magnificent Palace of Sargon. (Pages 42, 287–289, 365.)

Kiriath-sepher, a few miles southwest of Hebron. Here have been found Ashes of Joshua's fire, of Shishak's fire, of Nebuchadnezzar's fire; and Grain Pits of the time of the Judges: (See pages 51, 163, 172, 211, 221.)

Kish, at east edge of Babylon. Here Langdon (1928–29), found the Flood Deposit, Pre-Flood Writing, and a Pre-Flood Chariot. (Pages 44, 62, 78.)

Lachish, 15 miles west of Hebron. Here were found the famous "Lachish Letters." Also Alphabetic writing of 1500 B.C. Also the Ashes of Joshua's fire, and of Nebuchadnezzar's fire. (Pages 54, 163, 211, 315, 316.)

Lagash, 60 miles north of Eridu. Excavated by Sarzec (1877–1901). First Hamitic kingdom after the Flood. Great Library center. Vast quantities of primitive Inscriptions found. (Pages 46, 48, 86.)

Larsa, about 40 miles northwest of Eridu. Home of 4th Pre-Flood king. Weld-Blundell Expedition (1922) found the "Weld Prism," first known Outline of World History. (See pages 49, 66, 72.)

Megiddo, called also Armageddon, about 10 miles southwest of Nazareth. Excavated by Oriental Institute. Evidence of Israel's struggle with Canaanites. Solomon's Stables. Baal Worship. (Pages 172, 191, 199, 206.)

Mersin, near Tarsus. Excavated by Garstang, of Neilson Expedition. Most complete architectural remains of Halaf culture yet found.

Mizpah, 6 miles northwest of Jerusalem. W. F. Bade, of Pacific School of Religion, found (1932), Jaazaniah's Seal. (See page 317.)

Moab. Albright (1929), found mounds along east border, with ruins of cities which indicated a well settled region 2000 B.C. (See page 97.)

Nineveh, 300 miles north of Babylon. Ruins discovered by Rich (1820). Layard (1845–51), discovered the Great Library of Assurbanipal. George Smith (1872), found the Creation Tablets, and Flood Tablets. Mallowan (1932–33), found what may have been a Flood Deposit. In the Jonah Mound, Layard found the ruins of Esarhaddon's Palace. The Palaces of Sennacherib and Assurbanipal were found in the Koyunjik Mound. (Pages 42, 62, 76, 80, 365, 369, 370.)

Nippur, also called Calneh, one of Nimrod's cities, about 100 miles northwest of traditional Garden of Eden, Eridu. Excavated by Peters, Haynes, and Hilprecht, of University Museum, between 1888 and

1900. Vast libraries of primitive inscriptions were found, including the Creation Tablets. (See pages 48, 62.)

Obeid, also called Al-Ubeid. 4 miles west of Ur. Here (1923), was found, by Woolley, the Oldest Historical Document known. (Page 46.)

On, also called Heliopolis, in Egypt, a few miles northeast of Cairo. Obelisk standing in Abraham's day is still there. Petrie (1912), discovered ruins of what was thought to have been Joseph's Palace. (Pages 92, 107.)

Oxyrhynchus, in Egypt, south of Memphis. Grenfell and Hunt (1895–97), found here great quantities of Papyri manuscripts. (See page 752.)

Pergamum. Site of One of the Seven Churches. Excavated by a German Expedition. Ruins of what may have been "Satan's Throne." (Page 703.)

Persepolis, capital of the Persian Empire. Excavated by Oriental Institute. Ruins of Palace of Xerxes, Esther's husband, laid bare.

Pithom, in Egypt, northeast of Memphis. Built by Israelite slave labor. Naville (1883), and Kyle (1908), found bricks with straw and without straw, illustrating Exodus 5:10–19. (See page 120.)

Ras Shamra, also called Ugarit, at northeast corner of Mediterranean Sea, near Antioch. A French Expedition (1929–), found vast libraries, in many languages, and earliest Alphabet yet known. (Pages 54, 55.)

Rosetta, in Egypt, near Alexandria, where the Rosetta Stone, key to ancient Egyptian language, was found (1799. See page 52).

Samaria, in central Palestine. A Harvard University Expedition (1908–10, 1931–), found the ruins of Omri's Palace, and of Ahab's Ivory House, and some of Jezebel's Cosmetic Saucers. (Pages 197, 199, 206.)

Sardis, site of one of the Seven Churches of Revelation. Excavated by Princeton University (1909–14). Found the ruins of a Christian Church, and of a temple of Cybele (Diana).

Serabit, or Serabit-el-Khadim, 50 miles northwest of Mt. Sinai. Here (1905), Petrie found the earliest Alphabetic Writing then known, of about 1800 B.C., made 400 years before the days of Moses. (See pages 54, 127.)

Shechem, about 5 miles southeast of Samaria. Albright and Garstang found sherds of 2000 B.C., indicating that it was actually existent in Abraham's day. Sellin (1913–14; 1926–28), found inscriptions of the pre-Israel period, indicating the use of writing by the common people; also indications of Shechem's destruction by Abimelech, as told in Judges 9, and ruins of the temple of Baal (Judges 9:4. Pages 54, 100, 172.)

Shiloh, about 20 miles north of Jerusalem. A Danish Expedition (1922–31), found potsherds of 1200–1100 B.C., indicating Israelite culture, with no evidence of previous occupation. (See page 177.)

Sippar, also called Accad. About 30 miles north of Babylon. One of Nimrod's cities. Capital of 8th Pre-Flood king. Excavated by Rassam (1881), and by Scheil. Many primitive inscriptions were found, some of them very important, and a whole library. (See pages 48, 72, 87.)

Sodom and Gomorrah. Their possible location may be indicated by a discovery of Albright and Kyle (1924), at Bab-ed-Dra, at southeast corner of Dead Sea, with evidence of a dense population of 2500 B.C. to 2000 B.C. ending abruptly. (See pages 98, 99.)

Susa, also called Shushan, 200 miles east of Babylon. Winter residence of Persian kings. Site identified by Loftus (1852). Dieulafoy continued excavations (1884–86). Ruins of Palace of Xerxes, Esther's husband, were uncovered, illustrating details of the Story of Esther. M. J. de Morgan (1902), found Hammurabi's Code. (See pages 50, 236, 237.)

Tahpahnes, in northeast Egypt. Petrie (1886), found ruins, he thought, of the platform mentioned in Jeremiah 43:8. (See page 318.)

Tanis, in northeast Egypt. Here (1839), the Mummy of Shishak, who carried off Solomon's gold, was found. (See pages 191, 192, 221.)

Tell Billah, near Nineveh. Here was found the Gilgamesh Epic, containing the Babylonian Story of the Flood. (See page 76.)

Tepe Gawra, 12 miles north of Nineveh, 2 miles east of Khorsabad. A mound containing 26 cities, one above the other, abandoned before 1500 B.C. Bottom 20 cities are Pre-Historic. Excavated (1927–), by Speiser and Bache, of the University Museum and American School at Baghdad. They found, in the 8th level, the "Adam and Eve" Seal, and many relics of the earliest ages of man. (See page 69.)

Thebes. Wilkinson explored its wonders (1821–33). The Mummies were found (1871), in a tomb back of Thebes. Great Temple of Amon. Obelisk of Hatshepsut. Many marvels of ancient Egypt. (Pages 52, 53, 114, 117, 118.)

Ur, 12 miles north of Traditional Garden of Eden. Home of Abraham. Excavated by Woolley (1922–34), who found the Flood Deposit, Pre-Flood Seals, and laid bare Abraham's city. (Pages 44, 46, 47, 50, 51, 77, 87, 88.)

INDEX